MW00995936

# Fillmore Study Bible

# The New Testament

## Metaphysically Interpreted

TruthUnity Ministries

https://fillmore.bible

# Fillmore Study Bible

# The New Testament

## Metaphysically Interpreted



ISBN-13: 978-0-9841315-4-9

Library of Congress Control Number:

Front cover image: Charles Fillmore handwriting 1st Corinthians 2:9, Courtesy of Unity Archives.
Back cover image: Wood sculpture, Unity of Shreveport.

First Edition – January 2023

TruthUnity Ministries
PO Box 15
Timonium, Maryland 21094

https://www.truthunity.net/web

# The Fillmore Bible Society

The Fillmore Bible Society are collaborators who comb through dozens of metaphysical books written by Charles Fillmore and his students as well as over 70 years of Fillmore articles and sermons for metaphysical insights into the Bible. They edit and submit these insights as short annotations which are then applied to the text of the text of the World English Bible, a contemporary-language update of the American Standard Version of the Bible, both online and in print.

This collaboration project is managed by TruthUnity Ministries, which is the publisher of The Fillmore Study Bible. In time the Fillmore Bible Society will become free-standing with its own board, Editorial staff and peer-review committee.

Members of the Fillmore Bible Society include:

Rev. Dan Beckett. Mark, Colossians.

Mary Salama. Matthew, Corinthians 2, Thessalonians 1 & 2, Timothy 1 & 2, Titus, Peter 1 & 2, Jude.

Rev. Lisa Herklotz and Rev Jim Ernstsen. Revelation to John.

Thomas Scheinler. Acts, Galatians.

Rev. Mark Hicks. General Editor. John, Acts, Romans, Corinthians 1.

Susan St John. Hebrews.

Eddie Rodriguez. Obadiah, Jonah.

Rev. Michelle Vargas. Luke.

# The Fillmore Study Bible

The Fillmore Study Bible provides the reader with an introduction to metaphysical Bible interpretation by offering annotations and commentary from the works of Charles Fillmore and his students. Many Bible students learn their theology by reading the annotations and commentary of study Bibles. Study Bibles have a theological point of view, typically Catholic, Evangelical or Mainline Protestant. The Fillmore Study Bible makes this method of study available to the Metaphysical Christian.

Metaphysical Christianity is an authentic and distinct expression of the historic Christian faith that acknowledges and embraces the influence of Platonic and Stoic Greek philosophy in the early development of Christian theology. Much of this influence has been suppressed in orthodox Bible commentaries because metaphysical interpretation relies on an inner knowingness as authority for spiritual matters. The annotations included here embrace inner knowingness as authority.

This study bible uses the *World English Bible* translation, which is a contemporary-language update of the bible used by Charles Fillmore, the American Standard Version. The language of the WEB is not American nor British, but *contemporary, world* English, making the text pleasant to read for the broadest possible audience of global English speakers. The WEB differs from several contemporary-language translations by not adopting gender neutral language but it has provided footnotes when gender neutral language would be appropriate.

We believe that our present day culture of information, science and technology is ready to restore to it's spiritual teachings the perspectives of original thinkers who gave us not only mathematics, ethics, democracy and medicine, but also deep insights into the inner world of soul and Divine mind—the Greek metaphysicians. We also believe that contemporary Christianity needs a contemporary, global interpretation applied to a contemporary, global biblical text. The Fillmore Study Bible is our offering for addressing these spiritual needs.

# Table of Contents

# Introduction to *The New Testament*

Before taking up a study of the New Testament, it may be well to remind ourselves of our main purpose. Our purpose is to make a study *of* the New Testament—not to study *about* the New Testament. The difference should be clear. Many books have been written, and many more will be written about the New Testament; and undoubtedly some of these will prove helpful to the student. But with this multitude of books it is easily possible for the student to gather much information about the New Testament, and at the same time remain unfamiliar with the contents of the New Testament itself. Therefore in this Fillmore Study Bible our main emphasis will be upon the contents of the New Testament. The student will find that as one attains a good grasp of the contents of the New Testament, they will be attracted to helpful study books; but until this grasp is attained, the reading of many books may lead to confusion. Hence, the one necessary textbook is the New Testament.

A Study of the New Testament — Introduction by Herbert J. Hunt, former Dean of Bible Studies for the Unity School of Christianity.

# The Good News According to Matthew

Mount of Beatitudes seen from Capernaum, Berthold Werner, public domain.

## Introduction to Matthew

Matthew's Gospel has several outstanding features. To begin with, we have here a firsthand account of many of the events recorded—since Matthew (sometimes called Levi) was an actual disciple of Jesus. (See Matt. 9:9 and Luke 5:27.) Then, the style of writing in this Gospel indicates that the writer was a well-educated man, and accustomed to the best forms of public address. There are indications that Matthew wrote down many of the actual sayings of Jesus—possibly at the time of utterance, or shortly thereafter—and that these "sayings," transcribed onto small slips of parchment or papyrus, circulated freely among the early Christians. However, around A.D. 70 Matthew, or someone closely associated with him, put these "sayings" into connected form, adding the circumstances surrounding and leading to them, together with other important information, and thus forming our present Gospel according to Matthew.

Matthew's Gospel seems to have been written especially for the Jewish

Christians, and therefore it places emphasis upon the messiahship of Jesus. Indeed, the theme of this Gospel might be stated as: "Jesus, the Jewish Messiah." Matthew writes of Jesus as "King of the Jews"; shows that Jesus was connected with the royal line of David; and as a background for the birth of Jesus, he mentions kings, priests, wise men, and other exalted personages. Matthew makes frequent use of Old Testament quotations, and a characteristic phrase, repeated over and over again, is: "That it might be fulfilled." (See Matt. 1:22.)

Introduction to *The Good News According to Matthew* by Herbert J. Hunt, former Dean of Bible Studies for the Unity School of Christianity.

**Purpose of the letter.** The Gospel of Matthew was written by Matthew (Levi), one of the twelve disciples of Jesus Christ, around 48-50 A.D. Matthew writes to reveal Jesus Christ as "King of the Jews."

**Unique themes in Matthew.** Whereas Mark aims to present Jesus Christ as "the Suffering Servant" and Luke aims to present Him as "the Perfect Man," Matthew's aim is to present Jesus as "the King" - Israel's long awaited Messiah. So it is no wonder that Matthew mentions the word "Kingdom" 28 times and quotes the Old Testament Scriptures more than 60 times, in order to demonstrate that Jesus was the actual fulfilment of the words of the Jewish prophets.

**Metaphysically speaking.** Since the aim of Matthew is to reveal Jesus Christ as "King of the Jews," let us consider what that means metaphysically, on the level of our inner world.

According to Charles Fillmore, "king" (RW/king) refers to the executive faculty of "the will" in each one of us, as it is guided, governed, and directed by Spirit (RW/Spirit). And metaphysically speaking, "Jews" (MBD/Jews) represent our Spirit-tending thoughts. Thus, "King of the Jews" refers to a state of consciousness of an individual who is governed, led, and lives by Truth, at every level of their being, where the Word of the *I AM* is going forth as the ruling suggestion (RW/suggestion) in that individual's spirit, intellect, and general state of consciousness.

Therefore, in Matthew, the metaphysician will be able to perceive and track the stages of the ongoing process of regeneration as they relate to the unfolding of the Word of Truth within us, until it becomes the ruling authority in our consciousness, in other words the "King of *our* Jews". Here are the major stages of the movement of the *I AM* Word of Truth (Jesus) through us:

a. Its initiation within us (birth, baptism, and temptation) - Chapters 1-4
b. Its powerful impartations to reinstruct, heal, and transform us (Sermon on the Mount, miracles, discourses, parables) - Chapters 5-15
c. Its ability to endure and continue to disciple us, even in the face of all arising oppositional doubt, memories, and unbelief (Pharisees, scribes, Sadducees) - Chapters 16-22
d. Its ability to instruct and prepare our minds with foresight regarding

the signs of our transformation (a process that requires inevitable destruction of current patterns of error thinking - woes, predictions about temple destruction and the "end times") - Chapters 23-25

e. Its final necessary experiences before it resurrects a new state of consciousness within us ("handed over" transition phase, mocked by current state of consciousness, crucified in our attention, buried in our memory, resurrecting in the garden of our soul, appearing to us repeatedly, bringing joy, hope, confidence, and a new purpose-the "Great Commission") - Chapters 26-28

**Why we should read the Gospel of Matthew.** Matthew's Gospel reveals to us the inner opposition that may arise during our process of transmutation (overcoming), so that expecting it, we may pray and prepare as to how to best navigate through these stages and inner changes, that we may best cooperate and facilitate the resurrection of our next, next, and next states of consciousness, as the *I AM* Word of Truth continues to resurrect in us and abide as our King and Rule of life.

Introduction to *The Good News According to Matthew* by Mary Salama.

# MATTHEW 1

## The Genealogy of Jesus the Christ[1]

1:1 The book of the genealogy of Jesus Christ[1], the son of David, the son of Abraham.[2]

1:2 Abraham became the father of[3] Isaac. Isaac became the father of Jacob. Jacob became the father of Judah and his brothers. 1:3 Judah became the father of Perez and Zerah by Tamar. Perez became the father of Hezron. Hezron became the father of Ram. 1:4 Ram became the father of Amminadab. Amminadab became the father of Nahshon. Nahshon became the father of Salmon. 1:5 Salmon became the father of Boaz by Rahab. Boaz became the father of Obed by Ruth. Obed became the father of Jesse. 1:6 Jesse became the father of David the king.

David became the father of Solomon by her who had been the wife of Uriah. 1:7 Solomon became the father of Rehoboam. Rehoboam became the father of Abijah. Abijah became the father of Asa. 1:8 Asa became the father of Jehoshaphat. Jehoshaphat became the father of Joram. Joram became the father of Uzziah. 1:9 Uzziah became the father of Jotham. Jotham became the father of Ahaz. Ahaz became the father of Hezekiah. 1:10 Hezekiah became the father of Manasseh. Manasseh became the father of Amon. Amon became the father of Josiah. 1:11 Josiah became the father of Jechoniah and his brothers, at the time of the exile to Babylon.

1:12 After the exile to Babylon, Jechoniah became the father of Shealtiel. Shealtiel became the father of Zerubbabel. 1:13 Zerubbabel became the father of Abiud. Abiud became the father of Eliakim. Eliakim became the father of Azor.

1:14 Azor became the father of Sadoc.
Sadoc became the father of Achim.
Achim became the father of Eliud. 1:15
Eliud became the father of Eleazar.
Eleazar became the father of
Matthan. Matthan became the father
of Jacob. 1:16 Jacob became the
father of Joseph, the husband of
Mary, from whom was born Jesus[2],
who is called Christ. 1:17 So all the
generations from Abraham to David
are fourteen generations; from David
to the exile to Babylon fourteen
generations; and from the carrying
away to Babylon to the Christ,
fourteen generations.

1. See Luke 3:23-38

2. *the son of David, the son of Abraham.* David represents love and Abraham faith. These two faculties, when quickened in man, bring him into the Christ consciousness. The Christ in man is thus the offspring of love and faith.

3. *became the father of.* Metaphysically, this is from faith to Christ.

## The Birth of Jesus the Christ[1]

1:18 Now the birth of Jesus Christ[2]
was like this;[3] for after his mother,
Mary,[4] was engaged to Joseph,[5]
before they came together, she was
found pregnant by the Holy Spirit.[6]
1:19 Joseph, her husband, being a
righteous man, and not willing to
make her a public example, intended
to put her away secretly. 1:20 But
when he thought about these things,
behold, an angel of the Lord[7]
appeared to him in a dream, saying,
"Joseph, son of David,[8] don't be
afraid to take to yourself Mary, your
wife, for that which is conceived in
her is of the Holy Spirit. 1:21 She shall
bring forth a son. You shall call his
name Jesus, for it is he who shall
save his people from their sins."

1:22 Now all this has happened,
that it might be fulfilled which was
spoken by the Lord through the
prophet, saying,

1:23 "Behold, the virgin shall be with
child,
and shall bring forth a son.
They shall call his name
Immanuel;"[9]
which is, being interpreted,
"God with us."[3]

1:24 Joseph arose from his sleep,
and did as the angel of the Lord
commanded him, and took his wife
to himself; 1:25 and didn't know her
sexually until she had brought forth
her firstborn son. He named him
Jesus.

1. See Luke 1:26-38

2. *Jesus Christ.* The Christ is the perfect-idea man, whom God created, the real self of all men. Jesus Christ is the Christ self brought into perfect expression and manifestation. Christ is the Savior of mankind, the free, divine gift of God to us.

3. *was like this.* Everything first takes place in the mind. In truth it is in mind where real demonstrations find their impetus. Joseph and Mary's betrothal was to them such a sacred and holy thing that it stirred into activity the most spiritual forces of their souls, which forces perhaps had never been set into expression before, and their spiritual union was consummated. There followed such an outpouring of the Holy Spirit (which is God's Word in action) that Mary, through Joseph, was overshadowed by this heavenly power, and though she did not "know man" in a physical way, the initial germ seed was thereby projected, and she conceived and brought forth the child, Jesus.

4. *Mary.* Metaphysically interpreted within the soul, Mary, the Virgin mother, represents a pure state of mind that ponders spiritual things in her heart and believes in revelations from angels and messengers from God. Her imagination is so intense that she vitalizes the ultra-microscopic germs of life and they multiply in her body without external contact.

5. *Joseph.* Mary represents the soul; Joseph, intuitive wisdom. Joseph, "being

a righteous man," wished to do what was right without regard to his own interests, and he meditated on the course he should take. In meditation the mind is stilled and becomes receptive to the true ideas of universal Mind, in which all wisdom and knowledge abides. Joseph received guidance from the Lord in a dream following meditation.

6. *was found pregnant by the Holy Spirit.* The virgin birth is the awakening of the mind of man to the conception of the Christ Spirit as the only reality. The miraculous conception by which the Virgin Mary is held to have conceived without original sin. Joseph, not fully understanding the prophecy, "was minded to put her away privily," meaning that we do not in the first stages of the birth of Christ in us understand the process, and sometimes are moved to put it away from us. Joseph's soul (the name Joseph meaning "from perfection to perfection") is so heavily charged with divine life that it cannot express itself intelligently, because no union has yet taken place between it and the understanding, which union—when it is consumated—always equalizes and adjusts.

7. *an angel of the Lord.* An angel is a messenger of the Lord. Metaphysically, our angels are our spiritual perceptive faculties, which ever dwell in the presence of the Father.

8. *Joseph, son of David.* Wisdom is the outcome of love deeply and quietly held. We understand those whom we love. "Joseph [wisdom], thou son of David [love]." Together, wisdom and love form the mind of the Christ.

9. *they shall call his name Immanuel.* Immanuel means "God with us," but the metaphysician sees it as the consciousness that God is with us and that we are one with Him. The name thus means to him, "God within us."

Fillmore Study Bible annotations by Mark Hicks.

**World English Bible Footnotes:**

[1] v1:1. Messiah (Hebrew) and Christ (Greek) both mean "Anointed One"

[2] v1:16. "Jesus" means "Salvation."

[3] v1:23. Isaiah 7:14

# Matthew 2

## Visitation of the Wise Men

2:1 Now when Jesus① was born in
Bethlehem② of Judea in the days of
Herod the king, behold, wise men[4]
from the east③ came to Jerusalem,
saying, 2:2 "Where is he who is born
King of the Jews④? For we saw his
star in the east,⑤ and have come
to worship him." 2:3 When Herod the
king heard it, he was troubled,⑥ and
all Jerusalem with him. 2:4 Gathering
together all the chief priests and
scribes of the people, he asked them
where the Christ would be born. 2:5
They said to him, "In Bethlehem of
Judea, for thus it is written through
the prophet,

2:6 'You Bethlehem, land of Judah,
are in no way least among the princes of Judah:
for out of you shall come forth a governor,

who shall shepherd my people,
Israel.'"[5]

2:7 Then Herod secretly called the wise men, and learned from them exactly what time the star appeared.
2:8 He sent them to Bethlehem, and said, "Go and search diligently for the young child. When you have found him, bring me word, so that I also may come and worship him."

1. *Jesus.* The new man is called "Jesus" whose name means the same as the name "Jehovah," the I AM, the supreme will.

2. *was born in Bethlehem.* Bethlehem (house of bread) is the substance center where the spiritual or ideal man has his source. It represents the center of substance in our consciousness.

3. *Wise men from the east.* Symbolize the inner resources of the soul when it is stirred to the depths by a revelation of Truth. The East symbolizes the within, and the coming of the Wise Men signifies intuitive wisdom reverently seeking out the new ideal of life that is beginning in consciousness. The law governing spiritual consciousness and its development in the individual is as sure as the law that governs the stars or the planets in their courses. We have access to divine substance within the depths of our consciousness, and out or it we fashion a new ideal of life and a fuller, more abundant life.

4. *he that is born King of the Jews.* This is the ruling power of the spiritual consciousness when it first dawns on the mind and heart of the individual.

5. *we saw his star in the east.* When the Jesus ego first appears in the subconsciousness it is a mere spack of light, a "Star in the east." The star symbolizes intuition; the wise men were guided by intuition. Stars represent subjective and not fully understood guiding lights. They represent the inner realms of consciousness that, like books of life, have kept the records of past lives and held them in reserve for the great day when the soul would receive the supreme ego, Jesus. The star that pointed the way for the wise men was also in the East, and it typifies man's inner conviction of his divine sonship.

6. *when Herod the king heard it, he was troubled.* Herod represents the ruling power of the outer or personal consciousness. Metaphysically, "Son of a hero, heroic." When sense consciousness (Herod) rules, it dominates all intellectual, as well as ecclesiastical thoughts. These thoughts symbolise the chief priests and scribes of the people, all of which on this plane go to make up the intellectual man. The outer, personal, or sense consciousness (Herod) is disturbed by the first glimmering of a different consciousness in the mind and heart. The personal consciousness is jealous of its power and authority, and seeks to retain its dominion, whatever the cost.

## The Adoration of the Magi

2:9 They, having heard the king, went their way; and behold, the star, which they saw in the east, went before them, until it came and stood over where the young child was.
2:10 When they saw the star, they rejoiced with exceedingly great joy.❶
2:11 They came into the house and saw the young child with Mary, his mother, and they fell down and worshiped him. Opening their treasures, they offered to him gifts: gold, frankincense, and myrrh.
2:12 Being warned in a dream that they shouldn't return to Herod, they went back to their own country another way.❷

1. *When they saw the star, they rejoiced with exceeding great joy.* When the soul makes a spiritual demonstration there is great rejoicing. When one begins to have faith that he is destined to do the will of God, all the riches of wise experience—gifts of gold (riches of Spirit); frankincense, (the beauty of Spirit); and myrrh (the eternity of Spirit)—are bestowed upon the young child. When the wise thoughts from within bring their presents, there is great rejoicing and satisfaction in consciousness.

2. *they went back to their own country another way.* In this instance as in all others, the Lord is continually seeking to guide man into the higher ways of life, which always lead into the "country" of peace, wisdom and good will.

## The Escape to Egypt

2:13 Now when they had departed, behold, an angel of the Lord appeared to Joseph in a dream,[1] saying, "Arise and take the young child and his mother, and flee into Egypt, and stay there until I tell you, for Herod will seek the young child to destroy him."[2]

2:14 He arose and took the young child and his mother by night, and departed into Egypt, 2:15 and was there until the death of Herod; that it might be fulfilled which was spoken by the Lord through the prophet, saying, "Out of Egypt I called my son."[6]

1. *an angel of the Lord appeared to Joseph in a dream.* The Lord often speaks to this state of consciousness through what is commonly known as dreams and visions. Both the Wise-men and Joseph were guided by dreams. The message is thrown on the screen of the mind in the form of thought pictures, which the quickened soul readily interprets.

2. *flee into Egypt ... for Herod will seek the young child to destroy him.* It is wise to protect the new born spiritual consciousness from coming into contact with the personal ego, Herod. Under the guidance of Spirit no harm comes to it; it is taken down into the protected places of the subconsciousness (Egypt) until the personal ego destroys itself. When in the silence and in dreams we see a little child, we may know that the Christ body (Jesus) has begun to form in our subconscious minds. Then we should be watchful to see that the subtle desires of sense (Herod) do not rob the young child of its vitality and thus kill it out of consciousness. The young child must be cared for and fed daily with spiritual thoughts; otherwise it will pine away and we shall find ourselves back in the old sense state, with (Herod), sense consciousness in suprene control.

## The Massacre of the Infants

2:16 Then Herod, when he saw that he was mocked by the wise men, was exceedingly angry,[1] and sent out, and killed all the male children who were in Bethlehem and in all the surrounding countryside, from two years old and under, according to the exact time which he had learned from the wise men. 2:17 Then that which was spoken by Jeremiah the prophet was fulfilled, saying,

2:18 "A voice was heard in Ramah,
lamentation, weeping and
great mourning,
Rachel weeping for her children;
she wouldn't be comforted,
because they are no more."[7]

1. *Herod ... was exceedingly angry.* When the human self does not have its way it loses its temper, flies into a rage, is destructive and kills out many potentially good forces.

## The Return from Egypt

2:19 But when Herod was dead,[1] behold, an angel of the Lord appeared in a dream to Joseph in Egypt, saying, 2:20 "Arise and take the young child and his mother, and go into the land of Israel, for those who sought the young child's life are dead."

2:21 He arose and took the young child and his mother, and came into the land of Israel. 2:22 But when he heard that Archelaus[2] was reigning over Judea in the place of his father, Herod, he was afraid to go there. Being warned in a dream, he withdrew into the region of

Galilee,❸ 2:23 and came and lived in a city called Nazareth;❹ that it might be fulfilled which was spoken through the prophets❺: "He will be called a Nazarene."

1. *when Herod was dead.* Sense consciousness (Herod) is dead; therefore the new spiritual consciousness (the Christ child) is no longer in danger. It is free to express openly that which is real (Israel).

2. *Archelaus.* Represents a phase of the sense will (son of Herod the Great), or ruling power, in sense consciousness which was still dominant.

3. *Galilee.* Represents the life activity or soul energy of man acting in conjunction with substance.

4. *Nazareth.* A city of Galilee, means a sprout, a small thing held of slight significance, hence a term of reproach. It typifies the commonplace mind of man: but it is in the commonplace mind that the Christ ideal takes root and grows up in consciousness.

5. *that it might be fulfilled which was spoken through the prophets.* Throughout the gospel story of Jesus there runs continually a thread of fulfilled prophecy. To the casual reader who sees nothing beyond the literal narrative, it would seem sometimes that the parallelism is far-fetched. But it is seen that the fulfillment of prophecy takes place because prophecy is a foreknowledge of Truth to be demonstrated. The I AM has knowledge of all Truth, but to the natural man this knowledge comes dimly, — as a vague presentiment, a foreknowledge or prophecy of Truth to come. With the Christ man comes Truth—fulfillment.

---

Fillmore Bible Society annotations by Mark Hicks.

**World English Bible Footnotes:**

[4] v2:1. The word for "wise men" (magoi) can also mean teachers, scientists, physicians, astrologers, seers, interpreters of dreams, or sorcerers.

[5] v2:6. Micah 5:2

[6] v2:15. Hosea 11:1

[7] v2:18. Jeremiah 31:15

# Matthew 3

## The Proclamation of John the Baptist

3:1 In those days, John the Baptizer
came,❶ preaching in the wilderness
of Judea, saying, 3:2 "Repent,❷ for
the Kingdom of Heaven❸ is at hand!"
3:3 For this is he who was spoken of by
Isaiah the prophet, saying,

"The voice of one crying in the
wilderness,
make ready the way of the
Lord.
Make his paths straight."[8]

3:4 Now John himself wore clothing
made of camel's hair, with a leather
belt around his waist. His food was
locusts and wild honey. 3:5 Then
people from Jerusalem, all of Judea,
and all the region around the
Jordan❹ went out to him. 3:6 They

were baptized⑤[9] by him in the Jordan, confessing their sins. 3:7 But when he saw many of the Pharisees and Sadducees⑥ coming for his baptism,[10] he said to them, "You offspring of vipers,⑦ who warned you to flee from the wrath to come? 3:8 Therefore bring forth fruit worthy of repentance!⑧ 3:9 Don't think to yourselves, 'We have Abraham for our father,' for I tell you that God is able to raise up children to Abraham from these stones.

3:10 "Even now the axe lies at the root of the trees.⑨ Therefore, every tree that doesn't bring forth good fruit is cut down, and cast into the fire. 3:11 I indeed baptize[11] you in water for repentance,⑩ but he who comes after me is mightier than I, whose shoes I am not worthy to carry. He will baptize you in the Holy Spirit.⑪[12] 3:12 His winnowing fork is in his hand, and he will thoroughly cleanse his threshing floor. He will gather his wheat into the barn, but the chaff he will burn up with unquenchable fire."

1. *John the Baptizer came.* The voice of repentance within (John the Baptist) that leads to the appearance of the Word of Truth (Jesus) and immersion within our stream of consciousness (the Jordan). This is a continual immersion in a two-step baptism (John then Jesus) of denials and affirmations (denying the reality of the limiting condition/appearance and affirming a statement of Truth).

2. *Repent.* A turning from a belief in sin and error to a belief in God and righteousness; a reversal of mind and heart in the direction of the All Good.

3. *The Kingdom of heaven.* The realm of divine ideas, within human beings, producing their expression, perfect harmony.

4. *The Jordan.* Dispenser from above; flowing (river) of judgment; the stream of thought constantly flowing through the subconsciousness, made up of thoughts good, bad, and indifferent, the life flow of thought through the organism from head to feet. This thought stream has to be crossed before the Children of Israel can go over into the Promised Land (before the true, real thoughts of the organism can enter into the divine substance and life in the subconsciousness).

5. *They were baptized.* A time of making a commitment with the Lord of our Being by the cleansing power of denial, the activity of the faculty of renunciation in releasing old attitudes and beliefs (Jim Lewis).

6. *Pharisees and Sadducees.* Our inner doubts and unbeliefs.

7. *offspring of vipers.* The hypocritical attitude of some who merely pretended to change their way of thinking.

8. *fruit worthy of repentance!* Repentance: deliberately turning from a belief in error to an all-inclusive belief in God.

9. *the axe lies at the root of the trees.* Negative tendencies can become great trees of habit in the inner life. We are to rid ourselves completely of all negative mental growths.

10. *I baptize you in water for repentance.* We continue to immerse (baptize) ourselves in the Truth until we get that inner confirmation in our spirit and hear the Inner Voice (Spirit descending like a dove & the Voice out of heaven), the sense comes that we are "well-pleasing" to our Father in heaven.

11. *He will baptize you in the Holy Spirit.* an affirmative quickening of the spiritual nature, a positive acceptance of the Christ self in man. Fire symbolizes cleansing and purification. The fire of Spirit consumes error.

## The Baptism of Jesus

3:13 Then Jesus came from Galilee to the Jordan to John, to be baptized by him. 3:14 But John would have hindered him, saying, "I need to be baptized by you, and you come to me?"

3:15 But Jesus, answering, said to him, "Allow it now, for this is the fitting way① for us to fulfill all righteousness." Then he allowed him. 3:16 Jesus, when he was baptized, went up directly from the water: and behold, the heavens were opened to him.(2) He saw the Spirit of God descending as a dove, and coming on him. 3:17 Behold, a voice out of the heavens(3) said, "This is my beloved Son, with whom I am well pleased."

1. *this is the fitting way.* The baptism of John and the baptism of Jesus represent the two common steps in spiritual development: denial and affirmation, or the dropping of the old and laying hold of the new. Denial of error should precede affirmation of Truth. We should not focus our energies on denials, nor dwell too long on them; but rather, use them as the first step toward our affirmation of the good we desire to demonstrate.

2. *the heavens were opened to him.* From that moment, Jesus was completely aware of God's infinite love and of his heritage as God's Son.

3. *a voice out of the heavens.* Baptism of Jesus caused the ethers to vibrate with audible words of approval (Ed Rabel).

---

Fillmore Study Bible annotations by Mary Salama.

**World English Bible Footnotes:**

[8] v3:3. Isaiah 40:3

[9] v3:6. or, immersed

[10] v3:7. or, immersion

[11] v3:11. or, immerse

[12] v3:11. TR and NU add "and with fire"

# Matthew 4

## The Temptation of Jesus

4:1 Then Jesus was led up by the Spirit into the wilderness to be tempted(1) by the devil.(2) 4:2 When he had fasted forty days and forty nights, he was hungry afterward. 4:3 The tempter came and said to him, "If you are the Son of God,(3) command that these stones become bread."

4:4 But he answered,(4) "It is written, 'Man shall not live by bread alone, but by every word that proceeds out of the mouth of God.'"(5)[13]

4:5 Then the devil took him into the holy city. He set him on the pinnacle of the temple, 4:6 and said to him, "If you are the Son of God, throw yourself down, for it is written, 'He will put his angels in charge of you.' and,

'On their hands they will bear you up,
so that you don't dash your foot against a stone.'"[14]

4:7 Jesus said to him, "Again, it is written, 'You shall not test the Lord, your God.'"[15]

4:8 Again, the devil took him to

an exceedingly high mountain, and showed him all the kingdoms of the world, and their glory. 4:9 He said to him, "I will give you all of these things, if you will fall down and worship me."

4:10 Then Jesus said to him, "Get behind me,[16] Satan! For it is written, 'You shall worship the Lord your God, and you shall serve him only.'"[17]

4:11 Then the devil left him, and behold, angels came and served him.[6]

1. *Tempted.* Anything that causes us to think, feel, or act as if we were, separate and apart from God, the-All-Good.

2. *Devil (Satan).* Names for evil thinking or the temptation to follow wrong paths: a state of consciousness adverse to the good sense consciousness.

3. *If You are the Son of God.* The three temptations that come to the student of Truth are (1) to support himself by the spoken word divorced from physical effort (turn bread into stones); (2) The temptation of self-exaltation and ambition when he is urged to use his understanding of Divine law to gain power over his fellow men (throw Yourself down); (3) The temptation to make a display of his power before others (fall down and worship me).

4. *But he answered.* We meet and overcome our tests with denials and affirmations of Truth: "Man shall not live by bread alone." "Thou shalt not make trial of the Lord thy God." "Thou shalt worship the Lord thy God, and him only shalt thou serve." He thus established a pattern for us to follow.

5. *that proceeds out of the mouth of God.* Jesus met each temptation with a positive declaration of oneness with God.

6. *Angels came and served Him.* We triumph over temptation through denial and affirmation; by substituting good for apparent evil. "Overcome evil with good." The angels that minister to us are the true thoughts of universal Mind, the Mind of Christ.

## Jesus Begins His Ministry in Galilee

4:12 Now when Jesus heard that John[1] was delivered up, he withdrew into Galilee. 4:13 Leaving Nazareth, he came and lived in Capernaum,[2] which is by the sea, in the region of Zebulun and Naphtali, 4:14 that it might be fulfilled which was spoken through Isaiah the prophet, saying,

4:15 "The land of Zebulun and the
land of Naphtali,
toward the sea, beyond the
Jordan,
Galilee of the Gentiles,
4:16 the people who sat in darkness[3]
saw a great light,[4]
to those who sat in the region
and shadow of death,
to them light has dawned."[18]

4:17 From that time, Jesus began to preach, and to say, "Repent! For the Kingdom of Heaven is at hand."

1. *John.* When the spiritually quickened intellect (John) is cut off from actual expression (imprisoned), the spiritual I AM (Jesus) withdraws into Galilee (the consciousness of endless activity) in order to come into closer contact with God, the Source of all energy.

2. *Capernaum.* "Shelter of comfort "or "covering of compassion" symbolizes an inner conviction of the abiding compassion and restoring power of Being. When one enters the state of consciousness of Capernaum, a healing virtue pours out of the soul and transforms all discord into harmony.

3. *The people that sat in darkness.* Thoughts that lack spiritual illumination.

4. *saw a great light.* Light has come. The inner man becomes illumined; the spiritual I AM (Jesus) fearlessly goes forth and proclaims to all people (all states of consciousness); the redemption of the whole being through repenting and following the Lord (applying the spiritual law).

## Jesus Calls the First Disciples

[4:18] Walking by the sea of Galilee, he[19] saw two brothers: Simon, who is called Peter, and Andrew, his brother,(1) casting a net into the sea; for they were fishermen. [4:19] He said to them, "Come after me,(2) and I will make you fishers for men."(3)

[4:20] They immediately left their nets and followed him.(4) [4:21] Going on from there, he saw two other brothers, James the son of Zebedee, and John his brother,(5) in the boat with Zebedee their father, mending their nets. He called them. [4:22] They immediately left the boat and their father, and followed him.

1. *Simon Peter and Andrew, his brother.* Faith (Peter) and strength (Andrew); closely related spiritual qualities. Faith working by itself may be unstable or become weak, but when it is backed up by strength, it becomes undivided faith and accomplishes mighty works in the name and through the power of the Christ.

2. *Come after me.* We are to follow Jesus' example in accepting and living Truth and in always being receptive to God's light, wisdom, peace, power, and health. Then, through the I AM (Jesus) in us, we are enabled to do mighty works in the name of Jesus Christ.

3. *fishers for men.* That which draws people out of negative thoughts of life into positive spiritual thoughts. This change lays the foundation for spiritual power and for healing of mind, body, and affairs.

4. *They immediately left their nets and followed him.* Decision (nets) and positive action (followed him). Above all else our decisions should be guided by one prime consideration: What is God's will in this situation? What is for the highest good of all concerned? What does God want me to do?

5. *Peter, Andrew, James, and John.* The faculties of faith, strength, judgment, and love. We call forth these faculties in making right decisions.

## Jesus Ministers to Crowds of People

[4:23] Jesus went about in all Galilee, teaching in their synagogues, preaching the Good News of the Kingdom, and healing every disease and every sickness among the people. [4:24] The report about him went out into all Syria. They brought to him all who were sick, afflicted with various diseases and torments, possessed with demons, epileptics, and paralytics; and he healed them. [4:25] Great multitudes(1) from Galilee, Decapolis, Jerusalem, Judea and from beyond the Jordan followed him.

1. *Great multitudes...followed Him.* the multitude (of thoughts) come forth from the subconscious mind, and every disease is healed when Word is active in consciousness.

---

Fillmore Study Bible annotations by Mary Salama.

**World English Bible Footnotes:**

[13] v4:4. Deuteronomy 8:3

[14] v4:6. Psalm 91:11-12

[15] v4:7. Deuteronomy 6:16

[16] v4:10. TR and NU read "Go away" instead of "Get behind me"

[17] v4:10. Deuteronomy 6:13

[18] v4:16. Isaiah 9:1-2

[19] v4:18. TR reads "Jesus" instead of "he"

# Matthew 5

## The Beatitudes

5:1 Seeing the multitudes, he went up onto the mountain. When he had sat down, his disciples came to him.
5:2 He opened his mouth and taught them, saying,

5:3 "Blessed are(1) the poor in spirit,
for theirs is the Kingdom of Heaven.(2)[20]
5:4 Blessed are those who mourn,
for they shall be comforted.[21]
5:5 Blessed are the gentle,
for they shall inherit the earth.[22]
5:6 Blessed are those who hunger and thirst after righteousness,(3)
for they shall be filled.
5:7 Blessed are the merciful,
for they shall obtain mercy.(4)
5:8 Blessed are the pure in heart,(5)
for they shall see God.
5:9 Blessed are the peacemakers,(6)
for they shall be called children of God.
5:10 Blessed are those who have been persecuted for righteousness' sake,(7)
for theirs is the Kingdom of Heaven.

5:11 "Blessed are you when people reproach you, persecute you, and say all kinds of evil against you falsely, for my sake.
5:12 Rejoice, and be exceedingly glad, for great is your reward in heaven. For that is how they persecuted the prophets who were before you.

1. *Blessed are ...* To bless is to invoke good upon; to call forth the action of God; to confer God's good on something or someone. Blessedness or happiness is a matter of spiritual adjustment to life under the divine law.

2. *kingdom of heaven.* a state of consciousness in which mind, soul, and body are in harmony with Divine Mind.

3. *hunger and thirst after righteousness.* The desire to align one's life with what is right and lasting. *For they shall be filled.* This attitude of mind brings with it the blessing of fulfillment.

4. *for they shall obtain mercy.* Under Divine law, what we give out comes back to us multiplied.

5. *the pure in heart.* In consciousness, thought precedes the act, therefore, the impure thought leads to the impure act. With the thought fixed on the purity and oneness of the Mind of God, we become expressions of both purity and unity.

6. *the peacemakers.* A peacemaker shares the peace that he makes between other persons.

7. *persecuted for righteousness' sake.* Those who meet with opposition to spiritual development grow strong through mastering their difficulties and eventually gain the kingdom. Thus persecutions are often a blessing in disguise.

## Salt and Light

5:13 "You are the salt of the earth,❶ but if the salt has lost its flavor, with what will it be salted? It is then good for nothing, but to be cast out and trodden under the feet of men. 5:14 You are the light of the world.❷ A city located on a hill can't be hidden.❸ 5:15 Neither do you light a lamp, and put it under a measuring basket, but on a stand; and it shines to all who are in the house. 5:16 Even so, let your light shine before men; that they may see your good works, and glorify your Father who is in heaven.

1. *salt of the earth.* He who is true in himself and in his contacts with others imparts to life something of the same cleanness, sweetness, and zestful flavor that salt imparts to food.

2. *light of the world.* The faculties of all those whose understanding is quickened by the Christ consciousness are enlightened, and they in turn increase the wisdom and intelligence of their possessors.

3. *A city located on a hill can't be hidden.* Understanding, once acquired, cannot be concealed or lost.

## The Law and the Prophets

5:17 "Don't think that I came to destroy the law or the prophets. I didn't come to destroy, but to fulfill.❶ 5:18 For most certainly, I tell you, until heaven and earth pass away, not even one smallest letter[23] or one tiny pen stroke[24] shall in any way pass away from the law, until all things are accomplished. 5:19 Whoever, therefore, shall break one of these least commandments, and teach others to do so, shall be called least in the Kingdom of Heaven; but whoever shall do and teach them shall be called great in the Kingdom of Heaven.❷ 5:20 For I tell you that unless your righteousness exceeds that of the scribes and Pharisees,❸ there is no way you will enter into the Kingdom of Heaven.

1. *didn't come to destroy, but to fulfill.* Jesus proved that the law is a workable rule of lif by demonstrating the truth of it in His life and works. When we conform to this rule we keep or fulfill the law.

2. *great in the Kingdom of heaven.* One who helps his fellow men to behold Truth in all, and to realize that all men are God-like.

3. *Unless your righteousness exceeds that of the scribes and Pharisees.* Genuine righteousness is the desire to do right for the sake of the right and not for the sake of impressing others with our excellence.

## Concerning Anger

5:21 "You have heard that it was said to the ancient ones, 'You shall not murder;'❶[25] and 'Whoever shall murder shall be in danger of the judgment.' 5:22 But I tell you, that everyone who is angry❷ with his brother without a cause[26] shall be in danger of the judgment; and whoever shall say to his brother, 'Raca[27]!' shall be in danger of the council; and whoever shall say, 'You fool!' shall be in danger of the fire of Gehenna.[28]

5:23 "If therefore you are offering your gift at the altar, and there remember that your brother has anything against you, 5:24 leave your gift there before the altar, and go your way. First be reconciled to your brother, and then come and offer your gift. 5:25 Agree with your adversary quickly, while you are with him in the way; lest perhaps the prosecutor deliver you to the judge, and the judge deliver you to the officer, and you be cast into prison. 5:26 Most certainly I tell you, you shall by no means get out of there, until you have paid the last penny.[29]

1. *You shall not murder.* The body can be killed; this is the meaning of the original commandment. The inner life also can be "killed" by anger, scorn, or implacable hatred. Under the divine law the two are equal in gravity.

2. *Anger.* has the effect of destroying trust and confidence, friendship, good will, and other qualities that give life spiritual value. Margaret Sanford in the chapter on *The Law of Love, Healing Light* writes: "This judgment begins immediately. One of its first evidences is the failure of the prayer-power of the angry one. He will find that he cannot pray, no matter how hard he tries. He will also notice in his body the immediate results of anger... For the forces of spirit, mind and body are synchronized and ordered by the same inner control center, and that which affects one affects the others."

## Concerning Adultery

5:27 "You have heard that it was said, [30] 'You shall not commit adultery;'❶[31] 5:28 but I tell you that everyone who gazes at a woman to lust after her has committed adultery with her already in his heart. 5:29 If your right eye causes you to stumble, pluck it out❷ and throw it away from you. For it is more profitable for you that one of your members should perish, than for your whole body to be cast into Gehenna.[32] 5:30 If your right hand causes you to stumble, cut it off, and throw it away from you. For it is more profitable for you that one of your members should perish, than for your whole body to be cast into Gehenna.[33]

1. *shall not commit adultery.* Spiritually interpreted, "You shall not adulterate Truth." When this commandment is disregarded, Truth becomes illogical and irrelevant to the sense mind.

2. *Pluck it out.* The whole man is greater than his members.

## Concerning Divorce

5:31 "It was also said, 'Whoever shall put away his wife, let him give her a writing of divorce,'❶[34] 5:32 but I tell you that whoever puts away his wife, except for the cause of sexual immorality, makes her an adulteress; and whoever marries her when she is put away commits adultery.

1. *a writing of divorce.* "Jesus realized that almost all of His listeners and, later, readers would tend to think of marriage, divorce, sex on strictly literal, humanistic behavioristic terms. Mankind, in general, is not yet capable of thinking and feeling these things on metaphysical terms, because they are too important, intimate, and personal as literal things in our human life." - Ed Rabel, *1976 New Testament Lectures.*

## Concerning Oaths

5:33 "Again you have heard that it was said to them of old time, 'You shall not make false vows,❶ but shall perform to the Lord your vows,' 5:34

but I tell you, don't swear at all: neither by heaven, for it is the throne of God; 5:35 nor by the earth, for it is the footstool of his feet; nor by Jerusalem, for it is the city of the great King. 5:36 Neither shall you swear by your head, for you can't make one hair white or black. 5:37 But let your 'Yes' be 'Yes' and your 'No' be 'No.'[2] Whatever is more than these is of the evil one.

1. *false vows.* This is because violent speech gives false weight to words and is harmful to the thought and character of the speaker. It is altogether profitless and reveals lack of reverence as well as of understanding.

2. *And your 'No' be 'No'.* Simple affirmations and denials, "Yes" and "No" are clear and unmistakable words, symbols of sincerity. No one can misunderstand their meaning, and their power is sufficient for every occasion.

## Concerning Retaliation

5:38 "You have heard that it was said, 'An eye for an eye, and a tooth for a tooth.'[35] 5:39 But I tell you, don't resist him who is evil;[1] but whoever strikes you on your right cheek, turn to him the other also. 5:40 If anyone sues you to take away your coat, let him have your cloak also. 5:41 Whoever compels you to go one mile, go with him two. 5:42 Give to him who asks you, and don't turn away him who desires to borrow from you.

1. *Don't resist him who is evil.* Practicing nonresistance leaves our conscience free of self-condemnation, and it is of the utmost importance to have "a conscience void of offense toward God and men.

## Love for Enemies

5:43 "You have heard that it was said, 'You shall love your neighbor,[36] and hate your enemy.[37]' 5:44 But I tell you, love your enemies,[1] bless those who curse you, do good to those who hate you, and pray for those who mistreat you and persecute you, 5:45 that you may be children of your Father who is in heaven. For he makes his sun to rise on the evil and the good,[2] and sends rain on the just and the unjust. 5:46 For if you love those who love you, what reward do you have? Don't even the tax collectors do the same? 5:47 If you only greet your friends, what more do you do than others? Don't even the tax collectors do the same? 5:48 Therefore you shall be perfect,[3] just as your Father in heaven is perfect.

1. *Love your enemies.* by refusing to judge their conduct by worldly standards, by forgiving their "trespasses against" us, and by beholding them as children of God, the universal Father. The love we are to have is related to the Greek word *agape.* This term does not convey personal affection, such as that felt for our dear ones. It refers not to an emotion or sentiment, but to an attitude, to unselfish good will that is lifted above the personal level. Agape love recognizes the need of others and seeks to help them, regardless of what they have done. It does not approve of the wrongdoing but it sees the one who has done wrong as capable of being fine and good. It seeks to find and encourage the Christ in everyone.

2. *For He makes His sun to rise on the evil and the good.* Divine love is impersonal; it loves for the sake of loving.

3. *you shall be perfect.* Perfection is a state of mind that can be attained with the help of God

Fillmore Study Bible annotations by Mary Salama.

**World English Bible Footnotes:**

[20] v5:3. Isaiah 57:15; 66:2

[21] v5:4. Isaiah 61:2; 66:10,13

[22] v5:5. or, land. Psalm 37:11

[23] v5:18. literally, iota

[24] v5:18. or, serif

[25] v5:21. Exodus 20:13

[26] v5:22. NU omits "without a cause".

[27] v5:22. "Raca" is an Aramaic insult, related to the word for "empty" and conveying the idea of empty-headedness.

[28] v5:22. or, Hell

[29] v5:26. literally, kodrantes. A kodrantes was a small copper coin worth about 2 lepta (widow's mites)--not enough to buy very much of anything.

[30] v5:27. TR adds "to the ancients,"

[31] v5:27. Exodus 20:14

[32] v5:29. or, Hell

[33] v5:30. or, Hell

[34] v5:31. Deuteronomy 24:1

[35] v5:38. Exodus 21:24; Leviticus 24:20; Deuteronomy 19:21

[36] v5:43. Leviticus 19:18

[37] v5:43. not in the Bible, but see Qumran Manual of Discipline Ix, 21-26

# Matthew 6

## Do Good Anonymously

6:1 "Be careful that you don't do your charitable giving before men,(1) to be seen by them, or else you have no reward from your Father who is in heaven. 6:2 Therefore when you do merciful deeds, don't sound a trumpet before yourself, as the hypocrites do in the synagogues and in the streets, that they may get glory from men. Most certainly I tell you, they have received their reward. 6:3 But when you do merciful deeds, don't let your left hand know what your right hand does, 6:4 so that your merciful deeds may be in secret, then your Father who sees in secret will reward you openly.

1. *Don't do your charitable giving before men.* Doing good anonymously keeps the mind single and the intent pure.

## Make Union With Spirit[1]

6:5 "When you pray, you shall not be as the hypocrites, for they love to stand and pray in the synagogues and in the corners of the streets, that they may be seen by men. Most certainly, I tell you, they have received their reward. 6:6 But you, when you pray, enter into your inner chamber, and having shut your door, pray to your Father who is in secret,[2] and your Father who sees in secret will reward you openly. 6:7 In praying, don't use vain repetitions, as the Gentiles do; for they think that they will be heard for their much speaking. 6:8 Therefore don't be like them, for your Father knows what things you need, before you ask him.

6:9 Pray like this: 'Our Father[3] in heaven, may your name be kept holy. 6:10 Let your Kingdom come. Let your will be done, as in heaven,[4] so on earth. 6:11 Give us today our daily bread.[5] 6:12 Forgive us our debts, as we also forgive[6] our debtors. 6:13 Bring us not into temptation,[7] but deliver us from the evil one. For yours is the Kingdom, the power, and the glory forever. Amen.[38]'

6:14 "For if you forgive men their trespasses, your heavenly Father will also forgive you. 6:15 But if you don't forgive men their trespasses, neither will your Father forgive your trespasses.

1. See Mark 11:25; Luke 11:2-4

2. *Enter into your inner chamber.* Metaphysically understood, the "inner chamber" is the spiritual consciousness within the mind and soul of man, it is also called "the secret place of the Most High." *Having shut your door.* Shutting the door of the mind is closing out the thoughts of the outer world from one's consciousness. *Pray to your Father who is in secret.* The spiritual center within every one of us is hidden and secret from the outer consciousness. When we, in the silence, center our attention upon Spirit within us, we make contact with the universal Spirit in which we live, move, and have our being.

3. *Our Father.* The infinite wealth of the Lord's Prayer may be condensed into these two words.

4. *as in heaven, so on earth.* This is an acknowledgment that the will of the Infinite prevails in the realm of Divine Mind, and that it can be made to prevail in the physical and material realm also.

5. *our daily bread.* Our "daily bread" includes all our necessities; the satisfaction of all our hungers, whether physical, mental, or spiritual.

6. *as we also forgive.* By extending forgiveness to others we qualify ourselves to receive forgiveness of our shortcomings. Without a forgiving spirit we cannot receive or accept forgiveness of our sins.

7. *Bring us not into temptation.* Divine Mind does not bring us into temptation, but the sense mind can and does. This prayer is a plea that Divine Mind may dominate our consciousness and wholly fill us.

## Hold Fast To Your Desire For God

6:16 "Moreover when you fast, don't be like the hypocrites, with sad faces. For they disfigure their faces, that they may be seen by men to be fasting.[1] Most certainly I tell you, they have received their reward. 6:17 But you, when you fast, anoint your head, and wash your face; 6:18 so that you are not seen by men to be fasting, but by your Father who is in

secret, and your Father, who sees in
secret, will reward you.

1. *fasting.* Denial; abstinence from error thoughts, to the end that we may meditate on Truth and incorporate it into our consciousness of oneness with the Father (RW/fasting).

## The Heart Is With the Treasure[1]

6:19 "Don't lay up treasures for
yourselves on the earth, where moth
and rust consume, and where thieves
break through and steal; 6:20 but lay
up for yourselves treasures in
heaven,[2] where neither moth nor
rust consume, and where thieves
don't break through and steal; 6:21 for
where your treasure is, there your
heart will be also.[3]

1. See Luke 12:33-34

2. *treasures in heaven.* The rich store of true ideas and thoughts in mind and heart that, together with true actions, form the background of Christ-like character and individuality.

3. *there your heart will be also.* Whatever our thoughts are set upon comes to mean more to us than anything else, and feeling follows thought, clustering around the nucleus of ideas and ideals as bees about their queen. Thus the heart is with the treasure.

## The Lamp Of The Body Is The Eye[1]

6:22 "The lamp of the body is the
eye.[2] If therefore your eye is sound,
your whole body will be full of light.
6:23 But if your eye is evil, your whole
body will be full of darkness. If
therefore the light that is in you is
darkness, how great is the darkness!

1. See Luke 11:34-36

2. *The lamp of the body is the eye.* the eye typifies the ability of the mind to discern and understand the reality of Spirit that lies back of every form or symbol in the material world; to have an eye that is sound and single is to have a searching quality of mind with keen observation that selects only that which is good.

## The Thought of Divided Allegiance[1]

6:24 "No one can serve two
masters,[2] for either he will hate the
one and love the other; or else he
will be devoted to one and despise
the other. You can't serve both God
and Mammon.[3]

1. See Luke 16:13

2. *two masters.* No one can divide his allegiance between opposing ideals or beliefs and retain his individual integrity.

3. *You can't serve God and mammon.* People serve mammon who leave God out of their financial affairs and try to go it alone. Catherine Ponder, *Dynamic Laws of Prosperity*, Chapter 1.

## Do Not Worry[1]

6:25 Therefore, I tell you, don't be
anxious for your life: what you will
eat, or what you will drink; nor yet
for your body, what you will wear.

Isn't life more than food, and the body more than clothing? 6:26 See the birds of the sky, that they don't sow, neither do they reap, nor gather into barns. Your heavenly Father feeds them. Aren't you of much more value than they?

6:27 "Which of you, by being anxious, can add one moment[39] to his lifespan? 6:28 Why are you anxious about clothing? Consider the lilies of the field, how they grow. They don't toil, neither do they spin, 6:29 yet I tell you that even Solomon in all his glory was not dressed like one of these. 6:30 But if God so clothes the grass of the field, which today exists, and tomorrow is thrown into the oven, won't he much more clothe you, you of little faith?

6:31 "Therefore don't be anxious, saying, 'What will we eat?', 'What will we drink?' or, 'With what will we be clothed?' 6:32 For the Gentiles seek after all these things, for your heavenly Father knows that you need all these things. 6:33 But seek first God's Kingdom, and his righteousness; and all these things will be given to you as well.[2] 6:34 Therefore don't be anxious for tomorrow,[3] for tomorrow will be anxious for itself. Each day's own evil is sufficient.

1. See Luke 12:22-32; Luke 10:41

2. *But seek first.* We "seek God's Kingdom and His righteousness" by developing ideas and ideals in harmony with faith, love, wisdom, and the other faculties that we wish to express, and by expressing them consistently. *God's Kingdom.*The kingdom within ourselves; Jesus said, "The kingdom of God is within you"; it is the Christ consciousness, it is the inner realm of Spirit, where the Christ presence, the I AM, the Divine self of man, abides. *and his righteousness.* The right use of God-given attributes. *And all these things will be given to you as well.* As we put God first in our lives and obey His laws rightly, we attract additional blessings to fill all our needs and good desires.

3. *Therefore don't be anxious about tomorrow.* The spiritual and mental process of developing our Christ self does not supplant our physical efforts, but inspires and directs them rightly. Jesus was saying that the worrying is what is unnecessary, foolish, and useless.

---

Fillmore Study Bible annotations by Mary Salama.

**World English Bible Footnotes:**

[38] v6:13. NU omits "For yours is the Kingdom, the power, and the glory forever. Amen."

[39] v6:27. literally, cubit

# Matthew 7

## The Problem With Judging[1]

7:1 "Don't judge,[2] so that you won't be judged. 7:2 For with whatever judgment you judge, you will be judged; and with whatever measure you measure, it will be measured to you. 7:3 Why do you see the speck that is in your brother's eye, but don't consider the beam that is in your own eye? [7:4] Or how will you tell your brother, 'Let me remove the speck from your eye;' and behold, the beam is in your own eye? [7:5] You hypocrite! First remove the beam out of your own eye,[3] and then you can see clearly to remove the speck out of your brother's eye.

1. See Mark 4:24; Luke 6:37-38,41-42

2. *Don't judge.* Judging others is a habit of our personal human nature. Aside from the fact that the habit often works injustice to the one who is judged, it reacts also on we who judge by starting a vicious circle that brings back to us what we have sent out.

3. *First remove the beam out of your own eye.* By removing whatever obstructs our understanding of Truth. Prejudice, ignorance, preconceived opinions, doubt, worry, and materiality are some of these obstructions.

## Share Truth Appropriately

[7:6] "Don't give that which is holy to the dogs, neither throw your pearls before the pigs,[1] lest perhaps they trample them under their feet, and turn and tear you to pieces.

1. *Neither throw your pearls before the pigs.* We should always keep our sense of the fitness of things and refrain from displaying our understanding of Truth to those who are opposed to it or who are temperamentally indifferent to it and therefore unable to understand it.

## Ask and We Receive[1]

[7:7] "Ask, and it will be given you. Seek, and you will find. Knock,[2] and it will be opened for you.[3] [7:8] For everyone who asks receives.[4] He who seeks finds. To him who knocks it will be opened. [7:9] Or who is there among you, who, if his son asks him for bread, will give him a stone?[5] [7:10] Or if he asks for a fish, who will give him a serpent? [7:11] If you then, being evil, know how to give good gifts to your children, how much more will your Father who is in heaven give good things to those who ask him!

1. See Luke 11:9-13

2. *Ask/Seek/Knock.* Acts of Desire. Catherine Ponder, in *The Dynamic Laws of Prosperity*, Ch. 4, writes that desire is the first step in the creative law and that without desire mental imaging and constant affirming are ineffective.

3. *and it will be opened for you.* The command and its corollary show us that there is an inexhaustible supply in the invisible realm, which awaits our call upon it, and that its manifestation is dependent only on our understanding of what we are to do to bring it into manifestation.

4. *Everyone who asks receives.* This is the law of Divine receiving. Asking is desiring, and desire unfailingly draws to us what we persist in desiring. Under this law there is no such thing as failure.

5. *will give him a stone?* Unless what we ask for is truly the desire of our heart and our asking is backed up by faith, we "ask amiss" and receive accordingly. The outcome of our prayer is an index to our true desire.

## The Golden Rule

[7:12] Therefore whatever you desire for men to do to you, you shall also do to them;[1] for this is the law and the prophets.

> 1. *You shall also do to them.* Cause and effect underlie the Golden Rule insofar as others, in their dealings with us, naturally take their cue from our conduct toward them. Therefore we should act toward them as we would have them act toward us.

## The Narrow Gate of Truth

7:13 "Enter in by the narrow gate;[1] for wide is the gate and broad is the way that leads to destruction, and many are those who enter in by it. 7:14 How[40] narrow is the gate, and restricted is the way that leads to life! Few are those who find it.

> 1. *the narrow gate.* the habit of thinking and speaking daily what is in harmony with Truth and of denying error at all times. The broad gate is the habit of accepting both good and evil as real.

## The Fruit of True Ideas[1]

7:15 "Beware of false prophets,[2] who come to you in sheep's clothing, but inwardly are ravening wolves. 7:16 By their fruits you will know them. Do you gather grapes from thorns, or figs from thistles? 7:17 Even so, every good tree produces good fruit; but the corrupt tree produces evil fruit.[3] 7:18 A good tree can't produce evil fruit, neither can a corrupt tree produce good fruit. 7:19 Every tree that doesn't grow good fruit is cut down, and thrown into the fire.[4] 7:20 Therefore, by their fruits you will know them.

> 1. See Luke 6:43-44
>
> 2. *false prophets.* the deceptive thoughts that have been built up by erroneous desires. Outwardly they seem harmless, they present the appearance of being candid and open; inwardly they are ravenously thirsty for personal sensation and worldly gain.
>
> 3. *but the corrupt tree produces evil fruit.* Fruit is the fruition of ideas. An idea rooted in Truth brings forth love, joy, peace, plenty, and success; an adverse thought or one that is not rooted in Truth brings forth hatred, disappointment, lack, and bitterness.
>
> 4. *cut down, and thrown into the fire.* Changing a thought we perceive through spiritual discernment to be evil.

## Keep a Clear Consciousness[1]

7:21 Not everyone who says to me, 'Lord, Lord,' will enter into the Kingdom of Heaven; but he who does the will of my Father[2] who is in heaven. 7:22 Many will tell me in that day, 'Lord, Lord, didn't we prophesy in your name, in your name cast out demons, and in your name do many mighty works?'[3] 7:23 Then I will tell them, 'I never knew you. Depart from me, you who work iniquity.'[4]

> 1. See Luke 6:46; Luke 13:25-27
>
> 2. *but he who does the will of My Father.* Obedience is action based upon law. We may know that we are obedient to the Divine law by our feeling of oneness with God; by the trend of our thought Godward; by our willingness that God's will be done in us; by the soul's unfoldment; and by the body's showing forth the strength and purity of spiritual life and substance.
>
> 3. *in Your name do many mighty works.*

We may have understanding of the law of thought and through faith in the spoken word of Truth teach and heal in the name of the Lord, *yet fail to do the will of the Father in our own life*. This keeps us from entering the kingdom of heaven.

4. *you who work iniquity*. We may discern what will be the outcome of the error thoughts and actions of others and we may call their attention to it by prophesy. But to predict unwanted outcome by means of prophecy, declaring that unwanted outcome must come to pass, is to work iniquity.

## We Must Live The Truth That We Know[1]

7:24 "Everyone therefore who hears these words of mine, and does them, I will liken him to a wise man, who built his house on a rock.[2] 7:25 The rain came down, the floods came, and the winds blew, and beat on that house; and it didn't fall, for it was founded on the rock. 7:26 Everyone who hears these words of mine, and doesn't do them will be like a foolish man,[3] who built his house on the sand. 7:27 The rain came down, the floods came, and the winds blew, and beat on that house; and it fell--and great was its fall."

7:28 It happened, when Jesus had finished saying these things, that the multitudes were astonished at his teaching, 7:29 for he taught them with authority,[4] and not like the scribes.

1. See Luke 6:47-49. 5th Unity Principle: *Knowing and understanding the laws of life—also called truth—is not enough. A person must live the truth that he or she knows.*

2. *house on a rock*. A life that is founded upon Principle, which nothing can shake or remove from its solid basis of right and truth. The house built upon the sand is a superficial life that is without a sound spiritual foundation. Our responsibility is to learn the truth concerning what needs to be done and to follow up our knowledge by doing our part in accordance with the direction and instruction that we receive through the Christ.

3. *a foolish man*. A state of weakened faith when our will is functioning improperly. If we are to reveal ourselves as children of God we need the courage of our convictions and the will to do what we say we intend to do.

4. *for he taught them with authority*. Inspired by Spirit within. The Spirit of truth is the one and only authority in the study of Truth. See John 16:13 (RW/authority)

---

Fillmore Study Bible annotations by Mary Salama.

**World English Bible Footnotes:**

[40] v7:14. TR reads "Because" instead of "How"

# Matthew 8

## Leprosy Is Cleansed[1]

8:1 When he came down from the mountain, great multitudes followed him. 8:2 Behold, a leper[2] came to him and worshiped him, saying, "Lord, if you want to, you can make me clean."

8:3 Jesus stretched out his hand, and touched him, saying, "I want to. Be made clean." Immediately his leprosy was cleansed. 8:4 Jesus said to him, "See that you tell nobody, but go, show yourself to the priest, and offer the gift that Moses commanded,[3] as a testimony to them."

1. See Mark 1:40-44; Luke 5:12-14

2. *leper.* Leprosy here symbolizes substance so separated from the great central life Source that it has lost its vitality (stands afar off). This is caused by the impure relation of life activities in one who has by his error thoughts about life separated his life expressions from the one Source of life (MBD/lepers)

3. *the gift that Moses commanded.* Moses represents man's development in consciousness of the law of his being, from the negative side. Out of seemingly negative conditions comes the gift of new growth.

## The Centurion's Servant Is Healed[1]

8:5 When he came into Capernaum, a centurion came to him, asking him, 8:6 and saying, "Lord, my servant lies in the house paralyzed,[2] grievously tormented."

8:7 Jesus said to him, "I will come and heal him."

8:8 The centurion answered, "Lord, I'm not worthy for you to come under my roof. Just say the word, and my servant will be healed. 8:9 For I am also a man under authority, having under myself soldiers. I tell this one, 'Go,' and he goes; and tell another, 'Come,' and he comes; and tell my servant, 'Do this,' and he does it."

8:10 When Jesus heard it, he marveled, and said to those who followed, "Most certainly I tell you, I haven't found so great a faith, not even in Israel. 8:11 I tell you that many will come from the east and the west, and will sit down with Abraham, Isaac, and Jacob in the Kingdom of Heaven, 8:12 but the children of the Kingdom will be thrown out into the outer darkness. There will be weeping and gnashing of teeth." 8:13 Jesus said to the centurion, "Go your way. Let it be done for you as you have believed."[3] His servant was healed in that hour.

1. See Luke 7:1-10; Luke 13:28-29; John 4:46-54

2. *my servant lies in the house paralyzed.* Metaphysically interpreted, this passage is about the will (the centurion) and the body (the centurian's servant). The will must become amenable to the discipline of the higher self before the body can express the health that is its heritage under Divine law.

3. *Let it be done for you as you have believed.* Less metaphysically interpreted, this message is about spiritual healing. By speaking the word of Truth aloud or silently to the one who is in need of healing, and by knowing without doubt that the heal-

ing is now accomplished because the word of Truth is quick and powerful. Firm faith must be present in the mind of the one who speaks the word, and also in the mind of the one to be healed or in someone who is close to him.

## Jesus Heals at Peter's House[1]

8:14 When Jesus came into Peter's
house,[2] he saw his wife's mother
lying sick with a fever. 8:15 He
touched her hand,[3] and the fever
left her. She got up and served
him.[41] 8:16 When evening came, they
brought to him many possessed with
demons.[4] He cast out the spirits
with a word, and healed all who were
sick; 8:17 that it might be fulfilled
which was spoken through Isaiah the
prophet, saying: "He took our
infirmities, and bore our
diseases."[42]

1. See Mark 1:29-34; Luke 4:38-41

2. *Peter's house.* The leading characteristic of Peter (faith) before he is firmly established in spiritual consciousness is changeableness. He typifies that state of unsteadiness which fluctuates from the high spiritual to the material, yet with an ever recurring desire for Spirit and for the things of Spirit, which is bound to lead into the light. (MBD/Peter). Peter's house will show up again in Acts 11:11.

3. *He touched her hand, and the fever left her.* The I AM (here represented by Jesus) brings immediate healing to the one who is receptive to its power.

4. *They brought to Him many possessed with demons.* Demons, or evil spirits, are conditions of mind, or states of consciousness, that have been developed because one is using their creative power in an ignorant way, and thus bringing forth an ego or a personality of like character. The mind builds states of consciousness that become established in brain and body. In the new birth, the work of every overcomer is to cast out of himself the demons of sin and evil. We are empowered by the name of Jesus Christ to "cast out demons" (MBD/demons)

## Multitudes Follow Jesus[1]

8:18 Now when Jesus saw great
multitudes[2] around him, he gave the
order to depart to the other side.

8:19 A scribe came, and said to him,
"Teacher, I will follow you wherever
you go."

8:20 Jesus said to him, "The foxes
have holes, and the birds of the sky
have nests, but the Son of Man has
nowhere to lay his head."

8:21 Another of his disciples said to
him, "Lord, allow me first to go and
bury my father."

8:22 But Jesus said to him, "Follow
me, and leave the dead to bury their
own dead."[3]

1. See Mark 4:35; Luke 9:57-60

2. *multitudes.* Our own hungry thoughts; they want an influx of the truths of Spirit into our consciousness (MBD/multitude)

3. *Leave the dead to bury their own dead.* The dead are those who are unconscious of Truth.

## Jesus Stills the Wind and the Sea[1]

8:23 When he got into a boat,[2] his disciples followed him. 8:24 Behold, a violent storm came up on the sea, so much that the boat was covered with the waves, but he was asleep. 8:25 They came to him, and woke him up, saying, "Save us, Lord! We are dying!"

8:26 He said to them, "Why are you fearful, O you of little faith?"[3] Then he got up, rebuked the wind and the sea,[4] and there was a great calm.

8:27 The men marveled, saying, "What kind of man is this, that even the wind and the sea obey him?"

1. See Mark 4:35-41; Luke 8:22-25

2. *When He got into a boat.* The boat represents a positive thought. It is capable of floating on the water (the unstable mind). However when the subconsciousness is stirred by confusion and turmoil (violent storm) the positive thought is in danger of being engulfed.

3. *O you of little faith.* The I AM often expects more of its thought forces than they can accomplish. Jesus, in subsequent lessons, took his disciples or faculties aside and instructed them privately. Followers of Jesus find that the faculties are likely to be disconcerted over mental storms. To overcome this tendency, the faculties must be given special lessons with the attention directed upon the brain and nerve centers through which they function.

4. *rebuked the wind and the sea.* If we understand the truth that man has authority over all his emotions, we too, like Jesus, can rebuke the wind and sea of turbulent thoughts and emotions. The result is peace and harmony reign in mind and in body ... and there was a great calm.

## Jesus Heals the Two Men Possessed by Demons[1]

8:28 When he came to the other side, into the country of the Gergesenes,[43] two people possessed by demons[2] met him there, coming out of the tombs, exceedingly fierce, so that nobody could pass that way. 8:29 Behold, they cried out, saying, "What do we have to do with you, Jesus, Son of God? Have you come here to torment us before the time?" 8:30 Now there was a herd of many pigs feeding far away from them. 8:31 The demons begged him, saying, "If you cast us out, permit us to go away[3] into the herd of pigs."

8:32 He said to them, "Go!"

They came out,[4] and went into the herd of pigs: and behold, the whole herd of pigs rushed down the cliff into the sea, and died in the water. 8:33 Those who fed them fled, and went away into the city, and told everything, including what happened to those who were possessed with demons. 8:34 Behold, all the city came out to meet Jesus. When they saw him, they begged that he would depart from their borders.

1. See Mark 5:1-17; Luke 8:26-37

2. *Two people possessed by demons.* The negative traits of human nature which then assume personalities by suppressing negative emotions and thinking, which when suppressed become unconscious roles that can tear a person apart emotionally. (Ed Rabel *New Testament Bible Lectures*)

3. *Permit us to go away.* The accumulated negativity of the personality resists going back to formless substance and in panic seeks to enter the first vulnerable state of consciousness it can enter (Rabel)

4. *They came out.* Negative traits of human nature are recognized for what they are and we return in consciousness to an awareness of our true self, the unified Christ self, not the Legion of false personalities. (Rabel)

Fillmore Study Bible annotations by Mary Salama.

**World English Bible Footnotes:**

[41] v8:15. TR reads "them" instead of "him"

[42] v8:17. Isaiah 53:4

[43] v8:28. NU reads "Gadarenes"

# Matthew 9

## Jesus Heals a Paralyzed Will[1]

9:1 He entered into a boat, and crossed over, and came into his own city. 9:2 Behold, they brought to him a man who was paralyzed,[2] lying on a bed. Jesus, seeing their faith, said to the paralytic, "Son, cheer up! Your sins are forgiven you."

9:3 Behold, some of the scribes said to themselves, "This man blasphemes."[3]

9:4 Jesus, knowing their thoughts, said, "Why do you think evil in your hearts? 9:5 For which is easier, to say, 'Your sins are forgiven;'[4] or to say, 'Get up, and walk?' 9:6 But that you may know that the Son of Man has authority on earth to forgive sins..."[5] (then he said to the paralytic), "Get up, and take up your mat, and go up to your house."

9:7 He arose and departed to his house. 9:8 But when the multitudes saw it, they marveled and glorified God, who had given such authority to men.

1. See Mark 2:1-12; Luke 5:17-26

2. *paralyzed.* Because sickness is the effect of sin, healing cannot take place until the self-accusation of failure is forgiven and a fresh start made to receive and express the Truth. We who are paralyzed, who wish to be healed, must relax mind and body from the tensions of self-condemnation and despair that invade our mind in times of illness.

3. *This Man blasphemes.* The scribes here held that only God can forgive sin and did not perceive that forgiveness is God being expressed through man.

4. *Your sins are forgiven.* When we sin, we sin against ourselves, not against God. Sin means "missing the mark," the perfection of God being the mark. Since God is perfect Being, he cannot be offended.

5. *authority on earth to forgive sins.* The fact that the person whom we forgive is released from all consciousness of condemnation and is left free to realize the healing flow of the life energies within him is proof of our authority to forgive.

## Calling Forth the Will[1]

9:9 As Jesus passed by from there, he saw a man called Matthew[2] sitting at the tax collection office. He said to him, "Follow me." He got up and followed him. 9:10 It happened as he sat in the house, behold, many

tax collectors and sinners came and
sat down with Jesus and his disciples.
9:11 When the Pharisees③ saw it, they
said to his disciples, "Why does your
teacher eat with tax collectors and
sinners?"

9:12 When Jesus heard it, he said to
them, "Those who are healthy have
no need for a physician, but those
who are sick do. 9:13 But you go and
learn what this means: 'I desire
mercy, and not sacrifice,'[44] for I
came not to call the righteous, but
sinners to repentance.④[45]"

1. See Mark 2:14; Luke 5:27

2. *Matthew*. Metaphysically, the will, which plays a part in all forgiveness and in all healing. Matthew got up and followed Jesus because those who perceive their divinity will endeavor to call it forth into full expression.

3. *Pharisees*. Metaphysically, the formalized religious thoughts, which seek to interfere directly or indirectly with the word of Truth in ministering to those who are not yet spiritually illumined.

4. *I came not to call the righteous, but sinners to repentance*. Jesus does not call the self-righteous Pharisees but rather the will which follows after the conviction of power to rise.

## Fasting and Appropriating Spiritual Substance①

9:14 Then John's disciples came to
him, saying, "Why do we and the
Pharisees fast often, but your
disciples don't fast?"

9:15 Jesus said to them, "Can the
friends of the bridegroom mourn, as
long as the bridegroom is with
them?② But the days will come when
the bridegroom will be taken away
from them, and then they will fast.
9:16 No one puts a piece of unshrunk
cloth on an old garment; for the
patch would tear away from the
garment, and a worse hole is made.
9:17 Neither do people put new wine
into old wineskins,③ or else the skins
would burst, and the wine be spilled,
and the skins ruined. No, they put
new wine into fresh wineskins, and
both are preserved."

1. See Mark 2:18-22; Luke 5:33-39

2. *as long as the bridegroom is with them?* We do not fast from spiritual life and substance, which are appropriated when we have conscious union with our Christ nature.

3. *new wine into fresh wineskins*. This scripture teaches us the necessity of cleansing, harmonizing, and renewing our body temples (wine-skins) by knowing the truth of their infinite nature, that they may be able to contain the constant inflow of new spiritual life and power (the new wine) which is the experience of those who continue in truth. Our body temples must be renewed by our speaking to them words of Truth, that they may be made able to receive and hold the abundant, resurrecting Christ life. We do not overcome our errors by covering them in our consciousness and refusing to recognize them in any way. A right adjustment is made by uncovering them, by correcting them through exercise of the forgiving love of the Christ mind and by feasting upon words of Truth. (*Jesus' Soul Evolution* p.245)

## Two Methods of Spiritual Healing①

9:18 While he told these things to
them, behold, a ruler came and
worshiped him, saying, "My daughter
has just died, but come and lay your
hand on her, and she will live."

9:19 Jesus got up and followed him,
as did his disciples. 9:20 Behold, a
woman who had an issue of blood
for twelve years came behind him,
and touched the fringe[46] of his
garment; 9:21 for she said within

herself, "If I just touch his garment,[2] I will be made well."

9:22 But Jesus, turning around and seeing her, said, "Daughter, cheer up! Your faith has made you well." And the woman was made well from that hour.

9:23 When Jesus came into the ruler's house, and saw the flute players, and the crowd in noisy disorder, 9:24 he said to them, "Make room, because the girl isn't dead, but sleeping."[3] They were ridiculing him. 9:25 But when the crowd was put out, he entered in, took her by the hand, and the girl arose. 9:26 The report of this went out into all that land.

1. See Mark 5:21-43; Luke 8:40-56
2. *If I just touch his garment.* The woman who had been ill so many years touched the hem of Jesus' garment and was healed. Her faith was in the personality—she wanted to touch the healer. The same attitude is found among a class who this day want the healer to lay hands on them. A vitalizing virtue can be transferred from healer to patient, but it is not the highest form of healing and should be employed only in very rare cases. Jesus did not voluntarily use this method—the woman crept up behind Him and surreptitiously tapped the great aura of vitality that surrounded Him. (*Jesus' Soul Evolution* p.530-1)
3. *the girl isn't dead, but sleeping.* The bringing to life of Jairus's daughter was in line with the methods used by modern healers. Jesus said, "the damsel is not dead but sleepeth." The crowd laughed Him to scorn. Then admitting to the room only Peter, James, John, and the parents of the child, He reaffirmed the truth that the little girl was not dead but asleep. Taking her by the hand Jesus commanded her to arise, and her spirit returned and she arose immediately. (*Jesus' Soul Evolution* p.531-2)

## Two Men Believe in Jesus' Ability To Heal[1]

9:27 As Jesus passed by from there, two blind men followed him, calling out and saying, "Have mercy on us, son of David!" 9:28 When he had come into the house, the blind men came to him. Jesus said to them, "Do you believe that I am able to do this?"[2]

They told him, "Yes, Lord."

9:29 Then he touched their eyes, saying, "According to your faith be it done to you." 9:30 Their eyes were opened. Jesus strictly commanded them, saying, "See that no one knows about this." 9:31 But they went out and spread abroad his fame in all that land.

1. See Mark 10:46-52; Luke 18:35-43
2. *Do you believe that I am able to do this?* Jesus laid great store by faith. When the two blind men asked him for healing, he said, "Believe ye that I am able to do this?" Healers of every kind find that faith is necessary to success. (*Jesus' Soul Evolution* p.535)

## When the demon is cast out, the mute person speaks.[1]

9:32 As they went out, behold, a mute man who was demon possessed was brought to him. 9:33 When the demon was cast out, the mute man spoke.[2] The multitudes marveled, saying, "Nothing like this has ever been seen in Israel!"

9:34 But the Pharisees said, "By the prince of the demons, he casts out demons."

1. See Mark 3:22; Luke 11:14-15

2. *When the demon was cast out, the mute man spoke.* The casting of the devil out of the dumb man was considered the greatest of marvelous works. The man was not only dumb but possessed with a devil also. Jesus recognized all false conditions in the body as primarily false states of mind. He commanded them to "come out," and they obeyed. This method is being applied in many ways by healers in this day, and those, who scoffed and called these methods superstition are now acceptlng and using them because of their efficiency. (*Jesus' Soul Evolution* p.535-6)

## The Harvest of Thoughts Is Great, the Laborers Few[1]

9:35 Jesus went about all the cities
and the villages, teaching in their
synagogues, and preaching the Good
News of the Kingdom, and healing
every disease and every sickness
among the people. 9:36 But when he
saw the multitudes, he was moved
with compassion for them, because
they were harassed[47] and
scattered, like sheep without a
shepherd.[2] 9:37 Then he said to his
disciples, "The harvest indeed is
plentiful, but the laborers are few.
9:38 Pray therefore that the Lord of
the harvest will send out laborers
into his harvest."

1. See Mark 6:6b,34; Luke 8:1; Luke 10:2;John 4:35

2. *like sheep without a shepherd.* To know himself, man must open up the undiscovered country within himself. He must first appreciate the largeness of his God-given identity—the IAM. This step in spiritual evolution is represented by Jesus' going about through all the cities and villages, teaching, preaching, and helping. These movements of Jesus represent the I AM in its universal capacity as a teacher and harmonizer of its own mental and bodily conditions. But there is yet no organized harmony—the people (thoughts) "were scattered, as sheep not having a shepherd." The I AM must have agents to instruct the great throng of thoughts that surge about the consciousness—that is, the faculties of the mind must be spiritually disciplined and their right relations established, so that it will not be necessary for one's special attention to be directed toward faculties in order to have them in spiritual ways. They must be educated, and then they will do the Master's will obediently, whether he is consciously present or not. (*Jesus' Soul Evolution* p.538-9)

---

Fillmore Study Bible annotations by Mary Salama.

**World English Bible Footnotes:**

[44] v9:13. Hosea 6:6

[45] v9:13. NU omits "to repentance".

[46] v9:20. or, tassel

[47] v9:36. TR reads "weary" instead of "harassed"

# Matthew 10

## The Twelve Powers[1]

10:1 He called to himself his twelve disciples,[2] and gave them authority over unclean spirits, to cast them out, and to heal every disease and every sickness. 10:2 Now the names of the twelve apostles[3] are these. The first, Simon, who is called Peter; Andrew, his brother; James the son of Zebedee; John, his brother; 10:3 Philip; Bartholomew; Thomas; Matthew the tax collector; James the son of Alphaeus; Lebbaeus, whose surname was[48] Thaddaeus; 10:4 Simon the Canaanite; and Judas Iscariot, who also betrayed him.

1. See Mark 6:7; Mark 3:16-19; Luke 9:1; Luke 6:13-16

2. *He called to Himself His twelve disciples.* To call a disciple (or apostle) is mentally to recognize that disciple; it is to identify oneself with the intelligence working at a center: for example, judgment at the solar plexus.

3. *The names of the twelve apostles.* Jesus' twelve apostles are: Peter (faith); Andrew (strength); James, son of Zebedee (wisdom or judgment); John (love); Philip (power); Bartholomew (imagination); Thomas (understanding); Matthew (will); James (order); Simon the Cananaean (zeal); Thaddaeus (renunciation or elimination); and Judas (life conserver).

## The Mission of the Twelve Powers[1]

10:5 Jesus sent these twelve out, and commanded them, saying, "Don't go among the Gentiles, and don't enter into any city of the Samaritans.[2] 10:6 Rather, go to the lost sheep of the house of Israel.[3] 10:7 As you go, preach, saying, 'The Kingdom of Heaven is at hand!'[4] 10:8 Heal the sick, cleanse the lepers[49], and cast out demons. Freely you received, so freely give.[5] 10:9 Don't take any gold, nor silver, nor brass in your money belts. 10:10 Take no bag for your journey, neither two coats, nor shoes, nor staff: for the laborer is worthy of his food. 10:11 Into whatever city or village you enter, find out who in it is worthy; and stay there until you go on. 10:12 As you enter into the household, greet it. 10:13 If the household is worthy, let your peace come on it, but if it isn't worthy, let your peace return to you. 10:14 Whoever doesn't receive you, nor hear your words, as you go out of that house or that city, shake off the dust from your feet.[6] 10:15 Most certainly I tell you, it will be more tolerable for the land of Sodom and Gomorrah in the day of judgment than for that city.

1. See Mark 6:8-11; Luke 9:2-5

2. *Don't go among the Gentiles, and don't enter into any city of the Samaritans.* Our faculties exist in their purity in Divine Mind as ideas, and they should not be contaminated or adulterated. We are not to limit the activity of our faculties to the thought centers (Gentiles) or mix Truth with error (Samaritans).

3. *the lost sheep of the house of Israel.* Metaphysically, innate spiritual principles that we have lost contact with in the confusion of the material or sense life. When we begin the work of spiritualizing the mind, we redeem these principles (Israelites) by proclaiming the law in even the Egyptian darkness of materiality.

4. *The kingdom of heaven is at hand.* The inner spiritual reality, the Divine realm of perfection. It is always right at hand awaiting our recognition.

5. *Freely you received, so freely give.* We

must place our entire faith in Spirit; the living Word within us can and does demonstrate our every need, both physically and spiritually.

6. *shake off the dust from your feet.* When the I AM enters various states of consciousness, its work is to search out that which is worthy and establish spiritual supremacy therein, but if error is discovered which refuses to see the light, it should be left to its own destruction.

## Equanimity In Face of Persecution[1]

10:16 "Behold, I send you out as sheep in the midst of wolves.[2] Therefore be wise as serpents, and harmless as doves.[3] 10:17 But beware of men:[4] for they will deliver you up to councils, and in their synagogues they will scourge you. 10:18 Yes, and you will be brought before governors and kings for my sake, for a testimony to them and to the nations. 10:19 But when they deliver you up, don't be anxious how or what you will say, for it will be given you in that hour what you will say. 10:20 For it is not you who speak, but the Spirit of your Father who speaks in you.[5]

10:21 "Brother will deliver up brother to death, and the father his child. Children will rise up against parents, and cause them to be put to death. 10:22 You will be hated by all men for my name's sake, but he who endures to the end will be saved. 10:23 But when they persecute you in this city, flee into the next, for most certainly I tell you, you will not have gone through the cities of Israel, until the Son of Man has come.

10:24 "A disciple is not above his teacher, nor a servant above his lord.[6] 10:25 It is enough for the disciple that he be like his teacher, and the servant like his lord. If they have called the master of the house Beelzebul,[7] how much more those of his household!

1. See Mark 13:9-13; Luke 12:11-12; Luke 6:40; Luke 21:12-19

2. *as sheep in the midst of wolves.* Going forth in the consciousness of purity, innocence, guilelessness, and Divine obedience.

3. *Be wise as serpents, and harmless as doves.* Truth does not fight against opposing forces or endeavor to justify itself; it remains serene in the face of all circumstances, for it has all eternity in which to accomplish its purpose.

4. *But beware of men.* Spiritually unillumined thoughts that oppose Truth, and seek to negate or discredit it.

5. *The Spirit of your Father who speaks in you.* How God speaks to us today: in prayer we take with us a Word of Truth, go into the silence, contact God-Mind, then realize that Word of Truth until God-Mind satisfies the logic of our soul.

6. *A disciple is not above his teacher, nor a servant above his lord.* The Spirit of God is always greater than the disciples. We must let the Christ reveal one step at a time in order to go forward.

7. *Beelzebub.* The adverse belief that we have built up because of our mistaken idea that we are separate from God, a belief that gives rise to multitudes of thoughts in opposition to Truth.

## Keep Our Attention On Spirit[1]

10:26 Therefore don't be afraid of them, for there is nothing covered that will not be revealed;[2] and hidden that will not be known. 10:27 What I tell you in the darkness, speak in the light; and what you hear whispered in the ear, proclaim on the housetops. 10:28 Don't be afraid of those who kill the body, but are not able to kill the soul. Rather, fear him who is able to destroy both soul and body[3] in Gehenna.[50]

10:29 "Aren't two sparrows sold for an assarion coin[51]? Not one of them falls on the ground apart from your Father's will, 10:30 but the very hairs of your head are all numbered. 10:31 Therefore don't be afraid. You are of more value than many sparrows. 10:32 Everyone therefore who confesses me before men, him I will also confess before my Father[4] who is in heaven. 10:33 But whoever denies me before men, him I will also deny before my Father who is in heaven.

1. See Mark 4:22; Luke 12:2-9; Luke 8:17

2. *There is nothing covered that will not be revealed.* God Mind is everywhere present and God Mind is Divine intelligence, therefore, it is impossible to conceal anything from Spirit. (*Jesus' Soul Evolution* 540-559)

3. *Fear Him who is able to destroy both soul and body.* It is possible for our soul to get so material, so wrapped up in worldly affairs, that it entirely crowds out the spiritual.

4. *Everyone therefore who confesses Me before men, him I will also confess before My Father.* When we acknowledge our spiritual nature to ourselves and at the start of any activity we undertake, we open the way for that nature to receive in larger measure from the Father-our spiritual Source.

## Spiritual Relationships Superior to Human Relationships[1]

10:34 "Don't think that I came to send peace on the earth. I didn't come to send peace, but a sword.[2] 10:35 For I came to set a man at odds against his father, and a daughter against her mother, and a daughter-in-law against her mother-in-law. 10:36 A man's foes will be those of his own household.[52] 10:37 He who loves father or mother more than me is not worthy of me; and he who loves son or daughter more than me isn't worthy of me. 10:38 He who doesn't take his cross and follow after me, isn't worthy of me. 10:39 He who seeks his life will lose it; and he who loses his life for my sake will find it.

1. See Mark 8:34-35; Luke 12:51-53

2. *I didn't come to send peace, but a sword.* The human form of life is a stepping stone to the spiritual. The Spiritual man is not subject to the discord of human relationships; the one and only enduring relationship is among those who are related spiritually. (*Jesus' Soul Evolution* 540-559)

## Rewards of Living By Principle[1]

10:40 He who receives you receives me, and he who receives me receives him who sent me. 10:41 He who receives a prophet in the name of a prophet will receive a prophet's reward: and he who receives a righteous man in the name of a righteous man will receive a righteous man's reward. 10:42 Whoever gives one of these little ones just a cup of cold water to drink in the name of a disciple, most certainly I tell you he will in no way lose his reward."[2]

1. See Mark 9:37,41; Luke 10:16; John 12:44; John 13:20

2. *He will in no way lose his reward.* To follow Christ means to follow Principle. If we work from Principle, we are bound to win out. If we lose our life in service to others to the extent of forgetting our-

selves, we shall find the life everlasting.

Fillmore Study Bible annotations by Mary Salama.

**World English Bible Footnotes:**

[48] v10:3. NU omits "Lebbaeus, whose surname was"

[49] v10:8. TR adds ", raise the dead"

[50] v10:28. or, Hell.

[51] v10:29. An assarion is a small coin worth one tenth of a drachma or a sixteenth of a denarius (approximately the wages of one half hour of agricultural labor).

[52] v10:36. Micah 7:6

# Matthew 11

## The Imprisoned Intellect Questions Jesus(1)

11:1 It happened that when Jesus
had finished directing his twelve
disciples, he departed from there to
teach and preach in their cities. 11:2
Now when John(2) heard in the prison
the works of Christ, he sent two of
his disciples 11:3 and said to him, "Are
you he who comes, or should we look
for another?"

11:4 Jesus answered them, "Go and
tell John the things which you hear
and see: 11:5 the blind receive their
sight, the lame walk, the lepers are
cleansed, the deaf hear,[53] the dead
are raised up, and the poor have
good news preached to them.[54] 11:6
Blessed is he who finds no occasion
for stumbling in me."(3)

1. See Luke 7:18-23

2. *John*. Metaphysically, the forerunner of Jesus Christ. John signifies a high intellectual perception of Truth, but one not yet quickened of Spirit. He represents that attitude of mind in which we are zealous for the rule of Spirit. This attitude is not spiritual, but a perception of spiritual possibilities and an activity in making conditions in which Spirit may rule. This John-the-Baptist perception of Truth leads us to quarrel with evil as a reality, not having discerned the truth about its transitory character. Eventually, quarreling imprisons the intellect.

3. *no occasion for stumbling in Me*. In contrast to the intellect, the Christ does not quarrel with sin and evil in its many forms but rather asserts absolute spiritual dominion and heals these "plagues and evil spirits." The intellect, John, does not understand and when it sends out thoughts of doubt as to the identity of the miracle-worker, the reply of Christ is to behold the results.

## Jesus Praises the Intellect[1]

11:7 As these went their way, Jesus began to say to the multitudes concerning John, "What did you go out into the wilderness to see? A reed shaken by the wind? 11:8 But what did you go out to see? A man in soft clothing? Behold, those who wear soft clothing are in king's houses. 11:9 But why did you go out? To see a prophet? Yes, I tell you, and much more than a prophet. 11:10 For this is he, of whom it is written, 'Behold, I send my messenger before your face, who will prepare your way before you.'[55] 11:11 Most certainly I tell you, among those who are born of women there has not arisen anyone greater than John the Baptizer;[2] yet he who is least in the Kingdom of Heaven is greater than he.[3] 11:12 From the days of John the Baptizer until now, the Kingdom of Heaven suffers violence, and the violent take it by force.[56] 11:13 For all the prophets and the law prophesied until John. 11:14 If you are willing to receive it, this is Elijah, who is to come.[4] 11:15 He who has ears to hear, let him hear.

11:16 "But to what shall I compare this generation? It is like children sitting in the marketplaces, who call to their companions 11:17 and say, 'We played the flute for you, and you didn't dance. We mourned for you, and you didn't lament.' 11:18 For John came neither eating nor drinking, and they say, 'He has a demon.' 11:19 The Son of Man came eating and drinking, and they say, 'Behold, a gluttonous man and a drunkard, a friend of tax collectors and sinners!' But wisdom is justified by her children.[57]"

1. See Luke 7:24-35; Luke 16:16

2. *has not arisen anyone greater than John the Baptizer.* Jesus reveals that John the Baptist was the herald making straight the way of the Lord.

3. *is greater than he.* The least of our spiritual thoughts is greater than the mightiest reasoning of our intellect. Our intellectual concepts of things must give way to the understanding that comes from the Holy Spirit.

4. *this is Elijah, who is to come.* Elijah championed the cause of God with such enthusiasm that he became violent and destructive. This was the general state of religious affairs until the coming of the Christ.

## Woes To Self-Righteousness and False Sympathy[1]

11:20 Then he began to denounce the cities in which most of his mighty works had been done, because they didn't repent. 11:21 "Woe to you, Chorazin! Woe to you, Bethsaida! For if the mighty works had been done in Tyre and Sidon[2] which were done in you, they would have repented long ago in sackcloth and ashes. 11:22 But I tell you, it will be more tolerable for Tyre and Sidon on the day of judgment than for you. 11:23 You, Capernaum, who are exalted to heaven,[3] you will go down to Hades.[58] For if the mighty works had been done in Sodom which were done in you, it would have remained until this day. 11:24 But I tell you that it will be more tolerable for the land of Sodom, on the day of judgment, than for you."

1. See Luke 10:13-15

2. *Chorazin, Bethsaida, Tyre, Sidon.* Metaphysically, cities are symbols of fixed states of consciousness. Chorazin and Bethsaida are the self-righteous phase of consciousness, fixed in their ideas of what is religiously proper. Tyre and Sidon are openly wicked and stand a better chance before the law of adjustment because they

will admit their errors and repent. (*Jesus' Soul Evolution* 420-1)

3. *Capernaum, who are exalted to heaven.* Metaphysically, Capernaum is exalted unto heaven for its Christian sympathy but eventually brought down to hell (nothingness) because it mourns over the dead and joins with those who grieve. In Truth, human or false sympathy is a negative quality and as such is brought down when the works of Truth cast out the demons of sickness and raise the dead.

## Rest For the Weary Mind[1]

11:25 At that time, Jesus answered,
"I thank you, Father, Lord of heaven
and earth, that you hid these things
from the wise and understanding,
and revealed them to infants.[2] 11:26
Yes, Father, for so it was well-
pleasing in your sight. 11:27 All things
have been delivered to me by my
Father.[3] No one knows the Son,
except the Father; neither does
anyone know the Father, except the
Son,[4] and he to whom the Son
desires to reveal him.

11:28 "Come to me, all you who
labor and are heavily burdened, and I
will give you rest.[5] 11:29 Take my yoke
upon you,[6] and learn from me,[7] for
I am gentle and lowly in heart; and
you will find rest for your souls. 11:30
For my yoke is easy, and my burden
is light."[8]

1. See Luke 10:21-22

2. *revealed them to the infants.* Laws of Mind and Spirit are not made plain to the intellectually wise because such individuals would use them to further their personal ambitions.

3. *All things have been delivered to Me by My Father.* Understanding of all Truth is given to the Christ Mind by the Father.

4. *Neither does anyone know the Father, except the Son.* There can be no intermediary between God and humanity. In the absolute, or most intimate sense, God and humanity are one.

5. *I will give you rest.* We who strive to sustain the demands of the worldly standard are bidden to come to this meek and lowly Christ within and find rest.

6. *take My yoke upon you.* A yoke is a device for uniting two workers so that their combined strength may be applied to the same load.

7. *Learn from Me.* Let Divine intelligence and power flow through us.

8. *For my yoke is easy, and my burden is light.* Metaphysically, the yoke is the union with Christ, or with the high ideals of Spirit; the burden is taking on a right degree of responsibility: "For each one shall bear his or her own burden," meaning our own proper load. Service then becomes spiritual. (MBD/ulla)

---

Fillmore Study Bible annotations by Mary Salama.

**World English Bible Footnotes:**

[53] v11:5. Isaiah 35:5

[54] v11:5. Isaiah 61:1-4

[55] v11:10. Malachi 3:1

[56] v11:12. or, plunder it.

[57] v11:19. NU reads "actions" instead of "children"

[58] v11:23. or, Hell

# Matthew 12

## Sabbath Consciousness[1]

12:1 At that time, Jesus went on the Sabbath[2] day through the grain fields. His disciples were hungry and began to pluck heads of grain and to eat. 12:2 But the Pharisees, when they saw it, said to him, "Behold, your disciples do what is not lawful to do on the Sabbath."

12:3 But he said to them, "Haven't you read what David did, when he was hungry, and those who were with him; 12:4 how he entered into the house of God, and ate the show bread, which was not lawful for him to eat, neither for those who were with him, but only for the priests?[59] 12:5 Or have you not read in the law, that on the Sabbath day, the priests in the temple profane the Sabbath, and are guiltless? 12:6 But I tell you that one greater than the temple is here. 12:7 But if you had known what this means, 'I desire mercy, and not sacrifice,'[60] you would not have condemned the guiltless. 12:8 For the Son of Man is Lord of the Sabbath."[3]

1. See Mark 2:23-28; Luke 6:1-5

2. *Sabbath.* The consciousness that we have fulfilled the divine law in both thought and act; a state of mind that we enter or acquire when we go into the silence of our own soul, into the realm of Spirit. There we find true rest and peace. (MBD/sabbath)

3. *Lord of the Sabbath.* Divine Mind rests in a perpetual Sabbath and that which seems work is not work at all. When we become so at one with God-Mind as to feel it consciously we also recognize this eternal peace in which all things are accomplished. We then know that we are not subject to any condition whatsoever, but are "lord of the sabbath."

## The Withered Will[1]

12:9 He departed there, and went into their synagogue. 12:10 And behold there was a man with a withered hand.[2] They asked him, "Is it lawful to heal on the Sabbath day?" that they might accuse him.

12:11 He said to them, "What man is there among you, who has one sheep, and if this one falls into a pit on the Sabbath day, won't he grab on to it, and lift it out? 12:12 Of how much more value then is a man than a sheep! Therefore it is lawful to do good on the Sabbath day."[3] 12:13 Then he told the man, "Stretch out your hand." He stretched it out; and it was restored whole, just like the other. 12:14 But the Pharisees went out, and conspired against him, how they might destroy him.

1. See Mark 3:1-6; Luke 6:6-11

2. *withered hand.* The hand represents executive ability. By the power and understanding gained in the inner spiritual worship, we can free the mind from bondage to inefficiency. (*Jesus' Soul Evolution* 261)

3. *It is lawful to do good on the Sabbath.* Jesus observed the Sabbath but He claimed that it was a very grievous sin or error to allow the mind to be so blinded by manmade laws that it could not use reason and common sense logic. It is lawful to do good on the Sabbath, whether it consists in preaching in a pulpit, healing the sick, or in any other way saving men from ignorance and its results.

## Spiritual Man Does Not Fight[1]

12:15 Jesus, perceiving that,
withdrew from there.[2] Great
multitudes followed him; and he
healed them all, 12:16 and commanded
them that they should not make him
known: 12:17 that it might be fulfilled
which was spoken through Isaiah the
prophet, saying,

12:18 "Behold, my servant whom I have
chosen;
my beloved in whom my soul is
well pleased:
I will put my Spirit on him.
He will proclaim justice to the
nations.
12:19 He will not strive, nor shout;
neither will anyone hear his
voice in the streets.
12:20 He won't break a bruised reed.
He won't quench a smoking
flax,
until he leads justice to victory.
12:21 In his name, the nations will
hope."[61]

1. See Mark 3:7-12; Luke 6:7-19

2. *Jesus, perceiving that, withdrew from there.* Spiritual man does not fight, knowing that everything must be adjusted under Divine law. As for those who are prejudiced in their ideas, it is best to leave them to work out their own salvation. (*Jesus' Soul Evolution* 262)

## Don't Attribute Good Acts to Evil Causes[1]

12:22 Then one possessed by a
demon, blind and mute, was brought
to him and he healed him, so that
the blind and mute man both spoke
and saw. 12:23 All the multitudes were
amazed, and said, "Can this be the
son of David?" 12:24 But when the
Pharisees heard it, they said, "This
man does not cast out demons,
except by Beelzebul,[2] the prince of
the demons."

12:25 Knowing their thoughts, Jesus
said to them, "Every kingdom divided
against itself is brought to
desolation, and every city or house
divided against itself will not stand.
12:26 If Satan casts out Satan, he is
divided against himself. How then
will his kingdom stand? 12:27 If I by
Beelzebul cast out demons, by whom
do your children cast them out?
Therefore they will be your judges.
12:28 But if I by the Spirit of God cast
out demons, then the Kingdom of
God has come upon you.[3] 12:29 Or how
can one enter into the house of the
strong man, and plunder his goods,
unless he first bind the strong man?
Then he will plunder his house.

12:30 "He who is not with me is
against me, and he who doesn't
gather with me, scatters. 12:31
Therefore I tell you, every sin and
blasphemy will be forgiven men,[4]
but the blasphemy against the Spirit
will not be forgiven men. 12:32
Whoever speaks a word against the
Son of Man, it will be forgiven him;
but whoever speaks against the Holy
Spirit, it will not be forgiven him,
neither in this age, nor in that which
is to come.

1. See Mark 3:22-29; Luke 11:14-23; Luke 12:10

2. *except by Beelzebul, the prince of the demons.* Often when the Christ heals an error state of consciousness the Pharisaical thoughts within us refuse to see the words of the Christ, and begin quibbling and grumbling. They give credence to the "evil spirits," over which Beelzebul is supposed to rule.

3. *if I by the Spirit of God cast out demons, then the Kingdom of God has come upon you.* We should recognize and acknowledge the good wherever it is mani-

fest. If we see evil in good works it is proof that we have evil in our minds, and we cannot be wholly purified until we cast it out. Our work today is to spiritualize the external religious thought within us until they, too, are imbued with the Spirit of the Lord and behold the good and beautiful everywhere.

4. *the blasphemy against the Spirit will not be forgiven men.* The central idea in this scripture is the inconsistency and stubborn ignorance of attributing good acts to evil causes. Jesus said that the charge that good was done by evil was blasphemy, and that it was the sin against the Holy Spirit, which could not be forgiven. It is a very serious matter to attribute good works to evil sources because it betrays a deplorable lack of understanding of Truth. (*Jesus' Soul Evolution* 443-4)

## Words and Actions are the Fruit of Thought[1]

12:33 "Either make the tree good,
and its fruit good, or make the tree
corrupt, and its fruit corrupt; for the
tree is known by its fruit.[2] 12:34 You
offspring of vipers, how can you,
being evil, speak good things? For out
of the abundance of the heart,[3] the
mouth speaks. 12:35 The good man out
of his good treasure brings out good
things, and the evil man out of his
evil treasure[62] brings out evil
things. 12:36 I tell you that every idle
word[4] that men speak, they will give
account of it in the day of judgment.
12:37 For by your words you will be
justified,[5] and by your words you
will be condemned."

1. See Luke 6:43-45

2. *the tree is known by its fruit.* The quality and degree of our thought is revealed by our speech and actions. Words and actions are the fruit of thought. Every word and every combination of words has back of it an idea, and the power of the word is primarily in that idea. (*Jesus' Soul Evolution* 447)

3. *Out of the abundance of the heart, the mouth speaks.* Both good and evil are laid up in the heart or subconscious mind through the thought habits that we form and keep.

4. *Every idle word.* Idle words are words spoken with no underlying constructive purpose, but only for the pleasure or convenience of the passing moment. To say that a person is poor, sick, unhappy, unfortunate, or in danger of death or disaster is to speak contrary to what is true of him in Spirit, and is therefore to bear false witness against him.

5. *by your words you will be justified.* Our words and the thoughts behind them are formative. They are the vehicles through which ideas make themselves manifest. Constructive words work for our wellbeing. Negative words are destructive and harmful.

## Not By Signs, but By Spiritual Understanding[1]

12:38 Then certain of the scribes
and Pharisees answered, "Teacher,
we want to see a sign from you."[2]

12:39 But he answered them, "An
evil and adulterous generation seeks
after a sign, but no sign will be given
it but the sign of Jonah the prophet.
12:40 For as Jonah was three days and
three nights in the belly of the
whale, so will the Son of Man be
three days and three nights in the
heart of the earth. 12:41 The men of
Nineveh[3] will stand up in the
judgment with this generation, and
will condemn it, for they repented at
the preaching of Jonah; and behold,
someone greater than Jonah is here.
12:42 The queen of the south[4] will rise
up in the judgment with this
generation, and will condemn it, for
she came from the ends of the earth
to hear the wisdom of Solomon; and
behold, someone greater than

Solomon is here.

1. See Mark 8:11-12; Luke 11:16, 29-32

2. *We want to see a sign from You.* The religious thoughts pertaining to the realm of form (Pharisees) do not know that Truth comes into expression in the consciousness through understanding; they seek a sign in the external realm. No sign of the Presence of Christ can be given to such a consciousness, for the things of Spirit are spiritually discerned. Those who asked for a "sign" of the power of Truth were in a mixed or adulterated state of mind, and all the signs in the world would not have convinced them. (*Jesus' Soul Evolution* 451-53).

3. *The men of Nineveh.* Metaphysically, the potential thoughts of wisdom that have yet recognized that which is constructive from that which is not constructive.

4. *The queen of the south.* The subconscious mind, which is awakened in us when the wisdom of Spirit begins its work in our consciousness. This awakening stirs up both the good and the evil thoughts and we must choose or judge them, not by intellectual wisdom (Solomon), but by that "greater than Solomon," the Christ within.

## The Need For Positive Affirmation[1]

12:43 But the unclean spirit, when he is gone out of the man, passes through waterless places, seeking rest, and doesn't find it. 12:44 Then he says, 'I will return into my house from which I came out,' and when he has come back, he finds it empty, swept, and put in order. 12:45 Then he goes, and takes with himself seven other spirits more evil than he[2] is, and they enter in and dwell there. The last state of that man becomes worse than the first. Even so will it be also to this evil generation."

1. See Luke 11:24-26

2. *Then he goes, and takes with himself seven other spirits more evil than he.* Whenever we deny a negative condition we set up a mental vacuum. If a positive force is not set into activity immediately, still greater negation is encountered. One negative, unclean thought returns with seven others and the condition is worse than at the beginning. (*Jesus' Soul Evolution* 455)

## The True Family of Jesus[1]

12:46 While he was yet speaking to the multitudes, behold, his mother and his brothers stood outside, seeking to speak to him. 12:47 One said to him, "Behold, your mother and your brothers stand outside, seeking to speak to you."

12:48 But he answered him who spoke to him, "Who is my mother? Who are my brothers?"[2] 12:49 He stretched out his hand towards his disciples, and said, "Behold, my mother and my brothers! 12:50 For whoever does the will of my Father who is in heaven, he is my brother, and sister, and mother."[3]

1. See Mark 3:31-35; Luke 8:19-21

2. *Who is My mother? Who are My brothers?* The spiritual is stronger than any human connection. We who live under the light of Spirit are doing the will of the Father; we are the true family of Jesus Christ. (*Jesus' Soul Evolution* 459)

3. *my brother, and sister, and mother.* [The "family of God" are the thoughts of God. These thoughts are communicated to us by Jesus in the form of parables, precepts, promises, and healings. So the theme here of "the spiritual family" is carried forward into Chapter 13, where Jesus uses one parable after another to teach us about the Kingdom of Heaven.]

Fillmore Study Bible annotations by Mary Salama.

**World English Bible Footnotes:**

[59] v12:4. 1 Samuel 21:3-6
[60] v12:7. Hosea 6:6
[61] v12:21. Isaiah 42:1-4
[62] v12:35. TR adds "of the heart"

# MATTHEW 13

## Being a Sower of the Word[1]

13:1 On that day Jesus went out of
the house, and sat by the seaside. 13:2
Great multitudes gathered to him, so
that he entered into a boat, and sat,
and all the multitude stood on the
beach. 13:3 He spoke to them many
things in parables, saying, "Behold,
a farmer went out to sow.[2] 13:4 As
he sowed, some seeds[3] fell by the
roadside, and the birds came and
devoured them. 13:5 Others fell on
rocky ground, where they didn't have
much soil, and immediately they
sprang up, because they had no
depth of earth. 13:6 When the sun had
risen, they were scorched. Because
they had no root, they withered
away. 13:7 Others fell among thorns.
The thorns grew up and choked
them: 13:8 and others fell on good
soil,[4] and yielded fruit: some one
hundred times as much, some sixty,
and some thirty. 13:9 He who has ears
to hear, let him hear."

1. See Mark 4:1-9; Luke 8:4-8

2. *a farmer went out to sow.* Most people think that the Word referred to by Jesus is accomplished by preaching or talking with ecclesiastical authority, but nothing is said about his official capacity as a sower of good seed. Then whoever gives forth the true word is an authorized sower. Although the words we send forth may not all find reception in the minds of those who listen, we are to speak just as if we expect them to. The farmer always plants with the expectation of getting a crop, no matter how often he or she is disappointed.

3. *some seeds.* The seed is the Word of God. The spoken word has a special field of action in the realm of forms. Thought moves on the inner plane, where the vibratory forces have not crystallized into visible things.

4. *good soil, and yielded fruit: some one hundred times as much, some sixty, and some thirty.* The single idea of Truth which we implant in another mind may increase beyond all computation. (*Jesus' Soul Evolution* 475)

## The Purpose of the Parables[1]

13:10 The disciples came, and said
to him, "Why do you speak to them in
parables?"

13:11 He answered them, "To you it
is given to know the mysteries of the
Kingdom of Heaven,[2] but it is not
given to them. 13:12 For whoever has,
to him will be given, and he will have
abundance, but whoever doesn't

have, from him will be taken away
even that which he has. 13:13
Therefore I speak to them in
parables, because seeing they don't
see, and hearing, they don't hear,[3]
neither do they understand. 13:14 In
them the prophecy of Isaiah is
fulfilled, which says,

'By hearing you will hear,
and will in no way understand;
Seeing you will see,
and will in no way perceive:
13:15 for this people's heart has grown
callous,
their ears are dull of hearing,
they have closed their eyes;
or else perhaps they might
perceive with their eyes,
hear with their ears,
understand with their heart,
and should turn again;
and I would heal them.'[63]

13:16 "But blessed are your eyes, for
they see;[4] and your ears, for they
hear. 13:17 For most certainly I tell you
that many prophets and righteous
men desired to see the things which
you see, and didn't see them; and to
hear the things which you hear, and
didn't hear them.

1. See Mark 4:10-12,25; Luke 8:9-10,18

2. *The Kingdom of Heaven.* Heaven is a condition of the mind or a state of consciousness in which mind, soul, and body are in harmony with Divine Mind; a state of mind in which peace, love, and harmony fill the thought of the individual or of a group. Jesus knew the truth and gave the only description of heaven which we, immersed in the belief that forms are real, can understand—that is, by comparing it to the various conditions about us with which we are familiar.

3. *seeing they don't see, and hearing, they don't hear.* It is practically useless to try to spiritualize any state of consciousness before it is prepared to receive the quickening power of the Word. When we wholly on this plane of existence we are blind to spiritual things.

4. *But blessed are your eyes, for they see.* When we function in a negative state of consciousness, the soil of the mind is always shallow and unproductive or else rough and rocky, which makes his life tedious and hard. But when we sow the Seed in good soil (hear the Word and understand it) the results are satisfactory indeed. (*Jesus' Soul Evolution* 470-77)

## Being a Receiver of the Word[1]

13:18 "Hear, then, the parable of
the farmer. 13:19 When anyone hears
the word of the Kingdom, and doesn't
understand it, the evil one comes,
and snatches away that which has
been sown in his heart. This is what
was sown by the roadside.[2] 13:20 What
was sown on the rocky places,[3] this
is he who hears the word, and
immediately with joy receives it; 13:21
yet he has no root in himself, but
endures for a while. When oppression
or persecution arises because of the
word, immediately he stumbles. 13:22
What was sown among the thorns,[4]
this is he who hears the word, but
the cares of this age and the
deceitfulness of riches choke the
word, and he becomes unfruitful. 13:23
What was sown on the good ground,[5]
this is he who hears the word, and
understands it, who most certainly
bears fruit, and brings forth, some
one hundred times as much, some
sixty, and some thirty."

1. See Mark 4:13-20; Luke 8:11-15

2. *what was sown by the roadside.* The soil represents our consciousness. We may be totally unreceptive to truth, we may not understand it, we may be confused, defensive and always rejecting truth.

3. *the rocky places.* We may hear the word of truth and are happy to hear it because it will help us solve all our problems. However, when the pressures of life come along, we give in; we are not able to stick to our belief for we have no depth of consciousness.

4. *the thorns.* We hear the word of truth but use it selfishly to get things of the world; we are so materially minded that our greed chokes out the truth. The word of truth cannot grow in this type of consciousness. We must be willing to put aside all self-seeking.

5. *the good ground.* The good ground has variations, 30, 60, 100 which means that the good ground can be further developed. What seems to be negative and pessimistic to the human ego is that consciousness develops slowly, which is why a daily regimen of study and prayer are so essential. (Jim Lewis, *Biblical Favorites, Parable of the Sower*)

## When To Cleanse the Mind of Weeds

13:24 He set another parable before them, saying, "The Kingdom of Heaven❶ is like a man who sowed good seed in his field, 13:25 but while people slept, his enemy came and sowed darnel weeds❷[64] also among the wheat, and went away. 13:26 But when the blade sprang up and brought forth fruit, then the darnel weeds appeared also. 13:27 The servants of the householder came and said to him, 'Sir, didn't you sow good seed in your field? Where did this darnel come from?'

13:28 "He said to them, 'An enemy has done this.'

"The servants asked him, 'Do you want us to go and gather them up?'

13:29 "But he said, 'No,❸ lest perhaps while you gather up the darnel weeds, you root up the wheat with them. 13:30 Let both grow together until the harvest, and in the harvest time❹ I will tell the reapers, "First, gather up the darnel weeds, and bind them in bundles to burn them; but gather the wheat into my barn."'"

1. *The Kingdom of Heaven.* A condition where there shall remain only the good. (Jesus' Soul Evolution p.470-77)

2. *but while people slept, his enemy came and sowed darnel weeds.* Good seed are constructive, true thoughts and darnel weeds are destructive thoughts. The "enemy" that came and sowed the weeds is the sense consciousness, which sows them when we are not on the alert spiritually (while people slept).

3. *Do you want us to go and gather them up? But he said, No.* In the early stages of our spiritual development, it would be difficult for us to cleanse our mind thoroughly. If we attempted such cleansing, we might discard much that is good along with the evil.

4. *The harvest time.* When we have attained sufficient spiritual understanding (the harvest time) we can safely cleans our mind. Then we can cast out the destructive thoughts (bind and burn them) and preserve the positive good ideas (gather the wheat into my barn).

## The Power of a Small Thought of Truth❶

13:31 He set another parable before them, saying, "The Kingdom of Heaven is like a grain of mustard seed,❷ which a man took, and sowed in his field; 13:32 which indeed is smaller than all seeds. But when it is grown, it is greater than the herbs, and becomes a tree, so that the birds of the air come and lodge in its branches."

1. See Mark 4:30-32; Luke 13:18-19

2. *is like a grain of mustard seed.* The apparently small thought or idea of Truth (seed) has capacity to develop and expand in consciousness until it becomes the abiding place of a higher type of thoughts (birds of the air). (*Jesus' Soul Evolution* 487)

## The Parable of the Yeast[1]

13:33 He spoke another parable to them. "The Kingdom of Heaven is like yeast, which a woman[2] took, and hid in three measures[65] of meal, until it was all leavened."

1. See Luke 13:20-21

2. *is like yeast, which a woman.* Yeast, same as leaven, is Truth and Woman is soul. When a word of Truth seems to be hidden by the inner mind, it is not idle, but is quietly spreading from point to point. This process continues until the whole consciousness is vitalized by Spirit. People who have for years had this hidden word of Truth at work in them are quick to respond to a larger exposition of the Divine Law, and we recognize that they are ripe for the Truth. Those who can lay hold of these deep truths are awakened so they can see and hear spiritually as well as physically. Those who are not ready for the deep fundamental truths of Being take them literally instead of taking them symbolically. (*Jesus' Soul Evolution* 487)

## The Power of Parables[1]

13:34 Jesus spoke all these things in parables[2] to the multitudes; and without a parable, he didn't speak to them, 13:35 that it might be fulfilled which was spoken through the prophet, saying,

"I will open my mouth in
parables;
I will utter things hidden from
the foundation of the
world."[66]

1. See Mark 4:33-34

2. *Jesus spoke all these things in parables.* Parables are powerful because they lend themselves to meditation, in that they stir the imagination and make us see the story as an actual event. As we meditate on a parable our perception is quickened and we begin to see the underlying truth or spiritual principle that the story illustrates.

## Jesus Describes a World Cleansed of Weeds

13:36 Then Jesus sent the multitudes away, and went into the house. His disciples came to him, saying, "Explain to us the parable[1] of the darnel weeds of the field."

13:37 He answered them, "He who sows the good seed is the Son of Man, 13:38 the field is the world; and the good seed, these are the children of the Kingdom; and the darnel weeds are the children of the evil one. 13:39 The enemy who sowed them is the devil. The harvest is the end of the age, and the reapers are angels. 13:40 As therefore the darnel weeds are gathered up and burned with fire; so will it be at the end of this age.[2] 13:41 The Son of Man will send out his angels, and they will gather out of his Kingdom all things that cause stumbling, and those who do iniquity, 13:42 and will cast them into the furnace of fire. There will be weeping and the gnashing of teeth. 13:43 Then the righteous will shine forth like the sun in the Kingdom of their Father. He who has ears to hear, let him hear.

1. *Explain to us the parable.* The reapers or the angels are our helpful, constructive thoughts that gather in the good, and our devils or enemies symbolize our rebellious,

opposing thoughts—that gather in evil. If we are able to separate the "weeds" from our good thoughts, we will bring that peace and harmony which is ours in Spirit, right out into visibility, and the kingdom of heaven will be established in our mind and body.

2. *at the end of this age.* When enough people have thus been faithful, the earth itself will take on this peace and harmony and all violence will cease. Disease will be no more and death fall upon none. Our bodies will not grow old but increase in lightness and symmetry with every added spiritual thought until gravity no longer holds them to earth, and millions will build abodes in the air all about this beautiful planet. This is the kingdom of heaven to be established by humanity with this world as the center of operation. (*Jesus' Soul Evolution* 493)

## Parables of the Kingdom

13:44 "Again, the Kingdom of
Heaven is like a treasure hidden in
the field,[1] which a man found, and
hid. In his joy, he goes and sells all
that he has, and buys that field.

13:45 "Again, the Kingdom of
Heaven is like a man who is a
merchant seeking fine pearls,[2] 13:46
who having found one pearl of great
price, he went and sold all that he
had, and bought it.

13:47 "Again, the Kingdom of
Heaven is like a dragnet,[3] that was
cast into the sea, and gathered some
fish of every kind, 13:48 which, when
it was filled, they drew up on the
beach. They sat down, and gathered
the good into containers, but the bad
they threw away. 13:49 So will it be
in the end of the world.[4] The angels
will come forth, and separate the
wicked from among the righteous,
13:50 and will cast them into the
furnace of fire. There will be the
weeping and the gnashing of teeth."

13:51 Jesus said to them, "Have you
understood all these things?"

They answered him, "Yes, Lord."

13:52 He said to them, "Therefore,
every scribe who has been made a
disciple in the Kingdom of Heaven is
like a man who is a householder,[5]
who brings out of his treasure new
and old things." 13:53 It happened that
when Jesus had finished these
parables, he departed from there.

1. *treasure hidden in the field.* Our mind and heart are the field. They contain the hidden treasure of spiritual identity that we discover as we learn to know ourself as a child of God. The treasure hid in the field is the logical truth that all that is belongs to Being and can be brought forth by one who gives up the without and looks within for the real value.

2. *like a man who is a merchant seeking fine pearls.* We are the merchant who is seeking the jewel of the soul, or spiritual good, through exchange of thought, discussion, and argument. The pearl is pure spiritual understanding. When we know the great worth of spiritual understanding we gladly give up everything that would hinder our realization of it. We go and sell all. (*Jesus' Soul Evolution* 503)

3. *is like a dragnet.* The net represents the capacity or that state of mind that seeks for Truth in many places and gathers all kinds of thoughts, which then have to be tested; the good retained and the bad cast out.

4. *So will it be in the end of the world.* The end of the world represents the point in consciousness where the true thoughts are in the majority and the error thoughts have lost their power. This is the final consummation of the regenerative process and everything that has been stored up in consciousness is brought forth and becomes of visible, practical value to the person. This is represented by the "householder" who brings out of his treasure "new and old things." (*Jesus' Soul Evolution* 506)

5. *like a man who is a householder, who brings out.* The disciple of Truth has in

mind a rich store of ideas that can be brought forth at will or as the need arises.

We lay up this store by living consciously in touch with Divine Mind.

## The Rejection of Jesus at Nazareth[1]

13:54 Coming into his own
country,[2] he taught them in their
synagogue, so that they were
astonished, and said, "Where did this
man get this wisdom, and these
mighty works? 13:55 Isn't this the
carpenter's son? Isn't his mother
called Mary, and his brothers, James,
Joses, Simon, and Judas[67]? 13:56
Aren't all of his sisters with us?[3]
Where then did this man get all of
these things?" 13:57 They were
offended by him.

But Jesus said to them, "A prophet
is not without honor,[4] except in his
own country, and in his own house."
13:58 He didn't do many mighty works
there because of their unbelief.[5]

2. *Coming into His own country.* We are spiritual beings, and our natural estate or country is the kingdom of the heavens within. The synagogue is our spiritual consciousness in the soul.

3. *Aren't all of his sisters with us?* When the spiritual quickening is lacking, the prophet is frequently misunderstood. The auditors of Jesus tried to reduce Him to the level of His brothers and sisters.

4. *A prophet is not without honor, except in his own country.* A prophet is one who reads out of the thoughts of the present mind and can determine in what these thoughts are bound to culminate.

5. *He didn't do many mighty works there because of their unbelief.* In demonstration of spiritual power, faith is essential. In several instances mentioned in Jesus' ministry, He could do no mighty works because in those among whom He worked there was lack of faith.

1. See Mark 6:1-6; Luke 4:16-30

---

Fillmore Study Bible annotations by Mary Salama.

**World English Bible Footnotes:**

[63] v13:15. Isaiah 6:9-10

[64] v13:25. darnel is a weed grass (probably bearded darnel or lolium temulentum) that looks very much like wheat until it is mature, when the difference becomes very apparent.

[65] v13:33. literally, three sata. 3 sata is about 39 litres or a bit more than a bushel

[66] v13:35. Psalm 78:2

[67] v13:55. or, Judah

# Matthew 14

## The Death of John the Baptist

14:1 At that time, Herod[1] the tetrarch heard the report concerning Jesus, 14:2 and said to his servants, "This is John the Baptizer. He is risen from the dead. That is why these powers work in him." 14:3 For Herod had laid hold of John, and bound him, and put him in prison[2] for the sake of Herodias, his brother Philip's wife. 14:4 For John said to him, "It is not lawful for you to have her." 14:5 When he would have put him to death, he feared the multitude, because they counted him as a prophet. 14:6 But when Herod's birthday came, the daughter of Herodias danced among them and pleased Herod. 14:7 Whereupon he promised with an oath to give her whatever she should ask. 14:8 She, being prompted by her mother, said, "Give me here on a platter the head of John the Baptizer."

14:9 The king was grieved, but for the sake of his oaths, and of those who sat at the table with him, he commanded it to be given, 14:10 and he sent and beheaded John in the prison. 14:11 His head was brought on a platter, and given to the young lady: and she brought it to her mother. 14:12 His disciples came, and took the body, and buried it; and they went and told Jesus.

1. *At that time, Herod.* Herod, sense consciousness, rules on the plane of mortality. Under its rule man does not fulfill the law of his being. If allowed full rein he kills out John the Baptist, our repentant and redemptive state of mind, which is beginning its ministry of change and purification in our soul and body. The object of this Bible lesson about Herod and his killing of John the Baptist is to show the various steps leading up to the tragedy of sense dominion. (MBD/Herod)

2. *For Herod had laid hold of John, and bound him, and put him in prison.* If we are of haughty, domineering, self-sufficient will, we stand as Herod, the ruler in Judea. We are then married to the passions of the human soul, Herodias. She leads us into sense gratifications so deep, so degrading, that we cut off the head of John, the conscience that would have turned us into the highway of the good.

## Feeding the Five Thousand

14:13 Now when Jesus heard this, he withdrew from there in a boat, to a deserted place apart. When the multitudes heard it, they followed him on foot from the cities. 14:14 Jesus went out, and he saw a great multitude.[1] He had compassion on them, and healed their sick. 14:15 When evening had come, his disciples came to him, saying, "This place is deserted, and the hour is already late. Send the multitudes away, that they may go into the villages, and buy themselves food."

14:16 But Jesus said to them, "They don't need to go away. You give them something to eat."

14:17 They told him, "We only have here five loaves and two fish."[2]

14:18 He said, "Bring them here to me."[3] 14:19 He commanded the multitudes to sit down on the grass; and he took the five loaves and the two fish, and looking up to heaven, he blessed, broke and gave[4] the loaves to the disciples, and the disciples gave to the multitudes. 14:20 They all ate, and were filled.⑤ They took up twelve baskets full of that which remained left over from the broken pieces. 14:21 Those who ate⑥ were about five thousand men, besides women and children.

1. *a great multitude.* The multitude of thoughts (the people) have to be fed by the increasing spiritual word. The faculties (disciples), functioning through the intellect, are not at this period in full realization of the power and capacity of the I AM (Jesus) and so they do not see how so many mouths can be fed in an apparently desert place. If one listens to the intellect at this stage in development, there will be neglect of duty. (*Jesus' Soul Evolution* 577-79)

2. *five loaves and two fish.* Loaves represent the five senses that have taken form or become substance in consciousness (as feeling, tasting, smelling, hearing, seeing); fishes are ideas not yet in manifestation.

3. *"Bring them here to me."* Practical ways in which we may apply Jesus' methods of demonstrating supply: do not be discouraged by an appearance of lack; accept the Truth of unlimited spiritual substance as the source of all blessings; affirm that we have plenty for all our needs; never belittle present blessings; always bless and give thanks for the supply of good that is already evident, as well as that which we expect; multiply our supply by giving and sharing.

4. *Looking up to heaven, He blessed, broke and gave.* We cannot in our own power perform this miraculous increase, but when we look up to heaven and bless and give to our disciples, all our thoughts are fed by this Divine manna and there is an abundance left over.

5. *They all ate, and were filled.* Jesus understood and used the law of increase, so that formless substance was given form. He used the dynamic power of thought to break the bonds of atoms composing the few loaves and fish, and fed five thousand people.

6. *Those who ate.* Mental appropriation. The multitude to be fed is our thoughts. We partake of the word of God by affirmation, and so eat of the sustaining substance of Spirit.

## Jesus Walks on the Water

14:22 Immediately Jesus made the disciples get into the boat, and to go ahead of him to the other side, while he sent the multitudes away. 14:23 After he had sent the multitudes away, he went up into the mountain by himself to pray. When evening had come, he was there alone. 14:24 But the boat was now in the middle of the sea, distressed by the waves, for the wind was contrary. 14:25 In the fourth watch of the night,[68] Jesus came to them, walking on the sea.①[69] 14:26 When the disciples saw him walking on the sea, they were troubled, saying, "It's a ghost!"② and they cried out for fear. 14:27 But immediately Jesus spoke to them, saying "Cheer up! It is I![70] Don't be afraid."

14:28 Peter answered him and said, "Lord, if it is you, command me to come to you on the waters."

14:29 He said, "Come!"

Peter stepped down from the boat, and walked on the waters to come to Jesus.③ 14:30 But when he saw that the wind was strong, he was afraid,④ and beginning to sink, he cried out, saying, "Lord, save me!"⑤

14:31 Immediately Jesus stretched out his hand, took hold of him, and said to him, "You of little faith, why did you doubt?" 14:32 When they got up into the boat, the wind ceased.⑥ 14:33 Those who were in the boat came and worshiped him, saying, "You are truly the Son of God!"

1. *Jesus came to them, walking on the sea.* The race thoughts have formed a sea of thought, and to walk over it safely comes from understanding that God is Substance, the omnipresent energy that permeates all creation. Such an understanding of God establishes the mind firmly in faith and the feet walk surely over the sea of mind. (*Jesus' Soul Evolution* 583-90)

2. *They were troubled, saying, "It's a ghost!"* The Master Christ Mind seems an apparition when we try to walk the waves of life in our own personal strength. But the Christ Mind is not an apparition, rather a mighty power, and when we have faith in It, all the discordant elements of our lives are quieted and we reduce to harmony and wholeness everything our peace-giving thoughts touch.

3. *Peter ... walked on the waters to come to Jesus.* It is not necessary that we walk on material water to follow Jesus; these are lessons in spiritual overcoming.

4. *when he saw that the wind was strong, he was afraid.* Peter is faith in its various stages of development. When our faith in the power of Spirit to sustain us under all conditions is only partially developed, we are apt to sink into boisterous thought waves about us.

5. *Lord, save me!* We are often ambitious and start out bravely but are soon swept under by elements weak as water. When we begin to sink, we should cry out with faith "Lord, save me," and we will be raised up above the adverse conditions.

6. *the wind ceased.* When union is made between the Master Mind and the mind of man, consciousness realizes its true Self and the dominion which was man's from the beginning is restored to him.

## Jesus Heals the Sick in Gennesaret

14:34 When they had crossed over,
they came to the land of
Gennesaret.(1) 14:35 When the people
of that place recognized him,(2) they
sent into all that surrounding region,
and brought to him all who were sick,
14:36 and they begged him that they
might just touch the fringe[71] of his
garment. As many as touched it were
made whole.

1. *the land of Gennesaret.* Valley of riches; sea of Divine life. (MBD/Gennesaret)

2. *When the people of that place recognized Him.* We are related, both within the consciousness and without, to all creation through the Universal Life Principle. When we recognize our unity with the One life and with all life, we are on the way to true exaltation and rulership and abundant substance. (MBD)

---

Fillmore Study Bible annotations by Mary Salama.

**World English Bible Footnotes:**

[68] v14:25. The night was equally divided into four watches, so the fourth watch is approximately 3:00 A. M. to sunrise.

[69] v14:25. see Job 9:8

[70] v14:27. or, I AM!

[71] v14:36. or, tassel

# MATTHEW 15

## Tradition or Truth?

15:1 Then Pharisees and scribes
came to Jesus from Jerusalem,
saying, 15:2 "Why[1] do your disciples
disobey the tradition of the elders?[2]
For they don't wash their hands when
they eat bread."

15:3 He answered them, "Why do
you also disobey the commandment
of God because of your tradition? 15:4
For God commanded,[3] 'Honor your
father and your mother,'[72] and, 'He
who speaks evil of father or mother,
let him be put to death.'[73] 15:5 But
you say, 'Whoever may tell his father
or his mother, "Whatever help you
might otherwise have gotten from
me is a gift devoted to God," 15:6 he
shall not honor his father or mother.'
You have made the commandment of
God void because of your tradition.
15:7 You hypocrites[4]! Well did Isaiah
prophesy of you, saying,

15:8 'These people draw near to me
with their mouth,
and honor me with their lips;
but their heart is far from me.
15:9 And in vain do they worship me,
teaching as doctrine rules
made by men.'"[74]

1. *Pharisees and scribes came ... saying, "Why?"* Pharisees couldn't understand that Jesus was the son of God because they took the external. The understanding Jesus taught in this lesson comes from the development of our spiritual nature. Each one of us must know this for ourself. (Charles Fillmore, Mysteries of the Four Gospels, Things That Defile)

2. *The tradition of the elders.* With our personal nature, tradition holds the higher place, for back of it is the weight or authority of the race mind, and its hold on the race mind is unquestioned. When we think things through for ourselves our mind lays hold of the formless stuff of Divine substance and transforms it. By this thought process, which is the proper function of the mind in us, we discern the truth of the accumulated wisdom of humanity and are enabled to discard what does not concern us.

3. *For God commanded.* Our spiritual nature has reverence for the Divine law, not human tradition. Where tradition conflicts with the Divine law, our Christ nature sets aside tradition.

4. *You hypocrites!* Every tradition sooner or later is superseded by something else. For example, the scientific truths of one age become the exploded superstitions of the next, and new so-called scientific truths take their place.

## What Defiles the Consciousness?

15:10 He summoned the multitude,
and said to them, "Hear, and
understand. 15:11 That which enters
into the mouth doesn't defile[1] the
man; but that which proceeds out[2]
of the mouth, this defiles the man."

15:12 Then the disciples came, and
said to him, "Do you know that the
Pharisees were offended,[3] when
they heard this saying?"

15:13 But he answered, "Every plant
which my heavenly Father didn't
plant[4] will be uprooted. 15:14 Leave
them alone. They are blind guides
of the blind. If the blind guide the
blind, both will fall into a pit."

15:15 Peter answered him, "Explain

the parable to us."

15:16 So Jesus said, "Do you also still not understand? 15:17 Don't you understand that whatever goes into the mouth passes into the belly, and then out of the body?[5] 15:18 But the things which proceed out of the mouth come out of the heart,[6] and they defile the man. 15:19 For out of the heart come forth evil thoughts, murders, adulteries, sexual sins, thefts, false testimony, and blasphemies. 15:20 These are the things which defile the man; but to eat with unwashed hands doesn't defile the man."[7]

1. *That which enters into the mouth doesn't defile.* Harmful things which enter into us may hurt the body, but this type of harm is not the same as the defilement of the soul of which Jesus speaks. (Ed Rabel, *Things that Defile*)

2. *but that which proceeds out.* If there issue from the heart of impure thoughts, thoughts of false witness, murderous thoughts, revenge and so forth, it is because erroneous thinking has established these in our consciousness at some time and must eventually all be wiped out. (Charles Fillmore, Mysteries of the Four Gospels, Things That Defile)

3. *The Pharisees were offended.* The Pharisaical mind is within everyone to a greater or less degree

4. *Every plant which my heavenly Father didn't plant.* When we are not rooted in Truth, we become as plants that always seek and depend on their nourishment from other plants. Our consistent study of Truth keeps us "planted in the Father".

5. *passes into the belly, and then out of the body.* The faculty of renunciation eliminates old, worn-out ideas from the mind, and if poison ideas try to creep in, they are at once eliminated.

6. *the things that come out of the mouth come from the heart.* The heart is the inner or emotional nature, which harbors will, desire, and the individual and personal thought.

7. *eating with unwashed hands does not defile the man.* As we learn to control our thought processes and think constructively we lose our fear of contagion and become immune to outer contaminating influences.

## Don't Throw Your Energy to the Dogs of Sensation

15:21 Jesus went out from there, and withdrew into the region of Tyre and Sidon.[1] 15:22 Behold, a Canaanite woman came out[2] from those borders, and cried, saying, "Have mercy on me, Lord, you son of David! My daughter is severely demonized!"

15:23 But he answered her not a word.

His disciples came and begged him, saying, "Send her away;[3] for she cries after us."

15:24 But he answered, "I wasn't sent to anyone but the lost sheep of the house of Israel."[4]

15:25 But she came and worshiped him, saying, "Lord, help me."

15:26 But he answered, "It is not appropriate to take the children's bread and throw it to the dogs."

15:27 But she said, "Yes, Lord, but even the dogs eat the crumbs which fall[5] from their masters' table."

15:28 Then Jesus answered her, "Woman, great is your faith! Be it done to you even as you desire." And her daughter was healed from that hour.

1. *Tyre and Sidon.* Tyre means strength and Sidon means beast of prey. They represent the region in us which may be termed "body sensation". This realm has

not been illumined by Spirit and is considered too material to be worthy of spiritualization. This is the way nearly all people look upon the body and its sensations. (*Jesus' Soul Evolution* 607-12)

2. *a Canaanite woman came out.* She is unspiritualized love, natural to body. Her daughter is physical sensation, which has been sensualized by impure thoughts.

3. *Send her away.* At a certain stage in spiritual unfoldment, we may decide that a high spiritual thought force is too holy to operate in the lower forms of sense consciousness in order to redeem it. The disciples besought Jesus to send the woman away and thus refuse to heal her daughter.

4. *house of Israel.* Jesus' reply is that the whole person must be redeemed and that the "holier than thou" idea has no part of true Christianity.

5. *even the dogs eat the crumbs which fall.* Life is continuous throughout nature, a stream proceeding from the highest to the lowest. This understanding of the unity and purity of the One life brings healing to the demonized sense consciousness-*And her daughter was healed from that hour.*

## Truth Cures Countless Conditions

15:29 Jesus departed there, and
came near to the sea of Galilee; and
he went up into the mountain, and
sat there. 15:30 Great multitudes came
to him,❶ having with them the lame,
blind, mute, maimed, and many
others,❷ and they put them down at
his feet. He healed them,❸ 15:31 so
that the multitude wondered❹ when
they saw the mute speaking, injured
whole, lame walking, and blind
seeing--and they glorified the God of
Israel.

1. *Great multitudes came to Him.* The legions of thoughts that swarm the mind, seeking harmony. These thoughts are harmonized and unified by contact with the high spiritual consciousness of the I AM. (*Jesus' Soul Evolution* 615-22)

2. *lame, blind, mute, maimed, and many others.* Continuous thought about self and selfish interests throws the life force to the nerve centers and they become clogged, which we call "disease." The remedy is a quickening of the life flow in the body and an opening of the mind to Truth. Jesus "healed them all" because He purified and raised all the elements of His organism to a high rate of vibration, and so He was like a highly electrified magnet which could impart its power to other magnets in a state of partial inertia.

3. *He healed them.* All physical acts are first performed in the mind. There is an energy even finer than electricity through which the mind acts, when the mind concentrates upon Spirit there is an inflow of this finer force and the whole being (Spirit, soul, and body) is charged like a magnet.

4. *the multitude wondered.* All of the various thought entities that swarm the mind recognize the healing and uplifting work of the I AM.

## The Word of Truth Feeds Your 4,000

15:32 Jesus summoned his disciples
and said, "I have compassion on the
multitude, because they continue
with me now three days and have
nothing to eat. I don't want to send
them away fasting, or they might
faint on the way."

15:33 The disciples said to him,
"Where should we get so many loaves
in a deserted place as to satisfy so
great a multitude?"

15:34 Jesus said to them, "How
many loaves do you have?"

They said, "Seven, and a few small fish."

15:35 He commanded the multitude
to sit down on the ground; 15:36 and he
took the seven loaves and the fish.❶

He gave thanks and broke them, and gave to the disciples, and the disciples to the multitudes.[2] 15:37 They all ate, and were filled.[3] They took up seven baskets full of the broken pieces that were left over. 15:38 Those who ate were four thousand men, besides women and children. 15:39 Then he sent away the multitudes, got into the boat, and came into the borders of Magdala.

1. *the seven loaves and the fish.* The loaves symbolize universal substance, and fish represent ideas of increase. (*Jesus' Soul Evolution* 626-272)

2. *Then He gave them to the disciples, and the disciples gave them to the multitudes.* Truth is first established in our own consciousness, its Substance is then distributed throughout all the cells of our body through our twelve spiritual faculties. In this way, the body is fed and nourished with the living Word, the Bread from heaven.

3. *all ate and were filled.* Every need is supplied from the universal substance, through our power to realize and use it. Faith makes the substance tangible, and through the power of thought we form the substance into whatever we may need.

---

Fillmore Study Bible annotations by Mary Salama.

**World English Bible Footnotes:**

[72] v15:4. Exodus 20:12; Deuteronomy 5:16

[73] v15:4. Exodus 21:17; Leviticus 20:9

[74] v15:9. Isaiah 29:13

# Matthew 16

## Intellectual Understanding Demands a Sign

16:1 The Pharisees and Sadducees[1] came, and testing him, asked him to show them a sign from heaven. 16:2 But he answered them, "When it is evening, you say, 'It will be fair weather, for the sky is red.' 16:3 In the morning, 'It will be foul weather today, for the sky is red and threatening.' Hypocrites! You know how to discern the appearance of the sky, but you can't discern the signs of the times! 16:4 An evil and adulterous generation[2] seeks after a sign, and there will be no sign given to it, except the sign of the prophet Jonah." He left them, and departed.[3]

1. *Pharisees and Sadducees.* Intellectual understanding, narrowness, self-righteousness, hardness of heart, argumentativeness, crystallization in old religious rites and ceremonies. It is this state of consciousness that opposes and tries to tear down the constructive work of Spirit. The spiritual sign is always given, but can only be discerned by the spiritually quickened soul. (*Jesus' Soul Evolution* 630-34)

2. *evil and adulterous generation.* Those who have no spiritual discernment and believe only in the literal outworking of the law of cause and effect in the intellectual or manifest realm. Such persons have no understanding of the higher law of grace,

love, and mercy. To them is given "the sign of the prophet Jonah," the fulfillment of their belief that sinful man can expect only failure, bad luck, and ill conditions in body or affairs.

3. *He left them, and departed.* The I AM cannot remain in such a limited, doubting condition of mind, but departs quickly. There are Pharisees at every turn, tempting believers to do some great thing, like the healing instantly of some well-known case in their community, to the end that everybody may believe, but experienced healers knows the futility of such methods to convince people of Truth. Truth has entrance to the mind through the understanding.

## The Yeast of the Intellectual Understanding

16:5 The disciples came to the other side and had forgotten to take bread.(1) 16:6 Jesus said to them, "Take heed and beware of the yeast(2) of the Pharisees and Sadducees."

16:7 They reasoned among themselves, saying, "We brought no bread."(3)

16:8 Jesus, perceiving it, said, "Why do you reason among yourselves, you of little faith, 'because you have brought no bread?' 16:9 Don't you yet perceive, neither remember the five loaves for the five thousand, and how many baskets you took up?(4) 16:10 Nor the seven loaves for the four thousand, and how many baskets you took up? 16:11 How is it that you don't perceive that I didn't speak to you concerning bread?(5) But beware of the yeast of the Pharisees and Sadducees." 16:12 Then they understood that he didn't tell them to beware of the yeast of bread, but of the teaching of the Pharisees and Sadducees.

1. *The disciples came to the other side and had forgotten to take bread.* At this point, the I AM withdrews and departs to another side of consciousness. (*Jesus' Soul Evolution* 635-37)

2. *beware of the yeast.* Yeast (leaven) always means expansion. Whatever line of thought is received into consciousness goes on working until it is rooted out by another line of thinking or until it changes one's whole consciousness and manifests fully in the outer life.

3. *We brought no bread.* Beware of the limited thoughts. When we confine the Divine Law to the customary avenues of expression and scoff at anything beyond, we are letting the leaven of Herod work to our undoing. When the mind is raised up through affirmations of God's omnipresent substance and life, we are not only fed, but there is a surplus.

4. *how many baskets you took up?* It is not the outward demonstration that counts, but the increase of substance in mind and body that always follows the faithful application of the Law.

5. *I didn't speak to you concerning bread.* Jesus tried to get the attention of his people away from material things in order that they might realize the spiritual.

## Peter Affirms the Christ Nature of Jesus

16:13 Now when Jesus came into the parts of Caesarea Philippi, he asked his disciples, saying, "Who do men say that I, the Son of Man, am?" 16:14 They said, "Some say John the Baptizer, some, Elijah, and others, Jeremiah, or one of the prophets."

16:15 He said to them, "But who do you say that I am?"(1)

16:16 Simon Peter answered, "You are the Christ, the Son of the living God."(2)

16:17 Jesus answered him, "Blessed

are you, Simon Bar Jonah, for flesh and blood has not revealed this to you, but my Father who is in heaven.③ 16:18 I also tell you that you are Peter,[75] and on this rock[76] I will build my assembly,④ and the gates of Hades[77] will not prevail against it. 16:19 I will give to you the keys of the Kingdom of Heaven,⑤ and whatever you bind on earth will have been bound in heaven; and whatever you release on earth will have been released in heaven."⑥ 16:20 Then he commanded the disciples that they should tell no one that he is Jesus the Christ.

1. *Who do men say that I ... am?* "I am" expresses our identity. The I AM is the universal symbol of consciousness, and we who are conscious beings make use of it. Each of us thus affirms that we are the perfect idea of humanity in expression.

2. *You are the Christ, the Son of the living God.* Peter, the apostle of faith, acknowledged Jesus as the Christ, the Son of God.

3. *flesh and blood has not revealed this to you, but my Father who is in heaven.* Jesus tells Peter, in effect, that his answer has been prompted by the wisdom which comes only from our inner self.

4. *on this rock I will build my assembly.* Jesus names Peter appropriately, for Peter means "rock" and represents faith in God. Upon such faith is the church of Christ (spiritual consciousness) built.

5. *I will give to you the keys of the Kingdom of Heaven.* Constructive thoughts and words. These thoughts and words are affirmations and denials which guide, guard, direct, and develop our faculties, such as faith, love, wisdom, and strength.

6. *whatever you release on earth will have been released in heaven.* Through affirmations and denials we can loose ourselves from personal limitations and set free within us the power to accomplish all good. See footnote for Matt 18:18 for how this affects conflict with others.

## In the End, Truth Will Always Resurrect

16:21 From that time, Jesus began to show his disciples that he must go to Jerusalem and suffer many things from the elders, chief priests, and scribes,① and be killed,② and the third day be raised up.③ 16:22 Peter took him aside, and began to rebuke him, saying, "Far be it from you, Lord! This will never be done to you." 16:23 But he turned, and said to Peter, "Get behind me, Satan! You are a stumbling block to me, for you are not setting your mind on the things of God, but on the things of men."

1. *suffer many things from the elders, chief priests, and scribes.* The revelation that we are in fact the very children of the living God is too stupendous for even the illuminated one to comprehend and retain at once. Before this truth can become a constant factor in mind, we suffer many things at the hands of the "elders" and "chief priests" and "scribes," which represent the traditional beliefs and ruling religious ideas dominant in the mind.

2. *and be killed, and the third day be raised up.* Many of these beliefs have been fixed in mind from childhood and do not yield at once to the spiritual idea. Instead they assert their power to extinguish spiritual understanding for a season; it is "killed," but shall after "the third day be raised up."

3. *third day be raised up.* These three days are three movements of mind: perception, realization, and manifestation. The clear light of first perception is obscured, yet we know that changes are going on in consciousness, and if we are wise, we will accompany the Christ down into the tomb of matter within us and assist in every way in overcoming the hereditary sins of the flesh. Be raised up. Truth rises again to the conscious mind and establishes Itself.

## Self-denial Is Required for Transformation

16:24 Then Jesus said to his disciples, "If anyone desires to come after me, let him deny himself, and take up his cross,[1] and follow me. 16:25 For whoever desires to save his life will lose it, and whoever will lose his life for my sake will find it.[2] 16:26 For what will it profit a man, if he gains the whole world, and forfeits his life? Or what will a man give in exchange for his life?[3] 16:27 For the Son of Man will come in the glory of his Father with his angels, and then he will render to everyone according to his deeds. 16:28 Most certainly I tell you, there are some standing here who will in no way taste of death, until they see the Son of Man coming in his Kingdom."[4]

1. *take up his cross.* The personal self sets up counter currents which put life at cross-purposes with spiritual development. Steady, daily denial of the claims of the personal self constitutes our "cross."

2. *whoever will lose his life for My sake will find it.* In order that our spiritual nature may be supreme in consciousness, our mortal nature must be crucified.

3. *what will a man give in exchange for his life?* To gain spiritual life and spiritual consciousness we must concentrate our energies and our desires on winning through to the spiritual realm and making ourselves at home there. This means denying ourselves all indulgence in lesser interests and activities and recognizing only the claims of the higher.

4. *who will in no way taste of death, until they see the Son of Man coming in his Kingdom.* The loss of personal life is the only way to find eternal life. The acceptance of this mighty truth takes away the consciousness of death, and reveals the Son of God coming into His kingdom here and now.

---

Fillmore Study Bible annotations by Mary Salama.

**World English Bible Footnotes:**

[75] v16:18. Peter's name, Petros in Greek, is the word for a specific rock or stone.

[76] v16:18. Greek, petra, a rock mass or bedrock.

[77] v16:18. or, Hell

# Matthew 17

## The Transfiguration

17:1 After six days, Jesus took with him Peter, James, and John[1] his brother, and brought them up into a high mountain by themselves. 17:2 He was transfigured before them.[2] His face shone like the sun, and his garments became as white as the light.[3] 17:3 Behold, Moses and Elijah[4] appeared to them talking with him.

17:4 Peter answered, and said to Jesus, "Lord, it is good for us to be here. If you want, let's make three tents here: one for you, one for

Moses, and one for Elijah."

17:5 While he was still speaking, behold, a bright cloud overshadowed them. Behold, a voice came out of the cloud, saying, "This is my beloved Son, in whom I am well pleased. Listen to him."

17:6 When the disciples heard it, they fell on their faces, and were very afraid. 17:7 Jesus came and touched them and said, "Get up, and don't be afraid." 17:8 Lifting up their eyes, they saw no one, except Jesus alone.[5] 17:9 As they were coming down from the mountain, Jesus commanded them, saying, "Don't tell anyone what you saw,[6] until the Son of Man has risen from the dead."

17:10 His disciples asked him, saying, "Then why do the scribes say that Elijah must come first?"

17:11 Jesus answered them, "Elijah indeed comes first, and will restore all things, 17:12 but I tell you that Elijah has come already, and they didn't recognize him, but did to him whatever they wanted to. Even so the Son of Man will also suffer by them." 17:13 Then the disciples understood that he spoke to them of John the Baptizer.

1. *Jesus took with Him Peter, James, and John.* To pray effectively, one must have with him the three disciples: Peter (Faith), John (Love), James (Good Judgment).

2. *He was transfigured before them.* A lifting up of the soul; an example of the glory that is possible through the habitual uplifting of life and thought. Metaphysically, it is the supernatural change of appearance that takes place as we experience the full flow of Divine power through our being.

3. *as white as the light.* Jesus lives today in that body of glorified electricity in a kingdom that interpenetrates the earth and its environment. He called it the kingdom of the heavens.

4. *Moses and Elijah.* Two processes through which purified human beings demonstrate: the Mosaic or evolutionary process of nature (Moses) and the ability of the spiritual discerner of Truth (Elijah) to make conditions rapidly change on the mental plane, which are in due season worked out in substance. (*Jesus' Soul Evolution* 659-71)

5. *they saw no one, except Jesus alone.* The other two "separate" phases of our development (Moses and Elijah) blend into the One, the current state of our spiritual awareness (the One Jesus Christ self of you).

6. *Don't tell anyone what you saw.* Because of the inability of the mind to express the revelations of the spiritual.

## Jesus Cures a Boy with a Demon

17:14 When they came to the multitude, a man came to him, kneeling down to him, saying, 17:15 "Lord, have mercy on my son, for he is epileptic, and suffers grievously;[1] for he often falls into the fire, and often into the water. 17:16 So I brought him to your disciples, and they could not cure him."

17:17 Jesus answered, "Faithless and perverse generation! How long will I be with you? How long will I bear with you? Bring him here to me." 17:18 Jesus rebuked him, the demon went out[2] of him, and the boy was cured from that hour.

17:19 Then the disciples came to Jesus privately, and said, "Why weren't we able to cast it out?"

17:20 He said to them, "Because of your unbelief. For most certainly I tell you, if you have faith as a grain of mustard seed, you will tell this mountain, 'Move from here to there,' and it will move; and nothing will be impossible for you. 17:21 But this kind doesn't go out except by prayer and fasting."3

1. *he is epileptic, and suffers grievously.* Metaphysically, one in which the fleshly ego has assumed such proportions in the personality that it has lost even its physical poise and for the time being is a maniac. In this sense anyone who has lost physical poise has so suffered. (*Jesus' Soul Evolution* 672-77)

2. *Jesus rebuked him, the demon went out.* Jesus (the supreme Spiritual Entity) has power to restore the poise and equilibrium of the mind under Divine Law, and this accomplishes the so-called miracle of healing.

3. *except by prayer and fasting.* Jesus' disciples could not cast out the demons of personality. Through fasting and prayer, one may raise their spiritual power through denying their negative thoughts and affirming the positive.

## Jesus Again Foretells His Death and Resurrection

17:22 While they were staying in
Galilee,1 Jesus said to them, "The
Son of Man is about to be delivered
up2 into the hands of men, 17:23 and
they will kill him, and the third day
he will be raised up."3 They were
exceedingly sorry.

1. *Galilee.* Metaphysically, the soul's energy acting in conjunction with substance. Jesus' abiding in Galilee symbolizes a continual expression of the activity of Truth, which always brings about a realization of Christhood after personality has been denied and the praise of God has been set up. (*Jesus' Soul Evolution* 686-87)

2. *The Son of Man is about to be delivered up.* The experience one passes through, going from the natural to the spiritual consciousness.

3. *he will be raised up.* The transformation to the spiritual plane.

## Jesus and the Temple Tax

17:24 When they had come to
Capernaum,1 those who collected
the didrachma coins[78] came to
Peter, and said, "Doesn't your
teacher pay the didrachma?" 17:25 He
said, "Yes."

When he came into the house, Jesus anticipated him, saying, "What do you think, Simon? From whom do the kings of the earth2 receive toll or tribute? From their children, or from strangers?"

17:26 Peter said to him, "From
strangers."

Jesus said to him, "Therefore the
children are exempt. 17:27 But, lest
we cause them to stumble, go to the
sea, cast a hook, and take up the
first fish that comes up.3 When you
have opened its mouth, you will find
a stater coin.[79] Take that, and give
it to them for me and you."4

1. *Capernaum.* In individual consciousness, Capernaum is the coming into an understanding of the comforting power of Spirit. (*Jesus' Soul Evolution* 683-84)

2. *The kings of the earth.* Man-made difficulties and conditions which seem to dominate at the moment.

3. *Take up the first fish that comes up.* Fish are the idea of accumulation, of increasing, multiplying power. Jesus used fish to exemplify the fruitfulness of spiritual ideas. *When you have opened its mouth.* The piece of gold in the fish's mouth is the power of the true Word to increase the fruitfulness of nature.

4. *Take that, and give it to them for me and you.* Jesus and those who understand the Divine Law, although they are the Sons

of God and are free from earth's bondage, yet may conform to it in certain states of unfoldment.

---

Fillmore Study Bible annotations by Mary Salama.

**World English Bible Footnotes:**

[78] v17:24. A didrachma is a Greek silver coin worth 2 drachmas, about as much as 2 Roman denarii, or about 2 days' wages. It was commonly used to pay the half-shekel temple tax, because 2 drachmas were worth one half shekel of silver.

[79] v17:27. A stater is a silver coin equivalent to four Attic or two Alexandrian drachmas, or a Jewish shekel: just exactly enough to cover the half-shekel temple tax for two people.

# MATTHEW 18

## True Greatness

18:1 In that hour the disciples came
to Jesus, saying, "Who then is
greatest(1) in the Kingdom of
Heaven?"(2)

18:2 Jesus called a little child to
himself,(3) and set him in the midst
of them, 18:3 and said, "Most certainly
I tell you, unless you turn, and
become as little children, you will
in no way enter into the Kingdom
of Heaven. 18:4 Whoever therefore
humbles himself(4) as this little child,
the same is the greatest in the
Kingdom of Heaven. 18:5 Whoever
receives one such little child in my
name receives me,

1. *Who then is greatest.* In the spiritually quickened soul, through the activity of God Mind, the personal ego is also quickened and comes forth to assert its greatness. In our sane moments we realize that none is great save God, and that he who would be great must be servant of all. (*Jesus' Soul Evolution* 689-90)

2. *the Kingdom of Heaven.* The Kingdom of Heaven is a condition in which Divine Mind supplies ideals for all the thoughts of man's mind. The greatest in this Kingdom is he who is most humble and receptive to the Divine ideals.

3. *Jesus called a little child to Himself.* The little child is a meek and lowly attitude of mind that is receptive and obedient to spiritual Law and to perfect faith. The soul must possess these qualities in order that God Mind may find full, free, and unhampered expression through it.

4. *Whoever therefore humbles himself.* The humble, Christ-like spirit is necessary to those who desire to enter the presence of Divine Mind.

## Temptations to Sin

18:6 but whoever causes one of these little ones who believe in me to stumble, it would be better for him that[1] a huge millstone should be hung around his neck, and that he should be sunk in the depths of the sea. 18:7 "Woe to the world because of occasions of stumbling! For it must be that the occasions come, but woe to that person through whom the occasion comes! 18:8 If your hand or your foot causes you to stumble, cut it off, and cast it from you. It is better for you to enter into life maimed or crippled,[2] rather than having two hands or two feet to be cast into the eternal fire. 18:9 If your eye causes you to stumble, pluck it out,[3] and cast it from you. It is better for you to enter into life with one eye, rather than having two eyes to be cast into the Gehenna[80] of fire.

1. *it would be better for him that.* It is a dangerous thing to kill out innocent, childlike thoughts. It is better to be very negative; better to go to the very depths of the sea of mortality than to cause a single spiritual thought of childlike receptivity to be obstructed in consciousness.

2. *It is better for you to enter into life maimed or crippled.* Eliminate external impediments to spiritual progress and enter into spirituality at any cost. Physical handicaps are nothing in comparison with spiritual shortcomings.

3. *pluck it out.* The "eye" that should be plucked out is the lust for knowledge and power which blunts the sweet innocence of the little child within, and often leads to sins that have to be atoned for in the purifying fires of the soul.

## The Parable of the Lost Sheep

18:10 See that you don't despise one of these little ones, for I tell you that in heaven their angels always see the face of my Father who is in heaven. 18:11 For the Son of Man came to save that which was lost.

18:12 "What do you think? If a man has one hundred sheep,[1] and one of them goes astray,[2] doesn't he leave the ninety-nine, go to the mountains, and seek that which has gone astray? 18:13 If he finds it, most certainly I tell you, he rejoices over it more[3] than over the ninety-nine which have not gone astray. 18:14 Even so it is not the will of your Father who is in heaven that one of these little ones should perish.

1. *If a man has one hundred sheep.* The shepherd represents the Christ, the Master, redeeming and protecting our thoughts; the sheep represent our thoughts after they have been assembled and disciplined.

2. *and one of them goes astray.* An error thought that has separated itself from the Master and the fold. To conform to the standard set by Jesus Christ, the first great demonstration is to overcome the errors of the mind that are formed by wrong thinking.

3. *he rejoices over it more.* One may be ninety-nine per cent perfect and yet remain outside the Kingdom. We rejoice more over the restoration of "that one thought" than over all the thoughts that are secure in the good.

## Reproving Another Who Sins

18:15 "If your brother sins against you, go, show him his fault between you and him alone. If he listens to you, you have gained back your brother. 18:16 But if he doesn't listen, take one or two more with you, that at the mouth of two or three witnesses every word may be established.[81] 18:17 If he refuses to listen to them, tell it to the assembly. If he refuses to hear the assembly also, let him be to you as a Gentile or a tax collector. 18:18 Most certainly I tell you, whatever things you bind on earth[1] will have been bound in heaven, and whatever things you release on earth will have been released in heaven. 18:19 Again, assuredly I tell you, that if two of you will agree on earth concerning anything that they will ask, it will be done for them by my Father who is in heaven. 18:20 For where two or three are gathered together in my name,[2] there I am in the midst of them."

1. *whatever things you bind on earth.* How we affirm others is powerful. See footnote for Matt 16:19

2. *gathered together in my name.* When two or three are truly gathered together in the name of Jesus Christ, they inadvertently dwell in the realm of Absolute Principle, where Jesus Christ dwells, thus harmonizing their ideas with His understanding of Divine Mind. (*Jesus' Soul Evolution* 698)

## Forgiveness

18:21 Then Peter came and said to him, "Lord, how often shall my brother sin against me, and I forgive him?[1] Until seven times?"[2] 18:22 Jesus said to him, "I don't tell you until seven times, but, until seventy times seven.

1. *how often shall my brother sin against me, and I forgive him?* Forgiving offences to the uttermost is necessary in order that we may be God-like and bring down this Kingdom of the heavens unto the earth. (*Jesus' Soul Evolution* 702-04)

2. *Until seven times?* The measure of the wrong or injury done to us by another should not be taken into consideration; one is to forgive as often as one is offended, in order to keep the mind clear and unruffled.

## The Parable of the Unforgiving Servant

18:23 Therefore the Kingdom of Heaven is like a certain king,[1] who wanted to reconcile accounts with his servants. 18:24 When he had begun to reconcile, one was brought to him who owed him ten thousand talents.[82] 18:25 But because he couldn't pay, his lord commanded him to be sold, with his wife, his children, and all that he had, and payment to be made. 18:26 The servant therefore fell down and kneeled before him, saying, 'Lord, have patience with me, and I will repay you all!' 18:27 The lord of that servant, being moved with compassion, released him, and forgave him the debt.[2]

18:28 "But that servant went out, and found one of his fellow servants, who owed him one hundred denarii,[83] and he grabbed him, and took him by the throat, saying, 'Pay me what you owe!'

18:29 "So his fellow servant fell down at his feet and begged him, saying, 'Have patience with me, and I will repay you!' 18:30 He would not, but went and cast him into prison, until he should pay back that which was due. 18:31 So when his fellow servants saw what was done, they were exceedingly sorry, and came and told to their lord all that was done. 18:32 Then his lord called him in, and said to him, 'You wicked servant! I forgave you all that debt, because you begged me. 18:33 Shouldn't you also have had mercy on your fellow servant,[3] even as I had mercy on you?' 18:34 His lord was angry, and delivered him to the tormentors, until he should pay all that was due to him. 18:35 So my heavenly Father will also do to you, if you don't each forgive your brother from your hearts for his misdeeds."

1. *a certain king.* The king is the will of a man, all of whose other faculties are under its control. *Who wanted to reconcile accounts with his servants.*The servant is human nature, which as a rule is not under the dominion of the Divine will, but records every emotion, every thought, every word sent out by us. It is here that man incurs the great debt of "ten thousand talents".

2. *released him, and forgave him the debt.* The wisdom and love attributes of Being may be called into expression by man, and thus the great debt which man owes is paid by God.

3. *Shouldn't you also have had mercy on your fellow servant?* Impatience and the habit of harboring ill will and of exacting our due regardless of the needs or feelings of others, serve to bring back upon us the full load of our responsibility. We must enter into the consciousness of forgiveness if we would rise above personality and know the Divine.

---

Fillmore Study Bible annotations by Mary Salama.

**World English Bible Footnotes:**

[80] v18:9. or, Hell

[81] v18:16. Deuteronomy 19:15

[82] v18:24. Ten thousand talents represents an extremely large sum of money, equivalent to about 60,000,000 denarii, where one denarius was typical of one day's wages for agricultural labor.

[83] v18:28. 100 denarii was about one sixtieth of a talent.

# Matthew 19

## The Marriage Made in Heaven

19:1 It happened when Jesus had
finished these words, he departed
from Galilee, and came into the
borders of Judea beyond the Jordan.
19:2 Great multitudes followed him,
and he healed them there. 19:3
Pharisees came to him, testing him,
and saying, "Is it lawful for a man to
divorce his wife❶ for any reason?"

19:4 He answered, "Haven't you
read that he who made them from
the beginning made them male and
female,❷[84] 19:5 and said, 'For this
cause a man shall leave his father
and mother, and shall join to his
wife; and the two shall become one
flesh?'[85] 19:6 So that they are no
more two, but one flesh. What
therefore God has joined together,
don't let man tear apart."

19:7 They asked him, "Why then did
Moses command us to give her a bill
of divorce, and divorce her?"

19:8 He said to them, "Moses,
because of the hardness of your
hearts, allowed you to divorce your
wives, but from the beginning it has
not been so. 19:9 I tell you that
whoever divorces his wife, except for

sexual immorality, and marries another, commits adultery;[3] and he who marries her when she is divorced commits adultery."

19:10 His disciples said to him, "If this is the case of the man with his wife, it is not expedient to marry."

19:11 But he said to them, "Not all men can receive this saying, but those to whom it is given. 19:12 For there are eunuchs[4] who were born that way from their mother's womb, and there are eunuchs who were made eunuchs by men; and there are eunuchs who made themselves eunuchs for the Kingdom of Heaven's sake. He who is able to receive it, let him receive it."

1. *Is it lawful for a man to divorce his wife?* Jesus is always speaking on multi-dimensional levels and so here about the male and female natures of every individual, the marriage made in heaven, and the divorce which leads to mental and emotional imbalance. (Ed Rabel)

2. *made them male and female.* Spiritually interpreted, man symbolizes wisdom and woman symbolizes love. A true marriage under spiritual law brings about perfect unity in mind and body. These two must work together in order to fulfill the law. (*Jesus' Soul Evolution* 709)

3. *commits adultery.* Divine marriage is the union of harmonious soul. Whenever two Divinely married persons separate and seek other alliances, they break the Divine law. An alliance between persons who are not Divinely united is adultery and leads to corruption of spiritual life. (*Jesus' Soul Evolution* 710)

4. *there are eunuchs.* Metaphysically, a thought from which the capacity to increase life and its forms has been eliminated (MBD/Eunuch). There is a Divine asceticism which is recognized by Divine Mind and is one of the avenues through which the soul can be raised to pure spiritual consciousness. (*Jesus' Soul Evolution* 708). See Mark 10:1-12

## Jesus Blesses the Little Divine Ideas

19:13 Then little children[1] were brought to him, that he should lay his hands on them and pray; and the disciples rebuked them. 19:14 But Jesus said, "Allow the little children,[2] and don't forbid them to come to me; for the Kingdom of Heaven belongs to ones like these." 19:15 He laid his hands on them, and departed from there.

1. *little children.* Children represent thoughts of reality or the true ideas about Being that have to be brought out in every part of man's consciousness. (RW/children-of-israel)

2. *Allow the little children.* The matrix or realm of Divine ideas (the Kingdom of Heaven) lies all about us and within us. In order for our minds to be raised to its pure spiritual consciousness, we must make a place for these new and higher ideas (children) by taking a childlike attitude that is meek and receptive. (*Jesus' Soul Evolution* 712)

## The Truly Rich Young Man

19:16 Behold, one came to him and said, "Good teacher, what good thing shall I do, that I may have eternal life?"

19:17 He said to him, "Why do you call me good? No one is good but one, that is, God. But if you want to enter into life, keep the commandments."

19:18 He said to him, "Which ones?"

Jesus said, "'You shall not murder.' 'You shall not commit adultery.' 'You

shall not steal.' 'You shall not offer
false testimony.' 19:19 'Honor your
father and mother.'[86] And, 'You
shall love your neighbor as
yourself.'"[87]

19:20 The young man said to him,
"All these things I have observed from
my youth. What do I still lack?"

19:21 Jesus said to him, "If you want
to be perfect,❶ go, sell what you
have, and give to the poor, and you
will have treasure in heaven; and
come, follow me." 19:22 But when the
young man heard the saying, he went
away sad,❷ for he was one who had
great possessions. 19:23 Jesus said to
his disciples, "Most certainly I say to
you, a rich man will enter into the
Kingdom of Heaven❸ with difficulty.
19:24 Again I tell you, it is easier for a
camel to go through a needle's eye,
than for a rich man to enter into the
Kingdom of God."

19:25 When the disciples heard it,
they were exceedingly astonished,
saying, "Who then can be saved?"

19:26 Looking at them, Jesus said,
"With men this is impossible, but
with God all things are possible."

19:27 Then Peter answered,
"Behold, we have left everything,❹
and followed you. What then will we
have?"

19:28 Jesus said to them, "Most
certainly I tell you that you who have
followed me, in the regeneration
when the Son of Man will sit on the
throne of his glory, you also will sit
on twelve thrones, judging the
twelve tribes of Israel. 19:29 Everyone
who has left houses, or brothers, or
sisters, or father, or mother, or wife,
or children, or lands, for my name's
sake, will receive one hundred times,
and will inherit eternal life. 19:30 But
many will be last who are first;❺ and
first who are last.

1. *If you want to be perfect.* Jesus considered spiritual understanding of more importance than great riches, piety, and careful observance of the moral law. (*Jesus' Soul Evolution* 717)

2. *he went away sad.* The rich young man may be likened to personality. Personality is ambitious for eternal life and strives to attain it, but does not want to sacrifice the selfish attachment to things of sense. Personality may follow the commandments but there is one lack: it must give up its belief in the all-importance of earthly possessions.

3. *will enter into the Kingdom of Heaven.* All the powers of the mind must be developed Spirit-ward before we can rise to the higher consciousness called "heaven." If we trust in riches, trust in God is weakened, and this weakens our spiritual faculties. (*Jesus' Soul Evolution* 719)

4. *we have left everything.* Giving up all trust in the help of relations and earthly possessions and following the guidance of the higher self brings as a final reward a consciousness of the real, upon which these outer conditions rest. (*Jesus' Soul Evolution* 722)

5. *last who are first.* In the final test, those who seem least shall be given first place. Everywhere we see quiet spiritual workers who are laying up in the heavens of the mind a store of true thoughts that will eventually precipitate into visibility and make them spiritual lights. (*Jesus' Soul Evolution* 723)

---

Fillmore Study Bible annotations by .

**World English Bible Footnotes:**

[84] v19:4. Genesis 1:27

[85] v19:5. Genesis 2:24

[86] v19:19. Exodus 20:12-16; Deuteronomy 5:16-20

[87] v19:19. Leviticus 19:18

# Matthew 20

## Working Your Inner Vineyard

20:1 "For the Kingdom of Heaven is like a man who was the master of a household, who went out early in the morning to hire laborers for his vineyard.[1] 20:2 When he had agreed with the laborers for a denarius[88] a day, he sent them into his vineyard. 20:3 He went out about the third hour,[89] and saw others standing idle in the marketplace. 20:4 To them he said, 'You also go into the vineyard, and whatever is right I will give you.' So they went their way. 20:5 Again he went out about the sixth and the ninth hour,[90] and did likewise. 20:6 About the eleventh hour[91] he went out, and found others standing idle. He said to them, 'Why do you stand here all day idle?'

20:7 "They said to him, 'Because no one has hired us.'

"He said to them, 'You also go into the vineyard, and you will receive whatever is right.' 20:8 When evening had come,[2] the lord of the vineyard said to his manager, 'Call the laborers and pay them their wages, beginning from the last to the first.'

20:9 "When those who were hired at about the eleventh hour came, they each received a denarius.[3] 20:10 When the first came, they supposed that they would receive more; and they likewise each received a denarius. 20:11 When they received it, they murmured[4] against the master of the household, 20:12 saying, 'These last have spent one hour, and you have made them equal to us, who have borne the burden of the day and the scorching heat!'

20:13 "But he answered one of them, 'Friend, I am doing you no wrong. Didn't you agree with me for a denarius? 20:14 Take that which is yours, and go your way. It is my desire to give to this last just as much as to you. 20:15 Isn't it lawful for me to do what I want to with what I own? Or is your eye evil, because I am good?' 20:16 So the last will be first,[5] and the first last. For many are called, but few are chosen."

1. *To hire laborers for his vineyard.* Each one's vineyard is his consciousness and his faculties are the workers in it. In this parable Jesus teaches that God is no respecter of persons and gives to all who give themselves wholeheartedly to the living of Truth ideas.

2. *When evening had come.* Realization of eternal life does not necessarily come to us by the number of years that we study and practice Truth, but when we have completed preparation for it ("when even was come") by our diligence, devotion, and obedience to the Divine law.

3. *They each received a denarius.* Some of us grasp Truth principles quickly and apply them more faithfully than do others. Some (those who labored all day) may accept Truth ideas more slowly and take longer to use them effectively. But each receives from God that for which he agrees to work; that is, God provides all the blessings that our understanding and devotion allow us to accept and use rightly.

4. *They murmured.* Jealousy causes misery, warps one's perspective, and can affect one's health adversely. We can overcome jealousy by rejoicing in the love and

generosity of God, appreciating our own blessings, and remembering that God provides richly for all.

5. *The last will be first, and the first last.* In a sense every single one of us is an "eleventh hour" worker, since the gifts of God's love are so great that we could never actually earn them. The gifts of life, love, joy, power, and wisdom are ours because God loves us and because we have opened our minds and hearts to receive them.

## Error thoughts are Condemned to Death

20:17 As Jesus was going up to Jerusalem,[1] he took the twelve disciples aside, and on the way he said to them, 20:18 "Behold, we are going up to Jerusalem, and the Son of Man will be delivered to the chief priests and scribes, and they will condemn him to death,[2] 20:19 and will hand him over to the Gentiles to mock, to scourge, and to crucify; and the third day he will be raised up."

1. *Jesus was going up to Jerusalem.* We reach a place in our development where the old states of mind must be wholly erased and replaced with new and higher. When this takes place there is great commotion in mind. (*Jesus' Soul Evolution* 732)

2. *They will condemn Him to death.* The old and religious thoughts within us are full of condemnation and seek to "put to death" the new; but error, in its ignorance, only destroys itself.

## The Soul's Ambition to Sit at the Right and Left Hand of God

20:20 Then the mother of the sons[1] of Zebedee came to him with her sons, kneeling and asking a certain thing of him. 20:21 He said to her, "What do you want?"

She said to him, "Command that these, my two sons, may sit, one on your right hand, and one on your left hand, in your Kingdom."

20:22 But Jesus answered, "You don't know what you are asking. Are you able to drink the cup that I am about to drink, and be baptized with the baptism that I am baptized with?"

They said to him, "We are able."

20:23 He said to them, "You will indeed drink my cup, and be baptized with the baptism that I am baptized with, but to sit on my right hand and on my left hand is not mine to give; but it is for whom it has been prepared by my Father."[2]

20:24 When the ten heard it, they were indignant with the two brothers.

20:25 But Jesus summoned them, and said, "You know that the rulers of the nations lord it over them, and their great ones exercise authority over them. 20:26 It shall not be so among you, but whoever desires to become great among you shall be[92] your servant.[3] 20:27 Whoever desires to be first among you shall be your bondservant, 20:28 even as the Son of Man came not to be served, but to serve, and to give his life as a ransom for many."

1. *The mother of the sons.* The soul (the mother of Zebedee's sons) wants her offspring to have first place in the new kingdom. This ambition is evident when we think our abilities should be given due recognition in the spiritual kingdom, without considering our readiness and training in the spiritual law.

2. *Has been prepared by My Father.* Practicing the Divine Law by faith, before we even understand it, is what prepares us to understand it. This readiness is what places each one where he belongs.

3. *Shall be your servant.* As students of Truth, we must serve in the most menial duties before we are considered a safe custodian of the higher forces of the soul and mind. (*Jesus' Soul Evolution* 742-44)

## Truth Gives Sight to the Blind Soul

20:29 As they went out from
Jericho,(1) a great multitude followed
him.(2) 20:30 Behold, two blind men
sitting by the road, when they heard
that Jesus was passing by, cried out,
"Lord, have mercy on us, you son of
David!" 20:31 The multitude rebuked
them, telling them that they should
be quiet, but they cried out even
more, "Lord, have mercy on us, you
son of David!"

20:32 Jesus stood still, and called
them, and asked, "What do you want
me to do for you?"

20:33 They told him, "Lord, that our
eyes may be opened."(3)

20:34 Jesus, being moved with
compassion, touched their eyes; and
immediately their eyes received
their sight, and they followed him.

1. *As they went out from Jericho.* Jesus Christ (I AM) passed through Jericho (intellect) in His redemptive work. Jericho is the opposite of Jerusalem. One represents the spiritual; the other, the material.

2. *a great multitude followed Him.* As we proceed in our spiritual development, we become a leader of our multitude of thoughts.

3. *That our eyes may be opened.* The soul is always calling for more light, more understanding.

---

Fillmore Study Bible annotations by Mary Salama.

**World English Bible Footnotes:**

[88] v20:2. A denarius is a silver Roman coin worth 1/25th of a Roman aureus. This was a common wage for a day of farm labor.

[89] v20:3. Time was measured from sunrise to sunset, so the third hour would be about 9:00 AM.

[90] v20:5. noon and 3:00 P. M.

[91] v20:6. 5:00 PM

[92] v20:26. TR reads "let him be" instead of "shall be"

# Matthew 21

## Jesus' Triumphal Entry into our Life[1]

21:1 When they drew near to Jerusalem,[2] and came to Bethsphage,[93] to the Mount of Olives, then Jesus sent two disciples, 21:2 saying to them, "Go into the village that is opposite you, and immediately you will find a donkey tied, and a colt with her.[3] Untie them, and bring them to me. 21:3 If anyone says anything to you, you shall say, 'The Lord needs them,'[4] and immediately he will send them."

21:4 All this was done, that it might be fulfilled which was spoken through the prophet, saying,

21:5 "Tell the daughter of Zion,
behold, your King comes to you,
humble, and riding on a donkey,
on a colt, the foal of a donkey."[94]

21:6 The disciples went, and did just as Jesus commanded them, 21:7 and brought the donkey and the colt, and laid their clothes on them; and he sat on them. 21:8 A very great multitude spread their clothes on the road. Others cut branches from the trees, and spread them on the road. 21:9 The multitudes who went before him, and who followed kept shouting, "Hosanna[95] to the son of David! Blessed is he who comes in the name of the Lord! Hosanna in the highest!"[96][5]

21:10 When he had come into Jerusalem, all the city was stirred up, saying, "Who is this?" 21:11 The multitudes said, "This is the prophet, Jesus, from Nazareth of Galilee."

1. See Mark 11:1-11a; Luke 19:28-38; John 12:12-19

2. *drew near to Jerusalem.* The I AM, in order to overcome the personal self and gain dominion and power, draws near to the center of peace in man's heart (Jerusalem)

3. *and a colt with her.* The donkey and colt are the untrained animal forces that are in fact being held in check by the I AM.

4. *The Lord needs them.* We are not to crush or destroy our animal nature, but through the I AM (Jesus), we are to master it and make it serve us (He sat on them). The fact that Jesus rode the donkey was symbolical of His having conquered the forces in His own nature.

5. *Blessed is he who comes in the name of the Lord!* We honor the Christ Spirit that ruled in Jesus when we invite it to rule in our minds and hearts.

## The Word of God Cleanses Us[1]

21:12 Jesus entered into the temple of God,[2] and drove out all of those who sold and bought in the temple, and overthrew the money changers' tables and the seats of those who sold the doves. 21:13 He said to them, "It is written, 'My house shall be called a house of prayer,'[97] but you have made it a den of robbers![3]"[98]

21:14 The blind and the lame came to him in the temple, and he healed them. 21:15 But when the chief priests and the scribes saw the wonderful things that he did, and the children who were crying in the temple and saying, "Hosanna to the son of David!" they were indignant, 21:16 and said to him, "Do you hear what these are saying?"

Jesus said to them, "Yes. Did you never read, 'Out of the mouth of babes and nursing babies you have perfected praise?'"[99]

21:17 He left them, and went out of the city to Bethany,[4] and lodged there.

1. See Mark 11:15-17; Luke 19:45-46; John 2:13-17

2. *the temple of God.* The temple is our individual mind and body.

3. *den of robbers.* Destructive forces within us or that put our energies to unworthy uses. With His word, Jesus cast out these negations.

4. *Bethany.* The place of wailing, lamentation, affliction, and signifies the demonstration over these conditions (MBD/Bethany). Jesus' accomplishing many healings and teachings "in Bethany" is the power of the Word of Truth to both illuminate us as well as to give us victory during times of trouble.

## The Word frees us from Unfruitful Thought Trees[1]

21:18 Now in the morning, as he returned to the city, he was hungry. 21:19 Seeing a fig tree[2] by the road, he came to it, and found nothing on it but leaves. He said to it, "Let there be no fruit from you forever!"

Immediately the fig tree withered away. 21:20 When the disciples saw it, they marveled, saying, "How did the fig tree immediately wither away?"

21:21 Jesus answered them, "Most certainly I tell you, if you have faith, and don't doubt, you will not only do what was done to the fig tree, but even if you told this mountain, 'Be taken up and cast into the sea,' it would be done. 21:22 All things, whatever you ask in prayer, believing, you will receive."

1. See Mark 11:12-14,20-24

2. *a fig tree.* Among other things, figs or fig trees represent the seed of human beings, which in its original essence is mind energy (MBD/Almon-diblathaim). As a seed, so the tree and its fruit, so also, our thoughts are seeds that ought to bear fruitful trees. When the Word of Truth (Jesus) is active within us, It has the power to immediately cast out any unfruitful patterns of thinking.

## The Energy of Doubt Opposes the Authority of Spirit[1]

21:23 When he had come into the temple, the chief priests and the elders[2] of the people came to him as he was teaching, and said, "By what authority do you do these things? Who gave you this authority?"[3]

21:24 Jesus answered them, "I also will ask you one question, which if you tell me, I likewise will tell you by what authority I do these things. 21:25 The baptism of John, where was it from? From heaven or from men?"

They reasoned with themselves, saying, "If we say, 'From heaven,' he will ask us, 'Why then did you not believe him?' 21:26 But if we say, 'From men,' we fear the multitude, for all hold John as a prophet." 21:27 They answered Jesus, and said, "We don't know."

He also said to them, "Neither will I tell you[4] by what authority I do these things.

1. See Mark 11:27-33; Luke 20:1-8

2. *chief priests and the elders.* The religious thoughts in us that do not recognize that the authority of Spirit underlying our spiritual practices is far greater than their outward forms.

3. *Who gave you this authority?* The teacher of Truth must know Truth, be able to distinguish it from error, and be conscious of its essence within him. The authority of our inner conviction and knowledge is pre-eminent.

4. *Neither will I tell you.* The Christ in us has Divine authority and thus cannot be fettered or bound by the reasonings of the intellect.

## The Power of a Repentant Mind

21:28 But what do you think? A man had two sons, and he came to the first, and said, 'Son, go work today in my vineyard.' 21:29 He answered, 'I will not,' but afterward he changed his mind, and went. 21:30 He came to the second, and said the same thing. He answered, 'I go, sir,' but he didn't go.[1] 21:31 Which of the two did the will of his father?"[2]

They said to him, "The first."

Jesus said to them, "Most certainly I tell you that the tax collectors and the prostitutes are entering into the Kingdom of God before you. 21:32 For John came to you in the way of righteousness, and you didn't believe him, but the tax collectors and the prostitutes believed him. When you saw it, you didn't even repent afterward, that you might believe him.

1. *but he didn't go.* Individual worthiness is measured more by what we do than what we say. The first son at first rejects a spiritual standard of living, but later accepts it. The second son knows Truth ideas intellectually, but does not try to apply them.

2. *did the will of his father.* Those who live in error and change their ways are closer to spiritual understanding than are the religious "authorities" who ignore God's will. Our understanding of Truth and our ability to use it in every department of our life increases as we diligently and faithfully use the Truth that we know; this constitutes our entering into the Kingdom of God.

## The Principle of Honoring God's Faithful Tenants[1]

21:33 "Hear another parable. There was a man who was a master of a household,[2] who planted a vineyard, set a hedge about it, dug a winepress in it, built a tower, leased it out to farmers,[3] and went into another country. 21:34 When the season for the fruit drew near, he sent his servants[4] to the farmers, to receive his fruit. 21:35 The farmers took his servants, beat one, killed another, and stoned another. 21:36 Again, he sent other servants more than the first: and they treated them the same way. 21:37 But afterward he sent to them his son, saying, 'They will respect my son.' 21:38 But the farmers, when they saw the son, said among themselves, 'This is the heir. Come, let's kill him, and seize his inheritance.' 21:39 So they took him, and threw him out of the vineyard, and killed him. 21:40 When therefore the lord of the vineyard comes, what will he do to those farmers?"

21:41 They told him, "He will miserably destroy those miserable men, and will lease out the vineyard to other farmers,[5] who will give him the fruit in its season."

21:42 Jesus said to them, "Did you never read in the Scriptures,

'The stone which the builders
rejected,
the same was made the head
of the corner.
This was from the Lord.
It is marvelous in our
eyes?'[100]

21:43 "Therefore I tell you, the
Kingdom of God will be taken away
from you, and will be given to a
nation bringing forth its fruit. 21:44 He
who falls on this stone will be broken
to pieces, but on whoever it will fall,
it will scatter him as dust."

21:45 When the chief priests and the
Pharisees heard his parables, they
perceived that he spoke about them.
21:46 When they sought to seize him,
they feared the multitudes, because
they considered him to be a prophet.

1. See Mark 12:1-12; Luke 20:9-19

2. *master of a household.* The householder is God; his son is the Christ or Son of God (the Divine idea of us, in expression). The vineyard represents human beings in manifestation.

3. *farmers.* Our external religious thoughts and beliefs (scribes and Pharisees) can kill the messages sent us from God (servants).

4. *servants.* The servants of God are that which would keep us in the evolutionary process of developing understanding.

5. *other farmers.* We make space for the authority of intuitive Truth by letting go of external religious thoughts and beliefs.

Fillmore Study Bible annotations compiled by Mary Salama.

**World English Bible Footnotes:**

[93] v21:1. TR & NU read "Bethphage" instead of "Bethsphage"

[94] v21:5. Zechariah 9:9

[95] v21:9. "Hosanna" means "save us" or "help us, we pray."

[96] v21:9. Psalm 118:26

[97] v21:13. Isaiah 56:7

[98] v21:13. Jeremiah 7:11

[99] v21:16. Psalm 8:2

[100] v21:42. Psalm 118:22-23

# Matthew 22

## The Spiritual Wedding Feast[1]

22:1 Jesus answered and spoke
again in parables to them, saying,
22:2 "The Kingdom of Heaven is like a
certain king, who made a marriage
feast[2] for his son, 22:3 and sent out
his servants to call those who were
invited[3] to the marriage feast, but
they would not come. 22:4 Again he
sent out other servants, saying, 'Tell
those who are invited, "Behold, I

have made ready my dinner. My cattle and my fatlings are killed, and all things are ready. Come to the marriage feast!"' 22:5 But they made light of it, and went their ways, one to his own farm, another to his merchandise, 22:6 and the rest grabbed his servants, and treated them shamefully, and killed them. 22:7 When the king heard that, he was angry, and sent his armies, destroyed those murderers, and burned their city.

22:8 "Then he said to his servants, 'The wedding is ready, but those who were invited weren't worthy. 22:9 Go therefore to the intersections of the highways, and as many as you may find, invite to the marriage feast.' 22:10 Those servants went out into the highways, and gathered together as many as they found, both bad and good. The wedding was filled with guests. 22:11 But when the king came in to see the guests, he saw there a man who didn't have on wedding clothing[4], 22:12 and he said to him, 'Friend, how did you come in here not wearing wedding clothing?' He was speechless. 22:13 Then the king said to the servants, 'Bind him hand and foot, take him away, and throw him into the outer darkness; there is where the weeping and grinding of teeth will be.' 22:14 For many are called, but few chosen."[5]

1. See Luke 14:16-24

2. *king, who made a marriage feast.* The king is God. The marriage is the union of man with Spirit. A wedding feast stands for any occasion in our life, any type of situation in our life when we are being given an opportunity to partake of some spiritual, good, usually some new spiritual good.

3. *those who were invited.* The very large number of people who have made the union with Spirit are the first invited guests to the feast of the king. Strange yet true, these are most often the ones who are so taken up with exercising their superior abilities in material ways that they ignore the call of the Spirit. When we refuse God's invitations and make light of Spirit's messages (kill them), the price we pay is loss of the spiritual abundance God has for us.

4. *wedding clothing.* The most common meaning of garment is current attitude, toward self in general, toward the external, toward life events and other persons; so our prevailing or persistent attitude is our attitude-garment, becoming the garment of the moment, the garment being worn in any given situation. We put on the "wedding clothing" when we are clothed with right understanding of the Divine Principle and a careful conformity to it in thought and word.

5. *few chosen.* We prepare ourselves to "be chosen" for union with God by our practicing spiritual thinking and living.

## Paying Taxes to the Personal Will[1]

22:15 Then the Pharisees went and took counsel how they might entrap him in his talk. 22:16 They sent their disciples to him, along with the Herodians, saying, "Teacher, we know that you are honest, and teach the way of God in truth, no matter who you teach, for you aren't partial to anyone. 22:17 Tell us therefore, what do you think? Is it lawful to pay taxes to Caesar,[2] or not?"

22:18 But Jesus perceived their wickedness, and said, "Why do you test me, you hypocrites? 22:19 Show me the tax money."

They brought to him a denarius.

22:20 He asked them, "Whose is this image and inscription?"

22:21 They said to him, "Caesar's."

Then he said to them, "Give therefore to Caesar the things that are Caesar's, and to God the things that are God's."[3]

22:22 When they heard it, they
marveled, and left him,④ and went
away.

1. See Mark 12:13-17; Luke 20:20-26

2. *Caesar.* In consciousness, Caesar represents the tyrannical rule of the personal self unmodified by spiritual love and mercy and justice. Until the spiritual grows wise enough, sometimes we must even must make certain agreements with our unenlightened human will. Let us give the right amount of care and attention to external interests, but remain true to Spirit and to our highest Truth (the things that are God's).

3. *to God the things that are God's.* We are all stewards of Truth and of the riches of the inner kingdom. To be just stewards, we must spend these riches faithfully and use them aright.

4. *they marveled, and left Him.* Though at times it may seem we are at the mercy of our unmodified self-will (Caesar), our spiritual essence (Jesus) is outside the domain of Caesar, and the wisdom of our spiritual man is its very protection.

## Resurrection is Happening Now①

22:23 On that day Sadducees (those
who say that there is no resurrection)
came to him. They asked him, 22:24
saying, "Teacher, Moses said, 'If a
man dies, having no children, his
brother shall marry his wife, and
raise up seed for his brother.' 22:25
Now there were with us seven
brothers. The first married and died,
and having no seed left his wife to
his brother. 22:26 In like manner the
second also, and the third, to the
seventh. 22:27 After them all, the
woman died. 22:28 In the
resurrection② therefore, whose wife
will she be of the seven? For they all
had her."

22:29 But Jesus answered them,
"You are mistaken, not knowing the
Scriptures, nor the power of God. 22:30
For in the resurrection they neither
marry, nor are given in marriage, but
are like God's angels in heaven. 22:31
But concerning the resurrection of
the dead, haven't you read that
which was spoken to you by God,
saying, 22:32 'I am the God of Abraham,
and the God of Isaac, and the God of
Jacob?'[101] God is not the God of the
dead, but of the living." 22:33 When
the multitudes heard it, they were
astonished at his teaching.

1. See Mark 12:18-27; Luke 20:27-39

2. *In the resurrection.* The resurrection is the lifting up of the whole man (spirit, soul, and body) into the Christ consciousness. This is accomplished by the quickening power of the Holy Spirit which lifts up all the faculties of mind until they conform to the absolute ideas of Divine Mind. This renewal of the mind makes a complete transformation of the body so that every function works in Divine order and every cell becomes incorruptible and immortal. The resurrection is an organic change that takes place daily in all who are conforming their lives to the regenerating Truth of Jesus Christ.

## The Greatest Commandment①

22:34 But the Pharisees, when they
heard that he had silenced the
Sadducees, gathered themselves
together. 22:35 One of them, a lawyer,
asked him a question, testing him.
22:36 "Teacher, which is the greatest
commandment in the law?" 22:37 Jesus
said to him, "'You shall love the Lord
your God with all your heart, with
all your soul, and with all your
mind.'②[102] 22:38 This is the first and
great commandment. 22:39 A second
likewise is this, 'You shall love your
neighbor as yourself.'[103] 22:40 The

whole law and the prophets depend on these two commandments."

1. See Mark 12:28-31; Luke 10:25-28

2. *With all your mind.* Jesus confirms that the guarding of the thoughts of our minds with all our sincerity and strength is the most essential step to self-mastery and dominion. By continually setting our thoughts on the highest concept of the indwelling God, we are lifted into the realm of true thinking, where no wrong concepts of self or others are formed. (*Jesus' Soul Evolution* 981-82)

## Your Heritage is Divine, not "of David" (1)

22:41 Now while the Pharisees were
gathered together, Jesus asked them
a question, 22:42 saying, "What do you
think of the Christ? Whose son is he?"

They said to him, "Of David." (2)

22:43 He said to them, "How then
does David in the Spirit call him Lord,
saying,

22:44 'The Lord said to my Lord,
sit on my right hand,
until I make your enemies a
footstool for your
feet?'[104]

22:45 "If then David calls him Lord, (3)
how is he his son?"

22:46 No one was able to answer
him a word, neither did any man dare
ask him any more questions from that
day forth.

1. See Mark 12:35-37; Luke 20:21-44

2. *Of David.* Because of its limited range of perception, the intellect (the Pharisees) cannot conceive the formless, and so it attributes superior knowledge to some other man, hence the Pharisee's reply, "The son of David."

3. *David calls Him Lord.* The difference between the Divine and the human lineage of man is brought out in this question. Jesus did not give power to human heredity by tracing His descent through David, but showed that the Christ man, the Son of God, was the Higher Self or Lord, of David. David called upon the universal Lord to give power to his lord (spiritual consciousness). (*Jesus' Soul Evolution* 1003)

---

Fillmore Study Bible annotations by Mary Salama.

**World English Bible Footnotes:**

[101] v22:32. Exodus 3:6

[102] v22:37. Deuteronomy 6:5

[103] v22:39. Leviticus 19:18

[104] v22:44. Psalm 110:1

# MATTHEW 23

## Authentic Spirituality: Woes to Memories and Doubts❶

23:1 Then Jesus spoke to the multitudes and to his disciples,❷ 23:2 saying, "The scribes and the Pharisees sat on Moses' seat.❸ 23:3 All things therefore whatever they tell you to observe, observe and do, but don't do their works; for they say, and don't do. 23:4 For they bind heavy burdens that are grievous to be borne, and lay them on men's shoulders; but they themselves will not lift a finger to help them. 23:5 But all their works they do to be seen by men. They make their phylacteries[105] broad, enlarge the fringes[106] of their garments, 23:6 and love the place of honor at feasts, the best seats in the synagogues, 23:7 the salutations in the marketplaces, and to be called 'Rabbi, Rabbi' by men. 23:8 But don't you be called 'Rabbi,' for one is your teacher, the Christ,❹ and all of you are brothers. 23:9 Call no man on the earth your father, for one is your Father, he who is in heaven. 23:10 Neither be called masters, for one is your master, the Christ. 23:11 But he who is greatest among you will be your servant. 23:12 Whoever exalts himself will be humbled, and whoever humbles himself will be exalted.

23:13 "Woe to you,❺ scribes and Pharisees, hypocrites! For you devour widows' houses, and as a pretense you make long prayers. Therefore you will receive greater condemnation. [107]

23:14 "But woe to you, scribes and Pharisees, hypocrites! Because you shut up the Kingdom of Heaven against men; for you don't enter in yourselves, neither do you allow those who are entering in to enter. 23:15 Woe to you, scribes and Pharisees, hypocrites! For you travel around by sea and land to make one proselyte; and when he becomes one, you make him twice as much of a son of Gehenna[108] as yourselves.

23:16 "Woe to you, you blind guides, who say, 'Whoever swears by the temple, it is nothing; but whoever swears by the gold of the temple, he is obligated.' 23:17 You blind fools! For which is greater, the gold, or the temple that sanctifies the gold? 23:18 'Whoever swears by the altar, it is nothing; but whoever swears by the gift that is on it, he is obligated?' 23:19 You blind fools! For which is greater, the gift, or the altar that sanctifies the gift? 23:20 He therefore who swears by the altar, swears by it, and by everything on it. 23:21 He who swears by the temple, swears by it, and by him who was living in it. 23:22 He who swears by heaven, swears by the throne of God, and by him who sits on it.

23:23 "Woe to you, scribes and Pharisees, hypocrites! For you tithe mint, dill, and cumin,[109] and have left undone the weightier matters of the law: justice, mercy, and faith. But you ought to have done these, and not to have left the other undone. 23:24 You blind guides, who strain out a gnat, and swallow a camel!

23:25 "Woe to you, scribes and Pharisees, hypocrites! For you clean the outside of the cup and of the platter, but within they are full of extortion and unrighteousness.[110] 23:26 You blind Pharisee, first clean

the inside[6] of the cup and of the
platter, that its outside may become
clean also.

23:27 "Woe to you, scribes and
Pharisees, hypocrites! For you are
like whitened tombs, which
outwardly appear beautiful, but
inwardly are full of dead men's
bones, and of all uncleanness. 23:28
Even so you also outwardly appear
righteous to men, but inwardly you
are full of hypocrisy and iniquity.

23:29 "Woe to you, scribes and
Pharisees, hypocrites! For you build
the tombs of the prophets, and
decorate the tombs of the righteous,
23:30 and say, 'If we had lived in the
days of our fathers, we wouldn't have
been partakers with them in the
blood of the prophets.' 23:31 Therefore
you testify to yourselves that you are
children of those who killed the
prophets. 23:32 Fill up, then, the
measure of your fathers. 23:33 You
serpents, you offspring of vipers,
how will you escape the judgment of
Gehenna[111]? 23:34 Therefore, behold,
I send to you prophets, wise men,
and scribes. Some of them you will
kill and crucify; and some of them
you will scourge in your synagogues,
and persecute from city to city; 23:35
that on you may come all the
righteous blood shed on the earth,
from the blood of righteous Abel to
the blood of Zachariah son of
Barachiah, whom you killed between
the sanctuary and the altar.[7] 23:36
Most certainly I tell you, all these
things will come upon this
generation.

1. See Luke 11:47-51

2. *Jesus spoke to the multitudes and to His disciples.* Jesus (the indwelling Christ) is talking to His multitude of receptive thoughts (the multitude) and spiritual helpers (the disciples). In referring to those who love the chief places and seats, Jesus illustrated the effects of working in the outer instead of the within. (*Jesus' Soul Evolution* 1008)

3. *The Scribes and the Pharisees sat on Moses' seat.* Scribes are thoughts that come to us from other personalities or books. There is a faculty of mind that receives and transcribes upon the tablets of memory every wave of thought that touches the consciousness. Pharisees are thoughts that arise out of the subconsciousness, binding us to external forms of religion without giving us an understanding of their real meaning. (MBD/scribes)

4. *One is your Teacher, the Christ.* We are all enrolled in Jesus Christ's school and He is our Teacher.

5. *Woe to you.* Formalism in religious practices is not necessarily productive of spiritual progress and may in fact prevent the natural inflow of Spirit. If we are to be truly religious, we must give attention primarily to things of the Spirit. Jesus was warning them of the many woes and sorrows that would come if they persisted in living the outward life and continued to turn a deaf ear to the inspiration of Spirit.

6. *First clean the inside.* It is a law of Spirit that "as within, so without." Those who would grow spiritually must first deny or cleanse the mind of the false and limited beliefs of the sense man in order that they may become receptive to and unify themselves with Truth.

7. *The altar.* The place in consciousness where we are willing to give up the lower to the higher, the personal to the impersonal, the animal to the Divine. (*Jesus' Soul Evolution* 1023)

## Truth Cries Out in Our Soul[1]

23:37 "Jerusalem, Jerusalem,[2] who
kills the prophets, and stones those
who are sent to her! How often I
would have gathered your children
together, even as a hen gathers her
chicks under her wings, and you
would not! 23:38 Behold, your house is
left to you desolate. 23:39 For I tell
you, you will not see me from now
on, until you say, 'Blessed is he who
comes in the name of the Lord!'"[112]

1. See Luke 13:34-35
2. *Jerusalem, Jerusalem.* Jerusalem, "habitation of peace," is the love center in consciousness. It is the abode of the good and the pure, but error thoughts of the mind cause it to become the habitation of wickedness.

Fillmore Study Bible annotations by Mary Salama.

**World English Bible Footnotes:**

[105] v23:5. phylacteries (tefillin in Hebrew) are small leather pouches that some Jewish men wear on their forehead and arm in prayer. They are used to carry a small scroll with some Scripture in it. See Deuteronomy 6:8.

[106] v23:5. or, tassels

[107] v23:14. Some Greek manuscripts reverse the order of verses 13 and 14, and some omit verse 13, numbering verse 14 as 13.

[108] v23:15. or, Hell

[109] v23:23. cumin is an aromatic seed from Cuminum cyminum, resembling caraway in flavor and appearance. It is used as a spice.

[110] v23:25. TR reads "self-indulgence" instead of "unrighteousness"

[111] v23:33. or, Hell

[112] v23:39. Psalm 118:26

# Matthew 24

## The Transformation in Consciousness Foretold[1]

24:1 Jesus went out from the
temple,[2] and was going on his way.
His disciples came to him to show
him the buildings of the temple. 24:2
But he answered them, "Don't you
see all of these things? Most certainly
I tell you, there will not be left here
one stone on another, that will not
be thrown down."

1. See Mk 13.1-2; Lk 21.5-6.

2. *out from the temple.* We look to this chapter both as a prophecy and symbology of the regeneration process that takes place within us; the journey from the human to the Divine consciousness. The old is passing away and the new is being ushered in. Within ourselves, a temple represents material conditions, which Jesus taught would dissolve and disappear like a dream at the end of the age. (*Jesus' Soul Evolution* 1035-36)

## The Signs of the End of a Stage of Consciousness[1]

24:3 As he sat on the Mount of Olives, the disciples came to him privately, saying, "Tell us, when will these things be? What is the sign of your coming, and of the end of the age?"

24:4 Jesus answered them, "Be careful that no one leads you astray.[2] 24:5 For many will come in my name, saying, 'I am the Christ,'[3] and will lead many astray. 24:6 You will hear of wars and rumors of wars.[4] See that you aren't troubled, for all this must happen, but the end is not yet. 24:7 For nation will rise against nation, and kingdom against kingdom; and there will be famines, plagues, and earthquakes in various places. 24:8 But all these things are the beginning of birth pains.

1. See Mk 13.3-8; Lk 21.7-11.
2. *"Be careful that no one leads you astray."* because wisdom requires us to keep our thoughts constructive by contemplating life rather than death.
3. *"I am the Christ."* Jesus refutes the belief that the Christ will be found in this personality or in that one; the truth is that Christ must be formed in us. (*Jesus' Soul Evolution* 1039)
4. *wars and rumors of wars.* Wars represent mental states that disrupt peace and well-being of the body.

## The Regeneration Process Foretold[1]

24:9 Then they will deliver you up to oppression,[2] and will kill you. You will be hated by all of the nations for my name's sake. 24:10 Then many will stumble, and will deliver up one another, and will hate one another. 24:11 Many false prophets will arise, and will lead many astray. 24:12 Because iniquity will be multiplied, the love of many will grow cold. 24:13 But he who endures to the end, the same will be saved. 24:14 This Good News of the Kingdom will be preached in the whole world for a testimony to all the nations, and then the end will come.[3]

1. See Mk 13.9a, 13; Lk 21.12a, 17-19.
2. *oppression.* Oppression, or "great tribulation," means sacrifice; the giving up of things. We must be willing for the old to pass away in order for the new to come in (regeneration). (*Jesus' Soul Evolution* 1039)
3. *the end will come.* When we have the power to keep the mind stayed on Principle, refusing to be influenced by outer conditions, then the end (of our current state of consciousness) will come.

## Habits of Thinking that Lead to Desolation[1]

24:15 "When, therefore, you see the abomination of desolation,[113] which was spoken of through Daniel the prophet, standing in the holy place (let the reader understand), 24:16 then let those who are in Judea flee to the mountains. 24:17 Let him who is on the housetop not go down to take out things that are in his house. 24:18 Let him who is in the field not return back to get his clothes. 24:19 But woe to those who are with child and to nursing mothers[2] in those days![3] 24:20 Pray that your flight will not be in the winter, nor on a Sabbath,[4] 24:21 for then there will be great oppression, such as has not been from the beginning of the world

until now, no, nor ever will be. 24:22
Unless those days had been
shortened, no flesh would have been
saved. But for the sake of the chosen
ones, those days will be shortened.

24:23 "Then if any man tells you,
'Behold, here is the Christ,' or,
'There,' don't believe it. 24:24 For there
will arise false christs,5 and false
prophets, and they will show great
signs and wonders, so as to lead
astray, if possible, even the chosen
ones.

24:25 "Behold, I have told you
beforehand. 24:26 If therefore they tell
you, 'Behold, he is in the wilderness,'
don't go out; 'Behold, he is in the
inner chambers,' don't believe it. 24:27
For as the lightning flashes from the
east, and is seen even to the west,
so will be the coming of the Son of
Man. 24:28 For wherever the carcass
is, there is where the vultures[114]
gather together.

1. See Mk 13.14-23; Lk 17.23-24, 37; 21.20-24

2. *who are with child and to nursing mothers* This refers to those who live under the law of generation. This is the age of regeneration, and anyone living under the law of generation will meet with hazardous conditions. (*Jesus' Soul Evolution* 1037-38)

3. *in those days!* Spiritually interpreted, "those days" do not refer to some far off future date, but to man's own consciousness. When we are awakened to the truth about God and man and begin to practice that truth, then our material consciousness is nearing its last days of existence. Every day is the "last day" of the old way of thinking and the "beginning" of the new day. It is up to us to see that we do not give birth to material thoughts, words, and actions, for if we continue "nursing" grudges, fears, griefs, or inharmonies of any kind, we are depriving ourselves of the infinite blessings which each day holds for us. In order to enjoy each day's blessings, we must stop generating negative thoughts and instead regenerate ourselves in the way of Spirit.

4. *winter, nor on a Sabbath.* Winter and Sabbath are seasons of rest. In consciousness, there is a time to rest but there is also a time when one must be up and doing and not resting. There must be activity (inner work). (*Jesus' Soul Evolution* 1038-39)

5. *false christs.* Ideas in individual consciousness that are not true to Principle; a mixture of Spirit with matter. These ideas endeavor to deceive our most elect thoughts. In order to discern that which is true from that which is false, we must live very close to Spirit and seek the guidance of the Spirit of Truth, moment by moment. (*Jesus' Soul Evolution* 1041)

## The Coming of the Higher Consciousness1

24:29 But immediately after the
oppression of those days, the sun will
be darkened, the moon will not give
its light, the stars will fall from the
sky, and the powers of the heavens
will be shaken;2[115] 24:30 and then
the sign of the Son of Man will appear
in the sky. Then all the tribes of the
earth will mourn, and they will see
the Son of Man coming on the clouds
of the sky with power and great
glory. 24:31 He will send out his
angels3 with a great sound of a
trumpet, and they will gather
together his chosen ones from the
four winds, from one end of the sky
to the other.

1. See Mk 13.24-27; Lk 21.25-28.

2. *will be shaken.* This refers no doubt to the various experiences one goes through in regeneration. In passing from one step to another, one's existing consciousness is darkened by the inrush of universal (Higher or Divine) consciousness, but only for a season. Eventually the spiritual man must come into consciousness and the person raised up (great glory). (*Jesus' Soul Evolution* 1042)

3. *will send out His angels.* Angels symbolize thoughts direct from Divine Mind, whose nature is to draw to it the elect (our chosen, spiritual thoughts). Whereas up until now we had been getting spiritual information filtering through sense consciousness, we now will get it direct from

God. From the four winds. The east represents the within; the west, the manifest; the north, the cold intellect without the warmth of Spirit; and the south, life on the natural plane. (*Jesus' Soul Evolution* 1043-44)

## We Can Learn about Consciousness by Studying Nature[1]

24:32 "Now from the fig tree learn
this[2] parable. When its branch has
now become tender, and puts forth
its leaves, you know that the summer
is near. 24:33 Even so you also, when
you see all these things, know that
it is near,[3] even at the doors. 24:34
Most certainly I tell you, this
generation[116] will not pass away,
until all these things are
accomplished. 24:35 Heaven and earth
will pass away, but my words will not
pass away.[4]

1. See Mk 13.28-32; Lk 21.29-33.

2. *from the fig tree learn this.* Nature has its seasons, mind has its seasons. Just as we can predict effects that take place in nature by observing, studying, and understanding their underlying causes and the physical laws that govern them, we also, through consistent study and observation, can learn much about the nature of our minds and consciousness.

3. *know that it is near.* The ability to foretell the future is a desirable development of our perceptive powers to the extent that we are prepared to devote the full force of our thought and effort.

4. *my Words will not pass away.* Words of Truth will never "pass away," that is, become inapplicable to changed conditions or circumstances. The inner universe of causes, which we designate as Divine Mind, will always remain, since it is eternal and infinite, not subject to no limitations of either time or space.

## The Necessity for Watchfulness[1]

24:36 But no one knows of that day
and hour, not even the angels of
heaven, but my Father only. 24:37 "As
the days of Noah were, so will be the
coming of the Son of Man. 24:38 For as
in those days which were before the
flood they were eating and drinking,
marrying and giving in marriage,
until the day that Noah entered into
the ship, 24:39 and they didn't know
until the flood came, and took them
all away, so will be the coming of
the Son of Man. 24:40 Then two men
will be in the field: one will be taken
and one will be left; 24:41 two women
grinding at the mill, one will be
taken and one will be left. 24:42 Watch
therefore, for you don't know in what
hour your Lord comes. 24:43 But know
this, that if the master of the house
had known in what watch of the
night the thief was coming, he would
have watched,[2] and would not have
allowed his house to be broken into.
24:44 Therefore also be ready, for in an
hour that you don't expect, the Son
of Man[3] will come.

1. See Lk 17.26-27, 34-35; 12.39-40

2. *watch ... watch.* The repetition of the word "watch" points to the necessity of being continually on the alert, in this way, one is never to be taken by surprise but is ready for emergencies and able to meet them in a way that preserves poise and mental balance. Our I AM or Christ Spirit, rightly followed, keeps us alert and watchful, ready always to serve the highest. (See Luke 12:35-48)

3. *The Son of Man.* The Son of Man is the person that God created, our real Self.

## Our Consistent Obedience, the Faithful Servant[1]

24:45 "Who then is the faithful and wise servant,[2] whom his lord has set over his household,[3] to give them their food in due season? 24:46 Blessed is that servant whom his lord finds doing so when he comes. 24:47 Most certainly I tell you that he will set him over all that he has. 24:48 But if that evil servant should say in his heart, 'My lord is delaying his coming,' 24:49 and begins to beat his fellow servants, and eat and drink with the drunkards, 24:50 the lord of that servant will come in a day when he doesn't expect it, and in an hour when he doesn't know it, 24:51 and will cut him in pieces, and appoint his portion with the hypocrites. There is where the weeping and grinding of teeth will be.

1. See Lk 12.42-46.

2. *the faithful and wise servant.* Represents our soul, whose function it is to watch over, guard, and protect the body and nourish it with the Word of Truth.

3. *whom his lord has set over his household.* The "Lord" here is the higher Law of Life that is at work within us; the Spirit of Life that governs the human being. But if our soul becomes lethargic and our mind dulled by the ascendancy of sense desires, we become an evil servant, unresponsive to the calls of the Spirit.

---

Fillmore Study Bible annotations by Mary Salama.

**World English Bible Footnotes:**

[113] v24:15. Daniel 9:27; 11:31; 12:11

[114] v24:28. or, eagles

[115] v24:29. Isaiah 13:10; 34:4

[116] v24:34. The word for "generation" (genea) can also be translated as "race."

# MATTHEW 25

## Parable of the Virgin Senses of the Soul

25:1 "Then the Kingdom of Heaven[1] will be like ten virgins, who took their lamps, and went out to meet the bridegroom. 25:2 Five of them were foolish, and five were wise.[2] 25:3 Those who were foolish, when they took their lamps, took no oil with them, 25:4 but the wise took oil in their vessels with their lamps. 25:5 Now while the bridegroom delayed, they all slumbered and slept. 25:6 But at midnight there was a cry, 'Behold! The bridegroom is coming! Come out to meet him!' 25:7 Then all those virgins arose, and trimmed their lamps.[117] 25:8 The foolish said to the wise, 'Give us some of your oil, for our lamps are going out.' 25:9 But the wise answered, saying, 'What if there isn't enough for us and you? You go rather to those who sell, and buy for yourselves.' 25:10 While they went away to buy, the bridegroom came,[3] and those who were ready went in with him to the marriage feast, and the door was shut. 25:11 Afterward the other virgins also came, saying, 'Lord, Lord, open to us.' 25:12 But he answered, 'Most certainly I tell you, I don't know you.' 25:13 Watch therefore,[4] for you don't know the day nor the hour in which the Son of Man is coming.

1. *The kingdom of heaven* a state of consciousness in which soul and body are in harmony with Divine Mind. (*Jesus' Soul Evolution/Ten Bridesmaids*)

2. *foolish, and five were wise*. The ten virgins represent the senses. They are five in number but they have a twofold action. The outer are connected with the inner and both draw their supply from the same source. The eye has an inner eye, the ear an inner ear, feeling is more a matter of sympathy than of physical touch, tasting involves discrimination, and the sense of smell becomes the intuitive cognition of values.

3. *the bridegroom came*. The coming of the bridegroom, which is the subtle joining of spirit, soul, and body, is so deep in consciousness that we do not know when it takes place. We feel the result in a greater satisfaction and harmony, and this is in reality the forming in us of the kingdom of heaven. This kingdom is built up in human consciousness day by day, or rather, degree by degree; time is not a factor.

4. *Watch therefore*. The parable of the ten virgins is an object lesson in spiritual preparedness. To be prepared for the hour of union (marriage), we must remain mentally alert (constantly supplied with oil). The way to supply oil in the lamps is to affirm that the source of our seeing, hearing, smelling, feeling, and tasting is not material but spiritual understanding.

## Parable of the Soul's Talents [1]

25:14 "For it is like a man, going into another country, who called his own servants, and entrusted his goods to them.[2] 25:15 To one he gave five talents, to another two, to another one; to each according to his own ability. Then he went on his journey. 25:16 Immediately he who received the five talents went and traded with them, and made another five[3] talents. 25:17 In like manner he also who got the two gained another two. 25:18 But he who received the one went away and dug in the earth, and hid his lord's money.

25:19 "Now after a long time the lord of those servants came, and reconciled accounts with them. 25:20 He who received the five talents came and brought another five talents, saying, 'Lord, you delivered to me five talents. Behold, I have gained another five talents besides them.'

25:21 "His lord said to him, 'Well done,[4] good and faithful servant. You have been faithful over a few things, I will set you over many things. Enter into the joy of your lord.'

25:22 "He also who got the two talents came and said, 'Lord, you delivered to me two talents. Behold, I have gained another two talents besides them.'

25:23 "His lord said to him, 'Well done, good and faithful servant. You have been faithful over a few things, I will set you over many things. Enter into the joy of your lord.'

25:24 "He also who had received the one talent came and said, 'Lord, I knew you that you are a hard man, reaping where you did not sow, and gathering where you did not scatter. 25:25 I was afraid, and went away and hid your talent[5] in the earth.

Behold, you have what is yours.'

25:26 "But his lord answered him, 'You wicked and slothful servant. You knew that I reap where I didn't sow, and gather where I didn't scatter. 25:27 You ought therefore to have deposited my money with the bankers, and at my coming I should have received back my own with interest. 25:28 Take away therefore the talent from him, and give it to him who has the ten talents. 25:29 For to everyone who has will be given, and he will have abundance, but from him who doesn't have, even that which he has will be taken away. 25:30 Throw out the unprofitable servant into the outer darkness, where there will be weeping and gnashing of teeth.'

1. See Lk 19.12-27

2. *entrusted his goods to them.* The Divine Mind is "the man who entrusted His goods" to His servants and went "into another country." (*Jesus' Soul Evolution/The Talents*)

3. *made another five.* We have within us (our soul) both a capacity to increase our knowledge of Divine Mind, as well as to evolve and bring it forth (made another five.) The five talents also represent the five senses.

4. *Well done.* The right use of our senses and capacities to know God is commended by the Lord.

5. *hid your talent.* The cause of failure is not incapacity but failure to use the capacity one has. Potential capacity is really all that we possesses until we make these talents our very own by opening up their "inner" side.

## The Purification of the Imagi-Nations

25:31 "But when the Son of Man[1]

comes in his glory, and all the holy angels with him, then he will sit on the throne of his glory. 25:32 Before him all the nations will be gathered, and he will separate them one from another, as a shepherd separates the sheep from the goats.[2]

25:33 He will set the sheep on his right hand, but the goats on the left. 25:34 Then the King will tell those on his right hand, 'Come, blessed of my Father, inherit the Kingdom prepared for you from the foundation of the world; 25:35 for I was hungry, and you gave me food to eat; I was thirsty, and you gave me drink; I was a stranger, and you took me in; 25:36 naked, and you clothed me; I was sick, and you visited me; I was in prison, and you came to me.'

25:37 "Then the righteous[3]

will answer him, saying, 'Lord, when did we see you hungry, and feed you; or thirsty, and give you a drink? 25:38 When did we see you as a stranger, and take you in; or naked, and clothe you? 25:39 When did we see you sick, or in prison, and come to you?'

25:40 "The King will answer them, 'Most certainly I tell you, inasmuch as you did it to one of the least of these my brothers[118], you did it to me.' 25:41 Then he will say also to those on the left hand, 'Depart from me, you cursed, into the eternal fire which is prepared for the devil and his angels; 25:42 for I was hungry, and you didn't give me food to eat; I was thirsty, and you gave me no drink; 25:43 I was a stranger, and you didn't take me in; naked, and you didn't clothe me; sick, and in prison, and you didn't visit me.'

25:44 "Then they will also answer, saying, 'Lord, when did we see you hungry, or thirsty, or a stranger, or naked, or sick, or in prison, and didn't help you?'

[25:45] "Then he will answer them,
saying, 'Most certainly I tell you,
inasmuch as you didn't do it to one
of the least of these, you didn't do it
to me.' [25:46] These will go away into
eternal punishment[4]

but the righteous into eternal life."

1. *the Son of man.* The Son of *God* is Christ, the Divine Idea of Man. The Son of *man* is Adam, the manifestation of Christ. When it dawns upon us (the Son of man) that we are in reality Christ (the Son of God), a higher consciousness is born in us and we rule instead of being ruled. This is symbolically pictured as "he will sit on the throne of his glory." (*Jesus' Soul Evolution/Judgment of the Nations*)

2. *sheep from the goats.* The sheep represent our receptive, obedient, productive thoughts. The goats represent our aggressive, disobedient thoughts. When Divine understanding enters the mind, it quickens the discriminating faculty. Our standard becomes absolute Truth and requires us to deny all motives, thoughts, and acts that do not accord with it (the goats), and to affirm those in harmony with it (the sheep). Thus the sheep are separated from the goats.

3. *the righteous.* The appetites, passions, and thoughts are in fact righteous servants of mind and body; they minister to us while we are yet bound in sense consciousness. When the Higher Self (the Lord) comes into dominion and recognizes the service of these silent workers, they are surprised at being set at the right hand and are told that when they served the body, which is brother of the mind, they were at the same time serving the Christ.

4. *eternal punishment.* The goats (adverse states of thought) being sent into eternal punishment implies purification, which is not a punishment.

---

Fillmore Study Bible annotations by Mary Salama.

**World English Bible Footnotes:**

[117] v25:7. The end of the wick of an oil lamp needs to be cut off periodically to avoid having it become clogged with carbon deposits. The wick height is also adjusted so that the flame burns evenly and gives good light without producing a lot of smoke.

[118] v25:40. The word for "brothers" here may be also correctly translated "brothers and sisters" or "siblings."

# Matthew 26

## Plot to Release the Truth[1]

[26:1] It happened, when Jesus had
finished all these words, that he said
to his disciples, [26:2] "You know that
after two days the Passover[2] is
coming, and the Son of Man will be
delivered up to be crucified."

[26:3] Then the chief priests, the
scribes, and the elders of the people
were gathered together in the court
of the high priest, who was called
Caiaphas. [26:4] They took counsel
together that they might take Jesus
by deceit, and kill him.[3] [26:5] But they
said, "Not during the feast, lest a riot
occur among the people."

1. See Mark 14:1-2; Luke 22:1-2; John 11:47-53

2. *the Passover.* the passing over from one state of consciousness to another, preparing for a great awakening. The I Am Itself (Jesus) is the Passover Lamb. (MBD/ Passover)

3. *and kill Him.* When a new spiritual unfoldment (the Christ) takes place, the higher intellectual consciousness (symbolized by Caiaphas and his followers) plot to do away with this spiritual power. (*Jesus' Soul Evolution* 1083)

## Truth is Empowered when we Pour ourselves out in Loving Service to Others [1]

26:6 Now when Jesus was in Bethany, in the house of Simon the leper, 26:7 a woman came to him having an alabaster jar of very expensive ointment, and she poured it on his head as he sat at the table.[2] 26:8 But when his disciples saw this, they were indignant, saying, "Why this waste? 26:9 For this ointment might have been sold for much, and given to the poor."

26:10 However, knowing this, Jesus said to them, "Why do you trouble the woman? Because she has done a good work for me. 26:11 For you always have the poor with you; but you don't always have me. 26:12 For in pouring this ointment on my body, she did it to prepare me for burial. 26:13 Most certainly I tell you, wherever this Good News is preached in the whole world, what this woman has done will also be spoken of as a memorial of her."

1. See Mark 14:3-9; Luke 7:36-50; John 12:1-8

2. The anointing of Jesus' feet by "the woman having an alabaster jar of very expensive ointment" is the willingness of love to serve. As metaphysicians, our tendency may be to concentrate more upon our understanding of the Word of God, but we learn by experience that the cold science of mind without the warmth of the heart is a very chilly doctrine. (*Jesus' Soul Evolution* 1087-88)

## A Life of Praise Promises to Release the Truth [1]

26:14 Then one of the twelve, who was called Judas[2] Iscariot, went to the chief priests, 26:15 and said, "What are you willing to give me, that I should deliver him to you?" They weighed out for him thirty pieces of silver. 26:16 From that time he sought opportunity to betray him.

1. See Mark 14:10-11; Luke 22:3-6; John 11:57

2. *who was called Judas.* Among our disciples, or faculties, is one whose tendency is such that through it we are brought into condemnation and suffering. Self-appropriation (Judas) is the sin that brings tragedy. Judas represents the unredeemed life forces which are a thief and a destroyer and a betrayer. They deliver up Jesus for gratification of flesh desire (thirty pieces of silver). As in the days of Jesus, so it is today—misuse of the life faculty is deceiving the whole world, and even metaphysicians who are free in every other way are bound by its false reasoning. (*Jesus' Soul Evolution* 1090-91)

## The Mind's Passover [1]

26:17 Now on the first day of unleavened bread, the disciples came to Jesus, saying to him, "Where do you want us to prepare for you to eat the Passover?"[2]

26:18 He said, "Go into the city to a certain person, and tell him, 'The Teacher says, "My time is at hand. I will keep the Passover at your house with my disciples.""

26:19 The disciples did as Jesus commanded them, and they prepared the Passover. 26:20 Now when evening had come, he was reclining at the table with the twelve disciples. 26:21 As they were eating, he said, "Most certainly I tell you that one of you will betray me."

26:22 They were exceedingly sorrowful, and each began to ask him, "It isn't me, is it, Lord?"

26:23 He answered, "He who dipped his hand with me in the dish, the same will betray me. 26:24 The Son of Man goes, even as it is written of him, but woe to that man through whom the Son of Man is betrayed! It would be better for that man if he had not been born."

26:25 Judas, who betrayed him, answered, "It isn't me, is it, Rabbi?"

He said to him, "You said it."

1. See Mark 14:12-21; Luke 22:7-14,21-23; John 13:21-26

2. *the Passover*. This feast represents the passing from a lower to a higher consciousness. [A worthy question to bring to prayer often: "Lord, how would You have me pass through this season or experience in my life?"]

## Establishing a Life of Inner Communion [1]

26:26 As they were eating, Jesus took bread[2], gave thanks for[119] it, and broke it. He gave to the disciples, and said, "Take, eat; this is my body."[3] 26:27 He took the cup, gave thanks, and gave to them, saying, "All of you drink it,[4] 26:28 for this is my blood of the new covenant,[5] which is poured out for many[6] for the remission of sins.[7] 26:29 But I tell you that I will not drink of this fruit of the vine from now on, until that day when I drink it anew with you in my Father's Kingdom." 26:30 When they had sung a hymn,[8] they went out to the Mount of Olives.

1. See Mark 14:22-26; Luke 22:15-20,39; I Cor. 11:23

2. *bread, wine*. Bread represents the body of Christ, or Spirit [which is nonphysical and not yet formed substance]. Wine is the expressed life of the vine, a symbol of the very blood of life. We partake Spiritual communion whenever we appropriate (eat and drink) the Word of Truth, both in our minds and in our lives.

3. *body, blood*. The body is spiritual flesh or substance made permanent by the Word of God that Jesus spoke. His blood is Spirit life, the quickening element in creation. Both are of the universal essence or substance, which cannot be destroyed.

4. *Take, eat ... drink*. The appropriation or right use of substance is necessary to us in a threefold way: we must appropriate substance in the form of physical food, in the form of ideas, and in the form of spiritual aspirations and ideals.

5. *the new covenant*. The new covenant is the ultimate promise of God; the promise of spiritual freedom through Christ.

6. *poured out for many*. Through Jesus' experience on the cross, He lowered His consciousness to that of the race and

thereby was enabled to administer to the race a wonderful blood transfusion which we all understand so well implanted in both soul and body, the seed of eternal life here and now — the seed of Divine Substance, here and now.

7. *remission of sins.* The blood of Jesus Christ (the pure Christ life) takes away thirst for sin, and the world is saved through the absence of desire for sin. When we mentally appropriate the body and drink the blood of Jesus Christ, we become conscious of spiritual life and substance as the reality of being, and we are freed from the limiting thought of our flesh and blood bodies.

8. *sung a hymn.* Inasmuch as they make the mind receptive to Truth, the giving of thanks and singing of Psalms or hymns are all expressions that aid in the ushering in of spiritual consciousness.

## God anticipates our Denials [1]

26:31 Then Jesus said to them, "All
of you will be made to stumble
because of me tonight, for it is
written, 'I will strike the shepherd,
and the sheep of the flock will be
scattered.'[120] 26:32 But after I am
raised up, I will go before you into
Galilee."

26:33 But Peter answered him,
"Even if all will be made to stumble
because of you, I will never be made
to stumble."[2]

26:34 Jesus said to him, "Most
certainly I tell you that tonight,
before the rooster crows, you will
deny me three times."

26:35 Peter said to him, "Even if I
must die with you, I will not deny
you." All of the disciples also said
likewise.

1. See Mark 14:27-31; Luke 22:31-34; John 13:36-38

2. *I will never be made to stumble.* Peter here represents untried faith, which sometimes leads one into overconfidence through imperfect self-knowledge. All untried faculties are subject to the same defect: "All of the disciples also said likewise."

## Jesus Prays in Gethsemane[1]

26:36 Then Jesus came with them
to a place called Gethsemane,[2] and
said to his disciples, "Sit here, while
I go there and pray."[3] 26:37 He took
with him Peter and the two sons of
Zebedee,[4] and began to be
sorrowful and severely troubled. 26:38
Then he said to them, "My soul is
exceedingly sorrowful, even to
death. Stay here, and watch with
me."

26:39 He went forward a little, fell
on his face, and prayed, saying, "My
Father, if it is possible, let this cup
pass away from me; nevertheless,
not what I desire, but what you
desire."[5]

26:40 He came to the disciples, and
found them sleeping, and said to
Peter, "What, couldn't you watch
with me[6] for one hour? 26:41 Watch
and pray,[7] that you don't enter into
temptation. The spirit indeed is
willing, but the flesh is weak."[8]

26:42 Again, a second time he went
away, and prayed, saying, "My
Father, if this cup can't pass away
from me unless I drink it, your desire
be done." 26:43 He came again and
found them sleeping, for their eyes
were heavy. 26:44 He left them again,

went away, and prayed a third time, saying the same words. [26:45] Then he came to his disciples, and said to them, "Sleep on now, and take your rest. Behold, the hour is at hand, and the Son of Man is betrayed into the hands of sinners. [26:46] Arise, let's be going. Behold, he who betrays me is at hand."

1. See Mark 14:32-42; Luke 22:40-46; John 18:1

2. *Gethsemane.* Means "oil press." It symbolizes the place in consciousness where the finer essences of the spirit are pressed forth and raised to higher planes of expression.

3. *"Sit here, while I go there and pray."* In time of distress we turn instinctively to prayer for help. That Jesus brought all His faculties (disciples) with Him in this experience shows that we can meet our tests successfully, only as we apply all our powers to each as it arises.

4. *Peter and the two sons of Zebedee.* In a crisis, some faculties need to be quickened and active before all others. Jesus took with Him Peter, John, and James (faith, love, and judgment) to the place where He was to pray, leaving the other disciples seated a little distance away.

5. *not what I desire, but what You desire.* Jesus chose to unite His human will with the Divine will, and lose consciousness of the human in the deeper consciousness of the Divine.

6. *couldn't you watch with Me?* Faith (Peter) that is dulled by lack of daily exercise or application to spiritual ends is no better than skepticism; love (John) that is allowed to grow sluggish or self-centered instead of remaining alert and vigilant is of no value; and judgment (James) that ceases to function constructively is a liability instead of an asset.

7. *Watch and pray.* Remaining watchful and prayerful is especially helpful to us in times of testing, that we may avoid the temptation of slipping back into an easy acceptance of the race thought instead of relying stoutly on the spiritual foundation that God is sufficient to support us, no matter what we go through.

8. *"The spirit indeed is willing, but the flesh is weak."* This statement speaks to the necessity of spiritualizing the "flesh" or so-called "material mind" until we are schooled to rely completely on the higher power of God in all emergencies or trials.

## The Betrayal of our Inner Christ [1]

[26:47] While he was still speaking, behold, Judas,[2] one of the twelve, came, and with him a great multitude with swords and clubs, from the chief priest and elders of the people. [26:48] Now he who betrayed him gave them a sign, saying, "Whoever I kiss, he is the one. Seize him." [26:49] Immediately he came to Jesus, and said, "Hail, Rabbi!" and kissed him.[3]

[26:50] Jesus said to him, "Friend, why are you here?" Then they came and laid hands on Jesus, and took him. [26:51] Behold, one of those who were with Jesus stretched out his hand, and drew his sword, and struck the servant of the high priest, and struck off his ear. [26:52] Then Jesus said to him, "Put your sword back into its place, for all those who take the sword will die by the sword. [26:53] Or do you think that I couldn't ask my Father, and he would even now send me more than twelve legions of angels? [26:54] How then would the Scriptures be fulfilled that it must be so?"

[26:55] In that hour Jesus said to the multitudes, "Have you come out as against a robber with swords and clubs to seize me? I sat daily in the temple teaching, and you didn't arrest me. [26:56] But all this has happened, that the Scriptures of the prophets might be fulfilled."

1. See Mark 14:43-50; Luke 22:47-53; John 18:3-11

2. *Judas.* Our faculties are represented by the disciples of Jesus Christ. Among

them we have "a Judas" (life faculty). In its highest. In its highest office this faculty is Judah (spiritual appropriation through prayer and praise). Inverted in human consciousness, this faculty becomes Judas (acquisitiveness). In essence it is good, but in its personal sense and exercise, it brings about suffering and crucifixion. The life faculty (Judas) is redeemed by our first letting go of the idea that we possess anything, even the life and substance of our own physical organism. This renunciation constitutes part of the "remission of sins."

3. *kissed Him.* Every time we use the life and substance of Spirit to further sense demands, our personal I Am or Christ (Jesus) is betrayed anew into the hands of His enemies.

## The Word of God Stands Silent before our Inner High Priests [1]

Then all the disciples left him, and fled. 26:57 Those who had taken Jesus led him away to Caiaphas the high priest, where the scribes and the elders were gathered together. 26:58 But Peter followed him from a distance, to the court of the high priest,[2] and entered in and sat with the officers, to see the end. 26:59 Now the chief priests, the elders, and the whole council sought false testimony against Jesus, that they might put him to death; 26:60 and they found none. Even though many false witnesses came forward, they found none. But at last two false witnesses came forward, 26:61 and said, "This man said, 'I am able to destroy the temple of God, and to build it in three days.'"

26:62 The high priest stood up, and said to him, "Have you no answer? What is this that these testify against you?" 26:63 But Jesus held his peace. The high priest answered him, "I adjure you by the living God, that you tell us whether you are the Christ, the Son of God."

26:64 Jesus said to him, "You have said it. Nevertheless, I tell you, after this you will see the Son of Man sitting at the right hand of Power, and coming on the clouds of the sky."

26:65 Then the high priest tore his clothing, saying, "He has spoken blasphemy![3] Why do we need any more witnesses? Behold, now you have heard his blasphemy. 26:66 What do you think?"

They answered, "He is worthy of death!" 26:67 Then they spit in his face and beat him[4] with their fists, and some slapped him, 26:68 saying, "Prophesy to us, you Christ! Who hit you?"

1. See Mark 14:53-65; Luke 22:54-55,63-71; John 18:13-24

2. *the court of the high priest.* High Intellectual thoughts (the high priests) claim to be the Truth. We may know a great deal about Truth with our intellects, but when something comes that is beyond our understanding and we have to accept it on faith, [we may often find that we are preferring to follow Truth "from a distance."] (*Jesus' Soul Evolution* 1145)

3. *blasphemy.* When a purely spiritual thought is trying to replace an intellectual thought, it meets opposition on some ground or other. A leading significance of blasphemy is a tendency to think we can go too far in spiritualizing our thoughts and their environment.

4. *spit in His face and beat Him.* Spitting in Jesus' face and buffeting Him symbolizes utter disapproval and contempt of the spiritual Man.

## Our Moments of Denial (1)

26:69 Now Peter was sitting outside in the court, and a maid came to him, saying, "You were also with Jesus, the Galilean!"

26:70 But he denied it before them all,(2) saying, "I don't know what you are talking about."

26:71 When he had gone out onto the porch, someone else saw him, and said to those who were there, "This man also was with Jesus of Nazareth."

26:72 Again he denied it with an oath, "I don't know the man."

26:73 After a little while those who stood by came and said to Peter, "Surely you are also one of them, for your speech makes you known."

26:74 Then he began to curse and to swear, "I don't know the man!"

Immediately the rooster crowed.
26:75 Peter remembered the word which Jesus had said to him, "Before the rooster crows, you will deny me three times." He went out and wept bitterly.(3)

1. See Mark 14:66-72; Luke 22:55-62; John 18:25-27

2. *he denied it before them all.* Peter's action reveals how our faith is often tempted to waver when we face alarming situations, adversity, and persecutions. When our faith is not yet established so that we hold firmly to Truth in the face of great opposition, we fall from our high standard. [When we reach moments when the Truth seems to have failed us (in that moment, Jesus was appearing to be a failure and a fraud), we may be tempted to go along with the popular trend instead of being faithful to the Christ (he denied it).] (*Jesus' Soul Evolution* 1149)

3. *wept bitterly.* Until faith within us is identified with the Christ, we find that it is extremely vacillating. As a result, many times we weep bitterly.

---

Fillmore Study Bible annotations by Mary Salama.

**World English Bible Footnotes:**

[119] v26:26. TR reads "blessed" instead of "gave thanks for"

[120] v26:31. Zechariah 13:7

# Matthew 27

## The Word of Truth Brought to the Intellect (1)

27:1 Now when morning had come, all the chief priests and the elders of the people took counsel against Jesus to put him to death:(2) 27:2 and they bound him, and led him away, and delivered him up to Pontius Pilate,(3) the governor.

1. See Mk 15.1; Lk 22.66; 23.1; Jn 18.28.

2. *put Him to death.* The oppositional activity of the chief priests and elders to-

wards Jesus symbolizes the intellectual quibbling that goes on within us when we stand in a moment of new light (morning) yet are unable to lay hold of new inspiration because we are so steeped in intellectuality and more concerned with defending ourselves, and so we continue to oppose this new light (the Christ). (*Jesus' Soul Evolution* 1159)

3. *Pilate, the governor*. Pilate symbolizes the carnal will. He represents that in individual consciousness which has not caught the light sufficiently to depend wholly upon Spirit, but works to retain its worldly prestige. (MBD/Pilate)

## The Transformation of Judas: from self-acquisition to a life of praise

27:3 Then Judas,[1] who betrayed him, when he saw that Jesus was condemned, felt remorse, and brought back the thirty pieces of silver to the chief priests and elders, 27:4 saying, "I have sinned in that I betrayed innocent blood."

But they said, "What is that to us? You see to it."

27:5 He threw down the pieces of silver in the sanctuary, and departed. He went away and hanged himself. 27:6 The chief priests took the pieces of silver, and said, "It's not lawful to put them into the treasury, since it is the price of blood." 27:7 They took counsel, and bought the potter's field[2] with them, to bury strangers in. 27:8 Therefore that field was called "The Field of Blood" to this day. 27:9 Then that which was spoken through Jeremiah[121] the prophet was fulfilled, saying,

"They took the thirty pieces of
silver,
the price of him upon whom a
price had been set,
whom some of the children of
Israel priced,
27:10 and they gave them for the
potter's field,
as the Lord commanded
me."[122]

1. *Judas*. Judas, the last disciple Jesus called, symbolizes desire; appropriation; acquisitiveness. Exercised in its natural realm, it draws to us the supplies of the Universe, but when under the domination of the intellect, it oversteps the Law and becomes a destroyer. This brings about tragedy. Judas killed himself. (*Jesus' Soul Evolution* 1153)

2. *the potter's field*. the place in consciousness where we bury all dead, negative, impoverished thought forces. The potter's field also pertains to the redeeming blood of Jesus Christ in that Jesus lowered His consciousness to that of the race and "spilled His blood [in the field of the world]," in order to sow the seed of eternal life into the race consciousness.

## The Intellect Questions the Truth [1]

27:11 Now Jesus stood before the governor:[2] and the governor asked him, saying, "Are you the King of the Jews?"

Jesus said to him, "So you say."

27:12 When he was accused by the chief priests and elders, he answered nothing. 27:13 Then Pilate said to him, "Don't you hear how many things they testify against you?" 27:14 He gave him no answer, not even one word, so that the governor marveled greatly.

1. See Mk 15.2-5; Lk 23.2-3; Jn 18.29-38.

2. *the governor*. As our governor, the intellect questions: "Is there a ruling will over my religious nature?" But because the I AM within us (Jesus) is the Truth and so does not need to resort to outer methods of defending Itself, "He answered nothing." (*Jesus' Soul Evolution* 1160)

## With whom do we identify: Barabbas or Jesus? [1]

27:15 Now at the feast the governor was accustomed to release[2] to the multitude one prisoner, whom they desired. 27:16 They had then a notable prisoner, called Barabbas. 27:17 When therefore they were gathered together, Pilate said to them, "Whom do you want me to release to you? Barabbas, or Jesus, who is called Christ?" 27:18 For he knew that because of envy they had delivered him up.

27:19 While he was sitting on the judgment seat, his wife[3] sent to him, saying, "Have nothing to do with that righteous man, for I have suffered many things this day in a dream because of him." 27:20 Now the chief priests and the elders persuaded the multitudes to ask for Barabbas, and destroy Jesus. 27:21 But the governor answered them, "Which of the two do you want me to release to you?"

They said, "Barabbas!"

27:22 Pilate said to them, "What then shall I do to Jesus, who is called Christ?"

They all said to him, "Let him be crucified!"

27:23 But the governor said, "Why? What evil has he done?"

But they cried out exceedingly, saying, "Let him be crucified!"

1. See Mk 15.6-14; Lk 23.18-23; Jn 18.39-40.

2. *at the feast ... accustomed to release.* A feast symbolizes a notable event that people celebrate by eating and drinking to the glory of God—that is, spiritually partaking of Divine Substance. When we affirm spiritually, we release or deny error and materiality, here represented by the robber, Barabbas.

3. *his wife*. Pilate's wife symbolizes the soul having intuition, through which it is guided by the Holy Spirit in dreams. She represents that in consciousness that has in a measure received spiritual quickening and seeks to protect the Christ within, as best it can. The psychical nature may be spiritually awakened so that flashes of truth are revealed in dreams and visions, but have no enduring influence in consciousness. (*Jesus' Soul Evolution* 1169-70)

## Just take this Truth Away from Me! [1]

27:24 So when Pilate saw that nothing was being gained, but rather that a disturbance was starting, he took water, and washed his hands before the multitude, saying, "I am innocent[2] of the blood of this righteous person. You see to it."

27:25 All the people answered, "May his blood be on us, and on our children!"

27:26 Then he released to them Barabbas, but Jesus he flogged and delivered to be crucified.

1. See Mk 15.15; Lk 23.24-25; Jn 19.16.

2. *I am innocent*. The intellectual man would rather let the lower forces of being

(Barabbas) go free. Sometimes we want to simply wash our hands of the whole affair; we know that Truth is the right way ("this righteous Person") and yet like Pilate, we let the voice of the mob prevail and crucify our highest aspirations. (*Jesus' Soul Evolution* 1170)

## When our Inner Forces Mock the Truth [1]

27:27 Then the governor's soldiers took Jesus into the Praetorium, and gathered the whole garrison together against him. 27:28 They stripped him, and put a scarlet robe on him. 27:29 They braided a crown of thorns and put it on his head, and a reed in his right hand; and they kneeled down before him, and mocked him,[2] saying, "Hail, King of the Jews!" 27:30 They spat on him, and took the reed and struck him on the head. 27:31 When they had mocked him, they took the robe off of him, and put his clothes on him, and led him away to crucify him.[3]

1. See Mk 15.16-20; Jn 19.2-3.

2. *mocked Him.* Mockery is an exultation of the petty, personal self over the realities of love and Truth.

3. *to crucify Him.* The crucifixion is not a destructive process but a transformative process. The personal man (Jesus) has to give up entirely to the spiritual man (Christ). The crucifixion is a great victory, not a tragedy. (*Jesus' Soul Evolution* 1173)

## The Crossing Out of Error, to Truth [1]

27:32 As they came out, they found a man of Cyrene,[2] Simon by name, and they compelled him to go with them, that he might carry his cross. 27:33 They came to a place called "Golgotha,"[3] that is to say, "The place of a skull." 27:34 They gave him sour wine to drink mixed with gall. When he had tasted it, he would not drink. 27:35 When they had crucified him,[4] they divided his clothing among them, casting lots,[123] 27:36 and they sat and watched him there. 27:37 They set up over his head the accusation against him written, "THIS IS JESUS, THE KING OF THE JEWS."[5]

27:38 Then there were two robbers[6] crucified with him, one on his right hand and one on the left. 27:39 Those who passed by blasphemed him, wagging their heads, 27:40 and saying, "You who destroy the temple, and build it in three days, save yourself! If you are the Son of God, come down from the cross!"

27:41 Likewise the chief priests also mocking, with the scribes, the Pharisees,[124] and the elders, said, 27:42 "He saved others, but he can't save himself. If he is the King of Israel, let him come down from the cross now, and we will believe in him. 27:43 He trusts in God. Let God deliver him now, if he wants him; for he said, 'I am the Son of God.'" 27:44 The robbers also who were crucified with him cast on him the same reproach.

1. See Mk 15.21-32; Lk 23.26-43; Jn 19.17-27.

2. *a man of Cyrene.* Cyrene means wall; coldness (Cyrene, MBD). It refers to fixed (cold) states of thought in the realm of sense, and yet they are illumined to the measure they represent what we hope for and mentally see as possibilities in our lives. These thoughts in some degree help to relieve the pressure (carry the cross) brought to bear by the intellectual man. (*Jesus' Soul Evolution* 1175)

3. *a place called Golgotha.* "The place of

a skull," represents the place in consciousness where the intellect is crossed out to make way for the Spirit. In order to gain the supreme goal, God consciousness, it is necessary for the seeker after Truth to cross out the domination of the intellect or personal self and in its stead to permit the victorious Christ Spirit to have dominion. Jesus (the intellectual) was crucified at the place of the skull so that Christ (Truth) might become all in all.

4. *crucified Him.* As when ice is melted into water and water is changed into steam the essential elements are not only preserved and nothing is lost, but the power is much increased, so it is with each change that takes place in our unfoldment, each one a forward step until the spiritual man comes forth in us, in all His glory. The crucifixion represents the final erasure of error from consciousness. Every time we give up an error, there is a crucifixion. (*Jesus' Soul Evolution* 1174-75, 1182)

5. *"THIS IS JESUS, THE KING OF THE JEWS"* Signifies the universality of the Word that was and is to go forth to all the world, reaching people everywhere, in Spirit, soul, and body ("Hebrew, Greek, and Latin," or "religion, culture, and law").

6. *there were two robbers.* Represent the past and the future, which rob man of his peace and happiness; the one by means of regrets for unfulfilled promises, the other by means of apprehension for the future.

## Truth Releases Its Spirit in Us (1)

27:45 Now from the sixth hour[125]
there was darkness over all the
land(2) until the ninth hour.[126] 27:46
About the ninth hour Jesus cried with
a loud voice, saying, "Eli, Eli,
lima[127] sabachthani?" That is, "My
God, my God, why have you forsaken
me?"(3)[128]

27:47 Some of them who stood
there, when they heard it, said, "This
man is calling Elijah."

27:48 Immediately one of them ran,
and took a sponge, and filled it with
vinegar, and put it on a reed, and
gave him a drink. 27:49 The rest said,
"Let him be. Let's see whether Elijah
comes to save him."

27:50 Jesus cried again with a loud
voice, and yielded up his spirit. 27:51
Behold, the veil of the temple was
torn(4) in two from the top to the
bottom. The earth quaked and the
rocks were split. 27:52 The tombs were
opened, and many bodies of the
saints who had fallen asleep were
raised;(5) 27:53 and coming out of the
tombs after his resurrection, they
entered into the holy city and
appeared to many. 27:54 Now the
centurion, and those who were with
him watching Jesus, when they saw
the earthquake, and the things that
were done, feared exceedingly,
saying, "Truly this was the Son of
God."(6)

27:55 Many women were there
watching from afar, who had
followed Jesus from Galilee, serving
him. 27:56 Among them were Mary
Magdalene, Mary the mother of
James and Joses, and the mother of
the sons of Zebedee.

1. See Mk 15.33-41; Lk 23.44-49; Jn 19.25-30.

2. *"darkness over all the land"* The failure of understanding that settles upon the soul and casts its shadow upon mind and body in times of great trial.

3. *"My God, my God, why have you forsaken Me?"* Jesus' words here symbolize the struggle and the passing away of the very last of the natural state of consciousness in Jesus. Like all the other allegories of Jesus' life, the death on the cross is less important as a historical event than it is as a demonstration of an experience common to everyone passing from the human to the Divine. We have our crucifixions, deaths, and burials, yet none of them are real when we believe in the power of the One Life to save us to the uttermost. (*Jesus' Soul Evolution* 1189)

4. *the veil of the temple was torn.* The relinquishment of the soul to God is the final giving up of all human ambitions and aims. When this point is reached, the soul enters into glory ["beyond the veil" of materiality].

5. *saints who had fallen asleep were raised.* We have buried away in the subconscious mind saintly thoughts. [When the Word of Truth resurrects or expands within us (Jesus resurrected), so also do all the sleeping "saintly" thoughts within us awaken.]

6. *"Truly this was the Son of God."* Divine Law is always being fulfilled, even in circumstances of apparent lawlessness and cruelty. Divine Mind uses human instruments in its outworking of the law and no circumstance [or human mind] is beyond its transforming touch; it brings good out of what appears to be altogether evil.

## Truth Gets Buried Within Us [1]

27:57 When evening had come, a
rich man from Arimathaea, named
Joseph,[2] who himself was also Jesus'
disciple came. 27:58 This man went to
Pilate, and asked for Jesus' body.
Then Pilate commanded the body to
be given up. 27:59 Joseph took the
body, and wrapped it in a clean linen
cloth, 27:60 and laid it in his own new
tomb, which he had cut out in the
rock, and he rolled a great stone to
the door of the tomb, and departed.
27:61 Mary Magdalene was there, and
the other Mary,[3] sitting opposite the
tomb.

1. Mk 15.42-47; Lk 23.50-56; Jn 19.38-42

2. *Joseph of Arimathaea.* A high lofty state of consciousness that recognizes the Christ. His tomb represents an elevated, peaceful state of consciousness in which Jesus rested the three days previous to His resurrection. (*Jesus' Soul Evolution* 1194-95)

3. *and the other Mary.* [While the number of "Mary's" mentioned can be confusing, the point is that the naming of several different Mary's (representing a phase of the soul's evolution) at the crucifixion, death, and tomb of Jesus points to the fact that many phases of our soul support and stand witness to our own inner transformation and journey from error to Truth.]

## The Memory of Truth in Us is Well-Guarded

27:62 Now on the next day, which
was the day after the Preparation
Day, the chief priests and the
Pharisees were gathered together to
Pilate, 27:63 saying, "Sir, we remember
what that deceiver said while he was
still alive: 'After three days I will rise
again.' 27:64 Command therefore that
the tomb be made secure until the
third day, lest perhaps his disciples
come at night and steal him away,
and tell the people, 'He is risen from
the dead;' and the last deception will
be worse than the first."

27:65 Pilate said to them, "You have
a guard. Go, make it as secure as
you can."[1] 27:66 So they went with the
guard and made the tomb secure,
sealing the stone.

1. *make it as secure as you can.* The reasoning, intellectual man always endeavors to make sureness doubly sure. The tomb was sealed to guard against fraudulent methods to satisfy their distrustful nature. (*Jesus' Soul Evolution* 1197)

---

Fillmore Study Bible annotations by Mary Salama.

**World English Bible Footnotes:**

[121] v27:9. some manuscripts omit "Jeremiah"

[122] v27:10. Zechariah 11:12-13; Jeremiah 19:1-13; 32:6-9

[123] v27:35. TR adds "that it might be fulfilled which was spoken by the prophet: 'They divided my garments among them, and for my clothing they cast lots;'" [see Psalm 22:18 and John 19:24]

[124] v27:41. TR omits "the Pharisees"

[125] v27:45. noon

[126] v27:45. 3:00 P. M.

[127] v27:46. TR reads "lama" instead of "lima"

[128] v27:46. Psalm 22:1

# MATTHEW 28

## We are Resurrecting, Daily[1]

28:1 Now after the Sabbath, as it
began to dawn on the first day of
the week, Mary[2] Magdalene and the
other Mary came to see the tomb.
28:2 Behold, there was a great
earthquake, for an angel of the
Lord[3] descended from the sky, and
came and rolled away the stone[4]
from the door, and sat on it. 28:3 His
appearance was like lightning, and
his clothing white as snow. 28:4 For
fear of him, the guards shook, and
became like dead men. 28:5 The angel
answered the women, "Don't be
afraid,[5] for I know that you seek
Jesus, who has been crucified. 28:6 He
is not here, for he has risen,[6] just
like he said. Come, see the place
where the Lord was lying. 28:7 Go
quickly and tell his disciples, 'He has
risen from the dead,[7] and behold,
he goes before you into Galilee;
there you will see him.' Behold, I
have told you."

28:8 They departed quickly from
the tomb with fear and great joy,
and ran to bring his disciples word.
28:9 As they went to tell his disciples,
behold, Jesus met them, saying,
"Rejoice!"

They came and took hold of his
feet, and worshiped him.

28:10 Then Jesus said to them,
"Don't be afraid. Go tell my
brothers[129] that they should go into
Galilee, and there they will see me."

1. See Mk 16.1-8; Lk 24.1-12; Jn 20.1-18.

2. *as it began to dawn ... Mary.* Mary is the first part of our soul or consciousness to become aware of the resurrection of the Christ within us. A ray of light penetrates the soul as it perceives that love (the Christ) abides.

3. *an angel of the Lord.* A manifestation of the principle of denial and affirmation. This principle is needed and capable to rid our souls of fear ("For fear of him, the guards shook").

4. *the stone.* The stone may be likened to hard, heavy thoughts (such as prejudice, condemnation, and unbelief) that keep good from coming into manifestation.

5. *"Don't be afraid."* The principle of denial and affirmation, when clothed in the garment of Truth ("clothing as white as snow"), is a power strong enough to raise the body to renewed consciousness of life.

6. *He has risen.* We resurrect our body by putting a new mind into it, the Mind of Spirit. A resurrection takes place in us every time we rise to a realization of the perpetual in-dwelling life that connects us with the Father.

7. *He has risen from the dead.* The Christ life is a dynamic, not a static experience. Easter commemorates not only Jesus Christ's victory over death, but also the countless "minor resurrections" in your life and mine as we seek the true Christ consciousness that will eventually spiritualize the body.

## Intellectual Forces Report to the High Priest[1]

28:11 Now while they were going,
behold, some of the guards came
into the city, and told the chief
priests[2] all the things that had
happened. 28:12 When they were
assembled with the elders, and had
taken counsel, they gave a large
amount of silver to the soldiers, 28:13
saying, "Say that[3] his disciples came
by night, and stole him away while
we slept. 28:14 If this comes to the
governor's ears, we will persuade him
and make you free of worry." 28:15 So
they took the money and did as they
were told. This saying was spread
abroad among the Jews, and
continues until this day.

1. See Mt 27:62-66.

2. *guards came ... and told the chief priests.* The soldiers and the guards here represent forces within the consciousness that carry out the dictates of their superior, in this case the high priest (intellectuality). These forces become frightened and return to the priest in authority. (*Jesus' Soul Evolution* 1207)

3. *Say that.* When intellectual thoughts are trapped, they resort to falsehood and trickery to save themselves, which of course ends in defeat.

## The Commissioning of our Mind

28:16 But the eleven disciples went
into Galilee,[1] to the mountain
where Jesus had sent them. 28:17
When they saw him, they bowed
down to him, but some doubted.[2]
28:18 Jesus came to them and spoke to
them, saying, "All authority has been
given to me in heaven and on earth.
28:19 Therefore go, and make disciples
of all nations,[3] baptizing them in the
name of the Father and of the Son
and of the Holy Spirit, 28:20 teaching
them to observe all things[4] that I
commanded you. Behold, I am with
you always,[5] even to the end of the
age." Amen.

1. *went into Galilee.* Galilee symbolizes energy of life; life activity. "Galilee" associated with "mountain" symbolizes a high consciousness of life. This is where our mind meets with our Christ (where the disciples were to meet with Jesus).

2. *but some doubted.* The disciples represent our faculties. Our work is to train them to occupy the "kingdom of the heavens" within us. Some enter into it readily while others remain unmoved (some doubted).

3. *make disciples of all nations.* The authority of the Christ in us is to be exercised through the quickening of our countless faculties (making disciples of all the nations), exalting them to the consciousness of God in Christ and filling them with the Spirit.

4. *teaching them to observe all things.* We do not follow the Christ way except by our own will, and we must allow others the same opportunity. The Christ way presupposes that by teaching and example, others (the nations) will also learn to follow the Christ way of life gladly and of their own free will. To be taught the wisdom of keeping the Law is a very different thing

from being forced to keep it without understanding why.

5. *I am with you always.* These words assure us that we have the Power to live the perfect life by holding ourselves steadfastly in the Christ consciousness.

---

Fillmore Study Bible annotations by Mary Salama.

**World English Bible Footnotes:**

[129] v28:10. The word for "brothers" here may be also correctly translated "brothers and sisters" or "siblings."

# The Good News According to Mark

Fisherman in the Sea of Galilee, 1890-1900, Wikimedia Commons, public domain.

## Introduction to Mark

Mark is the shortest and earliest of the Gospels, and was written about A.D. 65. Mark (or John Mark, as he is sometimes called) is mentioned in other parts of the New Testament, and was associated with Barnabas and Paul on their first missionary journey (Acts 13:5). Later on, Mark attached himself to Peter, as interpreter and secretary—see I Peter 5:13. An early writer (about A.D. 140) gives the following information regarding the writing of Mark's Gospel:

"Mark, having become the interpreter of Peter, wrote down accurately everything that he remembered, without however recording in order what was either said or done by Christ. For neither did he hear the Lord, nor did he follow Him, but afterwards, as I said, attended Peter, who adapted his instructions to the needs of his hearers, but had no design of giving a connected account of the Lord's oracles (or words). So then Mark made no mistake while he thus wrote down some things as he remembered them; for he made it his one care not to omit anything that he heard, nor to set down any false statement therein" (Hastings, "Dictionary of the Bible," p. 579).

Mark's Gospel is written in a simple, straight-forward manner, and is notable for movement and dramatic effect in its descriptions. The word *straightway*, for example, occurs about fifty times. Actually, what we have in this Gospel bears all the marks of an eyewitness account—and this eyewitness seems to have many of those characteristics that we usually associate with Peter.

Introduction to *The Good News According to Mark* by Herbert J. Hunt, former Dean of Bible Studies for the Unity School of Christianity.

# Mark 1

## The Proclamation of John the Baptist[1]

1:1 The beginning of the Good
News of Jesus Christ,[2] the Son of
God. 1:2 As it is written in the
prophets,

"Behold, I send my messenger
before your face,
who will prepare your way
before you.[1]
1:3 The voice of one crying in the
wilderness,
'Make ready the way of the
Lord!
Make his paths straight!'"[2]

1:4 John[3] came baptizing[4][3] in
the wilderness and preaching the
baptism of repentance[5] for
forgiveness of sins. 1:5 All the country
of Judea and all those of Jerusalem
went out to him. They were baptized
by him in the Jordan river, confessing
their sins. 1:6 John was clothed with
camel's hair and a leather belt
around his waist. He ate locusts and
wild honey. 1:7 He preached, saying,
"After me comes he who is mightier
than I, the thong of whose sandals
I am not worthy to stoop down and
loosen. 1:8 I baptized you in[4]
water,[6] but he will baptize you in
the Holy Spirit."[7]

1. See Mt 3:1; Lk 3:1; Jn 1:19

2. *Jesus Christ* God's idea of man in expression; Christ is that idea in the absolute. (MBD/Jesus)

3. *John (the Baptist).* A high intellectual perception of Truth, but one not yet quickened of Spirit. He may also be said to be that innate principle in us all which ever seeks to do right. (MBD/John)

4. *baptizing*. water baptism symbolizes a cleansing process, the letting go of error. It is the first step in the realization of Truth. (MBD/baptism)

5. *repentance*. A change of mind; a transformation of the mind; change of thought and purpose. (MBD/repentance)

6. *water*. Water represents material cleansing, whereas fire represents spiritual cleansing. (MBD/water)

7. *Holy Spirit*. The law of God in action. It is the whole spirit of God and can be known by us only through our spiritual nature. (MBD/holy-spirit)

## The Baptism of Jesus[1]

[1:9] It happened in those days, that Jesus came from Nazareth of Galilee, and was baptized by John in the Jordan. [1:10] Immediately coming up from the water, he saw the heavens parting, and the Spirit descending on him like a dove.[2] [1:11] A voice came out of the sky, "You are my beloved Son, in whom I am well pleased."

1. See Mt 3:13; Lk 3:21; Jn 1:29.
2. *the heavens parting, and the Spirit descending on him like a dove.* The rending of the heavens means the opening of the mind to the fourth dimension; the descent of Spirit as a dove is the outpouring of innocence and peace.

## The Temptation of Jesus[1]

[1:12] Immediately the Spirit drove him out into the wilderness.[2] [1:13] He was there in the wilderness forty days tempted by Satan.[3] He was with the wild animals; and the angels[4] were serving him.

1. See Mt 4:1; Lk 4:1.
2. *wilderness.* In individual consciousness, the multitude of undisciplined and uncultivated thought (MBD/wilderness). In the wilderness of the subconscious mind one finds both angelic thoughts and wild, undisciplined animal thoughts. One finds ambitions, too, of various degrees of selfishness which must be dealt with.
3. *Satan.* The deceiving phase of mind in man that has fixed ideas in opposition to Truth (MBD/satan).
4. *angels.* Messengers of God; our spiritual perceptive faculties (MBD/angel).

## Truth Teaching Begins[1]

[1:14] Now after John was taken into custody, Jesus came into Galilee, preaching the Good News of the Kingdom of God,[2] [1:15] and saying, "The time is fulfilled, and the Kingdom of God is at hand! Repent, and believe in the Good News."

1. See Mt 4:12; Lk 4:12.
2. *kingdom of God.* The kingdom of God (also kingdom of heaven) is the realm of divine ideas, producing their expression, perfect harmony. That realm in man's consciousness where he knows and understands God (RW/kingdom).

## The 12 Powers of Man[1]

[1:16] Passing along by the sea of Galilee, he saw Simon and Andrew[2] the brother of Simon casting a net into the sea, for they were fishermen. [1:17] Jesus said to them, "Come after me, and I will make you into fishers for men."

[1:18] Immediately they left their nets, and followed him. [1:19] Going on a little further from there, he saw James the son of Zebedee, and John, his brother, who were also in the boat mending the nets. [1:20] Immediately he called them, and they left their father, Zebedee, in the boat with the hired servants, and went after him.

1. See Mt 4:18; Lk 5:1; Jn 1:35. See also 1 Kings 19:19.
2. *Simon, Andrew (and the other disci-*

*ples)* The disciples of Jesus represent, in mind analysis, the "Twelve Powers of Man," (MBD/disciples) sometimes referred to as the 12 faculties of mind (MBD/faculties). The 12 powers provide a system for soul growth. They are spiritual tools for creating a life that is, as the apostle Paul said, no longer storm-tossed by difficulties and challenges to your faith. Our minds can be a link to God through these 12 capacities: wisdom, love, strength, faith, imagination, order, understanding, will, power, zeal, release, and life itself. Based on the reality of the divine spark within all people, Charles Fillmore used the disciples of Jesus as exemplars of the 12 powers.

## The Man with an Unclean Spirit[1]

1:21 They went into Capernaum,[2] and immediately on the Sabbath day he entered into the synagogue and taught. 1:22 They were astonished at his teaching, for he taught them as having authority, and not as the scribes.[3] 1:23 Immediately there was in their synagogue a man with an unclean spirit,[4] and he cried out, 1:24 saying, "Ha! What do we have to do with you, Jesus, you Nazarene? Have you come to destroy us? I know you who you are: the Holy One of God!"

1:25 Jesus rebuked him, saying, "Be quiet, and come out of him!"

1:26 The unclean spirit, convulsing him and crying with a loud voice, came out of him. 1:27 They were all amazed, so that they questioned among themselves, saying, "What is this? A new teaching? For with authority he commands even the unclean spirits, and they obey him!" 1:28 The report of him went out immediately everywhere into all the region of Galilee and its surrounding area.

1. See Mt 7:28; Lk 4:31.

2. *Capernaum.* Village of consolation; shelter of comfort; covering of compassion; covering of repentance. The name thus indicates a cleansing of the mind, both conscious and subconscious. (MBD/Capernaum)

3. *scribes.* the thoughts that come to us from other personalities or from books, as opposed to from God (MBD/scribes).

4. *man with an unclean spirit.* The unclean spirit of doubt questions the necessity of loyalty to the Christ ideal. The doubter fears to identify himself with "the Holy One of God," lest he lose what makes his life dear to him-personality. But the Christ ideal, when steadfastly held, rebukes the unclean spirit of doubt and drives it out.

## The Healing Power of Faith and Strength[1]

1:29 Immediately, when they had come out of the synagogue, they came into the house of Simon and Andrew, with James and John.[2] 1:30 Now Simon's wife's mother lay sick with a fever, and immediately they told him about her. 1:31 He came and took her by the hand, and raised her up. The fever left her, and she served them. 1:32 At evening, when the sun had set, they brought to him all who were sick, and those who were possessed by demons. 1:33 All the city was gathered together at the door. 1:34 He healed many who were sick with various diseases, and cast out many demons. He didn't allow the demons to speak, because they knew him.

1. See Mt 8:14; Lk 4:38.

2. *they came into the house of Simon and Andrew, with James and John.* In individual consciousness, signifies the coming of the spiritual I AM into a firm, unyielding, enduring consciousness of faith

and strength (typified by Simon and Andrew), supported by the faculties of judgment and love (James and John). (MBD/Simon)

## A Preaching Tour in Galilee[1]

1:35 Early in the morning, while it was still dark, he rose up and went out, and departed into a deserted place, and prayed there. 1:36 Simon and those who were with him followed after him; 1:37 and they found him, and told him, "Everyone is looking for you."

1:38 He said to them, "Let's go elsewhere into the next towns, that I may preach there also, because I came out for this reason." 1:39 He went into their synagogues throughout all Galilee,[2] preaching and casting out demons.[3]

1. See Mt 4:23; Lk 4:42.

2. *He went into their synagogues throughout all Galilee.* Galilee represents the whole circuit of life activity in consciousness. The synagogues stand for brain and nerve centers where spiritual forces are at work.

3. *preaching and casting out demons.* When we enter into the consciousness of the spiritual life (Galilee) we speak words of Truth (preach) and deny away all conditions of error (demons).

## Truth Heals Error[1]

1:40 A leper came to him, begging him, kneeling down to him, and saying to him, "If you want to, you can make me clean."

1:41 Being moved with compassion,[2] he stretched out his hand, and touched him, and said to him, "I want to. Be made clean." 1:42 When he had said this, immediately the leprosy departed from him, and he was made clean. 1:43 He strictly warned him, and immediately sent him out, 1:44 and said to him, "See you say nothing to anybody, but go show yourself to the priest, and offer for your cleansing the things which Moses commanded,[3] for a testimony to them."

1:45 But he went out, and began to proclaim it much, and to spread about the matter, so that Jesus could no more openly enter into a city, but was outside in desert places: and they came to him from everywhere.

1. See Mt 8:1; Lk 5:12.

2. *compassion.* In the heart of God exists an eternal tenderness and mercy for His children (RW/compassion).

3. *go show yourself to the priest, and offer for your cleansing the things which Moses commanded.* When one is healed, his first duty should be to acknowledge the true source of his healing, which is God in consciousness.

---

Fillmore Study Bible annotations by Rev. Dan Beckett.

**World English Bible Footnotes:**

[1] v1:2. Malachi 3:1

[2] v1:3. Isaiah 40:3

[3] v1:4. or, immersing

[4] v1:8. The Greek word (en) translated here as "in" could also be translated as "with" in some contexts.

# Mark 2

## Healing and Forgiveness[1]

2:1 When he entered again into Capernaum[2] after some days, it was heard that he was in the house. 2:2 Immediately many were gathered together, so that there was no more room, not even around the door; and he spoke the word to them. 2:3 Four people came, carrying a paralytic to him. 2:4 When they could not come near to him for the crowd, they removed the roof where he was. When they had broken it up, they let down the mat that the paralytic was lying on. 2:5 Jesus,[3] seeing their faith, said to the paralytic, "Son, your sins are forgiven you."

2:6 But there were some of the scribes[4] sitting there, and reasoning in their hearts, 2:7 "Why does this man speak blasphemies like that? Who can forgive sins but God alone?"[5]

2:8 Immediately Jesus, perceiving in his spirit that they so reasoned within themselves, said to them, "Why do you reason these things in your hearts? 2:9 Which is easier, to tell the paralytic, 'Your sins are forgiven;' or to say, 'Arise, and take up your bed, and walk?' 2:10 But that you may know that the Son of Man has authority on earth to forgive sins"--he said to the paralytic-- 2:11 "I tell you, arise, take up your mat, and go to your house."[6]

2:12 He arose, and immediately took up the mat, and went out in front of them all; so that they were all amazed, and glorified God, saying, "We never saw anything like this!"

1. See Mt 9:1-8; Lk 5:17-26.

2. *Capernaum* Village of consolation; shelter of comfort; covering of compassion; covering of repentance. The name thus indicates a cleansing of the mind, both conscious and subconscious. (MBD/Capernaum)

3. *house, roof, Jesus* All physical healing is based upon the conception of the body as spiritually perfect. This ideal of bodily perfection is conceived in the top brain (the roof of the house). From that point it is let down to the body brain, the solar plexus where Jesus Christ, (the I AM) is functioning.

4. *scribes* Thoughts that come to us from other personalities or from books; external religious thoughts.

5. *Who can forgive sins but God alone?* The religious authorities overlooked the truth that men in their highest and best selves are sons of God, and as such they are endowed with divine attributes. Among these attributes is the power to forgive as God forgives, without reservation and without respect of persons. At heart all are one, even one with God.

6. *arise, take up your mat, and go to your house.* Initially, Jesus says the man's sins are forgiven, which stirs contentious discussions in the house. Looking at this Bible story metaphysically, we can see that the "helpers" might be spiritual characteristics (like faith, strength, wisdom, and zeal) or spiritual practices (like denials and affirmations). Whether the in-

dividual is "paralyzed" or "laying by the pool," we note the story is about an inability to take action based on what we in Unity call error thoughts (which other religions refer to as sin) or limiting beliefs. We must overcome any belief that the essence of who we are is broken or limited. See John 5:8. (Rev. Joy Wyler, *Radical Wholeness*)

## Divine Will in Action[1]

2:13 He went out again by the seaside. All the multitude came to him, and he taught them. 2:14 As he passed by, he saw Levi,[2] the son of Alphaeus, sitting at the tax office, and he said to him, "Follow me." And he arose and followed him.

2:15 It happened, that he was reclining at the table in his house, and many tax collectors and sinners sat down with Jesus and his disciples, for there were many, and they followed him. 2:16 The scribes and the Pharisees, when they saw that he was eating with the sinners and tax collectors,[3] said to his disciples, "Why is it that he eats and drinks with tax collectors and sinners?"

2:17 When Jesus heard it, he said to them, "Those who are healthy have no need for a physician, but those who are sick. I came not to call the righteous, but sinners to repentance."

1. See Mt 9:9-13; Lk 5:27-32.

2. *Levi (Matthew).* Matthew represents the decision-making part of the brain, the Divine Power of Will: the ability to choose, lead, and decide. See also "The Twelve Powers," Mark 1:16-20.

3. *eating with sinners and tax collectors.* When the I AM is awakened to its spiritual power It has to make contact with all types of thoughts in consciousness. Jesus proclaimed, "Agree with thine adversary quickly," that is, get acquainted with your shortcomings and through the application of your understanding of Truth they will be reformed.

## Abstinence from Error Thought[1]

2:18 John's disciples and the Pharisees were fasting,[2] and they came and asked him, "Why do John's disciples and the disciples of the Pharisees fast, but your disciples don't fast?"

2:19 Jesus said to them, "Can the groomsmen fast while the bridegroom is with them? As long as they have the bridegroom with them, they can't fast. 2:20 But the days will come when the bridegroom will be taken away from them, and then will they fast in that day. 2:21 No one sews a piece of unshrunk cloth on an old garment,[3] or else the patch shrinks and the new tears away from the old, and a worse hole is made. 2:22 No one puts new wine into old wineskins,[4] or else the new wine will burst the skins, and the wine pours out, and the skins will be destroyed; but they put new wine into fresh wineskins."

1. See Mt 9:14-17; Lk 5:33-39.

2. *fasting.* Abstinence from error thoughts, to the end that we may meditate upon spiritual truths and incorporate them into our consciousness of oneness with the Father. (MBD/Fasting)

3. *unshrunk cloth on an old garment.* This expression refers to new and untried truths injected into the mind of one who is wedded to old beliefs and practices.

4. *new wine into old wineskins.* Signifies the inspiration that springs afresh in the mind of the one who has given himself to the pursuit of the ideal.

## The Sabbath was made for us, not we for the Sabbath[1]

2:23 It happened that he was going on the Sabbath day through the grain fields, and his disciples began, as they went, to pluck the ears of grain. 2:24 The Pharisees said to him, "Behold, why do they do that which is not lawful on the Sabbath day?"[2]

2:25 He said to them, "Did you never read what David did, when he had need, and was hungry--he, and those who were with him? 2:26 How he entered into the house of God when Abiathar was high priest, and ate the show bread, which is not lawful to eat except for the priests, and gave also to those who were with him?"

2:27 He said to them, "The Sabbath was made for man, not man for the Sabbath.[3] 2:28 Therefore the Son of Man is lord even of the Sabbath."

1. See Mt 12:1-8; Lk 6:1-5.

2. *that which is not lawful on the Sabbath day.* Jesus and His disciples were not under the man-made law. They represent the law of Spirit, by which man transcends all laws of mortal man.

3. *The Sabbath was made for man, not man for the Sabbath.* For the natural man the day of rest is essential, but the spiritual man suits the occasion of the Sabbath to his needs.

Fillmore Study Bible annotations by Rev. Dan Beckett.

# Mark 3

## Healing of the Withered Consciousness[1]

3:1 He entered again into the synagogue,[2] and there was a man there who had his hand withered. 3:2 They watched him, whether he would heal him on the Sabbath day,[3] that they might accuse him. 3:3 He said to the man who had his hand withered, "Stand up." 3:4 He said to them, "Is it lawful on the Sabbath day to do good, or to do harm? To save a life, or to kill?" But they were silent. 3:5 When he had looked around at them with anger, being grieved at the hardening of their hearts, he said to the man, "Stretch out your hand." He stretched it out, and his hand was restored as healthy as the other. 3:6 The Pharisees went out, and immediately conspired with the Herodians[4] against him, how they might destroy him.

1. See Mt 12:9-14; Lk 6:6-11

2. *synagogue.* the mind of man, or the phase of man's mind that is given over to religious thought. In the new birth, or regeneration, the rebuilding of your consciousness begins in this synagogue or religious mentality. (MBD/synagogue)

3. *heal on the Sabbath day.* The work was not done outwardly but within His consciousness. There He realized divine compassion and understanding with the absolute authority of divine love. To hold oneself in this high consciousness of Truth is spiritual work of a high order.

4. *Herodians.* Thoughts that belong to our old-established religious ideas, but in character are very selfish and material,

even as Herod and the Romans were. They bitterly and actively oppose and seek to kill out of consciousness the higher Christ life and its ideals and activities. (MBD/Herodians)

## Inharmonious Thoughts Come for Healing[1]

3:7 Jesus withdrew to the sea with his disciples, and a great multitude followed him from Galilee, from Judea, 3:8 from Jerusalem, from Idumaea, beyond the Jordan, and those from around Tyre and Sidon.[2] A great multitude, hearing what great things he did, came to him. 3:9 He spoke to his disciples that a little boat should stay near him because of the crowd, so that they wouldn't press on him. 3:10 For he had healed many, so that as many as had diseases pressed on him that they might touch him. 3:11 The unclean spirits,[3] whenever they saw him, fell down before him, and cried, "You are the Son of God!" 3:12 He sternly warned them that they should not make him known.

1. See Mt 4:24-25; Mt 12:15-16; Lk 6:17-19.

2. *multitude (from Judea, Jerusalem, Idumaea, Tyre and Sidon).* The host of inharmonious thoughts that are seeking spiritual harmony. The different places from which the multitude came for healing bespeak the various characteristics of thought that throng to the place of vitality and energy represented by Jesus, I AM identified with Spirit.

3. *unclean spirits.* Error states of mind that vainly have been seeking satisfaction through the flesh. When these behold the true, spiritual man, they acknowledge him as the Son of God and they are healed.

## Our Power of Mind to Cast Out Discordant Thought[1]

3:13 He went up into the mountain, and called to himself those whom he wanted, and they went to him. 3:14 He appointed twelve,[2] that they might be with him, and that he might send them out to preach, 3:15 and to have authority to heal sicknesses and to cast out demons:[3] 3:16 Simon, to whom he gave the name Peter; 3:17 James the son of Zebedee; John, the brother of James, and he surnamed them Boanerges, which means, Sons of Thunder; 3:18 Andrew; Philip; Bartholomew; Matthew; Thomas; James, the son of Alphaeus; Thaddaeus; Simon the Zealot; 3:19 and Judas Iscariot, who also betrayed him.

1. See Mt 10:1-4; Lk 6:12-16.

2. *twelve.* The twelve apostles of Jesus are the twelve powers of mind, to which power is given to cast out all discordant thoughts. See also "The Twelve Powers," Mark 1:16-20.

3. *demons.* or evil spirits, are conditions of mind, or states of consciousness, that have been developed because our creative power has been used in an unwise or an ignorant way. The work of every overcomer is to cast out of herself or himself the demons of sin and evil, through the power and dominion of his indwelling Christ. (MBD/demons)

## We are Heir Only to the Good[1]

He came into a house. 3:20 The multitude came together again, so that they could not so much as eat bread. 3:21 When his friends heard it, they went out to seize him: for they said, "He is insane." 3:22 The scribes who came down from Jerusalem said, "He has Beelzebul," and, "By the prince of the demons he casts out the demons."

3:23 He summoned them, and said to them in parables, "How can Satan cast out Satan? 3:24 If a kingdom is divided against itself, that kingdom cannot stand. 3:25 If a house is divided against itself, that house cannot stand. 3:26 If Satan has risen up against himself, and is divided, he can't stand, but has an end. 3:27 But no one can enter into the house of the strong man to plunder, unless he first binds the strong man; and then he will plunder his house. 3:28 Most certainly I tell you, all sins of the descendants of man will be forgiven, including their blasphemies with which they may blaspheme; 3:29 but whoever may blaspheme against the Holy Spirit never has forgiveness, but is guilty of an eternal sin"[2] 3:30 -- because they said, "He has an unclean spirit."

1. See Mt 12:46-50; Lk 8:19-21.

2. *eternal sin.* The belief that God is the creator of disease or inharmony of any nature. As long as we abide in the conviction that God causes us to suffer, we close our mind against the inflow of God's gifts of health, prosperity and harmony. Our sins are forgiven when we cease to sin, and open our mind to the Truth that we are heir only to the good.

## Our Family in the Mental and Soul Realms[1]

3:31 His mother and his brothers came, and standing outside, they sent to him, calling him. 3:32 A multitude was sitting around him, and they told him, "Behold, your mother, your brothers, and your sisters[5] are outside looking for you."

3:33 He answered them, "Who are my mother and my brothers?" 3:34 Looking around at those who sat around him, he said, "Behold, my mother and my brothers![2] 3:35 For whoever does the will of God, the same is my brother, and my sister, and mother."

1. See Mt 12:22-32; Lk 11:14-23.

2. *Behold, my mother and my brothers!* Jesus taught that all who do the will of God are members of the same family, the Christ Body. Those who think alike and who delight in the same subjects are near kin in the mental and soul realms.

---

Fillmore Study Bible annotations by Rev. Dan Beckett.

**World English Bible Footnotes:**

[5] v3:32. TR omits "your sisters"

# Mark 4

## Divine Ideas Taking Root[1]

4:1 Again he began to teach by the seaside.[2] A great multitude was gathered to him, so that he entered into a boat[3] in the sea, and sat down. All the multitude were on the land by the sea. 4:2 He taught them many things in parables, and told them in his teaching, 4:3 "Listen! Behold, the farmer went out to sow, 4:4 and it happened, as he sowed, some seed fell by the road, and the birds[6] came and devoured it. 4:5 Others fell on the rocky ground, where it had little soil,[4] and immediately it sprang up, because it had no depth of soil. 4:6 When the sun had risen, it was scorched; and because it had no root, it withered away. 4:7 Others fell among the thorns, and the thorns grew up, and choked it, and it yielded no fruit. 4:8 Others fell into the good ground,[5] and yielded fruit, growing up and increasing. Some brought forth thirty times, some sixty times, and some one hundred times as much." 4:9 He said, "Whoever has ears[6] to hear, let him hear."

1. See Mt 13:1-9; Lk 8:4-8.
2. *sea.* The sea signifies universal Mind, that great realm of unexpressed and unformed thoughts and ideas that contains all-potentiality. (MBD/sea). *Water* in its different aspects can, depending on context, represent weakness and negativeness, cleansing, mental potentiality, and in some cases life, or vital energy. (MBD/water)
3. *boat.* A positive thought--a conveyance that is able to float upon the water (the unstable mind), and to bear up the disciples (the faculties of mind). The multitudes are the numberless thoughts that are seeking light, strength, and healing. (MBD/boat)
4. *soil (earth).* Represents the consciousness of the physical body. (RW/earth)
5. *good ground.* The receptive mind and the fertile bent of mind that is not content merely to hear a word of Truth but that must put the word to work and make it productive. The type of mind that increases the good is both receptive and retentive.
6. *ears.* The obedience and receptivity of the mind. (RW/ears). *Whoever has ears to hear, let him hear.* The Scriptures are historically fitted to the needs of the natural human being. There is, however, an inner meaning which is discerned by the spiritual consciousness in all of us. The spiritual ear is opened by an attitude of receptivity coupled with faith in the reality of things invisible. Thus faith and receptivity are the very foundation of spiritual growth. All true Scripture is based upon spiritual intelligence.

## Inner Truth Revealed

4:10 When he was alone, those who were around him with the twelve asked him about the parables.[1] 4:11 He said to them, "To you is given the mystery of the Kingdom of God, but to those who are outside, all things are done in parables, 4:12 that 'seeing they may see, and not perceive; and hearing they may hear, and not understand; lest perhaps they should turn again, and their sins should be forgiven them.'"[7]

4:13 He said to them, "Don't you understand this parable? How will you understand all of the parables? 4:14 The farmer sows the word. 4:15 The ones by the road are the ones where the word is sown; and when they have heard, immediately Satan comes, and takes away the word which has been sown in them. 4:16 These in like manner are those who are sown on the rocky places, who, when they have heard the word, immediately receive it with joy. 4:17 They have no root in themselves, but are short-lived. When oppression or persecution arises because of the word, immediately they stumble. 4:18 Others are those who are sown among the thorns. These are those who have heard the word, 4:19 and the cares of this age, and the deceitfulness of riches, and the lusts of other things entering in choke the word, and it becomes unfruitful. 4:20 Those which were sown on the good ground are those who hear the word, and accept it, and bear fruit, some thirty times, some sixty times, and some one hundred times."

1. *parables*. A parable is a narrative of a possible event of life, by which a truth is illustrated. In the Scripture a material illustration is often used to prove a spiritual truth. See v.33.

## Let Your Christ Light Shine[1]

4:21 He said to them, "Is the lamp[2] brought to be put under a basket[8] or under a bed? Isn't it put on a stand? 4:22 For there is nothing hidden, except that it should be made known; neither was anything made secret, but that it should come to light. 4:23 If any man has ears to hear, let him hear."

4:24 He said to them, "Take heed what you hear. With whatever measure you measure, it will be measured to you, and more will be given to you who hear. 4:25 For whoever has, to him will more be given, and he who doesn't have, even that which he has will be taken away from him."

1. See Mt 5:15; 7:2; 10:26; 13:12; 25:29; Lk 6:38; 8:16-18; 11:33; 12:2; 19:26.

2. *lamp (light)*. A symbol of intelligence. (MBD/light)

## The Emergence of Truth

4:26 He said, "The Kingdom of God[1] is as if a man should cast seed[2] on the earth, 4:27 and should sleep and rise night and day, and the seed should spring up and grow, he doesn't know how. 4:28 For the earth bears fruit: first the blade, then the ear, then the full grain in the ear. 4:29 But when the fruit is ripe, immediately he puts forth the sickle, because the harvest has come."

1. *kingdom of God*. The kingdom of God is a perfectly harmonious state of mind. That state of mind is susceptible of development in the mind of *every one*. Its growth is from the word or right thought "The seed is the word of God."

2. *seed*. The creative idea inherent in the Word. Its nature is inherited from its parent source, God. The "seed," that is, "the word of God," is the real man--not the external thinking personality that has consciousness of separation, but the internal Spirit center. (RW/seed)

## Divine Ideas Grow in Mind[1]

4:30 He said, "How will we liken the Kingdom of God? Or with what parable will we illustrate it? [4:31] It's like a grain of mustard seed, which, when it is sown in the earth, though it is less than all the seeds that are on the earth, [4:32] yet when it is sown, grows[2] up, and becomes greater than all the herbs, and puts out great branches, so that the birds of the sky can lodge under its shadow."

1. See Mt 13:31-32; Lk 13.18-19.

2. *grows.* What is mysterious about the increase of the kingdom in our consciousness since we ourselves must work toward its consummation? The miracle of growth is not yet wholly understood. We know some of the conditions under which it takes place, such as the preparing of the soil and the sowing of the seed. The growing is all done by the seed, and this still a miracle to us.

## How Truth is Conveyed[1]

[4:33] With many such parables[2] he spoke the word to them, as they were able to hear it. [4:34] Without a parable he didn't speak to them; but privately to his own disciples he explained everything.

1. See Mt 13:34-35.
2. *parables.* See v.10.

## The Peace of God[1]

[4:35] On that day, when evening had come, he said to them, "Let's go over to the other side." [4:36] Leaving the multitude, they took him with them, even as he was, in the boat. Other small boats were also with him. [4:37] A big wind[2] storm arose, and the waves beat into the boat, so much that the boat was already filled. [4:38] He himself was in the stern, asleep on the cushion, and they woke him up, and told him, "Teacher, don't you care that we are dying?"

[4:39] He awoke, and rebuked the wind, and said to the sea, "Peace![3] Be still!" The wind ceased, and there was a great calm. [4:40] He said to them, "Why are you so afraid? How is it that you have no faith?"

[4:41] They were greatly afraid, and said to one another, "Who then is this, that even the wind and the sea obey him?"

1. See Mt 8:23-27; Lk 8:22-25.

2. *wind.* Life currents that come from within and surround the whole being; the executive power of mind clearing the way to higher states of consciousness. (RW/wind)

3. *peace.* Harmony and tranquillity derived from awareness of the Christ consciousness. (RW/peace)

---

Fillmore Study Bible annotations by Rev. Dan Beckett.

**World English Bible Footnotes:**

[6] v4:4. TR adds "of the air"

[7] v4:12. Isaiah 6:9-10

[8] v4:21. literally, a modion, a dry measuring basket containing about a peck (about 9 litres)

# Mark 5

## Light Banishes Darkness[1]

5:1 They came to the other side of the sea, into the country of the Gadarenes.[2] 5:2 When he had come out of the boat, immediately there met him out of the tombs a man with an unclean spirit,[3] 5:3 who had his dwelling in the tombs. Nobody could bind him any more, not even with chains, 5:4 because he had been often bound with fetters and chains, and the chains had been torn apart by him, and the fetters broken in pieces. Nobody had the strength to tame him. 5:5 Always, night and day, in the tombs and in the mountains, he was crying out, and cutting himself with stones. 5:6 When he saw Jesus from afar, he ran and bowed down to him, 5:7 and crying out with a loud voice, he said, "What have I to do with you, Jesus, you Son of the Most High God? I adjure you by God, don't torment me." 5:8 For he said to him, "Come out of the man, you unclean spirit!"

5:9 He asked him, "What is your name?"

He said to him, "My name is Legion, for we are many." 5:10 He begged him much that he would not send them away out of the country. 5:11 Now there was on the mountainside a great herd of pigs[4] feeding. 5:12 All the demons[5] begged him, saying, "Send us into the pigs, that we may enter into them."

5:13 At once Jesus gave them permission. The unclean spirits came out and entered into the pigs. The herd of about two thousand rushed down the steep bank into the sea, and they were drowned in the sea. 5:14 Those who fed them fled, and told it in the city and in the country.

The people came to see what it was that had happened. 5:15 They came to Jesus, and saw him who had been possessed by demons sitting, clothed, and in his right mind, even him who had the legion; and they were afraid. 5:16 Those who saw it declared to them how it happened to him who was possessed by demons, and about the pigs. 5:17 They began to beg him to depart from their region.

5:18 As he was entering into the boat, he who had been possessed by demons begged him that he might be with him. 5:19 He didn't allow him, but said to him, "Go to your house, to your friends, and tell them what great things the Lord has done for you,[6] and how he had mercy on you."

5:20 He went his way, and began to proclaim in Decapolis[7] how Jesus had done great things for him, and everyone marveled.

1. See Mt 8:28-34; Lk 8:26-39.

2. *Gerasenes*. The word Gerasenes means "walled about," and it represents strongly organized thoughts of energy and power in the subconscious mind in man."

3. *man with an unclean spirit*. The man who was possessed of demons and dwelt in the tombs represents ignorant thoughts, as expressed in sense life. These thoughts were so complex and sensually (see Mark 5:9) strong that in their confusion they warred against one another to the point of utter exhaustion, inertia, death.

4. *pigs*. or swine, outpicture uncleanness and sensuality in a form that feeds on hypocrisy and pretensions of spirituality (the mountainside).

5. *demons*. See Mk 3:15

6. *and tell them what great things the Lord has done for you*. We can apply Truth right where we are, in our everyday routine. With no need to adjust ourselves to new circumstances or environment, we can apply our thought to our new blessings and by contemplating them in a spirit of thankfulness change our whole outlook on life.

7. *Decapolis (city)*. Cities represent fixed states of consciousness or aggregations of thoughts in the various nerve centers of the body. The presiding or central thought-meaning of a city is found in the significance of its name, combined with that of the person, tribe, country, or nation with which it is mentioned. (MBD/cities)

## The Healing Power of Faith[1]

5:21 When Jesus had crossed back over in the boat to the other side, a great multitude was gathered to him; and he was by the sea. 5:22 Behold, one of the rulers of the synagogue, Jairus[2] by name, came; and seeing him, he fell at his feet, 5:23 and begged him much, saying, "My little daughter is at the point of death. Please come and lay your hands on her, that she may be made healthy, and live."

5:24 He went with him, and a great multitude followed him, and they pressed upon him on all sides. 5:25 A certain woman, who had an issue of blood for twelve years, 5:26 and had suffered many things by many physicians, and had spent all that she had, and was no better, but rather grew worse, 5:27 having heard the things concerning Jesus, came up behind him in the crowd, and touched his clothes.[3] 5:28 For she said, "If I just touch his clothes,[4] I will be made well." 5:29 Immediately the flow of her blood was dried up, and she felt in her body that she was healed of her affliction.

5:30 Immediately Jesus, perceiving in himself that the power had gone out from him, turned around in the crowd, and asked, "Who touched my clothes?"

5:31 His disciples said to him, "You see the multitude pressing against you, and you say, 'Who touched me?'"

5:32 He looked around to see her who had done this thing. 5:33 But the woman, fearing and trembling, knowing what had been done to her, came and fell down before him, and told him all the truth.

5:34 He said to her, "Daughter, your faith has made you well. Go in peace, and be cured of your disease."

5:35 While he was still speaking, they came from the synagogue ruler's house saying, "Your daughter is dead. Why bother the Teacher any more?"

5:36 But Jesus, when he heard the message spoken, immediately said to the ruler of the synagogue, "Don't be afraid, only believe."[5] 5:37 He allowed no one to follow him, except Peter, James, and John[6] the brother of James. 5:38 He came to the synagogue ruler's house, and he saw an uproar, weeping, and great wailing. 5:39 When he had entered in, he said to them, "Why do you make an uproar and weep? The child is not dead, but is asleep."

5:40 They ridiculed him. But he, having put them all out, took the father of the child and her mother and those who were with him, and went in where the child was lying. 5:41 Taking the child by the hand, he said to her, "Talitha cumi;" which means, being interpreted, "Girl, I tell you, get up." 5:42 Immediately the girl rose up, and walked, for she was twelve years old. They were amazed with great amazement. 5:43 He strictly ordered them that no one should know this, and commanded that something should be given to her to eat.

1. See Mt 9:18-26; Lk 8:40-56.)

2. *Jairus*. Jairus means "shining" and "running water." Shining, metaphysically defined, means expressing light; running water represents activity of life.

3. *clothes (garment)*. The radiation or aura that surrounds the body. (RW/garment)

4. *touched his clothes*. Jesus was so charged with the thought of spiritual intelligence and life that His aura saturated His garments with dynamic power and strength. When the negative, weak mind of the woman touched, in faith, this mighty spiritual vibration, it flooded her with new life and she was healed.

5. *only believe*. As an object lesson in healing, we note the necessity of unwavering faith as a concomitant of the process. When the report came that the little maiden was dead Jesus said, "Only believe."

6. *Peter, James, and John*. What is essential to constructive thinking in the face of apparently complete limitation? The first essential is faith, which includes an absence of fear or distress; in other words, a positive attitude of mind. The thoughts should always be inspired by faith, judgment, and love (Peter, James, and John, the three disciples closest to Jesus).

Fillmore Study Bible annotations by Rev. Dan Beckett.

# Mark 6

## Lack of Faith Blocks Healing [1]

6:1 He went out from there. He came into his own country, and his disciples followed him. 6:2 When the Sabbath had come, he began to teach in the synagogue, and many hearing him were astonished, saying, "Where did this man get these things?" and, "What is the wisdom that is given to this man, that such mighty works come about by his hands? 6:3 Isn't this the carpenter, the son of Mary, and brother of James, Joses, Judah, and Simon? Aren't his sisters here with us?" They were offended at him.

6:4 Jesus said to them, "A prophet [2] is not without honor, except in his own country, and among his own relatives, and in his own house." 6:5 He could do no mighty work there, [3] except that he laid his hands on a few sick people, and healed them. 6:6 He marveled because of their unbelief.

1. See Mt 13:53-58; Lk 4:16-30.

2. *prophet*. A teacher, one who receives the inspiration of Spirit, an understanding of spiritual law, and imparts it to others. A prophet, in individual consciousness, is a thought that is in contact with Spirit, that receives revelations direct from the Holy Spirit; it knows and understands divine law and its working, therefore it warns and instructs the other thoughts. (MBD/prophet)

3. *He could do no mighty work there*. Why could Jesus do no mighty work in this place of unbelief, and why did He marvel

at that fact? In demonstration of spiritual power, Faith is essential. In several instances mentioned in Jesus' ministry, He could do no mighty works because in those among whom He worked there was lack of faith. He marveled at their unbelief because in His own consciousness He had a clear realization of the truths of being.

## God Provides[1]

He went around the villages teaching. 6:7 He called to himself the twelve, and began to send them out two by two; and he gave them authority over the unclean spirits.[2] 6:8 He commanded them that they should take nothing for their journey,[3] except a staff only: no bread, no wallet, no money in their purse, 6:9 but to wear sandals, and not put on two tunics. 6:10 He said to them, "Wherever you enter into a house, stay there until you depart from there. 6:11 Whoever will not receive you nor hear you, as you depart from there, shake off the dust[4] that is under your feet for a testimony against them. Assuredly, I tell you, it will be more tolerable for Sodom and Gomorrah in the day of judgment than for that city!" 6:12 They went out and preached that people should repent. 6:13 They cast out many demons, and anointed many with oil[5] who were sick, and healed them.

1. See Mt 10:1, 5-15; Lk 9:1-6

2. *unclean spirits.* What is one of the "unclean spirits" over which the Christ has power? The spirit of self-seeking and self-assertion. Wherever the self enters in no place is found for the pure love of God, compared with which the self is unclean.

3. *take nothing for their journey.* The disciples were to depend altogether on God for their supply, thus proving the constancy of their faith in the providing divine law.

4. *dust, shake off the.* To deny all seeming materiality. (RW/dust)

5. *oil, anointing.* The thought of love, which is poured over anything, making it holy or a perfect whole. (RW/oil)

## Sense Consciousness Begets Death[1]

6:14 King Herod[2] heard this, for his name had become known, and he said, "John the Baptizer[3] has risen from the dead, and therefore these powers are at work in him." 6:15 But others said, "He is Elijah."[4] Others said, "He is a prophet, or like one of the prophets." 6:16 But Herod, when he heard this, said, "This is John, whom I beheaded. He has risen from the dead." 6:17 For Herod himself had sent out and arrested John, and bound him in prison for the sake of Herodias, his brother Philip's wife, for he had married her. 6:18 For John said to Herod, "It is not lawful for you to have your brother's wife." 6:19 Herodias[5] set herself against him, and desired to kill him, but she couldn't, 6:20 for Herod feared John, knowing that he was a righteous and holy man, and kept him safe. When he heard him, he did many things, and he heard him gladly.

6:21 Then a convenient day came, that Herod on his birthday made a supper for his nobles, the high officers, and the chief men of Galilee. 6:22 When the daughter of Herodias[6] herself came in and danced, she pleased Herod and those sitting with him. The king said to the young lady, "Ask me whatever you want, and I will give it to you." 6:23 He swore to her, "Whatever you shall ask of me, I will give you, up to half of my kingdom."

6:24 She went out, and said to her mother, "What shall I ask?"

She said, "The head of John the Baptizer."

6:25 She came in immediately with haste to the king, and asked, "I want you to give me right now the head of John the Baptizer on a platter."

6:26 The king was exceedingly sorry, but for the sake of his oaths, and of his dinner guests, he didn't wish to refuse her. 6:27 Immediately the king sent out a soldier of his guard, and commanded to bring John's head, and he went and beheaded him in the prison, 6:28 and brought his head on a platter, and gave it to the young lady; and the young lady gave it to her mother.

6:29 When his disciples heard this, they came and took up his corpse, and laid it in a tomb.

1. See Mt 14:1-12; Lk 9:7-9
2. *Herod.* The ruling will of the physical, the ego in the sense consciousness. This ruling ego is temporal because it does not understand man's true origin or the law of man's being. It is narrow, jealous, destructive. Under its rule man does not fulfill the law of his being, and another ego must supplant the ego of sense. (MBD/Herod)
3. *John the Baptizer.* John the Baptist symbolizes the repentant state of mind necessary before purification of soul and body can be established.
4. *Elijah.* Represents the spiritual I AM of man's consciousness. Elijah on Mount Carmel (I Kings 18:19) represents the I AM in realization of its unfettered power. (MBD/Elijah)
5. *Herodias.* The passions of the human soul, the feminine side of sense thought. (MBD/Herodias)
6. *Daughter of Herodias.* The sex-sensation active in mortal consciousness.

## Faith in Action as Prosperity[1]

6:30 The apostles gathered themselves together to Jesus, and they told him all things, whatever they had done, and whatever they had taught. 6:31 He said to them, "You come apart into a deserted place,[2] and rest[3] awhile." For there were many coming and going, and they had no leisure so much as to eat. 6:32 They went away in the boat to a deserted place by themselves. 6:33 They[9] saw them going, and many recognized him and ran there on foot from all the cities. They arrived before them and came together to him. 6:34 Jesus came out, saw a great multitude, and he had compassion on them, because they were like sheep without a shepherd, and he began to teach them many things. 6:35 When it was late in the day, his disciples came to him, and said, "This place is deserted, and it is late in the day. 6:36 Send them away, that they may go into the surrounding country and villages, and buy themselves bread, for they have nothing to eat."

6:37 But he answered them, "You give them something to eat."

They asked him, "Shall we go and buy two hundred denarii[10] worth of bread, and give them something to eat?"

6:38 He said to them, "How many loaves[4] do you have? Go see."

When they knew, they said, "Five, and two fish."[5]

6:39 He commanded them that everyone should sit down in groups on the green grass. 6:40 They sat down in ranks, by hundreds and by fifties. 6:41 He took the five loaves and the two fish, and looking up to heaven, he blessed and broke the loaves, and he gave to his disciples to set before them, and he divided the two fish among them all. 6:42 They all ate, and were filled. 6:43 They took up twelve baskets full of broken pieces and also of the fish. 6:44 Those who ate the loaves were[11] five thousand men.

1. See Mt 14:13-21; Lk 9:10-17; Jn 6.1-13.

2. *deserted place*. metaphysically, a state in which conscious thought is suspended: a state in which we rest from the labor of affirming and denying and have "leisure ... to eat," or to let the recuperative power of the inner nature do its work.

3. *rest*. By relaxing in the consciousness of innate goodness and abiding there, we rest in God.

4. *loaves*. The loaves here referred to represent the nucleus or the seed from which abundance is to come forth. This nucleus is ample to satisfy all physical hunger and to meet any craving for the true understanding of life.

5. *Five, and two fish*. Five loaves and two fishes formed the nucleus that fed five thousand, with much more left over than the original amount. The nucleus that we start with may be all, but it can grow to truly astounding proportions, for the law of increase is subject to no limit in the mental or spiritual realm.

## Rise Above Troubled Thought[1]

6:45 Immediately he made his disciples get into the boat, and to go ahead to the other side, to Bethsaida,[2] while he himself sent the multitude away. 6:46 After he had taken leave of them, he went up the mountain[3] to pray.

6:47 When evening had come, the boat was in the midst of the sea, and he was alone on the land. 6:48 Seeing them distressed[4] in rowing, for the wind was contrary to them, about the fourth watch of the night he came to them, walking on the sea,[12] and he would have passed by them, 6:49 but they, when they saw him walking on the sea, supposed that it was a ghost, and cried out; 6:50 for they all saw him, and were troubled.[5] But he immediately spoke with them, and said to them, "Cheer up! It is I![13] Don't be afraid." 6:51 He got into the boat with them; and the wind ceased, and they were very amazed among themselves, and marveled; 6:52 for they hadn't understood about the loaves, but their hearts were hardened.

1. See Mt 14:22-33; Jn 6:15-21.

2. *Bethsaida*. A consciousness of increase of ideas, of gathering substance; a state of thought that is continually searching after new ideas, and endeavors to gain knowledge, by every possible means (house of fishing, place of hunting; place of nets; fishing town; hunting town). (MBD/Bethsaida)

3. *mountain*. Exaltation, a high plane of consciousness, a state of spiritual realization. (MBD/mountain)

4. *distressed*. We live in a sea of thought that is moved by every impulse of the mind. Only through faith in I AM can we walk safely.

5. *troubled*. The unawakened consciousness is troubled and afraid at the advent of the quickening Spirit.

## The Healing Power of the Christ[1]

6:53 When they had crossed over, they came to land at Gennesaret,[2] and moored to the shore. 6:54 When they had come out of the boat, immediately the people recognized him, 6:55 and ran around that whole region, and began to bring those who were sick, on their mats, to where they heard he was. 6:56 Wherever he entered, into villages, or into cities,

or into the country, they laid the
sick in the marketplaces, and begged
him that they might touch just the
fringe[14] of his garment;[3] and as
many as touched him were made
well.

1. See Mt 14:34-36.

2. *Gennesaret.* The "sea of life." We are related, both within the consciousness and without, to all creation through the Universal Life Principle.

3. *touch the fringe of his garment.* The Omnipotence of Spirit not only penetrates one's consciousness, but is everywhere present. If one but touches the "fringe of his garment" of Truth, he contacts a mighty healing power, and through faith in the Christ Principle is made whole. When we become conscious of righteousness and faithfulness in our mind and heart, we touch the Christ.

Fillmore Study Bible annotations by Rev. Dan Beckett.

**World English Bible Footnotes:**

[9] v6:33. TR reads "The multitudes" instead of "They"

[10] v6:37. 200 denarii was about 7 or 8 months wages for an agricultural laborer.

[11] v6:44. TR adds "about"

[12] v6:48. see Job 9:8

[13] v6:50. or, "I AM!"

[14] v6:56. or, tassel

# Mark 7

## The Authority of Spirit[1]

7:1 Then the Pharisees, and some
of the scribes[2] gathered together to
him, having come from Jerusalem.
7:2 Now when they saw some of his
disciples eating[3] bread with defiled,
that is, unwashed, hands, they found
fault. 7:3 (For the Pharisees, and all
the Jews, don't eat unless they wash
their hands and forearms, holding to
the tradition of the elders. 7:4 They
don't eat when they come from the
marketplace, unless they bathe
themselves, and there are many
other things, which they have
received to hold to: washings of
cups, pitchers, bronze vessels, and
couches.) 7:5 The Pharisees and the
scribes asked him, "Why don't your
disciples[4] walk according to the
tradition of the elders, but eat their
bread with unwashed hands?"

7:6 He answered them, "Well did
Isaiah prophesy of you hypocrites, as
it is written,

'This people honors me with their lips,
but their heart is far from me.
7:7 But in vain do they worship me,
teaching as doctrines the commandments of

men.'⑤[15]

7:8 "For you set aside the commandment of God, and hold tightly to the tradition of men--the washing of pitchers and cups, and you do many other such things." 7:9 He said to them, "Full well do you reject the commandment of God, that you may keep your tradition. 7:10 For Moses said, 'Honor your father and your mother;'[16] and, 'He who speaks evil⑥ of father or mother, let him be put to death.'[17] 7:11 But you say, 'If a man tells his father or his mother, "Whatever profit you might have received from me is Corban[18], that is to say, given to God;"' 7:12 then you no longer allow him to do anything for his father or his mother, 7:13 making void the word of God by your tradition, which you have handed down. You do many things like this."

7:14 He called all the multitude to himself, and said to them, "Hear me, all of you, and understand. 7:15 There is nothing from outside of the man, that going into him can defile him; but the things which proceed out of the man are those that defile the man. 7:16 If anyone has ears to hear, let him hear!"

7:17 When he had entered into a house away from the multitude, his disciples asked him about the parable. 7:18 He said to them, "Are you thus without understanding also? Don't you perceive that whatever goes into the man from outside can't defile him, 7:19 because it doesn't go into his heart, but into his stomach, then into the latrine, thus making all foods clean?" 7:20 He said, "That which proceeds out of the man, that defiles the man. 7:21 For from within, out of the hearts of men, proceed evil thoughts, adulteries, sexual sins, murders, thefts, 7:22 covetings, wickedness, deceit, lustful desires, an evil eye, blasphemy, pride, and foolishness. 7:23 All these evil things come from within, and defile the man."

1. See Mt 15:1-20.

2. *Pharisees, scribes.* The Pharisees represent that state of consciousness which is concerned with the formalities and customs of the external realm. The scribes represent fixed ideas built up in consciousness through adhering to tradition and superstition.

3. *eating.* Eating is symbolic of mental appropriation of thoughts of substance. "Thy words were found, and I did eat them; and thy words were unto me a joy and the rejoicing of my heart" (Jer. 15:16). (RW/eating)

4. *"Why don't your disciples..."* The significance of the attitude of the scribes and Pharisees is the overemphasis on the literal fulfillment of traditional religious custom which the attention from the spiritual meaning underlying all religious observance. "The letter killeth, but the Spirit giveth life."

5. *commandments of men.* The doctrines and precepts of men that have their foundation in personal opinion or traditional custom are profitless. To worship God is to conform to an entirely new principle and teaching. God is Spirit and must be worshiped in spirit and in truth.

6. *evil.* That which is not of God; unreality; error thought; a product of the fallen human consciousness; negation. (RW/evil)

## Healing Our Thoughts①

7:24 From there he arose, and went away into the borders of Tyre and Sidon.② He entered into a house, and didn't want anyone to know it, but he couldn't escape notice. 7:25 For a woman, whose little daughter had an unclean spirit, having heard of him, came and fell down at his feet. 7:26 Now the woman was a Greek, a Syrophoenician③ by race. She begged him that he would cast the demon out of her daughter. 7:27 But Jesus said to her, "Let the children[4] be filled first, for it is not appropriate to take the children's bread and throw it to the dogs."

7:28 But she answered him, "Yes, Lord. Yet even the dogs under the table eat the children's crumbs."

7:29 He said to her, "For this saying, go your way. The demon has gone out of your daughter."

7:30 She went away to her house, and found the child having been laid on the bed, with the demon gone out.

1. See Mt 15:21-28.

2. *Tyre and Sidon.* Tyre and Sidon symbolize the realm of sensation in man's consciousness. This realm must be consciously entered and spiritualized by the Christ.

3. *Syrophoenician.* The Syrophoenician woman signifies the intuitive perception of Truth reflected into the intellect from within the soul. (MBD/Syrophoenician)

4. *children.* The "children" typify the growing thoughts in consciousness. These thoughts should be given an upward trend, that they may bring forth the spiritualized body.

## Jesus Cures a Deaf Man[1]

7:31 Again he departed from the
borders of Tyre and Sidon, and came
to the sea of Galilee, through the
midst of the region of Decapolis. 7:32
They brought to him one who was
deaf and had an impediment in his
speech.[2] They begged him to lay his
hand[3] on him. 7:33 He took him aside
from the multitude, privately, and
put his fingers into his ears, and he
spat, and touched his tongue. 7:34
Looking up to heaven, he sighed, and
said to him, "Ephphatha!"[4] that is,
"Be opened!" 7:35 Immediately his ears
were opened, and the impediment
of his tongue was released, and he
spoke clearly. 7:36 He commanded
them that they should tell no one,
but the more he commanded them,
so much the more widely they
proclaimed it. 7:37 They were
astonished beyond measure, saying,
"He has done all things well. He
makes even the deaf hear, and the
mute speak!"

1. See Mt 15:29-31.

2. *deaf, speech impediment.* In the symbology of spiritual consciousness, "deaf" is a state of mind unreceptive (not listening) to the revealing Spirit. Similarly, a spiritual "speech impediment" indicates inactivity in expressing Truth. (This is not the same as the physical conditions of being deaf or mute, both of which occur naturally in some of God's children and as such are not deficiencies and do not need to be "fixed.")

3. *hand.* The hand is a symbol of activity or agency. The activity of the I AM (Jesus) brings spiritual power into play, spiritual power is the root of physical health.

4. *Ephphatha!.* An inner freeing, healing thought or word of the Christ that releases all tension in consciousness and opens the mind and the body to spiritual receptivity and wholeness. (MBD/Ephphatha)

---

Fillmore Study Bible annotations by Rev. Dan Beckett.

**World English Bible Footnotes:**

[15] v7:7. Isaiah 29:13

[16] v7:10. Exodus 20:12; Deuteronomy 5:16

[17] v7:10. Exodus 21:17; Leviticus 20:9

[18] v7:11. Corban is a Hebrew word for an offering devoted to God.

# Mark 8

## Spiritual Substance Made Manifest[1]

8:1 In those days, when there was a very great multitude, and they had nothing to eat, Jesus called his disciples to himself, and said to them, 8:2 "I have compassion on the multitude, because they have stayed with me now three days, and have nothing to eat. 8:3 If I send them away fasting to their home, they will faint on the way, for some of them have come a long way."

8:4 His disciples answered him, "From where could one satisfy these people with bread here in a deserted place?" 8:5 He asked them, "How many loaves do you have?" They said, "Seven."

8:6 He commanded the multitude to sit down on the ground, and he took the seven loaves. Having given thanks, he broke them, and gave them to his disciples to serve, and they served the multitude. 8:7 They had a few small fish.[2] Having blessed them, he said to serve these also. 8:8 They ate, and were filled. They took up seven baskets of broken pieces that were left over. 8:9 Those who had eaten were about four thousand.[3] Then he sent them away. 8:10 Immediately he entered into the boat with his disciples, and came into the region of Dalmanutha.

1. See Mt 15:32-39
2. *loaves and fishes.* The nucleus of divine substance or seed from which supply is to come forth and be made manifest.
3. *four thousand.* Is the supply of substance adequate to meet all demands that may be made upon it? Substance is infinite, therefore it can never be exhausted. However only those who learn to use the law of increase know how to draw upon substance at will.

## Lack of Spiritual Vision[1]

8:11 The Pharisees[2] came out and began to question him, seeking from him a sign from heaven, and testing him. 8:12 He sighed deeply in his spirit, and said, "Why does this generation[19] seek a sign?[3] Most certainly I tell you, no sign will be given to this generation." 8:13 He left them, and again entering into the boat, departed to the other side.

1. See Mt 16:1-4; Lk 11:29-32; cf. Mt 12:38-42; Lk 11:16; Jn 6:30.
2. *Pharisees.* The religious thoughts pertaining to the realm of form and do not know that Truth comes into expression in the consciousness through understanding, but seek a sign in the external realm.
3. *sign.* No sign of the presence of Christ can be given unto the pharisaical state of mind, for the things of Spirit are spiritually discerned.

## Beware the Seeds of Doubt[1]

8:14 They forgot to take bread; and they didn't have more than one loaf in the boat with them. 8:15 He warned them, saying, "Take heed:[2] beware of the yeast of the Pharisees and the yeast of Herod."

8:16 They reasoned with one another, saying, "It's because we have no bread."[3]

8:17 Jesus, perceiving it, said to them, "Why do you reason that it's because you have no bread? Don't you perceive yet, neither understand? Is your heart still hardened? 8:18 Having eyes, don't you see? Having ears, don't you hear? Don't you remember?[4] 8:19 When I broke the five loaves among the five thousand, how many baskets full of broken pieces did you take up?" They told him, "Twelve." 8:20 "When the seven loaves fed the four thousand, how many baskets full of broken pieces did you take up?" They told him, "Seven." 8:21 He asked them, "Don't you understand,[5] yet?"

1. See Mt 16:5-12; Lk 11:1; Jn 6:32-36.
2. *Take heed.* All the faculties of man's mind (the disciples) must be lifted out of the limited thoughts - leaven of the Pharisees and of Herod. The leaven of Herod symbolizes the demands of the selfish will.
3. *no bread.* The undeveloped faculties of mind, because they see not the outer manifestation of substance, are concerned with the evidence of lack.
4. *don't you see/hear/remember?* All the activities of mind must be centered in spiritual understanding in order to demonstrate the power of increase.
5. *understand.* The disciples did not understand that when the mind is raised through affirmations of God's substance and life, we are supplied abundantly in every expression, and there is always a surplus.

## Persistence in Expressing Truth[1]

8:22 He came to Bethsaida.[2] They brought a blind man to him, and begged him to touch him. 8:23 He took hold of the blind man by the hand, and brought him out[3] of the village. When he had spit on his eyes, and laid his hands on him, he asked him if he saw anything. 8:24 He looked up, and said, "I see men; for I see them like trees walking."

8:25 Then again[4] he laid his hands on his eyes. He looked intently, and was restored, and saw everyone clearly. 8:26 He sent him away to his house, saying, "Don't enter into the village,[5] nor tell anyone in the village."

1. See Jn 9:1-7.
2. *Bethsaida.* A consciousness of increase of ideas, of gathering substance; a state of thought that is continually searching after new ideas, and endeavors to gain knowledge, by every possible means. (MBD/Bethsaida)
3. *brought him out.* The Christ, exercising its power in consciousness, leads man out from the realm of mortal thoughts (the village) and anoints him with the healing energies of a regenerated mind.
4. *again.* If inability to understand is dominating the consciousness, persistent effort and patience in the use of the Word of Truth is necessary in order that all thought obstructions be dissolved from the mind.
5. *don't enter into the village.* When man enters into spiritual consciousness, he must daily withdraw his thoughts from the ordinary trend (the village), and center them in the Christ Mind.

## Two Planes of Consciousness[1]

[8:27] Jesus went out, with his disciples, into the villages of Caesarea Philippi.[2] On the way he asked his disciples, "Who do men say that I am?" [8:28] They told him, "John the Baptizer, and others say Elijah, but others: one of the prophets."[3]

[8:29] He said to them, "But who do you say that I am?"

Peter answered, "You are the Christ." [8:30] He commanded them that they should tell no one about him.[4]

1. See Mt 16:13-20; Lk 9:18-21.

2. *Caesarea Philippi.* Two planes of consciousness are in action here. The first, Caesarea Philippi, was a Roman town; it represents the abiding external personality; personal observation; the realm of appearances.

3. *They told him...* The first answers came from the first plane of consciousness, personal observation, the realm of appearances.

4. *Peter answered him...* he second answer came when Jesus appealed to the spiritual discernment, instead of to the personal observation, of His disciples. Peter, representing spiritual faith, saw within the personality and told what he perceived, "Thou art the Christ."

## Living From the Christ Within[1]

[8:31] He began to teach them that the Son of Man must suffer many things, and be rejected by the elders, the chief priests, and the scribes, and be killed, and after three days rise again. [8:32] He spoke to them openly. Peter took him, and began to rebuke him. [8:33] But he, turning around, and seeing his disciples, rebuked Peter, and said, "Get behind me, Satan![2] For you have in mind not the things of God, but the things of men."

[8:34] He called the multitude to himself with his disciples, and said to them, "Whoever wants to come after me, let him deny himself, and take up his cross, and follow me.[3] [8:35] For whoever wants to save his life will lose it; and whoever will lose his life for my sake and the sake of the Good News will save it.[4] [8:36] For what does it profit a man, to gain the whole world, and forfeit his life? [8:37] For what will a man give in exchange for his life? [8:38] For whoever will be ashamed of me and of my words in this adulterous and sinful generation, the Son of Man also will be ashamed of him, when he comes in the glory of his Father with the holy angels."[5]

1. See Mt 16:21-28; Lk 9:22-27.

2. *Get behind me Satan.* Get behind me Satan. Satan represents the deceiving phase of mind in man that has fixed ideas in opposition to Truth. (MBD/satan) See Mark 1:13.

3. *follow me.* It means denying the lower self, shouldering whatever handicap we may have, and living according to our best understanding of the truth of God.

4. *Save his life...* How does anyone save his life and yet lose it? By selfishly taking to himself all the good that he can command and turning a deaf ear to his brother's need he loses the larger life of service to others, with its attendant joy and satisfaction.

5. *...forfeit his life?* Our life on earth is a God-given opportunity to grow in spiritual stature and in the consciousness of things eternal. We gain nothing of lasting value and waste our divine opportunity ("forfeit" our "life") when we devote our energies to gaining material advancement or acquiring material possessions.

Fillmore Study Bible annotations by Rev. Dan Beckett.

**World English Bible Footnotes:**

[19] v8:12. The word translated "generation" here (genea) could also be translated "people," "race," or "family."

# Mark 9

## Living From the Christ Within (continued)

9:1 He said to them, "Most certainly
I tell you, there are some standing
here who will in no way taste death(1)
until they see the Kingdom of God
come with power."

1. *death*. The loss of this personal life is the only way to find eternal life. The acceptance of this mighty truth takes away the consciousness of death, and reveals the Son of God coming into his kingdom here and now.

## Radiating Spiritual Consciousness(1)

9:2 After six days Jesus took with
him Peter, James, and John, and
brought them up onto a high
mountain(2) privately by themselves,
and he was changed into another
form in front of them. 9:3 His clothing
became glistening, exceedingly
white,(3) like snow, such as no
launderer on earth can whiten them.
9:4 Elijah and Moses(4) appeared to
them, and they were talking with
Jesus.

9:5 Peter answered Jesus, "Rabbi,
it is good for us to be here. Let's
make three tents: one for you, one
for Moses, and one for Elijah." 9:6 For
he didn't know what to say, for they
were very afraid.

9:7 A cloud(5) came, overshadowing
them, and a voice came out of the
cloud, "This is my beloved Son. Listen
to him."

9:8 Suddenly looking around, they
saw no one with them any more,
except Jesus only.

1. See Mt 17:1-8; Lk 9:28-36.
2. *Peter, and James, and John onto a high mountain*. This represents the raising of faith (Peter), wisdom (James), and love (John) to spiritual consciousness, a state in which these faculties are mentally separated from the physical organism. (MBD/Peter, MBD/James, MBD/John)
3. *glistening, exceedingly white*. A symbol of the love, wisdom, and understanding of Divine Mind.
4. *Elijah and Moses*. In periods of spiritual exaltation the higher faculties are quickened. Elijah represents the ability to prophesy (MBD/Elijah); Moses represents understanding of the divine law (MBD/Moses). Their conversation with Jesus represents the expression of these abilities in the mind of man.
5. *cloud*. The cloud represents the obscured perception of man through which Jehovah is compelled to reveal Himself and identify His Son as the only begotten I AM.

## Divine Order[1]

9:9 As they were coming down from
the mountain,[2] he commanded them
that they should tell no one[3] what
things they had seen, until after the
Son of Man had risen from the dead.
9:10 They kept this saying to
themselves, questioning what the
"rising from the dead" meant.

9:11 They asked him, saying, "Why
do the scribes say that Elijah must
come first?"

9:12 He said to them, "Elijah indeed
comes first, and restores all things.
How is it written about the Son of
Man, that he should suffer many
things and be despised? 9:13 But I tell
you that Elijah has come, and they
have also done to him whatever they
wanted to, even as it is written about
him."

1. See Mt 17:9-13.
2. *mountain*. Exaltation, a high plane of consciousness, a state of spiritual realization. (MBD/mountain)
3. *tell no one*. We cannot express to others the meaning of spiritual experiences; we should attempt to explain them only to those who have spiritual understanding.

## Faith Conquers Error[1]

9:14 Coming to the disciples, he
saw a great multitude around them,
and scribes questioning them. 9:15
Immediately all the multitude, when
they saw him, were greatly amazed,
and running to him greeted him. 9:16
He asked the scribes, "What are you
asking them?"

9:17 One of the multitude
answered, "Teacher, I brought to you
my son, who has a mute spirit; 9:18
and wherever it seizes him, it throws
him down, and he foams at the
mouth, and grinds his teeth, and
wastes away. I asked your disciples
to cast it out, and they weren't able."

9:19 He answered him, "Unbelieving
generation, how long shall I be with
you? How long shall I bear with you?
Bring him to me."

9:20 They brought him to him, and
when he saw him, immediately the
spirit convulsed him, and he fell on
the ground, wallowing and foaming
at the mouth.

9:21 He asked his father, "How long
has it been since this has come to
him?"

He said, "From childhood. 9:22
Often it has cast him both into the
fire and into the water, to destroy
him. But if you can do anything, have
compassion on us, and help us."

9:23 Jesus said to him, "If you can
believe, all things are possible to him
who believes."

9:24 Immediately the father of the
child cried out with tears, "I believe.
Help my unbelief!"[2]

9:25 When Jesus saw that a
multitude came running together, he
rebuked the unclean spirit, saying to
him, "You mute and deaf spirit,[3] I
command you, come out of him, and
never enter him again!"

9:26 Having cried out, and
convulsed greatly, it came out of
him. The boy became like one dead;
so much that most of them said, "He
is dead." 9:27 But Jesus took him by
the hand, and raised him up; and he

arose.

9:28 When he had come into the house, his disciples asked him privately, "Why couldn't we cast it out?" 9:29 He said to them, "This kind can come out by nothing, except by prayer and fasting."

1. See Mt 17:14-20; Lk 9:37-43a.

2. *help my unbelief*. Faith and confidence on the part of an individual often calls out faith in another and reassures him.

3. *mute and deaf spirit*. In consciousness, deafness represents inability, or opposition to the word of Spirit; dumbness represents stubbornness in speaking the word of Spirit. These errors are cast out by prayer, that is, by making union with the mind of Spirit, which is open and receptive, and at the same time expressive. Regarding modern understanding of deafness, see annotation at Mark 7:32.

## The Coming Realization[1]

9:30 They went out from there, and passed through Galilee. He didn't want anyone to know it. 9:31 For he was teaching his disciples, and said to them, "The Son of Man is being handed over to the hands of men, and they will kill him; and when he is killed, on the third day he will rise again."

9:32 But they didn't understand[2] the saying, and were afraid to ask him.

1. See Mt 17:22-23; Lk 9:43b-45.

2. *didn't understand*. The disciples did not see that Jesus as the Son of man (symbol of the spiritual man as distinguished from the human) must die to the personal self and be resurrected into newness of life.

## A Lesson in Humility

9:33 He came to Capernaum, and when he was in the house he asked them, "What were you arguing among yourselves on the way?"

9:34 But they were silent, for they had disputed one with another on the way about who was the greatest.

9:35 He sat down, and called the twelve; and he said to them, "If any man wants to be first, he shall be last of all, and servant of all."[1] 9:36 He took a little child, and set him in the midst of them. Taking him in his arms, he said to them, 9:37 "Whoever receives one such little child in my name, receives me, and whoever receives me, doesn't receive me, but him who sent me."

1. *servant of all*. Whole-hearted service requires a detachment from the self that the self-centered person finds it difficult to accomplish.

## Partners in the Spirit[1]

9:38 John said to him, "Teacher, we saw someone who doesn't follow us casting out demons in your name; and we forbade him, because he doesn't follow us."

9:39 But Jesus said, "Don't forbid him, for there is no one who will do

a mighty work in my name, and be
able quickly to speak evil of me. 9:40
For whoever is not against us is on
our side. 9:41 For whoever will give
you a cup of water to drink in my
name, because you are Christ's, most
certainly I tell you, he will in no way
lose his reward.(2)

1. See Lk 9:49-50.

2. *in no way lose his reward.* In the Christ consciousness, fulfillment is the working out of principle, and principle admits of no exceptions. Therefore the smallest unselfish act done in this consciousness must bear fruit in character.

## Importance of the Inner Life(1)

9:42 Whoever will cause one of
these little ones who believe in me(2)
to stumble, it would be better for
him if he was thrown into the sea
with a millstone(3) hung around his
neck. 9:43 If your hand causes you to
stumble, cut it off. It is better for
you to enter into life maimed, rather
than having your two hands to go into
Gehenna,[20] into the unquenchable
fire, 9:44 'where their worm doesn't
die, and the fire is not quenched.' 9:45
If your foot(4) causes you to stumble,
cut it off. It is better for you to enter
into life lame, rather than having
your two feet to be cast into
Gehenna,[21] into the fire that will
never be quenched-- 9:46 'where their
worm doesn't die, and the fire is not
quenched.' 9:47 If your eye(5) causes
you to stumble, cast it out. It is
better for you to enter into the
Kingdom of God with one eye, rather
than having two eyes to be cast into
the Gehenna[22] of fire, 9:48 'where
their worm doesn't die, and the fire
is not quenched.'[23] 9:49 For everyone
will be salted with fire, and every
sacrifice will be seasoned with salt.(6)
9:50 Salt is good, but if the salt has
lost its saltiness, with what will you
season it? Have salt in yourselves,
and be at peace with one another."

1. See Mt 18:6-9; Lk 17:1-2.

2. *one of these little ones who believe in me.* Refers to the dawning of spiritual and soul qualities in one who has been absorbed in material thinking and living.

3. *millstone.* A seeming hindrance of an earthly nature; a heavy burden. (RW/millstone)

4. *hand, foot.* The importance of the inner life is emphasized by the teaching that it is better to lose a hand or a foot than to miss perfecting the expression of the inner life to its highest point. Love, sympathy, and faith are worth cultivating at any cost.

5. *eye.* More than the preservation of the physical sight, the inner vision or understanding of life is far more worthwhile than physical vision.

6. *salt.* The thoughts in man that understand, love, and obey Truth as Jesus taught and demonstrated it. (RW/salt)

---

Fillmore Study Bible annotations by Rev. Dan Beckett.

**World English Bible Footnotes:**

[20] v9:43. or, Hell

[21] v9:45. or, Hell

[22] v9:47. or, Hell

[23] v9:48. Isaiah 66:24

# Mark 10

## Marriage as Spiritual Union[1]

10:1 He arose from there and came into the borders of Judea[2] and beyond the Jordan.[3] Multitudes came together to him again. As he usually did, he was again teaching them. 10:2 Pharisees came to him testing him, and asked him, "Is it lawful for a man to divorce his wife?"

10:3 He answered, "What did Moses command you?"

10:4 They said, "Moses allowed a certificate of divorce to be written, and to divorce her."

10:5 But Jesus said to them, "For your hardness of heart, he wrote you this commandment. 10:6 But from the beginning of the creation, God made them male and female.[24] 10:7 For this cause a man will leave his father and mother, and will join to his wife, 10:8 and the two will become one flesh,[25] so that they are no longer two, but one flesh. 10:9 What therefore God has joined together, let no man separate."[4]

10:10 In the house, his disciples asked him again about the same matter. 10:11 He said to them, "Whoever divorces his wife, and marries another, commits adultery against her. 10:12 If a woman herself divorces her husband, and marries another, she commits adultery."

1. See Mt 19:1-9.
2. *Judea*. "the praise of Jehovah"; This is a key to the mental attitude in which the Christ consciousness will be opened to us—while we are praising the Lord. (MBD/Judea)
3. *Jordan*. There is a stream of thought constantly flowing through the subconsciousness (the south flowing), made up of thoughts good, bad, and indifferent, which is typified in Scripture by the river Jordan. (MBD/Jordan)
4. *separate*. Did Jesus sanction divorce? Jesus did not sanction the divorce of a man and a woman who are spiritually married. But, instead of living in spiritual unity, the majority of married persons live under the Mosaic dispensation (intellectuality). Their marriage is not of the Spirit. Jesus gave the cause of divorce among such persons as "hardness of heart."

## The Heart of a Child[1]

10:13 They were bringing to him little children, that he should touch them, but the disciples rebuked those who were bringing them. 10:14 But when Jesus saw it, he was moved with indignation, and said to them, "Allow the little children to come to me! Don't forbid them, for the Kingdom of God belongs to such as these.[2] 10:15 Most certainly I tell you, whoever will not receive the Kingdom of God like a little child, he will in no way enter into it." 10:16 He took them in his arms, and blessed them, laying his hands on them.

1. See Mt 19:13-15; Lk 18:15-17.
2. *such as these*. Why does the kingdom of God belong to little children? Because little children have trusting faith and singleness of heart, as well as obedience, humility, and teachableness; they are free from the self-righteousness that prevents the material-minded person from accepting Truth.

## Releasing Materiality[1]

10:17 As he was going out into the
way, one ran to him,[2] knelt before
him, and asked him, "Good Teacher,
what shall I do that I may inherit
eternal life?"

10:18 Jesus said to him, "Why do
you call me good? No one is good
except one--God. 10:19 You know the
commandments: 'Do not murder,' 'Do
not commit adultery,' 'Do not steal,'
'Do not give false testimony,' 'Do not
defraud,' 'Honor your father and
mother.'"[26]

10:20 He said to him, "Teacher, I
have observed all these things from
my youth."

10:21 Jesus looking at him loved
him, and said to him, "One thing you
lack. Go, sell whatever you have,[3]
and give to the poor, and you will
have treasure in heaven; and come,
follow me, taking up the cross."

10:22 But his face fell at that
saying, and he went away
sorrowful,[4] for he was one who had
great possessions. 10:23 Jesus looked
around, and said to his disciples,
"How difficult it is for those who have
riches to enter into the Kingdom of
God!"

10:24 The disciples were amazed at
his words. But Jesus answered again,
"Children, how hard is it for those
who trust in riches to enter into the
Kingdom of God! 10:25 It is easier for
a camel to go through a needle's eye
than for a rich man to enter into the
Kingdom of God."

10:26 They were exceedingly
astonished, saying to him, "Then who
can be saved?"

10:27 Jesus, looking at them, said,
"With men it is impossible, but not
with God, for all things are possible
with God."[5]

10:28 Peter began to tell him,
"Behold, we have left all, and have
followed you."

10:29 Jesus said, "Most certainly I
tell you, there is no one who has
left house, or brothers, or sisters,
or father, or mother, or wife, or
children, or land, for my sake, and
for the sake of the Good News, 10:30
but he will receive one hundred
times more now in this time, houses,
brothers, sisters, mothers, children,
and land, with persecutions; and in
the age to come eternal life. 10:31 But
many who are first will be last; and
the last first."

1. See Mt 19:16-30; Lk 18:18-30.

2. *one ran to him*. What does the person symbolize who came to Jesus to inquire the way to eternal life? He symbolizes personality or that in us which values the things that have form and shape.

3. *sell whatever you have*. What was Jesus' object in commanding the rich man to give his goods to the poor, and turn his attention toward God? The rich man needed to be set free from a responsibility that absorbed all his thought and attention in order that he might learn a surer approach to life.

4. *sorrowful*. Personality is disappointed because it cannot retain its belief in earthly possessions and at the same be conscious of spiritual things. It is ambitious for eternal life, but its belief in the supreme value of earthly possessions separates it from its real good.

5. *all things are possible with God*. Because the principle of All-Good cannot be exhausted. It is adequate to all demands made upon it in faith.

## The Coming Victory Over Death[1]

10:32 They were on the way, going up to Jerusalem; and Jesus was going in front of them, and they were amazed; and those who followed were afraid. He again took the twelve, and began to tell them the things that were going to happen to him. 10:33 "Behold, we are going up to Jerusalem. The Son of Man will be delivered to the chief priests and the scribes. They will condemn him to death, and will deliver him to the Gentiles.[2] 10:34 They will mock him, spit on him, scourge him, and kill him. On the third day he will rise again."

1. See Mt 20:17-28; Lk 18:31-34.

2. *Gentiles*. Worldly thoughts—thoughts pertaining to the external, or thoughts that function through the senses. The Gentile is the unregenerate state of mind in us. (MBD/Gentiles)

## Living in Service to Others

10:35 James and John, the sons of Zebedee, came near to him, saying, "Teacher, we want you to do for us whatever we will ask."

10:36 He said to them, "What do you want me to do for you?"

10:37 They said to him, "Grant to us that we may sit, one at your right hand, and one at your left hand, in your glory."[1]

10:38 But Jesus said to them, "You don't know what you are asking. Are you able to drink the cup that I drink, and to be baptized with the baptism that I am baptized with?"

10:39 They said to him, "We are able."

Jesus said to them, "You shall indeed drink the cup that I drink, and you shall be baptized with the baptism that I am baptized with; 10:40 but to sit at my right hand and at my left hand is not mine to give, but for whom it has been prepared."

10:41 When the ten heard it, they began to be indignant towards James and John.

10:42 Jesus summoned them, and said to them, "You know that they who are recognized as rulers over the nations lord it over them, and their great ones exercise authority over them. 10:43 But it shall not be so among you, but whoever wants to become great among you shall be your servant.[2] 10:44 Whoever of you wants to become first among you, shall be bondservant of all. 10:45 For the Son of Man also came not to be served, but to serve, and to give his life as a ransom for many."

1. *in your glory*. When James and John asked to be placed, one at the right and one at the left hand of Jesus when He came into His glory, they were in personal consciousness; personality thought that it could obtain a favor of a friend merely by asking.

2. *great...servant*. One becomes great through service because the same qualities are necessary for both: self-control, self detachment, self-discipline, and self-knowledge are products of the all-round development fostered by service. Greatness enters into them all.

## Persistence Leads to Healing (1)

10:46 They came to Jericho. As he went out from Jericho,(2) with his disciples and a great multitude, the son of Timaeus, Bartimaeus, a blind beggar, was sitting by the road. 10:47 When he heard that it was Jesus the Nazarene, he began to cry out, and say, "Jesus, you son of David, have mercy on me!" 10:48 Many rebuked him, that he should be quiet, but he cried out much more, "You son of David, have mercy on me!"

10:49 Jesus stood still, and said, "Call him."

They called the blind man, saying to him, "Cheer up! Get up. He is calling you!"

10:50 He, casting away his cloak, sprang up, and came to Jesus.

10:51 Jesus asked him, "What do you want me to do for you?"

The blind man said to him, "Rhabboni,[27] that I may see again."

10:52 Jesus said to him, "Go your way. Your faith has made you well." Immediately he received his sight,(3) and followed Jesus in the way.

1. See Mt 20:29-34; Lk 17:35-43.
2. *Jericho.* Jericho is the opposite of Jerusalem. One represents the spiritual; the other, the material. (MBD/Jericho)
3. *received his sight.* Faith that is blinded by the pollution of sense is without understanding of the purity of the Christ Spirit, but it persists in appealing to the power of that Spirit. The compassion of the Christ is so overpowering that it heals even where understanding is inactive. But healing means seeing, and he who receives the healing power of the Christ is cleansed of his pollution and gains spiritual understanding.

Fillmore Study Bible annotations by Rev. Dan Beckett.

**World English Bible Footnotes:**

[24] v10:6. Genesis 1:27

[25] v10:8. Genesis 2:24

[26] v10:19. Exodus 20:12-16; Deuteronomy 5:16-20

[27] v10:51. Rhabboni is a transliteration of the Hebrew word for "great teacher."

# Mark 11

## Jesus' Triumphal Entry into Jerusalem (1)

11:1 When they drew near to Jerusalem,(2) to Bethsphage[28] and Bethany,(3) at the Mount of Olives, he sent two of his disciples, 11:2 and said to them, "Go your way into the village that is opposite you.

Immediately as you enter into it, you will find a young donkey tied, on which no one has sat.[4] Untie him, and bring him. 11:3 If anyone asks you, 'Why are you doing this?' say, 'The Lord needs him;'[5] and immediately he will send him back here."

11:4 They went away, and found a young donkey tied at the door outside in the open street, and they untied him. 11:5 Some of those who stood there asked them, "What are you doing, untying the young donkey?" 11:6 They said to them just as Jesus had said, and they let them go.

11:7 They brought the young donkey to Jesus, and threw their garments on it, and Jesus sat on it. 11:8 Many spread their garments on the way,[6] and others were cutting down branches from the trees, and spreading them on the road. 11:9 Those who went in front, and those who followed, cried out, "Hosanna[29]! Blessed is he who comes in the name of the Lord![30][7] 11:10 Blessed is the kingdom of our father David that is coming in the name of the Lord! Hosanna in the highest!"

11:11 Jesus entered into the temple in Jerusalem. When he had looked around at everything, it being now evening, he went out to Bethany with the twelve.

1. See Mt 21:1-10; Lk 19:28-38; Jn 12:12-19.

2. In his journey towards peace, the follower of the Christ reaches a stage where he must assert his powers of mastery and dominion.

3. *Bethphage and Bethany.* Both names mean "house of figs," the former meaning also "house of unripe figs." Bethany means also "wailing, lamentation, affliction," from the sound of the wind in the foliage of the fig trees and from the "tears" (drops of gum that exude from the fruit). The significance of these meanings is that man, when he lacks self-dominion, is powerless to cope with life unaided. In this state his powers are not mature, but are as unripe fruit, without usefulness.

4. *Colt whereon no man ever yet sat.* We first train our faculties (disciples) to do our bidding. Next we transform the forces of our sense or animal nature (the "colt whereon no man ever yet sat").

5. The animal nature is meant to be brought into the service of the ideal self and to express their share of his self-realized destiny as a son of God.

6. *Spread their garments.* Praise and appreciation for the animal nature. The natural forces are not evil in themselves. They are evil only when they are misdirected.

7. *Who "cometh in the name of the Lord"* He who expresses the Christ Spirit through his right use of the I AM comes in the name of the Lord or divine law.

## Jesus Curses the Fig Tree[1]

11:12 The next day, when they had come out from Bethany, he was hungry. 11:13 Seeing a fig tree afar off having leaves, he came to see if perhaps he might find anything on it. When he came to it, he found nothing but leaves, for it was not the season for figs. 11:14 Jesus told it, "May no one ever eat fruit from you again!" and his disciples heard it.

1. See Mt 21:12-22; Lk 19:45-48; Jn 2:13-22.

## Jesus Cleanses the Temple[1]

11:15 They came to Jerusalem, and Jesus entered into the temple, and began to throw out those who sold and those who bought in the temple,[2] and overthrew the tables of the money changers, and the seats of those who sold the doves. 11:16 He would not allow anyone to carry a container through the temple. 11:17 He taught, saying to them, "Isn't it written, 'My house will be called a house of prayer for all the nations?'[31] But you have made it a den of robbers!"[3][32]

11:18 The chief priests and the scribes heard it, and sought how they might destroy him. For they feared him, because all the multitude was astonished at his teaching.

11:19 When evening came, he went out of the city.

1. See Mt 21:12-22;Lk 19:45-48; Jn 2:13-22.

2. *Casting out of the temple those that sold and bought.* In the regeneration one's mind is changed in regard to commercial transactions. The old thoughts of greed and gain must be cast out; even the very foundation (tables) must be overturned. "For other foundation can no man lay than that which is laid, which is Jesus Christ."

3. *a den of robbers.* Fear, greed, anger, malice, evil speaking, and other discordant and negative forces that enter into the body and rob it of health, peace, and all the other blessings that are its heritage under divine law.

## The Lesson from the Withered Fig Tree[1]

11:20 As they passed by in the morning, they saw the fig tree withered away from the roots. 11:21 Peter, remembering, said to him, "Rabbi, look! The fig tree which you cursed has withered away."

11:22 Jesus answered them, "Have faith in God. 11:23 For most certainly I tell you, whoever may tell this mountain, 'Be taken up and cast into the sea,' and doesn't doubt in his heart, but believes that what he says is happening; he shall have whatever he says. 11:24 Therefore I tell you, all things whatever you pray and ask for, believe that you have received them, and you shall have them.[2] 11:25 Whenever you stand praying, forgive, if you have anything against anyone; so that your Father, who is in heaven, may also forgive you your transgressions. 11:26 But if you do not forgive, neither will your Father in heaven forgive your transgressions."

1. See Mt 21:12-22;Lk 19:45-48; Jn 2:13-22.

2. The Prayer of Faith. See James 5:15.

## Jesus' Authority Is Questioned[1]

11:27 They came again to Jerusalem, and as he was walking in the temple, the chief priests, and the scribes, and the elders[2] came to him, 11:28 and they began saying to him, "By what authority do you do these things? Or who gave you this authority to do these things?"[3]

11:29 Jesus said to them, "I will ask you one question. Answer me, and I will tell you by what authority I do these things. 11:30 The baptism of John--was it from heaven, or from men? Answer me."

11:31 They reasoned with themselves, saying, "If we should say, 'From heaven;' he will say, 'Why then did you not believe him?' 11:32 If we should say, 'From men'"--they feared the people, for all held John to really be a prophet. 11:33 They answered Jesus, "We don't know."

Jesus said to them, "Neither do I tell you by what authority I do these things."[4]

1. See Mt 21:23-27;Lk 20:1-8.
2. The religious thoughts that follow strictly the forms and ceremonies of religion, but do not recognize that the authority of Spirit that underlies them is greater than the outward forms and ceremonies.
3. The teacher of Truth must know Truth, be able to distinguish it from error, and be conscious of its essence within him. The authority of man's inner conviction and knowledge is pre-eminent.
4. The Christ, having divine authority, cannot be fettered or bound by the reasonings of the intellect.

Fillmore Study Bible annotations compiled by Mark Hicks

**World English Bible Footnotes:**

[28] v11:1. TR & NU read "Bethphage" instead of "Bethsphage"

[29] v11:9. "Hosanna" means "save us" or "help us, we pray."

[30] v11:9. Psalm 118:25-26

[31] v11:17. Isaiah 56:7

[32] v11:17. Jeremiah 7:11

# Mark 12

## Abusing Truth[1]

12:1 He began to speak to them
in parables. "A man planted a
vineyard,[2] put a hedge around it,
dug a pit for the winepress, built a
tower, rented it out to a farmer, and
went into another country. 12:2 When
it was time, he sent a servant to the
farmer to get from the farmer his
share of the fruit of the vineyard.[3]
12:3 They took him, beat him, and sent
him away empty. 12:4 Again, he sent
another servant[4] to them; and they
threw stones at him, wounded him
in the head, and sent him away
shamefully treated. 12:5 Again he sent
another; and they killed him; and
many others, beating some, and
killing some. 12:6 Therefore still
having one, his beloved son, he sent
him last to them, saying, 'They will
respect my son.' 12:7 But those
farmers said among themselves, 'This
is the heir. Come, let's kill him, and
the inheritance will be ours.' 12:8 They
took him, killed him, and cast him
out of the vineyard. 12:9 What
therefore will the lord of the
vineyard do? He will come and
destroy the farmers, and will give
the vineyard to others. 12:10 Haven't
you even read this Scripture:

'The stone which the builders
rejected,
the same was made the head
of the corner.
12:11 This was from the Lord,
it is marvelous in our eyes'?"

[33]

12:12 They tried to seize him, but they feared the multitude; for they perceived that he spoke the parable against them. They left him, and went away.

1. See Mt 21:33-46; Lk 20:9-19

2. *vineyard.* The fruit of the vine is a symbol of life. Jesus said, "I am the vine." The vineyard represents the manifest human being, or humanity which was planted in perfection, and perfection is its destiny. (RW/vineyard)

3. *fruit of the vineyard.* "The fruits of the vineyard" represent the perfection of God expressed in the character of man. "Ye therefore shall be perfect as your heavenly Father is perfect."

4. *servant.* The servants who were sent for the fruits of the vineyard represent the spiritually illumined thoughts in human consciousness. They come expecting to find a welcome and a companionship in the our mind, but are destroyed by selfishness and ignorance.

## To Each Their Own[1]

12:13 They sent some of the Pharisees and of the Herodians to him, that they might trap him with words. 12:14 When they had come, they asked him, "Teacher, we know that you are honest, and don't defer to anyone; for you aren't partial to anyone, but truly teach the way of God. Is it lawful to pay taxes to Caesar, or not? 12:15 Shall we give, or shall we not give?"

But he, knowing their hypocrisy,[2] said to them, "Why do you test me? Bring me a denarius,[3] that I may see it."

12:16 They brought it.

He said to them, "Whose is this image and inscription?"

They said to him, "Caesar's."[4]

12:17 Jesus answered them, "Render to Caesar the things that are Caesar's, and to God the things that are God's."[5]

They marveled greatly at him.

1. See Mt 22:15-22; Lk 20:20-26.

2. *hypocrisy.* Jesus considered the Sadducees and the Pharisees hypocrites because they pretended to be what they were not. Secretly, they were trying to evade the taxes imposed by Caesar, but in asking Jesus whether or not they should pay tribute, they pretended they were honest.

3. *denarius.* After Jesus called for the tribute money He showed them the stamp of Caesar's face on the coin, signifying that the coin was identified with temporality and should be respected for what it was worth, but that we should not forget to put the thought of God into our monetary transactions.

4. *Caesar.* In consciousness Caesar represents the tyrannical rule of the personal will unmodified by spiritual love and mercy and justice.

5. *Render unto Caesar...things that are God's.* The secret of a harmonious life is to balance God and God manifest in one's thoughts and acts. Persons who become overzealous in religious observances are apt to treat with contempt temporal laws and conditions. This results in contention and discord between mind and body, and between the laws of God and the laws of human beings.

## God is Life[1]

12:18 There came to him Sadducees, who say that there is no resurrection.[2] They asked him, saying, 12:19 "Teacher, Moses wrote to us, 'If a man's brother dies, and leaves a wife behind him, and leaves no children, that his brother should take his wife, and raise up offspring for his brother.' 12:20 There were seven brothers. The first took a wife, and dying left no offspring. 12:21 The second took her, and died, leaving no children behind him. The third likewise; 12:22 and the seven took her and left no children. Last of all the woman also died. 12:23 In the resurrection, when they rise, whose wife will she be of them? For the seven had her as a wife."

12:24 Jesus answered them, "Isn't this because you are mistaken,❸ not knowing the Scriptures, nor the power of God? 12:25 For when they will rise from the dead, they neither marry, nor are given in marriage, but are like angels in heaven. 12:26 But about the dead, that they are raised; haven't you read in the book of Moses, about the Bush, how God spoke to him, saying, 'I am the God of Abraham,❹ the God of Isaac,❺ and the God of Jacob'❻[34]? 12:27 He is not the God of the dead, but of the living. You are therefore badly mistaken."

1. See Mt 22:23-33; Lk 20:27-40.

2. *resurrection.* The raising of man's mind and body from sense to spiritual consciousness. (MBD/resurrection)

3. *mistaken.* Jesus told the Sadducees that they knew not the Scriptures because, although they were familiar with the wording of the Scriptures, they did not understand the *meaning* of what they read. Without this understanding they did not really know the law or inner truth underlying the words.

4. *Abraham.* The power of the mind to reproduce its ideas in unlimited expression. This ability of the mind to make substance out of ideas is called faith. (MBD/Abraham)

5. *Isaac.* Divine sonship. Isaac, meaning laughter, signifies the joy of the new birth and the new life in Christ, which is the spiritual consciousness of relationship to God the Father. (MBD/Isaac)

6. *Jacob.* Jacob represents an idea of the I AM identity, through which the faculties of the mind receive their original inspirations. Jacob had twelve sons, to each of whom he gave an office and each of whom he blessed, or inspired, with his spiritual wisdom. (MBD/Jacob)

## Love Over All❶

12:28 One of the scribes❷ came, and heard them questioning together. Knowing that he had answered them well, asked him, "Which commandment is the greatest of all?"

12:29 Jesus answered, "The greatest is, 'Hear, Israel, the Lord our God, the Lord is one: 12:30 you shall love❸ the Lord your God with all your heart, and with all your soul, and with all your mind, and with all your strength.'[35] This is the first commandment. 12:31 The second❹ is like this, 'You shall love your neighbor as yourself.'[36] There is no other commandment greater than these."

12:32 The scribe said to him, "Truly, teacher, you have said well that he is one, and there is none other but he, 12:33 and to love him with all the heart, and with all the understanding, with all the soul, and with all the strength, and to love his neighbor as himself, is more important than all whole burnt offerings and sacrifices."

12:34 When Jesus saw that he answered wisely, he said to him, "You are not far from the Kingdom of God."❺ No one dared ask him any question after that.

1. See Mt 22:34-40; Lk 10.25-28.

2. *scribe.* The definition of the word scribe is "a copyist" or "a writer"; metaphysically considered, a scribe is the faculty within us that endeavors to engrave upon the tablets of the mind an interpretation of the Scriptures and of the law.

3. *love.* Love is the great unifying element. When our consciousness is saturated with love, it overflows into our body and into our affairs, and brings harmony into every hitherto discordant condition within and without.

4. *second.* After the love consciousness has been established in us, our next attitude should to make love the basis of all our relations, especially our relations with the persons and the things that are nearest to us, that is, our "neighbor." In this way we shall fulfill the law of God and demonstrate divine harmony within and without.

5. *You are not far from the Kingdom of God.* The scribe understood that loving God and his neighbor are our two chief duties, but his attitude showed that his interest was intellectual, not spiritual. He was not following what he understood to be essential.

## Of the House of David[1]

12:35 Jesus responded, as he taught in the temple, "How is it that the scribes say that the Christ is the son of David?[2] 12:36 For David himself said in the Holy Spirit,

'The Lord said to my Lord,
"Sit at my right hand,
until I make your enemies the
footstool of your
feet."'[37]

12:37 Therefore David himself calls him Lord, so how can he be his son?"

1. See Mt 22:41-46; Lk 20:41-44.

2. *David.* David is often referred to as a type of Christ. His life was a forerunner of that of the more perfect man, Jesus Christ, who was of the house of David. (MBD/David)

## Integrity Matters[1]

The common people heard him gladly. 12:38 In his teaching he said to them, "Beware of the scribes, who like to walk in long robes, and to get greetings in the marketplaces, 12:39 and the best seats in the synagogues, and the best places at feasts: 12:40 those who devour widows' houses, and for a pretense make long prayers.[2] These will receive greater condemnation."

1. See Lk 20:45-47.

2. *prayers.* In Truth, prayer is a means of connecting us with source, in order that we may know wisdom and use it in our life. To love Truth with all the heart, soul, mind, and strength is to do away, once and forever, with all that is not true in life.

## True Giving[1]

12:41 Jesus sat down opposite the treasury, and saw how the multitude cast money[2] into the treasury. Many who were rich cast in much. 12:42 A poor widow came, and she cast in two small brass coins,[38] which equal a quadrans coin.[39] 12:43 He called his disciples to himself, and said to them, "Most certainly I tell you, this poor widow gave[3] more than all those who are giving into the treasury, 12:44 for they all gave out of their abundance, but she, out of her poverty, gave all that she had to live on."

1. See Lk 21.1-4.

2. *cast money*. Personality delights in making a show of giving. It is prone to think it does much toward the maintenance of the body temple and toward the mind's religious worship; but until the intellect is quickened by Spirit and comes under the instruction of true wisdom, its gifts do not really count for much.

3. *gave*. How is true giving to be measured? True giving is measured by the love and substance and faith that the giver puts into the gift.

---

Fillmore Study Bible annotations by Rev. Dan Beckett.

**World English Bible Footnotes:**

[33] v12:11. Psalm 118:22-23

[34] v12:26. Exodus 3:6

[35] v12:30. Deuteronomy 6:4-5

[36] v12:31. Leviticus 19:18

[37] v12:36. Psalm 110:1

[38] v12:42. literally, lepta (or widow's mites). Lepta are very small brass coins worth half a quadrans each, which is a quarter of the copper assarion. Lepta are worth less than 1% of an agricultural worker's daily wages.

[39] v12:42. A quadrans is a coin worth about 1/64 of a denarius. A denarius is about one day's wages for an agricultural laborer.

# Mark 13

## The Body Temple[1]

13:1 As he went out of the temple,[2]

one of his disciples said to him, "Teacher, see what kind of stones and what kind of buildings!"

13:2 Jesus said to him, "Do you see these great buildings? There will not be left here one stone on another, which will not be thrown down."

13:3 As he sat on the Mount of Olives opposite the temple, Peter, James, John, and Andrew asked him privately, 13:4 "Tell us, when will these things[3]

be? What is the sign that these things are all about to be fulfilled?"

13:5 Jesus, answering, began to tell them, "Be careful that no one leads you astray. 13:6 For many will come in my name, saying, 'I am he![40]' and will lead many astray.

13:7 "When you hear of wars and

rumors of wars, don't be troubled. For those must happen, but the end is not yet. 13:8 For nation will rise against nation, and kingdom against kingdom. There will be earthquakes in various places. There will be famines and troubles. These things are the beginning of birth pains.

1. See Matt. 24.3-8; Luke 21.5-11

2. *temple.* The temple represents the body of man, its destruction represents the death of the body.

3. *these things.* Do wars, earthquakes, and famines serve as true portents of what is in store for us? Such calamities are not signs except in a negative sense. They show that humanity has not yet learned to exercise the dominion that it is capable of exercising, when it learns to develop the power that is its innate heritage.

## Spirit Always Triumphs[1]

13:9 But watch yourselves, for they will deliver you up to councils. You will be beaten in synagogues. You will stand before rulers and kings for my sake, for a testimony to them.
13:10 The Good News must first be preached to all the nations. 13:11 When they lead you away and deliver you up, don't be anxious beforehand, or premeditate what you will say, but say whatever will be given you in that hour. For it is not you who speak, but the Holy Spirit.

13:12 "Brother will deliver up brother to death, and the father his child. Children will rise up against parents, and cause them to be put to death. 13:13 You will be hated by all men for my name's sake, but he who endures to the end, the same will be saved.

1. See Matt. 24.9-14; Luke 21.12-19

## Spiritual Awareness[1]

13:14 But when you see the abomination of desolation,[41] spoken of by Daniel the prophet, standing where it ought not (let the reader understand), then let those who are in Judea flee to the mountains, 13:15 and let him who is on the housetop not go down, nor enter in, to take anything out of his house.
13:16 Let him who is in the field not return back to take his cloak. 13:17 But woe to those who are with child and to those who nurse babies in those days! 13:18 Pray that your flight won't be in the winter. 13:19 For in those days there will be oppression, such as there has not been the like from the beginning of the creation which God created until now, and never will be. 13:20 Unless the Lord had shortened the days, no flesh would have been saved; but for the sake of the chosen ones, whom he picked out, he shortened the days. 13:21 Then if anyone tells you, 'Look, here is the Christ!' or, 'Look, there!' don't believe it. 13:22 For there will arise false christs and false prophets,[2]

and will show signs and wonders, that they may lead astray, if possible, even the chosen ones. 13:23 But you watch.

1. See Matt. 24.15-24; Luke 21.20-24

2. *false prophets.* Deceptive thoughts that have been built up by error, selfish desires. Outwardly they present the appearance of being candid and open; inwardly they are ravenous for personal sensation and worldly gain. In order to attain their end they deceive even "the elect."

(MBD/false-prophets)

## Awakening

"Behold, I have told you all things beforehand. 13:24 But in those days, after that oppression, the sun will be darkened, the moon

will not give its light, 13:25 the stars will be falling from the sky, and the powers that are in the heavens will be shaken.[42] 13:26 Then they will see the Son of Man coming in clouds with great power and glory. 13:27 Then he will send out his angels, and will gather together his chosen ones from the four winds, from the ends of the earth to the ends of the sky.

1. See Matt. 24.29-31; Luke 21.25-28

2. *sun, moon.* The sun represents spiritual intelligence. Light is always a symbol of intelligence, and the sun, the supreme source of light in man's world, represents the highest form of intelligence, spiritual intelligence. The moon, which symbolizes the intellect, receives all its light from the spiritual intelligence. (MBD/sun)

## The Impermanent World of Form

13:28 "Now from the fig tree, learn this parable. When the branch has now become tender, and puts forth its leaves, you know that the summer is near; 13:29 even so you also, when you see these things coming to pass, know that it is near, at the doors. 13:30 Most certainly I say to you, this generation[43] will not pass away until all these things happen. 13:31 Heaven and earth will pass away, but my words will not pass away.

1. See Matt. 24.32-35; Luke 21.29-33

2. *heaven and earth.* If heaven and earth are destined to pass away, what is to remain to prove the truth of these principles? The inner universe of causes, which we designate as Divine Mind, will always remain, since it is eternal and infinite, subject to no limitations of either time or space.

## Spiritual Awareness

13:32 But of that day or that hour no one knows, not even the angels in heaven, nor the Son, but only the Father. 13:33 Watch, keep alert, and pray;

for you don't know when the time is.

13:34 "It is like a man, traveling to another country, having left his house, and given authority to his servants, and to each one his work, and also commanded the doorkeeper to keep watch. 13:35 Watch therefore, for you don't know when the lord of the house is coming, whether at evening, or at midnight, or when the rooster crows, or in the morning; 13:36 lest coming suddenly he might find you sleeping. 13:37 What I tell you, I tell all: Watch."

1. See Matt. 24.36-44; Luke 21.34-36

2. *watch, pray.* Why are prayer and watchfulness enjoined on us? Because they

connect us with inner springs of power and prepare us for whatever may come. Through prayer and watchfulness we learn to live life well and truly, and have no fear.

Fillmore Study Bible annotations by Rev. Dan Beckett.

**World English Bible Footnotes:**

[40] v13:6. or, "I AM!"

[41] v13:14. Daniel 9:17; 11:31; 12:11

[42] v13:25. Isaiah 13:10; 34:4

[43] v13:30. The word translated "generation" (genea) could also be translated "race," "family," or "people."

# Mark 14

## The Plot to Kill Jesus[1]

14:1 It was now two days before
the feast of the Passover[2] and the
unleavened bread, and the chief
priests and the scribes sought how
they might seize him by deception,
and kill him.[3] 14:2 For they said, "Not
during the feast, because there
might be a riot of the people."

1. See Matt. 26:1-5;Luke 22:1-2; John 11:47-53

2. *passover*. The Passover typifies the freeing of the spiritual man from the dominion of sense.

3. *seize him by deception, and kill him.* Explain. During such periods of transition the conservative ideas of the individual (the chief priests and scribes), actuated by fear of the Christ Spirit stirring in the heart, seek to suppress that Spirit, in order to keep the life unchanged and subject to its original allegiances.

## The Anointing at Bethany[1]

14:3 While he was at Bethany,[2] in
the house of Simon the leper,[3] as
he sat at the table, a woman came
having an alabaster jar of ointment
of pure nard--very costly. She broke
the jar, and poured it over his head.
14:4 But there were some who were
indignant among themselves, saying,
"Why has this ointment been wasted?
14:5 For this might have been sold for
more than three hundred denarii,[44]
and given to the poor."[4] They
grumbled against her.

14:6 But Jesus said, "Leave her
alone. Why do you trouble her?[5] She
has done a good work for me. 14:7
For you always have the poor with
you, and whenever you want to, you
can do them good; but you will not
always have me. 14:8 She has done
what she could. She has anointed my

body beforehand for the burying. [14:9]
Most certainly I tell you, wherever
this Good News may be preached
throughout the whole world, that
which this woman has done will also
be spoken of for a memorial of her."

1. See Matt. 26:6-13;Luke 22:1-2; John 11:47-53

2. *Bethany.* Means "fruitage." It represents a place in consciousness where our thoughts become established, and through which we can return whenever we so desire, and find a welcome.

3. *in the house of Simon the leper.* Leprosy is a disease of the body, the result of impure thoughts. Jesus was cleansing his consciousness of all impurity, and the woman with the alabaster cruse of ointment represents the activity of pure love.

4. *and given to the poor.* The poor represent thoughts of need, lack, insufficiency. The external mind sees these conditions, and its thought is that the first use of every good thing would be to meet the needs of the outer man. But through spiritual wisdom, we should often conserve spiritual substance for the building up of the new body in Christ.

5. *Why do you trouble her?* We are transformed by the renewing of our minds. The old thoughts die and pass away, and the cells of the organism follow. When we have the inner communion with Spirit, and the love consciousness is gradually built up, there is an outflow of a fine love essence which acts as a preservative. The pure substance of the body is thus being daily restored and forms the foundation of a new organism. This was symbolically described as preparing "my body beforehand for the burying."

## Judas Agrees to Betray Jesus[1]

[14:10] Judas[2] Iscariot, who was one
of the twelve, went away to the
chief priests, that he might deliver
him to them. [14:11] They, when they
heard it, were glad, and promised to
give him money. He sought how he
might conveniently deliver him.

1. See Matt. 26:14-16;Luke 22:3-6; John 11:57

2. *Judas.* Judas (the generative function) is a disciple of Jesus (the I AM). He is entrusted with the control and conservation of the life force or substance, under the direction of the I AM, or divine intelligence. But because he does not recognize or is unwilling to acknowledge the divinity of the I AM, he rebels and seeks to increase the expression of life in ways that are contrary to the divine law. In so doing he betrays the I AM, and the expression of life in the body is impaired or destroyed.

## The Passover with the Disciples[1]

[14:12] On the first day of unleavened
bread, when they sacrificed the
Passover, his disciples asked him,
"Where do you want us to go and
make ready that you may eat the
Passover?"

[14:13] He sent two of his disciples,[2]
and said to them, "Go into the city,
and there you will meet a man
carrying a pitcher of water. Follow
him, [14:14] and wherever he enters in,
tell the master of the house, 'The
Teacher says, "Where is the guest
room, where I may eat the Passover
with my disciples?"' [14:15] He will
himself show you a large upper room
furnished and ready. Make ready for
us there."

[14:16] His disciples went out, and
came into the city, and found things
as he had said to them, and they
prepared the Passover.[3]

[14:17] When it was evening he came
with the twelve. [14:18] As they sat and
were eating, Jesus said, "Most
certainly I tell you, one of you will
betray me[4]--he who eats with me."

[14:19] They began to be sorrowful, and to ask him one by one, "Surely not I?" And another said, "Surely not I?"

[14:20] He answered them, "It is one of the twelve, he who dips with me in the dish. [14:21] For the Son of Man goes, even as it is written about him, but woe to that man by whom the Son of Man is betrayed! It would be better for that man if he had not been born."

1. See Matt. 26:17-25;Luke 22:7-14,21-23; John 13:21-26

2. *He sent two of his disciples.* The faculties must be called into action, becoming obedient to the instruction of the Christ.

3. *they prepared the Passover.* Whatever makes the mind receptive to Truth prepares us to enter into spiritual consciousness. The "passing over" from sense consciousness to spiritual consciousness. This transition involves sacrifice. Clarification of the perceptive powers in that vision becomes an inner knowing rather than a seeing with the physical eyes.

4. *one of you will betray me.* Among our faculties, represented by the disciples of Jesus Christ, we have a Judas. In its highest office this faculty is Judah, spiritual appropriation through prayer and praise. Inverted in human consciousness, this faculty becomes Judas, acquisitiveness. In essence it is good, but in its personal sense and exercise, it brings about suffering and crucifixion.

## The Institution of the Lord's Supper[1]

[14:22] As they were eating, Jesus took bread,[2] and when he had blessed, he broke it, and gave to them, and said, "Take, eat. This is my body."

[14:23] He took the cup, and when he had given thanks, he gave to them. They all drank of it. [14:24] He said to them, "This is my blood of the new covenant, which is poured out for many.[3] [14:25] Most certainly I tell you, I will no more drink of the fruit of the vine, until that day when I drink it anew in the Kingdom of God."

1. See Matt. 26:26-30;Luke 22:15-20,39; I Cor. 11:23

2. *bread, the cup.* Of our partaking spiritually of the life and substance that Christ externalized and raised to Spiritual consciousness. Bread represents the body of Christ, which is spiritual substance. The "cup" is one of the symbols of the life principle, the quickening element in creation, the "blood" of Christ.

3. *poured out for many.* For remission of the world's sins, which is accomplished by the power of spiritual life to displace sin with a thirst for righteousness.

## Peter's Denial Foretold[1]

[14:26] When they had sung a hymn, they went out to the Mount of Olives.

[14:27] Jesus said to them, "All of you will be made to stumble[2] because of me tonight, for it is written, 'I will strike the shepherd, and the sheep will be scattered.'[45] [14:28] However, after I am raised up, I will go before you into Galilee."

[14:29] But Peter said to him, "Although all will be offended, yet I will not."[3]

[14:30] Jesus said to him, "Most certainly I tell you, that you today, even this night, before the rooster crows twice, you will deny me three times."

14:31 But he spoke all the more, "If
I must die with you, I will not deny
you." They all said the same thing.

1. See Matt. 26:31-36;Luke 22:31-34; John 13:36-38

2. *All of you will be made to stumble.* They were to fall away from Him because of their fear and spiritual immaturity. The Christ way of gratitude and thanksgiving, of recognition of God as the source of all things, is sometimes despised and rejected of men even today, and credit for success is given to lesser sources: initiative, perseverance, business ability, or personality.

3. *Peter said unto him ... yet I will not.* Peter here represents untried faith, which sometimes leads one into overconfidence through imperfect self-knowledge. All untried faculties are subject to the same defect: "In like manner also said they all."

## Jesus Prays in Gethsemane[1]

14:32 They came to a place which
was named Gethsemane.[2] He said to
his disciples, "Sit here, while I pray."
14:33 He took with him Peter, James,
and John, and began to be greatly
troubled and distressed. 14:34 He said
to them, "My soul is exceedingly
sorrowful, even to death. Stay here,
and watch."[3]

14:35 He went forward a little, and
fell on the ground, and prayed that,
if it were possible, the hour might
pass away from him. 14:36 He said,
"Abba, Father, all things are possible
to you. Please remove this cup from
me. However, not what I desire, but
what you desire."[4]

14:37 He came and found them
sleeping,[5] and said to Peter, "Simon,
are you sleeping? Couldn't you watch
one hour? 14:38 Watch and pray, that
you may not enter into temptation.
The spirit indeed is willing, but the
flesh is weak."[6]

14:39 Again he went away, and
prayed, saying the same words. 14:40
Again he returned, and found them
sleeping, for their eyes were very
heavy, and they didn't know what to
answer him. 14:41 He came the third
time, and said to them, "Sleep on
now, and take your rest. It is
enough.[7] The hour has come.
Behold, the Son of Man is betrayed
into the hands of sinners. 14:42 Arise,
let us be going. Behold, he who
betrays me is at hand."

1. See Matt. 26:36-46;Luke 22:40-46; John 18:1

2. *Gethsemane.* Jesus, representing the spiritual I Am, and his disciples, the faculties of mind, entering Gethsemane (meaning wine press and oil; a farm), typify these mind powers entering into the state of consciousness where the I Am goes through the final preparation for the supreme test, the crucifixion on the cross.

3. *watch.* While Jesus (the I AM) entered farther into the garden (deeper into spiritual consciousness), the disciples (faculties of mind) were bidden to watch in the "without" for the betrayer, Judas, the disciple with the consciousness adverse to the Truth.

4. *but what you desire.* In other words, Jesus was acknowledging God as the one and only Power, able to save from the coming experience, though it seemed inevitable.

5. *found them sleeping.* Because Judas, representing the Life faculty, no longer gave his support; consequently, they fell asleep.

6. *but the flesh is weak.* The Spirit, that in man which sees and knows from the God viewpoint, is always willing and ready to carry out the edicts of the I Am, but the flesh man, the mortal part of us, which sees from the limited viewpoint, and is not awakened to the larger vision, falls down, does not measure up to the spiritual standard.

7. *take your rest. It is enough.* Jesus had found the greater light; he had found that inner strength, that sustaining power through which he would be able to carry

out that Divine Plan, the Ideal Redemption of man, which he had been sent forth to accomplish, "to give his life a ransom for many," or in other words, to plant in the heart of humanity the seed of Divine Purity and Life everlasting.

## The Betrayal and Arrest of Jesus[1]

14:43 Immediately, while he was still speaking, Judas, one of the twelve, came--and with him a multitude with swords and clubs,[2] from the chief priests, the scribes, and the elders. 14:44 Now he who betrayed him had given them a sign, saying, "Whoever I will kiss, that is he. Seize him, and lead him away safely." 14:45 When he had come, immediately he came to him, and said, "Rabbi! Rabbi!" and kissed him.[3] 14:46 They laid their hands on him, and seized him. 14:47 But a certain one of those who stood by drew his sword, and struck the servant of the high priest, and cut off his ear.

14:48 Jesus answered them, "Have you come out, as against a robber,[4] with swords and clubs to seize me? 14:49 I was daily with you in the temple teaching, and you didn't arrest me. But this is so that the Scriptures might be fulfilled."

14:50 They all left him, and fled. 14:51 A certain young man followed him, having a linen cloth thrown around himself, over his naked body. The young men grabbed him, 14:52 but he left the linen cloth, and fled from them naked.

1. See Matt. 26:47-56;Luke 22:47-53; John 18:3-11

2. *multitude with swords and clubs.* The chief priests represent our natural religious tendencies; the scribes, our established religious thoughts. These desire to rule over the religious life by force, and to this end would destroy original truth as expressed in the Christ principle. Judas, representing appropriation, directs them to their selfish end.

3. *and kissed him.* This mark of greeting is also a token of love and allegiance. The Christ consciousness is the consciousness of divine love.

4. *Have you come out, as against a robber?* By willingly surrendering all that belongs to personality. One cannot be robbed of what one gives willingly. The acquisitive faculty is thus defeated.

## Jesus before the Council[1]

14:53 They led Jesus away to the high priest. All the chief priests, the elders, and the scribes came together with him.

14:54 Peter had followed him from a distance,[2] until he came into the court of the high priest.[3] He was sitting with the officers, and warming himself in the light of the fire. 14:55 Now the chief priests and the whole council sought witnesses against Jesus to put him to death, and found none. 14:56 For many gave false testimony against him, and their testimony didn't agree with each other. 14:57 Some stood up, and gave false testimony against him, saying, 14:58 "We heard him say, 'I will destroy this temple that is made with hands, and in three days I will build another made without hands.'" 14:59 Even so, their testimony did not agree.

14:60 The high priest stood up in the midst, and asked Jesus, "Have you no answer? What is it which these testify

against you?" 14:61 But he stayed quiet,
and answered nothing. Again the
high priest asked him, "Are you the
Christ, the Son of the Blessed?"

14:62 Jesus said, "I am. You will see
the Son of Man sitting at the right
hand of Power, and coming with the
clouds of the sky."

14:63 The high priest tore his
clothes, and said, "What further need
have we of witnesses? 14:64 You have
heard the blasphemy! What do you
think?" They all condemned him to be
worthy of death. 14:65 Some began to
spit on him, and to cover his face,
and to beat him with fists, and to tell
him, "Prophesy!" The officers struck
him with the palms of their hands.

1. See Matt 26:57-68;Luke 22:54-55,63-71; John 18:13-24

2. *Peter had followed him from a distance.* We often find our faith far out[stepped] by our efforts to live the abundant life. We need to keep our faith keyed to our present understanding, if we would avoid the stress and strain of fruitless striving.

3. *the high priest.* Represents each person's highest intellectual concept of religion.

## Peter Denies Jesus[1]

14:66 As Peter was in the courtyard
below, one of the maids of the high
priest[2] came, 14:67 and seeing Peter
warming himself, she looked at him,
and said, "You were also with the
Nazarene, Jesus!"

14:68 But he denied it, saying, "I
neither know, nor understand what
you are saying." He went out on the
porch, and the rooster crowed.

14:69 The maid saw him, and began
again to tell those who stood by,
"This is one of them." 14:70 But he
again denied it. After a little while
again those who stood by said to
Peter, "You truly are one of them, for
you are a Galilean, and your speech
shows it." 14:71 But he began to curse,
and to swear,[3] "I don't know this
man of whom you speak!" 14:72 The
rooster crowed the second time.
Peter remembered the word, how
that Jesus said to him, "Before the
rooster crows twice, you will deny
me three times." When he thought
about that, he wept.

1. See Matt. 26:69-75;Luke 22:55-62; John 18:25-27

2. *one of the maids of the high priest.* The maid represents spiritual intuition. She discerns that Peter (faith) belongs with Jesus and she proceeds to test him by saying, "Thou also wast with the Nazarene, even Jesus." Even when our faith in Truth wavers we intuitively connect our identity with that of the spiritual I AM, Jesus.

3. *he began to curse, and to swear.* Our minds work in a threefold manner. This trinity of thought action is metaphysically described as mind, idea, and manifestation. When we start thinking a wrong thought the natural tendency is to continue in the error state of consciousness, until the impetus of the thought is exhausted.

Fillmore Study Bible annotations compiled by Mark Hicks.

**World English Bible Footnotes:**

[44] v14:5. 300 denarii was about a years wages for an agricultural laborer.

[45] v14:27. Zechariah 13:7

# Mark 15

## The Christ and the Will[1]

15:1 Immediately in the morning the chief priests,[2] with the elders and scribes, and the whole council, held a consultation, and bound Jesus, and carried him away, and delivered him up to Pilate.[3] 15:2 Pilate asked him, "Are you the King of the Jews?"

He answered, "So you say."

15:3 The chief priests accused him of many things. 15:4 Pilate again asked him, "Have you no answer? See how many things they testify against you!"

15:5 But Jesus made no further answer, so that Pilate marveled.

1. See Matt. 27.1-2; Luke 23.1-5
2. *chief priests, with the elders and scribes.* The "chief priests with the elders and scribes" represent the conservative religious thoughts or instincts of man.
3. *Pilate.* Pilate, the governor, represents the will, the executive faculty of the mind.

## Unilluminated Will[1]

15:6 Now at the feast he used to release to them one prisoner, whom they asked of him. 15:7 There was one called Barabbas, bound with those who had made insurrection, men who in the insurrection had committed murder. 15:8 The multitude, crying aloud, began to ask him to do as he always did for them. 15:9 Pilate answered them, saying, "Do you want me to release to you the King of the Jews?" 15:10 For he perceived that for envy the chief priests had delivered him up. 15:11 But the chief priests stirred up the multitude, that he should release Barabbas[2] to them instead. 15:12 Pilate again asked them, "What then should I do to him whom you call the King of the Jews?"

15:13 They cried out again, "Crucify him!"

15:14 Pilate said to them, "Why, what evil has he done?"

But they cried out exceedingly, "Crucify him!"

15:15 Pilate, wishing to please[3] the multitude, released Barabbas to them, and handed over Jesus, when he had flogged[4] him, to be crucified.

1. See Matt. 27.11-23; Luke 23.13-25; John 18.28-40
2. *Barabbas.* Why was Barabbas released instead of Jesus? Barabbas represents the adverse consciousness, rebellion and hatred. The personal will gives way to such expressions as a matter of course, making little if any effort to discipline them. Truth is abandoned as of no consequence.
3. *wishing to please.* Why did Pilate wish to please the multitude? Pilate represents the human will, which occupies itself with the random thoughts that swarm through the mind of sense, undertaking to satisfy each in its turn.
4. *flogged.* Why was Jesus flogged before being delivered to the Jews? The outer ruling power (Pilate) flouts the spiritual power of Truth and subjects it to the extreme of abuse in order to remove any suggestion of blame attaching to the personal will.

## Jesus Stands in His Truth[1]

15:16 The soldiers led him away within the court, which is the Praetorium; and they called together the whole cohort. 15:17 They clothed him with purple, and weaving a crown of thorns, they put it on him. 15:18 They began to salute him, "Hail, King of the Jews!" 15:19 They struck his head with a reed, and spat on him, and bowing their knees, did homage to him. 15:20 When they had mocked him, they took the purple off of him, and put his own garments on him. They led him out to crucify him.

1. See Matt. 27.27-31; Luke 19.2-3

## New Life in Spirit[1]

15:21 They compelled one passing by, coming from the country, Simon of Cyrene, the father of Alexander and Rufus, to go with them, that he might bear his cross. 15:22 They brought him to the place called Golgotha,[2] which is, being interpreted, "The place of a skull." 15:23 They offered him wine mixed with myrrh[3] to drink, but he didn't take it.

15:24 Crucifying him, they parted his garments among them, casting lots[4] on them, what each should take. 15:25 It was the third hour,[46] and they crucified[5] him. 15:26 The superscription of his accusation was written over him, "THE KING OF THE JEWS." 15:27 With him they crucified two robbers; one on his right hand, and one on his left. 15:28 The Scripture was fulfilled, which says, "He was numbered with transgressors."

15:29 Those who passed by blasphemed him, wagging their heads, and saying, "Ha! You who destroy the temple, and build it in three days, 15:30 save yourself, and come down from the cross!"

15:31 Likewise, also the chief priests mocking among themselves with the scribes said, "He saved others. He can't save himself. 15:32 Let the Christ, the King of Israel, now come down from the cross, that we may see and believe him.[47]" Those who were crucified with him insulted him.

1. See Matt. 27.32-54; Luke 23.26-48; John 19.16b-37

2. *Golgotha*. What is the meaning of "Golgotha"? Golgotha means "place of the skull." The skull is the center of the intellect, which must be given over to the eternal ascendancy of Spirit. Jesus (the intellectual) was crucified at "the place of a skull" that Christ (Truth) might become all in all.

3. *wine mixed with myrrh*. What does the "wine mingled with myrrh" represent? Wine means life, and myrrh means bitterness. Jesus would not drink this bitterness of life; He merely tasted it, which means that He did not allow Himself to be swallowed up by the bitterness of death.

4. *casting lots*. What does the casting of lots for His garments represent? Garments represent the most external thought realm; casting lots for them means that those in the outer sense consciousness, in their ignorance, overlook spiritual things and gamble for the transitory things of externality.

5. *crucified*. The lesson of the crucifixion is a prophecy of a change in the real Christian's aspect toward life. The material concept of life which he has been living, must be killed and the new life in Spirit must be substituted.

## The Soul's Experience of the Eclipse of Truth[1]

15:33 When the sixth hour[48] had come, there was darkness[2] over the whole land until the ninth hour.[49] 15:34 At the ninth hour Jesus cried with a loud voice, saying, "Eloi, Eloi, lama sabachthani?" which is, being interpreted, "My God, my God,[3] why have you forsaken me?"[50]

15:35 Some of those who stood by, when they heard it, said, "Behold, he is calling Elijah."

15:36 One ran, and filling a sponge full of vinegar, put it on a reed, and gave it to him to drink, saying, "Let him be. Let's see whether Elijah[4] comes to take him down."

15:37 Jesus cried out with a loud voice, and gave up the spirit. 15:38 The veil[5] of the temple was torn in two from the top to the bottom. 15:39 When the centurion, who stood by opposite him, saw that he cried out like this and breathed his last, he said, "Truly this man was the Son of God!"

15:40 There were also women watching from afar, among whom were both Mary Magdalene, and Mary the mother of James the less and of Joses, and Salome; 15:41 who, when he was in Galilee, followed him, and served him; and many other women who came up with him to Jerusalem.

1. See Matt. 27.32-54; Luke 23.26-48; John 19.16b-37

2. *darkness. Darkness over the whole land until the ninth hour* signifies the feeling of desolation that the soul experiences, when in time of extreme crisis it temporarily loses its awareness of God.

3. *My God.* Why did Jesus cry with a loud voice, "My God, my God, why hast thou forsaken me?" The cry, "My God, my God, why hast thou forsaken me?" was the cry of the personal consciousness that believes in a personal God, who fails in the hour of trial. The "loud voice" represents the outer consciousness which is losing its hold on physical life.

4. *Elijah.* The meaning of the sentence *Let us see whether Elijah cometh to take him down* is that those on the natural plane of thought look for salvation through Elijah, or the highest expression of the natural man. Elijah does not save man. Man is saved through Christ; Jesus gave himself up to Spirit.

5. *veil.* What is the meaning of the rending of the veil of the temple from top to bottom? The temple represents the body, which loses its physical cohesion, when the tension of the mortal will relinquishes its hold on the invisible thought substance (veil).

## An Act of Kindness From High Consciousness[1]

15:42 When evening had now come, because it was the Preparation Day, that is, the day before the Sabbath, 15:43 Joseph of Arimathaea,[1] a prominent council member who also himself was looking for the Kingdom of God, came. He boldly went in to Pilate, and asked for Jesus' body. 15:44 Pilate marveled if he were already dead; and summoning the centurion, he asked him whether he had been dead long. 15:45 When he found out from the centurion, he granted the body to Joseph. 15:46 He bought a linen cloth, and taking him down, wound him in the linen cloth, and laid him in a tomb which had been cut out of a rock. He rolled a stone against the door of the tomb. 15:47 Mary Magdalene and Mary, the mother of Joses, saw where he was laid.

1. See Matt. 27.55-61; Luke 23.29-558; John 19.38-42

2. *Arimathaea.* The height; high place; highland. An aggregation of thoughts of a lofty character-a high state of consciousness in man (the height). (MBD/Arimathaea)

Fillmore Study Bible annotations by Rev. Dan Beckett.

**World English Bible Footnotes:**

[46] v15:25. 9:00 A. M.

[47] v15:32. TR omits "him"

[48] v15:33. or, noon

[49] v15:33. 3:00 PM

[50] v15:34. Psalm 22:1

# Mark 16

## Dynamic Life Revealed[1]

16:1 When the Sabbath was past,
Mary Magdalene,[2] and Mary the
mother of James, and Salome,[3]
bought spices, that they might come
and anoint him. 16:2 Very early[4] on
the first day of the week, they came
to the tomb[5] when the sun had
risen. 16:3 They were saying among
themselves, "Who will roll away the
stone from the door of the tomb for
us?" 16:4 for it was very big. Looking
up, they saw that the stone was
rolled back.

16:5 Entering into the tomb, they
saw a young man[6] sitting on the
right side, dressed in a white robe,
and they were amazed. 16:6 He said
to them, "Don't be amazed. You seek
Jesus, the Nazarene, who has been
crucified. He has risen.[7] He is not
here. Behold, the place where they
laid him! 16:7 But go, tell his disciples
and Peter, 'He goes before you into
Galilee. There you will see him, as he
said to you.'"

16:8 They went out,[51] and fled
from the tomb, for trembling and
astonishment had come on them.
They said nothing to anyone; for they
were afraid.

1. See Matt. 28.1-8; Luke 24.1-12; John 20.1-10

2. *Magdalene.* A thought exalting and magnifying strength in consciousness. (MBD/Magdalene, MBD/Magadan)

3. *Salome.* Represents the soul clothed in the thought of wholeness, soundness, love, peace, and Truth. (MBD/Salome)

4. *very early.* What is represented by the coming of Mary Magdalene and the other women to the tomb of Jesus "very early" in the morning? The women represent the various faculties of the individual soul; their coming early to the tomb, the fact that the soul is first to awake to the truth of resurrection. See also note at 16:9 below.

5. *tomb.* The tomb where Jesus was laid to rest represents an elevated, peaceful state of consciousness in which He rested the three days previous to His resurrection. (RW/tomb)

6. *young man.* The young man sitting on the right side, arrayed in a white robe represents the principles of affirmation and denial as a power strong enough to raise the body to new life.

7. *He has risen.* What is the significance of these words? The Christ life is a dynamic, not a static, experience. The body is to be transformed, regenerated by the Spirit. Jesus did not remain in "the place where they laid him" but went before the disciples "into Galilee," the high consciousness of life that He called "the kingdom of the heavens."

## The Christ First Appears to the Intuitive Perception of Truth[1]

16:9 Now when he had risen early on the first day of the week, he appeared first to Mary Magdalene,[2] from whom he had cast out seven demons. 16:10 She went and told those who had been with him, as they mourned and wept.[3] 16:11 When they heard that he was alive, and had been seen by her, they disbelieved.

16:12 After these things he was revealed in another form to two of them, as they walked, on their way into the country. 16:13 They went away and told it to the rest. They didn't believe them, either.

1. See Luke 24.9-11; 13-35

2. *he appeared first to Mary Magdalene.* See note on 16:2 above. See also RW/woman. There lingers in the mind the old idea that Spirit does not include the body in its redemptive process, but the body cries out for cleansing and purification. (MBD/woman)

3. *they mourned and wept.* Although their whole thought had been turned from personal love and attachment to the spiritual realm, they had not yet attained understanding of the great demonstration made by Jesus over death.

## The Christ in the World

16:14 Afterward he was revealed to the eleven themselves as they sat at the table, and he rebuked them for their unbelief and hardness of heart, because they didn't believe those who had seen him after he had risen. 16:15 He said to them, "Go into all the world, and preach the Good News to the whole creation. 16:16 He who believes and is baptized will be saved;[1] but he who disbelieves will be condemned.[2] 16:17 These signs will accompany those who believe: in my name they will cast out demons; they will speak with new languages; 16:18 they will take up serpents; and if they drink any deadly thing, it will in no way hurt them; they will lay hands on the sick, and they will recover."

1. *He who believes and is baptized will be saved.* What has baptism to do with salvation? Baptism represents denial, and it is necessary to deny that error has any power over us before we can be saved from the effects on mind and body of our former acceptance of error as true and unavoidable.

2. *condemned.* Who condemns the disbeliever? His disbelief condemns him to suffer the effects of his faith in negation.

## The Ascension of Jesus

16:19 So then the Lord Jesus, after he had spoken to them, was received up into heaven, and sat down at the right hand of God.[1] 16:20 They went out, and preached everywhere, the Lord working with them, and confirming the word by the signs that followed. Amen.

1. *right hand of God.* Why is Jesus represented as seated at the right hand of God? Symbolically this means that the Christ is the indispensable power or authority that avails to consummate our desire and efforts to unite with God in order to realize our true nature and being.

---

Fillmore Study Bible annotations by Rev. Dan Beckett.

**World English Bible Footnotes:**

[51] v16:8. TR adds "quickly"

# The Good News According to Luke

Mary's Well in Nazareth, Vasily Polenov, public domain.

## Introduction to Luke

Luke was not a disciple of Jesus, but was a convert of the apostle Paul. Thus, the information contained in Luke's Gospel is not of the firsthand type found in Matthew. Luke's information came through the apostle Paul and other early leaders, and through personal research. The "preface" to Luke's Gospel (Luke 1:1-4) indicates how careful and painstaking Luke was in compiling his Gospel; and it would appear that some part of the material was personally gathered during the two years Luke spent in the vicinity of Jerusalem, while Paul was in prison there. (See Acts 23-26.) This would be around A.D. 57-59—although the actual Gospel according to Luke was not completed and in circulation until around A.D. 70.

Luke, being himself a Gentile, wrote for Gentile Christians, and made his theme: "Jesus, the Saviour of Mankind." This universal viewpoint is readily recognized in "sending out the seventy" (Luke 10:1-20), the parable of the Good Samaritan (Luke 10:25-37), and many other passages. Also, when telling of the birth of Jesus, Luke (in contrast with Matthew) uses as a background the humble shepherds and the overcrowded inn, with the birth taking place in the outbuildings of the inn. This does not mean that the stories in Matthew and Luke should be regarded as contradictory. Rather, they are complementary, and together they make one complete picture; for Jesus was both the Messiah of the Jews and also the Saviour of mankind. The Gospel of Luke is written in such an interesting and helpful way, and contains so much of what is often termed "the human touch," that it has been designated "the most beautiful book in the world."

The above three Gospels – Matthew, Mark, and Luke – are sometimes referred to as "the Synoptic Gospels"; and the student should become familiar with this term. The word synoptic, as here used, means "seeing from the same general viewpoint." In other words, the Gospels of Matthew, Mark, and Luke cover similar ground, and have much in common. However, there are also some differences—and it is these similarities and differences that give rise to what is known to New Testament students as "the synoptic problem." This problem may be briefly stated as follows:

1. All three Gospels contain much similar material. Indeed, in many instances the same story is told in word-for-word fashion.
2. Practically the whole of Mark's Gospel is reproduced somewhere in Matthew or Luke.
3. However, some material is found in Matthew and Luke which does not appear in Mark.
4. Furthermore, in Matthew and also in Luke there are some stories which are peculiar to these Gospels. Matthew has some material which is found only in Matthew; while Luke also has material which is found only in Luke.

The "problem" is to find an explanation that will satisfactorily cover all the above points; and the suggested solution is briefly as follows:

1. Mark's was the first Gospel to be written (as noted above).
2. At the time when Mark's Gospel was first circulated there were in circulation some strips of parchment, or papyrus, on which appeared some "sayings" of Jesus. These "sayings" were highly prized by the early Christians, who seem to have used them freely at the early church gatherings; and these "sayings" are now technically known under the symbol "Q."
3. Thus, when Matthew and Luke started to write their Gospels, they would have had before them the completed Gospel of Mark, and also some collections of the "sayings of Jesus" ("Q"). The Gospel of Mark and these "sayings" were freely drawn upon by both Matthew and Luke. This would account for points 1, 2, and 3 of the "problem."
4. Both Matthew and Luke also had their own special sources of information—and the material thus at hand was incorporated by each in his Gospel. This would satisfactorily explain point 4.

The above brief explanation is given so that the student may not be confused by the similarities and differences found in the Synoptic Gospels. Of course, many other theories have been put forward from time to time; but what is given above seems to meet the situation.

Introduction to *The Good News According to Luke* by Herbert J. Hunt, former Dean of Bible Studies for the Unity School of Christianity.

# LUKE 1

## Dedication to Theophilus

1:1 Since many have undertaken to set in order a narrative concerning those matters which have been fulfilled among us, 1:2 even as those who from the beginning were eyewitnesses and servants of the word delivered them to us, 1:3 it seemed good to me also, having traced the course of all things accurately from the first, to write to you in order, most excellent Theophilus; 1:4 that you might know the certainty concerning the things in which you were instructed.[1]

1. *What is the meaning of the name Luke, and what is its significance in connection with the third Synoptic Gospel?* The name means "luminous," "enlightening," "instructing." The Book of Luke is a luminous record of events in the life of Jesus Christ, instructing and enlightening the reader in the way of Truth.

## The Birth of John the Baptist Foretold

1:5 There was in the days of Herod, the king of Judea, a certain priest named Zacharias,[1] of the priestly division of Abijah. He had a wife of the daughters of Aaron, and her name was Elizabeth.[2] 1:6 They were both righteous before God, walking blamelessly in all the commandments and ordinances of the Lord. 1:7 But they had no child,[3] because Elizabeth was barren, and they both were well advanced in years. 1:8 Now it happened, while he executed the priest's office before God in the order of his division, 1:9 according to the custom of the priest's office, his lot was to enter into the temple of the Lord[4] and burn incense.[5] 1:10 The whole multitude of the people were praying outside at the hour of incense.

1:11 An angel of the Lord appeared to him, standing on the right side of the altar of incense. 1:12 Zacharias was troubled when he saw him, and fear fell upon him. 1:13 But the angel said to him, "Don't be afraid, Zacharias, because your request has been heard, and your wife, Elizabeth, will bear you a son, and you shall call his name John.[6] 1:14 You will have joy and gladness; and many will rejoice at his birth. 1:15 For he will be great in the sight of the Lord, and he will drink no wine nor strong drink.[7] He will be filled with the Holy Spirit, even from his mother's womb. 1:16 He will turn many of the children of Israel to the Lord, their God. 1:17 He will go before him in the spirit and power of Elijah, 'to turn the hearts of the fathers to the children,' and the disobedient to the wisdom of the just; to make ready a people prepared for the Lord."

1:18 Zacharias said to the angel, "How can I be sure of this? For I am an old man, and my wife is well advanced in years."

1:19 The angel answered him, "I am Gabriel, who stands in the presence of God. I was sent to speak to you, and to bring you this good news. 1:20 Behold, you will be silent and not able to speak,[8] until the day that these things will happen, because you didn't believe my words, which will be fulfilled in their proper time."

1:21 The people were waiting for Zacharias, and they marveled that he delayed in the temple. 1:22 When he came out, he could not speak to them, and they perceived that he had seen a vision in the temple. He continued making signs to them, and remained mute. 1:23 It happened, when the days of his service were fulfilled, he departed to his house. 1:24 After these days Elizabeth, his wife, conceived,[9] and she hid herself five months, saying, 1:25 "Thus has the Lord done to me in the days in which he looked at me, to take away my reproach among men."

1. *Zacharias.* Zacharias represents in individual consciousness the spiritual phase of consciousness. Zacharias means "remembered by Jehovah." His work is in the temple. He is wedded to Elisabeth, who may be compared to the soul in the exalted state that it attains through living an entirely blameless, devoted life.

2. *Elizabeth.* The literal meaning of Elisabeth is "my God is my oath," or "a worshiper of God." The soul, in its adoration of God, is blameless, and its world is a world of innocence and peace.

3. *They had no child.* They had fallen into a belief in years; that they had failed to bring forth the fruit of mature spirituality, which is a consciousness of spiritual substance, life, and intelligence. The fruit of mature spirituality is symbolized by John, "the grace of the Lord." And it is this which every spiritual-minded individual is expected to bring forth.

4. *enter into the temple of the Lord.* The priest's entering into the temple represents spiritual meditation—metaphysically called "going into the silence." All extraneous thoughts, interests, and aspirations collect by degrees around the transmuting process ("the whole multitude of the people were praying at the hour of incense"). In deep concentration on the desired Truth of one's being, one becomes aware of the thought of the Lord (the angel, Gabriel). The thought that we as spiritual beings can control our destinies, and that we are even now making our lives what they are, at first instills fear. Zacharias was afraid of the angel. Humility of spirit hesitates to take to itself power that hitherto has been conceded to God only. However, the thought of God persistently held brings us the assurance that we are on the right road. The angel of the Lord stood "on the right side of the altar of incense."

5. *and burn incense.* The burning of the incense signifies the transmutation of the finer essences of the body. These essences are transmuted to what may be termed the fourth or radiant dimension, and a foundation is laid for an organism of permanent character. Paul calls it the "celestial body." This process takes place whenever the I AM makes union in the body with the Lord, or Higher Self.

6. *call him John.* John symbolizes the fruit of the union of the soul with spiritual consciousness. The union of soul and spiritual consciousness brings forth an ego that prepares the way for one greater than itself, the Christ of God, the highest expression of Divine Mind in man.

7. *strong drink.* The parentage of John the Baptist accounts for the statement that he would drink no wine or strong drink but would be "filled with the Holy Spirit, even from his mother's womb" in this respect, that when the soul is united with the spiritual consciousness the result of the union is dedication or consecration to God. John was so consecrated from before his birth. Consecration implies a concentration of all the thoughts and energies on the subject. Wine and strong drink scatter man's forces, making concentration impossible. It was therefore foreign to John's experience.

8. *not able to speak.* The work of the Spirit goes so far beyond what the mortal consciousness can grasp, that man is rendered dumb when the nature of spiritual life and its ways are proclaimed to him for the first time. These soul processes being unusual, even the spiritually minded do not understand what is taking place, and what the result will be, although assured by the messengers of the Lord of a propi-

tious outcome. Where no explanation can be offered, the natural attitude of the individual is one of silence.

9. *Elizabeth his wife conceived.* Elisabeth represents the soul, which, after many apparently fruitless experiences and a long-continued search for the way of life, conceives the idea of divine grace (John) as the law of man's being. In order to receive the blessing of a son something positive was required of Zacharias; namely the establishment of his faith in the invisible good as being present and active.

## The Birth of Jesus Foretold

1:26 Now in the sixth month, the
angel Gabriel was sent from God to
a city of Galilee, named Nazareth,
1:27 to a virgin pledged to be married
to a man whose name was Joseph,
of the house of David. The virgin's
name was Mary. 1:28 Having come in,
the angel said to her, "Rejoice, you
highly favored one! The Lord is with
you. Blessed are you among women!"

1:29 But when she saw him, she was
greatly troubled at the saying, and
considered what kind of salutation
this might be. 1:30 The angel said to
her, "Don't be afraid, Mary, for you
have found favor with God. 1:31
Behold, you will conceive in your
womb, and bring forth a son, and will
call his name 'Jesus.' 1:32 He will be
great, and will be called the Son of
the Most High. The Lord God will give
him the throne of his father, David,
1:33 and he will reign over the house
of Jacob forever. There will be no
end to his Kingdom."

1:34 Mary said to the angel, "How
can this be, seeing I am a virgin?"

1:35 The angel answered her, "The
Holy Spirit will come on you, and the
power of the Most High will
overshadow you.[1] Therefore also the
holy one who is born from you will
be called the Son of God. 1:36 Behold,
Elizabeth, your relative, also has
conceived a son in her old age; and
this is the sixth month with her who
was called barren. 1:37 For everything
spoken by God is possible."

1:38 Mary said, "Behold, the
handmaid of the Lord;[2] be it to me
according to your word."

1. *the power of the Most High will overshadow you.* As explained by the angel to Mary, we should not overlook the fact that this coming into activity of the Christ body is the result of an exalted idea sown in the mind and brought forth in the soul. Therefore, Mary, the soul, becomes devout and expectant and believes in the so-called miraculous as a possibility. Mary expected the birth of the Messiah as the Holy Spirit had promised. She was overshadowed by that high idea and it formed in her mind the seed that quickened into the cell and in due season there were aggregations of cells strong enough in their activity to attract the attention of the consciousness, and what is called the birth of Jesus took place.

2. *Behold, the handmaid of the Lord.* The word of God is all-powerful, all-potential, as is proved by the experience of Elisabeth in bringing forth John, and Mary in bringing forth Jesus.

## Mary Visits Elizabeth

The angel departed from her. 1:39
Mary arose in those days and went
into the hill country with haste, into
a city of Judah, 1:40 and entered into
the house of Zacharias and greeted
Elizabeth. 1:41 It happened, when
Elizabeth heard Mary's greeting, that
the baby leaped in her womb,[1] and
Elizabeth was filled with the Holy
Spirit. 1:42 She called out with a loud

voice, and said, "Blessed are you
among women, and blessed is the
fruit of your womb! 1:43 Why am I so
favored, that the mother of my Lord
should come to me? 1:44 For behold,
when the voice of your greeting
came into my ears, the baby leaped
in my womb for joy! 1:45 Blessed is
she who believed, for there will be a
fulfillment of the things which have
been spoken to her from the Lord!"

1. *the babe leaped in her womb.* This Scripture no doubt has an esoteric meaning; yet it is also historical. The power represented by Elisabeth on the intellectual plane corresponds to that represented by Mary on the spiritual plane. These thought forces are closely related. In truth Elisabeth represents the intellectual soul and Mary the spiritual soul. Being closely related, they are naturally drawn to each other. "The babe leaped in her womb" reveals a close soul sympathy between the two reincarnating souls, John and Jesus. The song of Mary is the expression of a soul that is convinced that it is working according to law, and that the blessings of the Most High are being poured out upon it.

## Mary's Song of Praise

1:46 Mary said,

"My soul magnifies the Lord.[1]
1:47 My spirit has rejoiced in God my Savior,
1:48 for he has looked at the humble state of his handmaid.
For behold, from now on, all generations will call me blessed.
1:49 For he who is mighty has done great things for me.
Holy is his name.
1:50 His mercy is for generations of generations on those who fear him.
1:51 He has shown strength with his arm.
He has scattered the proud in the imagination of their heart.
1:52 He has put down princes from their thrones.
And has exalted the lowly.
1:53 He has filled the hungry with good things.
He has sent the rich away empty.
1:54 He has given help to Israel, his servant, that he might remember mercy,
1:55 As he spoke to our fathers, to Abraham and his seed forever."

1:56 Mary stayed with her about
three months, and then returned to
her house.

1. *My soul magnifies the Lord.* The creative faculty of imagination. We habitually exercise this faculty either consciously or unconsciously. Imagination makes the soul the fertile side of our nature, out of which spring the issues of life. The soul has power to magnify whatever enters it. Since it is the seat of the emotions, which control man's happiness, it is important that we learn to magnify only that which is good and wholesome. It magnifies whatever is held in the conscious mind. In sense consciousness the soul magnifies trouble, disaster, and other negative thoughts, taking the good as a matter of course and leaving it to pass unacknowledged. In higher levels of consciousness the soul magnifies the good.

## The Birth of John the Baptist

1:57 Now the time that Elizabeth
should give birth was fulfilled, and
she brought forth a son.[1] 1:58 Her
neighbors and her relatives heard
that the Lord had magnified his

mercy towards her, and they
rejoiced with her. 1:59 It happened on
the eighth day, that they came to
circumcise the child; and they would
have called him Zacharias, after the
name of the father. 1:60 His mother
answered,[2] "Not so; but he will be
called John."

1:61 They said to her, "There is no
one among your relatives who is
called by this name." 1:62 They made
signs to his father, what he would
have him called.

1:63 He asked for a writing tablet,
and wrote, "His name is John."[3]

They all marveled. 1:64 His mouth
was opened immediately, and his
tongue freed, and he spoke, blessing
God. 1:65 Fear came on all who lived
around them, and all these sayings
were talked about throughout all the
hill country of Judea. 1:66 All who
heard them laid them up in their
heart, saying, "What then will this
child be?"[4] The hand of the Lord was
with him.

1. *she brought forth a son.* The fruit of spiritual consciousness in the innocent soul is a new idea, or outward expression, of grace and mercy. The new concept of grace and mercy frees the consciousness from undesirable thoughts habits, and the soul overflows with joy. This freeing thought has come from one's own mind; it is one's own son.

2. *And his mother answered.* The first thought is that the offspring of wisdom and love (Zacharias and Elisabeth) should be, like the father, an exponent of the divine law only, but mother love (Elisabeth) determines that John, meaning grace and mercy, shall be the dominant characteristic of their offspring.

3. *His name is John.* Deep in the soul is the conviction that a special function of Spirit performs the work of preparing us to free ourself from the clutch of sense. As long as we labor under a burden of condemnation, either that of our own conscience or the external censure of others, the way to achieve freedom is not open to us. Only when we perceive the truth that grace and mercy are included in the divine law as a very integral part of it do we find the voice of praise and blessing in our own heart. So the forerunner of freedom is the knowledge that grace and mercy are inalienable from the divine law, "His name is John."

4. *What then shall this child be?* "And fear came on all that dwelt round about them" does not necessarily mean a state of dread or anxiety in the mind. It means rather a consciousness of an idea not fully understood, but so all-pervading and so tenacious as to be instinctive. The understanding that grace and mercy are inseparable from the redeeming action of the higher law opens up a realm of boundless expectation. "What then shall this child be?"

## Zechariah's Prophecy

1:67 His father, Zacharias, was
filled with the Holy Spirit, and
prophesied,[1] saying,

1:68 "Blessed be the Lord, the God of
Israel,
for he has visited and worked
redemption[2] for his
people;
1:69 and has raised up a horn of
salvation for us in the
house of his servant David
1:70 (as he spoke by the mouth of
his holy prophets who
have been from of old),
1:71 salvation from our enemies,
and from the hand of all
who hate us;
1:72 to show mercy towards our
fathers,
to remember his holy
covenant,
1:73 the oath which he spoke to
Abraham, our father,
1:74 to grant to us that we, being
delivered out of the

hand of our enemies,
should serve him without fear,
1:75 In holiness and righteousness
before him all the days
of our life.
1:76 And you, child, will be called a
prophet❸ of the Most High,
for you will go before the face
of the Lord to make
ready his ways,
1:77 to give knowledge of
salvation❹ to his people
by the remission of their
sins,
1:78 because of the tender mercy of
our God,
whereby the dawn from on
high will visit us,
1:79 to shine on those who sit in
darkness and the shadow
of death;
to guide our feet into the way
of peace."

1:80 The child was growing, and becoming strong in spirit, and was in the desert until the day of his public appearance to Israel.

1. *and prophesied.* Zacharias, symbolizing a prophetic state of consciousness has here received the inspiration of Spirit according to his understanding of law and is here imparting that prophecy to all responding thoughts in consciousness.

2. *Redemption.* The "redemption" that the exaltation of reality brings is a quickening of the Christ concept in the heart. The expression of this concept leads to the establishing of peace among people of good will. It is the duty of everyone whose vision of the kingdom of heaven is a vision of the heart transformed. This transformation cannot take place in a heart that is disturbed or in a state of unrest.

3. *you, child, will be called a prophet.* Is it possible for us to become our own prophet? Yes. As we learn to recognize causes and relate them to their effects we can tell what will follow the setting in motion of a cause. We can, by our own efforts, develop clearer understanding. The desire and the will to do right brings enlightenment. The "sun of righteousness" makes the way clear to those who habitually walk by it's light.

4. *knowledge of salvation.* The Son of God was born under the law "that is not first which is spiritual, but that which is natural; then that which is spiritual." Evolution from sense to Spirit is under law, otherwise the command "Be ye transformed by the renewing of your mind" would be meaningless. Perfection creates after its kind, sometimes immediately, at other times by a gradual process; but in every case the divine will is that the race with its individuals shall "receive the adoption of sons."

Fillmore Study Bible annotations by Rev. Mark Hicks

# Luke 2

## The Birth of Jesus

2:1 Now it happened in those days, that a decree went out from Caesar Augustus❶ that all the world should be enrolled.❷ 2:2 This was the first enrollment made when Quirinius❸ was governor of Syria. 2:3 All went to enroll themselves, everyone to his own city. 2:4 Joseph also went up from Galilee, out of the city of Nazareth, into Judea, to the city of David, which is called Bethlehem, because he was of the house and family of David; 2:5 to enroll himself with Mary,[4] who was pledged to be married to him as wife, being pregnant.

2:6 It happened, while they were there, that the day had come that she should give birth.[5] 2:7 She brought forth her firstborn son, and she wrapped him in bands of cloth,[6] and laid him in a feeding trough[7], because there was no room for them in the inn.

1. *decree from Caesar Augustus.* It represents the arbitrary action of the will, ruling in selfishness and directed by human reason, to exercise domination over all the thoughts.

2. *all the world should be enrolled.* Despite the intention of Caesar, the enrollment was in the Christ consciousness—The expression of good will under the guidance of enlightened reason and understanding.

3. *Quirinius.* The name means "armed peace," and Quirinius signifies the ruling power in the egotistic, purely intellectual thought. The imposing of the will of the intellect on all people leads to recognition of the rule of force. The world believes that peace can be maintained only by military force. The state of armed peace now existing in the world is proof of the failure of this conception to bring real peace.

4. *Joseph, Mary.* Joseph and Mary represent wisdom and love, which have been ideas in mind, but are now to bring forth a manifestation in substance.

5. *and she gave birth.* The birth of the Christ takes place in the individual soul when the soul awakens to a realization of the truth that life is spiritual, not material. The Christ is the divine-idea human.

6. *and wrapped him in bands of cloth (swaddling clothes).* Swaddling clothes were bands of cloth in which it was customary to wrap young children. These swaddling clothes represent the confinement to the limitations of the physical nature ("manger") of this first emanation of Divine Life, "there being no room for them in the inn" (outer consciousness).

7. *and laid him in a feeding trough (manger).* A manger represents the animal life of the body in which the new life is first manifested. In humans this is the stomach. The inn represents the outer consciousness of spiritual things which cannot conceive, or give room to such an insignificant beginning of the great spiritual development of the soul. The instinct of the soul to express the life of God (the infant Jesus) enters into even the animal life and occupies it.

## The Shepherds and the Angels

2:8 There were shepherds in the same country staying in the field, and keeping watch by night over their flock.[1] 2:9 Behold, an angel of the Lord[2] stood by them, and the glory of the Lord shone around them, and they were terrified. 2:10 The angel said to them, "Don't be afraid, for behold, I bring you good news of great joy which will be to all the people. 2:11 For there is born to you, this day,[3] in the city of David,[4] a Savior, who is Christ the Lord.[5] 2:12 This is the sign to you:[6] you will find a baby wrapped in strips of cloth, lying in a feeding trough." 2:13 Suddenly, there was with the angel a multitude of the heavenly army praising God, and saying,

2:14 "Glory to God in the highest,
on earth peace, good will
toward men."[7]

2:15 It happened, when the angels went away from them into the sky, that the shepherds said one to another, "Let's go to Bethlehem, now, and see this thing that has happened, which the Lord has made known to us." 2:16 They came with haste, and found both Mary and Joseph, and the baby was lying in the feeding trough. 2:17 When they saw it, they publicized widely the saying which was spoken to them about this child. 2:18 All who heard it wondered at the things which were spoken to them by the shepherds. [2:19] But Mary kept all these sayings, pondering them in her heart.[8] [2:20] The shepherds returned, glorifying and praising God[9] for all the things that they had heard and seen, just as it was told them.

1. *shepherds, flocks, by night.* The flocks represent the divine natural forces in the subconscious, which are under the divine law of protection (shepherds), but obscure (night) to outer consciousness. Vigilance in watching our flocks (thoughts) makes us receptive to the spiritual side of existence. As the shepherds in Oriental countries have a name for every sheep, which is trained to come and go at command, so we should be familiar with our thoughts, and discipline them so thoroughly that they will be obedient to us when we send forth our desire. This familiarity with our mental realm leads to an acquaintance with the character, and gives one an opportunity to strengthen the weak points and transform the undesirable tendencies. It thus clears up and harmonizes the soul so that it is receptive to divine ideas.

2. *an angel of the Lord.* Angels are the thoughts in Divine Mind expressed to do a specific work. Christ is the sum total of the ideas of Divine Mind incarnating in man, while the angels are special thoughts expressed by Divine Mind, working in purity and untainted by matter or material limitations.

3. *there is born to you this day.* The spiritual birth of the Christ.

4. *city of David.* The City of David is Bethlehem, which means "house of bread", metaphysically, the substance center in our consciousness.

5. *who is Christ the Lord.* "Christ" signifies our divinity or our higher self born or realized in consciousness. God's idea of a perfect human being has always existed. It was before Adam, before David, and before Jesus. As Jesus explained in Matthew 22:41-45.

6. *And this is the sign to you:* The physical birth of Jesus, a sign of the spiritual birth of Christ."Jesus" signifies the Child who was brought into the manifest world.

7. *on earth peace, good will toward men.* The proclamation of peace on earth by the heavenly host symbolizes the calling together of a great multitude of angelic thoughts praising God and giving thanks for the great demonstration. The higher or heavenly realms of consciousness praise God for this evidence in the body (or earth) of a force that will restore peace and harmony.

8. *But Mary kept all these sayings, pondering them in her heart.* Mary represents the mother principle of the soul; by subjective thought and mediation the mother principle (Mary) builds the manifestation of the new realization of life (body of the babe).

9. *And the shepherds returned, glorifying and praising God.* The shepherds' return represents the spirit of devotion and praise, which should continue to exalt to spiritual consciousness all things that have been externally perceived.

## Jesus Is Named

[2:21] When eight days were fulfilled for the circumcision[1] of the child, his name was called Jesus, which was given by the angel before he was conceived in the womb.

1. *circumcision.* symbolical of the cutting off of mortal tendencies, and is indicative of purification and cleanliness. Under the law of Jesus Christ, circumcision is fulfilled in its spiritual meaning—the purification of the individual from the law of sin and death. We are circumcised in the true inner significance of the word only by being thoroughly purified in soul. Then the glory of the inner soul cleansing and purifying works out into the outer consciousness and the body and sets us free from all sensual, corruptible thoughts and activities. Thus we manifest wholeness and perfection throughout our being.

## Jesus Is Presented in the Temple

[2:22] When the days of their purification according to the law of

Moses were fulfilled, they brought him up to Jerusalem, to present him to the Lord 2:23 (as it is written in the law of the Lord, "Every male who opens the womb shall be called holy to the Lord"),[1] 2:24 and to offer a sacrifice according to that which is said in the law of the Lord, "A pair of turtledoves, or two young pigeons."[2]

2:25 Behold, there was a man in Jerusalem whose name was Simeon.① This man was righteous and devout, looking for the consolation of Israel, and the Holy Spirit was on him.② 2:26 It had been revealed to him by the Holy Spirit that he should not see death before he had seen the Lord's Christ.[3] 2:27 He came in the Spirit into the temple. When the parents brought in the child, Jesus, that they might do concerning him according to the custom of the law, 2:28 then he received him into his arms, and blessed God, and said,

2:29 "Now you are releasing your
servant, Master,
according to your word, in
peace;
2:30 for my eyes have seen your
salvation,
2:31 which you have prepared
before the face of all
peoples;
2:32 a light for revelation to the
nations,
and the glory of your people
Israel."

2:33 Joseph and his mother were marveling at the things which were spoken concerning him, 2:34 and Simeon blessed them, and said to Mary, his mother, "Behold, this child is set for the falling and the rising of many in Israel,③ and for a sign which is spoken against. 2:35 Yes, a sword will pierce through your own soul, that the thoughts of many hearts may be revealed."

2:36 There was one Anna,④ a prophetess, the daughter of Phanuel, of the tribe of Asher (she was of a great age, having lived with a husband seven years from her virginity, 2:37 and she had been a widow for about eighty-four years), who didn't depart from the temple, worshipping with fastings and petitions night and day. 2:38 Coming up at that very hour, she gave thanks to the Lord, and spoke of him to all those who were looking for redemption in Jerusalem.

1. *Simeon.* Simeon means "one who listens and obeys". The listening faculty of mind shows itself in the devout Christian as the mental state that looks for and expects spiritual guidance and instruction direct from God. Its meaning may be summed up in the word obedient.

2. *and the Holy Spirit was on him.* One who believes that God communes with us, and who opens the way to such communion by being obedient to every hint received in visions, or dreams, or from the "still small voice," is guided by the Holy Spirit.

3. *the falling and the rising of many in Israel.* Those who experience birth into the Christ consciousness find it necessary to readjust their religious convictions in many respects, discarding those which are no longer convincing in the light of spiritual understanding, and embracing instead ideas that are new to them but compelling in their reasonableness.

4. *Anna.* Anna, the prophetess, who had long been a worshiper in the Temple, represents a certain conservation of spiritual life that has been built up by devotion and faithfulness. This spiritual life is transmitted through many incarnations as an inheritance of the soul and is of great importance in forming the Christ body. Nothing is lost in the evolution of the soul.

## The Return to Galilee

2:39 When they had accomplished all things that were according to the law of the Lord, they returned into Galilee,[1] to their own city, Nazareth. 2:40 The child was growing, and was becoming strong in spirit, being filled with wisdom,[2] and the grace of God was upon him. 2:41 His parents went every year to Jerusalem at the feast of the Passover.

1. *returned into Galilee.* When the conscious and subconscious minds (Joseph and Mary) have united in carrying into effect in the body (temple) the freeing power of Spirit (all things that were according to the law of the Lord"), the mind comes down from its state of high exaltation and resumes the practical trend of everyday affairs ("they returned into Galilee, to their own city Nazareth"). Galilee means "circuit," and in this connection means that the normal round of life was again resumed.

2. *waxed strong, filled with wisdom.* As we consciously dwell upon the thought of the Christ Spirit within and submit ourself to it as our guiding principle, we grow in spiritual strength and gain true wisdom.

## The Boy Jesus in the Temple

2:42 When he was twelve years old, they went up to Jerusalem according to the custom of the feast, 2:43 and when they had fulfilled the days, as they were returning, the boy Jesus stayed behind in Jerusalem. Joseph and his mother didn't know it, 2:44 but supposing him to be in the company, they went a day's journey, and they looked for him among their relatives and acquaintances. 2:45 When they didn't find him,[1] they returned to Jerusalem, looking for him. 2:46 It happened after three days they found him in the temple, sitting in the midst of the teachers, both listening to them, and asking them questions. 2:47 All who heard him were amazed at his understanding and his answers. 2:48 When they saw him, they were astonished, and his mother said to him, "Son, why have you treated us this way? Behold, your father and I were anxiously looking for you."

2:49 He said to them, "Why were you looking for me? Didn't you know that I must be in my Father's house?" 2:50 They didn't understand the saying which he spoke to them. 2:51 And he went down with them, and came to Nazareth. He was subject to them, and his mother kept all these sayings in her heart. 2:52 And Jesus increased in wisdom and stature, and in favor with God and men.

1. *didn't find him.* Mary and Joseph thought that the boy Jesus was lost, and all of us have gone through this, when our thinking and feeling nature, Mary and Joseph, thought that the boy Jesus was lost. All of us have gone through this when our thinking and feeling nature, Mary and Joseph, thought that they had lost their spiritual awareness, but it is not lost. We can lose sight of it, but even when spiritual awareness is not working or functioning through us on the level of conscious awareness, it is in the temple about our Father's business, nevertheless; so do not ever think you can lose your spiritual awareness. Ed Rabel. New Testament Lectures, the Childhood of Jesus.

---

Fillmore Study Bible annotations by Rev. Mark Hicks.

**World English Bible Footnotes:**

[1] v2:23. Exodus 13:2,12

[2] v2:24. Leviticus 12:8

[3] v2:26. "Christ" (Greek) and "Messiah" (Hebrew) both mean "Anointed One"

# Luke 3

## John Proclaims Truth[1]

3:1 Now in the fifteenth year of the reign of Tiberius Caesar, Pontius Pilate being governor of Judea, and Herod being tetrarch of Galilee, and his brother Philip tetrarch of the region of Ituraea and Trachonitis, and Lysanias tetrarch of Abilene, 3:2 in the high priesthood of Annas and Caiaphas, the word of God[2] came to John, the son of Zacharias, in the wilderness.[3] 3:3 He came into all the region around the Jordan,[4] preaching the baptism of repentance[5] for remission of sins. 3:4 As it is written in the book of the words of Isaiah the prophet,

"The voice of one crying in the wilderness,
'Make ready the way of the Lord.
Make his paths straight.
3:5 Every valley will be filled.
Every mountain and hill will be brought low.
The crooked will become straight,
and the rough ways smooth.
3:6 All flesh will see God's salvation.'"[4][6]

3:7 He said therefore to the multitudes who went out to be baptized by him, "You offspring of vipers, who warned you to flee from the wrath[7] to come? 3:8 Bring forth therefore fruits worthy of repentance,[8] and don't begin to say among yourselves, 'We have Abraham for our father;' for I tell you that God is able to raise up children to Abraham from these stones! 3:9 Even now the axe also lies at the root of the trees. Every tree therefore that doesn't bring forth good fruit is cut down, and thrown into the fire."

3:10 The multitudes asked him, "What then must we do?"

3:11 He answered them, "He who has two coats, let him give to him who has none. He who has food, let him do likewise."

3:12 Tax collectors[9] also came to be baptized, and they said to him, "Teacher, what must we do?"

3:13 He said to them, "Collect no more than that which is appointed to you."

3:14 Soldiers[10] also asked him, saying, "What about us? What must we do?"

He said to them, "Extort from no one by violence, neither accuse anyone wrongfully. Be content with your wages."

3:15 As the people were in expectation, and all men reasoned in their hearts concerning John, whether perhaps he was the Christ, 3:16 John answered them all, "I indeed baptize you with water, but he comes who is mightier than I,[11] the latchet of whose sandals I am not worthy to loosen. He will baptize you in the Holy Spirit and fire, [3:17] whose fan is in his hand, and he will thoroughly cleanse his threshing floor, and will gather the wheat into his barn; but he will burn up the chaff with unquenchable fire."[12]

[3:18] Then with many other exhortations he preached good news to the people, [3:19] but Herod the tetrarch, being reproved by him for Herodias, his brother's[5] wife, and for all the evil things which Herod had done, [3:20] added this also to them all, that he shut up John in prison.

1. See Matthew 3:1-12; 14:3-4; Mark 1:2-8; Mark 6:17-18.

2. *word of God.* The Word of God is the divine Logos, God in His capacity as creative power, and includes all the potentialities of Being. It is the idea of God, the image and likeness of God, spiritual man. In it are all the possibilities, all the qualities, of God. (MBD/word)

3. *wilderness.* The wilderness represents in individual consciousness the multitude of undisciplined and uncultivated thoughts. (MBD/wilderness)

4. *came into all the region around the Jordan.* The name Jordan means "flowing of judgment" and represents the place in consciousness where we are willing to meet the result of our thoughts face to face. In this consciousness, zeal for the rule of Spirit or the principle that makes us desire to do right (John) accomplishes its best work.

5. *preaching the baptism of repentance for remission of sins.* The word translated "baptism" could have been better expressed as "immersion": the submerging of the whole mind into an enveloping spiritual atmosphere, which, when it is recognized, cleanses and purifies all the thoughts.

6. *All flesh will see God's salvation.* By the salvation of God is meant the power of the Infinite to change or transform imperfect forms of expression so that they may develop into perfection. All flesh, all humankind and every human's entire nature as an individual, is capable of advancing in spiritual consciousness and expressing greater degrees of perfection.

7. *wrath.* The "wrath of God" is really the working out of the law of Being destructively or inharmoniously for the individual who does not conform to the law but thinks and acts in opposition to it. (MBD/wrath)

8. *repentance.* To repent is, in the original Greek, to "change your mind." (RW/repentance)

9. *tax collectors (ASV, publicans).* The publicans represent the selfish thoughts.

10. *soldiers.* The soldiers represent the thoughts by which we demand our rights and try to enforce them by violence.

11. *he comes who is mightier than I.* The intellect asserts authority in its domain, but when it is spiritually illumined, it recognizes its limitations and yields to the supreme authority of the Christ.

12. *he will burn up the chaff with unquenchable fire.* The white heat of divine wisdom destroys all ignorance and folly in the heart of man, when he is filled with the Spirit of the Christ.

## Jesus' Consciousness is Spiritualized[1]

[3:21] Now it happened, when all the people were baptized,[2] Jesus also had been baptized, and was praying. The sky was opened, [3:22] and the Holy Spirit descended in a bodily form as a dove[3] on him; and a voice came out of the sky, saying "You are my beloved Son. In you I am well pleased."[4]

1. See Matthew 3:13-17; Mark 1:9-11.

2. *baptized.* The spiritual cleansing of the mind. Typifies the cleansing power and work of Spirit that redeems men from sin. It is the first step in the realization of Truth. When the baptizing power of the word is poured on a center in consciousness, it dissolves all material thought, and through this cleansing, purifying process, the individual is prepared to see and to discern spiritually. (RW/baptism)

3. *Dove.* Symbolizes peace of mind and confidence in divine law. The dove is nonresistant. In this state of consciousness we rest in Spirit. (RW/dove)

4. *You are my beloved Son. In you I am well pleased.* When Jesus dedicated Himself to His God-given ministry, the dedication was followed not only by the descent of the Holy Spirit, but also by the message of divine approval. In like manner, as we dedicate ourselves to God's service and are ready and willing to follow His directions, we also become aware of divine approval. (Herbert Hunt, Jesus Prepares for His Ministry.)

## From Adamic Consciousness to the Christ[1]

3:23 Jesus himself, when he began
to teach, was about thirty years old,
being the son (as was supposed) of
Joseph, the son of Heli, 3:24 the son of
Matthat, the son of Levi, the son of
Melchi, the son of Jannai, the son of
Joseph, 3:25 the son of Mattathias, the
son of Amos, the son of Nahum, the
son of Esli, the son of Naggai, 3:26 the
son of Maath, the son of Mattathias,
the son of Semein, the son of Joseph,
the son of Judah, 3:27 the son of
Joanan, the son of Rhesa, the son of
Zerubbabel, the son of Shealtiel, the
son of Neri, 3:28 the son of Melchi, the
son of Addi, the son of Cosam, the
son of Elmodam, the son of Er, 3:29
the son of Jose, the son of Eliezer,
the son of Jorim, the son of Matthat,
the son of Levi, 3:30 the son of
Simeon, the son of Judah, the son of
Joseph, the son of Jonan, the son of
Eliakim, 3:31 the son of Melea, the son
of Menan, the son of Mattatha, the
son of Nathan, the son of David, 3:32
the son of Jesse, the son of Obed,
the son of Boaz, the son of Salmon,
the son of Nahshon, 3:33 the son of
Amminadab, the son of Aram,[6] the
son of Hezron, the son of Perez, the
son of Judah, 3:34 the son of Jacob,
the son of Isaac, the son of Abraham,
the son of Terah, the son of Nahor,
3:35 the son of Serug, the son of Reu,
the son of Peleg, the son of Eber, the
son of Shelah, 3:36 the son of Cainan,
the son of Arphaxad, the son of
Shem, the son of Noah, the son of
Lamech, 3:37 the son of Methuselah,
the son of Enoch, the son of Jared,
the son of Mahalaleel, the son of
Cainan, 3:38 the son of Enos, the son
of Seth, the son of Adam, the son of
God.[2]

1. See Matthew 1:1-17. Nearly all these names are identified in the Metaphysical Bible Dictionary.

2. *the son of God.* This is not so much a genealogy of Jesus as it is of the Christ of Jesus. Note that the final sentence does not say *Son of Man.* Rather it says *Son of God.* That is because "Jesus represents God's idea of man in expression (Son of man); Christ is that idea in the absolute (Son of God). The Christ is the man that God created in His image and likeness, the perfect-idea man, and is the real self of all men." (MBD/Son of God).

---

Fillmore Study Bible annotations by: Rev. Michelle Vargas.

**World English Bible Footnotes:**

[4] v3:6. Isaiah 40:3-5

[5] v3:19. TR reads "brother Philip's" instead of "brother's"

[6] v3:33. NU reads "Admin, the son of Arni" instead of "Aram"

# Luke 4

## Jesus Overcomes Sense Consciousness[1]

4:1 Jesus, full of the Holy Spirit,[2] returned from the Jordan, and was led by the Spirit into the wilderness[3] 4:2 for forty days, being tempted[4] by the devil.[5] He ate nothing in those days. Afterward, when they were completed, he was hungry.[6] 4:3 The devil said to him, "If you are the Son of God, command this stone to become bread."[7]

4:4 Jesus answered him, saying, "It is written, 'Man shall not live by bread alone, but by every word of God.'"[7]

4:5 The devil, leading him up on a high mountain, showed him all the kingdoms of the world in a moment of time. 4:6 The devil said to him, "I will give you all this authority, and their glory, for it has been delivered to me; and I give it to whomever I want. 4:7 If you therefore will worship before me, it will all be yours."[8]

4:8 Jesus answered him, "Get behind me Satan! For it is written, 'You shall worship the Lord your God, and you shall serve him only.'"[8]

4:9 He led him to Jerusalem, and set him on the pinnacle of the temple, and said to him, "If you are the Son of God, cast yourself down[9] from here, 4:10 for it is written,

'He will put his angels in charge
of you, to guard you;'

4:11 and,

'On their hands they will bear you
up,
lest perhaps you dash your
foot against a stone.'"[9]

4:12 Jesus answering, said to him, "It has been said, 'You shall not tempt the Lord your God.'"[10]

4:13 When the devil had completed every temptation, he departed from him until another time.

1. See Matthew 4:1-11; Mark 1:12-13

2. *Holy Spirit.* The Holy Spirit is the abiding presence of God in, through, and around us.

3. *wilderness.* It is the soul experience wherein the undisciplined mind undergoes Spiritual discipline.

4. *being tempted.* Jesus' temptations in the wilderness symbolize the dominant attractions of sense consciousness that the developing soul has to meet.

5. *devil.* The Devil is the mass of adverse thoughts that have been built up in our consciousness through many generations of earthly experience and crystallized into what is termed the personal consciousness or carnal mind.

6. *he was hungry.* When we are intensely preoccupied with clarifying our spiritual understanding, we are scarcely conscious of the demands of the sense nature. Jesus was so absorbed in meditation and prayer that He did not feel hunger. After the forty days were completed, he hungered.

7. *command this stone to become bread.* Jesus' temptation to turn a stone into bread symbolizes our attempt to satisfy with materiality, the hunger of our soul for Spirit.

8. *it will all be yours.* Jesus' second temptation is symbolical of our desire to dominate people personally, to rule the world.

9. *cast yourself down from here.* The temptation to make a display of our power before others is a common one, but to yield to it puts us at the mercy of the personal consciousness in a most undesirable fashion.

## Jesus Begins His Ministry in Galilee

4:14 Jesus returned in the power of the Spirit into Galilee,[1] and news about him spread through all the surrounding area. 4:15 He taught in their synagogues, being glorified by all.

1. *Galilee*. Energy of life; life activity; soul energy; power, force, energy, acting in conjunction with substance.

## Truth Releases and Makes Whole[1]

4:16 He came to Nazareth,[2] where he had been brought up. He entered, as was his custom, into the synagogue on the Sabbath day, and stood up to read. 4:17 The book of the prophet Isaiah[3] was handed to him. He opened the book, and found the place where it was written,

4:18 "The Spirit of the Lord is on me,
because he has anointed me to preach good news to the poor.
He has sent me to heal the brokenhearted,[11]
to proclaim release to the captives,
recovering of sight to the blind,
to deliver those who are crushed,
4:19 and to proclaim the acceptable year of the Lord."[12][4]

4:20 He closed the book, gave it back to the attendant, and sat down. The eyes of all in the synagogue were fastened on him. 4:21 He began to tell them, "Today, this Scripture has been fulfilled in your hearing."[5]

4:22 All testified about him, and wondered at the gracious words which proceeded out of his mouth, and they said, "Isn't this Joseph's son?"

4:23 He said to them, "Doubtless you will tell me this parable, 'Physician, heal yourself! Whatever we have heard done at Capernaum, do also here in your hometown.'" 4:24 He said, "Most certainly I tell you, no prophet is acceptable in his hometown.[6] 4:25 But truly I tell you, there were many widows in Israel in the days of Elijah, when the sky was shut up three years and six months, when a great famine came over all the land. 4:26 Elijah was sent to none of them, except to Zarephath, in the land of Sidon, to a woman who was a widow. 4:27 There were many lepers in Israel in the time of Elisha the prophet, yet not one of them was cleansed,[7] except Naaman, the Syrian."

4:28 They were all filled with wrath[8] in the synagogue, as they heard these things. 4:29 They rose up, threw him out of the city, and led him to the brow of the hill that their city was built on, that they might throw him off the cliff. 4:30 But he, passing through the midst of them, went his way.

1. See Matthew 13:53-58; Mark 6:1-6a.
2. *Nazareth*. Nazareth represents the commonplace, the everyday things of life. The town of Nazareth, the home of Jesus, was a village of no distinction, evidently inferior in every way.
3. *Isaiah*. Isaiah represents that in us which discerns the reality, or the real character, of spiritual human, and which fearlessly proclaims it.
4. *the acceptable year of the Lord*. Jesus

felt the quickening of the Spirit within, and accepted the prophecy of greater things, regardless of poor environment. He proclaimed his mission to be the freeing of those in bondage to the thought of inferiority.

5. *this Scripture has been fulfilled in your hearing.* In Spirit all things are now fulfilled, and those who are spiritually quickened proclaim this truth regardless of appearances to the contrary. Pray believing that you have received, and you shall receive.

6. *no prophet is acceptable in his hometown.* The familiar acquaintance from childhood tends to emphasize personality, obscures our real Self and detracts from faith in Self.

7. *yet not one of them was cleansed.* Not everyone receives the benefits of God's abundance and healing power because many of us do not comply with the conditions laid down. In order to be heard by Spirit and to touch the substance and life of Spirit, we must have faith in spiritual things. To our faith we must add understanding.

8. *They were all filled with wrath.* Those who are still in mortal consciousness are not always lenient in their judgment of a prophet, especially when he tells them an unwelcome truth.

## Jesus Casts Out Error Consciousness[1]

4:31 He came down to Capernaum, a city of Galilee. He was teaching them on the Sabbath day, 4:32 and they were astonished at his teaching, for his word was with authority. 4:33 In the synagogue there was a man who had a spirit of an unclean demon,[2] and he cried out with a loud voice, 4:34 saying, "Ah! what have we to do with you, Jesus of Nazareth? Have you come to destroy us? I know you who you are: the Holy One of God!"

4:35 Jesus rebuked him, saying, "Be silent, and come out of him!" When the demon had thrown him down in their midst, he came out of him, having done him no harm.

4:36 Amazement came on all, and they spoke together, one with another, saying, "What is this word? For with authority and power he commands the unclean spirits, and they come out!" 4:37 News about him went out into every place of the surrounding region.

1. See Matthew 4:13; Matthew 7:28-29; Mark 1:21-28.

2. *demon.* Demons or devils are error states of mind that have to be lifted up by the quickening power of Spirit.

## Jesus Heals Many with Spiritual Truth[1]

4:38 He rose up from the synagogue, and entered into Simon's house. Simon's mother-in-law was afflicted with a great fever, and they begged him for her. 4:39 He stood over her, and rebuked the fever; and it left her. Immediately she rose up and served them.[2]

4:40 When the sun was setting, all those who had any sick with various diseases brought them to him; and he laid his hands on every one of them, and healed them.[3] 4:41 Demons also came out from many, crying out, and saying, "You are the Christ, the Son of God!" Rebuking them, he didn't allow them to speak, because they knew that he was the Christ.

1. See Matthew 8:14-17; 4.23; Mark 1:29-39.

2. *served them.* Simon's mother-in-law rose immediately and went about her work, when Jesus denied the power of fever to hold her.

3. *and healed them.* The real healing of the human body is based upon the understanding that we are Spirit-Mind, and always healthy at our spiritual source. Jesus knew the law of faith, and the power of the word to open the consciousness to the influx of Spirit-Mind. That power of the Highest heals all diseases, both of soul and of body. When faith is sufficiently strong to dissolve all adverse obsessions and to open the mind fully to the power of God, healing is instantaneous.

## Jesus Preaches the Good News of Truth

4:42 When it was day, he departed and went into an uninhabited place, and the multitudes looked for him, and came to him, and held on to him, so that he wouldn't go away from them. 4:43 But he said to them, "I must preach the good news of the Kingdom of God(1) to the other cities also. For this reason I have been sent." 4:44 He was preaching in the synagogues of Galilee.

1. *kingdom of God.* The Christ consciousness, kingdom of heaven. The kingdom of heaven is the realm of divine ideas, producing their expression, perfect harmony. It is within each of us. (RW/kingdom)

---

Fillmore Study Bible annotations by: Rev. Michelle Vargas.

**World English Bible Footnotes:**

[7] v4:4. Deuteronomy 8:3

[8] v4:8. Deuteronomy 6:13

[9] v4:11. Psalm 91:11-12

[10] v4:12. Deuteronomy 6:16

[11] v4:18. NU omits "to heal the brokenhearted"

[12] v4:19. Isaiah 61:1-2

# Luke 5

## Jesus Calls Forth the Powers of Hearing, Judgment, and Love(1)

5:1 Now it happened, while the multitude pressed on him and heard the word of God, that he was standing by the lake of Gennesaret.(2)
5:2 He saw two boats standing by the lake, but the fishermen had gone out of them, and were washing their nets.(3) 5:3 He entered into one of the boats, which was Simon's,(4) and asked him to put out a little from the land. He sat down and taught the multitudes from the boat. 5:4 When he had finished speaking, he said to Simon, "Put out into the deep,(5) and let down your nets for a catch."(6)

5:5 Simon answered him, "Master,
we worked all night, and took
nothing; but at your word I will let
down the net." 5:6 When they had
done this, they caught a great
multitude of fish, and their net was
breaking. 5:7 They beckoned to their
partners in the other boat, that they
should come and help them. They
came, and filled both boats, so that
they began to sink. 5:8 But Simon
Peter, when he saw it, fell down at
Jesus' knees, saying, "Depart from
me, for I am a sinful man, Lord." 5:9
For he was amazed, and all who were
with him, at the catch of fish which
they had caught; 5:10 and so also were
James[7] and John,[8] sons of Zebedee,
who were partners with Simon.

Jesus said to Simon, "Don't be
afraid. From now on you will be
catching people alive." 5:11 When they
had brought their boats to land, they
left everything, and followed him. 5:12

1. See Matthew 13:1-2; Matthew 4:18-22; Mark 4:1-2; Mark 1:16-20.

2. *Gennesaret.* Gennesaret (valley of riches) represents the sea of divine life. The universal life principle unites us with all creation, both within and without the consciousness.

3. *nets.* Fishermen represent gatherers of ideas in which there is great possibility of increase. The nets that gather these ideas are the traits of interest, attention, and application in the inquiring mind.

4. *Simon.* Simeon (Simon) means one who listens and obeys. (MBD/Simon)

5. *put out a little into the deep.* Many thoughts crowd the mind of the man in personal consciousness. To set them in order he employs a positive thought (a boat), and withdraws a little from personal things into the will of Spirit.

6. *for a catch.* The I AM directs us to entrust ourself to the universal life principle (the deep) and through meditation and prayer so fix our interest and attention on this principle and so apply ourself to it in expectation of receiving new light, that we will fill our mind with new ideas.

7. *James.* James the son of Zebedee is that disciple of Jesus Christ who represents the faculty of judgment in individual consciousness. (MBD/James)

8. *John.* John represents the spiritual faculty of love. (MBD/John)

## Jesus Cleanses a Man of His Error Thought[1]

It happened, while he was in one
of the cities, behold, there was a
man full of leprosy.[2] When he saw
Jesus, he fell on his face, and begged
him, saying, "Lord, if you want to,
you can make me clean."

5:13 He stretched out his hand, and
touched him, saying, "I want to. Be
made clean."

Immediately the leprosy left
him.[3] 5:14 He commanded him to tell
no one, "But go your way, and show
yourself to the priest, and offer for
your cleansing according to what
Moses commanded, for a testimony
to them." 5:15 But the report
concerning him spread much more,
and great multitudes came together
to hear, and to be healed by him of
their infirmities. 5:16 But he withdrew
himself into the desert, and prayed.

1. See Matthew 8:1-4; Mark 1:40-45.

2. *leprosy.* [In this context, leprosy may represent our error consciousness or error thoughts (otherwise known as "sin") and how they eat away at our lives. The leper asked Jesus to make him clean, and he was awakened to Truth when Jesus touched him.]

3. *the leprosy left him.* There is no record that any precautions were taken by Jesus Christ to avoid infection when He was engaged in healing the sick. He was without fear of evil, because He acknowledged only the power of the Highest, which is good.

## Jesus Removes the Burden of Error Consciousness from the Paralyzed Man[1]

5:17 It happened on one of those days, that he was teaching; and there were Pharisees[2] and teachers of the law sitting by, who had come out of every village of Galilee, Judea, and Jerusalem. The power of the Lord was with him to heal[3] them. 5:18 Behold, men brought a paralyzed man[4] on a cot, and they sought to bring him in to lay before Jesus.[5] 5:19 Not finding a way to bring him in because of the multitude, they went up to the housetop, and let him down through the tiles with his cot into the midst before Jesus. 5:20 Seeing their faith, he said to him, "Man, your sins[6] are forgiven you."

5:21 The scribes and the Pharisees began to reason, saying, "Who is this that speaks blasphemies? Who can forgive sins, but God alone?"

5:22 But Jesus, perceiving their thoughts, answered them, "Why are you reasoning so in your hearts? 5:23 Which is easier to say, 'Your sins are forgiven you;' or to say, 'Arise and walk?' 5:24 But that you may know that the Son of Man has authority on earth to forgive sins" (he said to the paralyzed man), "I tell you, arise, and take up your cot, and go to your house."

5:25 Immediately he rose up before them, and took up that which he was laying on, and departed to his house, glorifying God.[7] 5:26 Amazement took hold on all, and they glorified God. They were filled with fear, saying, "We have seen strange things today."

1. See Matthew 9:1-8; Mark 2:1-12.
2. *Pharisees*. In individual consciousness Pharisees represent thoughts that arise out of the subconsciousness, binding us to external forms of religion without giving us understanding of their real meaning. (MBD/Pharisees)
3. *heal*. To bring forth the perfect Christ human that exists within each of us. (RW/heal) See also RW/healing
4. *paralyzed man*. The paralyzed man represents one who has sinned against divine order and cut off the free flow of life in his body.
5. *before Jesus*. The attention should be centered at the highest point in consciousness, the housetop, and then let down into the body.
6. *sins*. The word, sin, which comes from the Greek, means missing the goal.
7. *glorifying God*. The realization of the perfection of human beings, as idealized by Divine Mind, will overcome all error and all bodily sickness.

## Jesus Calls Forth the Power of Will[1]

5:27 After these things he went out, and saw a tax collector named Levi[2] sitting at the tax office, and said to him, "Follow me!"

5:28 He left everything, and rose up and followed him.[3] 5:29 Levi made a great feast for him in his house. There was a great crowd of tax collectors and others who were reclining with them. 5:30 Their scribes and the Pharisees murmured against his disciples, saying, "Why do you eat and drink with the tax collectors and sinners?" 5:31 Jesus answered them, "Those who are healthy have no need for a physician, but those who are sick do. 5:32 I have not come to call the righteous, but sinners to repentance."

1. See Matthew 9:9-13; Mark 2:13-17.
2. *Levi*. Levi or Matthew represents the

will. His calling is important, because until the will is disciplined and taught to work in conjunction with faith, love, and spiritual judgment, man cannot fully exert his authority and dominion.

3. *followed him.* The appeal to come up higher or the call to spiritual living and selflessness is greater than any appeal to mere material success. When Jesus called Matthew, or Levi, to follow Him that disciple immediately left his work of collecting taxes or toll, and followed Jesus.

## The Parable of the New Wineskins[1]

5:33 They said to him, "Why do
John's disciples often fast and pray,
likewise also the disciples of the
Pharisees, but yours eat and drink?"[2]

5:34 He said to them, "Can you
make the friends of the bridegroom
fast, while the bridegroom is with
them? 5:35 But the days will come
when the bridegroom will be taken
away from them. Then they will fast
in those days." 5:36 He also told a
parable to them. "No one puts a
piece from a new garment on an old
garment, or else he will tear the
new, and also the piece from the
new will not match the old. 5:37 No
one puts new wine into old
wineskins, or else the new wine will
burst the skins, and it will be spilled,
and the skins will be destroyed. 5:38
But new wine must be put into fresh
wineskins, and both are preserved.
5:39 No man having drunk old wine
immediately desires new, for he
says, 'The old is better.'"

1. See Matthew 9:14-17; Mark 2:18-22.

2. *yours eat and drink.* We overcome our secret sins not by ignoring them, but by uncovering and correcting them. Jesus sat down to eat with publicans and sinners not because sin appealed to Him, but because He wished to help those men and reclaim them to right ways of living. The word of Truth seeks to redeem those who are spiritually in darkness.

---

Fillmore Study Bible annotations by: Rev. Michelle Vargas.

# Luke 6

## Jesus Teaches that People Are More Important than Laws[1]

6:1 Now it happened on the second
Sabbath[2] after the first, that he was
going through the grain fields. His
disciples plucked the heads of grain,
and ate, rubbing them in their hands.
6:2 But some of the Pharisees said to
them, "Why do you do that which is
not lawful to do on the Sabbath day?"

6:3 Jesus, answering them, said,
"Haven't you read what David[3] did
when he was hungry, he, and those
who were with him; 6:4 how he
entered into the house of God, and
took and ate the show bread, and
gave also to those who were with
him, which is not lawful to eat
except for the priests alone?" 6:5 He

said to them, "The Son of Man[4] is lord of the Sabbath."

1. See Matthew 12:1-8; Mark 2:23-28.
2. *Sabbath*. The Sabbath is a state of mind that we enter or acquire when we go into the silence of our own soul, into the realm of Spirit. There we find true rest and peace. (MBD/Sabbath)
3. *David*. David is often referred to as a type of Christ. His life was a forerunner of that of the more perfect human being, Jesus Christ, who was of the house of David. (MBD/David)
4. *Son of Man*. Jesus represents God's idea of man in expression (Son of man); Christ is that idea in the absolute (Son of God). The Christ is the man that God created in His image and likeness, the perfect-idea man, and is the real self of all men. (MBD/Son of Man)

## For Those With A Physical Limitation[1]

6:6 It also happened on another Sabbath that he entered into the synagogue[2] and taught. There was a man there, and his right hand[3] was withered.[4] 6:7 The scribes[5] and the Pharisees watched him, to see whether he would heal on the Sabbath, that they might find an accusation against him. 6:8 But he knew their thoughts; and he said to the man who had the withered hand, "Rise up, and stand in the middle." He arose and stood. 6:9 Then Jesus said to them, "I will ask you something: Is it lawful on the Sabbath to do good, or to do harm? To save a life, or to kill?" 6:10 He looked around at them all, and said to the man, "Stretch out your hand." He did, and his hand was restored as sound as the other. 6:11 But they were filled with rage, and talked with one another about what they might do to Jesus.

1. See Matthew 12:9-14; Mark 3:1-6.
2. *synagogue*. A Jewish synagogue was a little chapel, where any one could hear the law read out of the Hebrew Scriptures; or if he was a Rabbi he could read out of the law himself. There was a constant stream of people going and coming in the synagogue, and it fitly represents the mind of man, or the phase of man's mind that is given over to religious thought. In the new birth, or regeneration, the rebuilding of your consciousness begins in this synagogue or religious mentality. (MBD/synagogue)
3. *hand*. Represents executive ability; the doing of things; outer or manual power. (RW/hand)
4. *was withered*. James Dillet Freeman writes of Charles Fillmore: "He never accepted [his] withered leg as a handicap that he would have to put up with all the days of his life; he believed that his leg could be made whole and strong and perfect, and he worked in prayer to make it so. Those who knew him over a long period of time attest that as the years went by Charles's leg responded to the faith of the man, for they saw it grow in strength and vigor; they saw him discard cane and braces; they saw the leg become more nearly like the other. Charles Fillmore practiced the prayer that he taught. (Household of Faith p.156)
5. *scribes*. There is a faculty of the mind that receives and transcribes upon the tablets of memory every wave of thought that touches the consciousness, whether from the flesh or from Spirit. This faculty is Ezra the scribe; it may be exalted to a point where it will receive impressions from the spiritual side only. (MBD/scribes)

## Jesus Gathers to Him All the Faculties of Humankind[1]

6:12 It happened in these days, that he went out to the mountain[2] to pray, and he continued all night in prayer to God. 6:13 When it was day,[3] he called his disciples,[4] and from them he chose twelve, whom he also

named apostles:[5] 6:14 Simon, whom
he also named Peter;[6] Andrew,[7] his
brother; James;[8] John;[9] Philip;[10]
Bartholomew;[11] 6:15 Matthew;[12]
Thomas;[13] James, the son of
Alphaeus; Simon, who was called the
Zealot; 6:16 Judas the son of James;
and Judas Iscariot, who also became
a traitor.

1. See Matthew 10:1-4; Mark 13-19.

2. *mountain.* Exaltation, a high plane of consciousness, a state of spiritual realization. (MBD/mountain)

3. *when it was day,* When prayer and meditation have calmed our mind sufficiently for us to see all the factors involved in a problem and to view them dispassionately.

4. *disciples.* The disciples of Jesus represent, in mind analysis, the faculties. After one has been illumined by Truth, one desires to express it, to go forth in its ministry. This does not necessarily imply that all secular employment should be abandoned, but it does imply that the mind should make the dissemination of Truth the most important object of life. The various faculties of the mind have been occupied almost wholly in secular ways; now they are to be turned to spiritual ways. (MBD/disciples) Through the I AM anyone may identify with faith, strength, wisdom, love, zeal, and the other faculties that characterize the well-rounded character, and by recognizing and using, them consciously may express them more fully. (MBI/Luke 6:12-26, February 22, 1942)

5. *apostles.* Those sent forth; messengers; ambassadors; active spiritual thoughts. Jesus conferred this title on the Twelve whom He sent forth to teach and to heal. (RW/apostles)

6. *Simon, whom he also named Peter.* Simon (hearing), signifying his receptivity and ability to discern Truth, was changed by Jesus to Peter, or Cephas, which is the Greek for the word rock. This represents faith in God, strong, unwavering, and enduring. This faith ... is one of the first spiritual faculties to be called into expression by every one who would follow Jesus in the overcoming life. (MBD/Peter)

7. *Andrew.* The strength of the mind that is rejoiced greatly when it finds the inexhaustible Source of all strength. Andrew symbolizes the strength, while Simon Peter symbolizes the faith capacity, of the mind. When strength finds faith, and they are brothers consciously in the mind, a bond of unity is established that carries one along, even though one may encounter the most adverse experiences. (MBD/Andrew)

8. *James.* James the son of Zebedee is that disciple of Jesus Christ who represents the faculty of judgment in individual consciousness. We also call this faculty justice, discrimination; it is that quality in us which carefully weighs a question and draws a conclusion. (MBD/James)

9. *John.* The apostle John represents the spiritual faculty of love. He is known as the disciple whom Jesus loved, and love is the dominant theme of all his teachings and writings. (MBD/John)

10. *Philip.* The power faculty in humans. Philip means a lover of horses. He represents the faculty in us that, through love, masters the vital forces; hence we identify Philip as power. (MBD/Philip)

11. *Bartholomew.* The faculty of imagination. (MBD/Bartholomew)

12. *Matthew.* The will faculty in us. The will always enters into our decisions and the will makes the final choice to give up all and follow Jesus. The surrendering of the old ideas and conditions so that the greater increase of good may come into one's life is based on Matthew because Matthew represents the will. (MBD/Matthew)

13. *Thomas.* The disciple of Jesus Christ who represents the understanding faculty in us. Understanding and will function, or should function, in unison. (MBD/Thomas)

## Praise, Peace and Healing[1]

6:17 He came down with them, and
stood on a level place, with a crowd
of his disciples, and a great number
of the people from all Judea and
Jerusalem,[2] and the sea coast of
Tyre and Sidon, who came to hear
him and to be healed of their
diseases; 6:18 as well as those who
were troubled by unclean spirits, and
they were being healed.[3] 6:19 All the
multitude sought to touch him, for
power came out from him and healed

them all.

1. See Matthew 4:23-25.

2. *Judea and Jerusalem, Judea* means "the praise of Jehovah." This then is a key to the mental attitude in which the Christ consciousness will be opened to us-while we are praising the Lord. (MBD/Judaea) *Jerusalem* means habitation of peace. It is our abiding consciousness of spiritual peace, which is the result of continuous realizations of spiritual power tempered with spiritual poise and confidence. (MBD/Jerusalem)

3. *and they were being healed.* The first step in all spiritual healing is to believe, and the next step is openness and receptivity to the stream of healing life. Through the exercise of faith and our words, our spiritual quality is fused into unity with the power of Christ and the work is marvelously accomplished. (RW/healing)

## Happiness, Conditions and Consciousness[1]

6:20 He lifted up[2] his eyes to his disciples, and said,

"Blessed are you who are poor,[3]
for yours is the Kingdom of God.
6:21 Blessed are you who hunger now,[4]
for you will be filled.
Blessed are you who weep now,
for you will laugh.
6:22 Blessed are you when men shall hate you, and when they shall exclude and mock you, and throw out your name as evil,[5] for the Son of Man's sake.
6:23 Rejoice in that day, and leap for joy, for behold, your reward is great in heaven,[6] for their fathers did the same thing to the prophets.
6:24 "But woe to you who are rich![7]
For you have received your consolation.
6:25 Woe to you, you who are full now,
for you will be hungry.
Woe to you who laugh now,
for you will mourn and weep.[8]
6:26 Woe,[13] when[14] men speak well of you,
for their fathers did the same thing to the false prophets.

1. See Matthew 5:1-12.

2. *lifted up.* Lifted up in consciousness, resurrected. One who has discovered the Truth of Being is raised, lifted up in consciousness, resurrected daily out of their old, subconscious, negative thought condition into the one positive Reality. (RW/lifted up)

3. *poor.* Those who have denied personal consciousness. They are poor in the spirit of selfishness, but rich in the Spirit of Christ. (RW/poor)

4. *Blessed are you who hunger now.* Why are the hungry Blessed? Lack spurs us to seek supply, and "he that seeketh findeth." We who discover the divine law of abundance are blessed, whatever the road by which we approaches it.

5. *evil.* That which is not of God; unreality; error thought; a product of the fallen human consciousness; negation. (RW/evil)

6. *heaven.* The kingdom of heaven, or of the heavens, is a state of consciousness in which the soul and the body are in harmony with Divine Mind. (MBD/heaven)

7. *woe to you who are rich!* Why is woe pronounced upon those who know no lack and on those who are carefree and happy? A state of material well-being and absence of responsibility tend to make man conscious of externals only, so that he easily loses touch with the inner realm that is the real source of supply. When this occurs he soon falls again into the consciousness of lack and sorrow.

8. *mourn and weep.* Grief causes one to seek comfort from the God of all comfort, and since all supply is in God the grief-stricken make contact with joy and gladness and need sorrow no more.

## God Is Love, We Are Love[1]

6:27 "But I tell you who hear: love your enemies, do good to those who hate you, 6:28 bless those who curse you, and pray for those who mistreat you. 6:29 To him who strikes you on the cheek, offer also the other; and from him who takes away your cloak, don't withhold your coat also. 6:30 Give to everyone[2] who asks you, and don't ask him who takes away your goods to give them back again.

6:31 "As you would like people to do to you, do exactly so to them. 6:32 If you love those who love you, what credit is that to you? For even sinners love those who love them. 6:33 If you do good to those who do good to you, what credit is that to you? For even sinners do the same. 6:34 If you lend[3] to those from whom you hope to receive, what credit is that to you? Even sinners lend to sinners, to receive back as much. 6:35 But love your enemies, and do good, and lend, expecting nothing back; and your reward will be great, and you will be children of the Most High; for he is kind toward the unthankful and evil.

6:36 Therefore be merciful,
even as your Father is also
merciful.

1. See Matthew 5:43-48. The Sermon on the Mount represents a high spiritual understanding, expressing the law of the absolute. After a certain restoring work is done in the individual his mind must be taught Truth. In this lesson we find the higher self impressing upon the consciousness the law of love, which includes nonresistance and one's living up to the ideals that one would hold for other persons. We can love our enemies and do good to them that hate us if we realize the truth that God is love, and that all persons are various degrees of God in manifestation. In the silence of our own soul, we quicken the consciousness of divine love and realize it throughout our being; then we pour out love upon the world. (MBI/Luke 6:27-42)

2. *Give to everyone.* This verse is the essence of the Golden Rule, which many businessmen are seeking to carry out in the commercial world. It can be applied in every walk of life, and its effectiveness is being proved by those who use it.

3. *If you lend.* We should give in the consciousness of God's inexhaustible resource. We should measure everything that we give out, whether in thought or in things, by the standard of divine bounty, for: "With what measure ye mete it shall be measured to you again."

## Focus On Our Own Consciousness[1]

6:37 Don't judge,
and you won't be judged.[2]
Don't condemn,
and you won't be condemned.
Set free,
and you will be set free.

6:38 "Give, and it will be given to you:[3] good measure, pressed down, shaken together, and running over, will be given to you.[15] For with the same measure you measure it will be measured back to you."

6:39 He spoke a parable to them. "Can the blind guide the blind? Won't they both fall into a pit? 6:40 A disciple is not above his teacher, but everyone when he is fully trained will be like his teacher. 6:41 Why do you see the speck of chaff that is in your brother's eye, but don't consider the beam that is in your own eye? 6:42 Or how can you tell your brother,[4] 'Brother, let me remove the speck of chaff that is in your eye,' when you yourself don't see the beam that is in your own eye? You hypocrite! First remove the beam from your own eye, and then you can see clearly to remove the speck of chaff that is in your brother's eye.

1. See Matthew 7:1-5.

2. *Don't judge, and you won't be judged.* Goodness is man's natural expression; thus, his true judgments are always good. His goodness can be expressed, however, only when he is set free from limited concepts of justice. Obedience to the eternal principle of Absolute Good, which includes the moral law (high principles of human conduct) lifts man into a higher state of consciousness than does just the obedience to the moral law alone, the interpretation of which is given through Moses. (Unity Correspondence School Course, Judgments and Justice)

3. *Give, and it will be given to you.* "We are striving to educate the people on this question of giving and receiving, and show them that there is a Divine Law of equilibrium in matters financial, corresponding to the balance, poise and equilibrium that holds the suns and planets in space." Charles Fillmore, Tracts/Giving and Receiving.

4. *Or how can you tell your brother.* Until man sees clearly, he cannot make himself or his ideas clear to another. The inner vision of what is true and abiding must be cleared up before man can understand either his own life purposes or the needs of his neighbor.

## As Within, So Without[1]

6:43 For there is no good tree[2] that brings forth rotten fruit; nor again a rotten tree that brings forth good fruit. 6:44 For each tree is known by its own fruit. For people don't gather figs from thorns, nor do they gather grapes from a bramble bush. 6:45 The good man[3] out of the good treasure of his heart brings out that which is good, and the evil man out of the evil treasure of his heart brings out that which is evil, for out of the abundance of the heart, his mouth speaks.

1. See Matthew 7:15-20.

2. *tree.* Trees represent nerves, and nerves are expressions of thoughts of unity; they connect thought centers. (MBD/tree)

3. *The good man.* Good and evil impulses in the heart make their presence known in the outer life. Those who live a good life surrounds themselves with an atmosphere of goodness. Those whose subconscious life is evil impresses others as evil.

## We Build Our Foundation in God[1]

6:46 "Why do you call me, 'Lord, Lord,' and don't do the things which I say? 6:47 Everyone who comes to me, and hears my words, and does them, I will show you who he is like. 6:48 He is like a man[2] building a house, who dug and went deep, and laid a foundation on the rock. When a flood arose, the stream broke against that house, and could not shake it, because it was founded on the rock. 6:49 But he who hears, and doesn't do,[3] is like a man who built a house on the earth without a foundation, against which the stream broke, and immediately it fell, and the ruin of that house was great."

1. See Matthew 7:24-27.

2. *He is like a man.* Spiritual character is the rock-foundation of Being. Build yourself into God, and you will find yourself in heaven right here. Let go the little self and take hold of the Big Self. "Not my will, but thine be done."

3. *But he who hears, and doesn't do.* Storms of fear, hate, strife, cowardice, and other negative waves of feeling that sweep over us cannot avail to overcome us if we have established ourselves in the consciousness of the Christ.

Fillmore Study Bible annotations by: Rev. Michelle Vargas.

**World English Bible Footnotes:**

[13] v6:26. TR adds "to you"

[14] v6:26. TR adds "all"

[15] v6:38. literally, into your bosom.

# Luke 7

## The Power of Expectancy[1]

7:1 After he had finished speaking
in the hearing of the people, he
entered into Capernaum.[2] 7:2 A
certain centurion's[3] servant, who
was dear to him, was sick and at the
point of death. 7:3 When he heard
about Jesus, he sent to him elders
of the Jews, asking him to come and
save his servant. 7:4 When they came
to Jesus, they begged him earnestly,
saying, "He is worthy for you to do
this for him, 7:5 for he loves our
nation, and he built our synagogue
for us." 7:6 Jesus went with them.
When he was now not far from the
house, the centurion sent friends to
him, saying to him, "Lord, don't
trouble yourself, for I am not worthy
for you to come under my roof. 7:7
Therefore I didn't even think myself
worthy to come to you; but say the
word, and my servant will be healed.
7:8 For I also am a man placed under
authority, having under myself
soldiers. I tell this one, 'Go!' and he
goes;[4] and to another, 'Come!' and
he comes; and to my servant, 'Do
this,' and he does it."

7:9 When Jesus heard these things,
he marveled at him, and turned and
said to the multitude who followed
him, "I tell you, I have not found
such great faith,[5] no, not in Israel."
7:10 Those who were sent, returning
to the house, found that the servant
who had been sick was well.

1. See Matthew 8:5-13; John 4:46-54.

2. *Capernaum*. Capernaum refers to an inner conviction of the abiding compassion and restoring power of Being. When one enters this state of consciousness a healing virtue pours out of the soul and transforms all discord to harmony. (MBD/Capernaum)

3. *centurion*. Metaphysically, the centurion represents the will, whose servant, the body, is sick. Sickness results from a person's failure to blend their will with the divine will. (MBI/Luke-7, November 17, 1940)

4. *I tell this one, 'Go!' and he goes*. The centurion believed that Jesus could order about disease as he orders his soldiers: say to fever, palsy, Go! and it will go. Thus the intellect may not have faith in its own power to command disease, but its *expectancy of power on a higher plane will call it into action*. This is one of the peculiar laws of mind action, which is being proven everywhere by those who put it to the test. (MBI/Luke-7, April 15, 1906)

5. *great faith*. The central truth of this lesson is spiritual man's dominion over disease and death. The foundation of this dominion is faith.

## Inner Quickening Awakens the Soul To Newness Of

## Life

7:11 It happened soon afterwards, that he went to a city called Nain.[1] Many of his disciples, along with a great multitude, went with him. 7:12 Now when he drew near to the gate of the city, behold, one who was dead was carried out, the only son of his mother, and she was a widow. Many people of the city were with her. 7:13 When the Lord saw her, he had compassion on her, and said to her, "Don't cry." 7:14 He came near and touched the coffin, and the bearers stood still. He said, "Young man, I tell you, arise!"[2] 7:15 He who was dead sat up, and began to speak. And he gave him to his mother.

7:16 Fear took hold of all, and they glorified God, saying, "A great prophet has arisen among us!" and, "God has visited his people!" 7:17 This report went out concerning him in the whole of Judea, and in all the surrounding region.

1. *Nain.* Nain means proper; suitable. Human beings are the proper and suitable dwelling place for and the expresser of life and Truth and substance and the ways of Truth are pleasant to the consecrated soul. When the individual recognizes the abidingness of Truth, and acts on it by means of his I AM (Jesus), an inner quickening takes place and he is awakened to a newness of life and youth throughout his being. This is indicated by Jesus' raising the widow's son to life.

2. *Young man, I tell you, arise!* The raising of the widow's son represents those who have quickened and made alive the sleeping consciousness of their own souls. (MBI/Luke-7, April 15, 1906)

## The intellect is to prepare the way for the spiritual consciousness[1]

7:18 The disciples of John told him about all these things. 7:19 John, calling to himself two of his disciples, sent them to Jesus, saying, "Are you the one who is coming, or should we look for another?"[2] 7:20 When the men had come to him, they said, "John the Baptizer has sent us to you, saying, 'Are you he who comes, or should we look for another?'"

7:21 In that hour he cured many of diseases and plagues and evil spirits; and to many who were blind he gave sight. 7:22 Jesus answered them, "Go and tell John the things which you have seen and heard:[3] that the blind receive their sight, the lame walk, the lepers are cleansed, the deaf hear, the dead are raised up, and the poor have good news preached to them. 7:23 Blessed is he who is not offended by me."[4]

7:24 When John's messengers had departed, he began to tell the multitudes about John, "What did you go out into the wilderness to see? A reed shaken by the wind? 7:25 But what did you go out to see? A man clothed in soft clothing? Behold, those who are gorgeously dressed, and live delicately, are in kings' courts. 7:26 But what did you go out to see? A prophet? Yes, I tell you, and much more than a prophet. 7:27 This is he of whom it is written,

'Behold, I send my messenger
before your face,
who will prepare your way
before you.'[16][5]

7:28 "For I tell you, among those who are born of women there is not a greater prophet than John the Baptizer, yet he who is least in the Kingdom of God is greater than he."[6]

7:29 When all the people and the
tax collectors heard this, they
declared God to be just, having been
baptized with John's baptism. 7:30 But
the Pharisees and the lawyers
rejected the counsel of God, not
being baptized by him themselves.

7:31 [17]"To what then will I liken
the people of this generation? What
are they like? 7:32 They are like
children who sit in the marketplace,
and call one to another, saying, 'We
piped to you, and you didn't dance.
We mourned, and you didn't weep.'
7:33 For John the Baptizer came
neither eating bread nor drinking
wine, and you say, 'He has a demon.'
7:34 The Son of Man has come eating
and drinking, and you say, 'Behold,
a gluttonous man, and a drunkard; a
friend of tax collectors and sinners!'
7:35 Wisdom is justified by all her
children."[7]

1. See Matthew 11:2-19.

2. *Are you the one who is coming, or should we look for another?* John the Baptist represents the intellect who is so preoccupied with condemning evil and sin that the person is unable to discern the activity of Christ. Some people see evil in the world as a power so formidable that it paralyzes all their efforts and they accomplish nothing in the service of Truth. To them sin seems a reality, and they fight it and it fights back. In the end it imprisons those who stoop to quarrel with it. (MBI/Luke-7, November 11, 1912)

3. *Go and tell John the things which you have seen and heard.* The Christ does not strive with sin and evil in its many forms, but asserts absolute spiritual dominion over "plagues and evil spirits." When intellect (John) sends out its thought of doubt as to the identity of this miracle-worker, the reply is not one of argument, but of results. This is typical of that special development of the individual, there true reform begins.

4. "Blessed is he who is not offended by me." When we put no obstruction of intellectual methods or ways in doing the Spirit's work then we shall have blessings, or increase, in that which we are doing in the Christ way.

5. *Behold, I send my messenger before your face, who will prepare your way before you.* The intellect is to prepare the way for the spiritual consciousness, the Christ. The alert intellect that has been working toward the fulfillment of a divine ideal recognizes the development of spiritual consciousness and acknowledges its very first appearance, as John the Baptist recognized Jesus Christ. When the quickening by Spirit takes place in consciousness to the extent that the Christ is realized and felt and known, one depends on the inspiration of Spirit rather than on the reasonings of the intellectual person. (MBD/John)

6. *yet he who is least in the Kingdom of God is greater than he.* The least of the spiritual thoughts in human beings is greater than the mightiest reasoning of the intellect, and the intellectual concept of things must give way to the understanding that comes through the Holy Spirit. (MBD/John)

7. *Wisdom is justified by all her children.* For what do we look when we seek first the kingdom of God? We look for a state of mind in our selves that expresses in spiritual terms the things we have spiritually discerned.

## Love Conquers Sin[1]

7:36 One of the Pharisees[2] invited
him to eat with him. He entered into
the Pharisee's house,[3] and sat at the
table. 7:37 Behold, a woman in the
city who was a sinner, when she
knew that he was reclining in the
Pharisee's house, she brought an
alabaster jar of ointment. 7:38
Standing behind at his feet weeping,
she began to wet his feet[4] with her
tears, and she wiped them with the
hair of her head, kissed his feet, and
anointed them with the ointment.[5]
7:39 Now when the Pharisee who had
invited him saw it, he said to
himself, "This man, if he were a
prophet, would have perceived who
and what kind of woman this is who
touches him, that she is a sinner."

7:40 Jesus answered him, "Simon, I have something to tell you."

He said, "Teacher, say on."

7:41 "A certain lender had two debtors. The one owed five hundred
denarii, and the other fifty. 7:42 When they couldn't pay, he forgave them both. Which of them therefore will love him most?"

7:43 Simon answered, "He, I suppose, to whom he forgave the most."

He said to him, "You have judged
correctly." 7:44 Turning to the woman, he said to Simon, "Do you see this woman? I entered into your house, and you gave me no water for my feet, but she has wet my feet with her tears, and wiped them with the
hair of her head. 7:45 You gave me no kiss, but she, since the time I came in, has not ceased to kiss my
feet. 7:46 You didn't anoint my head with oil, but she has anointed my
feet with ointment. 7:47 Therefore I tell you, her sins, which are many, are forgiven, for she loved much. But to whom little is forgiven, the same
loves little." 7:48 He said to her, "Your sins are forgiven."[6]

7:49 Those who sat at the table with him began to say to themselves, "Who is this who even forgives sins?"

7:50 He said to the woman, "Your faith has saved you. Go in peace."

1. See Matthew 26:6-13; Mark 14:3-9; John 12:1-7. The woman with the alabaster jar of ointment symbolizes the repentant soul seeking the good. The inherent desire for good brings one to the feet (understanding) of the Christ consciousness, and gladness and joy (the anointing) naturally follow. (MBI/Luke-7, November 18, 1917)

2. *Pharisees.* A Pharisee is one who observes the forms, but neglects the spirit of religion. (MBI/Luke-7, April 22, 1906)

3. *Pharisee's house.* The house of the Pharisee represents the abiding consciousness of the intellect. It was here that Jesus, the I AM, came to instruct and to illumine spiritually. (MBI/Luke-7, February 15, 1931)

4. *feet.* Jesus signifies the I AM, and the feet represent that phase of the understanding which connects one with the outer, or manifest, world and reveals the right relationship toward worldly conditions in general. The washing of the disciples' feet by Jesus therefore typifies a cleansing process, or a denial of personality and materiality. (MBD/feet)

5. *ointment.* The fragrance of love with which understanding (feet) is often bathed. (RW/ointment) The anointing of Jesus' body by the woman is a portrayal of penance, the outpouring of the precious substance of love upon the divine body. (MBI/Luke-7, November 19, 1922)

6. *Your sins are forgiven.* Love is the greatest thing in the world. The intellect may entertain the divine man, and give him intellectual thoughts, but love pours out her substance upon him, and he is thereby transformed, purified, and lifted up.

---

Fillmore Study Bible annotations by: Rev. Michelle Vargas.

**World English Bible Footnotes:**

[16] v7:27. Malachi 3:1

[17] v7:31. TR adds "But the Lord said,"

# Luke 8

## Some Women Accompany Jesus

8:1 It happened soon afterwards, that he went about through cities and villages, preaching and bringing the good news of the Kingdom of God. With him were the twelve,[1] 8:2 and certain women[2] who had been healed of evil spirits and infirmities: Mary who was called Magdalene, from whom seven demons had gone out; 8:3 and Joanna, the wife of Chuzas, Herod's steward; Susanna;[3] and many others; who served them[18] from their possessions.

1. *With him were the twelve.* Jesus and his disciples represent the I AM and the twelve powers of man in each individual soul. By affirmation and prayer the I AM and the twelve spiritual powers are set into greater activity, and they begin their redeeming work in the different aggregations of thoughts, or "cities and villages."

2. *and certain women.* Women represent the feminine or substance side of the soul. The third person in the trinity is the Spirit of truth, the divine Shekinah, the "Shining One," the pure substance of God. All forms arise in this substance; it is the matrix of all forms and shapes in the universe, and it continues throughout their existence to be the source of their supply.

3. *Mary, Joanna, Susanna. Mary*: A lifting up of power in consciousness, and letting this greatly increased faculty be guided by the emotions and desires of the human soul (MBD/Magdalene). *Joanna*: the soul quality of intuition, discernment, which perceives the Truth that is expressed in the metaphysical explanation (MBD/Joanna). *Susanna*: purity of soul (white, shining, lily, pure, a woman follower of Jesus, one of those who ministered to His needs) (MBD/Susanna).

## The Parable of the Sower[1]

8:4 When a great multitude came together, and people from every city were coming to him, he spoke by a parable. 8:5 "The farmer went out to sow[2] his seed. As he sowed, some fell along the road,[3] and it was trampled under foot, and the birds of the sky devoured it. 8:6 Other seed fell on the rock,[4] and as soon as it grew, it withered away, because it had no moisture. 8:7 Other fell amid the thorns,[5] and the thorns grew with it, and choked it. 8:8 Other fell into the good ground,[6] and grew, and brought forth fruit one hundred times." As he said these things, he called out, "He who has ears to hear, let him hear!"

1. See Matthew 13:1-9, Mark 4:1-9

2. *The farmer went out to sow.* Everyone who thinks in accord with Truth and who speaks a good or a true word is a sower according to this parable, which implies that the seed to be sown is good seed.

3. *some fell along the road.* the mind that from force of long habit follows a beaten track and is unreceptive to new ideas. New and unfamiliar ideas falling into such a mind receive no attention (are trodden under foot).

4. *Other seed fell on the rock.* One whose mind is unretentive, like a sieve, may receive the word with interest and attention, but through lack of power to concentrate on one subject and keep the thought centered on it, he allows the word spoken to him to slip out of mind and be lost.

5. *Other fell amid the thorns.* The cares, riches, and pleasures of this life all serve to choke the word and prevent its coming to fruition. All serve to distract the thought from the truth that man seeks to instill into the mind.

6. *Other fell into the good ground.* The receptive and retentive type of mind. The fruits, or the crops obtained from these seeds, are conditioned by the character of the soil, or the type of mind, in which the seeds, or thoughts, find lodgment.

## The Purpose of the Parables[1]

8:9 Then his disciples asked him, "What does this parable mean?"

8:10 He said, "To you it is given to know the mysteries of the Kingdom of God, but to the rest in parables; that 'seeing they may not see, and hearing they may not understand.'[19][2]

1. See Isaiah 6:9, Matthew 13:14, Mark 4:12.

2. *seeing they may not see, and hearing they may not understand.* [Jesus] understood exactly what the conditions were on the invisible side of life, which is termed in His teaching the "kingdom of God" or the "kingdom of the heavens." We are trying to connect His teaching with modern science in order to show the parallel; but as He said in Mark 4:23, "if any man hath ears to hear, let him hear." This means that we must develop a capacity for understanding in terms of the atomic structure of the universe. Unless we have this spiritual capacity we do not understand. We think we have ears, but they are attuned to materiality. Atom-Smashing Power of Mind, (Thinking in the Fourth Dimension p.56)

## The Parable of the Sower Explained

8:11 Now the parable is this: The seed is the word of God.[1] 8:12 Those along the road are those who hear, then the devil comes, and takes away the word from their heart, that they may not believe and be saved. 8:13 Those on the rock are they who, when they hear, receive the word with joy; but these have no root, who believe for a while, then fall away in time of temptation. 8:14 That which fell among the thorns, these are those who have heard, and as they go on their way they are choked with cares, riches, and pleasures of life, and bring no fruit to maturity. 8:15 That in the good ground, these are such as in an honest and good heart, having heard the word, hold it tightly, and bring forth fruit with patience.

1. *the word of God.* the word of Truth. The soil in which the word is sown is the mind. The subconscious phase of mind is the universal substance that corresponds to the earthly soil. Many different kinds of seeds may be sown in the soil of the mind. A high thought is a seed sown in the soil of the kingdom of the mind. An intellectual thought is a seed sown on the intellectual plane. A sensual thought is a seed sown in the flesh. The fruits, or the crops obtained from these seeds, are conditioned by the character of the soil, or the type of mind, in which the seeds, or thoughts, find lodgment.

## A Lamp under a Jar

8:16 "No one, when he has lit a lamp, covers it with a container,[1] or puts it under a bed; but puts it on a stand, that those who enter in may see the light. 8:17 For nothing is hidden,[2] that will not be revealed; nor anything secret, that will not be known and come to light. 8:18 Be

careful therefore how you hear. For
whoever has, to him will be given;[3]
and whoever doesn't have, from him
will be taken away even that which
he thinks he has."

1. *covers it with a container.* See Matthew 5:15

2. *nothing is hidden, that will not be revealed.* Nothing ever can be hidden from Spirit. It is always best to uncover the whole inner consciousness to Spirit and to pray earnestly to be thoroughly cleansed from every taint of deception and error. (MBI/Acts 5:1-5)

3. *whoever has, to him will be given.* The Holy Spirit is always willing to give itself to us, always. God's good is always more than willing to give its action to us. Always more willing than we are. But, since we have been given the divine idea of freedom, we also are free if we so choose to reject our highest good. (Ed Rabel, Gospel Mysteries 2)

## The True Kindred of Jesus[1]

8:19 His mother and brothers came
to him, and they could not come near
him for the crowd. 8:20 It was told him
by some saying, "Your mother and
your brothers stand outside, desiring
to see you."

8:21 But he answered them, "My
mother and my brothers are these
who hear the word of God, and do
it."[2]

1. See Matthew 12:46-50, Mark 3:31-35

2. *My mother and my brothers are these who hear the word of God, and do it.* The spiritual is stronger than any human connection. We who live under the light of Spirit are doing the will of the Father; we are the true family of Jesus Christ. (Jesus' Soul Evolution 459)

## Jesus Calms a Storm[1]

8:22 Now it happened on one of
those days, that he entered into a
boat,[2] himself and his disciples, and
he said to them, "Let's go over to
the other side of the lake." So they
launched out. 8:23 But as they sailed,
he fell asleep. A wind[3] storm came
down on the lake, and they were
taking on dangerous amounts of
water. 8:24 They came to him, and
awoke him, saying, "Master, master,
we are dying!" He awoke, and
rebuked the wind and the raging of
the water, and they ceased, and it
was calm. 8:25 He said to them,
"Where is your faith?"[4] Being afraid
they marveled, saying one to
another, "Who is this, then, that he
commands even the winds and the
water, and they obey him?"

1. See Matthew 8:23-27, Mark 4:35-41.

2. *boat.* Metaphysically, a positive thought—a conveyance that is able to float upon the water (the unstable mind), and to bear up the disciples (the faculties of mind). The multitudes are the numberless thoughts that are seeking light, strength, and healing. (MBD/boat)

3. wind. Life currents that come from within and surround the whole being; the executive power of mind clearing the way to higher states of consciousness. (RW/wind)

4. *Where is your faith?* The perceiving power of the mind linked with the power to shape substance. Spiritual assurance; the power to do the seemingly impossible. It is a magnetic power that draws unto us our heart's desire from the invisible spiritual substance. Faith is a deep inner knowing that that which is sought is already ours for the taking. (RW/faith)

## Jesus Heals the Gerasene Demoniac[1]

8:26 They arrived at the country of the Gadarenes,[2] which is opposite Galilee. 8:27 When Jesus stepped ashore, a certain man out of the city who had demons for a long time[3] met him. He wore no clothes, and didn't live in a house, but in the tombs. 8:28 When he saw Jesus, he cried out, and fell down before him, and with a loud voice said, "What do I have to do with you, Jesus, you Son of the Most High God? I beg you, don't torment me!" 8:29 For Jesus was commanding the unclean spirit to come out of the man. For the unclean spirit had often seized the man. He was kept under guard, and bound with chains and fetters. Breaking the bands apart, he was driven by the demon into the desert.

8:30 Jesus asked him, "What is your name?"[4]

He said, "Legion,"[5] for many demons had entered into him. 8:31 They begged him that he would not command them to go into the abyss. 8:32 Now there was there a herd of many pigs[6] feeding on the mountain, and they begged him that he would allow them to enter into those. He allowed them. 8:33 The demons came out from the man, and entered into the pigs, and the herd rushed down the steep bank into the lake, and were drowned. 8:34 When those who fed them saw what had happened, they fled, and told it in the city and in the country.

8:35 People went out to see what had happened. They came to Jesus, and found the man from whom the demons had gone out, sitting at Jesus' feet, clothed and in his right mind; and they were afraid. 8:36 Those who saw it told them how he who had been possessed by demons was healed. 8:37 All the people of the surrounding country of the Gadarenes asked him to depart from them, for they were very much afraid. He entered into the boat, and returned. 8:38 But the man from whom the demons had gone out begged him that he might go with him, but Jesus sent him away, saying, 8:39 "Return to your house, and declare what great things God has done for you." He went his way, proclaiming throughout the whole city what great things Jesus had done for him.

1. See Matthew 8:28-34, Mark 5:1-20

2. *the country of the Gadarenes.* A symbol of the subconscious state of sin and evil. The energy of life (Galilee), when expressed on the lower levels, takes these forms.

3. *who had demons for a long time.* When we fall into a negative state of consciousness, we find ourself subject to countless fears. These are demons that must be overcome before we can know self-dominion.

4. *What is your name?* The hold of habitual error upon man is not easily loosened. Jesus, the directive will, did not immediately cast out the legion of demons from the possessed man. "He was commanding the unclean spirit to come out from the man," when He asked the man's name, and the man replied in the character of the demons instead.

5. *Legion.* The name Legion could identify anyone who is currently obsessed with the parts he lets play him in life. In other words, you are not playing a role consciously in this state; you become the toy of the roles who choose to play you. It is the surrendering to false personality and becoming subjective to the whims, the mental suggestions, the prevalent emotions running around. (Ed Rabel, New Testament Lectures, Jesus Heals the Gerasene Demoniac, pp.96-100)

6. *Pigs.* [The 1936 commentary says] Swine represent the lowest stratum of subconsciousness, which drops completely out of the life of man at the command of the higher self. [Ed Rabel has another perspective:] Nowadays you read this and the average person is hurt by it, why did Jesus involve himself in an incident where an innocent herd of swine would be forced to

commit suicide as they did? I can't take it any further in that direction. But there is a metaphysical, even more strongly, there is an occult factor here. Through man's consciousness he can directly infuse other forms of life and even natural phenomena with his emanations, now. If he is conscious and he knows who and what he is, what kind of emanations will he always be sure they are? Good, beneficial, uplifting emanations, that is the whole idea of pet ownership. The man in the parable was not aware of who or what he was; he was insane, he was possessed of negative roles, so after his healing, these demons that went from him did not go directly into the dissolving process which would have happened could he had been consciously using denials; in other words, the demon would then, as all negativity does, when you are rightly using denial, doesn't touch anybody else in its dissolving journey. But here we have a different case; here we have a man who was in such an extreme situation that he couldn't do his own denial.

## A Woman Healed and a Girl Restored to Life①

8:40 It happened, when Jesus returned, that the multitude welcomed him, for they were all waiting for him. 8:41 Behold, there came a man named Jairus, and he was a ruler of the synagogue. He fell down at Jesus' feet, and begged him to come into his house, 8:42 for he had an only daughter, about twelve years of age, and she was dying. But as he went, the multitudes pressed against him. 8:43 A woman who had a flow of blood for twelve years, who had spent all her living on physicians, and could not be healed by any, 8:44 came behind him, and touched the fringe[20] of his cloak,② and immediately the flow of her blood stopped. 8:45 Jesus said, "Who touched me?"

When all denied it, Peter and those with him said, "Master, the multitudes press and jostle you, and you say, 'Who touched me?'"

8:46 But Jesus said, "Someone did touch me, for I perceived that power has gone out of me." 8:47 When the woman saw that she was not hidden, she came trembling, and falling down before him declared to him in the presence of all the people the reason why she had touched him, and how she was healed immediately. 8:48 He said to her, "Daughter, cheer up. Your faith has made you well. Go in peace."

8:49 While he still spoke, one from the ruler of the synagogue's house came, saying to him, "Your daughter is dead. Don't trouble the Teacher."

8:50 But Jesus hearing it, answered him, "Don't be afraid. Only believe, and she will be healed."③

8:51 When he came to the house, he didn't allow anyone to enter in, except Peter, John, James, the father of the child, and her mother. 8:52 All were weeping and mourning her, but he said, "Don't weep. She isn't dead, but sleeping."

8:53 They were ridiculing him, knowing that she was dead. 8:54 But he put them all outside, and taking her by the hand, he called, saying, "Child, arise!"④ 8:55 Her spirit returned,⑤ and she rose up immediately. He commanded that something be given to her to eat. 8:56 Her parents were amazed, but he commanded them to tell no one what had been done.

1. See Matthew 9:20-22 Mark 5:24-34

2. *touched the fringe of his cloak.* It is good to think of Jesus as the living symbol of the conscious embodiment of a healing consciousness which is available to all of us; that is, the divine potential in all of us to develop a healing consciousness. In Jesus' case it had already been developed; it was there in total therefore, He was a

walking healing consciousness and people could tune in to Him just as you can tune in to your own Healing consciousness and get the results. This is different from thinking of Jesus as a supernatural person who had the gift to heal; don't equate healing with a gift that anyone is given, it is a valid consciousness that can be established and developed in any person. Through touching your spiritual awareness of healing, of the healing consciousness which is really within all of us, in any way to make a connection with it and it will bring forth a healing result, that is, that healing consciousness that we touch, make a connection with, does not need to be our own; it is there. (Ed Rabel, New Testament Lectures, Woman Who Touched Christ's Garment, pp.100-103)

3. *Only believe, and she will be healed.* Jesus saw deeper than those who were not spiritually awakened, and to him death was not what it seemed to them. They looked upon it as a total cessation of life, and the horror of it made them wail and beat their breasts. Jesus always saw that death was a very deep sleep, and so spoke of it in this as also in the case of Lazarus. It is so referred to almost universally in the Epistles — "Those who have fallen asleep." (MBI/Mark 5)

4. *Child, arise!* The healer needs to put out of the very atmosphere of room, as well as the patient's mind, all thoughts that believe in or fear death. Jesus put them all out of the house, and with Peter (faith), James (judgment), and John (love), went in and said unto the maiden, "Talithia cumi," Aramaic words, which are equivalent to "Rise, dear little maiden."

5. *Her spirit returned.* In the last quarter of a century this case of healing has been duplicated in various phases many times by modern metaphysicians but no special attention has been called to the cases, those who were witnesses having even doubted that the persons raised were really dead. And we rejoice to say that they were not dead—that there is no such thing as that awful condition of conscious oblivion which the sense mind sees and calls death. There is no loss of identity, no departure, no forgetfulness. All that ever was is here now in its varying states of consciousness. The true resurrection is to come to a realization of this — to know it in both its subjective and objective aspects.

---

Fillmore Study Bible annotations by: Rev. Mark Hicks

**World English Bible Footnotes:**

[18] v8:3. TR reads "him" instead of "them"

[19] v8:10. Isaiah 6:9

[20] v8:44. or, tassel

# Luke 9

## The Mission of the Twelve (1)

9:1 He called the twelve[21]
together, and gave them power and
authority over all demons, and to
cure diseases.(2) 9:2 He sent them
forth to preach the Kingdom of God,
and to heal the sick. 9:3 He said to
them, "Take nothing for your
journey(3)--neither staffs, nor wallet,
nor bread, nor money; neither have
two coats apiece. 9:4 Into whatever
house you enter, stay there, and
depart from there. 9:5 As many as
don't receive you, when you depart
from that city, shake off even the
dust from your feet(4) for a testimony
against them." 9:6 They departed, and

went throughout the villages, preaching the Good News, and healing everywhere.

1. See Matthew 10:5-15, Mark 6:6b-13; Luke 10:1-12.

2. *gave them power and authority over all demons, and to cure diseases.* When man's spiritual understanding is awakened, he discerns that he has faculties that he has not previously called into action; that through these faculties he can gain control of every condition of his mind; that through them he can cleanse all impure states of mind, and restore, heal, and harmonize ills both of mind and of body. (MBI/Matthew 10)

3. *Take nothing for your journey.* The new man is being erected in consciousness through his faculties and their staff, or dependence, must be upon Spirit. They must not depend on material resources (money), but they must have understanding (sandals) of the relation of spiritual ideas. (MBI/Mark 6)

4. *shake off even the dust from your feet.* Shaking the dust from under one's feet represents a denial of the contact of material thought in order that one may not be contaminated and limited in his free spiritual ministry. (MBI/Mark 6)

## Herod's Perplexity[1]

9:7 Now Herod[2] the tetrarch[3]
heard of all that was done by him;
and he was very perplexed, because
it was said by some that John had
risen from the dead, 9:8 and by some
that Elijah had appeared, and by
others that one of the old prophets
had risen again. 9:9 Herod said, "John
I beheaded,[4] but who is this, about
whom I hear such things?"[5] He sought
to see him.

1. See Matthew 14:1-2; Mark 6:14-16.

2. *Herod.* The family name of several Roman rulers of Judea (Matt. 2:1; Mark 6:14). Metaphysically, the ruling will of the physical, the ego in the sense consciousness. This ruling ego is temporal because it does not understand man's true origin or the law of man's being. (MBD/Herod)

3. *the tetrarch.* A Roman governor or ruler of the fourth part of a kingdom (Matt. 14:1). Metaphysically, a tetrarch, a ruler of the fourth part, indicates the very carnal thought that guides and directs the outer, manifest man, or body of man in its seemingly physical, corruptible state. The first three steps in bringing forth are purely spiritual—Father, Son, and Holy Spirit, or, mind, idea, and expression—but the fourth step, the outer manifestation, becomes very physical and material, apparently, whenever material thoughts and beliefs are given first place in the body-building consciousness of the individual. (MBD/tetrarch)

4. *John I beheaded.* We must be on our guard against this subtle sense mind and take tender care of the little, innocent, new idea that has been born deep down in the heart. We must not give it over to the keeping of Herod. We must nurture it, care for it, and hide it away. If necessary we should take it down into Egypt (darkness) when Herod seeks to kill it.

5. *who is this, about whom I hear such things?* [the question people always have asked about Jesus.] See v9:18 below.]

## Feeding the Five Thousand[1]

9:10 The apostles, when they had
returned, told him what things they
had done. He took them, and
withdrew apart to a deserted place
of a city called Bethsaida. 9:11 But the
multitudes, perceiving it, followed
him. He welcomed them, and spoke
to them of the Kingdom of God, and
he cured those who needed healing.
9:12 The day began to wear away; and
the twelve came, and said to him,
"Send the multitude away, that they
may go into the surrounding villages
and farms, and lodge, and get food,

for we are here in a deserted place."

9:13 But he said to them, "You give them something to eat."[2]

They said, "We have no more than five loaves and two fish, unless we should go and buy food for all these people." 9:14 For they were about five thousand men.

He said to his disciples, "Make them sit down in groups of about fifty each." 9:15 They did so, and made them all sit down. 9:16 He took the five loaves and the two fish, and looking up to the sky, he blessed them, and broke them, and gave them to the disciples to set before the multitude. 9:17 They ate, and were all filled. [3] They gathered up twelve baskets of broken pieces that were left over.

1. See Matthew 14:13-21; Mark 6:30-44; John 6:1-14.

2. *You give them something to eat.* To eat and drink is to appropriate; to become conscious of the food that "abideth unto eternal life," and to use it (RW/eat).

3. *They ate, and were all filled.* Eating is symbolical of mental appropriation of thoughts of substance. "Thy words were found, and I did eat them; and thy words were unto me a joy and the rejoicing of my heart" (Jer. 15:16). Supplying the physical needs does not solve the whole problem of hunger for man, for his hungers are as varied as his interests and desires. They include his thoughts and feelings as well as his physical needs. (RW/eating)

## Peter's Declaration about Jesus[1]

9:18 It happened, as he was praying alone, that the disciples[2] were with him, and he asked them, "Who do the multitudes say that I am?"[3]

9:19 They answered, "'John the Baptizer,' but others say, 'Elijah,'[4] and others, that one of the old prophets is risen again."

9:20 He said to them, "But who do you say that I am?"

Peter answered, "The Christ of God."[5]

1. See Matthew 16:13-23; Mark 8:27-33

2. *the disciples.* The disciples of Jesus represent, in mind analysis, the faculties. After one has been illumined by Truth, one desires to express it, to go forth in its ministry. (MBD/disciples)

3. *I am.* I AM is God's name in man; it is Jehovah, the indwelling Christ, the true spiritual man whom God made in His image and likeness. The outer, manifest man is the offspring of the I AM, or inner spiritual man. By use of I AM we link ourselves with outer seemings--or we make conscious union with the Father, with Spirit, with abiding life, wisdom, love, peace, substance, strength, power, Truth, the kingdom of the heavens within us. (MBD/I AM)

4. *Elijah.* The spiritual I AM of man's consciousness. Elijah on Mount Carmel (I Kings 18:19) represents the I AM in realization of its unfettered power. (MBD/Elijah)

5. *The Christ of God.* Christ is the divine-idea man. Jesus is the name that represents an individual expression of the Christ idea. Jesus Christ is the form of the name that is commonly applied to the man of Galilee who demonstrated perfection. Christ Jesus is the idea that is being expressed by men as the result of their faith in and understanding of Truth. (MBD/Christ)

## Jesus Foretells His Death and Resurrection[1]

9:21 But he warned them, and commanded them to tell this to no one, 9:22 saying, "The Son of Man must suffer many things, and be rejected

by the elders, chief priests, and
scribes, and be killed, and the third
day be raised up."

9:23 He said to all, "If anyone
desires to come after me,[2] let him
deny himself,[3] take up his
cross,[22][4] and follow me.[5] 9:24 For
whoever desires to save his life will
lose it, but whoever will lose his life
for my sake, the same will save it.[6]
9:25 For what does it profit a man if he
gains the whole world, and loses or
forfeits his own self? 9:26 For whoever
will be ashamed of me and of my
words, of him will the Son of Man
be ashamed, when he comes in his
glory, and the glory of the Father,
and of the holy angels. 9:27 But I tell
you the truth: There are some of
those who stand here, who will in no
way taste of death, until they see the
Kingdom of God."

1. See Matthew 16:24-28; Mark 8:34-9.1.

2. *If anyone desires to come after me.* When Jesus said these words He was speaking from His Christ or I AM Self. He meant that if anyone desires to come into the understanding, freedom, and abundance of life which the Christ consciousness affords, he must drop from consciousness ("deny himself") all error beliefs and accept the truth of himself as the beloved son of God with a divine inheritance. (Correspondence School Course, *Denials and Affirmations*, Annotations, Lesson 5)

3. *let him deny himself.* How do we bring our will closer into accord with the divine will? By daily denying the power or importance of self, by taking up our "cross," our realization that we have not yet demonstrated our innate perfection, and in following the Christ, who is the way to eternal life.

4. *take up his cross.* The crystallization of two currents of thought--the state of consciousness termed sense mind. The perpendicular bar symbolizes the inner current of divine life; the horizontal bar symbolizes the cross current of human limitation. The latter symbolizes the "mind of the flesh," also, and it burdens the body with its various erroneous beliefs. The center of action of this sense mind is in the brain, and there it has to be met in the final overcoming that the I AM undertakes: "The place called The place of a skull." (MBD/cross)

5. *and follow me.* To "follow me" is to live the laws of God in every phase of our experience. (*Denials and Affirmations*)

6. *whoever will lose his life for my sake, the same will save it.* How do we lose our life and at the same time save it? We "lose" our "life" (the petty, selfish, ineffectual life of the personal or outer man) by transferring our attention to the universal life of Spirit and becoming one with it. In so doing we learn the true meaning of life as an expression of divinity, and prove the eternal at the cost of the temporal.

## The Transfiguration[1]

9:28 It happened about eight days
after these sayings, that he took with
him Peter, John, and James,[2] and
went up onto the mountain to pray.[3]
9:29 As he was praying, the
appearance of his face was altered,
and his clothing became white and
dazzling.[4] 9:30 Behold, two men were
talking with him, who were Moses
and Elijah, 9:31 who appeared in glory,
and spoke of his departure,[23] which
he was about to accomplish at
Jerusalem.

9:32 Now Peter and those who were
with him were heavy with sleep,[5]
but when they were fully awake,
they saw his glory, and the two men
who stood with him. 9:33 It happened,
as they were parting from him, that
Peter said to Jesus, "Master, it is
good for us to be here. Let's make
three tents: one for you, and one
for Moses, and one for Elijah," not
knowing what he said.

9:34 While he said these things, a
cloud came and overshadowed
them,[6] and they were afraid as they
entered into the cloud. 9:35 A voice

came out of the cloud, saying, "This
is my beloved Son. Listen to him!"
9:36 When the voice came, Jesus was
found alone. They were silent, and
told no one in those days any of the
things which they had seen.

1. See Matthew 17:1-9; Mark 9:2-10.

2. *Peter, John, and James.* The faculties, Faith, Love and Judgment are not fully *awakened* but through the activity of these exalted spiritual forces they are *quickened*, and are able to receive that spiritual message which God always sends forth, when the assurance [that it was] fully complied with is brought into evidence. "He is my Son, my chosen: hear ye him."

3. *went up onto the mountain to pray.* The symbolical meaning of Jesus going up into the mountain to pray, accompanied by Peter, John and James means the I AM, supported by faith (Peter), love (John), and judgment (James), enters into that high spiritual understanding, the door to which realm can be unlocked only by prayer and the sincere desire of the soul to perform unselfish service for humanity.

4. *the appearance of his face was altered, and his clothing became white and dazzling.* The great spiritual work, which is about to take place, here spoken of freely is the crucifixion of Jesus (the I Am), at Jerusalem, or that spiritual process of Divine Love through which it is made possible for the Spirit of Truth (God manifest) to be born in every heart. What transformation here takes place? The countenance is changed, is fashioned anew, after the Divine Pattern. The whole being is immersed in the dazzling light of spiritual understanding and aspiration.

5. *Peter and those who were with him were heavy with sleep.* Our faculties have to be awakened out of inactivity [or "sleep."] This awakening is accomplished through prayer. Then the faculties join in the glorification of the whole man, spirit, soul, and body.

6. *While he said these things, a cloud came and overshadowed them.* What always follows a period of great spiritual activity? A period of seeming inaction and depression, the dormant season. It is the time when, to appearances, all seems lost. In truth, it is the period of change, when the old is giving way, and the new forces are collecting their energies preparatory to the germinating season, when the new off-shoots (mind gems) come forth into "livingness."

## Jesus Heals a Boy with a Demon[1]

9:37 It happened on the next day,
when they had come down from the
mountain, that a great multitude
met him. 9:38 Behold, a man from the
crowd called out, saying, "Teacher,
I beg you to look at my son, for he
is my only child. 9:39 Behold, a spirit
takes him,[2] he suddenly cries out,
and it convulses him so that he
foams, and it hardly departs from
him, bruising him severely. 9:40 I
begged your disciples to cast it out,
and they couldn't."

9:41 Jesus answered, "Faithless and
perverse generation, how long shall
I be with you and bear with you?[3]
Bring your son here."

9:42 While he was still coming, the
demon threw him down and
convulsed him violently. But Jesus
rebuked the unclean spirit, and
healed the boy, and gave him back
to his father. 9:43 They were all
astonished at the majesty of God.[4]

1. See Matthew 17:14-21; Mark 9:14-28.

2. *Behold, a spirit takes him.* In dealing with healing illustrations like this, [we need to] dispense once and for all with demonology and exorcism. They do exist only now in their symbolism, they are negative thoughts and feelings, destructive and blindly uncontrolled emotions. Exorcism is not called exorcism now; it is called mental or emotional healing. So let's get away from demons and entities. (Ed Rabel, New Testament Lectures, *Jesus Cures a Boy with a Demon*, pp.141-148)

3. *Faithless and perverse generation, how long shall I be with you?* What Jesus is trying to do here is to establish once and for all the validity of always believing that healing is possible. Upon what could we base our claim to that validity? Upon the

knowledge that health and life are ideas in divine mind, they are not matters of human opinion. They are first ideas in God Mind and all of God's divine ideas are now implanted in us as our divine inheritance. (Ed Rabel)

4. *They were all astonished at the majesty of God.* Divine ideas are real, they really are, and they are always here in all their fullness, in all their purity and splendor. If you and I commit our belief to any divine idea we are capable of recognizing and allow that connection then to proceed, the very essence, the very character, the very substance of whatever divine idea of combination will manifest in my world. (Ed Rabel)

## Jesus Again Foretells His Death[1]

But while all were marveling at all
the things which Jesus did, he said
to his disciples, 9:44 "Let these words
sink into your ears, for the Son of
Man will be delivered up into the
hands of men."[2] 9:45 But they didn't
understand this saying. It was
concealed from them, that they
should not perceive it, and they were
afraid to ask him about this saying.

1. See Matthew 17:22-23; Mark 9:30-32.

2. *the Son of Man will be delivered up into the hands of men.* We have a great mystery here which is never really cleared up. We assume that it refers to Jesus predicting his own trial and crucifixion... Now he is talking about himself, the Christ. Here again he is predicting or telling something that is going to happen; that a son of man is going to be delivered into the hands of men, he is going to be killed, and then is going to resurrect, but the way he says it certainly sounds as if he is talking about a third person, so we have a double question here. First of all, who is he really talking about here and just why? and secondly, why is there so much uncomprehension and fear on the part of the disciples? (Ed Rabel, New Testament Lectures, *Jesus Again Foretells His Death and Resurrection*, pp.148a-148b)

## True Greatness[1]

9:46 There arose an argument
among them about which of them
was the greatest. 9:47 Jesus,
perceiving the reasoning of their
hearts, took a little child, and set
him by his side, 9:48 and said to them,
"Whoever receives this little child in
my name receives me.[2] Whoever
receives me receives him who sent
me. For whoever is least among you
all, this one will be great."

1. See Matthew 18:1-5; Mark 9:33-37.

2. *Whoever receives this little child in my name receives me.* The famous psychologist, Piaget, wrote that the only normal mind is the child's mind. He might have added that the only way to happiness is the child's way because the child uses his mind properly. Imagination is the forefront of all natural thinking. We are not literal creatures with our thoughts imprisoned in facts alone. If this were so, we would hate games and sports and we certainly would not risk driving cars on the highway. Through the ages, man has turned to the excitement of adventure, surviving many risks since prehistoric times in attaining dominion over his environment. (Eric Butterworth Speaks: Essays on Abundant Living *The Secret of Living Happily* #20)

## Another Exorcist[1]

9:49 John answered, "Master, we
saw someone casting out demons in

your name,[2] and we forbade him, because he doesn't follow with us."

9:50 Jesus said to him, "Don't forbid him, for he who is not against us is for us."[3]

1. See Mark 9:38-40.

2. *in your name.* When we call upon the name of Jesus Christ, we are calling on the power of God because Jesus Christ is God incarnate. If we want to give our prayers spiritual authority, there's no greater authority in the spiritual realm than Jesus Christ. (May Rowland, *Jesus Christ, An Ever Present Reality*, clip 11)

3. *he who is not against us is for us.* In the light of Spirit there is no halfway place. When the movements of the mind turn towards the light, there is opened up in consciousness a fuller knowledge, a greater freedom. The way is made clear for the triumphant march of the Christ through the soul. See Luke 11:14-23 for more.

## A Samaritan Village Refuses to Receive Jesus

9:51 It came to pass, when the days were near that he should be taken up, he intently set his face to go to Jerusalem,[1] 9:52 and sent messengers before his face.[2] They went, and entered into a village of the Samaritans, so as to prepare for him. 9:53 They didn't receive him,[3] because he was traveling with his face set towards Jerusalem. 9:54 When his disciples, James and John, saw this, they said, "Lord, do you want us to command fire to come down from the sky, and destroy them,[4] just as Elijah did?"

9:55 But he turned and rebuked them,[5] "You don't know of what kind of spirit you are. 9:56 For the Son of Man didn't come to destroy men's lives, but to save them."

1. *he intently set his face to go to Jerusalem.* In the light of Spirit there is no halfway place. When the movements of the mind turn towards the light, there is opened up in consciousness a fuller knowledge, a greater freedom. The way is made clear for the triumphant march of the Christ through the soul.

2. *and sent messengers before his face.* Sending messengers before his face into the realm of mixed thoughts (the Samaritans) represents the projecting of spiritual thoughts ahead to prepare the way for what is to follow. For example, metaphysicians, when about to speak the words, "The Spirit of the Lord goes before and opens the way," project their spiritual consciousness ahead, and then utter the words.

3. *They didn't receive him.* The meaning of Samaria is "watch mountain;" it also signifies a mixed state of consciousness. [The Samaritans didn't receive Jesus because] old worldly thought is presented that one's enemies should be destroyed.

4. *Lord, do you want us to command fire to come down from the sky, and destroy them?* John's love was personal love, which jealously guards the prerogatives of the loved one and expresses violence and vindictiveness. Many years were required to effect the complete transformation to expressing humility and love.

5. *But he turned and rebuked them.* All destructive thoughts should be rebuked and another state of consciousness should be entered into, according to the example of Jesus and his disciples. We should turn our thought away from resentment and from all personal ill feelings, keeping it fixed on the constructive side. Calling down fire from heaven is not the Christ-like way to deal with petty discriminations and other personal ill feelings.

## Would-Be Followers of Jesus[1]

They went to another village. 9:57 As they went on the way, a certain man said to him, "I want to follow you wherever you go, Lord."

9:58 Jesus said to him, "The foxes have holes, and the birds of the sky have nests, but the Son of Man has no place to lay his head."②

9:59 He said to another, "Follow me!"

But he said, "Lord, allow me first to go and bury my father."

9:60 But Jesus said to him, "Leave the dead to bury their own dead,③ but you go and announce the Kingdom of God."

9:61 Another also said, "I want to follow you, Lord, but first allow me to bid farewell to those who are at my house."

9:62 But Jesus said to him, "No one, having put his hand to the plow, and looking back, is fit for the Kingdom of God."④

1. See Matthew 8:18-22.

2. *but the Son of Man has no place to lay his head.* Here Jesus is reminding us that human beings (Son of man) are evolving souls. As such, we have no fixed, final "resting place" in the universe. Every place we are in can be our right place, but none can be our permanent place. We are learning, growing, expanding units of consciousness. We are unfolding, evolving souls. (*USRS Bible Interpretation*, Lesson 7)

3. *Leave the dead to bury their own dead.* Only those who believe in the reality of death are concerned with proper burial of "the dead." Those who are in Truth do not believe in the reality of death; that is, as any sort of finality. Truth reveals that there are no "dead" that are to be buried. Only a corpse is buried; and a corpse is simply the remains of abandoned physical atoms and molecules, which is not the person. (*USRS Bible Interpretation*)

4. *No one, having put his hand to the plow, and looking back, is fit for the Kingdom of God.* The kingdom of God refers to the divine possibility, the kingdom of fulfillment. No one is fit for the fulfilling of his desires and ideals if he sets out on faith, carries with him the secret reservation, and then retreats back across the bridge in security, when he needs to. (Eric Butterworth Unity Podcast, *The All or None Law* #14)

Fillmore Study Bible annotations by: Rev. Mark Hicks.

**World English Bible Footnotes:**

[21] v9:1. TR reads "his twelve disciples" instead of "the twelve"

[22] v9:23. TR, NU add "daily"

[23] v9:31. literally, "exodus"

# Luke 10

## The Twelve Disciples and the Seven Senses①

10:1 Now after these things,② the
Lord also appointed seventy others,③
and sent them two by two ahead of
him[24]④ into every city and place,
where he was about to come. 10:2
Then he said to them, "The harvest
is indeed plentiful, but the laborers
are few.⑤ Pray therefore to the Lord

of the harvest, that he may send out laborers into his harvest. 10:3 Go your ways. Behold, I send you out as lambs among wolves.[6] 10:4 Carry no purse, nor wallet, nor sandals. Greet no one on the way. 10:5 Into whatever house you enter, first say, 'Peace be to this house.'[7] 10:6 If a son of peace is there, your peace will rest on him; but if not, it will return to you. 10:7 Remain in that same house, eating and drinking the things they give, for the laborer is worthy of his wages. Don't go from house to house. 10:8 Into whatever city you enter, and they receive you, eat the things that are set before you. 10:9 Heal the sick who are therein, and tell them, 'The Kingdom of God has come near to you.' 10:10 But into whatever city you enter, and they don't receive you, go out into its streets and say, 10:11 'Even the dust from your city that clings to us, we wipe off against you. Nevertheless know this, that the Kingdom of God has come near to you.' 10:12 I tell you, it will be more tolerable in that day for Sodom than for that city.

1. See Matthew 10:5-15, Mark 6:6b-13; Luke 9:1-5.

2. *Now after these things.* In the previous chapter we are told that Jesus sent out the twelve; this act represents the disciplining of the twelve spiritual faculties, upon which the whole character of man is founded. The Seventy stand in relation to the Twelve as body to the Spirit. The Spirit does not act directly upon the outer manifestation. It has its avenues of expression; these are the Twelve Disciples. But these also are not in direct touch with body, and it is part of the law of expression that they have other avenues through which the most outer physical is reached; these are the Seventy.

3. *the Lord also appointed seventy others.* The seventy represent the seven senses. We usually count but five senses: feeling, hearing, seeing, tasting, and smelling. There are, however, seven senses in all. The two additional ones are thinking and intuitive perception. The brain is the thinking organ, and the solar plexus the perceiving organ. In the individual consciousness the Lord represents the spiritual I AM as it sends disciplined thought forces into the exterior realms of the soul. The number seven represents completion on the natural plane of consciousness; the cipher added represents unlimited capacity.

4. *and sent them two by two ahead of him.* The ability to send and to receive thoughts, as the telegrapher sends and receives messages, is an undeveloped power of man. Through the solar plexus man can intuitively feel everything that he contacts. This intuitive feeling is soul perception, or intuition; in the unregenerate, it functions on the physical plane as instinct. These two powers must be disciplined and made to function through the Christ mind. Those who attempt to develop them without the sure guide of the super-mind will get mixed results, and will be held in darkness.

5. *The harvest is indeed plentiful, but the laborers are few.* The harvest is the fruition of the age-long experiences of the soul; the laborers are the forces of the soul that have been trained to serve. The laborers are few, because few have patiently borne the strain and the stress of life. They want the fruit of the harvest, but are not willing to work for it.

6. *I send you out as lambs among wolves.* This means that the general attitude should be one of nonresistance and unselfishness. We should not be ambitious for attainment of temporal possessions in mind, body, or affairs.

7. *first say, 'Peace be to this house.'* The work of the Spirit is to restore peace and harmony to the discordant thoughts and elements of mind and body. Hence, we should always send forth the thoughts of peace.

## Woes to Unrepentant Cities[1]

10:13 "Woe to you, Chorazin! Woe to you, Bethsaida![2] For if the mighty works had been done in Tyre and Sidon which were done in you, they would have repented long ago, sitting in sackcloth and ashes. 10:14 But it will be more tolerable for Tyre and Sidon in the judgment than for you. 10:15 You, Capernaum, who are exalted to heaven, will be brought down to Hades.[25] 10:16 Whoever listens to you listens to me, and whoever rejects you rejects me. Whoever rejects me rejects him who sent me."

1. Chorazin, Bethsaida and Capernaum are centres in the abdomen that are dominated by very physical thoughts. Their analysis is too intricate for this lesson. It is sufficient to give them a general treatment for conformity to the law.

2. *Chorazin, Bethsaida.* Bethsaida and Chorazin represent the state of mind that has a limited amount of Truth and believes that portion to be the full measure. This is the self-righteous phase of consciousness. The openly wanton and wicked cities of Tyre and Sidon stand a better chance in the day of judgment; that is, those who are wholly wrong will offer no excuse when their sins or shortcomings bring them before the law of adjustment; they will admit their errors and repent. But those who have a limited amount of Truth, which they hover over and declare to be the whole of Truth, are in danger of mental and spiritual crystallization. (MBD/Bethsaida)

## The Return of the Seventy[1]

10:17 The seventy returned with joy, saying, "Lord, even the demons[2] are subject to us in your name!"

10:18 He said to them, "I saw Satan[3] having fallen like lightning from heaven. 10:19 Behold, I give you authority to tread on serpents and scorpions, and over all the power of the enemy. Nothing will in any way hurt you. 10:20 Nevertheless, don't rejoice in this, that the spirits are subject to you, but rejoice that your names are written in heaven."[4]

1. See Matthew 11:25-27; Matthew 13:16-17.

2. *demons.* These are the discords of the body that yield to the word of Truth spoken in the consciousness of the Christ.

3. *Satan.* Satan is the "Devil," a state of mind formed by man's personal ideas of his power and completeness and sufficiency apart from God. Besides at times puffing up the personality, this satanic thought often turns about and, after having tempted one to do evil, discourages the soul by accusing it of sin. Summed up, it is the state of mind in man that believes in its own sufficiency independent of its creative Source. (MBD/Satan)

4. *but rejoice that your names are written in heaven.* Jesus is here saying something of great significance to those who have dedicated themselves to a life of spiritual Truth. He says that those who make a serious commitment to Spirit become known as INDIVIDUALS to the "heavenly hosts." Up to a certain level of consciousness, most persons are part of group consciousness (race consciousness.) They have individuality, but they do not really function entirely as individuals, so are not "known" (in a sense) as individuals on the higher levels of being.(*USRS Bible Interpretation*, Lesson 8)

## The Joy of Spiritualized Senses

10:21 In that same hour Jesus rejoiced in the Holy Spirit, and said, "I thank you, O Father, Lord of heaven and earth, that you have hidden these things[1] from the wise and understanding, and revealed them to little children. Yes, Father, for so it was well-pleasing in your sight."

10:22 Turning to the disciples, he said, "All things have been delivered to me by my Father.[2] No one knows who the Son is, except the Father, and who the Father is, except the Son, and he to whomever the Son desires to reveal him."

10:23 Turning to the disciples, he said privately, "Blessed are the eyes which see the things that you see,[3] 10:24 for I tell you that many prophets and kings desired to see the things which you see, and didn't see them, and to hear the things which you hear, and didn't hear them."

1. *I thank you ... that you have hidden these things.* Until enlightenment comes, the senses are lacking power to conceive or to impart the things of Spirit. But when the senses have been freed from the limitations of material thought and have proved their ability to fulfill the behests of the Christ mind, the higher mind rejoices and gives thanks.

2. *All things have been delivered to me by my Father.* It is through the spiritualized senses that we come into our true nature. Under the sure guidance of the Christ Spirit, every impulse of mind and body can be permeated with the true essence of Spirit (the Father can be revealed by the Son) and can be brought into full expression of good.

3. *Blessed are the eyes which see the things that you see.* Jesus represents the divine-human idea in expression. Anyone who is privileged to become aware of absolute good through the spiritualized senses, either that of seeing (perception) or hearing (receptivity), is blessed.

## The Parable of the Good Samaritan

10:25 Behold, a certain lawyer[1] stood up and tested him, saying, "Teacher, what shall I do to inherit eternal life?"[2]

10:26 He said to him, "What is written in the law? How do you read it?"

10:27 He answered, "You shall love the Lord your God with all your heart, with all your soul, with all your strength, and with all your mind;[26] and your neighbor as yourself."[27][3]

10:28 He said to him, "You have answered correctly. Do this, and you will live."

10:29 But he, desiring to justify himself, asked Jesus, "Who is my neighbor?"

10:30 Jesus answered, "A certain man was going down from Jerusalem to Jericho,[4] and he fell among robbers,[5] who both stripped him and beat him, and departed, leaving him half dead.[6] 10:31 By chance a certain priest was going down that way. When he saw him, he passed by on the other side. 10:32 In the same way a Levite[7] also, when he came to the place, and saw him, passed by on the other side. 10:33 But a certain Samaritan,[8] as he traveled, came where he was. When he saw him, he was moved with compassion,[9] 10:34 came to him, and bound up his wounds, pouring on oil and wine. He set him on his own animal, and brought him to an inn, and took care of him. 10:35 On the next day, when he departed, he took out two denarii, and gave them to the host, and said to him, 'Take care of him. Whatever you spend beyond that, I will repay you when I return.' 10:36 Now which of these three do you think seemed to be a neighbor to him who fell among the robbers?"

10:37 He said, "He who showed mercy on him."

Then Jesus said to him, "Go and do likewise."

1. *a certain lawyer.* The "certain lawyer" represents a phase of consciousness in which the law is understood and empha-

sized intellectually.

2. *what shall I do to inherit eternal life?* The intellect can reason and compare and arrive at conclusions, yet be dissatisfied, because such reasoning does not demonstrate continuity of life.

3. *and your neighbor as yourself.* See Matthew 22:34-40; Mark 12:28-34. The strong love to God is not the fulfillment of the law that leads up to eternal life; there is a manifest, or formed God, and with this also the initiate must make complete union; he must love his neighbor as himself. God-Life is in both the invisible and the visible, the formless and the formed, God and man. Our neighbor is the whole human family, and our duty is to aid them, and do unto them as we do unto ourselves.

4. *A certain man was going down from Jerusalem to Jericho.* This story shows what takes place in our consciousness, when we leave the spiritual realm (Jerusalem) for the material (Jericho). Such a change in our thinking and living exposes us to loss of peace and strips us of all the real values of life.

5. *and he fell among robbers.* He represents the body fallen under the power of uncontrolled appetites and desires.

6. *leaving him half dead.* Instead of being quick with vitalizing life, the abused body is left half dead and unconscious of the regenerative power of the Christ life. God is life, and wherever the pulse of life beats there God is. Man cannot give nor take life, but so long as he thinks he can slay the living, and so long as he proceeds to do so in man and beast, he will be at enmity with life.

7. *priest, Levite.* Stereotyped religious thoughts such as cause a person to keep the letter of the law without realizing its practical applicability or inner spiritual import.

8. *a certain Samaritan.* This is "Christ in you, the hope of glory." The idea of the Christ as an indwelling Spirit is not acceptable to the school of thought that conceives of the Christ as a magnified person only. "Jews have no dealings with Samaritans."

9. *he was moved with compassion.* Lay hold on eternal life, like the unconventional Samaritan. Have compassion upon the life in he body of every living creature, and especially in your own body. Declare life perpetually abiding in the organism. Bind up some of the wounds through which you are dissipating the life of your organism. Robbers are at work upon your body every day. They are the lusts of passion and appetite. Drive them off and bind up the wounds. Give life the sanctuary of your pure thought and pay the price through overcoming.

## Jesus Visits Martha and Mary

10:38 It happened as they went on
their way, he entered into a certain
village, and a certain woman named
Martha received him into her house.
10:39 She had a sister called Mary,(1)
who also sat at Jesus' feet,(2) and
heard his word. 10:40 But Martha was
distracted with much serving,(3) and
she came up to him, and said, "Lord,
don't you care that my sister left me
to serve alone? Ask her therefore to
help me."

10:41 Jesus answered her, "Martha,
Martha, you are anxious and troubled
about many things, 10:42 but one thing
is needed. Mary has chosen the good
part,(4) which will not be taken away
from her."

1. *Martha, Mary.* Martha and Mary represent the outer and the inner activities of love in the soul welcoming and entertaining the Christ principle and its manifestation, represented by Jesus Christ. Both of these states of consciousness are necessary.

2. *Mary, who also sat at Jesus' feet.* Mary's sitting at Jesus' feet represents the soul's learning the lessons of the law of life from the higher self.

3. *Martha was distracted with much serving.* Care should be taken not to allow an excess of activity in the outer or Martha consciousness, and thus disturb the inner love consciousness. It is in quiet receptivity that we draw our strength and power from Spirit.

4. *Mary has chosen the good part.* When the purpose to acquire ability to work under divine law is given first place in consciousness, the activity or service that fol-

lows becomes simple and easy.

---

Fillmore Study Bible annotations by: Rev. Mark Hicks

**World English Bible Footnotes:**

[24] v10:1. literally, "before his face"

[25] v10:15. Hades is the lower realm of the dead, or Hell.

[26] v10:27. Deuteronomy 6:5

[27] v10:27. Leviticus 19:18

# LUKE 11

## The Lord's Prayer 1

11:1 It happened, that when he
finished praying in a certain place,
one of his disciples said to him,
"Lord, teach us to pray, just as John
also taught his disciples."

11:2 He said to them, "When you
pray, say,

'Our Father in heaven,
may your name be kept holy. 2
May your Kingdom come. 3
May your will be done on
Earth, as it is in heaven.
11:3 Give us day by day our daily
bread. 4
11:4 Forgive us our sins,
for we ourselves also forgive
everyone who is
indebted to us.
Bring us not into temptation, 5
but deliver us from the evil
one.'" 6

1. See Matthew 6:9-13; 7.7-11.

2. *may your name be kept holy.* Are the words in which we express our prayers as important as the state of mind in which we pray? No. Faith and gratitude, acknowledgment of All-Power, and reverent expectation are more important than the words that we use, although these too are important and should be carefully chosen to express only Truth.

3. *May your Kingdom come.* How do we help to bring an answer to this prayer? The kingdom of Truth comes into manifestation in so far as we recognize and acknowledge it to be the foundation of the unmanifested world of spiritual Truth. We bring it into manifestation in our life and affairs by means of our faith.

4. *Give us day by day our daily bread.* How do we receive an adequate supply of our daily needs (our daily bread)? By realizing that all our needs are supplied from the universal storehouse, and by holding that the kingdom of Truth is now made manifest.

5. *Bring us not into temptation.* Does God ever bring us into temptation? No. We fall into temptation when we allow ourselves to lose consciousness of God within us as ever-present power, might, love, and wisdom. As long as we are conscious of God and trust actively in divine love, we cannot be tempted by evil.

6. *but deliver us from the evil one.* This phrase is not included in the ASV nor the NRSV. Footnote in NRSV says other ancient authorities add but rescue us from the evil one (or from evil)

## Perseverance in Prayer

11:5 He said to them, "Which of you, if you go to a friend at midnight, and tell him, 'Friend, lend me three loaves of bread, 11:6 for a friend of mine has come to me from a journey, and I have nothing to set before him,' 11:7 and he from within will answer and say, 'Don't bother me. The door is now shut, and my children are with me in bed. I can't get up and give it to you'? 11:8 I tell you, although he will not rise and give it to him because he is his friend, yet because of his persistence,[1] he will get up and give him as many as he needs.

11:9 "I tell you, keep asking, and it will be given you.[2] Keep seeking, and you will find. Keep knocking, and it will be opened to you. 11:10 For everyone who asks receives. He who seeks finds. To him who knocks it will be opened.

11:11 "Which of you fathers, if your son asks for bread, will give him a stone?[3] Or if he asks for a fish, he won't give him a snake instead of a fish, will he? 11:12 Or if he asks for an egg, he won't give him a scorpion, will he? 11:13 If you then, being evil, know how to give good gifts to your children, how much more will your heavenly Father give the Holy Spirit to those who ask him?"

1. *yet because of his persistence (importunity, ASV).* It is like the air — plenty of it right here all the time, but we must develop lung capacity. When you were first born, the first thing you did was to yell. The louder you yelled the better the doctor said your lung capacity was. That is the starter, and if you continue increasing the lung capacity and break right into the spirit side, you find you breathe deeply, not only of this atmosphere, but you will find you are being up lifted by a spiritual atmosphere, and that is what we are up against as individuals. Because through our innate freewill, we have developed a mental capacity something like the lung capacity and it is necessary in order to understand and receive largely from this great universal Mind, God-Mind, that we increase our minds, just as we increase our lungs. (*The Mysteries of The Four Gospels* Lesson Twelve, *Importunity*)

2. *keep asking, and it will be given you.* See Matthew 7:7. Why the necessity of the prayer or affirmation if it already is? In order that the creative law of the Word may be fulfilled. All things are in God as potentialities. It is man's share in the creative law to bring to manifestation the unmanifest.

3. *if your son asks for bread, will give him a stone?* Prayer is not supplication, nor begging, but a simple asking for, and affirmation of that which we know is waiting for us at the hands of our Father. The prayer which Jesus gave as a model is simplicity itself. There is none of that awe-inspiring "Oh, Thou!" which ministers affect in public prayer, but the ordinary informal request of a son to his father for things needed.

## Jesus and Beelzebul[1]

11:14 He was casting out a demon,[2] and it was mute. It happened, when the demon had gone out, the mute man spoke; and the multitudes marveled. 11:15 But some of them said, "He casts out demons by Beelzebul, the prince of the demons."[3] 11:16 Others, testing him, sought from him a sign from heaven. 11:17 But he, knowing their thoughts, said to them, "Every kingdom divided against itself is brought to desolation. A house divided against itself falls.[4] 11:18 If Satan also is divided against himself, how will his kingdom stand? For you say that I cast out demons by Beelzebul. 11:19 But if I cast out demons by Beelzebul, by whom do your children cast them out? Therefore will they be your judges. 11:20 But if I by the finger of God cast out demons, then the Kingdom of God has come to you.

11:21 "When the strong man, fully armed, guards his own dwelling, his goods are safe. 11:22 But when someone stronger attacks him and overcomes him, he takes from him his whole armor in which he trusted, and divides his spoils. 11:23 "He that is not with me is against me. He who doesn't gather with me scatters.

1. See Matthew 12:22-30, 43-45; Mark 3:22-27.

2. *He was casting out a demon.* There are many Truth students who have to learn to stop resisting the right use of denials. They say, "I do not need denials. I have affirmations." But, yet, they are not realizing the significance of the fact that in Jesus' ministry, so much of it consists in doing just what we say denial is supposed to do, cast out, overcome, get rid of. In our Bible text, He casts out a devil of dumbness and when examining His work through this same period, we find numerous instances of Him casting out devils, demons, getting rid of all kinds of afflictions and plagues which have invaded various individuals. (Ed Rabel, New Testament Lectures, *Jesus and Beelzebul*, pp.192-197)

3. *Beelzebul, the prince of the demons.* This adversary is self, the sense of separate identity, the sense of a separate, independent identity, which is a part of consciousness, and is the adversary to mankind; but he serves a purpose. Without him, we would not be given opportunities for choice. You would be, again, back in Eden, totally instinctive, totally obedient instinctively. By availing ourselves of freedom of choice, we are different from being totally obedient instinctively; therefore, our obedience has value. Then our obedience is creative rather than instinctive, as it was in Eden. (Rabel)

4. *A house divided against itself falls.* Jesus does not say a house divided shall fall, only that a house divided against itself will fall. This is a significant detail. In the Bible, you remember a house means an individual consciousness. You and I often have to divide a house or partition our consciousness for useful and constructive purposes, and then this causes greater growth and wider diversity of interest. But Jesus warned only of a house divided against itself. Now this consists of thinking or feeling or acting in ways which are actually working against our own consciousness of good, and we often mistake the end as being a total sanction for whatever means are used; but this is not correct. Only right means can bring right ends. (Rabel)

## The Return of the Unclean Spirit[1]

11:24 The unclean spirit, when he has gone out of the man, passes through dry places,[2] seeking rest, and finding none, he says, 'I will turn back to my house from which I came out.' 11:25 When he returns, he finds it swept and put in order. 11:26 Then he goes, and takes seven other spirits more evil than himself, and they enter in and dwell there. The last state of that man becomes worse than the first."[3]

1. See Matthew 12:43-45. [A continuation of the house which has been put in order by Beelzebul. It is swept and put in order, but dry.]

2. *dry places.* Metaphysically, a dry, barren, fruitless state of thought, signifying a belief in lack, lack of vitality, of substance, of strength, of power, and of increase of good (dried, parched, barren, lifeless, stubble, brush) (MBD/Phrygia).

3. *The last state of that man becomes worse than the first.* [The effect of using denials without hearing the Word of God and keeping it. The lesson continues with 11:27-28 below.] From the first part of this scripture we know that a house divided against itself will fall. We know that in unity alone is strength. But from Jesus' teaching in this particular Scripture, we glean it is far better to redeem, to transmute error rather than to pass it out. Lest if it return unto us, if we cast it out in an unpurified state. (Meditation by Cora Fillmore recorded in *The Mysteries of The Four Gospels* Lesson Ten, *Unity Interpretation of The Word*)

## True Blessedness

11:27 It came to pass, as he said
these things, a certain woman out
of the multitude lifted up her voice,
and said to him, "Blessed is the womb
that bore you,[1] and the breasts
which nursed you!"

11:28 But he said, "On the contrary,
blessed are those who hear the word
of God,[2] and keep it."

1. *Blessed is the womb that bore you.* The woman symbolizes the feminine thought on the mortal plane of consciousness. Perhaps with her face turned toward the light, she had been listening to Jesus' teachings and was filled with inspiration and she spoke from the the sense of natural parentage. But Jesus called her attention to the Spiritual parentage. The Blessed Mary was only the vehicle through whom Jesus was clothed with a material body, but his spiritual body ... how much greater is the Word of God that really creates all things!(Meditation by Cora Fillmore recorded in *The Mysteries of The Four Gospels* Lesson Ten, *Unity Interpretation of The Word*)

2. *On the contrary, blessed are those who hear the word of God.* The "Word of God" becomes confused with the Bible, because we are persistently taught by certain interpreters of Jesus Christ, that this written word, that is the Bible, is the word of God. Jesus didn't teach that. He taught that the WORD OF GOD was something superior, far superior, far greater in its grip (scope or grasp!!) and its power than the written word. But the majority of people take this to mean that because they keep the word of God and follow it and hear it and use the Scriptures as their guide, they are the ones who are spiritually minded. And in a measure this is true. But we want to call your attention to the fact that there is a creative principle right here present at all times and that it is possible for man to quicken that spiritual principle in himself and become the the LIVING, ACTIVE WORD OF GOD.

## The Sign of Jonah[1]

11:29 When the multitudes were
gathering together to him, he began
to say, "This is an evil[2] generation.[3]
It seeks after a sign. No sign will be
given to it but the sign of Jonah,
the prophet. 11:30 For even as Jonah
became a sign to the Ninevites, so
will also the Son of Man be to this
generation. 11:31 The Queen of the
South will rise up in the judgment
with the men of this generation, and
will condemn them: for she came
from the ends of the earth to hear
the wisdom of Solomon; and behold,
one greater than Solomon is here.
11:32 The men of Nineveh[4] will stand
up in the judgment with this
generation, and will condemn it: for
they repented at the preaching of
Jonah, and behold, one greater than
Jonah is here.

1. See Matthew 12.38-42; Mark 8.12.

2. *evil.* That which is not of God; unreality; error thought; a product of the fallen human consciousness; negation. (RW/evil)

3. *generation.* Metaphysically, procreation. The law of generation is undoubtedly the mystery of mysteries in human consciousness. Men have probed, with more or less success, all the secrets of nature, but of the origin of life they know comparatively nothing. It is only when the inquiring mind transcends the human and rises into the spiritual realm that light comes. (RW/generation)

4. *Queen of the South, men of Nineveh.* [See Matthew 12:41-42. Spiritually awakened states of consciousness which seek more than a sign.]

## The Light of the Body[1]

11:33 "No one, when he has lit a lamp, puts it in a cellar or under a basket, but on a stand, that those who come in may see the light. 11:34 The lamp of the body is the eye. Therefore when your eye is good, your whole body is also full of light; but when it is evil, your body also is full of darkness.[2] 11:35 Therefore see whether the light that is in you isn't darkness. 11:36 If therefore your whole body is full of light, having no part dark, it will be wholly full of light, as when the lamp with its bright shining gives you light."

1. See Matthew 5:15; 6.22-23; Mark 4:21.

2. *when [your eye] is evil, your body also is full of darkness.* It matters a great deal what one watches, or gives attention to. If one persists in recognizing that which appears to be evil and error, one cannot obtain abiding life and good. We are transformed into the Christ likeness by beholding Him, not by taking cognizance of the lesser self with its seeming limitations. "If thine eye be evil, thy whole body shall be full of darkness. If therefore the light that is in thee be darkness, how great is the darkness!" (Matthew 6:23). (MBD/Er)

## Jesus Denounces Pharisees and Lawyers[1]

11:37 Now as he spoke, a certain Pharisee asked him to dine with him. He went in, and sat at the table. 11:38 When the Pharisee saw it, he marveled that he had not first washed himself before dinner. 11:39 The Lord said to him, "Now you Pharisees cleanse the outside of the cup and of the platter, but your inward part is full of extortion and wickedness. 11:40 You foolish ones, didn't he who made the outside make the inside also? 11:41 But give for gifts to the needy those things which are within, and behold, all things will be clean to you. 11:42 But woe to you Pharisees![2] For you tithe mint and rue and every herb, but you bypass justice and the love of God. You ought to have done these, and not to have left the other undone. 11:43 Woe to you Pharisees! For you love the best seats in the synagogues, and the greetings in the marketplaces. 11:44 Woe to you, scribes and Pharisees, hypocrites! For you are like hidden graves, and the men who walk over them don't know it."[3]

11:45 One of the lawyers answered him, "Teacher, in saying this you insult us also."

11:46 He said, "Woe to you lawyers also![4] For you load men with burdens that are difficult to carry, and you yourselves won't even lift one finger to help carry those burdens. 11:47 Woe to you! For you build the tombs of the prophets, and your fathers killed them. 11:48 So you testify and consent to the works of your fathers. For they killed them, and you build their tombs. 11:49 Therefore also the wisdom of God said, 'I will send to them prophets and apostles; and some of them they will kill and persecute, 11:50 that the blood of all the prophets, which was shed from the foundation of the world, may be required of this generation; 11:51 from the blood of Abel to the blood of Zachariah, who perished between the altar and the sanctuary.' Yes, I tell you, it will be required of this generation. 11:52 Woe to you lawyers! For you took away the key of knowledge.[5] You didn't enter in yourselves, and those who were entering in, you hindered."

11:53 As he said these things to

them, the scribes and the Pharisees began to be terribly angry, and to draw many things out of him; 11:54 lying in wait for him, and seeking to catch him in something he might say, that they might accuse him.

1. See Matthew 23.1-36; Mark 12.38-40.

2. *woe to you Pharisees!* The Scriptural name of those who follow the letter of religion instead of the spirit. Those who interpret the Scriptures literally, those who personalize God, Christ, the Devil, and who localize heaven and hell, are the Pharisees of the present time. Spiritual things must be spiritually discerned and interpreted. It is the Pharisee in ourselves that causes us to love the forms and ceremonies of religion. It is the Pharisee in us that refuses to go deep into the consciousness and cleanse the inner man. It is the Pharisee in us that is ambitious for temporal honors, and that loves to be saluted with high-sounding titles. It is the Pharisaical thoughts that exalt and sustain personality.

3. *you are like hidden graves, and the men who walk over them don't know it.* the Pharisaic state of mind is filled with lifeless, outworn beliefs of which the person harboring them may not be conscious and which he may not express at all in words. Nevertheless these beliefs remain in the subconsciousness of the Pharisaic person and retard his spiritual progress.

4. *Woe to you lawyers also!* They represent the perceptive faculties that have a grasp of the law of life but that lack the imagination, good will, and generosity to extend their understanding to the whole man. He who knows what is good for him but who fails to pursue this good is burdened with a heavier load than he who does not know what is for his own good.

5. *For you took away the key of knowledge.* Those who do not admit that the mind of man is free always to delve beneath the surface and bring up new truth, interpreting it in terms intelligible to itself. Those who regard vision and the understanding of spiritual truth as belonging to a past age and who think these cannot be a present possession. All who think that the revelation of Truth is a closed chapter are tomb builders.

Fillmore Study Bible annotations by: Rev. Mark Hicks

# Luke 12

## A Warning against Hypocrisy (1)

12:1 Meanwhile, when a multitude of many thousands had gathered together, so much so that they trampled on each other, he began to tell his disciples first of all, "Beware of the yeast of the Pharisees, which is hypocrisy. 12:2 But there is nothing covered up, that will not be revealed, nor hidden, that will not be known. (2) 12:3 Therefore whatever you have said in the darkness will be heard in the light. What you have spoken in the ear in the inner chambers will be proclaimed on the housetops.

1. See Matthew 16:6, Mark 8:15

2. *But there is nothing covered up, that will not be revealed, nor hidden, that will not be known.* The one spiritual creative Mind is everywhere present and that that Mind knows. It has the Source of knowledge, and that Source is called Light, and that Light is interpenetrative, and we are told by those who study Light, that it is quickened within man, that our minds are effervescing currents of light; rays of light are always going forth... There is a habit in the human consciousness of concealing and that leads to the dropping of a curtain. When you think about concealing, you separate yourself from this light and pretty soon your eyes grow dim. This brings us

down to the practical teaching of Jesus Christ ... you can't hide. Murder will out. What you are thinking will come forth in language, affairs, face, form, everything, and especially in the eyes. (Meditation by Charles Fillmore recorded in *The Mysteries of The Four Gospels* Lesson Ten, *We Cannot Conceal Anything From Spirit*)

## Exhortation to Fearless Confession❶

12:4 "I tell you, my friends, don't be afraid of those who kill the body, and after that have no more that they can do.
12:5 But I will warn you whom you should fear. Fear him, who after he has killed, has power to cast into Gehenna.[28]❷ Yes, I tell you, fear him.

12:6 "Aren't five sparrows sold for two assaria coins[29]? Not one of them is forgotten by God.
12:7 But the very hairs of your head are all numbered.❸ Therefore don't be afraid. You are of more value than many sparrows.

12:8 "I tell you, everyone who confesses me before men, him will the Son of Man also confess before the angels of God;
12:9 but he who denies me in the presence of men will be denied in the presence of the angels of God.
12:10 Everyone who speaks a word against the Son of Man will be forgiven, but those who blaspheme against the Holy Spirit will not be forgiven.❹
12:11 When they bring you before the synagogues, the rulers, and the authorities, don't be anxious how or what you will answer, or what you will say;
12:12 for the Holy Spirit will teach you in that same hour what you must say."

1. See Matthew 10:26-33
2. *Gehenna.* Metaphysically, a region of lamentations; place of purifying fires; place of defilement. One does not have to die in order to go to hell, any more than one has to die to go to heaven. Both are states of mind, and conditions, which people experience as a direct outworking of their thoughts, beliefs, words, and acts. If one's mental processes are out of harmony with the law of man's being, they result in trouble and sorrow; mental as well as bodily anguish overtakes one, and this is hell. (MBD/hell)
3. *the very hairs of your head are all numbered.* You are, therefore, numbered. To be numbered is to be especially designated as having place, relation, importance, and necessity. If you are numbered, you are one of the factors that enter into the great problem of life. To number and to name mean one and the same thing. If you are numbered, you are therefore recorded in the annals of heaven, and the Omnipresent Father knows you by a name peculiar to Spirit. (Charles Fillmore sermon, *In The Name of the Lord*, November 1911)
4. *those who blaspheme against the Holy Spirit will not be forgiven.* The Holy Spirit is always willing to give itself to us, always. God's good is always more than willing to give its action to us. Always more willing than we are. But, since we have been given the divine idea of freedom, we also are free if we so choose to reject our highest good. To disbelieve in it, to mock it, to lie about it. That's called sin and blasphemy against our own highest good. If we are doing that, if we are rejecting our own highest good, Holy Spirit, then our highest good can't give itself to us. If we won't have it, then it can't give itself to us. (Ed Rabel, *Gospel Mysteries*, Why Shall blasphemy Against the Holy Spirit Not Be Forgiven?)

## The Parable of the Rich Fool

12:13 One of the multitude said to him, "Teacher, tell my brother to divide the inheritance with me."

12:14 But he said to him, "Man, who made me a judge or an arbitrator

over you?" 12:15 He said to them,
"Beware! Keep yourselves from
covetousness, for a man's life doesn't
consist of the abundance of the
things which he possesses."[1]

12:16 He spoke a parable to them,
saying, "The ground of a certain rich
man brought forth abundantly.[2] 12:17
He reasoned within himself, saying,
'What will I do, because I don't have
room to store my crops?' 12:18 He said,
'This is what I will do. I will pull down
my barns, and build bigger ones, and
there I will store all my grain and
my goods. 12:19 I will tell my soul,
"Soul, you have many goods laid up
for many years. Take your ease, eat,
drink, be merry."'

12:20 "But God said to him, 'You
foolish one, tonight your soul is
required of you.[3] The things which
you have prepared--whose will they
be?' 12:21 So is he who lays up treasure
for himself, and is not rich toward
God."[4]

1. *a man's life doesn't consist of the abundance of the things which he possesses.* In what does a man's life consist? The abundance of the things of God that man possesses makes his life a rich and satisfying experience. An abundance of the things of the world may impoverish instead of enriching him, if he sets his heart upon them and forgets to seek the true riches.

2. *The ground of a certain rich man brought forth abundantly.* The parable of the rich man whose ground brought forth plentifully represents what? The plentiful harvest of the rich man illustrates the principle of increase that is everywhere manifest as a result of concentration or devoted attention. The pulling down of the barns in order to build greater ones represents the greed of the selfish, self-centered soul that gives no thought to sharing, although sharing is the divine purpose of increase.

3. *tonight your soul is required of you.* In what sense is the rich man's soul required of him? He who sets his heart on material riches and lives to enjoy them to the exclusion of spiritual things forfeits his soul to materiality. Setting the heart on a thing brings into play the active vitality of the soul qualities.

4. *and is not rich toward God.* How do we become "rich toward God"? We become rich toward God through meditating upon God and communing with Him in daily prayer, and through setting our heart on the things that enlist the deepest interest of our mind and soul.

## Do Not Worry[1]

12:22 He said to his disciples,
"Therefore I tell you, don't be anxious
for your life,[2] what you will eat,
nor yet for your body, what you will
wear. 12:23 Life is more than food,
and the body is more than clothing.
12:24 Consider the ravens:[3] they don't
sow, they don't reap, they have no
warehouse or barn, and God feeds
them. How much more valuable are
you than birds![4] 12:25 Which of you by
being anxious can add a cubit to his
height? 12:26 If then you aren't able to
do even the least things, why are you
anxious about the rest? 12:27 Consider
the lilies,[5] how they grow. They
don't toil, neither do they spin; yet I
tell you, even Solomon in all his glory
was not arrayed like one of these.
12:28 But if this is how God clothes the
grass in the field, which today exists,
and tomorrow is cast into the oven,
how much more will he clothe you,[6]
O you of little faith? 12:29 Don't seek
what you will eat or what you will
drink; neither be anxious. 12:30 For the
nations of the world seek after all of
these things, but your Father knows
that you need these things. 12:31 But
seek God's Kingdom, and all these
things will be added to you.[7] 12:32
Don't be afraid, little flock, for it is
your Father's good pleasure to give
you the Kingdom.[8] 12:33 Sell that

which you have, and give gifts to the
needy. Make for yourselves purses
which don't grow old, a treasure in
the heavens that doesn't fail, where
no thief approaches, neither moth
destroys. 12:34 For where your
treasure is, there will your heart be
also.

1. See Matthew 6:25-34, 19-21.

2. *don't be anxious for your life, what you will eat, nor yet for your body, what you will wear.* We should have faith that all our needs will be met, when we make union in consciousness with the Spirit of infinite wisdom, love, and power.

3. *Consider the ravens.* Birds are considered to be creatures of instinct, which enables them to find the climate and food suited to them.

4. *How much more valuable are you than birds!* Man's instinct is less clearly defined than that of the birds, because he relies chiefly on reason, intuition, or faith in a higher power to put him in touch with limitless substance and so provide for his needs. Faith, reason, and intuition can be made instinctive in man as man consciously develops these powers. Man becomes a co-worker with God by readying himself through the exercise of faith, keeping his mind clear and untroubled, his feeling confident and serene, man works with God.

5. *Consider the lilies.* The members of the vegetable kingdom develop true to form because, being without consciousness, they offer no obstruction to their perfect unfolding. Man's development in the kingdom of the heavens should be much surer, since he can seek it consciously through faith.

6. *how much more will he clothe you.* The body is more than externalized thought. It is the instrument by means of which man proves his thought true or untrue and demonstrates his understanding of the principles of right living.

7. *But seek God's Kingdom, and all these things will be added to you.* By lending himself as a willing channel to Spirit, man adapts himself to such shifts and changes as he does not alter to suit himself. The nature of his equipment for mastering his environment, both mental and physical, frees him from handicaps and enables him to enter into eternal life consciousness, thus solving the question of survival.

8. *it is your Father's good pleasure to give you the Kingdom.* Problems are matters or situations that are difficult if not impossible of solution by the personal man. Through faith man solves his problems easily and to all appearance naturally.

## Watchful Slaves[1]

12:35 "Let your waist be girded and
your lamps burning. 12:36 Be like men
watching for their lord,[2] when he
returns from the marriage feast;
that, when he comes and knocks,
they may immediately open to him.
12:37 Blessed are those servants, whom
the lord will find watching when he
comes. Most certainly I tell you, that
he will dress himself, and make them
recline, and will come and serve
them.[3] 12:38 They will be blessed if he
comes in the second or third watch,
and finds them so. 12:39 But know this,
that if the master of the house had
known in what hour the thief was
coming, he would have watched, and
not allowed his house to be broken
into. 12:40 Therefore be ready also, for
the Son of Man is coming in an hour
that you don't expect him."

1. See Matthew 24:42-44; Mark 13.33-37.

2. *their lord.* The natural man's "lord" is the dominant desire or impulse that he serves, whether consciously or unconsciously. Christ becomes our Lord when we develop the Christ Spirit in our daily life and affairs, and express that Spirit in preference to any other.

3. *and will come and serve them.* This takes place when man becomes established in the spiritual consciousness.

## The Faithful or the Unfaithful Slave[1]

12:41 Peter said to him, "Lord, are you telling this parable to us, or to everybody?"

12:42 The Lord said, "Who then is the faithful and wise steward,[2] whom his lord will set over his household, to give them their portion of food at the right times? 12:43 Blessed is that servant whom his lord will find doing so when he comes. 12:44 Truly I tell you, that he will set him over all that he has. 12:45 But if that servant says in his heart, 'My lord delays his coming,' and begins to beat the menservants and the maidservants, and to eat and drink, and to be drunken, 12:46 then the lord of that servant will come in a day when he isn't expecting him, and in an hour that he doesn't know, and will cut him in two, and place his portion with the unfaithful. 12:47 That servant, who knew his lord's will, and didn't prepare, nor do what he wanted, will be beaten with many stripes,[3] 12:48 but he who didn't know, and did things worthy of stripes, will be beaten with few stripes. To whoever much is given, of him will much be required; and to whom much was entrusted, of him more will be asked.[4]

1. See Matthew 24:52-51; Mark 13:33-37. Faithfulness, watchfulness, readiness, are the keynotes of this lesson. The idea that Christ would come again at some future time was met by this series of parables and illustrations of the reward that always comes to those who are alert in taking advantage of the Now Opportunity.

2. *faithful and wise steward.* The steward represents the soul of man, whose function it is to watch over, guard, and protect the body, and nourish it with the word of Truth. Watching means preparation to receive the Christ idea.

3. *will be beaten with many stripes.* The natural or personal consciousness leads man to misuse his soul powers, and as a consequence the body is neglected or abused.

4. *to whom much was entrusted, of him more will be asked.* Jesus is not doing negative fortune telling, negative crystal ball gazing. He is describing factors that go into patterns of evolutions, that are, in a sense, inescapable; and especially this is typical of what we call in Unity, the final time period of a dispensation, of a world dispensation. Another term that can be used for that is an evolutionary life wave or a dispensation in more religious terms. When the final stages of these are entered into, there is always what is called tumult; a kind of chaos and confusion and things of a rather drastic and spectacular nature occur with more frequency and affect more and more people. Some of this, to those without understanding, and to those who still have the habit of negative reaction, to everything strange or unexpected, these can be very trying times; and people can be made very unhappy and fearful unnecessarily if they do not know the Truth, if they do not understand the principles behind all evolutionary activity. So Jesus is not trying to alarm us but only trying to alert us, and if we are alert with an understanding of His teachings, with at least some background of experience in practicing His teachings, then these vivid occurrences, which are typical of the end periods of dispensations, will not harm us. (Ed Rabel, New Testament Lectures, *Watch and Pray*, pp.280-283)

## Jesus the Cause of Division[1]

12:49 "I came to throw fire on the earth. I wish it were already kindled. 12:50 But I have a baptism to be baptized with,[2] and how distressed I am until it is accomplished! 12:51 Do you think that I have come to give peace in the earth? I tell you, no, but rather division. 12:52 For from now on, there will be five in one house divided,[3] three against two, and two against three. 12:53 They will be divided, father against son, and son

against father; mother against
daughter, and daughter against her
mother; mother-in-law against her
daughter-in-law, and daughter-in-
law against her mother-in-law."[4]

1. See Matthew 10:34-36; 16.2-3; 5.25-26; Mark 10:38. [The Fillmores never commented on this passage nor the passages that follow. But the commentary of Cora Fillmore in *The Mysteries of the Four Gospels* offers an insightful way that Spiritual Understanding lifts up life's burdens.]

2. *But I have a baptism to be baptized with.* [Jesus refers to] a state of consciousness into which He was developing. The cup that He drank represented the agony of soul and body in the transition, from the material plane to the spiritual plane of consciousness. The baptism with which He was baptized was the saturation of His mind and body with the diving life. (MBI/ Mark 10)

3. *from now on, there will be five in one house divided.* The Christ man doesn't enter into the human relationships. The Christ man has nothing to do with that. However, the language is of course in this text oriental. And we all know that the oriental language always uses very, very strong phrases. Today we don't find that we have to deny our human relationship, do we? The more we unfold the Christ in ourselves, the more the Christ is unfolded in families, among friends, the closer we will all draw together. (*The Mysteries of The Four Gospels* Lesson Two, *Not Peace But a Sword*)

4. *and daughter-in-law against her mother-in-law.* At the same time, we know that human relationship is temporary. Why? Because we have all lived thousands of lives upon the earth and no doubt we have had many different parents. There is only ONE ENDURING RELATIONSHIP and that is among those who are related spiritually. "Call no man on earth your father. One is your father, even God," are Jesus' own words. This grand truth, of course, breaks up the idea of human relationships, because while the human life, while the human sense of life is the steppingstones to the spiritual, yet when the human becomes spiritually quickened he enters under spiritual law. (Meditation by Cora Fillmore)

## Interpreting the Time[1]

12:54 He said to the multitudes also,
"When you see a cloud rising from the
west, immediately you say, 'A shower
is coming,' and so it happens. 12:55
When a south wind blows, you say,
'There will be a scorching heat,' and
it happens. 12:56 You hypocrites! You
know how to interpret the
appearance of the earth and the sky,
but how is it that you don't interpret
this time?[2]

1. See Matthew 16:3

2. *how is it that you don't interpret this time?* You know habit itself is stronger than nature. Let us get in the habit of making ourselves necessary to God. We may do thousands of things in the Silence. We may pour out healing blessings upon this one and that one—someone in need, no one else paying any attention to them, but the Lord always rewards. Let us remember that. If we are trying to unfold real spiritual qualities, let us do these things always for those [who] no one else is thinking about. We would reap a bountiful harvest. (Meditation by Cora Fillmore)

## Settling with Your Opponent[1]

12:57 Why don't you judge for
yourselves what is right?[2] 12:58 For
when you are going with your
adversary before the magistrate, try
diligently on the way to be released[3]
from him, lest perhaps he drag you to
the judge, and the judge deliver you
to the officer, and the officer throw
you into prison. 12:59 I tell you, you
will by no means get out of there,
until you have paid the very last
penny.[30]"

1. See Matthew 5:25-26.

2. *Why don't you judge for yourselves what is right?* It is the grand object of the race on the path of spiritual unfoldment. Strong and beautiful soul-faculties, these are all trying to unfold. Sometimes we get a down view. We attempt more than we can accomplish actually. However, occasionally we are thrown down in the life, we believe still this is the path of wonderful growth. (Meditation by Cora Fillmore)

3. *try diligently on the way to be released.* We are entering into a new kingdom here and now. Right now is our time for silent meditation. One presence, one power, one intelligence. The silent, scientific prayer is the very tool of heaven itself. (Meditation by Cora Fillmore)

---

Fillmore Study Bible annotations by: Rev. Mark Hicks

**World English Bible Footnotes:**

[28] v12:5. or, Hell

[29] v12:6. An assarion was a small copper coin worth about an hour's wages for an agricultural laborer.

[30] v12:59. literally, lepton. A lepton is a very small brass Jewish coin worth half a Roman quadrans each, which is worth a quarter of the copper assarion. Lepta are worth less than 1% of an agricultural worker's daily wages.

# Luke 13

## Repent or Perish

13:1 Now there were some present at the same time who told him about the Galileans,[1] whose blood Pilate[2] had mixed with their sacrifices. 13:2 Jesus answered them, "Do you think that these Galileans were worse sinners than all the other Galileans, because they suffered such things?[3] 13:3 I tell you, no, but, unless you repent, you will all perish in the same way.[4] 13:4 Or those eighteen, on whom the tower in Siloam fell, and killed them; do you think that they were worse offenders than all the men who dwell in Jerusalem? 13:5 I tell you, no, but, unless you repent, you will all perish in the same way."[5]

1. *Galileans.* Metaphysically, active life thoughts, illumined thoughts in the activity of life consciousness that exalt the Christ (MBD/Galileans)

2. *Pilate.* Metaphysically, the ruling principle of the sense plane, the carnal will. (MBD/Pilate) The carnal will destroys the active life thoughts, even while they are engaged in the refining process (sacrifice) by which matter is made to ascend to mind and mind to Spirit.

3. *Do you think that these Galileans were ... sinners ... because they suffered such things?* The error is inherent in the carnal will rather than in the thoughts of man, but until these thoughts are turned into constructive channels, they remain subject to the will of the lower or sense self.

4. *unless you repent, you will all perish in the same way.* Jesus perceives they are concerned about two recent tragedies in which a number of so called, apparently innocent victims were killed. Those who

are somewhat indoctrinated in the laws of consciousness would, then, start to surmise that something was in their consciousness that drew them to that place when that event occurred. What was it bad or wrong in their consciousness that caused them to be part of that? Jesus could see the futility of that kind of response or attitude. It is error. It is pernicious, so rather than "why those persons and not other persons", the real question should be, "why any person? Do these things have to happen?" So, Jesus says, "Repent". Change your way of thinking about why tragedies, accidents, happen, and why, this, that, when, those are involved. (Ed Rabel, New Testament Lectures, *Repent or Perish*, p.199)

5. *unless you repent, you will all perish in the same way*. [No condition and no tragedy—from the common cold to unspeakable abomination—is outside of the realm of God to be transformed into greater good—when we align with God and apply our Christ-like nature to the condition. We do not cause all conditions and we can not prevent all tragedies. But we have the capacity to respond to imperfect conditions and tragedies in transformative, divine ways—ways that transform them into all good. That is our claim. *Why Does God Allow Evil and Suffering?*]

## The Parable of the Barren Fig Tree[1]

13:6 He spoke this parable. "A
certain man had a fig tree[2] planted
in his vineyard, and he came seeking
fruit on it, and found none. 13:7 He
said to the vine dresser,[3] 'Behold,
these three years I have come
looking for fruit on this fig tree, and
found none. Cut it down. Why does
it waste the soil?' 13:8 He answered,
'Lord, leave it alone this year also,
until I dig around it, and fertilize it.
13:9 If it bears fruit, fine; but if not,
after that, you can cut it down.'"

1. See Matthew 7:15-20

2. *fig tree* What is symbolized by the barren fig tree? Thought activity that is not based on Truth and that is therefore unfruitful. (MBI/Matthew 7)

3. *vine dresser*. Who is the vinedresser? The Christ, whose mission is to save and redeem even those whom men deem unworthy. No matter how unproductive our life has been, the Father is infinitely patient with us, and through the Christ Mind in us gives us a new and enriched opportunity to fulfill our divine purpose.

## Jesus Heals a Crippled Woman

13:10 He was teaching in one of the
synagogues on the Sabbath day. 13:11
Behold, there was a woman who had
a spirit of infirmity eighteen years,[1]
and she was bent over, and could
in no way straighten herself up. 13:12
When Jesus saw her, he called her,
and said to her, "Woman, you are
freed from your infirmity." 13:13 He
laid his hands on her, and
immediately she stood up straight,
and glorified God.

13:14 The ruler of the synagogue,
being indignant because Jesus had
healed on the Sabbath, said to the
multitude, "There are six days in
which men ought to work. Therefore
come on those days and be healed,
and not on the Sabbath day!"

13:15 Therefore the Lord answered
him, "You hypocrites! Doesn't each
one of you free his ox or his donkey
from the stall on the Sabbath, and
lead him away to water? 13:16 Ought
not this woman, being a daughter of
Abraham, whom Satan had bound
eighteen long years, be freed from
this bondage on the Sabbath day?"

13:17 As he said these things, all his
adversaries were disappointed, and
all the multitude rejoiced for all the
glorious things that were done by
him.

1. *a woman who had a spirit of infirmity eighteen years.* The main point of this lesson is that we should be more active in our demonstrations and expect results. This woman who was healed after eighteen years of subjection to some idea, was immediately healed, she was made straight and glorified God. The followers of Jesus Christ in this day are not living up to their privileges. They are not realizing the power of their healing words. Jesus laid down the law that the healing word that you speak in the earth, that is from the material plane, would react upon the heavens, or the mental plane. The fact is, this so-called earthly or formed state is as fully subject to the power of the word as the free mental state. The word we speak, and when we speak that word, something occurs. We may not observe it, but in this lesson today, this woman was immediately straightened up. What was it that Jesus understood in the power of the word that accomplished this that had taken this woman eighteen years to fix in her mind and body the idea? It was probably family, or other burdens of some kind, but whatever it was, it was fixed in the mind and gradually translated into the body. (*The Mysteries of The Four Gospels* Lesson Two, *Healing the Woman Bowed Down Eighteen Years*)

## The Parable of the Mustard Seed[1]

13:18 He said, "What is the Kingdom
of God like?[2] To what shall I
compare it?[3] 13:19 It is like a grain of
mustard seed,[4] which a man took,
and put in his own garden. It grew,
and became a large tree, and the
birds of the sky lodged in its
branches."

1. See Matthew 13:31-33; Mark 4:30-32.

2. *What is the Kingdom of God like?* It is the inner consciousness of the Presence of God within us. The kingdom was fully established in Jesus. Biblical Favorites by Jim Lewis—The Mustard Seed

3. *To what shall I compare it?* The externalization of the Kingdom of God is one aspect of our purpose on earth. In order to do this, we must learn how to grow in dominion and mastery of existence. We cannot demonstrate the Kingdom of God if we have not first learned to be useful and dependable in the down-to-earth business of ordinary existence. Mr. Fillmore correctly states that the externalizing of God' s Kingdom is being accomplished "little by little." This is true, and we must learn to reconcile ourselves to this fact. Otherwise we become impatient and seek shortcuts and artificial methods. (Ed Rabel, Unity Metaphysics: *05 The Kingdom of God*—5D Externalization of The Kingdom Of God)

4. *It is like a grain of mustard seed.* The mustard seed comparison shows the capacity of the apparently small thought of Truth to develop in consciousness until it becomes the abiding place of a higher range of thoughts (birds of the air). (RW/mustard-seed)

## The Parable of the Yeast

13:20 Again he said, "To what shall
I compare the Kingdom of God?[1] 13:21
It is like yeast, which a woman took
and hid in three measures[31] of
flour, until it was all leavened."

1. *To what shall I compare the Kingdom of God?* It is a great mystery how these comparisons of heaven ever came to be construed as referring in any way to a locality in the skies. What relation to a city with streets of gold has a mustard seed, planted in the earth and springing forth into a tree, or a little cake of yeast fermenting a baking of bread? Heaven is a condition, to be brought about in the affairs of men, here on the earth. It is to grow from small beginnings, like the mustard seed or the yeast cake. His disciples were sent forth to sow the seed in a definite way, by carrying into the midst of men the signs that evidence the power of Spirit, through which the kingdom of heaven is to be established, right here on this planet. There is no basis for any other view. All the theories about a place called "heaven," are founded on John's symbolical description of New Jerusalem, which was a pic-

ture, in the imagination, of the fulfillment on earth of the very movement which Jesus inaugurated and which He described as having such small beginnings. This city, which John saw, is among men. Now that men are opening up the hidden resources of nature, in earth and in air, possibilities of achievement are dawning on them, and they see that human endeavor will yet make the earth a paradise. (Charles Fillmore, *The Kingdom of Heaven Is At Hand*)

## The Narrow Door[1]

13:22 He went on his way through cities and villages, teaching, and traveling on to Jerusalem. 13:23 One said to him, "Lord, are they few who are saved?"

He said to them, 13:24 "Strive to enter in by the narrow door,[2] for many, I tell you, will seek to enter in, and will not be able. 13:25 When once the master of the house has risen up, and has shut the door, and you begin to stand outside, and to knock at the door, saying, 'Lord, Lord, open to us!' then he will answer and tell you, 'I don't know you or where you come from.' 13:26 Then you will begin to say, 'We ate and drank in your presence, and you taught in our streets.'[3] 13:27 He will say, 'I tell you, I don't know where you come from. Depart from me, all you workers of iniquity.' 13:28 There will be weeping and gnashing of teeth, when you see Abraham, Isaac, Jacob, and all the prophets, in the Kingdom of God, and yourselves being thrown outside.[4] 13:29 They will come from the east, west, north, and south, and will sit down in the Kingdom of God. 13:30 Behold, there are some who are last who will be first, and there are some who are first who will be last."[5]

1. See Matthew 7:13-14, 22-23; Matthew 8.11-12; Matthew 19.30; Mark 10:31.

2. *Strive to enter in by the narrow door.* The open mind that measures all things by the gauge of Truth. This way is "straitened" because it requires that only Truth be recognized, and it rules out untruth or evil. (RW/narrow)

3. *'We ate and drank in your presence, and you taught in our streets.'* The easy, negative way by which men conform to sense consciousness and the pleasures of the world, with the result that their mind-muscle becomes soft and flabby. When trials come men find that they are not able to cope with them. (RW/gate,wide)

4. *and yourselves being thrown outside.* Now this door is expressing through every one of our faculties. The door of the Spirit in your eyes, in your ears, and in your mouth especially. It is expressed through the words that you speak and especially through the concentration and appreciation, let us say of that Something in you that you say is "I AM", your central identity. And there is really Spirit. And yet it is a very small proposition. It seems insignificant and narrow, and the multitudes in the midst of their scramble for the broad highway of externality, miss it. As Jesus said, "This master of the house will close the door sometime and then those who have lingered in the outer will say: We ate and drank in thy place, and thou didst teach in our streets." That's our outer consciousness. (*The Mysteries of The Four Gospels* Lesson Three, *The Door*)

5. *there are some who are last who will be first, and there are some who are first who will be last.* The disciples had a problem, just as we have a problem today. In the spiritually quickened soul, in the activity of this God-Mind we get some mighty realizations; strong, powerful insistent realizations. When we come out of them, it would seem as though that realization would transform the whole world and free those who are oppressed. It is not transformed! We feel we are truly the first in the kingdom. Now the truth of the business is that the personal ego within us has not been fully redeemed and it gets this quickening just the same as our spiritual nature, and it comes forth and assumes, or affirms, its personal greatness. Sometimes we spoil it by telling our friends how very strong we are spiritually, and how wonder-

ful we are spiritually. Sometimes we get a bit puffed up.(*The Mysteries of The Four Gospels* Lesson Seven, *Who Should Be the Greatest?*)

## The Lament over Jerusalem[1]

13:31 On that same day, some
Pharisees came, saying to him, "Get
out of here, and go away, for Herod
wants to kill you."[2]

13:32 He said to them, "Go and tell
that fox, 'Behold, I cast out demons
and perform cures today and
tomorrow, and the third day I
complete my mission. 13:33
Nevertheless I must go on my way
today and tomorrow and the next
day, for it can't be that a prophet
perish outside of Jerusalem.'

13:34 "Jerusalem, Jerusalem,[3] that
kills the prophets, and stones those
who are sent to her! How often I
wanted to gather your children
together, like a hen gathers her own
brood under her wings, and you
refused! 13:35 Behold, your house is
left to you desolate. I tell you, you
will not see me, until you say,
'Blessed is he who comes in the name
of the Lord!'"[32]

1. See Matthew 23:37-39.
2. *Get out of here ... for Herod wants to kill you.* Why was Jesus thus rejected? The Gospels indicate that the rejection of Jesus came about, not because He was something less than the Messiah the people expected, but because He proved Himself to be much more of a Messiah than the people actually wanted! People expected the Messiah to inaugurate a new kingdom; but Jesus declared: "The kingdom of God is [in the midst of you}." (See Luke 17:21, margin.) People expected the Messiah to change conditions in the land; but Jesus insisted that there must first be a change in the hearts of the people. (Herbert Hunt, A Study of the New Testament, *The Gathering Storm*)
3. *Jerusalem, Jerusalem* Jesus weeping over Jerusalem is the picture of a great love welling up in the heart and flowing out to all the earth—the love of the good Father for His erring and willful children. Such is the love of Christ for His own; such is the love of God through Christ for all creation. We may talk about the wisdom of God, but the love of God must be felt in the heart. It cannot be described, and one who has not felt it can have no concept of it from the descriptions of others. But the more we talk about love, the stronger it grows in the consciousness, and if we persist in thinking loving thoughts and speaking loving words, we are sure to bring into our experience the feeling of that great love that is beyond description—the very love of God. (Charles Fillmore, *Talks on Truth*, The Development of Divine Love)

---

Fillmore Study Bible annotations by: Rev. Mark Hicks

**World English Bible Footnotes:**

[31] v13:21. literally, three sata. 3 sata is about 39 litres or a bit more than a bushel

[32] v13:35. Psalm 118:26

# Luke 14

## Jesus Heals the Man with Dropsy

14:1 It happened, when he went into the house of one of the rulers of the Pharisees on a Sabbath to eat bread, that they were watching him. 14:2 Behold, a certain man who had dropsy[1] was in front of him. 14:3 Jesus, answering, spoke to the lawyers and Pharisees, saying, "Is it lawful to heal on the Sabbath?"

14:4 But they were silent.

He took him, and healed him, and let him go. 14:5 He answered them, "Which of you, if your son[33] or an ox[2] fell into a well, wouldn't immediately pull him out on a Sabbath day?"

14:6 They couldn't answer him regarding these things.

1. *a certain man who had dropsy*. Entering the Pharisee's house on the Sabbath day represents that state of mind in which one rests and meditates upon the right or wrong relation of certain thoughts to Divine principles. The Jesus Christ idea involves continual rest in Spirit, which manifests in harmonious activity without, while the Pharisee, looking to the letter and form of things, looks upon the Sabbath as a rest from outer activity, which leads to inertia and negation. This leads to inertia and negation, represented by the man with the dropsy, whom Jesus (I Am) heals.

2. *your son or an ox*. Your son or an ox represent physical strength. If your strength has fallen into a pit, or material bondage, you will lift it up in this consciousness of the perfection of all things in God's creation. The Pharisees are mute in the presence of these things, because they do not understand spiritual forces.

## Humility and Hospitality

14:7 He spoke a parable to those who were invited, when he noticed how they chose the best seats, and said to them, 14:8 "When you are invited by anyone to a marriage feast,[1] don't sit in the best seat, since perhaps someone more honorable than you might be invited by him, 14:9 and he who invited both of you would come and tell you, 'Make room for this person.' Then you would begin, with shame, to take the lowest place. 14:10 But when you are invited, go and sit in the lowest place, so that when he who invited you comes, he may tell you, 'Friend, move up higher.' Then you will be honored in the presence of all who sit at the table with you. 14:11 For everyone who exalts himself will be humbled, and whoever humbles himself will be exalted."

14:12 He also said to the one who had invited him, "When you make a dinner or a supper, don't call your friends, nor your brothers, nor your kinsmen, nor rich neighbors, or perhaps they might also return the favor, and pay you back. 14:13 But when you make a feast, ask the poor, the maimed, the lame, or the blind;[2] 14:14 and you will be blessed, because they don't have the resources to repay you. For you will be repaid in the resurrection of the righteous."

1. *marriage feast*. The feast on the Sabbath day is the inflow of Spiritual Substance, which we realize when we enter

the inner silence. A "marriage feast" is where there is a conscious union between soul and body in this silent influx of substance. Pride, ambition, and avarice are to be repressed and the spirit of true worth cultivated. When the selfish, ambitious thoughts perceive that there is an all-pervading thought-substance, upon which they can feed and grow fat and rich in all ways, they strive for first place. We should curb this selfishness and let the master of the feast, Divine Intelligence, bid to honorable places worthy thoughts.

2. *ask the poor, the maimed, the lame, or the blind.* We should build up our weak points, "the poor, the maimed, the lame and the blind," thus filling a vacuum in consciousness. If we fail to correct our errors, and give all our attention to the thoughts we take pride in, there will be an abnormal development, the excess acting and reacting upon itself.

## The Parable of the Great Dinner

14:15 When one of those who sat
at the table with him heard these
things, he said to him, "Blessed is
he who will feast in the Kingdom of
God!"[1]

14:16 But he said to him, "A certain
man made a great supper, and he
invited many people. 14:17 He sent out
his servant at supper time to tell
those who were invited, 'Come, for
everything is ready now.' 14:18 They all
as one began to make excuses.

"The first said to him, 'I have
bought a field,[2] and I must go and
see it. Please have me excused.'

14:19 "Another said, 'I have bought
five yoke of oxen,[3] and I must go try
them out. Please have me excused.'

14:20 "Another said, 'I have married
a wife,[4] and therefore I can't come.'

14:21 "That servant came, and told
his lord these things. Then the
master of the house, being angry,
said to his servant, 'Go out quickly
into the streets and lanes of the city,
and bring in the poor, maimed, blind,
and lame.'

14:22 "The servant said, 'Lord, it is
done as you commanded, and there
is still room.'[5]

14:23 "The lord said to the servant,
'Go out into the highways and
hedges,[6] and compel them to come
in, that my house may be filled. 14:24
For I tell you that none of those men
who were invited will taste of my
supper.'"[6]

1. *feast in the Kingdom of God!* The Great Supper typifies the feast of the pure Substance of Spirit ever accessible to the individual. Before one can partake fully of the Substance of Spirit there must be a willingness to turn the attention to the ideas of Spirit, to the exclusion of all outer attractions.

2. a field. The belief in materiality which prevents feasting on the pure Substance.

3. *five yoke of oxen.* The dependence of man upon the five senses for his satisfaction.

4. *a wife.* Centering the affections upon the things of the without; becoming lost in personal love.

5. *and there is still room.* These guests represent our inherent gifts which enable us to appropriate substance. If our inherent powers are not quickened by desire for the higher realm, they fail to build up our character or fit us to occupy the kingdom. We then excuse ourself from seeking the benefits of mind, soul, and spirit, and confines our desires to the purely material or physical.

6. *Go out into the highways and hedges.* The highways and hedges are well-worn thought habits. Notions of health, prosperity, peace, and harmony are all found in these mental grooves, and must be brought into line with the substance of true thought before man's life can be rounded out and made complete.

7. *none of those men who were invited*

*will taste of my supper*. The substance of Truth can be appreciated only by those who partake of it, because they are conscious of needing it. One who takes up the study of Truth idly, as a pastime, fails to get from it the value that is found by the one who comes to it because of some deep need.

## The Cost of Discipleship

[14:25] Now great multitudes were
going with him. He turned and said
to them, [14:26] "If anyone comes to me,
and doesn't hate❶ his own father,
mother, wife, children, brothers,
and sisters, yes, and his own life
also, he can't be my disciple. [14:27]
Whoever doesn't bear his own
cross,❷ and come after me, can't be
my disciple. [14:28] For which of you,
desiring to build a tower, doesn't
first sit down and count the cost,❸ to
see if he has enough to complete it?
[14:29] Or perhaps, when he has laid a
foundation, and is not able to finish,
everyone who sees begins to mock
him, [14:30] saying, 'This man began to
build, and wasn't able to finish.' [14:31]
Or what king, as he goes to
encounter another king in war, will
not sit down first and consider
whether he is able with ten thousand
to meet him who comes against him
with twenty thousand? [14:32] Or else,
while the other is yet a great way
off, he sends an envoy, and asks for
conditions of peace. [14:33] So therefore
whoever of you who doesn't renounce
all that he has, he can't be my
disciple.

1. *and doesn't hate*. The word "hate" is used here in a figurative sense to emphasize the necessity of complete loyalty to the spiritual side of life. We must "love" (give supreme allegiance to) only God: we must "hate" (consider of secondary importance) all else. In reality we are to love our neighbor as ourselves in order to keep the second great commandment of the law. We are not forbidden to love our better self, for in so doing we love life, which is of God. However, our first allegiance is to the ideal of the Christ.

2. *Whoever doesn't bear his own cross*. The cross that we must bear if we are to merit discipleship is faithful and loyal obedience to the divine law. We must remember to be what we desire to be, instead of following the impulses of the self, vacillating between sense and Spirit, between the human and the divine.

3. *doesn't first sit down and count the cost*. After we have begun the work of reconstructing our thought and conduct to bring them into harmony with the Christ mind, what must we do to bring the work to completion? We must give up all habits that conflict with the constructive work of the Christ (renounce all that we have). By so doing we are able to build up without interruption instead of alternating between constructive and destructive work.

## About Salt

[14:34] Salt❶ is good, but if the salt
becomes flat and tasteless, with
what do you season it? [14:35] It is fit
neither for the soil nor for the
manure pile. It is thrown out. He who
has ears❷ to hear, let him hear."

1. *salt*. The thoughts in man that understand, love, and obey Truth as Jesus taught and demonstrated it (RW/salt).

2. *ears*. the obedience and receptivity of the mind (RW/ears)

Fillmore Study Bible annotations by: Rev. Mark Hicks

**World English Bible Footnotes:**

[33] v14:5. TR reads "donkey" instead of "son"

# Luke 15

## The Parable of the Lost Sheep

15:1 Now all the tax collectors and sinners were coming close to him to hear him. 15:2 The Pharisees and the scribes murmured,[1] saying, "This man welcomes sinners, and eats with them."

15:3 He told them this parable. 15:4 "Which of you men, if you had one hundred sheep, and lost one of them, wouldn't leave the ninety-nine in the wilderness, and go after the one that was lost,[2] until he found it? 15:5 When he has found it, he carries it on his shoulders, rejoicing. 15:6 When he comes home, he calls together his friends and his neighbors, saying to them, 'Rejoice with me,[3] for I have found my sheep which was lost!' 15:7 I tell you that even so there will be more joy in heaven over one sinner who repents, than over ninety-nine righteous people who need no repentance.

1. *The Pharisees and the scribes murmured.* Man's self-righteous nature (scribes and Pharisees) objects to the undisciplined thoughts of the sense mind and desires to banish them without making an effort to redeem them. The Christ knows that this cannot be done successfully.

2. *Which of you ... wouldn't ... go after the one that was lost?* That there must be complete dedication of the thoughts to the ideal of Truth before one can claim the redeeming power of the Christ or enter into the kingdom. No stray thought can be allowed to remain out of the fold of constructive thinking.

3. *Rejoice with me.* There more joy over one sinner who repents than over ninety and nine just persons who need no repentance because changing the mind (repenting) requires effort and depth of purpose, whereas considering oneself good enough without making an effort to improve is the static condition under which man makes no progress.

## The Parable of the Lost Coin

15:8 Or what woman, if she had ten drachma[34] coins, if she lost one drachma coin, wouldn't light a lamp, sweep the house, and seek diligently until she found it? 15:9 When she has found it, she calls together her friends and neighbors, saying, 'Rejoice with me, for I have found the drachma which I had lost.'[1] 15:10 Even so, I tell you, there is joy in the presence of the angels of God over one sinner repenting."

1. *I have found the drachma which I had lost.* Finding the lost piece of silver by the woman represents the perfecting of the soul (woman) through diligent thought for the things of God.

## The Parable of the Prodigal Son and His Brother[1]

15:11 He said, "A certain man had two sons.[2] 15:12 The younger of them said to his father, 'Father, give me my share of your property.' He divided his livelihood between them.[3] 15:13 Not many days after, the younger son gathered all of this together and traveled into a far country.[4] There he wasted his property with riotous living. 15:14 When he had spent all of it, there arose a severe famine in that country, and he began to be in need.[5] 15:15 He went and joined himself to one of the citizens of that country, and he sent him into his fields to feed pigs. 15:16 He wanted to fill his belly with the husks[6] that the pigs ate, but no one gave him any. 15:17 But when he came to himself he said, 'How many hired servants of my father's have bread enough to spare, and I'm dying with hunger! 15:18 I will get up and go to my father,[7] and will tell him, "Father, I have sinned against heaven, and in your sight. 15:19 I am no more worthy to be called your son. Make me as one of your hired servants."'

15:20 "He arose, and came to his father.[8] But while he was still far off, his father saw him, and was moved with compassion, and ran, and fell on his neck, and kissed him. 15:21 The son said to him, 'Father, I have sinned against heaven, and in your sight. I am no longer worthy to be called your son.'

15:22 "But the father said to his servants, 'Bring out the best robe, and put it on him. Put a ring on his hand, and shoes on his feet. 15:23 Bring the fattened calf, kill it, and let us eat, and celebrate; 15:24 for this, my son, was dead, and is alive again.[9] He was lost, and is found.' They began to celebrate.[10]

15:25 "Now his elder son was in the field. As he came near to the house, he heard music and dancing. 15:26 He called one of the servants to him, and asked what was going on. 15:27 He said to him, 'Your brother has come, and your father has killed the fattened calf, because he has received him back safe and healthy.' 15:28 But he was angry, and would not go in. Therefore his father came out, and begged him. 15:29 But he answered his father, 'Behold, these many years I have served you, and I never disobeyed a commandment of yours, but you never gave me a goat, that I might celebrate with my friends. 15:30 But when this, your son, came, who has devoured your living with prostitutes, you killed the fattened calf for him.'

15:31 "He said to him, 'Son, you are always with me, and all that is mine is yours. 15:32 But it was appropriate to celebrate and be glad, for this, your brother, was dead, and is alive again. He was lost, and is found.'"

1. Jesus was giving a series of lessons on the subject of the repentance of sinners. In this parable he said: "I say unto you, there is joy in the presence of the angels of God over one sinner that repenteth." From this we understand that the man who had two sons is God.

2. *A certain man had two sons.* The two sons are soul consciousness and sense consciousness. Through the soul we are related to the Spirit, and through the sense to the flesh. These mental states are thought aggregations. All the thoughts of a spiritual character gravitate together and form a state of consciousness that is pervaded by Spirit, and perpetually sustained by the Divine Mind. This is the Spiritual Soul, or superconsciousness. The Human Soul thought aggregation finds its first pleasure in sense avenues. It is the exuberance of youth, where every human sense is flooded with life.

3. *He divided his livelihood between them.* These are the riches of God which are divided between the states of mind. These two souls, or states of thought, are referred to by Paul as the Spirit and the flesh at enmity, one warring against the other. It is not strictly correct to say that this higher plane of thought is the Spirit, but rather that it is the spiritual consciousness. The Spirit does not war against anybody or anything.

4. *traveled into a far country.* The mind

that revels in pleasures of sense, gradually finds itself centering about the things it thinks so much of. This is a law of thought action. What you think a great deal about, and like to do, you gradually become attached to it, and in due course the attachment becomes so strong that you separate yourself from everything else. The constant thought of man about sense objects and sense pleasures gradually sunders him from the spiritual, and he grows to believe that it does not exist. This is the journey into the "far country."

5. *he began to be in need.* But being detached in consciousness from the real sources of existence, the sense consciousness gradually uses up the life it has in the lusts of the flesh, and not knowing how to go within and draw from the original fount, there is a "mighty famine in that country, and he began to be in want."

6. *He wanted to fill his belly with the husks.* Then there is a still further descent into sense conditions. The sense soul attaches itself to the realm of flesh, and tries to get sustenance out of it. The original text here indicates that he literally glued himself to the selfish personality of the flesh consciousness. He fed the swinish nature with the husks of life, and got no soul satisfaction. When we get down into the animal, and try to feed our souls with its mere outer covering of Truth (husks), we starve. The human is eliminated until there is no man in it, "and no man gave unto him."

7. *I will get up and go to my father.* The coming to himself of the Human Soul is the awakening of understanding. Why should the body grow old and lose its life, "perish with hunger," when in the Father's house the hired servants have substance enough? The mind that has been groveling in sense must rise to a higher range of thought and go, or continually send its thought, in spiritual ways. This journey back to Spirit is not completed in a day, but is a gradual step by step traveling, sometimes over rough roads.

8. *He arose, and came to his father.* The moment the thought arises to the contemplation of Spirit, there is a union with the Divine Mind; his father "fell on his neck and kissed him." Confession of sin, or falling short, is good for the self-centred man. It opens the door to higher things, and mellows the soul.

9. *for this, my son, was dead, and is alive again.* He who is a slave to the senses is dead to all considerations of the spiritual truths of life. He cannot express his better nature because it is lost under the thick blanket of sense that envelops his thoughts.

10. *They began to celebrate.* When we make the unity between the outer sense and the inner Spirit there is great rejoicing, and the outer is flooded with vitality (robe), unending power is put into his hand (ring), and his understanding (feet) clothed upon. The "fatted calf " is the richness of strength always awaiting the needy soul. When all these relations have been established between the within and the without, there is rejoicing. The dead man of sense is made alive in the consciousness of Spirit; the lost is found. "And they began to be merry."

---

Fillmore Study Bible annotations by: Rev. Mark Hicks

**World English Bible Footnotes:**

[34] v15

# Luke 16

## The Parable of the Dishonest Manager

16:1 He also said to his disciples,
"There was a certain rich man❶ who
had a manager.❷ An accusation was
made to him that this man was
wasting his possessions.❸ 16:2 He
called him, and said to him, 'What is

this that I hear about you? Give an
accounting of your management, for
you can no longer be manager.'

16:3 "The manager said within
himself, 'What will I do,[4] seeing that
my lord is taking away the
management position from me? I
don't have strength to dig. I am
ashamed to beg. 16:4 I know what I
will do, so that when I am removed
from management, they may receive
me into their houses.' 16:5 Calling each
one of his lord's debtors to him,[5]
he said to the first, 'How much do
you owe to my lord?'[6] 16:6 He said,
'A hundred batos[35] of oil.' He said
to him, 'Take your bill, and sit down
quickly and write fifty.'[7] 16:7 Then
said he to another, 'How much do you
owe?' He said, 'A hundred cors[36] of
wheat.' He said to him, 'Take your
bill, and write eighty.'

16:8 "His lord commended the
dishonest manager because he had
done wisely, for the children of this
world are, in their own generation,
wiser than the children of the light.[8]
16:9 I tell you, make for yourselves
friends by means of unrighteous
mammon, so that when you fail, they
may receive you into the eternal
tents. 16:10 He who is faithful in a very
little is faithful also in much. He who
is dishonest in a very little is also
dishonest in much. 16:11 If therefore
you have not been faithful in the
unrighteous mammon, who will
commit to your trust the true riches?
16:12 If you have not been faithful in
that which is another's, who will give
you that which is your own? 16:13 No
servant can serve two masters, for
either he will hate the one, and love
the other; or else he will hold to one,
and despise the other. You aren't
able to serve God and mammon[37]."

1. *a certain rich man.* The different characters stand for our different aspects of ourselves at different times, different ways to think and feel and react, communicate. In this parable, we want to realize that the lord, the steward, and the debtors are all different aspects of each person's thinking, feeling, and being. (These annotations are from Ed Rabel, New Testament Lectures, p.220)

2. *who had a manager.* Now, in Jesus' parable, He refers to the lord as the rich man; and this rich man has a steward. The Lord of your being also has a steward, and the steward is your human self, the self of you, of which you are ordinarily aware and that you call "me".

3. *this man was wasting his possessions.* The Lord makes you one with all good; and the human level of your being serves as steward to the spiritual of your being, which is Lord. Now, this means, in effect, that we can humanly draw upon the substance of the good of our Lord and cause it to become forms, formed. We are to invest these forms into life, and as we do this lovingly, generously, and faithfully, then we are fulfilling our human role of wise stewardship

4. *What will I do?* We begin to feel very insecure and our life starts to feel burdensome and futile. This is good, that we do not like this, because it means that we are reawakening to the importance of our responsibility and privilege in wise and faithful stewardship.

5. *Calling each one of his lord's debtors to him.* Every person, of course, goes through periods in his life when, either by making mistakes or selfish behavior or unwise attitudes, causes debtor-factors to accumulate in his life. These debtor-factors in our life can be any place where good is no longer appearing.

6. *How much do you owe to my lord?* Notice what Jesus had this steward do, though, about his realization of his wastefulness and his mistakes, his debtor-factors. He does not try to ignore the debtors. He does not try to evade all his responsibility in this situation, but he does what to him seems the wisest and best thing to do in such a dilemma. He goes to each of his lord's recognized debtors, takes as much as payment from them as he can reasonably expect to get, and forgives the remainder of the debt.

7. *Take your bill ... and write fifty.* When you and I recognize our unwise stewardship and we also recognize the debtor-factor we have created, then we must remember as much truth as we can and realize that nothing is ever hopeless, and it is never too late. As human beings, we can always derive at least something good out of anything. A lot of people think you must

get that before you can extract the good out of anything. This is not true. Where we are now, in our human self-consciousness, we can extract something good out of anything, it does not matter what.

8. *the children of this world are, in their own generation, wiser than the children of the light*. Jesus is saying persons are all in different levels of understanding, of development. Some have greater degrees of awareness and skills than others and that those on what we would call, for the sake of analysis, lower stages of development, lower phases of unfoldment, who do the best they can in their limitations, are actually doing something greater than those with a great deal of know-how, who do what comes naturally anyhow.

## The Law and the Kingdom of God[1]

16:14 The Pharisees[2], who were
lovers of money, also heard all these
things, and they scoffed at him. 16:15
He said to them, "You are those who
justify yourselves in the sight of men,
but God knows your hearts. For that
which is exalted among men is an
abomination in the sight of God. 16:16
The law and the prophets were until
John. From that time the Good News
of the Kingdom of God is preached,
and everyone is forcing his way into
it. 16:17 But it is easier for heaven and
earth to pass away, than for one tiny
stroke of a pen in the law to fall. 16:18
Everyone who divorces his wife, and
marries another, commits adultery.
He who marries one who is divorced
from a husband commits adultery.

1. [This parable should be considered a preface to the next parable, *The Rich Man and Lazarus*]

2. A Pharisee observes the forms but neglects the spirit of religion. Henry Ward Beecher said: "A Pharisee is one who worships instruments. Whoever believes that churches, or books, or institutions, or customs, are more valuable than men is a Pharisee." (MBD/pharisees)

## The Rich Man and Lazarus[1]

16:19 "Now there was a certain rich
man, and he was clothed in purple
and fine linen, living in luxury every
day. 16:20 A certain beggar, named
Lazarus, was laid at his gate, full
of sores, 16:21 and desiring to be fed
with the crumbs that fell from the
rich man's table.[2] Yes, even the dogs
came and licked his sores. 16:22 It
happened that the beggar died, and
that he was carried away by the
angels to Abraham's bosom.[3] The
rich man also died, and was buried.
16:23 In Hades[38], he lifted up his
eyes, being in torment, and saw
Abraham far off, and Lazarus at his
bosom.[4] 16:24 He cried and said,
'Father Abraham, have mercy on me,
and send Lazarus, that he may dip
the tip of his finger in water, and
cool my tongue! For I am in anguish
in this flame.'

16:25 "But Abraham said, 'Son,
remember that you, in your lifetime,
received your good things, and
Lazarus, in like manner, bad things.
But now here he is comforted and
you are in anguish. 16:26 Besides all
this, between us and you there is
a great gulf fixed, that those who
want to pass from here to you are not
able, and that none may cross over
from there to us.'

16:27 "He said, 'I ask you therefore,
father, that you would send him to
my father's house; 16:28 for I have five
brothers, that he may testify to
them, so they won't also come into
this place of torment.'

16:29 "But Abraham said to him, 'They have Moses and the prophets. Let them listen to them.'

16:30 "He said, 'No, father Abraham, but if one goes to them from the dead, they will repent.'

16:31 "He said to him, 'If they don't listen to Moses and the prophets, neither will they be persuaded if one rises from the dead.'"

1. The meaning of this parable is that, when one who has built up a consciousness of love for material things, dies, he continues to long for those things, and has no means of satisfying his desire. This brings "torment." Lazarus, through his nonattachment to things, rests peacefully in the bosom of Abraham, Abraham representing the Father.

2. *desiring to be fed with the crumbs that fell from the rich man's table.* The inner man craves the sustenance of man's thought, even the least portion of the outer man's attention. These are the crumbs that fall from the rich man's table, but they do not avail to nourish or sustain the inner man.

3. *Abraham's bosom.* A Jewish name, not of heaven, but of the intermediate state of bliss, in which the souls of the just await the resurrection. Metaphysically the term means a state of faith in which man's soul rests safe and undisturbed from all thought of worldly trials and suffering.

4. *and saw Abraham far off, and Lazarus at his bosom.* As the worldly-minded man sees living in the same world with him some person whose mind is given to higher values, so after the death of the body the mind, which is eternal, discerns that certain states that the earthly consciousness has never penetrated afford rest and peace to those who have attained them. Perceiving this Truth is a different matter from attaining to it, for between the two states of consciousness there is a great gulf fixed.

---

Fillmore Study Bible annotations by: Rev. Mark Hicks

**World English Bible Footnotes:**

[35] v16:6. 100 batos is about 395 litres, 104 U. S. gallons, or 87 imperial gallons.

[36] v16:7. 100 cors = about 3,910 litres or 600 bushels.

[37] v16:13. "Mammon" refers to riches or a false god of wealth.

[38] v16:23. or, Hell

# Luke 17

## Some Sayings of Jesus

17:1 He said to the disciples, "It is impossible that no occasions of stumbling[1] should come, but woe to him through whom they come! 17:2 It would be better for him if a millstone were hung around his neck, and he were thrown into the sea, rather than that he should cause one of these little ones[2] to stumble. 17:3 Be careful. If your brother sins against you,[3] rebuke him. If he repents, forgive him. 17:4 If he sins against you seven times in the day, and seven times returns, saying, 'I repent,' you shall forgive him."[4]

17:5 The apostles said to the Lord,
"Increase our faith."[5]

17:6 The Lord said, "If you had faith
like a grain of mustard seed,[6] you
would tell this sycamore tree, 'Be
uprooted, and be planted in the sea,'
and it would obey you. 17:7 But who
is there among you,[7] having a
servant[8] plowing or keeping sheep,
that will say, when he comes in from
the field, 'Come immediately and sit
down at the table,' 17:8 and will not
rather tell him, 'Prepare my supper,
clothe yourself properly, and serve
me, while I eat and drink. Afterward
you shall eat and drink'? 17:9 Does he
thank that servant because he did
the things that were commanded?[9]
I think not. 17:10 Even so you also,
when you have done all the things
that are commanded you, say, 'We
are unworthy servants.[10] We have
done our duty.'"

1. *occasions of stumbling.* Occasions of stumbling come because the race consciousness, in which the majority of people live, makes such occasions inevitable. Occasions of stumbling will be done away entirely only when the whole race becomes conscious of spiritual reality.

2. *these little ones.* These little ones are people who have only a little understanding of Truth but a sincere desire to practice it as faithfully as possible.

3. *If your brother sins against you.* Our reaction when someone "sins" against us should be to take care that we do not in our turn offend the one who has offended us. We should make sure that our reaction is constructive and in harmony with divine law.

4. *you shall forgive him.* If someone offends us and does not ask forgiveness, should we continue to harbor resentment against him? The habit of harboring resentment is so hurtful to the mind that consideration of our own welfare, if nothing higher, should cause us to forgive everyone immediately, without waiting to be asked to do so.

5. *Increase our faith.* [Jesus tells them] that it is not a matter of how much [faith] you have [but rather] are you aware that you have it or not? That is all. The size, the quantity does not enter into it. Spirit has nothing to do with quantity or size. There are no dimensions in Spirit. In Spirit, the only thing that counts as far as a human being is concerned, is yea or nay, are you or aren't you, do you or don't you, will you or won't you; not how much or what size, or even what shape, but yea or nay. You either are aware of faith and what it is in you, or you are not. If you are aware of it, then being aware, of itself, is the how-to in using it; and it is strengthened. So the idea is not to worry about how much of any of these faculties you have, but are you working with them or not. Are they quickened? Do you understand what they are? (These annotations are from Ed Rabel, New Testament Lectures, pp.230-1)

6. *If you had faith like a grain of mustard seed.* Jesus uses the fancy illustration of transforming the sycamore tree from the soil into the sea. How? Charles Fillmore says that faith is our faculty which has the power of transforming energy from one plane of consciousness to another. It is the great firmnative [formative] principle of creation. In us, it is the faculty which also does this and is our direct connection with substance. When we use our faith faculty correctly, we make our affirmations of truth directly connected with substance, which brings forth results. If the faith faculty is in alignment with the faculty of power, then it results in the moving or transforming of energy from one plane of consciousness to another, and usually invisible or potential plane to the visible or the actual.

7. *who is there among you?* Jesus refers to the indwelling law of your highest good, your eternal unfoldment into greater degrees of goodness or awareness of goodness.

8. *having a servant.* So to do anything which increases your degree of awareness of goodness, to do anything which facilitates your encounter with your highest good, is called "serving the Lord".

9. *Does he thank that servant because he did the things that were commanded?* Jesus is showing us a false belief, which is that by doing what I have to do anyway, I am serving my Lord. But by doing only what you have to do, you are promulgating even exchange, in metaphysical terms. We are sustaining status quo when we do what we have to do because we have to do it.

10. *when you have done all the things that are commanded you, say, 'We are unworthy servants.* The only person who in-

creases his own highest good is the person who does and is more than he has to do, has to. In other words, he does his good as a matter of choice. He uses his freedom of will, his freedom of expression; and as a matter of choice, he does more than he has to, and in making that kind of a choice, he is serving his Lord. It is no longer even exchange. It is spiritual effort and growth.

## Jesus Cleanses Ten Lepers

[17:11] It happened as he was on his
way to Jerusalem, that he was
passing along the borders of Samaria
and Galilee.❶ [17:12] As he entered into
a certain village, ten men who were
lepers met him, who stood at a
distance. [17:13] They lifted up their
voices, saying, "Jesus, Master, have
mercy on us!"

[17:14] When he saw them, he said
to them, "Go and show yourselves to
the priests."❷ It happened that as
they went, they were cleansed. [17:15]
One of them, when he saw that he
was healed, turned back, glorifying
God with a loud voice. [17:16] He fell
on his face at Jesus' feet, giving him
thanks;❸ and he was a Samaritan.
[17:17] Jesus answered, "Weren't the ten
cleansed? But where are the nine?
[17:18] Were there none found who
returned to give glory to God, except
this stranger?" [17:19] Then he said to
him, "Get up, and go your way. Your
faith has healed you."❹

1. *was passing along the borders of Samaria and Galilee.* The Samaritan represents a state of consciousness that gives recognition to both good and "evil." In this case the consciousness of good prevailed over the evil, giving a quickened appreciation of benefits received and an awareness of the divine source from which the healing came. The nine Children of Israel represent formal religious thoughts, which means that they reckoned themselves the chosen of God and took their healing as a matter of course, without troubling to show what they felt.

2. *Go and show yourselves to the priests.* Jesus commanded them to obey the Mosaic law. His high consciousness of divine law, as He spoke to them, and the willing obedience of the lepers and their expectation of healing combined to restore them to health.

3. *giving him thanks.* What does the Christ Spirit indicate as the proper course for us to take when our prayer is answered? It inspires us to feel and express gratitude for all that we receive or expect to receive and to acknowledge God as the source of all our good.

4. *Your faith has healed you.* To what does the Christ give credit for the work of healing? To faith. Healing rests largely with the one who lacks health. If he keeps his vision fixed on health and steadily claims health instead of disease, in full faith that his words are heard, he will realize healing.

## The Coming of the Kingdom❶

[17:20] Being asked by the Pharisees
when the Kingdom of God would
come, he answered them, "The
Kingdom of God doesn't come with
observation;❷ [17:21] neither will they
say, 'Look, here!' or, 'Look, there!' for
behold, the Kingdom of God is within
you."❸

[17:22] He said to the disciples, "The
days will come, when you will desire
to see one of the days of the Son
of Man,❹ and you will not see it.
[17:23] They will tell you, 'Look, here!'
or 'Look, there!' Don't go away, nor
follow after them, [17:24] for as the
lightning, when it flashes out of the
one part under the sky, shines to the
other part under the sky; so will the
Son of Man be in his day. [17:25] But

first, he must suffer many things and
be rejected by this generation. 17:26
As it happened in the days of Noah,
even so will it be also in the days
of the Son of Man. 17:27 They ate,
they drank, they married, they were
given in marriage, until the day that
Noah entered into the ship, and the
flood came, and destroyed them all.
17:28 Likewise, even as it happened
in the days of Lot: they ate, they
drank, they bought, they sold, they
planted, they built; 17:29 but in the
day that Lot went out from Sodom,
it rained fire and sulfur from the sky,
and destroyed them all. 17:30 It will
be the same way in the day that the
Son of Man is revealed. 17:31 In that
day, he who will be on the housetop,
and his goods in the house, let him
not go down to take them away. Let
him who is in the field likewise not
turn back. 17:32 Remember Lot's wife!
17:33 Whoever seeks to save his life
loses it, but whoever loses his life
preserves it. 17:34 I tell you, in that
night there will be two people in one
bed. The one will be taken, and the
other will be left. 17:35 There will be
two grinding grain together. One will
be taken, and the other will be left."
17:36 [39]

17:37 They, answering, asked him,
"Where, Lord?"

He said to them, "Where the body is, there will the vultures also be gathered together."

1. See Luke 21:25-37

2. *The Kingdom of God doesn't come with observation.* Why is the coming of the kingdom of heaven "not with observation"? Because it is entered into consciously through right feeling, right thinking, and right acting. Only the last of these is visual, and since right feeling and right thinking precede right acting, the initial coming of the kingdom is unobserved by the senses.

3. *the Kingdom of God is within you.* [Note: the NRSV translates this as "the kingdom of God is among you" with a footnote "Or within".] There are many planes of life, one above or below another, yet not conflicting. All creation is based on life activity, or as it is called in physical science, rates of vibration. A certain activity in the life current forms worlds on a plane, which we may call the physical; a little increase in the vibratory rate makes another system, which we may designate as the psychical; a still higher rate makes a universe where spiritual ideas prevail. These are all interlaced and interblended in the presence around and within us, hence the 'Kingdom of God is within you', or 'among you', as one translator gives it. (Unity Metaphysics: 05 The Kingdom of God)

4. *one of the days of the Son of Man.* [Unity never commented on this passage. The following may be helpful.] The "Son of God" is Jehovah God, Christ, I AM, the composite Idea of God, the image of God, the Word of God, spiritual man, the ideal pattern of man in the Mind of God. This ideal is inherent in every man as his spiritual nature. The "Son of man" is the human being or manifest man quickened in awareness to the divinity of himself. He is becoming conscious of himself as a "Son of God," and is gradually expressing and manifesting his real nature. This state of becoming conscious of himself as a "Son of God" is metaphorically referred to as the "new birth," "rebirth," being "born again," being "born anew." (Unity Correspondence School, Series 2 - Lesson 3 - Annotation 20)

Fillmore Study Bible annotations by: Rev. Mark Hicks

**World English Bible Footnotes:**

[39] v17:36. Some Greek manuscripts add: "Two will be in the field: the one taken, and the other left."

# LUKE 18

## The Parable of the Widow and the Unjust Judge

18:1 He also spoke a parable to them that they must always pray,❶ and not give up, 18:2 saying, "There was a judge in a certain city who didn't fear God,❷ and didn't respect man. 18:3 A widow❸ was in that city, and she often came to him, saying, 'Defend me from my adversary!' 18:4 He wouldn't for a while, but afterward he said to himself, 'Though I neither fear God, nor respect man, 18:5 yet because this widow bothers me, I will defend her, or else she will wear me out by her continual coming.'"

18:6 The Lord said, "Listen to what the unrighteous judge says. 18:7 Won't God avenge his chosen ones, who are crying out to him day and night, and yet he exercises patience with them? 18:8 I tell you that he will avenge them quickly.❹ Nevertheless, when the Son of Man comes, will he find faith on the earth?"

1. *that they must always pray.* Not just audible words, but a prayerful attitude of mind; silent or audible speaking of words

2. *who didn't fear God.* Judge represents intellect, in this case stubborn in a continued way of thinking producing undesirable results

3. *widow.* a belief in lack; though not good in of itself, serves to call attention to judge, in this case, stubborn intellect. Also note the repeated action of the widow with the same declaration; affirmative prayer.

4. *he will avenge them quickly.* According to the original text, this verse should be translated: "And will not God grant justice to his chosen, who cry to him day and night, and have pity on them? He will, I tell you, grant them justice *instantly*."

## The Parable of the Pharisee and the Tax Collector

18:9 He spoke also this parable to certain people who were convinced of their own righteousness, and who despised all others. 18:10 "Two men went up into the temple to pray; one was a Pharisee,❶ and the other was a tax collector.❷ 18:11 The Pharisee stood and prayed to himself like this: 'God, I thank you, that I am not like the rest of men, extortioners, unrighteous, adulterers, or even like this tax collector. 18:12 I fast twice a week. I give tithes of all that I get.' 18:13 But the tax collector, standing far away, wouldn't even lift up his eyes to heaven, but beat his breast, saying, 'God, be merciful to me, a sinner!' 18:14 I tell you, this man went down to his house justified rather than the other; for everyone who exalts himself will be humbled, but he who humbles himself❸ will be exalted."

1. *Pharisee.* The "Pharisee" in consciousness is a selfish state of mind produced by the intellect. It is this self-satisfied mental attitude that causes man to lose sight of the real needs of soul and body, and finally results in dissolution of its own false structure, often at the expense of man's body. (MBD/Pharisees)

2. *tax collector.* (Publican, ASV). What in consciousness is a "publican"? In consciousness a "publican" is the spirit of meekness that opens us to the inflow of cleansing, illuminating Truth.

3. *he who humbles himself.* Those who humble themselves have reference to the crucifixion of personality. They are "far

away," but empty and receptive to the love and wisdom of God, while the consciousness is being illumined and the Christ within exalted.

## Jesus Blesses Little Children

18:15 They were also bringing their babies to him, that he might touch them. But when the disciples saw it, they rebuked them. 18:16 Jesus summoned them, saying, "Allow the little children to come to me, and don't hinder them, for the Kingdom of God belongs to such as these. 18:17 Most certainly, I tell you, whoever doesn't receive the Kingdom of God like a little child,❶ he will in no way enter into it."

1. See Matthew 19:13-15; Mark 10:13-16.

2. *like a little child.* "In entering upon this course of instruction, each of you should, so far as possible, lay aside, for the time being, all previous theories and beliefs ... If there is anything, as we proceed, which you do not understand or agree with, just let it lie passively in your mind until you have read the entire book ... for the time being, be willing to become as a little child." (Emilie Cady, *Lessons in Truth*, Lesson 1, Statement of Being).

## The Rich Ruler

18:18 A certain ruler asked him, saying, "Good Teacher, what shall I do to inherit eternal life?"❶

18:19 Jesus asked him, "Why do you call me good? No one is good, except one--God. 18:20 You know the commandments: 'Don't commit adultery,' 'Don't murder,' 'Don't steal,' 'Don't give false testimony,' 'Honor your father and your mother.'"[40]

18:21 He said, "I have observed all these things from my youth up."

18:22 When Jesus heard these things, he said to him, "You still lack one thing. Sell all that you have, and distribute it to the poor. You will have treasure in heaven. Come, follow me."

18:23 But when he heard these things, he became very sad, for he was very rich.

18:24 Jesus, seeing that he became very sad, said, "How hard it is for those who have riches to enter into the Kingdom of God! 18:25 For it is easier for a camel to enter in through a needle's eye, than for a rich man to enter into the Kingdom of God."

18:26 Those who heard it said, "Then who can be saved?"

18:27 But he said, "The things which are impossible with men are possible with God."

18:28 Peter said, "Look, we have left everything, and followed you."

18:29 He said to them, "Most certainly I tell you, there is no one who has left house, or wife, or brothers, or parents, or children, for the Kingdom of God's sake, 18:30 who will not receive many times more in this time, and in the world to come, eternal life."

1. *what shall I do to inherit eternal life?* Man already has inherited eternal life. Life is eternal, but no state of existence is eternal. Here is the point, to know the difference between the truth of eternal life, which never changes, and states of existence, which change constantly. Existence, itself, is a changeability. It is a

state, and many persons confuse their desire to know eternal life with their desire to prolong their current state of existence, and we can't have that because if it was possible and you succeeded in prolonging your current state of existence, you would be bored. Really you would be destroyed. You could not take it. Jesus realized, obviously, that many persons made this mistake. They think that because their current state of existence is pleasant that they want it extended into eternity, and Jesus, in His understanding, realized that that is not what you want at all. In fact, if you could have it, you would curse the day you gained it. What you really want is what you already have, eternal life, and you want a true consciousness of this; so, therefore, Jesus realized that anything at all, no matter how good or pleasant or desirable, which causes you to want your present state prolonged, is dangerous. (Ed Rabel, New Testament Lectures, pp.241)

## A Third Time Jesus Foretells His Death and Ressurection[1]

[18:31] He took the twelve aside, and said to them, "Behold, we are going up to Jerusalem, and all the things that are written through the prophets concerning the Son of Man[2] will be completed. [18:32] For he will be delivered up to the Gentiles, will be mocked, treated shamefully, and spit on. [18:33] They will scourge and kill him.[3] On the third day, he will rise again."

[18:34] They understood none of these things. This saying was hidden from them, and they didn't understand the things that were said.

1. See Cf. Matthew 20:17-19; Mark 10:32-34.

2. *Son of Man.* See annotation for Son of Man above, Luke 17:20. The Son of Man is the state of becoming conscious of ourself as a "Son of God".

3. *They will scourge and kill him.* Try to remember that in metaphysical language "self" means your present concept of you human personality, while soul means your total awareness, your awareness, of your being: Spirit, soul and body of your being, that is your totality, but your awareness of your total being is your soul and then *self is your present opinion of your human personality.* ... Here Jesus is very strongly implying that if we want to save ourselves a great deal of unhappiness and disappointment we can begin by giving up the notion that *self* must come first in all things. (Ed Rabel, New Testament Lectures, pp.241)

## Jesus Heals a Blind Beggar[1]

[18:35] It happened, as he came near Jericho,[2] a certain blind[3] man sat by the road, begging. [18:36] Hearing a multitude going by, he asked what this meant. [18:37] They told him that Jesus of Nazareth was passing by. [18:38] He cried out, "Jesus, you son of David, have mercy on me!" [18:39] Those who led the way rebuked him, that he should be quiet; but he cried out all the more, "You son of David, have mercy on me!"

[18:40] Standing still, Jesus commanded him to be brought to him. When he had come near, he asked him, [18:41] "What do you want me to do?"

He said, "Lord, that I may see again."

[18:42] Jesus said to him, "Receive your sight. Your faith has healed you."

[18:43] Immediately he received his sight, and followed him, glorifying God. All the people, when they saw it, praised God.

1. See Matthew 20:29-34; Matthew 9:27-31; Mark 10:46-52.

2. *Jericho.* Meta. The definitions of Jericho express relative terms; that is, they stand in a state of dependence on the Absolute. Jericho is the opposite of Jerusalem. One represents the spiritual; the other, the material. We often start from Jerusalem with high spiritual resolves, but are robbed by outlaw thoughts on the way (MBD/Jericho).

3. *blind.* Metaphysically, a darkened consciousness. When we are exalted and illumined in our thoughts, darkness disappears (MBD/blind eyes).

---

Fillmore Study Bible annotations by Rev. Mark Hicks and Eddie Rodriguez.

**World English Bible Footnotes:**

[40] v18:20. Exodus 20:12-16; Deuteronomy 5:16-20

# Luke 19

## Jesus and Zacchaeus

[19:1] He entered and was passing through Jericho. [19:2] There was a man named Zacchaeus.(1) He was a chief tax collector, and he was rich. [19:3] He was trying to see who Jesus was, and couldn't because of the crowd, because he was short. [19:4] He ran on ahead, and climbed up into a sycamore tree to see him, for he was to pass that way. [19:5] When Jesus came to the place, he looked up and saw him, and said to him, "Zacchaeus, hurry and come down, for today I must stay at your house."(2) [19:6] He hurried, came down, and received him joyfully. [19:7] When they saw it, they all murmured, saying, "He has gone in to lodge with a man who is a sinner."(3)

[19:8] Zacchaeus stood and said to the Lord, "Behold, Lord, half of my goods I give to the poor. If I have wrongfully exacted anything of anyone, I restore four times as much."

[19:9] Jesus said to him, "Today, salvation has come to this house, because he also is a son of Abraham. [19:10] For the Son of Man came to seek and to save that which was lost."(4)

1. Zacchaeus means "purified." He was small of stature and smaller still in his dealings with his fellows. Avarice had walled him in within the narrow limits of his own selfishness.

2. Jesus spoke kindly to Zacchaeus, engaged him in conversation, and spent the day as a guest in his home. As He talked He taught Zacchaeus the meaning of honesty, and His own manifest integrity impressed the chief publican.

3. Zacchaeus was honest with himself. He did not care what people thought of him but satisfied his curiosity at the expense of his dignity. He at least followed his impulses honestly, and when he became interested in goodness (incarnated in Jesus), he at once investigated goodness.

4. Avarice gives place to honesty, and the man is transformed from a petty trickster to an open-minded, fair-dealing citizen, intent on righting the wrongs that he has done in his ignorance.

## The Parable of the Ten Mina Coins

19:11 As they heard these things, he went on and told a parable, because he was near Jerusalem, and they supposed that the Kingdom of God would be revealed immediately. 19:12 He said therefore, "A certain nobleman went into a far country to receive for himself a kingdom,[1] and to return. 19:13 He called ten servants of his, and gave them ten mina coins,[2][41] and told them, 'Conduct business until I come.' 19:14 But his citizens hated him, and sent an envoy after him, saying, 'We don't want this man to reign over us.'

19:15 "It happened when he had come back again, having received the kingdom, that he commanded these servants, to whom he had given the money, to be called to him, that he might know what they had gained by conducting business.[3] 19:16 The first came before him, saying, 'Lord, your mina has made ten more minas.'

19:17 "He said to him, 'Well done, you good servant! Because you were found faithful with very little, you shall have authority over ten cities.'[4]

19:18 "The second came, saying, 'Your mina, Lord, has made five minas.'

19:19 "So he said to him, 'And you are to be over five cities.' 19:20 Another came, saying, 'Lord, behold, your mina, which I kept laid away in a handkerchief, 19:21 for I feared you, because you are an exacting man. You take up that which you didn't lay down, and reap that which you didn't sow.'

19:22 "He said to him, 'Out of your own mouth will I judge you, you wicked servant! You knew that I am an exacting man, taking up that which I didn't lay down, and reaping that which I didn't sow. 19:23 Then why didn't you deposit my money in the bank, and at my coming, I might have earned interest on it?' 19:24 He said to those who stood by, 'Take the mina away from him,[5] and give it to him who has the ten minas.'

19:25 "They said to him, 'Lord, he has ten minas!' 19:26 'For I tell you that to everyone who has, will more be given; but from him who doesn't have, even that which he has will be taken away from him. 19:27 But bring those enemies of mine who didn't want me to reign over them here, and kill them before me.'"

1. Christ, the Son of Divine Mind, is the nobleman. The kingdom in the far country, which he is to receive, is spiritual dominion.

2. *Servants, mina coins (pounds).* The servants represent the faculties, and the pounds represent the senses, which are dual in their expression. This incident represents the first quickening, or the first coming to our consciousness of the Christ, or spiritual self. The activity of the senses is under the direction of the faculties.

3. *What they had gained by conducting business.* At the second coming, or the second conscious realization of Christ, we are expected to increase the capacity of every faculty, on every plane of consciousness.

4. *have authority over ten cities.* We are given power and dominion over certain thought centers, of cities, and great increase in the ability to realize and demonstrate Spirit.

5. *Take the mina away from him.* The inaction results in atrophy and uselessness. "Take away from him the pound, and give

it unto him that hath the ten pounds."

## Jesus' Entry into Jerusalem

19:28 Having said these things, he went on ahead, going up to Jerusalem.

19:29 It happened, when he drew near to Bethsphage[42] and Bethany,❶ at the mountain that is called Olivet, he sent two of his disciples, 19:30 saying, "Go your way into the village on the other side, in which, as you enter, you will find a colt❷ tied, whereon no man ever yet sat. Untie it, and bring it. 19:31 If anyone asks you, 'Why are you untying it?' say to him: 'The Lord needs it.'"❸

19:32 Those who were sent went away, and found things just as he had told them. 19:33 As they were untying the colt, its owners said to them, "Why are you untying the colt?" 19:34 They said, "The Lord needs it." 19:35 They brought it to Jesus. They threw their cloaks on the colt, and set Jesus on them. 19:36 As he went, they spread their cloaks in the way. 19:37 As he was now getting near, at the descent of the Mount of Olives, the whole multitude of the disciples began to rejoice and praise God with a loud voice❹ for all the mighty works which they had seen, 19:38 saying, "Blessed is the King who comes in the name of the Lord![43] Peace in heaven, and glory in the highest!"

19:39 Some of the Pharisees❺ from the multitude said to him, "Teacher, rebuke your disciples!"

19:40 He answered them, "I tell you that if these were silent, the stones would cry out."❻

See Matt. 21:1-10; Mark 11:1-11a; John 12:12-19

1. These symbols indicate the centers where the life forces are gathered in the organism. They indicate not only subconscious spiritual potentialities, but also the houses, or cell centers, through which the forces work.

2. *colt*. A burden bearer, and we locate its house, or center, in the abdominal region. Unregenerate people never have sat upon or controlled this animal force, and in the natural order of expression it never has been directed in the right way.

3. *The Lord needs it*. In order to quicken and energize every cell in the organism, it is necessary that a fuller consciousness of the life force be realized.

4. The loud voice represents the outer manifestation through the power of the spoken word. By our words we should joyously express the evidences of life that well up within us.

5. *Pharisees*. The old conservative states of consciousness that would suppress the natural enthusiasm and joy of spirit.

6. *Stones would cry out*. Crystallized and stored-up forces of the organism, which are set free in regeneration, will react upon the nerve centers and will cause them to cry out in pain.

## Jesus Weeps over Jerusalem

19:41 When he drew near, he saw the city and wept over it, 19:42 saying, "If you, even you, had known today the things which belong to your peace! But now, they are hidden from your eyes. 19:43 For the days will come on you, when your enemies will throw up a barricade against you, surround you, hem you in on every side, 19:44 and will dash you and your children within you to the ground. They will not leave in you one stone on another,❶ because you didn't know the time of your visitation."

1. Jerusalem represents peace. Whoever does not realize peace in himself, but who consciously or unconsciously promotes discord in his environment and expresses it inwardly, has no understanding of peace. For him there is no true peace of mind.

## Jesus Cleanses the Temple

19:45 He entered into the temple, and began to drive out those who bought and sold in it, 19:46 saying to them, "It is written, 'My house is a house of prayer,'❶[44] but you have made it a 'den of robbers'!"❷[45]

19:47 He was teaching daily in the temple, but the chief priests and the scribes and the leading men among the people sought to destroy him. 19:48 They couldn't find what they might do, for all the people hung on to every word that he said.

1. *My house is a house of prayer.* The temple of our body consciousness should be constantly in touch with God through meditation and prayer.

2. *Den of robbers.* Through entertaining fears, worries, anxieties, doubts, suspicions, and other negative thoughts, we lose our peace of mind, and our body becomes a prey to destructive forces.

---

Fillmore Study Bible annotations compiled by Rev. Mark Hicks

**World English Bible Footnotes:**

[41] v19:13. 10 minas was more than 3 years' wages for an agricultural laborer.

[42] v19:29. TR, NU read "Bethpage" instead of "Bethsphage"

[43] v19:38. Psalm 118:26

[44] v19:46. Isaiah 56:7

[45] v19:46. Jeremiah 7:11

# Luke 20

## Who Is Giving You This Authority?

20:1 It happened on one of those days, as he was teaching the people in the temple and preaching the Good News, that the [46]priests and scribes came to him with the elders. 20:2 They asked him, "Tell us: by what authority do you do these things? Or who is giving you this authority?"❶

20:3 He answered them, "I also will ask you one question. Tell me: 20:4 the baptism of John, was it from heaven, or from men?"❷

20:5 They reasoned with
themselves, saying, "If we say, 'From
heaven,' he will say, 'Why didn't you
believe him?' 20:6 But if we say, 'From
men,' all the people will stone us,
for they are persuaded that John was
a prophet." 20:7 They answered that
they didn't know where it was from.

20:8 Jesus said to them, "Neither
will I tell you by what authority I do
these things."

1. *who is giving you this authority?* The Spirit of truth is the one and only authority in the study of Truth. See Matthew 7:29 and John 16:13 (RW/authority)

2. *the baptism of John, was it from heaven, or from men?* Jesus was trying to teach the chief priests and elders to do something for themselves. He told them He could not explain in definite language what to do from the plane of the natural man, symbolized by John the Baptist, but that they must use their inspiration. They had the same source of inspiration that He contacted—God. They should know for themselves that all authority is from God. ... Metaphysically interpreted, the indwelling Christ, symbolized by Jesus, is endeavoring to teach the highest religious thoughts in authority (the chief priests and elders) how to go to the one invisible Source and find out for themselves that all authority is from God (Jesus' Soul Evolution pp.797-8)

## Throwing Christ Out of the Vineyard

20:9 He began to tell the people
this parable. "A [47]man planted a
vineyard, and rented it out to some
farmers, and went into another
country for a long time. 20:10 At the
proper season, he sent a servant to
the farmers to collect his share of
the fruit of the vineyard. But the
farmers beat him, and sent him away
empty. 20:11 He sent yet another
servant, and they also beat him, and
treated him shamefully, and sent him
away empty. 20:12 He sent yet a third,
and they also wounded him, and
threw him out. 20:13 The lord of the
vineyard said, 'What shall I do? I will
send my beloved son.[1] It may be
that seeing him, they will respect
him.'

20:14 "But when the farmers saw
him, they reasoned among
themselves, saying, 'This is the heir.
Come, let's kill him, that the
inheritance may be ours.' 20:15 They
threw him out of the vineyard,[2] and
killed him. What therefore will the
lord of the vineyard do to them? 20:16
He will come and destroy these
farmers, and will give the vineyard to
others."

When they heard it, they said,
"May it never be!"

20:17 But he looked at them, and
said, "Then what is this that is
written,

'The stone which the builders
rejected,
the same was made the chief
cornerstone?'[48]
20:18 Everyone who falls on that stone
will be broken to pieces,
but it will crush whomever it
falls on to dust."

20:19 The chief priests and the
scribes sought to lay hands on him
that very hour, but they feared the
people--for they knew he had spoken
this parable against them.

1. *man:* God or Divine Mind. *vineyard:* the aggregation of religious ideas in the mind of man. *servants:* desire to keep the law and maintain a just balance between inner nature and expression through the enlightened faculties. *farmer:* the faculties that are given over to the dominance of the personal self. *beloved son:* the Christ or expression of perfect ideas in Divine Mind.

2. *threw him out of the vineyard.* By be-

ing put out of man's thought life or by being regarded as an impractical ideal without application to the practical affairs of everyday life, the natural or sense man suppresses or "kills" the Son of Christ by refusing to give it recognition or expression.

## Our Inner Spies

20:20 They watched him, and sent out spies,[1] who pretended to be righteous, that they might trap him in something he said, so as to deliver him up to the power and authority of the governor. 20:21 They asked him, "Teacher, we know that you say and teach what is right, and aren't partial to anyone, but truly teach the way of God. 20:22 Is it lawful for us to pay taxes to Caesar, or not?"

20:23 But he perceived their craftiness, and said to them, "Why do you test me?[2] 20:24 Show me a denarius. Whose image and inscription are on it?"

They answered, "Caesar's."

20:25 He said to them, "Then give to Caesar[3] the things that are Caesar's, and to God the things that are God's." 20:26 They weren't able to trap him in his words before the people. They marveled at his answer, and were silent.

1. *They watched him, and sent out spies.* The higher self is under continual suspicion of the sense self, which challenges every altruistic motive as ulterior instead.

2. *Why do you test me?* Old, established religious thoughts and beliefs are antagonistic toward Truth.

3. *give to Caesar.* We should recognize the demands of the external world in which we live, since we can transform it only by our life and example.

## Resurrection, Metaphysically Considered

20:27 Some of the Sadducees came to him, those who deny that there is a resurrection.[1] 20:28 They asked him, "Teacher, Moses wrote to us that if a man's brother dies having a wife, and he is childless, his brother should take the wife, and raise up children for his brother. 20:29 There were therefore seven brothers. The first took a wife, and died childless. 20:30 The second took her as wife, and he died childless. 20:31 The third took her, and likewise the seven all left no children, and died. 20:32 Afterward the woman also died. 20:33 Therefore in the resurrection whose wife of them will she be? For the seven had her as a wife."

20:34 Jesus said to them, "The children of this age marry, and are given in marriage. 20:35 But those who are considered worthy to attain to that age and the resurrection from the dead, neither marry, nor are given in marriage.[2] 20:36 For they can't die any more, for they are like the angels, and are children of God, being children of the resurrection. 20:37 But that the dead are raised, even Moses showed at the bush, when he called the Lord 'The God of Abraham, the God of Isaac, and the God of Jacob.'[49] 20:38 Now he is not the God of the dead, but of the living,[3] for all are alive to him."

20:39 Some of the scribes answered, "Teacher, you speak well." 20:40 They didn't dare to ask him any more questions.

1. *resurrection.* The resurrection is designating the state of consciousness which is completely above or greater than the current human level, even at the highest attainment.

2. *neither marry, nor are given in marriage.* Jesus indicates that on our next higher dimension of consciousness, in the resurrection, human relationships, such as cause us trouble in figuring out now, such as marital, will no longer be what they now seem to be.

3. *he is not the God of the dead, but of the living.* Jesus is asked a question, but it is based upon a low and faulty level of perception. Jesus simply cannot bring Himself to give the answer on that same level, so He gives the answer on a Truth level. (Ed Rabel NT Lectures, Questions about the Resurrection)

## Perfect Being and Divine Love

20:41 He said to them, "Why do they
say that the Christ❶ is David's son?
20:42 David❷ himself says in the book
of Psalms,

'The Lord said to my Lord,
"Sit at my right hand,
20:43 until I make your enemies the
footstool of your
feet."'[50]

20:44 "David therefore calls him
Lord, so how is he his son?"

1. *Christ.* The one complete idea of perfect human being in Divine Mind (MBD/Christ).

2. *David.* divine love individualized in human consciousness (MBD/David).

## Beware of the Accepted Authorities

20:45 In the hearing of all the
people, he said to his disciples,❶ 20:46
"Beware of the scribes,❷ who like to
walk in long robes, and love
greetings in the marketplaces, the
best seats in the synagogues, and the
best places at feasts; 20:47 who devour
widows' houses, and for a pretense
make long prayers: these will receive
greater condemnation."

1. *disciples.* Metaphysically, the faculties of mind.

2. *scribes.* Religious thoughts and beliefs of men which depend for their authority on their acceptance by leaders and masses; the trait that causes a man to crave and seek to gain the applause and esteem of others.

---

Fillmore Study Bible annotations by Rev. Mark Hicks.

**World English Bible Footnotes:**

[46] v20:1. TR adds "chief"

[47] v20:9. NU (in brackets) and TR add "certain"

[48] v20:17. Psalm 118:22

[49] v20:37. Exodus 3:6

[50] v20:43. Psalm 110:1

# Luke 21

## The Widow's Offering

21:1 He looked up, and saw the rich people[1] who were putting their gifts into the treasury. 21:2 He saw a certain poor widow[2] casting in two small brass coins.[51] 21:3 He said, "Truly I tell you, this poor widow put in more[3] than all of them, 21:4 for all these put in gifts for God from their abundance, but she, out of her poverty, put in all that she had to live on."

1. *rich people*. Thought forces that are active in accumulating material supply, and consequently have always a surplus.

2. *poor widow*. The affectional or divine love side of the individual, which has become separated from divine wisdom and consequently is impoverished.

3. *this poor widow put in more*. The widow gave all; she poured out all her love and substance, thereby exercising self-denial. The rich men gave of their bounty, making great display, but not in any way lessening their own comfort. That kind of giving amounts to but little in the sight of God.

## The Destruction of the Temple Foretold

21:5 As some were talking about the temple and how it was decorated with beautiful stones and gifts, he said, 21:6 "As for these things which you see, the days will come, in which there will not be left here one stone on another that will not be thrown down."[1]

1. *there will not be left here one stone on another that will not be thrown down*. The old is passing away and the new is being ushered in. Interpreted within ourselves a temple, as here referred to, represents material conditions, which Jesus taught would dissolve and disappear like a dream at the end of the age. No doubt today is the time to which He was looking forward. This whole chapter refers to regeneration. At the same time it has Its outer manifestation. Everything that takes place in the mind also expresses Itself in outer changes. It pictures man in his many experiences on the journey from the human to the divine consciousness. (*Jesus' Soul Evolution* p.1035-6)

## Signs and Persecutions

21:7 They asked him, "Teacher, so when will these things be? What is the sign that these things are about to happen?"

21:8 He said, "Watch out that you don't get led astray, for many will come in my name, saying, 'I am he[52],' and, 'The time is at hand.' Therefore don't follow them. 21:9 When you hear of wars and disturbances,[1] don't be terrified, for these things must happen first, but the end won't come immediately."

21:10 Then he said to them, "Nation will rise against nation, and kingdom against kingdom. 21:11 There will be great earthquakes, famines, and plagues in various places. There will be terrors and great signs from heaven. 21:12 But before all these things, they will lay their hands on you and will persecute you, delivering you up to synagogues and prisons, bringing you before kings and governors for my name's sake. 21:13 It will turn out as a testimony for you. 21:14 Settle it therefore in your hearts not to meditate beforehand how to answer, 21:15 for I will give you a mouth and wisdom which all your adversaries will not be able to withstand or to contradict. 21:16 You will be handed over even by parents, brothers, relatives, and friends. They will cause some of you to be put to death. 21:17 You will be hated by all men for my name's sake. 21:18 And not a hair of your head will perish.

21:19 "By your endurance you will win your lives.

1. *wars and disturbances,* Such things have nothing to do with “cosmic events, but result from men's belief in separation and their selfish lust for power and possessions. The end is not immediately connected with man's personal or selfish activities.

## The Destruction of Jerusalem Foretold

21:20 "But when you see Jerusalem surrounded by armies, then know that its desolation is at hand. 21:21 Then let those who are in Judea flee to the mountains. Let those who are in the midst of her depart. Let those who are in the country not enter therein. 21:22 For these are days of vengeance, that all things which are written may be fulfilled. 21:23 Woe to those who are pregnant and to those who nurse infants in those days![1] For there will be great distress in the land, and wrath to this people. 21:24 They will fall by the edge of the sword, and will be led captive into all the nations. Jerusalem will be trampled down by the Gentiles, until the times of the Gentiles are fulfilled.

1. *those days!* Spiritually interpreted, "those days" do not refer to some far off future date, but to man's own consciousness. When we are awakened to the truth about God and man, and begin to practice that that truth, then our material consciousness is nearlng its last days of existence. Every day is the "last day" of the old way of thinking and the "beginning" of the new day. (*Jesus' Soul Evolution* p.1035-6)

## The Coming of the Son of Man

21:25 There will be signs in the sun, moon, and stars; and on the earth anxiety of nations, in perplexity for the roaring of the sea and the waves; 21:26 men fainting for fear, and for expectation of the things which are coming on the world: for the powers of the heavens will be shaken. 21:27 Then they will see the Son of Man coming in a cloud with power and great glory.[1] 21:28 But when these things begin to happen, look up, and lift up your heads, because your redemption is near."

1. *glory.* Realization of divine unity; the blending and merging of man's mind with God-Mind. Glorification is the highest spiritual state of consciousness attainable by man. (RW/glory). *the Son of Man coming in a cloud with power and great glory.* Each one of us is a son of man, and our glory and power is in the keeping of the divine Logos. (*Teach Us To Pray* p.69)

## The Kingdom Of God Is Near

21:29 He told them a parable. "See the fig tree, and all the trees. 21:30 When they are already budding, you see it and know by your own selves that the summer is already near. 21:31 Even so you also, when you see these things happening, know that the Kingdom of God is near.[1] 21:32 Most certainly I tell you, this generation will not pass away until all things are accomplished. 21:33 Heaven and earth will pass away, but my words will by no means pass away.

1. *the Kingdom of God is near.* Heaven is a condition to be brought about in the affairs of men here on the earth. It is to grow from small beginnings, like the mustard seed or the yeast cake. His disciples were sent forth to sow the seed in a definite way, by carrying into the midst of men the signs that evidence the power of Spirit through which the kingdom of heaven is to be established, right here on this planet. There is no basis for any other view. Unity Tract; *The Kingdom of God Is At Hand.*

## Be Watchful All The Time

21:34 "So be careful, or your hearts will be loaded down with carousing, drunkenness, and cares of this life, and that day will come on you suddenly.[1] 21:35 For it will come like a snare on all those who dwell on the surface of all the earth. 21:36 Therefore be watchful all the time, praying that you may be counted worthy to escape all these things that will happen, and to stand before the Son of Man."

21:37 Every day Jesus was teaching in the temple, and every night he would go out and spend the night on the mountain that is called Olivet.[2]

21:38 All the people came early in the morning to him in the temple to hear him.

1. *that day will come on you suddenly.* The Christ comes again, as to Jesus, in the mind and heart of man, when he experiences birth into the consciousness of spiritual things.

2. *Olivet.* Mount of Olives; height yielding illuminating oil; high luminous principle; shining mount; exalted enlightenment. A mountain, or ridge of hills, near Jerusalem, to the east of the city. The ascension of Jesus Christ took place there (Acts 1:12),

---

Fillmore Study Bible annotations by Rev. Mark Hicks.

**World English Bible Footnotes:**

[51] v21:2. literally, "two lepta." 2 lepta was about 1% of a day's wages for an agricultural laborer.

[52] v21:8. or, I AM

# Luke 22

## The Plot to Kill Jesus

22:1 Now the feast of unleavened bread, which is called the Passover, drew near. 22:2 The chief priests and the scribes sought how they might put him to death, for they feared the people. 22:3 Satan[1] entered into Judas,[2] who was surnamed Iscariot, who was numbered with the twelve. 22:4 He went away, and talked with the chief priests and captains about how he might deliver him to them. 22:5 They were glad, and agreed to give him money. 22:6 He consented, and sought an opportunity to deliver him to them in the absence of the multitude.

See Matt. 26:1-5; Mark 14:1-2; John 11:47-53

1. *Satan* The deceiving phase of mind that has fixed ideas in opposition to Truth (adversary, lier in wait, accuser, opposer, hater, an enemy). Satan assumes various forms in our consciousness, among which may be mentioned egotism, a puffing up of the personality; and the opposite of this, self-deprecation, which admits the "accuser" into the consciousness. This "accuser" makes us believe that we are inherently evil.

2. *Judas.* Judas Iscariot—the custodian of life. This Judas represents the unredeemed life forces. He also typifies that in humanity which, though it has caught the higher vision of life, still resorts to underhanded methods in order to meet its obligations. Judas carried the money bag, and he betrayed Jesus for thirty pieces of silver.

## The Preparation of the Passover

22:7 The day of unleavened[1] bread came, on which the Passover[2] must be sacrificed. 22:8 He sent Peter and John, saying, "Go and prepare the Passover for us, that we may eat."

22:9 They said to him, "Where do you want us to prepare?"

22:10 He said to them, "Behold, when you have entered into the city, a man carrying a pitcher of water will meet you. Follow him into the house which he enters. 22:11 Tell the master of the house, 'The Teacher says to you, "Where is the guest room, where I may eat the Passover with my disciples?"' 22:12 He will show you a large, furnished upper room.[3] Make preparations there."

22:13 They went, found things as he had told them, and they prepared the Passover.

See Matt. 26:17-19; Mark 14:12-16

1. *leaven.* The law of increase observable throughout the entire creation is represented by leaven. *Unleavened bread.* The coming of a time when sincerity and truth shall form the mainspring of our life.

2. *passover.* The Passover is a symbol of our passing from sense to spiritual consciousness. It is therefore consistent with the giving up of pretense and duplicity for the sake of sincerity and truth.

3. *large, furnished upper room.* The mind with its exhaustless store of ideas.

## The Institution of the Lord's Supper

22:14 When the hour had come, he sat down with the twelve apostles. 22:15 He said to them, "I have earnestly desired to eat this Passover with you before I suffer, 22:16 for I tell you, I will no longer by any means eat of it until it is fulfilled in the Kingdom of God."[1] 22:17 He received a cup, and when he had given thanks, he said, "Take this, and share it among yourselves, 22:18 for I tell you, I will not drink at all again from the fruit of the vine, until the Kingdom of God comes."

22:19 He took bread, and when he had given thanks, he broke it,[2] and gave to them, saying, "This is my body which is given for you. Do this in memory of me."[3] 22:20 Likewise, he took the cup after supper, saying, "This cup is the new covenant in my blood,[4] which is poured out for you. 22:21 But behold, the hand of him who betrays me is with me on the table.[5] 22:22 The Son of Man indeed goes, as it has been determined, but woe to that man through whom he is betrayed!" 22:23 They began to question among themselves, which of them it was who would do this thing.

See Matt. 26:26-30; Mark 14:22-26; I Cor. 11:23

1. *until it is fulfilled in the kingdom of God.* The outer symbols used are inadequate to the spiritual appropriation of life and substance. Jesus, in his spiritual consciousness, could take no part in the material observance, but that he would soon be raised to a kingdom where he could partake of the real spiritual life and substance which the bread and wine represent. Those who observe the letter of the law in partaking of the Lord's supper do not receive the essence of spiritual life and substance. Spiritual things must be spiritually discerned and spiritually appropriated.

2. *he broke it.* Bread signifies the body of Christ or divine substance, and it is broken to indicate that we can appropriate it by degrees. No one can assimilate limitless substance, but each may partake of it according to their understanding or their mental and soul capacity.

3. *do this in remembrance of me.* The disciples had not yet been raised to spiritual consciousness; therefore, they needed the outer representation to lead men to the inner realization of the substance and life which the bread and the wine symbolize.

4. *the new covenant in my blood.* The promise of new life through the appropriation of the principle of the Christ in our life and daily activities.

5. *the hand of him who betrays me is with me on the table.* The betrayer is sense consciousness, whose hand or power enters into all outer manifestation.

## The Dispute about Greatness

22:24 There arose also a contention among them, which of them was considered to be greatest.[1] 22:25 He said to them, "The kings of the nations lord it over them, and those who have authority over them are called 'benefactors.' 22:26 But not so with you.[2] But one who is the greater among you, let him become as the younger, and one who is governing, as one who serves. 22:27 For who is greater, one who sits at the table, or one who serves? Isn't it he who sits at the table? But I am in the midst of you as one who serves. 22:28 But you are those who have continued with me in my trials. 22:29 I confer on you a kingdom, even as my Father conferred on me,[3] 22:30 that you may eat and drink at my table in my Kingdom. You will sit on thrones, judging the twelve tribes of Israel."[4]

See Matt. 20:24-28; Matt. 19:28; Mark 10:41-45

1. *was considered to be greatest*. Before we enter into this Gethsemane experience, self being still enthroned, there will be strife as to "who should be accounted greatest."

2. *not so with you* in the kingdom of heaven: but we that would attain to true spiritual greatness, let hus be least as to self: for spiritual eminence is attained by the Gethsemane victory over self by self-renunciation.

3. *even as my Father conferred on me*. What I have done in overcoming, you can do; and, as I have full dominion in my kingdom in the name of the Father, so shall you have full dominion in your kingdom in the name of Christ.

4. *the twelve tribes of Israel*. The number twelve represents spiritual fulfillment or perfection. The twelve tribes of Israel symbolize our twelve faculties, which we raise to perfection through the I AM.

## Jesus Predicts Peter's Denial

22:31 The Lord said, "Simon, Simon, behold, Satan(1) asked to have you, that he might sift you as wheat,(2)
22:32 but I prayed for you,(3) that your faith wouldn't fail. You, when once you have turned again, establish your brothers[53]."

22:33 He said to him, "Lord, I am ready to go with you both to prison and to death!"(4)

22:34 He said, "I tell you, Peter, the rooster will by no means crow today until you deny that you know me three times."

See Matt. 26:30-35; Mark 14:27-31; John 13:36-38

1. *Satan* (the adversary) represents fear in our personal mind, causing us to take thought for our own safety regardless of the claims of all others.

2. *sift you as wheat*. An unstable faith is largely due to our failure to identify himself with our spiritual source and draw upon divine strength in meeting temptation and tests that seem too much for us to meet successfully.

3. *but I prayed for you*. The Christ prayer of understanding will ultimately bring to our consciousness the pure "wheat" of True Being. When we reach this state of spiritual understanding, we shall be able to "strengthen the brethren." Only those who have passed through the great stages of overcoming know how to strengthen the weak, who have not made these demonstrations.

4. *I am ready to go with you both to prison and to death*. Simon has not yet learned the great lesson of self-renunciation: he is self-sufficient; we can never go with Christ "to prison and to death," until we demonstrate over self and self-will in Gethsemane; although with self exalted we may think we can demonstrate over "death"; self and spirit are antipodal; self must be dethroned.

## Purse, Bag, and Sword

22:35 He said to them, "When I sent you out without purse, and wallet, and shoes, did you lack anything?"

They said, "Nothing."

22:36 Then he said to them, "But now, whoever has a purse, let him take it,(1) and likewise a wallet. Whoever has none, let him sell his cloak, and buy a sword.
22:37 For I tell you that this which is written must still be fulfilled in me: 'He was counted with the lawless.'[54] For that which concerns me has an end."

[22:38] They said, "Lord, behold, here are two swords."

He said to them, "That is enough."

See Luke 9:3; Luke 10:4;

1. *But now, whoever has a purse, let him take it.* When you are alive to the Christ's voice, "sending you out" in his service, you will "lack nothing"; you will be provided for and defended. But when that voice is not heard within, and you are not alive to the spiritual, you had better carefully procure the things of worldly supply and defense

## Jesus Prays on the Mount of Olives

[22:39] He came out, and went, as his custom was, to the Mount of Olives.(1) His disciples also followed him. [22:40] When he was at the place, he said to them, "Pray that you don't enter into temptation."

[22:41] He was withdrawn from them about a stone's throw,(2) and he knelt down and prayed, [22:42] saying, "Father, if you are willing, remove this cup from me. Nevertheless, not my will, but yours, be done."

[22:43] An angel from heaven appeared to him, strengthening him. [22:44] Being in agony he prayed more earnestly.(3) His sweat became like great drops of blood falling down on the ground.

[22:45] When he rose up from his prayer, he came to the disciples, and found them sleeping because of grief, [22:46] and said to them, "Why do you sleep? Rise and pray that you may not enter into temptation."

1. *Mount of Olives.* The meaning of this name is "high luminous principle." And it represents the exaltation of divine love and wisdom in consciousness. The great work in the life of everyone is to incorporate the Christ mind in soul and body. The process of eliminating the old consciousness and entering into the new may be compared to the "wine press and oil," which is the meaning of Gethsemane.

2. *he was departed from them about a stone's throw.* The disciples represent the various faculties of the mind: faith, strength, judgment, love, power, imagination, understanding, will, order, zeal, elimination, and life. They are still under the law of sense.

3. *in an agony he prayed more earnestly;* From birth we are identified with sense consciousness, until it becomes ingrained in us. Separation from sense then causes us to suffer. The prayer that springs from overwrought emotion aroused by fear or apprehension does not prove effectual, unless faith in God proves stronger than the fear. Of itself agonizing does not make prayer effectual.

## The Betrayal and Arrest of Jesus

[22:47] While he was still speaking, behold, a multitude, and he who was called Judas, one of the twelve, was leading them. He came near to Jesus to kiss him. [22:48] But Jesus said to him, "Judas, do you betray the Son of Man with a kiss?"(1)

[22:49] When those who were around him saw what was about to happen, they said to him, "Lord, shall we strike with the sword?" [22:50] A certain one of them struck the servant of the high priest, and cut off his right ear.

[22:51] But Jesus answered, "Let me at least do this"--and he touched his ear, and healed him. [22:52] Jesus said to the chief priests, captains of the temple, and elders, who had come

against him, "Have you come out as
against a robber, with swords and
clubs? 22:53 When I was with you in
the temple daily, you didn't stretch
out your hands against me. But this
is your hour, and the power of
darkness."

See Matt. 26:47-56; Mark
14:43-50; John 18:3-11

1. *you betray the Son of man with a kiss?* Every time the life and substance of Spirit is used to further sense demands Jesus (the personal human being) is betrayed anew into the hands of His enemies.

## Peter Denies Jesus

22:54 They seized him, and led him
away, and brought him into the high
priest's house. But Peter followed
from a distance. 22:55 When they had
kindled a fire in the middle of the
courtyard, and had sat down
together, Peter sat among them. 22:56
A certain servant girl saw him as he
sat in the light, and looking intently
at him, said, "This man also was with
him."

22:57 He denied[1] Jesus, saying,
"Woman, I don't know him."

22:58 After a little while someone
else saw him, and said, "You also are
one of them!"

But Peter answered, "Man, I am
not!"

22:59 After about one hour passed,
another confidently affirmed, saying,
"Truly this man also was with him, for
he is a Galilean!"

22:60 But Peter said, "Man, I don't
know what you are talking about!"
Immediately, while he was still
speaking, a rooster crowed. 22:61 The
Lord turned, and looked at Peter.[2]
Then Peter remembered the Lord's
word, how he said to him, "Before
the rooster crows you will deny me
three times." 22:62 He went out, and
wept bitterly.

See Matt. 26:69-75; Mark
14:66-72; John 18:25-27

1. *he denied.* Peter denied the I AM (the Christ) instead of the limited personal self. Faith that is in the grip of fear is powerless to express itself truly.

2. *And the Lord turned, and looked upon Peter.* When we turn our attention within and examine our faith in the light of his I AM power, we sometimes find it deviating from its rightful center. A true disciple is always open to repentance. We may backslide and seem to be slipping spiritually, but our spiritual nature finally asserts its supremacy. The turning about of the Lord or the revealing of the face of the Lord represents discernment.

## The Mocking and Beating of Jesus

22:63 The men who held Jesus
mocked him and beat him. 22:64
Having blindfolded him, they struck
him on the face and asked him,
"Prophesy! Who is the one who struck
you?" 22:65 They spoke many other
things against him, insulting him.

## Jesus Before the Council

22:66 As soon as it was day, the
assembly of the elders of the people
was gathered together, both chief
priests and scribes, and they led him
away into their council, saying, 22:67
"If you are the Christ, tell us."

But he said to them, "If I tell you,
you won't believe, 22:68 and if I ask,
you will in no way answer me or let
me go. 22:69 From now on, the Son of
Man will be seated at the right hand
of the power of God."

22:70 They all said, "Are you then
the Son of God?"

He said to them, "You say it, because I am."

22:71 They said, "Why do we need
any more witness? For we ourselves
have heard from his own mouth!"

---

Fillmore Study Bible annotations compiled by Rev. Mark Hicks

**World English Bible Footnotes:**

[53] v22:32. The word for "brothers" here may be also correctly translated "brothers and sisters" or "siblings."

[54] v22:37. Isaiah 53:12

# Luke 23

## Jesus before Pilate

23:1 The whole company of them
rose up and brought him before
Pilate.(1) 23:2 They began to accuse
him, saying, "We found this man perverting the nation, forbidding paying taxes to Caesar, and saying that he himself is Christ, a king."

23:3 Pilate asked him, "Are you the
King of the Jews?"

He answered him, "So you say."

23:4 Pilate said to the chief priests
and the multitudes, "I find no basis
for a charge against this man." 23:5
But they insisted, saying, "He stirs up
the people, teaching throughout all Judea, beginning from Galilee even to this place."

1. *Pilate*. Metaphysically, the ruling principle of the sense plane, the carnal will. Pilate questioned the I AM, Jesus, "Art thou the King of the Jews?" Applying this to the each of us, we would say to ourself, "Is there a ruling will over my religious nature?" The personal will has no concept of the factors of that inner higher realm, and believes that it is the ruler of the whole person. It is jealous of any attempt to usurp its power, but when it is assured that the kingdom that the higher self would rule is "not of this world," it finds in that self no fault."

## Jesus before Herod

23:6 But when Pilate heard Galilee mentioned, he asked if the man was a Galilean. 23:7 When he found out that he was in Herod's jurisdiction, he sent him to Herod,[1] who was also in Jerusalem during those days.

23:8 Now when Herod saw Jesus, he was exceedingly glad, for he had wanted to see him for a long time, because he had heard many things about him. He hoped to see some miracle done by him. 23:9 He questioned him with many words, but he gave no answers. 23:10 The chief priests and the scribes stood, vehemently accusing him. 23:11 Herod with his soldiers humiliated him and mocked him. Dressing him in luxurious clothing, they sent him back to Pilate. 23:12 Herod and Pilate became friends with each other that very day, for before that they were enemies with each other.

1. *Herod.* Metaphysically, the ruling will of the physical, the ego in the sense consciousness. We who live in our appetites, in our passions, in our flesh, does not want anything but the flesh consciousness. Herod, sense consciousness, rules on the plane of mortality. If allowed full rein he kills out the repentant and redemptive state of mind, represented by John the Baptist, which is beginning its ministry of change and purification in soul and body. We must be on our guard against this subtle sense mind and take tender care of the little, innocent, new idea that has been born deep down in the heart. We must not give it over to the keeping of Herod. We must nurture it, care for it, and hide it away. If necessary we should take it down into Egypt (darkness) when Herod seeks to kill it. MBD/Herod.

## Jesus Sentenced to Death

23:13 Pilate called together the chief priests and the rulers and the people, 23:14 and said to them, "You brought this man to me as one that perverts the people, and see, I have examined him before you, and found no basis for a charge against this man concerning those things of which you accuse him. 23:15 Neither has Herod, for I sent you to him, and see, nothing worthy of death has been done by him. 23:16 I will therefore chastise him and release him."

23:17 Now he had to release one prisoner to them at the feast. 23:18 But they all cried out together, saying, "Away with this man! Release to us Barabbas!"-- 23:19 one who was thrown into prison for a certain revolt in the city, and for murder.

23:20 Then Pilate spoke to them again, wanting to release Jesus, 23:21 but they shouted, saying, "Crucify! Crucify him!"

23:22 He said to them the third time, "Why? What evil has this man done?[1] I have found no capital crime in him. I will therefore chastise him and release him." 23:23 But they were urgent with loud voices, asking that he might be crucified. Their voices and the voices of the chief priests prevailed. 23:24 Pilate decreed that what they asked for should be done. 23:25 He released him who had been thrown into prison for insurrection and murder, for whom they asked, but he delivered Jesus up to their will.

1. *What evil has this man done?* Charles Fillmore wrote in December 1906 "It is evident that Jesus ... expected to overcome death to the full and retain his physical body on the physical plane of consciousness. Before going to Jerusalem he had proclaimed that he could take his body temple up and lay it down at will, and that

if it were destroyed he could rebuild it in three days ... Here is where he evidently met more opposition than he anticipated. He had condemned the Pharisees severely, and the reaction of their thought was so great that he could not meet it... When Jesus met the full force of this, he was evidently stunned, and this accounts for his silence when questioned at the various trials to which he was subjected... The lesson for us is that we shall be on our guard against religious bigotry and especially the condemnation of those who differ from us, or are doing what we consider wrong. In the great overcoming of sins, which these final trials of Jesus symbolize, it is those of an ecclesiastical character that cause us most trouble. We think we shall be condemned for the sins of the flesh, but the verdict of Pilate, who represents the outer plane of consciousness, is that there is nothing in the man worthy of death." (MBI/Luke 23)

## The Crucifixion of Jesus

23:26 When they led him away, they grabbed one Simon of Cyrene, coming from the country, and laid on him the cross, to carry it after Jesus. 23:27 A great multitude of the people followed him, including women who also mourned and lamented him. 23:28 But Jesus, turning to them, said, "Daughters of Jerusalem, don't weep for me, but weep for yourselves and for your children. 23:29 For behold, the days are coming in which they will say, 'Blessed are the barren, the wombs that never bore, and the breasts that never nursed.' 23:30 Then they will begin to tell the mountains, 'Fall on us!' and tell the hills, 'Cover us.'[55] 23:31 For if they do these things in the green tree, what will be done in the dry?"

23:32 There were also others, two criminals, led with him to be put to death. 23:33 When they came to the place that is called The Skull,[1] they crucified him[2] there with the criminals,[3] one on the right and the other on the left.

23:34 Jesus said, "Father, forgive them, for they don't know what they are doing."

Dividing his garments[4] among them, they cast lots. 23:35 The people stood watching. The rulers with them also scoffed at him, saying, "He saved others. Let him save himself,[5] if this is the Christ of God, his chosen one!"

23:36 The soldiers also mocked him, coming to him and offering him vinegar, 23:37 and saying, "If you are the King of the Jews, save yourself!"

23:38 An inscription was also written over him in letters of Greek, Latin, and Hebrew:[6] "THIS IS THE KING OF THE JEWS."

23:39 One of the criminals who was hanged insulted him, saying, "If you are the Christ, save yourself and us!"

23:40 But the other answered, and rebuking him said, "Don't you even fear God, seeing you are under the same condemnation? 23:41 And we indeed justly, for we receive the due reward for our deeds, but this man has done nothing wrong." 23:42 He said to Jesus, "Lord, remember me when you come into your Kingdom."

23:43 Jesus said to him, "Assuredly I tell you, today you will be with me in Paradise."

1. *The place that is called the skull.* The place of the crucifixion being named a skull, which is the meaning of the Latin *Kranion*, translated Calvary, and Golgotha, skull in Aramaic, the language of the Jews in Palestine, is quite suggestive of the

place of the intellect, and points to a symbolism not hard to interpret. The seat of the conscious mind is the front brain, and it is here that the will has established its dominion.

2. *they crucified him.* Every time that the developing soul overcomes an error thought, there is a crucifixion. The error is cancelled. When all error has been overcome, the sense mind is completely erased and the body restored to spiritual perfection. This final cancellation of error is represented by the crucifixion of Jesus; which was the final and complete re1inquishament of the hold that error, represented by Judas, had upon His body.

3. *with the criminals.* The two malefactors represent the duality of good and evil that functions in human consciousness (1925). They also represent the past and the future. The past is full of regrets and accusations, but the future is hopeful and sees good ahead in spite of the great trial at hand (1906).

4. *dividing his garments.* The seamless garment is the consciousness of the indestructible unity of life and substance in the body entity. This consciousness inheres in the executive department of mind (soldiers).

5. *Let him save himself.* Jesus was acting out that which takes place in everyone who passes through regeneration. The carnal mind and its body of flesh must go through a transformation. Jesus said that this was done that the Scripture might be fulfilled. The Scripture veils in symbols and figures the law of mind and body regeneration.

6. *Greek, Latin and Hebrew.* The superscription written over Jesus signifies the rule of I AM in Spirit (Hebrew), soul (Greek), and body (Latin).

## The Death of Jesus

23:44 It was now about the sixth hour[56], and darkness came over the whole land[1] until the ninth hour.[57] 23:45 The sun was darkened,[2] and the veil of the temple was torn in two. 23:46 Jesus, crying with a loud voice, said, "Father, into your hands I commit my spirit!"[3] Having said this, he breathed his last.

23:47 When the centurion saw what was done, he glorified God, saying, "Certainly this was a righteous man." 23:48 All the multitudes that came together to see this, when they saw the things that were done, returned home beating their breasts. 23:49 All his acquaintances, and the women who followed with him from Galilee, stood at a distance, watching these things.

1. *darkness came over the whole land.* When error gives up its hold on the body, the bodily material consciousness is broken up, and the ignorance, evil, and error in which it functions envelop the whole land or body consciousness.

2. *The sun was darkened.* The sun, representing the light of Spirit, seems temporarily to fail. The veil of sense is rent preparatory to the coming forth of the new body in Christ.

3. *I commit my spirit.* Did Jesus die on the cross? No; Jesus gave up mortal consciousness with all its attachments, and merged himself into the mind of Spirit.

## The Burial of Jesus

23:50 Behold, a man named Joseph,[1] who was a member of the council, a good and righteous man 23:51 (he had not consented to their counsel and deed), from Arimathaea, a city of the Jews, who was also waiting for the Kingdom of God: 23:52 this man went to Pilate, and asked for Jesus' body. 23:53 He took it down, and wrapped it in a linen cloth, and laid him in a tomb that was cut in stone, where no one had ever been laid. 23:54 It was the day of the Preparation, and the Sabbath was drawing near. [23:55] The women, who had come with him out of Galilee, followed after, and saw the tomb, and how his body was laid. [23:56] They returned, and prepared spices and ointments. On the Sabbath they rested according to the commandment.

1. *Joseph.* of Arimathæa, signifies the imaging faculty functioning on a very high plane of consciousness (Arimathæa means a height). MBD/Joseph.

---

Fillmore Study Bible annotations by Rev. Mark Hicks.

**World English Bible Footnotes:**

[55] v23:30. Hosea 10:8

[56] v23:44. Time was counted from sunrise, so the sixth hour was about noon.

[57] v23:44. 3:00 PM

# Luke 24

## The Resurrection of Jesus

[24:1] But on the first day of the week, at early dawn, they and some others came to the tomb, bringing the spices which they had prepared. [24:2] They found the stone rolled away(1) from the tomb. [24:3] They entered in, and didn't find the Lord Jesus' body. [24:4] It happened, while they were greatly perplexed about this, behold, two men stood by them in dazzling clothing.(2) [24:5] Becoming terrified, they bowed their faces down to the earth.

They said to them, "Why do you seek the living among the dead? [24:6] He isn't here, but is risen. Remember what he told you when he was still in Galilee, [24:7] saying that the Son of Man must be delivered up into the hands of sinful men, and be crucified, and the third day rise again?"

[24:8] They remembered his words, [24:9] returned from the tomb, and told all these things to the eleven, and to all the rest. [24:10] Now they were Mary Magdalene,(3) Joanna, and Mary the mother of James. The other women with them told these things to the apostles. [24:11] These words seemed to them to be nonsense, and they didn't believe them. [24:12] But Peter got up and ran to the tomb. Stooping and looking in, he saw the strips of linen lying by themselves, and he departed to his home, wondering what had happened.(4)

1. *the stone rolled away.* The material concept of the body (represented by the stone) has been taken away.

2. *two men stood by them in dazzling clothing.* Represent spiritual thoughts of wisdom within the soul, thoughts which understand the resurrecting power of the Word.

3. *Now they were Mary Magdalene ...* The coming of the women at early dawn to the tomb represents the early awakening of the soul-feminine, through which the body is quickened into life.

4. *Peter ... wondering what had happened.* Faith (Peter) functions almost wholly in spiritual consciousness and does not readily comprehend that the body is essentially spiritual and is being raised into the fine essence of spiritual life.

## The Walk to Emmaus

24:13 Behold, two of them were going that very day to a village named Emmaus,[1] which was sixty stadia[58] from Jerusalem. 24:14 They talked with each other about all of these things which had happened. 24:15 It happened, while they talked and questioned together, that Jesus himself came near, and went with them. 24:16 But their eyes were kept from recognizing him. 24:17 He said to them, "What are you talking about as you walk, and are sad?"

24:18 One of them, named Cleopas,[2] answered him, "Are you the only stranger in Jerusalem who doesn't know the things which have happened there in these days?"

24:19 He said to them, "What things?"

They said to him, "The things concerning Jesus, the Nazarene, who was a prophet mighty in deed and word before God and all the people; 24:20 and how the chief priests and our rulers delivered him up to be condemned to death, and crucified him. 24:21 But we were hoping that it was he who would redeem Israel. Yes, and besides all this, it is now the third day since these things happened. 24:22 Also, certain women of our company amazed us, having arrived early at the tomb; 24:23 and when they didn't find his body, they came saying that they had also seen a vision of angels, who said that he was alive. 24:24 Some of us went to the tomb, and found it just like the women had said, but they didn't see him."

24:25 He said to them, "Foolish men, and slow of heart to believe in all that the prophets have spoken! 24:26 Didn't the Christ have to suffer these things and to enter into his glory?" 24:27 Beginning from Moses and from all the prophets, he explained to them in all the Scriptures the things concerning himself. 24:28 They drew near to the village, where they were going, and he acted like he would go further.

24:29 They urged him, saying, "Stay with us, for it is almost evening, and the day is almost over."

He went in to stay with them. 24:30 It happened, that when he had sat down at the table with them, he took the bread and gave thanks.[3] Breaking it, he gave to them. 24:31 Their eyes were opened, and they recognized him, and he vanished out of their sight. 24:32 They said one to another, "Weren't our hearts burning within us, while he spoke to us along the way, and while he opened the Scriptures to us?" 24:33 They rose up that very hour, returned to Jerusalem, and found the eleven gathered together, and those who were with them, 24:34 saying, "The Lord is risen indeed, and has appeared to Simon!" 24:35 They related the things that happened along the way, and how he was recognized by them in the breaking of the bread.

1. *Emmaus.* A place in consciousness

where the healing, restoring love and life and Truth of Spirit spring up and flow freely through our being (MBD/Emmaus).

2. *Cleopas.* Metaphysically, a faculty of mind not yet awakened fully to spiritual understanding. It has heard the Truth but has never affirmed as its own the Truth that Jesus taught. (MBD/Cleopas)

3. *he took the bread...* Through the blessing and breaking of bread his eyes were opened-his comprehension was cleared-and he realized the Truth as his own. *and gave thanks.* The bread represents the pure spiritual substance of the resurrected body, and it is appropriated by positive affirmations.

## Jesus Appears to His Disciples

24:36 As they said these things,
Jesus himself stood among them, and
said to them, "Peace be to you."[1]

24:37 But they were terrified[2] and
filled with fear, and supposed that
they had seen a spirit.

24:38 He said to them, "Why are
you troubled? Why do doubts arise in
your hearts? 24:39 See my hands and
my feet, that it is truly me. Touch
me and see, for a spirit doesn't have
flesh and bones, as you see that I
have." 24:40 When he had said this, he
showed them his hands and his feet.
24:41 While they still didn't believe for
joy, and wondered, he said to them,
"Do you have anything here to eat?"

24:42 They gave him a piece of a
broiled fish and some honeycomb.
24:43 He took them, and ate in front of
them. 24:44 He said to them, "This is
what I told you, while I was still with
you, that all things which are written
in the law of Moses, the prophets,
and the psalms, concerning me must
be fulfilled."[3]

24:45 Then he opened their minds,[4]
that they might understand the
Scriptures. 24:46 He said to them,
"Thus it is written, and thus it was
necessary for the Christ to suffer and
to rise from the dead the third day,
24:47 and that repentance and
remission of sins should be preached
in his name to all the nations,[5]
beginning at Jerusalem. 24:48 You are
witnesses of these things. 24:49
Behold, I send forth the promise of
my Father[6] on you. But wait in the
city of Jerusalem until you are
clothed with power from on high."

1. *Jesus himself stood among them, and said to them, "Peace be to you."* Standing "among them" represents the Christ presence abiding in the individual. With the Christ presence dominant in consciousness, the mind becomes peaceful and receptive.

2. *But they were terrified.* They think Jesus is dead and expect him to appear in ghostly form in which the spirits of the dead are supposed to come.

3. *must be fulfilled.* Truth, being eternal, is never lost, but is always made manifest.

4. *Then he opened their minds.* In order to interpret the Scriptures spiritually it is necessary that the mind have the quality usually called spiritual illumination. They learned what the Law, the Prophets, and the Psalms had to say concerning the Christ.

5. *should be preached in his name to all the nations.* That is, the entire consciousness, embracing mind, soul, and body. The "whole creation" of manifest and unmanifest being is to learn what insures its peace and to lay hold of the saving power of faith and concentrated denial (baptism).

6. *the promise of my Father.* the gift of the Holy Spirit, which is promised to us by reason of our potential capacity to express the divine. Luke again writes of this promise in Acts 1 and of its fulfillment in Acts 2.

## The Ascension of Jesus

24:50 He led them out as far as
Bethany,[1] and he lifted up his hands,
and blessed them. 24:51 It happened,
while he blessed them, that he
withdrew from them, and was
carried up into heaven.[2] 24:52 They
worshiped him, and returned to
Jerusalem with great joy, 24:53 and
were continually in the temple,
praising and blessing God. Amen.

1. *Bethany*. Bethany means "fruitage." Jesus' fulfillment of the spiritual law enabled Him to ascend into the pure realm of Spirit.

2. *carried up (ascended) into heaven*. The Ascension is the final step in attaining complete union with Divine Mind. Through the realization of His oneness with Divine Mind Jesus completely spiritualized His Physical body. Luke again writes of the ascension in Acts 1.

---

Fillmore Study Bible annotations by Rev. Mark Hicks.

**World English Bible Footnotes:**

[58] v24:13. 60 stadia = about 11 kilometers or about 7 miles.

# The Good News According to John

Last Supper, miniature from a Psalter, in Latin [Alsace (Strasbourg), c.1220-40]. Public Domain.

## Introduction to John

METAPHYSICAL BIBLE students recognize in the Gospel of John a certain spiritual quality that is not found in the other Gospels. Although this is not true of all Bible readers, it may be said that those who look for the mystical find it in the language of this book. The book is distinctive in this respect and is so successful in setting forth metaphysical truths that little interpretation is necessary. Only in a few instances does the original writing conceal the deep truths that the student seeks to discern. Written language is at best a reflection of inner ideas, and even though a teacher couples ideas and words as adroitly as Jesus does, elucidation is sometimes difficult.

Nevertheless ideas are catching, and this may be the best reason for publishing another book about this spirit-arousing Fourth Gospel. We are all heavily charged with ideas, and when these ideas are released they spring forth and pass from mind to mind, being "recorded" as they fly, and when they are expressed the whole race is lifted up—if the idea is charged with the uplifting Spirit. Jesus was God's idea of man made manifest in the flesh; so He was warranted in making that dynamic assertion, "I, if I be lifted up from the earth, will draw all men unto myself." Nowhere in all literature has this truth of the unity of God, man, and creation been so fearlessly expressed and affirmed by man as in the Book of John.

Here the question arises as to God's responsibility for all that appears in the flesh, both good and evil, which seems to confound our logic and understanding. We are in human consciousness the fruit of a tree that stemmed from the soil of Being. The laws instituted in the aeons and ages of the past still prevail in the present. Interpreting Being from a personal standpoint, we have ignored the principles and laws at the very foundation of all creation and substituted a personal God, and many contradictions have followed. Now through the unfoldment of the spiritual man implanted in us in the beginning we are discerning the unchangeable laws of the good and the absolute necessity of conforming to them.

So we see that Jesus taught plainly that God functions in and through man and nature instead of being a person somewhere in the skies; also that we demonstrate God by making His Spirit manifest in our life. "He that hath seen me hath seen the Father." Socrates was asked, "What is a good man?" He replied, "A man who does good." Again he was asked, "What is good?" "What the good man does," he replied.

No extended definition of good is necessary to those who follow Jesus; even converted savages understand good and do it. The universal desire among awakened Christians to love God and man is part of the law constantly operating through man when he finds his right relation to God.

The status of evil is that of a parasite. It has no permanent life of itself; its whole existence depends on the life it borrows from its parent, and when its connection with the parent is severed nothing remains. Apparent evil is the result of ignorance, and when the truth is presented the error disappears. Jesus called it a liar and the father of lies.

Men personalize good and evil in a multiplicity of Is and devils, but Truth students follow Jesus in recognizing the supreme Spirit in man as the "one God and Father of all."

Introduction to *Mysteries of John* by Charles Fillmore.

The Gospel of John stands in a class by itself, and is sometimes referred to as "the Spiritual Gospel." This term should not be regarded as a reflection on the Synoptic Gospels, nor is there any suggestion that they are not of a "spiritual" nature. Rather, the term Spiritual is intended to indicate that there are several marked differences between John's Gospel and the Synoptic Gospels.

(1) John's Gospel was, in all probability, written at Ephesus, sometime

between A.D. 90 and A.D. 120. This makes it of much later date than the Synoptic Gospels. The contents also indicate that John's Gospel was written for what might be termed "advanced students"—that is, those who were already familiar with the Synoptic Gospels.

(2) John's Gospel gives a great deal of what is usually termed "advanced teaching"—such as "the New Birth" (John 3), "the Bread of Life" (John 6), "the New Commandment" (John 15), to mention only a few such teachings. Then, there are the "I AM teachings"—"I am the light of the world" (John 8:12), "I am the resurrection, and the life" (John 11:25), and many similar passages. These "I AM teachings" do not appear in the Synoptic Gospels.

(3) John's Gospel does not contain parables, such as are found in the Synoptic Gospels. However, it will be noticed that the writer of John's Gospel frequently uses miracles to illustrate certain important teachings, instead of parables. Thus, we have the teaching, "I am the Light of the world"—and following is the account of healing the man born blind (John 8-9). Then there is the teaching, "I am the bread of life"—closely followed by the miracle of feeding the five thousand (John 6); and there are several other instances of this sort. Llowever, all this will be fully explained in a later lesson.

(4) The Synoptic Gospels record the Sermon on the Mount, in various forms—and this apparently covers teaching given during the earlier part of Jesus' ministry. In contrast with this, John's Gospel gives us the "Upper Room discourses" (John 14-17)—and these were given at the dose of Jesus' ministry.

Thus, John's Gospel gives us not only the "facts" of Jesus' ministry, but also the interpretation of many of His teachings and activities. Indeed, the writer of this Gospel sums up the entire record of the life and teachings of Jesus Christ in a clear statement of purpose: "These are written, that ye may believe that Jesus is the Christ, the Son of God; and that believing ye may have life in his name" (John 20:31).

Introduction to *The Good News According to John* by Herbert J. Hunt, former Dean of Bible Studies for the Unity School of Christianity.

# John 1

## The Prologue

1:1 In the beginning was the
Word,(1) and the Word was with God,
and the Word was God. 1:2 The same
was in the beginning with God. 1:3
All things were made through him.(2)
Without him was not anything made
that has been made. 1:4 In him was
life, and the life was the light of
men. 1:5 The light shines in the
darkness, and the darkness hasn't
overcome[1] it. 1:6 There came a man,
sent from God, whose name was

John. 1:7 The same came as a witness,
that he might testify about the
light,[3] that all might believe through
him. 1:8 He was not the light, but
was sent that he might testify about
the light. 1:9 The true light that
enlightens everyone was coming into
the world.[4]

1:10 He was in the world, and the
world was made through him, and
the world didn't recognize him. 1:11
He came to his own, and those who
were his own didn't receive him. 1:12
But as many as received him,[5] to
them he gave the right to become
God's children, to those who believe
in his name: 1:13 who were born not
of blood, nor of the will of the flesh,
nor of the will of man, but of God.

1:14 The Word became flesh,[6] and
lived among us. We saw his glory,
such glory as of the one and only
Son of the Father, full of grace and
truth. 1:15 John testified about him.
He cried out, saying, "This was he of
whom I said, 'He who comes after me
has surpassed me, for he was before
me.'" 1:16 From his fullness we all
received grace upon grace. 1:17 For
the law was given through Moses.
Grace and truth came through Jesus
Christ.[7] 1:18 No one has seen God at
any time. The one and only Son,[2]
who is in the bosom of the Father, he
has declared him.[8]

1. *In the beginning was the Word.* In pure metaphysics there is but one word, the Word of God. This is the original creative Word or thought of Being. It is the "God said" of Genesis. The Greek original refers to it in the 1st chapter of John as *logos. Logos* cannot be adequately translated into English. In the original it denotes wisdom, judgment, power, and in fact all the inherent potentialities of Being. This divine Logos was and always is in God; in fact it is God as creative power.

2. *All things were made through him.* Divine Mind creates under law; that is, spiritual law. Humans may get a comprehension of the creative process of Being by analyzing the action of one's own mind. First is mind, then the idea in mind of what the act is to be, then the act itself. Thus the Word and the divine process of creating are identical.

3. *that he might testify about the light.* Humans in their darkened, ignorant state dwell in a realm of material thoughts and perceives nothing higher until one arrives at the point of unfoldment where one is ready to receive understanding of the Christ Truth. The person then enters into the "John the Baptist" or intellectual perception of Truth. The intellectual perception of Truth by the natural man (John the Baptist) is not the true light (the Christ) but bears witness to the light and prepares the way for its dawning in consciousness.

4. *The true light that enlightens everyone was coming into the world.* The true light (the Christ or Word) that lights every man coming into the world is and ever has been in man. Even the outer man was formed and came into existence through it. Up to a certain stage in his unfolding man does not recognize this truth; now however this mystery, which is "Christ in you, the hope of glory," is being revealed to the race with more and more clarity and with greatly increased power.

5. *But as many as received him.* According to the 12th and 13th verses, the same truth that held good for Jesus will hold good for as many as receive Him (the Christ) and believe in His resurrecting power as Jesus believed in it.

6. *And the Word became flesh.* Jesus recognized this truth that the Christ, the divine-idea man or Word of God, was His true self and that He was consequently the Son of God. Because Jesus held to this perfect image of the divine man, the Christ or Word entered consciously into every atom of His being, even to the very cells of His outer organism, and transformed all His body into pure, immortal, spiritual substance and life. Thus "the Word became flesh." The resurrecting of His whole being included His body. Jesus entered alive and entire into the spiritual realm.

7. *grace and truth came through Jesus Christ.* The real saving, redeeming, transforming power came to man through the work that Jesus did in establishing for the race a new and higher consciousness in the earth. We can enter into that consciousness by faith in Him and by means of the inner spirit of the law that He taught and practiced.

8. *The one and only Son ... he has declared him.* Through the Christ in us we come into an understanding of the Father, since the Son (the Word) ever exists in

God, and Father and Son are one and are omnipresent in man and in the universe. Spirit Truth is discerned through Spirit only; not in outer ways or through intellectual perception do we come to know God.

## The Testimony of John

1:19 This is John's testimony, when the Jews sent priests and Levites from Jerusalem to ask him, "Who are you?"

1:20 He confessed, and didn't deny, but he confessed, "I am not the Christ."

1:21 They asked him, "What then? Are you Elijah?"

He said, "I am not."

"Are you the prophet?"

He answered, "No."

1:22 They said therefore to him, "Who are you? Give us an answer to take back to those who sent us. What do you say about yourself?"

1:23 He said, "I am the voice of one crying in the wilderness, 'Make straight the way of the Lord,'[3] as Isaiah the prophet said."

1:24 The ones who had been sent were from the Pharisees. 1:25 They asked him, "Why then do you baptize, if you are not the Christ, nor Elijah, nor the prophet?"

1:26 John answered them, "I baptize in water,[1] but among you stands one whom you don't know. 1:27 He is the one who comes after me, who is preferred before me, whose sandal strap I'm not worthy to loosen." 1:28 These things were done in Bethany beyond the Jordan, where John was baptizing.

1. *I baptize in water* In the regeneration two states of mind are constantly at work. First comes the cleansing or denial state, in which all the error thoughts are eliminated. This includes forgiveness for sins committed and a general clearing up of the whole consciousness. The idea is to get back into the pure, natural consciousness of Spirit. This state of mind is typified by John the Baptist, who came out of the wilderness a child of nature whose mission it was to make straight the way for One who was to follow.

## The Lamb of God

1:29 The next day, he saw Jesus coming to him, and said, "Behold, the Lamb of God, who takes away the sin of the world! 1:30 This is he of whom I said, 'After me comes a man who is preferred before me, for he was before me.' 1:31 I didn't know him, but for this reason I came baptizing in water: that he would be revealed to Israel." 1:32 John testified,[1] saying, "I have seen the Spirit descending like a dove out of heaven, and it remained on him. 1:33 I didn't recognize him, but he who sent me to baptize in water, he said to me, 'On whomever you will see the Spirit descending, and remaining on him, the same is he who baptizes in the Holy Spirit.'[2] 1:34 I have seen, and have testified that this is the Son of God."

1. *John testified.* Metaphysically interpreted, John the Baptist symbolizes in each individual the natural man, but with an illumined intellect. His face is turned toward the light in the measure that he recognizes and pays homage to the higher self within the individual. John baptized

with water all those who believed that Jesus was soon to make His appearance. This is a cleansing, purifying process, preparing the individual to see spiritually and to discern spiritually.

2. *baptizes in the Holy Spirit.* The Father-Mind is the living principle, the absolute, the unlimited. The Son is the living Word. "Word" is used to designate man's I AM identity. The Holy Spirit is the action or outpouring or activity of the living Word. This activity produces what may be termed the light of Spirit, the breath of God, the "personality" of Being. The outpouring of the Holy Spirit is the sign by which the natural man recognizes the divine. Jesus, who became the "Lamb of God" or perfect expression of God, baptized in the Holy Spirit.

## The First Disciples of Jesus

1:35 Again, the next day, John was standing with two of his disciples, 1:36 and he looked at Jesus as he walked, and said, "Behold, the Lamb of God!" 1:37 The two disciples heard him speak, and they followed Jesus. 1:38 Jesus turned, and saw them following, and said to them, "What are you looking for?"

They said to him, "Rabbi" (which is to say, being interpreted, Teacher), "where are you staying?"

1:39 He said to them, "Come, and see."

They came and saw where he was staying, and they stayed with him that day. It was about the tenth hour.[4] 1:40 One of the two who heard John, and followed him, was Andrew, Simon Peter's brother. 1:41 He first found his own brother, Simon, and said to him, "We have found the Messiah!"[1] (which is, being interpreted, Christ[5]). 1:42 He brought him to Jesus. Jesus looked at him, and said, "You are Simon[2] the son of Jonah. You shall be called Cephas" (which is by interpretation, Peter).

1. *We have found the Messiah.* When the conscious mind recognizes the Christ Mind, the various faculties gradually awaken and attach themselves to it. Andrew is the first apostle mentioned, and with him was one whose name is not given here but who is supposed to have been John (love). Love is modest and retiring, "seeketh not its own." Andrew represents the strength of the mind, which, greatly rejoiced when it finds the inexhaustible source of all strength, exclaims, "We have found the Messiah."

2. *You are Simon.* Strength is clearly related to substance (Simon), which in spirit we call faith. "Faith is the substance of things hoped for" (A.V.). What we hope for and mentally see as a possibility in our life comes into visibility, and we call it substantial.

## Jesus Calls Philip and Nathanael

1:43 On the next day, he was determined to go out into Galilee, and he found Philip. Jesus said to him, "Follow me." 1:44 Now Philip was from Bethsaida,[1] of the city of Andrew and Peter. 1:45 Philip found Nathanael, and said to him, "We have found him, of whom Moses in the law, and the prophets, wrote: Jesus of Nazareth, the son of Joseph."

1:46 Nathanael said to him, "Can any good thing come out of Nazareth?"

Philip said to him, "Come and see."

1:47 Jesus saw Nathanael coming to him, and said about him, "Behold, an Israelite indeed, in whom is no deceit!"

1:48 Nathanael said to him, "How do you know me?"

Jesus answered him, "Before Philip called you, when you were under the fig tree, I saw you."

1:49 Nathanael answered him, "Rabbi, you are the Son of God! You are King of Israel!"

1:50 Jesus answered him, "Because I told you, 'I saw you underneath the fig tree,' do you believe? You will see greater things than these!" 1:51 He said to him, "Most certainly, I tell you, hereafter you will see heaven opened,[2] and the angels of God ascending and descending on the Son of Man."

1. *Philip was from Bethsaida.* The name Philip means "lover of horses," and Philip is symbolic of the vigor, power, vitality, and energy of the mind. Philip, Andrew, and Peter are of the same "city," Bethsaida. The name Bethsaida means "house of fishing," and Bethsaida signifies a group of thoughts in consciousness that have as their central idea a belief in the increase of ideas and their expression and manifestation in outer form.

2. *You will see the heaven opened.* Among the apostles, Bartholomew represents the imagination. He is called Nathanael in the 1st chapter of John, where it is recorded that Jesus saw him under the fig tree, the inference being that He discerned Nathanael's presence before the latter came into visibility. This would indicate that images of people and things are projected into the imaging chamber of the mind and that by giving them attention one can understand their relation to outer things. Mind readers, clairvoyants, and dreamers have developed this capacity to varying degree. Consciousness is what is concerned with soul unfoldment both primarily, and secondarily and all the way! Forms are always manifestations of ideas. Whoever understands this can interpret the symbols shown him in dreams and visions, but lack of understanding of this law makes one a psychic without discernment. With this spiritual faculty it is possible for man to penetrate into the "fourth dimension" or what is usually called the "kingdom of the heavens" and to discern the trend of the spiritual forces. The angels of God are spiritual forces active in the Sons of God, the spiritually quickened.

---

Fillmore Study Bible annotations compiled by Rev. Mark Hicks.

**World English Bible Footnotes:**

[1] v1:5. The word translated "overcome" (katelaben) can also be translated "comprehended." It refers to getting a grip on an enemy to defeat him.

[2] v1:18. NU reads "God"

[3] v1:23. Isaiah 40:3

[4] v1:39. 4:00 PM.

[5] v1:41. "Messiah" (Hebrew) and "Christ" (Greek) both mean "Anointed One".

# John 2

## The Wedding at Cana

2:1 The third day, there was a marriage[1] in Cana[2] of Galilee. Jesus' mother was there. 2:2 Jesus also was invited, with his disciples, to the marriage. 2:3 When the wine ran out, Jesus' mother said to him, "They have no wine."

2:4 Jesus said to her, "Woman, what does that have to do with you and me? My hour has not yet come."

2:5 His mother said to the servants, "Whatever he says to you, do it." 2:6 Now there were six water pots of stone[3] set there after the Jews' manner of purifying, containing two or three metretes[6] apiece. 2:7 Jesus said to them, "Fill the water pots with water." They filled them up to the brim. 2:8 He said to them, "Now draw some out, and take it to the ruler of the feast."[4] So they took it. 2:9 When the ruler of the feast tasted the water now become wine, and didn't know where it came from (but the servants who had drawn the water knew), the ruler of the feast called the bridegroom, 2:10 and said to him, "Everyone serves the good wine first, and when the guests have drunk freely, then that which is worse. You have kept the good wine until now!" 2:11 This beginning of his signs Jesus did in Cana of Galilee, and revealed his glory; and his disciples believed in him.

2:12 After this, he went down to Capernaum,[5] he, and his mother, his brothers, and his disciples; and they stayed there a few days.

1. *a marriage.* Spiritually, a marriage represents the union of two dominant states of consciousness. Mary, the mother of Jesus, represents intuition, the spiritual soul, Eve, "the mother of all living." Jesus is the personal I AM and His apostles are the twelve faculties.

2. *in Cana.* Cana is a "place of reeds"; so is the larynx found in the body. The name Galilee means "to whirl"; air is rapidly forced through the larynx in speaking or singing. The apostles represent the dominant nerve centers, the spiritual symbolism of each being concealed in the name. Philip means "one who is fond of horses." The horse symbolizes vigor, vitality, power. Vigor or its opposite, weakness, is betrayed by the voice, so we designate Philip as the power faculty, and his place in body expression is in the larynx (at Cana).

3. *six waterpots of stone,* Six nerve centers in the body. Water may be compared to natural or human life, and wine to spiritual life. In the regeneration spirit and body are united, but before this union can be accomplished the exhausted natural life must be quickened with spirit (symbolized by the turning of water into wine).

4. *the ruler of the feast.* The supreme I AM, pronounced the transformed water to be superior to the best wine. This transformation of the negative, watery fluid of the organism into vitalizing Spirit is accomplished by adding to every word a spiritual idea. The idea of omnipresent life will then quicken the natural life in man, and it will make conscious contact with the one life and draw it out for the benefit of the many.

5. *went down to Capernaum* Capernaum designates or represents an inner conviction of the abiding compassion and restoring power of Being. When one enters this state of consciousness a healing virtue pours out of the soul and transforms all discord into harmony.

## Jesus Cleanses the Temple

2:13 The Passover of the Jews was at hand,❶ and Jesus went up to Jerusalem. 2:14 He found in the temple those who sold oxen, sheep, and doves, and the changers of money❷ sitting. 2:15 He made a whip of cords, and threw all out of the temple, both the sheep and the oxen; and he poured out the changers' money, and overthrew their tables. 2:16 To those who sold the doves, he said, "Take these things out of here! Don't make my Father's house a marketplace!" 2:17 His disciples remembered that it was written, "Zeal for your house will eat me up."❸[7]

2:18 The Jews therefore answered him, "What sign do you show us, seeing that you do these things?"

2:19 Jesus answered them, "Destroy this temple, and in three days I will raise it up."❹

2:20 The Jews therefore said, "Forty-six years was this temple in building, and will you raise it up in three days?" 2:21 But he spoke of the temple of his body. 2:22 When therefore he was raised from the dead, his disciples remembered that he said this, and they believed the Scripture, and the word which Jesus had said.

2:23 Now when he was in Jerusalem at the Passover, during the feast, many believed in his name, observing his signs which he did. 2:24 But Jesus didn't trust himself to them, because he knew everyone, 2:25 and because he didn't need for anyone to testify concerning man; for he himself knew what was in man.

1. *the passover of the Jews was at hand.* In individual consciousness, the "passover of the Jews" represents the time set aside for fasting and prayer, the cleansing and renewing of the body temple through denial and affirmation, making it ready for the coming of the Lord.

2. *"Those that sold oxen and sheep and doves" and "the changers of money"* are errors in the subconsciousness.

3. *Zeal for thy house will eat me up.* "Zeal," by its very nature, is intense activity. If allowed to take possession of the mind, it turns the attention to observance of forms, following the line of action that brings the appearance of greatest results, and the Spirit is lost sight of. To the Greek philosophers, passion (zeal) was a problem. That is because the ancients did not want to become a "beast." This contrasts with contemporary philosophy which is more concerned about becoming a "machine."

4. *and in three days.* The three degrees or parts of man's consciousness: spirit, soul and body. The spiritual I Am must establish its mastery in these before the Word of God is fulfilled and the perfect man brought forth.

---

Fillmore Study Bible annotations compiled by Rev. Mark Hicks.

**World English Bible Footnotes:**

[6] v2:6. 2 to 3 metretes is about 20 to 30 U. S. Gallons, 16 to 25 imperial gallons, or 75 to 115 litres.

[7] v2:17. Psalm 69:9

# John 3

## Nicodemus Visits Jesus

3:1 Now there was a man of the Pharisees named Nicodemus,[1] a ruler of the Jews.[2] 3:2 The same came to him by night, and said to him, "Rabbi, we know that you are a teacher[3] come from God, for no one can do these signs that you do, unless God is with him."

3:3 Jesus answered him, "Most certainly, I tell you, unless one is born anew,[4][8] he can't see the Kingdom of God."

3:4 Nicodemus said to him, "How can a man be born when he is old? Can he enter a second time into his mother's womb, and be born?"

3:5 Jesus answered, "Most certainly I tell you, unless one is born of water and spirit, he can't enter into the Kingdom of God! 3:6 That which is born of the flesh is flesh. That which is born of the Spirit is spirit. 3:7 Don't marvel that I said to you, 'You must be born anew.' 3:8 The wind[9] blows where it wants to, and you hear its sound, but don't know where it comes from and where it is going. So is everyone who is born of the Spirit."[5]

3:9 Nicodemus answered him, "How can these things be?"

3:10 Jesus answered him, "Are you the teacher of Israel, and don't understand these things? 3:11 Most certainly I tell you, we speak that which we know, and testify of that which we have seen, and you don't receive our witness. 3:12 If I told you earthly things and you don't believe, how will you believe if I tell you heavenly things? 3:13 No one has ascended into heaven, but he who descended out of heaven,[6] the Son of Man, who is in heaven. 3:14 As Moses lifted up the serpent in the wilderness, even so must the Son of Man be lifted up,[7] 3:15 that whoever believes in him should not perish, but have eternal life. 3:16 For God so loved the world,[8] that he gave his one and only Son, that whoever believes in him should not perish, but have eternal life. 3:17 For God didn't send his Son into the world to judge the world, but that the world should be saved through him. 3:18 He who believes in him is not judged. He who doesn't believe has been judged already,[9] because he has not believed in the name of the one and only Son of God. 3:19 This is the judgment, that the light has come into the world, and men loved the darkness rather than the light;[10] for their works were evil. 3:20 For everyone who does evil hates the light, and doesn't come to the light, lest his works would be exposed. 3:21 But he who does the truth comes to the light, that his works may be revealed, that they have been done in God."

1. *a man of the Pharisees named Nicodemus.* All "inheritance" of ideas and beliefs has a mental basis. We "inherit" some states of mind from our ancestors. An "inherited" or transmitted religion is a dark state, if there is no real understanding in it. This is the Nicodemus mentality. Nicodemus was a Pharisee and a ruler of the Jews. He represents the Pharisaical side of our mentality that observes the external forms of religion without understanding their real meaning.

2. *a ruler of the Jews.* This should be properly translated "a ruler of the

Judeans." Jesus was from Galilee, not from Judea. Much of the hostile language in the Gospel of John toward "the Jews" reflects hostility between the Galileans, of which was Jesus, and the Judeans, who were invested in temple sacrifice and conservative religious thought.

3. *We know that you are a teacher*. The Pharisees refused to be baptized by John. They did not consider that they needed the repentance that he demanded. They thought they were good enough to take the high places in the kingdom of God because of their popularly accepted religious supremacy.

4. *Except one be born anew*. The new birth is an uncertainty to the intellectual Christian, hence there has gradually evolved a popular belief that after death the souls of those who have accepted the church creed and have been counted Christians will undergo a change. But in His instructions to Nicodemus Jesus makes no mention of a resurrection after death as having any part in the new birth.

5. *The wind bloweth where it will*. Jesus cites the ever present though unseen wind as an illustration of those who are born of Spirit. The new birth is a change that comes here and now. It has to do with the present man, that he may be conscious of the "Son of man," who is the real I AM in each individual.

6. *but he that descended out of heaven*. There is but one real man, the ideal or spiritual man that God created. Jesus explains to Nicodemus the evolution of this spiritual man from his ideal to his manifest state. Man is fundamentally spiritual and so remains throughout his various manifestations. He comes out of heaven, manifests himself as a personality in the earth, and returns to heaven.

7. *even so must the Son of man be lifted up*. In these few words is summed up the fall of man from an Edenic state, where he had the constant inspiration of creative Mind, to a consciousness of matter and the desperate struggle of personality for existence. The natural man must evolve into the spiritual.

8. *for God so loved the world*. To believe in Jesus is to believe that in the regenerate state we are to be, like Him, "joint-heirs with Christ." This belief must then lead us to a desire and an effort to attain our inheritance, because then we know that there is no other thing in the universe worth striving for. Every person in his real, true self desires to be just as great and just as good as it is possible for him to be. The open door to the attainment of this objective is to believe in one's own divinity and then to raise oneself to its level by following the example of Jesus Christ. Eric Butterworth comments on this well-known verse in clip 16 of Eric Butterworth: Great Teachers – Meister Eckhart – the Eternal is forever begetting the only begotten:

9. *he that believeth not hath been judged already*. Salvation from the results of error thought begins at once when we have faith in the power of the Lord Jesus Christ to save us from the judgment. He comes to us in Spirit to do away with the effects of transgression of the law.

10. *men loved the darkness rather than the light*. World chaos results from the lack of spiritual light. We may plan peace and achieve it, but if this peace is not based on divine law, evolving love, and that law incorporated into the pact of peace as well as into the minds of those who sign that pact, we shall have no permanent peace.

## The Testimony of John the Baptist

3:22 After these things, Jesus came
with his disciples into the land of
Judea. He stayed there with them,
and baptized. 3:23 John also was
baptizing in Enon near Salim,[1]
because there was much water
there. They came, and were
baptized. 3:24 For John was not yet
thrown into prison. 3:25 There arose
therefore a questioning on the part
of John's disciples with some Jews
about purification. 3:26 They came to
John, and said to him, "Rabbi, he
who was with you beyond the Jordan,
to whom you have testified, behold,
the same baptizes, and everyone is
coming to him."

3:27 John answered, "A man can
receive nothing, unless it has been
given him from heaven. 3:28 You
yourselves testify that I said, 'I am
not the Christ,' but, 'I have been sent
before him.' 3:29 He who has the bride

is the bridegroom; but the friend of the bridegroom, who stands and hears him, rejoices greatly because of the bridegroom's voice. This, my joy, therefore is made full. 3:30 He must increase, but I must decrease.❷

1. *John also was baptizing*. John the Baptist represents the intellectual concept of Truth and his baptizing means a mental cleansing. The name Salim means "peace." "Near Salim" signifies the illumined consciousness of spiritual life and peace in the individual. The water refers to a natural rising in consciousness of the cleansing power of the thought and word of purification and life.

2. *He must increase, but I must decrease.* John the Baptist (representing the illumined intellect) decreases on the sense plane in proportion as the intellect is lifted up in Spirit and is in truth swallowed up in spiritual consciousness. The faculty decreases on one plane only to be reborn on a higher one. The illumined intellect wholly co-operates with Spirit, so there is a merging and blending of these powers until the mere intellect ceases to be mere intellect and is swallowed up in Spirit. This is the ideal unfoldment.

## The One Who Comes from Heaven

3:31 He who comes from above is above all. He who is from the Earth belongs to the Earth, and speaks of the Earth. He who comes from heaven is above all.❶ 3:32 What he has seen and heard, of that he testifies; and no one receives his witness. 3:33 He who has received his witness has set his seal to this, that God is true. 3:34 For he whom God has sent speaks the words of God; for God gives the Spirit without measure. 3:35 The Father loves the Son, and has given all things into his hand. 3:36 One who believes in the Son has eternal life, but one who disobeys[10] the Son won't see life, but the wrath of God remains on him."

1. *he who comes from heaven is above all.* In order to fulfill the divine law of his being man must realize that he is the Son of God in manifestation, that he came from above and is above all; also that in his evolution he leaves the earthly consciousness and ascends into the spiritual under a law of mind. "He that cometh from above is above all: he that is of the earth is of the earth, and of the earth he speaketh."

---

Fillmore Study Bible annotations compiled by Rev. Mark Hicks.

**World English Bible Footnotes:**

[8] v3:3. The word translated "anew" here and in John 3:7 (anothen) also means "again" and "from above".

[9] v3:8. The same Greek word (pneuma) means wind, breath, and spirit.

[10] v3:36. The same word can be translated "disobeys" or "disbelieves" in this context.

# John 4

## Jesus and the Woman from Samaria

4:1 Therefore when the Lord knew that the Pharisees had heard that Jesus was making and baptizing more disciples than John 4:2 (although Jesus himself didn't baptize, but his disciples), 4:3 he left Judea, and departed into Galilee. 4:4 He needed to pass through Samaria. 4:5 So he came to a city of Samaria, called Sychar, near the parcel of ground that Jacob gave to his son, Joseph. 4:6 Jacob's well was there.[1] Jesus therefore, being tired from his journey, sat down by the well. It was about the sixth hour[11]. 4:7 A woman of Samaria came[2] to draw water. Jesus said to her, "Give me a drink." 4:8 For his disciples had gone away into the city to buy food.

4:9 The Samaritan woman therefore said to him, "How is it that you, being a Jew,[3] ask for a drink from me, a Samaritan woman?" (For Jews have no dealings with Samaritans.)

4:10 Jesus answered her, "If you knew the gift of God, and who it is who says to you, 'Give me a drink,' you would have asked him, and he would have given you living water."

4:11 The woman said to him, "Sir, you have nothing to draw with, and the well is deep. From where then have you that living water? 4:12 Are you greater than our father, Jacob, who gave us the well, and drank of it himself, as did his children, and his livestock?"

4:13 Jesus answered her, "Everyone who drinks of this water will thirst again, 4:14 but whoever drinks of the water that I will give him will never thirst again; but the water that I will give him will become in him a well of water springing up to eternal life."

4:15 The woman said to him, "Sir, give me this water,[4] so that I don't get thirsty, neither come all the way here to draw."

4:16 Jesus said to her, "Go, call your husband, and come here."

4:17 The woman answered, "I have no husband."

Jesus said to her, "You said well, 'I have no husband,' 4:18 for you have had five husbands;[5] and he whom you now have is not your husband. This you have said truly."

4:19 The woman said to him, "Sir, I perceive that you are a prophet. 4:20 Our fathers worshiped in this mountain, and you Jews say that in Jerusalem is the place where people ought to worship."

4:21 Jesus said to her, "Woman, believe me, the hour comes, when neither in this mountain, nor in Jerusalem, will you worship the Father. 4:22 You worship that which you don't know. We worship that which we know; for salvation is from the Jews. 4:23 But the hour comes, and now is, when the true worshippers will worship the Father in spirit and truth, for the Father seeks such to be his worshippers. 4:24 God is spirit, and those who worship him must worship in spirit and truth."

4:25 The woman said to him, "I

know that Messiah comes," (he who is called Christ). "When he has come, he will declare to us all things."

4:26 Jesus said to her, "I am he, the one who speaks to you." 4:27 At this, his disciples came. They marveled that he was speaking with a woman; yet no one said, "What are you looking for?" or, "Why do you speak with her?" 4:28 So the woman left her water pot, and went away into the city, and said to the people, 4:29 "Come, see a man who told me everything that I did. Can this be the Christ?"

4:30 They went out of the city, and were coming to him. 4:31 In the meanwhile, the disciples urged him, saying, "Rabbi, eat."

4:32 But he said to them, "I have food to eat that you don't know about."[6]

4:33 The disciples therefore said one to another, "Has anyone brought him something to eat?"

4:34 Jesus said to them, "My food is to do the will of him who sent me, and to accomplish his work. 4:35 Don't you say, 'There are yet four months until the harvest?' Behold, I tell you, lift up your eyes, and look at the fields, that they are white for harvest already. 4:36 He who reaps receives wages, and gathers fruit to eternal life; that both he who sows and he who reaps may rejoice together. 4:37 For in this the saying is true, 'One sows, and another reaps.' 4:38 I sent you to reap that for which you haven't labored. Others have labored, and you have entered into their labor."

4:39 From that city many of the Samaritans believed in him because of the word of the woman, who testified, "He told me everything that I did." 4:40 So when the Samaritans came to him, they begged him to stay with them. He stayed there two days. 4:41 Many more believed because of his word. 4:42 They said to the woman, "Now we believe, not because of your speaking; for we have heard for ourselves, and know that this is indeed the Christ, the Savior of the world."

1. *Samaria, Sychar, Jacob.* THE NAME Samaria means "watchtower"; and Samaria represents that department of the objective consciousness which functions through the head. The name Sychar means "drunken," and the place symbolizes a confused state of mind. Sychar was located near the parcel of ground that Jacob gave to his son Joseph; physiologically it corresponds to the forehead, seat of intellectual perception. Here also is Jacob's well—inspiration through the intellect alone.

2. *A woman of Samaria.* The Samaritan woman represents the duality of the soul or subconsciousness. It is not the true source of wisdom, although many searchers after Truth fail to distinguish between its revelations and those of Spirit. In Hindu metaphysics it is known as the human and animal soul.

3. *How is it that you, being a Jew.* The questioning, analytical attitude taken by the woman at the well represents the tendency of intellect to argue: "I see no visible means whereby you can get the everlasting water of life. Are you greater than all the precedents and antecedents of intellectual inheritance and experience?" These assumptions of the spiritual-minded that they have a truth higher than human reason seem to be farfetched and ephemeral. These are but a few of the many questions and objections of the intellectually wise.

4. *give me this water.* The Samaritans claimed to be descendants of Jacob, and they used portions of the Hebrew Scriptures, but in the eyes of the Israelites the Samaritans were pretenders, not true followers of Jehovah. Thus spiritually enlightened people see in psychic and spiritistic phenomena and the revelations of that branch of occultism an imitation of Truth, without a true understanding of its relation to Spirit. But the soul must have Truth, and Christ recognizes the soul as worthy; hence this wonderful lesson of John 4:9-26 given to one auditor. The soul draws its life from both the earthly side

of existence (Jacob's well) and the spiritual (the Jew), but is destined to draw from a higher fount, omnipotent Spirit. Jesus asked the woman for a drink, which indicates the universality of the spiritual life, present in the Samaritan woman as well as in Jesus.

5. *you have had five husbands.* The five husbands to whom this soul had been attached are the five senses. Jesus, who represents Truth, discerned that the woman (soul) had not the understanding of the true, but was being guided by a psychic force, which was not her true husband.

6. *I have food to eat that you don't know about.* The natural man (represented by the disciples) thinks that the substance necessary for food must be put through the material process of planting and harvesting, but in Spirit the pure substance is always at hand ready to be appropriated by the inner consciousness. In states of high spiritual realization the desire for material food vanishes. Jesus fasted for forty days and "afterward hungered."

## Jesus Returns to Galilee

4:43 After the two days he went out from there and went into Galilee.
4:44 For Jesus himself testified that a prophet has no honor in his own country. 4:45 So when he came into Galilee, the Galileans received him, having seen all the things that he did in Jerusalem at the feast, for they also went to the feast.

## Jesus Heals an Official's Son

4:46 Jesus came therefore again to Cana of Galilee, where he made the water into wine. There was a certain nobleman whose son was sick at Capernaum. 4:47 When he heard that Jesus had come out of Judea into Galilee, he went to him, and begged him that he would come down and heal his son, for he was at the point of death. 4:48 Jesus therefore said to him, "Unless you see signs and wonders, you will in no way believe."

4:49 The nobleman said to him, "Sir, come down before my child dies."
4:50 Jesus said to him, "Go your way. Your son lives." The man believed the word[1] that Jesus spoke to him, and he went his way. 4:51 As he was now going down, his servants met him and reported, saying "Your child lives!"
4:52 So he inquired of them the hour when he began to get better. They said therefore to him, "Yesterday at the seventh hour,[12] the fever left him." 4:53 So the father knew that it was at that hour in which Jesus said to him, "Your son lives." He believed, as did his whole house. 4:54 This is again the second sign[2] that Jesus did, having come out of Judea into Galilee.

1. *The man believed the word.* Faith on the part of the patient or of someone connected with him is found to be an important factor in absent healing. This nobleman had faith that Jesus could heal his son, and when Jesus uttered the positive truth "Go thy way; thy son liveth," he "believed the word."

2. *The second sign.* Spiritual healing is so marvelous and so far beyond the range of human explanation that it may appear to be supernatural. We cannot explain it clearly, but this we know: When we attain oneness with the invisible force that moves the mind, a new and higher energy sweeps through us; the thought is ablaze, and even our spoken words seem alive. When the word or spiritualized thought is sent to a receptive mind, it is conducted like the oscillations of the wireless telegraph; there is a universal thought ether that carries the message.

Fillmore Study Bible annotations compiled by Rev. Mark Hicks.

**World English Bible Footnotes:**

[11] v4:6. noon
[12] v4:52. 1:00 P. M.

# John 5

## Jesus Heals on the Sabbath

5:1 After these things, there was a
feast of the Jews,[1] and Jesus went
up to Jerusalem.[2] 5:2 Now in
Jerusalem by the sheep gate,[3] there
is a pool, which is called in Hebrew,
"Bethesda,"[4] having five porches.[5]
5:3 In these lay a great multitude of
those who were sick, blind, lame,
or paralyzed, waiting for the moving
of the water; 5:4 for an angel of the
Lord went down at certain times into
the pool, and stirred up the water.
Whoever stepped in first after the
stirring of the water[6] was made
whole of whatever disease he had.
5:5 A certain man was there, who had
been sick for thirty-eight years. 5:6
When Jesus saw him lying there, and
knew that he had been sick for a long
time, he asked him, "Do you want to
be made well?"[7]

5:7 The sick man answered him,
"Sir, I have no one to put me into the
pool when the water is stirred up,
but while I'm coming, another steps
down before me."

5:8 Jesus said to him, "Arise, take
up your mat, and walk."[8]

5:9 Immediately, the man was
made well, and took up his mat and
walked.

Now it was the Sabbath on that
day.[9] 5:10 So the Jews said to him
who was cured, "It is the Sabbath.
It is not lawful for you to carry the
mat."[10]

5:11 He answered them, "He who
made me well, the same said to me,
'Take up your mat, and walk.'"

5:12 Then they asked him, "Who is
the man who said to you, 'Take up
your mat, and walk'?"

5:13 But he who was healed didn't
know who it was, for Jesus had
withdrawn, a crowd being in the
place.

5:14 Afterward Jesus found him in
the temple, and said to him, "Behold,
you are made well. Sin no more, so
that nothing worse happens to you."

5:15 The man went away, and told
the Jews that it was Jesus who had
made him well. 5:16 For this cause the
Jews persecuted Jesus, and sought to
kill him, because he did these things
on the Sabbath. 5:17 But Jesus
answered them, "My Father is still
working, so I am working, too." 5:18
For this cause therefore the Jews
sought all the more to kill him,
because he not only broke the
Sabbath, but also called God his own
Father, making himself equal with

God.

1. *The Jews.* In consciousness, the "Jews" represent those thoughts which recognize God as the Supreme Power. But they have not a working knowledge of the laws of being, which is attained through coming under the dominion and direction of Spiritual I Am (Jesus).

2. *Jerusalem.* The spiritual center in consciousness. It is called the "city of peace."

3. *Sheep gate.* The natural, innocent expression of spiritual life, and the "sheep gate'" is the channel through which this life flows into the organism.

4. *Pool of Bethesda.* That point in consciousness where we feel the flow of the cleansing life of the Spirit.

5. *Five porches.* The five-sense limitation, which does not realize the power of the Spirit. The porches are filled with the "sick, blind, halt and withered," or unregenerated ideas.

6. *Stirring of the water.* typifies the dependence of unawakened man upon certain slow, natural healing processes, which he calls "nature." The "multitude" of weak, sick, infirm thoughts and conditions in the mortal man have not received the quick, swift healing power of Spiritual I Am.

7. *Do you want to be made well?* This healing represents the power of the I Am (typified by Jesus) to restore the equilibrium of the organism through the activity of spiritual ideas in consciousness, independent of the healing methods utilized by the man of sense.

8. *Arise, take up your mat, and walk.* Jesus gives a simple directive here to take action and be accountable: Spirit calls our wholeness into action. Each of us creates a life that reflects our relationship with inner wholeness or a consciousness of outer limits and victimhood. When we stop blaming the outer world for unhappy conditions and instead recognize our wholeness, we claim the healing of "taking up our mat" and tap in to our spiritual power to take responsibility for our lives. (Rev. Joy Wyler, *Radical Wholeness*)

9. *It was the sabbath on that day.* "Sabbath" is not a day of the week. It is a state of mind entered into by a person, when he goes into the silence of his own soul, into the realm of Spirit. In this mental state healing becomes the normal, easy thing. Much of the healing that Jesus did was accomplished on the Jewish Sabbath.

10. *It is not lawful for you to carry the mat.* Here is pictured the activity of the letter (the Jews) and the Spirit (Jesus) of spiritual law. When man is really quickened of the Spirit he comes into the realization of the continuity of life in the organism, and is not limited by any laws of nature.

## The Authority of the Son

5:19 Jesus therefore answered
them, "Most certainly, I tell you, the
Son can do nothing of himself,[1] but
what he sees the Father doing. For
whatever things he does, these the
Son also does likewise. 5:20 For the
Father has affection for the Son, and
shows him all things that he himself
does. He will show him greater works
than these, that you may marvel. 5:21
For as the Father raises the dead and
gives them life, even so the Son also
gives life to whom he desires.[2] 5:22
For the Father judges no one, but he
has given all judgment to the Son, 5:23
that all may honor the Son,[3] even
as they honor the Father. He who
doesn't honor the Son doesn't honor
the Father who sent him.

5:24 "Most certainly I tell you, he
who hears my word, and believes him
who sent me, has eternal life, and
doesn't come into judgment, but has
passed out of death into life. 5:25 Most
certainly, I tell you, the hour comes,
and now is, when the dead will hear
the Son of God's voice; and those who
hear will live.[4] 5:26 For as the Father
has life in himself, even so he gave to
the Son also to have life in himself.
5:27 He also gave him authority to
execute judgment, because he is a
son of man. 5:28 Don't marvel at this,
for the hour comes, in which all that
are in the tombs will hear his voice,

5:29 and will come out; those who have done good, to the resurrection of life; and those who have done evil, to the resurrection of judgment.

1. *The Son can do nothing of himself.* The Father is the great source of all light and all understanding, and the Son is the idea that expresses the light and the wisdom of God.The Son is the idea of God-Mind, of man in his perfection. Under divine law man makes manifest what God has in His mind.

2. *So the Son also gives life to whom he desires.* The divine idea, the Christ, has been given eternal life and has the power to impart it to the Adam man. In addition to this He has been given judgment: He determines how the life shall be made manifest. The Father of life is a great river in the Garden of Eden, which represents man's innate capacity ready to obtain expression in all wisdom and understanding.

3. *That all may honor the Son.* We honor the Christ when we recognize it as having the authority of God. In its life-giving capacity it is equal to God and has the power of God. When that is enthroned in us which possesses spiritual identity we have the realization that we are speaking the word right from the Father. Jesus in this state of unfoldment proclaimed: "The words that I say unto you I speak not from myself: but the Father abiding in me doeth his works."

4. *The dead shall hear the Son of God's voice; and those who hear will live.* "The dead" are those who are spiritually asleep, who know nothing above or beyond the experiences of the physical nature. As they awaken to the reality of the divine nature within them, they are quickened to newness of life and enter into spiritual consciousness, where they really "live."

## Witnesses to Jesus

5:30 I can of myself do nothing.[1] As I hear, I judge, and my judgment is righteous; because I don't seek my own will, but the will of my Father who sent me.

5:31 "If I testify about myself, my witness is not valid. 5:32 It is another who testifies about me. I know that the testimony which he testifies about me is true. 5:33 You have sent to John, and he has testified to the truth. 5:34 But the testimony which I receive is not from man. However, I say these things that you may be saved. 5:35 He was the burning and shining lamp, and you were willing to rejoice for a while in his light. 5:36 But the testimony which I have is greater than that of John, for the works which the Father gave me to accomplish, the very works that I do, testify about me, that the Father has sent me. 5:37 The Father himself, who sent me, has testified about me. You have neither heard his voice at any time, nor seen his form. 5:38 You don't have his word living in you; because you don't believe him whom he sent.

5:39 "You search the Scriptures,[2] because you think that in them you have eternal life; and these are they which testify about me. 5:40 Yet you will not come to me, that you may have life. 5:41 I don't receive glory from men. 5:42 But I know you, that you don't have God's love in yourselves. 5:43 I have come in my Father's name, and you don't receive me. If another comes in his own name, you will receive him. 5:44 How can you believe, who receive glory from one another, and you don't seek the glory that comes from the only God?

5:45 "Don't think that I will accuse you to the Father. There is one who accuses you, even Moses, on whom you have set your hope. 5:46 For if you believed Moses, you would believe me; for he wrote about me. 5:47 But if you don't believe his writings, how will you believe my words?"

1. *I can of myself do nothing.* The divine law is our normal medium of expression. As

we awake to this truth, we cease to avail ourselves of the manmade law of self-defense, the practice of defending self-interest, and other habitual thought for the self, and concentrate our efforts on observing the right relations between ourselves and others, that Jesus designated as essential to a full grasp of the meaning of life. We still need to seek complete understanding of the Christ Spirit and the will to come to it as the source of our power.

2. *You search the scriptures.* The Scriptures alone are not sufficient to impart spiritual understanding. The Pharisees were inveterate students of the Hebrew Scriptures, but Jesus accused them repeatedly of lack of understanding. The Bible is a sealed book to one whose own spiritual understanding has not been quickened by the living Word. "The word is very nigh unto thee, in thy mouth, and in thy heart, that thou mayest do it." Jesus so identified Himself with the living Word that His words became, like it, creative. He submerged His personality in God-Mind until He became the expression of that Mind, the idea clothed in flesh.

Fillmore Study Bible annotations compiled by Rev. Mark Hicks.

# John 6

## Feeding the Five Thousand[1]

6:1 After these things, Jesus went away to the other side of the sea of Galilee, which is also called the Sea of Tiberias.[2] 6:2 A great multitude followed him, because they saw his signs which he did on those who were sick. 6:3 Jesus went up into the mountain,[3] and he sat there with his disciples. 6:4 Now the Passover, the feast of the Jews, was at hand. 6:5 Jesus therefore lifting up his eyes, and seeing that a great multitude was coming to him,[4] said to Philip,[5] "Where are we to buy bread, that these may eat?" 6:6 This he said to test him, for he himself knew what he would do.

6:7 Philip answered him, "Two hundred denarii worth of bread is not sufficient for them, that everyone of them may receive a little."

6:8 One of his disciples, Andrew, Simon Peter's brother, said to him, 6:9 "There is a boy here who has five barley loaves and two fish,[6] but what are these among so many?"

6:10 Jesus said, "Have the people sit down." Now there was much grass in that place.[7] So the men sat down, in number about five thousand. 6:11 Jesus took the loaves; and having given thanks,[8] he distributed to the disciples, and the disciples to those who were sitting down; likewise also of the fish as much as they desired. 6:12 When they were filled, he said to his disciples, "Gather up the broken pieces which are left over, that nothing be lost." 6:13 So they gathered them up, and filled twelve baskets[9] with broken pieces from the five barley loaves, which were left over by those who had eaten. 6:14 When therefore the people saw the sign which Jesus did, they said, "This is truly the prophet who comes into the world." 6:15 Jesus therefore, perceiving that they were about to come and take him by force, to make him king, withdrew again to the mountain by himself.[10]

1. The feeding of the five thousand is a symbolical representation of the steps taken and the ideas involved in supplying the outer, physical consciousness of man with inner, spiritual substance. Having quickened your idea of Power and Strength in Universal Spirit, you "sit down," or center your forces within, and begin to bless and give thanks. In Divine order you make connection with the Universal Mother, or Vital Energy of Being, and fill your whole consciousness with vitality. The surplus energy settles back into the various centers as reserve force. This is the "twelve baskets" which remained over.

2. *the other side of the sea of Galilee, which is also called the sea of Tiberias.* Galilee represents life activity, whose power is greatest on "the other side" or inner side. Tiberias means promptness and order. The real meaning of this passage of Scripture is that one who makes this demonstration must act in spiritual life with promptness and order.

3. *Jesus went up into the mountain* The I AM ascending to a high state of consciousness. When man enters into that high realization of his spiritual character, all his faculties (disciples) are lifted up with him.

4. *a great multitude was coming to him.* The multitude of thoughts living in material consciousness.

5. *Philip.* The power of the number "about five thousand" word. The word has not been used before to command spiritual increase sufficient to feed the hungry mentality, and it doubts its ability. But Jesus knows its capacity.

6. *Andrew, a boy here who has five barley loaves and two fish.* Andrew represents spiritual strength, which has great faith (Peter) in the increasing capacity (lad) of a few seeds of substance (loaves) and fishes (life).

7. *Make the people sit down, there was much grass.* Sitting represents a restful, expectant state of mind, and grass represents the consciousness of unfolding substance. Jesus' command symbolizes the I AM arranging receptive thought forces in just the order that will best enable them to receive spiritual inspiration.

8. *having given thanks, he distributed to the disciples.* Thanksgiving and praise are the key that opens the door into the great storehouse of spiritual ideas, the kingdom of the heavens. When this door is opened by one who understands and fulfills the righteous law of conserving and multiplying substance and life, a great flood of vitality flows to the whole consciousness of that one, and his every hungry thought is satisfied.

9. *filled twelve baskets.* The twelve centers of consciousness in the body. All the hungry thoughts are fed, and the overflow sinks back to the subconscious and fills these twelve centers, giving complete satisfaction within and without.

10. *Jesus ... withdrew again to the mountain by himself.* Those who are evolving spiritually know whether or not they are equal to certain demands made on them, and they withdraw to the within for further spiritual realization and power.

## Jesus Walks on the Water

6:16 When evening came, his
disciples went down to the sea, 6:17
and they entered into the boat, and
were going over the sea to
Capernaum. It was now dark, and
Jesus had not come to them.(1) 6:18
The sea was tossed by a great wind(2)
blowing. 6:19 When therefore they had
rowed about twenty-five or thirty
stadia,[13] they saw Jesus walking on
the sea,[14] and drawing near to the
boat; and they were afraid.(3) 6:20 But
he said to them, "It is I[15]. Don't
be afraid." 6:21 They were willing
therefore to receive him into the
boat.(4) Immediately the boat was at
the land where they were going.

1. *it was now dark, and Jesus had not yet come to them.* Lack of spiritual awareness.

2. *Wind.* Waves represent the ordinary ups and downs which every ordinary life characterizes. Wind refers to the way things are going or appearing in movement to the consciousness.

3. *and they were afraid.* Jesus at first is believed to be an apparition to the disciples; and this is the attitude of many people who for the first time hear these words "God is my help."

4. *They were willing therefore to receive him into the boat.* The first of the twelve to actually show willingness to believe is

Peter, Faith, the ability to say "yes" to Truth, the affirmative faculty and the faculty which connects us with the substance of Truth.

## The Bread from Heaven

6:22 On the next day, the multitude that stood on the other side of the sea saw that there was no other boat there, except the one in which his disciples had embarked, and that Jesus hadn't entered with his disciples into the boat, but his disciples had gone away alone. 6:23 However boats from Tiberias came near to the place where they ate the bread after the Lord had given thanks. 6:24 When the multitude therefore saw that Jesus wasn't there,[1] nor his disciples, they themselves got into the boats, and came to Capernaum, seeking Jesus. 6:25 When they found him on the other side of the sea, they asked him, "Rabbi, when did you come here?"

6:26 Jesus answered them, "Most certainly I tell you, you seek me, not because you saw signs, but because you ate of the loaves, and were filled. 6:27 Don't work for the food which perishes, but for the food which remains to eternal life,[2] which the Son of Man will give to you. For God the Father has sealed him."

6:28 They said therefore to him, "What must we do, that we may work the works of God?"

6:29 Jesus answered them, "This is the work of God, that you believe in him whom he has sent."[3]

6:30 They said therefore to him, "What then do you do for a sign, that we may see, and believe you? What work do you do? 6:31 Our fathers ate the manna in the wilderness.[4] As it is written, 'He gave them bread out of heaven[16] to eat.'"[17]

6:32 Jesus therefore said to them, "Most certainly, I tell you, it wasn't Moses who gave you the bread out of heaven, but my Father gives you the true bread out of heaven. 6:33 For the bread of God is that which comes down out of heaven, and gives life to the world."

6:34 They said therefore to him, "Lord, always give us this bread."

6:35 Jesus said to them, "I am the bread of life.[5] He who comes to me will not be hungry, and he who believes in me will never be thirsty. 6:36 But I told you that you have seen me, and yet you don't believe. 6:37 All those who the Father gives me will come to me. Him who comes to me I will in no way throw out. 6:38 For I have come down from heaven, not to do my own will, but the will of him who sent me. 6:39 This is the will of my Father who sent me, that of all he has given to me I should lose nothing, but should raise him up at the last day. 6:40 This is the will of the one who sent me, that everyone who sees the Son, and believes in him, should have eternal life; and I will raise him up at the last day."

6:41 The Jews therefore murmured concerning him, because he said, "I am the bread which came down out of heaven."[6] 6:42 They said, "Isn't this Jesus, the son of Joseph, whose father and mother we know? How then does he say, 'I have come down out of heaven?'"

6:43 Therefore Jesus answered them, "Don't murmur among yourselves. 6:44 No one can come to me unless the Father who sent me draws him, and I will raise him up in the last day. 6:45 It is written in the prophets, 'They will all be taught by God.'[18] Therefore everyone who hears from the Father, and has learned, comes to me. 6:46 Not that anyone has seen the Father, except he who is from God. He has seen the Father. 6:47 Most certainly, I tell you, he who believes in me has eternal life. 6:48 I am the bread of life. 6:49 Your fathers ate the manna in the wilderness, and they died. 6:50 This is the bread which comes down out of heaven, that anyone may eat of it and not die. 6:51 I am the living bread which came down out of heaven. If anyone eats of this bread, he will live forever. Yes, the bread which I will give for the life of the world is my flesh."

6:52 The Jews therefore contended with one another, saying, "How can this man give us his flesh to eat?"

6:53 Jesus therefore said to them, "Most certainly I tell you, unless you eat the flesh of the Son of Man and drink his blood, you don't have life in yourselves. 6:54 He who eats my flesh and drinks my blood has eternal life, and I will raise him up at the last day. 6:55 For my flesh is food indeed, and my blood is drink indeed. 6:56 He who eats my flesh and drinks my blood lives in me, and I in him. 6:57 As the living Father sent me, and I live because of the Father; so he who feeds on me, he will also live because of me. 6:58 This is the bread which came down out of heaven--not as our fathers ate the manna, and died. He who eats this bread will live forever." 6:59 These things he said in the synagogue, as he taught in Capernaum.

1. *Jesus wasn't there.* After feeding the multitude, Jesus retired to the mountain and spent the night in prayer. It is the universal testimony of those who are in the regeneration that they have to spend much time in prayer on the mount of spiritual realization. To pray all night is not unusual with one who is striving to make complete atonement with God.

2. *food which perishes, but for the food which remains to eternal life.* The proclamation of one who has found the real substance and source of supply . The outer consciousness strives for the things of sense.

3. *This is the work of God, that you believe in him whom he has sent.* To do this inner work that redeems the whole man and puts him in touch with spiritual realities, one must believe on, or have faith in, him "whom he hath sent." This one who is sent of God is Christ, Spiritual Man, the higher self of every man. We must believe that there is a Spirit in man that transcends the mortal, and that it has power to do all that we conceive possible to God. Thus God's work is done in us.

4. *manna in the wilderness.* Moses caused manna to fall from heaven to feed the Children of Israel. The body of Christ is a spiritual substance that we incorporate into consciousness through faith out of the heavens of mind. That the food we eat has a spiritual source is proved by those who fast in spiritual faith much longer and easier than those who are forced to starve.

5. *I am the bread of life.* The I AM is the living principle that enables us to make our desires manifest in whatever form we choose. To do this we recognize and draw upon universal substance.

6. *I am the bread which came down out of heaven.* The tendency of men to believe that some prophet or wise one has access to God which they have not must be refuted. The Jews counted the manna given to their ancestors by Moses as in some way having to do with their salvation. Jesus says, "The bread of God is he which cometh down from heaven." You must be your own high priest and prophet. God is the sustaining substance and life, manifesting through each soul; how, then, can he pass his resource to that soul through some human instrument? He cannot, and all dependence upon such helps is weakening and futile in the end. "I Am the bread of life." Whoever believes on the spiritual I Am as his Oversoul, and affirms it as his substance and life, shall never hunger nor thirst.

## The Words of Eternal Life

6:60 Therefore many of his disciples, when they heard this, said, "This is a hard saying! Who can listen to it?"

6:61 But Jesus knowing in himself that his disciples murmured at this, said to them, "Does this cause you to stumble? 6:62 Then what if you would see the Son of Man ascending to where he was before? 6:63 It is the spirit who gives life. The flesh profits nothing.[1] The words that I speak to you are spirit, and are life. 6:64 But there are some of you who don't believe." For Jesus knew from the beginning who they were who didn't believe, and who it was who would betray him. 6:65 He said, "For this cause have I said to you that no one can come to me, unless it is given to him by my Father."

6:66 At this, many of his disciples went back, and walked no more with him. 6:67 Jesus said therefore to the twelve, "You don't also want to go away, do you?"

6:68 Simon Peter answered him, "Lord, to whom would we go? You have the words of eternal life. 6:69 We have come to believe and know that you are the Christ, the Son of the living God."

6:70 Jesus answered them, "Didn't I choose you, the twelve, and one of you is a devil?" 6:71 Now he spoke of Judas, the son of Simon Iscariot, for it was he who would betray him, being one of the twelve.

1. *It is the spirit who gives life; the flesh profits nothing.* Being, the original fount, is an impersonal principle; but in its work of creation it puts forth an idea that contains all ideas: the Logos, Word, Christ, the Son of God, or spiritual man. This spiritual man or Christ or Word of God is the true inner self of every individual. Man therefore contains within himself the capacities of Being, and through his words uses the creative principle in forming his environment, good or bad. So we make our own heaven or hell.

---

Fillmore Study Bible annotations compiled by Rev. Mark Hicks.

**World English Bible Footnotes:**

[13] v6:19. 25 to 30 stadia is about 5 to 6 kilometers or about 3 to 4 miles

[14] v6:19. see Job 9:8

[15] v6:20. or, I AM

[16] v6:31. Greek and Hebrew use the same word for "heaven", "the heavens", "the sky", and "the air".

[17] v6:31. Exodus 16:4; Nehemiah 9:15; Psalm 78:24-25

[18] v6:45. Isaiah 54:13

# John 7

## The Unbelief of Jesus' Brothers

7:1 After these things, Jesus was walking in Galilee, for he wouldn't walk in Judea, because the Jews sought to kill him. 7:2 Now the feast of the Jews, the Feast of Booths, was at hand. 7:3 His brothers therefore said to him, "Depart from here, and go into Judea, that your disciples also may see your works which you do. 7:4 For no one does anything in secret, and himself seeks to be known openly. If you do these things, reveal yourself to the world." 7:5 For even his brothers didn't believe in him.

7:6 Jesus therefore said to them, "My time has not yet come, but your time is always ready.[1] 7:7 The world can't hate you, but it hates me, because I testify about it, that its works are evil. 7:8 You go up to the feast. I am not yet going up to this feast, because my time is not yet fulfilled."

7:9 Having said these things to them, he stayed in Galilee.

1. *My time has not yet come; but your time is always ready.* Jesus was developing his spiritual nature, which is under spiritual law. The Pharisaical Jews followed the letter of the law, which resists and seeks the destruction of the Christ. The Christ usually moves in secret. It does its spiritual work quietly instead of showing off. Some of the multitude thought Jesus was a good man; others thought He had led the people astray. This represents the quibbling of the lesser mind.

## Jesus at the Festival of Booths

7:10 But when his brothers had gone up to the feast, then he also went up, not publicly, but as it were in secret.[1] 7:11 The Jews therefore sought him at the feast, and said, "Where is he?" 7:12 There was much murmuring among the multitudes concerning him. Some said, "He is a good man." Others said, "Not so, but he leads the multitude astray." 7:13 Yet no one spoke openly of him for fear of the Jews. 7:14 But when it was now the midst of the feast, Jesus went up into the temple and taught.[2] 7:15 The Jews therefore marveled, saying, "How does this man know letters, having never been educated?"

7:16 Jesus therefore answered them, "My teaching is not mine, but his who sent me. 7:17 If anyone desires to do his will, he will know about the teaching, whether it is from God, or if I am speaking from myself. 7:18 He who speaks from himself seeks his own glory, but he who seeks the glory of him who sent him is true, and no unrighteousness is in him.[3] 7:19 Didn't Moses give you the law, and yet none of you keeps the law? Why do you seek to kill me?"

7:20 The multitude answered, "You have a demon! Who seeks to kill you?"

7:21 Jesus answered them, "I did one work, and you all marvel because of it. 7:22 Moses has given you circumcision (not that it is of Moses, but of the fathers), and on

the Sabbath you circumcise a boy.
7:23 If a boy receives circumcision on
the Sabbath, that the law of Moses
may not be broken, are you angry
with me, because I made a man
completely healthy on the Sabbath?
7:24 Don't judge according to
appearance, but judge righteous
judgment."

1. *then went he also up, not publicly, but as it were in secret.* Jesus' disciples wanted Him to go up to Jerusalem for one reason: to prove that He was the Christ, but He realized that He had not yet attained the necessary power. After they had departed He got more spiritual consciousness and was moved to go under the protection of Spirit, and in this state of mind the Jews could not lay their hands on Him or injure Him in any way.

2. *Jesus went up into the temple and taught.* Jesus, like all persons who are growing spiritually, felt the power within Him to be much stronger than He could manifest without. He wanted to prove to His friends that He was the Christ but doubted His ability.

3. *he who seeks the glory ... and no unrighteousness is in him.* He was not speaking from Himself for His own glory, but He was seeking the glory of Him that sent Him. Glory (doxa, Greek) is used repeatedly by John: Realization of divine unity; the blending and merging of man's mind with God-Mind (RW/glory).

## Is this the Christ?

7:25 Therefore some of them of
Jerusalem said, "Isn't this he whom
they seek to kill? 7:26 Behold, he
speaks openly, and they say nothing
to him. Can it be that the rulers
indeed know that this is truly the
Christ? 7:27 However we know where
this man comes from, but when the
Christ comes, no one will know
where he comes from."

7:28 Jesus therefore cried out in
the temple, teaching and saying,
"You both know me, and know where
I am from. I have not come of myself,
but he who sent me is true, whom
you don't know. 7:29 I know him,
because I am from him, and he sent
me."

7:30 They sought therefore to take
him; but no one laid a hand on him,
because his hour had not yet come.
7:31 But of the multitude, many
believed in him. They said, "When
the Christ comes, he won't do more
signs than those which this man has
done, will he?"

## Officers Are Sent to Arrest Jesus

7:32 The Pharisees heard the
multitude murmuring these things
concerning him, and the chief priests
and the Pharisees sent officers to
arrest him. 7:33 Then Jesus said, "I
will be with you a little while longer,
then I go to him who sent me. 7:34 You
will seek me, and won't find me; and
where I am, you can't come."[1]

7:35 The Jews therefore said among
themselves, "Where will this man go
that we won't find him? Will he go
to the Dispersion among the Greeks,
and teach the Greeks? 7:36 What is this
word that he said, 'You will seek me,
and won't find me; and where I am,
you can't come'?"

1. *where I am, you can't come.* The all-knowing Christ Mind can easily handle the Pharisaical mind that is following the letter of the law. The intellectual mind cannot understand the claim of the spiritual that it can go where it cannot be found by those present. The mind that functions in matter cannot comprehend a state in which matter can pass through matter.

## Rivers of Living Water

7:37 Now on the last and greatest day of the feast, Jesus stood and cried out, "If anyone is thirsty, let him come to me and drink!① 7:38 He who believes in me, as the Scripture has said, from within him will flow rivers of living water."② 7:39 But he said this about the Spirit, which those believing in him were to receive. For the Holy Spirit was not yet given, because Jesus wasn't yet glorified.③

1. *If anyone is thirsty, let him come to me and drink!* Jesus realized that man's real thirst is for Spirit and that this thirst can only be quenched through an outpouring of the Holy Spirit within the soul, which thrills one with new life and energy and vitality.

2. *from within him will flow rivers of living water.* If we have understanding faith we know that there is no cessation of life and that we have only to open our consciousness more and more to the Spirit of life in order to realize that from within flow rivers of living water.

3. *for the Spirit was not yet given; because Jesus wasn't yet glorified.* The Holy Spirit was in evidence before the time of Jesus, but He gave a new impetus to this indwelling helper and promised that the holy Comforter would be with us throughout all time.

## Division Among the People

7:40 Many of the multitude therefore, when they heard these words, said, "This is truly the prophet." 7:41 Others said, "This is the Christ." But some said, "What, does the Christ come out of Galilee? 7:42 Hasn't the Scripture said that the Christ comes of the seed of David,[19] and from Bethlehem,[20] the village where David was?" 7:43 So there arose a division in the multitude because of him.① 7:44 Some of them would have arrested him, but no one laid hands on him.

1. *So there arose a division in the multitude because of him.* When one is in a mixed state of consciousness there is always dissension and questioning. However when one is born anew into the Christ consciousness all things are made clear. "For all shall know me, From the least to the greatest of them." This quotation could be from several verses: Heb. 8:11, Jer. 31:34, Isa. 54:13

## The Unbelief of Those in Authority

7:45 The officers therefore came to the chief priests and Pharisees, and they said to them, "Why didn't you bring him?" 7:46 The officers answered, "No man ever spoke like this man!"①,④

7:47 The Pharisees therefore answered them,② "You aren't also led astray, are you? 7:48 Have any of the rulers believed in him, or of the Pharisees? 7:49 But this multitude that doesn't know the law is accursed."

7:50 Nicodemus (he who came to him by night, being one of them) said to them,③ 7:51 "Does our law judge a man, unless it first hears from him personally and knows what he does?"

7:52 They answered him, "Are you also from Galilee? Search, and see that no prophet has arisen out of Galilee.[21]"

7:53 Everyone went to his own house,

1. *Never man so spake.* The "chief priests" of the Pharisaical consciousness are the highest thoughts in authority in the Pharisaical hierarchy. The "officers" are thoughts that execute the law.

2. *The Pharisees therefore answered them.* However, when it reaches a certain state of unfoldment even the Pharisaical mind, which believes in the strict letter of the law, is open to conviction if it can entertain a higher truth safely.

3. *Nicodemus said to them.* This is proved by Nicodemus' spiritual conversion. The Pharisaical side of man's mind in its faithful adherence to religious forms eventually becomes aware of the presence of divine power.

4. *Never man so spake.* This truth was in evidence when the officers replied, "Never man so spake," revealing that the higher light of the Christ had found entrance into their consciousness.

---

Fillmore Study Bible annotations compiled by Rev. Mark Hicks.

**World English Bible Footnotes:**

[19] v7:42. 2 Samuel 7:12

[20] v7:42. Micah 5:2

[21] v7:52. See Isaiah 9:1 and Matthew 4:13-16.

# JOHN 8

## Men Who Cast Stones

8:1 but Jesus went to the Mount of Olives.[1] 8:2 Now very early in the morning, he came again into the temple, and all the people came to him. He sat down, and taught them. 8:3 The scribes and the Pharisees brought a woman taken in adultery. Having set her in the midst, 8:4 they told him, "Teacher, we found this woman in adultery, in the very act. 8:5 Now in our law, Moses commanded us to stone such.[22] What then do you say about her?"[2] 8:6 They said this testing him, that they might have something to accuse him of.

But Jesus stooped down, and wrote on the ground with his finger. 8:7 But when they continued asking him, he looked up and said to them, "He who is without sin among you, let him throw the first stone at her." 8:8 Again he stooped down, and with his finger wrote on the ground.

8:9 They, when they heard it, being convicted by their conscience, went out one by one,[3] beginning from the oldest, even to the last. Jesus was left alone with the woman where she was, in the middle. 8:10 Jesus, standing up, saw her and said, "Woman, where are your accusers? Did no one condemn you?"

8:11 She said, "No one, Lord."

Jesus said, "Neither do I condemn you. Go your way. From now on, sin no more."[4]

1. *Jesus went to the mount of Olives.* Jesus' going up into the Mount of Olives means the soul's ascending to the state

of consciousness where absolute Truth is manifest and from this high vantage point teaching a lesson in brotherly love to the intellectual faculties.

2. *what then do you say about her?* Sometimes the intellectual faculties imagine they are in supreme authority, as in this case, where the woman caught in adultery is presented as an example. "Now, spiritual man, what are you going to do about that?

3. *And they, when they heard it, went out one by one.* The intellectual faculties, thus trapped in their own conceit, slink away.

4. *Neither do I condemn you.* The final injunction. Thus the overcoming power of the Christ Mind is doing its perfect work.

## Jesus the Light of the World

8:12 Again, therefore, Jesus spoke to them, saying, "I am the light of the world.[23] He who follows me will not walk in the darkness, but will have the light of life."[1]

8:13 The Pharisees therefore said to him, "You testify about yourself.[2] Your testimony is not valid."

8:14 Jesus answered them, "Even if I testify about myself, my testimony is true, for I know where I came from, and where I am going;[3] but you don't know where I came from, or where I am going. 8:15 You judge according to the flesh. I judge no one. 8:16 Even if I do judge, my judgment is true, for I am not alone, but I am with the Father who sent me. 8:17 It's also written in your law that the testimony of two people is valid.[24] 8:18 I am one who testifies about myself, and the Father who sent me testifies about me."[4]

8:19 They said therefore to him, "Where is your Father?"

Jesus answered, "You know neither me, nor my Father. If you knew me, you would know my Father also." 8:20 Jesus spoke these words in the treasury, as he taught in the temple. Yet no one arrested him, because his hour had not yet come.[5]

1. *he that follows me ... will have the light of life.* The first lesson in spiritual development to be learned is that everyone has within him the light of divine understanding.

2. *You testify about yourself.* Those who do not recognize that they have this inner light are thinking intellectually instead of spiritually.

3. *I know where I came from, and where I am going.* The Christ light comes forth from God and under all circumstances is aware of its source.

4. *the Father who sent me testifies about me.* It places all judgment in the Father, knowing that its light is from that source alone. The intellectual man has no conception of this truth but depends more on man-made judgment.

5. *because his hour had not yet come.* Jesus (symbolizing the Christ) was working in the substance consciousness and under the light of Spirit and was master of the situation. Therefore no man took Him, because His hour was not yet come. He put all protection under God, who was ever-present as His witness and defense.

## Jesus Foretells His Death

8:21 Jesus said therefore again to them, "I am going away, and you will seek me, and you will die in your sins. Where I go, you can't come."

8:22 The Jews therefore said, "Will he kill himself, that he says, 'Where I am going, you can't come?'"

8:23 He said to them, "You are from beneath. I am from above. You are of this world. I am not of this world.[1] 8:24 I said therefore to you that you will die in your sins; for unless you believe that I am[25] he, you will die in your sins."

8:25 They said therefore to him, "Who are you?"[2]

Jesus said to them, "Just what I have been saying to you from the beginning. 8:26 I have many things to speak and to judge concerning you. However he who sent me is true; and the things which I heard from him, these I say to the world."

8:27 They didn't understand that he spoke to them about the Father.[3] 8:28 Jesus therefore said to them, "When you have lifted up the Son of Man, then you will know that I am he,[4] and I do nothing of myself, but as my Father taught me, I say these things. 8:29 He who sent me is with me. The Father hasn't left me alone, for I always do the things that are pleasing to him." 8:30 As he spoke these things, many believed in him.

1. *I am from above ... I am not of this world.* Jesus, symbolizing the I AM, the Christ, again is proclaiming Truth from the absolute standpoint.

2. *Who are you?* Through self-righteous adherence to outer forms man resists his true unfoldment or evolution.

3. *They didn't understand that he spoke to them about the Father.* The egotistical personality assumes that its world of phenomena is real and that all talk about disappearing into spirit is illusion. Sanctimoniousness develops from the belief that intellect can be spiritually sanctified.

4. *then you will know that I am he.* The spiritual mind (the I AM) is the Saviour and is working to come into evidence. It is working to redeem the self-righteous, Pharisaical, intellectual man. When this man has been lifted up, "then shall ye know that I am he, and that I do nothing of myself, but as the Father taught me. I speak these things."

## True Disciples

8:31 Jesus therefore said to those Jews who had believed him, "If you remain in my word, then you are truly my disciples. 8:32 You will know the truth, and the truth will make you free."[26]

8:33 They answered him, "We are Abraham's seed, and have never been in bondage to anyone. How do you say, 'You will be made free?'"

8:34 Jesus answered them, "Most certainly I tell you, everyone who commits sin is the bondservant of sin. 8:35 A bondservant doesn't live in the house forever.[1] A son remains forever. 8:36 If therefore the Son makes you free, you will be free indeed. 8:37 I know that you are Abraham's seed,[2] yet you seek to kill me, because my word finds no place in you. 8:38 I say the things which I have seen with my Father; and you also do the things which you have seen with your father."[3]

1. *A bondservant doesn't live in the house forever.* The "house" is man's body. No one who allows intemperate desires to rule his life and to gain expression through his thought and conduct can hope to remain long in the body or to experience in it any measure of true satisfaction.

2. *you are Abraham's seed.* As the chosen people, the Jews were in bondage to racial pride, and their intemperance in this regard was difficult to uproot.

3. *you also do the things which you have seen with your father.* Jesus in effect said, "If you live in the spirit of My teachings, you will become truly My disciples, and you will be freed from all your limitations through the understanding of Truth that comes to you as the result of your steadfastness."

## Jesus and Abraham

8:39 They answered him, "Our father is Abraham."[1]

Jesus said to them, "If you were Abraham's children, you would do the works of Abraham. 8:40 But now you seek to kill me, a man who has told you the truth,[2] which I heard from God. Abraham didn't do this. 8:41 You do the works of your father."

They said to him, "We were not born of sexual immorality. We have one Father, God."

8:42 Therefore Jesus said to them, "If God were your father, you would love me, for I came out and have come from God. For I haven't come of myself, but he sent me. 8:43 Why don't you understand my speech? Because you can't hear my word. 8:44 You are of your father, the devil, and you want to do the desires of your father. He was a murderer from the beginning, and doesn't stand in the truth, because there is no truth in him. When he speaks a lie, he speaks on his own; for he is a liar, and its father. 8:45 But because I tell the truth, you don't believe me. 8:46 Which of you convicts me of sin? If I tell the truth, why do you not believe me? 8:47 He who is of God hears the words of God. For this cause you don't hear, because you are not of God."

8:48 Then the Jews answered him, "Don't we say well that you are a Samaritan, and have a demon?"

8:49 Jesus answered, "I don't have a demon, but I honor my Father, and you dishonor me. 8:50 But I don't seek my own glory. There is one who seeks and judges. 8:51 Most certainly, I tell you, if a person keeps my word, he will never see death."

8:52 Then the Jews said to him, "Now we know that you have a demon. Abraham died, and the prophets; and you say, 'If a man keeps my word, he will never taste of death.' 8:53 Are you greater than our father, Abraham, who died? The prophets died. Who do you make yourself out to be?"

8:54 Jesus answered, "If I glorify myself, my glory is nothing. It is my Father who glorifies me, of whom you say that he is our God. 8:55 You have not known him, but I know him. If I said, 'I don't know him,' I would be like you, a liar. But I know him, and keep his word. 8:56 Your father Abraham rejoiced to see my day. He saw it, and was glad."

8:57 The Jews therefore said to him, "You are not yet fifty years old, and have you seen Abraham?"

8:58 Jesus said to them, "Most certainly, I tell you, before Abraham came into existence, I AM.[3][27]"

8:59 Therefore they took up stones to throw at him, but Jesus was hidden, and went out of the temple, having gone through the midst of them, and so passed by.

1. *Our father is Abraham.* Those who think of themselves as descended from human ancestors are in bondage to all the limitations of those ancestors. It is a falling short of the full stature of man to regard himself as descended from the human family. This is a sin that keeps the majority of men in bondage to sense consciousness.

2. *you seek to kill me, a man who has told you the truth.* It seems incredible that men should seek to destroy and kill out of their thoughts this super-conscious mind, but such is the self-sufficiency of ignorance identified with human lineage. Mortality has failed generation after generation, yet men cling to it as the summum bonum of existence, and antagonize the

Spirit.

3. *before Abraham came into existence, I am.* It is hard for the intellect to realize the spiritual "I AM THAT I AM." It always argues back and forth, endeavoring to prove that the intellect itself is the highest authority.

---

Fillmore Study Bible annotations compiled by Rev. Mark Hicks.

**World English Bible Footnotes:**

[22] v8:5. Leviticus 20:10; Deuteronomy 22:22

[23] v8:12. Isaiah 60:1

[24] v8:17. Deuteronomy 17:6; 19:15

[25] v8:24. or, I AM

[26] v8:32. Psalm 119:45

[27] v8:58. or, I am

# John 9

## A Man Born Blind Receives Sight

9:1 As he passed by, he saw a man blind from birth. 9:2 His disciples asked him, "Rabbi, who sinned, this man or his parents, that he was born blind?"[1]

9:3 Jesus answered, "Neither did this man sin, nor his parents; but, that the works of God might be revealed in him.[2] 9:4 I must work the works of him who sent me, while it is day.[3] The night is coming, when no one can work. 9:5 While I am in the world, I am the light of the world." 9:6 When he had said this, he spat on the ground, made mud with the saliva, anointed the blind man's eyes with the mud,[4] 9:7 and said to him, "Go, wash in the pool of Siloam" (which means "Sent").[5] So he went away, washed, and came back seeing. 9:8 The neighbors therefore, and those who saw that he was blind before, said, "Isn't this he who sat and begged?" 9:9 Others were saying, "It is he." Still others were saying, "He looks like him."

He said, "I am he." 9:10 They therefore were asking him, "How were your eyes opened?"

9:11 He answered, "A man called Jesus made mud, anointed my eyes, and said to me, 'Go to the pool of Siloam, and wash.' So I went away and washed, and I received sight."

9:12 Then they asked him, "Where is he?"

He said, "I don't know."

1. *who sinned, this man or his parents, that he was born blind?* The inquiry indicates a previous incarnation of the man in the flesh body, where it is possible he may

have sinned.

2. *that the works of God might be revealed in him.* The perfect ideas of a perfect man-Idea in Divine Mind. Jesus' response says that everyone is born with a clean slate and with a unique path for revealing their own divinity. Every condition we deem as adversity is an opportunity to reveal the depth of power, wisdom, and love in our true nature. "God's work revealed in him" describes the work of everyone—it's not a special charge to individuals with physical challenges or disabilities. (Rev. Joy Wyler, *Radical Wholeness.*)

3. *We must work the works of him that sent me, while it is day.* When the inspiration of God moves us and we respond and do His will, we have the "day," or the light, and we should act upon our inspiration. On the other hand, if we neglect to do the will of Him that sent us, we shall sink into darkness, ignorance, "night."

4. *anointed the blind man's eyes with the mud (clay, ASV).* Clay represents materiality. This is to be washed away before the material-minded person can see with the eye of the mind or use his innate powers of discernment.

5. *wash in the pool of Siloam.* Siloam means "sent," "sending forth, or putting away." To wash in Siloam is to deny all belief in materiality and affirm the spiritual nature of all substance.

## The Pharisees Investigate the Healing

9:13 They brought him who had
been blind❶ to the Pharisees. 9:14 It
was a Sabbath when Jesus made the
mud and opened his eyes. 9:15 Again
therefore the Pharisees also asked
him how he received his sight. He
said to them, "He put mud on my
eyes, I washed, and I see."

9:16 Some therefore of the
Pharisees said, "This man is not from
God, because he doesn't keep the
Sabbath."❷ Others said, "How can a
man who is a sinner do such signs?"
There was division among them. 9:17
Therefore they asked the blind man
again, "What do you say about him,
because he opened your eyes?"

He said, "He is a prophet."

9:18 The Jews therefore did not
believe concerning him, that he had
been blind, and had received his
sight, until they called the parents
of him who had received his sight,
9:19 and asked them, "Is this your son,
who you say was born blind? How
then does he now see?"

9:20 His parents answered them,
"We know that this is our son, and
that he was born blind; 9:21 but how
he now sees, we don't know; or who
opened his eyes, we don't know. He
is of age. Ask him. He will speak for
himself." 9:22 His parents said these
things because they feared the Jews;
for the Jews had already agreed that
if any man would confess him as
Christ, he would be put out of the
synagogue. 9:23 Therefore his parents
said, "He is of age. Ask him."

9:24 So they called the man who
was blind a second time, and said to
him, "Give glory to God. We know
that this man is a sinner."

9:25 He therefore answered, "I don't
know if he is a sinner. One thing I do
know: that though I was blind, now I
see."

9:26 They said to him again, "What
did he do to you? How did he open
your eyes?"

9:27 He answered them, "I told you
already, and you didn't listen. Why
do you want to hear it again? You
don't also want to become his
disciples, do you?"

9:28 They insulted him and said,
"You are his disciple, but we are

disciples of Moses. [9:29] We know that
God has spoken to Moses. But as for
this man, we don't know where he
comes from."

[9:30] The man answered them, "How
amazing! You don't know where he
comes from, yet he opened my eyes.
[9:31] We know that God doesn't listen
to sinners, but if anyone is a
worshipper of God, and does his will,
he listens to him.[28] [9:32] Since the
world began it has never been heard
of that anyone opened the eyes of
someone born blind. [9:33] If this man
were not from God, he could do
nothing."

[9:34] They answered him, "You were
altogether born in sins, and do you
teach us?" They threw him out.(3)

1. Unity Bible commentary says that the main theme of this lesson is the teaching of the quickening of spiritual discernment, that is, how to see with the inner eye. The Ed Rabel commentary says "the works of God are needed here, not an analysis of how it came about." We should not ask "why did this happen" but rather "how can we heal."

2. *This man is not from God, because because he doesn't keep the Sabbath.* The Pharisees regarded the keeping of the Sabbath day as a commandment to be observed in the letter. They did not understand spiritually.

3. *They threw him out.* The Pharisees (traditional faith) casts out (one whose spiritual vision has been quickened) because faith that is rooted in tradition has nothing in common with Truth for Truth's sake. Its foundation is the authority of past leaders and thinkers, not Truth itself.

## Spiritual Blindness

[9:35] Jesus heard that they had
thrown him out, and finding him, he
said, "Do you believe in the Son of
God?"(1)

[9:36] He answered, "Who is he, Lord,
that I may believe in him?"

[9:37] Jesus said to him, "You have
both seen him, and it is he who
speaks with you."

[9:38] He said, "Lord, I believe!" and
he worshiped him.(2)

[9:39] Jesus said, "I came into this
world for judgment, that those who
don't see may see; and that those
who see may become blind."

[9:40] Those of the Pharisees who
were with him heard these things,
and said to him, "Are we also blind?"

[9:41] Jesus said to them, "If you
were blind, you would have no sin;
but now you say, 'We see.' Therefore
your sin remains.

1. *Do you believe in the Son of God?* Jesus had awakened the man's intellectual understanding, but the awakening was not complete until the man had been grounded in the divine Sonship.

2. *And he worshipped him.* Was Jesus referring here to his own personality? It is quite evident that Jesus was instructing the man to have faith in his indwelling Lord. This is borne out by the answer which the man gave in verse 38: "Lord, I believe."

---

Fillmore Study Bible annotations compiled by Rev. Mark Hicks.

**World English Bible Footnotes:**

[28] v9:31. Psalm 66:18, Proverbs 15:29; 28:9

# John 10

## Jesus the Good Shepherd

10:1 "Most certainly, I tell you, one who doesn't enter by the door into the sheep fold,[1] but climbs up some other way, the same is a thief and a robber.[2] 10:2 But one who enters in by the door is the shepherd of the sheep. 10:3 The gatekeeper opens the gate for him, and the sheep listen to his voice.[3] He calls his own sheep by name, and leads them out. 10:4 Whenever he brings out his own sheep, he goes before them, and the sheep follow him, for they know his voice. 10:5 They will by no means follow a stranger, but will flee from him; for they don't know the voice of strangers." 10:6 Jesus spoke this parable to them, but they didn't understand what he was telling them.

10:7 Jesus therefore said to them again, "Most certainly, I tell you, I am the sheep's door. 10:8 All who came before me are thieves and robbers, but the sheep didn't listen to them. 10:9 I am the door. If anyone enters in by me, he will be saved, and will go in and go out, and will find pasture. 10:10 The thief only comes to steal, kill, and destroy. I came that they may have life, and may have it abundantly. 10:11 I am the good shepherd.[4][29] The good shepherd lays down his life for the sheep. 10:12 He who is a hired hand, and not a shepherd, who doesn't own the sheep, sees the wolf coming, leaves the sheep, and flees. The wolf snatches the sheep, and scatters them.[5] 10:13 The hired hand flees because he is a hired hand, and doesn't care for the sheep. 10:14 I am the good shepherd. I know my own, and I'm known by my own; 10:15 even as the Father knows me, and I know the Father. I lay down my life for the sheep.[6] 10:16 I have other sheep, which are not of this fold.[7][30] I must bring them also, and they will hear my voice. They will become one flock with one shepherd. 10:17 Therefore the Father loves me, because I lay down my life,[31] that I may take it again. 10:18 No one takes it away from me, but I lay it down by myself. I have power to lay it down, and I have power to take it again. I received this commandment from my Father."

10:19 Therefore a division arose again among the Jews because of these words. 10:20 Many of them said, "He has a demon, and is insane! Why do you listen to him?" 10:21 Others said, "These are not the sayings of one possessed by a demon. It isn't possible for a demon to open the eyes of the blind, is it?"[32]

1. *the door into the sheep fold.* The sheepfold represents the mind with its thoughts; the door represents the I AM consciousness.

2. *climbs up some other way, the same is a thief and a robber.* All forces that come into our consciousness in any other way than through our own I AM are thieves and robbers. No man can be saved from the limitations and mistakes of ignorance except through his own volition.

3. *the sheep listen to his voice.* Man learns to control his thought life through attention, study, and practice as well as through prayer. When his thoughts become orderly and obedient to his will, it is then that the sheep hear his voice.

4. *I am the good shepherd.* The good shepherd is the Christ, I AM, or the individual I AM, Christed, illumined, lighted by the understanding of Truth. Man is saved by the Good-Shepherding of his thought powers, or by his learning to think in har-

mony with divine law and thereafter controlling his thoughts accordingly.

5. *The wolf snatches the sheep, and scatters them.* Wolves represent worldly thoughts, always wanting and never finding, always hungry and never satisfied, restless, searching here and there and everywhere for Truth. These thoughts are let into the consciousness by the hireling, the personal ego, and the result is a scattered state of mind.

6. *I lay down my life for the sheep.* This means that the high spiritual I AM lets itself become identified with the limitations of self-consciousness that it may lift all up to the spiritual plane. "I lay down my life, that I may take it again."

7. *I have other sheep, which are not of this fold.* Our temporal Gentile thoughts and states of consciousness, which we have considered not included in the divine plan of perfection for us. A non-metaphysical interpretation by Ed Rabel mentions that Jesus may be indicating sheep from another world or dimension.

## Jesus is rejected by the Jews

10:22 It was the Feast of the Dedication[33] at Jerusalem. 10:23 It was winter, and Jesus was walking in the temple, in Solomon's porch. 10:24 The Jews therefore came around him and said to him, "How long will you hold us in suspense? If you are the Christ, tell us plainly."(1)

10:25 Jesus answered them, "I told you, and you don't believe. The works that I do in my Father's name, these testify about me. 10:26 But you don't believe, because you are not of my sheep, as I told you. 10:27 My sheep hear my voice, and I know them, and they follow me. 10:28 I give eternal life to them.(2) They will never perish, and no one will snatch them out of my hand. 10:29 My Father, who has given them to me, is greater than all. No one is able to snatch them out of my Father's hand. 10:30 I and the Father are one."(3)

10:31 Therefore Jews took up stones again to stone him. 10:32 Jesus answered them, "I have shown you many good works from my Father. For which of those works do you stone me?"

10:33 The Jews answered him, "We don't stone you for a good work, but for blasphemy: because you, being a man, make yourself God."

10:34 Jesus answered them, "Isn't it written in your law, 'I said, you are gods?'[34] 10:35 If he called them gods, to whom the word of God came (and the Scripture can't be broken), 10:36 do you say of him whom the Father sanctified and sent into the world, 'You blaspheme,' because I said, 'I am the Son of God?' 10:37 If I don't do the works of my Father, don't believe me. 10:38 But if I do them, though you don't believe me, believe the works; that you may know and believe that the Father is in me, and I in the Father."

10:39 They sought again to seize him, and he went out of their hand. 10:40 He went away again beyond the Jordan into the place where John was baptizing at first, and there he stayed.(4) 10:41 Many came to him. They said, "John indeed did no sign, but everything that John said about this man is true." 10:42 Many believed in him there.

1. *If you are the Christ, tell us plainly.* In this Scripture Jesus symbolizes the I AM or Christ, and the Jews symbolize our high-brow intellectual thoughts, which hold to the letter of the law to such an extent that they cannot let the spiritual word expand in and through the consciousness.

2. *I give eternal life to them.* By identifying ourselves only with true thoughts and ideas and proving both in our daily life, we

give them vitality and permanence.

3. *I and the Father are one.* We may use it in the same form in which Jesus stated it, or we may say, "I am one with Divine Mind, and I think divine thoughts."

4. *he went away again beyond the Jordan ... and there he stayed.* After the Christ has done a positive work it always withdraws to an inner state of consciousness in order to replenish its power before it goes forth to achieve again. Into this state of consciousness opposing intellect cannot find entrance.

---

Fillmore Study Bible annotations compiled by Rev. Mark Hicks.

**World English Bible Footnotes:**

[29] v10:11. Isaiah 40:11; Ezekiel 34:11-12,15,22

[30] v10:16. Isaiah 56:8

[31] v10:17. Isaiah 53:7-8

[32] v10:21. Exodus 4:11

[33] v10:22. The "Feast of the Dedication" is the Greek name for "Hanukkah," a celebration of the rededication of the Temple.

[34] v10:34. Psalm 82:6

# John 11

## The Death of Lazarus

11:1 Now a certain man was sick, Lazarus from Bethany,[1] of the village of Mary and her sister, Martha.[2] 11:2 It was that Mary who had anointed the Lord with ointment, and wiped his feet with her hair, whose brother, Lazarus, was sick. 11:3 The sisters therefore sent to him, saying, "Lord, behold, he for whom you have great affection is sick." 11:4 But when Jesus heard it, he said, "This sickness is not to death, but for the glory of God, that God's Son may be glorified by it." 11:5 Now Jesus loved Martha, and her sister, and Lazarus. 11:6 When therefore he heard that he was sick, he stayed two days in the place where he was. 11:7 Then after this he said to the disciples, "Let's go into Judea again."

11:8 The disciples told him, "Rabbi, the Jews were just trying to stone you, and are you going there again?"

11:9 Jesus answered, "Aren't there twelve hours of daylight? If a man walks in the day, he doesn't stumble, because he sees the light of this world. 11:10 But if a man walks in the night, he stumbles, because the light isn't in him." 11:11 He said these things, and after that, he said to them, "Our friend, Lazarus, has fallen asleep, but I am going so that I may awake him out of sleep."[3]

11:12 The disciples therefore said, "Lord, if he has fallen asleep, he will recover."

11:13 Now Jesus had spoken of his death, but they thought that he spoke of taking rest in sleep. 11:14 So Jesus said to them plainly then, "Lazarus is dead.④ 11:15 I am glad for your sakes that I was not there,⑤ so that you may believe. Nevertheless, let's go to him."

11:16 Thomas therefore, who is called Didymus,⑥[35] said to his fellow disciples, "Let's go also, that we may die with him."

1. *Now a certain man was sick, Lazarus.* Lazarus is the ruling thought in the intellect; the name means court of God. At its center it is good; we could not draw to ourselves the potentialities of Being without this accumulative faculty, but its fault is in piling up thoughts and things on the material plane. When man lets his intellect spend all his energies in money getting, he is sowing the seeds of a long sleep in matter.

2. *Mary and her sister Martha.* The human love, Mary, and the natural life, Martha, are sisters to this intellect, and although they, like all women, have faith in the Spirit, they allow themselves to fall under the mortal law thought, and believe in the reality of death. The whole world is under the hypnotism of this material belief, and it is making tombs for thousands every day.

3. *I am going so that I may awake him out of sleep.* The lifting up of the whole man, spirit, soul, and body, into the Christ consciousness of power.

4. *Lazarus is dead.* The meaning of "Lazarus" is "God is helper." When man fails to recognize God as the one Helper and the one support of his life, spiritual understanding becomes weak in him and he sinks into materiality. To all intents, he is dead to the truth of his own being.

5. *I am glad for your sakes that I was not there.* Jesus, who represents the I AM in each individual, is always glad of the opportunity to develop a greater faith in the disciples, or the twelve faculties of man.

6. *Thomas ... who is called Didymus.* The phase of understanding represented by Thomas is that which includes reason and intellectual perception. Thomas did not understand that life is eternal, but did understand the truth that made Jesus fearless in the face of danger, and was loyal enough to his Master to be willing to die with Him if necessary.

## Jesus the Resurrection and the Life

11:17 So when Jesus came, he found that he had been in the tomb four days already. 11:18 Now Bethany was near Jerusalem, about fifteen stadia[36] away. 11:19 Many of the Jews had joined the women around Martha and Mary, to console them concerning their brother. 11:20 Then when Martha heard that Jesus was coming, she went and met him, but Mary stayed in the house.① 11:21 Therefore Martha said to Jesus, "Lord, if you would have been here, my brother wouldn't have died. 11:22 Even now I know that, whatever you ask of God, God will give you." 11:23 Jesus said to her, "Your brother will rise again."

11:24 Martha said to him, "I know that he will rise again in the resurrection at the last day."

11:25 Jesus said to her, "I am the resurrection② and the life. He who believes in me will still live, even if he dies.③ 11:26 Whoever lives and believes in me will never die.④ Do you believe this?"

11:27 She said to him, "Yes, Lord. I have come to believe that you are the Christ, God's Son, he who comes into the world."

1. *Martha ... went and met him, but Mary stayed in the house.* Martha represents the part of the soul that is preoccupied with externals. Mary was preoccupied with the inner realities of thought and understanding. Martha ministered to His physical needs. Mary allowed Him to minister to her spiritual needs. His physical

presence was not essential to her. When He drew near she "still sat in the house."

2. *the resurrection at the last day ... I am the resurrection.* Jesus denies the belief that the resurrection of the dead occurs "at the last day." The resurrection is an occurrence in the present. It is an inner awakening, not an external fact. The "I" is the "Word" that was made flesh, the eternal truth of life. The eternal, the primordial, that existed in the beginning, rose again in Lazarus.

3. *He who believes in me will still live, even if he dies.* This statement sets forth man's uninterrupted consciousness of individual identity with Christ regardless of life, death, or other limiting circumstance. Man cannot lose his identity as a son of God.

4. *Whoever lives and believes in me will never die.* The restorative and renewing functions are adequate to the perfect health, strength, and youthfulness of the body. The mind first lets go its hold upon the idea of eternal youth, and the body follows the action of the mind.

## Jesus Weeps

11:28 When she had said this, she went away, and called Mary, her sister, secretly, saying, "The Teacher is here, and is calling you."

11:29 When she heard this, she arose quickly, and went to him. 11:30 Now Jesus had not yet come into the village, but was in the place where Martha met him. 11:31 Then the Jews who were with her in the house, and were consoling her, when they saw Mary, that she rose up quickly and went out, followed her, saying, "She is going to the tomb to weep there." 11:32 Therefore when Mary came to where Jesus was, and saw him, she fell down at his feet, saying to him, "Lord, if you would have been here, my brother wouldn't have died."

11:33 When Jesus therefore saw her weeping, and the Jews weeping who came with her, he groaned in the spirit, and was troubled,[1] 11:34 and said, "Where have you laid him?"

They told him, "Lord, come and see."

11:35 Jesus wept.

11:36 The Jews therefore said, "See how much affection he had for him!" 11:37 Some of them said, "Couldn't this man, who opened the eyes of him who was blind, have also kept this man from dying?"

1. *Jesus ... groaned in the spirit and was troubled.* There is very strong reason for believing that Lazarus was the rich young ruler referred to in Mark 10:17-22, whom Jesus loved, and whom he bade to sell all he had and follow him, but who had "much possessions," and could not give them up. Lazarus is the ruling thought in the intellect; the name means court of God. At its center it is good; we could not draw to ourselves the potentialities of Being without this accumulative faculty, but its fault is in piling up thoughts and things on the material plane. Jesus loves this young man, but groans in spirit and weeps over his sense sleep and entombment in matter.

## Jesus Raises Lazarus to Life

11:38 Jesus therefore, again groaning in himself, came to the tomb. Now it was a cave, and a stone lay against it.[1] 11:39 Jesus said, "Take away the stone."[2]

Martha, the sister of him who was dead, said to him, "Lord, by this time there is a stench, for he has been dead four days."

11:40 Jesus said to her, "Didn't I tell

you that if you believed, you would see God's glory?"

11:41 So they took away the stone from the place where the dead man was lying.[37] Jesus lifted up his eyes, and said, "Father, I thank you that you listened to me. 11:42 I know that you always listen to me, but because of the multitude that stands around I said this, that they may believe that you sent me." 11:43 When he had said this, he cried with a loud voice, "Lazarus, come out!"[3]

11:44 He who was dead came out, bound hand and foot with wrappings, and his face was wrapped around with a cloth.

Jesus said to them, "Free him, and let him go."

1. *Now it was a cave, and a stone lay against it.* The cave represents the darkness of materiality, and the stone that "lay against it" represents that which seals the thought that youth has come to an end.

2. *Jesus said, Take away the stone.* Jesus makes a denial of the thought that material conditions can confine life.

3. *Lazarus, come out!* The treatment for this sleep in matter is silent asking, then audible commanding. This is the formula given by Jesus, and it is found very effective by Christian healers. Then give perfect freedom: "Free him, and let him go."

## The Plot to Kill Jesus

11:45 Therefore many of the Jews, who came to Mary and saw what Jesus did, believed in him. 11:46 But some of them went away to the Pharisees, and told them the things which Jesus had done. 11:47 The chief priests therefore and the Pharisees gathered a council, and said, "What are we doing? For this man does many signs. 11:48 If we leave him alone like this, everyone will believe in him, and the Romans will come and take away both our place and our nation."

11:49 But a certain one of them, Caiaphas, being high priest that year, said to them, "You know nothing at all, 11:50 nor do you consider that it is advantageous for us that one man should die for the people, and that the whole nation not perish." 11:51 Now he didn't say this of himself, but being high priest that year, he prophesied that Jesus would die for the nation, 11:52 and not for the nation only, but that he might also gather together into one the children of God who are scattered abroad. 11:53 So from that day forward they took counsel that they might put him to death. 11:54 Jesus therefore walked no more openly among the Jews, but departed from there into the country near the wilderness, to a city called Ephraim. He stayed there with his disciples.

11:55 Now the Passover of the Jews was at hand. Many went up from the country to Jerusalem before the Passover, to purify themselves. 11:56 Then they sought for Jesus and spoke one with another, as they stood in the temple, "What do you think--that he isn't coming to the feast at all?" 11:57 Now the chief priests and the Pharisees had commanded that if anyone knew where he was, he should report it, that they might seize him.

Fillmore Study Bible annotations compiled by Rev. Mark Hicks.

**World English Bible Footnotes:**

[35] v11:16. "Didymus" means "Twin"

[36] v11:18. 15 stadia is about 2.8 kilometers or 1.7 miles

[37] v11:41. NU omits "from the place where the dead man was lying."

# JOHN 12

## Mary Anoints Jesus

12:1 Then six days before the Passover, Jesus came to Bethany,[1] where Lazarus was, who had been dead, whom he raised from the dead. 12:2 So they made him a supper there. Martha served, but Lazarus was one of those who sat at the table with him.[2] 12:3 Mary, therefore, took a pound[38] of ointment of pure nard, very precious, and anointed the feet of Jesus,[3] and wiped his feet with her hair. The house was filled with the fragrance of the ointment.[4] 12:4 Then Judas Iscariot,[5] Simon's son, one of his disciples, who would betray him, said, 12:5 "Why wasn't this ointment sold for three hundred denarii,[39] and given to the poor?" 12:6 Now he said this, not because he cared for the poor, but because he was a thief, and having the money box, used to steal what was put into it. 12:7 But Jesus said, "Leave her alone. She has kept this for the day of my burial. 12:8 For you always have the poor with you, but you don't always have me."

1. *Bethany*. "A place of fruits" and is realized in the subconscious. When man is quickened of the Spirit, he gets a certain result in mind and body, which is the fruit of his thought.

2. *Martha served; but Lazarus sat*. Signifies the giving and receiving of the forces that feed us on the invisible side of life. The "supper" is the consciousness of sustenance for the physical man.

3. *Mary ... anointed the feet of Jesus*. Anointing of the feet represents the willingness of love to serve. Love is the fruit of devotion and thanksgiving expressed by Mary.

4. *and the house was filled with the fragrance of the ointment*. Every emotion has a corresponding emanation. When we do a loving, unselfish thing, or even think an unselfish thought, there pours forth from the solar plexus a real substance. Those who are sensitive to odors often catch its sweet perfume, and think it comes from some external source.

5. *Judas Iscariot*. The sense consciousness of man. Its satisfaction is in personal gains and it is continually opposed to the outpouring of Love. Judas is transformed and redeemed, when all pertaining to personality is surrendered and the substance of Love is poured into consciousness. Love overcomes all selfishness and transforms the sense man into his pure and original state. The quickening life of Spirit anoints the whole body and resurrects it into newness of life and substance, thus begetting the new creature in Christ Jesus.

## The Plot to Kill Lazarus

12:9 A large crowd therefore of the Jews learned that he was there, and they came, not for Jesus' sake only, but that they might see Lazarus also, whom he had raised from the dead. 12:10 But the chief priests conspired to put Lazarus to death also, 12:11 because on account of him many of the Jews went away and believed in Jesus.

## Jesus' Triumphal Entry into Jerusalem

12:12 On the next day a great multitude had come to the feast. When they heard that Jesus was coming to Jerusalem,[1] 12:13 they took the branches of the palm trees, and went out to meet him, and cried out, "Hosanna[40]! Blessed is he who comes in the name of the Lord,[41] the King of Israel!"

12:14 Jesus, having found a young donkey, sat on it. As it is written, 12:15 "Don't be afraid, daughter of Zion. Behold, your King comes, sitting on a donkey's colt."[42] 12:16 His disciples didn't understand these things at first, but when Jesus was glorified, then they remembered that these things were written about him, and that they had done these things to him. 12:17 The multitude therefore that was with him when he called Lazarus out of the tomb, and raised him from the dead, was testifying about it. 12:18 For this cause also the multitude went and met him, because they heard that he had done this sign. 12:19 The Pharisees therefore said among themselves, "See how you accomplish nothing. Behold, the world has gone after him."

1. *Jesus was coming to Jerusalem.* Jesus' riding into Jerusalem represents progressive unfoldment, the fulfillment of the time when the I AM is to take control and lift all our animal forces into the spiritual realm of mastery, purity, and peace. Jerusalem means "habitation of peace," and represents spiritual consciousness.

## Some Greeks Wish to See Jesus

12:20 Now there were certain Greeks[1] among those that went up to worship at the feast.[2] 12:21 These, therefore, came to Philip, who was from Bethsaida[3] of Galilee, and asked him, saying, "Sir, we want to see Jesus." 12:22 Philip came and told Andrew, and in turn, Andrew came with Philip, and they told Jesus. 12:23 Jesus answered them, "The time has come for the Son of Man to be glorified. 12:24 Most certainly I tell you, unless a grain of wheat falls into the earth and dies, it remains by itself alone. But if it dies, it bears much fruit.[4] 12:25 He who loves his life will lose it. He who hates his life in this world will keep it to eternal life. 12:26 If anyone serves me, let him follow me. Where I am, there will my servant also be. If anyone serves me, the Father will honor him.

1. *Now there were certain Greeks.* Greeks represent intellectual reasoning, and the "certain Greeks" mentioned in the text of today's lesson represent that branch of modern scientific thought which interprets the universe in terms understandable to both science and religion.

2. *at the feast.* A feast represents appropriation in a large measure, or the laying hold of divine potentialities.

3. *Bethsaida.* ("house of fishing," "place of nets") represents a consciousness of in-

crease of ideas, of gathering of substance. It also represents a mental state of continual search after new ideas, and of endeavor to gain them by every means possible. This approach is typical of both science and religion in that both seek Truth with complete lack of self-interest.

4. *but if it dies, it bears much fruit.* The possibility of increase in the spiritual realm depends on disinterestedness or unselfishness. The life that is lived to and for itself alone must be given up in favor of the larger life that is lived for all, before man can deepen and enrich his life consciousness.

## Jesus Speaks about His Death

12:27 "Now my soul is troubled.
What shall I say? 'Father, save me
from this time?' But for this cause I
came to this time. 12:28 Father, glorify
your name!"[1]

Then there came a voice out of the sky, saying, "I have both glorified it, and will glorify it again."

12:29 The multitude therefore, who
stood by and heard it, said that it had
thundered. Others said, "An angel
has spoken to him."

12:30 Jesus answered, "This voice
hasn't come for my sake, but for your
sakes. 12:31 Now is the judgment of
this world. Now the prince of this
world will be cast out.[2] 12:32 And I,
if I am lifted up from the earth, will
draw all people to myself." 12:33 But
he said this, signifying by what kind
of death he should die. 12:34 The
multitude answered him, "We have
heard out of the law that the Christ
remains forever.[43] How do you say,
'The Son of Man must be lifted up?'
Who is this Son of Man?"

12:35 Jesus therefore said to them,
"Yet a little while the light is with
you. Walk while you have the light,
that darkness doesn't overtake you.
He who walks in the darkness doesn't
know where he is going. 12:36 While
you have the light, believe in the
light, that you may become children
of light."

1. *Father, glorify your name!* The natural man when in trouble prays, "Father, save me from this hour." God's name is glorified when man brings his intellectual reasonings into contact with the Spirit of truth and permeates his reason with the wisdom that is from above, God's name is glorified; that is, the good of mankind is increased.

2. *now will the prince of this world be cast out.* Ignorance and superstition rule the race mind. With the dawn of a better understanding of life and the part that man is fitted to play in it, these negative states disappear.

## The Unbelief of the People

Jesus said these things, and he
departed and hid himself from them.
12:37 But though he had done so many
signs before them, yet they didn't
believe in him, 12:38 that the word of
Isaiah the prophet might be fulfilled,
which he spoke,

"Lord, who has believed our
report?
To whom has the arm of the
Lord been revealed?"[44]

12:39 For this cause they couldn't
believe, for Isaiah said again,

12:40 "He has blinded their eyes and
he hardened their heart,
lest they should see with their
eyes,

and perceive with their heart,
and would turn,
and I would heal them."[45]

12:41 Isaiah said these things when
he saw his glory, and spoke of
him.[46] 12:42 Nevertheless even of the
rulers many believed in him, but because of the Pharisees they didn't confess it, so that they wouldn't be put out of the synagogue, 12:43 for they loved men's praise more than God's praise.

## Summary of Jesus' Teachings

12:44 Jesus cried out and said,
"Whoever believes in me, believes
not in me, but in him who sent me.
12:45 He who sees me sees him who
sent me.(1) 12:46 I have come as a light
into the world, that whoever
believes in me may not remain in
the darkness. 12:47 If anyone listens
to my sayings, and doesn't believe,
I don't judge him. For I came not
to judge the world, but to save the
world. 12:48 He who rejects me, and
doesn't receive my sayings, has one
who judges him. The word that I
spoke, the same will judge him in the
last day. 12:49 For I spoke not from
myself, but the Father who sent me,
he gave me a commandment, what I
should say, and what I should speak.
12:50 I know that his commandment
is eternal life. The things therefore which I speak, even as the Father has said to me, so I speak."

1. *He who sees me sees him who sent me.* Jesus (symbolizing the indwelling Christ) declares to the whole soul consciousness that the preponderance of power is spiritual. Spiritual character is the rock foundation of Being; therefore He is urging the multitude of thoughts to realize that their redemption comes through decreeing their oneness with Spirit and that the will of God is active in consciousness.

---

Fillmore Study Bible annotations compiled by Rev. Mark Hicks.

**World English Bible Footnotes:**

[38] v12:3. a Roman pound of 12 ounces, or about 340 grams

[39] v12:5. 300 denarii was about a year's wages for an agricultural laborer.

[40] v12:13. "Hosanna" means "save us" or "help us, we pray."

[41] v12:13. Psalm 118:25-26

[42] v12:15. Zechariah 9:9

[43] v12:34. Isaiah 9:7; Daniel 2:44 (but see also Isaiah 53:8)

[44] v12:38. Isaiah 53:1

[45] v12:40. Isaiah 6:10

[46] v12:41. Isaiah 6:1

# John 13

## Jesus Washes the Disciples' Feet

13:1 Now before the feast of the Passover,[1] Jesus, knowing that his time had come[2] that he would depart from this world to the Father, having loved his own who were in the world, he loved them to the end. 13:2 After supper, the devil having already put into the heart of Judas Iscariot, Simon's son, to betray him,[3] 13:3 Jesus, knowing that the Father had given all things into his hands,[4] and that he came forth from God, and was going to God, 13:4 arose from supper, and laid aside his outer garments. He took a towel, and wrapped a towel around his waist. 13:5 Then he poured water into the basin, and began to wash the disciples' feet,[5] and to wipe them with the towel that was wrapped around him. 13:6 Then he came to Simon Peter. He said to him, "Lord, do you wash my feet?"

13:7 Jesus answered him, "You don't know what I am doing now, but you will understand later."

13:8 Peter said to him, "You will never wash my feet!"

Jesus answered him, "If I don't wash you, you have no part with me."[6]

13:9 Simon Peter said to him, "Lord, not my feet only, but also my hands and my head!"

13:10 Jesus said to him, "Someone who has bathed only needs to have his feet washed, but is completely clean. You are clean, but not all of you." 13:11 For he knew him who would betray him, therefore he said, "You are not all clean."[7] 13:12 So when he had washed their feet, put his outer garment back on, and sat down again, he said to them, "Do you know what I have done to you? 13:13 You call me, 'Teacher' and 'Lord.' You say so correctly, for so I am. 13:14 If I then, the Lord and the Teacher, have washed your feet, you also ought to wash one another's feet.[8] 13:15 For I have given you an example, that you also should do as I have done to you. 13:16 Most certainly I tell you, a servant is not greater than his lord,[9] neither one who is sent greater than he who sent him. 13:17 If you know these things, blessed are you if you do them. 13:18 I don't speak concerning all of you. I know whom I have chosen. But that the Scripture may be fulfilled, 'He who eats bread with me has lifted up his heel against me.'[47] 13:19 From now on, I tell you before it happens, that when it happens, you may believe that I am he. 13:20 Most certainly I tell you, he who receives whomever I send, receives me; and he who receives me, receives him who sent me."

1. *Now before the feast of the passover.* In spiritual evolution the Passover represents the passing of the soul consciousness from one plane to another without death of the body. The Passover is typified as a feast, because Spirit uplifts and transmutes both soul and body to spiritual essence.

2. *knowing that his time had come.* Jesus had overcome materiality, and was about to be translated into completely spiritual consciousness.

3. *the devil having already put into the heart of Judas Iscariot ... to betray him.* Judas represents the life consciousness in the soul. The devil is the personal mind, which believes that it is sustained by ma-

terial food. The belief that the body lives upon the food that it eats is responsible for material or sense consciousness, Satan.

4. *Jesus, knowing that the Father had given all the things into his hands.* The overcomer, represented by Jesus, must know that the Father has given all things into his hands; that he is Spirit; that he came forth from God, and now identifies himself with God. The overcomer then proceeds to wash his disciples' feet, which means that metaphysically he denies all sense of materiality in understanding.

5. *Then he ... began to wash the disciples' feet.* Jesus is the I Am, and the feet represent spiritual understanding, especially that phase of spiritual understanding which connects with the manifest world, and which reveals the right relationship towards worldly conditions in general. The "washing," therefore, typifies a cleansing process, or a denial of personality and materiality.

6. *If I don't wash you, you have no part with me.* Peter, representing faith, like all the other faculties of the mind, must be freed from identification with material things. The faith of the unregenerate man functions in sense consciousness, and before such faith can attain spiritual ideas, the hold of matter and of material sensation must be dissolved.

7. *You are not all clean.* Because Judas (Life) was not established in the purity and the freedom of Spirit, the whole man was not yet redeemed.

8. *you also ought to wash one another's feet.* When we have purified our own souls and lifted them to spiritual consciousness, we should then extend the same purifying service to others, that they too may be lifted up.

9. *a servant is not greater than his lord.* There had been contention among the disciples as to who would sit at the Master's right, and who at his left, in the kingdom. Jesus was wiping out this strife, thus bringing home to his followers that truth that he, who willingly performs lowly, humble service for others with no thought for personal distinction, the same is greatest in God's kingdom.

## Jesus Foretells His Betrayal

13:21 When Jesus had said this, he
was troubled in spirit, and testified,
"Most certainly I tell you that one of
you will betray me."

13:22 The disciples looked at one
another, perplexed about whom he
spoke. 13:23 One of his disciples, whom
Jesus loved, was at the table,
leaning against Jesus' breast. 13:24
Simon Peter therefore beckoned to
him, and said to him, "Tell us who it
is of whom he speaks."

13:25 He, leaning back, as he was,
on Jesus' breast, asked him, "Lord,
who is it?"

13:26 Jesus therefore answered, "It
is he to whom I will give this piece
of bread when I have dipped it." So
when he had dipped the piece of
bread, he gave it to Judas, the son of
Simon Iscariot. 13:27 After the piece of
bread, then Satan entered into him.

Then Jesus said to him, "What you
do, do quickly."

13:28 Now no man at the table knew
why he said this to him. 13:29 For some
thought, because Judas had the
money box, that Jesus said to him,
"Buy what things we need for the
feast," or that he should give
something to the poor. 13:30
Therefore, having received that
morsel, he went out immediately. It
was night.

## The New Commandment

13:31 When he had gone out, Jesus
said, "Now the Son of Man has been
glorified, and God has been glorified
in him. 13:32 If God has been glorified

in him, God will also glorify him in himself, and he will glorify him immediately. 13:33 Little children, I will be with you a little while longer. You will seek me, and as I said to the Jews, 'Where I am going, you can't come,' so now I tell you. 13:34 A new commandment I give to you,[1] that you love one another, just like I have loved you;[2] that you also love one another. 13:35 By this everyone will know that you are my disciples,[3] if you have love for one another."[4]

1. *A new commandment I give to you.* The new commandment of Jesus Christ is based on the impersonal principle of love for love's sake, regardless of the attitude of those who are loved.

2. *just like I have loved you.* Jesus loved His disciples by seeing them as spiritually perfect. The I AM sees man's faculties as perfect also. Faith is unfailing, love divine, strength inexhaustible, judgment flawless, understanding perfect, will good, imagination true, power always sufficient, appropriation selfless, zeal always in order, wisdom unceasing, order divine.

3. *By this everyone will know that you are my disciples.* Although love is invisible, its effects are plainly manifest. The love of the Christ, when fully exerted, has power to protect its object, and it stirs those who receive it to express the ideals that are held of them. Those who express the love of the Christ and those who receive it are alike outstanding.

4. *if you have love for one another.* With reference to the faculties, the spiritual nature and relationship of the faculties is made manifest when they are developed harmoniously and expressed in unity.

## Jesus Foretells Peter's Denial

13:36 Simon Peter said to him, "Lord, where are you going?"

Jesus answered, "Where I am going, you can't follow now, but you will follow afterwards."[1]

13:37 Peter said to him, "Lord, why can't I follow you now? I will lay down my life for you."[2]

13:38 Jesus answered him, "Will you lay down your life for me? Most certainly I tell you, the rooster won't crow until you have denied me three times.

1. *Where I am going ... you will follow afterwards.* Jesus (the I Am), though sure of spiritual guidance, was carefully making preparations to travel over new, untried ground, the object of which was to open the way into the kingdom, that realm of Divine Ideas, which would make the path easier, not only for his disciples, but for all humanity. He knew that his disciples (faculties of mind) had a work to do before they were strong enough to follow and to enter therein.

2. *Peter said ... I will lay down my life for you.* The leading characteristic of Peter (Faith) before he is firmly established in spiritual consciousness is changeableness. He typifies that state of unsteadiness which fluctuates from the high spiritual to the material, yet with an ever recurring desire for Spirit and for the things of Spirit, which is bound to always lead into the light.

---

Fillmore Study Bible annotations compiled by Rev. Mark Hicks.

**World English Bible Footnotes:**

[47] v13:18. Psalm 41:9

# John 14

## Jesus the Way to the Father

[14:1] "Don't let your heart be troubled. Believe in God. Believe also in me. [14:2] In my Father's house are many homes.[1] If it weren't so, I would have told you. I am going to prepare a place for you. [14:3] If I go and prepare a place for you, I will come again, and will receive you to myself; that where I am, you may be there also. [14:4] Where I go, you know, and you know the way."[2]

[14:5] Thomas[3] said to him, "Lord, we don't know where you are going. How can we know the way?"

[14:6] Jesus said to him, "I am the way, the truth, and the life.[4] No one comes to the Father, except through me. [14:7] If you had known me, you would have known my Father also. From now on, you know him, and have seen him."

[14:8] Philip[5] said to him, "Lord, show us the Father, and that will be enough for us."

[14:9] Jesus said to him, "Have I been with you such a long time, and do you not know me, Philip? He who has seen me has seen the Father. How do you say, 'Show us the Father?' [14:10] Don't you believe that I am in the Father, and the Father in me? The words that I tell you, I speak not from myself; but the Father who lives in me does his works. [14:11] Believe me that I am in the Father, and the Father in me; or else believe me for the very works' sake. [14:12] Most certainly I tell you, he who believes in me, the works that I do, he will do also;[6] and he will do greater works than these, because I am going to my Father. [14:13] Whatever you will ask in my name, that will I do, that the Father may be glorified in the Son. [14:14] If you will ask anything in my name, I will do it.

1. *In my Father's house are many homes.* "Many mansions" means many abiding places. "Mansion" comes from the Latin manere, to remain. The meaning of Jesus was that He was making a permanent abiding place for those who believed in His teaching and accepted Him for what He really was—God manifest. The idea usually held out is that Jesus was preceding His disciples to heaven, where He would await and welcome them. But there is no such meaning in the text. The permanent abiding place to which Jesus invites His friends is "prepared" by Him: He makes the place Himself, in fact He is the place. "Where I am, there ye may be also.

2. *Where I go, you know, and you know the way.* Jesus meant that those who find the inner spiritual kingdom know Him, and that they also know the way to reach Him wherever they may be.

3. *Thomas.* Thomas means "twins." Spiritually considered, Thomas is understanding, whose twin is Matthew, the will. Intellectual understanding assures us of the truth of our sense impressions. It says, "Seeing is believing."

4. *I am the way, and the truth, and the life.* Jesus talked from the I AM standpoint. The I AM in man is the center of attention and is the open door into the kingdom of God. When man in the silence centers his attention on his spiritual I AM, realizing that he is pure being, he finds his way to the Father's house.

5. *Philip.* Philip represents the power of the Word. The I AM in man is the open door into the kingdom of God. The power faculty must, by acknowledgement that the word of the I AM spoken through it is not of the mortal but of God, be raised to realization of the omnipresence of Spirit.

6. *he who believes in me, the works that I do, he will do also.* This is the greatest promise to all people who have faith in the spiritual man in this lesson.

## The Promise of the Holy Spirit

14:15 If you love me, keep my commandments. 14:16 I will pray to the Father, and he will give you another Counselor,[1][48] that he may be with you forever,-- 14:17 the Spirit of truth,[2] whom the world can't receive; for it doesn't see him, neither knows him. You know him, for he lives with you, and will be in you. 14:18 I will not leave you orphans. I will come to you. 14:19 Yet a little while, and the world will see me no more; but you will see me. Because I live, you will live also.[3] 14:20 In that day you will know that I am in my Father, and you in me, and I in you. 14:21 One who has my commandments, and keeps them, that person is one who loves me. One who loves me will be loved by my Father, and I will love him, and will reveal myself to him."

14:22 Judas (not Iscariot) said to him, "Lord, what has happened that you are about to reveal yourself to us, and not to the world?"

14:23 Jesus answered him, "If a man loves me, he will keep my word. My Father will love him, and we will come to him, and make our home with him. 14:24 He who doesn't love me doesn't keep my words. The word which you hear isn't mine, but the Father's who sent me. 14:25 I have said these things to you, while still living with you. 14:26 But the Counselor, the Holy Spirit, whom the Father will send in my name,[4] he will teach you all things, and will remind you of all that I said to you. 14:27 Peace I leave with you. My peace I give to you;[5] not as the world gives, give I to you. Don't let your heart be troubled, neither let it be fearful. 14:28 You heard how I told you, 'I go away, and I come to you.' If you loved me, you would have rejoiced, because I said 'I am going to my Father;' for the Father is greater than I. 14:29 Now I have told you before it happens so that, when it happens, you may believe. 14:30 I will no more speak much with you, for the prince of the world comes, and he has nothing in me. 14:31 But that the world may know that I love the Father, and as the Father commanded me, even so I do. Arise, let us go from here.

1. *Counselor (Comforter, ASV).* The Counselor, the Advocate, the Spirit of truth is omnipresent as divine wisdom and power, which are brought into active touch with our consciousness through our believing in Him. In "the world"—on the phenomenal side—we cannot know this guide and helper, but having learned the truth about the omnipresence of Spirit, with all the abundance of life, love, Truth, and intelligence through which it is made manifest, we at once begin to realize that the Mighty One dwells with us, and "shall be in you."

2. *the Spirit of truth.* The universal world teacher who comes to every disciple of Jesus as a guide, director, comforter, and executive power. When we call upon Christ to be with us in our hours of trial, or to help us make some demonstration, it is "the Spirit of truth" that responds; in other words, "the Spirit of truth" is the executive of the Christ. In the early stages of our work this "Spirit of truth" seems to be external to us, but as we continue our unfoldment in the Christ consciousness we become more and more aware of spiritual Truth as an indwelling presence.

3. *because I live, you shall live also.* With this expansion of the sense of our divine identity comes a perception of our unity with the Father, and the absolute identity of our sense-limited I with the universal I AM, the Christ.

4. *But the Counselor, the Holy Spirit, whom the Father will send in my name.* The Father is principle. The Son is this Father principle revealed in a creative plan. The Holy Spirit is the executive power of both Father and Son. The Holy Spirit is not all of Being, nor the fullness of Christ, but an emanation or "breath" sent forth to do a divine work. Thus circumscribed, the Holy Spirit may in a sense be said to take on the characteristics of personality, but personality that for capacity transcends all man's conceptions. The Holy Spirit was before the time of Jesus. However Jesus' life

and demonstration gave a new impetus to it. The Holy Spirit or Spirit of truth is man's one sure guide in his spiritual ongoing. An outpouring of the Holy Spirit always brings peace and infinite faith in the Father through the Son.

5. My peace I give to you. The peace of Christ (based on consciousness and compassion) is not the peace of Rome (Pax Romana, peace based on power and domination) nor the peace of Judeo-Christian tradition (Justice, peace based on law).

---

Fillmore Study Bible annotations compiled by Rev. Mark Hicks.

**World English Bible Footnotes:**

[48] v14:16. Greek Parakleton: Counselor, Helper, Intercessor, Advocate, and Comfortor.

# JOHN 15

## Jesus the True Vine

[15:1] "I am the true vine, and my Father is the farmer. [15:2] Every branch in me that doesn't bear fruit,❶ he takes away. Every branch that bears fruit, he prunes, that it may bear more fruit. [15:3] You are already pruned clean because of the word which I have spoken to you. [15:4] Remain in me,❷ and I in you. As the branch can't bear fruit by itself, unless it remains in the vine, so neither can you, unless you remain in me. [15:5] I am the vine. You are the branches. He who remains in me, and I in him, the same bears much fruit,❸ for apart from me you can do nothing. [15:6] If a man doesn't remain in me, he is thrown out as a branch, and is withered;❹ and they gather them, throw them into the fire, and they are burned. [15:7] If you remain in me, and my words remain in you, you will ask whatever you desire,❺ and it will be done for you.❻

[15:8] "In this is my Father glorified, that you bear much fruit; and so you will be my disciples. [15:9] Even as the Father has loved me, I also have loved you. Remain in my love. [15:10] If you keep my commandments,❼ you will remain in my love;❽ even as I have kept my Father's commandments, and remain in his love. [15:11] I have spoken these things to you, that my joy may remain in you, and that your joy may be made full.

[15:12] "This is my commandment, that you love one another, even as I have loved you. [15:13] Greater love has no one than this, that someone lay down his life for his friends. [15:14] You are my friends, if you do whatever I command you. [15:15] No longer do I call you servants, for the servant doesn't know what his lord does. But I have called you friends,❾ for everything that I heard from my Father, I have made known to you. [15:16] You didn't choose me, but I chose you, and appointed you, that you should go and bear fruit, and that your fruit should remain; that whatever you will ask of the Father in my name, he may give it to you.❿ [15:17] "I command these things to you, that you may love one another.

1. *true vine, husbandman, branch, fruit.* Metaphysically stated, the Father is the God-Mind; Jesus is the individual incarnation of that Mind, here called the true vine. "Every branch in me" means the faculties of mind, and the "fruit" is the thought.

2. *Remain (abide, ASV) in me.* "Abiding in the Word" is a conscious centering of the Mind in the depths of one's being, thus keeping up connection with the Father within.

3. *He who remains in me, and I in him, the same bears much fruit.* The natural effect of "abiding in the Word" is to liberate the forces of one's Being through which perfection is attained, and to cease from external efforts.

4. *and is withered.* An unused faculty atrophies and withers away.

5. *ask whatever you desire.* Desire: A promise from God, God tapping at the door of your consciousness with His infinite supply. LIT/Faith.

6. *and it will be done for you.* In order to receive that which we ask, the I Am must be centered in the Realm of Ideas (Divine Mind) within, in faith and understanding.

7. *If you keep my commandments.* Commanding, controlling and directing every thought according to the harmonious law of love to one another.

8. *you will remain in my love.* Love dissolves all negative, reactionary tendencies, and makes progress possible for us. Love also brings joy in its wake, and sets the mind and heart free to see and appreciate the good.

9. *No longer do I call you servants ... but I have called you friends.* Jesus knew definitely that henceforth the apostles were to do the works of Him that sent them. As co-workers with Him, He called them "friends." In all His ministry Jesus taught freedom of the individual. We are not "servants" but agents free to do as we will.

10. *whatever you will ask of the Father in my name, he may give it to you.* The Father does not give things per se. The Father responds to our asking by imparting more of His qualities into us that result in our connection and acceptance of His divine ideas. Then these will take myriad channels or modes of expression to finalize at what we call the right answer, the desired blessing. Another meaning of asking in the name of Jesus Christ would be to align yourself with the givingness part of God's nature. Remember that God is givingness itself, or let us say that givingness itself is one of the divine ideas in God-Mind. It is a beautiful idea, givingness.—Ed Rabel

## The World's Hatred

15:18 If the world hates you, you
know that it has hated me before it
hated you. 15:19 If you were of the
world, the world would love its own.
But because you are not of the
world, since I chose you out of the
world, therefore the world hates
you. 15:20 Remember the word that I
said to you: 'A servant is not greater
than his lord.'[49] If they persecuted
me, they will also persecute you. If
they kept my word, they will keep
yours also. 15:21 But all these things
will they do to you for my name's
sake, because they don't know him
who sent me. 15:22 If I had not come
and spoken to them, they would not
have had sin; but now they have no
excuse for their sin. 15:23 He who
hates me, hates my Father also. 15:24
If I hadn't done among them the
works which no one else did, they
wouldn't have had sin. But now have
they seen and also hated both me
and my Father. 15:25 But this
happened so that the word may be
fulfilled which was written in their
law, 'They hated me without a
cause.'[50]

15:26 "When the Counselor[51] has
come,[1] whom I will send to you from
the Father, the Spirit of truth, who
proceeds from the Father, he will
testify about me. 15:27 You will also
testify, because you have been with
me from the beginning.

1. *But when the Counselor (Comforter, ASV) is come.* The Counselor or Holy Spirit is the law of God in action and when thought of in this way it appears to have personality. From this truth the Hebrews got their conception of the personal, tribal God. The functions ascribed to the Holy Counselor or Holy Spirit or Spirit of truth imply distinct personal subsistence: He is said to speak, search, select, reveal, reprove, testify, lead, comfort, distribute to every man, know the deep things of God, and He can be known by man only through his spiritual nature.

---

Fillmore Study Bible annotations compiled by Rev. Mark Hicks.

**World English Bible Footnotes:**

[49] v15:20. John 13:16

[50] v15:25. Psalms 35:19; 69:4

[51] v15:26. Greek Parakletos: Counselor, Helper, Advocate, Intercessor, and Comfortor.

# John 16

## The World's Hatred (continued)

16:1 "These things have I spoken to
you, so that you wouldn't be caused
to stumble. 16:2 They will put you out
of the synagogues. Yes, the time
comes that whoever kills you will
think that he offers service to God.
16:3 They will do these things[52]
because they have not known the
Father, nor me.❶ 16:4 But I have told
you these things, so that when the
time comes, you may remember that
I told you about them.

1. *They will do these things because they have not known the Father, nor me.* The Pharisaical or worldly state of mind has no conception of the higher realm within but thinks it governs the whole man and is jealous of any attempt to usurp its power. Hence persecution follows.

## Work of the Spirit

I didn't tell you these things from
the beginning, because I was with
you. 16:5 But now I am going to him
who sent me, and none of you asks
me, 'Where are you going?' 16:6 But
because I have told you these things,
sorrow has filled your heart. 16:7
Nevertheless I tell you the truth: It is
to your advantage that I go away,❶
for if I don't go away, the Counselor
won't come to you. But if I go, I will
send him to you. 16:8 When he has
come, he will convict the world
about sin, about righteousness, and
about judgment;❷ 16:9 about sin,
because they don't believe in me; 16:10
about righteousness, because I am
going to my Father, and you won't
see me any more; 16:11 about
judgment, because the prince of this

world has been judged.

16:12 "I have yet many things to tell you, but you can't bear them now.[3] 16:13 However when he, the Spirit of truth, has come, he will guide you into all truth,[4] for he will not speak from himself; but whatever he hears, he will speak. He will declare to you things that are coming. 16:14 He will glorify me, for he will take from what is mine, and will declare it to you. 16:15 All things whatever the Father has are mine; therefore I said that he takes[53] of mine, and will declare it to you.

1. *It is to your advantage that I go away.* Jesus realized that, so long as He remained manifest in material form to His followers, they would continue to focus all their attention on Him in a personal way, that thus they would fail to recognize the Spirit of truth within themselves. In order to overcome as Jesus overcame, it was necessary that they should consciously know the power and presence of Spirit; hence arose the necessity that Jesus disappear from their mortal vision.

2. *The Counselor ... will convict the world about sin, about righteousness, and about judgment.* The Spirit of truth quickens the conscience of man, which, as Paul says, has been seared over as with a hot iron. Spirit then reveals the right way to think and to live. Sinlessness is taught in the Bible and man must demonstrate it. When ill-temper, vanity, greed, selfishness, or error of any other kind appears, it should be denied, and the love, unselfishness, purity, uprightness, and integrity of the higher self should be affirmed, until the Christ righteousness is fully realized and demonstrated.

3. *I have yet many things to tell you, but you can't bear them now.* The only reason why there is Truth we do not know yet, is that there is no reason why we have to know certain things yet. There are certain things that we once knew but have forgotten and for the reason that we no longer need that knowledge. That knowledge has been incorporated into other knowledge. Nothing is lost in Spirit, but forms come and go. It is the essence of knowledge which matters, not the current factual form of knowledge which one must preserve forever. It is the essence of knowledge that will be preserved forever.—Ed Rabel

4. *will guide you into all truth.* For Metaphysical Christians, authority the Spirit of truth is the one and only authority in the study of Truth. See Matthew 7:29 (RW/authority)

## Sorrow Will Turn into Joy

16:16 A little while, and you will not see me. Again a little while, and you will see me." 16:17 Some of his disciples therefore said to one another, "What is this that he says to us, 'A little while, and you won't see me, and again a little while, and you will see me;' and, 'Because I go to the Father?'" 16:18 They said therefore, "What is this that he says, 'A little while?' We don't know what he is saying."

16:19 Therefore Jesus perceived that they wanted to ask him, and he said to them, "Do you inquire among yourselves concerning this, that I said, 'A little while, and you won't see me, and again a little while, and you will see me?' 16:20 Most certainly I tell you, that you will weep and lament, but the world will rejoice. You will be sorrowful, but your sorrow will be turned into joy.[1] 16:21 A woman, when she gives birth, has sorrow, because her time has come. But when she has delivered the child, she doesn't remember the anguish any more, for the joy that a human being is born into the world. 16:22 Therefore you now have sorrow, but I will see you again, and your heart will rejoice, and no one will take your joy away from you.

16:23 "In that day you will ask me no questions.[2] Most certainly I tell you, whatever you may ask of the

Father in my name, he will give it to you. [16:24] Until now, you have asked nothing in my name. Ask, and you will receive, that your joy may be made full.

1. *but your sorrow will be turned into joy*. Spiritual perception reveals to us that we are not persons but ideas in the cosmic Mind. Jesus knew that the hour for His crucifixion was approaching. Crucifixion means the giving up of the whole personality. This was the demonstration that the Master was facing. However, He knew His spiritual power, and He was well aware that He would rise from the dead, would again be with His disciples, and would be more able than ever to instruct them in the mysteries of Being. "I will see you again."

2. *in that day you will ask me no questions.* The apostles would have unfolded to the point where they would understand the laws of Spirit and would be able to read out of the law for themselves.

## Peace for the Disciples

[16:25] I have spoken these things to you in figures of speech.(1) But the time is coming when I will no more speak to you in figures of speech, but will tell you plainly about the Father. [16:26] In that day you will ask in my name; and I don't say to you, that I will pray to the Father for you, [16:27] for the Father himself loves you, because you have loved me, and have believed that I came forth from God. [16:28] I came out from the Father, and have come into the world. Again, I leave the world, and go to the Father."(2)

[16:29] His disciples said to him, "Behold, now you speak plainly, and speak no figures of speech. [16:30] Now we know that you know all things, and don't need for anyone to question you. By this we believe that you came forth from God."

[16:31] Jesus answered them, "Do you now believe? [16:32] Behold, the time is coming, yes, and has now come, that you will be scattered, everyone to his own place, and you will leave me alone. Yet I am not alone, because the Father is with me. [16:33] I have told you these things, that in me you may have peace. In the world you have oppression; but cheer up! I have overcome the world."

1. *figures of speech (dark sayings, ASV).* The figures of speech, or "dark sayings", refers to the darkened consciousness that cannot see the true light. But this Scripture indicates that "the night is far spent, and the day is at hand." The apostles are coming into a great illumination and will be able to go direct to the Father for light and guidance and power. Hitherto the apostles have been students. Now they are to come into a consciousness in which they can tap the great universal reservoir and receive therefrom.

2. *I came out from the Father, and have come into the world. Again, I leave the world, and go to the Father.* Where did He come from? What was his pre-natal state and where did He go to? Where did He go from the transition? Jesus does not explain or elaborate. He simply calls his pre-incarnation state the Father, and He leaves it up to our intuitive understanding to guess what this means.—Ed Rabel

---

Fillmore Study Bible annotations compiled by Rev. Mark Hicks.

**World English Bible Footnotes:**

[52] v16:3. TR adds "to you"

[53] v16:15. TR reads "will take" instead of "takes"

# John 17

## Jesus Prays for His Disciples

17:1 Jesus said these things, and lifting up his eyes to heaven, he said, "Father, the time has come. Glorify your Son, that your Son may also glorify you; 17:2 even as you gave him authority over all flesh, he will give eternal life to all whom you have given him. 17:3 This is eternal life,[1] that they should know you, the only true God, and him whom you sent, Jesus Christ.[2] 17:4 I glorified you on the earth. I have accomplished the work which you have given me to do. 17:5 Now, Father, glorify me with your own self with the glory which I had with you before the world existed.

17:6 I revealed your name to the people whom you have given me out of the world.[3] They were yours, and you have given them to me. They have kept your word. 17:7 Now they have known that all things whatever you have given me are from you, 17:8 for the words which you have given me I have given to them,[4] and they received them, and knew for sure that I came forth from you, and they have believed that you sent me. 17:9 I pray for them. I don't pray for the world, but for those whom you have given me, for they are yours. 17:10 All things that are mine are yours, and yours are mine, and I am glorified in them.[5] 17:11 I am no more in the world, but these are in the world, and I am coming to you. Holy Father, keep them through your name which you have given me, that they may be one, even as we are. 17:12 While I was with them in the world, I kept them in your name. Those whom you have given me I have kept. None of them is lost, except the son of destruction,[6] that the Scripture might be fulfilled. 17:13 But now I come to you, and I say these things in the world, that they may have my joy made full in themselves. 17:14 I have given them your word. The world hated them, because they are not of the world, even as I am not of the world. 17:15 I pray not that you would take them from the world, but that you would keep them from the evil one. 17:16 They are not of the world even as I am not of the world. 17:17 Sanctify them in your truth. Your word is truth.[54] 17:18 As you sent me into the world, even so I have sent them into the world. 17:19 For their sakes I sanctify myself, that they themselves also may be sanctified in truth.

17:20 Not for these only do I pray, but for those also who believe in me through their word, 17:21 that they may all be one; even as you, Father, are in me, and I in you, that they also may be one in us;[7] that the world may believe that you sent me. 17:22 The glory which you have given me, I have given to them; that they may be one, even as we are one;[8] 17:23 I in them, and you in me, that they may be perfected into one; that the world may know that you sent me, and loved them, even as you loved me. 17:24 Father, I desire that they also whom you have given me be with me where I am, that they may see my glory, which you have given me,[9] for you loved me before the foundation of the world.

17:25 Righteous Father, the world hasn't known you, but I knew you; and these knew that you sent me. 17:26 I made known to them your name, and will make it known; that the love with which you loved me may be in them, and I in them."

1. *And this is eternal life.* Eternal life rests in the understanding that Spirit identifies and manifests itself in its idea, perfect man, through which manifest man is educated, empowered, and invested with divinity.

2. *that they should know you, the only true God, and him whom you sent, Jesus Christ.* Jesus was asking for a full and complete unification of His consciousness with that of the Father. Jesus realized that He had been given all authority over the flesh. He was holding the realization not only for His own glorification but also for that of His disciples.

3. *I revealed (manifested, ASV) your name to the people whom you have given me out of the world.* God's name is I AM. Man's name is I AM. When man thinks about God as omnipresent Spirit, he merges his I AM into spiritual I AM, and this conjunction exalts and glorifies both man and God.

4. *for the words which you have given me I have given unto them.* All thoughts and words emanate from the one Logos or living Word. When man opens his consciousness for the inflow of the Logos, in Spirit he receives everything that God has to give.

5. *All things that are mine are yours, and yours are mine, and I am glorified in them.* Jesus made the great renunciation by giving up himself and all his possessions to Spirit. Then he realized that he had made unity with God, that all that God had belonged to him, and that he was exalted, joyous, happy in the possession of the ideas that lay back of and within all things.

6. *None of them is lost, except the son of destruction (perdition, ASV).* The "son of destruction" is the adverse consciousness that man builds through thinking that he has existence apart from God. This thought or adversary or carnal mind must perish before man can be wholly reconciled to God. The Scripture represents the truth, which is fulfilled in man's life, when he destroys all thought of separation from God.

7. *even as you, Father, are in me, and I in you, that they also may be one in us.* The Holy Spirit is the consciousness of unity or perfect communion with God. As mind, idea, and expression are one, so man is one with God and Christ. Mind is the source of the idea, which becomes manifest in expression.

8. *I have given to them; that they may be one.* The following commentary is from an authoritative source within the Orthodox Church: *The Greek Fathers took these and similar texts in their literal sense, and dared to speak of man's "deification" (in Greek, theosis). If man is to share in God's glory, they argued, he is to be "perfectly one" with God, this means in effect that man must be "deified": he is called to become by grace what God is by nature. Accordingly Saint Athanasius summed up the purpose of the Incarnation by saying: "God became man that we might be made god" (On the Incarnation, 54).* [Source: Ware, Timothy, *The Orthodox Church* (Penguin, 2015), 20. ]

9. *that they may see my glory, which you have given me.* The glory of Jesus Christ was His complete unification with the Father, through which He did always the things that were pleasing to God. Divine Mind is well pleased with the perfect idea or son of the Father.

Fillmore Study Bible annotations compiled by Rev. Mark Hicks.

**World English Bible Footnotes:**

[54] v17:17. Psalm 119:142

# John 18

## The Betrayal and Arrest of Jesus

18:1 When Jesus had spoken these words,❶ he went out with his disciples over the brook Kidron,❷ where there was a garden, into which he and his disciples entered. 18:2 Now Judas, who betrayed him, also knew the place, for Jesus often met there with his disciples. 18:3 Judas then, having taken a detachment of soldiers and officers from the chief priests and the Pharisees, came there with lanterns, torches, and weapons.❸ 18:4 Jesus therefore, knowing all the things that were happening to him, went forth, and said to them, "Who are you looking for?"

18:5 They answered him, "Jesus of Nazareth."

Jesus said to them, "I am he."❹

Judas also, who betrayed him, was standing with them. 18:6 When therefore he said to them, "I am he," they went backward, and fell to the ground.

18:7 Again therefore he asked them, "Who are you looking for?"

They said, "Jesus of Nazareth."

18:8 Jesus answered, "I told you that I am he. If therefore you seek me, let these go their way," 18:9 that the word might be fulfilled which he spoke, "Of those whom you have given me, I have lost none."[55]

18:10 Simon Peter therefore, having a sword, drew it, and struck the high priest's servant, and cut off his right ear.❺ The servant's name was Malchus. 18:11 Jesus therefore said to Peter, "Put the sword into its sheath. The cup which the Father has given me, shall I not surely drink it?"❻

1. *When Jesus had spoken these words.* The I AM must demonstrate that it is Spirit, omnipresent, omniscient, and omnipotent. The first step in this demonstration is to send forth the words of consummation, just as it had taken place. Jesus spoke such words in the previous chapter, John 17. Then these words spoken from the powerful standpoint of the I AM set up counter thought vibrations in the consciousness and there is unusual commotion. Because of this chemicalization which frequently takes place in consciousness, some people refrain from "high statements," but high places spiritually cannot be attained by the fainthearted. When you perceive the Truth, speak the words regardless of consequences.

2. *he went out with his disciples over the brook Kidron.* Kidron means "turbid stream" and it represents the current of confused thoughts that sometimes pour in upon us when we try to go into the silence. The "garden" locates the current in the world of universal thought. When Jesus went "over the brook Kidron" and entered the garden of Gethsemane, He passed in His own consciousness from the without to the within.

3. *Judas ... came there with lanterns and torches and weapons.* Judas, who knows the place, and takes advantage of its darkness to capture the I AM. He comes with a "band" (combative thoughts) and "officers from the chief priests and Pharisees" (the ideas of priestly authority and religious guidance from the standpoint of the letter), "lanterns, torches, and weapons" (light of the intellect, torch of reason, and force of circumstances).

4. *Jesus said to them, I am he.* Jesus boldly stands forth and says, "Whom seek ye? They answered him, Jesus of Nazareth. Jesus saith unto them, I AM." (The word "he" [in "I AM he"] is not in the original Greek, and should be omitted, not only here, but in nearly every place in the scripture where Jesus uses I AM).

5. *Simon Peter ... struck the high priest's servant, and cut off his right ear.* Your faith (Peter) in the righteousness of your cause may lead you to combat the thoughts of the ruling religious powers, and in your impetuosity you resent their counsel ("Malchus," counselor), and deny their capacity to receive Truth ("cut off his right ear"), but good judgment and a broad comprehension of the divine overcoming, through which you are passing, causes you to adopt pacific means.

6. *The cup which the Father has given me, shall I not surely drink it?* The consciousness of eternal life. This must be attained through an utter crossing out or crucifixion of the personal self, both on its objective and subjective planes of volition; hence "they lead him away," that other processes of the divine law might be carried out.

## Jesus before the High Priest

18:12 So the detachment, the
commanding officer, and the officers
of the Jews, seized Jesus and bound
him,[1] 18:13 and led him to Annas
first,[2] for he was father-in-law to
Caiaphas, who was high priest[3] that
year. 18:14 Now it was Caiaphas who
advised the Jews that it was
expedient that one man should
perish for the people.

1. *So the detachment, the commanding officer, and the officers of the Jews, seized Jesus and bound him.* The detachment and the commanding officer, and the officers of the Jews are found in the intellectual realm, and it is before this tribunal that the Christ appears, to be tested and tried.

2. *and led him to Annas first.* Annas was a leading factor in the persecutions at the time of the ministry and crucifixion of Jesus. He represents intellectual opposition to spiritual Truth.

3. *he was father-in-law to Caiaphas, who was high priest.* His son-in-law Caiaphas, the high priest, represents a ruling religious thought force that is also entirely intellectual. He belongs to the religious world of forms and ceremonies, the "letter" of the word. The ruthlessness of these men shows how a merely formal religion will persecute and attempt to kill the inner Christ Spirit and all that pertains to it.

## Peter Denies Jesus

18:15 Simon Peter followed Jesus,
as did another disciple.[1] Now that
disciple was known to the high
priest, and entered in with Jesus into
the court of the high priest; 18:16 but
Peter was standing at the door
outside. So the other disciple, who
was known to the high priest, went
out and spoke to her who kept the
door, and brought in Peter.[2] 18:17
Then the maid who kept the door
said to Peter, "Are you also one of
this man's disciples?"

He said, "I am not."[3]

18:18 Now the servants and the
officers were standing there, having
made a fire of coals, for it was cold.
They were warming themselves.
Peter was with them, standing and
warming himself.

1. *Simon Peter followed Jesus, as did another disciple.* Jesus' disciples (the faculties of the I Am) were not strong enough to sustain him through this trial. They fled, all but two. One disciple, supposed to be John, was able to follow, enter in, and support the Master. Peter (Faith) followed afar off.

2. *the other disciple ... brought in Peter.* John (Love) is able to bring Peter (Faith) into closer touch with the Master. The spiritual warmth of love draws into closer proximity the faculty of faith, proving that

these powers are closely allied with each other.

3. *He said, I am not.* Peter is not to be condemned for denying Jesus. He had not yet unfolded to that spiritual degree where he was able to face seemingly strong adversity and stand firm.

## The High Priest Questions Jesus

18:19 The high priest therefore asked Jesus about his disciples, and about his teaching.[1] 18:20 Jesus answered him, "I spoke openly to the world. I always taught in synagogues, and in the temple, where the Jews always meet. I said nothing in secret. 18:21 Why do you ask me? Ask those who have heard me what I said to them. Behold, these know the things which I said."

18:22 When he had said this, one of the officers standing by slapped Jesus with his hand, saying, "Do you answer the high priest like that?"

18:23 Jesus answered him, "If I have spoken evil, testify of the evil; but if well, why do you beat me?"

18:24 Annas sent him bound to Caiaphas, the high priest.

1. *The high priest therefore asked Jesus of his disciples, and of his teaching.* The high priest who questioned Jesus symbolizes a form of religious thoughts in man that follows the set rule of the letter of the law with little or no thought of its inner spiritual importance. Jesus (here representing the Christ) sets forth the Truth in plain, concise language, which however has no significance for the person functioning on the natural-religious plane of existence.

## Peter Denies Jesus Again

18:25 Now Simon Peter was standing and warming himself. They said therefore to him, "You aren't also one of his disciples, are you?"

He denied it, and said, "I am not."

18:26 One of the servants of the high priest, being a relative of him whose ear Peter had cut off, said, "Didn't I see you in the garden with him?"

18:27 Peter therefore denied it again, and immediately the rooster crowed.

## Jesus before Pilate

18:28 They led Jesus therefore from Caiaphas into the Praetorium.[1] It was early, and they themselves didn't enter into the Praetorium, that they might not be defiled, but might eat the Passover. 18:29 Pilate therefore went out to them, and said, "What accusation do you bring against this man?"

18:30 They answered him, "If this man weren't an evildoer, we wouldn't have delivered him up to you."[2]

18:31 Pilate therefore said to them, "Take him yourselves, and judge him according to your law."

Therefore the Jews said to him, "It is not lawful for us to put anyone to death," 18:32 that the word of Jesus might be fulfilled, which he spoke, signifying by what kind of death he should die.

18:33 Pilate therefore entered again into the Praetorium, called Jesus, and said to him, "Are you the King of the Jews?"

18:34 Jesus answered him, "Do you say this by yourself, or did others tell you about me?"

18:35 Pilate answered, "I'm not a Jew, am I? Your own nation and the chief priests delivered you to me. What have you done?"

18:36 Jesus answered, "My Kingdom is not of this world. If my Kingdom were of this world, then my servants would fight, that I wouldn't be delivered to the Jews. But now my Kingdom is not from here."

18:37 Pilate therefore said to him, "Are you a king then?"[3]

Jesus answered, "You say that I am a king. For this reason I have been born, and for this reason I have come into the world, that I should testify to the truth. Everyone who is of the truth listens to my voice."

18:38 Pilate said to him, "What is truth?"

1. *They lead Jesus therefore from Caiaphas into the Praetorium.* The Praetorium symbolizes a state of despotism, where force and cruelty and tyranny exist. The Jews, symbolizing intellectual spirituality, would because of their religious traditions turn the Jesus over to barbarians to be crucified.

2. *If this man weren't an evildoer, we wouldn't have delivered him up to you.* The Jewish priesthood taught persecution as the unavoidable heritage of their race; even Jesus told His followers that they would suffer persecution when they taught His doctrine. Although it is true that the spiritual mind and the mortal are at war, metaphysicians see that the persecution of the Jews in every land is the result of the affirmation of the law of persecution by those with the power of the word.

3. *Are you a king then?* The Jews and the high priests and the officers who represent intellectual religious thought forces continued to work for Jesus' execution because they realized within their hearts that He was indeed a King, and they feared His spiritual power.

## Jesus Sentenced to Death

When he had said this, he went out again to the Jews, and said to them, "I find no basis for a charge against him. 18:39 But you have a custom, that I should release someone to you at the Passover. Therefore do you want me to release to you the King of the Jews?"

18:40 Then they all shouted again, saying, "Not this man, but Barabbas!"[1] Now Barabbas was a robber.

1. *Not this man, but Barabbas!* Barabbas represents the adverse consciousness (rebellion and hatred) to which man gives himself when he allows himself to oppose the Christ. Man gives free rein to this adverse consciousness when he would destroy the Christ or true spiritual I AM in himself, since it is through the Christ alone that an overcoming can be gained over the Adversary. This adverse state of thought (Barabbas) is of its father the Devil.

---

Fillmore Study Bible annotations compiled by Rev. Mark Hicks.

**World English Bible Footnotes:**

[55] v18:9. John 6:39

# John 19

## Jesus Sentenced to Death (continued)

19:1 So Pilate then took Jesus, and flogged him. 19:2 The soldiers twisted thorns into a crown, and put it on his head, and dressed him in a purple garment. 19:3 They kept saying, "Hail, King of the Jews!" and they kept slapping him.

19:4 Then Pilate went out again, and said to them, "Behold, I bring him out to you, that you may know that I find no basis for a charge against him."

19:5 Jesus therefore came out, wearing the crown of thorns and the purple garment. Pilate said to them, "Behold, the man!"

19:6 When therefore the chief priests and the officers saw him, they shouted, saying, "Crucify! Crucify!"

Pilate said to them, "Take him yourselves, and crucify him,[1] for I find no basis for a charge against him."

19:7 The Jews answered him, "We have a law, and by our law he ought to die, because he made himself the Son of God."

19:8 When therefore Pilate heard this saying, he was more afraid. 19:9 He entered into the Praetorium again, and said to Jesus, "Where are you from?"[2] But Jesus gave him no answer. 19:10 Pilate therefore said to him, "Aren't you speaking to me? Don't you know that I have power to release you, and have power to crucify you?"

19:11 Jesus answered, "You would have no power at all against me, unless it were given to you from above.[3] Therefore he who delivered me to you has greater sin."

19:12 At this, Pilate was seeking to release him, but the Jews cried out, saying, "If you release this man, you aren't Caesar's friend! Everyone who makes himself a king speaks against Caesar!"

19:13 When Pilate therefore heard these words, he brought Jesus out, and sat down on the judgment seat at a place called "The Pavement," but in Hebrew, "Gabbatha." 19:14 Now it was the Preparation Day of the Passover, at about the sixth hour.[56] He said to the Jews, "Behold, your King!"

19:15 They cried out, "Away with him! Away with him! Crucify him!"

Pilate said to them, "Shall I crucify your King?"

The chief priests answered, "We have no king but Caesar!"

19:16 So then he delivered him to them to be crucified.

1. *Take him yourselves, and crucify him.* The contest for supremacy between the

intellectual forces, represented by Pilate, and the pseudo-spiritual, represented by the Jews, is portrayed here. Both contenders realize that it is a momentous occasion, and they seek to shift the responsibility for the destruction of the coming King Jesus and His rule.

2. *Where are you from?* The personal will (Pilate) is nonplused and fearful, when its efforts to exercise domination over the I AM (Jesus) are unavailing. Lacking spiritual understanding, the personal will does not understand the nature of its challenge to its domination that is made by Truth

3. *You would have no power at all against me, unless it were given to you from above.* The authority of the personal will, while absolute in degree, does not extend to the world of Spirit, in which the I AM dwells. God is the source of all power, and the attempts of the personal will to vanquish the I AM at the behest of the religious thoughts (Jews) represent a misuse of divine power.

## The Crucifixion of Jesus

So they took Jesus and led him away. 19:17 He went out, bearing his cross, to the place called "The Place of a Skull,"① which is called in Hebrew, "Golgotha," 19:18 where they crucified him,② and with him two others, on either side one, and Jesus in the middle. 19:19 Pilate wrote a title also, and put it on the cross. There was written, "JESUS OF NAZARETH, THE KING OF THE JEWS." 19:20 Therefore many of the Jews read this title, for the place where Jesus was crucified was near the city; and it was written in Hebrew, in Latin, and in Greek.③ 19:21 The chief priests of the Jews therefore said to Pilate, "Don't write, 'The King of the Jews,' but, 'he said, I am King of the Jews.'"

19:22 Pilate answered, "What I have written, I have written."

19:23 Then the soldiers, when they had crucified Jesus, took his garments④ and made four parts, to every soldier a part; and also the coat. Now the coat was without seam, woven from the top throughout.⑤ 19:24 Then they said to one another, "Let's not tear it, but cast lots for it to decide whose it will be," that the Scripture might be fulfilled, which says,

> "They parted my garments among them.
> For my cloak they cast lots."[57]

Therefore the soldiers did these things. 19:25 But there were standing by the cross of Jesus his mother, and his mother's sister, Mary the wife of Clopas, and Mary Magdalene. 19:26 Therefore when Jesus saw his mother, and the disciple whom he loved standing there, he said to his mother, "Woman, behold your son!" 19:27 Then he said to the disciple, "Behold, your mother!" From that hour, the disciple took her to his own home.

19:28 After this, Jesus, seeing[58] that all things were now finished, that the Scripture might be fulfilled, said, "I am thirsty." 19:29 Now a vessel full of vinegar was set there; so they put a sponge full of the vinegar on hyssop, and held it at his mouth. 19:30 When Jesus therefore had received the vinegar, he said, "It is finished." He bowed his head, and gave up his spirit.⑥

1. *place of a skull.* The crucifixion took place at Golgotha, "The place of a skull" (the front brain, the seat of the will and conscious understanding, the throne of the mind, where all ideas are tested and either enthroned or cast out). In the crucifixion of Jesus both Pilate and the Jews (both the intellect and the ruling spiritual ideas) unite in casting out the claim that man is the Son of God.

2. *they crucified him.* The crucifixion

symbolizes the final and full erasure of personality from consciousness. When man is willing to surrender himself to the Christ Mind, he begins the crucifixion. Every time that he gives up a false belief in the name of Christ it is destroyed in his consciousness. When all the errors that constitute the carnal mind are destroyed, Satan is wholly cast out and Judas is redeemed.

3. *it was written in Hebrew, and in Latin, and in Greek*. The fact that the title, "JESUS OF NAZARETH, THE KING OF THE JEWS, was written in three languages signifies that the Jesus Christ Truth—life, perfection, immortality, expressed and demonstrated throughout man, even to his outer organism—must be recognized and acknowledged by man on all three planes of his consciousness. He must accept this Truth and the Christ must rule in his superconscious mind, his conscious mind, and his subconscious mind. The Hebrew language refers here to the spiritual, or superconscious phase of mind in man; Latin to the subconscious; and Greek to the conscious, reasoning mind.—MBD/Latin

4. *The soldiers ... took his garments*. The soldiers represent the thoughts that fight against the elemental forces: earth, air, fire, and water. The garments represent the thoughts that protect the body against those forces.

5. *the coat was without seam, woven from the top throughout*. Although Jesus (representing the spiritual man) was not allowed to establish His conscious rule in the front brain, He left a great unified doctrine of truth (represented by the seamless garment that the soldiers found they could not separate).

6. *he said, "It is finished." He bowed his head, and gave up his spirit*. The popular thought, based upon theology, that Jesus died upon the cross for our sins, is not reasonable, nor true. It is a libel upon the goodness of God that He would demand the death of his beloved son in such a horrible manner, to appease His anger toward the balance of the sinners in the human family. Again, how could the death of one man atone for the sins of billions of others? Is the death of a criminal in any way an atonement for his crime, or does it help other men to be better? As we emerge from barbaric methods, we abolish capital punishment in all its forms.

It is quite evident that theology has not understood the true character of Jesus' death. Instead of dying upon the cross like the two thieves that were crucified with him, he simply passed through the human consciousness of death and came out fully alive on the other side. Jesus became alive again, was glorified, and, as is plainly taught in the Scriptures, transcended to quickening life and substance for all who will eat it and drink it. This is a great mystery to the sense man, but he who sees beyond the veil knows positively that the body of Jesus is right here in our midst radiant with eternal life.

Then Jesus did not die upon the cross to save men from their sins, but he lived. This is an important distinction, and clears up points that have always been stumbling blocks to those who wanted a reasonable theology. What we all need is a way to overcome death. We do not want anyone to die for us. There is, and always has been, enough of that sort of atonement. Thousands of men and women have heroically died for their friends and country. But who among them all has been so heroic and powerful as to master that great and "last enemy to be overcome," death itself? None save Jesus.

Then we should quit wailing over the agony of the cross; quit looking for the Master, like Mary in the tomb, quit talking about the death and departure of Jesus, and realize the Truth, that Jesus went through the appearance called death to demonstrate for us its powerlessness in the presence of one who had made the atonement with the Father.

We are to take up our cross, square our likes by the rectitude of Truth, both in Spirit and in the material world, and then we shall follow Jesus in the crucifixion of the world, the flesh and the devil, and overcome as he overcame. This supreme attainment is not only possible to all men, but must be accomplished by all who expect to perpetuate their conscious existence.—Unity May 28, 1905

## Jesus' Side is Pierced

19:31 Therefore the Jews, because
it was the Preparation Day, so that
the bodies wouldn't remain on the
cross on the Sabbath (for that
Sabbath was a special one), asked
of Pilate that their legs might be
broken,[1] and that they might be
taken away. 19:32 Therefore the

soldiers came, and broke the legs of
the first, and of the other who was
crucified with him; 19:33 but when
they came to Jesus, and saw that he
was already dead, they didn't break
his legs. 19:34 However one of the
soldiers pierced his side with a spear,
and immediately blood and water
came out. 19:35 He who has seen has
testified, and his testimony is true.
He knows that he tells the truth, that
you may believe. 19:36 For these things
happened, that the Scripture might
be fulfilled, "A bone of him will not
be broken."[59] 19:37 Again another
Scripture says, "They will look on him
whom they pierced."❷[60]

1. *asked of Pilate that their legs might be broken.* Crushing the bones destroyed the last vestige of life in the body.

2. *They will look on him whom they pierced.* This whole Scripture reveals how those established in the intellect will seek to kill out the Christ, and also how they are ultimately defeated in His victory over death.

## The Burial of Jesus

19:38 After these things, Joseph of
Arimathaea, being a disciple of
Jesus, but secretly for fear of the
Jews, asked of Pilate that he might
take away Jesus' body. Pilate gave
him permission. He came therefore
and took away his body. 19:39
Nicodemus, who at first came to
Jesus by night, also came bringing a
mixture of myrrh and aloes, about a
hundred pounds.[61] 19:40 So they took
Jesus' body, and bound it in linen
cloths with the spices, as the custom
of the Jews is to bury. 19:41 Now in the
place where he was crucified there
was a garden. In the garden was a
new tomb in which no man had ever
yet been laid. 19:42 Then because of
the Jews' Preparation Day (for the
tomb was near at hand) they laid
Jesus there.❶

1. *they laid Jesus there.* Arimathea represents an aggregation of thoughts of lofty character, a high state of consciousness in man. Joseph represents a state of consciousness in which we increase in character along all lines. We not only grow into a broader understanding but we also increase in vitality and substance. Jesus' resting in Joseph's tomb symbolizes the truth that Jesus was resting in the consciousness of vitality and substance, was growing into a broader understanding, and was in truth gathering strength for the great demonstration over death to follow.

---

Fillmore Study Bible annotations compiled by Rev. Mark Hicks.

**World English Bible Footnotes:**

[56] v19:14. noon

[57] v19:24. Psalm 22:18

[58] v19:28. NU, TR read "knowing" instead of "seeing"

[59] v19:36. Exodus 12:46; Numbers 9:12; Psalm 34:20

[60] v19:37. Zechariah 12:10

[61] v19:39. 100 Roman pounds of 12 ounces each, or about 72 pounds, or 33 Kilograms.

# John 20

## The Resurrection of Jesus

[20:1] Now on the first day of the week, Mary Magdalene went early, while it was still dark, to the tomb, and saw the stone taken away from the tomb. [20:2] Therefore she ran and came to Simon Peter, and to the other disciple whom Jesus loved, and said to them, "They have taken away the Lord out of the tomb, and we don't know where they have laid him!"

[20:3] Therefore Peter and the other disciple went out, and they went toward the tomb. [20:4] They both ran together. The other disciple outran Peter,[1] and came to the tomb first. [20:5] Stooping and looking in, he saw the linen cloths lying, yet he didn't enter in. [20:6] Then Simon Peter came, following him, and entered into the tomb. He saw the linen cloths lying, [20:7] and the cloth that had been on his head, not lying with the linen cloths, but rolled up in a place by itself. [20:8] So then the other disciple who came first to the tomb also entered in, and he saw and believed. [20:9] For as yet they didn't know the Scripture, that he must rise from the dead. [20:10] So the disciples went away again to their own homes.

1. *the other disciple outran Peter*. The passage was written by John, who is presumably "the other disciple." John represents love, which through its affections is more closely attached to the physical than is faith (Peter); consequently love (John) precedes faith (Peter) in the desire to find the physical (body of Jesus).

## Jesus Appears to Mary Magdalene

[20:11] But Mary was standing outside at the tomb weeping. So, as she wept, she stooped and looked into the tomb, [20:12] and she saw two angels in white sitting, one at the head, and one at the feet,[1] where the body of Jesus had lain. [20:13] They told her, "Woman, why are you weeping?"

She said to them, "Because they have taken away my Lord, and I don't know where they have laid him." [20:14] When she had said this, she turned around and saw Jesus[2] standing, and didn't know that it was Jesus.

[20:15] Jesus said to her, "Woman, why are you weeping? Who are you looking for?"

She, supposing him to be the gardener, said to him, "Sir, if you have carried him away, tell me where you have laid him, and I will take him away."

[20:16] Jesus said to her, "Mary."

She turned and said to him, "Rhabbouni!" which is to say, "Teacher!"

[20:17] Jesus said to her, "Don't touch me,[3] for I haven't yet ascended to my Father; but go to my brothers, and tell them, 'I am ascending to my Father and your Father, to my God and your God.'"

[20:18] Mary Magdalene came and told the disciples that she had seen

the Lord,[4] and that he had said
these things to her.

1. *two angels in white sitting, one at the head, and one at the feet.* The two angels at Jesus' tomb symbolize our spiritual perceptions, which are always consciously in the presence of God, the perceptions which from that high spiritual state are able to make known to us that which is vital. The angel at the head "where the body of Jesus had lain" represents high spiritual perception, and the angel at the foot represents understanding in relation to the world without.

2. *she turned around and saw Jesus.* Instead of looking without, we look within and find that there is no reality in the thought of absence; that in the inner recesses of the soul all things are omnipresent, but we know not "that it was Jesus."

3. *Jesus said to her, "Don't touch me."* Jesus did not want the sorrowing Mary (thought) to touch him, because it would pull him down into the darkness and ignorance of mortality. The spiritual mind does not grieve over anything, nor look to matter and the limitations of the flesh for life eternal. The most effective consolation we can get and give to others under grief, is to deny the human belief in death and separation. This dissipates the flood of sorrow-thoughts that submerge the souls of those who mourn.

4. *Mary Magdalene came and told the disciples that she had seen the Lord.* Mary Magdalene, the soul-feminine, is the connecting link between the I AM and the body. Love, cleansed of all impurity, is able to perceive spiritually, and therefore beholds the risen Lord. It then spreads the glad tidings among the disciples (the twelve powers of man) that the Lord Jesus is not dead, but has entered into a higher spiritual state.

## Jesus Appears to the Disciples

20:19 When therefore it was
evening, on that day, the first day of
the week, and when the doors were
locked where the disciples were
assembled, for fear of the Jews,
Jesus came and stood in the midst,
and said to them, "Peace be to you."

20:20 When he had said this, he
showed them his hands and his
side.[1] The disciples therefore were
glad when they saw the Lord. 20:21
Jesus therefore said to them again,
"Peace be to you. As the Father has
sent me, even so I send you." 20:22
When he had said this, he breathed
on them, and said to them, "Receive
the Holy Spirit! 20:23 Whoever's sins
you forgive, they are forgiven them.
Whoever's sins you retain, they have
been retained."

1. *he showed them his hands and his side.* After the dissolution of the carnal consciousness, represented by the crucifixion, the body takes up its activities in the psychical or astral realm, where it functions until it is sufficiently purified to enter into the kingdom of the heavens, or the fourth dimension. Metaphysicians who are in the regeneration and are putting out of mind the errors of carnality find that their bodies gradually become more refined, more ethereal in texture and in feeling, and under certain conditions they realize the unreality, of material environment. This is not the true spiritual estate, but is one degree toward it. When we fully enter the spiritual estate our bodies will be raised so high in radiation as to become invisible to physical sight. Such is the body of Jesus.

## Jesus and Thomas

20:24 But Thomas, one of the
twelve, called Didymus,[1] wasn't with
them when Jesus came.[2] 20:25 The
other disciples therefore said to him,
"We have seen the Lord!"

But he said to them, "Unless I see
in his hands the print of the nails,

and put my hand into his side, I will not believe."

[20:26] After eight days again his disciples were inside, and Thomas was with them. Jesus came, the doors being locked, and stood in the midst, and said, "Peace be to you." [20:27] Then he said to Thomas, "Reach here your finger, and see my hands. Reach here your hand, and put it into my side. Don't be unbelieving, but believing."(3)

[20:28] Thomas answered him, "My Lord and my God!"(4)

[20:29] Jesus said to him, "Because you have seen me,[62] you have believed. Blessed are those who have not seen, and have believed."(5)

1. *But Thomas, one of the twelve, called Didymus.* Thomas represents one of the twelve faculties through which man, the I AM, functions. He symbolizes the intellect. Intellect or reason connects the inner world of thought with the outer world of action. Didymus signifies the same as Thomas: "twain," "double," "twin." On the constructive side the intellect functions as understanding; on the negative side as doubt and futile questioning.

2. *was not with them when Jesus came.* Intellectual perception is slower than the other faculties to perceive the truth of the resurrection life. It is much slower than faith or love. "Thomas ... was not with them when Jesus came." The intellect is the last of man's faculties to comprehend the supremacy of spiritual law over natural law. It must be convinced on its own plane of thought that the body has been raised after it was put to death.

3. *Don't be unbelieving, but believing.* The great truth which spiritual understanding reveals to us is that the resurrection of the body from death is not to be confined to Jesus Christ alone, but that all men may unfold this same ability by following the teachings of Jesus Christ. The resurrection of Jesus also takes place in consciousness. Every time that man raises his realization of the perpetual indwelling life flow to the spiritual standard, he is connected with the indwelling Christ. Through the power of the living Word he enters into the realization of a new and higher life activity than that of the physical.

4. *My Lord and my God!* When the intellect is quickened to the degree that it can comprehend the spiritual, it may be convinced of the authenticity of a spiritual demonstration.

5. *Blessed are those who have not seen, and have believed.* When man becomes conscious of the fact that he does not have to depend upon intellectual reasoning to know and to understand the things of Spirit, he is doubly blessed. He has the power to draw on spiritual inspiration from within, which enables him to bring quickly into the manifest realm his desired demonstrations.

## The Purpose of this Book

[20:30] Therefore Jesus did many other signs in the presence of his disciples, which are not written in this book; [20:31] but these are written, that you may believe that Jesus is the Christ,(1) the Son of God, and that believing you may have life in his name.(2)

1. *but these are written, that you may believe that Jesus is the Christ* The question often is asked whether or not we believe that Jesus rose from the dead with the same flesh body in which He walked the earth and, if so, what became of that body. The school of "high criticism" is openly attacking Bible occurrences that it cannot account for under natural law. The historical account makes clear that the flesh body that had been crucified was the body that Jesus had after His resurrection. That Jesus knew how to restore life to dead organs is evidenced by His healing of paralytics, blind people, and in three cases by raising those who had died. He had spent whole nights in prayer, and through the intensity of His devotions had made union with Divine Mind. This union was so full and so complete that His whole being was flooded with spiritual life, power, and substance and the wisdom to use them in

divine order. In this manner He projected the divine-body idea, and through it His mortal body was transformed into an immortal body where it exists to this day as a body of ethereal substance directed and controlled by His thought and mind force.

2. *and that believing you may have life in his name.* Having a body of spiritually electrified atoms, Jesus is able to quicken the bodies of people who attract His presence by believing in Him; He radiates a glorious life that energizes those who believe in His power. By positive affirmations we must all appropriate this same Christ life, substance, and Truth as ours individually and as the very foundation and substance of our body.

Fillmore Study Bible annotations compiled by Rev. Mark Hicks.

**World English Bible Footnotes:**

[62] v20:29. TR adds " Thomas,"

# John 21

## Jesus Appears to Seven Disciples

21:1 After these things, Jesus revealed himself again to the disciples at the sea of Tiberias. He revealed himself this way. 21:2 Simon Peter, Thomas called Didymus, Nathanael of Cana in Galilee, and the sons of Zebedee, and two others of his disciples were together. 21:3 Simon Peter said to them, "I'm going fishing."

They told him, "We are also coming with you." They immediately went out, and entered into the boat. That night, they caught nothing. 21:4 But when day had already come, Jesus stood on the beach, yet the disciples didn't know that it was Jesus. 21:5 Jesus therefore said to them, "Children, have you anything to eat?"

They answered him, "No."

21:6 He said to them, "Cast the net on the right side of the boat, and you will find some."[1] They cast it therefore, and now they weren't able to draw it in for the multitude of fish. 21:7 That disciple therefore whom Jesus loved said to Peter, "It's the Lord!"

So when Simon Peter heard that it was the Lord, he wrapped his coat around him (for he was naked), and threw himself into the sea. 21:8 But the other disciples came in the little boat (for they were not far from the land, but about two hundred cubits[63] away), dragging the net full of fish. 21:9 So when they got out on the land, they saw a fire of coals there, and fish laid on it, and bread.[2] 21:10 Jesus said to them, "Bring some of the fish which you have just caught."

21:11 Simon Peter went up, and drew the net to land, full of great fish, one hundred fifty-three; and even though there were so many, the net wasn't torn.

[21:12] Jesus said to them, "Come and eat breakfast."[3]

None of the disciples dared inquire of him, "Who are you?" knowing that it was the Lord.

[21:13] Then Jesus came and took the bread, gave it to them, and the fish likewise. [21:14] This is now the third time that Jesus was revealed to his disciples,[4] after he had risen from the dead.

1. *Cast the net on the right side of the boat, and you will find some.* Man's mind is the net that catches thoughts, which are the basis of external conditions. The sea is the mental realm in which man exists. The net of man's thought works hard and long in the darkness of human understanding and gains but little, but once the Christ Mind is perceived and obeyed the net is cast on the "right side," and success follows. The "right side" is the side on which man realizes the truth that inexhaustible resources are always present and can be made manifest by those who exercise their faith in that direction.

2. *fish laid on it, and bread.* The bread and fish that Jesus provided on the shore represents the supply of Spirit for the needs of the body. Not only does the Father provide for man in the natural world, as by the draught of fishes, but in the invisible world of substance are elements that correspond to the material things. Bread symbolizes the substance of the omnipresent Christ body and fish the capacity of increase that goes with it. Whoever seeks supply through Spirit and submits his cause to the law of justice and righteousness always succeeds. The reason why men fail to demonstrate the many promises of divine support is that they cling to some selfish or unjust thought.

3. *Jesus said to them, Come and eat breakfast.* Eating is a symbol of the appropriation of spiritual substance and life. One fasts from thinking, when one allows the thoughts to drift aimlessly in the race stream of consciousness, merely registering impressions from the outer world with no attempt to understand what underlies them or get at the truth of any subject. One breaks one's fast by mentally assimilating each idea that presents itself, considering the substance of Truth on which it rests, and understanding it.

4. *This is now the third time that Jesus was revealed (manifested, ASV) to the disciples.* The third appearance of Jesus to the disciples corresponds to the third phase of man's being. Man is threefold: Spirit, soul, and body. On His first manifestation to the disciples Jesus "breathed on them, and saith unto them, Receive ye the Holy Spirit." On the second He convinced Thomas of the truth of the Resurrection. On the third He satisfied the physical hunger of the disciples.

## Jesus and Peter

[21:15] So when they had eaten their breakfast, Jesus said to Simon Peter, "Simon, son of Jonah, do you love me more[1] than these?"

He said to him, "Yes, Lord; you know that I have affection for you."

He said to him, "Feed my lambs."
[21:16] He said to him again a second time, "Simon, son of Jonah, do you love me?"

He said to him, "Yes, Lord; you know that I have affection for you."

He said to him, "Tend my sheep."

[21:17] He said to him the third time, "Simon, son of Jonah, do you have affection for me?"

Peter was grieved because he asked him the third time, "Do you have affection for me?" He said to him, "Lord, you know everything. You know that I have affection for you."

Jesus said to him, "Feed my sheep.[2] [21:18] Most certainly I tell you, when you were young, you dressed yourself, and walked where you wanted to. But when you are old, you will stretch out your hands, and another will dress you, and carry you where you don't want to go."[3]

21:19 Now he said this, signifying by what kind of death he would glorify God. When he had said this, he said to him, "Follow me."

1. *love me more?* Faith must be established in love and must work by love; and every faculty of man must be established in love and work by love if perfect harmony and good are to be realized. Faith established in love and working by love will remain steadfast at all times, under all circumstances; it will be our sustaining power during our every hour of need.

2. *Feed my sheep.* After first providing them food, Jesus three times commanded Peter, "Feed my lambs" and "Feed my sheep." Sheep represent thoughts, and we see in this admonition the importance of thinking the thoughts of the Christ and of doing the works that these thoughts enjoin. We are to follow the Christ in thought, word, and deed.

3. *when you are old, you will stretch out your hands, and another will dress you, and carry you where you don't want to go.* In the first spiritual illumination there is much enthusiasm, and while we are in this state of consciousness, great works are often accomplished. Later, when the true spiritual understanding begins to unfold, when we are older in Truth, we learn to rely more and more on the Principle, until we can say with Jesus, "The Father abiding in me doeth his works."

## Jesus and the Beloved Disciple

21:20 Then Peter, turning around, saw a disciple following. This was the disciple whom Jesus sincerely loved, the one who had also leaned on Jesus' breast at the supper and asked, "Lord, who is going to betray You?" 21:21 Peter seeing him, said to Jesus, "Lord, what about this man?"

21:22 Jesus said to him, "If I desire that he stay until I come, what is that to you? You follow me."[1] 21:23 This saying therefore went out among the brothers[64], that this disciple wouldn't die. Yet Jesus didn't say to him that he wouldn't die, but, "If I desire that he stay until I come, what is that to you?" 21:24 This is the disciple who testifies about these things, and wrote these things. We know that his witness is true. 21:25 There are also many other things which Jesus did,[2] which if they would all be written, I suppose that even the world itself wouldn't have room for the books that would be written.

1. *what is that to you? You follow me.* most of us have been indoctrinated to take that statement to support the idea that it is none of your business what the other guy does. But it could also mean, how important is this to you? How concerned are you?—Ed Rabel

2. *And there are also many other things which Jesus did.* In the Gospels that we have, there are more things we are not told than what we are told. But the important thing is what we are told, to take that, not to worry about the things Jesus said and did which have not been written down but give the entire attention and understanding to what has been written down.—Ed Rabel

---

Fillmore Study Bible annotations compiled by Rev. Mark Hicks.

**World English Bible Footnotes:**

[63] v21:8. 200 cubits is about 100 yards or about 91 meters

[64] v21:23. The word for "brothers" here may be also correctly translated "brothers and sisters" or "siblings."

# The Acts of the Apostles

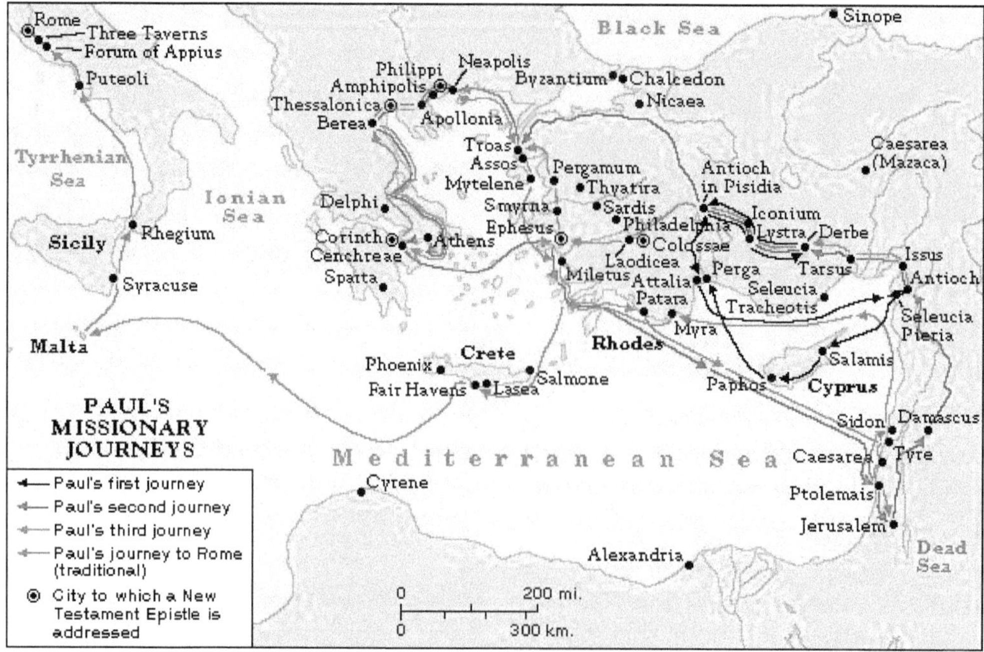


Turkish Language Class, https://www.turkishclass.com/picture_1928. Used by permission.

## Introduction to Acts

(1) Author: Luke, the "beloved physician," is generally recognized as the author of Acts. Both the Gospel of Luke and Acts contain similar dedications (shown in the opening verses), and both mention "Theophilus"—who was probably a patron of Luke. The opening verse of Acts also makes mention of "the first book" (or "former treatise")—and this evi- dently refers to the Gospel of Luke. Many similarities, both of style and technical phrases used, will also be noted. The date of writing is usually placed at around A.D. 85. The metaphysical meaning of the name Luke is: "luminous; light-giving; enlightening; instructing" (Metaphysical Bible Dictionary/Luke)—and it is easy to recognize the significance of this interpretation when reading the Gospel of Luke, or the book of Acts.

(2) Purpose: At first reading, the book of Acts appears to consist of two main sections: the first section dealing with the activities of Peter, and the second section describing the activities of Paul. The New Testament also contains evidence of factional divisions in the early church—some Christians

recognizing the leadership of Peter, with others looking to Paul for guidance. Because of this, some early New Testament commentators suggested the possibility of there being originally two books of "Acts," which were later combined. However, in all of Luke's writings there is a marked tendency to minimize all controversial matters; hence, it seems much more likely that Luke's purpose in writing this book was to draw the factions together, and to show that the two apostles, although outwardly differing, were one in their great purpose and in their loyalty to Jesus Christ.

(3) Special feature: When writing his Gospel, Luke had to depend upon other persons, or written documents, for the needed information. But in writing Acts, Luke was able to report several important happenings at first hand, for he was actually present and took part in some of the activities mentioned. The reader is able to recognize many of these first- hand reports through Luke's use of the pronoun we—indicating that the writer was present on those occasions. Further reference will be made to this in later lessons.

(4) A problem: The reader will notice that the book of Acts ends rather abruptly, mentioning Paul's imprisonment at Rome, but giving no further details. Other parts of the New Testament indicate that there were important happenings during and after Paul's imprisonment; but no mention is made of these in Acts. The question therefore arises as to whether Luke planned to write a third volume—and if this volume was completed, what became of it? Possibly it was Luke's intention to write about later happenings, but there seems no indication that such a book was ever written. The probability is that Luke died, or was imprisoned and executed, before this project could be put into operation. However, in a later lesson we shall be able to trace something of what this projected volume might have contained.

*Introduction to Acts of the Apostles* by Herbert J. Hunt, former Dean of Bible Studies for the Unity School of Christianity.

# Acts 1

## The Promise of the Holy Spirit

1:1 The first book I wrote, Theophilus,[1] concerned all that Jesus began both to do and to teach,[2] 1:2 until the day in which he was received up, after he had given commandment through the Holy Spirit to the apostles whom he had chosen. 1:3 To these he also showed himself alive after he suffered, by many proofs, appearing to them over a period of forty days, and speaking about God's Kingdom.[3] 1:4 Being assembled together with them, he commanded them, "Don't depart from Jerusalem,[4] but wait for the promise of the Father, which you heard from me. 1:5 For John indeed baptized in water, but you will be baptized in the Holy Spirit[5] not many days from now."

1. *Theophilus.* Theophilus means "lover of God," and the metaphysical meaning is

"divine love" or "spiritual unity."

2. *to do and to teach.* Jesus finished the training of His disciples in the fundamental principles of expressing the Christ, but His work of expressing those principles was only begun. We are to carry on this work to completion.

3. *about God's Kingdom.* Jesus began to make manifest the kingdom of God or realm of spiritual truth *here and now*. This kingdom is a kingdom of spiritual consciousness.

4. *Don't depart from Jerusalem.* Jerusalem represents peace, without which the Holy Spirit finds no lodgment in our mind or heart. We must first be established in the consciousness of peace.

5. *baptized in the Holy Spirit.* Holy Spirit baptism is an absolute prerequisite for expression of the Christ. John's baptism is a symbol of self-denial or a washing away of wrong habits of thinking and living. The Holy Spirit baptism is a symbol of the burning up of all such dross in the fire of a living zeal for Truth, and an opening of the mind to the light of new and living ideas. The second baptism pours a flood of life-giving thoughts into the mind, so that the entire life undergoes a transformation and a reconstruction.

## The Last Words of Jesus

1:6 Therefore, when they had
come together, they asked him,
"Lord, are you now restoring the
kingdom to Israel?"[1]

1:7 He said to them, "It isn't for
you to know times or seasons which
the Father has set within his own
authority. 1:8 But you will receive
power[2] when the Holy Spirit has
come upon you. You will be
witnesses to me in Jerusalem, in all
Judea and Samaria, and to the
uttermost parts of the earth."[3]

1. *are you now restoring the kingdom to Israel?* Jesus had already restored the kingdom to Israel, the kingdom of spiritual consciousness, of which men have allowed themselves to become unaware. His work was complete. Jesus adapted the teaching to the needs of the age to which He gave it. After the Resurrection He gave the apostles further instructions, and each successive age has interpreted His teaching to fit its peculiar needs. While true in an absolute sense, the teaching of Jesus Christ is also adaptable to changing worldly conditions.

2. *you will receive power.* Metaphysical Christians proclaim the faith *of* Jesus rather than the faith *about* Jesus. If Christianity were about the worship of the person of Jesus there would be no need for empowerment of his disciples.

3. *to the uttermost parts of the earth.* The empowerment of disciples leads to world harmony which is achieved first by claiming it as already here, realizing that it is one of the eternal realities, and next by working faithfully to bring it into manifestation.

## The Ascension of Jesus

1:9 When he had said these things,
as they were looking, he was taken
up,[1] and a cloud received him out
of their sight.[2] 1:10 While they were
looking steadfastly into the sky as
he went, behold, two men stood by
them in white clothing, 1:11 who also
said, "You men of Galilee, why do
you stand looking into the sky? This
Jesus, who was received up from you
into the sky will come back in the
same way as you saw him going into
the sky."[3]

1. *he was taken up (ascended).* See Luke 24:51. We who have entered into the Jesus Christ discipline are daily mentally going through the crucifixion, death, burial, resurrection and ascension of the "Person in Christ." This new person is born of a Divine

Idea through the overshadowing of the Holy Spirit, and this Idea is that we are each a spiritual being. Therefore the Ascension is the final step in attaining complete union with Divine Mind. Through the realization of His oneness with Divine Mind Jesus completely spiritualized His Physical body.

2. *and a cloud received him out of their sight*. The Lord does not enter directly into our material activities. Spirit imparts to our consciousness the Word, "When he had said these things." "As they were looking" represents that there was an intelligent perception of Truth, followed by a withdrawal, "he was taken up"; then a seeming obscurity and a darkening of the consciousness, "and a cloud received him out of their sight." This all describes in symbols the impartation by the Lord of His power and His Word, which we take and use in the manifest world.

3. *will come back in the same way as you saw him going into the sky*. After a great spiritual illumination we find our minds and hearts reaching out for heavenly things until we almost forget our practical life. We continue to look steadfastly into heaven "until the two men in white apparel" (consciousness of Spirit within and without) call our attention to the fact that this New Man in Christ has not left us but will return in the same manner that he went, that is, in consciousness.

## Harmony among the Disciples

1:12 Then they returned to Jerusalem from the mountain called Olivet,❶ which is near Jerusalem, a Sabbath day's journey away. 1:13 When they had come in, they went up into the upper room,❷ where they were staying; that is Peter, John, James, Andrew, Philip, Thomas, Bartholomew, Matthew, James the son of Alphaeus, Simon the Zealot, and Judas the son of James. 1:14 All these with one accord❸ continued steadfastly in prayer and supplication, along with the women, and Mary the mother of Jesus, and with his brothers.

1:15 In these days, Peter stood up in the midst of the disciples (and the number of names was about one hundred twenty), and said, 1:16 "Brothers, it was necessary that this Scripture should be fulfilled, which the Holy Spirit spoke before by the mouth of David concerning Judas, who was guide to those who took Jesus. 1:17 For he was numbered with us, and received his portion in this ministry. 1:18 Now this man obtained a field with the reward for his wickedness, and falling headlong, his body burst open, and all his intestines gushed out. 1:19 It became known to everyone who lived in Jerusalem that in their language that field was called 'Akeldama,' that is, 'The field of blood.' 1:20 For it is written in the book of Psalms,

'Let his habitation be made
desolate.
Let no one dwell therein;'[1]

and,

'Let another take his office.'[2]

1:21 "Of the men therefore who have accompanied us all the time that the Lord Jesus went in and out among us, 1:22 beginning from the baptism of John, to the day that he was received up from us, of these one must become a witness with us of his resurrection."

1:23 They put forward two, Joseph called Barsabbas, who was surnamed Justus, and Matthias. 1:24 They prayed, and said, "You, Lord, who know the hearts of all men, show which one of these two you have chosen 1:25 to take part in this ministry and apostleship from which Judas fell away, that he might go to his own place." 1:26 They drew lots for them, and the lot fell on Matthias, and he was numbered with the eleven apostles.

1. *Olivet*. Mount of Olives; height yielding illuminating oil; high luminous principle; shining mount; exalted enlightenment. A mountain, or ridge of hills, near Jerusalem, to the east of the city. Jesus often went to the Mount of Olives. A mountain always signifies an exalted state of mind, a high place in consciousness, while olives and olive trees signify the Spirit of love (the Mount of Olives was so named because of the many olive trees that grew on it), and illumination bespeaks light, understanding. Olive oil is symbolical of the Holy Spirit; also of peace and love. (MBD/Olivet).

2. *up into the upper room*. That high state of mind we assume in thinking about spiritual things. It may be attained through prayer, or going into the silence with true words, or in spiritual meditation.

3. *All these with one accord*. Where do we do our first missionary work? We begin in ourself, and as we patiently and persistently carry the message of Truth into every department of our being, including our mind, body, and affairs, we experience conversion in the fullest sense.

---

Fillmore Study Bible annotations by Mark Hicks

**World English Bible Footnotes:**

[1] v1:20. Psalm 69:25

[2] v1:20. Psalm 109:8

# Acts 2

## The Coming of the Holy Spirit

2:1 Now when the day of Pentecost[1] had come, they were all with one accord in one place.[2] 2:2 Suddenly there came from the sky a sound like the rushing of a mighty wind, and it filled all the house[3] where they were sitting. 2:3 Tongues like fire appeared and were distributed to them, and one sat on each of them.[4] 2:4 They were all filled with the Holy Spirit,[5] and began to speak with other languages, as the Spirit gave them the ability to speak.

2:5 Now there were dwelling in Jerusalem Jews, devout men,[6] from every nation under the sky. 2:6 When this sound was heard, the multitude came together, and were bewildered, because everyone heard them speaking in his own language. 2:7 They were all amazed and marveled, saying to one another, "Behold, aren't all these who speak Galileans? 2:8 How do we hear, everyone in our own native language? 2:9 Parthians, Medes, Elamites, and people from Mesopotamia, Judea, Cappadocia, Pontus, Asia, 2:10 Phrygia, Pamphylia, Egypt, the parts of Libya around Cyrene, visitors from Rome, both Jews and proselytes, 2:11 Cretans and Arabians: we hear them speaking in our languages the mighty works of God!" 2:12 They were all amazed, and were perplexed, saying one to another, "What does this mean?" 2:13 Others, mocking, said, "They are filled with new wine."

1. *Pentecost.* Metaphysically, an unfoldment of the spiritual mind when the ideas that we have meditated upon and accepted as true, spring forth into consciousness, becoming living realities in our lives, instead of mere mental concepts. In this awakening we get the fruits of the ideas that we have planted in our minds; we have escaped from the darkness (Egypt), and have entered into light (Promised Land).

2. *they were all with one accord in one place.* A conjunction between the thinking mind, or what we term normal consciousness, and the superconscious or spiritual mind. When this connection is made there is a descent into the body of spiritual energies that produce a great and unusual commotion.

3. *a sound like the rushing of a mighty wind, and it filled all the house.* An inrush of spiritiual energy from the Spirit, which will fill the whole body.

4. *Tongues like fire ... sat on each of them.* When we are assembled in a high state of spiritual illumination, we mentally touch omnipresent Intelligence to the degree that whatever is spoken is instantly transmitted to each faculty.

5. *filled with the Holy Spirit.* To be quickened by the Holy Spirit is to "have a conscience void of offense toward God and men always." This is not a negative state, for it is one that is reached through unflagging zeal.

6. *devout men.* There dwell within us many "devout men," or subjective thoughts, of which we are totally unconscious until this Holy Spirit descends into our minds and we see good in the depths of our being that we never saw before. Then our Word of instruction and enlightenment goes into these darkened comers of our realm, and we preach the gospel of Jesus Christ to all the people or thoughts that are there congregated, and they "all hear in our own tongues the mighty works of God."

## The First Recorded Christian Sermon

2:14 But Peter, standing up(1) with
the eleven, lifted up his voice, and
spoke out to them, "You men of
Judea, and all you who dwell at
Jerusalem, let this be known to you,
and listen to my words. 2:15 For these
aren't drunken, as you suppose,
seeing it is only the third hour of the
day[3]. 2:16 But this is what has been
spoken through the prophet Joel:

2:17 'It will be in the last days, says God,
that I will pour out my Spirit on all flesh.
Your sons and your daughters will prophesy.
Your young men will see visions.
Your old men will dream dreams.
2:18 Yes, and on my servants and on my handmaidens in those days,
I will pour out my Spirit, and they will prophesy.
2:19 I will show wonders in the sky above,
and signs on the earth beneath;
blood, and fire, and billows of smoke.
2:20 The sun will be turned into darkness,
and the moon into blood,
before the great and glorious day of the Lord comes.
2:21 It will be, that whoever will call on the name of the Lord will be saved.'[4]

2:22 "Men of Israel, hear these
words! Jesus of Nazareth, a man(2)
approved by God to you by mighty
works and wonders and signs which
God did by him in the midst of you,
even as you yourselves know, 2:23 him,
being delivered up by the
determined counsel and
foreknowledge of God, you have

taken by the hand of lawless men, crucified and killed; 2:24 whom God raised up,[3] having freed him from the agony of death, because it was not possible that he should be held by it. 2:25 For David says concerning him,

'I saw the Lord always before my face,
For he is on my right hand, that I should not be moved.
2:26 Therefore my heart was glad, and my tongue rejoiced.
Moreover my flesh also will dwell in hope;
2:27 because you will not leave my soul in Hades[5],
neither will you allow your Holy One to see decay.
2:28 You made known to me the ways of life.
You will make me full of gladness with your presence.'[6]

2:29 "Brothers, I may tell you freely of the patriarch David, that he both died and was buried, and his tomb is with us to this day. 2:30 Therefore, being a prophet, and knowing that God had sworn with an oath to him that of the fruit of his body, according to the flesh, he would raise up the Christ to sit on his throne, 2:31 he foreseeing this spoke about the resurrection of the Christ, that neither was his soul left in Hades[7], nor did his flesh see decay. 2:32 This Jesus God raised up, to which we all are witnesses. 2:33 Being therefore exalted by the right hand of God, and having received from the Father the promise of the Holy Spirit, he has poured out this,[4] which you now see and hear. 2:34 For David didn't ascend into the heavens, but he says himself,

'The Lord said to my Lord, "Sit by my right hand,
2:35 until I make your enemies a footstool for your feet."'[8]

2:36 "Let all the house of Israel therefore know certainly that God has made him both Lord and Christ, this Jesus whom you crucified."

1. *Peter, standing up.* Peter no longer denies the Master, but in a strong, forceful, straightforward manner makes clear to "whosoever will" the Jesus Christ way of redemption. Peter, typifying faith and spiritual understanding, is the sure foundation (the rock) upon which the Christ Church is based.

2. *Jesus of Nazareth, a man.* Jesus represents God's idea of man in expression. Christ is that idea in the absolute. "Jesus of Nazareth, a man" became the Lord Christ as attested by the Resurrection.

3. *whom God raised up.* Jesus kept the law of the indwelling God, the law of life, so completely that death could not overcome Him. By identifying Himself always with divine being He raised His consciousness to the divine. Thus God (life) raised Him up.

4. *Being therefore exalted...* Jesus became Lord through mastering the law of Being and Christ through bringing into manifestation the principle by which he identified Himself with perfect man. *he has poured out this.* God's idea of man in expression becomes the Christ through the directive power of the Spirit or hand of God actively functioning within man.

## The First Converts

2:37 Now when they heard this, they were cut to the heart, and said to Peter and the rest of the apostles, "Brothers, what shall we do?"

2:38 Peter said to them, "Repent, and be baptized, every one of you, in the name of Jesus Christ for the forgiveness of sins, and you will receive the gift of the Holy Spirit.[1] 2:39 For to you is the promise, and to your children, and to all who are

far off, even as many as the Lord
our God will call to himself." 2:40 With
many other words he testified, and
exhorted them, saying, "Save
yourselves from this crooked
generation!"

2:41 Then those who gladly
received his word were baptized.
There were added that day about
three thousand souls. 2:42 They
continued steadfastly in the apostles'
teaching and fellowship, in the
breaking of bread, and prayer.[2]

1. *Repent, baptized, receive the Holy Spirit.* To repent is to change the mind; to give up error for Truth. Baptism washes away the old state of thought and dissolves all negative conditions, that we may be ready to receive the power of the Holy Spirit.

2. *the breaking of bread, and prayer.* Stirring the inner substance into action in the consciousness, and concentrating the mind upon it as the real possession.

## Life among the Believers

2:43 Fear came on every soul, and
many wonders and signs were done
through the apostles. 2:44 All who
believed were together, and had all
things in common.[1] 2:45 They sold
their possessions and goods, and
distributed them to all, according as
anyone had need. 2:46 Day by day,
continuing steadfastly with one
accord in the temple, and breaking
bread at home, they took their food
with gladness and singleness of
heart, 2:47 praising God, and having
favor with all the people. The Lord
added to the assembly[2] day by day
those who were being saved.

1. *had all things in common.* It is possible for people to live in a community, and have all things in common if they "believe" that all things belong to God, and that men are merely his stewards, working for the common good of all. The whole world must eventually become an organized co-operation, based upon the understanding and application of the laws stated by Jesus Christ.

2. *assembly (church).* Metaphysically, the church is a harmonious aggregation of spiritual ideas in the mind of the individual. Less metaphysically, the Church of Christ is the great brotherhood which Jesus Christ established in Spirit. It is not made of creeds and forms, nor is it contained in walls of wood and stone. Its temple is the heart of man.

---

Fillmore Study Bible annotations by Mark Hicks

**World English Bible Footnotes:**

[3] v2:15. about 9:00 AM

[4] v2:21. Joel 2:28-32

[5] v2:27. or, Hell

[6] v2:28. Psalm 16:8-11

[7] v2:31. or, Hell

[8] v2:35. Psalm 110:1

# Acts 3

## Peter Heals a Lame Beggar

3:1 Peter and John[1] were going up into the temple at the hour of prayer, the ninth hour[9]. 3:2 A certain man who was lame from his mother's womb[2] was being carried, whom they laid daily at the door of the temple which is called Beautiful,[3] to ask gifts for the needy of those who entered into the temple. 3:3 Seeing Peter and John[4] about to go into the temple, he asked to receive gifts for the needy. 3:4 Peter, fastening his eyes on him, with John, said, "Look at us." 3:5 He listened to them, expecting to receive something from them. 3:6 But Peter said, "Silver and gold have I none, but what I have, that I give you. In the name of Jesus Christ of Nazareth, get up and walk!" 3:7 He took him by the right hand, and raised him up. Immediately his feet and his ankle bones received strength. 3:8 Leaping up, he stood, and began to walk. He entered with them into the temple, walking, leaping, and praising God.[5] 3:9 All the people saw him walking and praising God. 3:10 They recognized him, that it was he who used to sit begging for gifts for the needy at the Beautiful Gate of the temple. They were filled with wonder and amazement at what had happened to him.

1. *Peter and John.* Peter (Faith) and John (Love) went "up into the temple at the hour of prayer." Their minds were lifted up by prayer.

2. *lame from his mother's womb.* Metaphysically, one who has not affirmed his spiritual strength (the sustaining influence of spiritual ideas that permeate his being) through the living Christ. His understanding needs to be lifted up and adjusted. The feet represent a phase of the understanding.

3. *the door of the temple which is called Beautiful.* Metaphysically, spiritual understanding. The door opens when we pray and praise.

4. *Seeing Peter and John.* There must be faith on the part of the one who is to be healed that the power of the Christ to restore him lies in himself, and that he can call it forth. Faith (Peter) and love (John) are the avenues of health.

5. *leaping, and praising God.* He immediately praised God and practiced walking. He was not afraid to trust himself to his feet but accepted the gift of health and strength.

## Peter Speaks in Solomon's Portico

3:11 As the lame man who was healed held on to Peter and John, all the people ran together to them in the porch that is called Solomon's,[1] greatly wondering. 3:12 When Peter saw it, he responded to the people, "You men of Israel, why do you marvel at this man? Why do you fasten your eyes on us, as though by our own power or godliness we had made him walk? 3:13 The God of Abraham, Isaac, and Jacob, the God of our fathers, has glorified his Servant Jesus, whom you delivered up, and denied in the presence of Pilate, when he had determined to release him. 3:14 But you denied the Holy and Righteous One, and asked for a murderer to be granted to you, 3:15 and killed the Prince of life, whom God raised from the dead, to which we are witnesses. 3:16 By faith in his name, his name has made this man strong, whom you see and know.

Yes, the faith which is through him has given him this perfect soundness in the presence of you all.

3:17 "Now, brothers[10], I know that you did this in ignorance, as did also your rulers. 3:18 But the things which God announced by the mouth of all his prophets, that Christ should suffer, he thus fulfilled.

3:19 "Repent therefore, and turn again, that your sins may be blotted out, so that there may come times of refreshing from the presence of the Lord, 3:20 and that he may send Christ Jesus, who was ordained for you before, 3:21 whom heaven must receive until the times of restoration of all things,[2] which God spoke long ago by the mouth of his holy prophets. 3:22 For Moses indeed said to the fathers, 'The Lord God will raise up a prophet for you from among your brothers, like me. You shall listen to him in all things whatever he says to you. 3:23 It will be, that every soul that will not listen to that prophet will be utterly destroyed from among the people.'[11] 3:24 Yes, and all the prophets from Samuel and those who followed after, as many as have spoken, they also told of these days. 3:25 You are the children of the prophets, and of the covenant which God made with our fathers, saying to Abraham, 'In your seed will all the families of the earth be blessed.'[12] 3:26 God, having raised up his servant, Jesus, sent him to you first, to bless you, in turning away everyone of you from your wickedness."

1. *Solomon.* Metaphysically, the state of mind that is established in consciousness when the soul is unified with wisdom and love (MBD/solomon).

2. *until the times of restoration of all things.* The restoration of all things is the work of the "church of Christ." It is of the utmost importance, then, that each of us diligently seek truth, obey it, and be able to do our work as a member of the "body." The work of restoration begins in us; we aspire to realize consciously our unity with God. Gradually our thoughts begin to shape ourselves aright and as we acquire the true perspective, we become conscious of others who are working along the same way, having the same aspirations. We perceive our oneness with others who have consecrated themselves unto the Lord, and our sense of unity becomes deepened. Unity Correspondence School Lesson 4, *Body of Christ.*

---

Fillmore Study Bible annotations by Mark Hicks

**World English Bible Footnotes:**

[9] v3:1. 3:00 PM

[10] v3:17. The word for "brothers" here may be also correctly translated "brothers and sisters" or "siblings."

[11] v3:23. Deuteronomy 18:15,18-19

[12] v3:25. Genesis 22:18; 26:4

# ACTS 4

## Peter and John Defend Their Authority

4:1 As they spoke to the people, the priests and the captain of the temple and the Sadducees came to them, 4:2 being upset because they taught the people and proclaimed in Jesus the resurrection from the dead.[1] 4:3 They laid hands on them, and put them in custody until the next day, for it was now evening. 4:4 But many of those who heard the word believed, and the number of the men came to be about five thousand.

4:5 It happened in the morning, that their rulers, elders, and scribes were gathered together in Jerusalem. 4:6 Annas the high priest was there, with Caiaphas, John, Alexander, and as many as were relatives of the high priest. 4:7 When they had stood them in the middle of them, they inquired, "By what power, or in what name, have you done this?"[2]

4:8 Then Peter, filled with the Holy Spirit, said to them, "You rulers of the people, and elders of Israel, 4:9 if we are examined today concerning a good deed done to a crippled man, by what means this man has been healed, 4:10 be it known to you all, and to all the people of Israel, that in the name of Jesus Christ of Nazareth,[3] whom you crucified, whom God raised from the dead, in him does this man stand here before you whole. 4:11 He is 'the stone which was regarded as worthless by you, the builders, which has become the head of the corner.'[4][13] 4:12 There is salvation in none other, for neither is there any other name under heaven, that is given among men, by which we must be saved!"

4:13 Now when they saw the boldness of Peter and John, and had perceived that they were unlearned and ignorant men, they marveled. They recognized that they had been with Jesus. 4:14 Seeing the man who was healed standing with them, they could say nothing against it. 4:15 But when they had commanded them to go aside out of the council, they conferred among themselves, 4:16 saying, "What shall we do to these men?[5] Because indeed a notable miracle has been done through them, as can be plainly seen by all who dwell in Jerusalem, and we can't deny it. 4:17 But so that this spreads no further among the people, let's threaten them, that from now on they don't speak to anyone in this name." 4:18 They called them, and commanded them not to speak at all nor teach in the name of Jesus.

4:19 But Peter and John answered them, "Whether it is right in the sight of God to listen to you rather than to God, judge for yourselves, 4:20 for we can't help telling the things which we saw and heard."

4:21 When they had further threatened them, they let them go, finding no way to punish them, because of the people; for everyone glorified God for that which was done. 4:22 For the man on whom this miracle of healing was performed was more than forty years old.

1. *proclaimed in Jesus the resurrection from the dead.* The resurrection of spiritual truth from the materialism of the present time. We need to resurrect our faculties as individuals and at the same time to undertake the resurrection of the same

spiritual faculties in society.

2. *By what power, or in what name, have you done this?* Everyone who believes in the power of the indwelling Christ to heal disease and establish harmony in human beings is authorized to speak the word. The metaphysician believes that since Jesus Christ of Nazareth demonstrated the power of God and healed many who were weak in understanding, we can do the same.

3. *in the name of Jesus Christ of Nazareth.* We identify ourself in the inner realm by means of the I AM, and among human beings by our name. Through the right use of the I AM we build up character, and when others hear our name they identify it with the character they have given it. Thus a name has power to characterize the one who bears it.

4. *the head of the corner (cornerstone).* The spiritual I AM, which many have case aside, is the very cornerstone of our character. The Christ in Jesus was the cornerstone of his character.

5. *What shall we do to these men?* When a new relation between God and humanity is revealed, and the priest or minister who has ruled hitherto as mediator between humanity and the far away Deity is found to be superfluity, there is an uproar in consciousness. Metaphysically, the conventional thoughts lay hands on the illuminated ones and cast them into prison, or darkness and bondage. It is well to be informed about these movements of the mind, for may may thereby be saved much perplexity.

## Believers Pray With Boldness

4:23 Being let go, they came to their own company, and reported all that the chief priests and the elders had said to them. 4:24 When they heard it, they lifted up their voice to God with one accord, and said, "O Lord, you are God, who made the heaven, the earth, the sea, and all that is in them; 4:25 who by the mouth of your servant, David, said,

'Why do the nations rage,
and the peoples plot a vain thing?
4:26 The kings of the earth take a stand,
and the rulers take council together,
against the Lord, and against his Christ[14].'[15]

4:27 "For truly, in this city against your holy servant, Jesus, whom you anointed, both Herod and Pontius Pilate, with the Gentiles and the people of Israel, were gathered together 4:28 to do whatever your hand and your council foreordained to happen. 4:29 Now, Lord, look at their threats, and grant to your servants to speak your word with all boldness, 4:30 while you stretch out your hand to heal; and that signs and wonders may be done through the name of your holy Servant Jesus." 4:31 When they had prayed, the place was shaken where they were gathered together. They were all filled with the Holy Spirit, and they spoke the word of God with boldness. ❶

1. *they spoke the word of God with boldness.* It is from God through Jesus Christ that all spiritual healing comes. No one has yet done the "greater works" that Jesus foretold, but the fact that he foresaw their accomplishment encourages our faith in the possibility of these surpassing deeds.

## A Community of Grace Emerges

4:32 The multitude of those who believed were of one heart and soul. Not one of them claimed that anything of the things which he possessed was his own, but they had all things in common. 4:33 With great power, the apostles gave their testimony of the resurrection of the Lord Jesus. Great grace was on them all.❶ [4:34] For neither was there among them any who lacked, for as many as were owners of lands or houses sold them, and brought the proceeds of the things that were sold, [4:35] and laid them at the apostles' feet, and distribution was made to each, according as anyone had need. [4:36] Joses, who by the apostles was surnamed Barnabas❷ (which is, being interpreted, Son of Encouragement), a Levite, a man of Cyprus by race, [4:37] having a field, sold it, and brought the money and laid it at the apostles' feet.

1. *Great grace was on them all.* The progress of such a community today would depend on two things: the unselfishness of its members, and confidence that the directive head of the community was guided by Jesus Christ. The apostles vigorously proclaimed the resurrection of the Lord Jesus Christ, who was the head of all their work.

2. *Barnabas.* Metaphysically, Barnabas is the imagination brought into expression through association with the word (Paul) (MBD/barnabas).

Fillmore Study Bible annotations by Mark Hicks

**World English Bible Footnotes:**

[13] v4:11. Psalm 118:22

[14] v4:26. Christ (Greek) and Messiah (Hebrew) both mean Anointed One.

[15] v4:26. Psalm 2:1-2

# Acts 5

## The Self-Deception of Ananias and Sapphira

[5:1] But a certain man named Ananias, with Sapphira, his wife, sold a possession, [5:2] and kept back❶ part of the price, his wife also being aware of it, and brought a certain part, and laid it at the apostles' feet. [5:3] But Peter said, "Ananias, why has Satan filled your heart to lie to the Holy Spirit, and to keep back part of the price of the land? [5:4] While you kept it, didn't it remain your own? After it was sold, wasn't it in your power? How is it that you have conceived this thing in your heart? You haven't lied to men, but to God." [5:5] Ananias, hearing these words, fell down and died. Great fear came on all who heard these things. [5:6] The young men arose and wrapped him up, and they carried him out and buried him. [5:7]

About three hours later, his wife, not knowing what had happened, came in. [5:8] Peter answered her, "Tell me whether you sold the land for so much." She said, "Yes, for so much." [5:9] But Peter asked her, "How is it that you have agreed together to tempt the Spirit of the Lord? Behold, the feet of those who have buried your husband are at the door, and they will carry you out." [5:10] She fell down immediately at his feet, and died. The young men came in and found her dead, and they carried her out and buried her by her husband. [5:11] Great fear came on the whole assembly,[2] and on all who heard these things.

1. *kept back.* Self-deception is the chief theme of today's lesson. The deceptive belief (Ananias) that we can attain all the blessings of Spirit and at the same time retain our hold upon worldly ways and things, is a very subtle mortal error which causes the would-be disciple much misery. Nothing ever can be hidden from Spirit. It is always best to uncover the whole inner consciousness to Spirit and to pray earnestly to be thoroughly cleansed from every taint of deception and error.

2. *Great fear came on the whole assembly.* In a literal sense, the incident of Ananias and Sapphira is harsh and unchristian. The Spirit of truth leads sinners into all truth, not by frightening them to death, but by guiding them into the way of righteousness and peace. In a metaphysical sense this lesson is valuable, for it shows that a clean choice must be made between the life of deception and the Christ life of straightforwardness, through faith in the Spirit of truth within the heart.

## The Apostles Heal Many

[5:12] By the hands of the apostles[1] many signs and wonders were done among the people. They were all with one accord in Solomon's porch. [5:13] None of the rest dared to join them, however the people honored them. [5:14] More believers were added to the Lord, multitudes of both men and women. [5:15] They even carried out the sick into the streets, and laid them on cots and mattresses, so that as Peter came by, at the least his shadow might overshadow some of them. [5:16] Multitudes also came together from the cities around Jerusalem, bringing sick people, and those who were tormented by unclean spirits: and they were all healed.[2]

1. *apostles.* Those sent forth; messengers; ambassadors; active spiritual thoughts. Jesus conferred this title on the Twelve whom He sent forth to teach and to heal (RW/apostles).

2. *and they were all healed.* Metaphysically, the apostles come together at Solomon's porch (place of the soul unified with wisdom and love) for Peter (Faith) to heal the the multitudes (many thoughts).

## The Freeing Power Of Truth

[5:17] But the high priest rose up, and all those who were with him (which is the sect of the Sadducees), and they were filled with jealousy, [5:18] and laid hands on the apostles,[1] and put them in public custody. [5:19] But an angel of the Lord opened the prison doors by night, and brought them out, and said, [5:20] "Go stand and speak in the temple to the people all the words of this life."

[5:21] When they heard this, they entered into the temple about daybreak, and taught. But the high priest came, and those who were with him, and called the council together, and all the senate of the children of Israel, and sent to the prison to have them brought. [5:22] But the officers who came didn't find them in the prison. They returned and reported, [5:23] "We found the prison shut and locked, and the guards standing before the doors, but when we opened them, we found no one inside!"

5:24 Now when the high priest, the captain of the temple, and the chief priests heard these words, they were very perplexed about them and what might become of this. 5:25 One came and told them, "Behold, the men whom you put in prison are in the temple, standing and teaching the people." 5:26 Then the captain went with the officers, and brought them without violence, for they were afraid that the people might stone them.

5:27 When they had brought them, they set them before the council. The high priest questioned them, 5:28 saying, "Didn't we strictly command you not to teach in this name? Behold, you have filled Jerusalem with your teaching, and intend to bring this man's blood on us."

5:29 But Peter and the apostles answered, "We must obey God rather than men.[2] 5:30 The God of our fathers raised up Jesus, whom you killed, hanging him on a tree. 5:31 God exalted him with his right hand to be a Prince and a Savior, to give repentance to Israel, and remission of sins. 5:32 We are His witnesses of these things; and so also is the Holy Spirit, whom God has given to those who obey him."

5:33 But they, when they heard this, were cut to the heart, and determined to kill them. 5:34 But one stood up in the council, a Pharisee named Gamaliel,[3] a teacher of the law, honored by all the people, and commanded to put the apostles out for a little while. 5:35 He said to them, "You men of Israel, be careful concerning these men, what you are about to do. 5:36 For before these days Theudas rose up, making himself out to be somebody; to whom a number of men, about four hundred, joined themselves: who was slain; and all, as many as obeyed him, were dispersed, and came to nothing. 5:37 After this man, Judas of Galilee rose up in the days of the enrollment, and drew away some people after him. He also perished, and all, as many as obeyed him, were scattered abroad. 5:38 Now I tell you, withdraw from these men, and leave them alone. For if this counsel or this work is of men, it will be overthrown. 5:39 But if it is of God, you will not be able to overthrow it, and you would be found even to be fighting against God!"

5:40 They agreed with him. Summoning the apostles, they beat them and commanded them not to speak in the name of Jesus, and let them go. 5:41 They therefore departed from the presence of the council, rejoicing that they were counted worthy to suffer dishonor for Jesus' name.

5:42 Every day, in the temple and at home, they never stopped teaching and preaching Jesus, the Christ.

1. *the Sadducees ... laid hands on the apostles.* Many conflicts take place in the mind between the old and the new lines of thought. The new encroaches upon the old, and occupies its field as teacher and leader. There is reaction again and again, and we sometimes think it would be best to crush out entirely these revolutionary truths which are making such powerful headway in the consciousness. Some people are too cautious to become real Christians. They dare not let go the teachings of their forefathers for fear they may be led into some heresy, and lose their chance of getting into heaven.

2. *Peter and the apostles answered We must obey God rather than men.* In all religious matters we should exercise faith and love and judgment. These faculties give balance and poise to the developing soul. In the life of Jesus they were represented by Peter (faith), John (love), and James (judgment). These three apostles were present with Jesus in the performance of all his outstanding works.

3. *one stood up in the council, a Pharisee named Gamaliel.* Gamaliel, the "doctor of the law" who advocates that Truth be test-

ed by its fruits, was a leader among the most conservative Pharisees; he recommended common sense and reason. Prejudice and bigotry often blind us to real merit. There is in every one that spirit of fairness which will give every idea a chance to prove itself. Gamaliel's words are the conclusion of every well-balanced mind, and we should listen to every doctrine with this good judgment to the front. (MBD/gamaliel)

---

Fillmore Study Bible annotations by Mark Hicks

# Acts 6

## New Converts Claim Injustice

6:1 Now in those days, when the number of the disciples was multiplying, a complaint arose from the Hellenists[16]❶ against the Hebrews, because their widows were neglected in the daily service. 6:2 The twelve summoned the multitude of the disciples and said, "It is not appropriate for us to forsake the word of God and serve tables.❷ 6:3 Therefore select from among you, brothers, seven men of good report, full of the Holy Spirit and of wisdom, whom we may appoint over this business. 6:4 But we will continue steadfastly in prayer and in the ministry of the word."

6:5 These words pleased the whole multitude. They chose Stephen, a man full of faith and of the Holy Spirit, Philip, Prochorus, Nicanor, Timon, Parmenas, and Nicolaus, a proselyte of Antioch; 6:6 whom they set before the apostles. When they had prayed, they laid their hands on them. 6:7 The word of God increased and the number of the disciples multiplied in Jerusalem exceedingly. A great company of the priests were obedient to the faith.

1. *a complaint arose from the Hellenists.* The Hellenists represent new converts to the faith. Until selfishness is overcome, a sense of injustice arises in mind at every indication that the purely spiritual interests of life are receiving more attention and more sustaining power than the other worth-while interests of the individual. New converts are always careful to insure their own rights.
2. *It is not appropriate for us to forsake the word of God and serve tables.* We owe loyalty to the Ideal of perfection, and should harmonize all our powers and faculties to that end.

## Arguing with Entrenched Beliefs

6:8 Stephen,❶ full of faith and power, performed great wonders and signs among the people. 6:9 But some of those who were of the synagogue called "The Libertines," and of the Cyrenians, of the Alexandrians,❷ and of those of Cilicia and Asia arose, disputing with Stephen. 6:10 They weren't able to withstand the wisdom and the Spirit by which he spoke. 6:11 Then they secretly induced men to say, "We have heard him speak blasphemous words against Moses and God." 6:12 They stirred up the people, the elders, and the scribes,③ and came against him and seized him, and brought him in to the council, 6:13 and set up false witnesses who said, "This man never stops speaking blasphemous words④ against this holy place and the law. 6:14 For we have heard him say that this Jesus of Nazareth will destroy this place, and will change the customs which Moses delivered to us." 6:15 All who sat in the council, fastening their eyes on him, saw his face like it was the face of an angel.

1. *Stephen.* Means "crowned"; in this lesson the symbolical meaning of the name is that reason has been crowned or illumined with spiritual truth.

2. *Libertines, and the Cyrenians, and the Alexandrians.* Represent fixed states of thought in the realm of sense, which object to any new inspiration that may try to establish itself in consciousness.

3. *The elders, and the scribes.* The elders symbolize leading Pharisaical religious thoughts which are classed as having authority; the scribes symbolize that in our consciousness which records the standard beliefs of our inherited religious tendencies.

4. *blasphemous words.* The cry of "blasphemy" is always made by those who are put to rout by the Truth—it is their last resort. It is never wise to insist upon our own opinion or conviction when arguing with those of opposite beliefs. It antagonizes others instead of converting them.

Fillmore Study Bible annotations by Thomas Scheinler and Mark Hicks

**World English Bible Footnotes:**

[16] v6:1. The Hellenists used Greek language and culture, even though they were also of Hebrew descent.

# Acts 7

## Stephen's Speech to the Council

7:1 The high priest said, "Are these things so?"

7:2 He said, "Brothers and fathers, listen. The God of glory appeared to our father Abraham,① when he was in Mesopotamia, before he lived in Haran, 7:3 and said to him, 'Get out of your land, and from your relatives, and come into a land which I will show you.'[17]② 7:4 Then he came out of the land of the Chaldaeans, and lived in Haran. From there, when his father was dead, God moved him into this land, where you are now living.③ 7:5 He gave him no inheritance in it, no, not so much as to set his foot on. He promised that he would give it to him for a possession, and to his seed after him, when he still had no child. 7:6 God spoke in this way: that his seed would live as aliens in a strange land, and that they would be enslaved and mistreated for four hundred years. 7:7 'I will judge the nation to which they will be in bondage,' said God, 'and after that will they come out, and serve me in this place.'[18] 7:8 He gave him the covenant of circumcision. So

Abraham became the father of Isaac,
and circumcised him the eighth day.
Isaac became the father of Jacob,
and Jacob became the father of the
twelve patriarchs.

7:9 "The patriarchs, moved with
jealousy against Joseph, sold him
into Egypt. God was with him, 7:10
and delivered him out of all his
afflictions, and gave him favor and
wisdom before Pharaoh,④ king of
Egypt. He made him governor over
Egypt and all his house. 7:11 Now a
famine came over all the land of
Egypt and Canaan, and great
affliction. Our fathers found no food.
7:12 But when Jacob heard that there
was grain in Egypt, he sent out our
fathers the first time. 7:13 On the
second time Joseph was made known
to his brothers, and Joseph's race
was revealed to Pharaoh. 7:14 Joseph
sent, and summoned Jacob, his
father, and all his relatives, seventy-
five souls. 7:15 Jacob went down into
Egypt, and he died, himself and our
fathers, 7:16 and they were brought
back to Shechem, and laid in the
tomb that Abraham bought for a
price in silver from the children of
Hamor of Shechem.

7:17 "But as the time of the promise
came close which God had sworn to
Abraham, the people grew and
multiplied in Egypt, 7:18 until there
arose a different king, who didn't
know Joseph. 7:19 The same took
advantage of our race, and
mistreated our fathers, and forced
them to throw out their babies, so
that they wouldn't stay alive. 7:20 At
that time Moses was born, and was
exceedingly handsome. He was
nourished three months in his
father's house. 7:21 When he was
thrown out, Pharaoh's daughter took
him up, and reared him as her own
son.⑤ 7:22 Moses was instructed in all
the wisdom of the Egyptians. He was
mighty in his words and works. 7:23
But when he was forty years old, it
came into his heart to visit his
brothers[19], the children of Israel.
7:24 Seeing one of them suffer wrong,
he defended him, and avenged him
who was oppressed, striking the
Egyptian. 7:25 He supposed that his
brothers understood that God, by his
hand, was giving them deliverance;
but they didn't understand.

7:26 "The day following, he
appeared to them as they fought,
and urged them to be at peace again,
saying, 'Sirs, you are brothers. Why
do you wrong one another?' 7:27 But he
who did his neighbor wrong pushed
him away, saying, 'Who made you a
ruler and a judge over us? 7:28 Do you
want to kill me, as you killed the
Egyptian yesterday?'[20] 7:29 Moses
fled at this saying, and became a
stranger in the land of Midian, where
he became the father of two sons.

7:30 "When forty years were
fulfilled, an angel of the Lord
appeared to him in the wilderness
of Mount Sinai, in a flame of fire in
a bush. 7:31 When Moses saw it, he
wondered at the sight. As he came
close to see, a voice of the Lord
came to him, 7:32 'I am the God of
your fathers, the God of Abraham,
the God of Isaac, and the God of
Jacob.'[21] Moses trembled, and
dared not look. 7:33 The Lord said to
him, 'Take your sandals off of your
feet, for the place where you stand
is holy ground. 7:34 I have surely seen
the affliction of my people that is
in Egypt, and have heard their
groaning. I have come down to
deliver them. Now come, I will send
you into Egypt.'[22]

7:35 "This Moses, whom they
refused, saying, 'Who made you a
ruler and a judge?'--God has sent him
as both a ruler and a deliverer by
the hand of the angel who appeared
to him in the bush. 7:36 This man led
them out, having worked wonders
and signs in Egypt, in the Red Sea,

and in the wilderness for forty years.
7:37 This is that Moses, who said to the
children of Israel, 'The Lord our God
will raise up a prophet for you from
among your brothers, like me.[23]'[24]
7:38 This is he who was in the assembly
in the wilderness with the angel that
spoke to him on Mount Sinai, and
with our fathers, who received living
oracles to give to us, 7:39 to whom
our fathers wouldn't be obedient, but
rejected him, and turned back in
their hearts to Egypt, 7:40 saying to
Aaron, 'Make us gods that will go
before us, for as for this Moses, who
led us out of the land of Egypt, we
don't know what has become of
him.'[25] 7:41 They made a calf in
those days, and brought a sacrifice to
the idol, and rejoiced in the works
of their hands. 7:42 But God turned,
and gave them up to serve the army
of the sky,[26] as it is written in the
book of the prophets,

'Did you offer to me slain animals
and sacrifices
forty years in the wilderness,
O house of Israel?
7:43 You took up the tent of Moloch,
the star of your god Rephan,
the figures which you made to
worship.
I will carry you away[27]
beyond Babylon.'

7:44 "Our fathers had the tent of
the testimony in the wilderness,
even as he who spoke to Moses
commanded him to make it
according to the pattern that he had
seen; 7:45 which also our fathers, in
their turn, brought in with Joshua
when they entered into the
possession of the nations, whom God
drove out before the face of our
fathers, to the days of David, 7:46 who
found favor in the sight of God, and
asked to find a habitation for the God
of Jacob. 7:47 But Solomon built him
a house. 7:48 However, the Most High
doesn't dwell in temples made with
hands, as the prophet says,

7:49 'heaven is my throne,
and the earth a footstool for
my feet.
What kind of house will you build
me?' says the Lord;
'or what is the place of my
rest?
7:50 Didn't my hand make all these
things?'[28]

7:51 "You stiff-necked and
uncircumcised in heart and ears, you
always resist the Holy Spirit! As your
fathers did, so you do. 7:52 Which of
the prophets didn't your fathers
persecute? They killed those who
foretold the coming of the Righteous
One, of whom you have now become
betrayers and murderers. 7:53 You
received the law as it was ordained
by angels, and didn't keep it!"

1. *Abraham.* The power of the mind to reproduce its ideas in unlimited expression. This ability of the mind to make substance out of ideas is called faith. (MBD/Abraham)

2. *come into a land which I will show you.* The new conception of substance that the spiritually quickened man discerns when he is stirred to religious activity. This land is found by everyone who obeys his impulse to rise higher in consciousness. It is our assurance of the reality of the things of Spirit.

3. *God moved him into this land, where you are now living.* For his unswerving faith in God. Abram had a vision of what a faith consistently held makes possible, and discerned the blessings that were in store for him if he would throw the full weight of his faith on Jehovah.

4. *God was with him ... and gave him favor and wisdom before Pharaoh.* We may take hold of events with the aid of faith and shape their course more nearly to our liking. More important still, we may remake ourselves with the aid of divine love and power.

5. *Pharaoh's daughter took him up, and reared him as her own son.* The ark in which Moses was placed was symbolic of the ark of love and trust. Love and trust always find a way out of difficulty. Pharaoh's daughter was an instrument of God. Through her, Moses (representing the progressive law of evolution working in the

soul) was "instructed in all the wisdom of the Egyptians; and he was mighty in his words and works." God is the one and only power in the universe.

## The Stoning of Stephen

7:54 Now when they heard these things, they were cut to the heart, and they gnashed at him with their teeth. 7:55 But he, being full of the Holy Spirit, looked up steadfastly into heaven, and saw the glory of God, and Jesus standing on the right hand of God, 7:56 and said, "Behold, I see the heavens opened, and the Son of Man standing at the right hand of God!"

7:57 But they cried out with a loud voice, and stopped their ears, and rushed at him with one accord. 7:58 They threw him out of the city, and stoned him.[1] The witnesses placed their garments at the feet of a young man named Saul. 7:59 They stoned Stephen as he called out, saying, "Lord Jesus, receive my spirit!" 7:60 He kneeled down, and cried with a loud voice, "Lord, don't hold this sin against them!" When he had said this, he fell asleep.

1. *They threw him out of the city, and stoned him.* The manner of presenting Truth rests with each individual. Those who want to continue as ministers of Truth and make a lasting impression on their hearers should be wise and should not stir up antagonism in the friends they are seeking to convert. The old method of employing accusations, condemnations, and common scoldings is not effective in getting the attention of others. Such methods have always ended in tragedies, of which the stoning of Stephen is an outstanding example.

---

Fillmore Study Bible annotations by Tom Scheinler and Mark Hicks

**World English Bible Footnotes:**

[17] v7:3. Genesis 12:1

[18] v7:7. Genesis 15:13-14

[19] v7:23. The word for "brothers" here and where the context allows may be also correctly translated "brothers and sisters" or "siblings."

[20] v7:28. Exodus 2:14

[21] v7:32. Exodus 3:6

[22] v7:34. Exodus 3:5,7-8,10

[23] v7:37. TR adds "You shall listen to him."

[24] v7:37. Deuteronomy 18:15

[25] v7:40. Exodus 32:1

[26] v7:42. This idiom could also be translatted "host of heaven," or "angelic beings," or "heavenly bodies."

[27] v7:43. Amos 5:25-27

[28] v7:50. Isaiah 66:1-2

# Acts 8

## Saul Ravages the Assembly

8:1 Saul was consenting to his death. A great persecution arose against the assembly which was in Jerusalem in that day. They were all scattered abroad throughout the regions of Judea and Samaria, except for the apostles. 8:2 Devout men buried Stephen, and lamented greatly over him. 8:3 But Saul ravaged the assembly,[1] entering into every house, and dragged both men and women off to prison.

1. *Saul ravaged the assembly.* Saul represents the action of the will in attaining that which man desires. Stephen (crowned) represents the illumined intellect under the influence of the Holy Spirit but not yet fully impregnated with that Spirit. The will, which leads man to cling to the formalism of his inherited faith, resists the promptings of the Holy Spirit, and man is unresponsive to the call of the higher influence.

## Philip Preaches in Samaria

8:4 Therefore those who were scattered abroad went around preaching the word. 8:5 Philip[1] went down to the city of Samaria,[2] and proclaimed to them the Christ. 8:6 The multitudes listened with one accord to the things that were spoken by Philip, when they heard and saw the signs which he did. 8:7 For unclean spirits came out of many of those who had them. They came out, crying with a loud voice. Many who had been paralyzed and lame were healed. 8:8 There was great joy in that city.

8:9 But there was a certain man, Simon[3] by name, who used to practice sorcery in the city, and amazed the people of Samaria, making himself out to be some great one, 8:10 to whom they all listened, from the least to the greatest, saying, "This man is that great power of God." 8:11 They listened to him, because for a long time he had amazed them with his sorceries. 8:12 But when they believed Philip preaching good news concerning the Kingdom of God and the name of Jesus Christ, they were baptized, both men and women. 8:13 Simon himself also believed. Being baptized, he continued with Philip. Seeing signs and great miracles occurring, he was amazed.

8:14 Now when the apostles who were at Jerusalem heard that Samaria had received the word of God, they sent Peter and John[4] to them, 8:15 who, when they had come down, prayed for them, that they might receive the Holy Spirit; 8:16 for as yet he had fallen on none of them. They had only been baptized in the name of Christ Jesus. 8:17 Then they laid their hands on them,[5] and they received the Holy Spirit. 8:18 Now when Simon saw that the Holy Spirit was given through the laying on of the apostles' hands, he offered them money, 8:19 saying, "Give me also this power, that whoever I lay my hands on may receive the Holy Spirit." 8:20 But Peter said to him, "May your silver perish with you, because you thought you could obtain the gift of God with money! 8:21 You have neither part nor lot in this matter, for your heart isn't right before God. 8:22 Repent therefore of this, your wickedness, and ask God if perhaps the thought of your heart may be forgiven you. 8:23 For I see that you are in the gall of bitterness and in the bondage of iniquity."

8:24 Simon answered, "Pray for me to the Lord, that none of the things which you have spoken happen to me."

8:25 They therefore, when they had testified and spoken the word of the Lord, returned to Jerusalem, and preached the Good News to many villages of the Samaritans.

1. *Philip*. Philip exercises his power through the spiritual Word, which is outwardly made manifest in speech. The scattering of the disciples throughout these two regions signifies that the spiritually illumined thoughts of man may permeate his intellectual perception and quicken him to a new appreciation of the value of praise.

2. *Went down to the city of Samaria*. The Samaritans were a race of people who were a mixture of Assyrian and Hebrew. They claimed to be the descendants of Abraham and taught the books of Moses, but they were not recognized by the Jews as followers of the Jewish religion. Metaphysically, Samaria represents a state of consciousness in which both Truth and error are mixed, with Truth predominating.

3. *Simon, the sorcerer*. The ambition of personality to handle the power of Spirit, without paying the price through faith and love.

4. *Peter and John*. Peter represents faith, and John, love. These powers of the mind open the way for the descent of the Holy Spirit into all mixed states of consciousness.

5. *They laid their hands on them*. A movement prayer, in which the executive power of Faith and Love does its work, directing the spiritual forces, and through which action this state of consciousness receives the blessing of blessings, the baptism of the Holy Spirit. Metaphysically speaking, we lay on hands when we affirm the presence and power of Spirit in the flesh. Physically speaking, the hands represent execution or the direct contact of Spirit with body. The body is permeated by a material consciousness, and the materially minded require a sign or outer manifestation of the power of Spirit before they will receive it. Many Christian healers lay their hands on their patients, and some anoint them with oil.

## Philip, the Ethiopian Eunuch and Stillness

8:26 But an angel of the Lord spoke to Philip, saying, "Arise, and go toward the south[1] to the way that goes down from Jerusalem to Gaza. This is a desert."

8:27 He arose and went; and behold, there was a man of Ethiopia, a eunuch of great authority under Candace,[2] queen of the Ethiopians, who was over all her treasure, who had come to Jerusalem to worship. 8:28 He was returning and sitting in his chariot, and was reading the prophet Isaiah.

8:29 The Spirit said to Philip, "Go near, and join yourself to this chariot."[3]

8:30 Philip ran to him, and heard him reading Isaiah the prophet, and said, "Do you understand what you are reading?"

8:31 He said, "How can I, unless someone explains it to me?" He begged Philip to come up and sit with him. 8:32 Now the passage of the Scripture which he was reading was this,

"He was led as a sheep to the
slaughter.
As a lamb before his shearer is
silent,

so he doesn't open his mouth.
8:33 In his humiliation, his judgment
was taken away.
Who will declare His
generation?
For his life is taken from the
earth."[29]

8:34 The eunuch answered Philip,
"Who is the prophet talking about?[4]
About himself, or about someone
else?"

8:35 Philip opened his mouth, and
beginning from this Scripture,
preached to him Jesus. 8:36 As they
went on the way, they came to some
water, and the eunuch said, "Behold,
here is water. What is keeping me
from being baptized?"

8:37 [30] 8:38 He commanded the
chariot to stand still,[5] and they both
went down into the water, both
Philip and the eunuch, and he
baptized him.

8:39 When they came up out of the
water, the Spirit of the Lord caught
Philip away, and the eunuch didn't
see him any more, for he went on
his way rejoicing. 8:40 But Philip was
found at Azotus. Passing through, he
preached the Good News to all the
cities, until he came to Caesarea.

1. *Go toward the south.* In Scriptural symbology, east means within; west, without; north, above; south, below. The Christ truth is a germinal idea upon which all bodily regeneration depends. The divine idea of man's perfection, when held in mind first quickens the brain cells at the very crown of the head; from that point it descends into the body, doing its quickening and regenerating work as it goes, until the whole body is redeemed. Gaza means strength which has been depleted (desert).

2. *Ethiopia, Candace, the eunuch.* Ethiopia symbolizes the abdominal region of the body; Candace, the divine feminine; the eunuch, the masculine principle which has lost its spiritual life.

3. *Go ... and join yourself to this chariot.* The chariot represents the body.

4. *Who is the prophet talking about?* Isaiah was prophesying the coming of the spiritual man and pointing out some of the experiences through which he would pass in rejuvenating the body. That man's body consciousness may be lifted up, the spiritual ego, Christ, must descend to the level of the body consciousness and temporarily be subjected to humiliation, desertion, and apparent death.

5. *He commanded the chariot to stand still.* Spiritual processes are accomplished in the silence of the inner man. When one has attained the ability to be still, he is ready for the cleansing, quickening flood of spiritual life.

---

Fillmore Study Bible annotations by Thomas Scheinler and Mark Hicks

**World English Bible Footnotes:**

[29] v8:33. Isaiah 53:7,8

[30] v8:37. TR adds "Philip said, 'If you believe with all your heart, you may.' He answered, 'I believe that Jesus Christ is the Son of God.'"

# Acts 9

## The Conversion of Saul

9:1 But Saul, still breathing threats and slaughter[1] against the disciples of the Lord, went to the high priest, 9:2 and asked for letters from him to the synagogues of Damascus, that if he found any who were of the Way, whether men or women, he might bring them bound to Jerusalem. 9:3 As he traveled, it happened that he got close to Damascus,[2] and suddenly a light from the sky shone around him.[3] 9:4 He fell on the earth, and heard a voice saying to him, "Saul, Saul, why do you persecute me?"

9:5 He said, "Who are you, Lord?"

The Lord said, "I am Jesus, whom you are persecuting.[31][4] 9:6 But[32] rise up, and enter into the city, and you will be told what you must do."

9:7 The men who traveled with him stood speechless, hearing the sound, but seeing no one. 9:8 Saul arose from the ground, and when his eyes were opened, he saw no one. They led him by the hand, and brought him into Damascus. 9:9 He was without sight for three days, and neither ate nor drank.

9:10 Now there was a certain disciple at Damascus named Ananias. The Lord said to him in a vision, "Ananias!"

He said, "Behold, it's me, Lord."

9:11 The Lord said to him, "Arise, and go to the street which is called Straight, and inquire in the house of Judah[33] for one named Saul, a man of Tarsus. For behold, he is praying, 9:12 and in a vision he has seen a man named Ananias coming in, and laying his hands on him, that he might receive his sight."

9:13 But Ananias answered, "Lord, I have heard from many about this man, how much evil he did to your saints at Jerusalem. 9:14 Here he has authority from the chief priests to bind all who call on your name."

9:15 But the Lord said to him, "Go your way, for he is my chosen vessel to bear my name before the nations and kings, and the children of Israel. 9:16 For I will show him how many things he must suffer for my name's sake."

9:17 Ananias departed, and entered into the house. Laying his hands on him,[5] he said, "Brother Saul, the Lord, who appeared to you on the road by which you came, has sent me, that you may receive your sight, and be filled with the Holy Spirit." 9:18 Immediately something like scales fell from his eyes, and he received his sight. He arose and was baptized. 9:19 He took food and was strengthened.

1. *Saul, still breathing threats and slaughter.* Saul represents the will and its dominance over the mind and heart of man. When it is man's will to destroy those who disagree with him and to uphold his convictions through strife, spiritual perception is impossible to man.

2. *He got close to Damascus.* Damascus ("activity"; "alertness" in respect to trade or possessions), refers to the capacity of the intellect to engender strife and warring thoughts and conditions.

3. *Suddenly a light from the sky shone around him.* Transformation of the unbridled will to spiritual understanding.

4. *I am Jesus, whom you are persecuting.* "I am Jesus" represents God's idea of man in expression, a will that transcends every other.

5. *Ananias ... laying his hands on him.* Saul received the Pentecostal baptism the same as those disciples in the "upper room" in Jerusalem. It was so intense that he could not assimilate it and the Lord sent him a healer in Ananias, who laid hands on him and helped him to equalize the tremendous spiritual energy that had descended suddenly into soul and body. This experience is quite common in this day among Truth workers, and we often find it necessary to help one another get poise and mastery of the higher forces. The body is often slow in responding to the swift vibrations of light, and a dazed condition of mind follows a special spiritual baptism. One who has attained poise and mastery is most acceptable in such cases and helps to restore sight to blinded eyes.

## Saul Preaches in Damascus

Saul stayed several days with the disciples who were at Damascus. 9:20 Immediately in the synagogues he proclaimed the Christ,[1] that he is the Son of God. 9:21 All who heard him were amazed, and said, "Isn't this he who in Jerusalem made havoc of those who called on this name? And he had come here intending to bring them bound before the chief priests!"

9:22 But Saul increased more in strength, and confounded the Jews who lived at Damascus, proving that this is the Christ.

1. *Immediately in the synagogues he proclaimed the Christ.* Conversion does not mean bestowal of the Holy Spirit. The baptism of the Holy Spirit follows the spiritual and moral change called conversion that a person undergoes when he comes in contact the Christ consciousness. This baptism was Saul's authorization of apostleship. By it he was empowered to do God's work.

## Saul Finds Safety

9:23 When many days were fulfilled, the Jews conspired together to kill him, 9:24 but their plot became known to Saul. They watched the gates both day and night that they might kill him, 9:25 but his disciples took him by night,[1] and let him down through the wall, lowering him in a basket.

1. *But his disciples took him by night.* Nonresistance is the most effective method of obtaining safety. The disciples of Saul took him by night and let him down through the wall in a basket, which represents withdrawal of the will from its combative attitude. Saul's escape to Jerusalem (peace) carries out the idea of spiritual harmony which should be the ideal of every Christian.

## Saul in Jerusalem

9:26 When Saul had come to Jerusalem, he tried to join himself to the disciples; but they were all afraid of him, not believing that he was a disciple. 9:27 But Barnabas took him, and brought him to the apostles, and declared to them how he had seen the Lord in the way, and that he had spoken to him, and how at Damascus he had preached boldly in the name of Jesus. 9:28 He was with them entering into[34] Jerusalem, 9:29 preaching boldly in the name of the Lord. He spoke and disputed against the Hellenists,[35][1] but they were seeking to kill him. 9:30 When the brothers[36] knew it, they brought him down to Caesarea, and sent him off to Tarsus.[2] 9:31 So the assemblies throughout all Judea and Galilee and Samaria had peace, and were built up. They were multiplied, walking in the fear of the Lord and in the comfort of the Holy Spirit.

1. *He spoke and disputed against the Hellenists.* We see in Saul, or Paul, the religious zealot, with marked ability, energy, and spirituality, having the qualities necessary to success in teaching and preaching the Gospel of Jesus Christ, yet lacking one thing necessary to its full-rounded exposition—love. Paul saw love as the greatest asset of a Christian, but a close study of his life shows that he did not use it to overcome his enemies.

2. *And sent him off to Tarsus.* Metaphysically, Tarsus is a group of thoughts in man's consciousness of an intellectual character and bordering on, becoming blended with, the more deeply inspirational phase of understanding that we recognize as being spiritual (MBD/Tarsus).

## The Healing of Aeneas

9:32 It happened, as Peter went throughout all those parts, he came down also to the saints who lived at Lydda. 9:33 There he found a certain man named Aeneas,[1] who had been bedridden for eight years, because he was paralyzed. 9:34 Peter said to him, "Aeneas, Jesus Christ heals you. Get up and make your bed!" Immediately he arose. 9:35 All who lived at Lydda and in Sharon saw him, and they turned to the Lord.

1. *Aeneas* That which is praiseworthy arises—full of thankfulness and gratitude, no longer bound by cross currents of criticism, faultfinding and weakness—and in the name of Jesus Christ proclaims life and health and freedom; all strife is turned into constructive, spiritual activity; all desert places in consciousness receive the redeeming power of the living Word (MBD/Aeneas).

## Peter raises the I AM in Tabitha

9:36 Now there was at Joppa a certain disciple named Tabitha,[1] which when translated, means Dorcas.[37] This woman was full of good works and acts of mercy which she did. 9:37 It happened in those days that she fell sick, and died. When they had washed her, they laid her in an upper chamber. 9:38 As Lydda was near Joppa, the disciples, hearing that Peter was there, sent two men[38] to him, imploring him not to delay in coming to them. 9:39 Peter got up and went with them. When he had come, they brought him into the upper chamber. All the widows stood by him weeping, and showing the coats and garments which Dorcas had made while she was with them. 9:40 Peter put them all out, and kneeled down and prayed. Turning to the body, he said, "Tabitha, get up!"[2] She opened her eyes, and when she saw Peter, she sat up. 9:41 He gave her his hand, and raised her up. Calling the saints and widows, he presented her alive. 9:42 And it became known throughout all Joppa, and many believed in the Lord. 9:43 It happened, that he stayed many days in Joppa with one Simon, a tanner.

1. *Tabitha.* Tabitha symbolizes a graceful, feminine force that has failed to appreciate that good works such as caring for the needy, ministering to the sick, and clothing the naked do not fulfill the law of love. This power is active in doing good in its limited consciousness, but it gradually fades away. One may use his substance and power in doing good according

to worldly standards, yet starve the soul.
2. *Tabitha, get up!* The I AM in Tabitha responded to his command. Her body responded to the direction of the I AM in her.

---

Fillmore Study Bible annotations by Thomas Scheinler and Mark Hicks

**World English Bible Footnotes:**

[31] v9:5. TR adds "It's hard for you to kick against the goads."

[32] v9:6. TR omits "But"

[33] v9:11. or, Judas

[34] v9:28. TR and NU add "and going out"

[35] v9:29. The Hellenists were Hebrews who used Greek language and culture.

[36] v9:30. The word for "brothers" here and where the context allows may also be correctly translated "brothers and sisters" or "siblings."

[37] v9:36. "Dorcas" is Greek for "Gazelle."

[38] v9:38. Reading from NU, TR; MT omits "two men"

# Acts 10

## Peter and Cornelius

10:1 Now there was a certain man in Caesarea, Cornelius by name, a centurion of what was called the Italian Regiment, 10:2 a devout man, and one who feared God with all his house, who gave gifts for the needy generously to the people, and always prayed to God. 10:3 At about the ninth hour of the day[39], he clearly saw in a vision an angel of God coming to him, and saying to him, "Cornelius!"

10:4 He, fastening his eyes on him, and being frightened, said, "What is it, Lord?"

He said to him, "Your prayers and your gifts to the needy have gone up for a memorial before God. 10:5 Now send men to Joppa, and get Simon, who is surnamed Peter. 10:6 He lodges with one Simon, a tanner, whose house is by the seaside.[40]"

10:7 When the angel who spoke to him had departed, Cornelius called two of his household servants and a devout soldier of those who waited on him continually. 10:8 Having explained everything to them, he sent them to Joppa. 10:9 Now on the next day as they were on their journey, and got close to the city, Peter went up on the housetop to pray at about noon. 10:10 He became hungry and desired to eat, but while they were preparing, he fell into a trance. 10:11 He saw heaven opened and a certain container descending to him, like a great sheet let down by four corners on the earth, 10:12 in which were all kinds of four-footed animals of the earth, wild animals, reptiles, and birds of the sky. 10:13 A voice came to him, "Rise, Peter, kill and eat!"

10:14 But Peter said, "Not so, Lord; for I have never eaten anything that is common or unclean."

10:15 A voice came to him again the second time, "What God has cleansed, you must not call unclean."② 10:16 This was done three times, and immediately the vessel was received up into heaven. 10:17 Now while Peter was very perplexed in himself what the vision which he had seen might mean, behold, the men who were sent by Cornelius, having made inquiry for Simon's house, stood before the gate, 10:18 and called and asked whether Simon, who was surnamed Peter, was lodging there. 10:19 While Peter was pondering the vision, the Spirit said to him, "Behold, three[41] men seek you. 10:20 But arise, get down, and go with them, doubting nothing; for I have sent them."

10:21 Peter went down to the men, and said, "Behold, I am he whom you seek. Why have you come?"

10:22 They said, "Cornelius, a centurion, a righteous man③ and one who fears God, and well spoken of by all the nation of the Jews, was directed by a holy angel to invite you to his house, and to listen to what you say." 10:23 So he called them in and lodged them. On the next day Peter arose and went out with them, and some of the brothers from Joppa accompanied him. 10:24 On the next day they entered into Caesarea. Cornelius was waiting for them, having called together his relatives and his near friends. 10:25 When it happened that Peter entered, Cornelius met him, fell down at his feet, and worshiped him. 10:26 But Peter raised him up, saying, "Stand up! I myself am also a man." 10:27 As he talked with him, he went in and found many gathered together. 10:28 He said to them, "You yourselves know how it is an unlawful thing for a man who is a Jew to join himself or come to one of another nation, but God has shown me that I shouldn't call any man unholy or unclean.④ 10:29 Therefore also I came without complaint when I was sent for. I ask therefore, why did you send for me?"

10:30 Cornelius said, "Four days ago, I was fasting until this hour, and at the ninth hour,[42] I prayed in my house, and behold, a man stood before me in bright clothing, 10:31 and said, 'Cornelius, your prayer is heard, and your gifts to the needy are remembered in the sight of God. 10:32 Send therefore to Joppa, and summon Simon, who is surnamed Peter. He lodges in the house of Simon a tanner, by the seaside. When he comes, he will speak to you.' 10:33 Therefore I sent to you at once, and it was good of you to come. Now therefore we are all here present in the sight of God to hear all things that have been commanded you by God."

1. *Peter and Cornelius* Peter represents man's inner spiritual vision, and Cornelius represents the outer illumination. Both of them are brought together in Christ. Peter was shown by his vision that God had cleansed Cornelius, who had been earnestly seeking Truth; therefore Cornelius should no longer be called common or unclean.

2. *What God has cleansed, you must not call unclean.* Many people construe Peter's vision to be a lesson pertaining to food, and especially indicating that all animals were made for human consumption. There is no truth in this. Peter's vision pertains to the truth that people of all nations, all races, have one origin, God. God is the Father of all, and all have the same access to Him and to His good.

3. *Cornelius ... a righteous man.* Cornelius represents pride of rank and position. Cornelius however was a devout believer in God and was given to prayer. This spiritual exercise neutralized worldly pride. Cornelius was waiting for Peter, having called together his kinsman and his near friends to hear the message with him.

4. *God has shown me that I shouldn't call any man unholy or unclean.* Tolerance has never been mastered by the race as a whole. Lacking tolerance, nations set themselves up as superior to other nations, racial intolerance still exists, and even certain persons in the same nation or society feel superiority to their fellow men. Real progress in civilization awaits the dawn of a new era in tolerance.

## Gentiles Hear the Good News

10:34 Peter opened his mouth and said, "Truly I perceive that God doesn't show favoritism;[1] 10:35 but in every nation he who fears him and works righteousness is acceptable to him. 10:36 The word which he sent to the children of Israel, preaching good news of peace[2] by Jesus Christ--he is Lord of all-- 10:37 that spoken word you yourselves know, which was proclaimed throughout all Judea, beginning from Galilee, after the baptism which John preached; 10:38 even Jesus of Nazareth, how God anointed him with the Holy Spirit and with power, who went about doing good and healing all who were oppressed by the devil, for God was with him. 10:39 We are witnesses of everything he did both in the country of the Jews, and in Jerusalem; whom they also[43] killed, hanging him on a tree. 10:40 God raised him up the third day, and gave him to be revealed, 10:41 not to all the people, but to witnesses who were chosen before by God,[3] to us, who ate and drank with him after he rose from the dead. 10:42 He commanded us to preach to the people and to testify that this is he who is appointed by God as the Judge of the living and the dead. 10:43 All the prophets testify about him, that through his name everyone who believes in him will receive remission of sins."[4]

1. *God doesn't show favoritism.* Peter was a Jew and had been taught that the Jews were the elect of God, his favorite children, his chosen people. Now Peter received a new revelation and perceived that all offspring of God had the same opportunities—that the God attributes were given in equal measure to all alike.

2. *Preaching good news of peace.* That God is the one God, and that all men are brothers, because all are children of the one God.

3. *Not to all the people, but to witnesses who were chosen before by God.* The resurrected body of Jesus was functioning on a higher plane of vibration than that on which the bodies of other people were functioning at that time; it is probable that he could not be seen by those who were not illumined.

4. *Through his name everyone who believes in him will receive remission of sins.* Jesus' followers were conscious of making immediate contact with the spirituality of Jesus, and their faith was so stimulated that they had the absolute assurance that they could do miracles by proclaiming Jesus Christ as their coworker. His name and his power are still operative and marvelous things are being done in his name.

## Gentiles Receive the Holy Spirit

10:44 While Peter was still speaking these words, the Holy Spirit fell on all those who heard the word.[1] 10:45 They of the circumcision who believed were amazed, as many as came with Peter, because the gift of the Holy Spirit was also poured out on the Gentiles.[2] 10:46 For they heard them speaking in other languages and magnifying God.

Then Peter answered, 10:47 "Can any man forbid the water, that these who have received the Holy Spirit as well as we should not be baptized?" 10:48 He commanded them to be baptized in the name of Jesus Christ. Then they asked him to stay some days.

1. *The Holy Spirit fell on all those who heard the word.* The tongue of tolerance, of justice and mercy, of kindliness and understanding, of compassion and helpfulness, of praise and thanksgiving is the tongue that expresses the Holy Spirit.

2. *The Holy Spirit was also poured out on the Gentiles.* Unity of spirit will do this. "He made of one every nation of men to dwell on all the face of the earth."

---

Fillmore Study Bible annotations by Thomas Scheinler and Mark Hicks

**World English Bible Footnotes:**

[39] v10:3. 3:00 PM

[40] v10:6. TR adds "This one will tell you what it is necessary for you to do."

[41] v10:19. Reading from TR and NU. MT omits "three"

[42] v10:30. 3:00 P. M.

[43] v10:39. TR omits "also"

# Acts 11

## Peter Shares His Dream in Jerusalem

11:1 Now the apostles and the brothers[44] who were in Judea heard that the Gentiles had also received the word of God. 11:2 When Peter had come up to Jerusalem, those who were of the circumcision contended with him, 11:3 saying, "You went in to uncircumcised men, and ate with them!"

11:4 But Peter began, and explained to them in order, saying, 11:5 "I was in the city of Joppa praying, and in a trance I saw a vision:[1] a certain container descending, like it was a great sheet let down from heaven by four corners. It came as far as me. 11:6 When I had looked intently at it, I considered, and saw the four-footed animals of the earth, wild animals, creeping things, and birds of the sky. 11:7 I also heard a voice saying to me, 'Rise, Peter, kill and eat!'[2] 11:8 But I said, 'Not so, Lord, for nothing unholy or unclean has ever entered into my mouth.' 11:9 But a voice answered me the second time out of heaven, 'What God has cleansed, don't you call unclean.' 11:10 This was done three times, and all were drawn up again into heaven. 11:11 Behold, immediately three men stood before the house where I was, having been sent from Caesarea[3] to me. 11:12 The Spirit told me to go with them, without discriminating. These six brothers also accompanied me, and we entered into the man's house. 11:13 He told us how he had seen the angel standing in his house, and saying to him, 'Send to Joppa, and get Simon, whose surname is Peter, 11:14 who will speak to you words by which you will be saved, you and all your house.' 11:15 As I began to speak, the Holy Spirit fell on them, even as on us at the beginning. 11:16 I remembered the word of the Lord, how he said, 'John indeed baptized in water, but you will be baptized in the Holy Spirit.' 11:17 If then God gave to them the same gift as us, when we believed in the Lord Jesus Christ, who was I, that I could withstand God?"

11:18 When they heard these things, they held their peace, and glorified God, saying, "Then God has also granted to the Gentiles repentance to life!"[4]

1. *In a trance I saw a vision.* Dreams and visions fall into two classes. First (Peter's vision) are those which occur during sleep without conscious volition on man's part. These are subconscious visions of faith. Through faith man comes in contact with higher realms of thought than he is capable of reaching otherwise. In the second class (Cornelius' vision in Acts 10:4) falls conscious vision or the power to foresee and understand events and to enjoy an unusual degree of perceptive ability. Such are conscious visions of intellect.

2. *Rise, Peter, kill and eat!* A careful translation of the command, "kill and eat," is given in Ferrar Fenton's *Complete Bible in Modern English* as "sacrifice and eat." To sacrifice is to consecrate and dedicate to the superconscious mind all life as divine life. This is not a command to kill animals for food. Peter himself explains that he finally understood the vision to mean that he should accept the Gentiles as worthy of Holy Spirit baptism.

3. *three men ... from Caesarea.* Caesarea represents the intellect, and the three men the spirit, soul and body of man under the dominance of intellect.

4. *God has also granted to the Gentiles repentance to life!* This lesson assures that the unregenerate state of mind in us (the Gentiles), which includes worldly thoughts, thoughts pertaining to externals, or thoughts that function through the senses, can be regenerated and transformed by words of faith if we give ourselves wholeheartedly to the habit of thinking and speaking them exclusively.

## The Church in Antioch

11:19 They therefore who were scattered abroad by the oppression that arose about Stephen traveled as far as Phoenicia, Cyprus, and Antioch, speaking the word to no one except to Jews only. 11:20 But there were some of them, men of Cyprus and Cyrene, who, when they had come to Antioch, spoke to the Hellenists,[45] preaching the Lord Jesus. 11:21 The hand of the Lord was with them, and a great number believed and turned to the Lord.[1] 11:22 The report concerning them came to the ears of the assembly which was in Jerusalem. They sent out Barnabas to go as far as Antioch, 11:23 who, when he had come, and had seen the grace of God, was glad. He exhorted them all, that with purpose of heart they should remain near to the Lord. 11:24 For he was a good man, and full of the Holy Spirit and of faith, and many people were added to the Lord.

11:25 Barnabas went out to Tarsus to look for Saul.[2] 11:26 When he had found him, he brought him to Antioch. It happened, that for a whole year they were gathered together with the assembly, and taught many people. The disciples were first called Christians in Antioch.

[11:27] Now in these days, prophets came down from Jerusalem to Antioch. [11:28] One of them named Agabus stood up, and indicated by the Spirit that there should be a great famine all over the world,[3] which also happened in the days of Claudius. [11:29] As any of the disciples had plenty, each determined to send relief to the brothers who lived in Judea; [11:30] which they also did, sending it to the elders by the hands of Barnabas and Saul.

1. *The Hellenists ... believed and turned to the Lord.* The nonreligious (the Hellenists were nonreligious from the Jewish standpoint) gladly received the word of the Lord. The Jews symbolize our religious thoughts, the Hellenists our worldly thoughts. One normally connects the word of Truth with the religious rather than with the worldly in consciousness. However the intellect (represented in this lessson by the Hellenists) follows the religious nature (the Jews) in responding to the Spirit of truth.

2. *Barnabus, Paul.* Paul represents the will, and Barnabas, the understanding. They had both been baptized by the Lord and were ready for the ministry.

3. *Prophets ... from Jerusalem ... indicated by the Spirit that there should be a great famine all over the world* A great work has been accomplished by the disciples in converting both Jews and Gentiles. This work, in the outer sense, symbolizes rapid appropriation of life and substance, which, under the law of action and reaction, brings seeming depletion in the outer realms of consciousness.

---

Fillmore Study Bible annotations by Thomas Scheinler and Mark Hicks

**World English Bible Footnotes:**

[44] v11:1. The word for "brothers" here and where context allows may also be correctly translated "brothers and sisters" or "siblings."

[45] v11:20. A Hellenist is someone who keeps Greek customs and culture.

# Acts 12

## James Killed and Peter Imprisoned

[12:1] Now about that time, Herod[1] the king stretched out his hands to oppress some of the assembly. [12:2] He killed James, the brother of John, with the sword. [12:3] When he saw that it pleased the Jews, he proceeded to seize Peter also. This was during the days of unleavened bread. [12:4] When he had arrested him, he put him in prison, and delivered him to four squads of four soldiers each to guard him, intending to bring him out to the people after the Passover. [12:5] Peter therefore was kept in the prison,[2] but constant prayer was made by the assembly to God for him.

1. *Herod.* The ruling will of the physical man, the ego in the sense consciousness. By his manner of living the physical man reveals the basis of his face as wholly material.

2. *Peter therefore was kept in the prison*

The hold of materiality on man's faith is strong. In the grip of materiality man cannot realize his nature as a son of God or exercise the powers that are his by divine right. These he should be able to discern and use through faith. In the natural man faith is chained to material power and worldly prestige (two soldiers), and all its avenues of expression (prison doors) are closed and guarded against spiritual influences.

## Peter Delivered from Prison

12:6 The same night when Herod
was about to bring him out, Peter
was sleeping between two soldiers,
bound with two chains. Guards in
front of the door kept the prison.
12:7 And behold, an angel of the Lord
stood by him, and a light shone in
the cell. He struck Peter on the side,
and woke him up, saying, "Stand up
quickly!" His chains fell off from his
hands.❶ 12:8 The angel said to him,
"Get dressed and put on your
sandals." He did so. He said to him,
"Put on your cloak, and follow me."
12:9 And he went out and followed
him. He didn't know that what was
being done by the angel was real, but
thought he saw a vision. 12:10 When
they were past the first and the
second guard, they came to the iron
gate that leads into the city, which
opened to them by itself. They went
out, and went down one street, and
immediately the angel departed
from him.

12:11 When Peter had come to
himself, he said, "Now I truly know
that the Lord has sent out his angel
and delivered me out of the hand
of Herod, and from everything the
Jewish people were expecting." 12:12
Thinking about that, he came to the
house of Mary,❷ the mother of John
whose surname was Mark, where
many were gathered together and
were praying. 12:13 When Peter
knocked at the door of the gate, a
maid named Rhoda came to answer.
12:14 When she recognized Peter's
voice, she didn't open the gate for
joy, but ran in, and reported that
Peter was standing in front of the
gate.

12:15 They said to her, "You are
crazy!" But she insisted that it was
so. They said, "It is his angel." 12:16
But Peter continued knocking. When
they had opened, they saw him, and
were amazed. 12:17 But he, beckoning
to them with his hand to be silent,
declared to them how the Lord had
brought him out of the prison. He
said, "Tell these things to James, and
to the brothers."❸ Then he departed,
and went to another place.

12:18 Now as soon as it was day,
there was no small stir among the
soldiers about what had become of
Peter. 12:19 When Herod had sought
for him, and didn't find him, he
examined the guards, and
commanded that they should be put
to death. He went down from Judea
to Caesarea, and stayed there.

1. *His chains fell off from his hands.* The release of Peter from prison by an angel comes under the head of the supernatural. The church classes it with the miracles. Sound reason would find a lawful cause for the incident and take away superstition on the one hand and skepticism on the other. Man sets into action any of the three realms of his being, spirit, soul, and body, by concentrating his thought upon them. If he thinks only of the body, the physical senses encompass all of his existence. If mind and emotion are cultivated he adds soul to his consciousness. If he rises to the Absolute and comprehends Spirit, he rounds out the God-man.

2. *He came to the house of Mary.* When Peter is set at liberty, his first act is to go to the house of Mary and make known to them the wondrous works of the Lord.

Greater faith, a more enduring strength, and an indescribable awe, tempered with a deep reverence for the things of spirit, spread throughout the consciousness, which tend to make more secure that unalterable foundation, the rock upon which the church is founded.

3. *Tell these things to James, and to the brothers*. There is new enlightenment and clear power of discernment in all the other faculties when faith is set free from material bondage. Peter instructed his fellow Christians to "tell these things to James [judgment], and to the brothers [twelve powers of man]."

## The Death of Herod

12:20 Now Herod was very angry
with the people of Tyre and Sidon.
They came with one accord to him,
and, having made Blastus,❶ the
king's personal aide, their friend,
they asked for peace, because their
country depended on the king's
country for food. 12:21 On an
appointed day, Herod dressed
himself in royal clothing, sat on the
throne, and gave a speech to them.
12:22 The people shouted, "The voice
of a god, and not of a man!" 12:23
Immediately an angel of the Lord
struck him, because he didn't give
God the glory, and he was eaten by
worms and died.

12:24 But the word of God grew and
multiplied. 12:25 Barnabas and Saul
returned to[46] Jerusalem, when they
had fulfilled their service, also taking
with them John whose surname was
Mark.

1. *Blastus*. A chamberlain of King Herod Agrippa's. He was a friend to "them of Tyre and Sidon". Sense man's belief that the mortal will, or the ruling ego of the sense man (Herod), causes life and its awakening ideas of good to germinate and to come to fruition in consciousness (shoot, sprout, that buds). This belief brings forth no fruit (Blastus was a eunuch) because it is a false one. God (unformed Spirit) alone is the origin of all life, understanding, growth, unfoldment. and attainment of good. The human will cannot attempt to put itself in the place of God without bringing about disastrous results (MBD/Blastus).

---

Fillmore Study Bible annotations by Thomas Scheinler and Mark Hicks

**World English Bible Footnotes:**

[46] v12:25. TR reads "from" instead of "to"

# Acts 13

## Barnabas and Saul Commissioned

13:1 Now in the assembly that was
at Antioch❶ there were some
prophets and teachers: Barnabas,
Simeon who was called Niger, Lucius
of Cyrene, Manaen the foster brother
of Herod the tetrarch, and Saul.❷ 13:2
As they served the Lord and fasted,
the Holy Spirit said, "Separate

Barnabas and Saul for me,[3] they sent them away. for the work to which I have called them." 13:3 Then, when they had fasted and prayed and laid their hands on them,[4] they sent them away.

1. *the assembly that was at Antioch.* The church that was established at Antioch symbolizes and assembling of spiritual thoughts. The church at Antioch represents the first establishment of the Christ consciousness in man.

2. *Barnabas, Simeon, Lucius, of Cyrene, Manaen and Saul.* Five interpreters of Spirit to the outer or sense consciousness. Barnabas signifies "son of consolation." His original name was Joseph, which represents the imagination. Renamed Barnabas by the disciples, he still represents the imagination, but now it is brought into expression through association with the word of Truth (Paul). Symeon, who was called Niger, represents hearing or expectation; Lucius ("light") represents understanding; Manaen ("comforter," "consoler") represents the activity of the Holy Spirit in individual consciousness in its role of comforter or consoler. Saul ("demanded," "asked for") represents the action of the will entertaining that which it desires, in this case through the spoken word. Barnabas and Saul were chosen for missionary work among the Gentiles because of their superior qualifications for the task, mainly their firm faith, loyalty, courage, and resourcefulness, as well as their zeal for Truth. The will and imagination illumined by the Christ turn all the thoughts toward Truth.

3. *Separate Barnabas and Saul for me.* [This is the start of Paul's first missionary journey.]

4. *when they had fasted and prayed and laid their hands on them.* Metaphysically interpreted, fasting means the denial of all thoughts that limit the growth of the soul to material sources. Prayer is the affirmation of the reality of spiritual things. The laying on of hands represents the impartation of the power of the word, and sending them away is the freedom that we give our thoughts in the unlimited realms of the absolute.

## Saul and Barnabas Encounter a Sorcerer

13:4 So, being sent out by the Holy Spirit, they went down to Seleucia.[1] From there they sailed to Cyprus. 13:5 When they were at Salamis, they proclaimed the word of God in the Jewish synagogues. They had also John as their attendant.[2] 13:6 When they had gone through the island to Paphos, they found a certain sorcerer[3], a false prophet, a Jew, whose name was Bar Jesus, 13:7 who was with the proconsul, Sergius Paulus, a man of understanding.[4] This man summoned Barnabas and Saul, and sought to hear the word of God. 13:8 But Elymas the sorcerer (for so is his name by interpretation) withstood them, seeking to turn aside the proconsul from the faith. 13:9 But Saul, who is also called Paul, filled with the Holy Spirit, fastened his eyes on him, 13:10 and said, "Full of all deceit and all cunning, you son of the devil, you enemy of all righteousness, will you not cease to pervert the right ways of the Lord? 13:11 Now, behold, the hand of the Lord is on you, and you will be blind, not seeing the sun for a season!"

Immediately a mist and darkness fell on him. He went around seeking someone to lead him by the hand. 13:12 Then the proconsul, when he saw what was done, believed, being astonished at the teaching of the Lord.

1. *they went down to Seleucia.* The two disciples passed through Seleucia without lingering there because Seleucia means "beaten by waves," "troubled." The will and inspired imagination or understanding do not allow the mind to remain in a troubled state but pass on at once to a fair, unbiased state of mind (Cyprus means "fairness").

2. *they proclaimed the word of God in the Jewish synagogues. They had also John as their attendant.*The synagogues of the Jews represent aggressions of religious

thoughts based upon Truth, thoughts that have not yet received the inspiration of the Holy Spirit; that is, the whole truth. The presence of John as an attendant represents that this inspiration was accomplished through love.

3. *sorcerer*. Elymas is magician, corrupter. He represents the mortal thought which tries to counterfeit the working of the Spirit. When the mind resists the Truth mental resistance closes the doors and windows of the mind, and shuts out the light of Spirit. Then the darkness of ignorance pervades the consciousness; and there is dependence on external leadings.

4. *Sergius Paulus, a man of understanding*. When the personal consciousness is rendered inoperative the reasoning faculty (the proconsul), observing the effect of Spirit, perceives the power of the Higher Self (the Lord), accepts Truth, and becomes a willing disciple.

## Paul and Barnabas in Antioch of Pisidia

13:13 Now Paul and his company set sail from Paphos, and came to Perga in Pamphylia. John departed from them and returned to Jerusalem. 13:14 But they, passing on from Perga, came to Antioch of Pisidia.① They went into the synagogue on the Sabbath day, and sat down. 13:15 After the reading of the law and the prophets, the rulers of the synagogue sent to them, saying, "Brothers, if you have any word of exhortation for the people, speak."

13:16 Paul stood up, and beckoning with his hand said, "Men of Israel, and you who fear God, listen.② 13:17 The God of this people[47] chose our fathers, and exalted the people when they stayed as aliens in the land of Egypt, and with an uplifted arm, he led them out of it. 13:18 For a period of about forty years he put up with them in the wilderness. 13:19 When he had destroyed seven nations in the land of Canaan, he gave them their land for an inheritance, for about four hundred fifty years. 13:20 After these things he gave them judges until Samuel the prophet. 13:21 Afterward they asked for a king, and God gave to them Saul the son of Kish, a man of the tribe of Benjamin, for forty years. 13:22 When he had removed him, he raised up David to be their king, to whom he also testified, 'I have found David the son of Jesse, a man after my heart, who will do all my will.' 13:23 From this man's seed, God has brought salvation[48] to Israel according to his promise, 13:24 before his coming, when John had first preached the baptism of repentance to Israel.[49]③ 13:25 As John was fulfilling his course, he said, 'What do you suppose that I am? I am not he. But behold, one comes after me the sandals of whose feet I am not worthy to untie.' 13:26 Brothers, children of the stock of Abraham, and those among you who fear God, the word of this salvation is sent out to you. 13:27 For those who dwell in Jerusalem, and their rulers,④ because they didn't know him, nor the voices of the prophets which are read every Sabbath, fulfilled them by condemning him. 13:28 Though they found no cause for death, they still asked Pilate to have him killed. 13:29 When they had fulfilled all things that were written about him, they took him down from the tree, and laid him in a tomb. 13:30 But God raised him from the dead, 13:31 and he was seen for many days by those who came up with him from Galilee to Jerusalem, who are his witnesses to the people. 13:32 We bring you good news of the promise made to the fathers, 13:33 that God has fulfilled the same to us, their children, in that he raised up Jesus. As it is also written in the second psalm,

'You are my Son.
Today I have become your

father.'[50]

13:34 "Concerning that he raised him up from the dead, now no more to return to corruption, he has spoken thus: 'I will give you the holy and sure blessings of David.'[51] 13:35 Therefore he says also in another psalm, 'You will not allow your Holy One to see decay.'[52] 13:36 For David, after he had in his own generation served the counsel of God, fell asleep, and was laid with his fathers, and saw decay. 13:37 But he whom God raised up saw no decay. 13:38 Be it known to you therefore, brothers[53], that through this man is proclaimed to you remission of sins, 13:39 and by him everyone who believes is justified from all things,[5] from which you could not be justified by the law of Moses. 13:40 Beware therefore, lest that come on you which is spoken in the prophets:

13:41 'Behold, you scoffers, and
wonder, and perish;
for I work a work in your days,
a work which you will in no
way believe, if one
declares it to you.'"[54]

13:42 So when the Jews went out of the synagogue, the Gentiles begged that these words might be preached to them the next Sabbath. 13:43 Now when the synagogue broke up, many of the Jews and of the devout proselytes followed Paul and Barnabas; who, speaking to them, urged them to continue in the grace of God. 13:44 The next Sabbath almost the whole city was gathered together to hear the word of God. 13:45 But when the Jews saw the multitudes, they were filled with jealousy, and contradicted the things which were spoken by Paul,[6] and blasphemed.

13:46 Paul and Barnabas spoke out boldly, and said, "It was necessary that God's word should be spoken to you first. Since indeed you thrust it from you, and judge yourselves unworthy of eternal life, behold, we turn to the Gentiles. 13:47 For so has the Lord commanded us, saying,

'I have set you as a light for the
Gentiles,[7]
that you should bring salvation
to the uttermost parts
of the earth.'"[55]

13:48 As the Gentiles heard this, they were glad, and glorified the word of God. As many as were appointed to eternal life believed. 13:49 The Lord's word was spread abroad throughout all the region. 13:50 But the Jews stirred up the devout and prominent women and the chief men of the city, and stirred up a persecution against Paul and Barnabas, and threw them out of their borders. 13:51 But they shook off the dust of their feet against them,[8] and came to Iconium. 13:52 The disciples were filled with joy with the Holy Spirit.

1. *Antioch of Pisidia.* Another city named Antioch. Metaphysically, Antioch means "formulated theology." This state of mind in us must be Christianized thoroughly. Our ideas of God and of man's relation to him must undergo a great change before we can begin uplifting and unifying the whole man - spirit, soul, and body - in life. In Acts 14:8-20 the formulated theology that Antioch represents takes on a spirit of antagonism and opposition (MBD/Antioch).

2. *Men of Israel, and you who fear God, listen.* The sermon was delivered and Antioch (withstanding, lasting) of Pisidia (pitchy, clinging, tenacious), a province in Asia (a state of consciousness impregnated by old, material, outworn ideas which must be discarded by the one who would progress spiritually).

3. *when John had first preached the baptism of repentance to Israel.* John baptized his followers, and his baptism represents denial. Baptism symbolizes the getting rid of the limited thoughts that encumber and darken the understanding, in preparation for the entering of the Christ light.

4. *those who dwell in Jerusalem, and*

*their rulers.* The religious life of man, especially the formal beliefs that a man holds in order to be in conformity with the ideas of others in his class, are represented by the phrase "those who dwell in Jerusalem, and their rulers." When a man's faith is bound up in the husks of formalism and he has no understanding of the indwelling Christ and its power, he fulfills the law negatively, and the result is adversity and suffering for him.

5. *everyone who believes is justified from all things.* When faith in the indwelling Christ is claimed and called into active expression, it enables man to overcome all the adversaries that might otherwise wear down his resistance and conquer him.

6. *they were filled with jealousy, and contradicted the things which were spoken by Paul.* The Jews represent traditional beliefs and opinions based on the authority of custom. This state of mind is opposed to all innovation and resists all change.

7. *light of the Gentiles.* The understanding that man's whole nature - spirit, soul, and body—is subject to the action of Divine Mind, and can be lifted up and transformed into the image of perfection by its power.

8. *they shook off the dust of their feet against them.* Shaking the dust off one's feet means the denying of material and mental beliefs and the affirming of the image-and-likeness-of-God consciousness, which brings one to Iconium (I-AM-age).

Fillmore Study Bible annotations by Mark Hicks

**World English Bible Footnotes:**

[47] v13:17. TR, NU add "Israel"

[48] v13:23. TR, NU read "a Savior, Jesus" instead of "salvation"

[49] v13:24. TR, NU read "to all the people of Israel" instead of "to Israel"

[50] v13:33. Psalm 2:7

[51] v13:34. Isaiah 55:3

[52] v13:35. Psalm 16:10

[53] v13:38. The word for "brothers" here and where the context allows may also be correctly translated "brothers and sisters" or "siblings."

[54] v13:41. Habakkuk 1:5

[55] v13:47. Isaiah 49:6

# Acts 14

## Paul and Barnabas in Iconium

14:1 It happened in Iconium❶ that they entered together into the synagogue of the Jews, and so spoke that a great multitude both of Jews and of Greeks believed. 14:2 But the disbelieving[56] Jews stirred up and embittered the souls of the Gentiles against the brothers.❷ 14:3 Therefore they stayed there a long time, speaking boldly in the Lord, who testified to the word of his grace, granting signs and wonders to be done by their hands. 14:4 But the multitude of the city was divided. Part sided with the Jews, and part with the apostles. 14:5 When some of both the Gentiles and the Jews, with their rulers, made a violent attempt to mistreat and stone them, 14:6 they became aware of it, and fled to the cities of Lycaonia, Lystra, Derbe,[3] and the surrounding region. 14:7 There they preached the Good News.

1. *Iconium.* The name Iconium means "imagelike," "yielding." It signifies a group of thoughts of an imaging and receptive character, tending to negativeness in the emotional nature. It is susceptible to both good and error.

2. *Jews stirred up and embittered the souls of the Gentiles against the brothers.* Man's formal religious thoughts and convictions (Jews) influence his worldly or secular thoughts (Gentiles), and make them inimical to the Christ ideal ("the brethren").

3. *Lycaonia, Lystra, Derbe.* These towns represent various phases of the realm of feeling in man. Lystra represents the emotional nature swayed by the undisciplined, devouring, unredeemed thoughts of the animal man.

## Paul and Barnabas in Lystra and Derbe

14:8 At Lystra[1] a certain man sat, impotent in his feet,[2] a cripple from his mother's womb, who never had walked. 14:9 He was listening to Paul speaking, who, fastening eyes on him, and seeing that he had faith to be made whole, 14:10 said with a loud voice, "Stand upright on your feet!"[3] He leaped up and walked. 14:11 When the multitude saw what Paul had done, they lifted up their voice, saying in the language of Lycaonia, "The gods have come down to us in the likeness of men!"[4] 14:12 They called Barnabas "Jupiter," and Paul "Mercury," because he was the chief speaker. 14:13 The priest of Jupiter, whose temple was in front of their city, brought oxen and garlands to the gates, and would have made a sacrifice along with the multitudes. 14:14 But when the apostles, Barnabas and Paul, heard of it, they tore their clothes, and sprang into the multitude, crying out, 14:15 "Men, why are you doing these things?[5] We also are men of like passions with you, and bring you good news, that you should turn from these vain things to the living God, who made the sky and the earth and the sea, and all that is in them; 14:16 who in the generations gone by allowed all the nations to walk in their own ways. 14:17 Yet he didn't leave himself without witness, in that he did good and gave you[57] rains from the sky and fruitful seasons, filling our hearts with food and gladness."

14:18 Even saying these things, they hardly stopped the multitudes from making a sacrifice to them. 14:19 But some Jews from Antioch and Iconium came there, and having persuaded the multitudes, they stoned Paul, and dragged him out of the city,[6] supposing that he was dead. 14:20 But as the disciples stood around him, he rose up, and entered into the city. On the next day he went out with Barnabas to Derbe.

1. *At Lystra* Lycaonia means "wolfland," and represents the wild, uncultured, emotional, passionate, animal nature in man. The like Lycaonians were nature worshipers. They assigned gods to almost all natural objects - earth, air, wood, water - and men who exhibited superior ability were supposed to be incarnations of these gods. When we allow our emotions and passions to dominate us we are swayed by emotions and passions and give way to the surface activity of the soul, we lose poise and detach ourselves from the quiet,

peaceful inflow of Spirit.

2. *impotent in his feet.* The feet are those members of the body which contact the earth. They are also that upon which we stand; metaphysically, the feet represent our understanding of earthly things, that is the feet express the relation which the consciousness bears to substance.

3. *Stand upright on your feet!* The essential for healing in such cases is that the patient shall have faith that he can be made whole. If he has faith, then the word of Truth, expressed through the will (represented by Paul), gives the audible treatment spoken by Paul.

4. *The gods have come down to us in the likeness of men!* The "multitude" saying in the speech of Lycaonia means that all the undisciplined, unredeemed, and unconverted thoughts of the consciousness believed that something had been accomplished outside of natural law, and desired to make gods of the personalities through which the work was done. The deification of one person by another is the expression of the emotional, animal mentality. When this emotional nature is released from the subconscious it is likely to pour out a flood of praise and adoration one moment and a whirlwind of censure the next.

5. *Men, why are you doing these things?* In some schools of metaphysics the emotional and passionate nature is classified as the animal soul. When we feel the surge of this emotional and passionate enthusiasm, what discipline should we give it? [Rather than deifying others,] we should raise the natural man to the throne of dominion and realize that the emotional and passionate nature must be restrained and disciplined by the superconscious or Christ mind.

6. *they stoned Paul, and dragged him out of the city.* In ministering spiritually a worker must keep in mind the one Presence and the one Power, otherwise while engaged in the work of dissolving adverse thoughts and conditions he arouses antagonism and meets with opposition. Opposition comes from the personal consciousness and cannot be successfully overcome by counteropposition. It must be met by spiritual means.

## The Return to Antioch

14:21 When they had preached the Good News to that city, and had made many disciples, they returned to Lystra, Iconium, and Antioch, 14:22 confirming the souls of the disciples, exhorting them to continue in the faith, and that through many afflictions we must enter into the Kingdom of God. 14:23 When they had appointed elders for them in every assembly, and had prayed with fasting, they commended them to the Lord, on whom they had believed.

14:24 They passed through Pisidia, and came to Pamphylia. 14:25 When they had spoken the word in Perga, they went down to Attalia. 14:26 From there they sailed to Antioch, from where they had been committed to the grace of God[1] for the work which they had fulfilled. 14:27 When they had arrived, and had gathered the assembly together, they reported all the things that God had done with them,[2] and that he had opened a door of faith to the nations. 14:28 They stayed there with the disciples for a long time.

1. *the grace of God.* [This is the conclusion of Paul's first missionary journey.] The grace of God signifies the constructive power of divine love that infolds those to whom it is committed and that prospers all labors that are undertaken in the spirit of impersonal benevolence and co-operative goodwill.

2. *they reported all the things that God had done with them.* As the work of God their work contained nothing of personality.

---

Fillmore Study Bible annotations by Mark Hicks

**World English Bible Footnotes:**

[56] v14:2. or, disobedient

[57] v14:17. TR reads "us" instead of "you"

# Acts 15

## The Council of Apostles and Elders in Jerusalem

15:1 Some men came down from Judea and taught the brothers, "Unless you are circumcised❶ after the custom of Moses, you can't be saved." 15:2 Therefore when Paul and Barnabas had no small discord and discussion with them, they appointed Paul and Barnabas, and some others of them, to go up to Jerusalem to the apostles and elders about this question. 15:3 They, being sent on their way by the assembly, passed through both Phoenicia and Samaria, declaring the conversion of the Gentiles. They caused great joy to all the brothers.[58] 15:4 When they had come to Jerusalem, they were received by the assembly and the apostles and the elders, and they reported all things that God had done with them.

15:5 But some of the sect of the Pharisees who believed rose up, saying, "It is necessary to circumcise them, and to command them to keep the law of Moses."❷

15:6 The apostles and the elders were gathered together to see about this matter.❸ 15:7 When there had been much discussion, Peter rose up and said to them, "Brothers, you know that a good while ago God made a choice among you, that by my mouth the nations should hear the word of the Good News, and believe. 15:8 God, who knows the heart, testified about them, giving them the Holy Spirit, just like he did to us. 15:9 He made no distinction between us and them, cleansing their hearts by faith.❹ 15:10 Now therefore why do you tempt God, that you should put a yoke on the neck of the disciples which neither our fathers nor we were able to bear? 15:11 But we believe that we are saved through the grace of the Lord Jesus,[59] just as they are."

15:12 All the multitude kept silence, and they listened to Barnabas and Paul reporting what signs and wonders God had done among the nations through them. 15:13 After they were silent, James answered, "Brothers, listen to me. 15:14 Simeon has reported how God first visited the nations, to take out of them a people for his name. 15:15 This agrees with the words of the prophets. As it is written,

15:16 'After these things I will return.<br>
I will again build the tent of David, which has fallen.<br>
I will again build its ruins.<br>
I will set it up,<br>
15:17 That the rest of men may seek after the Lord;<br>
All the Gentiles who are called by my name,<br>
Says the Lord, who does all these things.[60]<br>
15:18 All his works are known to God from eternity.'

15:19 "Therefore my judgment is that we don't trouble those from among the Gentiles who turn to God,

15:20 but that we write to them that they abstain from the pollution of idols, from sexual immorality, from what is strangled, and from blood. 15:21 For Moses from generations of old has in every city those who preach him, being read in the synagogues every Sabbath."

1. *Unless you are circumcised.* Circumcision is symbolical of the cutting off of mortal tendencies, and is indicative of purification and cleanliness. Under the law of Jesus Christ, circumcision is fulfilled in its spiritual meaning—the purification of the individual from the law of sin and death. One is circumcised in the true inner significance of the word only by being thoroughly purified in soul. Then the glory of the inner soul cleansing and purifying works out into the outer consciousness and the body and sets one free from all sensual, corruptible thoughts and activities. Thus man becomes a new creature in Christ Jesus, he manifests wholeness and perfection throughout his being (MBD/circumcision).

2. *It is necessary to circumcise them, and to command them to keep the law of Moses.* The bonds of custom and tradition are often very difficult to break, for inbred religious convictions take deeper root in the soul than almost anything else. Religious rites and customs are of spiritual value only to the extent that we perceive and are inspired by their inner spiritual meaning. Observing them merely from a sense of duty does not help us to grow spiritually.

3. *The apostles and the elders were gathered together to see about this matter.* Apostles and elders represent the individual's developed faculties after they have been brought under the control of the higher self and made to function as an undivided whole. [This chapter resolves some conflicts that emerged from Paul's first missionary journey. It may represent our state of consciousness after our first study of Truth.]

4. *He made no distinction between us and them, cleansing their hearts by faith.* Faith appeals to the conviction of man (the heart). In fact faith and conviction are one and the same thing. He whose faith is in principles holds to them and sees ceremonies as unimportant. Baptism with water is a rite, but the baptism of the Holy Spirit is a flooding of the whole mind, heart and soul, with the presence and power of divine love, and with this, rites and ceremonies have nothing to do.

## Elders and Apostles Write to Gentile Believers

15:22 Then it seemed good to the apostles and the elders, with the whole assembly, to choose men out of their company, and send them to Antioch with Paul and Barnabas: Judas called Barsabbas, and Silas, chief men among the brothers.[61] 15:23 They wrote these things by their hand:

"The apostles, the elders, and the brothers, to the brothers who are of the Gentiles[1] in Antioch, Syria, and Cilicia: greetings. 15:24 Because we have heard that some who went out from us have troubled you with words,[2] unsettling your souls, saying, 'You must be circumcised and keep the law,' to whom we gave no commandment; 15:25 it seemed good to us, having come to one accord, to choose out men and send them to you with our beloved Barnabas and Paul, 15:26 men who have risked their lives for the name of our Lord Jesus Christ. 15:27 We have sent therefore Judas and Silas, who themselves will also tell you the same things by word of mouth. 15:28 For it seemed good to the Holy Spirit, and to us, to lay no greater burden on you than these necessary things: 15:29 that you abstain from things sacrificed to idols, from blood, from things strangled, and from sexual immorality,[3] from which if you keep yourselves, it will be well with you. Farewell."

15:30 So, when they were sent off, they came to Antioch. Having gathered the multitude together, they delivered the letter. 15:31 When they had read it, they rejoiced over

the encouragement. 15:32 Judas and
Silas,[4] also being prophets
themselves, encouraged the brothers
with many words, and strengthened
them. 15:33 After they had spent some
time there, they were sent back with
greetings from the brothers to the
apostles. 15:34 [62] 15:35 But Paul and
Barnabas stayed in Antioch, teaching
and preaching the word of the Lord,
with many others also.

1. *to the brothers who are of the Gentiles.* The early Christians were divided into two classes: the Christian Jews and the Gentile Christians, who accepted Jesus as their saviour, but refused to submit to the peculiar rites of Jewish life. In our individual consciousness a similar division is at first set up. The form of words in which a truth is stated seems of great importance to us, and we cannot understand how there can be so many statements in apparently diverse words, of exact principles. The Jewish thought is the intellectual perception, which is usually wedded to certain set ways of expressing Truth, and gives careful attention that the same idea be stated in exactly the same way every time. If allowed to dominate, this Jew forms a religious caste, which separates itself from its fellows in factions and sects, based upon the form of Truth, instead of its essence.

2. *some who went out from us have troubled you with words.* Peace is the normal condition of the inner spiritual church, from which thoughts of peace (apostles and elders) go out as delegates to the outer or Gentile consciousness, represented by Antioch, Syria, and Cilicia. This conference symbolizes the drawing together in conscious unity of all the intelligent directive powers of the spiritual self around the standard of peace and harmony.

3. *abstain from things sacrificed to idols, from blood, from things strangled, and from sexual immorality.* Historically, the things mentioned accompanied pagan religious rites, which had been carried over into the worship of the new Christian church, and from which its members were advised to abstain. Metaphysically, we are to withdraw our thought from all lifeless things and not unite ourself to any illusion of sense.

4. *Judas and Silas; Paul and Barnabas.* Judas (appropriation), Silas (sturdiness), Paul (will) and Barnabas (imagination) were sent to the Gentile Christians with a list of what were deemed fundamentals of the Christ faith at that time. We see the qualities represented by the four delegates as fundamentals of the true way today.

## Paul and Barnabas Separate

15:36 After some days Paul said to
Barnabas, "Let's return now and
visit[1] our brothers in every city in
which we proclaimed the word of the
Lord, to see how they are doing."
15:37 Barnabas planned to take John,
who was called Mark, with them also.
15:38 But Paul didn't think that it was
a good idea to take with them
someone who had withdrawn from
them in Pamphylia, and didn't go
with them to do the work. 15:39 Then
the contention grew so sharp that
they separated from each other.
Barnabas took Mark[2] with him, and
sailed away to Cyprus, 15:40 but Paul
chose Silas,[3] and went out, being
commended by the brothers to the
grace of God. 15:41 He went through
Syria and Cilicia, strengthening the
assemblies.

1. *Let's return now and visit.* [This is the start of Paul's second missionary journey.] Metaphysicians find that in soul development they have to go over the same ground again and again. Regeneration is reeducation, not only of the conscious mind, but also of the subconscious mind, and those who follow Jesus find that they must visit often the various cities and villages (centers and sub-centers throughout the organism), speaking the word with love, zeal, wisdom, power, and all other qualities that enter into the Logos, or embodied mind of God.

2. *Barnabas took Mark.* The name "John Mark" means God's gift. John Mark represented a certain spiritual receptivity, meekness, and obedience. Metaphysically, Cyprus is a fair, frank, honest, just, unbiased state of mind (fairness) established in a degree of substance (a measure of corn);

thus it draws to one very favorable and desirable conditions. Barnabas was a native of Cyprus (Acts 4:36), and Cyprus in the individual consciousness is in close touch with intellectual reasonings (the Greeks) and formulated theology (Antioch). (MBD/ Cyprus).

3. *Paul chose Silas.* The will (Paul) is dominating and dictatorial; it has little patience with the as yet unestablished meekness of John Mark. Because meekness has failed on former occasions to stabilize itself in certain mixed states of mind (Pamphylia), the will refuses to have anything to do with it. Silas means "woody, a forest." Silas represents the spirit of the pioneer, who is willing to suffer the hardships that come to one who overcomes materiality by force, instead of by meekness and love. The meanings of the names of the cities which Paul and Silas visited, Cilicia (rolling), Derbe (sting), Lystra (dissolving), indicate that the work of the two required great effort and that it was not altogether pleasant. Forceful thoughts often stir up opposition, while gentle thoughts bring a peaceful victory.

---

Fillmore Study Bible annotations by Mark Hicks

**World English Bible Footnotes:**

[58] v15:3. The word for "brothers" here and where the context allows may also be correctly translated "brothers and sisters" or "siblings."

[59] v15:11. TR adds "Christ"

[60] v15:17. Amos 9:11-12

[61] v15:22. The word for "brothers" here and where the context allows may also be correctly translated "brothers and sisters" or "siblings."

[62] v15:34. Some manuscripts add: But it seemed good to Silas to stay there.

# Acts 16

## Timothy Joins Paul and Silas

16:1 He came to Derbe and Lystra:(1)
and behold, a certain disciple was
there, named Timothy,(2) the son of a
Jewess who believed; but his father
was a Greek. 16:2 The brothers who
were at Lystra and Iconium gave a
good testimony about him. 16:3 Paul
wanted to have him go out with him,
and he took and circumcised him
because of the Jews(3) who were in
those parts; for they all knew that
his father was a Greek. 16:4 As they
went on their way through the cities,
they delivered the decrees to them
to keep which had been ordained by
the apostles and elders who were at
Jerusalem. 16:5 So the assemblies
were strengthened in the faith, and
increased in number daily.

1. *Derbe and Lystra.* [Two cities that would oppose Paul's mission.]

2. *Timothy.* Timothy means honoring or worshiping God. Timothy's father was a Greek and his mother was a Jewess. In

this duality of parentage, two streams of thought enter into the ego: the spiritual from his mother and the intellectual from his father.

3. *he took and circumcised him because of the Jews.* Circumcision symbolizes the cutting off of the thought of physical generation, to the end that the attentions may be turned to spiritual generation. In his zeal for Truth, Paul admitted that he was all things to all men for the sake of Christ. To conciliate the Jews and to make the worship of God wholly spiritual, Paul sought to eliminate every carnal thought and to sanctify Timothy to purity and to Truth.

## Troas: Paul Yields to the Word of Truth

16:6 When they had gone through
the region of Phrygia and Galatia,
they were forbidden by the Holy
Spirit to speak the word in Asia.[1] 16:7
When they had come opposite Mysia,
they tried to go into Bithynia, but the
Spirit didn't allow them. 16:8 Passing
by Mysia, they came down to Troas.
16:9 A vision appeared to Paul in the
night.[2] There was a man of
Macedonia standing, begging him,
and saying, "Come over into
Macedonia[3] and help us." 16:10 When
he had seen the vision, immediately
we sought to go out to Macedonia,[4]
concluding that the Lord had called
us to preach the Good News to them.

1. *they were forbidden by the Holy Spirit to speak the word in Asia.* Paul and Silas represent man's use of the word of God to awaken the body centers to spiritual consciousness. Certain centers are so unreceptive to spiritual quickening that it would be unprofitable to work in them. The meanings of some of the cities mentioned in today's lesson show the character of those cities: Phrygia means "torrid, barren, dry;" Galatia, "white but lifeless;" Asia, "muddy, boggy;" Mysia, "abominable, criminal;" Bithynia, "violent precipitation."

2. *A vision appeared to Paul in the night.* We are guided by Spirit through visions, dreams, and direct inspiration of Spirit. In this lesson Paul had a dream-vision. He interpreted the meaning as a call from God to preach the Gospel in Macedonia. Paul symbolizes the converted will illumined by the Word. He represents that in man which turns from the set, unyielding letter of the law to the uplifting, life-giving, directing power of the spirit of the law.

3. *Come over into Macedonia.* Paul and his companions entering Europe is symbolical of opening up in the consciousness the Word of Truth, where it had never before been realized. The body is pervaded by a life and intelligence, which has formed a little world of its own. It has no knowledge of the higher, life of the Spirit. It has to be regenerated, born from above. The spiritual spark is carried by the Converted Will, (Paul) and it has to meet obstacles of various kinds. The lands and towns through which Paul passed represent some of these. For instance, Phrygia means dry, barren; Galatia, white, but lifeless; Asia, muddy, boggy. The Holy Ghost forbade Paul speaking the Word there. When guided by the Spirit, we are led to develop along the lines of least resistance and where the conditions are most favorable. We should not be discouraged when we strike the barren places, nor waste our time in trying to quicken the localities that are at present too negative to respond. It is the experience of those who regenerate the body, that a certain fiery element is necessary to give action to the watery negative parts. This is referred to in this lesson. Macedonia means burning adoration, and is representative of that enthusiasm and energy of Spirit which sets the whole man aflame. It is necessary that this phase of the consciousness be cultivated, because without it a certain passivity sets in that is content with the battle only half won.

4. *immediately we sought to go out to Macedonia.* Paul's obedience to the guidance of Spirit stands out in bold relief. When the light shone about him and Jesus spoke out of the clear sky to him, he asked quickly what the Lord wanted him to do; then he promptly did it. When in the temple he fell in a trance and saw the Lord standing by telling him to make haste and get out of Jerusalem quickly, he obeyed. When in a vision or dream at night the man of Macedonia was beseeching him to "come over and help us," Paul made no delay, but proceeded at once to go and preach the gospel as requested.

## Philippi: The Divine Feminine Perceives Truth

16:11 Setting sail therefore from Troas, we made a straight course❶ to Samothrace, and the day following to Neapolis; 16:12 and from there to Philippi, which is a city of Macedonia, the foremost of the district, a Roman colony. We were staying some days in this city.

16:13 On the Sabbath day we went forth outside of the city by a riverside, where we supposed there was a place of prayer, and we sat down, and spoke to the women who had come together. 16:14 A certain woman named Lydia, a seller of purple, of the city of Thyatira,❷ one who worshiped God, heard us; whose heart the Lord opened to listen to the things which were spoken by Paul. 16:15 When she and her household were baptized, she begged us, saying, "If you have judged me to be faithful to the Lord, come into my house,❸ and stay." So she persuaded us.

1. *we made a straight course.* Troas ("penetrated," "perforated") symbolizes the dawning of spiritual consciousness in man. When this takes place, man's will (Paul) and determination (Silas) cause him to make a straight course to Samothrace ("height of Thrace" ), a high, noble state of thought, at first intellectual rather than spiritual. Thence he reaches a new center of action (Neapolis), and at last, realizes power (Philippi) to remake his life by the Christ ideal.

2. *Lydia, Thyatira.* Lydia means "a dispenser of blessings." The Lydia in our lesson represents the divine feminine, which pours forth the power of good in all its attributes: health, power, joy, prosperity. Thyatira means *burning incense*; it represents the intense desire of the soul for the higher expressions of life. [Since she was the first convert in Europe,] this reveals that the soul, symbolized by the woman, is quicker than the intellect (man) to catch the spark of zeal, when a new idea enters the mind.

3. *come into my house, and stay.* When we have a realization that our words are charged with spiritual power, we can immerse certain centers of consciousness, not only in our own bodies but in the bodies of others. This is spiritual baptism. When we have faith in this spiritual quickening of life in the body temple, it becomes an abiding consciousness.

## Prayer and Singing Opens Prison Doors

16:16 It happened, as we were going to prayer, that a certain girl having a spirit of divination❶ met us, who brought her masters much gain by fortune telling. 16:17 Following Paul and us, she cried out, "These men are servants of the Most High God, who proclaim to us the way of salvation!" 16:18 She was doing this for many days.

But Paul, becoming greatly annoyed, turned and said to the spirit, "I command you in the name of Jesus Christ to come out of her!"❷ It came out that very hour. 16:19 But when her masters saw that the hope of their gain was gone,❸ they seized Paul and Silas, and dragged them into the marketplace before the rulers. 16:20 When they had brought them to the magistrates, they said, "These men, being Jews, are agitating our city, 16:21 and set forth customs which it is not lawful for us to accept or to observe, being Romans."

16:22 The multitude rose up together against them, and the magistrates tore their clothes off of them, and commanded them to be beaten with rods. 16:23 When they had laid many stripes on them, they threw them into prison, charging the

jailer to keep them safely, 16:24 who,
having received such a command,
threw them into the inner prison,
and secured their feet in the
stocks.[4]

16:25 But about midnight Paul and
Silas were praying and singing hymns
to God,[5] and the prisoners were
listening to them. 16:26 Suddenly there
was a great earthquake, so that the
foundations of the prison were
shaken; and immediately all the
doors were opened, and everyone's
bonds were loosened. 16:27 The jailer,
being roused out of sleep and seeing
the prison doors open, drew his
sword and was about to kill himself,
supposing that the prisoners had
escaped. 16:28 But Paul cried with a
loud voice, saying, "Don't harm
yourself, for we are all here!"

16:29 He called for lights and sprang
in, and, fell down trembling before
Paul and Silas, 16:30 and brought them
out and said, "Sirs, what must I do to
be saved?"

16:31 They said, "Believe in the Lord
Jesus Christ, and you will be saved,
you and your household." 16:32 They
spoke the word of the Lord to him,
and to all who were in his house.

16:33 He took them the same hour
of the night, and washed their
stripes, and was immediately
baptized, he and all his household.
16:34 He brought them up into his
house, and set food before them,
and rejoiced greatly, with all his
household, having believed in God.

16:35 But when it was day, the
magistrates sent the sergeants,
saying, "Let those men go."

16:36 The jailer reported these
words to Paul, saying, "The
magistrates have sent to let you go;
now therefore come out, and go in
peace."

16:37 But Paul said to them, "They
have beaten us publicly, without a
trial, men who are Romans, and have
cast us into prison! Do they now
release us secretly? No, most
certainly, but let them come
themselves and bring us out!"[6]

16:38 The sergeants reported these
words to the magistrates, and they
were afraid when they heard that
they were Romans, 16:39 and they
came and begged them. When they
had brought them out, they asked
them to depart from the city. 16:40
They went out of the prison, and
entered into Lydia's house. When
they had seen the brothers, they
encouraged them, and departed.

1. *a certain girl having a spirit of divination.* This "maid" represents man's belief in a realm in which the unknown and the past and the future may be revealed. Belief in the occult is the result of ignorance and superstition. Victor Hugo said: "There are no occult truths; all is luminous." The superstition that centers in the occult should be denied out of consciousness, in the name of Truth.

2. *I command you in the name of Jesus Christ to come out of her!* Paul and Silas represent the will and the understanding engaged in their work of cleansing the consciousness. Paul had cast the demon of "divination" out of the damsel, who "brought her masters much gain by soothsaying."

3. *her masters saw that the hope of their gain was gone.* Her masters represent acquisitiveness, greed, and selfishness, which seek gain through the use of occult or psychic forces. Like Simon Magus, they would buy the power of the Holy Ghost and use it for selfish ends.

4. *threw them into the inner prison, and secured their feet in the stocks.* The intellectual powers that have tried to hold this seemingly occult faculty as a source of material profit are enraged and endeavor to throw into bondage the freeing powers of Spirit, represented by Paul and Silas.

5. *Paul and Silas were praying and singing hymns to God.* Spiritualized mind forces are always joyous, full of praise and thanksgiving, with no consciousness of opposition. This dynamic power shatters the error forces, throwing open the prison

doors and giving the spiritual will and understanding greater freedom of expression.

6. *let them come themselves and bring us out!* Paul never missed an opportunity to make a convert. Instead of escaping from the jail and the jailer, he remained and converted the whole family. When, through the power of the Spirit, you have made a demonstration, do not leave it incomplete, but bring into spiritual harmony all the factors entering into the problem.

---

Fillmore Study Bible annotations by Mark Hicks

# Acts 17

## Thessalonica: An Immature Desire for Truth

17:1 Now when they had passed through Amphipolis and Apollonia,[1] they came to Thessalonica,[2] where there was a Jewish synagogue. 17:2 Paul, as was his custom, went in to them, and for three Sabbath days reasoned with them from the Scriptures, 17:3 explaining and demonstrating that the Christ had to suffer and rise again from the dead, and saying, "This Jesus, whom I proclaim to you, is the Christ."

17:4 Some of them were persuaded, and joined Paul and Silas, of the devout Greeks a great multitude,[3] and not a few of the chief women. 17:5 But the unpersuaded Jews took along[63] some wicked men from the marketplace, and gathering a crowd, set the city in an uproar. Assaulting the house of Jason, they sought to bring them out to the people. 17:6 When they didn't find them, they dragged Jason and certain brothers[64] before the rulers of the city,[4] crying, "These who have turned the world upside down have come here also, 17:7 whom Jason has received. These all act contrary to the decrees of Caesar, saying that there is another king, Jesus!" 17:8 The multitude and the rulers of the city were troubled when they heard these things. 17:9 When they had taken security from Jason[5] and the rest, they let them go.

1. *when they had passed through Amphipolis and Apollonia.* Truth passes through several stages in entering the mind: first doubt, then examination, then a great desire for the Truth, then acceptance. These are represented by the Gentile cities—Amphipolis, Apollonia, and Thessalonica—through which Paul passed, and Beroea where "they received the word with all readiness of mind." (MBD/Apollonia)

2. *they came to Thessalonica.* Thessalonica (its ancient name, Thermæ, meaning hot springs), a city of Macedonia from which Paul was driven by persecution by the Jews there, represents the burning or heated zeal of the soul in its desire for Truth, but at this phase of unfoldment it is without a sufficient thinking balance to give tolerance and wisdom. (MBD/Thessalonica)

3. *of the devout Greeks a great multitude.* The Greeks represent the intellect. They were accustomed to engaging in logical argument and disputations and took delight in matching their wits with an adversary. The Jews trusted more the traditions of the fathers, in which their feelings were involved; therefore, they were more difficult to reach and convince than the Greeks.

4. *they dragged Jason and certain broth-*

*ers before the rulers of the city.* We can see why Paul and Silas stirred up so much contention. Paul represents the true pioneer. He dearly loved to meet the opposition and discuss the proposition. His writings bristle with suggestions of war, and in one way or another he is constantly admonishing Christians to "put on the whole armor of God." To him soul development was a war between the Spirit and the flesh. That subtle thought of war in Paul had its effect in this work. He argued, exhorted and contended, and the result was a reaction upon them of that sort of thought. It may be that certain fixed states of human thought have to be met that way and that the "fighting person" has his place among the pioneers of religion.

5. *When they had taken security from Jason.* Jason means deliverer, healer, he who cures, Jehovah delivers; he represents the I AM in its first stages of growth in the higher law. He is hauled before the rulers and accused of setting up a new king in opposition to Cæsar. He is called upon to give security for the brethren; that is, he heals the breach between the opposing forces in the consciousness by making concessions for the time being. He sends away the fiery Paul and the psalm-singing Silas, and harmony is restored. We should not be too full of zeal in our spiritual ongoing. We are apt to become fanatical and disagreeable and make ourselves obnoxious. Pour oil on your troubled waters by now and then going into the silence and holding for harmony (slipping away in the night).

## Beroea: A Consciousness Ready for Truth

17:10 The brothers immediately
sent Paul and Silas away by night to
Beroea.[1] When they arrived, they
went into the Jewish synagogue.[2]
17:11 Now these were more noble than
those in Thessalonica, in that they
received the word with all readiness
of the mind, examining the
Scriptures daily to see whether these
things were so. 17:12 Many of them
therefore believed; also of the
prominent Greek women, and not a
few men. 17:13 But when the Jews of
Thessalonica had knowledge that the
word of God was proclaimed by Paul
at Beroea also, they came there
likewise, agitating the multitudes.
17:14 Then the brothers immediately
sent out Paul to go as far as to the
sea, and Silas and Timothy still
stayed there. 17:15 But those who
escorted Paul brought him as far as
Athens. Receiving a commandment
to Silas and Timothy that they should
come to him very quickly, they
departed.

1. *to Beroea* At Beroea, while there is the same desire for Truth as in Thessalonica, there is also a readiness to look into that which differs from the old established religious thought. So Beroea signifies the zeal of the soul in religious matters, tempered by good judgment, tolerance, and intelligent willingness to examine all thoughts presented to it, that the real Truth may be discerned and received into consciousness. By understanding is any phase of man's consciousness watered so that the Truth may take root and grow and bring forth fruit.

2. *they went into the Jewish synagogue.* The fact that he always looked for a synagogue and taught the Jews first shows that spiritual truth gains by being taught in surroundings that are in harmony with it. His teaching the Jews first emphasizes our responsibility to enlighten that part of our mind which is busy with religious convictions and traditions.

## Athens: Our Intellectual Center

17:16 Now while Paul waited for
them at Athens,[1] his spirit was
provoked within him as he saw the
city full of idols. 17:17 So he reasoned
in the synagogue with the Jews and
the devout persons, and in the
marketplace every day with those
who met him. 17:18 Some of the
Epicurean and Stoic philosophers[2]
also[65] were conversing with him.

Some said, "What does this babbler want to say?"

Others said, "He seems to be advocating foreign deities," because he preached Jesus and the resurrection.

17:19 They took hold of him, and brought him to the Areopagus,[3] saying, "May we know what this new teaching is, which is spoken by you? 17:20 For you bring certain strange things to our ears. We want to know therefore what these things mean." 17:21 Now all the Athenians and the strangers living there spent their time in nothing else, but either to tell or to hear some new thing.

17:22 Paul stood in the middle of the Areopagus, and said, "You men of Athens, I perceive that you are very religious in all things.[4] 17:23 For as I passed along, and observed the objects of your worship, I found also an altar with this inscription: 'TO AN UNKNOWN GOD.' What therefore you worship in ignorance,[5] this I announce to you. 17:24 The God who made the world and all things in it, he, being Lord of heaven and earth, doesn't dwell in temples made with hands, 17:25 neither is he served by men's hands, as though he needed anything, seeing he himself gives to all life and breath, and all things. 17:26 He made from one blood every nation of men to dwell on all the surface of the earth, having determined appointed seasons, and the boundaries of their dwellings, 17:27 that they should seek the Lord, if perhaps they might reach out for him and find him, though he is not far from each one of us. 17:28 'For in him we live, and move, and have our being.'[6] As some of your own poets have said, 'For we are also his offspring.' 17:29 Being then the offspring of God, we ought not to think that the Divine Nature is like gold, or silver, or stone, engraved by art and design of man. 17:30 The times of ignorance therefore God overlooked. But now he commands that all people everywhere should repent, 17:31 because he has appointed a day in which he will judge the world in righteousness by the man whom he has ordained; of which he has given assurance to all men, in that he has raised him from the dead."

17:32 Now when they heard of the resurrection of the dead, some mocked; but others said, "We want to hear you again concerning this."

17:33 Thus Paul went out from among them. 17:34 But certain men joined with him, and believed, among whom also was Dionysius the Areopagite, and a woman named Damaris,[7] and others with them.

1. *while Paul waited for them at Athens.* Athens represents our intellectual center. Paul waiting at Athens represents the spiritual will waiting for the opportunity to set into action the spiritual Word in the chief seat of intellectual learning.

2. *Epicurean and Stoic philosophers.* The Epicureans represent an aggregation of thoughts whose philosophy is that love of pleasure and enjoyment leads into abiding peace and health. The Stoic philosophers represent the direct opposite of the Epicureans. The Stoics believe that indifference in both pleasure and pain is the highest attainment of man.

3. *brought him to the Areopagus.* Areopagus, or Mars' hill, was a rocky hill in Athens; on it the court of justice was held. It symbolizes the place in consciousness where all kinds of thoughts are received and judged as to their truth. Areopagus means "court of justice," or that place in consciousness where all the different aggregations of thought forces get a hearing, and (according to the light manifested in consciousness) a righteous judgment.

4. *You men of Athens, I perceive that you are very religious in all things.* Paul, the spiritual will, in introducing himself, made it clear that he did not worship the idols of gold or silver or stone, but called Athenians' attention to their altar dedicated to "An Unknown God," thereby avoiding all

cause for offense. At the same time, he awakened in his listeners a desire to know something of the real God, which their idol typified.

5. *What therefore you worship in ignorance.* Paul did not call the Athenians ignorant. This is a mistranslation. What he did say was, "Whom ye worship, not understanding his name, attributes and nature, him I set forth." God is Spirit. Spirit is not form nor condition, but formless. The character of God as Absolute Being cannot be comprehended by the intellect. The Truth, therefore, makes a total denial of all beliefs about God of a temporal character.

6. *For in him we live, and move, and have our being.* A splendid treatment for the realization of Omnipresence. The One Life permeates every fiber of our organism; we move in it and it moves in us; our true being is involved in this One Essence and Cause of all. *We believe that we live, move, and have our being in God-Mind; also that God-Mind lives, moves, and has being in us, to the degree of our consciousness (Unity Statement of Faith, #17).*

7. *Dionysius the Areopagite, and a woman named Damaris.* Dionysius and Damaris are two converts from Paul's speech. Metaphysically, Damaris is soul in its relation to the intellect (Athens symbolizes the intellect, and a woman refers to the soul). The soul is more closely unified (wife, joined) with our intellectual thoughts and activities than most persons realize. When we think that we have reasoned a thing out entirely with our head, and that we are acting altogether from a reasoning standpoint, it would surprise us if we could see how much we have been guided all along by the intuitions, affections, emotions, and desires of the soul. (MBD/Damaris).

Fillmore Study Bible annotations by Mark Hicks

**World English Bible Footnotes:**

[63] v17:5. TR reads "And the Jews who were unpersuaded, becoming envious and taking along" instead of "But the unpersuaded Jews took along"

[64] v17:6. The word for "brothers" here and where the context allows may be also correctly translated "brothers and sisters" or "siblings."

[65] v17:18. TR omits "also"

# Acts 18

## Athens to Corinth: From Intellect to Love

18:1 After these things Paul
departed from Athens, and came to
Corinth.(1) 18:2 He found a certain Jew
named Aquila, a man of Pontus by
race, who had recently come from
Italy, with his wife Priscilla,(2)
because Claudius had commanded all
the Jews to depart from Rome. He
came to them, 18:3 and because he
practiced the same trade, he lived
with them and worked, for by trade
they were tent makers.(3) 18:4 He
reasoned in the synagogue every
Sabbath, and persuaded Jews and
Greeks.(4) 18:5 But when Silas and
Timothy came down from Macedonia,

Paul was compelled by the Spirit,[5] testifying to the Jews that Jesus was the Christ. 18:6 When they opposed him and blasphemed,[6] he shook out his clothing and said to them, "Your blood be on your own heads! I am clean. From now on, I will go to the Gentiles!"[7]

18:7 He departed there, and went into the house of a certain man named Justus, one who worshiped God, whose house was next door to the synagogue. 18:8 Crispus,[8] the ruler of the synagogue, believed in the Lord with all his house. Many of the Corinthians, when they heard, believed and were baptized. 18:9 The Lord said to Paul in the night by a vision, "Don't be afraid, but speak and don't be silent; 18:10 for I am with you, and no one will attack you to harm you, for I have many people in this city."

18:11 He lived there a year and six months, teaching the word of God among them. 18:12 But when Gallio was proconsul of Achaia, the Jews with one accord rose up against Paul and brought him before the judgment seat, 18:13 saying, "This man persuades men to worship God contrary to the law."

18:14 But when Paul was about to open his mouth, Gallio said to the Jews, "If indeed it were a matter of wrong or of wicked crime, you Jews, it would be reasonable that I should bear with you; 18:15 but if they are questions about words and names and your own law, look to it yourselves. For I don't want to be a judge of these matters." 18:16 He drove them from the judgment seat.

18:17 Then all the Greeks laid hold on Sosthenes, the ruler of the synagogue, and beat him before the judgment seat. Gallio didn't care about any of these things.

1. *Paul departed from Athens, and came to Corinth.* In individual consciousness, Paul's going from Athens to Corinth means the withdrawal of the power of the Word from the intellectual center (Athens) and its entrance into the love center (Corinth). Corinth means "lovely, beautiful." The Corinth of Paul's time contained a temple of Venus, which was dedicated to the worship of love. Corinth represents the love center in man's consciousness, around which all his thoughts of love are grouped. It was to the Corinthians that Paul wrote his matchless poem on love (I Cor. 13).

2. *Priscilla, Aquila.* The heart center, the solar plexus, instead of being pervaded by thoughts of peace and harmony and a just appreciation of the divine law, is perverted to the basest thoughts and the most violent passions. But the patient, sustaining power within, is not wholly thwarted. When the body is lacerated, he sets his builders to work and they patch up the holes. We call this *the healing force of nature.* Metaphysically, Priscilla is the feminine or receptive phase of the healing forces of nature that are always at work rebuilding the body and repairing the ravages of ignorant man. Aquila, husband of Priscilla, is the positive phase of these forces. These healing forces of nature are very old, in so far as man's idea of time refers to age. They have been present and active since manifest creation began. God has ever been in every atom of His universe as unifying, constructive life, energy, love, intelligence, power, substance, and progressive influence (MBD/Priscilla, MBD/Aquila).

3. *for by trade they were tent makers.* Priscilla and Aquila were Christians, and tentmakers by trade. Paul abode and worked with them in Corinth. Aquila and Priscilla represent the masculine and the feminine forces that construct the body (tent). Through the work of these forces, aided by the word of Truth (Paul) the redemption of the body (tent) is wrought. They work and cooperate with Paul (the power of the Word) in building the body.

4. *He reasoned in the synagogue every Sabbath, and persuaded Jews and Greeks.* The word of Truth appeals to the higher understanding as well as to the intellect, and is accepted by the whole man, when he is free from religious bias.

5. *when Silas and Timothy came down from Macedonia, Paul was compelled by the Spirit.* Silas represents perception from on high, Timothy zeal, Macedonia the fervor of the soul. Under the influence of exalted thought the word of Truth (Paul) is impelled to proclaim that Jesus (I AM ) is

the Christ, the saving power.

6. *they opposed him and blasphemed.* When one is rooted and rounded in certain religious dogmas, and especially in the teaching that the Messiah, or the anointed of God, is come again in the flesh, one opposes such teachings and calls them blasphemy, because one does not understand their spiritual import.

7. *I will go to the Gentiles!* When there is plain evidence of non-receptivity, it is wise to withdraw and begin the education of the external realms of thought.

8. *Justus, Crispus.* Justus (ASV, Titus Justus) denotes the body consciousness. The word of Truth, by being spoken from the body consciousness, reaches many worldly thoughts (Gentiles). Crispus, who "believed in the Lord with all his house" indicates that Truth encompasses the whole man, more especially the love of man's soul.

## Cenchreae: Paul Returns With a Vow

18:18 Paul, having stayed after this many more days, took his leave of the brothers,[66] and sailed from there for Syria, together with Priscilla and Aquila. He shaved his head in Cenchreae,[1] for he had a vow.[2] 18:19 He came to Ephesus, and he left them there; but he himself entered into the synagogue, and reasoned with the Jews. 18:20 When they asked him to stay with them a longer time, he declined; 18:21 but taking his leave of them, and saying, "I must by all means keep this coming feast in Jerusalem, but I will return again to you if God wills," he set sail from Ephesus.

18:22 When he had landed at Caesarea, he went up and greeted the assembly, and went down to Antioch.[3] 18:23 Having spent some time there, he departed, and went through the region of Galatia, and Phrygia, in order, establishing all the disciples.

1. *He shaved his head in Cenchreae.* Cenchreae, a harbor of Corinth. There was a Christian assembly in the place, and Phoebe was a deaconess in this church (Rom. 16:1). Metaphysically, Cenchreae means *small grains*, and, like the mustard seed of Jesus' parable, it signifies the fact that the Truth established in the consciousness of man is at first similar to a very tiny seed (the word is the seed). We should not therefore despise nor look upon as insignificant any beginning of light and Truth that comes to us or to others, no matter how small it may seem. (MBD/Cenchreae).

2. *for he had a vow.* In Cenchreae, either Paul or Aquila (the text is not quite clear) had "shorn his head...for he had a vow." [The vow taken is likely Nazirite, the vow also taken by Samson and by John the Baptist. This passage may be related to the next, regarding Apollos, a disciple of John. It is not clear why Unity never commented on this metaphysically rich passage of scripture. See MBD/Nazirite, MBD/Samson and MBD/John ]

3. *went down to Antioch.* [The close of Paul's second missionary journey.]

## Ministry of Apollos

18:24 Now a certain Jew named Apollos,[1] an Alexandrian by race, an eloquent man, came to Ephesus. He was mighty in the Scriptures. 18:25 This man had been instructed in the way of the Lord; and being fervent in spirit, he spoke and taught accurately the things concerning Jesus, although he knew only the baptism of John. 18:26 He began to speak boldly in the synagogue. But when Priscilla and Aquila heard him,[2] they took him aside, and explained to him the way of God more accurately.

18:27 When he had determined to pass over into Achaia, the brothers encouraged him, and wrote to the disciples to receive him. When he had come, he greatly helped those who had believed through grace; 18:28 for he powerfully refuted the Jews, publicly showing by the Scriptures that Jesus was the Christ.

1. *Apollos.* Apollos means "destroyer", "the sun." The Apollos mentioned in this lesson was a Jew, who had been converted to the teaching of John the Baptist, and who was zealous in getting rid of error. The intellectual conception of Truth tends to make one hard and destructive in one's judgments.

2. *when Priscilla and Aquila heard him.* Priscilla ("old") and Aquila ("eagle") represent the patient, sustaining power within man, that we are in the habit of calling the healing forces of nature. These healing forces have been in evidence since manifest creation began.

---

Fillmore Study Bible annotations by Mark Hicks

**World English Bible Footnotes:**

[66] v18:18. The word for "brothers" here and where the context allows may also be correctly translated "brothers and sisters" or "siblings."

# Acts 19

## Ephesus: A City of Desire

19:1 It happened that, while Apollos was at Corinth,(1) Paul, having passed through the upper country, came(2) to Ephesus,(3) and found certain disciples.(4) 19:2 He said to them, "Did you receive the Holy Spirit when you believed?"

They said to him, "No, we haven't even heard that there is a Holy Spirit."

19:3 He said, "Into what then were you baptized?"

They said, "Into John's baptism."

19:4 Paul said, "John indeed baptized with the baptism of repentance, saying to the people that they should believe in the one who would come after him, that is, in Jesus."

19:5 When they heard this, they were baptized in the name of the Lord Jesus. 19:6 When Paul had laid his hands on them, the Holy Spirit came on them, and they spoke with other languages and prophesied. 19:7 They were about twelve men in all. 19:8 He entered into the synagogue, and spoke boldly for a period of three months,(5) reasoning and persuading about the things concerning the Kingdom of God.

19:9 But when some were hardened and disobedient, speaking evil of the Way before the multitude, he departed from them, and separated the disciples, reasoning daily in the school of Tyrannus.[6] 19:10 This continued for two years, so that all those who lived in Asia heard the word of the Lord Jesus, both Jews and Greeks.

1. *Apollos was at Corinth.* Apollos remains in Corinth because the word of Truth that is sown in the body by Paul does not always bear fruit immediately. Faith and understanding (Apollos) must be brought to bear on it before it can develop properly.

2. *Paul came.* Paul sows the word of Truth (seed) in all parts of the body to which Apollos will provide a true, practical understanding of faith and understanding as they are needed to refresh, encourage, and aid the new Truth thoughts to reach fruition.

3. *to Ephesus.* Ephesus means "desirable." The city founded at least one thousand years before Christ, was at one time the chief point in Asia. Asia represents the inner realm, and the importance of the power of desire is clearly indicated in this symbology. Desire may be fixed on the things of sense or materiality as well as on the things of the inner realm. The work of the Christ is to transform it until it becomes righteous desire and faithfully expresses the inner realm of Spirit.

4. *and found certain disciples.* Ephesus was famed for its arts; the temple of Diana was there, and many craftsmen made up the city's inhabitants. This all shows its prevailing mental state, and symbolizes a certain center of consciousness in the body of a man. Some people think it far-fetched to claim that a city or place on the earth has any relation to man's mind. The fact is that all places are representative of the mind. The prevailing idea in the race mind at any age of its history may be told by the character of its cities. The American people are picturing in their cities what exists in their minds, and we readily locate the intellectual, governmental, artistic, manufacturing, etc. cities of our country. If we take this country as a whole and call it a man, we can easily locate the head, the heart, the stomach, etc.; in fact, every part of the man may be found in a representative city.

5. *spoke boldly for a period of three months.* The three months denote spirit, soul, and body, man's threefold avenues of expression; A synagogue represents the established religious consciousness inbred in us by tradition and inheritance. When the illumined will enters into this consciousness, it meets resistance even when man's desire is for Truth.

6. *school of Tyrannus (lecture hall of Tyrannus, NRSV).* The name Tyrannus ("tyrant," "ruling prince") represents the rule of desire in the individual. Paul's work in the school of Tyrannus represents the word of Truth continuing its work in the spiritually awakening individual through his inner desire for the things of Spirit. This work goes on even though for a time the individual may repudiate the higher message of Truth, because his mind is filled with preconceived, established religious beliefs.

## The Denial of Magical Arts in Ephesus

19:11 God worked special miracles by the hands of Paul, 19:12 so that even handkerchiefs or aprons were carried away from his body to the sick, and the evil spirits went out. 19:13 But some of the itinerant Jews, exorcists, took on themselves to invoke over those who had the evil spirits the name of the Lord Jesus,[1] saying, "We adjure you by Jesus whom Paul preaches." 19:14 There were seven sons of one Sceva,[2] a Jewish chief priest, who did this.

19:15 The evil spirit answered, "Jesus I know, and Paul I know, but who are you?" 19:16 The man in whom the evil spirit was leaped on them, and overpowered them, and prevailed against them, so that they fled out of that house naked and wounded. 19:17 This became known to all, both Jews and Greeks, who lived at Ephesus. Fear fell on them all, and the name of the Lord Jesus was magnified. 19:18 Many also of those who had believed came, confessing, and declaring their deeds. 19:19 Many of those who practiced magical arts brought their books together and burned them❸ in the sight of all. They counted the price of them, and found it to be fifty thousand pieces of silver.[67] 19:20 So the word of the Lord was growing and becoming mighty.

1. *some of the itinerant Jews, exorcists, took on themselves to invoke over those who had the evil spirits the name of the Lord Jesus.* Ephesus was given up to idolatry, superstition and general materialism. So we find in unregenerate man that this center is given up to physical and mortal ideas, and must be raised to the spiritual through the impregnating power of the Word. Hence Paul spent three years preaching the Gospel in Ephesus. The word of Truth cast out evil spirits and healed the sick at Ephesus, and this was imitated by strolling Jew exorcists. They used the same formulas that Paul did, but they had not been converted, or not totally purified, and the evil spirits turned upon them and overpowered them so that they fled. We find people who want to be healed without repentance; they want to be freed from the penalty of error, but do not wish to do right. These ask for word formulas, magic, and they create a demand for the exorcists that imitate the Truth, but are not in the understanding of that change of heart and thought which must accompany all true healing.

2. *seven sons of one Sceva.* Sceva, the Jew, means an established instrument and refers to the fixed state of mind which prevails in the physical consciousness. The "seven sons" are the seven centers of thought and action in the body.

3. *Many of those who practiced magical arts brought their books together and burned them.* The burning of the books of those who practiced magical arts means the total denial of all formulas and aids that are not based in the understanding of Truth. Ministry of the word of Truth includes denial of error.

## Chemicalization in Ephesus

19:21 Now after these things had ended, Paul determined in the spirit, when he had passed through Macedonia and Achaia, to go to Jerusalem, saying, "After I have been there, I must also see Rome."

19:22 Having sent into Macedonia two of those who served him, Timothy and Erastus, he himself stayed in Asia for a while. 19:23 About that time there arose no small stir concerning the Way. 19:24 For a certain man named Demetrius,❶ a silversmith, who made silver shrines of Artemis,❷ brought no little business to the craftsmen, 19:25 whom he gathered together, with the workmen of like occupation, and said, "Sirs, you know that by this business we have our wealth. 19:26 You see and hear, that not at Ephesus alone, but almost throughout all Asia, this Paul has persuaded and turned away many people, saying that they are no gods, that are made with hands. 19:27 Not only is there danger that this our trade come into disrepute, but also that the temple of the great goddess Artemis will be counted as nothing, and her majesty destroyed, whom all Asia and the world worships."

19:28 When they heard this they were filled with anger,❸ and cried out, saying, "Great is Artemis of the Ephesians!" 19:29 The whole city was filled with confusion,❹ and they rushed with one accord into the theater, having seized Gaius and Aristarchus, men of Macedonia, Paul's companions in travel. 19:30 When Paul wanted to enter in to the people, the disciples didn't allow him. 19:31 Certain also of the Asiarchs, being his friends, sent to him and begged him not to venture into the theater. 19:32 Some therefore cried one thing, and some another, for the assembly was in confusion. Most of them didn't know why they had come together. 19:33 They brought Alexander out of the multitude, the Jews putting him forward. Alexander

beckoned with his hand, and would
have made a defense to the people.
19:34 But when they perceived that he
was a Jew, all with one voice for a
time of about two hours cried out,
"Great is Artemis of the Ephesians!"

19:35 When the town clerk had
quieted the multitude, he said, "You
men of Ephesus, what man is there
who doesn't know that the city of the
Ephesians is temple keeper of the
great goddess Artemis, and of the
image which fell down from Zeus?
19:36 Seeing then that these things
can't be denied, you ought to be
quiet, and to do nothing rash. 19:37 For
you have brought these men here,
who are neither robbers of temples
nor blasphemers of your goddess. 19:38
If therefore Demetrius and the
craftsmen who are with him have a
matter against anyone, the courts
are open,[5] and there are proconsuls.
Let them press charges against one
another. 19:39 But if you seek anything
about other matters, it will be
settled in the regular assembly. 19:40
For indeed we are in danger of being
accused concerning this day's riot,
there being no cause. Concerning it,
we wouldn't be able to give an
account of this commotion." 19:41
When he had thus spoken, he
dismissed the assembly.

1. Demetrius. A silversmith at Ephesus who stirred up a great tumult against Paul and the doctrine of Christ. He did this because he feared that the Truth would take away his business and he would thus lose materially (MBD/Demetrius).

2. Artemus (Diana, ASV). Artemus was the fertility goddess of the heathen world, and was associated in men's thought with the moon. The moon exerts an influence upon the whole earth, and in like manner desire is a trait common to all men. Asia represents the within, and desire reaches to man's consciousness.

3. *When they heard this they were filled with anger.* When the God of Spirit is proclaimed, the consciousness that believes in and profits from the concept of a personal God, makes an uproar and almost causes a riot, because of injury to the industry which has been built up by material religion. Demetrius, the silversmith, represents the mentality that is sending forth thoughts and images of a material God. The idea that substance is wholly material represented by Demetrius, the silversmith.

4. *The whole city was filled with confusion.* Thoughts are things, and people fill their minds with thought substance. When new ideas are entertained, if the subject matter is of a more spiritual character than the ideas previously entertained, the old ideas resist. This process is sometimes called chemicalization. It should be feared. It denotes a thorough repentance or change of mind.

5. *If therefore Demetrius and the craftsmen who are with him have a matter against anyone, the courts are open.* The riot of Demetrius and his fellow workers symbolizes the battle of materiality against spirituality, in which self-interest seeks to enforce its will against reason and the good of all, without regard for truth or right. The individual's right of expression must be kept within the bounds of law and order, otherwise confusion and anarchy result, and society is placed on an unstable basis. The only time when it is permissible for a person to be a law unto himself is when he rises to a consciousness of the Christ and becomes selfless. The personal self must be subordinate to the good of the whole society. The good of all is paramount to the good of the personal self, and it should be so accepted. As we take the larger view of law, we see that authority is necessary to the maintenance of the social order and this in turn is necessary to individual security.

Fillmore Study Bible annotations by Mark Hicks

**World English Bible Footnotes:**

[67] v19:19. The 50,000 pieces of silver here probably referred to 50,000 drachmas. If so, the value of the burned books was equivalent to about 160 man-years of wages for agricultural laborers.

# Acts 20

## Paul Goes to Macedonia and Greece[1]

20:1 After the uproar had ceased,
Paul sent for the disciples, took leave
of them, and departed to go into
Macedonia.[2] 20:2 When he had gone
through those parts, and had
encouraged them with many words,
he came into Greece.[3] 20:3 When he
had spent three months there, and a
plot was made against him by Jews
as he was about to set sail for Syria,
he determined to return through
Macedonia. 20:4 These accompanied
him as far as Asia: Sopater[4] of
Beroea; Aristarchus[5] and Secundus[6]
of the Thessalonians; Gaius[7] of
Derbe; Timothy[8]; and Tychicus[9] and
Trophimus[10] of Asia. 20:5 But these
had gone ahead, and were waiting
for us at Troas. 20:6 We sailed away
from Philippi after the days of
Unleavened Bread, and came to
them at Troas in five days, where we
stayed seven days.

1. See Acts 16:9, Acts 17:19

2. *Macedonia*. Fervor, intensity, and vehemence are required in order to carry the great and beautiful message of Truth over seeming hindrances to the different centers and states of consciousness (represented by the cities and nations through which Paul journeyed and preached). Macedonia signifies the enthusiasm and the energy of Spirit, which set the whole man aflame. It is necessary that this phase of the consciousness be cultivated, because without it a passivity sets in that makes one content with the battle only half won. (MBD/Macedonia)

3. *Greece*. The intellect in man. Athens, the capital of Greece, and the birthplace of Plato, was a great center for learning throughout the then known world. In man's consciousness Athens refers to the intellectual center. (MBD/Greece)

4. *Sopater*. The spiritually awakened or illumined understanding, that perceives the saving power of Spirit and defends the cause (as by argument, reasoning) of the true Source of all (MBD/Sopater)

5. *Aristarchus*. Spiritual power, authority, and soul fervor--the very Christ of God or Divine Mind itself (best ruler, best leader, supreme beginning, first principle (MBD/Aristarchus)

6. *Secundus*. A secondary attitude of thought (second) that is necessary to promote the acceptance and growth of Truth in the whole being of man. It is an attitude of thought that approves of Truth and is willing to do all in its power to further the activity of the word of Truth (Paul) in the consciousness (MBD/Secundus)

7. *Gaius*. The acceptance by the body consciousness (of the earth, earthy man) of the truth pertaining to the divine law, or Lord. This acceptance of Truth by the seemingly earthy phase of man's being works with Paul (the activity of the word of Truth) in bringing about the redemption of the body (MBD/Gaius)

8. *Timothy*. A Christian convert, who helped Paul much in his ministry. Metaphysically, inspired reason united with faith and zeal (MBD/Timothy)

9. *Tychicus*. A belief in fate (fortuitous, fateful, chance, fortunate). Converted to Christian faith, this belief would take on a strong assurance of good as being ever present and demonstrable. One who learns the divine law is not subject to fate. He makes his own destiny by his use of divine law. (MBD/Tychicus)

10. *Trophimus*. Metaphysically, a thought or expression of desire. Desire in man is fundamentally spiritual; it is the foundation quality of all growth and unfoldment, and when it expresses in the higher, spiritual understanding it is fed and supported by true spiritual life and substance. (MBD/Trophimus)

## Paul's Farewell Visit to Troas[1]

20:7 On the first day of the week,
when the disciples were gathered
together to break bread, Paul talked
with them, intending to depart on
the next day, and continued his
speech until midnight. 20:8 There
were many lights in the upper
chamber where we[68] were gathered
together. 20:9 A certain young man
named Eutychus[2] sat in the window,
weighed down with deep sleep. As
Paul spoke still longer, being
weighed down by his sleep, he fell
down from the third story, and was
taken up dead. 20:10 Paul went down,
and fell upon him, and embracing
him said, "Don't be troubled, for his
life is in him."

20:11 When he had gone up, and had
broken bread,[3] and eaten, and had
talked with them a long while, even
until break of day, he departed. 20:12
They brought the boy in alive, and
were greatly comforted.

1. *Troas.* A phase of thought by which Spirit can find its way into consciousness more easily than by other ways (penetrated, bored through). (MBD/Troas). See Acts 16:6.

2. *Eutychus.* The understanding that the youthful energies of the organism can be quickened into new life again even after they appear to be utterly dead, after such a renewal appears to be hopeless. Man is indeed fortunate in having the word of Truth (indicated here by Paul) always at hand, since by the word of Truth he can speak his whole being into newness and fullness of life at will. (MBD/Eutychus)

3. *bread.* Universal substance (MBD/bread).

## The Voyage from Troas to Miletus

20:13 But we who went ahead to
the ship set sail for Assos,[1] intending
to take Paul aboard there, for he
had so arranged, intending himself to
go by land. 20:14 When he met us at
Assos, we took him aboard, and came
to Mitylene[2]. 20:15 Sailing from there,
we came the following day opposite
Chios. The next day we touched at
Samos[3] and stayed at Trogyllium,[4]
and the day after we came to
Miletus.[5] 20:16 For Paul had
determined to sail past Ephesus, that
he might not have to spend time in
Asia; for he was hastening, if it were
possible for him, to be in Jerusalem
on the day of Pentecost.

1. *Assos.* An intellectual state of consciousness that is willing to examine into the truth (Apollonia), and is therefore drawing near to (approaching) an understanding of it. (MBD/Assos)

2. *Mitylene, Chios.* A place in consciousness wherein the word of Truth (Paul) enters and does a much needed (pressing, meaning urgent) cleansing and purifying; thus error is diminished (curtailing) and the individual is made ready for the next step, which is signified by Chios, where Paul went from Mitylene. Chios means open, and is representative of an open, unobstructed attitude of mind. (MBD/Mitylene).

3. *Samos.* The state of thought that Samos and Samothrace symbolize is intellectual rather than spiritual, since their location is in the Grecian Archipelago and Greece refers to the intellect. (MBD/Samothrace)

4. *Trogyllium* An analyzing and assimilating of ideas; a conscious taking on of substance (eating place, place of fruits, nuts, vegetables), by means of the word of Truth, represented here by Paul. (MBD/Trogyyllium)

5. *Miletus.* Miletus, meaning red, scarlet, refers to the seemingly material life in the organism of the individual. Purest wool, from the fact that only the purest of wool could take the scarlet dye, points to the true substance of life as lying back of and existing in the apparently material and corruptible, which seem to be in the ascendancy at this stage of individual unfold-

ment: "Trophimus I left at Miletus sick," Paul said (II Tim. 4:20). (MBD/Miletus)

## Paul Speaks to the Ephesian Elders

20:17 From Miletus he sent to Ephesus, and called to himself the elders of the assembly.[1] 20:18 When they had come to him, he said to them, "You yourselves know, from the first day that I set foot in Asia, how I was with you all the time,[2] 20:19 serving the Lord with all humility, with many tears, and with trials which happened to me by the plots of the Jews; 20:20 how I didn't shrink from declaring to you anything that was profitable, teaching you publicly and from house to house, 20:21 testifying both to Jews and to Greeks repentance toward God, and faith toward our Lord Jesus.[69] 20:22 Now, behold, I go bound by the Spirit to Jerusalem, not knowing what will happen to me there; 20:23 except that the Holy Spirit testifies in every city, saying that bonds and afflictions wait for me. 20:24 But these things don't count;[3] nor do I hold my life dear to myself, so that I may finish my race with joy, and the ministry which I received from the Lord Jesus, to fully testify to the Good News of the grace of God.

20:25 "Now, behold, I know that you all, among whom I went about preaching the Kingdom of God, will see my face no more. 20:26 Therefore I testify to you this day that I am clean from the blood of all men, 20:27 for I didn't shrink from declaring to you the whole counsel of God. 20:28 Take heed, therefore, to yourselves, and to all the flock, in which the Holy Spirit has made you overseers, to shepherd the assembly of the Lord and[70] God which he purchased with his own blood. 20:29 For I know that after my departure, vicious wolves will enter in among you,[4] not sparing the flock. 20:30 Men will arise from among your own selves, speaking perverse things, to draw away the disciples after them. 20:31 Therefore watch, remembering that for a period of three years I didn't cease to admonish everyone night and day with tears. 20:32 Now, brothers,[71] I entrust you to God, and to the word of his grace, which is able to build up, and to give you the inheritance among all those who are sanctified. 20:33 I coveted no one's silver, or gold, or clothing. 20:34 You yourselves know that these hands served my necessities,[5] and those who were with me. 20:35 In all things I gave you an example, that so laboring you ought to help the weak, and to remember the words of the Lord Jesus, that he himself said, 'It is more blessed to give than to receive.'" [6]

20:36 When he had spoken these things, he knelt down and prayed with them all. 20:37 They all wept a lot, and fell on Paul's neck and kissed him, 20:38 sorrowing most of all because of the word which he had spoken, that they should see his face no more. And they accompanied him to the ship.

1. *the elders of the assembly.* The elders signify the intelligent, directive powers of the spiritual self. Paul's calling the elders together represents a drawing together in conscious unity of the spiritual powers, to the end that peace and harmony may be established in the life.

2. *how I was with you all the time.* Paul reminds the elders of the consistency of his life among them which represents the creative word of Truth that is always present when the directive powers are assembled.

3. *these things don't count.* Self-control is a most necessary part of our spiritual education, and not only that self-control which shows as outward calmness and dispassion, but also control of our very thoughts and feelings, so that with Paul, we can truly say from our heart, "None of these things move me. (KJV)" (1892 Unity Tract, *None of These Things Move Me*, Annie Rix Militz)

4. *vicious wolves will enter in among you.* One should never put fear into the mind of another, or mention impending danger, without also emphasizing the saving power of God. After telling his followers that grievous wolves would enter the flock and that even among themselves men would arise, speaking perverse things, he said, "I entrust you to God, and to the word of his grace, which is able to build up, and to give you the inheritance among all those who are sanctified."

5. *You yourselves know that these hands served my necessities.* Paul was a tentmaker and labored at his trade to support himself and companions, while he preached the Gospel to the people. We think that Paul should have taught Truth and looked to God for his supply and support without laboring with his hands.

6. *It is more blessed to give than to receive.* This quotation which Paul attributes to Jesus is nowhere else recorded in the Scriptures.

---

Fillmore Study Bible annotations by Mark Hicks

**World English Bible Footnotes:**

[68] v20:8. TR reads "they" instead of "we"

[69] v20:21. TR adds "Christ"

[70] v20:28. TR, NU omit "the Lord and"

[71] v20:32. The word for "brothers" here and where the context allows may also be correctly translated "brothers and sisters" or "siblings."

# Acts 21

## Paul's Journey to Jerusalem[1]

21:1 When it happened that we had parted from them and had set sail, we came with a straight course to Cos,[2] and the next day to Rhodes, and from there to Patara.
21:2 Having found a ship crossing over to Phoenicia, we went aboard, and set sail.
21:3 When we had come in sight of Cyprus, leaving it on the left hand, we sailed to Syria, and landed at Tyre, for there the ship was to unload her cargo.
21:4 Having found disciples, we stayed there seven days. These said to Paul through the Spirit, that he should not go up to Jerusalem.
21:5 When it happened that we had accomplished the days, we departed and went on our journey. They all, with wives and children, brought us on our way until we were out of the city. Kneeling down on the beach, we prayed.
21:6 After saying goodbye to each other, we went on board the ship, and they returned home again.

[21:7] When we had finished the voyage from Tyre, we arrived at Ptolemais. We greeted the brothers, and stayed with them one day. [21:8] On the next day, we, who were Paul's companions, departed, and came to Caesarea.

We entered into the house of Philip the evangelist, who was one of the seven, and stayed with him. [21:9] Now this man had four virgin daughters who prophesied. [21:10] As we stayed there some days, a certain prophet named Agabus[3] came down from Judea. [21:11] Coming to us, and taking Paul's belt, he bound his own feet and hands, and said, "Thus says the Holy Spirit: 'So will the Jews at Jerusalem bind the man who owns this belt, and will deliver him into the hands of the Gentiles.'"

[21:12] When we heard these things, both we and they of that place begged him not to go up to Jerusalem. [21:13] Then Paul answered, "What are you doing, weeping and breaking my heart? For I am ready not only to be bound, but also to die at Jerusalem for the name of the Lord Jesus."

[21:14] When he would not be persuaded, we ceased, saying, "The Lord's will be done."

[21:15] After these days we took up our baggage and went up to Jerusalem.[4] [21:16] Some of the disciples from Caesarea also went with us, bringing one Mnason of Cyprus, an early disciple, with whom we would stay.

1. *Paul's Journey to Jerusalem.* The central truth of today's lesson is the going to Jerusalem at all hazards. Jerusalem is the center of the spiritual consciousness, the very acme of high perception. It requires more than ordinary courage for the apostle of Jesus Christ, the *I Am*, to go up to Jerusalem. We sometimes call it making "high statements." We know that we shall have to prove our words and that old states of consciousness both within and without will rise up in arms against us.

2. *Cos, Rhodes, Phoenicia, Cyprus, and Caesarea.* Each of these places symbolizes certain pleasant phases of consciousness in man who is seeking the highest; but they are not, strictly speaking, on the spiritual plane. Cos means summit; Rhodes, roses; Phoenicia, land of palm trees; Cyprus, fairness; Caesarea, dominant world power.

3. *Agabus.* Agabus symbolizes that in us which perceives the different forces working in the soul, at what point of contact these forces are liable to clash, and the evident outcome. This is known in man's consciousness as the power of prophecy.

4. *We took up our baggage and went up to Jerusalem.* Jerusalem is the faculty of love in consciousness, and also the "place of peace." As Jerusalem often was and still continues to be a center of turmoil and strife, so the heart of man often is a stranger to the peace that under divine law is his for the claiming. "Taking up our baggage and going to Jerusalem" is something we all need to do ;).

## Paul Visits James at Jerusalem

[21:17] When we had come to Jerusalem, the brothers received us gladly. [21:18] The day following, Paul went in with us to James; and all the elders were present. [21:19] When he had greeted them, he reported one by one the things which God had worked among the Gentiles through his ministry.[1] [21:20] They, when they heard it, glorified God. They said to him, "You see, brother, how many thousands there are among the Jews of those who have believed, and they are all zealous for the law. [21:21] They have been informed about you, that you teach all the Jews who are among the Gentiles to forsake Moses, telling them not to circumcise their children neither to walk after the customs. [21:22] What then? The assembly must certainly meet, for they will hear that you have come.

21:23 Therefore do what we tell you. We have four men who have taken a vow. 21:24 Take them, and purify yourself with them, and pay their expenses for them, that they may shave their heads. Then all will know that there is no truth in the things that they have been informed about you, but that you yourself also walk keeping the law. 21:25 But concerning the Gentiles who believe, we have written our decision[2] that they should observe no such thing, except that they should keep themselves from food offered to idols, from blood, from strangled things, and from sexual immorality." 21:26 Then Paul took the men, and the next day, purified himself and went with them into the temple, declaring the fulfillment of the days of purification, until the offering was offered for every one of them.

1. *[Paul] reported one by one the things which God had worked among the Gentiles through his ministry.* This is the idea which has seized Paul, and he is determined to reconcile Jew and Gentile. This is the object of his journey to Jerusalem. In applying this to our individual consciousness we find that there is a separation between our religious thoughts and our worldly thoughts. The Jews represent the religious thoughts, and the Gentiles the worldly thoughts.

2. *concerning the Gentiles who believe, we have written our decision.* The broad Truth of the Holy Spirit enters the mind and begins to break down this wall of separation between the religious thoughts and the worldly thoughts. It perceives that the principles involved in the Fatherhood of God must go to the uttermost parts of the mind and body and unify them in the Spirit.

## Paul Arrested in the Temple

21:27 When the seven days were almost completed, the Jews from Asia,[1] when they saw him in the temple, stirred up all the multitude and laid hands on him, 21:28 crying out, "Men of Israel, help! This is the man who teaches all men everywhere against the people, and the law, and this place. Moreover, he also brought Greeks into the temple, and has defiled this holy place!" 21:29 For they had seen Trophimus, the Ephesian, with him in the city, and they supposed that Paul had brought him into the temple.

21:30 All the city was moved, and the people ran together. They seized Paul and dragged him out of the temple.[2] Immediately the doors were shut. 21:31 As they were trying to kill him, news came up to the commanding officer of the regiment that all Jerusalem was in an uproar. 21:32 Immediately he took soldiers and centurions, and ran down to them. They, when they saw the chief captain and the soldiers, stopped beating Paul. 21:33 Then the commanding officer came near, arrested him, commanded him to be bound with two chains,[3] and inquired who he was and what he had done. 21:34 Some shouted one thing, and some another, among the crowd. When he couldn't find out the truth because of the noise, he commanded him to be brought into the barracks.

21:35 When he came to the stairs, it happened that he was carried by the soldiers because of the violence of the crowd; 21:36 for the multitude of the people followed after, crying out, "Away with him!"[4]

1. *Jews from Asia.* The Jews from Asia represent man's inmost and most tenaciously held religious convictions. The "people" are symbols of our thoughts, either original or gleaned from random outside sources. The law is another name for the worldly authority that we acknowledge as the guide of our actions.

2. *They seized Paul and dragged him out of the temple.* The sense man shuts Truth

out of his body consciousness by refusing to see that desire may be made a spiritual force.

3. *two chains.* The first chain is the chain of identity. Through the I AM man identifies himself with what he thinks is true of him, but which is often true only in appearance. The sense man therefore cherishes mistaken identity. The second chain is that of past action or experience (what man has done). Both these things bind man to temporal things.

4. *Away with him!* In this process the Truth, represented by Paul, meets with opposing thoughts from many directions. Jerusalem is the citadel of crystallized thoughts about religious matters, and the Truth must enter into it and speak the word that frees. The many warnings Paul received of obstacles to be overcome did opt deter him from going right forward. When we see danger and allow it to terrify us, we are not yet equal to the highest spiritual outpouring of power. When we are warned of danger, and are not deterred nor fearful, but take advantage of the warning to be wary, then we are sure to win.

## Paul Defends Himself

21:37 As Paul was about to be
brought into the barracks, he asked
the commanding officer, "May I speak
to you?" He said, "Do you know
Greek? 21:38 Aren't you then the
Egyptian, who before these days
stirred up to sedition and led out into
the wilderness the four thousand
men of the Assassins?"

21:39 But Paul said, "I am a Jew,[1]
from Tarsus in Cilicia,[2] a citizen of
no insignificant city. I beg you, allow
me to speak to the people."[3]

21:40 When he had given him
permission, Paul, standing on the
stairs, beckoned with his hand to the
people. When there was a great
silence, he spoke to them in the
Hebrew language, saying,

1. *I am a Jew.* In this statement we see an acknowledgment that faith is essentially a spiritual, not a material, faculty; that its rightful function is to transform material existence into a higher and more enduring quality of life.

2. *from Tarsus in Cilicia.* A city represents an aggregation of thoughts. Paul identified himself with his city as well as with his nation. Tarsus ("tranquillity," "pleasantness") represents a group of thoughts of an intellectual character in our consciousness, a group that blends with the more deeply inspirational phase of understanding that is spiritual.

3. *allow me to speak to the people.* Paul was not wise. Religious partisans do not argue, they dogmatize. What they have been taught is their authority and they are not open to reason or logic. Hence, to argue with one bound mentally in some religious sect creates antagonism and anger, and history proves that the heretic was never allowed to argue his case; his destruction was instantly demanded.

Fillmore Study Bible annotations by Mark Hicks

# Acts 22

## Paul Defends Himself (continued)

22:1 "Brothers and fathers, listen to the defense which I now make to you."

22:2 When they heard that he spoke to them in the Hebrew language,[1] they were even more quiet. He said, 22:3 "I am indeed a Jew,[2] born in Tarsus of Cilicia, but brought up in this city at the feet of Gamaliel, instructed according to the strict manner of the law of our fathers, being zealous for God, even as you all are this day. 22:4 I persecuted this Way to the death, binding and delivering into prisons both men and women. 22:5 As also the high priest and all the council of the elders testify, from whom also I received letters to the brothers, and traveled to Damascus to bring them also who were there to Jerusalem in bonds to be punished.

1. *Hebrew language.* Paul's listeners were Hebrews, a name representing a passing over, from the purely physical or material thought to a higher conception of religious truth. Though still under the law of sin and death, they were nevertheless spiritually developed enough to be responsive to the word of Truth in man's mind.

2. *I am indeed a Jew.* Paul was born a Jew, which means that the word of Truth is innately connected with the religious instinct in man. He was also born a Roman, which considered in connection with his imprisonment in Rome, shows that the will usurps complete authority when it is allowed to control man. But Paul was converted to the way of the Christ, thus symbolizing man's voluntary allegiance to Truth over and above all compulsory loyalties.

## Paul Tells of His Conversion

22:6 It happened that, as I made my journey, and came close to Damascus, about noon, suddenly there shone from the sky a great light around me.[1] 22:7 I fell to the ground, and heard a voice saying to me, 'Saul, Saul, why are you persecuting me?'[2] 22:8 I answered, 'Who are you, Lord?' He said to me, 'I am Jesus of Nazareth, whom you persecute.'

22:9 "Those who were with me indeed saw the light and were afraid, but they didn't understand the voice of him who spoke to me. 22:10 I said, 'What shall I do, Lord?' The Lord said to me, 'Arise, and go into Damascus. There you will be told about all things which are appointed for you to do.' 22:11 When I couldn't see for the glory of that light, being led by the hand of those who were with me, I came into Damascus. 22:12 One Ananias,[3] a devout man according to the law, well reported of by all the Jews who lived in Damascus, 22:13 came to me, and standing by me said to me, 'Brother Saul, receive your sight!'[4] In that very hour I looked up at him. 22:14 He said, 'The God of our fathers has appointed you to know his will, and to see the Righteous One, and to hear a voice from his mouth. 22:15 For you will be a witness for him to all men of what you have seen and heard. 22:16 Now why do you wait? Arise, be baptized, and wash away your sins, calling on the name of the Lord.'

1. *a great light around me.* Saul received a spiritual baptism like that received by the disciples who were in the upper room in Jerusalem on the day of Pentecost. This spiritual baptism was so intense that he could not assimilate the tremendous spiritual energy that had come to him.

2. *Saul, Saul, why are you persecuting me?* The word "Saul" means "wished" or "affirmed"; in one of its phases it represents activity of mind called the will. In man's evolution, King Saul, with his boundless ambition and erratic judgment, represents the last stand of the human will. An almost exact parallel is found in the life of Saul of Tarsus.

3. *Ananias.* The Lord sent him a healer in the person of Ananias, who laid hands on him and helped him to equalize the spiritual energy which had descended suddenly into his soul and his body. Similar experiences are quite common in this day among Truth workers; often they find it necessary to help one another to master their higher forces.

4. *Brother Saul, receive your sight!* The vision was a vision only to those who accompanied Saul; to Saul it was a real occurrence. Jesus actually talked to him out of the fourth dimension or out of what modern scientists call the luminiferous ether.

## Paul Sent to the Gentiles

22:17 "It happened that, when I had returned to Jerusalem, and while I prayed in the temple, I fell into a trance, 22:18 and saw him saying to me, 'Hurry and get out of Jerusalem quickly, because they will not receive testimony concerning me from you.' 22:19 I said, 'Lord, they themselves know that I imprisoned and beat in every synagogue those who believed in you. 22:20 When the blood of Stephen, your witness, was shed, I also was standing by, and consenting to his death, and guarding the cloaks of those who killed him.'

22:21 "He said to me, 'Depart, for I will send you out far from here to the Gentiles.'"[1]

1. *Depart, for I will send you out far from here to the Gentiles.* Stephen was zealous for the new religion; Saul was equally zealous for the old. The zeal of Saul carried him away to other lands. On the road he meditated and opened up the superman in himself and was converted to Christianity.

## Paul and the Roman Tribune

22:22 They listened to him until he said that; then they lifted up their voice, and said, "Rid the earth of this fellow, for he isn't fit to live!"[1]

22:23 As they cried out, and threw off their cloaks, and threw dust into the air, 22:24 the commanding officer commanded him to be brought into the barracks, ordering him to be examined by scourging, that he might know for what crime they shouted against him like that.[2] 22:25 When they had tied him up with thongs, Paul asked the centurion who stood by, "Is it lawful for you to scourge a man who is a Roman, and not found guilty?"

22:26 When the centurion heard it, he went to the commanding officer and told him, "Watch what you are about to do, for this man is a Roman!"

22:27 The commanding officer came and asked him, "Tell me, are you a Roman?"

He said, "Yes."

22:28 The commanding officer answered, "I bought my citizenship for a great price."

Paul said, "But I was born a Roman."

22:29 Immediately those who were about to examine him departed from him, and the commanding officer also was afraid when he realized that he was a Roman, because he had bound him.

1. *Rid the earth of this fellow, for he isn't fit to live!* Paul had been high in Jewish ecclesiastical circles and he took it for granted that his friends would readily believe him. The organized Christian institutions of today do not accept special spiritual revelations from their followers.

2. *he might know for what crime they shouted against him like that.* The universal tendency of all ideas in the mind of man is toward crystallization. Our religious institutions represent the crystallization of former spiritual revelations.

## Paul before the Council

22:30 But on the next day, desiring to know the truth about why he was accused by the Jews, he freed him from the bonds, and commanded the chief priests❶ and all the council❷ to come together, and brought Paul down and set him before them.

1. *the chief priests* The descendants of Levi represent thoughts that spring from and belong to the love faculty in individual consciousness. As ministers and priests in the Temple and in the Temple worship they signify our natural religious tendencies, not necessarily spiritual. (MBD/Levites)

2. *the council.* The whole consciousness (MBD/council).

---

Fillmore Study Bible annotations by Mark Hicks

# Acts 23

## Paul before the Council (continued)

23:1 Paul, looking steadfastly at the council, said, "Brothers, I have lived before God in all good conscience until this day."

23:2 The high priest, Ananias,❶ commanded those who stood by him to strike him on the mouth.

23:3 Then Paul said to him, "God will strike you, you whitewashed wall! Do you sit to judge me according to the law, and command me to be struck contrary to the law?"

23:4 Those who stood by said, "Do you malign God's high priest?"

23:5 Paul said, "I didn't know, brothers, that he was high priest. For it is written, 'You shall not speak evil
of a ruler of your people.'"[72] 23:6 But
when Paul perceived that the one part were Sadducees and the other Pharisees, he cried out in the council, "Men and brothers, I am a Pharisee,❷ a son of Pharisees. Concerning the hope and resurrection of the dead I am being

judged!"

23:7 When he had said this, an argument arose between the Pharisees and Sadducees, and the assembly was divided. 23:8 For the Sadducees say that there is no resurrection, nor angel, nor spirit; but the Pharisees confess all of these. 23:9 A great clamor arose, and some of the scribes of the Pharisees part stood up, and contended, saying, "We find no evil in this man. But if a spirit or angel has spoken to him, let's not fight against God!"

23:10 When a great argument arose, the commanding officer, fearing that Paul would be torn in pieces by them, commanded the soldiers to go down and take him by force from among them, and bring him into the barracks.

23:11 The following night, the Lord stood by him, and said, "Cheer up, Paul, for as you have testified about me at Jerusalem, so you must testify also at Rome."

1. *Ananias.* The high priest Ananias symbolizes a still different phase of character in man. He represents the hypocrisy that inheres in the intellectual, religious, ruling mind in man when it is governed by the letter of the word, outer forms, and ceremonies, instead of being given over to real spiritual Truth (MBD/Ananias).

2. *I am a Pharisee.* You will have more trouble with your sectarian thoughts (Pharisees and chief priests) than with all others. They are very close to the spiritual realm in your consciousness, and therefore more powerful than the more material thoughts (John 7:32). The old-established religious thoughts belonging to the intellectual domain never miss an opportunity to reason with and to dispute every true, spiritual idea that is presented to the consciousness. This is symbolized by the Pharisees, who would keep only the letter of the law. When the spirit of the law is taught it overthrows the outer forms and ceremonies that belong to the letter; so they who are strict in observing the letter usually oppose the spirit of the law. The Truth that the higher self is always bringing to every part of the individual is missed by the pharisaical phase of consciousness.

## The Plot to Kill Paul

23:12 When it was day, some of the Jews banded together, and bound themselves under a curse, saying that they would neither eat nor drink until they had killed Paul. 23:13 There were more than forty people who had made this conspiracy. 23:14 They came to the chief priests and the elders, and said, "We have bound ourselves under a great curse, to taste nothing until we have killed Paul. 23:15 Now therefore, you with the council inform the commanding officer that he should bring him down to you tomorrow, as though you were going to judge his case more exactly. We are ready to kill him before he comes near."

23:16 But Paul's sister's son heard of their lying in wait,[1] and he came and entered into the barracks and told Paul. 23:17 Paul summoned one of the centurions, and said, "Bring this young man to the commanding officer, for he has something to tell him."

23:18 So he took him, and brought him to the commanding officer, and said, "Paul, the prisoner, summoned me and asked me to bring this young man to you, who has something to tell you."

23:19 The commanding officer took him by the hand, and going aside, asked him privately, "What is it that you have to tell me?"

23:20 He said, "The Jews have agreed to ask you to bring Paul down to the council tomorrow, as though intending to inquire somewhat more accurately concerning him. 23:21 Therefore don't yield to them, for more than forty men lie in wait for him, who have bound themselves under a curse neither to eat nor to drink until they have killed him. Now they are ready, looking for the promise from you." 23:22 So the commanding officer let the young man go, charging him, "Tell no one that you have revealed these things to me."

1. *But Paul's sister's son heard of their lying in wait.* Paul was seemingly surrounded by enemies who were banded together for the purpose of killing him, but there was a higher power working for his safety. He may have made mistakes, and he may have been obstinate in his insistence upon going to Jerusalem in the face of the warning of the Holy Spirit, but this did not prevent the Lord from protecting him.

## Paul Sent to Felix the Governor

23:23 He called to himself two of the centurions, and said, "Prepare two hundred soldiers to go as far as Caesarea, with seventy horsemen, and two hundred men armed with spears, at the third hour of the night[73]." 23:24 He asked them to provide animals, that they might set Paul on one, and bring him safely to Felix the governor.[1] 23:25 He wrote a letter like this:

23:26 "Claudius Lysias to the most excellent governor Felix: Greetings.

23:27 "This man was seized by the Jews, and was about to be killed by them, when I came with the soldiers and rescued him, having learned that he was a Roman. 23:28 Desiring to know the cause why they accused him, I brought him down to their council. 23:29 I found him to be accused about questions of their law, but not to be charged with anything worthy of death or of imprisonment. 23:30 When I was told that the Jews lay in wait for the man, I sent him to you immediately, charging his accusers also to bring their accusations against him before you. Farewell."

23:31 So the soldiers, carrying out their orders, took Paul and brought him by night to Antipatris. 23:32 But on the next day they left the horsemen to go with him, and returned to the barracks. 23:33 When they came to Caesarea and delivered the letter to the governor, they also presented Paul to him. 23:34 When the governor had read it, he asked what province he was from. When he understood that he was from Cilicia, he said, 23:35 "I will hear you fully when your accusers also arrive." He commanded that he be kept in Herod's palace.

1. *bring him safely to Felix the governor* Paul wanted to go to Rome to preach the Truth, and the conspiracy of the Jews to kill him was paving the way for the fulfillment of that desire. When you are following the Spirit and seeking to do the will of the Lord to the very best of your ability, count all your experiences as steppingstones to your good. The central truth of this lesson is that what we are loyal to in the heart, or within, will finally make itself manifest in the without.

---

Fillmore Study Bible annotations by Mark Hicks

**World English Bible Footnotes:**

[72] v23:5. Exodus 22:28

[73] v23:23. about 9:00 PM

# Acts 24

## Paul before Felix at Caesarea

24:1 After five days, the high priest, Ananias,[1] came down with certain elders[2] and an orator, one Tertullus.[3] They informed the governor against Paul. 24:2 When he was called, Tertullus began to accuse him, saying, "Seeing that by you we enjoy much peace, and that excellent measures are coming to this nation, 24:3 we accept it in all ways and in all places, most excellent Felix, with all thankfulness. 24:4 But, that I don't delay you, I entreat you to bear with us and hear a few words. 24:5 For we have found this man to be a plague, an instigator of insurrections among all the Jews throughout the world, and a ringleader of the sect of the Nazarenes. 24:6 He even tried to profane the temple, and we arrested him.[74] 24:7 [75] 24:8 [76]By examining him yourself you may ascertain all these things of which we accuse him."

24:9 The Jews also joined in the attack, affirming that these things were so.

1. *Ananias.* Represents the hypocrisy that inheres in the intellectual, religious, ruling mind in man when it is governed by the letter of the word, outer forms, and ceremonies, instead of being given over to real spiritual Truth (MBD/Ananias).

2. *certain elders.* The assembling of elders signifies a drawing together in conscious unity of all the intelligent directive powers of the spiritual self, to the standard of peace and harmony. This process may take place without the conscious mind's understanding its import. The whole consciousness is made up of objective and subjective thoughts and their results. Like a chemical solution, they go through changes on the subjective side that are observed in their outer appearance only, and but dimly understood. (MBD/elders)

3. *Tertullus.* Expression in an outer, sense way, and incited by the outer, established religious ideas of the intellect in man (diminutive of Tertius, little third, minor third, one who came with the elders of the Jews to testify against Paul (MBD/Tertullus).

## Paul's Defense before Felix

24:10 When the governor had beckoned to him to speak, Paul answered, "Because I know that you have been a judge of this nation for many years, I cheerfully make my defense,[1] 24:11 seeing that you can recognize that it is not more than twelve days since I went up to worship at Jerusalem. 24:12 In the temple they didn't find me disputing with anyone or stirring up a crowd, either in the synagogues, or in the city. 24:13 Nor can they prove to you the things of which they now accuse me. 24:14 But this I confess to you, that after the Way, which they call a sect, so I serve the God of our fathers,[2] believing all things which

are according to the law, and which
are written in the prophets; 24:15
having hope toward God, which these
also themselves look for, that there
will be a resurrection of the dead,
both of the just and unjust. 24:16
Herein I also practice always having
a conscience void of offense toward
God and men. 24:17 Now after some
years, I came to bring gifts for the
needy to my nation, and offerings;
24:18 amid which certain Jews from
Asia found me purified in the temple,
not with a mob, nor with turmoil. 24:19
They ought to have been here before
you, and to make accusation, if they
had anything against me. 24:20 Or else
let these men themselves say what
injustice they found in me when I
stood before the council, 24:21 unless
it is for this one thing that I cried
standing among them, 'Concerning
the resurrection of the dead I am
being judged before you today!'"

24:22 But Felix, having more exact
knowledge concerning the Way,[3]
deferred them, saying, "When Lysias,
the commanding officer, comes
down, I will decide your case." 24:23
He ordered the centurion that Paul
should be kept in custody, and should have some privileges, and not to forbid any of his friends to serve him or to visit him.

1. *I cheerfully make my defense.* It is absolutely impossible for man to be set free from the hard conditions that bind him by appealing to temporal helps. All the ills that beset us have their origin in the mind. There is no other source, and we must go to that source to make permanent adjustment. If we are not getting our rights, it is because we are not declaring God our advocate. Mind moves matter and the moulding power of the world will be found only in mind.

2. *after the Way ... so I serve the God of our fathers.* [Paul's defense appealed to the Law and the Prophets instead of to the living Christ]. When we have grasped the idea that Christ lives here and now, and only waits our acknowledgment to make himself manifest in our lives, we have taken that first step in the demonstration. Every spiritual Demonstration depends upon our acknowledgment of the Christ as the real self. When we acknowledge ourselves to be anything less than spiritually perfect, we are taking side with the adversary and we will surely find the Christ light growing dimmer and dimmer.

3. *the Way.* The I AM in man, the open door to the kingdom of God. See Christ and Jesus. (RW/Way)

## Paul Held in Custody

24:24 But after some days, Felix
came with Drusilla, his wife, who was
a Jewess, and sent for Paul, and
heard him concerning the faith in
Christ Jesus. 24:25 As he reasoned
about righteousness, self-control,
and the judgment to come, Felix was
terrified,[1] and answered, "Go your
way for this time, and when it is
convenient for me, I will summon
you." 24:26 Meanwhile, he also hoped
that money would be given to him
by Paul, that he might release him.
Therefore also he sent for him more
often, and talked with him. 24:27 But
when two years were fulfilled, Felix
was succeeded by Porcius Festus,
and desiring to gain favor with the
Jews, Felix left Paul in bonds.[2]

1. *Felix was terrified.* Felix represents the twin faculties, the will and the understanding, functioning in mortal consciousness. Paul's words of Truth did not move the relaxation of the will, but disturbed the understanding, which was "terrified."

2. *Felix left Paul in bonds.* In claiming the protection of Roman citizenship, when he was arrested, Paul found the truth here stated exemplified in his experience. He gave his case to the Romans and took it out of the hands of God. The result of his servitude is shown in the years of imprisonment which be had to endure. When he and Silas were in prison and prayed and sang psalms, the doors were opened and they were immediately set free. That was wholehearted dependence, and the results

show what powerful agencies were brought to bear as a result of that concentration.

Fillmore Study Bible annotations by Mark Hicks

**World English Bible Footnotes:**

[74] v24:6. TR adds "We wanted to judge him according to our law,"

[75] v24:7. TR adds "but the commanding officer, Lysias, came by and with great violence took him out of our hands,"

[76] v24:8. TR adds "commanding his accusers to come to you."

# Acts 25

## Paul Appeals to the Emperor

25:1 Festus therefore, having come into the province, after three days went up to Jerusalem from Caesarea. 25:2 Then the high priest and the principal men of the Jews informed him against Paul, and they begged him, 25:3 asking a favor against him, that he would summon him to Jerusalem; plotting to kill him on the way. 25:4 However Festus answered that Paul should be kept in custody at Caesarea, and that he himself was about to depart shortly. 25:5 "Let them therefore," said he, "that are in power among you go down with me, and if there is anything wrong in the man, let them accuse him."

25:6 When he had stayed among them more than ten days, he went down to Caesarea, and on the next day he sat on the judgment seat, and commanded Paul to be brought. 25:7 When he had come, the Jews who had come down from Jerusalem stood around him, bringing against him many and grievous charges which they could not prove, 25:8 while he said in his defense, "Neither against the law of the Jews, nor against the temple, nor against Caesar, have I sinned at all."

25:9 But Festus, desiring to gain favor with the Jews, answered Paul and said, "Are you willing to go up to Jerusalem, and be judged by me there concerning these things?"

25:10 But Paul said, "I am standing before Caesar's judgment seat, where I ought to be tried. I have done no wrong to the Jews, as you also know very well. 25:11 For if I have done wrong, and have committed anything worthy of death, I don't refuse to die; but if none of those things is true that they accuse me of, no one can give me up to them. I appeal to Caesar!"[1]

25:12 Then Festus, when he had conferred with the council, answered, "You have appealed to Caesar. To Caesar you shall go."[2]

1. *I appeal to Caesar!* You must not look to Caesar for justification. "Thou shalt keep him in perfect peace, whose mind is stayed on Thee" (Isaiah 26:3). The Spirit will surely take care of you in any contingency. You have nothing to fear: for you have learned that "there is no evil." To "appeal unto Caesar" is to forget this basic doctrine of your faith. You, who are "in the world but not of it," should not court its favor and approbation. Such a course is inconsistent with your high calling and trust.

2. *You have appealed to Caesar. To Caesar you shall go.* In true metaphysics all actors are to be found within; and therefore this lesson is the picturing under the symbology of history, of the struggle going on within your own breast, as you undertake to carry out the principles of Christ in opposition to your old religious thought and that of the world. The old material consciousness will continue to assert itself, until a higher, the Spiritual consciousness, is established. So great and venomous is the hostility of the old religious thought that you take umbrage under the thought as the less of two evils; this is "appealing unto Caesar," which is not the correct thing to do. But the Christian should ever make his appeal to the Spirit, which is always a "very present help in every time of need."

## Festus Consults King Agrippa

25:13 Now when some days had passed, Agrippa the King and Bernice arrived at Caesarea, and greeted Festus. 25:14 As he stayed there many days, Festus laid Paul's case before the king, saying, "There is a certain man left a prisoner by Felix; 25:15 about whom, when I was at Jerusalem, the chief priests and the elders of the Jews informed me, asking for a sentence against him. 25:16 To whom I answered that it is not the custom of the Romans to give up any man to destruction, before the accused has met the accusers face to face, and has had opportunity to make his defense concerning the matter laid against him. 25:17 When therefore they had come together here, I didn't delay, but on the next day sat on the judgment seat, and commanded the man to be brought. 25:18 Concerning whom, when the accusers stood up, they brought no charge of such things as I supposed; 25:19 but had certain questions against him about their own religion, and about one Jesus, who was dead, whom Paul affirmed to be alive.[1] 25:20 Being perplexed how to inquire concerning these things, I asked whether he was willing to go to Jerusalem and there be judged concerning these matters. 25:21 But when Paul had appealed to be kept for the decision of the emperor, I commanded him to be kept until I could send him to Caesar."

25:22 Agrippa said to Festus, "I also would like to hear the man myself."

"Tomorrow," he said, "you shall hear him."

1. *whom Paul affirmed to be alive.* The Jews represent the religious thoughts that crystallize in certain fixed forms. Crystallization of beliefs permits no new ideas to enter in but rejects them as a matter of course. The idea that fulfillment [resurrection] had actually come was too good to accept as true, and the Jews preferred to keep fulfillment indefinitely in the future. The resurrection from the dead strained their faith to the breaking point.

## Paul Brought before Agrippa

25:23 So on the next day, when Agrippa and Bernice had come with great pomp, and they had entered into the place of hearing with the commanding officers and principal men of the city, at the command of Festus, Paul was brought in. [25:24] Festus said,❶ "King Agrippa, and all men who are here present with us, you see this man, about whom all the multitude of the Jews petitioned me, both at Jerusalem and here, crying that he ought not to live any longer. [25:25] But when I found that he had committed nothing worthy of death, and as he himself appealed to the emperor I determined to send him. [25:26] Of whom I have no certain thing to write to my lord. Therefore I have brought him forth before you, and especially before you, King Agrippa, that, after examination, I may have something to write. [25:27] For it seems to me unreasonable, in sending a prisoner, not to also specify the charges against him."

1. *Festus said.* Paul imprisoned at Caesarea symbolizes Truth confined to the intellect. It seems paradoxical to say that so great and powerful a thing as Truth can be confined or hampered by so small and weak a thing as the intellect, yet observation and experience proves that it can. In this connection we should distinguish between a Statement of Truth, which Paul represents, and the Whole Truth, which is the Holy Ghost. The statement of Truth goes before and opens the mind for the advent of the larger realization to follow.

Fillmore Study Bible annotations by Mark Hicks

# Acts 26

## Paul Defends Himself before Agrippa

[26:1] Agrippa said to Paul, "You may speak for yourself."

Then Paul stretched out his hand, and made his defense. [26:2] "I think myself happy, King Agrippa, that I am to make my defense before you this day❶ concerning all the things that I am accused by the Jews, [26:3] especially because you are expert in all customs and questions which are among the Jews. Therefore I beg you to hear me patiently.

[26:4] "Indeed, all the Jews know my way of life from my youth up, which was from the beginning among my own nation and at Jerusalem; [26:5] having known me from the first, if they are willing to testify, that after the strictest sect of our religion I lived a Pharisee. [26:6] Now I stand here to be judged for the hope of the promise made by God to our fathers, [26:7] which our twelve tribes, earnestly serving night and day, hope to attain. Concerning this hope I am accused by the Jews, King Agrippa! [26:8] Why is it judged incredible with you, if God does raise the dead?

[26:9] "I myself most certainly thought that I ought to do many things contrary to the name of Jesus of Nazareth.❷ [26:10] This I also did in Jerusalem. I both shut up many of the saints in prisons, having received authority from the chief priests, and when they were put to death I gave my vote against them. [26:11] Punishing them often in all the synagogues, I tried to make them blaspheme. Being exceedingly enraged against them, I persecuted them even to foreign cities.

1. *I think myself happy ... that I am to make my defense before you this day.* Why was Saul inclined to be argumentative and contentious? Because his zeal, which was great, was divorced from spiritual understanding. He identified himself with the Pharisees, who represent the external forms of faith in contrast with the essence of faith itself, namely the Spirit of truth.

2. *Jesus of Nazareth.* The metaphysical meaning of the name Jesus of Nazareth means "offshoot, guarded; defended," and the name Jesus means "Saviour, Deliverer." Jesus is the Saviour, and the Christ is the I AM in man. The I AM guards and defends the common everyday life of man, until it takes on the likeness and substance of spiritual truth and saves man from the disillusionment and frustrations that he experiences in sense consciousness

## Paul Tells of His Conversion[1]

26:12 "Whereupon as I traveled to
Damascus with the authority and
commission from the chief priests,
26:13 at noon, O King, I saw on the way
a light from the sky, brighter than
the sun, shining around me and those
who traveled with me. 26:14 When we
had all fallen to the earth, I heard
a voice saying to me in the Hebrew
language, 'Saul, Saul, why are you
persecuting me?[2] It is hard for you to
kick against the goads.'[3]

26:15 "I said, 'Who are you, Lord?'

"He said, 'I am Jesus, whom you
are persecuting. 26:16 But arise, and
stand on your feet, for I have
appeared to you for this purpose: to
appoint you a servant and a witness
both of the things which you have
seen, and of the things which I will
reveal to you;[4] 26:17 delivering you
from the people, and from the
Gentiles, to whom I send you, 26:18
to open their eyes, that they may
turn from darkness to light and from
the power of Satan to God, that they
may receive remission of sins and an
inheritance among those who are
sanctified by faith in me.'

1. See Acts 9:1

2. *Saul, Saul, why are you persecuting me?* Is it reasonable to teach that Jesus spoke to Paul out of the heavens as one personality speaks to another? Jesus lives in the ether, which is an interpenetrating, radiant realm of substance, more rarefied than the earth or its atmosphere, yet which has real existence. Jesus has manifested Himself to His followers many times from this kingdom of the heavens, and it is quite reasonable to believe that He spoke to Paul as stated in the Scripture.

3. *kick against the goads.* Zeal for God was the "goad" against which Saul was kicking, a zeal that reacted upon him later when, in preaching Christ, he was persecuted by the Jews as relentlessly as he had persecuted others.

4. *"But arise, and stand on your feet, for I have appeared to you for this purpose: to appoint you a servant (minister, ASV) and a witness both of the things which you have seen, and of the things which I will reveal to you."* Catherine Ponder writes this passage in the ASV inspired her to become a minister. *A Prosperity Love Story* p.38

## Paul Tells of His Preaching

26:19 "Therefore, King Agrippa, I
was not disobedient to the heavenly
vision,[1] 26:20 but declared first to
them of Damascus, at Jerusalem, and
throughout all the country of Judea,
and also to the Gentiles, that they
should repent and turn to God, doing
works worthy of repentance. 26:21 For
this reason the Jews seized me in
the temple, and tried to kill me. 26:22
Having therefore obtained the help
that is from God, I stand to this day

testifying both to small and great,
saying nothing but what the prophets
and Moses said would happen, 26:23
how the Christ must suffer, and how,
by the resurrection of the dead, he
would be first to proclaim light both
to these people and to the Gentiles."

1. *I was not disobedient to the heavenly vision.* Does the will have a part in effecting the transformation? Yes, the change is a voluntary one. No one is transformed against his will. Saul's conversion seems to have been an exception to this rule. Was it actually so? Although it seemed not to be so, Saul's conversion was voluntary. As soon as he saw the light and heard the voice of Jesus, he acknowledged the authority of the Speaker by his words, "Who art thou, Lord?" His willingness to obey equaled his perception of his Lord.

## Paul Appeals to Agrippa to Believe

26:24 As he thus made his defense,
Festus said with a loud voice, "Paul,
you are crazy![1] Your great learning
is driving you insane!"

26:25 But he said, "I am not crazy,
most excellent Festus, but boldly
declare words of truth and
reasonableness. 26:26 For the king
knows of these things, to whom also
I speak freely. For I am persuaded
that none of these things is hidden
from him, for this has not been done
in a corner. 26:27 King Agrippa, do you
believe the prophets? I know that you
believe."

26:28 Agrippa said to Paul, "With a
little persuasion are you trying to
make me a Christian?"[2]

26:29 Paul said, "I pray to God, that
whether with little or with much, not
only you, but also all that hear me
this day, might become such as I am,
except for these bonds."

26:30 The king rose up with the
governor, and Bernice, and those
who sat with them. 26:31 When they
had withdrawn, they spoke one to
another, saying, "This man does
nothing worthy of death or of bonds."
26:32 Agrippa said to Festus, "This man
might have been set free if he had
not appealed to Caesar."[3]

1. *Paul, you are crazy!* When the illuminated Christian preaches the Gospel in demonstration of the Spirit, worldly wisdom calls it "madness" or "fanaticism." But "words of Truth" are "words of soberness," the very opposite of madness.

2. *Are you trying to make me a Christian?* As Festus represents the transient joys of the external life, his brother-in-law, Agrippa, shows the close association that this sort of pleasure has with pain. So long as we are enjoying ourselves in the sense life, our ears are usually dull to Truth: Festus was not moved by Paul's eloquent appeal. But pain brings us very close to an acceptance of the higher way: Agrippa was almost persuaded to believe. Most of those who are now studying Truth became interested because of an urgent need for physical healing, for release from inharmony. (MBD/Agrippa)

3. *This man might have been set free if he had not appealed to Caesar.* We have spoken of Festus and Agrippa as representing worldly thought. In fact they are semi-religious and assume to have authority over the spiritual. If you "appeal unto Caesar" instead of Christ, you must remain bound in prison; you have not the consciousness of freedom. You may preach the gospel in Rome; but it will be under bondage. Sometimes Christians undertake to settle a church controversy by the courts. This is "appealing unto Caesar" and it never brings spiritual freedom, only spiritual bondage.

Fillmore Study Bible annotations by Mark Hicks

# Acts 27

## Paul Sails for Rome

27:1 When it was determined that we should sail for Italy, they delivered Paul and certain other prisoners to a centurion[1] named Julius, of the Augustan band. 27:2 Embarking in a ship of Adramyttium, which was about to sail to places on the coast of Asia, we put to sea; Aristarchus, a Macedonian of Thessalonica, being with us. 27:3 The next day, we touched at Sidon. Julius treated Paul kindly, and gave him permission to go to his friends and refresh himself. 27:4 Putting to sea from there, we sailed under the lee of Cyprus, because the winds were contrary. 27:5 When we had sailed across the sea which is off Cilicia and Pamphylia, we came to Myra, a city of Lycia. 27:6 There the centurion found a ship of Alexandria sailing for Italy, and he put us on board. 27:7 When we had sailed slowly many days, and had come with difficulty opposite Cnidus, the wind not allowing us further, we sailed under the lee of Crete, opposite Salmone. 27:8 With difficulty sailing along it we came to a certain place called Fair Havens, near the city of Lasea.

27:9 When much time had passed and the voyage was now dangerous,[2] because the Fast had now already gone by, Paul admonished them, 27:10 and said to them, "Sirs, I perceive that the voyage will be with injury and much loss, not only of the cargo and the ship, but also of our lives." 27:11 But the centurion gave more heed to the master and to the owner of the ship than to those things which were spoken by Paul. 27:12 Because the haven was not suitable to winter in, the majority advised going to sea from there, if by any means they could reach Phoenix, and winter there, which is a port of Crete, looking northeast and southeast.

1. *they delivered Paul and certain other prisoners to a centurion.* Paul and Silas were released from prison on a former occasion by the angel of the Lord, and Peter had a similar experience. The Bible gives many examples of the interposition of the power of the Lord to set aside material bonds, when it is invoked. But it must be invoked. The law does not work unless man works it, or with his mind touches the button that sets going the machinery that does the work. If we lose faith in the higher law, or decide that it is expedient to adopt the lower, we get results according to the ability of the method under which we have placed ourselves.

2. *the voyage was now dangerous.* The illuminated Christian, who "dwells in the secret place of the Most High," dwells safely with a guarantee of immunity from everything that assails others, who know not God as their sure defense. But unless one finds the secret understanding of that "secret place" the manifestations of evil from an unfriendly environment may threaten and disturb him sometimes even more than the man of the world. For the world knows not your joys, therefore they think you are peculiar and fanatical.

## The Storm at Sea

27:13 When the south wind blew softly, supposing that they had obtained their purpose, they weighed anchor and sailed along Crete, close to shore. 27:14 But before long, a stormy wind beat down from shore,[1] which is called Euroclydon.[77] 27:15 When the ship

was caught, and couldn't face the
wind, we gave way to it, and were
driven along. 27:16 Running under the
lee of a small island called Clauda,
we were able, with difficulty, to
secure the boat. 27:17 After they had
hoisted it up, they used cables to
help reinforce the ship. Fearing that
they would run aground on the Syrtis
sand bars, they lowered the sea
anchor, and so were driven along.
27:18 As we labored exceedingly with
the storm, the next day they began
to throw things overboard.[2] 27:19 On
the third day, they threw out the
ship's tackle with their own hands.
27:20 When neither sun nor stars shone
on us for many days, and no small
storm pressed on us, all hope that we
would be saved was now taken away.

27:21 When they had been long
without food, Paul stood up in the
middle of them, and said, "Sirs, you
should have listened to me, and not
have set sail from Crete, and have
gotten this injury and loss. 27:22 Now
I exhort you to cheer up, for there
will be no loss of life among you, but
only of the ship. 27:23 For there stood
by me this night an angel, belonging
to the God whose I am and whom
I serve, 27:24 saying, 'Don't be afraid,
Paul. You must stand before Caesar.
Behold, God has granted you all
those who sail with you.' 27:25
Therefore, sirs, cheer up! For I
believe God, that it will be just as
it has been spoken to me. 27:26 But
we must run aground on a certain
island."[3]

27:27 But when the fourteenth night
had come, as we were driven back
and forth in the Adriatic Sea, about
midnight the sailors surmised that
they were drawing near to some
land. 27:28 They took soundings, and
found twenty fathoms.[78] After a
little while, they took soundings
again, and found fifteen fathoms.[79]
27:29 Fearing that we would run
aground on rocky ground, they let
go four anchors from the stern, and
wished for daylight. 27:30 As the sailors
were trying to flee out of the ship,
and had lowered the boat into the
sea, pretending that they would lay
out anchors from the bow, 27:31 Paul
said to the centurion and to the
soldiers, "Unless these stay in the
ship, you can't be saved." 27:32 Then
the soldiers cut away the ropes of
the boat, and let it fall off.

27:33 While the day was coming on,
Paul begged them all to take some
food, saying, "This day is the
fourteenth day that you wait and
continue fasting, having taken
nothing. 27:34 Therefore I beg you to
take some food,[4] for this is for your
safety; for not a hair will perish from
any of your heads." 27:35 When he had
said this, and had taken bread, he
gave thanks to God in the presence
of all, and he broke it, and began
to eat. 27:36 Then they all cheered
up, and they also took food. 27:37 In
all, we were two hundred seventy-six
souls on the ship. 27:38 When they had
eaten enough, they lightened the
ship, throwing out the wheat into the
sea.

1. *A stormy wind beat down from shore.* Having "appealed unto Caesar" at first you start out beautifully: "the south wind blows softly"; you "suppose you have attained your purpose." But, since you have committed your cause to the law of mortal thought, the merciless "euroclydon" is liable to swoop down on you any moment. You are threatened with the "lee shore" of "Clauda" on the one hand and the quicksands of "Syrtis" on the other. For self-preservation you seem to be "steering between the rook, Scylla, and the whirlpool, Charybdis."

2. *began to throw things overboard.* How the disobedient soul is tempest-tossed on the sea of mortal thought, while he looks unto Caesar for justice; until you loose your valuable cargo of Spiritual riches, the consciousness of abundant Good.

3. *But we must run aground on a certain island.* Fasting, if enforced, denotes denials. By your denial of hopelessness you are able to "stand forth in the midst," and

make your strong affirmation of hope and cheer. Through the enlightening visions of truth you affirm hope and cheer and the indestructibility of life. You also affirm the destruction of the false reasoning that carries you to Caesar. For only after this "ship of Alexandria" (Egypt) is destroyed, can you save "all them that are with you." This leaves you stranded "on a certain island" of unreclaimed thought in the broad sea of mortal thought.

4. *take some food.* Symbolical of the affirmative state of mind. *Two hundred seventy-six souls* Mathematical accuracy, law, and order prevail in Spirit.

## The Shipwreck

27:39 When it was day, they didn't recognize the land,[1] but they noticed a certain bay with a beach, and they decided to try to drive the ship onto it. 27:40 Casting off the anchors, they left them in the sea, at the same time untying the rudder ropes. Hoisting up the foresail to the wind, they made for the beach.[2] 27:41 But coming to a place where two seas met, they ran the vessel aground. The bow struck and remained immovable, but the stern began to break up by the violence of the waves.

27:42 The soldiers' counsel was to kill the prisoners, so that none of them would swim out and escape. 27:43 But the centurion, desiring to save Paul, stopped them from their purpose, and commanded that those who could swim should throw themselves overboard first to go toward the land; 27:44 and the rest should follow, some on planks, and some on other things from the ship. So it happened that they all escaped safely to the land.

1. *they didn't recognize the land.* Day represents a certain degree of light or understanding which establishes one in a new state of consciousness with which he is not familiar.

2. *Anchors, rudder ropes, foresail wind, beach.* What is represented by casting off the anchors and leaving them in the sea, loosening the bands of the rudder, hoisting up the foresail to the wind, and making for the beach? One who in time of stress and storm fulfills the law through affirmation and denial and begins to see his way out of trouble, should deny everything that anchors him to the old, and should loose every mental and material bond.

Fillmore Study Bible annotations by Mark Hicks

**World English Bible Footnotes:**

[77] v27:14. Or, "a northeaster."

[78] v27:28. 20 fathoms = 120 feet = 36.6 meters

[79] v27:28. 15 fathoms = 90 feet = 27.4 meters

# Acts 28

## Paul on the Island of Malta

28:1 When we had escaped, then they[80] learned that the island was called Malta.[1] 28:2 The natives showed us uncommon kindness; for they kindled a fire, and received us all, because of the present rain, and because of the cold. 28:3 But when Paul had gathered a bundle of sticks and laid them on the fire, a viper came out because of the heat, and fastened on his hand. 28:4 When the natives saw the creature hanging from his hand, they said one to another, "No doubt this man is a murderer, whom, though he has escaped from the sea, yet Justice has not allowed to live." 28:5 However he shook off the creature into the fire, and wasn't harmed. 28:6 But they expected that he would have swollen or fallen down dead suddenly, but when they watched for a long time and saw nothing bad happen to him, they changed their minds, and said that he was a god.[2]

28:7 Now in the neighborhood of that place were lands belonging to the chief man of the island, named Publius, who received us, and courteously entertained us for three days. 28:8 It happened that the father of Publius lay sick of fever and dysentery. Paul entered in to him, prayed, and laying his hands on him, healed him.[3] 28:9 Then when this was done, the rest also who had diseases in the island came, and were cured. 28:10 They also honored us with many honors, and when we sailed, they put on board the things that we needed.

1. *Malta.* Malta refers to the sweetness (honey), joy, and agreeable, pleasant feeling that are sensed deeply by the individual when in his overcoming he has experienced some great deliverance from error and has entered into the peace, content, and satisfaction that follow such an experience in overcoming. (MBD/Melita)

2. *They ... said that he was a god.* The inhabitants of the island supposed of course that the poison of the viper that fastened upon Paul's hand would soon produce the usual results, and their surprise was great, when he was not in the least harmed. They concluded that he was a god. This conclusion is almost identical with that of modern Christians. They tell us that it was a miraculous intervention of God. Instead of inquiring into the state of mind and body, which would cause a follower of Jesus to have power to heal himself and others, they rest in easy ignorance and say; "miraculous," "one of the gods."

3. *Paul ... healed him.* There is no miracle connected with this ability in man to overcome negative conditions. We all possess powers that we know not of, and we will always remain in ignorance of them, until we are willing to learn the law by which they are brought into expression. The Devil is an assumed name; his real cognomen is "Ignorant Personality." This worthy invents names for things he does not understand and good people fall into his trap. He invented "miraculous" and said it designated what God did by special intervention, and what man could not understand. This is a great lie. God never performed a miracle. God does all his works according to law. The universe would be a chaos of contending elements if God should depart from the uniform law in its control. Then whatever has been done by any man at any time can be done now.

## Paul Arrives at Rome

28:11 After three months, we set sail in a ship of Alexandria which had wintered in the island, whose sign was "The Twin Brothers."[1] 28:12

Touching at Syracuse, we stayed
there three days. 28:13 From there we
circled around and arrived at
Rhegium. After one day, a south wind
sprang up, and on the second day we
came to Puteoli, 28:14 where we found
brothers,[81] and were entreated to
stay with them for seven days. So
we came to Rome. 28:15 From there
the brothers, when they heard of us,
came to meet us as far as The Market
of Appius and The Three Taverns.
When Paul saw them, he thanked
God, and took courage. 28:16 When we
entered into Rome, the centurion
delivered the prisoners to the
captain of the guard, but Paul was
allowed to stay by himself with the
soldier who guarded him.

1. "After three months", in the fullness of time, having by demonstration made helping friends of external mortal thought, you enter another "ship of Alexander", still "going to Caesar." A "ship", or a chariot, because it carries you along, is your reasoning: and a "ship of Alexandria" (Egyptian) is mortal-mind reasoning, which cannot carry you to Jerusalem, the Spiritual, but carries you to Rome, the worldly. To resort to human expedients for protection or healing is sailing in "a ship of Alexandria"; as in insuring against accidents, instead of realizing your absolute safety from accidents in the "secret place" of Being. Alas! How many sail in this mortal-mind ship "whose sign is the Twin Brothers," Good and Evil. These Twin Brothers, Realities (to mortal mind), are the controlling "sign" at the very prow of the ship of human reasoning. Such reasoning carries one farther and farther from Jerusalem, and nearer and nearer to Rome.

## Paul and Jewish Leaders in Rome

28:17 It happened that after three
days Paul called together those who
were the leaders of the Jews.[1] When
they had come together, he said to
them, "I, brothers, though I had done
nothing against the people, or the
customs of our fathers, still was
delivered prisoner from Jerusalem
into the hands of the Romans, 28:18
who, when they had examined me,
desired to set me free, because
there was no cause of death in me.
28:19 But when the Jews spoke against
it, I was constrained to appeal to
Caesar, not that I had anything about
which to accuse my nation. 28:20 For
this cause therefore I asked to see
you and to speak with you. For
because of the hope of Israel I am
bound with this chain."

28:21 They said to him, "We neither
received letters from Judea
concerning you, nor did any of the
brothers come here and report or
speak any evil of you. 28:22 But we
desire to hear from you what you
think. For, as concerning this sect, it
is known to us that everywhere it is
spoken against."

1. *Paul called together those who were the leaders of the Jews.* Paul called the Jews together at Rome and explained to them that he had, so far as he knew, done nothing against the religion of the fathers, "yet was delivered prisoner from Jerusalem into the hands of the Romans." We often justify ourselves in this way when environments seem to hold us. We argue that we have been true to the science, yet we are bound hand and foot; why is this? We forget that we have appealed to Caesar in the beginning, and that the law which we then invoked is still working. But in spite of bonds, we go on declaring the Truth. The conservative element rebels against any expansion of the doctrine which it has accepted, and without investigation puts the customary hearsay stamp of counterfeit upon it: "this sect we know is everywhere spoken against".

## Paul Preaches in Rome

28:23 When they had appointed him
a day, many people came to him at

his lodging. He explained to them,
testifying about the Kingdom of God,
and persuading them concerning
Jesus, both from the law of Moses
and from the prophets, from morning
until evening. 28:24 Some believed the
things which were spoken, and some
disbelieved.[1] 28:25 When they didn't
agree among themselves, they
departed after Paul had spoken one
word, "The Holy Spirit spoke rightly
through Isaiah, the prophet, to our
fathers, 28:26 saying,

'Go to this people, and say,
in hearing, you will hear,
but will in no way understand.
In seeing, you will see,
but will in no way perceive.
28:27 For this people's heart has grown
callous.
Their ears are dull of hearing.
Their eyes they have closed.
Lest they should see with their
eyes,
hear with their ears,
understand with their heart,
and would turn again,
and I would heal them.'[82]

28:28 "Be it known therefore to you,
that the salvation of God is sent to
the nations. They will also listen."

28:29 When he had said these
words, the Jews departed, having a
great dispute among themselves.

28:30 Paul stayed two whole years
in his own rented house, and
received all who were coming to him,
28:31 preaching the Kingdom of God,
and teaching the things concerning
the Lord Jesus Christ with all
boldness, without hindrance.

1. *Some believed the things which were spoken, and some disbelieved.* Truth advances by degrees. Do not be discouraged if your work is slowly accepted. Go right on, as did Paul, teaching and preaching the Lord Jesus Christ, and the harvest will eventually come. The indomitable persistence of a single mind daily sending out its concentrated force, is said by occultists to be the most potent power in the world. If your philosophy is based upon Truth do not fear but what it will demonstrate, if you persist in affirming it, and refuse to dilute it for the sake of popular demand. Because people disbelieve is no sign that your statements are error. Every new statement of Truth has been hooted by the masses. What is accepted as true today in nearly every avenue of science and religion was ridiculed when it was set forth. When Jesus declared himself the Messiah, the Jews laughed at him in scorn. If Jesus in our day should tramp from town to town, and associate with the class that he did in Palestine, how many would believe in him? The church that owes its origin to his words would he the most sarcastic in its sneers, and the people that bow in adoration before the ideal pictures which art has produced, would laugh in his humble face. "Judge not according to appearances" (John 7:24).

---

Fillmore Study Bible annotations by Mark Hicks

**World English Bible Footnotes:**

[80] v28:1. NU reads "we"

[81] v28:14. The word for "brothers" here and where context allows may also be correctly translated "brothers and sisters" or "siblings."

[82] v28:27. Isaiah 6:9-10

# Paul's Letter to the Romans

Christ and the Apostles in the Heavenly Jerusalem, apse mosaic, early fifth century, Rome, Santa Pudenziana. Public domain.

## Introduction to Romans

When the projected visit to Rome had taken definite shape in Paul's mind, he immediately concerned himself with preparations for the journey. One very important preliminary step was the writing of a care-fully-worded letter, which was then dispatched to Rome. Fortunately this letter has been preserved and given a prominent place in the New Testament, where it is familiarly known as "Paul's Epistle to the Romans." This Epistle should now be given careful consideration. Perhaps the best method of study will be to present and discuss some important questions relating to the Epistle as a whole, and then proceed to an examination of the contents.

(A) What was Paul's purpose in writing this Epistle? As stated, this Epistle formed part of Paul's preparations for his visit to Rome. On previous journeys, Paul had gone directly to the various synagogues and delivered his message without previous communication. Consequently, the "good news" concerning the Messiah came as a surprise to many synagogue members, and they were not prepared to receive a teaching so much at variance with their traditions. Then followed acrimonious discussions, and the final rejection of Paul and his message. Paul of course made some converts at the synagogues, but he also stirred up much bitter opposition from those who did not accept his teaching. Therefore, for this new venture he determined upon a different method of approach. Not only did Paul give advance notice of his coming, but he also sent a carefully-prepared resume of his teaching, so that upon his arrival his hearers would be acquainted with the basic principles of the Gospel message. Paul hoped that, in this way, many of the former misunderstandings would be avoided, and that both he and his message would receive a favorable reception at Rome.

(B) To whom was the Epistle addressed? Traditionally, this Epistle has always been regarded as addressed to "the Church at Rome" – and few further questions have been raised. However, several modern writers have pointed out that there is nothing in the New Testament to indicate the existence of an organized Christian church in Rome at that time. If there had been a congregation at Rome, Paul would not have been under the necessity of explaining the Christian teaching – for the church membership would have been acquainted with the fundamentals of their faith; nor would they have needed any persuasion from Paul to become Christians. Furthermore, Paul clearly states the basic purpose of this missionary enterprise: "To preach the Gospel not where Christ has already been named, lest I should build on another man's foundation . . (Rom. 15:20). Throughout his ministry, Paul went only to "virgin territory" – and it would seem strange indeed if he changed his procedure for this journey. Possibly, therefore, this preparatory Epistle was sent to friends of Aquila and Priscilla, residing in Rome, and through them to the officers of the Jewish synagogue at Rome. The Epistle bears testimony to this possibility, since all Paul's arguments are couched in terms which would be understood and appreciated by persons well-versed in Jewish traditions. The procedure would also be in harmony with Paul's own teaching, frequently used in this Epistle: "To the Jew first." It is also significant that when Paul finally arrived at Rome, he immediately communicated with the Jewish leaders there.

(C) What important teaching is contained in this Epistle? The theme of the Epistle to the Romans is usually stated as "justification by faith." The word justification, as here used, is a Jewish legal term. For Jewish people in those days, life's greatest attainment was to receive the divine pronouncement that they were "just," or "righteous"; and they were thus enabled to enter into fellowship with God. But to attain this "justification," a man was required to fulfill all the commands of the Mosaic law, without violation, either by commission or omission. Unfortunately the law contained so many detailed regulations that few persons–if any–could measure up to the required standard. Now Paul proclaimed that this greatly desired state of justification, together with the ensuing fellowship with God, is attainable through faith in Jesus Christ. This teaching is clearly set forth through such statements as "The just shall live by faith" (Rom. 1:17 A.V.) and "Therefore, being justified by faith, we have peace with God through our Lord Jesus Christ" (Rom. 5:1 A.V.).

(D) How is this teaching presented? In the main section of the Epistle the theme mentioned above is carefully explained, amplified, and illustrated, so that it may be clearly understood by the readers. First, the apostle states that all men are separated from God by reason of sin. This applies to the Gentiles, who are convicted by conscience, and also to the Jews, who stand convicted by their law. (See Rom. 1:18 through 3:20.) Then Paul declares that the only way to reconciliation with God is through Jesus Christ. Justification is not attained through the "works of the law," but through righteousness imparted by the Christ Spirit. Nothing, then, can separate the believer from the love of God (Rom. 3:21 through 8:39).

But the apostle recognizes that this new teaching may give rise to a poignant question. Jewish readers would be likely to inquire: Does all this mean that God has now abandoned Israel? Paul answers: Not necessarily! It means, rather, that God has prepared a plan for the salvation of both Jews and Gentiles. For the present, Jews may be regarded as "marking time" until the way is fully opened for the Gentiles. (See Rom. 9:1 through 11:36.)

Then follows what may be termed the practical application of the teaching. The apostle points out that through the acceptance of this new teaching, both Jews and Gentiles may now enter into a new and better relationship, both with God and their fellow men. The readers are urged not to be "conformed to this world," but to be "transformed by the renewing of your mind." The section concludes with some personal explanations, and a loving benediction. (See Rom. 12:1 through 15:33.)

Chapter sixteen should not be regarded as belonging to the Epistle to the Romans. The opening section of Romans clearly indicates that, at the time of writing, Paul had no personal connections with the people at Rome; but in this sixteenth chapter he sends greetings to many close friends. It will also be noticed that greetings are sent to Aquila and Priscilla—who, at that time, were living at Ephesus. Chapter sixteen may have been the closing section of another letter, written by Paul, and sent to Ephesus about the same time as the writing of the Epistle to the Romans.

Introduction to *Paul's Letter to the Romans* by Herbert J. Hunt, former Dean of Bible Studies for the Unity School of Christianity.

# Romans 1

## Salutation

[1:1] Paul, a servant of Jesus
Christ,❶ called to be an apostle, set
apart for the Good News of God, [1:2]
which he promised before through
his prophets in the holy Scriptures,
[1:3] concerning his Son, who was born
of the seed of David according to the
flesh, [1:4] who was declared to be the
Son of God with power, according
to the Spirit of holiness, by the
resurrection from the dead, Jesus
Christ our Lord, [1:5] through whom we
received grace and apostleship,❷ for
obedience of faith among all the
nations, for his name's sake; [1:6]
among whom you are also called to
belong to Jesus Christ; [1:7] to all who
are in Rome,❸ beloved of God, called
to be saints: Grace to you and peace

from God our Father and the Lord
Jesus Christ.

1. *a servant of Jesus Christ.* The especial office of the word of truth, which Paul represents, is to make Christ Spirit manifest.

2. *grace and apostleship.* The grace that we receive is in proportion to the measure of the Christ consciousness that we attain and is the result of that consciousness. The measure of our apostleship is our ability to translate our understanding and love into service.

3. *Rome.* Rome represents the head, in contrast to Jerusalem, which represents the heart. These words represent the will, which must be reached and converted before the teaching of the Christ can become effectual.

## Prayer of Thanksgiving

1:8 First, I thank my God through
Jesus Christ for all of you, that your
faith is proclaimed throughout the
whole world.(1) 1:9 For God is my
witness, whom I serve in my spirit(2)
in the Good News of his Son, how
unceasingly I make mention of you
always in my prayers, 1:10 requesting,
if by any means now at last I may
be prospered by the will of God to
come to you. 1:11 For I long to see
you, that I may impart to you some
spiritual gift, to the end that you
may be established; 1:12 that is, that I
with you may be encouraged in you,
each of us by the other's faith, both
yours and mine.

1:13 Now I don't desire to have you
unaware, brothers, that I often
planned to come to you, and was
hindered so far, that I might have
some fruit among you also, even as
among the rest of the Gentiles. 1:14
I am debtor both to Greeks and to
foreigners,(3) both to the wise and to
the foolish. 1:15 So, as much as is in
me, I am eager to preach the Good
News to you also who are in Rome.

1. *proclaimed throughout the whole world.* Because the spiritualized intellect has power to influence and change the life as the emotional nature, unaided by the intellect, cannot do.

2. *whom I serve in my spirit.* By laying hold of the substance of Truth and making it his own.

3. *to Greeks and to foreigners.* Greeks represent man's intellectual reasonings, foreigners his uncultivated, unillumined thoughts. To these as well as to his understanding and his ignorance (the wise and the foolish) he owes the gift of the insight and wisdom of the Christ mind.

## The Power of the Good News of Christ (Gospel)

1:16 For I am not ashamed of the
Good News of Christ, for it is the
power of God for salvation(1) for
everyone who believes; for the Jew
first, and also for the Greek.(2) 1:17 For
in it is revealed God's righteousness
from faith to faith. As it is written,
"But the righteous shall live by
faith."[1]

1. *salvation.* Salvation is for the whole of man, for his outer organism as well as for his soul; but not all persons, nor all our individual thoughts, are ready for Truth when it is first proclaimed though all will come to perfect understanding in due season. As we daily declare Truth over and over to ourselves, our thoughts and faculties and the very cells of our body will awaken, until finally we shall be fully resurrected into the Christ consciousness.

2. *the Jew first, and also for the Greek.* The Jews symbolize our religious thoughts and the Gentiles symbolize our worldly thoughts. Paul was determined to reconcile the Jew and the Gentile (Acts 21:13, 19). We find that there is a separation between our religious thoughts and our

worldly thoughts. We have built up a Sunday religion and thrown around it a wall of sacredness. In it are rites and ceremonies and sacrifices according to a standard fixed by some sect, whose teachings about God we have accepted as true. Then the broad Truth of the Holy Spirit enters the mind and begins to break down this wall of separation between the religious thoughts and the worldly thoughts. It perceives that the principles involved in the Fatherhood of God must go to the uttermost parts of the mind and the body and unify them in Spirit. MBD/Jews

## The Guilt of Humankind

1:18 For the wrath of God is revealed from heaven against all ungodliness and unrighteousness of men, who suppress the truth in unrighteousness, 1:19 because that which is known of God is revealed in them, for God revealed it to them. 1:20 For the invisible things of him since the creation of the world are clearly seen, being perceived through the things that are made,[1] even his everlasting power and divinity; that they may be without excuse. 1:21 Because, knowing God, they didn't glorify him as God, neither gave thanks, but became vain in their reasoning, and their senseless heart was darkened.

1:22 Professing themselves to be wise, they became fools, 1:23 and traded the glory of the incorruptible God for the likeness of an image of corruptible man, and of birds, and four-footed animals, and creeping things. 1:24 Therefore God also gave them up in the lusts of their hearts to uncleanness, that their bodies should be dishonored among themselves, 1:25 who exchanged the truth of God for a lie, and worshiped and served the creature rather than the Creator, who is blessed forever. Amen.

1:26 For this reason, God gave them up to vile passions. For their women changed the natural function into that which is against nature. 1:27 Likewise also the men, leaving the natural function of the woman, burned in their lust toward one another, men doing what is inappropriate with men, and receiving in themselves the due penalty of their error. 1:28 Even as they refused to have God in their knowledge, God gave them up to a reprobate mind, to do those things which are not fitting; 1:29 being filled with all unrighteousness, sexual immorality, wickedness, covetousness, maliciousness; full of envy, murder, strife, deceit, evil habits, secret slanderers, 1:30 backbiters, hateful to God, insolent, haughty, boastful, inventors of evil things, disobedient to parents, 1:31 without understanding, covenant breakers, without natural affection, unforgiving, unmerciful; 1:32 who, knowing the ordinance of God, that those who practice such things are worthy of death, not only do the same, but also approve of those who practice them.

1. *perceived through the things that are made.* "After the practice of self-knowledge, this consideration of the creatures is the first thing in order upon this spiritual road to the knowledge of God; by means of them, the soul considers His greatness and excellence."-John of the Cross, The Faults of Beginners

Fillmore Study Bible annotations by Mark Hicks

**World English Bible Footnotes:**

[1] v1:17. Habakkuk 2:4

# Romans 2

## The Problem in Judging Others

2:1 Therefore you are without excuse, O man, whoever you are who judge. For in that which you judge another, you condemn yourself. For you who judge practice the same things. 2:2 We know that the judgment of God is according to truth against those who practice such things. 2:3 Do you think this, O man who judges those who practice such things, and do the same, that you will escape the judgment of God? 2:4 Or do you despise the riches of his goodness, forbearance, and patience, not knowing that the goodness of God leads you to repentance? 2:5 But according to your hardness and unrepentant heart you are treasuring up for yourself wrath in the day of wrath, revelation, and of the righteous judgment of God; 2:6 who "will pay back to everyone according to their works:"[2] 2:7 to those who by patience in well-doing❶ seek for glory, honor, and incorruptibility, eternal life; 2:8 but to those who are self-seeking, and don't obey the truth, but obey unrighteousness, will be wrath and indignation, 2:9 oppression and anguish, on every soul of man who works evil, to the Jew first, and also to the Greek.

2:10 But glory, honor, and peace go to every man who works good, to the Jew first, and also to the Greek. 2:11 For there is no partiality with God.❷ 2:12 For as many as have sinned without law will also perish without the law. As many as have sinned under the law will be judged by the law. 2:13 For it isn't the hearers of the law who are righteous before God, but the doers of the law will be justified 2:14 (for when Gentiles who don't have the law do by nature the things of the law, these, not having the law, are a law to themselves, 2:15 in that they show the work of the law written in their hearts, their conscience testifying with them, and their thoughts among themselves accusing or else excusing them) 2:16 in the day when God will judge the secrets of men, according to my Good News, by Jesus Christ.

1. *by patience in well-doing.* Restitution in each individual must be complete, and no one can compare himself with another at any stage of the process. We have all lost consciousness of the divine image and we must all be restored to its likeness. We cannot hasten the restoration work except "by patience in well-doing," holding fast to the saving grace and power of Jesus Christ to help us on the way.—Lesson 4, Unity Correspondence School Course.

2. *no partiality with God.* The scriptural authority for the notion of God as unchanging principle is highly reinforced. "The fundamental basis of practical Christianity is that God is principle" (Meyer p. 30).

## The Jews and the Law

2:17 Indeed you bear the name of a Jew, and rest on the law, and glory in God, 2:18 and know his will, and approve the things that are excellent, being instructed out of the law, 2:19 and are confident that you yourself are a guide of the blind, a light to those who are in darkness, 2:20 a corrector of the foolish, a teacher of babies, having in the law the form of knowledge and of the truth. 2:21 You therefore who teach another, don't you teach yourself? You who preach that a man shouldn't steal, do you steal? 2:22 You who say a man shouldn't commit adultery. Do you commit adultery? You who abhor idols, do you rob temples? 2:23 You who glory in the law, through your disobedience of the law do you dishonor God? 2:24 For "the name of God is blasphemed among the Gentiles because of you,"[3] just as it is written. 2:25 For circumcision indeed profits, if you are a doer of the law, but if you are a transgressor of the law, your circumcision has become uncircumcision. 2:26 If therefore the uncircumcised keep the ordinances of the law, won't his uncircumcision be accounted as circumcision? 2:27 Won't the uncircumcision which is by nature, if it fulfills the law, judge you, who with the letter and circumcision are a transgressor of the law? 2:28 For he is not a Jew who is one outwardly, neither is that circumcision which is outward in the flesh; 2:29 but he is a Jew who is one inwardly, and circumcision is that of the heart,[1] in the spirit not in the letter; whose praise is not from men, but from God.

1. *circumcision is that of the heart.* Let us understand with Paul that the true baptism, like the true circumcision, is not that "which is outward of the flesh;" but the true baptism "is that of the heart, in the Spirit, and not in the letter; whose praise is not of men, but of God"—John L. Chesnutt, *Walk in the Light* p12.

---

Fillmore Study Bible annotations by Mark Hicks

**World English Bible Footnotes:**

[2] v2:6. Psalm 62:12; Proverbs 24:12

[3] v2:24. Isaiah 52:5; Ezekiel 36:22

# Romans 3

## The Jews and the Law (continued)

3:1 Then what advantage does the Jew[1] have? Or what is the profit of circumcision? 3:2 Much in every way! Because first of all, they were entrusted with the oracles of God. 3:3 For what if some were without faith? Will their lack of faith nullify the faithfulness of God? 3:4 May it

never be! Yes, let God be found true,
but every man a liar. As it is written,

"That you might be justified in
your words,
and might prevail when you
come into judgment."[4]

3:5 But if our unrighteousness
commends the righteousness of God,
what will we say? Is God unrighteous
who inflicts wrath? I speak like men
do. 3:6 May it never be! For then how
will God judge the world? 3:7 For if
the truth of God through my lie
abounded to his glory, why am I also
still judged as a sinner? 3:8 Why not
(as we are slanderously reported,
and as some affirm that we say), "Let
us do evil, that good may come?"
Those who say so are justly
condemned.

1. *What advantage does the Jew have?* The Hebrews surely represent the thoughts in man that have come up out of the purely material and passed over to a higher concept of God and of His laws, into a closer and clearer relationship with God. These thoughts are, however, still under law, the law of sin and death; for true freedom, spiritual understanding and realization, life and peace, come only by the still higher way—which is the Christ method, the way taught and demonstrated by Jesus Christ.—MBD: Hebrew

## None Is Righteouus

3:9 What then? Are we better than
they? No, in no way. For we
previously warned both Jews and
Greeks,[1] that they are all under sin.
3:10 As it is written,

"There is no one righteous;
no, not one.
3:11 There is no one who
understands.
There is no one who seeks
after God.
3:12 They have all turned aside.
They have together become
unprofitable.
There is no one who does good,
no, not, so much as one."[5]
3:13 "Their throat is an open tomb.
With their tongues they have
used deceit."[6]
"The poison of vipers is under
their lips;"[7]
3:14 "Whose mouth is full of cursing
and bitterness."[8]
3:15 "Their feet are swift to shed
blood.
3:16 Destruction and misery are in
their ways.
3:17 The way of peace, they
haven't known."[9]
3:18 "There is no fear of God before
their eyes."[10]

3:19 Now we know that whatever
things the law says, it speaks to those
who are under the law, that every
mouth may be closed, and all the
world may be brought under the
judgment of God. 3:20 Because by the
works of the law, no flesh will be
justified in his sight. For through the
law comes the knowledge of sin.

1. *both Jews and Greeks.* The Jews symbolize our religious thoughts and the Gentiles symbolize our worldly thoughts. Paul was determined to reconcile the Jew and the Gentile (Acts 21:13, 19).-MBD/Jews: Paul's Epistle to the Romans is more about reconciling Jews and Greeks (a 1st century concern) than it is about Sin and Grace (a 16th century concern).

## Righteousness through Faith[1]

3:21 But now apart from the law, a righteousness of God has been

revealed,[2] being testified by the law
and the prophets; 3:22 even the
righteousness of God through faith in
Jesus Christ to all and on all those
who believe. For there is no
distinction, 3:23 for all have sinned,
and fall short of the glory of God;
3:24 being justified freely by his grace
through the redemption that is in
Christ Jesus; 3:25 whom God set forth
to be an atoning sacrifice[11],
through faith in his blood, for a
demonstration of his righteousness
through the passing over of prior
sins, in God's forbearance; 3:26 to
demonstrate his righteousness at this
present time; that he might himself
be just, and the justifier of him who
has faith in Jesus.

3:27 Where then is the boasting?[3] It
is excluded. By what manner of law?
Of works? No, but by a law of faith.
3:28 We maintain therefore that a man
is justified by faith apart from the
works of the law.[4] 3:29 Or is God the
God of Jews only? Isn't he the God of
Gentiles also?[5] Yes, of Gentiles also,
3:30 since indeed there is one God who
will justify the circumcised by faith,
and the uncircumcised through faith.
3:31 Do we then nullify the law
through faith? May it never be! No,
we establish the law.

1. *Righteousness through Faith.* Man as the offspring of God is a composite idea of all that God is. Spiritually he is the creative law of God in action. A person must have a consciousness of his spiritual identity, a certain integrity to hold him firm and steady amid the winds and waves of negative thought. This Is illustrated in the case of a person who is misunderstood, as Jesus was. When condemnation comes upon anyone from without, he is apt to be beaten down In humiliation and grief unless he has a strong consciousness of his own spiritual integrity. If this consciousness is very strong, if he has great faith in his righteousness—not the righteousness of the limited personal man, but of the Christ indwelling—he can go safely through such an experience, often unmoved by it. This is a very practical demonstration of faith.—Unity Correspondence School Series 2, Lesson 8: Faith

2. *a righteousness of God has been revealed.* "Apart from the law," which is a predetermined standard, "a righteousness of God hath been manifested". Faith in the Christ within man quickens his perceptive faculties. As he learns to believe in himself as a sharer of the divine nature, which is infinite in love, wisdom and power, he draws on the qualities that arouse his faith still more fully, and they enlighten him according to his need. Man can know this righteousness of God and manifest it also. The fact that it is in harmony with the standard set by the thinkers and seers of early times (the Mosaic law) and with the law of cause and effect (the Prophets) is strong corroborative evidence of its truth. Man's inner conviction is further evidence on this point.

3. *Where then is the boasting?* There exists a higher and better order than man has seen manifested in the natural world or has proved in its fullness. He accepts this order as true in faith, though still unmanifest to the eye of flesh. The habit of looking to something higher than himself, for strength and wisdom develops in him humility, thus excluding self-conceit or "glorying."

4. *apart from the works of the law.* The works of faith include the exercising of man's inner vision in such a way as to show him that spiritual strength sufficient for all his needs is to be had for the taking; also the keeping of the inner eye single, so that he sees good only. As he does these works they justify his course by proving it the law of life and well-being.

5. *Isn't he not God of the Gentiles also?* Since faith is a universal law of man's being, it can be applied by all alike regardless of forms and ceremonies. "He shall justify the circumcision by faith, and the uncircumcision through faith." The religious instinct (Jews) and the external interests (Gentiles) are both subject to this law.

Fillmore Study Bible annotations by Mark Hicks

**World English Bible Footnotes:**

[4] v3:4. Psalm 51:4

[5] v3:12. Psalms 14:1-3; 53:1-3; Ecclesiastes 7:20

[6] v3:13. Psalm 5:9

[7] v3:13. Psalm 140:3

[8] v3:14. Psalm 10:7

[9] v3:17. Isaiah 59:7-8

[10] v3:18. Psalm 36:1

[11] v3:25. or, a propitiation

# Romans 4

## The Example of Abraham

4:1 What then will we say that Abraham, our forefather, has found according to the flesh? 4:2 For if Abraham was justified by works, he has something to boast about, but not toward God. 4:3 For what does the Scripture say? "Abraham believed God, and it was accounted to him for righteousness."❶[12] 4:4 Now to him who works, the reward is not counted as grace, but as debt. 4:5 But to him who doesn't work, but believes in him who justifies the ungodly, his faith is accounted for righteousness. 4:6 Even as David also pronounces blessing on the man to whom God counts righteousness apart from works,

4:7 "Blessed are they whose
iniquities are forgiven,
whose sins are covered.
4:8 Blessed is the man whom the
Lord will by no means
charge with sin."[13]

4:9 Is this blessing then pronounced on the circumcised, or on the uncircumcised also? For we say that faith was accounted to Abraham for righteousness. 4:10 How then was it counted? When he was in circumcision, or in uncircumcision? Not in circumcision, but in uncircumcision. 4:11 He received the sign of circumcision, a seal of the righteousness of the faith which he had while he was in uncircumcision, that he might be the father of all those who believe, though they be in uncircumcision, that righteousness might also be accounted to them. 4:12 The father of circumcision to those who not only are of the circumcision, but who also walk in the steps of that faith of our father Abraham, which he had in uncircumcision.

1. *and it was accounted to him for righteousness.* St. Paul was in conflict with the Jews in regard to circumcision, trying to convince them of the falsity of their idea of circumcision of the flesh. Paul had awakened to the consciousness of circumcision of the heart from all fleshly-carnal claims, fleshly ties that stand between us and Divinity. In the degree of our awakening to the Christ, we are born into the higher consciousness of existence and no longer seek our own selfish ends, but seek our neighbor's interests and welfare as our own.-Unity magazine Sept 1907.

## God's Promise Realized through Faith

4:13 For the promise to Abraham and to his seed that he should be heir of the world wasn't through the law, but through the righteousness of faith.[1] 4:14 For if those who are of the law are heirs, faith is made void, and the promise is made of no effect. 4:15 For the law works wrath, for where there is no law, neither is there disobedience. 4:16 For this cause it is of faith, that it may be according to grace, to the end that the promise may be sure to all the seed, not to that only which is of the law, but to that also which is of the faith of Abraham, who is the father of us all. 4:17 As it is written, "I have made you a father of many nations."[14] This is in the presence of him whom he believed: God, who gives life to the dead, and calls the things that are not, as though they were. 4:18 Who in hope believed against hope, to the end that he might become a father of many nations, according to that which had been spoken, "So will your seed be."[15] 4:19 Without being weakened in faith, he didn't consider his own body, already having been worn out, (he being about a hundred years old), and the deadness of Sarah's womb. 4:20 Yet, looking to the promise of God, he didn't waver through unbelief, but grew strong through faith, giving glory to God, 4:21 and being fully assured that what he had promised, he was able also to perform. 4:22 Therefore it also was "reckoned to him for righteousness."[16] 4:23 Now it was not written that it was accounted to him for his sake alone, 4:24 but for our sake also, to whom it will be accounted, who believe in him who raised Jesus, our Lord, from the dead, 4:25 who was delivered up for our trespasses, and was raised for our justification.

1. *but through the righteousness of faith.* Abraham represents the awakening of faith in God, in man's consciousness. In Romans 4:11, 13, we are told that he is "the father of all them that believe."-Unity April 1928

---

Fillmore Study Bible annotations by Mark Hicks

**World English Bible Footnotes:**

[12] v4:3. Genesis 15:6

[13] v4:8. Psalm 32:1-2

[14] v4:17. Genesis 17:5

[15] v4:18. Genesis 15:5

[16] v4:22. Genesis 15:6

# Romans 5

## Results of Justification

5:1 Being therefore justified by
faith,[1] we have peace with God[2]
through our Lord Jesus Christ; 5:2
through whom we also have our
access by faith into this grace in
which we stand. We rejoice in hope
of the glory of God. 5:3 Not only this,
but we also rejoice in our
sufferings,[3] knowing that suffering
works perseverance; 5:4 and
perseverance, proven character; and
proven character, hope: 5:5 and hope
doesn't disappoint us, because God's
love has been poured out into our
hearts through the Holy Spirit who
was given to us.

5:6 For while we were yet weak,
at the right time Christ died for the
ungodly.[4] 5:7 For one will hardly die
for a righteous man. Yet perhaps for
a righteous person someone would
even dare to die. 5:8 But God
commends his own love toward us,
in that while we were yet sinners,
Christ died for us.[5] 5:9 Much more
then, being now justified by his
blood,[6] we will be saved from God's
wrath through him. 5:10 For if, while
we were enemies, we were
reconciled to God through the death
of his Son, much more, being
reconciled, we will be saved by his
life.[7] 5:11 Not only so, but we also
rejoice in God through our Lord Jesus
Christ, through whom we have now
received the reconciliation.

1. *justified by faith*. Having our course proved right without the actual experience of furnishing the proof ourselves. Faith requires us to hold to a higher and better order than we can yet prove. Faith proves itself to us in the form of inner conviction, which no argument or external happening can shake.

2. *we have peace with God*. To have one's course proved right beyond all question brings peace of mind. Serene faith in God and the daily following up of one's understanding bring one into consciousness of the grace of God.

3. *rejoice in our sufferings*. The Christ consciousness turns all things to our final benefit. Since the Christ consciousness is constructive power it must bring good into our life, no matter through what avenue it comes.

4. *Christ died for the ungodly*. The ungodly are those who live entirely outside the Christ consciousness after they have once come to know its saving power.

5. *Christ died for us*. Christ dies in the sinner, because sin thrusts the one who sins outside the Christ consciousness, so that it seems to him no longer to exist.

6. *justified by his blood*. Salvation through the blood of Christ is presented to the mind in two phases: first, as justification, and second, as an actual cleansing power introduced into the mind and body of man... The blood is life. The Adam blood must be shed (denied away) and the blood or life of the risen Christ must be substituted in every individual.-Unity, July 1915

7. *we were reconciled to God through the death of his Son, much more, being reconciled, we will be saved by his life*. The terms, "Jesus" and "Christ," have come to be used synonymously by many professed Christians. But a distinction must be perceived in order to get a true understanding of Jesus Christ. Christ, the man of God, restored the divine life to the purified body, of Jesus. Thus Jesus *died* for us and Christ *lived* for us.-Weekly Unity, January 20, 1929. It is not by a dead Jesus that we are saved, but by a resurrected living Christ.-Unity, December 1914.

## Adam and Christ

[5:12] Therefore, as sin entered into the world through one man, and death through sin; and so death passed to all men,[1] because all sinned. [5:13] For until the law, sin was in the world; but sin is not charged when there is no law. [5:14] Nevertheless death reigned from Adam until Moses, even over those whose sins weren't like Adam's disobedience, who is a foreshadowing of him who was to come.

[5:15] But the free gift isn't like the trespass. For if by the trespass of the one the many died, much more did the grace of God, and the gift by the grace of the one man, Jesus Christ, abound to the many. [5:16] The gift is not as through one who sinned: for the judgment came by one to condemnation, but the free gift came of many trespasses to justification. [5:17] For if by the trespass of the one, death reigned through the one; so much more will those who receive the abundance of grace and of the gift of righteousness reign in life through the one, Jesus Christ.

[5:18] So then as through one trespass, all men were condemned; even so through one act of righteousness, all men were justified to life. [5:19] For as through the one man's disobedience many were made sinners, even so through the obedience of the one, many will be made righteous. [5:20] The law came in besides, that the trespass might abound; but where sin abounded, grace abounded more exceedingly; [5:21] that as sin reigned in death, even so grace might reign through righteousness to eternal life through Jesus Christ our Lord.

1. *so death passed to all men.* Death is the absence of the life idea from the body consciousness, thus leaving the body to go to corruption. In Romans 5:12 and 19, it is written that through disobedience sin entered into the world and death by sin. In the second and third chapters of Genesis we see that the disobedience was in eating of the tree of the knowledge of good and evil, or, in other words, believing in a power of evil as well as good, thus setting up a false god and attributing a part of the One Power (God) to evil.-Unity, February 1915.

---

Fillmore Study Bible annotations by Mark Hicks

# Romans 6

## Dying and Rising with Christ

[6:1] What shall we say then? Shall we continue in sin, that grace may abound? [6:2] May it never be! We who died to sin, how could we live in it any longer? [6:3] Or don't you know that all we who were baptized into Christ Jesus were baptized into his death? [6:4] We were buried therefore with him through baptism to death, that just like Christ was raised from the dead through the glory of the Father, so we also might walk in newness of life.

6:5 For if we have become united with him in the likeness of his death, we will also be part of his resurrection; 6:6 knowing this, that our old man was crucified with him, that the body of sin might be done away with, so that we would no longer be in bondage to sin. 6:7 For he who has died has been freed from sin. 6:8 But if we died with Christ, we believe that we will also live with him; 6:9 knowing that Christ, being raised from the dead, dies no more. Death no more has dominion over him! 6:10 For the death that he died, he died to sin one time; but the life that he lives, he lives to God. 6:11 Thus consider yourselves also to be dead to sin, but alive to God in Christ Jesus our Lord.

6:12 Therefore don't let sin reign in your mortal body, that you should obey it in its lusts. 6:13 Neither present your members to sin as instruments of unrighteousness, but present yourselves to God, as alive from the dead, and your members as instruments of righteousness to God. 6:14 For sin will not have dominion over you. For you are not under law, but under grace.

## Slaves of Righteousness

6:15 What then? Shall we sin, because we are not under law, but under grace? May it never be! 6:16 Don't you know that to whom you present yourselves as servants to obedience, his servants you are whom you obey;[1] whether of sin to death, or of obedience to righteousness? 6:17 But thanks be to God, that, whereas you were bondservants of sin, you became obedient from the heart to that form of teaching whereunto you were delivered. 6:18 Being made free from sin, you became bondservants of righteousness.[2] 6:19 I speak in human terms because of the weakness of your flesh, for as you presented your members as servants to uncleanness and to wickedness upon wickedness, even so now present your members as servants to righteousness for sanctification.

6:20 For when you were servants of sin, you were free in regard to righteousness. 6:21 What fruit then did you have at that time in the things of which you are now ashamed? For the end of those things is death.[3] 6:22 But now, being made free from sin, and having become servants of God, you have your fruit of sanctification,[4] and the result of eternal life. 6:23 For the wages of sin is death,[5] but the free gift of God is eternal life in Christ Jesus our Lord.

1. *his servants you are whom you obey.* In claiming the protection of Roman citizenship, when he was arrested, Paul found the truth here stated exemplified in his experience. He gave his case to the Romans and took it out of the hands of God. The result of his servitude is shown in the years pf imprisonment which be had to endure. [But] when he and Silas were in prison and prayed and sang psalms, the doors were opened and they were immediately set free. MBI, Acts 24-Unity October 1909.

2. *Being made free from sin, you became bondservants of righteousness.* In the moral viewpoint we must serve either sin or righteousness. When we are freed from the one, we embrace the other.

3. *the end of those things is death.* The fruit of sin is death.

4. *you have your fruit of sanctification.* Righteousness, or right living, leads to consciousness of eternal life. This is the greatest profit that can accrue to anyone.

5. *the wages of sin is death* Sin is the consciousness of separation. And the one and only solution to the one basic problem is to reestablish a sense of oneness, to get recentered in the divine flow.-Eric Butter-

worth, *The Universe Is Calling*, 153.

---

Fillmore Study Bible annotations by Mark Hicks

# Romans 7

## An Analogy from Marriage

7:1 Or don't you know, brothers[17] (for I speak to men who know the law), that the law has dominion over a man for as long as he lives?[1] 7:2 For the woman that has a husband is bound by law to the husband while he lives, but if the husband dies, she is discharged from the law of the husband. 7:3 So then if, while the husband lives, she is joined to another man, she would be called an adulteress. But if the husband dies, she is free from the law, so that she is no adulteress, though she is joined to another man. 7:4 Therefore, my brothers, you also were made dead to the law through the body of Christ,[2] that you would be joined to another, to him who was raised from the dead, that we might bring forth fruit to God.[3] 7:5 For when we were in the flesh, the sinful passions which were through the law, worked in our members to bring forth fruit to death. 7:6 But now we have been discharged from the law, having died to that in which we were held; so that we serve in newness of the spirit, and not in oldness of the letter.

1. *that the law has dominion over a man for as long as he lives.* Paul is referring to the law of sin and death, which is temporary. Compare to law of God (7:22), which is eternal.

2. *made dead to the law through the body of Christ;* We are free of the (carnal) law of sin and death because we are members of the (spiritual) body of Christ.

3. *that you would be joined to another...that we might bring forth fruit to God.* Christ came so that we may bear the fruit of oneness (joined to another).

## The Law and Sin

7:7 What shall we say then? Is the law sin? May it never be! However, I wouldn't have known sin, except through the law. For I wouldn't have known coveting, unless the law had said, "You shall not covet."[18] 7:8 But sin, finding occasion through the commandment, produced in me all kinds of coveting. For apart from the law, sin is dead. 7:9 I was alive apart from the law once, but when the commandment came, sin revived, and I died.[1] 7:10 The commandment, which was for life, this I found to be for death; 7:11 for sin, finding occasion through the commandment, deceived me, and through it killed me. 7:12 Therefore the law indeed is holy, and the commandment holy, and righteous, and good.

7:13 Did then that which is good become death to me? May it never be! But sin, that it might be shown to be sin, by working death to me through that which is good; that through the commandment sin might become exceeding sinful.

1. *I was alive apart from the law once, but when the commandment came, sin revived, and I died.* The ego personality has been groomed and molded from youth and believes it's the ruler of the Soul. Then when the I AM has been revived, spiritual warfare breaks out in the mind and body, leading the individual to believe they are wretched; instead of the Truth, that they've been misguided and egotistical to God's Law and the Ideal Person which is Christ in you. That Revelation helped changed my life, Thank you Truth Unity for your teaching (This commentary is from a TruthUnity visitor).

## The Inner Conflict

7:14 For we know that the law is spiritual, but I am fleshly, sold under sin. 7:15 For I don't know what I am doing.[1] For I don't practice what I desire to do; but what I hate, that I do. 7:16 But if what I don't desire, that I do, I consent to the law that it is good. 7:17 So now it is no more I that do it, but sin which dwells in me. 7:18 For I know that in me, that is, in my flesh, dwells no good thing. For desire is present with me, but I don't find it doing that which is good. 7:19 For the good which I desire, I don't do; but the evil which I don't desire, that I practice. 7:20 But if what I don't desire, that I do, it is no more I that do it, but sin which dwells in me. 7:21 I find then the law, that, to me, while I desire to do good, evil is present. 7:22 For I delight in God's law[2] after the inward man, 7:23 but I see a different law in my members,[3] warring against the law of my mind, and bringing me into captivity under the law of sin which is in my members. 7:24 What a wretched man I am![4] Who will deliver me out of the body of this death? 7:25 I thank God through Jesus Christ, our Lord! So then with the mind, I myself serve God's law, but with the flesh, the sin's law.

1. *For I don't know what I am doing.*. Paul switches to present tense in vv14-25 and this section is the basis for the General Confession in liturgical and evangelical: *ALMIGHTY and most merciful Father, We have erred and strayed from thy ways ... And there is no health in us.* Unity rejects this theology.

2. *For I delight in God's law.* The law of God is the orderly working out of the principle of Being, or the divine ideals, into expression and manifestation throughout creation (MBD/Law).

3. *a different law in my members.* The law of sin and death. See 8:2: *For the law of the Spirit of life in Christ Jesus made me free from the law of sin and of death.*

4. *What a wretched man I am!* Unity never provided commentary on any of part of this chapter, most likely because: *If, through the power of our thought and word, we affirm the opposite of life and talk about the absence of life, we rob the body cells of their natural element. This treatment will eventually bring death to the organism. Let us not say, "I am tired"; "I am weak"; "I am sick." Rather, let us say, "I am strong"; "I am well"; "I am alive with the life of God now and forevermore."* (RW/Death)

Fillmore Study Bible annotations by Mark Hicks

**World English Bible Footnotes:**

[17] v7:1. The word for "brothers" here and where context allows may also be correctly translated "brothers and sisters" or "siblings."

[18] v7:7. Exodus 20:17; Deuteronomy 5:21

# Romans 8

## Life in the Spirit

8:1 There is therefore now no condemnation to those who are in Christ Jesus, who don't walk according to the flesh, but according to the Spirit.[19] 8:2 For the law of the Spirit of life in Christ Jesus(1) made me free from the law of sin and of death.(2) 8:3 For what the law couldn't do, in that it was weak through the flesh, God did, sending his own Son in the likeness of sinful flesh and for sin, he condemned sin in the flesh; 8:4 that the ordinance of the law might be fulfilled in us, who walk not after the flesh, but after the Spirit. 8:5 For those who live according to the flesh set their minds on the things of the flesh, but those who live according to the Spirit, the things of the Spirit. 8:6 For the mind of the flesh is death, but the mind of the Spirit is life and peace; 8:7 because the mind of the flesh is hostile towards God; for it is not subject to God's law, neither indeed can it be.

8:8 Those who are in the flesh can't please God. 8:9 But you are not in the flesh but in the Spirit, if it is so that the Spirit of God dwells in you. But if any man doesn't have the Spirit of Christ, he is not his. 8:10 If Christ is in you, the body is dead because of sin, but the spirit is alive because of righteousness. 8:11 But if the Spirit of him who raised up Jesus from the dead dwells in you, he who raised up Christ Jesus from the dead will also give life to your mortal bodies through his Spirit who dwells in you.(3)

8:12 So then, brothers, we are debtors, not to the flesh, to live after the flesh. 8:13 For if you live after the flesh, you must die; but if by the Spirit you put to death the deeds of the body, you will live. 8:14 For as many as are led by the Spirit of God,(4) these are children of God. 8:15 For you didn't receive the spirit of bondage again to fear, but you received the Spirit of adoption, by whom we cry, "Abba[20]! Father!" 8:16 The Spirit himself testifies with our spirit that we are children of God; 8:17 and if children, then heirs; heirs of God, and joint heirs with Christ; if indeed we suffer with him, that we may also be glorified with him.

1. *law of the Spirit of life in Christ Jesus* is the activity of the principle of Absolute Good in man's consciousness. When active in the hearts of men it will inspire them to turn to God for guidance, so that divine wisdom and love will be expressed in the earth. Each person will be as conscious of all the family of God as he is of "self" and he will be divinely alive to the purpose and needs of his fellow men. Series 1 - Lesson 6 - Annotation 18

2. *law of sin and of death* is the operation of a secondary or a mental law that man has put into activity by the wrong use of his power to think and feel. It is the operation of the mental law of cause and effect based on an error belief... The mental law of cause and effect, while it shows the justice of God, has no saving power of itself. Series 1 - Lesson 6 - Annotation 17

3. *through his Spirit who dwells in you.* Few Christians realize the vital truth in this statement by Paul, although it is but one of many of like character to be found in his writings. Paul taught that what Spirit did for Jesus it would do for all who follow

Him and adopt His methods of spiritual self-development. Jesus Christ Heals 193.

4. *For as many as are led by the Spirit of God, these are sons of God.* When we become conscious of our oneness with God we are in the "spiritual body" and, being "led by the Spirit," are, therefore, sons of God, God beings. It is while we are in this consciousness of identity with the Christ within us that healing for others or for ourselves takes place, that inspiration is born, or that illumination enlightens us. Unity January 1932

## Future Glory

8:18 For I consider that the sufferings of this present time are not worthy to be compared with the glory which will be revealed toward us. 8:19 For the creation waits with eager expectation for the children of God to be revealed.(1) 8:20 For the creation was subjected to vanity, not of its own will, but because of him who subjected it, in hope 8:21 that the creation itself also will be delivered from the bondage of decay into the liberty of the glory of the children of God. 8:22 For we know that the whole creation groans and travails in pain together until now. 8:23 Not only so, but ourselves also, who have the first fruits of the Spirit, even we ourselves groan within ourselves, waiting for adoption, the redemption of our body. 8:24 For we were saved in hope, but hope that is seen is not hope. For who hopes for that which he sees? 8:25 But if we hope for that which we don't see, we wait for it with patience.

8:26 In the same way, the Spirit also helps our weaknesses, for we don't know how to pray as we ought. But the Spirit himself makes intercession for us(2) with groanings which can't be uttered. 8:27 He who searches the hearts knows what is on the Spirit's mind, because he makes intercession for the saints according to God.

8:28 We know that all things work together for good(3) for those who love God, to those who are called according to his purpose. 8:29 For whom he foreknew, he also predestined to be conformed to the image of his Son, that he might be the firstborn among many brothers.[21] 8:30 Whom he predestined, those he also called. Whom he called, those he also justified. Whom he justified, those he also glorified.

1. *expectation for the children of God to be revealed.* Spiritual evolution is the unfolding of the Spirit of God into expression. The Christ or Son of God evolution in man is plainly taught in the New Testament as the supreme attainment of every man. Metaphysical meaning of evolution (rw)

2. *the Spirit himself makes intercession for us.* A subtle clue that immanent Spirit makes an intercession to the transcendent Father. Everyone who depends upon the enabling power of the Holy Spirit learns through prayer that he gains what he seeks, when his desire is toward God and the direction of his thought is inclined toward what is right. Every prayer that is in harmony with Truth ("according to the will of God") is an intercession of the Holy Spirit become active in man. As one element of the Trinity, the Holy Spirit makes union with Divine Mind (The Father), and is heard.

3. *all things work together for good.* The very circumstances in your life that seem heartbreaking evils will turn to joy before your very eyes if you will steadfastly refuse to see anything but God in them. Bondage or Liberty, Which? 35. Refer to Ed Rabel Nothing But Good and Mysteries of Genesis Joseph Sold into Slavery: the faculty of imagination, if it has been trained and disciplined, will work for the good of man even in the darkened realm of sense (Egypt). Though the purpose in selling Joseph into Egypt was error, the result proved to be good.

*God's perfect life floods my being now and I am made whole.*

## God's Love in Christ Jesus

[8:31] What then shall we say about these things? If God is for us, who can be against us? [8:32] He who didn't spare his own Son, but delivered him up for us all, how would he not also with him freely give us all things? [8:33] Who could bring a charge against God's chosen ones? It is God who justifies. [8:34] Who is he who condemns? It is Christ who died, yes rather, who was raised from the dead, who is at the right hand of God, who also makes intercession for us.

[8:35] Who shall separate us from the love of Christ? Could oppression, or anguish, or persecution, or famine, or nakedness, or peril, or sword? [8:36] Even as it is written, "For your sake we are killed all day long. We were accounted as sheep for the slaughter."[22] [8:37] No, in all these things, we are more than conquerors through him who loved us. [8:38] For I am persuaded, that neither death, nor life, nor angels, nor principalities, nor things present, nor things to come, nor powers, [8:39] nor height, nor depth, nor any other created thing, will be able to separate us from the love of God,[1] which is in Christ Jesus our Lord.

1. *will be able to separate us from the love of God.* God cannot be separated from His creation because, as these lessons have already emphasized, He is the cause of all creation, the source from which it comes forth. He is the life, substance, and intelligence that maintains and sustains man and the universe. Lessons In Truth - Lesson 2 - Annotation 8

---

Fillmore Study Bible annotations by Mark Hicks

**World English Bible Footnotes:**

[19] v8:1. NU omits "who don't walk according to the flesh, but according to the Spirit"

[20] v8:15. Abba is an Aramaic word for father or daddy, often used affectionately and respectfully in prayer to our Father in heaven.

[21] v8:29. The word for "brothers" here and where context allows may also be correctly translated "brothers and sisters" or "siblings."

[22] v8:36. Psalm 44:22

# Romans 9

## God's Election of Israel

[9:1] I tell the truth in Christ. I am not lying, my conscience testifying with me in the Holy Spirit,[1] [9:2] that I have great sorrow and unceasing pain in my heart. 9:3 For I could wish that I myself were accursed from Christ for my brothers' sake, my relatives according to the flesh, 9:4 who are Israelites;[2] whose is the adoption, the glory, the covenants, the giving of the law, the service, and the promises; 9:5 of whom are the fathers, and from whom is Christ as concerning the flesh,[3] who is over all, God, blessed[4] forever. Amen.

9:6 But it is not as though the word of God has come to nothing. For they are not all Israel, that are of Israel. 9:7 Neither, because they are Abraham's seed, are they all children. But, "In Isaac will your seed be called."[23] 9:8 That is, it is not the children of the flesh who are children of God, but the children of the promise[5] are counted as a seed. 9:9 For this is a word of promise, "At the appointed time I will come, and Sarah will have a son."[24] 9:10 Not only so, but Rebecca also conceived by one, by our father Isaac. 9:11 For being not yet born, neither having done anything good or bad, that the purpose of God according to election might stand, not of works, but of him who calls, 9:12 it was said to her, "The elder will serve the younger."[25] 9:13 Even as it is written, "Jacob I loved, but Esau I hated."[26]

9:14 What shall we say then? Is there unrighteousness with God? May it never be! 9:15 For he said to Moses, "I will have mercy on whom I have mercy, and I will have compassion on whom I have compassion."[27] 9:16 So then it is not of him who wills, nor of him who runs, but of God who has mercy. 9:17 For the Scripture says to Pharaoh, "For this very purpose I caused you to be raised up, that I might show in you my power, and that my name might be proclaimed in all the earth."[28] 9:18 So then, he has mercy on whom he desires, and he hardens whom he desires.

1. *testifying with me in the Holy Spirit.* The Holy Spirit is authority on the gospel of Jesus. It is the only authority that Jesus ever recognized, and whoever attempts to set forth His gospel from any other standpoint is in the letter and not the spirit. No man can know what Jesus' doctrine is except he gets it direct from the one and only custodian. It is not to come secondhand, but each for himself must receive it from the Holy Spirit, which is sent by the Father in the name of the Son. Revealing Word, Holy Spirit

2. *Israelites.* The illumined thoughts in consciousness, which are undergoing spiritual discipline. They are the total of our religious thoughts. MBD, Israelites

3. *from whom is Christ concerning the flesh* See the alternative translation in NRSV. Some scholars would end the sentence here and then begin a new sentence "May he who is god over all be blessed forever." This is important because it appropriately separates the Christ, or Messiah, from the transcendent God.

4. *Christ ... who is over all, God blessed.* When we enter into spiritual consciousness, do we find that all our former religious beliefs and prejudices are at once transformed? In spiritual consciousness we, either surrender our "conscious prejudices and narrow religious beliefs, or we allow them to be transformed. Our subconscious beliefs and prejudices take longer to reach and influence. Romans 9 Metaphysical Bible Interpretation

5. *children of the promise.* God has prepared a plan for the salvation of both Jews and Gentiles. For the present, Jews may be regarded as "marking time" until the way is fully opened for the Gentiles. Herbert Hunt 6. Paul's Journey to Rome

## God's Wrath and Mercy

9:19 You will say then to me, "Why does he still find fault? For who withstands his will?" 9:20 But indeed, O man, who are you to reply against God? Will the thing formed ask him who formed it, "Why did you make me like this?"[29] 9:21 Or hasn't the potter a right over the clay, from the

same lump to make one part a vessel
for honor, and another for dishonor?
9:22 What if God, willing to show his
wrath, and to make his power
known, endured with much patience
vessels of wrath made for
destruction, 9:23 and that he might
make known the riches of his glory on
vessels of mercy, which he prepared
beforehand for glory, 9:24 us, whom
he also called, not from the Jews
only, but also from the Gentiles? 9:25
As he says also in Hosea,

"I will call them 'my people,'
which were not my people;
and her 'beloved,' who was not
beloved."[30]

9:26 "It will be that in the place
where it was said to them,
'You are not my people,'
There they will be called
'children of the living
God.'"[31]

9:27 Isaiah cries concerning Israel,

"If the number of the children of
Israel are as the sand of the
sea,
it is the remnant who will be
saved;

9:28 for He will finish the work and
cut it short in
righteousness,
because the LORD will make a
short work upon the
earth."[32]

9:29 As Isaiah has said before,

"Unless the Lord of Armies(1)[33]
had left us a seed,
we would have become like
Sodom,
and would have been made
like Gomorrah."(2)[34]

1. *Lord of Armies (Sabaoth in ASV)*. or "Jehovah of hosts," in individual consciousness is that the Jehovah, Christ, true I AM in one, is Lord of--has dominion over--all the host of thoughts, forces, and activities in one's whole organism, in mind (heaven) and body (earth).

2. *Gomorrah*. A state of mind in man that is adverse to the law of Spirit. It is submerged in sense and is very tyrannical in its nature. (See SODOM.)

## Israel's Unbelief

9:30 What shall we say then? That
the Gentiles, who didn't follow after
righteousness, attained to
righteousness, even the
righteousness which is of faith; 9:31
but Israel, following after a law of
righteousness, didn't arrive at the
law of righteousness. 9:32 Why?
Because they didn't seek it by faith,
but as it were by works of the law.
They stumbled over the stumbling
stone; 9:33 even as it is written,

"Behold, I lay in Zion a
stumbling(1) stone(2) and a
rock of offense;
and no one who believes in
him will be
disappointed."(3)[35]

1. *a stone of stumbling*. Isaiah 8:14. Stumbling because of reliance on law instead of Jesus Christ.

2. *I lay in Zion a stone*. Isaiah 28:16. The stone is Jesus Christ.

3. *no one who believes in him will be disappointed (shall not be put to shame)*. See discussion of grace in The Master Key To Every Kingdom: Grace by Crichton Russ Boatwright.

---

Fillmore Study Bible annotations by Mark Hicks

**World English Bible Footnotes:**

[23] v9:7. Genesis 21:12
[24] v9:9. Genesis 18:10,14
[25] v9:12. Genesis 25:23
[26] v9:13. Malachi 1:2-3
[27] v9:15. Exodus 33:19
[28] v9:17. Exodus 9:16
[29] v9:20. Isaiah 29:16; 45:9
[30] v9:25. Hosea 2:23
[31] v9:26. Hosea 1:10
[32] v9:28. Isaiah 10:22-23
[33] v9:29. Greek: Sabaoth (for Hebrew: Tze'va'ot)
[34] v9:29. Isaiah 1:9
[35] v9:33. Isaiah 8:14; 28:16

# Romans 10

## Israel's Unbelief (continued)

10:1 Brothers, my heart's desire and my prayer to God is for Israel, that they may be saved. 10:2 For I testify about them that they have a zeal for God, but not according to knowledge. 10:3 For being ignorant of God's righteousness, and seeking to establish their own righteousness, they didn't subject themselves to the righteousness of God. 10:4 For Christ is the fulfillment[36] of the law for righteousness❶ to everyone who believes.

1. *For Christ is the fulfillment (end, ASV) of the law for righteousness.* Harper Study Bible says "It is not certain whether end means termination or goal; the latter is the more probable." This Unity commentary agrees with HSB that "end" means "goal": The law unto righteousness, or law of right thinking, right speaking, and right acting, is *wholly fulfilled* in the Christ consciousness. As we believe in the power of true thought and persist in putting our faith into practice, we realize that "with the heart man believeth unto righteousness; and with the mouth confession is made unto salvation."

## Salvation Is for All

10:5 For Moses writes about the righteousness of the law, "The one who does them will live by them."[37] 10:6 But the righteousness which is of faith says this, "Don't say in your heart,❶ 'Who will ascend into heaven?'[38] (that is, to bring Christ down); 10:7 or, 'Who will descend into the abyss?'[39] (that is, to bring Christ up from the dead.)" 10:8 But what does it say? "The word is near you, in your mouth, and in your heart;❷"[40] that is, the word of faith, which we preach:❸ 10:9 that if you will confess

with your mouth that Jesus is Lord,
and believe in your heart that God
raised him from the dead, you will
be saved. 10:10 For with the heart, one
believes unto righteousness;❹ and
with the mouth confession is made
unto salvation. 10:11 For the Scripture
says, "Whoever believes in him will
not be disappointed."❺[41]

10:12 For there is no distinction
between Jew and Greek; for the
same Lord is Lord of all, and is rich
to all who call on him. 10:13 For,
"Whoever will call on the name of the
Lord will be saved."[42] 10:14 How then
will they call on him in whom they
have not believed? How will they
believe in him whom they have not
heard? How will they hear without
a preacher? 10:15 And how will they
preach unless they are sent? As it is
written:

"How beautiful are the feet of
those who preach the Good
News of peace,
who bring glad tidings❻ of
good things!"[43]

10:16 But they didn't all listen to
the glad news. For Isaiah says, "Lord,
who has believed our report?"[44] 10:17
So faith comes by hearing, and
hearing by the word of God. 10:18 But
I say, didn't they hear? Yes, most
certainly,

"Their sound went out into all the
earth,
their words to the ends of the
world."[45]

10:19 But I ask, didn't Israel know?
First Moses says,

"I will provoke you to jealousy
with that which is no
nation,
with a nation void of
understanding I will
make you angry."[46]

10:20 Isaiah is very bold, and says,

"I was found by those who didn't
seek me.
I was revealed to those who
didn't ask for me."[47]

10:21 But as to Israel he says, "All
day long I stretched out my hands
to a disobedient and contrary
people."[48]

1. *say in your heart*. As used in Scripture, the word heart represents the subconscious mind (Revealing Word, heart).

2. *in your mouth, and in your heart*. The Christ ideal can be realized by every man and woman.

3. *the word of faith, which we preach*. The function of words is to express thought, and the word of faith expresses our thought of God and our belief in Him. God dwells in us as thought.

4. *for with the heart one believes unto righteousness*. Through faith in the I AM, man puts his emotions in order. This done, he sees reason as a surer guide for action than feeling. Faith in the ideals of right, love, and Truth enables him to transform his heart, the symbolic seat of emotion, into a center of right thinking.

5. *Whosoever believes in him shall not be disappointed (put to shame, ASV)*. Whoever really believes in God and Jesus Christ is as good as his professed word. Faithful thinking and speaking of Truth lead to faithful living in harmony with thought and word, for real faith is practical and can be applied to everyday living.

6. *the feet ... who bring glad tidings*. The accomplishing of needed service. Words unaccompanied by appropriate action lack the faith that moves mountains of doubt and difficulty.

---

Fillmore Study Bible annotations by Mark Hicks

**World English Bible Footnotes:**

[36] v10:4. or, completion, or end
[37] v10:5. Leviticus 18:5
[38] v10:6. Deuteronomy 30:12
[39] v10:7. Deuteronomy 30:13
[40] v10:8. Deuteronomy 30:14
[41] v10:11. Isaiah 28:16
[42] v10:13. Joel 2:32
[43] v10:15. Isaiah 52:7
[44] v10:16. Isaiah 53:1
[45] v10:18. Psalm 19:4
[46] v10:19. Deuteronomy 32:31
[47] v10:20. Isaiah 65:1
[48] v10:21. Isaiah 65:2

# Romans 11

## Israel's Rejection Is Not Final

11:1 I ask then, did God reject his
people? May it never be! For I also
am an Israelite,[1] a descendant of
Abraham, of the tribe of Benjamin.[2]
11:2 God didn't reject his people,
which he foreknew. Or don't you
know what the Scripture says about
Elijah? How he pleads with God
against Israel: 11:3 "Lord, they have
killed your prophets, they have
broken down your altars; and I am
left alone, and they seek my life."[49]
11:4 But how does God answer him?
"I have reserved for myself seven
thousand men, who have not bowed
the knee to Baal."[50] 11:5 Even so then
at this present time also there is a
remnant according to the election of
grace. 11:6 And if by grace, then it is
no longer of works; otherwise grace
is no longer grace. But if it is of
works, it is no longer grace;
otherwise work is no longer work.

11:7 What then? That which Israel
seeks for, that he didn't obtain, but
the chosen ones obtained it, and the
rest were hardened. 11:8 According as
it is written, "God gave them a spirit
of stupor, eyes that they should not
see, and ears that they should not
hear, to this very day."[51] 11:9 David
says,

"Let their table be made a snare,
and a trap,
a stumbling block, and a
retribution to them.
11:10 Let their eyes be darkened, that
they may not see.
Bow down their back
always."[52]

1. *I also am an Israelite.* Israelite: The illumined thoughts in consciousness, which are undergoing spiritual discipline.

2. *of the tribe of Benjamin.* Benjamin: established in consciousness express as strong, courageous, and conquering thoughts ("mighty men of valor").

## The Salvation of the Gentiles

11:11 I ask then, did they stumble that they might fall? May it never be! But by their fall salvation has come to the Gentiles, to provoke them to jealousy. 11:12 Now if their fall is the riches of the world, and their loss the riches of the Gentiles; how much more their fullness? 11:13 For I speak to you who are Gentiles.[1] Since then as I am an apostle to Gentiles, I glorify my ministry; 11:14 if by any means I may provoke to jealousy those who are my flesh, and may save some of them. 11:15 For if the rejection of them is the reconciling of the world, what would their acceptance be, but life from the dead? 11:16 If the first fruit is holy, so is the lump. If the root is holy, so are the branches. 11:17 But if some of the branches were broken off, and you, being a wild olive,[2] were grafted in among them, and became partaker with them of the root and of the richness of the olive tree; 11:18 don't boast over the branches. But if you boast, it is not you who support the root, but the root supports you. 11:19 You will say then, "Branches were broken off, that I might be grafted in." 11:20 True; by their unbelief they were broken off, and you stand by your faith. Don't be conceited, but fear; 11:21 for if God didn't spare the natural branches, neither will he spare you. 11:22 See then the goodness and severity of God. Toward those who fell, severity; but toward you, goodness, if you continue in his goodness; otherwise you also will be cut off. 11:23 They also, if they don't continue in their unbelief, will be grafted in, for God is able to graft them in again. 11:24 For if you were cut out of that which is by nature a wild olive tree, and were grafted contrary to nature into a good olive tree, how much more will these, which are the natural branches, be grafted into their own olive tree?

1. *Gentiles.* Worldly thoughts-thoughts pertaining to the external, or thoughts that function through the senses. The Gentile is the unregenerate state of mind in us.

2. *you, being a wild olive.* The exalting of divine wisdom and love in consciousness (Mount of Olives, height yielding illuminating oil, high luminous principle) ... *didst become partaker with them of the root of the fatness of the olive tree.* In Romans 11:17 we read of "the fatness of the olive tree," and it is a well-known fact that love is a great attracter of substance, of true riches. (MBD/Olivet)

## All Israel Will Be Saved

11:25 For I don't desire you to be ignorant, brothers,[53] of this mystery, so that you won't be wise in your own conceits, that a partial hardening has happened to Israel, until the fullness of the Gentiles has come in, 11:26 and so all Israel will be saved. Even as it is written,

"There will come out of Zion the
Deliverer,
and he will turn away
ungodliness from Jacob.
11:27 This is my covenant to them,
when I will take away their
sins."[54]

11:28 Concerning the Good News, they are enemies for your sake. But concerning the election, they are beloved for the fathers' sake. 11:29 For the gifts[1] and the calling of God are irrevocable. 11:30 For as you in time past were disobedient to God, but now have obtained mercy by their disobedience, 11:31 even so these also have now been disobedient, that by the mercy shown to you they may also obtain mercy. 11:32 For God has shut up all to disobedience, that he might have mercy on all.

11:33 Oh the depth of the riches both of the wisdom and the knowledge of God! How unsearchable are his judgments, and his ways past tracing out!

11:34 "For who has known the mind of
the Lord?
Or who has been his
counselor?"[55]
11:35 "Or who has first given to him,
and it will be repaid to him
again?"[56]

11:36 For of him, and through him, and to him, are all things. To him be the glory for ever! Amen.

1. *Gifts.* The gifts that the Wise Men of the East brought to Jesus represent qualities of mind given by divine wisdom.

---

Fillmore Study Bible annotations by Mark Hicks

**World English Bible Footnotes:**

[49] v11:3. 1 Kings 19:10,14

[50] v11:4. 1 Kings 19:18

[51] v11:8. Deuteronomy 29:4; Isaiah 29:10

[52] v11:10. Psalm 69:22,23

[53] v11:25. The word for "brothers" here and where context allows may also be correctly translated "brothers and sisters" or "siblings."

[54] v11:27. Isaiah 59:20-21; 27:9; Jeremiah 31:33-34

[55] v11:34. Isaiah 40:13

[56] v11:35. Job 41:11

# Romans 12

## The New Life in Christ

12:1 Therefore I urge you, brothers, by the mercies of God, to present your bodies a living sacrifice,[1] holy, acceptable to God, which is your spiritual service. 12:2 Don't be conformed[2] to this world, but be transformed by the renewing of your mind,[3] so that you may prove what is the good, well-pleasing, and perfect will of God. 12:3 For I say, through the grace that was given me, to every man who is among you, not to think of himself more highly than he ought to think; but to think reasonably, as God has apportioned to each person a measure of faith. 12:4 For even as we have many members in one body, and all the members don't have the same function, 12:5 so we, who are many, are one body in Christ, and individually members one of another. 12:6 Having gifts differing according to the grace that was given to us,[4] if prophecy, let us prophesy according to the proportion of our faith; 12:7 or service, let us give ourselves to service; or he who teaches, to his teaching; 12:8 or he who exhorts, to his exhorting: he who gives, let him do it with liberality; he who rules, with diligence; he who shows mercy, with cheerfulness.[5]

1. *a living sacrifice.* The sacrifice consists in devoting the body to spiritual service, transforming it meanwhile, by renewing the mind at the one source and by thinking of his body as filled with life, health, and strength, and always identifying it in thought with that which is perfect.

2. *Don't be conformed (fashioned, ASV).* In Greek, "conformed" or "fashioned" is syschēmatizō, Strong's 4964, to conform one's self (i.e. one's mind and character) to another's pattern, (fashion one's self according to)

3. *transformed by the renewing of your mind.* Of ourselves we cannot, by taking thought, add one cubit to our stature, but by thinking of the Christ and claiming the power of the Christ in all that we do, we do express a higher degree of power than we have known before.

4. *gifts differing according to the grace that was given to us.* To that for which we have especial aptitude. Each one should develop his "gift", or that which he does best and most gladly.

5. *prophecy, service ...* [These are known as gifts of the Spirit. An alternative list of gifts of the Spirit is given in First Corinthians 12:28-30. They are not the same as the fruits of the Spirit given in Galatians 5:22-23. The fruits of the Spirit are those precious qualities of the soul that lift us up into the very heart of God. By their presence we know we abide in Him and He abides in us. The gifts of the Spirit, on the other hand, according to Paul, are the means, the tools by which we can bring the precious fruits down to our fellow men when we use them rightly. (Glenn Clark, *The Holy Spirit*) See annotations in Corinthians and Galatians for additional commentary.]

## Marks of the True Christian

12:9 Let love be without hypocrisy.[1] Abhor that which is evil. Cling to that which is good. 12:10 In love of the brothers be tenderly affectionate one to another; in honor preferring one another; 12:11 not lagging in diligence; fervent in spirit; serving the Lord; 12:12 rejoicing in hope; enduring in troubles; continuing steadfastly in prayer; 12:13 contributing to the needs of the saints; given to hospitality. 12:14 Bless those who persecute you; bless, and don't curse. 12:15 Rejoice with those who rejoice. Weep with those who weep.[2] 12:16 Be of the same mind one toward another. Don't set your mind on high things, but associate with the humble. Don't be wise in your own conceits. 12:17 Repay no one evil for evil. Respect what is honorable in the sight of all men. 12:18 If it is possible, as much as it is up to you, be at peace with all men. 12:19 Don't seek revenge yourselves, beloved, but give place to God's wrath.[3] For it is written, "Vengeance belongs to me; I will repay, says the Lord."[57] 12:20 Therefore

"If your enemy is hungry, feed him.
If he is thirsty, give him a drink;
for in doing so, you will heap coals of fire on his head."[58]

12:21 Don't be overcome by evil, but overcome evil with good.

1. *Let love be without hypocrisy.* Love is the essence of truth and sincerity, and, when love fills our heart, there is no room in it for hypocrisy.

2. *weep with those who weep.* Should we actually "weep with them that weep"? No,

we should avoid negativeness at all times, but we can always be understanding and considerate and hold a constructive attitude of mind toward those who are troubled.

3. *give place to God's wrath.* It is possible to entrust all our problems and social relations to the divine law, knowing that we need not take matters into our own hands in order to secure our rights. Cause and effect are here represented, as "the wrath of God."

---

Fillmore Study Bible annotations by Mark Hicks

**World English Bible Footnotes:**

[57] v12:19. Deuteronomy 32:35

[58] v12:20. Proverbs 25:21-22

# Romans 13

## Being Subject to Authorities

13:1 Let every soul be in subjection to the higher authorities,[1] for there is no authority except from God, and those who exist are ordained by God. 13:2 Therefore he who resists the authority, withstands the ordinance of God; and those who withstand will receive to themselves judgment. 13:3 For rulers are not a terror to the good work, but to the evil. Do you desire to have no fear of the authority? Do that which is good, and you will have praise from the same, 13:4 for he is a servant of God to you for good. But if you do that which is evil, be afraid, for he doesn't bear the sword in vain; for he is a servant of God, an avenger for wrath to him who does evil. 13:5 Therefore you need to be in subjection, not only because of the wrath, but also for conscience' sake. 13:6 For this reason you also pay taxes, for they are servants of God's service, attending continually on this very thing. 13:7 Give therefore to everyone what you owe: taxes to whom taxes are due; customs to whom customs; respect to whom respect; honor to whom honor.

1. *Let every soul be in subjection to the higher authorities (powers, ASV).* See Unity Bible Lesson Commentary for Romans 13. Unity published commentary on Romans 13:1-7 each presidential election cycle in the United States: November 1928, October 1932, November 1936, November 1944. Unity's consistent message is: *(1) We should make ourselves subject to the authority of the indwelling Spirit of God.* Jesus said: I do nothing of myself, but as the Father taught me; I speak these things." Individually, each of us is responsible for making our life full, rich, and satisfying, a life under law. Individually and collectively we are responsible for raising the level of the race consciousness until it reaches there permanently. *(2) What follows when we make ourselves obedient to God is a demonstration that God is love, and the law of love overcomes the world.* We obtain universal peace on earth and permanent well-being by holding in mind persistently a vision of universal understanding, universal harmony, and universal peace by declaring it to be now realized, and by working faithfully toward the realization of it. *(3) Temporal rulers represent the ruling principle of divine law, and in the degree that we become obedient to that*

*law their authority to us is divine.* Man, exercising his own judgment and ignoring the divine law, forms an adverse state of mind. Through its activity he sets up an independent kingdom which sooner or later comes to an end, with the result that he calls down upon himself what in the Old Testament is termed the vengeance of Jehovah.

## Love for One Another

13:8 Owe no one anything, except to love one another; for he who loves his neighbor has fulfilled the law.(1) 13:9 For the commandments, "You shall not commit adultery," "You shall not murder," "You shall not steal," "You shall not give false testimony," "You shall not covet,"[59][60] and whatever other commandments there are, are all summed up in this saying, namely, "You shall love your neighbor as yourself."[61] 13:10 Love doesn't harm a neighbor. Love therefore is the fulfillment of the law.(2)

1. *for he who loves his neighbor has fulfilled the law.* Through love, the energies of Being are stirred up, both in the lover and the Universal, and as equilibrium of forces is thus established.

2. *love therefore is the fulfilment of the law.* Other commandments are fulfilled through loving one's neighbors as oneself. Love works good to our neighbor, and makes the sins of murder, adultery, theft, and covetousness against him imporrible. He who loves what is honest, true, just, pure, and good is fortified against gross social sins.

## An Urgent Appeal

13:11 Do this, knowing the time, that it is already time for you to awaken out of sleep, for salvation is now nearer to us than when we first believed. 13:12 The night is far gone, and the day is near. Let's therefore throw off the works of darkness, and let's put on the armor of light.(1) 13:13 Let us walk properly, as in the day;(2) not in reveling and drunkenness, not in sexual promiscuity and lustful acts, and not in strife and jealousy. 13:14 But put on the Lord Jesus Christ,(3) and make no provision for the flesh,(4) for its lusts.

1. *the armor of light.* The protective influence of a true understanding in man's mind of his own well-being, including all that promotes it.

2. *walk becomingly, as in the day.* Our habitual behavior is to be intelligent instead of being merely a dim out-picturing of sense desires. When we realize that a certain course is right and good, we are to follow it faithfully.

3. *put on the Lord Jesus Christ.* By realizing that through claiming our dominion and mastership, we rise to newness of life in our I AM selfhood. As we do this we put on the perfect idea/conception of Divine Mind.

4. *make not provision for the flesh.* We are to make provision for faith in our divine nature. As children of God, we are to provide for suitable expression of our divine qualities and leave behind us all provision for externals.

---

Fillmore Study Bible annotations by Mark Hicks

**World English Bible Footnotes:**

[59] v13:9. TR adds "You shall not give false testimony,"

[60] v13:9. Exodus 20:13-15,17; Deuteronomy 5:17-19,21

[61] v13:9. Leviticus 19:18

# Romans 14

## Do Not Judge Another

14:1 Now accept one who is weak in faith, but not for disputes over opinions. 14:2 One man has faith to eat all things, but he who is weak eats only vegetables.[1] 14:3 Don't let him who eats despise him who doesn't eat. Don't let him who doesn't eat judge him who eats, for God has accepted him. 14:4 Who are you who judge another's servant? To his own lord he stands or falls. Yes, he will be made to stand, for God has power to make him stand.

14:5 One man esteems one day as more important. Another esteems every day alike. Let each man be fully assured in his own mind. 14:6 He who observes the day, observes it to the Lord; and he who does not observe the day, to the Lord he does not observe it. He who eats, eats to the Lord, for he gives God thanks. He who doesn't eat, to the Lord he doesn't eat, and gives God thanks. 14:7 For none of us lives to himself, and none dies to himself. 14:8 For if we live, we live to the Lord. Or if we die, we die to the Lord. If therefore we live or die, we are the Lord's. 14:9 For to this end Christ died, rose, and lived again, that he might be Lord of both the dead and the living.

14:10 But you, why do you judge your brother? Or you again, why do you despise your brother? For we will all stand before the judgment seat of Christ. 14:11 For it is written,

"'As I live,' says the Lord, 'to me
every knee will bow.
Every tongue will confess to
God.'"[62]

14:12 So then each one of us will give account of himself to God.

1. *One man has faith to eat all things, but he who is weak eats only vegetables.* See the Metaphysical Bible Interpretations and the commentary for v21 below. For the Fillmores, "man is healthier and clearer in mind, when he subsists on a strictly vegetarian diet ... there is no occasion for taking the life of birds or animals for food."

## Do Not Make Another Stumble

14:13 Therefore let's not judge one another any more, but judge this rather, that no man put a stumbling block in his brother's way, or an occasion for falling. 14:14 I know, and am persuaded in the Lord Jesus, that nothing is unclean of itself; except that to him who considers anything to be unclean, to him it is unclean. 14:15 Yet if because of food your brother is grieved, you walk no longer in love. Don't destroy with

your food him for whom Christ died.
14:16 Then don't let your good be
slandered, 14:17 for the Kingdom of
God is not eating and drinking, but
righteousness, peace, and joy in the
Holy Spirit. 14:18 For he who serves
Christ in these things is acceptable
to God and approved by men. 14:19 So
then, let us follow after things which
make for peace, and things by which
we may build one another up. 14:20
Don't overthrow God's work for food's
sake. All things indeed are clean,
however it is evil for that man who
creates a stumbling block by eating.
14:21 It is good to not eat meat, drink
wine, nor do anything by which your
brother stumbles, is offended, or is
made weak.[1]

14:22 Do you have faith? Have it to
yourself before God. Happy is he who
doesn't judge himself in that which
he approves. 14:23 But he who doubts
is condemned if he eats, because it
isn't of faith; and whatever is not of
faith is sin.

14:24 [63]

1. *nor do anything by which your brother stumbles, is offended, or is made weak.* See the Metaphysical Bible Interpretations and the commentary for v2 above. The commentaries imply that judging people who eat meat is a bigger problem than eating meat itself. For Paul, this verse is not about vegetarianism nor about a plant-based diet. Rather, this passage is about the judgement of the wealthy toward the poor. Paul is critical of those who refrain from eating meat because they are restricted by religious custom—fear of eating meat that had been sacrificed to pagan rituals. Eating such food was a necessity for the poor—distributing sacrificed meat was a form of "government assistance" of the day. The wealthy could refrain from eating such food. Paul is addressing the judgment of the wealthy regarding the poor.

Fillmore Study Bible annotations by Mark Hicks

**World English Bible Footnotes:**

[62] v14:11. Isaiah 45:23

[63] v14:26. WEB places Romans 16:25-27 here after 14:23 as verses 24-26. This edition has them moved to 16:25-27 in conformity to ASV and NRSV.

# Romans 15

## Please Others, Not Yourselves

15:1 Now we who are strong ought
to bear the weaknesses of the weak,
and not to please ourselves. 15:2 Let
each one of us please his neighbor
for that which is good, to be building
him up. 15:3 For even Christ didn't
please himself. But, as it is written,
"The reproaches of those who
reproached you fell on me."[64] 15:4
For whatever things were written
before were written for our learning,
that through patience and through
encouragement of the Scriptures we
might have hope. 15:5 Now the God
of patience and of encouragement
grant you to be of the same mind one

with another[1] according to Christ Jesus, 15:6 that with one accord you may with one mouth glorify the God and Father of our Lord Jesus Christ.

1. *be of the same mind one with another* In ail those activities which have been termed "unfinished business," Paul symbolized divine order. This is a feature that is frequently overlooked. Many important metaphysical meanings have already been recognized in connection with Paul's earlier activities, but it is equally important to note how Paul continually sought to establish order in the churches he founded. Herbert Hunt, *Correspondence School Study of the New Testament*, 148.

## The Gospel for Jews and Gentiles Alike

15:7 Therefore accept one another, even as Christ also accepted you,[65] to the glory of God. 15:8 Now I say that Christ has been made a servant of the circumcision for the truth of God, that he might confirm the promises given to the fathers, 15:9 and that the Gentiles might glorify God for his mercy. As it is written,

"Therefore will I give praise to
you among the Gentiles,
and sing to your name."[66]

15:10 Again he says,

"Rejoice, you Gentiles, with his
people."[67]

15:11 Again,

"Praise the Lord, all you Gentiles!
Let all the peoples praise
him."[68]

15:12 Again, Isaiah says,

"There will be the root of Jesse,
he who arises to rule over the
Gentiles;
in him the Gentiles will
hope."[69]

15:13 Now may the God of hope fill you with all joy and peace in believing, that you may abound in hope, in the power of the Holy Spirit.

## Paul's Reason for Writing So Boldly

15:14 I myself am also persuaded about you, my brothers[70], that you yourselves are full of goodness, filled with all knowledge, able also to admonish others. 15:15 But I write the more boldly to you in part, as reminding you, because of the grace that was given to me by God, 15:16 that I should be a servant of Christ Jesus to the Gentiles,[1] serving as a priest the Good News of God, that the offering up of the Gentiles[2] might be made acceptable, sanctified by the Holy Spirit. 15:17 I have therefore my boasting[3] in Christ Jesus in things pertaining to God. 15:18 For I will not dare to speak of any things except those which Christ worked through me,[4] for the obedience of the Gentiles, by word and deed, 15:19 in the power of signs and wonders,[5] in the power of God's Spirit; so that from Jerusalem, and around as far as to Illyricum,[6] I have fully preached the Good News of Christ; 15:20 yes, making it my aim to preach the Good News, not where Christ was already named,[7] that I might not build on another's foundation. 15:21 But, as it is written,

"They will see, to whom no news
of him came.
They who haven't heard will
understand."[71]

1. *a servant of Christ Jesus to the Gentiles* Paul, first called Saul, represents the regenerated or illumined will. Under the direction of the illumined will (Paul), our worldly thoughts (Gentiles) are lifted up and spiritualized, as we learn to harmonize them with Truth through the power of the Holy Spirit.

2. *the offering up of the Gentiles* The Gentiles, whose "offering up" is "sanctified by the Holy Spirit," represent our worldly thoughts, the unregenerate state of mind in us. These are to be transformed by the word of Truth (the preaching of Paul).

3. *I have therefore my boasting (glorying, ASV)* The will has power "in things pertaining to God" to convert the worldly thoughts and to turn worldliness to holiness.

4. *For I will not dare to speak of any things except those which Christ worked through me* No negative mental reaction should be allowed by anyone who wishes to demonstrate power.

5. *in the power of signs and wonders* "Signs and wonders" become possible in the experience of the one who is filled with the Holy Spirit. When a worldly-minded person shows interest in spiritual matters and begins to reform his thinking and his speech, it is a sign of the Holy Spirit's indwelling.

6. *from Jerusalem, and around as far as to Illyricum* The outer extreme of Paul's ministry—from theological to barbaric minds.

7. *not where Christ was already named.* Metaphysically interpreted, the last four verses of our lesson teach the carrying of the word of Christ to those parts of our organisms to which it has never been taken before. Every atom of our being that is still in darkness must be illumined by the Word and given new life and truth.

## Paul's Plan to Visit Rome

15:22 Therefore also I was hindered these many times from coming to you,[1] 15:23 but now, no longer having any place in these regions, and having these many years a longing to come to you, 15:24 whenever I journey to Spain,[2] I will come to you. For I hope to see you on my journey,[3] and to be helped on my way there by you, if first I may enjoy your company for a while. 15:25 But now, I say, I am going to Jerusalem, serving the saints. 15:26 For it has been the good pleasure of Macedonia and Achaia to make a certain contribution for the poor among the saints who are at Jerusalem. 15:27 Yes, it has been their good pleasure, and they are their debtors. For if the Gentiles have been made partakers of their spiritual things, they owe it to them also to serve them in fleshly things. 15:28 When therefore I have accomplished this, and have sealed to them this fruit, I will go on by way of you to Spain. 15:29 I know that, when I come to you, I will come in the fullness of the blessing of the Good News of Christ.

15:30 Now I beg you, brothers, by our Lord Jesus Christ, and by the love of the Spirit, that you strive together with me in your prayers to God for me, 15:31 that I may be delivered from those who are disobedient in Judea, and that my service which I have for Jerusalem may be acceptable to the saints; 15:32 that I may come to you in joy through the will of God, and together with you, find rest. 15:33 Now the God of peace be with you all. Amen.

1. *I was hindered these many times from coming to you* The entry of Paul and his companions into Europe is symbolical of opening up in the consciousness the word of Truth where it had never before been realized.

2. *journey to Spain* Spain was often used to indicate the regions at the ends of the earth.

3. *For I hope to see you on my journey* Spiritual leaders are especially needed to show us the way to world peace and good will at the present time, instead of await-

ing the slow process of transforming persons one by one into the likeness of Christ. Leaders possessed of spiritual power are needed to convert the world to the conviction that good will and brotherhood are possible on a universal scale, and that, if the world is to be formed into the kingdom of God everyone must set about doing his part in the great work now.

Fillmore Study Bible annotations by Mark Hicks

**World English Bible Footnotes:**

[64] v15:3. Psalm 69:9

[65] v15:7. TR reads "us" instead of "you"

[66] v15:9. 2 Samuel 22:50; Psalm 18:49

[67] v15:10. Deuteronomy 32:43

[68] v15:11. Psalm 117:1

[69] v15:12. Isaiah 11:10

[70] v15:14. The word for "brothers" here and where context allows may also be correctly translated "brothers and sisters" or "siblings."

[71] v15:21. Isaiah 52:15

# Romans 16

## Personal Greetings

16:1 I commend to you Phoebe,(1) our sister, who is a servant[72] of the assembly that is at Cenchreae,(2) 16:2 that you receive her in the Lord, in a way worthy of the saints, and that you assist her in whatever matter she may need from you, for she herself also has been a helper of many, and of my own self.

16:3 Greet Prisca and Aquila,(3) my fellow workers in Christ Jesus, 16:4 who for my life, laid down their own necks; to whom not only I give thanks, but also all the assemblies of the Gentiles. 16:5 Greet the assembly that is in their house. Greet Epaenetus, my beloved, who is the first fruits of Achaia to Christ. 16:6 Greet Mary, who labored much for us. 16:7 Greet Andronicus(4) and Junias,(5) my relatives and my fellow prisoners, who are notable among the apostles, who also were in Christ before me. 16:8 Greet Amplias, my beloved in the Lord. 16:9 Greet Urbanus, our fellow worker in Christ, and Stachys, my beloved. 16:10 Greet Apelles,(6) the approved in Christ. Greet those who are of the household of Aristobulus. 16:11 Greet Herodion, my kinsman. Greet them of the household of Narcissus,(7) who are in the Lord. 16:12 Greet Tryphaena and Tryphosa, who labor in the Lord. Greet Persis, the beloved, who labored much in the Lord. 16:13 Greet Rufus, the chosen in the Lord, and

his mother and mine. 16:14 Greet
Asyncritus, Phlegon, Hermes,
Patrobas, Hermas, and the
brothers[73] who are with them. 16:15
Greet Philologus and Julia, Nereus
and his sister, and Olympas, and all
the saints who are with them. 16:16
Greet one another with a holy kiss.
The assemblies of Christ greet you.

1. *Phoebe.* A "servant" or "deaconess" of the church at Cenchreæ in Corinth. Metaphysically, the pure Christ light and love radiating throughout the consciousness: bright; shining; brilliant; radiant; pure.

2. *Cenchreae.* Signifies, like the mustard seed of Jesus' parable, the fact that the Truth established in the consciousness of man is at first similar to a very tiny seed (the word is the seed). We should not therefore despise nor look upon as insignificant any beginning of light and Truth that comes to us or to others, no matter how small it may seem.

3. *Prisca and Aquila* Priscilla, the feminine or receptive phase of the healing forces of nature that are always at work rebuilding the body and repairing the ravages of ignorant man. Aquila, husband of Priscilla, is the positive phase of these forces.

4. *Andronicus* was "of note among the apostles," and "in Christ before me," means that man was ideally perfect in the Christ mind from the beginning, before he ever exercised his free will in a perverse way.

5. *Junias* The inner, ever renewing vital force of the subjective mind. This vital force, along with the word of Truth (Paul), is held in bondage and is kept from doing its perfect renewing, vitalizing work in the organism of man, when man lets his spiritually unawakened intellect rule in consciousness instead of being open to and guided by the inspiration and understanding of the Christ.

6. *Apelles, the approved in Christ* That in man which follows the inner leading of Spirit onward and upward (called, set apart) to the exclusion of lesser, sense promptings and desires. This brings about a realization of the approval of the inner Christ.

7. *household of Narcissus* Mental inertia, or a thought tendency belonging to the intellect of man, the head (Rome), that tends to inertia of perhaps both mind and body (narcotic, stupefying). The family, or thoughts that lie nearest in relation to this cause of apathy and inaction, have been quickened and awakened by Truth (the household of Narcissus are "in the Lord"), thus the whole condition is in process of redemption.

## Final Instructions

16:17 Now I beg you, brothers, look
out for those who are causing the
divisions and occasions of stumbling,
contrary to the doctrine which you
learned, and turn away from them.
16:18 For those who are such don't
serve our Lord, Jesus Christ, but
their own belly; and by their smooth
and flattering speech, they deceive
the hearts of the innocent. 16:19 For
your obedience has become known to
all. I rejoice therefore over you. But I
desire to have you wise in that which
is good, but innocent in that which is
evil. 16:20 And the God of peace will
quickly crush Satan under your feet.
The grace of our Lord Jesus Christ be
with you.

16:21 Timothy, my fellow worker,
greets you, as do Lucius, Jason, and
Sosipater, my relatives. 16:22 I,
Tertius, who write the letter, greet
you in the Lord. 16:23 Gaius, my host
and host of the whole assembly,
greets you. Erastus, the treasurer of
the city, greets you, as does Quartus,
the brother.

## Final Doxology

16:25 Now to him who is able to
establish you according to my Good

News and the preaching of Jesus Christ, according to the revelation of the mystery which has been kept secret through long ages, 16:26 but now is revealed, and by the Scriptures of the prophets, according to the commandment of the eternal God, is made known for obedience of faith to all the nations; 16:27 to the only wise God, through Jesus Christ, to whom be the glory forever! Amen.[74]

---

Fillmore Study Bible annotations by Mark Hicks

**World English Bible Footnotes:**

[72] v16:1. or, deacon

[73] v16:14. The word for "brothers" here and where context allows may also be correctly translated "brothers and sisters" or "siblings."

[74] v16:25. WEB places Romans 16:25-27 at the end of chapter 14, and numbers these verses 14:24-26. These verses are placed here to conform to ASV and NRSV. WEB verse 16:24 "The grace of our Lord Jesus Christ be with you all! Amen." has been removed.

# Paul's First Letter to the Corinthians

Ruins of ancient Corinth. Public Domain.

## Introduction to Paul's First Letter to the Corinthians

Toward the close of Paul's ministry at Ephesus, the apostle received very disturbing news regarding conditions in the church at Corinth. It was reported that there were dissensions in matters of doctrine, immorality among the membership, and many other irregularities quite inconsistent with Christian principles. Paul immediately wrote a strongly-worded letter of admonition, calling upon the Corinthians to amend their ways. Unfortunately, this letter is now lost; but Paul clearly refers to it in a later message. (See I Cor. 5:9-11.) In any event, it would appear from what transpired later that this letter of admonition was completely ignored by the Corinthians.

However, a short time later some of the leaders and teachers in the Corinthian Church wrote to Paul—not mentioning his letter of admonition, but urgently seeking answers to some important questions concerning

Christian conduct and doctrine. Apparently these questions had arisen in instruction classes or religious discussions at Corinth, and the local teachers had been unable to furnish satisfactory answers. Paul immediately replied by sending to them what we now term the Paul's First Letter to the Corinthians.

Introduction to *Paul's First Letter to the Corinthians* by Herbert J. Hunt, former Dean of Bible Studies for the Unity School of Christianity.

**Purpose of the letter.** In about 53 CE, three years after founding the church in Corinth, Paul writes to them in an attempt to restore harmony and unity among many different fractions. It was a cosmopolitan, somewhat crass city, located not far from Athens, filled with a cross-section of people, and this was reflected in the church, where there was a great deal of jealousy and animosity. Paul writes to bring unity and harmony.

**Popular appeal of the letter.** In this letter we have two of Paul's best known chapters. First is chapter twelve, where Paul says that the church is one body with many members who have a variety of spiritual gifts, which are "activated by the one and the same Spirit" (12:11). This may be a metaphysical expression of the church's faculty of order, by which it establishes harmony, balance, right adjustment, and right sequence of action (among the various gifts). Second is chapter thirteen, where Paul talks about the gift of love. When he writes that that love "bears all things, believes all things, hopes all things, endures all things" we may be hearing Paul's understanding of the church's expression of the faculty of strength, by which it has steadfastness, dependability, stability, and capacity for endurance.

**Metaphysical Ministry.** Besides these two well-known chapters, Metaphysical Christians will find three important ideas in the letter. First is Charles Fillmore's identification of himself as a modern day Apostle Paul and what it says about metaphysical ministry. The commentary for 4:12 reads "He who once manifested as Paul the apostle is now expressing himself through another personality, right here in America." He continues, "So if we assert that he who was once called Paul is among us, teaching and healing in a humble way, do not let these illusions of ecclesiastical education darken your understanding." The ministry of Paul and Charles Fillmore have four common characteristics, based on Jesus' sending forth the twelve disciples in Matthew 10: a ministry of healing, freely given; a vocation without any credentials or social status except having been commissioned by Jesus Christ; a reliance on freely-given love offerings; and a total disregard of rejection by critics. Charles Fillmore returns to this formula for ministry in chapter 9, verse 14. Commenting on "those who proclaim the Good News should live from the Good News," he says, "The disciples of Jesus were not to take scrip or purse, but they were to meet the spiritual needs of those to whom they went."

**Spiritual unfoldment, metaphysically understood.** The second important idea is an almost unnoticeable formula for spiritual unfoldment tucked away in chapter six, verse 11. Paul writes "but you were washed. But you were sanctified. But you were justified..." Calvinist theology holds that we are first justified by faith then sanctified by grace which slowly washes us of the effects of sin. But Paul in 6:12 and Charles Fillmore in his commentary place justification after sanctification and sanctification after washing (denial). In other words, justification is the end of a process, metaphysically known as "regeneration", rather than the beginning of a process of reunion with God, which makes no sense to a metaphysician. The Unity commentary of October 29, 1939 reads: *"Washed" is another word for "denied." A "sanctified" person is a person set apart or completely dedicated to God in thought, word, and act. "Justified" has to do with a person's vindication by faith in his indwelling Lord.*

**Harmony in spiritual worship.** The third important metaphysical concept is the balance of masculine and feminine activity in the inner workings of the soul. Paul's regrettable admonitions in chapter seven, "Directions concerning Marriage", chapter 11, "Head Coverings", and chapter 14, "Orderly Worship" run counter to our modern sensibilities of gender equality. The metaphysical Christian commentary offers a healthy way to approach these troublesome passages in a way that liberal biblical criticism and Evangelical biblical literalism are unable to provide. The key to the metaphysical approach is that "worship" is not an external ritual that takes place in a church but rather an internal process which takes place in the soul, where all persons, men and women, have both thinking and feeling processes. Paul's passages in the letter offer valuable insight into how these thinking and feeling processes need to be in harmony. Further insight is obtained from biblical commentary by Jim Lewis about speaking in tongues, a feeling process, and the gift of prophecy, a thinking process.

**Other insights.** Many additional verses and annotations provide new insights into the letter from Paul, such as verse 6:15, declaring that our body (not only our soul) is a member of Christ; verse 7:21 declaring that if we get an opportunity to be free, use it; and verse 7:28, declaring that there is no need for sexual shame (oppression of the flesh).

**Realized eschatology.** Chapter 15 provides a capstone for Paul's letter, declaring that Jesus Christ appeared to Cephas, then to the twelve; that Jesus did not leave the earth, but he did leave the consciousness of material conditions, which we call the earth. He is still in our midst in his eternal body, dwelling in another form.

Introduction to *Paul's First Letter to the Corinthians* by Rev. Mark Hicks.

# First Corinthians 1

## Salutation

1:1 Paul, called to be an apostle[1]
of Jesus Christ through the will of
God, and our brother Sosthenes,[2]
1:2 to the assembly of God which is at
Corinth;[3] those who are sanctified
in Christ Jesus, called to be saints,[1]
with all who call on the name of our
Lord Jesus Christ in every place, both
theirs and ours:

1:3 Grace to you and peace from
God our Father and the Lord Jesus
Christ.

1:4 I always thank my God

concerning you, for the grace of God which was given you in Christ Jesus; 1:5 that in everything you were enriched in him, in all speech and all knowledge; 1:6 even as the testimony of Christ was confirmed in you: 1:7 so that you come behind in no gift; waiting for the revelation of our Lord Jesus Christ; 1:8 who will also confirm you until the end, blameless in the day of our Lord Jesus Christ. 1:9 God is faithful, through whom you were called into the fellowship of his Son, Jesus Christ, our Lord.

1. *called to be an apostle, called to be saints.* The call in each case corresponds to the urge that man feels to give up his petty personal will by merging it in the will of God. The higher will is identified with the perfect-man idea, Jesus Christ.

2. *Sosthenes.* (sound strength; secure in strength) represents the idea of Christ as the saving, redeeming principle in man and as the unfailing strength of man's life. The name is fittingly associated with the word of Truth (Paul).

3. *Corinth.* (ornament, beauty), forty miles to the west of Athens, contained the Greek temple of Venus, which was dedicated to the worship of love. So we discern that it was at the love center in consciousness that the Truth sought to do a work. Paul here is referred to as the word of Truth, and Corinth is the love center. Paul wrote his matchless poem on love to the Corinthians. But this center was largely given over to licentiousness. Under the guise of religion, more than a thousand courtesans were attached to the temple of Venus at Corinth as assistants, says secular history. So the need of purification, and of the lifting up of the affections here at the love center in human consciousness, is very great when the word of Truth first enters to do its redeeming work. MBD/ Corinth

## Divisions in the Church

1:10 Now I beg you, brothers,[1] through the name of our Lord, Jesus Christ, that you all speak the same thing and that there be no divisions among you, but that you be perfected together in the same mind and in the same judgment.❶ 1:11 For it has been reported to me concerning you, my brothers, by those who are from Chloe's household,❷ that there are contentions among you.❸ 1:12 Now I mean this, that each one of you says, "I follow Paul," "I follow Apollos," "I follow Cephas," and, "I follow Christ." 1:13 Is Christ divided? Was Paul crucified for you? Or were you baptized into the name of Paul? 1:14 I thank God that I baptized none of you, except Crispus and Gaius, 1:15 so that no one should say that I had baptized you into my own name. 1:16 (I also baptized the household of Stephanas; besides them, I don't know whether I baptized any other.) 1:17 For Christ sent me not to baptize, but to preach the Good News❹--not in wisdom of words, so that the cross of Christ wouldn't be made void.

1. *speak the same thing, in the same mind, in the same judgment.* The first manifestation of unity in Christ is in word ("that ye all speak the same thing"), the second in mind, and the third in judgment ("that ye be perfected together in the same mind and in the same judgment").

2. *Chloe's household.* The household of Chloe represents spiritual thoughts of life and love that are increasing, harmoniously. Such thoughts quickly divine cross-currents that arise from a contentious frame of mind.

3. *contentions among you.* They are divided among themselves over the subject of their entrance into the faith, that some who had come in through his preaching felt superior to others who had been converted by Apollos, that still others who held to the views of Cephas looked down on the brethren who had come into Christianity through other avenues. These thoughts are quick to sense the cross currents of a divided or contentious attitude of mind. They communicate the news of this inharmony

to the word of Truth (Paul), so that by the activity of the word the cross currents may be eliminated and the love consciousness reestablished in the harmony of the Christ Spirit.

4. *For Christ sent me not to baptize, but to preach the Good News.* Paul's ministry signifies the word of Truth in its work throughout the consciousness and the organism of man.

## Christ the Power and Wisdom of God

1:18 For the word of the cross❶ is foolishness to those who are dying, but to us who are saved it is the power of God. 1:19 For it is written,

> "I will destroy the wisdom of the wise,
> I will bring the discernment of the discerning to nothing."[2]

1:20 Where is the wise? Where is the scribe? Where is the lawyer of this world? Hasn't God made foolish the wisdom of this world? 1:21 For seeing that in the wisdom of God, the world through its wisdom didn't know God, it was God's good pleasure through the foolishness of the preaching to save those who believe. 1:22 For Jews ask for signs, Greeks seek after wisdom,❷ 1:23 but we preach Christ crucified; a stumbling block to Jews, and foolishness to Greeks, 1:24 but to those who are called, both Jews and Greeks, Christ is the power of God and the wisdom of God. 1:25 Because the foolishness of God is wiser than men, and the weakness of God❸ is stronger than men. 1:26 For you see your calling, brothers, that not many are wise according to the flesh, not many mighty, and not many noble; 1:27 but God chose the foolish things of the world that he might put to shame those who are wise. God chose the weak things of the world, that he might put to shame the things that are strong; 1:28 and God chose the lowly things of the world, and the things that are despised, and the things that are not, that he might bring to nothing the things that are: 1:29 that no flesh should boast before God. 1:30 But of him, you are in Christ Jesus, who was made to us wisdom from God, and righteousness and sanctification, and redemption: 1:31 that, according as it is written, "He who boasts, let him boast in the Lord."[3]

1. *word of the cross.* The word of denial of the personal self, or the sense nature, which virtually everyone, in ignorance of this true self, has built up as the substructure of his life.

2. *For Jews ask for signs, Greeks seek after wisdom.* The signs that the Jews demanded and the wisdom sought by the Greeks were both attempts to arrive at understanding of our essential unity.

3. *foolishness of God, weakness of God.* These expressions serve to heighten the contrast between divine wisdom and worldly wisdom, divine power and personal power. The slightest degree of divine wisdom expressed by man is better than the highest degree of intellectual development he may make, and with power and might.

---

Fillmore Study Bible annotations compiled by Rev. Mark Hicks.

**World English Bible Footnotes:**

[1] v1:10. The word for "brothers" here and where context allows may also be correctly translated "brothers and sisters" or "siblings."

[2] v1:19. Isaiah 29:14

[3] v1:31. Jeremiah 9:24

# First Corinthians 2

## Proclaiming Christ Crucified

2:1 When I came to you, brothers, I didn't come with excellence of speech or of wisdom,(1) proclaiming to you the testimony of God. 2:2 For I determined not to know anything among you, except Jesus Christ, and him crucified. 2:3 I was with you in weakness, in fear, and in much trembling. 2:4 My speech and my preaching were not in persuasive words of human wisdom, but in demonstration of the Spirit and of power,(2) 2:5 that your faith wouldn't stand in the wisdom of men, but in the power of God.

1. *I didn't come with excellence of speech or of wisdom.* When he first came among them, Paul had made no display of worldly wisdom or oratory, but had determined to rely entirely on the power of the Christ consciousness to save men by crossing out all the counter-currents of personality.

2. *demonstration of the Spirit and of power.* Paul "crossed out" weakness, fear, and "much trembling" by dropping all personality out of mind and being conscious of the Christ only. In this way he demonstrated the power of the Holy Spirit.

## The True Wisdom of God

2:6 We speak wisdom, however, among those who are full grown; yet a wisdom not of this world, nor of the rulers of this world, who are coming to nothing. 2:7 But we speak God's wisdom in a mystery, the wisdom that has been hidden, which God foreordained before the worlds for our glory, 2:8 which none of the rulers of this world has known. For had they known it, they wouldn't have crucified the Lord of glory. 2:9 But as it is written,

"Things which an eye didn't see,
and an ear didn't hear,
which didn't enter into the heart of man,
these God has prepared for those who love him."(1)[4]

2:10 But to us, God revealed them through the Spirit. For the Spirit searches all things, yes, the deep things of God.(2) 2:11 For who among men knows the things of a man, except the spirit of the man, which is in him? Even so, no one knows the things of God, except God's Spirit. 2:12 But we received, not the spirit of the world, but the Spirit which is from God, that we might know the things that were freely given to us by God. 2:13 Which things also we speak, not in words which man's wisdom teaches, but which the Holy Spirit teaches, comparing spiritual things with spiritual things.

2:14 Now the natural man doesn't receive the things of God's Spirit, for they are foolishness to him, and he can't know them, because they are spiritually discerned. 2:15 But he who is spiritual discerns all things, and he himself is judged by no one. 2:16 "For who has known the mind of the Lord, that he should instruct him?"[5] But we have Christ's mind.(3)

1. *God has prepared for those who love him.* We have never seen, nor heard, nor even imagined all the marvelous, amazingly fascinating things that God will do for those who love Him, trust Him, and put His principles into practice-*Thought Conditioners* #34, Norman Vincent Peale.

2. *For the Spirit (pneuma) searches all things, yes, the deep things of God.* Paul uses the word pneuma (spirit) several ways, but he usually speaks of Spirit as a power which is available to everyone.

3. *But we have Christ's mind.* Man merges his consciousness with the Absolute through harmonizing all his ideas with the unlimited ideas of the Christ Mind. This is accomplished through understanding Divine Mind and its Laws. Man becomes conscious of Divine Mind through appropriating or thinking upon the ideas of Divine Mind.

---

Fillmore Study Bible annotations compiled by Rev. Mark Hicks.

**World English Bible Footnotes:**

[4] v2:9. Isaiah 64:4

[5] v2:16. Isaiah 40:13

# First Corinthians 3

## On Divisions in the Corinthian Church(1)

3:1 Brothers, I couldn't speak to you as to spiritual, but as to fleshly, as to babies in Christ.(2) 3:2 I fed you with milk, not with meat; for you weren't yet ready. Indeed, not even now are you ready, 3:3 for you are still fleshly. For insofar as there is jealousy, strife, and factions among you, aren't you fleshly, and don't you walk in the ways of men? 3:4 For when one says, "I follow Paul," and another, "I follow Apollos," aren't you fleshly?

3:5 Who then is Apollos, and who is Paul, but servants through whom you believed; and each as the Lord gave to him? 3:6 I planted. Apollos watered.(3) But God gave the increase.(4) 3:7 So then neither he who plants is anything, nor he who waters, but God who gives the increase. 3:8 Now he who plants and he who waters are the same, but each will receive his own reward according to his own labor. 3:9 For we are God's fellow workers. You are God's farming, God's building.

3:10 According to the grace of God which was given to me, as a wise master builder I laid a foundation,(5) and another builds on it. But let each man be careful how he builds on it. 3:11 For no one can lay any other foundation than that which has been laid, which is Jesus Christ.(6) 3:12 But if anyone builds on the foundation with

gold, silver, costly stones, wood,
hay, or stubble;⑦ 3:13 each man's work
will be revealed. For the Day will
declare it, because it is revealed in
fire; and the fire itself will test what
sort of work each man's work is. 3:14
If any man's work remains which he
built on it, he will receive a reward.
3:15 If any man's work is burned, he
will suffer loss, but he himself will be
saved, but as through fire.

3:16 Don't you know that you are a
temple of God, and that God's Spirit
lives in you? 3:17 If anyone destroys
the temple of God, God will destroy
him;⑧ for God's temple is holy, which
you are.

3:18 Let no one deceive himself. If
anyone thinks that he is wise among
you in this world, let him become a
fool, that he may become wise.

3:19 For the wisdom of this world
is foolishness with God. For it is
written, "He has taken the wise in
their craftiness."[6] 3:20 And again,
"The Lord knows the reasoning of the
wise, that it is worthless."[7] 3:21
Therefore let no one boast in men.
For all things are yours, 3:22 whether
Paul, or Apollos, or Cephas, or the
world, or life, or death, or things
present, or things to come. All are
yours, 3:23 and you are Christ's, and
Christ is God's.⑨

1. *On Divisions in the Corinthian Church.* This is a lengthy letter and in it Paul discusses a variety of subjects. The first and most pressing was the unification of four factions that had arisen in the church, that is, those who follow Paul, Cephas (Peter), Apollos, and others who took the name of Christ. He reminds them that the Gospel is the good tidings of salvation through Christ to all. Christian teachers are divinely appointed and should work in harmony. One teacher should not be selected to the exclusion of others. How important is it for us to remember this! Each one has his own work to do in life, and in God's sight it is equal importance to that done by any person. The Lord will always give the increase if we are faithful to our given task. *Be Ye Transformed*, Elizabeth Sand Turner, p.95

2. *As to babies in Christ.* The surest sign of the mental maturity in man or woman is the habit of self-reliance and quiet confidence.

3. *Apollos watered.* Apollos represents a phase of understanding that, under intellectual thought, is likely to be hard and destructive because of zeal to put away error, apart from the loving thought of the Christ. Understanding waters the growing Truth, and so helps it along to fruition.

4. *God gave the increase.* The realization that all things come of God and that one must look to Him and accept in faith all that one asks for or desires. The increasing, life-giving power of Truth is Spirit.

5. *I laid a foundation.* Self-reliance is invaluable to man in building a Christ-like character because only a competent workman can erect a building in a workmanlike manner. One must know one's work and must know that one knows it.

6. *foundation than that which has been laid, which is Jesus Christ.* The perfect Christ foundation is laid in the ideal of every man's being, as he exists in Divine Mind. No other than this can be laid, but men build diverse superstructures upon it, each according to his bent.

7. *wood, hay, or stubble* Negative thoughts that are of little, if any, value in character building and that fail to endure. For the most part they are not in any respect building material.

8. *If anyone destroys the temple of God, God will destroy him.* God is working in us to bring into expression our perfect Self. To hinder this unfoldment would be sinning against God, defeating His plan.

9. *you are Christ's, and Christ is God's.* The foundation of all spiritual truth is Jesus Christ and His doctrine.

---

Fillmore Study Bible annotations compiled by Rev. Mark Hicks.

**World English Bible Footnotes:**

[6] v3:19. Job 5:13

[7] v3:20. Psalm 94:11

# First Corinthians 4

## The Ministry of the Apostles

4:1 So let a man think of us as Christ's servants, and stewards of God's mysteries. 4:2 Here, moreover, it is required of stewards, that they be found faithful. 4:3 But with me it is a very small thing that I should be judged by you, or by man's judgment. Yes, I don't judge my own self. 4:4 For I know nothing against myself. Yet I am not justified by this, but he who judges me is the Lord. 4:5 Therefore judge nothing before the time, until the Lord comes, who will both bring to light the hidden things of darkness, and reveal the counsels of the hearts. Then each man will get his praise from God.

4:6 Now these things, brothers, I have in a figure transferred to myself and Apollos for your sakes, that in us you might learn not to think beyond the things which are written, that none of you be puffed up against one another. 4:7 For who makes you different? And what do you have that you didn't receive? But if you did receive it, why do you boast as if you had not received it?

4:8 You are already filled. You have already become rich. You have come to reign without us. Yes, and I wish that you did reign, that we also might reign with you. 4:9 For, I think that God has displayed us, the apostles, last of all, like men sentenced to death. For we are made a spectacle to the world, both to angels and men. 4:10 We are fools for Christ's sake, but you are wise in Christ. We are weak, but you are strong. You have honor, but we have dishonor. 4:11 Even to this present hour we hunger, thirst, are naked, are beaten, and have no certain dwelling place. 4:12 We toil, working with our own hands.[1] When people curse us, we bless. Being persecuted, we endure. 4:13 Being defamed, we entreat. We are made as the filth of the world, the dirt wiped off by all, even until now.

1. *We toil, working with our own hands.* "He who once manifested as Paul the apostle is now expressing himself through another personality, right here in America. It should be remembered, in discussing this character, that the real Paul and the ideal which the world today holds of Paul, are not the same. The illusions of hero worship are beyond all reason, and especially so when the hero has been sainted and a religious halo thrown about his character and his writings. A calm, unbiased perusal of Paul's history, as recorded in his writings, will convince any one, who is not hypnotized by ecclesiastical assumptions, that he lacked much of being the saint that the church thinks him. As one of the early church fathers, his lot was hard—that of the disseminator of new and strange doctrines utterly opposed to those popularly accepted by the people. From the day that he adopted the ministry of Jesus Christ he was despised and persecuted, except by a few followers ... So if we assert that he who was once called Paul is among us, teaching and healing in a humble way, do not let these illusions of ecclesiastical education darken your understanding. Our word today that we know Paul is just as good as his was nineteen hundred years ago that he had seen and talked with Jesus of Nazareth, who was supposed to be

> dead." *Paul Is Now Here*, Charles Fillmore, Unity, August 1924.

## Fatherly Admonition

4:14 I don't write these things to shame you, but to admonish you as my beloved children. 4:15 For though you have ten thousand tutors in Christ, yet not many fathers. For in Christ Jesus, I became your father through the Good News. 4:16 I beg you therefore, be imitators of me.[1] 4:17 Because of this I have sent Timothy to you, who is my beloved and faithful child in the Lord, who will remind you of my ways which are in Christ, even as I teach everywhere in every assembly. 4:18 Now some are puffed up, as though I were not coming to you. 4:19 But I will come to you shortly, if the Lord is willing. And I will know, not the word of those who are puffed up, but the power. 4:20 For the Kingdom of God is not in word, but in power.[2] 4:21 What do you want? Shall I come to you with a rod, or in love and a spirit of gentleness?

> 1. *be imitators of me.* As children imitate the parents because they know no one else so well, so followers of the Christ express the word of Truth wholeheartedly, because they know no other expression.
>
> 2. *For the Kingdom of God is not in word, but in power.* The kingdom of God is revealed through a man's *consciousness* of power, rather than through the words he speaks. The latter may be empty, but power is self-revealing, and cannot be hidden. At some point, Unity's teachers began to focus on the language used in prayer rather than the the consciousness from which we pray. That is a most unfortunate mistake because the kingdom of God is not in word, but in the power of consciousness.

Fillmore Study Bible annotations compiled by Rev. Mark Hicks.

# First Corinthians 5

## Sexual Immorality Defiles the Church

5:1 It is actually reported that there is sexual immorality among you, and such sexual immorality as is not even named among the Gentiles, that one has his father's wife. 5:2 You are puffed up, and didn't rather mourn, that he who had done this deed might be removed from among you.

5:3 For I most certainly, as being absent in body but present in spirit, have already, as though I were present, judged him who has done this thing. 5:4 In the name of our Lord Jesus Christ, you being gathered together, and my spirit, with the power of our Lord Jesus Christ, 5:5 are to deliver such a one to Satan for the destruction of the flesh, that the spirit may be saved in the day of the Lord Jesus.

5:6 Your boasting is not good. Don't

you know that a little yeast leavens
the whole lump?❶ 5:7 Purge out the
old yeast,❷ that you may be a new
lump, even as you are unleavened.
For indeed Christ, our Passover, has
been sacrificed in our place. 5:8
Therefore let us keep the feast, not
with old yeast, neither with the yeast
of malice and wickedness, but with
the unleavened bread of sincerity
and truth.

1. *a little yeast leavens the whole lump.* The "leaven" represents limited thoughts. When we allow the finer forces of the body to go to fulfill lust and appetite, we are letting the leaven work to our undoing. When the mind is raised up through affirmations of God's omnipresent substance and life, we are not only fed but there is a surplus. MBD/Leaven.

2. *Purge out the old yeast.* Whatever line of thought is received into consciousness goes on working until it is rooted out by another line of thinking or until it changes one's whole consciousness and manifests fully in the outer life. (cf. Matthew 13:33, Mark 8:15)

## Sexual Immorality Must Be Judged

5:9 I wrote to you in my letter to
have no company with sexual
sinners; 5:10 yet not at all meaning
with the sexual sinners of this
world,❶ or with the covetous and
extortioners, or with idolaters; for
then you would have to leave the
world. 5:11 But as it is, I wrote to
you not to associate with anyone who
is called a brother who is a sexual
sinner, or covetous, or an idolater,
or a slanderer, or a drunkard, or an
extortioner. Don't even eat with such
a person.❷ 5:12 For what have I to
do with also judging those who are
outside?❸ Don't you judge those who
are within? 5:13 But those who are
outside, God judges. "Put away the
wicked man from among
yourselves."[8]

1. *yet not at all meaning with the sexual sinners of this world.* The distinction is drawn between "sexual sinners *of this world*" and "sexual sinners" who are fellow Christians. The latter are to be avoided more than the former for the reason that fellows in Christ are moved by the same spirit, and without faithfulness to the ideal of purity and honesty there can be no spiritual unity among so-called fellows. The standard of perfection is to be upheld without wavering.

2. *Don't even eat with such a person.* Eating symbolizes the appropriation of substance, and no one can appropriate the substance of both Truth and falsity.

3. *For what have I to do with also judging those who are outside? Don't you judge those who are within?* We are not to judge others those who are outside but is to busy ourselves with clearing up our inner conflicts.

---

Fillmore Study Bible annotations compiled by Rev. Mark Hicks.

**World English Bible Footnotes:**

[8] v5:13. Deuteronomy 17:7; 19:19; 21:21; 22:21; 24:7

# First Corinthians 6

## Lawsuits among Believers

6:1 Dare any of you, having a matter against his neighbor, go to law before the unrighteous, and not before the saints? 6:2 Don't you know that the saints will judge the world? And if the world is judged by you, are you unworthy to judge the smallest matters? 6:3 Don't you know that we will judge angels? How much more, things that pertain to this life? 6:4 If then, you have to judge things pertaining to this life, do you set them to judge who are of no account in the assembly? 6:5 I say this to move you to shame. Isn't there even one wise man among you who would be able to decide between his brothers? 6:6 But brother goes to law with brother, and that before unbelievers!

6:7 Therefore it is already altogether a defect in you, that you have lawsuits one with another. Why not rather be wronged? Why not rather be defrauded? 6:8 No, but you yourselves do wrong, and defraud, and that against your brothers.

6:9 Or don't you know that the unrighteous will not inherit the Kingdom of God?[1] Don't be deceived. Neither the sexually immoral, nor idolaters, nor adulterers, nor male prostitutes, nor homosexuals, 6:10 nor thieves, nor covetous, nor drunkards, nor slanderers, nor extortioners, will inherit the Kingdom of God. 6:11 Such were some of you, but you were washed. But you were sanctified. But you were justified[2] in the name of the Lord Jesus, and in the Spirit of our God.

1. *will inherit the Kingdom of God.* Ten classes of those whose conduct is negative are mentioned as unable to inherit the kingdom of God. Those who do inherit the kingdom are those who enter consciously into the kingdom and through faithful affirmation of their divine nature develop power to express the better part and leave behind the lesser. Those who abandon themselves to the appeals of the sense consciousness or who make a fetish of externals and neglect to develop the inner life, cannot inherit what does not in any real sense belong to them.

2. *Washed, sanctified, justified.* "Washed", metaphysically, is denial of error and its effects. A "sanctified" person is a person set apart or completely dedicated to God in thought, word, and act. "Justified" has to do with a person's vindication by faith in his indwelling Lord. Note the the Fillmore commentary has *justification following sanctification.* Anyone who devotes himself to the ideal of the perfect life in and through the Spirit of the Christ is sanctified or set apart and dedicated to the service of God. "Justification" follows "sanctification" in that to be accepted as being right and as doing right can be only "in the name of the Lord Jesus, and in the Spirit of our God." Any claim that rests merely on personal excellence is without supporting evidence or foundation in Truth.

## Glorify God in Body and Spirit

6:12 "All things are lawful for me," but not all things are expedient. "All things are lawful for me," but I will not be brought under the power of anything. 6:13 "Foods for the belly, and the belly for foods," but God will bring to nothing both it and them. But the body is not for sexual immorality, but for the Lord; and the Lord for the body. 6:14 Now God raised up the Lord, and will also raise us up by his power. 6:15 Don't you know that your bodies are members of Christ?[1] Shall I then take the members of Christ, and make them members of a prostitute? May it never be! 6:16 Or don't you know that he who is joined to a prostitute is one body? For, "The two," says he, "will become one flesh."[9] 6:17 But he who is joined to the Lord is one spirit. 6:18 Flee sexual immorality! "Every sin that a man does is outside the body," but he who commits sexual immorality sins against his own body. 6:19 Or don't you know that your body is a temple of the Holy Spirit which is in you, which you have from God? You are not your own, 6:20 for you were bought with a price. Therefore glorify God in your body[2] and in your spirit, which are God's.

1. *Don't you know that your bodies are members of Christ?* Our bodies are members, not only our souls.

2. *Therefore glorify God in your body.* The body is "a temple of the Holy Spirit" and in order to glorify God, one must have a pure and healthy body, through which God's life and light and beauty may express. Paul's assertion is in line with the text given in Genesis when God blessed humanity in the beginning.

Fillmore Study Bible annotations compiled by Rev. Mark Hicks.

**World English Bible Footnotes:**

[9] v6:16. Genesis 2:24

# First Corinthians 7

## Directions concerning Marriage

7:1 Now concerning the things about which you wrote to me: it is good for a man not to touch a woman. 7:2 But, because of sexual immoralities, let each man have his own wife, and let each woman have her own husband.[1] 7:3 Let the husband render to his wife the affection owed her, and likewise also the wife to her husband. 7:4 The wife doesn't have authority over her own body, but the husband. Likewise also the husband doesn't have authority over his own body, but the wife. 7:5 Don't deprive one another, unless it is by consent for a season, that you may give yourselves to fasting and prayer, and may be together again, that Satan doesn't tempt you because of your lack of self-control. 7:6 But this I say by way of concession, not of commandment. 7:7 Yet I wish that all men were like me. However each man has his own gift from God, one of this kind, and another of that kind.

7:8 But I say to the unmarried and to widows, it is good for them if they remain even as I am. 7:9 But if they don't have self-control, let them marry. For it's better to marry than to burn.

7:10 But to the married I command--not I, but the Lord--that the wife not leave her husband 7:11

(but if she departs, let her remain unmarried, or else be reconciled to her husband), and that the husband not leave his wife.

7:12 But to the rest I--not the Lord--say, if any brother has an unbelieving wife, and she is content to live with him, let him not leave her. 7:13 The woman who has an unbelieving husband, and he is content to live with her, let her not leave her husband. 7:14 For the unbelieving husband is sanctified in the wife, and the unbelieving wife is sanctified in the husband. Otherwise your children would be unclean, but now they are holy. 7:15 Yet if the unbeliever departs, let there be separation. The brother or the sister is not under bondage in such cases, but God has called us in peace.[2] 7:16 For how do you know, wife, whether you will save your husband? Or how do you know, husband, whether you will save your wife?

1. *woman, wife, marriage*. Although this chapter is addressing practical matters, a metaphysical interpretation should note that we are "made up of many men and many women, because the masculine and feminine qualities are equally distributed and they all work together in harmony when divine order is established." "Taking a wife" represents a unification of the I AM with the affections. Spiritually, "marriage" represents the union of two dominant states of consciousness. When we open the door of the mind by consciously affirming the presence and power of the divine I AM in our midst, there is a marriage or union of the higher forces in being with the lower and we find that we are quickened in every part; the life of the I AM has been poured out for us. See: MBD/woman, RW/wife and RW/marriage.

2. *God has called us in peace*. "The eye of the storm is a center of calm in the midst of outer chaos. The peace of God centers me in a place of absolute peace and tranquility. The spirit of God within me is peace—peace that soothes and comforts me when I need it most. So if events in my life seem out of control or if others are trying to pull me into a whirlpool of activities that may not be what I want or need to do, I let God's peace shine on me and on each situation. Then I know what to do and how to respond to both opportunities and challenges. I am poised and calm as I stay focused on the spirit of God within, the spirit of peace and love and harmony that will always bless me. Sheltered in God's presence, I have peace in mind and heart." *Daily Word*, April 18, 2000.

## The Life That the Lord Has Assigned

7:17 Only, as the Lord has distributed to each man, as God has called each, so let him walk. So I command in all the assemblies. 7:18 Was anyone called having been circumcised? Let him not become uncircumcised. Has anyone been called in uncircumcision? Let him not be circumcised. 7:19 Circumcision is nothing, and uncircumcision is nothing, but the keeping of the commandments of God. 7:20 Let each man stay in that calling in which he was called.

7:21 Were you called being a bondservant? Don't let that bother you, but if you get an opportunity to become free, use it.[1] 7:22 For he who was called in the Lord being a bondservant is the Lord's free man. Likewise he who was called being free is Christ's bondservant. 7:23 You were bought with a price. Don't become bondservants of men. 7:24 Brothers, let each man, in whatever condition he was called, stay in that condition with God.

1. *if you get an opportunity to become free, use it*. "The very first step in this process that we're calling the art of thinking, is to know that no matter what happens in your world, no matter what happens out there, no matter what you read in the papers, no matter what is taking

place around you or to you, you always have a choice. You always have a choice. You don't have to be angry. You don't have to be unhappy. You don't have to be worried. You don't have to be fearful. You can choose to think positively or creatively if that's the way you want. You can become the master instead of the slave. Oh, it's not easy. Now, let's not kid ourselves. It's not easy to take possession of our mind. To change from being a reflex thinker to a creative thinker it takes a lot of discipline, and will, and commitment because we've been thinking in the other way so long, but we can do so." Eric Butterworth, You Always Have a Choice, *Practical Metaphysics*, clip 32 (audio), page 61 (text).

## The Unmarried and the Widows

7:25 Now concerning virgins,[1] I have no commandment from the Lord, but I give my judgment as one who has obtained mercy from the Lord to be trustworthy. 7:26 I think that it is good therefore, because of the distress that is on us, that it is good for a man to be as he is. 7:27 Are you bound to a wife? Don't seek to be freed. Are you free from a wife? Don't seek a wife. 7:28 But if you marry, you have not sinned. If a virgin marries, she has not sinned. Yet such will have oppression in the flesh,[2] and I want to spare you. 7:29 But I say this, brothers: the time is short, that from now on, both those who have wives may be as though they had none; 7:30 and those who weep, as though they didn't weep; and those who rejoice, as though they didn't rejoice; and those who buy, as though they didn't possess; 7:31 and those who use the world, as not using it to the fullest. For the mode of this world passes away.

7:32 But I desire to have you to be free from cares. He who is unmarried is concerned for the things of the Lord, how he may please the Lord; 7:33 but he who is married is concerned about the things of the world, how he may please his wife. 7:34 There is also a difference between a wife and a virgin. The unmarried woman cares about the things of the Lord, that she may be holy both in body and in spirit. But she who is married cares about the things of the world--how she may please her husband. 7:35 This I say for your own profit; not that I may ensnare you, but for that which is appropriate, and that you may attend to the Lord without distraction.

7:36 But if any man thinks that he is behaving inappropriately toward his virgin, if she is past the flower of her age, and if need so requires, let him do what he desires. He doesn't sin. Let them marry. 7:37 But he who stands steadfast in his heart, having no necessity, but has power over his own heart, to keep his own virgin, does well. 7:38 So then both he who gives his own virgin in marriage does well, and he who doesn't give her in marriage does better.

7:39 A wife is bound by law for as long as her husband lives; but if the husband is dead, she is free to be married to whoever she desires, only in the Lord. 7:40 But she is happier if she stays as she is, in my judgment, and I think that I also have God's Spirit.

1. *Now concerning virgins.* Again, Paul is dealing with practical issues. But virgins, spiritually considered, is found in Matthew 25, the Parable of the the Ten Bridesmaids. Spiritually, virgins represent the senses. "They are five in number, but have a twofold action--five in the inner realm, and five in the outer world. The way to supply oil for the lamps of the virgins, even of the foolish ones, is to affirm that the life source, Spirit, from which comes the power of hearing, smelling, feeling, see-

ing, and tasting, is not material but spiritual." MBD/virgins.

2. *oppression in the flesh.* "Virginity, like purity, is a state of mind and of heart, and may exist even when the body has been violated. And though there have been sexual mistakes and people have lived in sexual indulgence for years, yet if the mind is pure and there is a complete turning away from the old life, the desire of one's heart and the determined training of the mind out of the old lustful thinking, will result in that virginity of mind and heart which is one with the original purity of the Divine Self." Annie Rix Miltz, *Generation and Regeneration, The Riches of Virginity.*

---

Fillmore Study Bible annotations compiled by Rev. Mark Hicks.

# First Corinthians 8

## Food Offered to Idols

8:1 Now concerning things sacrificed to idols:[1] We know that we all have knowledge. Knowledge puffs up, but love builds up. 8:2 But if anyone thinks that he knows anything, he doesn't yet know as he ought to know. 8:3 But if anyone loves God, the same is known by him.

8:4 Therefore concerning the eating of things sacrificed to idols, we know that no idol is anything in the world,[2] and that there is no other God but one. 8:5 For though there are things that are called "gods," whether in the heavens or on earth; as there are many "gods" and many "lords;" 8:6 yet to us there is one God, the Father, of whom are all things, and we for him; and one Lord, Jesus Christ, through whom are all things, and we live through him.

8:7 However, that knowledge isn't in all men. But some, with consciousness of the idol until now, eat as of a thing sacrificed to an idol, and their conscience, being weak, is defiled.[3] 8:8 But food will not commend us to God.[4] For neither, if we don't eat, are we the worse; nor, if we eat, are we the better. 8:9 But be careful that by no means does this liberty of yours become a stumbling block to the weak.[5] 8:10 For if a man sees you who have knowledge sitting in an idol's temple, won't his conscience, if he is weak, be emboldened to eat things sacrificed to idols? 8:11 And through your knowledge, he who is weak perishes, the brother for whose sake Christ died. 8:12 Thus, sinning against the brothers, and wounding their conscience when it is weak, you sin against Christ. 8:13 Therefore, if food causes my brother to stumble, I will eat no meat forevermore, that I don't cause my brother to stumble.

1. *Now concerning things sacrificed to idols.* Paul had been asked in a letter received from the Corinthian church whether or not one might eat meat, which had first been offered to idols. His letter in this chapter was a discourse along this line. Corinth formerly had been idolatrous, but had been converted to Christianity.

2. *we know that no idol is anything in the world.* If one understands that there is no reality in idols, that they have no power, and that there is but one God, who is through all and in all, he is safe in whatever he does.

3. *their conscience, being weak, is de-*

*filed.* Paul teaches that one who understands the truth should be an example in all that he does, to the end that those who are weak shall be strengthened and fortified by his good example; that conscience is really the rule or law for man's acts.

4. *But food will not commend us to God.* Man in his spiritual identity is one with God. The union is not broken by material things. However, man's body is the temple of God and should be kept clean and pure, free from the lusts of the flesh.

5. *But be careful that by no means does this liberty of yours become a stumbling block to the weak.* Paul gives a warning to Christian metaphysicians who feel their spiritual dominion and power over food and drink. Paul's final affirmation is verse 13: "if food causes my brother to stumble, I will eat no meat forevermore."

Fillmore Study Bible annotations compiled by Rev. Mark Hicks.

# First Corinthians 9

## The Rights of an Apostle

9:1 Am I not free? Am I not an apostle?[1] Haven't I seen Jesus Christ, our Lord? Aren't you my work in the Lord? 9:2 If to others I am not an apostle, yet at least I am to you;[2] for you are the seal of my apostleship in the Lord.

9:3 My defense to those who examine me is this. 9:4 Have we no right to eat and to drink? 9:5 Have we no right to take along a wife who is a believer, even as the rest of the apostles, and the brothers of the Lord, and Cephas? 9:6 Or have only Barnabas and I no right to not work? 9:7 What soldier ever serves at his own expense? Who plants a vineyard, and doesn't eat of its fruit? Or who feeds a flock, and doesn't drink from the flock's milk?

9:8 Do I speak these things according to the ways of men? Or doesn't the law also say the same thing? 9:9 For it is written in the law of Moses, "You shall not muzzle an ox while it treads out the grain."[10] Is it for the oxen that God cares, 9:10 or does he say it assuredly for our sake? Yes, it was written for our sake, because he who plows ought to plow in hope, and he who threshes in hope should partake of his hope. 9:11 If we sowed to you spiritual things, is it a great thing if we reap your fleshly things? 9:12 If others partake of this right over you, don't we yet more?

Nevertheless we did not use this right, but we bear all things, that we may cause no hindrance to the Good News of Christ. 9:13 Don't you know that those who serve around sacred things eat from the things of the temple, and those who wait on the altar have their portion with the altar? 9:14 Even so the Lord ordained that those who proclaim the Good News should live from the Good News.[3]

9:15 But I have used none of these things, and I don't write these things that it may be done so in my case; for I would rather die, than that anyone should make my boasting void. 9:16 For if I preach the Good News, I have nothing to boast about; for necessity is laid on me; but woe is to me, if I don't preach the Good News. 9:17 For if I do this of my own will, I have a reward. But if not of my own will, I have a stewardship entrusted to me. 9:18 What then is my reward? That, when I preach the Good News, I may present the Good News of Christ without charge, so as not to abuse my authority in the Good News.

9:19 For though I was free from all, I brought myself under bondage to all, that I might gain the more. 9:20 To the Jews I became as a Jew, that I might gain Jews; to those who are under the law, as under the law, that I might gain those who are under the law; 9:21 to those who are without law, as without law (not being without law toward God, but under law toward Christ), that I might win those who are without law. 9:22 To the weak I became as weak, that I might gain the weak. I have become all things to all men, that I may by all means save some. 9:23 Now I do this for the sake of the Good News, that I may be a joint partaker of it.

9:24 Don't you know that those who run in a race all run, but one receives the prize?[4] Run like that, that you may win. 9:25 Every man who strives in the games exercises self-control in all things.[5] Now they do it to receive a corruptible crown, but we an incorruptible. 9:26 I therefore run like that, as not uncertainly. I fight like that, as not beating the air, 9:27 but I beat my body and bring it into submission, lest by any means, after I have preached to others, I myself should be rejected.

1. *Am I not an apostle?* Metaphysically, apostles are "one sent forth; messengers; ambassadors; active spiritual thoughts." Jesus conferred this title on the Twelve whom He sent forth to teach and to heal ... The Grand Man, Christ, has twelve powers of fundamental ideas, represented in the history of Jesus by the Twelve Apostles.

2. *If I am not an apostle to others, at least I am to you.* Metaphysically interpreted, this chapter may be the Apostle in Paul speaking to the sense consciousness in Paul.

3. *those who proclaim the Good News should live from the Good News.* "For confirmation of the truth of the statement that they who serve in the Gospel should live of the Gospel, we refer you to the words that Jesus spoke to the twelve, and to the seventy whom he sent out to preach and make practical his teachings. These disciples of Jesus were not to take scrip or purse, but they were to meet the spiritual needs of those to whom they went; they were to heal the sick, to preach the glad tidings of the kingdom of heaven at hand. They were to accept graciously, in a true Christian spirit, such things as were provided by those to whom they ministered. Those who receive blessings are more richly blessed if they in turn give to their benefactors. Although Paul taught the same truth, on this subject, that Jesus had taught, the truth that was commanded in the law of Moses, yet he himself did not follow it, at least not with all the churches or people to whom he preached and ministered. Yet he continued to do the same things, though, as he intimated (verse 15), the more he did for people, taking nothing from them in return, the less was he appreciated and loved by them. Paul's determination to accept nothing from the Corinthians for his services to them, increased his own sufferings and hardships and really cheated them out of the abundant good that would have come to them through their obeying the divine law of giving and receiving." *Unity*, Tithing, July 1925, pp3-4.

4. *those who run in a race all run, but one receives the prize.* The race that every man must run is that journey from sense consciousness to spiritual consciousness; through this process the corruptible flesh puts on incorruption. He is crowned with eternal life, come the fruits of the Spirit, love, joy, peace, light, gentleness, and unlimited abundance.

5. *Every man who strives in the games exercises self-control in all things.* To exercise spiritual self-control requires mastery and dominion not only over the physical and the sense planes of consciousness, but also control over every thought, word and act. This can be attained only through a conscious union with the Spirit of God within man, which is Christ.

Fillmore Study Bible annotations compiled by Rev. Mark Hicks.

**World English Bible Footnotes:**

[10] v9:9. Deuteronomy 25:4

# First Corinthians 10

## Warnings from Israel's History

10:1 Now I would not have you ignorant, brothers, that our fathers were all under the cloud, and all passed through the sea; 10:2 and were all baptized into Moses in the cloud and in the sea; 10:3 and all ate the same spiritual food; 10:4 and all drank the same spiritual drink. For they drank of a spiritual rock that followed them, and the rock was Christ.① 10:5 However with most of them, God was not well pleased, for they were overthrown in the wilderness.

10:6 Now these things were our examples, to the intent we should not lust after evil things, as they also lusted. 10:7 Neither be idolaters, as some of them were. As it is written, "The people sat down to eat and drink, and rose up to play."[11] 10:8 Neither let us commit sexual immorality, as some of them committed, and in one day twenty-three thousand fell. 10:9 Neither let us test the Lord, as some of them tested, and perished by the serpents. 10:10 Neither grumble, as some of them also grumbled, and perished by the destroyer. 10:11 Now all these things happened to them by way of example, and they were written for our admonition, on whom the ends of the ages have come. 10:12 Therefore let him who thinks he stands be careful that he doesn't fall. 10:13 No temptation has taken you except what is common to man. God is faithful, who will not allow you to be tempted above what you are able, but will with the temptation also make the way of escape,② that you may be able to endure it.

10:14 Therefore, my beloved, flee from idolatry. 10:15 I speak as to wise men. Judge what I say. 10:16 The cup of blessing which we bless, isn't it a sharing of the blood of Christ? The bread which we break, isn't it a sharing of the body of Christ? 10:17 Because there is one loaf of bread, we, who are many, are one body; for we all partake of the one loaf of bread. 10:18 Consider Israel according to the flesh. Don't those who eat the sacrifices participate in the altar?

10:19 What am I saying then? That a thing sacrificed to idols is anything, or that an idol is anything? 10:20 But I say that the things which the Gentiles sacrifice, they sacrifice to demons, and not to God, and I don't desire that you would have fellowship with demons. 10:21 You can't both drink the cup of the Lord and the cup of demons. You can't both partake of the table of the Lord, and of the table of demons. 10:22 Or do we provoke the Lord to jealousy? Are we stronger than he?

1. *For they drank of a spiritual rock that followed them, and the rock was Christ.* Jesus said to Peter, "Thou art Peter, and upon this rock I will build my church." Peter means a stone, and symbolizes the faith faculty in man; "this rock" is the indwelling Christ, and the "church" is spiritual consciousness. See MBD/pedahzur.

2. *the way of escape.* "The seed of Truth is sown in consciousness by memorizing promises of God and statements of Truth. We may read passages that are uplifting, but unless the subconscious takes hold of the Truth that is read and makes it part of one's soul and body consciousness, the good seed take no deep root and they wither away. For this reason it is good to dwell upon Words of Truth until they are firmly fixed in memory. If they are once learned with deep faith and interest, they are like leaven; they work in the mind and body, quickening and nourishing the whole inner man. Then, too, in time of trial, or more properly speaking, in time of discipline, they come to consciousness, bringing comfort and cheer and healing when things in the outer seem to have failed." *Unity*, February 1915, Sowing the Seed, p.101.

## Do All to the Glory of God

10:23 "All things are lawful for
me,"[1] but not all things are
profitable.[2] "All things are lawful for
me," but not all things build up. 10:24
Let no one seek his own, but each
one his neighbor's good. 10:25
Whatever is sold in the butcher shop,
eat, asking no question for the sake
of conscience, 10:26 for "the earth is
the Lord's, and its fullness."[12] 10:27
But if one of those who don't believe
invites you to a meal, and you are
inclined to go, eat whatever is set
before you, asking no questions for
the sake of conscience. 10:28 But if
anyone says to you, "This was offered
to idols," don't eat it for the sake of
the one who told you, and for the
sake of conscience. For "the earth is
the Lord's, and all its fullness." 10:29
Conscience, I say, not your own, but
the other's conscience.[3] For why is
my liberty judged by another
conscience? 10:30 If I partake with
thankfulness, why am I denounced
for that for which I give thanks?

10:31 Whether therefore you eat,
or drink, or whatever you do, do all
to the glory of God.[4] 10:32 Give no
occasions for stumbling, either to
Jews, or to Greeks, or to the
assembly of God; 10:33 even as I also
please all men in all things, not
seeking my own profit, but the profit
of the many, that they may be saved.

1. *All things are lawful for me.* Paul places himself in the Absolute, and recognizes that man is above the law when he realizes and acts from the standpoint of his spiritual selfhood. The Absolute is not bound by the relative; the Lawmaker is above the law. Men often catch sight of this truth and proceed to carry it out in their lives. They say, "It does not matter what we do; we can dissolve the results of our acts by denial, and stop the working out of the law." Many crimes have been committed in the name or this kind of reasoning. "The end justifies the means, is based upon it. Regular confessions for sins that are committed with the expectation of confession and forgiveness, are in line with it, and the modern metaphysical practices of bringing about external results to prove the power of the "science," are based upon an evasion of the law.

2. *but not all things are profitable.* We must take into consideration the rights of others. "Let no man seek his own, but each his neighbor's good." If this law were always applied, there would be no interference with human liberty. We should beware how, in our zeal to help people, we interfere with their liberty. Not only should we discern the law in the Absolute, but also its relation in the lives of those who are in the consciousness of the relative.

3. *eat whatever is set before you, asking no questions for the sake of ... the other's conscience.* An intelligent application of the Law cultivates a right spirit, makes one broad-minded, forgiving, tactful and harmonious in all the affairs of life. Cultivat-

ing the Christ spirit makes one positive in Truth. And to all that seems incomplete from his viewpoint he quietly says, "suffer it to be so now," at the same time keeping himself poised in his spiritual mastery.

4. *do all to the glory of God.* The teaching which harmonizes these seeming variances, is found in the admonition: "Do all to the glory of God." If we are truly seeking to conform to the Divine Law, and to glorify the Spirit in manifestation, we shall not go far wrong. One should have as an ideal the Absolute Truth and should endeavor to fulfill the Law in all activities. In applying the Law, Divine Wisdom and Love should decide all things. *Unity*, September 1921, Sunday Lesson, pp.234-5.

---

Fillmore Study Bible annotations compiled by Rev. Mark Hicks.

**World English Bible Footnotes:**

[11] v10:7. Exodus 32:6

[12] v10:26. Psalm 24:1

# First Corinthians 11

## Do All to the Glory of God (continued)

11:1 Be imitators of me, even as I also am of Christ.

## Head Coverings[1]

11:2 Now I praise you, brothers,[2] that you remember me in all things, and hold firm the traditions, even as I delivered them to you. 11:3 But I would have you know that the head of every man is Christ, and the head of the woman[3] is the man, and the head of Christ is God. 11:4 Every man praying or prophesying,[4] having his head covered, dishonors his head. 11:5 But every woman praying or prophesying with her head unveiled dishonors her head. For it is one and the same thing as if she were shaved. 11:6 For if a woman is not covered, let her also be shorn. But if it is shameful for a woman to be shorn or shaved, let her be covered. 11:7 For a man indeed ought not to have his head covered, because he is the image and glory of God, but the woman is the glory of the man. 11:8 For man is not from woman, but woman from man; 11:9 for neither was man created for the woman, but woman for the man. 11:10 For this cause the woman ought to have authority on her head, because of the angels.

11:11 Nevertheless, neither is the woman independent of the man, nor the man independent of the woman, in the Lord.[5] 11:12 For as woman came from man, so a man also comes through a woman; but all things are from God. 11:13 Judge for yourselves. Is it appropriate that a woman pray to God unveiled? 11:14 Doesn't even nature itself teach you that if a man

has long hair, it is a dishonor to him?
11:15 But if a woman has long hair,
it is a glory to her, for her hair is
given to her for a covering. 11:16 But
if any man seems to be contentious,
we have no such custom, neither do
God's assemblies.

1. This difficult passage should be read together with all of chapter 14. There, Paul reveals an inner truth about masculine and feminine phases of the soul in the dynamics of inner stillness. Paul will pick up the discussion in chapter 14 where he considers the inner dynamics of speaking in tongues, prophecy and orderly worship.

2. *brothers.* This gender specific translation is gender neutral in other modern translations.

3. *man, woman.* Man is "an idea in Divine Mind; the epitome of being. The apex of God's creation, created in His image and likeness" (RW/man). Woman is "the feminine phase of man... She signifies the intuitive perception of Truth reflected into the intellect from the soul. She also represents the unspiritualized love that is natural to the body" (RW/woman).

4. *praying or prophesying.* This difficult pericope may be interpreted metaphysically and the interpreter should note that Paul is addressing the inner dynamic of masculine and feminine phases of the soul while in the silence.

5. *in the Lord.* In the higher state of consciousness.

## Abuses at the Lord's Supper

11:17 But in giving you this
command, I don't praise you, that
you come together not for the better
but for the worse. 11:18 For first of
all, when you come together in the
assembly, I hear that divisions exist
among you, and I partly believe it.
11:19 For there also must be factions
among you, that those who are
approved may be revealed among
you. 11:20 When therefore you
assemble yourselves together, it is
not the Lord's supper that you eat.[1]
11:21 For in your eating each one takes
his own supper first. One is hungry,
and another is drunken. 11:22 What,
don't you have houses to eat and to
drink in? Or do you despise God's
assembly, and put them to shame
who don't have? What shall I tell you?
Shall I praise you? In this I don't
praise you.

1. *it is not the Lord's supper that you eat.* The Lord's supper symbolizes the *appropriation* of spiritual life and spiritual substance by the twelve central faculties of man (the twelve disciples). Eating is symbolical of mental appropriation of thoughts of substance. "Thy words were found, and I did eat them; and thy words were unto me a joy and the rejoicing of my heart" (Jer. 15:16) (RW/eating).

## The Institution of the Lord's Supper

11:23 For I received from the Lord
that which also I delivered to you,
that the Lord Jesus on the night in
which he was betrayed took bread.[1]
11:24 When he had given thanks, he
broke it, and said, "Take, eat. This
is my body, which is broken for you.
Do this in memory of me."[2] 11:25 In
the same way he also took the cup,[3]
after supper, saying, "This cup is the
new covenant in my blood.[4] Do this,
as often as you drink, in memory of
me." 11:26 For as often as you eat this
bread and drink this cup, you
proclaim the Lord's death[5] until he
comes.

Cf. Matt. 26:26-30; Mark 14:22-26; Luke 22:15-20,39

1. *bread.* Represents the "flesh of

Christ," divine substance. It is the outer form of the inner substance.

2. *do this in memory of me.* Everything that is done for the sake of attaining the Christ consciousness in an outer as well as an inner sense is "in remembrance" of Him, the perfect expression of the Christ idea. We take these mighty ideas into the silence and really clothe these ideas with life and substance. We have a mighty work to do here. We must actualize these ideas and realize each of these ideas is a mighty magnet functioning in God-Mind. Thus we are transforming the soul and really unfolding the divine spiritual body.

3. *the cup.* The cup of which Jesus drank was the cup of new spiritual life. When man affirms spiritual life, he must be prepared to incorporate that life in soul and in body. This incorporation is not always an easy task, because man's faculties are often inert and indifferent to spiritual ideas.

4. *new covenant in my blood.* Blood of divine life, the quickening element in creation. "The blood is the life." The Children of Israel were commanded to pour out the blood of animals offered in sacrifice and by no means to drink it. Jesus, on the contrary, said that, unless we ate His flesh and drank His blood, we had no life in us. We are to drink, to take within ourselves, the Spirit of life that animated Him, and come into an awareness of eternal life through this Spirit.

5. *proclaim the Lord's death.* Spiritual communion. Through spiritually eating the body of Jesus Christ and spiritually drinking His blood, we appropriate in consciousness the imperishable substances of Spirit, and we drink of the waters of eternal life. When the mind continues in this process it will eventually raise the whole body out of death into life; then man will realize what Jesus meant when He said, "Verily, verily, I say unto you, If a man keep my word, he shall never see death."

## Partaking of the Supper Unworthily

11:27 Therefore whoever eats this
bread or drinks the Lord's cup in a
manner unworthy❶ of the Lord will
be guilty of the body and the blood of
the Lord. 11:28 But let a man examine
himself, and so let him eat of the
bread, and drink of the cup. 11:29 For
he who eats and drinks in an
unworthy manner eats and drinks
judgment to himself, if he doesn't
discern the Lord's body. 11:30 For this
cause many among you are weak and
sickly, and not a few sleep.❷ 11:31 For
if we discerned ourselves, we
wouldn't be judged.❸ 11:32 But when
we are judged, we are punished by
the Lord, that we may not be
condemned with the world. 11:33
Therefore, my brothers, when you
come together to eat, wait one for
another. 11:34 But if anyone is hungry,
let him eat at home, lest your coming
together be for judgment. The rest I
will set in order whenever I come.

1. *in an manner unworthy.* Jesus said: "Watch and pray, that ye enter not into temptation." Prayer keeps the mind active along spiritual lines. When one's attention is directed to high ideals, the consciousness becomes so alive with spirituality that error thoughts are cast out and one is not tempted by the sensations of the flesh.

2. *not a few sleep.* When man affirms spiritual life, he must be prepared to incorporate that life in soul and in body. This incorporation is not always an easy task, because man's faculties are often inert and indifferent to spiritual ideas.

3. *if we discerned ourselves, we wouldn't be judged.* We obtain the best results by a daily going into the silence, and in the name of the great God-Demonstrator, Jesus Christ, appropriate and assimilate the substance and life of Spirit.

Fillmore Study Bible annotations compiled by Rev. Mark Hicks

# First Corinthians 12

## Spiritual Gifts

12:1 Now concerning spiritual things, brothers, I don't want you to be ignorant. 12:2 You know that when you were heathen[13], you were led away to those mute idols, however you might be led. 12:3 Therefore I make known to you that no man speaking by God's Spirit says, "Jesus is accursed." No one can say, "Jesus is Lord," but by the Holy Spirit. 12:4 Now there are various kinds of gifts, but the same Spirit.[1]

12:5 There are various kinds of service, and the same Lord. 12:6 There are various kinds of workings, but the same God, who works all things in all.[2] 12:7 But to each one is given the manifestation of the Spirit for the profit of all. 12:8 For to one is given through the Spirit the word of wisdom, and to another the word of knowledge, according to the same Spirit; 12:9 to another faith, by the same Spirit; and to another gifts of healings, by the same Spirit; 12:10 and to another workings of miracles; and to another prophecy; and to another discerning of spirits; to another different kinds of languages; and to another the interpretation of languages. 12:11 But the one and the same Spirit works all of these,[3] distributing to each one separately as he desires.

Cf. Ephesians 4:7-13

1. *Now there are various kinds of gifts, but the same Spirit.* Those whose "gifts" or inherent talents are diverse and show the same Spirit. All may have the same Spirit, the desire to know the truth and to live accordingly, irrespective of differences in inherent talents or traits. Truth belongs everywhere, and no legitimate activity or bent can be outside its field.

2. *There are various kinds of workings, but the same God, who works all things in all.* God has given all His attributes to man; it rests with each individual whether he expresses them or not. God is no respecter of persons.

3. *But the one and the same Spirit works all of these.* Emilie Cady, in Chapter 11 of Lessons in Truth, Spiritual Gifts, writes, "Thus Paul enumerates some of the free "gifts" of the Spirit to those who will not limit the manifestations of the Holy One." She believes the important thing is not *discovering* our gifts but rather *accepting* them. We limit our gifts by not fully trusting God, who "worketh ... as he will."

## One Body with Many Members

12:12 For as the body is one, and has many members, and all the members of the body, being many, are one body; so also is Christ.[1] 12:13 For in one Spirit we were all baptized into one body, whether Jews or Greeks, whether bond or free; and were all given to drink into one Spirit. 12:14 For the body is not one member, but many. 12:15 If the foot would say, "Because I'm not the hand, I'm not part of the body," it is not therefore not part of the body. 12:16 If the ear would say, "Because I'm not the eye, I'm not part of the body," it's not therefore not part of the body. 12:17 If the whole body were an eye, where would the hearing be? If the whole were hearing, where would the smelling be? 12:18 But now God has set the members, each one of them, in the body, just as he desired. 12:19

If they were all one member, where would the body be? 12:20 But now they are many members, but one body.[2] 12:21 The eye can't tell the hand, "I have no need for you," or again the head to the feet, "I have no need for you." 12:22 No, much rather, those members of the body which seem to be weaker are necessary. 12:23 Those parts of the body which we think to be less honorable, on those we bestow more abundant honor; and our unpresentable parts have more abundant propriety; 12:24 whereas our presentable parts have no such need. But God composed the body together, giving more abundant honor to the inferior part,[3] 12:25 that there should be no division in the body, but that the members should have the same care for one another. 12:26 When one member suffers, all the members suffer with it. Or when one member is honored, all the members rejoice with it.

12:27 Now you are the body of Christ, and members individually.[4] 12:28 God has set some in the assembly: first apostles, second prophets, third teachers, then miracle workers, then gifts of healings, helps, governments, and various kinds of languages.[4] 12:29 Are all apostles? Are all prophets? Are all teachers? Are all miracle workers? 12:30 Do all have gifts of healings? Do all speak with various languages? Do all interpret? 12:31 But earnestly desire the best gifts. Moreover, I show a most excellent way to you.

1. *For as the body is one ... so also is Christ.* Christ likened to the body because the Christ is the embodiment of all divine ideas, such as intelligence, life, love, substance, and strength. The Christ, the perfect man idea existing eternally in Divine Mind, is the true, spiritual, higher, self of every individual. This self is an entity as truly as the physical body is an entity.

2. *now they are many members, but one body.* There is only one body of the universe, each individual being a member of that body. Therefore, the body of Christ cannot attain a perfect expression until each member, each individual, is spiritually quickened, and puts on the Christ perfection.

3. *But God composed the body together, giving more abundant honor to the inferior part.* As the "single eye" sheds its rays of light through the whole body, through Christ, so God's love yoked with wisdom, penetrates into every part and tempers and binds together all its members.

4. *Now you are the body of Christ, and members individually.* Our bodies are fashioned after the Christ body. As each cell of our body has within it the potentialities of the whole body, so are we potential Christs, and our bodies may be raised to the universal Christ body and become fit members of it, through following the law of God as did Jesus.

5. *God has set some in the assembly...* [These are typically called gifts of the Spirit but they are really a list of those who possess gifts of the Spirit. An alternative list of gifts of the Spirit is given in Romans 12:6-8. They are not the same as the fruits of the Spirit given in Galatians 5:22-23. See annotations in Romans and Galatians for additional commentary.]

Fillmore Study Bible annotations compiled by Rev. Mark Hicks

**World English Bible Footnotes:**

[13] v12:2. or Gentiles

# First Corinthians 13

## The Gift of Love

13:1 If I speak with the languages of men and of angels,[1] but don't have love, I have become sounding brass, or a clanging cymbal. 13:2 If I have the gift of prophecy,[2] and know all mysteries and all knowledge; and if I have all faith, so as to remove mountains, but don't have love, I am nothing.[3] 13:3 If I dole out all my goods to feed the poor, and if I give my body to be burned,[4] but don't have love, it profits me nothing.

1. *tongues of men and angels.* The "tongues of men" represent the expressions of intellectual knowledge; the tongues of "angels" represent the expressions of spiritual truths.

2. *the gift of prophecy.* Metaphysically, the ability to foretell the outcome of mental causes. When intuition is developed, it enables its possessor to perceive the connection between cause, and effect and to grasp the underlying truth of conditions and knowledge beyond the average person's power to understand. The one whose intuitive powers are developed gains the power of prophecy through observation. "That which hath been (in cause) is that which shall be (in effect)."

3. *don't have love, I am nothing.* God is love, so humans are love. Without love the I AM is nothing, no matter how great one's feats of faith.

4. *body to be burned.* Being a martyr.

13:4 Love is patient[1] and is kind;[2] love doesn't envy.[3] Love doesn't brag, is not proud,[4] 13:5 doesn't behave itself inappropriately,[5] doesn't seek its own way,[6] is not provoked,[7] takes no account of evil;[8] 13:6 doesn't rejoice in unrighteousness, but rejoices with the truth;[9] 13:7 bears all things,[10] believes all things,[11] hopes all things, endures all things.[12]

1. *is patient.* A steady, quiet confidence in the Divine law of love.

2. *kind.* Returning good for evil. Gentleman and ladylike.

3. *doesn't envy.* Generous. Unless one gives oneself with the gift, love is not involved. Nothing is gained from mere giving. To be acceptable the gift must be made in the spirit of love.

4. *doesn't brag, is not proud.* Not boastful or arrogant.

5. *doesn't behave itself inappropriately.* Courteous, not rude.

6. *doesn't seek its own way.* Unselfish, does not insist on its own way.

7. *not provoked.* Of good temper, not irritable or resentful.

8. *takes no account of evil.* Pure in heart. Love does not condone or ignore evil, but by recognizing only the good as real and true, it calls forth the good, and leaves what appears to be evil to vanish, as darkness vanishes with the coming of light.

9. *rejoices with (in, ASV) the truth.* Joyful.

10. *bears all things.* Unresentful.

11. *believes all things.* Trusting, give your cloak to he who asks for your coat.

12. *endures all things.* Never fails. Source: Charles Fillmore lesson August 24, 1919, Social Responsibility.

13:8 Love never fails. But where there are prophecies, they will be done away with. Where there are various languages, they will cease. Where there is knowledge, it will be done away with. 13:9 For we know in part, and we prophesy in part; 13:10 but when that which is complete has come, then that which is partial will be done away with. 13:11 When I was a child, I spoke as a child, I felt as a child, I thought as a child. Now that I have become a man, I have put away childish things. 13:12 For now we see in a mirror, dimly, but then face to face.[1] Now I know in part, but then I will know fully, even as I was also fully known. 13:13 But now faith, hope, and love remain[2]--these three. The greatest of these is love.[3]

1. *For now we see in a mirror, dimly, but then face to face.* To see through a glass darkly, means to see through the obstructed vision of the mortal; but to see "face to face," means to see with spiritual vision, which is unobstructed, perfect.

2. *faith, hope, and love remain (abideth, ASV).* Faith and hope lead to divine love in the heart, and love in turn helps us attain perfection as the Father is perfect.

3. *the greatest of these is love.* Love is love greater than faith or hope because its full expression includes faith and hope, as well as love.

Fillmore Study Bible annotations compiled by Rev. Mark Hicks

# First Corinthians 14

## Gifts of Prophecy and Tongues

14:1 Follow after love, and earnestly desire spiritual gifts,[1] but especially that you may prophesy.[2] 14:2 For he who speaks in another language[3] speaks not to men, but to God; for no one understands; but in the Spirit he speaks mysteries. 14:3 But he who prophesies speaks to men for their edification, exhortation, and consolation. 14:4 He who speaks in another language edifies himself, but he who prophesies edifies the assembly.[4] 14:5 Now I desire to have you all speak with other languages, but rather that you would prophesy. For he is greater who prophesies than he who speaks with other languages, unless he interprets, that the assembly may be built up.

14:6 But now, brothers,[14] if I come to you speaking with other languages, what would I profit you, unless I speak to you either by way of revelation, or of knowledge, or of prophesying, or of teaching? 14:7 Even things without life, giving a voice, whether pipe or harp, if they didn't give a distinction in the sounds, how would it be known what is piped or harped? 14:8 For if the trumpet gave an uncertain sound, who would prepare himself for war? 14:9 So also you, unless you uttered by the tongue words easy to understand, how would it be known what is spoken?[5] For you would be speaking into the air. 14:10 There are, it may be, so many kinds of sounds in the world, and none of them is without meaning. 14:11 If then I don't know the meaning of the sound, I would be to him who speaks a foreigner, and he who speaks would be a foreigner to me. 14:12 So also you, since you are zealous for spiritual gifts, seek that you may abound to the building up of the assembly.

14:13 Therefore let him who speaks in another language pray that he may interpret. 14:14 For if I pray in another language, my spirit prays, but my understanding is unfruitful. 14:15 What is it then? I will pray with the spirit, and I will pray with the understanding also.[6] I will sing with the spirit, and I will sing with the understanding also. 14:16 Otherwise if you bless with the spirit, how will he who fills the place of the unlearned say the "Amen" at your giving of thanks, seeing he doesn't know what you say? 14:17 For you most certainly give thanks well, but the other person is not built up. 14:18 I thank my God, I speak with other languages more than you all. 14:19 However in the assembly I would rather speak five words with my understanding, that I might instruct others also, than ten thousand words in another language.

14:20 Brothers, don't be children in thoughts, yet in malice be babies, but in thoughts be mature.[7] 14:21 In the law it is written, "By men of strange languages and by the lips of strangers I will speak to this people. Not even thus will they hear me, says the Lord."[15] 14:22 Therefore other languages are for a sign, not to those who believe, but to the unbelieving;[8] but prophesying is for a sign, not to the unbelieving, but to those who believe. 14:23 If therefore the whole assembly is assembled together and all speak with other languages, and unlearned or unbelieving people come in, won't they say that you are crazy? 14:24 But if all prophesy, and someone unbelieving or unlearned comes in, he is reproved by all, and he is judged by all. 14:25 And thus the secrets of his heart are revealed. So he will fall down on his face and worship God, declaring that God is among you indeed.

1. *desire spiritual gifts.* See: Lessons In Truth, Spiritual Gifts.

2. *especially that you may prophesy.* A prophet, in individual consciousness, is a thought that is in contact with Spirit, that receives revelations direct from the Holy Spirit; it knows and understands divine law and its working, therefore it warns and instructs the other thoughts (MBD/prophet). All humanity is given the gift of prophecy. "Whenever we become still enough to listen deeply we shall begin to feel the prophet faculty stirring" (Frances Foulks, *Prophecy-Yesterday and Today*, *Unity*, August 1938).

3. *speaks in another language (speak in a tongue, NRSV).* Symbolizes increased ability to express Truth clearly and freely (RW/tongues).

4. *he who prophesies edifies the assembly.* The purpose of prophecy is to edify. The assembly may be metaphysically interpreted as our thinking. Prophesies should edify our thinking.

5. *unless you uttered by the tongue words easy to understand, how would it be known what is spoken?* in a position to explain it clearly to others (other thoughts). Scattered thoughts only bring scattered presentation of plans. (How I Used Truth Annotations, Lesson 9, Annotation 10).

6. *I will pray with the spirit, and I will pray with the understanding (the mind, NRSV) also.* A clear indicator that this chapter reveals more about the internal dynamic of prayer than about the practice of speaking in tongues. "God has given all of his transcending powers to man, and it rests with us whether we will express them or not. We may connect ourselves with the light of God or with the outer darkness, or with the realm of reflected light. There are many philosophies but only one truth; that is light, Divine understanding. The light of truth resolves everything into ideas. Those in understanding look upon the phenomenal world and interpret it from the ideas it represents, and not as it appears." Unity, September 2, 1917.

7. *don't be children in thoughts ... but in thoughts be mature.* Jim Lewis cautions about the phenomenon of glossolalia: "The speaking in tongues is a phenomenon that developed in the early church after Jesus left. Jesus never spoke in this manner nor

did His followers while He was here. It was associated with what they believed to be the Holy Spirit Baptism and was looked upon as a sign that the individual had become possessed by the Holy Spirit. It was believed that the Holy Spirit was an entity that came into a person and possessed him. This made the person feel good because he saw it as a sign that he was accepted by God. We should keep in mind that the speaking in tongues is not the most important part of the phenomenon; rather, the Holy Spirit Baptism is most important" (Jim Lewis, The Mystical Teachings of Christianity, Speaking in Tongues). See more from Jim Lewis below.

8. *other languages are for a sign ... to the unbelieving.* Charles Fillmore cautions about those who claim spiritual mastery: "Certain persons called 'masters' have forged ahead of the race in their understanding and use of some of the powers of mind and have in personal egotism set up little kingdoms and put themselves on thrones. These so-called 'masters' and members of occult brotherhoods are attracting susceptible minds away from the "straight and narrow path" and leading them to believe that there is a short cut into the kingdom" (Charles Fillmore, Jesus Christ Heals, 19-20)

## Orderly Worship[1]

[14:26] What is it then, brothers? When you come together, each one of you has a psalm, has a teaching, has a revelation, has another language, has an interpretation. Let all things be done to build each other up. [14:27] If any man speaks in another language, let it be two, or at the most three, and in turn; and let one interpret.[2] [14:28] But if there is no interpreter, let him keep silent in the assembly, and let him speak to himself, and to God. [14:29] Let the prophets speak, two or three, and let the others discern. [14:30] But if a revelation is made to another sitting by, let the first keep silent. [14:31] For you all can prophesy one by one, that all may learn, and all may be exhorted. [14:32] The spirits of the prophets are subject to the prophets, [14:33] for God is not a God of confusion, but of peace.

As in all the assemblies of the saints, [14:34] let your wives keep silent in the assemblies, for it has not been permitted for them to speak; but let them be in subjection, as the law also says. [14:35] If they desire to learn anything, let them ask their own husbands at home, for it is shameful for a woman to chatter in the assembly.[3] [14:36] What? Was it from you that the word of God went out? Or did it come to you alone?[4]

[14:37] If any man thinks himself to be a prophet, or spiritual, let him recognize the things which I write to you, that they are the commandment of the Lord. [14:38] But if anyone is ignorant, let him be ignorant. [14:39] Therefore, brothers, desire earnestly to prophesy, and don't forbid speaking with other languages. [14:40] Let all things be done decently and in order.

1. This chapter should be read together with chapter 11:2-16, Head Coverings. Charles Fillmore, who perceived himself to be a modern Paul, found in these difficult passages helpful ideas about the inner dynamics of prayer (orderly internal worship). The Fillmores often referred to the feeling nature as a feminine quality, found equally in men as well as women. If so, reading Jim Lewis would indicate that speaking in tongues is a feminine process; prophecy, the interpretation of tongues, is a masculine process, again equally shared by women and men.

2. *If any man speaks in another language ... let one interpret.* Spiritually interpreted, Paul may be conveying that feelings, once expressed in the consciousness mind, need to be interpreted by the thinking nature. Although he is not specifically talking about an internal process of prayer, Jim Lewis writes about glossolalia in such a way that it conveys such a concern: "Speaking in tongues is a vocal attempt to

express one's deepest or highly repressed feelings. These expressions are often incoherent. The person is quite emotional and temporarily loses self-control. It is believed by him and those who favor this phenomenon that the individual is actually possessed by God, the Holy Spirit."

3. *for it is shameful for a woman to chatter in the assembly.* We can read this painful passage as a warning to not allow our feelings to "chatter" in the assembly of our thinking. Jim Lewis continues, "Be very, very careful of being involved in group emotional experiences. These groups are widespread today and are led, in most cases, by well-meaning people. Even when it seems that these group experiences are for good purposes, however, we must recognize that some are offered by not-so-well-meaning individuals. Uncontrolled emotion can get us into difficulty faster than anything else."

4. *Was it from you that the word of God went out? Or did it come to you alone?* We should be expressing the word of God, not the word of masculine intellect nor the word of feminine feeling. As Jim Lewis concludes: "In order to attain spiritual mastery as Jesus taught it, one must have balanced control and expression of his thoughts and feelings. This point is brought out in the mystical teachings of Paul. In the first part of I Corinthians, the eleventh chapter, he states, "Christ is the head of man and man is the head of woman." He should have stopped there, for in his attempt to give a literal interpretation to a spiritual idea he received, he gets carried away—he mixes the spiritual with a literal interpretation. Christ is the guiding intelligence within all of us, for it is the Spirit of God within us. The intellect, man, should always be responsive and obedient to this guiding intelligence, and man, the intellect, should always control the emotional nature, woman. When the emotional nature influences the intellect, the person often has trouble, becoming involved in undesirable circumstances."

Fillmore Study Bible annotations compiled by Rev. Mark Hicks.

**World English Bible Footnotes:**

[14] v14:6. The word for "brothers" here and where context allows may also be correctly translated "brothers and sisters" or "siblings."

[15] v14:21. Isaiah 28:11-12

# First Corinthians 15

## The Resurrection of Christ

15:1 Now I declare to you, brothers, the Good News which I preached to you, which also you received, in which you also stand, 15:2 by which also you are saved, if you hold firmly the word which I preached to you--unless you believed in vain.

15:3 For I delivered to you first of all that which I also received:[1] that Christ died for our sins according to the Scriptures, 15:4 that he was buried, that he was raised on the third day[2] according to the Scriptures, 15:5 and that he appeared to Cephas, then to the twelve.[3] 15:6 Then he appeared to over five hundred brothers at once, most of whom remain until now, but some have also fallen asleep. 15:7 Then he appeared to James, then to all the apostles, 15:8 and last of all, as to the child born at the wrong time, he appeared to me also. 15:9 For I am the least of the apostles, who is not worthy to be called an apostle, because I persecuted the assembly of God. 15:10 But by the grace of God I am what I am. His grace which was bestowed on me was not futile, but I worked more than all of them; yet not I, but the grace of God which was with me.[4] 15:11 Whether then it is I or they, so we preach, and so you believed.

1. *that which I also received.* Jesus Christ overcame all the sins of the flesh, saved His body from the tomb, and raised it to eternal life.

2. *raised on the third day.* Christian metaphysicians see that His overcoming, the Resurrection, was not a miracle, but rather the outworking and fulfillment of divine law. Through faith and understanding they are overcoming many of the ills of mind and body, and they know by analogy that the final demonstration of the law will be perfect health, that is, continuous life in the body, spiritualized.

3. *He appeared to Cephas, then to the twelve.* Jesus did not leave the earth, but He did leave the consciousness of material conditions, which men call the earth. He is still in our midst in His eternal body, dwelling in another form.

4. *the grace of God which was with me.* Paul was not given grace because he worked more abundantly than others, but because he was ignorant of the law.

## The Resurrection of the Dead

15:12 Now if Christ is preached, that he has been raised from the dead, how do some among you say that there is no resurrection of the dead?[1] 15:13 But if there is no resurrection of the dead, neither has Christ been raised.[2] 15:14 If Christ has not been raised, then our preaching is in vain, and your faith also is in vain. 15:15 Yes, we are found false witnesses of God, because we testified about God that he raised up Christ, whom he didn't raise up, if it is so that the dead are not raised. 15:16 For if the dead aren't raised, neither has Christ been raised. 15:17 If Christ has not been raised, your faith is vain; you are still in your sins. 15:18 Then they also who are fallen asleep in Christ have perished. 15:19 If we have only hoped in Christ in this life, we are of all men most pitiable.

15:20 But now Christ has been raised from the dead. He became the first fruits of those who are asleep.[3] 15:21 For since death came by man, the resurrection of the dead also came by man. 15:22 For as in Adam all die,[4] so also in Christ all will be made alive. 15:23 But each in his own order: Christ the first fruits, then those who are Christ's, at his coming. 15:24 Then the end comes, when he will deliver up the Kingdom to God, even the Father; when he will have abolished all rule and all authority and power.[5] 15:25 For he must reign until he has put all his enemies under his feet. 15:26 The last enemy that will be abolished is death. 15:27 For, "He put all things in subjection under his feet."[16] But when he says, "All things are put in subjection," it is evident that he is excepted who subjected all things to him. 15:28 When all things have been subjected to him, then the Son will also himself be subjected to him who subjected all things to him, that God may be all in all. 15:29 Or else what will they do who are baptized for the dead? If the dead aren't raised at all, why then are they baptized for the dead? 15:30 Why do we also stand in jeopardy every hour? 15:31 I affirm, by the boasting in you which I have in Christ Jesus our Lord, I die daily. 15:32 If I fought with animals at Ephesus for human purposes, what does it profit me? If the dead are not raised, then "let us eat and drink, for tomorrow we die."[17] 15:33 Don't be deceived! "Evil companionships corrupt good morals." 15:34 Wake up righteously, and don't sin, for some have no knowledge of God. I say this to your shame.

1. *no resurrection of the dead?* If preachers say Jesus was resurrected from the dead then it must follow that all those who apply Jesus' teachings will be resurrected also.

2. *neither has Christ been raised.* If the law of resurrection were not universal, it would not have been possible for Jesus Christ to resurrect his body.

3. *the first fruits of those who are asleep.* Paul affirms that Jesus Christ was the first fruits of them that had fallen asleep for lack of the constant inflow of new life from the fountainhead. Christ is the principle that quickens the life of Spirit in man. The sense mind is dead to spiritual values, but the Christ awakens it to them.

4. *For in Adam all die.* When one's thoughts are out of harmony with divine law, cross currents are set up. In the Scriptures this condition is called sin. Sin results in death. The Adamic man, the natural man, broke the consciousness that the life current connected him with the parent life; Jesus Christ restored that union.

5. *abolished all rule and all authority and power.* By establishing the Spirit of truth as the sole guide to conduct in human relations, the authority and dominion of earthly rulers will give place to the authority and dominion of God in Christ.

## The Resurrection Body

15:35 But someone will say, "How are the dead raised?" and, "With what kind of body do they come?" 15:36 You foolish one, that which you yourself sow is not made alive unless it dies. 15:37 That which you sow, you don't sow the body that will be, but a bare grain, maybe of wheat, or of some other kind. 15:38 But God gives it a body even as it pleased him, and to each seed a body of its own. 15:39 All flesh is not the same flesh, but there is one flesh of men, another flesh of animals, another of fish, and another of birds. 15:40 There are also celestial bodies, and terrestrial bodies; but the glory of the celestial differs from that of the terrestrial. 15:41 There is one glory of the sun, another glory of the moon, and another glory of the stars; for one star differs from another star in glory.(1)

15:42 So also is the resurrection of the dead. It is sown in corruption; it is raised in incorruption. 15:43 It is sown in dishonor; it is raised in glory. It is sown in weakness; it is raised in power. 15:44 It is sown a natural body; it is raised a spiritual body. There is a natural body and there is also a spiritual body.(2)

15:45 So also it is written, "The first man, Adam, became a living soul."[18] The last Adam became a life-giving spirit.(3) 15:46 However that which is spiritual isn't first, but that which is natural, then that which is spiritual. 15:47 The first man is of the earth, made of dust. The second man is the Lord from heaven. 15:48 As is the one made of dust, such are those who are also made of dust; and as is the heavenly, such are they also that are heavenly. 15:49 As we have borne the image of those made of dust, let's[19] also bear the image of the heavenly.

15:50 Now I say this, brothers,[20] that flesh and blood can't inherit the Kingdom of God;(4) neither does corruption inherit incorruption. 15:51 Behold, I tell you a mystery.(5) We will not all sleep, but we will all be changed, 15:52 in a moment,(6) in the twinkling of an eye, at the last

trumpet. For the trumpet will sound,
and the dead will be raised
incorruptible, and we will be
changed. 15:53 For this corruptible
must put on incorruption,(7) and this
mortal must put on immortality.(8)
15:54 But when this corruptible will
have put on incorruption, and this
mortal will have put on immortality,
then what is written will happen:

"Death is swallowed up in
victory."(9)[21]
15:55 "Death, where is your sting?(10)
Hades[22], where is your
victory?"[23]

15:56 The sting of death is sin, and
the power of sin is the law. 15:57 But
thanks be to God, who gives us the
victory through our Lord Jesus Christ.
15:58 Therefore, my beloved brothers,
be steadfast, immovable, always
abounding in the Lord's work,
because you know that your labor is
not in vain in the Lord.

1. *glories of the sun, moon, and stars.* Spiritual life is greater than the material. Whereas the soul clings to material existence and fears the unconsciousness of the material that death brings, consciousness of spiritual life overcomes all such fear.

2. *spiritual body.* See II Corinthians 5:1, *a house not made with hands*, annotation 1.

3. *life-giving spirit.* A living soul is the individual consciousness of the self as one of the race in thought, feeling, and expression. The life-giving spirit is the expression of the Christ consciousness or idea of God.

4. *Flesh and blood can't inherit the kingdom of God.* We are to develop consciousness of more than flesh and blood and thus put ourselves in contact with eternal life here and now.

5. *I tell you a mystery.* The mystery of immortality, that eternal life subsists here and now as well as on the other side of death.

6. *we shall all be changed, in a moment.* The change is one of consciousness.

7. *this corruptible must put on incorruption.* The corruptible body is that which is subject to decay. When it is transformed into the spiritual body, it becomes incorruptible and is forever enduring (RW/corruptible).

8. *mortal ... put on immortality.* By entering into and expressing the Spirit of the Christ we develop a consciousness of eternal life in the mind and heart.

9. *death swallowed up in victory.* When the victory of the resurrection life is grasped and firmly held in faith, death is forgotten (swallowed up).

10. *where is your sting?* resurrection has removed the fear of death as the inevitable end of life.

Fillmore Study Bible annotations compiled by Rev. Mark Hicks

**World English Bible Footnotes:**

[16] v15:27. Psalm 8:6

[17] v15:32. Isaiah 22:13

[18] v15:45. Genesis 2:7

[19] v15:49. NU, TR read "we will" instead of "let's"

[20] v15:50. The word for "brothers" here and where context allows may also be correctly translated "brothers and sisters" or "siblings."

[21] v15:54. Isaiah 25:8

[22] v15:55. or, Hell

[23] v15:55. Hosea 13:14

# First Corinthians 16

## The Collection for the Saints

16:1 Now concerning the collection for the saints, as I commanded the assemblies of Galatia, you do likewise. 16:2 On the first day of the week, let each one of you save, as he may prosper, that no collections be made when I come. 16:3 When I arrive, I will send whoever you approve with letters to carry your gracious gift to Jerusalem. 16:4 If it is appropriate for me to go also, they will go with me.

## Plans for Travel

16:5 But I will come to you when I have passed through Macedonia, for I am passing through Macedonia. 16:6 But with you it may be that I will stay, or even winter, that you may send me on my journey wherever I go. 16:7 For I do not wish to see you now in passing, but I hope to stay a while with you, if the Lord permits. 16:8 But I will stay at Ephesus until Pentecost, 16:9 for a great and effective door has opened to me, and there are many adversaries.

16:10 Now if Timothy comes, see that he is with you without fear, for he does the work of the Lord, as I also do. 16:11 Therefore let no one despise him. But set him forward on his journey in peace, that he may come to me; for I expect him with the brothers.

16:12 Now concerning Apollos, the brother, I strongly urged him to come to you with the brothers; and it was not at all his desire to come now; but he will come when he has an opportunity.

## Final Messages and Greetings

16:13 Watch! Stand firm in the faith! Be courageous! Be strong![1] 16:14 Let all that you do be done in love.

16:15 Now I beg you, brothers (you know the house of Stephanas, that it is the first fruits of Achaia, and that they have set themselves to serve the saints), 16:16 that you also be in subjection to such, and to everyone who helps in the work and labors. 16:17 I rejoice at the coming of Stephanas, Fortunatus, and Achaicus; for that which was lacking on your part, they supplied. 16:18 For they refreshed my spirit and yours. Therefore acknowledge those who are like that.

16:19 The assemblies of Asia greet you. Aquila and Priscilla greet you much in the Lord, together with the assembly that is in their house.[2] 16:20 All the brothers greet you. Greet one another with a holy kiss.

16:21 This greeting is by me, Paul, with my own hand. 16:22 If any man doesn't love the Lord Jesus Christ, let him be accursed[24]. Come, Lord![25] 16:23 The grace of the Lord Jesus Christ be with you. 16:24 My love to all of you in Christ Jesus. Amen.

1. *Watch! Stand firm in the faith! Be courageous! Be strong!* This verse is often quoted as an affirmation in metaphysical writings, for example: "Much of human difficulty is due to the fact that man has become inactive and submissive to conditions and circumstances which are born of human ignorance. There comes a time when he must arouse himself to positive action if he would shake off these shackles of human bondage." EV Ingraham, *Prayer-It's Practice and It's Answer*, 159

2. *the assembly (church, ASV, NRSV) that is in their house.* An aggregation of healing, constructive thoughts that gather around the healing forces of nature, attracted by the truth that these forces serve.

Fillmore Study Bible annotations compiled by Rev. Mark Hicks.

**World English Bible Footnotes:**

[24] v16:22. Greek: anathema.

[25] v16:22. Aramaic: Maranatha!

# Paul's Second Letter to the Corinthians

Ruins of ancient Corinth. Public Domain.

## Introduction to Paul's Second Letter to the Corinthians

When the Corinthian Christians received Paul's Epistle (which we now know as First Corinthians), it might be supposed that they forthwith amended their erroneous ways, and conformed to Paul's instructions. But this was not the case. News soon reached Paul (who was still in Ephesus) that conditions in Corinth were rapidly deteriorating, and that the converts were conducting themselves in ways unbecoming to Christians. Paul hurriedly departed from Ephesus and sailed to Corinth, determined to set things right.

Paul's first meeting with the Corinthians brought a rude shock to the apostle. It must be remembered that several years had passed since Paul had established the church, and during the intervening period Apollos and other teachers had been active among the converts, with the Judaizersalso making inroads into the congregation. Consequently Paul's authority at Corinth was questioned, and his leadership repudiated. Indeed, the Corinthians refused to listen to the apostle—much less obey his commands! Paul was therefore compelled to withdraw from the meeting without accomplishing his purpose, and indications are that he retired heartbroken to a suburb of Corinth.

But Paul was by no means vanquished. He immediately wrote a very strongly-worded letter, and instructed his young helper Titus to carry it to the rebellious converts. This letter, with its present-day designation, forms the first of two parts in Second Corinthians, known as "The Letter of Sharp Remonstrance." Unfortunately, several parts of this letter are now lost. However, two fragments still remain, and through these we are able to trace something of Paul's turmoil of mind, together with his continuing love for the erring converts. These fragments are embedded in chapters 6 and 10 of Second Corinthians.

When Titus arrived at Corinth with Paul's "letter of sharp remonstrance," as mentioned above, a miracle happened. Whether this miracle was brought about by Paul's letter, or whether Titus' persuasive abilities produced the result, must remain a matter of conjecture. (Possibly Paul's prayers and the activity of the Holy Spirit should also be taken into consideration.) Certain it is that the Corinthians completely repented, both of their evil ways and of their shameful behavior toward Paul. Furthermore, they immediately disciplined the wrongdoers, and then asked Titus to return to Paul and entreat his forgiveness for their hostile attitudes and actions. Paul, on his part, was overjoyed when he received the good news, but for some reason he was unable to return to Corinth at that time. However, he immediately wrote a loving and appreciative letter, which was carried to the repentant Corinthians by Titus. Fortunately we now have this letter in its entirety, incorporated in Second Corinthians; and, giving it the present-day designation, it forms Section Two: "The Letter of Loving Reconciliation."

Introduction to *Paul's Second Letter to the Corinthians* by Herbert J. Hunt, former Dean of Bible Studies for the Unity School of Christianity.

**Purpose of the letter.** Historically, the apostle Paul likely wrote this letter near the end of AD 56, possibly in the city of Philippi, in order to turn the Corinthian church away from false teachers who were spreading heresy, challenging Paul's authority and fomenting many divisions and quarrels in the church.

Paul defends his ministry by sharing details about the many persecutions he himself had endured for the sake of Christ, including the thorn in the flesh that kept him dependent upon God. He then says that as he has forgiven those who have been critical of him so should the congregation forgive those who have brought suffering in their church. He encourages them to forgive one another when offenses arise, and to give generously to the cause of Christ; this is how unity is preserved - unity among each other and personal unity with Christ.

**Corinth and the message of 2 Corinthians, in consciousness.** Metaphysically, Corinth means ornament or beauty. It is the love center in consciousness where Truth seeks to do a work. Paul is typically interpreted as the Will, our capacity to manage the eleven other spiritual powers. Paul's state of consciousness in 2 Corinthians is elevated enough so that it no longer imposes its own human will, but rather serves the Will of God, as revealed by the Word of God (Christ).

Closely associated with the Will is our faculty of Spiritual Understanding-our capacity to comprehend the revelation of the Word, the truth lying back of physical events. This is what makes Paul an evangelist: a quickened Will that is now listening to the Word and is now strong enough to carry the Word of God throughout our consciousness (throughout Europe and Asia).

Which brings us to the relation of people and places in metaphysical interpretation. Metaphysically interpreting the epistles is often about "what happens when Paul goes to ...?" The places, like Athens or Corinth, are states of consciousness. Paul is Will that is listening to the Word. All these stories are about what happens when an enlightened Will "goes to" a particular state of consciousness.

**Metaphysical structure of the letter.** Metaphysically interpreted, the Second Letter of Paul to the Corinthians is a letter about overcoming the difficulties of ministry and overcoming the difficulties of living the Christian life. We can see Paul overcoming these difficulties with three prominent themes. In chapters one through seven, Paul overcomes his challenges *by forgiveness with spiritual understanding*: he lets go and releases error thoughts, pride, and resistance to sufferings because "momentary, light affliction is producing for us an eternal weight of glory far beyond all comparison."

In chapters eight and nine, Paul urges the Corinthians to overcome their difficulties *by generous giving*: sending an offering to the believers in Judea because if they gave generously they would also "reap generously" (9:6) in Truth and in their inner life. In the final four chapters, ten through thirteen, Paul describes reaping a better life *by having a new awareness of and connection to the inner Christ and the Presence and Power of God's Holy Spirit*.

*Introduction to Paul's Second Letter to the Corinthians* by Mary Salama.

# SECOND CORINTHIANS 1

## Salutations from the Regenerated Will!

1:1 Paul,(1) an apostle of Christ
Jesus through the will of God, and
Timothy(2) our brother, to the
assembly of God which is at
Corinth,(3) with all the saints who are
in the whole of Achaia: 1:2 Grace to
you and peace(4) from God our Father
and the Lord Jesus Christ.

1. *Paul, an apostle of Christ Jesus through the will of God.* Our minds have 13 characters: 12 powers and 1 Christ. Paul is the will. The regenerated Paul is a will that serves Christ. The will is the executive that manages the 11 other powers. Thus, as Paul evangelized the world for Christ, so does our regenerated will evangelize our inner world and consciousness, disseminating the Word through our consciousness. Cultivating a firebrand will

that listens to the Word is essential to the process of our transmutation.

2. *Timothy* Timothy was "the son of a Jewess that believed; but his father was a Greek." A Greek symbolizes intellectual reasoning. "A Jewess that believed" symbolizes our faith in God and our love for Him. Timothy therefore represents an idea in us that has its inception in a union between our intellectual reasoning and our inner spiritual qualities of faith and love. So we understand Timothy to symbolize inspired reason united with faith and zeal. (MBD/Timothy)

3. *Corinth* Corinth is "ornament; ornamentation; beauty." Corinth was home to the Greek temple of Venus so we discern that Corinth is the love center in consciousness, and it is where the Word of Truth working through the regenerated will (Paul) now seeks to do a work. Paul wrote his matchless poem on love to the Corinthians. (MBD/Corinth)

4. *Grace and peace ... from God our Father and the Lord Jesus Christ.* The regenerated will acknowledges and affirms to our consciousness that grace and peace come to us from God alone (our Father, Source), through the activity of Truth within (Lord Jesus Christ).

## The God of all Comfort

1:3 Blessed be the God and Father of our Lord Jesus Christ, the Father of mercies and God of all comfort; 1:4 who comforts us in all our affliction, that we may be able to comfort those who are in any affliction, through the comfort with which we ourselves are comforted by God. 1:5 For as the sufferings of Christ abound to us, even so our comfort also abounds through Christ. 1:6 But if we are afflicted, it is for your comfort and salvation.[1] If we are comforted, it is for your comfort, which produces in you the patient enduring of the same sufferings which we also suffer. 1:7 Our hope for you is steadfast, knowing that, since you are partakers of the sufferings, so also are you of the comfort.[2] 1:8 For we don't desire to have you uninformed, brothers,[1] concerning our affliction which happened to us in Asia, that we were weighed down exceedingly, beyond our power, so much that we despaired even of life. 1:9 Yes, we ourselves have had the sentence of death within ourselves, that we should not trust in ourselves, but in God who raises the dead, 1:10 who delivered us out of so great a death, and does deliver; on whom we have set our hope that he will also still deliver us; 1:11 you also helping together on our behalf by your supplication; that, for the gift bestowed on us by means of many, thanks may be given by many persons on your behalf.

1. *comfort and salvation.* The belief that Jesus in an outer way atoned for our sins is not salvation. Salvation is based solely on an inner overcoming, a change in consciousness. It is a cleansing of the mind, through Christ, from thoughts of evil. (RW/Salvation)

2. *partakers of the sufferings, so also ... of the comfort.* [To suffer is to allow, to permit, to "let it be so for now." To the degree we are willing to "suffer" change, we will in likewise experience transformations in consciousness and receive the cleansing that produces in us great strength and comfort, with which we can then turn around and comfort/strengthen others.]

## A Regenerated Will Opens Our Way

1:12 For our boasting is this: the testimony of our conscience,[1] that in holiness and sincerity of God, not in fleshly wisdom but in the grace of God we behaved ourselves in the world, and more abundantly toward you. 1:13 For we write no other things to you, than what you read or even acknowledge, and I hope you will acknowledge to the end; 1:14 as also you acknowledged us in part, that we are your boasting, even as you also are ours, in the day of our Lord Jesus.(2)

1:15 In this confidence, I was determined to come first to you, that you might have a second benefit; 1:16 and by you to pass into Macedonia,(3) and again from Macedonia to come to you, and to be sent forward by you on my journey to Judea.(4) 1:17 When I therefore was thus determined, did I show fickleness? Or the things that I purpose, do I purpose according to the flesh, that with me there should be the "Yes, yes" and the "No, no?" 1:18 But as God is faithful, our word toward you was not "Yes and no." 1:19 For the Son of God, Jesus Christ, who was preached among you by us, by me, Silvanus, and Timothy, was not "Yes and no," but in him is "Yes." 1:20 For however many are the promises of God, in him is the "Yes."(5) Therefore also through him is the "Amen," to the glory of God through us.

1:21 Now he who establishes us with you in Christ, and anointed us, is God; 1:22 who also sealed us, and gave us the down payment of the Spirit in our hearts. 1:23 But I call God for a witness to my soul, that I didn't come to Corinth to spare you. 1:24 Not that we have lordship over your faith, but are fellow workers with you for your joy. For you stand firm in faith.

1. *our conscience.* Whoever has sat at the feet of his own inner convictions has been aware of God's presence (RW/conscience). A sensitive and responsive conscience is a valuable tool for one who desires to grow and learn by receiving the protective foresight of Spirit; the path of least suffering.

2. *in the day of our Lord Jesus.* Days and nights, in Scripture, are symbols describing degrees of unfoldment: night being ignorance, and day understanding. As the Word of Truth (the Lord Jesus) moves through us, new degrees of understanding (days) are unfolded. The "last day" is the last degree of understanding, and though many stifle the voice of conscience for years, maybe for ages, eventually understanding (its day) comes.

3. *into Macedonia.* The enthusiasm and the energy of Spirit, which are required in order to carry the great and beautiful message of Truth over seeming hindrances to our different centers and states of consciousness. (MBD/Macedonia)

4. *to Judea.* The southern division of Palestine; from the Scriptural name Judah, meaning "the praise of Jehovah." Judea is a key to the mental attitude in which the Christ consciousness will be opened to us--while we are praising the Lord [and illustrating the progression of our regenerated will].

5. *in Him is the "Yes."* When we are led by the Spirit of God, we can be confident that we are always being guided in the direction of highest good, the "yes".]

---

Fillmore Study Bible annotations compiled by Mary Salama.

**World English Bible Footnotes:**

[1] v1:8. The word for "brothers" here and where context allows may also be correctly translated "brothers and sisters" or "siblings."

# SECOND CORINTHIANS 2

## A Regenerated Will Opens Our Way (continued)

2:1 But I determined this for myself, that I would not come to you again in sorrow.[1] 2:2 For if I make you sorry, then who will make me glad but he who is made sorry by me? 2:3 And I wrote this very thing to you, so that, when I came, I wouldn't have sorrow from them of whom I ought to rejoice; having confidence in you all, that my joy[2] would be shared by all of you. 2:4 For out of much affliction and anguish of heart I wrote to you with many tears, not that you should be made sorry, but that you might know the love that I have so abundantly for you.

1. *sorrow.* [Paul's travel is blocked by] distressed states of mind; mental attitudes that keep us from God's good (RW/anxiety). See note on Troas below.

2. *joy.* On the other hand, when God is expressing through us His perfect Ideals, we experience this spiritual flow as happy states of mind; joy and gladness are strength-giving. (RW/joy)

## Giving Up the False for the True

2:5 But if any has caused sorrow, he has caused sorrow, not to me, but in part (that I not press too heavily) to you all. 2:6 Sufficient to such a one is this punishment[1] which was inflicted by the many; 2:7 so that on the contrary you should rather forgive him and comfort him, lest by any means such a one should be swallowed up with his excessive sorrow.[2] 2:8 Therefore I beg you to confirm your love[3] toward him. 2:9 For to this end I also wrote, that I might know the proof of you, whether you are obedient in all things.[4] 2:10 Now I also forgive whomever you forgive anything. For if indeed I have forgiven anything, I have forgiven that one for your sakes[5] in the presence of Christ, 2:11 that no advantage may be gained over us by Satan; for we are not ignorant of his schemes.

1. *this punishment.* We do not receive punishment from an outside force. We punish ourselves by holding false thoughts. We escape from punishment as soon as we align our thought with that of God. (RW/punishment)

2. *excessive sorrow.* [Sorrow, as a state of consciousness, is a problem only when it is excessive. See note 4 below.]

3. *your love.* In reality there is only one love; when we express divine love in limited ways we make a separation in consciousness and our expression of love is personal instead of universal. (MBD/love)

4. *obedient in all things.* [Obedient in all states of consciousness.] Things are thoughts lowered in vibration to the level of sense perception. The things that appear are the formulations of our ideas of ourself and God. Back of everything is a thought. If we still the senses we will perceive the thought behind the things. (RW/things)

5. *forgiven that one for your sakes.* A process of giving up the false for the true; erasing sin and error from the mind and body. It is through forgiveness that true spiritual healing is accomplished. (RW/forgiveness)

## From Anxiety to Triumph in Christ

2:12 Now when I came to Troas[1] for the Good News of Christ, and when a door was opened to me in the Lord, 2:13 I had no relief for my spirit, because I didn't find Titus, my brother,[2] but taking my leave of them, I went out into Macedonia.[3] 2:14 Now thanks be to God, who always leads us in triumph in Christ, and reveals through us the sweet aroma of his knowledge in every place. 2:15 For we are a sweet aroma of Christ to God, in those who are saved,[4] and in those who perish;[5] 2:16 to the one a stench from death to death; to the other a sweet aroma from life to life. Who is sufficient for these things? 2:17 For we are not as so many, peddling the word of God. But as of sincerity, but as of God, in the sight of God, we speak in Christ.

1. *Troas.* Troas is a phase of thought by which Spirit can find its way into consciousness more easily than by other ways. It was while in this city, after having been forbidden by the Holy Spirit to preach in some other places, that Paul received his vision of the man of Macedonia. (MBD/Troas)

2. *Titus, my brother.* A pleasing, agreeable, and honorable attitude of mind (pleasant, honorable, titled, renowned) that accompanies the word of Truth in its restoring work throughout the human organism and consciousness. (MBD/Titus)

3. *Macedonia* When our thoughts turn adoringly toward God, spiritual zeal and enthusiasm are awakened and these set our whole consciousness into constructive activity. (MBD/Macedonia)

4. *those who are saved.* Those who are restored to their spiritual birthright; regaining conscious possession of their God-given attributes. (RW/salvation)

5. *those who perish.* Through believing in error and dissipating the life substance, the mind loses hold of its consciousness of life and enters into negation, and dissolution takes place. The result is death of the body temple. (RW/death)

Fillmore Study Bible annotations compiled by Mary Salama.

# Second Corinthians 3

## Ministers of a New Perspective

3:1 Are we beginning again to commend ourselves? Or do we need, as do some, letters of commendation to you or from you? 3:2 You are our letter, written in our hearts, known and read by all men; 3:3 being revealed that you are a letter of Christ,[1] served by us, written not with ink, but with the Spirit of the living God; not in tablets of stone, but in tablets that are hearts of flesh.

3:4 Such confidence we have through Christ toward God; 3:5 not that we are sufficient of ourselves, to account anything as from ourselves; but our sufficiency is from God;[2] 3:6 who also made us sufficient as servants of a new covenant; not of the letter, but of the Spirit. For the letter kills, but the Spirit gives life.[3]

3:7 But if the service of death, written engraved on stones, came with glory, so that the children of Israel could not look steadfastly on the face of Moses[4] for the glory of his face; which was passing away: 3:8 won't service of the Spirit be with much more glory?[5] 3:9 For if the service of condemnation has glory, the service of righteousness exceeds much more in glory. 3:10 For most certainly that which has been made glorious has not been made glorious in this respect, by reason of the glory that surpasses. 3:11 For if that which passes away was with glory, much more that which remains is in glory.

3:12 Having therefore such a hope, we use great boldness of speech, 3:13 and not as Moses, who put a veil on his face,[6] that the children of Israel wouldn't look steadfastly on the end of that which was passing away. 3:14 But their minds were hardened, for until this very day at the reading of the old covenant the same veil remains, because in Christ it passes away. 3:15 But to this day, when Moses is read, a veil lies on their heart. 3:16 But whenever one turns to the Lord, the veil is taken away. 3:17 Now the Lord is the Spirit and where the Spirit of the Lord is, there is liberty. 3:18 But we all, with unveiled face beholding as in a mirror the glory of the Lord, are transformed[7] into the same image from glory to glory,[8] even as from the Lord, the Spirit.

1. *you are a letter of Christ.* letters of commendation bring death, but living letters bring life.

2. *Our sufficiency is of God.* The Spirit of the living God within us, fed ever from the Fountainhead, is not only the giver of all good gifts, the supplier of all supply, but is the gift itself. We must come right up to this point. The giver and the gift are one. Emilie Cady, All Sufficiency In All Things.

3. *For the letter kills, but the Spirit gives life.* See Rom 7.6-11; Rom 8.2

4. *Moses.* Moses symbolizes this progressive or drawing-out process, which works from within outward; as applied to the universe, the progression is the upward trend of all things, the evolutionary law; as applied to the individual, the progression is the development in consciousness of the law of our being, (MBD/Moses)

5. *glory.* Realization of divine unity; the blending and merging of man's mind with God-Mind. (RW/glory)

6. *who put a veil on his face.* The full Truth is too powerful to behold and so Its totality remains "veiled" from us, but It is revealed to us by the Spirit in stages, ever urging us forward to greater expressions of inherent abilities. (RW/Moses)

7. *are transformed.* Same as transfiguration, is a supernatural change of appearance that takes place as we experience the full flow of Divine power through our being. (RW/transfiguration)

8. *from glory to glory.* Our destiny is to go from glory to glory. We are destined to bring forth God's perfect pattern and we must eventually reach this supreme goal. (RW/destiny)

---

Fillmore Study Bible annotations compiled by Mary Salama.

# Second Corinthians 4

## Living in Christ Consciousness

4:1 Therefore seeing we have this ministry, even as we obtained mercy, we don't faint. 4:2 But we have renounced the hidden things of

shame, not walking in craftiness, nor
handling the word of God deceitfully;
but by the manifestation of the truth
commending ourselves to every
man's conscience in the sight of God.
4:3 Even if our Good News is veiled,
it is veiled in those who perish; 4:4
in whom the god of this world has
blinded the minds of the unbelieving,
that the light of the Good News of
the glory of Christ, who is the image
of God, should not dawn on them.
4:5 For we don't preach ourselves, but
Christ Jesus as Lord, and ourselves
as your servants for Jesus' sake;① 4:6
seeing it is God who said, "Light will
shine out of darkness,"②[2] who has
shone in our hearts, to give the light
of the knowledge of the glory of God
in the face of Jesus Christ.

4:7 But we have this treasure in
clay vessels, that the exceeding
greatness of the power may be of
God, and not from ourselves. 4:8 We
are pressed on every side, yet not
crushed; perplexed, yet not to
despair; 4:9 pursued, yet not
forsaken; struck down, yet not
destroyed; 4:10 always carrying in the
body the putting to death of the Lord
Jesus, that the life of Jesus may also
be revealed in our body. 4:11 For we
who live are always delivered to
death for Jesus' sake, that the life
also of Jesus may be revealed in our
mortal flesh. 4:12 So then death works
in us, but life in you.

4:13 But having the same spirit of
faith,③ according to that which is
written, "I believed, and therefore
I spoke."[3] We also believe, and
therefore also we speak; 4:14 knowing
that he who raised the Lord Jesus
will raise us also with Jesus, and will
present us with you. 4:15 For all things
are for your sakes, that the grace,
being multiplied through the many,
may cause the thanksgiving to
abound to the glory of God.

1. *ourselves as your servants for Jesus' sake.* Living the life of the Christ means first of all a life of service.

2. *Light will shine out of darkness.* We study consciousness because it is one of the unseen things in which life itself is involved and through which it is expressed.

3. *But having the same spirit of faith.* To live the life of the Christ we must have unity of mind; we must be one with the Christ, one with God, and one with others who have the same aspiration. Unity involves the Christ consciousness of God and the brotherhood of man.

## Living a Life of Overcoming①

4:16 Therefore we don't faint, but
though our outward man is decaying,
yet our inward man is renewed day
by day.② 4:17 For our light affliction,
which is for the moment,③ works for
us more and more exceedingly an
eternal weight of glory; 4:18 while we
don't look at the things which are
seen, but at the things which are not
seen.④ For the things which are seen
are temporal, but the things which
are not seen are eternal.⑤

1. *Overcoming.* Overcoming is dealing with the problems of life with spiritual understanding and demonstrating over error through the keeping of spiritual laws (RW/overcoming).

2. *our inward man is renewed day by day.* By communing consciously with the indwelling Spirit of power and by renewing the mind in the Word of Truth, we renew the inward person.

3. *our light affliction, which is for the moment.* Affliction "works for us more and more exceedingly an eternal weight of glory" by training us to look beyond the apparent to the real, beyond the external to the reality of the inner life, and also by teaching us to recognize cause in effects.

4. *things which are not seen.* We can do this with our mental gifting and capacity to develop powers of perception and reflec-

tion, to correlate ideas, and to enter into the universal Mind or Spirit.

5. *eternal*. Without beginning or end; timeless; everlasting in duration (RW/eternal). "The eternal God is thy dwelling-place" (Deut. 33:27).

---

Fillmore Study Bible annotations compiled by Mary Salama.

**World English Bible Footnotes:**

[2] v4:6. Genesis 1:3

[3] v4:13. Psalm 116:10

# SECOND CORINTHIANS 5

## Assurance of a New Body-Mind

5:1 For we know that if the earthly
house of our tent is dissolved, we
have a building from God, a house
not made with hands,[1] eternal, in
the heavens. 5:2 For most certainly in
this we groan, longing to be clothed
with our habitation which is from
heaven; 5:3 if so be that being clothed
we will not be found naked. 5:4 For
indeed we who are in this tent do
groan,[2] being burdened; not that we
desire to be unclothed, but that we
desire to be clothed, that what is
mortal may be swallowed up by life.
5:5 Now he who made us for this very
thing is God, who also gave to us the
down payment of the Spirit.

5:6 Therefore, we are always
confident and know that while we
are at home in the body, we are
absent from the Lord; 5:7 for we walk
by faith, not by sight. 5:8 We are of
good courage, I say, and are willing
rather to be absent from the body,
and to be at home with the Lord. 5:9
Therefore also we make it our aim,
whether at home or absent,[3] to be
well pleasing to him. 5:10 For we must
all be revealed before the judgment
seat of Christ; that each one may
receive the things in the body,
according to what he has done,
whether good or bad.

1. *we have a building from God, a house not made with hands.* Those who understand the subconscious become aware of an invisible thought body that is the pattern upon which the visible body is based. This is the *spiritual body*, which endures after the material body is dissolved. See I Corinthians 15:44, *spiritual body*.

2. *we who are in this tent do groan.* This Scripture passage brings out the thought that the ideal body will clothe itself again in the process known as reincarnation. However, it is possible for man to cooperate with divine law and re-create out of the heavens of the mind a heavenly or Christ body! Paul teaches that our souls are groaning for this new *body consciousness*, groaning for the when that which is mortal shall be swallowed up of life.

3. *whether at home or absent.* If we abide in the consciousness of flesh alone we are absent from or unconscious of Spirit. We should be conscious of the Lord and at the same time abide in the body.

## In Christ, We Are a New Creation

5:11 Knowing therefore the fear of the Lord, we persuade men, but we are revealed to God; and I hope that we are revealed also in your consciences. 5:12 For we are not commending ourselves to you again, but speak as giving you occasion of boasting on our behalf, that you may have something to answer those who boast in appearance, and not in heart. 5:13 For if we are beside ourselves, it is for God. Or if we are of sober mind, it is for you. 5:14 For the love of Christ constrains us; because we judge thus, that one died for all, therefore all died. 5:15 He died for all,[1] that those who live should no longer live to themselves, but to him who for their sakes died and rose again.

5:16 Therefore we know no one after the flesh from now on. Even though we have known Christ after the flesh, yet now we know him so no more. 5:17 Therefore if anyone is in Christ, he is a new creation.[2] The old things have passed away. Behold, all things have become new. 5:18 But all things are of God, who reconciled us to himself through Jesus Christ, and gave to us the ministry of reconciliation;[3] 5:19 namely, that God was in Christ reconciling the world to himself, not reckoning to them their trespasses, and having committed to us the word of reconciliation. 5:20 We are therefore ambassadors on behalf of Christ,[4] as though God were entreating by us. We beg you on behalf of Christ, be reconciled to God. 5:21 For him who knew no sin he made to be sin on our behalf; so that in him we might become the righteousness of God.[5]

1. *He died for all.* Paul is interpreting the metaphysical meaning of the death of Jesus. The real man did not die on the cross; only the personal man died. In order to reap the reward of Jesus' sacrifice of personality for us we must cease to worship or look to the personal man Jesus for salvation.

2. *Therefore if anyone is in Christ, he is a new creation.* By giving up His personality, Jesus made it possible for all who enter into his consciousness to give up their personalities and to live with him in spiritual consciousness. In all our ways we must seek to realize the spiritual nature of Christ; to put on Christ in thought and in act.

3. *ministry of reconciliation.* Reconciliation is the atonement between God and man through Christ; the uniting of our consciousness with the higher consciousness. (RW/atonement)

4. *ambassadors on behalf of Christ.* We are ambassadors in the sense that we represent the Christ to others, and as we daily grow in our understanding of the Christ Spirit and the knowledge of what we can accomplish by our faithful expression of it, others will increasingly see that Spirit in us.

5. *the righteousness of God.* We become "righteous" by developing perfection harmoniously and consistently in all our faculties.

---

Fillmore Study Bible annotations compiled by Mary Salama.

# Second Corinthians 6

## Our Inner Ministry of Reconciliation

6:1 Working together, we entreat also that you not receive the grace of God in vain, 6:2 for he says,

> "At an acceptable time I listened
> to you,
> in a day of salvation I helped
> you."[4]

Behold, now is the acceptable time. Behold, now is the day of salvation.[1] 6:3 We give no occasion of stumbling in anything, that our service may not be blamed, 6:4 but in everything commending ourselves, as servants of God, in great endurance, in afflictions, in hardships, in distresses, 6:5 in beatings, in imprisonments, in riots, in labors, in watchings, in fastings; 6:6 in pureness,[2] in knowledge, in patience, in kindness, in the Holy Spirit, in sincere love, 6:7 in the word of truth, in the power of God; by the armor of righteousness on the right hand and on the left, 6:8 by glory and dishonor, by evil report and good report; as deceivers, and yet true; 6:9 as unknown, and yet well known; as dying, and behold, we live; as punished, and not killed; 6:10 as sorrowful, yet always rejoicing; as poor, yet making many rich; as having nothing, and yet possessing all things.

6:11 Our mouth is open to you, Corinthians. Our heart is enlarged. 6:12 You are not restricted by us, but you are restricted by your own affections.[3] 6:13 Now in return, I speak as to my children, you also be open wide.

1. *the day of salvation.* Every day is "a day of salvation" because every day we can set about immediately to accomplish the real work that needs to be done. An actual beginning of the task before us is better than visionary daydreaming or criticizing existing conditions without making an effort to improve them.

2. *in pureness.* Purity of thought and life, knowledge, long-suffering, kindness, the Holy Spirit, unfeigned love, the word of Truth, and the power of God ensure our success in developing the Christ consciousness under adverse conditions.

3. *restricted by your own affections.* Nothing can limit us but our own lack of will or devotion to our task. If we hold ourselves in the consciousness of Divine love (*be open wide*), we cannot be separated from it.

## The Temple of the Living God

6:14 Don't be unequally yoked[1] with unbelievers, for what fellowship have righteousness and iniquity? Or what fellowship has light with darkness?[2] 6:15 What agreement has Christ with Belial? Or what portion has a believer with an unbeliever?

6:16 What agreement has a temple of God with idols? For you are a temple of the living God. Even as God said, "I will dwell in them, and walk in them; and I will be their God, and they will be my people."[5] 6:17 Therefore,

> "'Come out from among them,
> and be separate,'[3] says the
> Lord.
> 'Touch no unclean thing.
> I will receive you.[6]

6:18 I will be to you a Father.
You will be to me sons and daughters,'

says the Lord Almighty."[7]

1. *Don't be unequally yoked.* Love must be separated from sense and self and be made selfless before its spiritual quality becomes evident.

2. *what fellowship has light with darkness?* The key to true fellowship is the sharing of thought in harmony and accord. Those whose beliefs are in harmony with one another's know fellowship and peace of mind.

3. *"Come out from among them, and be separate."* Our transmutation to higher states of consciousness requires that we undergo processes of separation, but we should not to fear the loss of any zest for life. In fact, we find that the opposite is true. Whether in work or play, thoughts or musings, we find that love enters into all of life, gives it meaning, and finds expression through all.

---

Fillmore Study Bible annotations compiled by Mary Salama.

**World English Bible Footnotes:**

[4] v6:2. Isaiah 49:8

[5] v6:16. Leviticus 26:12; Jeremiah 32:38; Ezekiel 37:27

[6] v6:17. Isaiah 52:11; Ezekiel 20:34,41

[7] v6:18. 2 Samuel 7:14; 7:8

# SECOND CORINTHIANS 7

## Our Regenerate Will Rejoices When Our Soul Repents

7:1 Having therefore these
promises, beloved, let us cleanse
ourselves from all defilement of flesh
and spirit, perfecting holiness[1] in
the fear of God.

7:2 Open your hearts to us. We
wronged no one. We corrupted no
one. We took advantage of no one.
7:3 I say this not to condemn you, for
I have said before, that you are in
our hearts to die together and live
together. 7:4 Great is my boldness of
speech toward you. Great is my
boasting on your behalf. I am filled
with comfort. I overflow with joy in
all our affliction.

7:5 For even when we had come
into Macedonia, our flesh had no
relief, but we were afflicted on
every side. Fightings were outside.
Fear was inside. 7:6 Nevertheless, he
who comforts the lowly, God,
comforted us by the coming of Titus;
7:7 and not by his coming only, but
also by the comfort with which he
was comforted in you, while he told
us of your longing, your mourning,
and your zeal for me; so that I
rejoiced still more.

7:8 For though I made you sorry
with my letter, I do not regret it,
though I did regret it. For I see that
my letter made you sorry, though

just for a while. 7:9 I now rejoice, not that you were made sorry, but that you were made sorry to repentance. For you were made sorry in a godly way, that you might suffer loss by us in nothing. 7:10 For godly sorrow works repentance[2] to salvation, which brings no regret. But the sorrow of the world works death. 7:11 For behold, this same thing, that you were made sorry in a godly way, what earnest care it worked in you. Yes, what defense, indignation, fear, longing, zeal, and vengeance! In everything you demonstrated yourselves to be pure in the matter. 7:12 So although I wrote to you, I wrote not for his cause that did the wrong, nor for his cause that suffered the wrong, but that your earnest care for us might be revealed in you in the sight of God. 7:13 Therefore we have been comforted.[3]

In our comfort we rejoiced the more exceedingly for the joy of Titus, because his spirit has been refreshed by you all. 7:14 For if in anything I have boasted to him on your behalf, I was not disappointed. But as we spoke all things to you in truth, so our glorying also which I made before Titus was found to be truth. 7:15 His affection is more abundantly toward you, while he remembers all of your obedience, how with fear and trembling you received him. 7:16 I rejoice[4] that in everything I am of good courage concerning you.

1. *perfecting holiness.* We "perfect holiness" by steadfastly fixing our thoughts to what is true, pure, just, lovely, and of good report; denying all that would defile either flesh or spirit; and calling to our aid "the fear of God" (the eager and reverent keeping of the Divine law).

2. *Godly sorrow works repentance.* Repentance is a turning from a belief in sin and error to a belief in God and righteousness; a reversal of mind and heart in the direction of the All-Good. When we repent, we break with mortal thought and ascend into a spiritual thought realm, the kingdom of God. (RW/repentance)

3. *Therefore we have been comforted.* The Holy Spirit is He who gives comfort and cheer and reveals the Truth of God to us (RW/comforter), [therefore, comfort (a state of inner rest) becomes to us a proof of the presence and activity of the Spirit of God within us.]

4. *I rejoice* [Joy, comfort, confidence, and courage, are also among the fruit of repentance. Such a positive inner state is essential for the laying hold of and flourishing of a new state of consciousness.]

Fillmore Study Bible annotations compiled by Mary Salama.

# Second Corinthians 8

## The Importance of Generosity

8:1 Moreover, brothers, we make known to you the grace of God[1] which has been given in the assemblies of Macedonia; 8:2 how that in much proof of affliction the abundance of their joy and their deep poverty abounded to the riches of their liberality.[2] 8:3 For according to their power, I testify, yes and beyond their power, they gave of their own accord, 8:4 begging us with much entreaty to receive this grace and the fellowship in the service to the saints. 8:5 This was not as we had hoped, but first they gave their own selves to the Lord, and to us through the will of God.[3] 8:6 So we urged Titus, that as he made a beginning before, so he would also complete in you this grace. 8:7 But as you abound in everything, in faith, utterance, knowledge, all earnestness, and in your love to us, see that you also abound in this grace.

1. *the grace of God* The power of God manifesting through man, in love instead of in personal dominance. Macedonia represents zeal and enthusiasm, both of which are necessary before one can give according to the Divine law of increase. Zeal and enthusiasm move us to give of ourselves to a cause that enlists our love and interest. When this is done, the law of increase operates to empower us to give of our own substance, even the giving of our creative effort.

2. *deep poverty abounded to the riches of their liberality.* Paul is endeavoring to impress upon his listeners that there is a definite spiritual law back of giving to the Lord's work. Through the operation of this law, the Macedonians perceived with joy that their poverty had turned into riches.

3. *but first they gave their own selves to the Lord, and to us through the will of God.* This Scripture passage reveals that the first step in giving or tithing to the Lord is to dedicate oneself to Spirit [and to the] ministry of the Gospel, and to resolve to carry forward the good work; not only to give a tithe of one's time to prayer and meditation and the reading of the Gospel of Jesus Christ, but to make a complete consecration of oneself to the Lord's work.

## We are Designed to Give!

8:8 I speak not by way of commandment, but as proving through the earnestness of others the sincerity also of your love. 8:9 For you know the grace of our Lord Jesus Christ, that, though he was rich, yet for your sakes he became poor,[1] that you through his poverty might become rich. 8:10 I give a judgment in this: for this is expedient for you,[2] who were the first to start a year ago, not only to do, but also to be willing. 8:11 But now complete the doing also, that as there was the readiness to be willing, so there may be the completion also out of your ability. 8:12 For if the readiness is there, it is acceptable according to what you have, not according to what you don't have. 8:13 For this is not that others may be eased and you distressed, 8:14 but for equality. Your abundance[3] at this present time supplies their lack, that their abundance also may become a supply for your lack; that there may be equality. 8:15 As it is written, "He who gathered much had nothing left over, and he who gathered little had no lack."[8][4]

1. *He became poor.* Jesus rested on the law of self-sacrifice. By giving up the claims of the personal self and becoming "poor", Jesus realized the greater Self of the Christ and became rich in spiritual power. As we follow Him and put aside personality, we also will realize the same power that He commanded and share the same riches.

2. *this is expedient for you.* We benefit much from eagerly seeking and following our inner impulse to help others. Seeking ways to serve others is not only effective at applying our minds to constructive thinking, which could lead to our own spiritual progress, but it can also heal the conditions and causes that underlie poverty, strife, materiality and other negative influences that retard the human race as a whole.

3. *abundance.* In this lesson, Paul writes much of abundance and riches. These words have a special import in metaphysical unfoldment in the sense that if one desires prosperity, the words, "riches," "opulence," and "abundance," are good words to hold in one's mind. When we keep our minds charged with the thoughts that opulence and abundance are flowing to us from Divine Mind, we will never lack any good thing, and our [spiritual] gifts will

carry increase wherever we go.

4. See Ex 16.18.

## Serving Others Supports the Race and Our Own Regeneration!

8:16 But thanks be to God, who puts the same earnest care for you into the heart of Titus. 8:17 For he indeed accepted our exhortation, but being himself very earnest, he went out to you of his own accord.[1] 8:18 We have sent together with him the brother whose praise in the Good News is known through all the assemblies. 8:19 Not only so, but who was also appointed by the assemblies to travel with us in this grace, which is served by us to the glory of the Lord himself, and to show our readiness. 8:20 We are avoiding this, that any man should blame us concerning this abundance which is administered by us. 8:21 Having regard for honorable things, not only in the sight of the Lord, but also in the sight of men. 8:22 We have sent with them our brother, whom we have many times proved earnest in many things, but now much more earnest, by reason of the great confidence which he has in you. 8:23 As for Titus, he is my partner and fellow worker for you. As for our brothers, they are the apostles of the assemblies, the glory of Christ. 8:24 Therefore show the proof of your love to them in front of the assemblies, and of our boasting on your behalf.

1. *he went out to you of his own accord.* The best gift we can give is our good will, because it is most potent to bring the kingdom of heaven into manifestation here and now. Also our faith, which we give to the world by putting it into our daily thought and work, and making all that we do expressive of our deepest convictions.

---

Fillmore Study Bible annotations compiled by Mary Salama.

**World English Bible Footnotes:**

[8] v8:15. Exodus 16:8

# Second Corinthians 9

## Administering Your Gifts

9:1 It is indeed unnecessary for me to write to you concerning the service to the saints,[1] 9:2 for I know your readiness, of which I boast on your behalf to them of Macedonia, that Achaia has been prepared for a year past. Your zeal has stirred up very many of them. 9:3 But I have sent the brothers that our boasting on your behalf may not be in vain in this respect, that, just as I said, you may be prepared, 9:4 so that I won't by any means, if there come with me any of Macedonia and find you unprepared, we (to say nothing of you) should be disappointed in this confident boasting. 9:5 I thought it necessary therefore to entreat the brothers that they would go before to you, and arrange ahead of time the generous gift that you promised before, that the same might be ready as a matter of generosity, and not of greediness.[2]

1. *service to the saints.* "The saints" here refers to the Grecian Jews, who represent new converts to the faith. Until selfishness is overcome, a sense of injustice arises in mind at every indication that the purely spiritual interests of life are receiving more attention and more sustaining power than our other "worth-while" interests of the individual. In individual consciousness, we should meet situations of this kind by always being nonresistant toward new states of consciousness that are forming and declare perfect freedom for them. The Spirit of truth, which is in each soul ever working to harmonize and to uplift, calls into executive authority the most enlightened of these thought forces and they are given the right to share in the management and distribution of the inflowing spiritual substance. Thus peace is established.

2. *as a matter of generosity, and not of greediness.* It has taken human beings centuries to learn the lesson of unselfish generosity. It is not yet learned; it is still a lesson. Paul found it imperative to urge the early Christians to make generous donations to the support of workers. We must learn to give in the spirit of unselfish love and enthusiasm before we can hope to receive in like manner or degree from the Giver of "every good gift and every perfect gift."

## The Cheerful Giver

9:6 Remember this: he who sows sparingly will also reap sparingly. He who sows bountifully will also reap bountifully.[1] 9:7 Let each man give according as he has determined in his heart; not grudgingly, or under compulsion; for God loves a cheerful giver.[2] 9:8 And God is able to make all grace abound to you, that you, always having all sufficiency in everything, may abound to every good work. 9:9 As it is written,

> "He has scattered abroad, he has given to the poor.
> His righteousness remains forever."[9]

9:10 Now may he who supplies seed to the sower and bread for food, supply and multiply your seed for sowing, and increase the fruits of your righteousness; 9:11 you being enriched in everything to all liberality, which works through us thanksgiving to God. 9:12 For this service of giving that you perform not only makes up for lack among the saints, but abounds also through many givings of thanks to God; 9:13 seeing that through the proof given by this service, they glorify God for the obedience of your confession to the Good News of Christ, and for the liberality of your contribution to them and to all; 9:14 while they themselves also, with supplication on your behalf, yearn for you by reason of the exceeding grace of God in you. 9:15 Now thanks be to God for his unspeakable gift![3]

1. *will also reap bountifully.* When one is right with God, all one's acts will be right. When such an individual receives bountifully, naturally he will give forth bountifully. Every gift will be full of love and free from all grudging feelings. "He who sows bountifully will also reap bountifully."

2. *God loves a cheerful giver.* He who has a generous heart is in harmony with Divine law. In this state of harmony we are receptive to Divine love and the other blessings that free will, rightly exercised, obtains for us.

3. *His unspeakable gift!* If a person knows the law, he knows that he must first give himself to the Lord. Then by giving of his substance with abounding faith in God's abundance, he is conscious of receiving a

blessing. The blessing is magnified and increased in the thought atmosphere of his mind, and he receives not only spiritually, but also in seemingly material ways.

Fillmore Study Bible annotations compiled by Mary Salama.

**World English Bible Footnotes:**

[9] v9:9. Psalm 112:

# Second Corinthians 10

## Our Inner Battle

10:1 Now I Paul, myself, entreat you by the humility and gentleness of Christ; I who in your presence am lowly among you, but being absent am of good courage toward you. 10:2 Yes, I beg you that I may not, when present, show courage with the confidence with which I intend to be bold against some, who consider us to be walking according to the flesh.[1] 10:3 For though we walk in the flesh, we don't wage war according to the flesh; 10:4 for the weapons of our warfare are not of the flesh, but mighty before God to the throwing down of strongholds,[2] 10:5 throwing down imaginations and every high thing that is exalted against the knowledge of God, and bringing every thought into captivity to the obedience[3] of Christ; 10:6 and being in readiness to avenge all disobedience, when your obedience will be made full.

10:7 Do you look at things only as they appear in front of your face? If anyone trusts in himself that he is Christ's, let him consider this again with himself, that, even as he is Christ's, so also we are Christ's. 10:8 For though I should boast somewhat abundantly concerning our authority,[4] (which the Lord gave for building you up, and not for casting you down) I will not be disappointed, 10:9 that I may not seem as if I desire to terrify you by my letters. 10:10 For, "His letters," they say, "are weighty and strong, but his bodily presence is weak, and his speech is despised." 10:11 Let such a person consider this, that what we are in word by letters when we are absent, such are we also in deed when we are present.

10:12 For we are not bold to number or compare ourselves with some of those who commend themselves. But they themselves, measuring themselves by themselves, and comparing themselves with themselves, are without understanding. 10:13 But we will not boast[5] beyond proper limits, but within the boundaries with which God appointed to us, which reach even to you. 10:14 For we don't stretch ourselves too much, as though we didn't reach to you. For we came even as far as to you with the Good News of Christ, 10:15 not boasting beyond proper limits in other men's labors, but having hope that as your faith grows, we will be abundantly enlarged by you in our sphere of influence,(6) 10:16 so as to preach the Good News even to the parts beyond you, not to boast in what someone else has already done. 10:17 But "he who boasts, let him boast in the Lord."[10] 10:18 For it isn't he who commends himself who is approved, but whom the Lord commends.

1. *flesh.* Mortal consciousness expressing itself through appetite. It is overcome by denying that appetite is physical and by affirming it to be spiritual. (RW/flesh)

2. *strongholds.* A strongly fortified aggregation of rebellious, oppressing, thieving, destroying thoughts in man's consciousness. (MBD/Ashdod)

3. *obedience.* Spiritual obedience comes through understanding our relation to God. When we show forth wisdom and purity and the perfect Principle that is God, we are obedient to Him. (RW/obedience)

4. *concerning our authority.* Authority is power; mastery; or dominion. It is inspired by Spirit within (the Lord). The Spirit of truth is the one and only authority in the study of Truth. [Right use of our authority is to submit it to Spirit, in doing so, this power then aids our Spirit-led will (Paul) to build us up along our process of regeneration.] (RW/authority)

5. *But we will not boast.* Boasting is never in good taste. A statement of fact is allowable when some misrepresentation is distorting the truth and destroying the possibility of our future usefulness by challenging our qualifications or impugning our motives or intentions. Such a state of fact is not boasting; it enables others to arrive at a better understanding of the matter. Our deeds are always more convincing than our words. Deeds are the ultimate proof of our faiths and intentions.

6. *but having hope that as your faith grows, we will be abundantly enlarged by you in our sphere of influence.* [Knowing that our journey in Christ Consciousness takes time to unfold, our regenerated will holds an inner light for us as our faith grows, our will for God accordingly gains more influence within us.]

Fillmore Study Bible annotations compiled by Mary Salama.

**World English Bible Footnotes:**

[10] v10:17. Jeremiah 9:24

# Second Corinthians 11

## Our Will and False Thoughts

11:1 I wish that you would bear with me in a little foolishness, but indeed you do bear with me. 11:2 For I am jealous over you with a godly jealousy. For I married you to one husband, that I might present you as a pure virgin to Christ. 11:3 But I am afraid that somehow, as the serpent deceived Eve in his craftiness, so your minds might be corrupted from the simplicity that is in Christ.(1) 11:4 For if he who comes preaches another Jesus, whom we did not preach, or if you receive a different spirit, which you did not receive, or a different "good news", which you did not accept, you put up with that well enough. 11:5 For I reckon that I am not at all behind the very best apostles. 11:6 But though I am unskilled in speech, yet I am not unskilled in knowledge. No, in every way we have been revealed to you in all things.

11:7 Or did I commit a sin in humbling myself that you might be exalted, because I preached to you God's Good News[2] free of charge? 11:8 I robbed other assemblies, taking wages from them that I might serve you. 11:9 When I was present with you and was in need, I wasn't a burden on anyone, for the brothers, when they came from Macedonia, supplied the measure of my need. In everything I kept myself from being burdensome to you, and I will continue to do so. 11:10 As the truth of Christ is in me, no one will stop me from this boasting in the regions of Achaia. 11:11 Why? Because I don't love you? God knows.

11:12 But what I do, that I will do, that I may cut off occasion from them that desire an occasion, that in which they boast, they may be found even as we. 11:13 For such men are false apostles,[3] deceitful workers, masquerading as Christ's apostles. 11:14 And no wonder, for even Satan masquerades as an angel of light. 11:15 It is no great thing therefore if his servants also masquerade as servants of righteousness, whose end will be according to their works.

1. *the simplicity that is in Christ.* Simplicity (purity, ASV) of the Christ Mind—The deep purity and mighty strength of the Christ Mind are made manifest in us as we develop spiritually. Instead of consciously and unconsciously tempting one another in sense ways, these qualities in each will incite in the other holy aspirations to fulfill the law of righteousness. (RW/purity)

2. *God's Good News.* The gospel of Jesus is that every man can become God incarnate. It is not alone a gospel of right living, but also shows the way into dominion and power equal to and surpassing that of Jesus of Nazareth. (RW/Gospel)

3. *false apostles.* Deceptive thoughts that have been built up by error, selfish desires. Outwardly they present the appearance of being candid and open; inwardly they are ravenous for personal sensation and worldly gain. In order to attain their end they deceive even "the elect." (MBD/false-prophets)

## The Value of Inner Trials

11:16 I say again, let no one think me foolish. But if so, yet receive me as foolish, that I also may boast a little. 11:17 That which I speak, I don't speak according to the Lord, but as in foolishness, in this confidence of boasting. 11:18 Seeing that many boast after the flesh, I will also boast.[1] 11:19 For you bear with the foolish gladly, being wise. 11:20 For you bear with a man, if he brings you into bondage, if he devours you, if he takes you captive, if he exalts himself, if he strikes you on the face. 11:21 I speak by way of disparagement,[2] as though we had been weak.

Yet however any is bold (I speak in foolishness), I am bold also. 11:22 Are they Hebrews? So am I. Are they Israelites? So am I. Are they the seed of Abraham? So am I. 11:23 Are they servants of Christ? (I speak as one beside himself) I am more so; in labors more abundantly,[3] in prisons more abundantly, in stripes above measure, in deaths often. 11:24 Five times from the Jews I received forty stripes minus one. 11:25 Three times I was beaten with rods. Once I was stoned. Three times I suffered shipwreck. I have been a night and a day in the deep. 11:26 I have been in travels often, perils of rivers, perils of robbers, perils from my countrymen, perils from the Gentiles, perils in the city, perils in the wilderness, perils in the sea, perils among false brothers; 11:27 in labor and travail, in watchings often, in hunger and thirst, in fastings often, and in cold and nakedness.

11:28 Besides those things that are outside,[4] there is that which presses on me daily, anxiety for all the assemblies. 11:29 Who is weak, and I am not weak?[5] Who is caused to stumble, and I don't burn with indignation? 11:30 If I must boast, I will boast of the things that concern my weakness. 11:31 The God and Father of the Lord Jesus Christ, he who is blessed forevermore, knows that I don't lie. 11:32 In Damascus the governor under Aretas the king guarded the city of the Damascenes desiring to arrest me. 11:33 Through a window I was let down in a basket by the wall, and escaped his hands.

1. *I will also boast.* See commentary for 2 Cor 10:13.

2. *I speak by way of disparagement.* Communicating to us through our own inner voice and regenerated will, the Word of Truth (which Paul here represents) endures, and is neither strengthened nor weakened by the opposition of our sense consciousness.

3. *in labors more abundantly.* Paul's summing up of his many troubles and years of service in the cause of Christ is valuable for us because it brings home to us a realization of what the indomitable Spirit can accomplish, and it inspires us to emulate Paul's example of endurance, perseverance, and faithfulness.

4. *Besides those things that are outside.* The giving of material things unaccompanied by a helpful thought or word is futile. We should always accompany our gifts with some substantial thought or word. Whether toward others or toward ourselves, to give with the idea that it is almsgiving and that the one receiving the gift is in great need, increases the lack and sows broadcast the need of additional charity. Giving without wisdom is nonproductive of good.

5. *Who is weak, and I am not weak?* Inner trials can become a source of weakness, but only when we yield to them. When pressed by inner trials, the best thing for us to do is to develop a constructive viewpoint and affirm that what we see in Spirit is now manifest and is done.

---

Fillmore Study Bible annotations compiled by Mary Salama.

# Second Corinthians 12

## Receiving Divine Visions & Revelations

12:1 It is doubtless not profitable for me to boast. For I will come to visions and revelations[1] of the Lord. 12:2 I know a man in Christ, fourteen years ago (whether in the body, I don't know, or whether out of the body, I don't know; God knows), such a one caught up into the third heaven.[2] 12:3 I know such a man (whether in the body, or outside of the body, I don't know; God knows), 12:4 how he was caught up into Paradise, and heard unspeakable words, which it is not lawful for a man to utter.

1. *visions and revelations of the Lord.* Ministers of the orthodox churches in this day preach often of Paul's conversion, and lay special stress upon his obedience to the heavenly vision, yet if a member of any of these congregations should arise in prayer meeting and relate such an experience, he would be sung down or ejected from the church. But Paul did have visions, and he was not timid in relating them. When Jesus stood by him in the dreams of the night and told him not to be afraid but to go on to Rome, Paul boldly told about it. When he was "caught up into Paradise,

and heard unspeakable words," he did not hesitate to relate the experience, regardless of the ridicule that was sure to follow.

2. *the third heaven ... Paradise*. There is a kingdom, interpenetrating the world in which we live, inhabited by Christ and the "saints in glory." This is the "heaven" of Jesus and "Paradise" of Paul. When the superconscious or spiritual part of our mind is lighted by the higher understanding, we find our head and heart in heaven, although our body may still be here on earth.

## Our "Thorn": a Window for God's Grace

12:5 On behalf of such a one I will boast, but on my own behalf I will not boast, except in my weaknesses. 12:6 For if I would desire to boast, I will not be foolish; for I will speak the truth. But I refrain, so that no man may think more of me than that which he sees in me, or hears from me. 12:7 By reason of the exceeding greatness of the revelations, that I should not be exalted excessively, there was given to me a thorn in the flesh, a messenger of Satan to torment me, that I should not be exalted excessively. 12:8 Concerning this thing, I begged the Lord three times that it might depart from me. 12:9 He has said to me, "My grace[1] is sufficient for you,[2] for my power is made perfect in weakness."[3] Most gladly therefore I will rather glory in my weaknesses, that the power of Christ may rest on me. 12:10 Therefore I take pleasure in weaknesses, in injuries, in necessities, in persecutions, in distresses, for Christ's sake. For when I am weak, then am I strong.[4]

1. *My grace*. The word grace is only mentioned in the Gospels seven times: once in Luke and six times in John. Jesus never spoke the word grace in the Gospels except for this once, when He spoke it to Paul when He appeared to him in this vision. (Debbie Tyson, *Grace Awakening*, Grace in the Bible)

2. *is sufficient for you*. Agnes Sanford tells of a woman who was not able to be healed from an incurable disease. Rather, she was told that her strength was made perfect in weakness and that His strength was sufficient for her. Sanford writes, "She interpreted 'My strength is made perfect in weakness' to mean that in her weakness His strength would be made perfect. She does her own work, teaches classes, starts prayer groups, attends conferences heals the sick and comforts the sorrowing by renewing her strength through His Strength every day." *The Healing Light*, pp49-50.

3. *made perfect in weakness*. The power that is "made perfect in weakness" has the capacity to renew our inner forces and faculties, enabling us to endure calmly for the time what we are unable to remove immediately. [By holding fast to the Truth we know during our challenges, we can tap into] the Divine power of the Christ, which touches the problem and dissolves it, or brings peace to replace stress and tension.

4. *For when I am weak, then am I strong*. "There is an allness in every illness"—Eric Butterworth.

## Paul's Concern for the Corinthian Church

12:11 I have become foolish in boasting. You compelled me, for I ought to have been commended by you, for in nothing was I inferior to the very best apostles,[1] though I am nothing. 12:12 Truly the signs of an apostle were worked among you in all patience, in signs and wonders and mighty works. 12:13 For what is there in which you were made inferior to the rest of the assemblies, unless it is that I myself was not a burden to you? Forgive me this wrong.

12:14 Behold, this is the third time

I am ready to come to you, and I will not be a burden to you; for I seek not your possessions, but you. For the children ought not to save up for the parents, but the parents for the children. 12:15 I will most gladly spend and be spent for your souls. If I love you more abundantly, am I loved the less? 12:16 But be it so, I did not myself burden you. But, being crafty, I caught you with deception. 12:17 Did I take advantage of you by anyone of them whom I have sent to you? 12:18 I exhorted Titus,[2] and I sent the brother with him. Did Titus take any advantage of you? Didn't we walk in the same spirit? Didn't we walk in the same steps?

12:19 Again, do you think that we are excusing ourselves to you? In the sight of God we speak in Christ. But all things, beloved, are for your edifying. 12:20 For I am afraid that by any means, when I come, I might find you not the way I want to, and that I might be found by you as you don't desire; that by any means there would be strife, jealousy,[3] outbursts of anger, factions, slander, whisperings, proud thoughts, riots; 12:21 that again when I come my God would humble me before you, and I would mourn for many of those who have sinned before now, and not repented of the uncleanness and sexual immorality and lustfulness which they committed.

1. *the very best apostles.* In consciousness, our apostles are our active spiritual thoughts. Jesus conferred this title on the twelve whom He sent forth to teach and to heal, they were: Peter (faith); Andrew (strength); James son of Zebedee (wisdom or judgment); John (love); Philip (power); Bartholomew (imagination); Thomas (understanding); Matthew (will); James (order); Simon the Cananaean (zeal); Thaddaeus (renunciation or elimination); and Judas (life conserver). (RW/apostles)

2. *I exhorted Titus.* In consciousness, Titus is a pleasing, agreeable, and honorable attitude of mind. This attitude is sent forth by the Spirit to support our will (Paul) in accomplishing the work of regeneration within us. (RW/Titus)

3. *jealousy.* A form of mental bias that blinds the judgment and causes one to act without weighing the consequences. The remedy is a dismissal of the negative thoughts that cause one to be jealous, followed by a fuller trust in the great all-adjusting power of God. (RW/jealousy)

---

Fillmore Study Bible annotations compiled by Mary Salama.

# Second Corinthians 13

## Affirming our Power & Victory

13:1 This is the third time I am coming to you. "At the mouth of two or three witnesses shall every word be established."[1][11] 13:2 I have said beforehand, and I do say beforehand, as when I was present the second time, so now, being absent, I write to those who have sinned before now, and to all the rest, that, if I come again, I will not spare; 13:3 seeing that you seek a proof of Christ who speaks in me; who toward you is not weak, but is powerful in you. 13:4 For he was crucified through weakness, yet he lives through the power of God. For we also are weak in him, but we will live with him through the power of God toward you.

13:5 Test your own selves, whether
you are in the faith.[2] Test your own
selves. Or don't you know as to your
own selves, that Jesus Christ is in
you?--unless indeed you are
disqualified. 13:6 But I hope that you
will know that we aren't disqualified.

13:7 Now I pray to God that you
do no evil; not that we may appear
approved, but that you may do that
which is honorable, though we are as
reprobate. 13:8 For we can do nothing
against the truth, but for the truth.
13:9 For we rejoice when we are weak
and you are strong. And this we also
pray for, even your perfecting.[3] 13:10
For this cause I write these things
while absent, that I may not deal
sharply when present, according to
the authority which the Lord gave me
for building up, and not for tearing
down.

1. *At the mouth of two or three witnesses shall every word be established.* While we believe that there is an outer interpretation to all prophecy, we know that there is also an inner interpretation, and since this is the more necessary in our overcoming we always seek to give the Scriptures an individual meaning or explanation. (RW/witnesses)

2. *Test your own selves, whether you are in the faith.* To demonstrate Truth is to effect a change of consciousness. This includes the elimination of error and the establishment of Truth. (RW/demonstrate)

3. *for the truth, your perfecting.* The basic principle of Truth is that the mind of each individual may be consciously unified with Divine Mind through the indwelling Christ. By affirming at-one-ment with God-Mind, we eventually realize that perfect mind which was in Christ Jesus. (RW/truth)

## Absolute Encouragement and Blessing!

13:11 Finally, brothers, rejoice. Be
perfected, be comforted, be of the
same mind, live in peace, and the
God of love and peace will be with
you. 13:12 Greet one another with a
holy kiss. 13:13 All the saints greet you.
13:14 The grace of the Lord Jesus
Christ,[1] the love of God,[2] and the
fellowship of the Holy Spirit,[3] be
with you all.[4] Amen.

1. *grace of the Lord Jesus Christ.* Aid from God in the process of regeneration. (RW/grace)

2. *love of God.* The power that joins and binds in divine harmony the universe and everything in it; the great harmonizing principle known to humanity. (RW/love)

3. *fellowship of the Holy Spirit.* (Communion, ASV) Sharing the deep aspirations of our heart with the indwelling Father and hearing His "still small voice" (RW/communion)

4. *"grace, love, fellowship" be with you all.* Order is to be restored to our confused thoughts by consecutive stages of realization, not all at once.

---

Fillmore Study Bible annotations compiled by Mary Salama.

**World English Bible Footnotes:**

[11] v13:1. Deuteronomy 19:15

# Paul's Letter to the Galatians

The Separation of Saints Peter and Paul, Giovanni Lanfranco (1582-1647). Public Domain.

## Introduction to Paul's Letter to the Galatians

The disturbed state of affairs indicated by the term "Galatian Controversy" forms the historical background of Paul's Epistle to the Galatians; and if this Epistle is to be properly understood, some knowledge of what was taking place at the time of writing is absolutely necessary. Unfortunately, the New Testament gives little detailed information on the subject. Consequently, many differing accounts of these happenings have been put forward, and even the time and place of Paul's writing have been variously stated. However, this lesson will present what appears the most reasonable explanation of what took place, giving the happenings in the chronological order which best harmonizes with other activities of Paul.

(1)The disturbing news: When Paul reached Antioch, at the close of his second missionary journey, disturbing news awaited him. It would appear that, during the apostle's long absence, emissaries of the "Judaizing party" had visited the Christian groups in Galatia, denouncing Paul as an impostor, and declaring that all Gentiles—if they desired to become Christians—must submit to the ordinances of Judaism, including circumcision. Some time earlier, this matter had been taken up by the Apostles at the Jerusalem council (as discussed in Lesson Three), and a decision favorable to the Gentiles had been rendered; but during Paul's prolonged absence in Europe this decision had been thrust aside, and many Gentile converts had been intimidated into submission. Thus much of Paul's work among the Gentiles had been nullified, and the converts had surrendered their newly-gained freedom.

(2) The churches affected: The term Galatians, as here used, refers to the Christian groups formed by Paul and Barnabas on their first missionary journey. Thus, the churches concerned in this Galatian controversy would be those of Antioch (in Pisidia), Iconium, Lystra,and Derbe.

(3) Paul's twofold action: Paul first dictated the strongly-worded letter, which we now refer to as the Epistle to the Galatians, and dispatched it to the above-mentioned churches. The apostle's purpose in writing is clearly indicated in the Epistle. First, he sought to vindicate his claim to apostleship—averring that his appointment was not "from men or through man, but through Jesus Christ and God the Father" (Gal. 1:1). Then he plunged into the important business of reconverting those Gentile Christians who had been so basely deceived by the "Judaizers," and winning them back into experiences of Christian freedom. Paul further instructed his converts in the right use of this Christian freedom—their actions being no longer restricted by the limitations of the law, but enlarged through the working of Christian love.

Then, following the writing and dispatching of this Epistle, Paul hurriedly departed from his headquarters at Antioch (in Syria), and revisited the Christian groups in Galatia. During this visit Paul gave the converts further instructions along lines laid down in his Epistle, together with whatever additional guidance was necessary. Evidently Paul's efforts to reestablish his Galatian converts in Christian freedom were successful, for after a short stay with them, he departed from Galatia and journeyed westward as far as Ephesus, where some important work awaited his coming. Paul's activities in Ephesus will be discussed later in this lesson.

(4) Historical significance: It is true that Paul wrote his Epistle to the Galatians in order to vindicate his apostleship, and to win back the misguided Galatian converts. But history clearly shows that the Epistle to the Galatians should also be recognized as a combined "Declaration of Independence" and "Magna Charta" of Christian freedom. For at the time of writing something more than the ceremonial status of a few Galatian converts was at stake. The real points at issue were: Should Christians in general submit to the bondage of the Mosaic law, or should they find their freedom in Jesus Christ? Should the Christian Church continue as a subsidiary of Judaism, or should it now be regarded as a completely independent organization? The apostle took a stand for freedom and independence. Of course, all this controversy was not settled at that time. Nevertheless, Paul's Epistle to the Galatians, and his courageous actions, should be recognized as important milestones along the road which ultimately led to Christian freedom and the separation between Judaism and Christianity.

(5) Metaphysical meaning: The Roman province of Galatia derived its name from the Gauls, who invaded that section of Asia Minor in preChristian

times. Thus, the term Galatia meant "the territory occupied by Gaulish immigrants"; and it also tended to emphasize the fact that the inhabitants were of comparatively recent arrival (or to use a modern term, they were "newcomers"). In a somewhat similar way, the Gentile Christians in Galatia should be recognized as recent converts, who were not yet fully established in the Christian teaching. Later on, Paul termed some of his newly-fledged converts "babes in Christ" (I Cor. 3:1-3). Apparently it was because of this spiritual immaturity that the Gentile converts in Galatia so easily surrendered their Christian freedom to the "Judaizers." Applying what is indicated above to present-day experiences, it would seem that the Epistle to the Galatians has special reference to the dangers associated with spiritual immaturity. Like the Galatians, persons who are not well-grounded in Truth may easily become involved in erroneous teaching, and soon lose whatever measure of freedom they have gained. Possibly, it was some recollection of this Galatian experience which later caused Paul to write: "Therefore, take the whole armor of God, that you may be able to withstand in the evil day, and having done all, to stand" (Eph. 6:13).

Another important present-day message from Galatians is to be recognized in Paul's oft-quoted admonition: "For freedom has Christ set us free; stand fast therefore, and do not submit again to a yoke of slavery" (Gal. 5:1). Religious freedom is a precious heritage. But this freedom, when once attained, must also be maintained, and its maintenance calls for constant vigilance. Jesus made clear what our attitude must be in this respect, when He said: "Watch and pray that you may not enter into temptation" (Matt. 26:41). Paul's words, given in a later epistle, are also significant: "Pray at all times in the Spirit. . . keep alert with all perseverance" (Eph. 6:18).

Introduction to *Paul's Letter to the Galatians* by Herbert J. Hunt, former Dean of Bible Studies for the Unity School of Christianity.

*In the first sentence of his letter, Paul declares that his authority as an apostle is not found in tradition, nor scripture, nor reason nor experience.* It may be claimed that the rest of the letter is an elaboration on that inspired statement in Christian scripture (1:1-5)

Paul's first assertion is that there is only one Gospel or Good News. As we will see, this means in the world of religion and spirituality there are some absolutes. There may be disagreements about what is absolute and what is relative. However Paul's point is that *it is perfectly fine for a spiritual tradition to assert Truth in such a way that denies the validity of some erroneous spiritual assertions* (1:6-10).

Paul's letter addresses problems that emerged when the ministry and message of Jesus, a Jew grounded in the Jewish covenant and legal traditions, was received by Gentiles, who had no covenant with the Jewish God nor any legal requirement to keep the Jewish law. That the Gospel of Jesus would take root in a non-Jewish, hellenistic culture surprised everyone. It not only took root, the mission and message of Jesus exhibited great spiritual power among the Gentiles. So the story of Paul's letter to the Galatians begins with understanding that since the Good News for a particular people and culture could come to serve an entirely different people and culture then *Truth transcends culture* (1:11-24).

The acceptance of the ministry and message of Jesus in the Gentile world surprised even the Apostle Paul, who was responsible for evangelizing in Damascus and Arabia, places known metaphysically as centers of Gentile intellectual and worldly thoughts. In fact, so surprised was Paul that he and his friends convened a private meeting in Jerusalem with Peter, James and John, the core of Jewish Christian leadership, to make sure they were in agreement about how to understand non-Jewish Christianity. According to Paul, the Jewish Christian leadership extended the right hand of fellowship to Paul and his companions. So it was agreed that while there would be *one Gospel* but that there would also be *separate ministries*-one for the Gentiles and another ministry for the Jews (2:1-10).

It was not long before disagreements arouse between Gentile Christians and Jewish Christians about religious practices and orthodox teachings. The disagreements exploded when Peter, the Jewish Christian leader, visited Antioch, the center of Gentile Christian practice. Peter had shared fellowship meals with the Gentile converts there, but he ceased when people from his own religious circle showed up and accused him of impropriety. *It's a painful story that illustrates how people who were at one time religiously marginalized will often exhibit spiritual elitism when they become religiously prominent* (2:11-14).

Paul makes an astonishing statement when reflecting on what had happened. People believed then, as they do now, that Jesus somehow saves each of us in some way. But the church has never clarified exactly how salvation works. Some theologians say Jesus paid a ransom to the devil. Others say he paid an atonement to God. Others hold that Jesus just showed the way to a better way to live. *Astonishingly, Paul doesn't talk so much about Jesus as much as he talks about himself.* He writes, "I have been crucified with Christ, and it is no longer I that live, but Christ living in me. That life which I now live in the flesh, I live by faith in the Son of God, who loved me, and gave himself up for me." (2:15-21).

*So Paul's solution to how the ministry and message of Jesus might serve Gentiles as well as Jews is to remove that ministry and message away from the culture and place it within each individual Gentile and Jew.* It is Paul who is crucified, crucified with Christ, but with Christ who lives *in him*. Paul says that this Christ within supplies the Spirit to you and me and works miracles among each one of us (3:1-13).

*Having removed the ministry and message of Jesus away from culture, Paul then moves it away from any particular covenant with God.* He does so by declaring that the covenant with Abraham is one seed, which is Christ. Metaphysically, "one seed" is a euphemism for Principle, a singular metaphysical rule or Idea by which we are able to gain true spiritual heritage and possess riches of the kingdom of God (3:15-18).

*The hostile disagreements between Jewish Christians and Gentile Christians have now been resolved. We are no longer concerned about culture nor covenant* because, as Paul says, "There is neither Jew nor Greek, there is neither slave nor free man, there is neither male nor female; for you are all one in Christ Jesus" (3:19-29).

Introduction to *Paul's Letter to the Galatians* by Rev. Mark Hicks.

# Galatians 1

## Greeting from Our Spirit of Truth

1:1 Paul,① an apostle (not from
men, neither through man, but
through Jesus Christ,② and God the
Father,③ who raised him from the
dead),④ 1:2 and all the brothers[1]
who are with me, to the assemblies
of Galatia:

1:3 Grace to you and peace from
God the Father, and our Lord Jesus
Christ, 1:4 who gave himself for our
sins, that he might deliver us out of
this present evil⑤ age, according to
the will of our God and Father-- 1:5 to
whom be the glory forever and ever.
Amen.

1. *Paul.* Metaphysically, Paul is the word of the Spirit of truth. The converted Paul (formerly Saul, the will) becomes, by the power of the word, the most active thought in the establishment of good throughout our being. (MBD/Paul)

2. *Jesus Christ. Jesus* is God's idea of man in expression (MBD/Jesus). *Christ* is the idea in the absolute (MBD/Christ). Jesus Christ was the type man, which includes all the mental phases through which man passes in demonstrating life's problems.

3. *God the Father.* God is not person but principle, the underlying unchangeable truth. God is personal to us when we recognize Him within us as our indwelling life, intelligence, love, and power. (RW/God)

4. *dead.* the outer symbol of mental negation or spiritual inertia. (RW/death)

5. *evil.* That which is not God; unreality; error thought; a product of the fallen human consciousness; negation. (RW/evil)

## There Is Only One Gospel

1:6 I marvel that you are so quickly
deserting him who called you in the
grace of Christ to a different "good
news";① 1:7 and there isn't another
"good news." Only there are some
who trouble you, and want to pervert
the Good News of Christ. 1:8 But even
though we, or an angel② from
heaven, should preach to you any
"good news" other than that which
we preached to you, let him be
cursed. 1:9 As we have said before,
so I now say again: if any man③
preaches to you any "good news"
other than that which you received,
let him be cursed. 1:10 For am I now
seeking the favor of men, or of God?
Or am I striving to please men? For if
I were still pleasing men, I wouldn't
be a servant of Christ.

1. *Good News-"Gospel".* The Good news of Jesus is that every man can become God incarnate. It is now universally identified with Jesus' mission. (RW/gospel)

2. *angel.* A messenger of God. (MBD/angel)

3. *man, humanity.* An idea in Divine Mind; the epitome of being. The apex of God's creation, created in God's image and likeness. We appear unlike God because we, through disobedience, fell into sin. Through accepting race thoughts, we have adopted wrong ideas about ourself and our relation to our source. We have believed we are unlike and separate from God. (RW/man)

## Truth Transcends Culture

1:11 But I make known to you, brothers, concerning the Good News which was preached by me, that it is not according to man. 1:12 For neither did I receive it from man, nor was I taught it, but it came to me through revelation of Jesus Christ.

1:13 For you have heard of my way of living in time past in the Jews' religion, how that beyond measure I persecuted the assembly of God, and ravaged it. 1:14 I advanced in the Jews' religion beyond many of my own age among my countrymen, being more exceedingly zealous for the traditions of my fathers. 1:15 But when it was the good pleasure of God, who separated me from my mother's womb, and called me through his grace, 1:16 to reveal his Son in me, that I might preach him among the Gentiles,[1] I didn't immediately confer with flesh and blood, 1:17 nor did I go up to Jerusalem to those who were apostles before me, but I went away into Arabia.[2] Then I returned to Damascus.

1:18 Then after three years I went up to Jerusalem[3] to visit Peter,[4] and stayed with him fifteen days. 1:19 But of the other apostles I saw no one, except James, the Lord's brother. 1:20 Now about the things which I write to you, behold, before God, I'm not lying. 1:21 Then I came to the regions of Syria[5] and Cilicia. 1:22 I was still unknown by face to the assemblies of Judea which were in Christ, 1:23 but they only heard: "He who once persecuted us now preaches the faith that he once tried to destroy." 1:24 And they glorified God in me.

1. *Gentiles.* Worldly thoughts-thoughts pertaining to the external, or thoughts that function through the senses. The Gentile is the unregenerate state of mind in us. (MBD/Gentiles)

2. *Arabia.* Metaphysically, an outer, or Gentile, state of consciousness that is its wild, ignorant undisciplined, and unsettled nature is destructive in its tendency and is unproductive of good. (MBD/Arabia)

3. *Jerusalem.* The spiritual center in consciousness. In us, it is the abiding consciousness of spiritual peace. (RW/Jerusalem)

4. *Peter.* The spiritual faculty of faith. (MBD/Peter)

5. *Syria.* Metaphysically, the intellect, intellectual pride (highland, swelling up). Egotistic purely intellectual thought. The Syria thoughts of the intellectual realm that have no understanding of the real (Israel) come down and seek to kill the spiritual thoughts of the heart. (MBD/Syria)

---

Fillmore Study Bible annotations compiled by Thomas Scheinler.

**World English Bible Footnotes:**

[1] v1:2. The word for "brothers" here and where context allows may also be correctly translated "brothers and sisters" or "siblings."

# Galatians 2

## The Fellowship of Jewish and Gentile Christianity

2:1 Then after a period of fourteen years I went up again to Jerusalem[1] with Barnabas,[2] taking Titus also with me. 2:2 I went up by revelation, and I laid before them the Good News which I preach among the Gentiles, but privately before those who were respected, for fear that I might be running, or had run, in vain. 2:3 But not even Titus, who was with me, being a Greek, was compelled to be circumcised. 2:4 This was because of the false brothers secretly brought in, who stole in to spy out our liberty which we have in Christ Jesus, that they might bring us into bondage; 2:5 to whom we gave no place in the way of subjection, not for an hour, that the truth of the Good News might continue with you. 2:6 But from those who were reputed to be important (whatever they were, it makes no difference to me; God doesn't show partiality to man)--they, I say, who were respected imparted nothing to me, 2:7 but to the contrary, when they saw that I had been entrusted with the Good News for the uncircumcision, even as Peter with the Good News for the circumcision 2:8 (for he who appointed Peter to the apostleship of the circumcision appointed me also to the Gentiles); 2:9 and when they perceived the grace that was given to me, James and Cephas and John,[3] they who were reputed to be pillars, gave to me and Barnabas the right hand of fellowship, that we should go to the Gentiles, and they to the circumcision. 2:10 They only asked us to remember the poor--which very thing I was also zealous to do.

1. *went up again to Jerusalem.* Jerusalem, in humanity, represents the abiding consciousness of spiritual peace, which is the result of continuous realizations of spiritual power tempered with spiritual poise and confidence. It represents the habitation of peace, or the dwelling place of peace. (MBD/Jerusalem)

2. *Barnabas, Paul.* Barnabas and Paul are chosen for missionary work among the Gentiles because of their superior qualifications for the task, mainly their firm faith, loyalty, courage, and resourcefulness, as well as their zeal for Truth. The will (Paul) and imagination (Barnabas) illumined by the Christ turn all the thoughts toward Truth.

3. *James and Cephas and John.* [Judgment, Faith and Love are pillars of the church (orthodox religion) that give the right hand of fellowship to transformed will and quickened imagination (metaphysical religion).] The right hand of fellowship is the seal of approval that evidences the bond of harmony and union between those of the same mind.

## An Example of Spiritual Elitism.

2:11 But when Peter came to Antioch,[1] I resisted him to his face, because he stood condemned. 2:12 For before some people came from James, he ate with the Gentiles. But when they came, he drew back and separated himself, fearing those who were of the circumcision.[2] 2:13 And the rest of the Jews[3] joined him in his hypocrisy; so that even Barnabas was carried away with their hypocrisy. 2:14 But when I saw that they didn't walk uprightly according to the truth of the Good News, I said to Peter before them all, "If you, being a Jew, live as the Gentiles do, and not as the Jews do, why do you compel the Gentiles to live as the Jews do?[4]

1. *when Peter came to Antioch.* The church that was established at Antioch symbolizes an assembling of spiritual thoughts, the first establishment of our awareness of Christ consciousness. (MBI/Acts 13) [It was there that followers of Jesus were first called "Christians". So Antioch represents a state of mind guided by "formulated theology" instead of spiritual understanding. Peter in the Antioch state of mind has abandoned the right hand of fellowship established in Jerusalem.] The Antioch state of mind must be *thoroughly* Christened. (MBD/Antioch)

2. *fearing those who were of the circumcision.* Our ideas of God and of our relation to God must undergo a great change before we can begin uplifting and unifying the whole person (Jew and Gentile). Peter did not know that circumcision, spiritually, signifies the setting free of the individual from the law of sin and death. (RW/circumcision)

3. *Gentiles, Jews.* The Jews symbolize our religious thoughts and the Gentiles symbolize our worldly thoughts. Gentiles are worldly thoughts pertaining to the external, or thoughts that function through the senses. Jews in their highest aspect symbolize divine ideas, or spiritual consciousness. Each individual has a formless mind and a formed mind, and these two minds seem in the present race consciousness to be hostile one to the other. (MBD/Jews)

4. *why do you compel the Gentiles to live as the Jews do?* The lesson here is that a spiritually immature Peter, captive to the Antioch state of formalized theology, fears being set free from the law of sin and death.

## The Transformation of the Soul

2:15 "We, being Jews by nature, and not Gentile sinners, 2:16 yet knowing that a man is not justified by the works of the law but through faith in Jesus Christ,[1] even we believed in Christ Jesus, that we might be justified by faith in Christ, and not by the works of the law, because no flesh will be justified by the works of the law. 2:17 But if, while we sought to be justified in Christ, we ourselves also were found sinners, is Christ a servant of sin? Certainly not! 2:18 For if I build up again those things which I destroyed, I prove myself a law-breaker. 2:19 For I, through the law, died to the law, that I might live to God. 2:20 I have been crucified with Christ,[2] and it is no longer I that live, but Christ living in me. That life which I now live in the flesh, I live by faith in the Son of God, who loved me, and gave himself up for me. 2:21 I don't make void the grace of God.[3] For if righteousness is through the law, then Christ died for nothing!"

1. *not justified by the works of the law but through faith in Jesus Christ.* [Paul came to his understanding of "justification by grace through faith" because of his inability to achieve a perfect expression by will and intellect. He was a good Pharisee, but he knew that his life was not sufficient to achieve the full expression of his true nature. The will is one of the Twelve Powers, our decision making faculty that moves the other faculties into action. The problem with the will is that it cannot see the reality of Divine ideas. So Paul's mission was to conquer the will and intellect and to place it in service to his Christ nature. Paul's discovery is that the it is the faculty of faith, our ability to perceive the reality of the oneness of God and the flow of Divine ideas, that enables us to achieve perfect expression. (Divine Ideas in Paul's Writings)]

2. *I have been crucified with Christ...* [An important message for strong-willed persons: First, it is Paul (the will) who is crucified. Second, the will is not crucified alone, but rather crucified *with Christ*. Third, the will is transformed, not in its status before God (it still lives "in the flesh") but rather in its new reliance on faith. Finally, the will is now, possibly for the first time, aware of being loved.]

3. *make void the grace of God.* We make void the grace of God by refusing to ex-

press divine goodness (ideas), which is the fundamental principle of Being. Everyone can do good and thus prove that the Christ is risen in our mind and heart. It is not enough to understand spiritual teachings.

We must live the Truth we know. (Unity Principle #5)

---

Fillmore Study Bible annotations compiled by Thomas Scheinler.

# Galatians 3

## First Steps to Spiritual Consciousness

3:1 Foolish Galatians,[1] who has bewitched you not to obey the truth, before whose eyes Jesus Christ was openly set forth among you as crucified? 3:2 I just want to learn this from you. Did you receive the Spirit by the works of the law, or by hearing of faith? 3:3 Are you so foolish? Having begun in the Spirit, are you now completed in the flesh? 3:4 Did you suffer so many things in vain, if it is indeed in vain? 3:5 He therefore who supplies the Spirit to you, and works miracles among you,[2] does he do it by the works of the law, or by hearing of faith?

3:6 Even as Abraham[3] "believed God, and it was counted to him for righteousness." 3:7 Know therefore that those who are of faith, the same are children of Abraham. 3:8 The Scripture, foreseeing that God would justify the Gentiles by faith, preached the Good News[4] beforehand to Abraham, saying, "In you all the nations will be blessed."[2] 3:9 So then, those who are of faith are blessed with the faithful Abraham.

3:10 For as many as are of the works of the law are under a curse. For it is written, "Cursed is everyone who doesn't continue in all things that are written in the book of the law, to do them."[3] 3:11 Now that no man is justified by the law before God is evident, for, "The righteous will live by faith."[4][5] 3:12 The law is not of faith, but, "The man who does them will live by them."[5]

3:13 Christ redeemed us from the curse of the law, having become a curse for us. For it is written, "Cursed is everyone who hangs on a tree,"[6][6] 3:14 that the blessing of Abraham might come on the Gentiles through Christ Jesus; that we might receive the promise of the Spirit through faith.

1. *Foolish Galatians.* Galatians, represents the thoughts to the Galatia state of consciousness. (Galatia signifies a state of thought that is not yet ready for the operation of the word of truth.) (MBD/Galatia)

2. *works miracles among you.* Miracles are events that take lace as a result of the operation of higher unknown law. All things happenings are the result of cause and can be explained under the law of cause and effect. (MBD/miracles)

3. *Abraham.* Abraham is the power of the mind to reproduce its ideas in unlimited expression. (MBD/Abraham) Metaphysically, Abraham represents the first step in our redemption from mortal to spiritual consciousness. (Elizabeth Sand Turner/*Let*

*There Be Light*)

4. *Good News*. The Good news of Jesus is that each of us can become God incarnate. It is not alone a gospel of right living, but also shows the way into dominion and power equal to and surpassing that of Jesus of Nazareth. (RW/Gospel)

5. *The righteous will live by faith*. Righteousness is a state of harmony established in consciousness through the right use of God-given attributes. (RW/righteousness)

6. *Cursed is everyone who hangs on a tree*. See Deuteronomy 21:22-23. [Don't let your mistakes hang on a tree. Let go and bury them.]

## A Covenant, Metaphysically Understood

3:15 Brothers, speaking of human terms, though it is only a man's covenant,[1] yet when it has been confirmed, no one makes it void, or adds to it. 3:16 Now the promises were spoken to Abraham and to his seed. He doesn't say, "To seeds," as of many, but as of one, "To your seed,"[7] which is Christ. 3:17 Now I say this. A covenant confirmed beforehand by God in Christ, the law, which came four hundred thirty years after, does not annul, so as to make the promise of no effect. 3:18 For if the inheritance is of the law, it is no more of promise; but God has granted it to Abraham by promise.

1. *covenant*. The covenant of the Bible represents the principles or rules by which men are able to gain their true spiritual heritage and possess the riches of the kingdom of God. All God's children are promised perfect health, prosperity, peace, light, and happiness, but it is necessary for us to abide by the spiritual law if we would gain the blessings of Spirit. (MBD/covenant)

## A New Understanding of Divine Law

3:19 What then is the law?[1] It was added because of transgressions, until the seed should come to whom the promise has been made. It was ordained through angels by the hand of a mediator. 3:20 Now a mediator is not between one, but God is one.

3:21 Is the law then against the promises of God? Certainly not! For if there had been a law given which could make alive, most certainly righteousness would have been of the law. 3:22 But the Scriptures imprisoned all things under sin, that the promise by faith in Jesus Christ might be given to those who believe.

3:23 But before faith came, we were kept in custody under the law, confined for the faith which should afterwards be revealed. 3:24 So that the law has become our tutor to bring us to Christ, that we might be justified by faith. 3:25 But now that faith has come, we are no longer under a tutor. 3:26 For you are all children of God, through faith in Christ Jesus. 3:27 For as many of you as were baptized[2] into Christ have put on Christ. 3:28 There is neither Jew nor Greek, there is neither slave nor free man, there is neither male nor female;[3] for you are all one in Christ Jesus.[4] 3:29 If you are Christ's, then you are Abraham's seed and heirs according to promise.

1. *What then is the law?* Jesus taught a new understanding of divine law. He acknowledged mechanical cause and effect, but he knew it was possible to "fulfill the law" by transcending its strictly mechanical repetition. This can be done only by certain changes of consciousness. One of these changes is to let go of the insistence of "even-exchanges" in life all the time.

Another change is to be willing to forgive sin instead of insisting on punishment for sin. Grace is the name given to the aspect of divine law which does not deal in "even-exchanging," but in the increase of good through greater giving. Ed Rabel/Metaphysics 1, The Divine Paradox, Law/Grace

2. *baptized.* The spiritual cleansing of the mind, the first step in the realization of truth. (RW/baptism)

3. *There is neither Jew nor Greek.* Often blessings may seem to come to us through human instrumentality, but back of appearances is the unalterable law of God and it is only as we conform our lives to the Christ standard that the gifts of the kingdom can come to us.

4. *for you are all one in Christ Jesus.* On what principle does the law of Christ operate? The principle of unity. "Ye all are the man in Christ Jesus."

Fillmore Study Bible annotations compiled by Thomas Scheinler.

**World English Bible Footnotes:**

[2] v3:8. Genesis 12:3; 18:18; 22:18

[3] v3:10. Deuteronomy 27:26

[4] v3:11. Habakkuk 2:4

[5] v3:12. Leviticus 18:5

[6] v3:13. Deuteronomy 21:23

[7] v3:16. Genesis 12:7; 13:15; 24:7

# Galatians 4

## The Birth and and Expression of Divine Law

4:1 But I say that so long as the
heir is a child, he is no different from
a bondservant, though he is lord of
all; 4:2 but is under guardians and
stewards until the day appointed by
the father. 4:3 So we also, when we
were children, were held in bondage
under the elemental principles of the
world. 4:4 But when the fullness of
the time came,(1) God sent out his
Son,(2) born to a woman, born under
the law, 4:5 that he might redeem
those who were under the law,(3) that
we might receive the adoption of
children. 4:6 And because you are
children, God sent out the Spirit of
his Son into your hearts, crying,
"Abba,[8] Father!" 4:7 So you are no
longer a bondservant, but a son; and
if a son, then an heir of God through
Christ.

1. *when the fullness of the time came.* We cannot enter into spiritual consciousness until we meet and fulfill the conditions that govern it. When we do this "the fulness of the time" comes for us, and we enter naturally.

2. *God sent out his Son, born to a woman, born under the law.* God's Son is the Christ, the perfect idea of humanness or ideal of perfection in our soul. *Woman* represents our soul, and *the law* is the law of the Spirit of life in Christ.

3. *that he might redeem those who were*

*under the law.* Do outer conditions always conform to inner conditions? Not always immediately. Inner conditions are conditions of the mind and heart. Outer conditions become manifest according to the pattern of the inner.

## Paul Appeals to Our Higher Consciousness

4:8 However at that time, not knowing God, you were in bondage to those who by nature are not gods. 4:9 But now that you have come to know God, or rather to be known by God, why do you turn back again to the weak and miserable elemental principles,[1] to which you desire to be in bondage all over again? 4:10 You observe days, months, seasons, and years. 4:11 I am afraid for you, that I might have wasted my labor for you. 4:12 I beg you, brothers, become as I am, for I also have become as you are. You did me no wrong, 4:13 but you know that because of weakness of the flesh I preached the Good News to you the first time. 4:14 That which was a temptation to you in my flesh, you didn't despise nor reject; but you received me as an angel of God, even as Christ Jesus.[2]

4:15 What was the blessing you enjoyed? For I testify to you that, if possible, you would have plucked out your eyes and given them to me. 4:16 So then, have I become your enemy by telling you the truth? 4:17 They zealously seek you in no good way. No, they desire to alienate you, that you may seek them. 4:18 But it is always good to be zealous in a good cause,[3] and not only when I am present with you.

4:19 My little children, of whom I am again in travail until Christ is formed in you[4]-- 4:20 but I could wish to be present with you now, and to change my tone, for I am perplexed about you.

1. *the weak and miserable elemental principles.* [The natural law of cause and effect. Also mentioned in v.3]

2. *but you received me as an angel of God, even as Christ Jesus.* [An early expression of *I Behold the Christ in You.*]

3. *always good to be zealous in a good cause.* Zeal is intensity, ardor, enthusiasm; the inward fire of the soul that urges man onward, regardless of the intellectual mind of caution and conservatism (RW/zeal).

4. *until Christ is formed in you.* Christ is a living presence, not a personality. *Can Christ Prevent War?*, Unity Magazine Dec. 1937

## We are Born in Freedom

4:21 Tell me, you that desire to be under the law, don't you listen to the law? 4:22 For it is written that Abraham had two sons, one by the handmaid,[1] and one by the free woman.[2] 4:23 However, the son by the handmaid was born according to the flesh, but the son by the free woman was born through promise. 4:24 These things contain an allegory, for these are two covenants. One is from Mount Sinai, bearing children to bondage, which is Hagar. 4:25 For this Hagar is Mount Sinai in Arabia, and answers to the Jerusalem[3] that exists now, for she is in bondage with her children. 4:26 But the Jerusalem that is above is free, which is the mother of us all. 4:27 For it is written,

"Rejoice, you barren who don't
bear.
Break forth and shout, you
that don't travail.

> For more are the children of
> the desolate than of her
> who has a husband."[9]

4:28 Now we, brothers, as Isaac
was, are children of promise.[4] 4:29
But as then, he who was born
according to the flesh persecuted
him who was born according to the
Spirit, so also it is now. 4:30 However
what does the Scripture say? "Throw
out the handmaid and her son, for
the son of the handmaid will not
inherit with the son of the free
woman."[10] 4:31 So then, brothers, we
are not children of a handmaid, but
of the free woman.

1. *one by the handmaid.* Hagar, the natural soul. It is a stranger to the awakened spiritual phase of the soul, in that its thoughts and emotions are sensual and are likely to be selfish and unholy, thus producing fear and uncertainty (wanderer). (MBD/Hagar) [The first born from the handmaid is our birth to its highest nature in physical form. Hence, we are above the animals yet still a servant to the physical realm.]

2. *one by the free woman.* Sarah, The soul, the affectional, emotional part of the man. It is the daughter of the king (princess) and should never be allowed to unite in any way with matter or with material conditions. (MBD/Sarah) [The Son born from the free woman, represents us in our highest nature. Our true nature is connected to and working with God/Mind. We are in high, free spiritual consciousness.]

3. *Arabia, Jerusalem. Arabia*, an outer, or Gentile, state of consciousness that in its wild, ignorant undisciplined, and unsettled nature is destructive in its tendency and is unproductive of good (MBD/Arabia) *Jerusalem*, the spiritual center in consciousness. In man it is the abiding consciousness of spiritual peace. (MBD/Jerusalem)

4. *we ... as Isaac was, are children of promise.* Isaac, meaning laughter, signifies the joy of the new birth and new life in Christ. (MBD/Isaac)

Fillmore Study Bible annotations compiled by Thomas Scheinler.

**World English Bible Footnotes:**

[8] v4:6. Abba is a Greek spelling for the Aramaic word for "Father" or "Daddy" used in a familiar, respectful, and loving way.

[9] v4:27. Isaiah 54:1

[10] v4:30. Genesis 21:10

# Galatians 5

## The Nature of Christian Freedom

5:1 Stand firm therefore in the
liberty by which Christ has made us
free, and don't be entangled again
with a yoke of bondage. 5:2 Behold,
I, Paul,[1] tell you that if you receive
circumcision, Christ will profit you
nothing. 5:3 Yes, I testify again to
every man who receives
circumcision, that he is a debtor to
do the whole law. 5:4 You are
alienated from Christ, you who
desire to be justified by the law. You
have fallen away from grace.[2] 5:5 For
we, through the Spirit, by faith wait

for the hope of righteousness. 5:6 For in Christ Jesus neither circumcision[3] amounts to anything, nor uncircumcision, but faith[4] working through love.[5] 5:7 You were running well! Who interfered with you that you should not obey the truth? 5:8 This persuasion is not from him who calls you. 5:9 A little yeast grows through the whole lump. 5:10 I have confidence toward you in the Lord that you will think no other way. But he who troubles you will bear his judgment, whoever he is.

5:11 But I, brothers, if I still preach circumcision, why am I still persecuted? Then the stumbling block of the cross has been removed. 5:12 I wish that those who disturb you would cut themselves off. 5:13 For you, brothers, were called for freedom. Only don't use your freedom for gain to the flesh, but through love be servants to one another.[6] 5:14 For the whole law is fulfilled in one word,[7] in this: "You shall love your neighbor as yourself."[11] 5:15 But if you bite and devour one another, be careful that you don't consume one another.

1. *Paul.* Metaphysically, Paul is the word of the Spirit of truth. The converted Paul (formerly Saul, the will) becomes, by the power of the word, the most active thought in the establishment of good throughout our being. (MBD/Paul)

2. *You have fallen away from grace.* Jesus taught a new understanding of divine law. He acknowledged mechanical cause and effect, but he knew it was possible to "fulfill the law" by transcending its strictly mechanical repetition. This can be done only by certain changes of consciousness. One of these changes is to let go of the insistence of "even-exchanges" in life all the time. Another change is to be willing to forgive sin instead of insisting on punishment for sin. Grace is the name given to the aspect of divine law which does not deal in "even-exchanging," but in the increase of good through greater giving. (Ed Rabel/Metaphysics 1, The Divine Paradox, Law/Grace).

3. *circumcision.* The cutting off mortal tendencies; indicative of purification and cleanliness under divine law. (RW/circumcision)

4. *faith.* The perceiving power of the mind linked with the power to shape substance. Spiritual assurance: the power to do the seemingly impossible. (RW/faith)

5. *love.* The pure essence of Being that binds together the whole human family. Of all the attributes of God, love is undoubtedly the most beautiful. In Divine Mind, love is the power that joins and binds in divine harmony the universe and everything in it; the great harmonizing principle known to man. (RW/love)

6. *Only don't use your freedom for gain to the flesh, but through love be servants to one another.* Rites, ceremonies, and laws for the conduct of Christians are necessary for discipline and, faithfully followed, hold sense consciousness in check. When the liberty of Christ is revealed and we discern that it is no longer necessary for us to be bound to the observance of the church ritual, we are likely to go to the other extreme, letting license instead of the higher wisdom of Christ, lead him.

7. *the whole law is fulfilled in one word.* How does the divine law as perceived by Moses compare with the law of Christ? The Mosaic law is largely negative in form, as is evidenced by "Thou shall not" often repeated. The law of Christ is affirmative: "Thou shalt love thy neighbor". In this verse Paul gives the Golden Rule which Jesus taught through in a slightly different form.

## The Works of the Flesh

5:16 But I say, walk by the Spirit,[1] and you won't fulfill the lust of the flesh. 5:17 For the flesh lusts against the Spirit, and the Spirit against the flesh;[2] and these are contrary to one another, that you may not do the things that you desire. 5:18 But if you are led by the Spirit, you are not under the law.[3] 5:19 Now the works of the flesh are obvious, which are: adultery, sexual immorality, uncleanness, lustfulness, 5:20 idolatry,

sorcery, hatred, strife, jealousies,
outbursts of anger, rivalries,
divisions, heresies, 5:21 envyings,
murders, drunkenness, orgies, and
things like these; of which I forewarn
you, even as I also forewarned you,
that those who practice such things
will not inherit the Kingdom of God.

1. *walk by the Spirit.* Spirit is God as the moving force in the universe; Principle as the breath of life in all creation; the principle of life; creative intelligence and life (RW/Spirit). To walk by the Spirit is to think love, joy, peace, long-suffering, kindness, goodness, faithfulness, meekness, self control.

2. *For the flesh lusts against the Spirit, and the Spirit against the flesh.* Lust is sense consciousness, which causes human beings to be tempted (RW/lust). There should be no strife between Spirit and the flesh. We should not build up a thought of strife anywhere, especially not in our own thought world. Jesus said, "Agree with thine adversary." Animal trainers say that it is very much easier to love animals into obedience than to ship them into obedience. For the same reason a Christian metaphysician trains his animal nature to obey him through love. Firmness is necessary to such training, but resentment is not, nor is the fear of punishment.

3. *But if you are led by the Spirit, you are not under the law.* Many of the Galatian followers of Christ were Jews, who believed that their salvation depended upon their observing the rites of the Jewish religion, especially the rite of circumcision. In this lesson Paul was expounding his favorite text, "Where the Spirit of the Lord is, there is liberty." Real Christians do not live under human law but under grace. A higher mental and spiritual atmosphere envelops the whole life activity of those who put on Christ. All religious and natural laws, by reason of their inherent inefficiency, cease to affect the life of him who enters into the love of God, which is also called grace.

## The Fruit of the Spirit

5:22 But the fruit of the Spirit❶ is
love, joy, peace, patience, kindness,
goodness, faith,[12] 5:23 gentleness,
and self-control.❷ Against such
things there is no law.❸ 5:24 Those
who belong to Christ have crucified
the flesh❹ 5:25 If we live by the Spirit,
let's also walk by the Spirit.❺ 5:26 Let's
not become conceited, provoking
one another, and envying one
another.

1. *fruit of the Spirit.* These are proofs of the Spirit. Whoever exhibits these qualities in their daily living possesses and is possessed by the Spirit in the measure in which they expresses them. [They are not the same as the gifts of the Spirit given in Romans 12:6-8 and First Corinthians 12:8-10.]

2. *Love:* the pure essence of Being that binds together the whole human family (RW/love). The practical application of charity was probably the most potent single cause of Christian success (Henry Chadwick, *The Penguin History of the (Early) Church*). *Joy:* the happiness of God expressed through God's perfect idea—human beings (RW/joy). *Peace:* harmony and tranquillity derived from awareness of the Christ consciousness (RW/peace). *Patience:* an attitude of mind characterized by poise, inner calmness, and quiet endurance, especially in the face of trying conditions. Patience has its foundation in faith, and it is perfected only in those who have unwavering faith in God (RW/patience). *Kindness:* the kindness of God is revealed to us as we give it active expression (MBI/Colossians 3). *Goodness:* (NRSV, generosity) there is always a saving grace in divine goodness; and if we have ever done a kind act, it has been preserved in the careful records of memory and will come forth when we most need it (RW/goodness). *Faithfulness:* faithfulness "perceives" the good that we desire to demonstrate (show forth in our outer life), and it keeps us on the goal toward its attainment (Correspondence School Course, Series 1, Lesson 3, Annotation 13). *Gentleness:* the Christ Spirit of gentleness wins the heart of a transgressor, whereas censure and harshness fail to reach him (MBI/Galatians 6). *Self-control:* The capacity to direct one's behavior in right ways. One who tries to establish self-control through will power and suppression never accom-

plishes permanent results. Self-control is accomplished when all the forces of man come in touch with the divine will and understanding (RW/self-control).

3. *Against such things there is no law.* See comment for Galatians 5:18.

4. *crucified the flesh.* [Traditional Christianity says the fruits are a sign or outcome of the work of Spirit within a human being. Whether that Spirit is a transcendent Holy Spirit or the Spirit of the Metaphysical Trinity of Man (Spirit, Soul, Body) is unclear. Chrysostom believed it was the inner Spirit at work. He wrote, "For if the statement mentions the flesh and the Spirit, where is the soul? Is Paul then speaking of soulless beings? For if the evil belongs to the flesh and the good to the Spirit, then the soul would be superfluous. Not at all; for the ordering of the passions is the work of the soul and concerns the soul. The soul is situated in the middle of the struggle between virtue and vice. If the soul uses the body as it should, it makes itself more spiritual." (*Homily on Galatians*). How does the soul "order the passions"? According to Ed Rabel, it does so by proper use of the Twelve Powers. He writes, "Joy is not one of the twelve faculties, but joy is one of the fruits of the spirit or rewards one gets for using the twelve powers correctly. Peace is not one of the twelve faculties; peace is a fruit of the spirit and the reward one gets for using the twelve faculties. But the twelve faculties themselves are what Mr. Fillmore says they are; they are the originals; they are the Divine Ideas embodied into human nature as faculties and can be expressed by man through his human nature to serve the Christ." (Ed Rabel, Old Testament Lectures, p.44)]

5. *If we live by the Spirit, let's also walk by the Spirit.* A person can allow his feelings alone to absorb his faculties, remaining either too indolent or too different to express them clearly or fully. The Spirit is quenched by this subserviences to the opinions of others or by spiritual laziness. The Spirit is not a mood to be enjoyed selfishly; it is a motivating principle or power.

Fillmore Study Bible annotations compiled by Thomas Scheinler and Rev. Mark Hicks.

**World English Bible Footnotes:**

[11] v5:14. Leviticus 19:18

[12] v5:22. or, faithfulness

# Galatians 6

## True Christian Responsibility

[6:1] Brothers, even if a man is
caught in some fault, you who are
spiritual must restore such a one in
a spirit of gentleness; looking to
yourself so that you also aren't
tempted. [6:2] Bear one another's
burdens, and so fulfill the law of
Christ. [6:3] For if a man thinks himself
to be something when he is nothing,
he deceives himself. [6:4] But let each
man test his own work, and then he
will take pride in himself and not in
his neighbor. [6:5] For each man will
bear his own burden.❶ [6:6] But let him
who is taught in the word share all
good things with him who teaches.
[6:7] Don't be deceived. God is not
mocked, for whatever a man sows,
that he will also reap.❷ [6:8] For he
who sows to his own flesh will from
the flesh reap corruption. But he who
sows to the Spirit❸ will from the

Spirit reap eternal life. 6:9 Let us not be weary in doing good, for we will reap in due season, if we don't give up. 6:10 So then, as we have opportunity, let's do what is good toward all men, and especially toward those who are of the household of the faith.

1. *Bear one another's burdens; For each man will bear his own burden.* We bear one another's burdens by realizing that the Christ in each one of us is the great burden bearer for all. "Come unit me, all ye that labor and are heavy laden, and I will give you rest." If Christ is the great burden bearer, what is the meaning of the 5th verse? We cannot lay the responsibility for our acts upon other persons. But Christ saves us all from the thought of personal responsibility. "Christ redeemed us from the curse of the law."

2. *God is not mocked, for whatever a man sows, that he will also reap.* We deceive ourselves when we imagine that we can think thoughts or speak words without getting definite results in mind, body and affairs. Everything that occurs in our lives is the result of some thought sown in the substance of the mind. "The seed is the word of God."

3. *sows to his own flesh; sows to the Spirit.* Sowing to one's own flesh is thinking that the flesh is the source of life, intelligence, and power. We sow to the Spirit by thinking about spiritual life, affirming it as the source of our eternal existence and conforming our conduct to that affirmation.

## Cutting Off or Restoration?

6:11 See with what large letters I write to you with my own hand. 6:12 As many as desire to look good in the flesh, they compel you to be circumcised; only that they may not be persecuted for the cross of Christ. 6:13 For even they who receive circumcision don't keep the law themselves, but they desire to have you circumcised, that they may boast in your flesh. 6:14 But far be it from me to boast, except in the cross of our Lord Jesus Christ, through which the world has been crucified to me, and I to the world. 6:15 For in Christ Jesus neither is circumcision anything, nor uncircumcision, but a new creation.[1] 6:16 As many as walk by this rule, peace and mercy be on them, and on God's Israel. 6:17 From now on, let no one cause me any trouble, for I bear the marks of the Lord Jesus branded on my body.

6:18 The grace of our Lord Jesus Christ be with your spirit, brothers. Amen.

1. *For in Christ Jesus neither is circumcision anything, nor uncircumcision, but a new creation.* [Circumcision is the will cutting off mortal tendencies; a new creation is a full restoration of the the divine human being.]

---

Fillmore Study Bible annotations compiled by Thomas Scheinler.

# Paul's Letter to the Ephesians

Temple of Hadrianus in Ephesus, Turkey. Wikipedia Commons. Public Domain.

## Introduction to Ephesians

As a background for this Epistle, it should be realled that Paul, during his third missionary journey, spent nearly three years at Ephesus. The indications are that a sizable Christian group was built up during this period. (See Acts 19.) The New Testament also makes it clear that Paul held the Ephesian converts in high regard, for while the apostle was on his way to Jerusalem, in preparation for his journey to Rome, he arranged a special meeting with the elders of the Ephesian Church. (See Acts 20:17-37.) However, when the Epistle to the Ephesians was written, Paul had completed his projected journey, and was being held under house arrest at Rome. Why, then, did Paul feel called upon to write to his converts at Ephesus at that time? What had transpired at Ephesus to give rise to this Epistle?

Apparently the Epistle arose out of a visit made by one of Paul's converts, a man named Epaphras. Epaphras' home was in Colossae (Asia Minor), but he was also well acquainted with the membership and activities of the Christian group at Ephesus. When Epaphras journeyed to Rome on some personal business, he sought out Paul, and acquainted the apostle with the latest developments among the Christian groups in Asia Minor. In regard to the work at Ephesus, he reported that the friendly relationship between Jewish and Gentile Christians, which Paul had so effectively promoted, was rapidly deteriorating. Also, since Paul's arrest and imprisonment there was a lack of Christian leadership at Ephesus. Aquila and Priscilla were good persons, but they did not possess the qualifications to deal with arising difficulties in the church; consequently, there was considerable disorder there. Furthermore, the converts were becoming confused regarding the Christian doctrine and its practical application. The Ephesians scarcely knew what they were supposed to believe, and many of them were starting to formulate their own doctrines.

Paul sought to meet this situation by writing his Epistle to the Ephesians. First he endeavored to restore harmony between the Jewish and Gentile Christians at Ephesus—giving full recognition to the freedom of the Gentiles, but also reminding them of their indebtedness to "the commonwealth of Israel" (Eph. 2:12). Then the authoritative statements given in the Epistle provided the needed leadership for the church at Ephesus. The Ephesians would recognize that Paul was still at the head of affairs, and they could unhesitatingly follow his directions. Also in this Epistle Paul gave a simple, clear exposition of the Christian teaching—telling the Ephesians what they should believe, and how they should conduct themselves, so that there need be no further con- fusion regarding the meaning and purpose of the Gospel message. The following special features of this Epistle should be carefully noted.

STYLE: The writing in Paul's Epistle to the Ephesians is quite informal, and stands in marked contrast to the formal style used in his Epistle to the Romans. This is understandable. Paul was well acquainted with the leaders at Ephesus, while they in turn regarded the apostle as both spiritual leader and personal friend. Consequently the Epistle reads like a friendly letter, and the various matters are dealt with just as they came uppermost in the apostle's mind. For this reason, it is not advisable to attempt a formal outline of the Epistle to the Ephesians, as was done with the Epistle to the Romans. However, this difficulty will be dealt with later on in the lesson.

MATURE VIEWPOINT: Earlier in the lesson reference was made to Paul's spiritual development, as indicated in his Epistles of the Imprisonment. An actual instance or two will make this clear. In his Epistles to the Thessalonians and Corinthians, Paul writes of resurrection in the future tense—associating this with the Second Coming of the Lord. But in Ephesians, Paul refers to resurrection as a present experience. (See Eph. 2:1-6.) Note how he writes: "even when we were dead . . . [God] made us alive together with Christ. . . and raised us up with him" (Eph. 2:5-6). He further urges that "we may no longer be children . . . Rather. . . grow up in every way unto him who is the head, into Christ" (Eph. 4:14-15). Of course these statements may be interpreted as having reference to Christian baptism, or something similar, but the teaching is clearly of more advanced character than that given in Paul's earlier Epistles.

METAPHYSICAL MEANING: In an earlier lesson, Ephesus was explained as meaning "desirable," or "appealing." Ephesus symbolizes "that central building faculty of the consciousness, called desire." (MBD/Ephesus) The application of this desire to physical things, or experiences, led to those disturbing conditions during Paul's ministry at Ephesus. (See Acts 19:23-41.) But this desire may also be for spiritual attainments or experiences. Paul recognized that the great desire of his Ephesian converts was for this spiritual development. He thought of them as desiring to know "what are the riches of his glorious inheritance, and what is the immeasurable greatness of his power in us who believe" (Eph. 1:18-19). Therefore the apostle, in this Epistle, clearly presented the necessary steps to betaken in quickening and developing spiritual consciousness—through which would come the fulfillment of this high desire. All these steps are clearly indicated, and may be now set forth in order, together with what we may regard as the main theme of the Epistle.

THEME: ATTAinING AND MAINTANING SPIRITUAL CONSCIOUSNESS

First Step: The Awakening. "Awake, O sleeper, and arise from the dead, and Christ shall give you light" (Eph. 5:14). In all probability, Paul was here quoting from a familiar early church hymn—but the wording seems most appropriate. This awakening is sometimes referred to as an inner quickening, or spiritual illumination.

Second Step: The Practice of Prayer. The student should read again the prayer given in Ephesians 3:14-21—especially noting how the apostle prays that "Christ may dwell in your hearts through faith" (Eph. 3:17)—quite an advance over the far-off conception given in Paul's earlier Epistles! In giving this prayer, Paul is setting an example for his converts. Later in the Epistle he urges them to "Pray at all times in the Spirit, with all prayer and supplication . . . making supplication for all the saints, and also for me" (Eph. 6:18-19). The student should also read Paul's earlier prayer, as recorded in the opening chapter of the Epistle. (See Eph. 1:16-23.)

Third Step: Daily Christian Living. "Lead a life worthy of the calling to which you have been called" (Eph. 4:1); "Be imitators of God, as beloved children. And walk in love, as Christ loved us" (Eph. 5:2). The apostle then gives detailed directions for Christian living, covering many daily activities. (See Eph.4:17-32; 5:1-33; 6:1-9.)

Fourth Step: Needful Spiritual Protection. "Therefore, take the whole armor of God, that you may be able to withstand in the evil day, and having done all, to stand" (Eph. 6:13). Every piece of the Christian's protective armor should be carefully checked, and its use and metaphysical significance noted. (See Eph. 6:10-20.)

Fifth Step: Right Use of Spiritual Gifts. "And his gifts were . . . for the equipment of the saints, for the work of the ministry, for the building up of the body of Christ" (Eph. 4:11-12). In this connection, it will be helpful to refer back to Paul's earlier discus- sion of spiritual gifts, given in First Corinthians, Chapters 12,13, and 14.

Sixth Step: The Christian's Objective. The converts are urged to press onward in all this spiritual development, "until we all attain to the unity of the faith and the knowledge of the Son of God, to mature manhood, to the measure of the stature of the fullness of Christ" (Eph. 4:13).

Introduction to *Paul's Letter to the Ephesians* by Herbert J. Hunt, former

Dean of Bible Studies for the Unity School of Christianity.

Ephesians and Colossians have similar vocabulary and similar structure. While most scholars believe they were written after Paul's death by a disciple, the both have much in common with Philippians and Philemon, letters that also reflect the zeal, power, love and wisdom, for both letters convey the essential spiritual principle of oneness and unity, both in the church and in consciousness.

Ephesians appears to be a compilation of Paul's thought, filled with short, beautiful passages commenting on the oneness and unity of the church: "for by grace you have been saved (2:8)," "For he is our peace (2:14)," "creating a new humanity in place of the two, thus making peace (2:15)," "making every effort to maintain the unity of the Spirit in the bond of peace (4:2)." It may be that, after the destruction of the Temple and the final split between Judaism and Christianity, the writer is attempting to unify Jewish-Christians and Gentile-Christians.

Both Ephesians and Colossians describe a oneness and unity in consciousness with repeated reference to the term mystery, such as "the mystery that has been hidden throughout the ages and generations but has now been revealed to his saints. To them God chose to make known how great among the Gentiles are the riches of the glory of this mystery, which is Christ in you, the hope of glory" (Col. 1:26-27). The mystic is "one who has intimate, firsthand acquaintance with God ... Jesus was the greatest mystic of all ages" (Revealing Word, mystic). Many scholars believe that these references were subtle arguments against the encroachment of Gnosticism in the church, which taught a form of duality.

Introduction to *Paul's Letter to the Ephesians* by Rev. Mark Hicks.

# Ephesians 1

## Salutation

1:1 Paul, an apostle of Christ Jesus
through the will of God,
to the saints who are at Ephesus,(1)
and the faithful in Christ Jesus: 1:2
Grace to you and peace from God our
Father and the Lord Jesus Christ.

1. *Ephesus* Metaphysically, Ephesus is the central building faculty of the consciousness called desire. In its physical aspect Ephesus symbolizes the stomach. In its mental aspect it symbolizes the ganglionic center at the pit of the stomach, which controls and directs all the organs pertaining to digestion and assimilation. (MBD/ Ephesus)

## Spiritual Blessings in Christ

1:3 Blessed be the God and Father of our Lord Jesus Christ, who has blessed us with every spiritual blessing in the heavenly places in Christ; 1:4 even as he chose us in him before the foundation of the world, that we would be holy and without blemish before him in love; 1:5 having predestined us for adoption as children through Jesus Christ to himself, according to the good pleasure of his desire, 1:6 to the praise of the glory of his grace, by which he freely bestowed favor on us in the Beloved, 1:7 in whom we have our redemption through his blood,[1] the forgiveness of our trespasses, according to the riches of his grace, 1:8 which he made to abound toward us in all wisdom and prudence, 1:9 making known to us the mystery of his will, according to his good pleasure which he purposed in him 1:10 to an administration of the fullness of the times, to sum up all things in Christ, the things in the heavens, and the things on the earth, in him;[2] 1:11 in whom also we were assigned an inheritance, having been foreordained according to the purpose of him who works all things after the counsel of his will; 1:12 to the end that we should be to the praise of his glory, we who had before hoped in Christ: 1:13 in whom you also, having heard the word of the truth, the Good News of your salvation,--in whom, having also believed, you were sealed with the Holy Spirit of promise, 1:14 who is a pledge of our inheritance, to the redemption of God's own possession, to the praise of his glory.

1. *redemption through his blood.* Christ is the Word of God, and the life of the Word must he a form of energy far transcending any life current that inheres in blood. Blood represents life, but it is only the vehicle that carries life through the body, not the life itself. See 1 John 5:7

2. *to sum up all things in Christ, the things in the heavens, and the things on the earth, in him.* As the one great harmonizer, peace-giver, and health-giver, Jesus Christ teaches that love, in its universal application, will harmonize the world and will give it peace, health, and happiness.

## Paul's Prayer

1:15 For this cause I also, having heard of the faith in the Lord Jesus which is among you, and the love which you have toward all the saints, 1:16 don't cease to give thanks for you, making mention of you in my prayers, 1:17 that the God of our Lord Jesus Christ, the Father of glory, may give to you a spirit of wisdom and revelation in the knowledge of him; 1:18 having the eyes of your hearts[1] enlightened, that you may know what is the hope of his calling, and what are the riches of the glory of his inheritance in the saints, 1:19 and what is the exceeding greatness of his power toward us who believe, according to that working of the strength of his might 1:20 which he worked in Christ, when he raised him from the dead, and made him to sit at his right hand in the heavenly places, 1:21 far above all rule, and authority, and power, and dominion, and every name that is named, not only in this age, but also in that which is to come. 1:22 He put all things in subjection under his feet, and gave him to be head over all things for the assembly, 1:23 which is his body, the fullness of him who fills all in all.[1]

1. *which is his body, the fullness of him*

*who fills all in all.* Is there a parallel between the sowing and the growth of the seeds in the ground and the development in the earth of the church of Christ? Yes, a very close parallel. The word of God is the seed; the soil is the mind; the growth is the development of the idea; the harvest is the fulfillment in the body.

Fillmore Study Bible annotations by Rev. Mark Hicks.

**World English Bible Footnotes:**

[1] v1:18. TR reads "understanding" instead of "hearts"

# Ephesians 2

## From Death to Life

2:1 You were made alive when you were dead in transgressions and sins, 2:2 in which you once walked according to the course of this world, according to the prince of the powers of the air, the spirit who now works in the children of disobedience; 2:3 among whom we also all once lived in the lust of our flesh, doing the desires of the flesh and of the mind, and were by nature children of wrath, even as the rest. 2:4 But God, being rich in mercy,(1) for his great love with which he loved us, 2:5 even when we were dead through our trespasses,(2) made us alive together with Christ(3) (by grace you have been saved), 2:6 and raised us up with him, and made us to sit with him in the heavenly places in Christ Jesus,(4) 2:7 that in the ages to come he might show the exceeding riches of his grace in kindness toward us in Christ Jesus; 2:8 for by grace you have been saved(5) through faith,(6) and that not of yourselves; it is the gift of God, 2:9 not of works, that no one would boast. 2:10 For we are his workmanship,(7) created in Christ Jesus for good works, which God prepared before that we would walk in them.

1. *being rich in mercy.* God as "mercy" is the constant pouring forth of infinite goodness and riches in all qualities that are Godlike. "Grace" is the expression of God qualities in man.

2. *dead through our trespasses.* We are "dead through our trespasses" when we are blinded by the realm of effects, the appearances of inharmony, and the teachings of sin and death as man's inheritance.

3. *made us alive together with Christ.* We are made "alive together with Christ" by renewing our minds. We must behold the eternal Truth that we may realize our Sonship, put on Christ.

4. *the heavenly places in Christ Jesus.* The Christ consciousness "affords" states of joy, peace, and ineffable bliss to those who enter into it. All these are heavenly "places" or conditions of mind and soul.

5. *by grace you have been saved.* Grace is good will; favor; disposition to show mercy; aid from God in the process of regeneration (RW/grace). Jesus taught a new understanding of divine law. He acknowledged mechanical cause and effect, but he knew it was possible to "fulfill the law" by transcending its strictly mechanical repetition. This can be done only by certain changes of consciousness. One of these changes is to let go of the insistence of "even-exchanges" in life all the time. Another change is to be willing to forgive sin

instead of insisting on punishment for sin. Grace is the name given to the aspect of divine law which does not deal in "even-exchanging," but in the increase of good through greater giving. Ed Rabel, Metaphysics 1/The Divine Paradox, Law/Grace. Compare Colossians 2:8, elements of the world

6. *through faith.* Is faith a gift, or must we work for it? Faith is an innate faculty and in this sense is a gift of God; but we must develop our gifts, if we expect them to serve us in time of need.

7. *For we are his workmanship.* The perfect-man idea is the pattern of our true nature. For we are his workmanship, created in Christ Jesus for good works.

## One in Christ

2:11 Therefore remember that once
you, the Gentiles[1] in the flesh,[2]
who are called "uncircumcision" by
that which is called "circumcision,"
(in the flesh, made by hands); 2:12
that you were at that time separate
from Christ, alienated from the
commonwealth of Israel, and
strangers from the covenants of the
promise, having no hope and without
God in the world. 2:13 But now in
Christ Jesus you who once were far
off are made near in the blood of
Christ. 2:14 For he is our peace,[3] who
made both one, and broke down the
middle wall of partition, 2:15 having
abolished in the flesh the hostility,[4]
the law of commandments contained
in ordinances, that he might create
in himself one new man of the two,
making peace; 2:16 and might
reconcile them both in one body to
God through the cross, having killed
the hostility thereby. 2:17 He came
and preached peace[5] to you who
were far off and to those who were
near. 2:18 For through him we both
have our access in one Spirit to the
Father. 2:19 So then you are no longer
strangers and foreigners, but you are
fellow citizens with the saints, and of
the household of God, 2:20 being built
on the foundation of the apostles and
prophets,[6] Christ Jesus himself
being the chief cornerstone; 2:21 in
whom the whole building, fitted
together, grows into a holy temple in
the Lord; 2:22 in whom you also are
built together for a habitation of God
in the Spirit.

1. *Gentiles.* Metaphysically, Gentiles are worldly thoughts—thoughts pertaining to the external, or thoughts that function through the senses. The Gentile is the unregenerate state of mind in us. (MBD/Gentiles)

2. *in the flesh.* flesh, carnal or sensual is a malformation of the substance idea of Being. It must be transformed by right conception of divine perfection before the mortal can put on the immortal. Physically, flesh is mortal consciousness expressing itself through appetite. It is overcome by denying that appetite is physical and by affirming it to be spiritual. (RW/flesh)

3. *For he is our peace.* Scriptures [such as this and the following] must be given spiritual interpretation because the Spirit is back of the letter. "For the letter killeth, but the spirit giveth life" (II Cor. 3:6).

4. *having abolished in the flesh the hostility (ASV, emnity).* The enmity that Jesus Christ abolished was the enmity existing between the Spirit and the flesh.

5. *He came and preached peace.* Did Jesus bring peace upon the earth? No. Paul is referring to that peace of mind which comes to those who are in close cooperation with the Christ principles in their own consciousness. We follow Jesus in establishing peace by making peace among the discords and inharmonies of the mind of the flesh, and raising this state of consciousness to the Christ mind.

6. *being built on the foundation of the apostles and prophets.* How is the building faculty of desire illustrated in this lesson? The last three verses show desire as the great builder, its final work that of "a holy temple in the Lord" or the regenerate man, body, soul, and mind.

Fillmore Study Bible annotations by Rev. Mark Hicks.

# Ephesians 3

## Paul's Ministry to the Gentiles

3:1 For this cause I, Paul, am the prisoner of Christ Jesus on behalf of you Gentiles, 3:2 if it is so that you have heard of the administration of that grace of God which was given me toward you; 3:3 how that by revelation the mystery was made known to me,[1] as I wrote before in few words, 3:4 by which, when you read, you can perceive my understanding in the mystery of Christ; 3:5 which in other generations was not made known to the children of men, as it has now been revealed to his holy apostles and prophets in the Spirit; 3:6 that the Gentiles are fellow heirs, and fellow members of the body, and fellow partakers of his promise in Christ Jesus through the Good News, 3:7 of which I was made a servant, according to the gift of that grace of God which was given me according to the working of his power. 3:8 To me, the very least of all saints, was this grace given, to preach to the Gentiles the unsearchable riches of Christ,[2] 3:9 and to make all men see what is the administration[2] of the mystery which for ages has been hidden in God, who created all things through Jesus Christ; 3:10 to the intent that now through the assembly the manifold wisdom of God might be made known to the principalities and the powers in the heavenly places, 3:11 according to the eternal purpose which he purposed in Christ Jesus our Lord; 3:12 in whom we have boldness and access in confidence through our faith in him. 3:13 Therefore I ask that you may not lose heart at my troubles for you, which are your glory.

1. *mystery was made known to me.* See Colossians 1:26-27; Colossians 2:2. [Unity never commented on this verse however the Fillmore spiritual path is based on development of the soul so that one becomes aware of the Christ presence within, our hope of glory. That we can rejoice in our sufferings for a noble cause is the mystery of Christ.]

2. *the unsearchable riches of Christ.* [Apparently this is a euphemism for spiritual substance.] The "things of God" can never be depleted or exhausted. No matter to what extent they are drawn upon, the riches of the Christ remain as infinite as before. Whoever trusts spiritual substance become manifest in his life as he trusts the Christ proves God and the existence of spiritual law.

## Prayer for the Readers[1]

3:14 For this cause, I bow my knees to the Father of our Lord Jesus Christ, 3:15 from whom every family in heaven and on earth is named, 3:16 that he would grant you, according to the riches of his glory, that you may be strengthened with power through his Spirit in the inward man;[2] 3:17 that Christ may dwell in your hearts through faith; to the end that you, being rooted and grounded in love, 3:18 may be strengthened to comprehend with all the saints what is the breadth and length and height

and depth, 3:19 and to know Christ's
love which surpasses knowledge, that
you may be filled with all the fullness
of God.③ 3:20 Now to him who is able
to do exceedingly abundantly above
all that we ask or think,④ according
to the power that works in us, 3:21
to him be the glory in the assembly
and in Christ Jesus to all generations
forever and ever. Amen.

1. *What are the outstanding ideas in this lesson?* The outstanding ideas are love, faith, and thanksgiving, for which the apostle Paul praised and gave thanks.

2. *What sort of expression is appropriate to us, when we are "strengthened with power through his Spirit in the inward man"?* The expression that someone has made clear in these words: "Power of any sort, whether of wealth or intellect or social position, or accident brings duty, the duty of truth, the duty of fairness, the duty of courtesy, the duty of sanity; a duty to the weak not to oppress them; a duty to the credulous, not to mislead them; a duty to one's friends, not to flatter or cajole them; a duty to one's enemies, not to malign them; a duty to the rich, not to be a sycophant; a duty to the poor, not to be a demagogue." - *The Life and Speeches of Charles Brantley Aycock.*

3. *that you may be filled with all the fullness of God.* Do our blessings come from God direct or do they come through man? "God is Spirit." When we dwell in "his Spirit in the inward man," we receive our blessings direct from God. That reception may come in our own temporal life or it may come to us through others, but it has its initial source in God mind.

4. *above all that we ask or think.* Does God's protecting love, as taught by Jesus, include animals? God is love. God is the universal principle that unifies and harmonizes life and substance in all its forms. Jesus said, "Go ye into all the world, and preach the gospel to every creature" (Mark 16:15). It is written in Isaiah: "And the wolf shall dwell with the lamb... (Isaiah 11:6)

---

Fillmore Study Bible annotations by Rev. Mark Hicks.

**World English Bible Footnotes:**

[2] v3:9. TR reads "fellowship" instead of "administration"

# Ephesians 4

## Unity in the Body of Christ

4:1 I therefore, the prisoner in the
Lord, beg you to walk worthily of the
calling with which you were called,
4:2 with all lowliness and humility,
with patience, bearing with one
another in love; 4:3 being eager to
keep the unity of the Spirit in the
bond of peace. 4:4 There is one body,
and one Spirit, even as you also were
called in one hope of your calling;①
4:5 one Lord, one faith, one baptism,
4:6 one God and Father of all, who is
over all, and through all, and in us
all. 4:7 But to each one of us was the
grace given according to the measure
of the gift of Christ.② 4:8 Therefore
he says, "When he ascended on high,
he led captivity captive, and gave
gifts to men."[3] 4:9 Now this, "He
ascended," what is it but that he also
first descended into the lower parts
of the earth?③ 4:10 He who descended
is the one who also ascended far
above all the heavens, that he might

fill all things.

4:11 He gave some to be apostles;
and some, prophets; and some,
evangelists; and some, shepherds[4]
and teachers;[4] 4:12 for the perfecting
of the saints,[5] to the work of
serving, to the building up of the
body of Christ; 4:13 until we all attain
to the unity of the faith, and of the
knowledge of the Son of God, to a
full grown man, to the measure of
the stature of the fullness of Christ;[6]
4:14 that we may no longer be
children, tossed back and forth and
carried about with every wind of
doctrine, by the trickery of men, in
craftiness, after the wiles of error;
4:15 but speaking truth in love, we
may grow up in all things into him,
who is the head, Christ; 4:16 from
whom all the body, being fitted and
knit together through that which
every joint supplies, according to the
working in measure of each
individual part, makes the body
increase to the building up of itself in
love.[7]

1. *as you also were called in one hope of your calling.* What is the goal of every one who accepts the Gospel of Jesus Christ? The goal of every one is Godlikeness. Jesus Christ is the perfect pattern for all and we must become like Him; therefore a great transformation is to take place in our minds and in our bodies. As we grow more Christlike we shall grow nearer the true "unity of the faith" that exists only in spiritual understanding and practice.

2. *But to each one of us was the grace given according to the measure of the gift of Christ.* How can the social problems of crime, lack, and unemployment be solved? The combined power of the spiritual ideas brought to bear on these problems by the concerted actions of a nuclear group of workers in Christ will cause the full solution to develop (*Unity*, May 12 1935).

3. *He ascended ... he also first descended into the lower parts of the earth.* [Ascending and descending are movements between the higher and lower dimensions. God's Reach, part 1]

4. *He gave some to be apostles; and some, prophets; and some, evangelists; and some, shepherds and teachers.* Metaphysically interpreted, these Gospel messengers are man's inner faculties and powers quickened and inspired by Spirit to do a constructive, uplifting, redeeming work in consciousness, to the end that man may become wholly enlightened and perfected.

5. *for the perfecting of the saints.* The goal of every one is Godlikeness. Jesus Christ is the perfect pattern for all and we must become like Him; therefore a great transformation is to take place in our minds and in our bodies.

6. *until we all attain ... to the measure of the stature of the fullness of Christ.* Paul is writing about the perfect Christ body in each individual, not about the manifest church of Christ.

7. *makes the body increase to the building up of itself in love.* In verse 16 Paul emphasizes in a physiological descriptor that he means the body of the personal man

## The Old Life and the New

4:17 This I say therefore, and
testify in the Lord, that you no longer
walk as the rest of the Gentiles also
walk, in the futility of their mind,
4:18 being darkened in their
understanding, alienated from the
life of God, because of the ignorance
that is in them, because of the
hardening of their hearts; 4:19 who
having become callous gave
themselves up to lust, to work all
uncleanness with greediness. 4:20 But
you did not learn Christ that way;[1]
4:21 if indeed you heard him, and were
taught in him, even as truth is in
Jesus: 4:22 that you put away, as
concerning your former way of life,
the old man,[2] that grows corrupt
after the lusts of deceit; 4:23 and that
you be renewed in the spirit of your
mind, 4:24 and put on the new man,[3]
who in the likeness of God has been
created in righteousness and holiness
of truth.

1. *But you did not learn Christ that way.* Mental discipline is necessary for self-control is reached only through mental discipline. One whose mind is undisciplined cannot be truly religious snce order is heaven's first law, no one can have a true understanding of religion until he learns to order his own mind.

2. *old man.* Metaphysically, the old man is the sense man, the Adam man, the personal man. This is the man who sees himself as an imperfect, limited, mortal being rather than as perfect spirit, soul, and body. This is man before he receives the new life that is in Christ. (MBD/old-man)

3. *new man.* Metaphysically, the "new man" is born of a divine idea through the overshadowing of the Holy Spirit. This idea is that man is a spiritual being. He is a "holy thing," as Mary (the soul) was informed. (MBD/new-man). *How may we "put on the new man," that is, bring forth "Jesus Christ" in ourselves?* The first step is to "put away" the "old man" of lust, limitation, etc, through denial of his reality. The second step is to accept the Truth of our being in faith; then, through understanding, to set about diligently to live the Truth in thought, in word, in deed.

## Rules for the New Life

4:25 Therefore, putting away falsehood, speak truth① each one with his neighbor. For we are members of one another. 4:26 "Be angry, and don't sin."[5] Don't let the sun go down on your wrath,② 4:27 neither give place to the devil. 4:28 Let him who stole steal no more; but rather let him labor, working with his hands the thing that is good,③ that he may have something to give to him who has need. 4:29 Let no corrupt speech proceed out of your mouth, but such as is good for building up as the need may be, that it may give grace to those who hear. 4:30 Don't grieve the Holy Spirit of God,④ in whom you were sealed for the day of redemption. 4:31 Let all bitterness, wrath, anger, outcry, and slander, be put away from you, with all malice. 4:32 And be kind to one another, tenderhearted, forgiving each other, just as God also in Christ forgave you.

1. *putting away falsehood, speak truth.* Deny out of mind all falsity in all social relationships.

2. *Don't let the sun go down on your wrath.* All bitterness, wrath, anger, clamor, railing, and malice, and every thought or emotion that is negative in its effect on the mind or body should be ruled out.

3. *working with his hands the thing that is good.* We can dignify all work by realizing that we are not serving man, but serving God. If you are weary of your work, ask the Lord to show you wherein you are serving Him; then rejoice in what you are doing.

4. *Don't grieve the Holy Spirit of God.* How does man sometimes grieve the Holy Spirit? Man often questions the Truth that comes from the inner kingdom. Thus he suppresses his God-given thoughts, and grieves the Holy Spirit. He wants some external authority to sanction his teaching, forgetting that every religious doctrine was in its beginning expressed by some so-called unauthorized one. (MBI/Acts 4)

---

Fillmore Study Bible annotations by Rev. Mark Hicks.

**World English Bible Footnotes:**

[3] v4:8. Psalm 68:18

[4] v4:11. or, pastors

[5] v4:26. Psalm 4:4

# Ephesians 5

## Overcoming an Empty Life

5:1 Be therefore imitators of God,
as beloved children. 5:2 Walk in love,
even as Christ also loved you, and
gave himself up for us, an offering
and a sacrifice to God for a sweet-
smelling fragrance. 5:3 But sexual
immorality, and all uncleanness, or
covetousness,[1] let it not even be
mentioned among you, as becomes
saints; 5:4 nor filthiness, nor foolish
talking, nor jesting, which are not
appropriate; but rather giving of
thanks.

5:5 Know this for sure, that no
sexually immoral person, nor unclean
person, nor covetous man, who is an
idolater, has any inheritance in the
Kingdom of Christ and God.

5:6 Let no one deceive you with
empty words.[2] For because of these
things, the wrath of God comes on
the children of disobedience. 5:7
Therefore don't be partakers with
them. 5:8 For you were once darkness,
but are now light in the Lord. Walk
as children of light, 5:9 for the fruit
of the Spirit is in all goodness and
righteousness and truth, 5:10 proving
what is well pleasing to the Lord.
5:11 Have no fellowship with the
unfruitful works of darkness, but
rather even reprove them. 5:12 For the
things which are done by them in
secret, it is a shame even to speak
of. 5:13 But all things, when they are
reproved, are revealed by the light,
for everything that reveals is light.
5:14 Therefore he says, "Awake, you
who sleep, and arise from the dead,
and Christ will shine on you."

5:15 Therefore watch carefully how
you walk, not as unwise, but as wise;
5:16 redeeming the time, because the
days are evil. 5:17 Therefore don't be
foolish, but understand what the will
of the Lord is. 5:18 Don't be drunken
with wine, in which is dissipation,
but be filled with the Spirit,[3] 5:19
speaking to one another in psalms,
hymns, and spiritual songs; singing,
and singing praises in your heart to
the Lord; 5:20 giving thanks always
concerning all things in the name of
our Lord Jesus Christ, to God, even
the Father; 5:21 subjecting yourselves
one to another in the fear of Christ.

1. *sexual immorality, uncleanness, covetousness.* We fail to master our intemperate appetites because of lack of light, or understanding of this law. To suppress a living desire is like bottling up a constantly expanding energy which is liable at any time to explode. Suppression is not overcoming, but human intervention. Desire is good at the point of origin, but in the intemperate has gone wrong; it must be set right. This is quickly accomplished through the transforming power of true thoughts and words. When such reformation is adopted, we are healed of our false appetite for all time, and it will never break forth again, no matter how great the temptation.

2. *Let no one deceive you with empty words.* Empty words are words that are void of Truth. Such words leave a vacuum in the mind which is reflected into the body, and man wants something to fill the emptiness. Seeking to supply this want, and not knowing the real resource, man becomes intemperate in eating and drinking. True words have in them the Substance of Spirit and this Substance fills the vacuum made by empty words, and gives the satisfaction which man constantly desires.

3. *Don't be drunken with wine, in which is dissipation, but be filled with the Spirit.* Words filled with the Substance of Spirit can be applied in a practical way whenever the appetite demands gratification. Instead of eating and drinking intemperate-

ly, eat living words; that is, take them into your consciousness by affirmation. One who is tempted to yield to false appetite will find freedom and satisfaction through the use of these statements: "I have the mind of Christ;" "I know the Truth and the Truth makes me free." "I no longer seek the sense gratification, but am satisfied with living Substance of the body of Christ." - "My flesh is meat indeed, and my blood is drink indeed."

## A Household Code for Harmonious Families, Churches and Businesses[1]

5:22 Wives, be subject to your own
husbands, as to the Lord. 5:23 For the
husband is the head of the wife,[2]
and Christ also is the head of the
assembly, being himself the savior of
the body. 5:24 But as the assembly is
subject to Christ, so let the wives
also be to their own husbands in
everything.

5:25 Husbands, love your wives,
even as Christ also loved the
assembly,[3] and gave himself up for
it; 5:26 that he might sanctify it,
having cleansed it by the washing of
water with the word, 5:27 that he
might present the assembly to
himself gloriously, not having spot or
wrinkle or any such thing; but that it
should be holy and without blemish.
5:28 Even so husbands also ought to
love their own wives as their own
bodies. He who loves his own wife
loves himself.[4] 5:29 For no man ever
hated his own flesh; but nourishes
and cherishes it, even as the Lord
also does the assembly; 5:30 because
we are members of his body, of his
flesh and bones. 5:31 "For this cause a
man will leave his father and mother,
and will be joined to his wife. The
two will become one flesh."[6][5] 5:32
This mystery is great, but I speak
concerning Christ and of the
assembly. 5:33 Nevertheless each of
you must also love his own wife even
as himself; and let the wife see that
she respects her husband.

1. *Household Code.* A social media meme which encouraged Stoicism for keeping a peaceful order in Roman and Greek households. Later inserted in Christian scripture to defend the Jesus movement from pagan criticism of disorderly egalitarianism. See metaphysical interpretations at Ephesians 5:22-6:9, Colossians 3:18-4:1, Titus 2:1-10 and 1 Peter 2:18-3:1-8.

2. *For the husband is the head of the wife, and Christ also is the head of the assembly.* In today's lesson Paul compares the wife to the church. In verse 32 he calls the relation between Christ and the church a great mystery. What does spiritual discernment reveal this mystery to be? The church represents the body. Christ represents Divine Mind that directs and controls the body. The relation between the body and Divine Mind is mystical; it is not understood by the natural man.

3. *Christ also loved the assembly, and gave himself up for it.* How does the Christ in each person give itself up, to the end that the person's body may be purified? Our bodies are cleansed by the Christ mind through the word of denial. Deny all forms of bodily impurity, in the name of Christ. Your body is the temple of the living God. Take the Christ thought of purity and truth down into your body; raise the lower nature through your consciousness of the higher. In this way you will glorify the body (church) and in spiritual consciousness you will present it, "holy and without blemish." to God.

4. *He who loves his own wife loves himself.* Does this interpretation of the great mystery, which Paul says is here involved, imply that husbands should love their wives less? When men understand that their bodies represent the feminine qualities of being, they will, by giving more love to their bodies, increase their capacity to love; the final result will be that they will have greater love for their wives.

5. *will be joined to his wife, the two will become one flesh.* What mystical truth is involved in the statement that a man "will

be joined to his wife, the two will become one flesh"? When the love bond is harmonious and pure between husband and wife, they build a bond invisible, yet real in body consciousness. This bond may be compared to the ligaments that joined the Siamese twins and made them seem as one. Married couples who love each other devotedly grow to look alike. This fact proves that, as Paul said, "the two shall become one flesh."

---

Fillmore Study Bible annotations by Rev. Mark Hicks.

**World English Bible Footnotes:**

[6] v5:31. Genesis 2:24

# Ephesians 6

## Children and Parents❶

6:1 Children, obey your parents in
the Lord,❷ for this is right. 6:2 "Honor
your father and mother,"❸ which is
the first commandment with a
promise: 6:3 "that it may be well with
you, and you may live long on the
earth."[7]

6:4 You fathers, don't provoke your
children❹ to wrath, but nurture
them in the discipline and instruction
of the Lord.

1. A continuation of the Household code explained in the previous chapter.

2. *parents in the Lord.* "Parents in the Lord" means parents from whom the Spirit of the Christ emanates.

3. *Honor your father and mother.* How shall the child be taught to honor his father, and his mother? Teach the child the truth, that God is the one Father-Mother Spirit, from which we all come forth, in which we live and move and, have our being, to which we should be eternally thankful for all things. This teaching will quicken a sense of gratitude in the child, and he will manifest it in honor and in gratitude his earthly parents. The parents' duty is to deport themselves so as to merit the honor their children pay them, thus making the duty of the children a joy, instead of a burden.

4. *don't provoke your children.* How can we keep the teachings of this lesson in regard to husbands, wives, children, and parents? By seeking the inner meaning of commandment and proving it our life.

## Slaves and Masters❶

6:5 Servants, be obedient to those
who according to the flesh are your
masters, with fear and trembling, in
singleness of your heart, as to Christ;
6:6 not in the way of service only
when eyes are on you, as men
pleasers; but as servants of Christ,
doing the will of God from the heart;
6:7 with good will doing service, as
to the Lord, and not to men;❷ 6:8
knowing that whatever good thing
each one does, he will receive the

same again from the Lord, whether he is bound or free.

6:9 You masters, do the same things to them, and give up threatening,[3] knowing that he who is both their Master and yours is in heaven,[4] and there is no partiality with him.

1. A continuation of the Household code explained in the previous chapter.

2. *with good will doing service, as to the Lord, and not to men.* Paul emphasizes service to the Lord instead of to others.

3. *give up threatening.* Do Truth students want their employees to obey with fear and trembling? Truth students have the co-operation of their employees, in the spirit of obedience to God and Christ. "For one is your master, even the Christ."

4. *knowing that he who is both their Master and yours is in heaven.* From a spiritual viewpoint we are all equal and of equal importance under the divine law. Divine Mind does not recognize any official station or position.

## Metaphysical Strength

6:10 Finally, be strong in the Lord,[1]
and in the strength of his might. 6:11
Put on the whole armor of God, that you may be able to stand against the wiles of the devil.[2] 6:12 For our wrestling is not against flesh and blood, but against the principalities, against the powers, against the world's rulers of the darkness of this age, and against the spiritual forces of wickedness in the heavenly places. 6:13 Therefore, put on the whole armor of God,[3] that you may be able to withstand in the evil day, and, having done all, to stand. 6:14
Stand therefore, having the utility belt of truth buckled around your waist, and having put on the breastplate of righteousness,[4] 6:15
and having fitted your feet with the preparation of the Good News of peace;[5] 6:16 above all, taking up the shield of faith,[6] with which you will be able to quench all the fiery darts of the evil one. 6:17 And take the helmet of salvation, and the sword of the Spirit,[7] which is the spoken word of God; 6:18 with all prayer and requests, praying at all times in the Spirit, and being watchful to this end in all perseverance and requests for all the saints: 6:19 on my behalf, that utterance may be given to me in opening my mouth, to make known with boldness the mystery of the Good News, 6:20 for which I am an ambassador in chains; that in it I may speak boldly, as I ought to speak.

1. *be strong in the Lord.* Our greatest source of strength is in our understanding of our spiritual character and of our relation to spiritual source, God.

2. wiles of the devil. Our greatest temptations to err are found in our own unfolding consciousness. The root cause of our desires are not evil. Desire is Spirit's urge to a larger unfoldment. Mistakes and evil conditions are the results of action taken without the guidance of divine wisdom. When we have accumulated many different error thoughts in consciousness, a complex state of mind is the result. In the Scriptures these aggregations of error thoughts are named the adversary, Satan, the devil.

3. *the whole armor of God.* The realization that the omnipresent Spirit of good is our resource and that we have nothing to fear when we trust in and are guided by Spirit, that is, God.

4. *the breastplate of righteousness.* A union of love and wisdom. When our judgment is tempered with love, we vanquish the adversary and cast out all fear.

5. *fitted your feet with the preparation of the Good News of peace.* The feet represent understanding of our most material activities. It is mostly in the outer activities of life that we are tempted to acts of resistance. It is there that we combat and oppose invasions. To meet these seeming oppositions we should always practice the gospel of peace and good will, loving our neighbors as ourselves.

6. *shield of faith.* Faith is inner confidence in the all-providing Spirit of good. When we are nonresistant and send out only thoughts of peace and love and good will, the fiery darts of opposition and evil that may be sent in our direction fall harmless at our feet.

7. *sword of the Spirit.* We wield the sword of the Spirit by speaking true words and affirming Truth in the face of error. When evil presses upon our consciousness and tries to make us believe that it is real and powerful, we should affirm the truth that there is no reality in evil, no power in evil, because God is good and good is all.

## An Assurance of God's Ever Presence

6:21 But that you also may know my
affairs, how I am doing, Tychicus,[1]
the beloved brother and faithful
servant in the Lord, will make known
to you all things; 6:22 whom I have
sent to you for this very purpose,
that you may know our state, and
that he may comfort your hearts.

6:23 Peace be to the brothers, and
love with faith, from God the Father
and the Lord Jesus Christ. 6:24 Grace
be with all those who love our Lord
Jesus Christ with incorruptible love.
Amen.

1. *Tychicus.* A Christian, and a fellow worker of Paul's, "faithful minister". Metaphysically, a belief in fate (fortuitous, fateful, chance, fortunate). Converted to Christian faith, this belief would take on a strong assurance of good as being ever present and demonstrable. One who learns the divine law is not subject to fate. He makes his own destiny by his use of divine law (MBD/Tychicus).

---

Fillmore Study Bible annotations by Rev. Mark Hicks.

**World English Bible Footnotes:**

[7] v6:3. Deuteronomy 5:16

# Paul's Letter to the Philippians

Ancient Philippi, ruins of Basilica B, Christopher Steinle, CC Attribution.

## Introduction to Philippians

When Paul eventually reached Rome, instead of being thrust into a prison cell, he was placed under "house arrest"; and this form of imprisonment continued for about two years. During this period, Paul also wrote several outstanding epistles. Four of these have been preserved, and they now form part of our New Testament. Possibly Paul wrote several other epistles but the four which remain are the Epistle to the Ephesians; the Epistle to the Philippians; the Epistle to the Colossians; and the Epistle to Philemon. These are usually termed "Paul's Epistles of the Imprisonment," since they are regarded as having been written by the apostle during the period of his imprisonment at Rome.

It will be noticed that these Epistles of the Imprisonment differ considerably from the earlier letters of Paul. These differences are discernible even from a casual reading. The style of writing differs to a marked degree, and several points of Christian doctrine are presented in an entirely different manner. Because of these differences, several New Testament commentators have ventured to question the Pauline authorship of the Epistles of the

Imprisonment.

Now, while it is not the purpose of these lessons to enter into controversy of this sort, one very important point should be emphasized here—for this furnishes the key to the situation. When studying Paul's writings, we should always take into account the apostle's spiritual development. Unfortunately Paul's Epistles are not given in chronological order in the New Testament, but are arranged according to size, or supposed importance. When these Epistles are placed in proper chronological sequence the various stages of Paul's spiritual progress are clearly revealed.

Thus in the earlier Epistles (Thessalonians, Galatians, Corinthians, Romans) we trace the progress of the enthusiastic convert and untiring missionary. Then came Paul's arrest and imprisonment at Jerusalem and Caesarea, which brought about a period of compulsory inactivity. Paul could no longer travel from place to place, nor could he engage in strenuous religious controversies. However, this period also furnished Paul with ample time and opportunity to "be still, and know," and to make fresh contact with his Lord; and all this, in turn, led the apostle into a deeper spiritual experience—such as was not possible during his missionary activities. Indeed, it would seem that during this period Paul experienced what has been termed his "second conversion." The first conversion, at Damascus, was followed by Paul's extensive missionary activities; this second conversion led the apostle into a deeper understanding of the teaching of Jesus Christ. Paul was literally trans- formed by the renewing of his mind.

**Purpose of the Epistle:** The Epistle to the Philippians may be regarded as a somewhat elaborate "thank you" letter. It would appear that when the news regarding Paul's imprisonment at Rome reached Philippi, Lydia and her associates immediately decided to send a gift to the apostle. This was not the first time for the Philippians to act in this helpful way; they ministered to Paul's needs when he was at Thessalonica, and other places. (See Phil. 4:14-16.) This gift—probably consisting of money, food, and other helpful articles—was placed in the hands of a trustworthy convert named Epaphroditus; and he then journeyed to Rome. Paul was deeply touched when the gift arrived, and his heart overflowed with gratitude.

Unfortunately Epaphroditus soon after his arrival at Rome became very sick, and was "near to death" (Phil. 2:7); but through Paul's strenuous efforts and earnest prayers, he was finally restored. Paul also recognized that Epaphroditus was suffering from "homesickness," for the Epistle mentions that "he has been longing for you all, and has been distressed" (Phil. 2:26). Thus when Epaphroditus had regained his strength, Paul made arrangements for the messenger's return to Philippi, sending with him this specially written letter of appreciation and thanksgiving, which we now term "Paul's Epistle to the Philippians." It should be noted that this Epistle contains not only Paul's thanks to Lydia and her fellow-workers, but also some very important teaching—not only applying to the Philippian converts, but also helpful and inspiring to present-day readers.

Introduction to *Paul's Letter to the Philippians* by Herbert J. Hunt, former Dean of Bible Studies for the Unity School of Christianity.

Many scholars today believe that both this letter to the Philippians and the letter to Philemon were written when Paul was in prison in Ephesus, after his third missionary journey, perhaps around 52 CE. Both letters refer to the presence of Epaphras and both letters are exceptionally heart-centered in tone. Perhaps no other letter of Paul is more frequently quoted in New Thought churches than this letter to the Philippians. This is for two reasons.

Paul is in chains, but he only sees the positive and good. He writes, "the things which happened to me have turned out rather to the progress of the Good News so that it became evident to the whole praetorian guard, and to all the rest, that my bonds are in Christ" (1:13) and declares that "Christ will be magnified in my body, whether by life, or by death" (1:20). Obviously, Paul is expressing zeal, which is the faculty of enthusiasm, intensity and exuberance that provides our inner urge to progress and our our motivation to achieve.

Many verses in Philippians have found their way into New Thought affirmations, such as "I am confident the one who began a good work among you will bring it to completion" (1:6), "Let the same mind be in you that was in Christ Jesus" (2:5), "Do not worry about anything, but in everything by prayer and thanksgiving let your requests be made known to God" (4:6), "The peace of God, which surpasses all understanding, will guard your hearts and your minds in Christ Jesus" (4:7), "Whatever is is true, whatever is honorable, whatever is just, whatever is pure, whatever is pleasing, whatever is commendable, if there is any excellence and if there is anything worthy of praise, think about these things" (4:8), and "I can do all things through him who strengthens me" (4:13). Affirmations are expressions of the faculty of power, which enables us to have authority over our own emotions (feelings), inspirations, and thoughts and to bring forth Divine ideas.

Introduction to *Paul's Letter to the Philippians* by Rev. Mark Hicks.

# PHILIPPIANS 1

## Salutation

1:1 Paul and Timothy, servants of Jesus Christ;

To all the saints in Christ Jesus who are at Philippi,(1) with the overseers[1] and servants[2]: 1:2 Grace to you, and peace from God, our Father, and the Lord Jesus Christ.

1. *Philippi* was a city in Macedonia where the proconsul or governor of Macedonia lived. It is therefore the center of the executive faculty of that in us signified by Macedonia: burning adoration. It is necessary to stir up this fiery power in the man when he gets into negative states of consciousness. The vision of the man imploring, "Come over into Macedonia, and help us," is the discernment of this inner fervor, which needs stirring up. A certain fiery fervor is necessary in order to establish faith and persistency in barren, weak states of consciousness, such as those suggested by Phrygia, Galatia, and Asia. (cf. Acts 16:6-10.)

## Paul's Prayer for the Philippians①

1:3 I thank my God whenever I
remember you, 1:4 always in every
request of mine on behalf of you all
making my requests with joy, 1:5 for
your partnership[3] in furtherance of
the Good News from the first day
until now; 1:6 being confident of this
very thing, that he who began a good
work in you will complete it until the
day of Jesus Christ. 1:7 It is even right
for me to think this way on behalf
of all of you, because I have you in
my heart, because, both in my bonds
and in the defense and confirmation
of the Good News, you all are
partakers with me of grace. 1:8 For
God is my witness, how I long after
all of you in the tender mercies of
Christ Jesus.

1:9 This I pray, that your love may
abound yet more and more in
knowledge and all discernment; 1:10
so that you may approve the things
that are excellent; that you may be
sincere and without offense to the
day of Christ; 1:11 being filled with
the fruits of righteousness, which are
through Jesus Christ, to the glory and
praise of God.

1. *Paul's purpose is to encourage.* Paul (the word of Truth) first commends those who are seeking to live the Christ life and gives thanks for the spiritual progress they have already made. Then he affirms his faith that the good work already begun in them will be perfected, and he encourages them to persevere in it. Finally he gives further instruction as regards the importance of constructive thinking.

## Paul's Present Circumstances

1:12 Now I desire to have you know,
brothers,[4] that the things which
happened to me have turned out
rather to the progress of the Good
News; 1:13 so that it became evident
to the whole praetorian guard, and
to all the rest, that my bonds① are
in Christ; 1:14 and that most of the
brothers in the Lord, being confident
through my bonds, are more
abundantly bold to speak the word
of God without fear. 1:15 Some indeed
preach Christ even out of envy and
strife, and some also out of good
will. 1:16 The former insincerely
preach Christ from selfish ambition,
thinking that they add affliction to
my chains; 1:17 but the latter out of
love, knowing that I am appointed
for the defense of the Good News.

1:18 What does it matter? Only that
in every way, whether in pretense
or in truth, Christ is proclaimed. I
rejoice in this, yes, and will rejoice.
1:19 For I know that this will turn out
to my salvation, through your
supplication and the supply of the
Spirit② of Jesus Christ, 1:20 according
to my earnest expectation and hope,
that I will in no way be disappointed,
but with all boldness, as always, now
also Christ will be magnified in my
body, whether by life, or by death.
1:21 For to me to live is Christ, and to
die is gain.③ 1:22 But if I live on in the
flesh, this will bring fruit from my
work; yet I don't make known what I
will choose. 1:23 But I am in a dilemma
between the two, having the desire
to depart and be with Christ, which
is far better. 1:24 Yet, to remain in the
flesh is more needful for your sake.
1:25 Having this confidence, I know
that I will remain, yes, and remain
with you all, for your progress and
joy in the faith, 1:26 that your
rejoicing may abound in Christ Jesus
in me through my presence with you
again.

1:27 Only let your manner of life be

worthy of the Good News of Christ, that, whether I come and see you or am absent, I may hear of your state, that you stand firm in one spirit,(4) with one soul striving for the faith of the Good News; 1:28 and in nothing frightened by the adversaries, which is for them a proof of destruction, but to you of salvation, and that from God. 1:29 Because it has been granted to you on behalf of Christ, not only to believe in him, but also to suffer on his behalf, 1:30 having the same conflict which you saw in me, and now hear is in me.

1. *bonds.* The one who notwithstanding his failure to surmount limitations keeps faith in the principles of Truth and courage to persevere in his efforts undiminished, is an example to those in need of courage to follow the Way.

2. *supply of the Spirit.* The Spirit of Jesus Christ is infinite and omnipresent, but each one determines for himself the measure of his realization of it through earnest expectation and hope as well as prayer. The prayers of others for him also increase his receptivity to the Christ Spirit provided he is conscious of them and desires the help they bring him.

3. *to live is Christ and to die is gain.* To teach Truth by example, as Jesus taught it in His works is truly to live. To heal the sick, cleanse the lepers, raise the dead, cast out devils, these are some of the greater works always present to be dealt with by man after the Christ method.

4. *stand firm in one spirit.* Metaphysically, the exhortation to "stand firm in one spirit, with one soul striving" signifies that the individual is to unify soul and spirit or to harmonize his powers in order to realize the "fulness of Christ."

---

Fillmore Study Bible annotations by Mark Hicks.

**World English Bible Footnotes:**

[1] v1:1. or, superintendents, or bishops

[2] v1:1. Or, deacons

[3] v1:5. The word translated "partnership" (koinonia) also means "fellowship" and "sharing."

[4] v1:12. The word for "brothers" here and where context allows may also be correctly translated "brothers and sisters" or "siblings."

# PHILIPPIANS 2

## Imitating Christ's Humility

2:1 If there is therefore any exhortation in Christ, if any consolation of love, if any fellowship of the Spirit, if any tender mercies and compassion, 2:2 make my joy full, by being like-minded, having the same love, being of one accord, of one mind; 2:3 doing nothing through rivalry or through conceit, but in humility, each counting others better than himself; 2:4 each of you not just looking to his own things, but each of you also to the things of others.

2:5 Have this in your mind,[1] which was also in Christ Jesus, 2:6 who, existing in the form of God, didn't consider equality with God a thing to be grasped, 2:7 but emptied himself, taking the form of a servant, being made in the likeness of men. 2:8 And being found in human form, he humbled himself, becoming obedient to death, yes, the death of the cross. 2:9 Therefore God also highly exalted him, and gave to him the name which is above every name; 2:10 that at the name of Jesus every knee should bow,[2] of those in heaven, those on earth, and those under the earth, 2:11 and that every tongue should confess that Jesus Christ is Lord,[3] to the glory of God the Father.

1. *Have this in your mind.* That which we identify with, we become. cf. Rom. 12:2.

2. *every knee should bow.* The writer of Philippians follows up the statement that forms today's Golden Text with the words "That in the name of Jesus every knee should bow, of things in heaven and things on earth and things under the earth." Metaphysically, the name Jesus represents the "I" in man, the self, the directive power, raised to di vine understanding and power—the I am. It is this I in each man that holds all else in him under its domin ion and power. This high entity controls the working of his mind ("things in heaven") as well as his emo tions and his overt actions ("things on earth"), and it also has under its direction the subconscious impulses of which the conscious mind is often unaware ("things under the earth"). This high motivating and identifying principle of man "is he that shall save his people from their sins." Unity 1934-05

3. *Jesus is Lord.* Paul's true mission is not just converting Jews or Gentiles, but rather converting all of Rome, for Rome symbolized a world order that could not stand in light of the new world order (of oneness) established by Christ. According to Marcus Borg, when Paul declares that "Jesus is Lord" he is implicitly declaring that "Caesar is not Lord," neither are the masters of slaves, and that there is no distinction between Jew and Gentile. But all of these, including Caesar, are part of the one reign of Jesus Christ. Borg, Marcus. *Reading the Bible Again for the First Time* (2001). New York: Harper Collins. See Divine Ideas in Paul's Writings, Bible Interpretation - Acts to Revelation.

## Shining as Lights in the World

2:12 So then, my beloved, even as you have always obeyed, not only in my presence, but now much more in my absence, work out your own salvation[1] with fear and trembling. 2:13 For it is God who works in you[2] both to will and to work, for his good pleasure. 2:14 Do all things without murmurings and disputes, 2:15 that you may become blameless and harmless, children of God without blemish in the midst of a crooked and perverse generation, among whom you are seen as lights in the world, 2:16 holding up the word of life; that I may have something to boast in the day of Christ, that I didn't run in vain nor labor in vain. 2:17 Yes, and if I am poured out on the sacrifice[3] and service of your faith, I rejoice, and rejoice with you all. 2:18 In the same way, you also rejoice, and rejoice with me.

1. *Work out your own salvation.* We have been learning how to do the outworking, but have now come to a point where we must learn more of how to place ourselves in an attitude where we can each be conscious of the divine inner working. cf Lessons in Truth Lesson 9, Annotation 10.

2. *God who works in you.* The work of regeneration cannot come through the personal self. When we consciously desire to unify ourself with Him, our life is no longer ours but His, and we may rest assured that He will not let us out of His care and keeping. *Be Ye Transformed* 151.

3. *if I am poured out the sacrifice.* If you have a thought of love and good will, you set free invisible emanations that are impregnated with these ideas. ... This is the inner meaning of offering sacrifices to the Lord

## Timothy and Epaphroditus

[2:19] But I hope in the Lord Jesus to send Timothy to you soon, that I also may be cheered up when I know how you are doing. [2:20] For I have no one else like-minded, who will truly care about you. [2:21] For they all seek their own, not the things of Jesus Christ.[1] [2:22] But you know the proof of him, that, as a child serves a father, so he served with me in furtherance of the Good News. [2:23] Therefore I hope to send him at once, as soon as I see how it will go with me. [2:24] But I trust in the Lord that I myself also will come shortly. [2:25] But I counted it necessary to send to you Epaphroditus,[2] my brother, fellow worker, fellow soldier, and your apostle and servant of my need; [2:26] since he longed for you all, and was very troubled, because you had heard that he was sick. [2:27] For indeed he was sick, nearly to death, but God had mercy on him; and not on him only, but on me also, that I might not have sorrow on sorrow. [2:28] I have sent him therefore the more diligently, that, when you see him again, you may rejoice, and that I may be the less sorrowful. [2:29] Receive him therefore in the Lord with all joy, and hold such in honor, [2:30] because for the work of Christ he came near to death, risking his life to supply that which was lacking in your service toward me.

1. *not the things of Jesus Christ.* Macedonia represents the business mind and Philippi means getting gain, which is the chief motive of business. It is very natural that in this place (state of consciousness) there is "no man likeminded, who will care truly for your state. And so Timothy was sent to the assembly of believers at Philippi. The thoughts wherein love of gain is uppermost need Timothy (inspired reason united with faith) to instruct them concerning spiritual substance and life (the true riches) and their use.

2. *Epaphroditus.* A message of love and peace that is sent by the word of Truth (Paul) to the enlightened thoughts of the states of mind that Philippi and Colossæ signify in individual consciousness.

---

Fillmore Study Bible annotations by Mark Hicks.

# Philippians 3

## Breaking with the Past

[3:1] Finally, my brothers, rejoice in the Lord. To write the same things to you, to me indeed is not tiresome, but for you it is safe. [3:2] Beware of the dogs, beware of the evil workers, beware of the false circumcision. [3:3] For we are the circumcision, who worship God in the Spirit, and rejoice in Christ Jesus, and have no confidence in the flesh;[1] [3:4] though I myself might have confidence even in the flesh. If any other man thinks that he has confidence in the flesh, I yet more: [3:5] circumcised the eighth day, of the stock of Israel, of the tribe of Benjamin, a Hebrew of Hebrews; concerning the law, a Pharisee; [3:6] concerning zeal, persecuting the assembly; concerning the righteousness which is in the law, found blameless.

3:7 However, what things were gain to me, these have I counted loss for Christ. 3:8 Yes most certainly, and I count all things to be loss for the excellency of the knowledge of Christ Jesus, my Lord, for whom I suffered the loss of all things, and count them nothing but refuse,(2) that I may gain Christ 3:9 and be found in him, not having a righteousness of my own, that which is of the law, but that which is through faith in Christ, the righteousness which is from God by faith;(3) 3:10 that I may know him, and the power of his resurrection, and the fellowship of his sufferings, becoming conformed to his death; 3:11 if by any means I may attain to the resurrection from the dead.

1. *no confidence in the flesh.* When we keep the Christ thought foremost in all we think and do, we shall come out victorious.

2. *count them noting but refuse.* The apostle warns against those who are trying to bring Gentile converts under the Mosaic Law. At one time he himself had been proud of his Jewish heritage, but now he is willing to put all behind him for a greater goal. *Be Ye Transformed* 130.

3. *righteousness which is from God by faith.* We can have no absolute assurance that we are right, except as we place our faith in divine wisdom and claim its enlightenment in our mind. As we look to this higher wisdom to express itself in and through us and trust it to do so, we find that our understanding becomes clear and that we see what is right in every instance.

## Pressing toward the Goal

3:12 Not that I have already obtained, or am already made perfect; but I press on, if it is so that I may take hold of that for which also I was taken hold of by Christ Jesus. 3:13 Brothers, I don't regard myself as yet having taken hold, but one thing I do. Forgetting the things which are behind, and stretching forward to the things which are before, 3:14 I press on toward the goal(1) for the prize of the high calling of God in Christ Jesus. 3:15 Let us therefore, as many as are perfect, think this way. If in anything you think otherwise, God will also reveal that to you. 3:16 Nevertheless, to the extent that we have already attained, let us walk by the same rule. Let us be of the same mind. 3:17 Brothers, be imitators together of me, and note those who walk this way, even as you have us for an example. 3:18 For many walk, of whom I told you often, and now tell you even weeping, as the enemies of the cross of Christ, 3:19 whose end is destruction, whose god is the belly, and whose glory is in their shame, who think about earthly things. 3:20 For our citizenship is in heaven, from where we also wait for a Savior, the Lord Jesus Christ; 3:21 who will change the body of our humiliation to be conformed to the body of his glory,(2) according to the working by which he is able even to subject all things to himself.

1. *I press on toward the goal...* A 3-part formula for healing: (1) Letting go of the past (by changing one's thinking), (2) leaning into the problem and (3) press on to the full expression of your Christ nature. See Luke 5:24 and Dealing With Stress Through Spiritual Methods.

2. *conformed to the body of his glory.* This all has been interpreted that after we are dead we will go to heaven. But this is all in the Now. Our bodies are now in this heavenly state so the only death of which we have any evidence is the death of the body. *Hidden Man of the Bible*, lesson 6, page 7

Fillmore Study Bible annotations by Mark Hicks.

# Philippians 4

## Exhortations

4:1 Therefore, my brothers,
beloved and longed for, my joy and
crown, so stand firm in the Lord, my
beloved. 4:2 I exhort Euodia, and I
exhort Syntyche, to think the same
way in the Lord. 4:3 Yes, I beg you
also, true yokefellow, help these
women, for they labored with me in
the Good News, with Clement[1] also,
and the rest of my fellow workers,
whose names are in the book of life.
4:4 Rejoice in the Lord always! Again
I will say, Rejoice![2] 4:5 Let your
gentleness[3] be known to all men.
The Lord is at hand. 4:6 In nothing be
anxious, but in everything, by prayer
and petition with thanksgiving, let
your requests be made known to
God. 4:7 And the peace of God, which
surpasses all understanding, will
guard your hearts and your thoughts
in Christ Jesus.

4:8 Finally, brothers, whatever
things[4] are true, whatever things
are honorable, whatever things are
just, whatever things are pure,
whatever things are lovely, whatever
things are of good report; if there is
any virtue, and if there is any praise,
think about these things. 4:9 The
things which you learned, received,
heard, and saw in me:[5] do these
things, and the God of peace will be
with you.

1. *Clement*. Metaphysically, the gentle, soothing, releasing (tender, merciful mild, kind) quality of the word in its calming, equalizing, healing activities in the consciousness. Although Clement of Alexandria lived much later, his temperament aligns well with this interpretation, particularly in comparison to Origen, who followed him.

2. *again I will say, Rejoice!* We were created to be happy and we should render praise to God regardless of moods or events.

3. *gentleness (forbearance).* To forbear to enforce one's "rights" is a splendid exercise in the development of the higher will.

4. *whatever things...* If we turn our thoughts away from the outer appearance and toward the spiritual, dwelling on the good in ourself and others, all the apparent evil will first drop out of your thoughts and then out of our life. Verse 8 in chapter 4 is complete in itself, requires no metaphysical interpretation and will always be an up-to-date guide for people in all moral and religious states of consciousness.

5. *learned, received, heard, and saw in me:* Paul represents the word of the Spirit of truth. The converted Paul (formerly Saul, the will) becomes, by the power of the word, the most active thought in the establishment of good throughout our being.

## Gratitude for the Philippians' Gift

4:10 But I rejoice in the Lord
greatly, that now at length you have
revived your thought for me; in
which you did indeed take thought,
but you lacked opportunity. 4:11 Not
that I speak in respect to lack, for
I have learned in whatever state I
am, to be content in it. 4:12 I know
how to be humbled, and I know also
how to abound. In everything and in
all things I have learned the secret[1]
both to be filled and to be hungry,
both to abound and to be in need.
4:13 I can do all things through Christ,
who strengthens me. 4:14 However
you did well that you shared in my
affliction. 4:15 You yourselves also
know, you Philippians, that in the

beginning of the Good News, when
I departed from Macedonia, no
assembly shared with me in the
matter of giving and receiving but
you only. 4:16 For even in Thessalonica
you sent once and again to my need.
4:17 Not that I seek for the gift, but
I seek for the fruit that increases to
your account.[2] 4:18 But I have all
things, and abound. I am filled,
having received from Epaphroditus
the things that came from you, a
sweet-smelling fragrance, an
acceptable and well-pleasing
sacrifice to God. 4:19 My God will
supply[3] every need of yours
according to his riches in glory in
Christ Jesus.[4] 4:20 Now to our God
and Father be the glory forever and
ever! Amen.

1. *I have learned the secret.* The possession of poise and equanimity under extremes, whether of good or ill.

2. *that increases to your account.* The law of Giving and Receiving. In exchange for light, and guidance into spiritual knowledge, the followers of the apostle of the Christ gladly gave of their support and sustenance.

3. *my God will supply.* A study of the Bible reveals the fact that God intends that His children shall have an abundance of the good things of life.

4. *according to his riches in glory in Christ Jesus.* "God is a ceaseless flow of substance, and no matter what the extent of the need, Universal substance can easily supply it. But there is one thing God cannot do. God cannot supply lack. This is because lack is a state of mind, and the condition cannot be remedied until the state of mind is altered. Eric Butterworth, *Spiritual Economics*, p14.

## Final Greetings and Benediction

4:21 Greet every saint in Christ
Jesus. The brothers who are with me
greet you. 4:22 All the saints greet
you, especially those who are of
Caesar's household. 4:23 The grace of
the Lord Jesus Christ be with you all.
Amen.

Fillmore Study Bible annotations by Mark Hicks.

# Paul's Letter to the Colossians

Bifolio from Paul's Letter to the Romans, the end of Paul's Letter to the Philippians and the beginning of Paul's Letter to the Colossians, from a codex containing the Pauline Epistles. Greek on papyrus. Egypt, c. 200 AD. Wikipedia Commons. Public Domain.

## Introduction to Colossians

The Epistle to the Colossians is closely related to Paul's Epistle to the Ephesians. Even a casual reading reveals many similarities, and some passages in the two Epistles are almost identical; but there are also several marked differences. The following details will furnish a helpful background for the study of this Epistle.

**The church at Colossae:** Some New Testament commentators state that Paul was not the founder of the Christian group at Colossae. This opinion is based mainly on Paul's statement that some of the converts "have not seen my face" (Col. 2:1); and it is also pointed out that the phraseology in this Epistle is not as intimate as that used in Ephesians. However, it seems clear that there were many of Paul's converts at Colossae, and also that the entire church membership acknowledged the spiritual leadership of the apostle. All of Paul's instructions and admonitions, as given in this Epistle, are couched in terms which indicate recognized authority.

**Purpose of the Epistle:** This Epistle (like the one to the Ephesians) arose out of the report made by Epaphras, when he visited Paul at Rome. Epaphras stated that while the Jewish and Gentile Christians at Colossae were not always in agreement, their main problem was this: The converts at Colossae were becoming confused by certain Gnostic teachings which were then creeping into the church. It should be mentioned here that, while Gnosticism did not fully develop until much later, some earlier forms of this teaching wrought considerable havoc in the early Church. Paul, therefore, sternly warned the converts not to be led astray: "See to it that no one makes a prey of you by philosophy and empty deceit, according to human tradition, according to the elemental spirits of the universe, and not according to Christ" (Col. 2:8). In this and other emphatic passages, the apostle sends forth the ringing challenge: Is it to be Gnosticism, or is it to be Christ? Paul also gives some clearly stated directions for Christian living—as in the Epistle to the Ephesians.

**The mature viewpoint:** In the Introduction to Philippians, reference was made to Paul's spiritual development as indicated in these Epistles. The Epistle to the Colossians contains a number of passages which show a marked development of thought, as compared with the teaching given in Paul's earlier Epistles. Note the following: "He has delivered us from the dominion of darkness and transferred us to the kingdom of his beloved Son" (Col. 1:13); "And you, who were dead . . . God made alive together with him . . . having canceled the bond which stood against us . . . nailing it to the cross" (Col. 2:13-14); "If then you have been raised with Christ, seek the things that are above . . . for . . . your life is hid with Christ in God" (Col. 3:1-3).

**Regarding Laodicea:** Laodicea, Hierapolis, and Colossae were neighboring cities, situated on the Lycus river in Asia Minor, and Christian groups had been formed in all three. Reference is made to an "Epistle to the Laodiceans," which was to be shared with the converts at Colossae, while the Colossians were likewise to share their Epistle with the Laodiceans. (See Col. 4:16.) No trace of an Epistle to the Laodiceans now remains; but many commentators are of the opinion that this may have been a duplicate of the Epistle to the Ephesians. The heading of Ephesians indicates that it was intended to be circulated among several churches.

**Metaphysical meaning:** The name Colossae is usually explained as meaning "punishment," "correction," or "discipline" (MBD/Colossae). This may have reference to wrongdoing, which is followed by retributive punishment. This is in accord with the law of cause and effect. Possibly, therefore, the destruction of Colossae by earthquake shortly after this Epistle was written may be regarded as more than a coincidence! However, there is another and more helpful way of interpreting Colossae.

The Colossian Christians, when thinking or speaking of Jesus Christ (Messiah), were accustomed to using both past and future tenses. They looked backward when recalling happenings connected with His ministry in the Holy Land; they looked forward to the event of His Second Coming. So engrossed were they with these two viewpoints that they overlooked an important teaching of Jesus: "I am with you always" (Matt. 28:20). Paul also, during his ministry, followed along similar lines in his preaching. But when the apostle was led into a deeper spiritual understanding he recognized the presence of Jesus Christ in all Christian activities and experiences. Hence when Paul wrote this Epistle, he sought to bring about an important "correction" in the Colossians' way of thinking and speaking. Past and future events had a rightful place in Christian doctrine; but now Paul would have his converts put the major emphasis upon present-day experience: the converts should realize that their Lord was with them, and within them, in all their activities. Thus Paul wrote to the Colossians in his emphatic way, saying, "God chose to make known . . . this mystery, which is Christ in you, the hope of glory" (Col. 1:27).

This Epistle to the Colossians has its present-day application, for this "correction" should also be made in our consciousness. There is need to emphasize what may be termed "the Gospel in the present tense." This applies especially to the recognition of the Christ presence in all our activities and experience. Jesus said, "Where two or three are gathered together in my name, there am I in the midst of them" (Matt. 18:20). Also in His "marching orders" to the disciples, Jesus said, "Go therefore and make disciples of all nations . . . and lo, I am with you always" (Matt. 28:19-20). The "correction," therefore, may be thought of as a new alignment of our thinking. This does not mean the exclusion of the past and future phases of Christian teaching, but it does place new emphasis on a present experience of "Christ in you, the hope of glory."

*Introduction to Paul's Letter to the Colossians* by Herbert J. Hunt, former Dean of Bible Studies for the Unity School of Christianity.

# Colossians 1

## Greeting

1:1 Paul,❶ an apostle of Christ
Jesus through the will of God, and
Timothy our brother, 1:2 to the saints
and faithful brothers[1] in Christ at
Colossae: Grace to you and peace
from God our Father, and the Lord
Jesus Christ.

1. *Paul.* Paul represents the word of the Spirit of truth. The converted Paul (formerly Saul, the will) becomes, by the power of the word, the most active thought in the establishment of good throughout our being. (MBD/Paul)

## Paul Thanks God for the Colossians

1:3 We give thanks to God the
Father of our Lord Jesus Christ,
praying always for you, 1:4 having
heard of your faith❷ in Christ Jesus,
and of the love which you have
toward all the saints, 1:5 because of
the hope❷ which is laid up for you
in the heavens, of which you heard
before in the word of the truth❸ of
the Good News, 1:6 which has come to
you; even as it is in all the world❹
and is bearing fruit and growing, as
it does in you also, since the day
you heard and knew the grace of God
in truth; 1:7 even as you learned of

Epaphras our beloved fellow servant,
who is a faithful servant of Christ on
our behalf, 1:8 who also declared to us
your love in the Spirit.

1:9 For this cause, we also, since
the day we heard this, don't cease
praying and making requests for you,
that you may be filled with the
knowledge of his will in all spiritual
wisdom[5] and understanding,[6] 1:10
that you may walk worthily of the
Lord, to please him in all respects,
bearing fruit in every good work, and
increasing in the knowledge of God;
1:11 strengthened with all power,[7]
according to the might of his glory,
for all endurance and perseverance
with joy; 1:12 giving thanks to the
Father, who made us fit to be
partakers of the inheritance of the
saints in light; 1:13 who delivered us
out of the power of darkness, and
translated us into the Kingdom of the
Son of his love; 1:14 in whom we have
our redemption,[2][8] the forgiveness
of our sins;

1. *faith*. Faith in God is the substance of existence. To have faith *in* God is to have the faith *of* God. We must have faith in God as our Father and source of all the good we desire. (RW/faith)

2. *hope*. Hope is the expectation of good in the future. It is a quality (good as far as it goes) of sense mind because it is subject to time. (RW/hope)

3. *truth*. The basic principle of Truth is that the mind of each individual may be consciously unified with Divine Mind through the indwelling Christ. By affirming at-one-ment with God-Mind, we eventually realize that perfect mind which was in Christ Jesus. (RW/truth)

4. *world*. A state of consciousness formed through the belief in the reality of things external. It leads one to follow standards of living based on man's opinions rather than on Truth. The world is overcome by our denying that it has any power over us and affirming freedom in Christ. (RW/world)

5. *wisdom*. Intuitive knowing; spiritual intuition; the voice of God within as the source of our understanding; mental action based on the Christ Truth within. (RW/wisdom)

6. *understanding*. God is supreme knowing. That in humans which comprehends is understanding; it knows and comprehends in wisdom. (RW/understanding)

7. *power*. In mind, power is increased through exalted ideas. These show us the relation between the world without and the mind within, and we find that they are parallel. (RW/power)

8. *redemption*. The process by which the life and substance of our lesser self are brought to conform to the standards of our spiritual self. (RW/redemption)

## Christ Consciousness is Ultimate Source

1:15 who is the image of the
invisible[1] God, the firstborn of all
creation. 1:16 For by him all things[2]
were created, in the heavens and on
the earth, things visible and things
invisible, whether thrones or
dominions or principalities or
powers; all things have been created
through him, and for him. 1:17 He is
before all things, and in him all
things are held together. 1:18 He is the
head of the body, the assembly[3],
who is the beginning, the firstborn
from the dead; that in all things he
might have the preeminence. 1:19 For
all the fullness was pleased to dwell
in him; 1:20 and through him to
reconcile all things to himself, by
him, whether things on the earth, or
things in the heavens, having made
peace[4] through the blood[5] of his
cross.[6]

1:21 You, being in past times
alienated and enemies in your mind
in your evil[7] works, 1:22 yet now he
has reconciled in the body of his
flesh through death, to present you
holy and without blemish and
blameless before him, 1:23 if it is so
that you continue in the faith,
grounded and steadfast, and not

moved away from the hope of the Good News which you heard, which is being proclaimed in all creation under heaven; of which I, Paul, was made a servant.

1. *invisible*. The invisible is reality that cannot be seen, touched, or comprehended by any of the outer senses. In this realm a great and mighty work is being accomplished. (RW/invisible)

2. *things*. The things that appear are the formulations of our ideas of self and God. Back of everything is a thought. If we will still the senses then we will perceive the thought behind the things. (RW/things)

3. *assembly (ASV, church)*. To establish the church, or *ecclesia*, of God in humankind, a new state of consciousness must be formed. We must gain an understanding of God as Spirit, and also must understand our own relation to Spirit. (MBD/church)

4. *peace*. Harmony and tranquility derived from awareness of the Christ consciousness. (RW/peace)

5. *blood (of Christ)*. Spiritual energy that purifies and redeems human beings by pouring into them life currents of a new and purer stream. This divine energy cleanses the consciousness of dead works to enable people to serve the living God. (RW/blood)

6. *cross*. The cross is not a burden as commonly understood, but a symbol of the forces in humans adjusted in their right relation. (RW/cross)

7. *evil*. That which is not of God; unreality; error thought; a product of the fallen human consciousness; negation. (RW/evil)

## Christ in You

1:24 Now I rejoice in my sufferings[1] for your sake, and fill up on my part that which is lacking of the afflictions of Christ in my flesh for his body's sake, which is the assembly;
1:25 of which I was made a servant, according to the stewardship of God which was given me toward you, to fulfill the word of God,
1:26 the mystery which has been hidden for ages[2] and generations. But now it has been revealed to his saints,
1:27 to whom God was pleased to make known what are the riches of the glory[3] of this mystery among the Gentiles, which is Christ in you, the hope of glory;[4]
1:28 whom we proclaim, admonishing every man and teaching every man in all wisdom, that we may present every man perfect in Christ Jesus;
1:29 for which I also labor, striving according to his working, which works in me mightily.

1. *rejoice in my sufferings*. Patience and long-suffering are connected with joy as the natural result of the realization that we have developed patience and long-suffering, and that we are no longer subject to the peevishness, irritability, and short-tempered moods of sense. The possession of self-control is in itself a joy.

2. *mystery which has been hidden for ages*. See Colossians 2:2; Ephesians 3:9. [Unity never commented on this verse however the Fillmore spiritual path is based on development of the soul so that one becomes aware of the Christ presence within, our hope of glory. That we can rejoice in our sufferings for a noble cause is the mystery of Christ. See 4:2.]

3. *glory*. Realization of divine unity; the blending and merging of our mind with God-Mind. (RW/glory)

4. *Christ in you, the hope of glory*. How is our life transformed? By the renewing of our mind on the Christ pattern. Such renewal transforms our life completely, giving us a clear view of the work that we can do as our contribution to the uplift of humanity.

---

Fillmore Study Bible annotations compiled by Rev. Dan Beckett.

**World English Bible Footnotes:**

[1] v1:2. The word for "brothers" here and where context allows may also be correctly translated "brothers and sisters" or "siblings."

[2] v1:14. TR adds "through his blood,"

# Colossians 2

## Paul's Greeting

2:1 For I desire to have you know how greatly I struggle for you, and for those at Laodicea,[1] and for as many as have not seen my face in the flesh; 2:2 that their hearts may be comforted, they being knit together in love, and gaining all riches of the full assurance of understanding, that they may know the mystery of God,[2] both of the Father and of Christ, 2:3 in whom are all the treasures of wisdom[3] and knowledge[4] hidden. 2:4 Now this I say that no one may delude you with persuasiveness of speech. 2:5 For though I am absent in the flesh, yet am I with you in the spirit, rejoicing and seeing your order, and the steadfastness of your faith in Christ.

1. *Laodicea.* Metaphysically, this town represents a phase of the judgment faculty in the individual, which bases its understanding, its decisions, on outer seemings and intellectual reasonings. (MBD/Laodicea)

2. *mystery of God.* See annotation for Colossians 1:26 and Ephesians 3:9.

3. *wisdom.* Intuitive knowing; spiritual intuition; the voice of God within as the source of our understanding; mental action based on the Christ Truth within. (RW/wisdom)

4. *knowledge/knowing.* There is in humankind a knowing capacity transcending intellectual knowledge. Nearly everyone has at some time touched this hidden wisdom and has been more or less astonished at its revelations. The knowing that man receives from the direct fusion of the Mind of God with his mind is real spiritual knowing. (RW/knowing)

## Remain Steadfast in Faith[1]

2:6 As therefore you received Christ Jesus, the Lord, walk in him, 2:7 rooted and built up in him, and established in the faith, even as you were taught, abounding in it in thanksgiving. 2:8 Be careful that you don't let anyone rob you through his philosophy and vain deceit, after the tradition of men, after the elements of the world,[2] and not after Christ. 2:9 For in him all the fullness of the Godhead dwells bodily, 2:10 and in him you are made full, who is the head of all principality and power; 2:11 in whom you were also circumcised with a circumcision not made with hands, in the putting off of the body of the sins of the flesh, in the circumcision of Christ; 2:12 having been buried with him in baptism, in which you were also raised with him through faith in the working of God, who raised him from the dead. 2:13 You were dead through your trespasses and the uncircumcision of your flesh. He made you alive together with him, having forgiven us all our trespasses, 2:14 wiping out the handwriting in ordinances which was against us; and he has taken it out of the way, nailing it to the cross; 2:15

having stripped the principalities and the powers, he made a show of them openly, triumphing over them in it.

2:16 Let no man therefore judge you in eating, or in drinking, or with respect to a feast day or a new moon or a Sabbath day, 2:17 which are a shadow of the things to come; but the body is Christ's.[3] 2:18 Let no one rob you of your prize by a voluntary humility and worshipping of the angels, dwelling in the things which he has not seen, vainly puffed up by his fleshly mind, 2:19 and not holding firmly to the Head, from whom all the body, being supplied and knit together through the joints and ligaments, grows with God's growth.

1. [This passage is more historical than metaphysical. Paul is warning his listeners against the teachings of Peter and James, who believed that in order to be Christian, one must be Jewish first. Paul disagreed. Hence the pushback in the references to circumcision and dietary restrictions.]

2. *elements of the world (NRSV, elemental spirits of the universe).* [Most likely a reference to the law of cause and effect.] Jesus taught a new understanding of divine law. He acknowledged mechanical cause and effect, but he knew it was possible to "fulfill the law" by transcending its strictly mechanical repetition. This can be done only by certain changes of consciousness. One of these changes is to let go of the insistence of "even-exchanges" in life all the time. Another change is to be willing to forgive sin instead of insisting on punishment for sin. Grace is the name given to the aspect of divine law which does not deal in "even-exchanging," but in the increase of good through greater giving. Ed Rabel, Metaphysics 1/The Divine Paradox, Law/Grace. Compare Ephesians 2:5, "by grace you have been saved".

3. *the body is Christ's.* Greek, sōma. The outer expression of consciousness; the precipitation of the thinking part of man. God created the idea of the body of man as a self-perpetuating, self-renewing organism, which man reconstructs into his personal body. God creates the body idea, or divine idea, and man, by his thinking, makes it manifest. As God created man in His image and likeness by the power of His word, so man, as God's image and likeness, projects his body by the same power. (RW/body)

## Know Nothing of the Lesser Self

2:20 If you died with Christ from the elements of the world,[1] why, as though living in the world, do you subject yourselves to ordinances,[2] 2:21 "Don't handle, nor taste, nor touch" 2:22 (all of which perish with use), according to the precepts and doctrines of men? 2:23 Which things indeed appear like wisdom in self-imposed worship, and humility,[3] and severity to the body; but aren't of any value against the indulgence of the flesh.

1. *elements of the world.* See 2:8 above.

2. *ordinances.* Do forms, ceremonies, or special localities have power to make God known to us? These things are unknown in the realm of Spirit. Satisfaction is found by the Christ-minded in the formless life and substance. (MBI/Colossians 3, June 2, 1935)

3. *humility.* True humility is needed very much in the Christ-centered individual. The true Christian is humble. He knows the nothingness of the lesser self in man and the allness of Christ. (RW/humility)

---

Fillmore Study Bible annotations compiled by Rev. Dan Beckett.

# Colossians 3

## The Peace of the Christ

3:1 If then you were raised together with Christ, seek the things that are above,[1] where Christ is, seated on the right hand of God. 3:2 Set your mind on the things that are above, not on the things that are on the earth. 3:3 For you died, and your life is hidden with Christ in God. 3:4 When Christ, our life,[2] is revealed, then you will also be revealed with him in glory. 3:5 Put to death therefore your members which are on the earth: sexual immorality, uncleanness, depraved passion, evil desire, and covetousness, which is idolatry; 3:6 for which things' sake the wrath of God comes on the children of disobedience. 3:7 You also once walked in those, when you lived in them; 3:8 but now you also put them all away: anger, wrath, malice, slander, and shameful speaking out of your mouth. 3:9 Don't lie to one another, seeing that you have put off the old man with his doings, 3:10 and have put on the new man, who is being renewed in knowledge after the image of his Creator, 3:11 where there can't be Greek and Jew, circumcision and uncircumcision, barbarian, Scythian, bondservant, freeman; but Christ is all, and in all.

3:12 Put on therefore, as God's chosen ones, holy and beloved, a heart of compassion, kindness, lowliness, humility, and perseverance; 3:13 bearing with one another, and forgiving each other, if any man has a complaint against any; even as Christ forgave you, so you also do.

3:14 Above all these things, walk in love, which is the bond of perfection. 3:15 And let the peace of God[3] rule in your hearts, to which also you were called in one body; and be thankful. 3:16 Let the word of Christ[4] dwell in you[5] richly; in all wisdom teaching and admonishing one another with psalms, hymns, and spiritual songs, singing with grace in your heart to the Lord.

3:17 Whatever you do, in word or in deed, do all in the name of the Lord Jesus, giving thanks to God the Father, through him.

1. *things that are above.* What are the things that are above? Whatever uplifts mind, body, or soul belongs to the things that are above.

2. *our life.* Is it possible to "let the peace of Christ rule in your hearts" regardless of external conditions? It is. By staying the mind on God and the things that are above and by expressing only what is in the mind, we can be at peace regardless of conditions or circumstances. Compare with Isaiah 26.3: "Thou wilt keep him in perfect peace, whose mind is stayed on thee; because he trusteth in thee."

3. *peace of God (ASV, peace of Christ.).* Is it possible to "let the peace of Christ rule in your hearts" regardless of external conditions? It is. By staying the mind on God and the things that are above and by expressing only what is in the mind, we can be at peace regardless of conditions or circumstances. "Thou wilt keep him in perfect peace, whose mind is stayed on thee; because he trusteth in thee" (Isaiah 26:3)

4. *word of Christ.* Does our word commit us as definitely as our deed? Our spoken word is as clear an expression of ourselves as our deeds. "Whatsoever ye do in word or in deed" puts both in the class of acts of will.

5. *dwell in you.* Explain how we learn to recognize the Spirit of truth as indwelling. Through meditating on the Spirit of truth, believing in it as the fundamental reality of our being, expecting its guidance, di-

recting toward it the desire of our heart, and focusing our thoughts upon it, we learn to recognize it as indwelling.

## A Household Code To Get In the Flow of Life[1]

3:18 Wives, be in subjection to your husbands, as is fitting in the Lord.

3:19 Husbands,[2] love your wives, and don't be bitter against them.

3:20 Children, obey your parents in all things, for this pleases the Lord.

3:21 Fathers,[3] don't provoke your children, so that they won't be discouraged.

3:22 Servants, obey in all things those who are your masters according to the flesh, not just when they are looking, as men pleasers, but in singleness of heart, fearing God. 3:23 And whatever you do, work heartily, as for the Lord,[4] and not for men, 3:24 knowing that from the Lord you will receive the reward of the inheritance; for you serve the Lord Christ. 3:25 But he who does wrong will receive again for the wrong that he has done, and there is no partiality.

1. *Household Code.* A social media meme which encouraged Stoicism for keeping a peaceful order in Roman and Greek households. Later inserted in Christian scripture to defend the Jesus movement from pagan criticism of disorderly egalitarianism. See metaphysical interpretations at Ephesians 5:22-6:9, Colossians 3:18-4:1, Titus 2:1-10 and 1 Peter 2:18-3:1-8.

2. *Wives, Husbands.* Love is not to be found. It's not a matter of finding the right person, but being the right person. Unless we know this, we will tend to place all kinds of unreal expectations on a relationship even before it happens... It's important to get back to basics, you are a wonderful, capable, beautiful person in your transcended self. This is the root of you, this is the heart of you. You may not know it, you may frustrate it, this is what you are... And your basic need is not to be loved but to love. (Eric Butterworth Unity Podcast #67/On Forming Relationships.)

3. *Children, Fathers.* In the creative flow of life, God is the true parent. Gibran says, "Your children are not your children. They are sons and daughters of life's longing for itself. They come through you but not from you..." Thus, the parent must honor the father-mother principle of life by keeping a true perspective in the role of parenthood. (Eric Butterworth Speaks #70/How To Break the 5th Commandment)

4. Servants, masters; work heartily, as for the Lord. Eric Butterworth has said, "The chains that bind us in life are forged in our own thoughts of self-limitation. Freedom is our inheritance, but ours is the responsibility to "stir up the gift of God," to get our faith lifted, and to work up a spontaneous enthusiasm for life. Emerson says, "Nothing great was ever achieved without enthusiasm." Actually, we are born with enthusiasm. It is that "spark of celestial fire" at the core of our being. The apathetic life simply has the flame turned down—and it can be turned up whenever one cares to do so... You may say, "Enthusiasm is fine, but with my problems what do I have to be enthusiastic about?" This is the great fallacy. Enthusiasm is not a response, but a cause. The enthusiastic person does not act in that way because things are going well. Things go well because he is enthusiastic. Get the fire turned on and your consciousness tuned in by working with a realization such as this one: "I am alive, awake, alert, joyous, and enthusiastic about life." (Eric Butterworth Speaks #70/The "High Way" to Freedom)

Fillmore Study Bible annotations compiled by Rev. Dan Beckett and Mark Hicks.

# Colossians 4

## Live in Harmony

4:1 Masters,[1] give to your servants
that which is just and equal, knowing
that you also have a Master in
heaven.

4:2 Continue steadfastly in prayer,
watching therein with thanksgiving;[2]
4:3 praying together for us also, that
God may open to us a door for the
word, to speak the mystery of
Christ,[3] for which I am also in bonds;
4:4 that I may reveal it as I ought
to speak. 4:5 Walk in wisdom toward
those who are outside,[4] redeeming
the time. 4:6 Let your speech always
be with grace,[5] seasoned with salt,
that you may know how you ought to
answer each one.

1. Masters. [Here, and in 3:22-25 above, the same Greek word, *kurios*, is used for both masters and the Lord, reinforcing the conclusion in v24 that, regardless of who we serve "according to the flesh", we are always "serving, [spiritually], the Lord Christ."]

2. *Continue steadfastly in prayer, watching therein with thanksgiving*. Charles Fillmore says that thanksgiving means rendering our grateful thoughts to God for His manifold blessings. Not to say "thank you" is uncouth. (Life of Prayer II/Lesson 1/Understanding)

3. *the mystery of Christ*. See annotation for 1:26 and 2:2 above.

4. *Walk in wisdom toward those who are outside*. [Unity, as a movement, is a sacred canopy. Charles Fillmore wrote,] "there is need of a church organization that can interpret and demonstrate the spiritual realities back of the church symbols. All Christians could join such a church with out breaking their present religious affiliations. Unity in Spirit and practice is the ideal Christian Church Universal, and it offers to people everywhere a spiritual church membership in which Christ will demonstrate his power to save his people here and now from the ills of mind, body, and affairs." (Unity, May 1924, Unity Church Universal)

5. Let your speech always be with grace. Does our word commit us as definitely as our deed? Our spoken word is as clear as expression of ourselves as our deeds. "Whatsoever ye do in word or in deed" puts both in the class of acts of will. See 3:16 above.(MBI/Colossians 3, June 2, 1935)

## Paul's Beloved Community

4:7 All my affairs will be made
known to you by Tychicus, the
beloved brother, faithful servant,
and fellow bondservant in the Lord.
4:8 I am sending him to you for this
very purpose, that he may know your
circumstances and comfort your
hearts, 4:9 together with Onesimus,
the faithful and beloved brother,
who is one of you. They will make
known to you everything that is going
on here. 4:10 Aristarchus, my fellow
prisoner greets you, and Mark, the
cousin of Barnabas (concerning whom
you received commandments, "if he
comes to you, receive him"), 4:11 and
Jesus who is called Justus, who are
of the circumcision. These are my
only fellow workers for the Kingdom
of God, men who have been a
comfort to me.

4:12 Epaphras, who is one of you, a
servant of Christ, salutes you, always
striving for you in his prayers, that
you may stand perfect and complete

in all the will of God. 4:13 For I testify
about him, that he has great zeal
for you, and for those in Laodicea,
and for those in Hierapolis. 4:14 Luke,
the beloved physician,[1] and Demas
greet you. 4:15 Greet the brothers who
are in Laodicea, and Nymphas, and
the assembly that is in his house.
4:16 When this letter has been read
among you, cause it to be read also
in the assembly of the Laodiceans;
and that you also read the letter
from Laodicea. 4:17 Tell Archippus,
"Take heed to the ministry which you
have received in the Lord, that you
fulfill it."

4:18 The salutation of me, Paul,
with my own hand: remember my
bonds.[2] Grace be with you. Amen.[3]

1. *Luke, the beloved physician.* Paul refers to Luke as “the beloved physician.” Metaphysically this would indicate that Luke belongs especially to that phase of the intelligence which has to do with keeping the body well; as a missionary, Luke carries the healing message to all parts of the body. Paul and Luke working together symbolize the converted will and spiritual illumination united in presenting the healing ministry of Jesus Christ to the entire being. (MBI/Colossians 4, September 16, 1923)

2. *remember my bonds.* See annotation for 1:26 and 2:2 above.

3. *Amen.* Anyone can prove the therapeutic power of a spiritual thought by mentally affirming day after day, say for thirty days, that he is filled with divine life and divine energy. At the end of that time he will have the evidence of the truth of the idea in a stronger life-flow in his organism. Thus the observance of true religion and an extension of its truths into the conscious, everyday thought, will eventually be recognized by man as the one and only source of his health. All healing methods that do not take the spiritual man into consideration are temporal and transitory. There is but one way to attain wholeness, and that is the way of the spiritual man, mystically called Jesus Christ. (MBI/Colossians 4)

---

Fillmore Study Bible annotations compiled by Rev. Dan Beckett and Mark Hicks.

# Paul's First Letter to the Thessalonians

Ancient marketplace in Thessaloniki. Wikipedia Commons. Public Domain.

## Introduction to Paul's First Letter to the Thessalonians

### Overview of Paul's First Letter to the Thessalonians

While Paul was waiting at Athens for Silas and Timothy to arrive, he became deeply concerned about his converts at Thessalonica. As already mentioned, a very close relationship had developed between Paul and his Thessalonian converts during his three-weeks-plus stay with them; and now he desired to know how they were faring. Were they standing fast in the Christian teaching? Or was the pressure of persecution proving too much for them? The suspense was more than he could bear. (See I Thess. 3:1.) When Silas and Timothy at length reached Athens, Paul instructed them to return at once to Thessalonica, so that they could bring him a firsthand report of the situation there. Meanwhile, Paul himself pressed on to Corinth, bidding Silas and Timothy join him there when they returned.

The report that was brought to Paul at Corinth was a very encouraging one. The converts at Thessalonica continued to hold Paul in highest esteem, and they were holding fast in their faith, despite much bitter persecution. However, one problem had arisen, and this was sorely disturbing the converts. Some of the Christians at Thessalonica had died since Paul's departure; in some instances this was the result of the persecutions, while other converts had passed away through natural causes. But Paul, during his ministry at Thessalonica, had taught that the Messiah would be soon returning, and His coming would be the time of fulfilling all the glorious expectations of Jewish teaching. This important question therefore arose: Would death rob these dear departed ones of all the joys and glories of the Second Coming? Indeed, many of the converts were saying, "How can this promised Parousia be a joyous event to us, unless we can share it with our dear ones?" Paul thereupon dictated his First Epistle to the Thessalonians, which was carried by Timothy to Thessalonica. This Epistle contains the apostle's answer to the converts' all-important question. Actually, the Epistle is a great message of assurance, stressing two outstanding points.

1. Paul assures the Thessalonian converts of his deepest regard for them, and highly commends them for their steadfastness in the face of such bitter persecution.
2. Paul further assures the converts that death will not rob their dear ones of the joy and glory associated with the Second Coming. Indeed, those who have died "in Christ" are to be given first place in meeting the returning Lord. The details of this outstanding passage should be carefully studied:

> "But we would not have you ignorant, brethren, concerning those who are asleep, that you may not grieve as others do who have no hope. For since we believe that Jesus died and rose again, even so through Jesus, God will bring with him those who have fallen asleep. For this we declare to you by the word of the Lord, that we who are alive, who are left until the coming of the Lord, shall not precede those who have fallen asleep. For the Lord himself will descend from heaven with a cry of command, with the archangel's call, and with the sound of the trumpet of God. And the dead in Christ will rise first; then we who are alive, who are left, shall be caught up together with them in the clouds to meet the Lord in the air; and so we shall be always with the Lord. Therefore, comfort one another with these words" (I Thess. 4:13-18).

Introduction to *Paul's First Letter to the Thessalonians* by Herbert J. Hunt, former Dean of Bible Studies for the Unity School of Christianity.

For our will (Saul) to be transfigured into a Spirit-led will (Paul), an experience of the light of Truth ("beatific vision" on the road to Damascus) is needed.

For this experience to be had, our will (Saul) must be made ready to receive this Light through a period of study of Scripture/Truth. This time and study will awaken one's innate zeal for Truth (Timothy) and build up our current "rugged state of consciousness" (Silas) as we increase in understanding.

Our transformed Spirit-led will moves throughout our being (Macedonia), interfacing with our various cities/aggregations of thoughts and beliefs. In areas where we have studied much and gained deeper understanding (Berea), we have more receptivity to the Spirit's prompts and leadings, whereas in areas or issues where we have not yet sufficient understanding and zeal, we remain tossing to and fro like billowy waves (Thessalonica).

Therefore, the bridge between the parts of our consciousness that are able to discern the will of God and Truth and those parts that are not, is a shift in understanding. We can facilitate this shift in our understanding by spending more time in the studying of the Word of Truth and conversations with God. These practices awaken in us more zeal for Truth (Timothy) and more understanding (Silas), which are needed to support our Spirit-led will (Paul) as it moves through our aggregated thought centers (cities) spreading the Word of Truth (evangelizing the nations).

### 3 Key Themes in 1st Thessalonians

1. **Encouragement to persevere:** When your inner church soul is suffering serious persecutions (error thoughts or circumstances of life), this is the time to praise ... to praise God for His Presence and power, and to praise yourself for your patient endurance and dedication to continue in faith, hope, and love.
2. **Hope for the return of Christ:** Whether in times of crisis or times of peace, we have the opportunity and access to return our awareness, over and over again, to the Christ, the Truth, the Word of God. This is our hope, our connection, the anchor for our soul.
3. **Keep increasing your love for fellow believers:** Love is an inner quality that sees good everywhere and in everybody. It insists that all is good, and by refusing to see anything but good it causes that quality finally to appear uppermost in itself, and in all things. (RW/love)

Introduction to *Paul's First Letter to the Thessalonians* by Rev. Mark Hicks.

# First Thessalonians 1

## Our Inner Church

1:1 Paul, Silvanus, and Timothy,[1] to the assembly[2] of the Thessalonians[3] in God the Father and the Lord Jesus Christ: Grace to you and peace from God our Father and the Lord Jesus Christ.

1. See 2 Thessalonians 1:1-2

2. *Paul, Silvanus, and Timothy.* Paul represents the will, which is an important factor in expressing the Christ actively in the life. Understanding (represented by Silvanus) and zeal or the inspired reason united with faith (Timothy) must cooperate with the will, if man would express the

Christ fully.

3. *Assembly or "church."* The true church is an aggregation of spiritual ideas in individual consciousness. To establish a new aggregation of spiritual ideas of God within us, a new state of consciousness must first be formed. (MBD/church), thus, every "inner church" begins as a mental perception and by degrees establishes itself in the whole consciousness.

4. *Thessalonians*. Thessalonica's ancient name was *Thermæ*, because of the many hot springs that were there), a city of Macedonia (the enthusiasm and energy of Spirit that set the whole of our being aflame), from which Paul (our Spirit-led will) is driven away by our lack of discernment of Spirit/Truth (persecution by the Jews). Thessalonica in us is that phase of our unfoldment that lacks sufficient thinking balance to give tolerance and wisdom [to Spirit's leading or to that which arises in our lives] (billowy, tossed by the waves).(MBD/Thessalonica)

## Spiritual Power

1:2 We always give thanks to God for all of you, mentioning you in our prayers, 1:3 remembering without ceasing your work of faith and labor of love and patience of hope❶ in our Lord Jesus Christ, before our God and Father. 1:4 We know, brothers[1] loved by God, that you are chosen, 1:5 and that our Good News came to you not in word only, but also in power, and in the Holy Spirit, and with much assurance.❷ You know what kind of men we showed ourselves to be among you for your sake. 1:6 You became imitators of us, and of the Lord, having received the word in much affliction, with joy of the Holy Spirit, 1:7 so that you became an example to all who believe in Macedonia and in Achaia. 1:8 For from you the word of the Lord has been declared, not only in Macedonia and Achaia, but also in every place your faith toward God has gone out; so that we need not to say anything. 1:9 For they themselves report concerning us what kind of a reception we had from you; and how you turned to God from idols, to serve a living and true God,❸ 1:10 and to wait for his Son from heaven, whom he raised from the dead--Jesus, who delivers us from the wrath to come.

1. *Faith and labor of love and patience of hope*. By the right exercise of these qualities we realize a consciousness of power that fills us with confidence and courage, and assures our success.

2. *And with much assurance*. Understanding, love, and power come to us as we gain deeper and firmer faith in the Christ.

3. *How you turned to God from idols, to serve a living and true God*. When we turn our faith Godward and look for that which is perfect in all that concerns us, steadily refusing to recognize imperfection, we become conscious of the ideal expression of good (Jesus), and learn to depend upon its regenerative influence.

---

Fillmore Study Bible annotations compiled by Mary Salama.

**World English Bible Footnotes:**

[1] v1:4. The word for "brothers" here and where context allows may also be correctly translated "brothers and sisters" or "siblings."

# First Thessalonians 2

## Truth and Love in Ministry

2:1 For you yourselves know, brothers, our visit to you wasn't in vain, 2:2 but having suffered before and been shamefully treated, as you know, at Philippi, we grew bold in our God to tell you the Good News of God in much conflict. 2:3 For our exhortation is not of error, nor of uncleanness, nor in deception. 2:4 But even as we have been approved by God to be entrusted with the Good News, so we speak; not as pleasing men, but God, who tests our hearts.[1] 2:5 For neither were we at any time found using words of flattery, as you know, nor a cloak of covetousness (God is witness), 2:6 nor seeking glory from men (neither from you nor from others), when we might have claimed authority as apostles of Christ. 2:7 But we were gentle among you, like a nursing mother cherishes her own children.

2:8 Even so, affectionately longing for you, we were well pleased to impart to you, not the Good News of God only, but also our own souls,[2] because you had become very dear to us. 2:9 For you remember, brothers, our labor and travail; for working night and day, that we might not burden any of you, we preached to you the Good News of God. 2:10 You are witnesses with God, how holy, righteously, and blamelessly we behaved ourselves toward you who believe. 2:11 As you know, we exhorted, comforted, and implored every one of you, as a father does his own children,[3] 2:12 to the end that you should walk worthily of God, who calls you into his own Kingdom and glory. 2:13 For this cause we also thank God without ceasing, that, when you received from us the word of the message of God, you accepted it not as the word of men, but, as it is in truth, the word of God, which also works in you who believe. 2:14 For you, brothers, became imitators of the assemblies of God which are in Judea in Christ Jesus; for you also suffered the same things from your own countrymen, even as they did from the Jews; 2:15 who killed both the Lord Jesus and their own prophets, and drove us out, and didn't please God, and are contrary to all men; 2:16 forbidding us to speak to the Gentiles that they may be saved; to fill up their sins always. But wrath has come on them to the uttermost.

1. *So we speak; not as pleasing men, but God, who tests our hearts.* As recorded in Acts 16 and Acts 17, Paul and Silas had been run out of town by wealthy Gentiles and prominent Jews for casting out evil spirits and speaking truth. Many temptations are set before the followers of Jesus, one of the strongest being the desire to trim Truth to please the people. Covetousness, money-getting, is another temptation. Many teachers and preachers suppress absolute truth, because it may offend some of their wealthy supporters.

2. *Impart to you, not the Good News of God only, but also our own souls.* Paul was aggressive, yet affectionate and loving. Through love our thoughts and our words of Truth are charged with an abundance of growth. Jesus said that his words were Spirit and life. When our words are charged with Spirit and life and our hearts overflow with love, our words impregnate receptive souls; in this way seeds of the new birth are sown in receptive soil.

3. *We exhorted, comforted, and implored every one of you, as a father does his own children.* Paul's labor among them was pure, sincere, unselfish, and truly righteous. Interpreting this part of our lesson metaphysically, we perceive the necessity of one's being undivided in thought

and belief, when he speaks the Christ Truth into the individual consciousness.

## Paul's Great Desire

2:17 But we, brothers, being
bereaved of you for a short season,
in presence, not in heart, tried even
harder to see your face with great
desire,(1) 2:18 because we wanted to
come to you--indeed, I, Paul, once
and again--but Satan hindered us. 2:19
For what is our hope, or joy, or
crown of rejoicing? Isn't it even you,
before our Lord Jesus[2] at his
coming? 2:20 For you are our glory and
our joy.

1. *With great desire* Desire is a deep and onward impulse. It springs from deep within our Being and it has enduring power. Deep desire is essential to spiritual growth. It is desire—earnest and intense—that draws the whole being up out of mortality and its transient joys into the power to appreciate and to receive real spiritual blessings. The inspiration of the Holy Spirit is continually urging us to forsake earthly things and desire that which is of heaven. The desire to excel should be encouraged and cultivated in the right direction. It is in all of us. (RW/desire)

---

Fillmore Study Bible annotations compiled by Mary Salama.

**World English Bible Footnotes:**

[2] v2:19. TR adds "Christ"

# First Thessalonians 3

## Paul's Great Desire (continued)

3:1 Therefore, when we couldn't
stand it any longer, we thought it
good to be left behind at Athens
alone, 3:2 and sent Timothy, our
brother and God's servant in the
Good News of Christ, to establish
you, and to comfort you concerning
your faith; 3:3 that no one be moved
by these afflictions. For you know
that we are appointed to this task.
3:4 For most certainly, when we were
with you, we told you beforehand
that we are to suffer affliction, even
as it happened, and you know. 3:5
For this cause I also, when I couldn't
stand it any longer, sent that I might
know your faith,(1) for fear that by
any means the tempter had tempted
you, and our labor would have been
in vain.

1. When I couldn't stand it any longer, sent that I might know your faith. [Our being anchored and grounded in the knowledge (faith) that God is working all things for good, can sometimes become shaken when we are going through stages of our transmutation (times of testing, temptation). When we feel that we have reached a point where we "can't stand it any longer," we need to encourage ourselves by reestablishing our minds back in the Word of Truth.]

## Spiritual Fellowship

3:6 But when Timothy came just
now to us from you, and brought us
glad news of your faith and love, and
that you have good memories of us
always, longing to see us, even as
we also long to see you;[1] 3:7 for this
cause, brothers, we were comforted
over you in all our distress and
affliction through your faith. 3:8 For
now we live, if you stand fast in the
Lord. 3:9 For what thanksgiving can
we render again to God for you, for
all the joy with which we rejoice for
your sakes before our God; 3:10 night
and day praying exceedingly that we
may see your face, and may perfect
that which is lacking in your faith?
3:11 Now may our God and Father
himself, and our Lord Jesus Christ,
direct our way to you; 3:12 and the
Lord make you to increase and
abound in love one toward another,
and toward all men, even as we also
do toward you, 3:13 to the end he
may establish your hearts blameless
in holiness before our God and
Father, at the coming of our Lord
Jesus with all his saints.

1. Have good memories of us always, longing to see us Good, the Absolute; the incomparable; that which is Godly in its character (RW/good). [We have been given the ability to stir up longing for God, for good, for holiness, and so on. We do this by purposefully calling the good, the Absolute, to memory.]

---

Fillmore Study Bible annotations compiled by Mary Salama.

# First Thessalonians 4

## A Life Best-Fitting for Oneness with God

4:1 Finally then, brothers, we beg
and exhort you in the Lord Jesus,
that as you received from us how
you ought to walk and to please God,
that you abound more and more.[1] 4:2
For you know what instructions we
gave you through the Lord Jesus. 4:3
For this is the will of God: your
sanctification, that you abstain from
sexual immorality, 4:4 that each one
of you know how to possess himself
of his own vessel in sanctification
and honor, 4:5 not in the passion of
lust, even as the Gentiles who don't
know God; 4:6 that no one should take
advantage of and wrong a brother
or sister in this matter; because the
Lord is an avenger in all these things,
as also we forewarned you and
testified. 4:7 For God called us not for
uncleanness, but in sanctification. 4:8
Therefore he who rejects this doesn't
reject man, but God, who has also
given his Holy Spirit to you.

4:9 But concerning brotherly
love,[2] you have no need that one
write to you. For you yourselves are
taught by God to love one another,
4:10 for indeed you do it toward all the
brothers who are in all Macedonia.
But we exhort you, brothers, that
you abound more and more; 4:11 and
that you make it your ambition to
lead a quiet life, and to do your own
business, and to work with your own

hands, even as we instructed you; 4:12 that you may walk properly toward those who are outside, and may have need of nothing.

1. Walk and to please God, that you abound more and more. [When we practice and apply living by the Words of Truth and guidance of the Spirit's Inner Voice, we walk in the way of aligning with God, and when we walk (live) in this way, we abound more and more, in every good thing, even in our ability to continue walking the narrow path.]

2. *But concerning brotherly love.* In practical Christianity every man, who aspires to the highest attainment in the Christian life, "needs not" to be taught of man the doctrine of "brotherly love," because in finding God he finds Divine Love; and this Eternal Principle springs forth from the heart of love in spontaneity to every man, his brother.

## The Resurrection of Those Who Have Died

4:13 But we don't want you to be ignorant,[1] brothers, concerning those who have fallen asleep,[2] so that you don't grieve like the rest, who have no hope. 4:14 For if we believe that Jesus died and rose again, even so God will bring with him those who have fallen asleep in Jesus.[3] 4:15 For this we tell you by the word of the Lord, that we who are alive, who are left to the coming of the Lord, will in no way precede those who have fallen asleep.[4] 4:16 For the Lord himself will descend from heaven with a shout, with the voice of the archangel, and with God's trumpet. The dead in Christ will rise first,[5] 4:17 then we who are alive, who are left, will be caught up together with them in the clouds,[6] to meet the Lord in the air. So we will be with the Lord forever. 4:18 Therefore comfort one another with these words.

1. *We don't want you to be ignorant.* Paul's teaching of the resurrection of the body was an entirely new idea to Gentile converts and therefore they were confused about the parousia, or Second Coming of Christ. What would be the state of those who had died before hearing the Christ message, and what would happen to those who were alive when He came? (Be Ye Transformed 87).

2. *Concerning those who have fallen asleep.* The Resurrection is the great doctrine of the Christ, which has its basis in the truth that man is Spiritual and not material, and continues to live, though the external manifestation may perish. In this Christian doctrine we "sorrow not for them which are asleep, as other who have no hope" of anything beyond the physical manifestation of life.

3. *God will bring with him those who have fallen asleep in Jesus.* For the reappearance of Jesus after his death is proof positive that man does not die, that death is a delusion; for "them that sleep in Jesus," as immortal Spiritual beings, have a resurrection from this appearance of death to the consciousness of life. The continuation of the living Spiritual man in an unseen Spiritual body is accomplished by the power of the Divine within.

4. *We who are alive ... will in no way precede those who have fallen asleep.* Therefore, "In the day when the Son of man is revealed," when we shall see with unbeclouded vision, we shall understand that those, who on the physical plane demonstrated immortality, shall not take precedence over those who make the same demonstration through laying down the physical.

5. *The dead in Christ will rise first.* For the first in the demonstration of life are "the dead in Christ," they who "lay down their lives for Christ's sake." "He that loseth his life for my sake, shall keep it unto life eternal," shall not lose it at all, but shall make the demonstration of Life Eternal. This was the inspiration of the martyrs.

6. *Then we who are alive ... will be caught up together with them in the clouds.* In realization, ascending above material ideas, until material conceptions disappear as fully as to those who have laid down the body.

Fillmore Study Bible annotations compiled by Mary Salama.

# First Thessalonians 5

## The Resurrection of Those Who Have Died (continued)

5:1 But concerning the times and the seasons,(1) brothers, you have no need that anything be written to you. 5:2 For you yourselves know well that the day of the Lord(2) comes like a thief in the night. 5:3 For when they are saying, "Peace and safety," then sudden destruction will come on them, like birth pains on a pregnant woman; and they will in no way escape. 5:4 But you, brothers, aren't in darkness, that the day should overtake you like a thief. 5:5 You are all children of light, and children of the day.(3) We don't belong to the night, nor to darkness, 5:6 so then let's not sleep, as the rest do, but let's watch and be sober. 5:7 For those who sleep, sleep in the night, and those who are drunk are drunk in the night. 5:8 But let us, since we belong to the day, be sober, putting on the breastplate of faith and love, and, for a helmet, the hope of salvation. 5:9 For God didn't appoint us to wrath, but to the obtaining of salvation through our Lord Jesus Christ, 5:10 who died for us, that, whether we wake or sleep, we should live together with him. 5:11 Therefore exhort one another, and build each other up, even as you also do.

1. *But concerning the times and the seasons.* But in making this greatest of demonstrations “times and seasons” are not to be considered; immortality is not a condition to develop into, but a realization of that which already is and ever was.

2. *The day of the Lord.* A “day,” or state of realization, instantaneously “comes,” not by “times and seasons” but in eternity, in the measureless Now. “Now is the accepted time, now is the day of salvation,” the moment of realization. Instantaneity is the “thief” that steals away “times and seasons.”

3. *You are all children of light, and children of the day.* They who understand something of the hidden springs of conduct and character are “of the day,” while those who lack self-understanding are of “the night” and cannot steer a straight course in temperate living.

## The Coming of the Lord

5:12 But we beg you, brothers, to know those who labor among you, and are over you in the Lord, and admonish you, 5:13 and to respect and honor them in love for their work's sake.

Be at peace among yourselves.(1) 5:14 We exhort you, brothers, admonish the disorderly, encourage the fainthearted, support the weak, be patient toward all. 5:15 See that no one returns evil for evil to anyone, but always follow after that which is good, for one another, and for all.

5:16 Rejoice always.(2) 5:17 Pray without ceasing.(3) 5:18 In everything give thanks, for this is the will of God in Christ Jesus toward you. 5:19 Don't

quench the Spirit. 5:20 Don't despise
prophesies. 5:21 Test all things, and
hold firmly that which is good.[4] 5:22
Abstain from every form of evil.

5:23 May the God of peace himself
sanctify you completely. May your
whole spirit, soul, and body[5] be
preserved blameless at the coming of
our Lord Jesus Christ.

5:24 He who calls you is faithful,
who will also do it. 5:25 Brothers, pray
for us. 5:26 Greet all the brothers with
a holy kiss. 5:27 I solemnly command
you by the Lord that this letter be
read to all the holy brothers.

5:28 The grace[6] of our Lord Jesus
Christ be with you. Amen.

1. *Be at peace among yourselves.* It requires patience and perseverance to master all the thoughts that make up the various planes of consciousness in each of us. There are the "unruly" thoughts that have not yet learned the law of order. Then there are the "feeble-minded" thoughts, those that believe in inability and inefficiency. Here is where we must rise in Spirit and affirm the might and power of the I Am, which is the image and likeness of the Omnipresent God.

2. *Rejoice always.* In order to keep ourselves continuously in the Christ consciousness we should abide in the thought of God and express the faculties that help us to enter into this consciousness.

3. *Pray without ceasing.* There are activities of the Spirit which the intellectual man may not have discerned, and among them is the inner flame that constantly recognizes the presence and power of God, and a certain concentration of the mind within the devotee quickens the brain centers in the organism, until they constantly quiver with the vibrations of the Spirit.

4. *Test all things, and hold firmly that which is good.* The Christ stirs us to "prove all things" and "hold fast that which is good." The authority of the Christ is native to each individual. Only the good is to remain unchanged.

5. *Spirit, soul, and body.* This is the biblical reference for the metaphysical trinity of human beings. The greek word for body is *soma*, not *sarx* (flesh).

6. *Grace.* Good will; favor; disposition to show mercy; aid from God in the process of regeneration (RW/grace).

---

Fillmore Study Bible annotations compiled by Mary Salama.

# Paul's Second Letter to the Thessalonians

Overlooking modern Thessaloniki seafront from Old Town. Wikipedia Commons. Public Domain.

## Introduction to Second Thessalonians

### Overview of Paul's Second Letter to the Thessalonians

As already mentioned in the Introduction to Paul's First Letter to the Thessalonians, this letter of assurance was carried to the Thessalonians by Timothy. But soon Timothy returned to Paul with a newly-arisen problem. Some of the Thessalonian converts had become so enamored with the promise of this Second Coming that they were neglecting the ordinary duties of life, and idly awaiting the Messianic return. Paul immediately dispatched a second letter (Second Thessalonians), couched in stern terms, telling the converts that there must first be a "falling away," and that the Lord would not appear until the appointed time. Meanwhile, the apostle commands that there shall be no idleness or wasting of time among the converts, for "if any one will not work, let him not eat" (II Thess. 3:10).

Introduction to *Paul's Second Letter to the Thessalonians* by Herbert J. Hunt, former Dean of Bible Studies for the Unity School of Christianity.

Paul had heard that the church at Thessalonica was getting sidetracked with inaccurate reports about the Day of the Lord, and so he writes this letter in order to comfort them, to correct the false reports, and to deal with the issue of idleness arising amidst some of them and was causing problems.

Metaphysically, in a world that is constantly feeding us a stream of negative reports and beliefs, our minds can get sidetracked and lose sight of the Truth of God's Presence and power, and the Truth of who we are. This loss of focus is disturbing to our souls (our minds, our wills, our emotions) and is in need of correction, especially to return our attention back into focus and protect us from the problems (ex. fear, doubt, confusion, etc.) that usually result from idle thinking.

### 3 Key Themes in 2nd Thessalonians

1. **Encouragement to continue maturing:** We are to daily, continually, encourage ourselves to continue in our journey of transmutation and onward evolution.
2. **Correct error thoughts:** The sooner we catch error thoughts at their onset and bring ourselves back to focus, with a Word of Truth, the better off we are.
3. **Accountability:** Lest we fall into spiritual idleness, let us effort to maintain a state of watchfulness over our thoughts and feelings. Remaining and returning ourselves to the Word of God and the awareness of the Presence of God is a safekeeping for us along our journey of spiritual transmutation.

Introduction to *Paul's Second Letter to the Thessalonians* by Rev. Mark Hicks.

# Second Thessalonians 1

## A Billowy Church, Tossed by the Waves[1]

1:1 Paul, Silvanus, and Timothy,[2]
to the assembly of the
Thessalonians[3] in God our Father,
and the Lord Jesus Christ: 1:2 Grace to
you and peace from God our Father
and the Lord Jesus Christ.

1. See 1 Thessalonians 1:1-2
2. *Paul, Silvanus, and Timothy*. Paul represents the will, which is an important factor in expressing the Christ actively in the life. Understanding (represented by Silvanus) and zeal or the inspired reason united with faith (Timothy) must cooperate with the will, if man would express the Christ fully.
3. *Thessalonians*. Thessalonica's ancient name was *Thermæ*, because of the many hot springs that were there), a city of

Macedonia (the enthusiasm and energy of Spirit that set the whole of our being aflame), from which Paul (our Spirit-led will) is driven away by our lack of discernment of Spirit/Truth (persecution by the Jews). Thessalonica in us is that phase of our unfoldment that lacks sufficient thinking balance to give tolerance and wisdom [to Spirit's leading or to that which arises in our lives] (billowy, tossed by the waves).(MBD/Thessalonica)

## Where Faith Grows

1:3 We are bound to always give
thanks to God for you, brothers,[1]
even as it is appropriate, because
your faith grows exceedingly, and
the love of each and every one of
you towards one another abounds;
1:4 so that we ourselves boast about
you in the assemblies① of God for
your patience and faith in all your
persecutions and in the afflictions
which you endure.

1. *Assembly or "church."* The true church is an aggregation of spiritual ideas in individual consciousness. To establish a new aggregation of spiritual ideas of God within us, a new state of consciousness must first be formed. (MBD/church), thus, every "inner church" begins as a mental perception and by degrees establishes itself in the whole consciousness.

## What is Righteous Judgement?

1:5 This is an obvious sign of the
righteous judgment① of God, to the
end that you may be counted worthy
of the Kingdom of God, for which you
also suffer. 1:6 Since it is a righteous
thing with God to repay affliction to
those who afflict you, 1:7 and to give
relief to you who are afflicted with
us, when the Lord Jesus is revealed
from heaven with his mighty angels
in flaming fire, 1:8 giving vengeance
to those who don't know God, and
to those who don't obey the Good
News of our Lord Jesus, 1:9 who will
pay the penalty: eternal destruction
from the face of the Lord and from
the glory of his might, 1:10 when he
comes to be glorified in his saints,
and to be admired among all those
who have believed (because our
testimony to you was believed) in
that day.

1:11 To this end we also pray
always for you, that our God may
count you worthy of your calling, and
fulfill every desire of goodness and
work of faith, with power; 1:12 that
the name of our Lord Jesus[2] may
be glorified in you, and you in him,
according to the grace of our God
and the Lord Jesus Christ.

1. *Righteous judgment of God.* The word "judgment" (krisis) is not the same as the word "condemnation" (kata-krisis), neither does "to judge" (krino) always mean "to damn" (kata-krino). A judge may pronounce a thing good and may give his word in favor of the one brought before him. This distinction between judgment and condemnation has not always been regarded by the translators of the Bible; often they have used "condemnation" and "damnation" where the true word is "judgment." See John 5:29, 2 Thessalonians 2:12, where "damnation" should be "judgment"; and John 5:24, also 3:17-19, where "condemnation" should be "judgment." Not only are we not to condemn—to pronounce evil against any one or any thing, and to mete out punishment but also we are not to sit in judgment, neither to declare for nor against. In other words, we are to cease eating of that forbidden tree which causes us to see double, the tree of the knowledge of good and evil. We are to know only that Good which has no opposite. We stop our ears from hearing of evil, and shut our eyes from see-

ing it (Is. 33:15). We judge not after the sight of mortal eyes, neither reprove after the hearing of the ears (Is 11:3). We judge not according to appearances, but judge righteous judgment, which is to see all things with those pure eyes that behold only God. There is no judgment in the Kingdom of Heaven. The Father judgeth no man, but hath committed all judgment unto the Son, who says of himself, "I judge no man." "I came not to judge the world, but to save the world." (Annie Rix Militz: The Sermon on the Mound—an Interpretation, p.94-96)

---

Fillmore Study Bible annotations compiled by Mary Salama.

**World English Bible Footnotes:**

[1] v1:3. The word for "brothers" here and where context allows may also be correctly translated "brothers and sisters" or "siblings."

[2] v1:12. TR adds "Christ"

# SECOND THESSALONIANS 2

## Lawlessness: a Disorderly State of Consciousness

2:1 Now, brothers, concerning the coming of our Lord Jesus Christ,[1] and our gathering together to him, we ask you 2:2 not to be quickly shaken in your mind, nor yet be troubled, either by spirit, or by word, or by letter as from us, saying that the day of Christ had come. 2:3 Let no one deceive you in any way. For it will not be, unless the departure comes first, and the man of sin is revealed, the son of destruction, 2:4 he who opposes and exalts himself against all that is called God or that is worshiped; so that he sits as God in the temple of God, setting himself up as God. 2:5 Don't you remember that, when I was still with you, I told you these things? 2:6 Now you know what is restraining him, to the end that he may be revealed in his own season. 2:7 For the mystery of lawlessness already works. Only there is one who restrains now, until he is taken out of the way. 2:8 Then the lawless one[2] will be revealed, whom the Lord will kill with the breath of his mouth, and destroy by the manifestation of his coming; 2:9 even he whose coming is according to the working of Satan with all power and signs and lying wonders, 2:10 and with all deception of wickedness for those who are being lost, because they didn't receive the love of the truth, that they might be saved. 2:11 Because of this, God sends them a working of error,[3] that they should believe a lie; 2:12 that they all might be judged who didn't believe the truth, but had pleasure in unrighteousness.

1. *Concerning the coming of our Lord Jesus Christ, and our gathering together to him.* Paul was unprepared for the effect that his words regarding the Second Coming would have upon the Thessalonians. Some in the church were discouraged. They interpreted his words as meaning that Jesus Christ would come again in the near future, and they doubted whether

they could possibly develop in themselves the spiritual qualities that would make them worthy to receive Him. Others gave up their ordinary pursuits and depended upon the more stable members of the Christian group for their livelihood, placidly awaiting the return of the Lord who would carry them into heaven. Paul assures them that the Second Coming is not to be expected immediately. His explanation is somewhat obscure, implying that what he calls "restraining" power (evil) must run its course before the great event would take place. To the conscientious and loyal believers, Paul says that they need only stand firm and continue in well-doing. To those who were shrinking their responsibilities, he reminds them that he, Silas, and Timothy had worked to earn a living so as not to be a burden on anyone, and they should do likewise. "For even when we were with you, we gave you this command: If anyone will not work, let him not eat" (II Thess. 3:10). (Be Ye Transformed 88-89).

2. *The lawless one.* The adversarial consciousness in mind. (MBD/Belial).

3. *God sends them a working of error.* "Error" are thoughts, with their corresponding words and acts, that are not in harmony with Divine Mind. Error thoughts have no foundation in absolute Truth. They originate in the intellect. Such thoughts are eliminated by one's denying their reality and power, and affirming the Truth of Being; then their outer expressions and manifestations disappear also. (MBD/error).

## Salvation and Sanctification

2:13 But we are bound to always
give thanks to God for you, brothers
loved by the Lord, because God
chose you from the beginning for
salvation❶ through sanctification❷ of
the Spirit and belief in the truth; 2:14
to which he called you through our
Good News, for the obtaining of the
glory of our Lord Jesus Christ. 2:15 So
then, brothers, stand firm, and hold
the traditions which you were taught
by us, whether by word, or by letter.

2:16 Now our Lord Jesus Christ
himself, and God our Father, who
loved us and gave us eternal comfort
and good hope through grace, 2:17
comfort your hearts and establish
you in every good work and word.

1. *Salvation.* Salvation is the process or state of our regaining conscious possession of our God-given attributes. (RW/salvation).

2. *Sanctification.* Sanctification is the putting on of the nature of God and rising to the plane of dominion that gives man peace and satisfaction (RW/sanctification). "This is the will of God, even your sanctification" (I Thess. 4:3).

Fillmore Study Bible annotations compiled by Mary Salama.

# SECOND THESSALONIANS 3

## Request for Prayer

3:1 Finally, brothers, pray for us,
that the word of the Lord may spread
rapidly and be glorified,❶ even as
also with you; 3:2 and that we may be
delivered from unreasonable and evil

men; for not all have faith. [3:3] But the Lord is faithful, who will establish you, and guard you from the evil one. [3:4] We have confidence in the Lord concerning you, that you both do and will do the things we command. [3:5] May the Lord direct your hearts into the love of God, and into the patience of Christ.

1. *That the word of the Lord may spread rapidly and be glorified.* "The Lord" is referred to as "Jehovah" (YHWH) in the Old Testament and as "Christ" in the New Testament; both represent our spiritual being. When we enter into "our lordship," we rule. We rule over ourselves, our thoughts, our body, our environment, and over all the creatures and creations of the earth. (MBD/Lord).

## Warning against Inner Idleness

[3:6] Now we command you, brothers, in the name of our Lord Jesus Christ, that you withdraw yourselves from every brother who walks in rebellion, and not after the tradition which they received from us. [3:7] For you know how you ought to imitate us. For we didn't behave ourselves rebelliously among you, [3:8] neither did we eat bread from anyone's hand without paying for it, but in labor and travail worked night and day,① that we might not burden any of you; [3:9] not because we don't have the right, but to make ourselves an example to you,② that you should imitate us. [3:10] For even when we were with you, we commanded you this: "If anyone will not work, neither let him eat."③ [3:11] For we hear of some who walk among you in rebellion, who don't work at all, but are busybodies.④ [3:12] Now those who are that way, we command and exhort in the Lord Jesus Christ, that with quietness they work, and eat their own bread.

[3:13] But you, brothers, don't be weary in doing well. [3:14] If any man doesn't obey our word in this letter, note that man, that you have no company with him, to the end that he may be ashamed. [3:15] Don't count him as an enemy, but admonish him as a brother.

1. *But in labor and travail worked night and day.* In consciousness, to "work" is to erase persistent forms of negative manifestations [and lackful interpretations] through the increased use of denials and affirmations as often necessary. (RW/work). This is our inner, continual work in our journey of transfiguration.

2. *To make ourselves an example to you.* The love of Christ gives us a sense of responsibility toward others. We realize that we are to owe no one anything but to love one another, and love leads us to help others by an example of service. The nature of love is to serve.

3. *If anyone will not work, neither let him eat.* The true object of all work is to express the powers of one's being and to benefit mankind. (RW/work). This command comes from within, from our regenerated, Spirit-led will (Paul) and it is in accordance with Divine Law; it is a new rendering of the decree "By the sweat of your face will you eat bread" (Gen 3:19). Our sense-mind considers work to be a curse, but in Truth, work is actually a blessing in disguise.

4. *Some who walk among you in rebellion, who don't work at all, but are busybodies.* To busy oneself telling others what is their duty or trying to influence their course of action is to be "in rebellion" or a "busybody"; concerning oneself with what does not concern us. We give best when we give service and withhold unasked advice on the service of others.

## Final Greetings and Benediction

[3:16] Now may the Lord of peace himself give you peace at all times in all ways. The Lord be with you all.

3:17 The greeting of me, Paul, with
my own hand, which is the sign in
every letter:[1] this is how I write. 3:18
The grace of our Lord Jesus Christ be
with you all. Amen.

1. *Which is the sign in every letter.* [A possible allusion to an esoteric sign or message.]

---

Fillmore Study Bible annotations compiled by Mary Salama.

# PAUL'S FIRST LETTER TO TIMOTHY

Saints Timothy and Titus. Unknown church. Courtesy: America Needs Fatima website.

## INTRODUCTION TO PAUL'S FIRST LETTER TO TIMOTHY

**The Pastoral Letters.** The term pastoral is frequently used in connection with Paul's Epistles to Timothy and Titus. Originally the word had reference to shepherds and their activities, but later was used in connection with Christian ministers and their congregations. Thus, the Pastoral Epistles are to be recognized as letters from the Chief Shepherd (Paul) to his under-shepherds (Timothy and Titus), and dealing with matters relating to their congregations. These Pastoral Epistles make interesting and helpful reading, especially where recognition is given to their background. Many statements given in these Epistles are frequently quoted, and they have practical application to modern conditions.

Timothy had been installed as minister of the church at Ephesus. It will be readily recognized that this ministry was no easy task. The church had been in existence for several years, and some of the officials there had assisted Paul in the early struggles toward establishment. However things were not going well at Ephesus, and therefore Paul had decided to put Timothy in charge of affairs. But Timothy was a young man, and he found it difficult to secure the full cooperation of the church officials. Some of these officials were much older than Timothy, and apparently they resented Paul's action in placing him at the head of affairs. Timothy therefore wrote an urgent letter to Paul—who was then starting out upon his missionary journey in North Africa—seeking advice regarding this unpleasant situation at Ephesus.

Paul's reply was intended to put fresh heart into Timothy. The apostle urged his young friend to hold fast to "sound doctrine" (I Tim. 1:10),to "wage the good warfare" (I Tim. 1:18), to exercise great care in appointing new church officials, and to maintain Christian discipline (I Tim. 3:1-13). Explicit directions were given regarding church activities, and then Paul urged Timothy to "Command and teach these things. Let no one despise your youth ... Do not neglect the gift you have . . . Practice these duties . . . Take heed to yourself and your teaching; hold to that, for by so doing you will save yourself and your hearers" (I Tim. 4:11-16).

Metaphysically, the name Timothy is said to mean "worshiping God, honoring God" (MBD/Timothy). This indicates that there is something in our consciousness which recognizes and honors God; and, at the same time, this something is also recognized and honored by God. This "something" may be readily identified through a careful study of the New Testament passages relating to Timothy. Paul mentions that "sincere faith . . . dwells in you" (II Tim. 1:5). Paul also recognized that Timothy possessed what may be termed executive ability. Hence Timothy was selected by Paul as a trusted messenger to the converts at Philippi (See Phil. 2:22-23); and later on Paul placed Timothy in charge of the church at Ephesus (I Tim. 1:3). However, the indications are that Timothy's faith and ability became somewhat ineffective because of an inherent timidity, or fear. Timothy did well when Paul was close at hand, but when left to work on his own account he was far from successful. Thus we find Paul urging Timothy to "fight the good fight of the faith" (I Tim. 6:12); to "rekindle the gift of God that is within you" (II Tim. 1:6); and then Paul sought to reassure Timothy by reminding him that "God did not give us a spirit of timidity but a spirit of power and love and self-control" (II Tim. 1:7). Timothy, therefore, may be interpreted in terms of inspiration, and also of warning. Our spiritual and physical powers are to be used to honor God; but we shall be honored by God only as we overcome timidity and "aim at righteousness, godliness, faith, love, steadfastness, gentleness" (I Tim. 6:11).

*Introduction to Paul's First Letter to Timothy* by Herbert J. Hunt, former Dean of Bible Studies for the Unity School of Christianity.

# First Timothy 1

## An Acknowledgement of Christ in Me

1:1 Paul, an apostle of Christ Jesus according to the commandment of God our Savior, and Christ Jesus our hope;❶ 1:2 to Timothy,❷ my true child in faith: Grace, mercy, and peace, from God our Father and Christ Jesus our Lord.

1. *our hope.* Hope is the expectation of good in the future, but because hope is a quality (good as far as it goes) of sense mind, it is subject to time. On the other hand, faith is the certain knowledge that our good is ours right now. Faith is of God and goes beyond time and space. (RW/hope)

2. *Paul ... to Timothy.* Paul is our Spirit-inspired or regenerated will. Timothy is our inspired reason united with faith, also zeal. (MBD/Timothy). [As metaphysicians, we interpret the entire Bible and its Holy Scriptures as unfolding within our own consciousness. Thus, the conversations taking place between Paul and Timothy (our will and our zeal for God) are conversations we have with ourselves, within ourselves. Such self-talk is especially important during times of challenge and the onset of negative thoughts (false teachers), when we most need to encourage and recommit ourselves to continue in the Word and Spirit.]

## Beware of Error/Negative Thoughts

1:3 As I urged you when I was going
into Macedonia, stay at Ephesus that
you might command certain men not
to teach a different doctrine, 1:4
neither to pay attention to myths and
endless genealogies, which cause
disputes, rather than God's
stewardship, which is in faith-- 1:5 but
the goal of this command is love,
out of a pure heart and a good
conscience and unfeigned faith; 1:6
from which things some, having
missed the mark, have turned aside
to vain talking; 1:7 desiring to be
teachers of the law, though they
understand neither what they say,
nor about what they strongly
affirm.(1)

1:8 But we know that the law(2) is
good, if a man uses it lawfully, 1:9 as
knowing this, that law is not made
for a righteous man, but for the
lawless and insubordinate, for the
ungodly and sinners, for the unholy
and profane, for murderers of
fathers and murderers of mothers,
for manslayers, 1:10 for the sexually
immoral, for homosexuals,(3) for
slave-traders, for liars, for perjurers,
and for any other thing contrary to
the sound doctrine; (4) 1:11 according
to the Good News of the glory of the
blessed God, which was committed
to my trust.

1. *affirm.* to hold steadfast in mind or to speak aloud a statement of Truth. (RW/affirm). [As teachers of Truth (to ourselves as well as to others), we must apply ourselves to gain understanding about what we affirm as well as the process of affirmation, in and of itself.]

2. *the Law.* The Law of God is the orderly working out of the principle of Being, or the Divine ideals, into expression and manifestation throughout creation. The law of mind action may be described in three steps: mind, idea, manifestation. First, there must be mind; second, everything exists first as an idea in mind; third, the inherent power and intelligence in the idea causes it to act or express, and when it is expressed we have the manifestation. (MBD/law)

3. *for the sexually immoral, for homosexuals.* "The orientation of the libido is not the determining factor, rather, it is the mode or the effect it will have on your life." (Ed Rabel, *1975 Old Testament Lectures, Sodom and Gomorrah*, Sodom and Gomorrah

4. *contrary to the sound doctrine.* [Reminding ourselves and affirming the Law of God is always beneficial, but especially for anything contrary to the sound doctrine.]

## Thank Goodness for Mercy!!

1:12 And I thank him who enabled me, Christ Jesus our Lord, because he counted me faithful, appointing me to service; 1:13 although I was before a blasphemer,[1] a persecutor, and insolent. However, I obtained mercy, because I did it ignorantly in unbelief. 1:14 The grace of our Lord abounded exceedingly with faith and love which is in Christ Jesus. 1:15 The saying is faithful and worthy of all acceptance, that Christ Jesus came into the world to save sinners; of whom I am chief. 1:16 However, for this cause I obtained mercy, that in me first, Jesus Christ might display all his patience, for an example of those who were going to believe in him for eternal life. 1:17 Now to the King eternal, immortal, invisible, to God who alone is wise, be honor and glory forever and ever. Amen.

1:18 This instruction I commit to you, my child[2] Timothy, according to the prophecies which led the way to you, that by them you may wage the good warfare; 1:19 holding faith and a good conscience; which some having thrust away made a shipwreck concerning the faith; 1:20 of whom is Hymenaeus and Alexander; whom I delivered to Satan,[3] that they might be taught not to blaspheme.

1. *a blasphemer.* Impious or irreverent thoughts toward God, such as sickness, poverty, death. (RW/blasphemy) [Such thoughts make us feel "cut off" rom our Source, and so as with Paul, because it is "out of ignorance and unbelief" that we think in these ways, it is only by the mercy of God that we are restored back to right thinking.]

2. *my child.* As God joins parent and child in a bond that cannot be broken, so we are joined with Divine Mind in a union that cannot be denied, disproved, or annulled. (Second Timothy Unity Bible Lessons, June 1939)

3. *Satan.* The deceiving phase of mind in man that has fixed ideas in opposition to Truth. From egotism to self-deprecation, Satan assumes various forms in our human consciousness (MBD/Satan). [However, our Spirit-led will (Paul) delivers us from negative thoughts (Hymenaeus and Alexander) belonging to deceiving states of mind (Satan), in order that these error thoughts which oppose the Truth may be "taught not to blaspheme" (disciplined to not oppose the Truth).]

Fillmore Study Bible annotations compiled by Mary Salama.

# First Timothy 2

## Instructions concerning Prayer

2:1 I exhort therefore, first of all, that petitions, prayers,[1] intercessions, and givings of thanks,[2] be made for all men: 2:2 for kings and all who are in high places; that we may lead a tranquil and quiet life in all godliness and reverence. 2:3 For this is good and acceptable in the sight of God our Savior; 2:4 who desires all people to be saved and come to full knowledge of the truth. 2:5 For there is one God, and one mediator between God and men, the man Christ Jesus, 2:6 who

gave himself as a ransom for all;[3]
the testimony in its own times;[4] 2:7
to which I was appointed a preacher
and an apostle (I am telling the truth
in Christ, not lying), a teacher of the
Gentiles in faith and truth.

2:8 I desire therefore that the men
in every place pray, lifting up holy
hands without anger and doubting. 2:9
In the same way, that women also
adorn themselves in decent
clothing,[5] with modesty and
propriety; not just with braided hair,
gold, pearls, or expensive clothing;
2:10 but (which becomes women
professing godliness) with good
works. 2:11 Let a woman[6] learn in
quietness with all subjection. 2:12 But
I don't permit a woman to teach, nor
to exercise authority over a man, but
to be in quietness.[7] 2:13 For Adam
was first formed, then Eve. 2:14 Adam
wasn't deceived, but the woman,
being deceived, has fallen into
disobedience; 2:15 but she will be
saved through her childbearing,[8] if
they continue in faith, love, and
sanctification with sobriety.

1. *petitions, prayers.* Prayer is our communion with God and, as such, is the most highly accelerated mind action known. It steps up mental action until our consciousness synchronizes with the Christ Mind. (RW/prayer) [In prayer, we bring forth our urgent appeals to the Father and make ourselves open to receive the exchanging of our personal desires and ideas for the Desires and Ideas of the Christ Mind. We do well to cultivate the habit of referring all things, in the moment they arise, to God in prayer.]

2. *intercessions, and giving of thanks.* Everyone who depends upon the enabling power of the Holy Spirit learns through prayer that we gain what we seek, when our desire is toward God and the direction of God's thought is inclined toward what is right. Every prayer that is in harmony with Truth ("according to the will of God") is an intercession of the Holy Spirit become active in us. (MBI/Romans 8) True thanksgiving may be likened to rain falling upon ready soil, refreshing it and increasing its productiveness. (RW/thanksgiving) [Thanksgiving is the necessary accompaniment of prayer; it ought never be absent from our devotions. Thankful words, prayed in faith, will eventually produce a change in our minds and hearts.]

3. *who gave himself as a ransom for all.* [Ransom to the devil, never to God. God is all good, everywhere present and He has no need to be paid. However the devil, our lower consciousness, needs to be sacrificed. Christianity has no consensus about how atonement works. New Thought Christianity rejects the *satisfaction theory* (Jesus is my substitute) and embraces the *moral influence theory*]

4. *the testimony in its own times.* Time is the limitation of our human consciousness of space. Time is the measure we give to passing events. The only power in time is what we impart to it. When we get into the understanding of the Absolute, we will be liberated from all bondages and limitations of time. (RW/time).

5. *women also adorn themselves in decent clothing.* A warning to not allow our feelings to be preoccupied with frivolous and external matters (indecent clothing and adornments), but rather, to ensure that our emotional capacities are always adorned with words of Truth (decent clothing).

6. *Let a woman.* Every department of our being has its distinct thought center, so we are made up of many men and many women (MBD/woman). When Paul speaks about "women" and "the woman," metaphysically, these words are describing the feminine phase of our being. In the Greek, "woman" signifies the intuitive perception of Truth reflected into the intellect from the soul. (RW/woman) We know that Adam is the basic ability to think; and from this basic ability to think, the Lord God or the Lord of our Being has extended or expanded another dimension of the ability to think, and it is now woman, or the ability to feel. These two components shall cleave together and become one. (Ed Rabel, *Old Testament Lectures*, Man and Woman).

7. *be in quietness.* Jim Lewis says, "Be very, very careful of being involved in group (or personal) emotional experiences. [Our very own emotional experiences can be very deceptive - limiting us when it would be best to move forward, at other times urging us to rush in before prayerful consideration. We must learn to recognize and discern these inner fluctuations and bring them under the authority of the Word of Truth, lest they get us into difficulty faster than anything else (fall into disobedience)." *Mystical Teachings of*

*Christianity*, Speaking in Tongues.

8. *she will be saved through her childbearing*. [If men and women are our thoughts and feelings, then children are our afterthoughts and meta-feelings, and when our emotions (women) "continue in faith, love and the conscious putting on of the nature of God," they are able to bring forth the thoughts and will of the Spirit (childbearing).]

---

Fillmore Study Bible annotations compiled by Mary Salama.

# First Timothy 3

## Qualifications for our Inner Overseers

3:1 This is a faithful saying: if a man seeks the office of an overseer[1],① he desires a good work. 3:2 The overseer therefore must be without reproach, the husband of one wife, temperate, sensible, modest, hospitable, good at teaching; 3:3 not a drinker,② not violent, not greedy for money, but gentle, not quarrelsome, not covetous; 3:4 one who rules his own house well, having children in subjection with all reverence; 3:5 (but if a man doesn't know how to rule his own house, how will he take care of the assembly of God?) 3:6 not a new convert, lest being puffed up he fall into the same condemnation as the devil. 3:7 Moreover he must have good testimony from those who are outside, to avoid falling into reproach and the snare of the devil.

1. *an overseer*. [This is our judgement faculty, which is always at work within us, providing the appropriate guiding of our attention to ensure our alignment with and receptivity to "visitations" of Spirit]

2. ... *not a drinker*. [Spending time with God in study and prayer strengthens our good judgement (overseer), keeping us free from inner criticism (without reproach), singularly committed (husband of one wife), temperate, sensible, modest, hospitable to the Word of Truth; not drunk on negative thoughts (not a drinker), not violating the Truth (not violent), and so on.]

## Qualifications for our Inner Deacons

3:8 Servants[2]①, in the same way, must be reverent, not double-tongued, not addicted to much wine, not greedy for money; 3:9 holding the mystery of the faith in a pure conscience.② 3:10 Let them also first be tested; then let them serve[3] if they are blameless. 3:11 Their wives in the same way must be reverent, not slanderers, temperate, faithful in all things. 3:12 Let servants[4] be husbands of one wife, ruling their children and their own houses well. 3:13 For those who have served well[5] gain for themselves a good standing, and great boldness in the faith which is in Christ Jesus.

1. *Servants*. Here specifically referring to

deacons. In the Greek, a deacon is "one who [speedily] executes the commands of another, especially of a master" (www.biblehub.com), but in consciousness, servants are the elemental forces of Being, ever at hand to carry out our demands. (MBD/servants). [Our "deacon" energies and capacities serve us best when they are reverent, stable, not wasteful in repetition or deceit (not double-tongued), free from being distracted by manifestations (much wine), and are free to hold the mystery of the Truth in our consciousness. By these measures, we can test and refine our inner deacons, servant energies.]

2. *a pure conscience.* [Taken at its surface level, conscience is that] accusing state of mind that refuses to remit past sins and keeps one in a state of self-condemnation and remorse. However, whoever has felt the prick of conscience has been spoken to by the Holy Spirit, and whoever has sat at the feet of his own inner convictions has been aware of God's presence, [and so in that regard, this "inner accuser" is our very best friend and "serves us well".] (RW/conscience)

## Our Inner Church: the Secret Assembly Line Behind our Conviction

3:14 These things I write to you,
hoping to come to you shortly; 3:15
but if I wait long, that you may know
how men ought to behave themselves
in the house of God, which is the
assembly of the living God,(1) the
pillar and ground of the truth. 3:16
Without controversy, the mystery of
godliness is great:

God was revealed in the flesh,
justified in the spirit,
seen by angels,
preached among the nations,
believed on in the world,
and received up in glory.(2)

1. *the assembly of the living God.* Assembly, in other versions, "church." The true or inner church is an aggregation of spiritual ideas in individual consciousness. The church of God begins its activity within us as a mental perception which must go through certain processes before it is established in the whole consciousness. Its work is subjective first; that is, it is a silent interior planting of spiritual ideas, which do not make themselves manifest at once, but work like leaven, and in time transform the individual. (MBD/church) [Seen this way, "the church" can be seen as a process; a verb and not a noun. We are always in the process of "churching" or "assembling" a new state of consciousness.]

2. *flesh, spirit, angels, nations, world, glory.* God is revealed to us through apparent or materialized conditions (flesh). These appearances are corrected by the Mind of God within us (justified in the Spirit), discerned by our spiritual perceptive faculties, which ever dwell in the presence of the Father (seen by angels). The Divine Truth is then proclaimed throughout our aggregations of thoughts held in mind (preached among the nations) and a deposit of faith (belief) is made into our current state of consciousness which has been formed through the belief in the reality of things external (the inner world). The process of our inner churching is made complete with our attaining a realization of Divine unity (glory); the blending and merging of our mind with God-Mind. (MBD/flesh, spirit, angels, world, RW/nations, glory)

---

Fillmore Study Bible annotations compiled by Mary Salama.

**World English Bible Footnotes:**

[1] v3:1. or, superintendents, or bishops

[2] v3:8. or, Deacons.

[3] v3:10. or, serve as deacons

[4] v3:12. or, deacons

[5] v3:13. or, served well as deacons

# First Timothy 4

## The Remedy for Unnecessary Abstinences: The Word of God and prayer

4:1 But the Spirit says expressly that in later times some will fall away from the faith, paying attention to seducing spirits and doctrines of demons,[1] 4:2 through the hypocrisy of men who speak lies, branded in their own conscience as with a hot iron; 4:3 forbidding marriage and commanding to abstain from foods which God created to be received with thanksgiving by those who believe and know the truth. 4:4 For every creature of God is good,[2] and nothing is to be rejected, if it is received with thanksgiving. 4:5 For it is sanctified through the word of God and prayer.[3]

1. *demons.* Demons or evil spirits, are conditions of mind or states of consciousness that have been developed because our creative power having been misused in an unwise or ignorant way. If in thought or in word we use our creative power ignorantly, we bring forth an ego or a personality of like character. The mind builds states of consciousness that become established in brain and body. Both good and evil are found in the unregenerate man, but in the new birth, evil and all its works must be cast out. [Demons are powerless thoughts that oppose our Christ nature and Its plan and unfolding in us, therefore], the work of every overcomer is to cast out of him or herself the demons of sin and evil, through the power and dominion of their indwelling Christ. (MBD/demons)

2. *every creature of God is good.* See Genesis 1:31: "God saw everything that He had made, and, behold, it was very good."

3. *sanctified through the word of God and prayer.* [It is the Word of God combined with words of thankfulness, spoken or prayed out of our own mouths, that has the power to make holy and pure any situation or condition that lies before us. We are most like our heavenly Father when we label (call) all things: "This too, is very good!"]

## A Good Minister of the Word of Truth

4:6 If you instruct the brothers of these things, you will be a good servant[1] of Christ Jesus, nourished in the words of the faith, and of the good doctrine which you have followed. 4:7 But refuse profane and old wives' fables. Exercise yourself toward godliness.[2] 4:8 For bodily exercise has some value, but godliness has value in all things,[3] having the promise of the life which is now, and of that which is to come. 4:9 This saying is faithful and worthy of all acceptance. 4:10 For to this end we both labor and suffer reproach, because we have set our trust in the living God, who is the Savior of all men, especially of those who believe.[4] 4:11 Command and teach these things.

4:12 Let no man despise your youth; but be an example to those who believe, in word, in your way of life, in love, in spirit, in faith, and in purity. 4:13 Until I come, pay attention to reading, to exhortation, and to teaching. 4:14 Don't neglect the gift that is in you,[5] which was given to you by prophecy, with the laying on of the hands of the elders. 4:15 Be diligent in these things. Give yourself wholly to them, that your progress may be revealed to all. 4:16 Pay attention to yourself, and to your teaching.[6] Continue in these things, for in doing this you will save both yourself and those who hear you.

1. *a good servant.* We are good servants and ministers of Christ Jesus when we keep and practice the Word of Truth and principles of faith to ourselves. When we prove the Word of Truth in our own experience, we are then qualified and able to present It to others with conviction, zeal, and understanding.

2. *exercise yourself toward godliness.* We do this by keeping our mind fixed on the good, regardless of appearances, and by expressing what is good in words and deeds.

3. *godliness has value in all things.* Because godliness is the consciousness of the spiritual nature back of all things, thus, a consciousness of godliness helps the person who has it to be able to see the true reality beneath surface appearances.

4. *especially of those who believe.* The life principle that animates all men is the living God. Those who recognize this principle as Divine and entrust themselves to it in all things are saved from the evils that befall those who, lacking this faith, have no ground upon which to base their confidence.

5. *Don't neglect the gift that is in you.* To be effective, a natural or innate gift must be cultivated. When we are diligent in cultivating our inner gift, which is Christ in us, our "progress may be revealed to all."

6. *Pay attention to yourself, and to your teaching.* [As teachers of Truth to ourselves and to others, we cannot afford to look upon our personal progress] or teaching as a matter of routine. Relaxing our interest and teaching from the old springs of inspiration is fatal to the success of a teacher of Truth. The way of Truth is the living way. "*Continue* in these things, for in doing this you will save both yourself and those who hear you." The result of our meditating profoundly on Truth is that we become so in harmony with It, that our life reveals it, to all.

---

Fillmore Study Bible annotations compiled by Mary Salama.

# First Timothy 5

## Guidelines for Refining our Inner Church

5:1 Don't rebuke an older man, but exhort him as a father; the younger men as brothers; 5:2 the elder[1] women as mothers; the younger as sisters, in all purity.

5:3 Honor widows who are widows indeed.[2] 5:4 But if any widow has children or grandchildren, let them learn first to show piety towards their own family, and to repay their parents, for this is[6] acceptable in the sight of God. 5:5 Now she who is a widow indeed, and desolate, has her hope set on God, and continues in petitions and prayers night and day. 5:6 But she who gives herself to pleasure is dead while she lives. 5:7 Also command these things, that they may be without reproach. 5:8 But if anyone doesn't provide for his own, and especially his own household, he has denied the faith, and is worse than an unbeliever.

5:9 Let no one be enrolled as a widow under sixty years old, having been the wife of one man, 5:10 being approved by good works, if she has brought up children, if she has been hospitable to strangers, if she has washed the saints' feet, if she has relieved the afflicted, and if she has diligently followed every good work. 5:11 But refuse younger widows, for when they have grown wanton against Christ, they desire to marry; 5:12 having condemnation, because they have rejected their first pledge. 5:13 Besides, they also learn to be idle, going about from house to house. Not only idle, but also gossips and busybodies, saying things which they ought not. 5:14 I desire therefore that the younger widows marry, bear children, rule the household, and give no occasion to the adversary for reviling. 5:15 For already some have turned aside after Satan. 5:16 If any man or woman who believes has widows, let them relieve them, and don't let the assembly be burdened; that it might relieve those who are widows indeed.

5:17 Let the elders who rule well be counted worthy of double honor, especially those who labor in the word and in teaching.[3] 5:18 For the Scripture says, "You shall not muzzle the ox when it treads out the grain."[7][4] And, "The laborer is worthy of his wages."[8]

5:19 Don't receive an accusation against an elder, except at the word of two or three witnesses. 5:20 Those who sin, reprove in the sight of all,[5] that the rest also may be in fear. 5:21 I command you in the sight of God, and Christ Jesus, and the chosen angels, that you observe these things without prejudice, doing nothing by partiality. 5:22 Lay hands hastily on no one, neither be a participant in other men's sins. Keep yourself pure.[6] 5:23 Be no longer a drinker of water only, but use a little wine[7] for your stomach's sake and your frequent infirmities.

5:24 Some men's sins are evident, preceding them to judgment, and some also follow later. 5:25 In the same way also there are good works that are obvious, and those that are otherwise can't be hidden.

1. *older, elder.* Our "elders" are all of the intelligent, directive powers of our spiritual self. The refining of our "elder" directive powers is a process that may take place without our conscious mind's understanding its import. Like a chemical solution, the directive powers of our spiritual self go through changes (being rebuked and exhorted) on the subjective side that are observed in their outer appearance only, and but dimly understood. (MBD/elders)

2. *Honor widows who are widows indeed.* Widows represent half-truths. These half-truths see the external of Truth but reject the real or inner spirit of it; thus they are in lack. Half-truths are bereft of worldly protection and power, [therefore, Paul's encouraging us to "honor them," is to restore them to the full Truth.] It is our own responsibility to correct the errors or half-truths in our consciousness (MBD/widow)

3. *elders ... who labor in the word and in teaching.* [The intelligent, directive powers of our spiritual self (our elders) are ceaselessly at work within us, doing the work of regenerating our consciousness.]

4. *You shall not muzzle the ox* See (Deut 25:4): the minister, who treads out the grain of Truth, should be supported by the ministry.

5. *Those who sin, reprove in the sight of all.* When we become aware that we have departed from the Truth, Spirit encourages us to offer a sincere repentance (in the sight of all) in order that our entire consciousness (the rest also) may remain in positive fear.

6. *Keep yourself pure.* To be pure in consciousness is to be completely free from all anxiety, resentment, selfishness, lust, and every other form of antichrist thought and

feeling. (RW/pure, purity)

7. *but use a little wine.* [If we wish to regenerate the body, we must listen to the wisdom of the body and allow its essence to blend with our thinking and feeling nature.] Metaphysically, wine is the vitality that forms the connecting link between soul and body. It represents an all-pervading, free essence that is generated from the nerve substance, or water of life. The wine of life, or vitality of the organism, must be available before a blending of thoughts, or of soul and body (wedding), can be made successfully. When the new Christ life comes into a mind where old beliefs concerning the body have been held, the body is transformed into its innate spiritual perfection. (RW/wine)

---

Fillmore Study Bible annotations compiled by Mary Salama.

**World English Bible Footnotes:**

[6] v5:4. TR adds "good and"

[7] v5:18. Deuteronomy 25:4

[8] v5:18. Luke 10:7; Leviticus 19:13

# First Timothy 6

## Honor the One, True Master

6:1 Let as many as are
bondservants under the yoke count
their own masters(1) worthy of all
honor, that the name of God and the
doctrine not be blasphemed. 6:2
Those who have believing masters,
let them not despise them, because
they are brothers,(2) but rather let
them serve them, because those who
partake of the benefit are believing
and beloved. Teach and exhort these
things.

1. *their own masters.* Jesus Himself tells us, "Neither be called masters, for one is your master, the Christ" (Matthew 23:10). The more we allow ourselves to be mastered by our indwelling Christ, the more we demonstrate mastery and dominion in our ability to persistently think thoughts of power and strength in the absolute principle of Truth. (RW/mastery)

2. *they are brothers.* The five seemingly material avenues of sense expression. (MBD/brethren) [Our energies, faculties, and capacities are our brothers and bondservants. Heretofore we may have allowed them to take us captive, but we now know that they can serve us in our journey of spiritual regeneration.]

## Temporary versus True Riches

6:3 If anyone teaches a different
doctrine, and doesn't consent to
sound words,(1) the words of our Lord
Jesus Christ, and to the doctrine
which is according to godliness, 6:4 he
is conceited, knowing nothing, but
obsessed with arguments, disputes,
and word battles, from which come

envy, strife, reviling, evil suspicions,
6:5 constant friction② of people of corrupt minds and destitute of the truth, who suppose that godliness is a means of gain. Withdraw yourself from such.[9]

6:6 But godliness with contentment
is great gain. 6:7 For we brought
nothing into the world, and we
certainly can't carry anything out. 6:8
But having food and clothing, we will
be content with that. 6:9 But those
who are determined to be rich fall into a temptation and a snare and many foolish and harmful lusts, such as drown men in ruin and
destruction. 6:10 For the love of money③ is a root of all kinds of evil. Some have been led astray from the faith in their greed, and have pierced themselves through with many sorrows.

1. *Sound words.* Sound words are an indication of sound judgment, reasonableness and impartiality; they inspire trust and confidence in the one who hears them and give them a desire to express their convictions.

2. *constant friction.* [There are thoughts that cause constant friction within us. When such thoughts arise, we are to gently but quickly "withdraw yourself from such" and return our attention to "sound words, the words of our Lord Jesus Christ."]

3. *the love of money.* Love of money shows that personality is in control of the life, whereas true prosperity is founded on a consciousness of the unfailing riches of the inner realm. A person may have great material wealth and still feel poor, as does the miser, but no one who is conscious of All-Good as omnipresent feels otherwise than rich. No one can love money for its own sake and at the same time possess the true riches.

## The Good Fight of Faith: Keep Focused on Your True Purpose

6:11 But you, man of God, flee
these things, and follow after righteousness, godliness, faith, love,
patience, and gentleness. 6:12 Fight
the good fight of faith.① Lay hold of the eternal life② to which you were called, and you confessed the good confession in the sight of many
witnesses. 6:13 I command you before
God, who gives life to all things, and before Christ Jesus, who before Pontius Pilate testified the good
confession, 6:14 that you keep the
commandment without spot,③ blameless, until the appearing of our
Lord Jesus Christ; 6:15 which in its own
times he will show, who is the blessed and only Ruler, the King of
kings, and Lord of lords; 6:16 who
alone has immortality, dwelling in unapproachable light; whom no man has seen, nor can see: to whom be honor and eternal power. Amen.

1. *the good fight of faith.* The ceaseless effort to transform the lower nature into the higher through the power of the Christ.

2. *lay hold of the eternal life.* When we allow our will to support our understanding that the life of the Christ is hidden in our soul and that it can be called forth by our faithfully following the urge to lift up our minds to the standard of the perfect.

3. *keep the commandment without spot.* A reference to the expression of the Divine idea of God's perfect human within each individual, as each one of us succeeds in laying hold of the life eternal. That it does not refer to a physical reappearance of Jesus is evident in the description of the glorified Jesus Christ as "King of kings, and Lord of lords ... whom no man hath seen, nor can see." Jesus Christ is no longer visible to the eye of sense. "Even though we have known Christ after the flesh, yet now we know Him so no more."

## Feeling Heavy? Renounce!

[6:17] Charge those who are rich in this present world that they not be haughty, nor have their hope set on the uncertainty of riches,(1) but on the living God, who richly provides us with everything to enjoy; [6:18] that they do good, that they be rich in good works, that they be ready to distribute,(2) willing to communicate; [6:19] laying up in store for themselves a good foundation against the time to come, that they may lay hold of eternal life.

1. *the uncertainty of riches.* [True richness is having what we need when we need it, and the very knowing of this Truth is also a source of great enrichment for our minds and souls.] Our own Spirit-led will (Paul) charges and reminds us to beware of setting our hope on uncertain and temporary things, but that we should rather set our minds upon God, "who richly provides us with everything to enjoy."

2. *be ready to distribute.* The apostle urges those who have wealth to "be rich in good works," also to distribute their riches. [In consciousness, when our will is led by the Spirit of God, it prompts us of what we need to let go of, renounce, distribute, in order that we may move forward more easily and joyfully on our journey of spiritual regeneration.]

## Guard Your Guard

[6:20] Timothy, guard that(1) which is committed to you, turning away from the empty chatter and oppositions of the knowledge which is falsely so called; [6:21] which some professing have erred concerning the faith. Grace be with you.(2) Amen.

1. *Timothy, guard that.* Our zeal for God is our enthusiasm and commitment to Truth. This zeal is a strong protector for the Truth that is within us. We support and protect our zeal for God by turning our attention "away from the empty chatter and oppositions" of negative thoughts that if otherwise left to roam about freely, would corrupt our minds.

2. *Grace be with you.* On our journey of regeneration, we have with us the favor and aid of God (RW/grace). By our meditating on the truth of life as it is in Divine Mind and attempting to give that truth expression in all that we do, the gift of grace stirs our zeal for God (Timothy). Keeping the spiritual side of life in our minds arouses in us the power and desire to express the best that is in us, and such expression increases as we continue to practice it. (MBI/2 Timothy 1)

---

Fillmore Study Bible annotations compiled by Mary Salama.

**World English Bible Footnotes:**

[9] v6:5. NU omits "Withdraw yourself from such."

# Paul's Second Letter to Timothy

The Martyrdom of Saint Timothy - Walters Museum, Baltimore. Public Domain.

## Introduction to Paul's Second Letter to Timothy

This letter is one of three grouped together as the Pastoral Letters. Go to the Introduction to Paul's First Letter to Timothy for Dr. Hunt's introduction to the Pastoral Letters.

This Epistle is now generally recognized as Paul's final message, and was written during the closing days of the apostle's ministry. Paul was arrested, probably at Nicopolis, and then taken to Rome and thrust into a dungeon to await sentence and execution. It is significant, therefore, that this closing message should be addressed to the young man whom Paul lovingly designated as "my son" (II Tim. 2:1).

The Second Letter to Timothy contains two main ideas, which are expressed in various ways and emphasized throughout the Letter. First, Paul sought by every means at his command to impart new strength, courage, and endurance to Timothy. Mention has already been made regarding Timothy's apparent inability to cope with difficult situations, especially when he was called upon to act without the assistance of Paul. This second message may be regarded as adding emphasis to what had been written in the First Letter. However, Paul now recognized that the time of his departure had come, and he sought to prepare Timothy for those strenuous days ahead when the young helper would be called upon to stand alone. Hence the urgent appeal to "be steady, endure suffering, do the work of an evangelist, fulfil your ministry" (II Tim. 4:5).

Second, Paul desired that Timothy should come with all speed to Rome. This request appears twice (II Tim. 4:9 and 21), and may also be read between the lines in several other places in the Epistle. Timothy was also requested to bring with him "the cloak . . . the books . . . and . . . the parchments" (II Tim. 4:13). It is easy to understand why the cloak would be needed in the cold, damp, Roman prison; but we may wonder what was back of the urgent call for the books and parchments. Perhaps the answer is to be found in the brief statement, "Luke alone is with me" (II Tim. 4:11). At that time, Luke had collected considerable material for his projected Gospel, and also for the *Book of Acts*. It seems possible, therefore, that during this period of imprisonment Paul had been urging Luke to carry through this literary undertaking with all speed, and the books and parchments may have been needed to complete these important records. Thus Paul's final thought was to carry the Gospel message even farther afield than had been possible through his missionary journeys, using the writings of Luke for this purpose.

"I HAVE FINISHED MY COURSE." Something of great historical importance happened during the period of Paul's final missionary activities. At that time, Nero was the Roman emperor, and he had already begun a persecution of the Christians. Then came the great fire of Rome, when a large section of the city was destroyed (A.D. 64). History attributes the fire to the foolish actions of Nero, but Nero blamed the Christians for the catastrophe. This happening immediately brought about a great change in Roman policy. Heretofore, the Romans had tolerated various religious beliefs among the nations that constituted the empire; but following the fire, a decision was made to stamp out Christianity. The fire, of course, was the excuse for this action; but the real cause was that Rome was beginning to fear Christianity. Already Christians everywhere were proclaiming Jesus Christ as "King of kings"—and the Romans regarded this as a growing threat to the empire. Consequently a bitter persecution was launched against the Christians, and many of them were arrested and put to death.

Among the Christian leaders arrested at that time was Peter, who was then conducting his ministry in Rome, as already mentioned. Paul, who was wintering at Nicopolis, was also arrested and taken to Rome under heavy guard, where he was thrust into prison. This would be around A.D. 67. There seems a possibility that the two apostles were lodged in the same prison at this time. Prior to this, there was considerable disagreement between Peter and Paul, as already intimated; but there is a tradition that during this period of imprisonment the two apostles were brought together, and there was a complete reconciliation. There is a further story which tells how Peter managed to gain temporary freedom, but feeling that an escape in this way might be regarded as a second denial of his Lord, he returned to the prison, and shortly afterward was crucified. An early writer tells how Peter, deeming himself unworthy of the same form of execution as his Lord, begged his executioners to reverse the cross; so Peter was crucified head downward.

An element of mystery surrounds the close of Paul's active career. It seems unlikely that Paul was crucified. His Roman citizenship would have saved him from such an indignity. Possibly, too Paul's Roman citizenship secured for him some sort of formal trial, for he makes reference to his "first defense" (II Tim. 4:16); but this may have been a mere preliminary to his final sentencing. Some early writers state that Paul was executed at Rome, while others indicate that he was taken some distance outside the city, and there beheaded. Some of Paul's own statements suggest other possibilities. When writing to the Corinthians, at an earlier period, Paul declared, "Death is swallowed up in victory" (I Cor. 15:54); and when writing to the Philippians, his prayer was, "that I may know . . . the power of his resurrection . . . that if possible I may attain the resurrection from the dead" (Phil. 3:10-11). Many students of the New Testament have wondered if these expressions of Paul's faith were literally fulfilled in his closing days. Again and again the question has been asked: "Did Paul, at that time, in some way attain his freedom?" Such questions are difficult to answer, but one thing is certain: Paul attained immortality through the apostolic work he accomplished in the name of Jesus Christ. Paul belongs to that noble group of whom it was written, "They may rest from their labors, for their deeds follow them" (Rev. 14:13). Some of Paul's enduring contributions to Christianity were:

(1) Paul made "disciples of all nations," and carried the Gospel message to the ends of the then-known world. Above all other early leaders, Paul had worldwide vision; he carried the Gospel not only to the Jews, but also to the Gentiles. Matthew wrote the words of Jesus, "Go therefore and make disciples of all nations" (Matt. 28:19), but Paul carried out this command.

(2) Paul organized and established churches in Asia, Europe, and North Africa, thus making for permanence in the Christian work. Paul also inspired and instructed others to carry forward this Christian work—Timothy, Titus, Luke, and others.

(3) Paul proclaimed and emphasized the universality of the Gospel message. For him, Jesus was not only the Messiah of the Jews, but also the Christ, the Savior of the world.

(4) Paul gave us the major part of our New Testament. Thirteen Epistles were written directly by Paul; and the Gospel of Luke and the Book of Acts also owe their existence, very largely to the inspiration and materials supplied by Paul.

(5) Paul freed Christianity from ceremonial bondage. It should be recalled that prior to the work of Paul, Christianity functioned entirely within the bounds of Judaism. Even when Christian teaching began to expand into other areas, many of the early leaders sought to force the converts to accept the ceremonialism of the Jews. But Paul took his stand for religious freedom. He wrote, "For freedom Christ has set us free; stand fast therefore, and do not submit again to a yoke of slavery" (Gal. 5:1). Paul's Epistle to the Galatians has frequently been termed, "Christianity's declaration of independence."

Referring back to Paul's statements regarding knowing "the power of his resurrection," as mentioned above, the following quotation sounds a positive and practical note which will bring this lesson to a close:

"The resurrection is the raising up of the whole man—spirit, soul, and body—into the Christ consciousness of life and wholeness . . . Resurrection is accomplished by the quickening power of the Holy Spirit. Every time we rise into the realization of eternal, indwelling life, making union with the Father-Mind, the resurrection of Jesus takes place within us. All thoughts of limitation and inevitable obedience to material law are left to the tomb of materiality . . . Today the light of Truth is illumining my mind, and I rise up in the majesty of my divine sonship and proclaim myself to be the child of the Most High, free from all belief in sin, sickness, and death. I affirm: 'In unity with Christ I realize that I am resurrected into the life, light, and power of God.'" (*Keep a True Lent* 197)

Introduction to *Paul's Second Letter to Timothy* by Herbert J. Hunt, former Dean of Bible Studies for the Unity School of Christianity.

# Second Timothy 1

## Greeting Truth

1:1 Paul, an apostle❶ of Jesus
Christ through the will of God,
according to the promise of the life
which is in Christ Jesus, 1:2 to
Timothy,❷ my beloved child: Grace,
mercy, and peace,❸ from God the
Father and Christ Jesus our Lord.

1:3 I thank God, whom I serve as
my forefathers did, with a pure
conscience.❹ How unceasing is my
memory of you in my petitions, night
and day 1:4 longing to see you,
remembering your tears,❺ that I may
be filled with joy; 1:5 having been
reminded of the unfeigned faith that
is in you; which lived first in your
grandmother Lois, and your mother
Eunice, and, I am persuaded, in you
also.

1:6 For this cause, I remind you
that you should stir up the gift of
God❻ which is in you through the
laying on of my hands. 1:7 For God
didn't give us a spirit of fear,❼ but of
power, love, and self-control.❽

1. *an apostle* To be an "apostle" or one "sent out" by the Spirit to do the Spirit's evangelizing work, one must have first received the Spirit's "power from on high," and this endowment is "the promise of the life which is in Jesus Christ." In order to be efficient, our apostleship must be "by the will of God," that is, we must be "meek and lowly of heart;" we must in Gethsemane have laid down the self-will and consented to do the Father's will. "Not my will but Thy will" is the lesson to be learned in Gethsemane.

2. *Timothy*. Metapysically, Timothy is our inspired reason united with faith; also zeal. (MBD/Timothy)

3. *Grace, mercy, and peace*. This salutation fixes the thought of both the reader and the writer of this letter on a high level.

4. *with a pure conscience*. Even when persecuting Christians, Paul believed that he was serving God. Thus, we are wise when we do the best we know to do, until the regenerating power of the Holy Spirit reveals to us the higher things of the Spirit.

5. *remembering your tears*. When our brothers and sisters are "in tears" of sorrow and suffering, like Paul, we must have constant "remembrance" of them, holding them up, "night and day" in Divine perfection, that we also "may be filled with joy"

as we see them coming into the truth of their Being.

6. *stir up the gift of God.* The gift of God which we are to stir up is our innate spiritual ego, the image and likeness implanted within us in the beginning. This stirring up is accomplished by casting out all fear and affirming the power of the word. Faith is renewed by giving concentrated thought, interest, and attention to the things of God.

7. *spirit of fear.* Fearfulness is a state of mind. Fearfulness is a parasite; it drives away Divine guidance and produces weakness of the heart. (RW/fearfulness)

8. *self-control.* The habit of concentrating or centering our thoughts on the contemplation of Truth requires discipline of a high order, for the mind during meditation is prone to wander instead of coming to a focus.

## Empowering Zeal for Truth

1:8 Therefore don't be ashamed of the testimony of our Lord,[1] nor of me his prisoner; but endure hardship for the Good News according to the power of God, 1:9 who saved us and called us with a holy calling, not according to our works, but according to his own purpose and grace, which was given to us in Christ Jesus before times eternal, 1:10 but has now been revealed by the appearing of our Savior, Christ Jesus, who abolished death, and brought life and immortality to light through the Good News. 1:11 For this, I was appointed[2] as a preacher, an apostle, and a teacher of the Gentiles. 1:12 For this cause I also suffer these things.

Yet I am not ashamed, for I know him whom I have believed, and I am persuaded that he is able to guard that which I have committed to him against that day.

1. *the testimony of our Lord.* The inner experience or conviction of Truth that comes to us when we practice concentrating the full power of our thinking on the things that transcend our present knowledge.

2. *For this, I was appointed.* Our first field of conquest is our own life, not the material universe, and our first work in self-development is the overcoming of fear.

## Holding Fast to the Power of Truth

1:13 Hold the pattern[1] of sound words which you have heard from me, in faith and love[2] which is in Christ Jesus. 1:14 That good thing which was committed to you, guard through the Holy Spirit[3] who dwells in us.

1:15 This you know, that all who are in Asia[4] turned away from me; of whom are Phygelus and Hermogenes. 1:16 May the Lord grant mercy to the house of Onesiphorus, for he often refreshed me, and was not ashamed of my chain, 1:17 but when he was in Rome, he sought me diligently, and found me 1:18 (the Lord grant to him to find the Lord's mercy in that day); and in how many things he served at Ephesus, you know very well.

1. *hold the Pattern.* "The Pattern" is the Divine incarnation of Jesus is the divine pattern (Jesus AS the Divine pattern) for all men who are seeking the Christ way of life. (RW/pattern)

2. *in faith and love.* Timothy was of mixed parentage and therefore represents an idea that has its beginning in a union of the intellectual reasoning (a Greek father) with the inner spiritual qualities of faith and love (a Jewess mother).

3. *guard through the Holy Spirit.* Life is the gift that all humans share and it is our responsibility to guard it through the Holy Spirit.

4. *all who are in Asia.* A state of consciousness impregnated by old, decayed, worn-out, material ideas that should have been left behind long ago by the one who would progress spiritually. (MBD/Asia)

---

Fillmore Study Bible annotations compiled by Mary Salama.

# Second Timothy 2

## Be Diligent in the Word of Truth

2:1 You therefore, my child,[1] be strengthened in the grace that is in Christ Jesus. 2:2 The things which you have heard from me among many witnesses, commit the same to faithful men, who will be able to teach others also. 2:3 You therefore must endure hardship,[2] as a good soldier of Christ[3] Jesus. 2:4 No soldier on duty entangles himself in the affairs of life, that he may please him who enrolled him as a soldier. 2:5 Also, if anyone competes in athletics, he isn't crowned unless he has competed by the rules. 2:6 The farmers who labor must be the first to get a share of the crops. 2:7 Consider what I say, and may the Lord give you understanding in all things.

2:8 Remember Jesus Christ, risen from the dead, of the seed of David, according to my Good News, 2:9 in which I suffer hardship to the point of chains as a criminal. But God's word isn't chained. 2:10 Therefore I endure all things for the chosen ones' sake, that they also may obtain the salvation which is in Christ Jesus with eternal glory. 2:11 This saying is faithful:

"For if we died with him,
we will also live with him.
2:12 If we endure,
we will also reign with him.
If we deny him,
he also will deny us.
2:13 If we are faithless,
he remains faithful.
He can't deny himself."

1. *You therefore, my child.* Paul's referring to Timothy as child implies that we must have the consciousness of the power of the Holy Spirit and not ignore its work in our lives, because it is this very Divine energy that is going to transmute us and the world and is that which enables us to speak the right Word "grace, mercy and peace" at the right time, to others.

2. *must endure hardship.* Hardship gives us greater strength and makes victory possible for us. We give ourselves to total service. We unfit ourselves for meeting hardship by complaints, self-pity, resentment, rash conduct, or reckless defiance. We fortify ourselves with inner strength by holding ourselves in the Spirit of the Christ.

3. *a good soldier of Christ Jesus.* One who sees active service in the cause of Truth and who is obedient always to its Principles, who surrenders the personal consciousness with its standard of personal rights and submits to the dominion of Universal consciousness instead.

## Approved and Disapproved Thoughts

2:14 Remind them of these things, charging them in the sight of the Lord, that they don't argue about words, to no profit, to the subverting of those who hear.

2:15 Give diligence to present yourself approved by God, a workman who doesn't need to be ashamed, properly handling the Word of Truth. 2:16 But shun empty chatter, for they will proceed further in ungodliness, 2:17 and their word will consume like gangrene, of whom is Hymenaeus and Philetus; 2:18 men who have erred concerning the truth, saying that the resurrection is already past, and overthrowing the faith of some. 2:19 However God's firm foundation stands, having this seal, "The Lord knows those who are his,"[1] and, "Let every one who names the name of the Lord[2] depart from unrighteousness." 2:20 Now in a large house there are not only vessels of gold and of silver, but also of wood and of clay. Some are for honor, and some for dishonor. 2:21 If anyone therefore purges himself from these, he will be a vessel for honor,❶ sanctified, and suitable for the master's use, prepared for every good work.

2:22 Flee from youthful lusts;❷ but pursue righteousness, faith, love, and peace with those who call on the Lord out of a pure heart. 2:23 But refuse foolish and ignorant questionings, knowing that they generate strife. 2:24 The Lord's servant must not quarrel, but be gentle towards all, able to teach, patient, 2:25 in gentleness correcting those who oppose him: perhaps God may give them repentance leading to a full knowledge of the truth, 2:26 and they may recover themselves out of the devil's snare, having been taken captive by him to his will.

1. *a vessel for honor.* A vessel with the potential to provide us with a unique and necessary gift to increase our mastery.

2. *flee from youthful lusts.* To flee from immature thoughts and "pursue right-use-ness" by turning our attention to thoughts that build up our faith, love and peace, rather than thoughts that generate inner strife.

---

Fillmore Study Bible annotations compiled by Mary Salama.

**World English Bible Footnotes:**

[1] v2:19. Numbers 16:5

[2] v2:19. TR reads "Christ" instead of "the Lord"

# Second Timothy 3

## How to Deal with Error Thoughts

3:1 But know this, that in the last days,❶ grievous times will come. 3:2

For men will be[2] lovers of self,
lovers of money, boastful, arrogant,
blasphemers, disobedient to parents,
unthankful, unholy, 3:3 without
natural affection, unforgiving,
slanderers, without self-control,
fierce, no lovers of good, 3:4 traitors,
headstrong, conceited, lovers of
pleasure rather than lovers of God;
3:5 holding a form of godliness, but
having denied the power thereof.
Turn away from these, also. 3:6 For
of these are those who creep into
houses, and take captive[3] gullible
women loaded down with sins, led
away by various lusts, 3:7 always
learning, and never able to come to
the knowledge of the truth. 3:8 Even
as Jannes and Jambres opposed
Moses, so do these also oppose the
truth;[4] men corrupted in mind,
reprobate concerning the faith. 3:9
But they will proceed no further. For
their folly will be evident to all men,
as theirs also came to be.

1. *the last days.* The last degrees of understanding. (MBD/day)

2. *For men will be.* Thought forms and images that are self-indulgent, focused on material appearances, disobedient, lacking in gratitude, unholy, unappreciative, out of control, fierce, reckless; thoughts that betray our trust, are stubborn, conceited; thoughts that promise pleasure but have no power to deliver it.

3. *those who creep into houses, and take captive.* Thoughts (men) that creep into the mind (houses) and take captive our emotional attention (women).

4. *these also oppose the Truth.* Negative thoughts that oppose Truth, and corrupt the mind fail to pass the test of faith. If we catch these thoughts and bring them to the Light of God, they "will proceed no further".

## Paul's Charge to Timothy

3:10 But you did follow my
teaching, conduct, purpose, faith,
patience, love, steadfastness, 3:11
persecutions, and sufferings: those
things that happened to me at
Antioch, Iconium, and Lystra. I
endured those persecutions. Out of
them all the Lord delivered me. 3:12
Yes, and all who desire to live godly
in Christ Jesus will suffer
persecution.[1] 3:13 But evil men and
impostors will grow worse and worse,
deceiving and being deceived. 3:14 But
you remain in[2] the things which you
have learned and have been assured
of, knowing from whom you have
learned them. 3:15 From infancy, you
have known the sacred writings
which are able to make you wise for
salvation[3] through faith, which is in
Christ Jesus. 3:16 Every writing
inspired by God[3] is profitable[4] for
teaching, for reproof, for correction,
and for instruction which is in
righteousness, 3:17 that the man of
God may be complete, thoroughly
equipped[5] for every good work.

1. *will suffer persecution.* We must allow for the Truth to aggressively chase after us.

2. *remain in.* Continuing in learning the doctrines of Truth.

3. *wise for salvation.* When Spirit reveals to us the interior meaning of the sacred writings, we are made wise for salvation.

4. *Every writing inspired by God is profitable.* At the time Paul wrote this letter, the sacred writings of the New Testament were not yet in existence. The only sacred writings were parts of the Old Testament. Consequently the sacred writings referred to by Paul are the word of Truth which is revealed by the Spirit of Truth promised by Jesus in John 16:13: "However when he, the Spirit of Truth, has come, he will guide you into all Truth."

5. *complete, thoroughly equipped.* The study of Scripture instructs us in the knowledge of our own Being. This knowledge perfects and equips us to express our innate Divine powers and to be of benefit to the entire human family.

Fillmore Study Bible annotations compiled by Mary Salama.

**World English Bible Footnotes:**

[3] v3:16. literally, God-breathed

# Second Timothy 4

## Open Your Mouth and Preach to Yourself!

4:1 I command you therefore before God and the Lord Jesus Christ, who will judge the living and the dead[1] at his appearing and his Kingdom: 4:2 preach the word;[2] be urgent in season and out of season; reprove, rebuke, and exhort, with all patience and teaching. 4:3 For the time will come when they will not listen to the sound doctrine, but, having itching ears,[3] will heap up for themselves teachers after their own lusts; 4:4 and will turn away their ears from the truth, and turn aside to fables. 4:5 But you be sober in all things, suffer hardship, do the work of an evangelist, and fulfill your ministry.

4:6 For I am already being offered, and the time of my departure has come. 4:7 I have fought the good fight. I have finished the course. I have kept the faith. 4:8 From now on, there is stored up for me the crown of righteousness,[4] which the Lord, the righteous judge, will give to me on that day; and not to me only, but also to all those who have loved his appearing.

1. *judge the living and the dead.* Our thoughts are brought to judgment. The thoughts of life (the living) and the thoughts of "the dead" are tried by the Truth, and only those thoughts that are in harmony with Truth will be permitted into the kingdom of God within us

2. *preach the Word.* The Word of Truth must be declared constantly, "in season and out of season." When we grow lax in this respect, we will find ourselves falling back into mortal thought and material ways.

3. *itching ears.* When our minds come to that place where our "ears itch" for new teachings and fuller explanations of the mysteries of the doctrine, let us beware of falling into the habit of distracting ourselves by seeking out one more new teacher or new teaching and remind ourselves that the Truth is capable of revealing itself to us, by the guidance of the Holy Spirit: "However when He, the Spirit of Truth, has come, He will guide you into all Truth" (Jn 16:13).

4. *the crown of righteousness.* The fulfilling of the Divine Law and the resurrection of the body; a new state of mind every time we overcome some mortal error.

## The Overactive Will, Wears Us Out!

4:9 Be diligent to come to me soon, 4:10 for Demas left me, having loved this present world, and went to Thessalonica; Crescens to Galatia, and Titus to Dalmatia.[1] 4:11 Only Luke is with me.[2] Take Mark, and bring him with you,[3] for he is useful to

me for service. 4:12 But I sent Tychicus
to Ephesus. 4:13 Bring the cloak that
I left at Troas with Carpus when you come, and the books, especially the
parchments. 4:14 Alexander, the
coppersmith, did much evil to me. The Lord will repay him according to
his works, 4:15 of whom you also must
beware; for he greatly opposed our words.

1. *and Titus to Dalmatia.* Those ideas in us that believe in the material world as the source of our happiness and well-being cannot go on with us in our spiritual development. Paul also eliminated Crescens ("increasing") and Titus ("pleasant"), which refer to thoughts that are degenerating in consciousness, or falling away from a realization of Truth into foolish and deceitful ways.

2. *Only Luke is with me.* Luke means luminous. When one ceases to cling to material things, the luminous state of mind becomes abiding.

3. *Take Mark and bring him with you.* Mark served those whom he accompanied. He looked after the supplying of their daily needs while they preached and taught the people. Thus he also represents the substance idea in the overcomer, and is very useful in many ways in ministering to our spiritual faculties in their redeeming work throughout our being.

## Our Inner Lord is Faithful

4:16 At my first defense, no one
came to help me, but all left me.❶
May it not be held against them. 4:17
But the Lord stood by me, and strengthened me, that through me the message might be fully proclaimed, and that all the Gentiles might hear;❷ and I was delivered out
of the mouth of the lion. 4:18 And the
Lord will deliver me from every evil work, and will preserve me for his heavenly Kingdom;❸ to whom be the glory forever and ever. Amen.

1. *all left me.* The departure of Paul's several companions is appropriate when we consider the states of mind these persons reveal; they represent limited thoughts that must be put away before one can ascend to a higher state of consciousness.

2. *that all the Gentiles might hear.* By the aid of the One sustaining Power with and within us, we are able to teach the Truth to our Gentile thoughts.

3. *Kingdom.* The Divine presence that delivers us from every untruthful thought (every evil) and brings us into a realization of perfect harmony, health, and joy.

## Divine Grace is Our Sure Guide

4:19 Greet Prisca and Aquila, and
the house of Onesiphorus. 4:20 Erastus
remained at Corinth, but I left
Trophimus at Miletus sick. 4:21 Be
diligent to come before winter. Eubulus salutes you, as do Pudens, Linus, Claudia, and all the
brothers.❶ 4:22 The Lord Jesus Christ
be with your spirit. Grace❷ be with you. Amen.

1. *all the brothers.* Metaphysically, "brothers" are the five seemingly material avenues of sense expression (MBD/brethren).

2. *Grace.* Grace is good will; favor; disposition to show mercy; aid from God in the process of regeneration. (RW/grace)

---

Fillmore Study Bible annotations compiled by Mary Salama.

# PAUL'S LETTER TO TITUS

Saint Paul writing. From an early 9th century manuscript version of Saint Paul's letters. The manuscript is ascribed to the Monastery of St. Gallen under the scribe Wolfcoz. The picture follows an early medieval tradition of depicting the author of a text. It is believed to be one of the earliest depictions of Saint Paul in European art. The inscription says: "S(AN)C(TU)S PAULUS" and "sedet hic scripsit" ("he sits here and writes"). Public Domain.

## INTRODUCTION TO PAUL'S LETTER TO TITUS

This letter is one of three grouped together as the Pastoral Letters. Go to the Introduction to Paul's First Letter to Timothy for Dr. Hunt's introduction to the Pastoral Letters.

Titus had become the presiding elder, or minister, of the Christian groups in Crete. Titus was a much stronger type than Timothy, and therefore he took charge of affairs in Crete in a masterly way. There was no necessity for him to call upon Paul for moral support of organizational directions, as did Timothy. Nevertheless, when Paul had occasion to communicate with Titus later on, the apostle included in his Epistle some valuable advice pertaining to the work at Crete.

Titus was a Greek, and was converted by Paul, probably on the first missionary journey. There is a possibility that Titus acted as Paul's personal assistant during the first journey, replacing John Mark, who left the expedition at Perga and returned to Jerusalem. Certain it is that Titus returned with Paul to Antioch, and later played an important part in the proceedings of the first Jerusalem council. (See Galatians 2:1-3 and Acts 15:1-21.) However, Paul selected Timothy as personal assistant for the second missionary journey, since this was the type of work suitable for a younger man. Later, when Paul urgently needed assistance in connection with the "Corinthian controversy," he called upon Titus, and Titus was eminently successful in restoring order in the Corinthian church.

Apparently the Letter to Titus was written when Paul was heading for Nicopolis, on the last stage of the apostle's final missionary journey. At that time, Paul was well aware of the Roman Emperor's hostile activities, and also the difficult situation which now confronted the Christian church. Therefore, Titus was urged to be on the alert for "marching orders," and to be prepared to join Paul on short notice. Possibly Titus went to Nicopolis, in accord with Paul's instructions; and then, following Paul's arrest, journeyed with the apostle to Rome.

Metaphysically interpreted, Titus represents "a pleasing, agreeable, and honorable attitude of mind . . . that accompanies the word of Truth in its restoring work throughout the organism and the consciousness of man" (MBD/Titus). All this is readily recognized when studying the activities of Titus, as recorded in the New Testament. Titus had overcome all timidity, and whatever spiritual and physical' powers he possessed, he used them fully in the service of his Lord. Titus worked under the direction of Paul, but he was also fully aware of his own indwelling Christ; and this enabled him to carry through several important assignments with complete success. It was through the efforts of Titus that order was fully restored among the rebelling Corinthians; and when Paul took Titus to Crete, the Christian groups there readily responded to his leadership. Thus, interpreted in the light of present-day needs, Titus symbolizes that spirit in us which responds to every call of Christian duty, puts fear aside, and fully recognizes that "I can do all things in him who strengthens me" (Phil. 4:13). The Titus spirit within us enables us to become fully competent "ambassadors for Christ" (II Cor. 5:20), and we unhesitatingly declare:

"I'll go where You want me to go, dear Lord,
  Over mountain, or plain, or sea;
I'll say what You want me to say, dear Lord,
  I'll be what You want me to be."
    —(Unity Song Selections 256)

*Introduction to Paul's Letter to Titus* by Herbert J. Hunt, former Dean of Bible Studies for the Unity School of Christianity.

# Titus 1

## A Salutation of Affirmation

1:1 Paul,[1] a servant of God, and an apostle of Jesus Christ, according to the faith of God's chosen ones, and the knowledge of the truth which is according to godliness, 1:2 in hope of eternal life, which God, who can't lie, promised before time began; 1:3 but in his own time revealed his word in the message with which I was entrusted according to the commandment of God our Savior;[2] 1:4 to Titus,[3] my true child according to a common faith: Grace, mercy, and peace from God the Father and the Lord Jesus Christ our Savior.

1. *Paul*. Our will, after it has been regenerated and is now a Spirit-led will.

2. *our Savior*. The Christ Mind is our Savior. Through the Christ Mind we find salvation from poverty, sickness, sin, and death. (RW/Saviour)

3. *Titus*. A pleasing, agreeable, and honorable attitude of mind that accompanies the regenerated will (Paul) in its restoring work throughout the organism and the consciousness of man (MBD/Titus).

## Titus in Crete: Look out for Your Honorable, Agreeable Mind in a Sensual World

1:5 I left you in Crete[1] for this reason, that you would set in order the things that were lacking, and appoint elders in every city, as I directed you; 1:6 if anyone is blameless, the husband of one wife, having children who believe, who are not accused of loose or unruly behavior. 1:7 For the overseer must be blameless, as God's steward; not self-pleasing, not easily angered, not given to wine, not violent, not greedy for dishonest gain; 1:8 but given to hospitality, as a lover of good, sober minded, fair, holy, self-controlled; 1:9 holding to the faithful word which is according to the teaching, that he may be able to exhort in the sound doctrine, and to convict those who contradict him.

1:10 For there are also many unruly men, vain talkers and deceivers, especially those of the circumcision,[2] 1:11 whose mouths must be stopped; men who overthrow whole houses, teaching things which they ought not, for dishonest gain's sake. 1:12 One of them, a prophet of their own, said, "Cretans are always liars, evil beasts, and idle gluttons."

1:13 This testimony is true. For this cause, reprove them sharply, that they may be sound in the faith, 1:14 not paying attention to Jewish fables and commandments of men who turn away from the truth. 1:15 To the pure, all things are pure;[3] but to those who are defiled and unbelieving, nothing is pure; but both their mind and their conscience are defiled. 1:16 They profess that they know God, but by their works they deny him, being abominable, disobedient, and unfit for any good work.

1. *Crete*. Carnal, cutoff, fleshly, Crete is the material, sensual, worldly consciousness in us, as opposed to the spiritual. (MBD/Crete)

2. *circumcision.* [In his letters to the Romans and the Galatians, Paul criticized the idea that circumcision is a sign of righteousness. This historical criticism is reinforced by the metaphysical assertion that true circumcision] is symbolic of the cutting off of mortal tendencies and is indicative of purification and cleanliness. We are truly circumcised only by being thoroughly purified in soul, at which time the glory of our cleansed and purified inner soul works its way out into our outer consciousness and body, setting us free from all sensual, corruptible thoughts and activities. Thus we become a new creature in Christ Jesus, and we manifest wholeness and perfection throughout our entire being. (RW/circumcision)

3. *To the pure, all things are pure.* [Cynical statements such as "nothing is pure" are a sign of our turning away from Truth. As we turn our minds back to the Commandments and to true confessions (profess that we are one with God), this is the inner work that restores our consciousness back to an attitude of mind that says, "All things are pure."]

Fillmore Study Bible annotations compiled by Mary Salama.

# Titus 2

## A Household Code for Mentoring Others[1]

2:1 But say the things which fit
sound doctrine,[2] 2:2 that older men
should be temperate, sensible, sober
minded, sound in faith, in love, and
in patience:[3]

2:3 and that older women likewise
be reverent in behavior, not
slanderers nor enslaved to much
wine, teachers of that which is good;
2:4 that they may train the young
women[4] to love their husbands, to
love their children, 2:5 to be sober
minded, chaste, workers at home,
kind, being in subjection to their own
husbands, that God's word may not
be blasphemed.[5]

2:6 Likewise, exhort the younger
men[6] to be sober minded; 2:7 in all
things showing yourself an example
of good works; in your teaching
showing integrity, seriousness,
incorruptibility, 2:8 and soundness of
speech that can't be condemned;
that he who opposes you may be
ashamed, having no evil thing to say
about us.

2:9 Exhort servants to be in
subjection to their own masters,[7]
and to be well-pleasing in all things;
not contradicting; 2:10 not stealing,
but showing all good fidelity; that
they may adorn the doctrine of God,
our Savior, in all things.

1. *Household Code.* A social media meme which encouraged Stoicism for keeping a peaceful order in Roman and Greek households. Later inserted in Christian scripture to defend the Jesus movement from pagan criticism of disorderly egalitarianism. See metaphysical interpretations at Ephesians 5:22-6:9, Colossians 3:18-4:1, Titus 2:1-10 and 1 Peter 2:18-3:1-8.

2. *say the things which fit sound doctrine.* We must be careful to carry out this central idea of Paul's in its right place, that is, the mind. The true remedy for all that ails us is to "speak the sound doctrine in faith, in love, in patience." That sound doctrine is that God is Spirit, everywhere present as life substance and intelligence; that that Omnipresent substance, when taken into the consciousness, satisfies all the desires of the senses. As teach-

ers of Truth, our first step is to preach this sound doctrine to ourselves, until we are examples of sobriety, moderation, and purity.

3. *sound in faith, in love, in patience.* If all Christians in the world would take this text daily and follow it in thought and in expressed deeds, intemperance (greed, excess, immoderation) would soon be a thing of the past.

4. *older women; young women. Older women,* [the disciplined aspects of] soul, supply us with qualities that are capable of developing qualities in *young women,* [the inexperienced aspects of] soul, such as love of the Word and Spirit (love their husbands),] earnestness (sober-mindedness), purity, industry, kindness, and humility.

5. *that God's word may not be blasphemed.* The best preparation for the work of teaching others is for us to make sure of our own ground, to know our own mind, and to know God as the Source of all good.

6. *older men, younger men.* Older men, our trained intellect is in fact capable of developing praiseworthy qualities in younger men, our undisciplined intellect.

7. *Exhort servants to be in subjection to their own masters.* Here we have an appeal for the tempering of gluttony, which enslaves us to the multitude of passions. Temperance means self-control along all lines. An unruly appetite is apt to break out in any direction. The vibrations of lustful thought, though outwardly hidden, will poison the minds of those near and far who are not armored with Christian purity. The remedy is: Analyze your own sense man and purify him. Give him that satisfaction which all are seeking: the pure substance of Omnipresent Spirit.

## We are Made Whole by God's Grace

2:11 For the grace of God has
appeared, bringing salvation① to all
men, 2:12 instructing us to the intent
that, denying ungodliness and
worldly lusts,② we would live
soberly, righteously, and godly in this
present world; 2:13 looking for the
blessed hope and appearing of the
glory of our great God and Savior,
Jesus Christ; 2:14 who gave himself for
us, that he might redeem us from
all iniquity, and purify for himself
a people for his own possession,
zealous for good works.

2:15 Say these things and exhort
and reprove with all authority. Let
no man despise you.

1. *For the grace of God has appeared, bringing salvation.* Grace is aid from God in the process of regeneration (RW/grace). [Our consciousness of the Word of Truth and submission to the guidance of Spirit prepare us to perceive and receive the Divine aid of grace, which we so very much need on our spiritual regeneration journey.]

2. *denying ungodliness and worldly lusts.* This denial should be practiced daily, not only for ourselves, but for all people. Then affirm, "The grace of God hath appeared bringing salvation to everyone." This treatment applied in the silence with "faith, love and patience" will reform you and your loved one quicker than any other method, and upon this system rests the reformation of the whole world.

Fillmore Study Bible annotations compiled by Mary Salama and Mark Hicks.

# Titus 3

## Continually Renew Your Thinking

3:1 Remind them to be in subjection to rulers and to authorities,[1] to be obedient, to be ready for every good work, 3:2 to speak evil of no one, not to be contentious, to be gentle, showing all humility toward all men. 3:3 For we were also once foolish, disobedient, deceived, serving various lusts and pleasures, living in malice and envy, hateful, and hating one another. 3:4 But when the kindness of God our Savior and his love toward mankind appeared, 3:5 not by works of righteousness, which we did ourselves, but according to his mercy, he saved us, through the washing of regeneration and renewing by the Holy Spirit,[2] 3:6 whom he poured out on us richly, through Jesus Christ our Savior; 3:7 that, being justified by his grace, we might be made heirs according to the hope of eternal life.[3]

1. *be in subjection to rulers and authorities.* The Christ follower cooperates with authorities instead of antagonizing them, thus maintaining peace instead of stirring up strife, and at the same time he reaps the rewards of self-discipline.

2. *renewing by the Holy Spirit.* We are saved from the evils of sense and selfish self-centeredness through entering into the regeneration and surrendering ourselves to the guidance of the Holy Spirit.

3. *heirs according to the hope of eternal life.* As we develop consciousness of spiritual realities, we are made heirs of the kingdom of God and our hope of eternal life is heightened by our new understanding that it exists now, as surely as it will exist in the future.

## Avoid Superficial Thoughts

3:8 This saying is faithful, and concerning these things I desire that you affirm confidently, so that those who have believed God may be careful to maintain good works.[1] These things are good and profitable to men; 3:9 but shun foolish questionings, genealogies, strife, and disputes about the law; for they are unprofitable[2] and vain. 3:10 Avoid a factious man after a first and second warning; 3:11 knowing that such a one is perverted, and sins, being self-condemned.[3]

1. *maintain good works.* Because faith follows the law of expression, our belief in All-Good will naturally express outwardly as good works.

2. *but shun foolish questionings; for they are unprofitable.* All superficial views of life and of God, and all that turns our attention away from the inner truth of Being and tends it to focus on externals, these are all unprofitable to us and we are to avoid, reject, and turn our attention away from them. If indulged in, they lead to unprofitable expression.

3. *being self-condemned.* Self-condemnation is a sin in so far as it keeps us from reaching the mark set by our ideal and our aspirations.

## Self-affirmations for our Inner Renewal

3:12 When I send Artemas[1] to you, or Tychicus,[2] be diligent to come

to me to Nicopolis,[3] for I have
determined to winter there. [3:13] Send
Zenas, the lawyer, and Apollos on
their journey speedily, that nothing
may be lacking for them. [3:14] Let our
people also learn to maintain good
works for necessary uses, that they
may not be unfruitful.

[3:15] All who are with me greet you.
Greet those who love us in faith.
Grace be with you all. Amen.

1. *Artemas. Artemas*, gift of perfection; gift of wholeness. A follower of Jesus Christ, whom Paul was thinking of sending to Crete to take the place of Titus, so that Titus could come to Paul at Nicopolis. (MBD/Artemas)

2. *Tychicus. Tychicus*, whom Paul considered sending to Crete to relieve Titus instead of sending Artemas, represents a belief in fate. Paul seems to have been undecided as to whether it would be best to leave this carnal state of consciousness (Crete) to its fate (Tychicus) for a time, or to send Artemas to it; that is, to seek at that time, through a further use of true, sound words of wholeness and perfection (gift of perfection, gift of wholeness), to lift this carnal state of mind to the spiritual plane. Converted to Christian faith, this belief in fate would take on a strong assurance of good as being ever present and demonstrable. One who learns the divine law is not subject to fate. He makes his own destiny by his use of divine law. (MBD/Tychicus)

3. *Nicopolis*. "city of victory." In consciousness, this is a realization of victory for Truth. Here, our regenerated will (Paul) urges in us a pleasing, agreeable, and honorable attitude of mind (Titus) to "be diligent to come forth", in order to assist us in our attaining victory and mastery over lesser error thoughts and beliefs. (MBD/Nicopolis)

---

Fillmore Study Bible annotations compiled by Mary Salama.

# Paul's Letter to Philemon

Rembrandt, "Saint Paul at His Writing Desk," ca. 1629. Public Domain.

## Introduction to Philemon

In order to understand this Epistle, some background information is necessary; we should know something about the persons involved, and also Paul's purpose in writing. The following details will be found helpful.

Philemon was a wealthy member of the church at Colossae, and had been converted through Paul's preaching. The Epistle indicates that a warm friendship existed between the apostle and his convert. As was customary in those days, Philemon owned several slaves; among these was a young man named Onesimus. But this young man robbed his master probably taking money and clothing—and had sought his freedom by running away from what he regarded as his house of bondage. In those days, if a runaway slave was caught he was severely beaten, and this punishment often resulted in death. But Onesimus was not caught. Apparently he made his way to the nearest seaport, and after stowing away on a waiting ship, he finally arrived at Rome.

It would appear that sometime during Paul's imprisonment at Rome, he needed a messenger who could also perform other personal duties; and the apostle was able to secure the services of a bright young man, who happened to be in the vicinity seeking employment. Paul became very fond of this young man, and soon brought about his conversion. Then the young man confessed that he was Onesimus, the runaway slave of Paul's friend Philemon—and at the same time begged Paul to keep him as his own personal slave. However, Paul saw that this was a dangerous thing to do, since discovery would lead to imprisonment, perhaps death, for the young man.

Paul therefore wrote a letter to the young man's master, Philemon, making Onesimus the bearer of the letter; and the apostle called upon a trusted worker, Tychicus, to accompany the runaway slave to Colossae. It will be recalled that Tychicus carried the Epistle to the Colossians, and his presence would guarantee the safe arrival of Onesimus. (See Col. 4:7-9.) In his letter, Paul reminded Philemon of his conversion, with its rich spiritual experiences, and his indebtedness to the apostle in this regard. Paul then suggested that Philemon could repay this debt— at least, in part—by freeing Onesimus, and receiving him, not merely as a returning slave, but as a Christian brother.

The Epistle to Philemon should be carefully read, and the reader should note how Paul presents his extraordinary request, and how he advances his arguments, step by step, in a sure and loving way. Note how Paul makes himself responsible for the repayment of whatever was stolen by Onesimus—"Charge that to my account"—but at the same time subtly reminds Philemon of his own indebtedness to the writer of the Epistle. (See verses 18-20.) A request presented in this masterly way could not be denied!

Metaphysical meaning: As a starting point, it will be well to note the meaning of the names: *Onesimus* means "useful," or "helpful"; *Paul* represents "the freeing word of Truth"; and *Philemon* may be interpreted as "loving," or "affectionate." Careful thought should be given to the following details:

1. Onesimus was a slave. This reminds us that there are times when we may enter into some sort of bondage-bondage of habit, error thought, lack, limitation, and so on. Under such circumstances, instead of being "useful," we may become "useless"-and instead of being "helpful," we may feel "helpless."
2. Onesimus tried to escape from his bondage. We may seek to do likewise. However, like Onesimus, we soon discover that we do not gain freedom by attempting to run away from our bondage. Actually, bondage is a state of consciousness; and we carry our consciousness with us wherever we go.
3. Onesimus came into contact with Paul. This was a very important step in the young man's quest for freedom—although at first glance, this may appear as a "lucky break." However, the young man was willing to listen to, and be guided by, the apostle. We too make real progress when we listen to and receive the word of Truth. Long ago, Jesus said, "You will know the truth, and the truth will make you free" (John 8:32). The study of Truth helps us to realize that we are sons of God, not slaves; and when this freeing word of Truth is established within our consciousness, the outer manifestation of freedom soon follows.
4. Onesimus was sent back to Colossae. At first glance, this may seem

> like an anticlimax to the story. However, it should be noted that Onesimus' return brought about a complete change in his status; for he was no longer to function as a slave, but was to be regarded as a beloved brother in Christ. Similarly, there are times when we must return to our "Colossae"—the places, persons, or conditions that we associate with our bondage. But, like Onesimus, we shall find that things are different—because we are different! When we realize the truth regarding ourself, we are then able to see Truth operating in persons and conditions around us. "Philemon" is no longer an exacting taskmaster, for we now recognize him as being "loving," "affectionate"! Truly, Christ in us is our hope of glory.

At this point, inquiry may be made regarding Paul's activities after writing the Epistles discussed above. Was he released from his imprisonment? What otherwise befell him? Unfortunately, the Book of Acts closes with Paul's imprisonment at Rome, and the reader is left in doubt. However, there are several indications in other parts of the New Testament of Paul's further meaningful activities and writings, and these will form the subject of the next lesson.

Introduction to *Paul's Letter to Philemon* by Herbert J. Hunt, former Dean of Bible Studies for the Unity School of Christianity.

When Paul writes, presumably in about 52 CE, to Philemon ("phi-LEE-mon"), who has been wronged in some way by Onesimus ("o-NEE-see-mus"), he uses his best persuasive abilities, wisdom and love. The traditional view that Onesimus is a run-away slave may be true, but it is disputed by some scholars today. Regardless, Onesimus is in debt to Philemon and Paul writes to get Philemon to forgive the debt.

The Metaphysical Bible Dictionary says that Philemon represents "a thought that belongs to the love nature in man, and becomes deeply attached to the Christ Truth" and Turner says, "the epistle expresses to the fullest the apostle's compassionate spirit" (:135). Obviously, Paul is appealing to the love faculty of Philemon, which is the attracting, harmonizing, unifying faculty of mind; it is the constructive, building force of Spirit and our power to comprehend Oneness.

When Paul writes "formerly he was useless to you, but now he is indeed useful both to you and to me" (1:11) and "if he has wronged you in any way, or owes you anything, charge that to my account" (1:18)," Paul is appealing to Philemon's faculty of judgment, which is the faculty by which we appraise, evaluate, and discern in order to make correct decisions.

Introduction to *Paul's Letter to Philemon* by Mary Salama.

# Philemon 1

## The Word addresses a friend of Truth

1:1 Paul, a prisoner[1] of Christ Jesus, and Timothy our brother,

to Philemon,[2] our beloved fellow worker, 1:2 to the beloved Apphia, to Archippus, our fellow soldier, and to the assembly in your house:

1:3 Grace to you and peace[3] from God our Father and the Lord Jesus Christ.

1. *Paul, a prisoner*. In this letter, Paul represents the Word; the prison represents the center from which the will rules. When the will imprisons the Word, the activity of the Spirit seems inhibited.

2. *Philemon*. Philemon was the owner of Onesimus, a slave. Philemon bad been converted to Christianity by Paul; his name means *friendship*; he was a friend of Truth. Philemon (*loving, affectionate*) represents a thought that belongs to the love nature in man and that becomes devoted to the Christ Truth. This thought is established in substance and power (Philemon was wealthy and influential).

3. *grace, peace*. Grace: see verse 25 below; peace: harmony and tranquillity derived from awareness of the Christ consciousness. (RW/peace)

## Paul Appeals to Higher Consciousness

1:4 I thank my God always, making mention of you in my prayers, 1:5 hearing of your love, and of the faith which you have toward the Lord Jesus, and toward all the saints; 1:6 that the fellowship of your faith may become effective,[1] in the knowledge of every good thing which is in us in Christ Jesus. 1:7 For we have much joy and comfort in your love, because the hearts of the saints have been refreshed through you, brother.[2]

1. *may become effective*. Paul recalls Philemon's reputation for faith both as an individual follower of the Christ and as a member of the entire Christian brotherhood. The inference is that Philemon will wish to sustain his reputation as a follower of the Christ.

2. *refreshed through you, brother*. The mind of Christ refreshes the heart by leading its possessor to forgive fully and freely in order to get the wrong out of mind as quickly as possible and so permit the expressing of good will, knowing also that the harboring of grudges injures the one who harbors them, as well as the one against whom they are directed.

## Paul's Plea for Oneness

1:8 Therefore, though I have all boldness in Christ to command you that which is appropriate, 1:9 yet for love's sake I rather beg,[1] being such a one as Paul, the aged, but also a prisoner of Jesus Christ. 1:10 I beg you for my child, whom I have become the father of in my chains, Onesimus,[1] 1:11 who once was useless to you, but now is useful to you and to me. 1:12 I am sending him back. Therefore receive him, that is, my own heart, 1:13 whom I desired to keep with me, that on your behalf he might serve me in my chains for

the Good News. 1:14 But I was willing
to do nothing without your consent,
that your goodness would not be as
of necessity, but of free will. 1:15 For
perhaps he was therefore separated
from you for a while, that you would
have him forever, 1:16 no longer as
a slave,❷ but more than a slave, a
beloved brother, especially to me,
but how much rather to you, both in
the flesh and in the Lord.

1:17 If then you count me a partner,
receive him as you would receive
me. 1:18 But if he has wronged you at
all, or owes you anything, put that
to my account. 1:19 I, Paul, write this
with my own hand: I will repay it (not
to mention to you that you owe to
me even your own self besides). 1:20
Yes, brother, let me have joy from
you in the Lord. Refresh my heart
in the Lord. 1:21 Having confidence
in your obedience, I write to you,
knowing that you will do even
beyond what I say.

1:22 Also, prepare a guest room for
me, for I hope that through your
prayers I will be restored to you.❸

1. *for love's sake I rather beg.* Paul appeals to love and cooperation instead of commanding. Inspiring others toward goodness of their own free will is the highest form of influence possible. Our best course is to show others that the Divine will is for one's highest good, and to try to inspire others to align their will with it.

2. *no longer as a slave, but ... a beloved brother.* Paul's appeal to Philemon for clemency towards Onesimus the slave is based on the Truth that in spite of certain limitations in the activity of the Word, it can, through the forgiving love of God, bring about freedom in some planes of consciousness.

3. *restored to you.* Paul asked Philemon to prepare to receive him, expecting Philemon's prayers to effect his release from prison.

## Affirming a Change in Consciousness

1:23 Epaphras,❶ my fellow prisoner
in Christ Jesus, greets you, 1:24 as do
Mark, Aristarchus, Demas, and Luke,
my fellow workers. 1:25 The grace❷ of
our Lord Jesus Christ be with your
spirit. Amen.

1. *Epaphras ... greets you.* Epaphras: the loving message of the Christ and its action in the Colossæ and Rome states of mind. (MBD/Epaphras)

2. *grace.* Grace is a change in consciousness that lets go of the insistence of "even-exchanges" in life all the time. Ed Rabel-Metaphysics 1, *The Divine Paradox, Law/Grace*

---

Fillmore Study Bible annotations by Mary Salama.

**World English Bible Footnotes:**

[1] v1:10. Onesimus means "useful."

# The Letter to the Hebrews

Giusto de' Menabuoi, Paradise, Padua Baptistry's frescoed dome, 1375-1378, Public Domain.

## Introduction to The Letter to the Hebrews

It should be recalled that in the early days the Christian church was mainly Jewish in membership. The Apostles were Jews, and their converts were drawn for the most part from the synagogues. For a brief period these converts maintained what may be termed dual membership. They attended the Christian assemblies and received Christian instruction, but they also maintained their connection with the Jewish synagogues. However, the Jewish leaders soon called a halt to these proceedings, and the Jewish Christians were compelled to choose between membership in the Christian church and membership in the synagogue. If they desired to be "in" with a Christian group, they were ruled as definitely "out" as regards their connection with the synagogue.

During the early period of Christian activity, this excommunication from the synagogue did not greatly concern the Jewish Christians. Their enthusiasm for the new teaching, coupled with Christian fellowship—and above all, their belief in the speedy return of their Lord—enabled them to accept without question whatever hardships they were called upon to endure. But with the passing of the years, their hopes regarding the return of the Lord were not fulfilled, and their enthusiasm began to wane.

Then came the persecutions, in which Jewish Christians suffered severely because of their beliefs. Small wonder, therefore, that many of these Jewish Christians began to have second thoughts regarding their severance from the synagogues. In those days the synagogue was regarded as the center of the community, and excommunication meant being cut off from practically all the worthwhile things of life. Therefore during this period (approximately A.D. 70-85) there was a marked defection of Jewish Christians from the church.

Thus it was that a very important New Testament book was written in an effort to stem this tide of defection and to win back those who had already defected—the book we now know as "the Epistle to the Hebrews." This Epistle is an outstanding literary work, in which the writer presents Christian teaching as superior to all the Jewish beliefs and traditions. He does not detract from Judaism in any way, but points out in various ways the superiority of Christianity as compared with Judaism. He indicates that Judaism is good, but Christianity is by far the better way. He therefore urges all Jewish Christians who may be wavering in their faith, or losing their earlier enthusiasm, to press forward, and "run perseverance the race that is set before us. looking to Jesus the pioneer and perfecter of our faith" (Hebrews 12:2).

**Author of the Epistle:** In most modern versions of the New Testament, the Epistle to the Hebrews is given without the author's name. But the King James Version still follows an old Eastern tradition, and attaches Paul's name to the Epistle. Possibly this tradition had its origin in a praiseworthy desire to insure an undisputed place in the New Testament for such an outstanding piece of Christian literature.

Martin Luther is credited with the suggestion that possibly Apollos (see Acts 18:24 and I Corinthians 1:12) was the author of Hebrews, and there are several indications, both in the Epistle and elsewhere, which support this suggestion. Apollos was an Alexandrian Jew—possibly educated at the University of Alexandria; and Hebrews is written in what is termed the Alexandrian style. Apollos is described in the New Testament as "an eloquent man, well versed in the scriptures" (Acts 18:24), and this description would apply to the writer of Hebrews. Furthermore, Apollos spent considerable time at Ephesus and Corinth, and possibly this was the area first affected by the defecting Jewish Christians. It would certainly appear, therefore, that Apollos was a man well qualified for this important piece of work.

**Date of the Epistle:** The main purpose of Hebrews, together with its contents, indicates that the Epistle was written about A.D. 80, or shortly thereafter.

**Metaphysical notes:** Problems of defection were not peculiar to the early church. Defections of various sorts continued throughout Christian history, with individuals or groups drifting back to their former ways of thinking and living. Even today, there are persons whose enthusiasm for high ideals and Truth principles tends to wane, and then there is a noticeable falling off in their interest and activities as regards spiritual things. Thus the entire theme, besides many passages in the Epistle to the Hebrews, may be regarded as having important present-day application. We can still profit by the admonition to "run with perseverance the race that is set before us," and to "lift your drooping hands and strengthen your weak knees, and make straight paths for your feet" (Hebrews 12:1-12).

Also, the method of presentation used in this Epistle is one that can be profitably followed today. It will be noted that the writer does not condemn the older forms of religion, but places emphasis upon the advantages of the new way. He recognizes that many of the old forms and customs were good for former times; but he then points out that the new revelation through Jesus Christ is infinitely superior, and leads to higher spiritual developments. Such a method of presentation does not arouse antagonism, but opens the way for a fair consideration of all the new possibilities.

The word *Hebrews* is also significant. This word has been explained as indicating persons who have pressed onward, or have passed over, to regions beyond. All of this is exemplified in the call and activities of Abraham, when the Lord said to him, "Go from your country and your kindred and your father's house to the land that I will show you" (Genesis 12:1). Metaphysically, "The Hebrews surely represent the thoughts in man that have come up out of the purely material and passed over to a higher concept of God and His laws, into a closer and clearer relationship with God. These thoughts are, however, still under law, the law of sin and death; for true freedom, spiritual understanding and realization, life and peace, come only by the still higher way—which is the Christ method, the way taught and demonstrated by Jesus Christ" (MBD/Hebrew).

Then, in all this "passing over," recognition must be given to the work of faith. Jesus said, "Do not judge by appearances, but judge with right judgment" (John 7:24)—and we are enabled to "judge right judgment" by the perceptive power of faith. Under these circumstances, we are not disturbed nor dismayed by appearances, but we press forward to "receive as an inheritance" wherein is that "city which has foundations, whose builder and maker is God" (Hebrews 11:8-10).

Introduction to *The Letter to the Hebrews* by Herbert J. Hunt, former Dean of Bible Studies for the Unity School of Christianity.

# Hebrews 1

## The Christ Within Moves Us From Idea To Action

[1:1] God,[1] having in the past
spoken to the fathers through the
prophets at many times and in
various ways, [1:2] has at the end of
these days spoken to us by his Son,[2]
whom he appointed heir of all things,
through whom also he made the
worlds. [1:3] His Son is the radiance
of his glory, the very image of his
substance, and upholding all things

by the word of his power,❸ when he had by himself made purification for our sins, sat down on the right hand of the Majesty on high;
1:4 having become so much better than the angels,❹ as he has inherited a more excellent name than they have.

1. *God.* God is the great source of all things, the generator which gives origin. (RW/God)

2. *has spoken to us by his Son.* Christ used in place of "Son of God" is the spiritual self of every individual, our Divine Mind or the Christ within each of us. Christ is the is the one complete idea of perfect human in Divine Mind. As the perfect human, they are the embodiment of all divine ideas. (RW/Son of God)

3. *by the word of his power.* The revelation of the order of the power humanity exerts to change energy from one plane of consciousness to another, from thought to the more concrete plane in word. (RW/power)

4. *angels.* See 1:5 below.

## Our Inner Christ Moves Us From Idea To Action

1:5 For to which of the angels❶ did he say at any time,

"You are my Son.
Today have I become your father?"[1]❷

and again,

"I will be to him a Father,
and he will be to me a Son?"[2]

1:6 Again, when he brings in the firstborn into the world he says, "Let all the angels of God worship him."
1:7 Of the angels he says,

"Who makes his angels winds,
and his servants a flame of fire."[3]

1:8 But of the Son he says,

"Your throne, O God, is forever and ever.
The scepter of uprightness is the scepter of your Kingdom.
1:9 You have loved righteousness,❸
and hated iniquity;
therefore God, your God, has anointed you with the oil of gladness above your fellows."[4]

1:10 And,

"You, Lord, in the beginning, laid the foundation of the earth.
The heavens are the works of your hands.
1:11 They will perish, but you continue.
They all will grow old like a garment does.
1:12 As a mantle, you will roll them up,
and they will be changed;
but you are the same.
Your years will not fail."[5]

1:13 But which of the angels has he told at any time,

"Sit at my right hand,
until I make your enemies the footstool of your feet?"[6]

1:14 Aren't they all serving spirits, sent out to do service for the sake of those who will inherit salvation?❹

1. *angels.* A messenger of God or the projection into our consciousness of a spiritual idea. (RW/angel)

2. *today I have become your Father.* Identifies God as Father and suggests a relationship with humans that is "closer

than breathing and nearer than hands and feet." (RW/Father)

3. *Righteousness.* A state of our natural harmony established in consciousness through the right use of God-given attributes. Love is a state of righteousness. (RW/righteousness)

4. *Salvation.* Salvation is the freely given restitution of humanity to its birthright, freeing us from limitations that have plagued our existence as a result of following our senses instead of the Christ within. By following the Christ Mind within, our minds can be cleansed of erroneous thoughts and we are freed from all limitations. (RW/salvation)

---

Fillmore Study Bible annotations compiled by Susan St. John.

**World English Bible Footnotes:**

[1] v1:5. Psalm 2:7

[2] v1:5. 2 Samuel 7:14; 1 Chronicles 17:13

[3] v1:7. Psalm 104:4

[4] v1:9. Psalm 45:6-7

[5] v1:12. Psalm 102:25-27

[6] v1:13. Psalm 110:1

# Hebrews 2

## Be Sure To Concentrate On God's Salvation (1)

2:1 Therefore we ought to pay
greater attention to the things that
were heard, (2) lest perhaps we drift
away. 2:2 For if the word spoken
through angels proved steadfast, and
every transgression and disobedience
received a just recompense; 2:3 how
will we escape if we neglect so great
a salvation (3)--which at the first
having been spoken through the
Lord, was confirmed to us by those
who heard; 2:4 God also testifying
with them, both by signs and
wonders, by various works of power,
and by gifts of the Holy Spirit,
according to his own will? (4)

1. The centering of the attention on a particular idea is the nucleus of a spiritual confidence or faith. Concentration forms a mental magnet in the mind to which thought substance rushes like iron filings, bringing the forces, whether mental or physical, to a common purpose.

2. *things that were heard.* Thoughts lowered in vibration to the level of sense perception. The things that appear are the formulations of our ideas of ourself and God. Behind everything is a thought. We must still the senses to perceive the higher vibration of thought. (RW/things)

3. *how will we escape if we neglect so great a salvation.* The belief that Jesus in an outer way atoned for our sins is not salvation. Salvation is based solely on an inner overcoming, a change in consciousness. It is a cleansing of the mind, through Christ, from thoughts that take us away from our spiritual birthright to regain conscious possession of our God-given attributes. It comes as the result of redemption; the change from sin to righteousness. Salvation comes to us as a free gift from God.

It embodies a knowledge of God that frees us from all limitations and points the way by which mind and body may be lifted up to the spiritual place of consciousness. (RW/salvation)

4. *according to his own will.* Truth is simple and easily mastered principle. Complexity arises because of the variety of ways in which men apply these principles, which in turn depends on the varying degrees of their understanding.

# Exaltation Through Honouring Suffering

2:5 For he didn't subject the world to come, of which we speak, to angels. 2:6 But one has somewhere testified, saying,

"What is man, that you think of him?
Or the son of man, that you care for him?
2:7 You made him a little lower than the angels.
You crowned him with glory and honor.[7]
2:8 You have put all things in subjection under his feet."[8]

For in that he subjected all things to him, he left nothing that is not subject to him. But now we don't see all things subjected to him, yet. 2:9 But we see him who has been made a little lower than the angels, Jesus, because of the suffering of death crowned with glory and honor, that by the grace of God he should taste of death for everyone.

2:10 For it became him, for whom are all things, and through whom are all things, in bringing many children to glory, to make the author of their salvation perfect through sufferings.❶ 2:11 For both he who sanctifies and those who are sanctified are all from one, for which cause he is not ashamed to call them brothers[9], 2:12 saying,

"I will declare your name to my brothers.
In the midst of the congregation I will sing your praise."[10]

2:13 Again, "I will put my trust in him."[11] Again, "Behold, here I am with the children whom God has given me."[12] 2:14 Since then the children have shared in flesh and blood, he also himself in like manner partook of the same, that through death he might bring to nothing him who had the power of death, that is, the devil, 2:15 and might deliver all of them who through fear of death❷ were all their lifetime subject to bondage. 2:16 For most certainly, he doesn't give help to angels, but he gives help to the seed of Abraham. 2:17 Therefore he was obligated in all things to be made like his brothers, that he might become a merciful and faithful high priest in things pertaining to God, to make atonement for the sins of the people. 2:18 For in that he himself has suffered being tempted, he is able to help those who are tempted.

1. *made perfect through sufferings.* It has been said the only complete catastrophe is the catastrophe from which we learn nothing. There's a growth possibility in every experience. To whatever the experience is, much as you hesitate to express it, it's your divine appointment. Don't miss it through indulging, and resistance, and self-pity. Some persons look at God through their troubles. Other persons look at their troubles through God. If you look at your troubles through God, it's to begin with a basic premise God is the ground of your being, realizing that God the good is all-present, omnipresent, all-knowing. Truth is, when you set a course of righteousness for yourself, you tend to invariably run into what (are called) the crosscurrents of your own static thought.

This is dramatized in the form of the adversary. Some folks fail to understand that when you set a new course for yourself, such as you begin to study the truth, begin to work out, spiritual consciousness in your life, sometimes for a while things get worse, you stir up a lot of stuff. Consciousness begins to rebel. You have a kind of a crosscurrent within yourself, both against this what I call the force of inertia that pulls against you. You're trying to go in one direction, it's pulling you back in the other because it wants to go the way it always has been. So you set up all these crosscurrents in consciousness. Despite the suffering, there is within it the opportunity for growth and betterment. (Eric Butterworth Unity Podcast #75, "Why Doesn't God?")

2. *deliver all them who through fear of death.* Death is always the result of a failure to recognize God as the source of wisdom and life. When the soul falls short in this respect, it sings and there is a physical dissolution that is but the outer symbol or mental negation or spiritual inertia. The dissolution of the body is the "second death". The first death is where the consciousness has lost sight of spiritual wisdom and sunk into the belief that God is absent from humanity and the universe. If we allow ourselves to live in the senses and fail to recognize our spiritual selfhood and our relation to Being—we are already virtually dying. We are only minimally alive when we are more in the senses than the spirit on the animal plane, because the senses will fail before long. (RW/dying)

---

Fillmore Study Bible annotations compiled by Susan St. John.

**World English Bible Footnotes:**

[7] v2:7. TR adds "and set him over the works of your hands"

[8] v2:8. Psalm 8:4-6

[9] v2:11. The word for "brothers" here and where context allows may also be correctly translated "brothers and sisters" or "siblings."

[10] v2:12. Psalm 22:22

[11] v2:13. Isaiah 8:17

[12] v2:13. Isaiah 8:18

# Hebrews 3

## Moses the Emerging, Christ the Expressing

3:1 Therefore, holy brothers,[1] partakers of a heavenly calling, consider the Apostle and High Priest of our confession, Jesus;[2] 3:2 who was faithful to him who appointed him, as also was Moses[3] in all his house. 3:3 For he has been counted worthy of more glory than Moses, inasmuch as he who built the house has more honor than the house. 3:4 For every house is built by someone; but he who built all things is God. 3:5 Moses indeed was faithful in all his house as a servant,[4] for a testimony of those things which were afterward to be spoken, 3:6 but Christ[5] is faithful as a Son over his house; whose house we are, if we hold fast our confidence and the glorying of our hope[6] firm to the end.

1. *holy brothers.* [and sisters!]

2. *Jesus.* The Man of Nazareth, son of Mary; the Saviour of mankind according to present-day Christian belief. Metaphysically He is the I AM in man, the self, the directive power, raised to divine understanding and power-the I AM identity. (RW/Jesus)

3. *Moses.* Moses means drawing out, extracting, i.e., from the water, representing humanity's development in consciousness of the law of their being, from the negative side, but with great possibility. As always, in the Kingdom of God, our of seemingly negative conditions comes the new growth. (MBD/Moses)

4. *servant.* The elemental force of Being, ever at hand to carry out one's demands. (MBI/John 2)

5. *Christ.* The incarnating principle of the God-man; the perfect idea of God; the divine human which unfolds into the true person, perfect, and blessed with eternal life by measuring up to the divine standard, fulfilling the law of righteousness. Christ abides in each person as their potential perfection; the only begotten Child of God; living Principle working in humanity. (RW/Christ)

6. *Hope.* The expectation of good in the future. It is a quality of sense mind because it is subject to time. It is of human-mind, and not of God as is Faith which goes beyond time and space. (RW/hope)

## Warning Against Conscious Or Subconscious Barriers

3:7 Therefore, even as the Holy Spirit says,

"Today if you will hear his voice,
3:8 don't harden your hearts, as in the provocation,[1]
like as in the day of the trial in the wilderness,
3:9 where your fathers tested me by proving me,
and saw my works for forty[2] years.
3:10 Therefore I was displeased with that generation,
and said, 'They always err in their heart,
but they didn't know my ways;'
3:11 as I swore in my wrath,
'They will not enter into my rest.'"[13]

3:12 Beware, brothers, lest perhaps there be in any one of you an evil heart of unbelief,[3] in falling away from the living God; 3:13 but exhort one another day by day, so long as it is called "today;" lest any one of you be hardened by the deceitfulness of sin. 3:14 For we have become partakers of Christ, if we hold fast the beginning of our confidence firm to the end: 3:15 while it is said,

"Today if you will hear his voice,
don't harden your hearts, as in the rebellion."[14]

3:16 For who, when they heard, rebelled? No, didn't all those who came out of Egypt by Moses? 3:17 With whom was he displeased forty years? Wasn't it with those who sinned, whose bodies fell in the wilderness?[4] 3:18 To whom did he swear that they wouldn't enter into his rest, but to those who were disobedient? 3:19 We see that they were not able to enter in because of unbelief.

1. *as in the provocation.* Provocation in Greek (parapikrasmos) means "rebellion against God". Rebellion is an open defiance and resistance to an authority to which one owes allegiance when one believes they are not being fairly governed. In rebellion against tragedies of this earthly plane, we must recognize that our own thoughts and words are the cause of the conditions and not an imposition by their true authority, God. (RW/rebellion)

2. *forty.* completeness; as long as it takes. (MBD/forty days and forty nights)

3. *Unbelief.* Belief is an inner acceptance of an idea that can function consciously or subconsciously. Many false individual and race beliefs operate in the subconscious. We must watch for the false Belief in the notion of separateness and our resistance

to the belief in the Christ as the only true source of expression. (RW/belief)

4. *wilderness.* The wilderness represents in individual consciousness the multitude of undisciplined and uncultivated thoughts. (RW/wilderness)

---

Fillmore Study Bible annotations compiled by Susan St. John.

**World English Bible Footnotes:**

[13] v3:11. Psalm 95:7-11

[14] v3:15. Psalm 95:7-8

# Hebrews 4

## The Rest That God Promised

4:1 Let us fear therefore, lest
perhaps anyone of you should seem
to have come short of a promise of
entering into his rest. 4:2 For indeed
we have had good news preached to
us, even as they also did, but the
word they heard didn't profit them,
because it wasn't mixed with faith
by those who heard.(1) 4:3 For we who
have believed do enter into that rest,
even as he has said, "As I swore in
my wrath, they will not enter into my
rest;"[15](2) although the works were
finished from the foundation of the
world. 4:4 For he has said this
somewhere about the seventh day,
"God rested on the seventh day from
all his works;"[16] 4:5 and in this place
again, "They will not enter into my
rest."[17]

4:6 Seeing therefore it remains
that some should enter therein, and
they to whom the good news was
before preached failed to enter in
because of disobedience, 4:7 he again
defines a certain day, today, saying
through David so long a time
afterward (just as has been said),

"Today if you will hear his voice,
don't harden your hearts."[18]

4:8 For if Joshua had given them
rest, he would not have spoken
afterward of another day. 4:9 There
remains therefore a Sabbath rest for
the people of God.(3) 4:10 For he who
has entered into his rest has himself
also rested from his works, as God
did from his. 4:11 Let us therefore give
diligence to enter into that rest, lest
anyone fall after the same example
of disobedience. 4:12 For the word of
God is living, and active, and sharper
than any two-edged sword, and
piercing even to the dividing of soul
and spirit, of both joints and
marrow, and is able to discern the
thoughts and intentions of the heart.
4:13 There is no creature that is
hidden from his sight, but all things
are naked and laid open before the
eyes of him with whom we have to
do.

1. *Because it wasn't mixed with faith by those who heard.* Good News is not profitable, and so does not lead to rest, unless

mixed with faith—a deep inner knowing that that which is sought is already ours for the taking (See Hebrews 11:1). Without variation, faith brings results that appear miraculous, but are simply inspired by the faith of each of us. (RW/faith). Greek "pistis" (πιστιν) "state of believing on the basis of the reliability of the one trusted" (*A Greek-English Lexicon of the New Testament* 818).

2. *As I swore in my wrath, they will not enter into my rest.* The individual who does not conform to the law but thinks and acts in opposition to it cannot rest because the "wrath of God" is really the working out of the law of Being destructively or inharmoniously (MBD/wrath).

3. *A Sabbath rest for the people of God.* The Sabbath is a state of mind that a person enters or acquires when they goes into the silence of their own soul, into the realm of Spirit. There they find true rest and peace. The 'seventh day' means the seventh or perfect stage of one's spiritual unfoldment where a person finds rest and peace. The Sabbath can be enjoyed at any hour. People show their lack of understanding and limit their happiness by confining the Sabbath to any one of the days of the week (MBD/sabbath).

## Jesus the Great High Priest

4:14 Having then a great high
priest,① who has passed through the
heavens,② Jesus, the Son of God, let
us hold tightly to our confession.③ 4:15
For we don't have a high priest who can't be touched with the feeling of our infirmities, but one who has been in all points tempted like we are, yet
without sin. 4:16 Let us therefore draw near with boldness to the throne of grace,④ that we may receive mercy, and may find grace for help in time of need.

1. *Great high priest.* Jesus dedicated Himself to the cause of Truth.

2. *Who has passed through the heavens.* Jesus permeated the entire realm of thought and interpreted the highest (the thought of God) as love. He entered the realm of spiritual power and learned its law, so that He controlled it and expressed it.

3. *Our confession.* Greek homologias (ὁμολογίας) "expression of allegiance, agreement" (*Greek-English Lexicon of the New Testament* 709).

4. *The throne of grace.* The high consciousness of love and power that is found in Divine Mind. In this consciousness all power abides, and we avail ourselves of it by claiming it through Christ.

---

Fillmore Study Bible annotations compiled by Susan St. John.

**World English Bible Footnotes:**

[15] v4:3. Psalm 95:11

[16] v4:4. Genesis 2:2

[17] v4:5. Psalm 95:11

[18] v4:7. Psalm 95:7-8

# Hebrews 5

## Jesus the Great High Priest (continued)

5:1 For every high priest, being taken from among men, is appointed for men in things pertaining to God, that he may offer both gifts and sacrifices for sins. 5:2 The high priest can deal gently with those who are ignorant and going astray,[1] because he himself is also surrounded with weakness. 5:3 Because of this, he must offer sacrifices for sins for the people, as well as for himself. 5:4 Nobody takes this honor on himself, but he is called by God, just like Aaron was. 5:5 So also Christ didn't glorify himself to be made a high priest, but it was he who said to him,

> "You are my Son.
> Today I have become your
> father."[19]

5:6 As he says also in another place,

> "You are a priest forever,
> after the order of
> Melchizedek."[20]

5:7 He, in the days of his flesh, having offered up prayers and petitions with strong crying and tears to him who was able to save him from death, and having been heard for his godly fear, 5:8 though he was a Son, yet learned obedience by the things which he suffered. 5:9 Having been made perfect, he became to all of those who obey him the author of eternal salvation, 5:10 named by God a high priest after the order of Melchizedek.[2]

1. *The high priest can deal gently with those who are ignorant and going astray.* "Jesus symbolized the indwelling Christ which withdraws to the superconscious Mind. Sitting at the right hand of God symbolizes the executive power of the indwelling Christ. From this high vantage point, it is enabled to work with the disciples (man's faculties) and aid them in all ways." (*The Story of Jesus Soul Evolution*, Charles Fillmore, Dec 1947, pg 1242).

2. *After the order of Melchizedek.* See Hebrews 7:11-28. The divine will established in man in righteousness, justice, and peace (king of righteousness, king of justice, king of Salem, Salem meaning peace). Melchizedek really refers to the Christ mind or superconsciousness, that which when ruling in man's consciousness establishes and maintains right doing, perfect adjustment, peace, and perfection (MBD/Melchizedek).

## Warning against Falling Away

5:11 About him we have many words to say, and hard to interpret, seeing you have become dull of hearing. 5:12 For when by reason of the time you ought to be teachers, you again need to have someone teach you the rudiments of the first principles of the oracles of God. You have come to need milk, and not solid food.[1] 5:13 For everyone who lives on milk is not experienced in the word of righteousness, for he is a baby. 5:14 But solid food is for those who are full grown, who by reason of use have their senses exercised to discern good and evil.

1. *You have come to need milk, and not solid food.* Milk the simplest form of food and represents the truths which are easily discerned and appropriated. "Solid food"

represents the deeper truths which require study, meditation and concentration order that they may be ap propriated and assimilated the mind. Paul here reproves those who continue to feed on milk when they should be partaking of solid food, and imparting to others the Word of Life. Notice that he says to these milk-fed Hebrews, "You have become sluggish hearers." This the condition that come to all who neglect the eating of the word of God, the Bread of Life. Their spiritual ears become dulled and they cannot hear the higher truths.

One must either move forward or slip backward. "Babes Christ" must grow up to the full stature of manhood Christ Jesus (*Unity*, July 1915).

2. *Have their senses exercised to discern good and evil.* By declaring our senses to be spiritual and by speaking the increasing word of the I AM to every one of them, we multiply their capacities and give them a sustaining vigor and vitality. This is done through the simple word of the I AM, backed up by the realization of its spiritual power (RW/senses).

---

Fillmore Study Bible annotations compiled by Susan St. John.

**World English Bible Footnotes:**

[19] v5:5. Psalm 2:7

[20] v5:6. Psalm 110:4

# Hebrews 6

## From First Principles to Perfection

[6:1] Therefore leaving the doctrine of the first principles❶ of Christ, let us press on to perfection❷--not laying again a foundation of repentance❸ from dead works, of faith toward God, [6:2] of the teaching of baptisms, of laying on of hands, of resurrection of the dead, and of eternal judgment. [6:3] This will we do, if God permits. [6:4] For concerning those who were once enlightened and tasted of the heavenly gift, and were made partakers of the Holy Spirit, [6:5] and tasted the good word of God,❹ and the powers of the age to come, [6:6] and then fell away, it is impossible to renew them again to repentance; seeing they crucify the Son of God for themselves again, and put him to open shame. [6:7] For the land which has drunk the rain that comes often on it, and brings forth a crop suitable for them for whose sake it is also tilled, receives blessing from God; [6:8] but if it bears thorns and thistles, it is rejected and near being cursed, whose end is to be burned.

[6:9] But, beloved, we are persuaded of better things for you, and things that accompany salvation, even though we speak like this. [6:10] For God is not unrighteous, so as to forget your work and the labor of love which you showed toward his name, in that you served the saints, and still do serve them. [6:11] We desire that each one of you may show the same diligence to the fullness of hope even to the end,❺ [6:12] that you won't be sluggish, but imitators of those who through faith and patience inherited the promises.

1. *First principles.* Greek: *Logion* (λογίων) "saying, teaching" (*Greek-English Lexicon of the New Testament*, pg 598)

2. *Let us press on to perfection.* A state of consciousness completely free from any negation by affirming the truth of being for man (Divine mind) as the law of our being (RW/perfection).

3. *Repentance.* Change one's mind, change of thought to allow humans to do away with the 'shortcoming attitude' about the nature of ourselves. To open the opportunity to align with God mind that sees humans in perfection (MBD/repentance).

4. *And tasted the good word of God.* Hebrews 6:4-6 refers to people who have left behind the first principles of the doctrine of Christ, and have gone on unto perfection. The heavenly gift of which they have tasted is the Life of God within their bodies, for they understand and are seeking to demonstrate the redemption of the whole man, which includes the body. They have tasted the powers of the world to come, that they have quickened within themselves the God-qualities or spiritual powers, even to the extent of bringing forth the Christ Child—the New Birth. (*Unity*, July 1917).

5. *We desire that each one of you may show the same diligence to the fullness of hope even to the end.* Christian people have, for centuries, been staying in the beginning of the Christ word and doctrine. Over and over again, they have been laying the foundation of repentance, but they have never gone on in the overcoming life until they reached perfection. (*Unity*, November 1921, p.461).

## The Certainty of God's Promise

6:13 For when God made a promise
to Abraham, since he could swear by
none greater, he swore by himself,
6:14 saying, "Surely blessing I will bless
you,❶ and multiplying I will multiply
you."[21] 6:15 Thus, having patiently
endured, he obtained the promise.
6:16 For men indeed swear by a
greater one, and in every dispute of
theirs the oath is final for
confirmation. 6:17 In this way God,
being determined to show more
abundantly to the heirs of the
promise the immutability of his
counsel, interposed with an oath; 6:18
that by two immutable things,❷ in
which it is impossible for God to lie,
we may have a strong
encouragement, who have fled for
refuge to take hold of the hope set
before us. 6:19 This hope we have as
an anchor of the soul, a hope both
sure and steadfast and entering into
that which is within the veil; 6:20
where as a forerunner Jesus entered
for us, having become a high priest
forever after the order of
Melchizedek.

1. *Surely blessing I will bless you.* Blessing imparts the quickening spiritual power that produces growth and increase (RW/blessing). Spiritual quickening is the wakening of the whole person to what they are in the sight of God, making them wide awake, and full of their truthful power (RW/quickening).

2. *Immutable things.* Greek ἀμετάθετος, ametethatos. Unchangeable, unalterable (Greek-English Lexicon, pg 53).

---

Fillmore Study Bible annotations compiled by Susan St. John.

**World English Bible Footnotes:**

[21] v6:14. Genesis 22:17

# Hebrews 7

## The Priestly Order of Melchizedek

7:1 For this Melchizedek, king of Salem,[1] priest of God Most High, who met Abraham returning from the slaughter of the kings and blessed him, 7:2 to whom also Abraham divided a tenth part of all (being first, by interpretation, king of righteousness, and then also king of Salem, which is king of peace; 7:3 without father, without mother, without genealogy, having neither beginning of days nor end of life, but made like the Son of God), remains a priest continually.

7:4 Now consider how great this man was, to whom even Abraham, the patriarch,[2] gave a tenth out of the best spoils. 7:5 They indeed of the sons of Levi who receive the priest's office have a commandment to take tithes[3] of the people according to the law, that is, of their brothers, though these have come out of the body of Abraham, 7:6 but he whose genealogy is not counted from them has accepted tithes from Abraham, and has blessed him who has the promises. 7:7 But without any dispute the lesser is blessed by the greater. 7:8 Here people who die receive tithes, but there one receives tithes of whom it is testified that he lives. 7:9 We can say that through Abraham even Levi, who receives tithes, has paid tithes, 7:10 for he was yet in the body of his father when Melchizedek met him.

1. *Melchizedek, king of Salem.* "King of Salem," and "priest of God Most High," who "brought forth bread and wine" for Abram on his return from the slaughter of the heathen kings who had taken Lot captive (Gen. 14:18; Heb. 7). Of Jesus Christ it was said that He should be a priest forever, after the order of Melchizedek (Psalms 110:4; Heb. 5:6). (MBD/Melchizedek)

2. *Abraham, the patriarch.* The power of the mind to reproduce its ideas in unlimited expression. The ability of the mind to make substance out of ideas, called faith. Abraham represents humanity's faith of God understanding that our faith is the 'father/Abraham' of manifested thoughts an acts. Abraham represents the early development of humanity's development of consciousness from the 'Adam man' (MBD/Abraham).

3. *Tithes.* The understanding of agreement that God and humanity are in partnership regarding their finances. It acknowledges God as our source of supply and it is the surest way to demonstrate 'plenty' because it exemplifies God's own law and way of giving (RW/tithe, RW/tithing).

## Another Priest, Like Melchizedek

7:11 Now if there was perfection through the Levitical priesthood (for under it the people have received the law), what further need was there for another priest to arise after the order of Melchizedek, and not be called after the order of Aaron? 7:12 For the priesthood being changed, there is of necessity a change made also in the law. 7:13 For he of whom these things are said belongs to another tribe, from which no one has officiated at the altar. 7:14 For it is evident that our Lord has sprung out of Judah, about which tribe Moses spoke nothing concerning priesthood.

7:15 This is yet more abundantly evident, if after the likeness of Melchizedek there arises another priest,① 7:16 who has been made, not after the law of a fleshly commandment, but after the power of an endless life: 7:17 for it is testified,

"You are a priest forever,
according to the order of
Melchizedek."[22]

7:18 For there is an annulling of a foregoing commandment because of its weakness and uselessness 7:19 (for the law made nothing perfect), and a bringing in of a better hope, through which we draw near to God. 7:20 Inasmuch as he was not made priest without the taking of an oath 7:21 (for they indeed have been made priests without an oath), but he with an oath by him that says of him,

"The Lord swore and will not
change his mind,
'You are a priest forever,
according to the order of
Melchizedek.'"[23]

7:22 By so much, Jesus has become the collateral of a better covenant.② 7:23 Many, indeed, have been made priests, because they are hindered from continuing by death. 7:24 But he, because he lives forever, has his priesthood unchangeable. 7:25 Therefore he is also able to save to the uttermost those who draw near to God through him, seeing that he lives forever to make intercession for them.

7:26 For such a high priest was fitting for us: holy, guiltless, undefiled, separated from sinners, and made higher than the heavens; 7:27 who doesn't need, like those high priests, to offer up sacrifices daily, first for his own sins, and then for the sins of the people. For he did this once for all, when he offered up himself.③ 7:28 For the law appoints men as high priests who have weakness, but the word of the oath which came after the law appoints a Son forever who has been perfected.

1. *There arises another priest.* Melchizedek really refers to the Christ mind or superconsciousness, that which when ruling in man's consciousness establishes and maintains right doing, perfect adjustment, peace, and perfection. This priest "has been made, not after the law of a fleshly commandment, but after the power of an endless life." (MBD/Melchizedek)

2. *Jesus has become the collateral of a better covenant.* A covenant is an agreement that represents the principles of rules by which men are able to gain their true spiritual heritage and possess the riches of the kingdom of God (MBD/covenant).

3. *For he did this once for all, when he offered up himself.* The Christ covers all our imperfections with His high consciousness, but at the same time requires of us the sacrifice or putting away of sense consciousness, with its demands, and dedication to the wholeness of Truth.

---

Fillmore Study Bible annotations compiled by Susan St. John.

**World English Bible Footnotes:**

[22] v7:17. Psalm 110:4

[23] v7:21. Psalm 110:4

# HEBREWS 8

## Mediator of a Better Covenant

8:1 Now in the things which we are
saying, the main point is this. We
have such a high priest, who sat
down on the right hand of the throne
of the Majesty in the heavens, 8:2 a
servant of the sanctuary, and of the
true tabernacle, which the Lord
pitched, not man. 8:3 For every high
priest is appointed to offer both gifts
and sacrifices. Therefore it is
necessary that this high priest also
have something to offer. 8:4 For if he
were on earth, he would not be a
priest at all, seeing there are priests
who offer the gifts according to the
law; 8:5 who serve a copy and shadow
of the heavenly things,[1] even as
Moses was warned by God when he
was about to make the tabernacle,[2]
for he said, "See, you shall make
everything according to the pattern
that was shown to you on the
mountain."[24] 8:6 But now he has
obtained a more excellent ministry,
by so much as he is also the mediator
of a better covenant,[3] which on
better promises has been given as
law. 8:7 For if that first covenant had
been faultless, then no place would
have been sought for a second. 8:8 For
finding fault with them, he said,

"Behold, the days come," says the Lord,
"that I will make a new covenant with the house of Israel and with the house of Judah;
8:9 not according to the covenant that I made with their fathers,
in the day that I took them by the hand to lead them out of the land of Egypt;
for they didn't continue in my covenant,
and I disregarded them," says the Lord.
8:10 "For this is the covenant that I will make with the house of Israel.
After those days," says the Lord;
"I will put my laws into their mind,
I will also write them on their heart.[4]
I will be their God,
and they will be my people.
8:11 They will not teach every man his fellow citizen,[25]
and every man his brother, saying, 'Know the Lord,'
for all will know me,
from the least of them to the greatest of them.
8:12 For I will be merciful to their unrighteousness.
I will remember their sins and lawless deeds no more."[26]

8:13 In that he says, "A new
covenant," he has made the first
old.[5] But that which is becoming old
and grows aged is near to vanishing
away.

1. *a copy and shadow of the heavenly things.* [An imperfect expression of a divine Idea].

2. *tabernacle* The temporal body of humans; when in the wilderness of sense, humans worship God in a 'tent/tabernacle' or transitory state of mind, which manifests a perishable body. However, this flimsy body holds all the furnishings of the great temple that is to be built. The BODY OF EVERY HUMAN is a promise of an imperishable temple. (RW/tabernacle)

3. *covenant.* see Hebrews 7:22 (MBD/covenant)

4. *I will put my laws into their mind, I*

*will also write them on their heart.* An allusion to Jeremiah 31:33.

5. *In that he says, "A new covenant," he has made the first old.* Humanly speaking, a last will sets aside all wills previously made, rendering them void and of no effect. The divine will differs from the human will in this respect, for the last will of God, which we call the New Testament, does not invalidate the first, but rather fulfills it.

---

Fillmore Study Bible annotations compiled by Susan St. John.

**World English Bible Footnotes:**

[24] v8:5. Exodus 25:40

[25] v8:11. TR reads "neighbor" instead of "fellow citizen"

[26] v8:12. Jeremiah 31:31-34

# Hebrews 9

## The Physical Consciousness and the Divine within Humans

9:1 Now indeed even the first[27] covenant had ordinances of divine service, and an earthly sanctuary.[1] 9:2 For a tabernacle was prepared. In the first part were the lampstand, the table, and the show bread; which is called the Holy Place. 9:3 After the second veil was the tabernacle which is called the Holy of Holies, 9:4 having a golden altar of incense, and the ark of the covenant overlaid on all sides with gold, in which was a golden pot holding the manna, Aaron's rod that budded, and the tablets of the covenant; 9:5 and above it cherubim of glory overshadowing the mercy seat, of which things we can't speak now in detail.

9:6 Now these things having been thus prepared, the priests[2] go in continually into the first tabernacle, accomplishing the services, 9:7 but into the second the high priest alone, once in the year, not without blood, which he offers for himself, and for the errors of the people. 9:8 The Holy Spirit is indicating this, that the way into the Holy Place wasn't yet revealed while the first tabernacle was still standing; 9:9 which is a symbol of the present age, where gifts and sacrifices are offered that are incapable, concerning the conscience, of making the worshipper perfect; 9:10 being only (with meats and drinks and various washings) fleshly ordinances, imposed until a time of reformation.

9:11 But Christ[3] having come as a high priest of the coming good things, through the greater and more perfect tabernacle, not made with hands, that is to say, not of this creation, 9:12 nor yet through the blood[4] of goats and calves, but through his own blood, entered in once for all into the Holy Place, having obtained eternal redemption.

9:13 For if the blood of goats and bulls,[5] and the ashes of a heifer sprinkling those who have been defiled, sanctify to the cleanness of the flesh: 9:14 how much more will the blood of Christ,[6] who through the eternal Spirit offered himself without blemish to God, cleanse your conscience from dead works to serve the living God?

9:15 For this reason he is the mediator of a new covenant,[7] since a death has occurred for the redemption of the transgressions that were under the first covenant, that those who have been called may receive the promise of the eternal inheritance. 9:16 For where a last will and testament is, there must of necessity be the death of him who made it. 9:17 For a will is in force where there has been death, for it is never in force while he who made it lives. 9:18 Therefore even the first covenant has not been dedicated without blood. 9:19 For when every commandment had been spoken by Moses to all the people according to the law, he took the blood of the calves and the goats, with water and scarlet wool and hyssop, and sprinkled both the book itself and all the people, 9:20 saying, "This is the blood of the covenant which God has commanded you."[28]

9:21 Moreover he sprinkled the tabernacle and all the vessels of the ministry in like manner with the blood. 9:22 According to the law, nearly everything is cleansed with blood, and apart from shedding of blood there is no remission.[8]

1. *sanctuary*. The secret place within man's being where he has a rendezvous with God (RW/sanctuary)

2. *priests*. Metaphysically, priests represent thoughts that spring from and belong to the love faculty in individual consciousness. As ministers and priests in the Temple and in the Temple worship they signify our natural religious tendencies, not necessarily spiritual. (MBD/Levites)

3. *Christ*. Metaphysically, Christ is the divine-idea man (MBD/Christ).

4. *blood*. Blood expresses a spiritual principle, resting on pure ideals (no combinations of components), but is manifested in mind and body, and used to purify the mind and heal the body. See v22: "nearly everything is cleansed with blood". (RW/blood)

5. *blood of goats and bulls*. Animal sacrifice is symbolical of what takes place in man when the lower sense life (represented by animals) is given up (sacrificed). When man enters into the higher understanding of life, for which the Christ stands, the lower "atones" for the higher. Man's powers and faculties are thus brought into harmony.

6. *blood of Christ*. The life contained in God's Word. It is spiritual energy that purifies and redeems humans by pouring into our life currents a new and purer stream, cleansing the consciousness of dead works to enable humanity to serve the LIVING GOD. (RW/blood of Christ)

7. *mediator of a new covenant*. Jesus proved anew that, by loving the things of spiritual significance and seeking to express them, man enters into a vital relation with God and finds the satisfaction that is "life indeed." This bringing of life and immortality to light gave men a new understanding of God and led them to enter into a new relation with him.

8. *apart from shedding of blood there is no remission*. When the life of the flesh (the ways of error) is abandoned (shed), the power of the Spirit "remits" sin by enabling men to lay hold of the higher life. One can establish oneself in the consciousness of the Christ only when one has abandoned the old sense consciousness altogether.

## The Divine nature of Humanity releases the energy of error

9:23 It was necessary therefore that the copies of the things in the heavens should be cleansed with these; but the heavenly things themselves with better sacrifices[1] than these. 9:24 For Christ hasn't entered into holy places made with hands, which are representations of the true, but into heaven itself,[2] now to appear in the presence of God for us; 9:25 nor yet that he should offer himself often, as the high priest enters into the holy place year by year with blood not his own, 9:26 or else he must have suffered often since the foundation of the world. But now once at the end of the ages, he has been revealed to put away sin by the sacrifice of himself. 9:27 Inasmuch as it is appointed for men to die once,[3] and after this, judgment,[4] 9:28 so Christ also, having been offered once to bear the sins of many, will appear a second time,[5] without sin, to those who are eagerly waiting for him for salvation.

1. *sacrifice.* The refining process of releasing the Godliness energy into their appropriate places in human mind an body carrying out the ascension of matter to mind and mind to Spirit. (RW/sacrifice)

2. *For Christ ... into heaven itself.* [The writer implies that the atoning work of Jesus was not rising from the dead but rather ascending into heaven. If so, the same may be said of the followers of Jesus. (MH)]

3. *Inasmuch as it is appointed for men to die once.* [Unity, teaching reincarnation, never commented on this verse. In the final chapter of Emilie Cady's *God A Present Help* (1912 edition, never published by Unity), Emilie Cady says "Since there is but One Life in the universe, and that Life is the Eternal God who is without beginning or end, how can there be any reality in death?" (MH)]

4. *and after this, judgment.* The description of the Last Judgment, as given in the Gospels, has been used to terrify men and women and thus compel them to unite with the church; but in this day of enlightenment people are not so easily led or driven by fear. They ask for understanding. When they seek light concerning the judgment it is given, and they learn that the judgment is all a matter of divine law. They find that for every departure from this law they must suffer, not in some future time of great tribulation, not in a great judgment after death, but in this life—here and now (MBD/judgment)

5. *a second time.* (1) From the spiritual viewpoint there is no such thing as time in the way that man has come to regard it (MBD/time). (2) ["Time in this culture is the unfoldment of an event, or and therefore has no particular duration except that the event is completed. The participants decide when the event is done." *ESL Foreign to Familiar: A Guide to understanding Hot and Cold-Climate cultures,* Sarah Lanier, 77-83. (SSJ)]. (3) [Time and Space are only necessary so that spiritual beings may have a human experience (God's Reach, Glenn Clark, p.206) (MH)]

---

Fillmore Study Bible annotations compiled by Susan St. John.

**World English Bible Footnotes:**

[27] v9:1. TR adds "tabernacle"

[28] v9:20. Exodus 24:8

# Hebrews 10

## Releasing Error Makes Perfect

10:1 For the law, having a shadow of the good to come, not the very image of the things, can never with the same sacrifices year by year, which they offer continually, make perfect those who draw near.[1] 10:2 Or else wouldn't they have ceased to be offered, because the worshippers, having been once cleansed, would have had no more consciousness of sins? 10:3 But in those sacrifices there is yearly reminder of sins. 10:4 For it is impossible that the blood of bulls and goats should take away sins. 10:5 Therefore when he comes into the world, he says,

"Sacrifice and offering you didn't
desire,[2]
but you prepared a body for
me;[3]
10:6 You had no pleasure in whole
burnt offerings and
sacrifices for sin.
10:7 Then I said, 'Behold, I have
come (in the scroll of
the book it is written of
me)
to do your will, O God.'"[29]

10:8 Previously saying, "Sacrifices and offerings and whole burnt offerings and sacrifices for sin you didn't desire, neither had pleasure in them" (those which are offered according to the law), 10:9 then he has said, "Behold, I have come to do your will." He takes away the first, that he may establish the second, 10:10 by which will we have been sanctified through the offering of the body of Jesus Christ once for all.

10:11 Every priest indeed stands day by day serving and often offering the same sacrifices, which can never take away sins, 10:12 but he, when he had offered one sacrifice for sins forever, sat down on the right hand of God;[4] 10:13 from that time waiting until his enemies are made the footstool of his feet.[5] 10:14 For by one offering he has perfected forever those who are being sanctified. 10:15 The Holy Spirit also testifies to us, for after saying,

10:16 "This is the covenant that I will
make with them:
'After those days,' says the
Lord,
'I will put my laws on their heart,
I will also write them on their
mind;'"[30]

then he says,

10:17 "I will remember their sins and
their iniquities no
more."[31]

10:18 Now where remission of these is, there is no more offering for sin.

1. *make perfect those who draw near.* [Transformed from a shadow of God to an image of God. See RW/image. (MH)]

2. *Sacrifice and offering you didn't desire.* Burnt offering transmutation of physical forces to the next higher plane of action, a process of body refinement. (MBD/offering)

3. *but you prepared a body for me.* A freewill offering, that could be a distinguishing factor for the actions of Jesus, is a law of life in that there is acknowledgment what is freely received (life) can be freely given to realize the highest good of humanity. Giving measures receiving: "Freely ye received, freely give" (Matt. 10:8) RW/offering, freewill.

4. *on the right hand of God.* The directive and executive power of Divine Mind.

The Christ commands this.

5. *from that time waiting until his enemies are made the footstool of his feet.* An allusion to Psalm 110.

## A Call to Persevere

10:19 Having therefore, brothers, boldness to enter into the holy place by the blood of Jesus, 10:20 by the way which he dedicated for us, a new and living way, through the veil, that is to say, his flesh; 10:21 and having a great priest over the house of God, 10:22 let's draw near with a true heart in fullness of faith,[1] having our hearts sprinkled from an evil conscience, and having our body washed with pure water, 10:23 let us hold fast the confession of our hope without wavering; for he who promised is faithful.

10:24 Let us consider how to provoke one another to love and good works,[2] 10:25 not forsaking our own assembling together, as the custom of some is, but exhorting one another; and so much the more, as you see the Day approaching.[3] 10:26 For if we sin willfully after we have received the knowledge of the truth, there remains no more a sacrifice for sins, 10:27 but a certain fearful expectation of judgment, and a fierceness of fire which will devour the adversaries. 10:28 A man who disregards Moses' law dies without compassion on the word of two or three witnesses.[4] 10:29 How much worse punishment, do you think, will he be judged worthy of, who has trodden under foot the Son of God, and has counted the blood of the covenant with which he was sanctified an unholy thing, and has insulted the Spirit of grace? 10:30 For we know him who said, "Vengeance belongs to me," says the Lord, "I will repay."[32] Again, "The Lord will judge his people."[33] 10:31 It is a fearful thing to fall into the hands of the living God.

10:32 But remember the former days, in which, after you were enlightened, you endured a great struggle with sufferings; 10:33 partly, being exposed to both reproaches and oppressions; and partly, becoming partakers with those who were treated so. 10:34 For you both had compassion on me in my chains, and joyfully accepted the plundering of your possessions, knowing that you have for yourselves a better possession and an enduring one in the heavens. 10:35 Therefore don't throw away your boldness, which has a great reward. 10:36 For you need endurance so that, having done the will of God, you may receive the promise.

10:37 "In a very little while,
he who comes will come, and
will not wait.
10:38 But the righteous will live by
faith.
If he shrinks back, my soul has
no pleasure in him."[34]

10:39 But we are not of those who shrink back to destruction, but of those who have faith to the saving of the soul.

1. *fulness of faith.* From *Revealing Word* we learn that Faith empowers us to do what may seem impossible to our human mind. It draws us from our deep inner knowing and, once beginning to energize the Christ energy, is the stabilizing factor that keeps us on the path to perfection. (RW/faith)

2. *Let us consider how to provoke one another to love and good works.* As we become so firmly established in our consciousness of Truth that we can associate with others yet remain unswayed by their human, changeable thoughts and emo-

tions, we become great powers for good in helping to establish the race thought in Truth. Our presence uplifts and steadies others—the crowd in which we mingle. "Ye are the salt of the earth, Ye are the light of the world."

3. *as you see the Day approaching*. The time of fulfillment, manifest wholeness and perfection having come out of human limitation, expressing the Christ consciousness more fully. At this point we may feel the need to be with other people even more to share the most perfect consciousness, drawn by the love in us.

4. *A man who disregards Moses' law dies without compassion on the word of two or three witnesses*. If a person stays by himself, keeps his religious views to himself, and does not share his inspirations and joys with others, if he never listens to the opinions and convictions of others, nor considers them, he becomes narrow and one-sided.

Fillmore Study Bible annotations compiled by Susan St. John.

**World English Bible Footnotes:**

[29] v10:7. Psalm 40:6-8

[30] v10:16. Jeremiah 31:33

[31] v10:17. Jeremiah 31:34

[32] v10:30. Deuteronomy 32:35

[33] v10:30. Deuteronomy 32:36; Psalm 135:14

[34] v10:38. Habakkuk 2:3-4

# Hebrews 11

## The Meaning of Faith

11:1 Now faith(1) is assurance(2) of
things hoped for, proof of things not
seen.(3) 11:2 For by this, the elders
obtained testimony. 11:3 By faith, we
understand that the universe has
been framed by the word of God,(4) so
that what is seen has not been made
out of things which are visible.

1. *Faith*. The perceiving power of the mind linked with the power to shape substance; Spiritual assurance; the power to do the seemingly impossible. It is a magnetic power that draws unto us our heart's desire from the invisible spiritual substance. Faith is a deep inner knowing that that which is sought is already ours for the taking. (RW/faith). It is the spiritual foundation of that which humanity is meant to bring forth. We become conscious of and increases our faith through prayer (affirmation of eternal Truth that has not yet come into consciousness) and by acting on the deepest impulses of our soul (RW/prayer). When we fail to exercise faith we become bound by fear, falling short of our capacity to use God-given faculties and powers, seemingly standing still, which amounts to stagnation, death.

2. *assurance*. [In the original Greek, *assurance* is *hypostasis*. While it is figuratively rendered as *assurance* in the ASV, WEB, and NRSV, the term is translated literally in the King James version as *substance*, and it literally means the Real spiritual essence, substance or divine idea behind all manifest things. From this well-known understanding in metaphysical reli-

gion, we see faith as our capacity to shape substance as we need and desire and that which provides confidence about humankinds place in the Cosmos. (MH)]

3. *things not seen* [External realities beyond the physical senses.]

4. *the universe has been framed by the word of God.* Faith makes clear to us what science has lately proved, namely that the manifest creation has come into being from the realm of the unmanifest or invisible. The universal life energy or "word of God" is the motive power or divine will that causes all manifestation.

## The Examples of Abel, Enoch, and Noah

11:4 By faith, Abel offered to God a
more excellent sacrifice than Cain,[1]
through which he had testimony
given to him that he was righteous,
God testifying with respect to his
gifts; and through it he, being dead,
still speaks. 11:5 By faith, Enoch[2] was
taken away, so that he wouldn't see
death, and he was not found,
because God translated him. For he
has had testimony given to him that
before his translation he had been
well pleasing to God. 11:6 Without
faith it is impossible to be well
pleasing to him, for he who comes
to God must believe that he exists,
and that he is a rewarder of those
who seek him.[3] 11:7 By faith, Noah,[4]
being warned about things not yet
seen, moved with godly fear,
prepared a ship for the saving of his
house, through which he condemned
the world, and became heir of the
righteousness which is according to
faith.

1. *Abel, Cain.* Abel is the mind that controls the animal functions; more closely related to spiritual consciousness than the physical (MBD/Abel). Cain is the power of the mind to reproduce its ideas in unlimited expression; rulership by centralized power (MBD/Cain). Abel believed that God is worshipped most truly in the highest realm of man's consciousness. The animal kingdom, since it is composed of sentient creatures endowed with the faculties of sensation and perception, is higher than the nonsentient plants of the vegetable kingdom. Abel therefore offered to God in symbolic form a higher consciousness than did Cain.

2. *Enoch.* Entrance into and instruction in a new state of thought and understanding, a new spiritual consciousness, a new life in Christ (MBD/Enoch). The grandson of Adam, Enoch proved through faithfully living in God consciousness that the curse pronounced upon Adam "Dust thou art, and unto dust thou shalt return" is not a universal law to which all men are subject, but that it applies only to the disobedient. Enoch translated his body from flesh to Spirit, and did not return to dust.

3. *He who comes to God must believe that he exists, and that he is a rewarder of those who seek him.* ("diligently" seek him, ASV). Concentrated attention of the mind on an idea of any kind is equal to prayer and will make available the spiritual principle that is its source in proportion to the intensity and continuity of the mental effort. (Jesus Christ Heals, p48)

4. *Noah.* The consciousness at rest and obedience from which our learning from our enthusiasm for things of sense, grows; a state of consciousness where 'race' thoughts (generations of error) are cleansed. (MBD/Noah) Noah rested in faith, using it as a guide to future conduct, and through relying upon the divine assurance so gained, developed foresight and foreknowledge of things to come. He was therefore able to survive the flood, when all those without such foresight perished.

## The Faith of Abraham

11:8 By faith, Abraham,[1] when he
was called, obeyed to go out to the
place which he was to receive for
an inheritance. He went out, not

knowing where he went. 11:9 By faith, he lived as an alien in the land of promise, as in a land not his own, dwelling in tents, with Isaac and Jacob, the heirs with him of the same promise. 11:10 For he looked for the city which has the foundations, whose builder and maker is God.[2] 11:11 By faith, even Sarah herself received power to conceive, and she bore a child when she was past age, since she counted him faithful who had promised. 11:12 Therefore as many as the stars of the sky in multitude, and as innumerable as the sand which is by the sea shore, were fathered by one man, and him as good as dead.

11:13 These all died in faith, not having received the promises, but having seen[35] them and embraced them from afar, and having confessed that they were strangers and pilgrims on the earth. 11:14 For those who say such things make it clear that they are seeking a country of their own.[3] 11:15 If indeed they had been thinking of that country from which they went out, they would have had enough time to return. 11:16 But now they desire a better country, that is, a heavenly one. Therefore God is not ashamed of them, to be called their God, for he has prepared a city for them.

11:17 By faith, Abraham, being tested, offered up Isaac. Yes, he who had gladly received the promises was offering up his one and only son; 11:18 even he to whom it was said, "In Isaac will your seed be called;"[36] 11:19 concluding that God is able to raise up even from the dead. Figuratively speaking, he also did receive him back from the dead. 11:20 By faith, Isaac blessed Jacob[4] and Esau, even concerning things to come. 11:21 By faith, Jacob, when he was dying, blessed each of the sons of Joseph, and worshiped, leaning on the top of his staff. 11:22 By faith, Joseph, when his end was near, made mention of the departure of the children of Israel; and gave instructions concerning his bones.

1. *Abraham.* The power of the mind to reproduce its ideas in unlimited expressions (MBD/Abraham).

2. *For he looked for the city which has the foundations, whose builder and maker is God.* We owe to Abraham our first clear knowledge of the true God, His spiritual and holy nature, and the undivided devotion that we are to render Him. He was made great, first by his faith in God. Next, he was great in patience, in working toward the realization of his hopes and desires. He lived at peace with the Canaanites, among whom he was a stranger. He built up a Godlike character and realized the joy of achievement in the spiritual realm. These attainments all fitted him to become the founder and the inspiration of an enduring people.

3. *seeking a country of their own.* Paul says we seek a country from which we came forth, and to which we shall return. We are travelers that have wandered away from home and have not found our wanderings pleasant. The outer man looks upon the home he is seeking as a place fixed in the heavens, but a fuller realization of Truth shows that this home is in the place Jesus pointed out—"the kingdom of God is within you." Having once established yourself in this place it is an easy matter to externalize it. (Temple Talks, Series 3, Chapter 4, Obedience)

4. *By faith, Isaac blessed Jacob.* How did Isaac and Jacob develop faith? Both these men used faith to steady and clarify their vision of character and were able to discern what their sons and grandsons would become in later years.

## The Faith of Moses

11:23 By faith, Moses, when he was born,[1] was hidden for three months by his parents, because they saw that he was a beautiful child, and they were not afraid of the king's commandment. 11:24 By faith, Moses, when he had grown up, refused to be called the son of Pharaoh's daughter, 11:25 choosing rather to share ill treatment with God's people, than to enjoy the pleasures of sin for a time; 11:26 accounting the reproach of Christ greater riches than the treasures of Egypt; for he looked to the reward. 11:27 By faith, he left Egypt,(2) not fearing the wrath of the king; for he endured, as seeing him who is invisible. 11:28 By faith, he kept the Passover, and the sprinkling of the blood, that the destroyer of the firstborn should not touch them.

1. *Moses, when he was born.* Moses means drawing out, extracting, i. e., from the water. The birth of Moses represents man's development in consciousness of the law of his being, from the negative side. Water represents universal negation; but water also represents the great possibility. Out of seemingly negative conditions comes the new growth. When we are in what seems Egyptian darkness, and weak as water, we are ripe for the higher understanding. The thoughts that rule in the darkness are bent upon putting out all the children of light, but if we are of the house of faith, as were Moses' parents, then our desire to bring forth the higher consciousness will find a protector. We must care for the infant thought of Truth and surround it with the ark of love and trust, right in the midst of its seeming enemies. (MBD/Moses)

2. *By faith, he left Egypt.* Moses' fleeing to the wilderness represents the discipline that we must undergo when we have sought the exalted One. Horeb means solitude, that is, we have to go into the solitude of the within and lead our flock of thoughts to the back of the wilderness, where dwells the exalted One, the divine I AM, whose kingdom is good judgment. There we are in training forty years, or until we arrive at a four-sided or balanced state of mind.

## The Faith of Other Israelite Heroes

11:29 By faith, they passed through the Red Sea as on dry land. When the Egyptians tried to do so, they were swallowed up. 11:30 By faith, the walls of Jericho fell down,(1) after they had been encircled for seven days. 11:31 By faith, Rahab the prostitute, didn't perish with those who were disobedient, having received the spies in peace.

11:32 What more shall I say? For the time would fail me if I told of Gideon, Barak, Samson, Jephthah, David, Samuel, and the prophets; 11:33 who, through faith subdued kingdoms, worked out righteousness, obtained promises, stopped the mouths of lions,[37] 11:34 quenched the power of fire,[38] escaped the edge of the sword,[39] from weakness were made strong, grew mighty in war, and caused foreign armies to flee.(2) 11:35 Women received their dead by resurrection.[40] Others were tortured, not accepting their deliverance, that they might obtain a better resurrection. 11:36 Others were tried by mocking and scourging, yes, moreover by bonds and imprisonment. 11:37 They were stoned.[41] They were sawn apart. They were tempted. They were slain with the sword.[42] They went around in sheep skins and in goat skins; being destitute, afflicted, ill-treated 11:38 (of whom the world was not worthy), wandering in deserts, mountains, caves, and the holes of the earth.

11:39 These all, having had testimony given to them through their faith, didn't receive the promise,(3) 11:40 God having provided some better thing concerning us, so that apart from us they should not be made perfect.

1. *By faith, the walls of Jericho fell down.* Moses, the law, ever urges man forward to greater expressions of inherent

abilities, but the law requires adherence to certain principles, as it urges the children of the real to go forward. Moses, in Joshua 1:1,2, represents the evolutionary force of new ideas that have grown in the subconsciousness until they have lifted Israel (our true, spiritual thoughts) out of the depths of sense (Egyptian) bondage into a higher life expression. He has led the new ideas safely through the wilderness of our untried and undisciplined mind to the border of Canaan; then he gives up his leadership to Joshua.

2. *who, through faith subdued kingdoms ... and caused foreign armies to flee.* What quality in the mind causes men to persist in doing that which to the sense perception seems impossible? A short name for it is faith. Faith is the assurance of hope. Columbus began with hope, which gradually strengthened in his mind, until it became substance, which is the ultimate of every idea one firmly believes in and assiduously cultivates. Faith, then, is not confined to religion, but has to do with every department of life. Faith is one of the fundamental ideas in Divine Mind and is made active in man's consciousness in whatsoever place he may elect to put it. It works in small things as well as great—take your choice. If you want to remove mountains, you must have the faith of God. A very small quantity of that kind of faith will do it, according to the teaching of Jesus.

3. *didn't receive the promise.* What "advantage has the believer in God over the materialist or the unbeliever? The believer is convinced that all creation rests on a spiritual foundation and that the manifest comes out of the unmanifest—that invisible realm of causation, which is completely charged with the creative principle of life or "word of God." The materialist, or unbeliever, having no such faith on which to stand, lacks understanding of the source or first cause of life. He rejects the firm foundation of faith.

---

Fillmore Study Bible annotations compiled by Susan St. John.

**World English Bible Footnotes:**

[35] v11:13. TR adds "and being convinced of"

[36] v11:18. Genesis 21:12

[37] v11:33. Daniel 6:22-23

[38] v11:34. Daniel 3:1-30

[39] v11:34. 1 Kings 19:1-3; 2 Kings 6:31-7:20

[40] v11:35. 1 Kings 19:1-3; 2 Kings 6:31-7:20

[41] v11:37. 2 Chronicles 24:20-21

[42] v11:37. Jeremiah 26:20-23; 1 Kings 19:10

# Hebrews 12

## The Example of Jesus

12:1 Therefore let us also, seeing
we are surrounded by so great a
cloud of witnesses,❶ lay aside every
weight and the sin which so easily
entangles us, and let us run with
patience the race that is set before
us, 12:2 looking to Jesus, the author❷
and perfecter❸ of faith,❹ who for

the joy that was set before him endured the cross, despising its shame, and has sat down at the right hand of the throne of God.

12:3 For consider him who has endured such contradiction of sinners against himself, that you don't grow weary, fainting in your souls. 12:4 You have not yet resisted to blood, striving against sin; 12:5 and you have forgotten the exhortation which reasons with you as with children,

"My son, don't take lightly the
chastening of the Lord,
nor faint when you are
reproved by him;
12:6 For whom the Lord loves, he
chastens,5
and scourges every son whom
he receives."[43]

12:7 It is for discipline that you endure. God deals with you as with children, for what son is there whom his father doesn't discipline? 12:8 But if you are without discipline, of which all have been made partakers, then are you illegitimate, and not children. 12:9 Furthermore, we had the fathers of our flesh to chasten us, and we paid them respect. Shall we not much rather be in subjection to the Father of spirits, and live? 12:10 For they indeed, for a few days, punished us as seemed good to them; but he for our profit, that we may be partakers of his holiness. 12:11 All chastening seems for the present to be not joyous but grievous; yet afterward it yields the peaceful fruit of righteousness to those who have been exercised thereby.

12:12 Therefore, lift up the hands that hang down and the feeble knees,[44] 12:13 and make straight paths for your feet,[45]6 so that which is lame may not be dislocated, but rather be healed.

1. *a cloud of witnesses.* [See the painting, Giusto de' Menabuoi, Paradise, Padua Baptistry's frescoed dome, 1375-1378, at the start of Fillmore Study Bible: Hebrews. The cloud of witnesses speak from a higher dimension. (MH)]

2. *the author.* [Greek term for *author* is *archēgos*, meaning the chief leader, prince, one that takes the lead in any thing and thus affords an example, a predecessor in a matter, pioneer. You may recognize the word archetype coming from this word. In metaphysical Christianity, we refer to *archēgos* as the *Wayshower.* (MH)]

3. *and perfecter.* [Greek term for perfecter is teleiōtēs, meaning finisher, a perfecter, one who has in his own person raised faith to its perfection and so set before us the highest example of faith. (MH)]

4. *of faith.* See previous chapter.

5. *For whom the Lord loves, he chastens, and scourges every son whom he receives.* Law is the orderly working out of the Principle, or Principle in action. When people do not work in harmony with the Principle they build up error states of consciousness. These later manifest in the body and affairs in many inharmonious ways, such as sickness, pain, discord, strife, poverty and death. This explains the text in Hebrews 12:6, "Whom the Lord loveth he chasteneth and scourgeth every son whom he receiveth." If people did not reap the result of their error in suffering, they would never seek the kingdom of God, or right ideas, that they might come into right relation with the Great Principle of Being. When we understand the Principle and work from it, in harmony with the Law, all things will be possible to us. (Unity, September 1918, p.232).

6. *make straight paths for your feet.* [An allusion to Isaiah 40.] When we steadfastly hold in mind a conviction that what we believe in exists and is to become visible, we attract unseen energized substance to us and give it the form of our conviction. Conviction is the mold in which unseen substance crystallizes and becomes visible.

## Warnings against Rejecting God's Grace

12:14 Follow after peace with all men,1 and the sanctification

without which no man will see the
Lord, 12:15 looking carefully lest there
be any man who falls short of the
grace of God; lest any root of
bitterness springing up trouble you,
and many be defiled by it; 12:16 lest
there be any sexually immoral
person, or profane person, like
Esau,② who sold his birthright for
one meal. 12:17 For you know that
even when he afterward desired to
inherit the blessing, he was rejected,
for he found no place for a change
of mind though he sought it diligently
with tears.

12:18 For you have not come to a
mountain that might be touched,③
and that burned with fire, and to
blackness, darkness, storm, 12:19 the
sound of a trumpet, and the voice
of words; which those who heard it
begged that not one more word
should be spoken to them, 12:20 for
they could not stand that which was
commanded, "If even an animal
touches the mountain, it shall be
stoned[46];"[47] 12:21 and so fearful was
the appearance, that Moses said, "I
am terrified and trembling."[48]

12:22 But you have come to Mount
Zion,④ and to the city of the living
God, the heavenly Jerusalem, and to
innumerable multitudes of angels,
12:23 to the general assembly and
assembly of the firstborn who are
enrolled in heaven, to God the Judge
of all, to the spirits of just men made
perfect, 12:24 to Jesus, the mediator
of a new covenant,[49] and to the
blood of sprinkling that speaks better
than that of Abel.

12:25 See that you don't refuse him
who speaks. For if they didn't escape
when they refused him who warned
on the Earth, how much more will we
not escape who turn away from him
who warns from heaven, 12:26 whose
voice shook the earth then, but now
he has promised, saying, "Yet once
more I will shake not only the earth,
but also the heavens."[50] 12:27 This
phrase, "Yet once more," signifies the
removing of those things that are
shaken, as of things that have been
made, that those things which are
not shaken may remain. 12:28
Therefore, receiving a Kingdom that
can't be shaken, let us have grace,
through which we serve God
acceptably, with reverence and awe,
12:29 for our God is a consuming
fire.[51]⑤

1. *Follow after peace with all men.* Harmony and tranquillity derived from awareness of the Christ consciousness. Until world peace is based on the divine law of love and this law incorporated into the pact of peace as well as into the minds of those who sign the pact, there will be no permanent peace. (RW/peace)

2. *Esau.* The body or physical vigour. In the immature consciousness the natural human is moved by desire. Appetite and passion are satisfied regardless of the higher law. The feeling of our inward rebellion when we are changing our modes of thought. (MBD/Esau)

3. *For you have not come to a mountain that might be touched.* An allusion to Mount Sinai, Exodus 20:18-21.

4. *But you have come to Mount Zion.* a A fortified hill that David took from the Jebusites. David built his palace there (II Sam. 5:7), and the place was called the city of David. Later Zion became a part of the city of Jerusalem. In referring to the Holy City, the New Jerusalem, Zion symbolizes spiritual consciousness. Metaphysically, Zion is Love's abode in the phase of the subjective consciousness where high, holy thoughts and ideals abide. (MBD/Zion)

5. *consuming fire.* Symbolizes cleansing and purification, the fire of the Spirit of reality. The whole universe is alive with a divine, living spiritual energy that consumes all the rubbish of sense and materiality, burning eternally when it meets rubbish. The fire consumes only when it meets anything unlike itself. In purified humanity is manifested as eternal life. (RW/fire)

---

Fillmore Study Bible annotations compiled by Susan St. John.

**World English Bible Footnotes:**

[43] v12:6. Proverbs 3:11-12
[44] v12:12. Isaiah 35:3
[45] v12:13. Proverbs 4:26
[46] v12:20. TR adds "or shot with an arrow" [see Exodus 19:12-13]
[47] v12:20. Exodus 19:12-13
[48] v12:21. Deuteronomy 9:19
[49] v12:24. Jeremiah 31:31
[50] v12:26. Haggai 2:6
[51] v12:29. Deuteronomy 4:24

# Hebrews 13

## Service Well-Pleasing to God

13:1 Let brotherly love continue. 13:2 Don't forget to show hospitality to strangers, for in doing so, some have entertained angels[1] without knowing it. 13:3 Remember those who are in bonds, as bound with them; and those who are ill-treated, since you are also in the body. 13:4 Let marriage[2] be held in honor among all, and let the bed be undefiled: but God will judge the sexually immoral and adulterers.[3]

13:5 Be free from the love of money,[4] content with such things as you have, for he has said, "I will in no way leave you, neither will I in any way forsake you."[52] 13:6 So that with good courage we say,

"The Lord is my helper. I will not
fear.
What can man do to me?"[53]

13:7 Remember your leaders, men who spoke to you the word of God, and considering the results of their conduct, imitate their faith. 13:8 Jesus Christ is the same yesterday, today, and forever.[5] 13:9 Don't be carried away by various and strange teachings, for it is good that the heart be established by grace, not by food, through which those who were so occupied were not benefited.

13:10 We have an altar from which those who serve the holy tabernacle have no right to eat. 13:11 For the bodies of those animals, whose blood is brought into the holy place by the high priest as an offering for sin, are burned outside of the camp.[54] 13:12 Therefore Jesus also, that he might sanctify the people through his own blood, suffered outside of the gate. 13:13 Let us therefore go out to him outside of the camp, bearing his reproach. 13:14 For we don't have here an enduring city, but we seek that which is to come.[6] 13:15 Through him, then, let us offer up a sacrifice of praise to God[55] continually, that is, the fruit of lips which proclaim allegiance to his name. 13:16 But don't forget to be doing good and sharing,

for with such sacrifices God is well
pleased.

13:17 Obey your leaders[7] and
submit to them, for they watch on
behalf of your souls, as those who
will give account, that they may do
this with joy, and not with groaning,
for that would be unprofitable for
you.

13:18 Pray for us,[8] for we are
persuaded that we have a good
conscience, desiring to live
honorably in all things. 13:19 I strongly
urge you to do this, that I may be
restored to you sooner.

1. *angels.* A messenger of God; a projection into the consciousness of the spiritual idea direct from the Fountainhead. The word of truth in which is centered the power of God to overcome all limited beliefs and conditions. (RW/angel)

2. *marriage.* Metaphysically, marriage between two dominant states of consciousness; a union of the higher forces in being with the lower and we are quickened in every part. Higher consciousness is poured out for us. (RW/marriage)

3. *sexually immoral and adulterers.* (Sexually immoral, fornicator, ASV): One who debases the spiritual nature (RW/fornication). Adulterer: One who mixes thought, errors that have existence in unrepented feelings, have not come under the authority of the Spiritual self (I AM) (RW/adultery).

4. *Be free from the love of money.* If the mind is free from attachment to money or love of it, and lovingly concentrated on the divine substance, there is never failure in the demonstration. (Keep a True Lent, p.106)

5. *yesterday, today, and forever.* [An often-used phrase that God is abiding, eternal, and unchangeable. It's message is to trust God. In this passage, the writer is saying to beware looking to politics (verse 7) or faddish religion (verse 9) to solve problems. "Divine law worked yesterday, is working today, and will work forever to bring about order and balance in all things" (Unity Correspondence Course, Series 2, Lesson 11, Annotation 7, *What is the sure way to establish justice in one's affairs?*)(MH)]

6. *For we don't have here an enduring city, but we seek that which is to come.* [A city whose builder and maker is God. See Heb. 11:10.]

7. Obey your leaders. [Trust you minister.]

8. Pray for us. [and see your minister as a friend.]

## Benediction

13:20 Now may the God of peace,
who brought again from the dead the
great shepherd of the sheep with the
blood of an eternal covenant, our
Lord Jesus, 13:21 make you complete[1]
in every good work to do his will,
working in you that which is well
pleasing in his sight, through Jesus
Christ, to whom be the glory forever
and ever. Amen.

1. *complete.* Perfect, ASV. See Heb. 12:3.

## Final Exhortation and Greetings

13:22 But I exhort you, brothers,
endure the word of exhortation, for
I have written to you in few words.
13:23 Know that our brother Timothy
has been freed,[1] with whom, if he
comes shortly, I will see you. 13:24
Greet all of your leaders and all the
saints. The Italians greet you. 13:25
Grace be with you all. Amen.

1. *Timothy has been freed.* Metaphysically, Timothy is inspired reason united with faith (Paul). [See the Introduction. The church is coming under attack.]

Fillmore Study Bible annotations compiled by Susan St. John.

**World English Bible Footnotes:**

[52] v13:5. Deuteronomy 31:6
[53] v13:6. Psalm 118:6-7
[54] v13:11. Leviticus 16:27
[55] v13:15. Psalm 50:23

# THE LETTER FROM JAMES

James the Just (brother of Jesus). Russian Icon. Public Domain.

## INTRODUCTION TO THE LETTER FROM JAMES

Nowadays there is a tendency to regard Christian churches of the early days as ideal institutions, with all members working together in love, peace, and harmony. This makes a beautiful picture, but it is far from being accurate. In point of fact, the New Testament indicates that there were many dissensions and disturbances within the early Christian groups and at a comparatively early date there appeared a very helpful document dealing with this problem. This document is now known as *The Epistle of James*, and all its five chapters deal with problems arising within Christian groups or churches. The general theme of this Epistle may be stated as: "The practical application of Christian principles," with the subtitle: "Internal dissensions and disturbances— their cause and cure." The Epistle of James should, therefore, be studied from this viewpoint, keeping well in mind that many of the problems and solutions set forth have present-day application.

**The Author:** The writer of this Epistle declares himself to be "James (Heb. Jacob), a servant of God and of the Lord Jesus Christ" (James 1:1). This James is usually regarded as James, the brother of Jesus, and was referred to in the early church as "James the Just." Apparently James did not accept the Christian teaching during the active ministry of Jesus, but was converted at the time of the Resurrection. (See I Cor. 15:7.) Following the Ascension, James became the head, or presiding elder, of the Apostolic Council at Jerusalem, and the New Testament has several references to his activities while occupying this important position. (See Galatians 1:19; Acts 15:4-29; 21:17-19.) This Epistle of James was written, probably, shortly before A.D. 66.

**The Readers:** In the opening verse of the Epistle of James the "readers" are referred to as "the twelve tribes in the Dispersion" (James 1:1). But since the writer was concerned with Christian converts rather than the tribes of Israel, this must be regarded as a figure of speech. The thought was that just as the Israelites were dispersed throughout various parts of the world, so had the Christian groups extended far beyond the bounds of the Holy Land. The "readers," therefore, included Christian converts in Syria, Asia Minor, Europe, and possibly North Africa.

**The Dissensions and Disturbances:** The Epistle of James indicates that the writer was familiar with the functioning of the various church groups, and was also aware of the dissensions and disturbances which, from time to time, arouse therein. He therefore sought to deal with the various situations by pointing out the causes of the troubles, and then indicating the remedies. It will be noted that James, as presiding elder of the Apostolic Council, inserted a note of authority into his Epistle, as he urged the readers to take all necessary action to restore peace and harmony within the Christian groups concerned.

Introduction to *The Letter from James* by Herbert J. Hunt, former Dean of Bible Studies for the Unity School of Christianity.

The Letter from James is intended to be read in Jewish-Christian communities, written sometime after 75 CE. A quick reading gives the impression that it's a stern admonishment to a life of good works. A closer look will bring to mind many similarities with Jesus' teachings in the Sermon on the Mount because, like Jesus, the writer appears to be calling us to a standard of perfection. But the writer also gives us the key to moral perfection, which is the metaphysical concept of wisdom. Read this way, the letter of James becomes much more valuable. How does wisdom lead to perfection?

Metaphysically, wisdom is a spiritual understanding of our inner Truth. More specifically, wisdom provides us the ability to discriminate between what is in our best interest and what is not for us. Similar to the ability of our body to intuitively know that which is nutritionally best to eat, wisdom is an ability of our soul to know intuitively that which is the correct decision. The writer makes three key points about wisdom: wisdom is a gift from God (1:5), it is always rooted in a consciousness of faith (1:6) and it operates, without exception, when we chose to do any act of generosity (1:17). In other words, when we chose, in faith, to live a life of perfect oneness with God and love of our neighbor, wisdom will inexplicably appear. The key is making the decision in faith for oneness and love, and not attempting to figure out ahead of time how such a decision may be implemented - the way will be known.

Introduction to *The Letter from James* by Mary Salama.

# James 1

## Salutation

[1:1] James,❶ a servant of God and of the Lord Jesus Christ, to the twelve tribes which are in the Dispersion:❷ Greetings.

1. *James.* James is the English equivalent of Jacob (the "supplanter"). Metaphysically, the name represents judgment in individual consciousness, or justice and discrimination. In His statement, "For judgment came I into this world, that they that see not may see" Jesus showed that spiritual judgment is a necessary part of man's development.

2. *twelve tribes which are of the Dispersion.* The twelve faculties of man, and the fact that they were dispersed shows that the faculties of the natural man are scattered through want of discipline and understanding.

## Faith and Wisdom

[1:2] Count it all joy, my brothers[1],
when you fall into various
temptations, [1:3] knowing that the
testing of your faith produces
endurance. [1:4] Let endurance have its
perfect work,❶ that you may be
perfect and complete, lacking in
nothing.

[1:5] But if any of you lacks
wisdom,❷ let him ask of God, who
gives to all liberally and without
reproach; and it will be given to him.
[1:6] But let him ask in faith, without
any doubting, for he who doubts is
like a wave of the sea, driven by
the wind and tossed. [1:7] For let that
man not think that he will receive
anything from the Lord. [1:8] He is a
double-minded man,❸ unstable in all
his ways.

1. *Let endurance (patience, ASV) have its perfect work.* He who withstands temptation gains patience through using his faith as a bulwark against tests. The Spartans not only welcomed the customary trials that come to the natural man, but invented additional hardships with which to wrestle, in the belief that, in surmounting obstacles, man develops nobler character.

2. *Wisdom.* Wisdom is essential to the exercise of good judgment, as well as to the gaining of patience. The wise man does not give way to impatience.

3. *a doubleminded man.* Spiritual discrimination causes a man to affirm his true estate under divine law, regardless of appearances. The affirmation "Ye are gods" is understood by the metaphysician to be true of each man in the ideal sense.

## Poverty and Riches

[1:9] But let the brother in humble
circumstances glory in his high
position; [1:10] and the rich, in that he
is made humble, because like the
flower in the grass, he will pass
away. [1:11] For the sun arises with the
scorching wind, and withers the

grass, and the flower in it falls, and the beauty of its appearance perishes. So also will the rich man fade away in his pursuits.

## Trial and Temptation

1:12 Blessed is the man who endures temptation,[1] for when he has been approved, he will receive the crown of life, which the Lord promised to those who love him. 1:13 Let no man say when he is tempted, "I am tempted by God," for God can't be tempted by evil,[2] and he himself tempts no one. 1:14 But each one is tempted, when he is drawn away by his own lust, and enticed. 1:15 Then the lust, when it has conceived, bears sin; and the sin, when it is full grown, brings forth death. 1:16 Don't be deceived, my beloved brothers.

1:17 Every good gift and every perfect gift is from above, coming down from the Father of lights,[3] with whom can be no variation, nor turning shadow.[4] 1:18 Of his own will he brought us forth by the word of truth, that we should be a kind of first fruits of his creatures.[5]

1. *Blessed is the man who endures temptation.* Temptation affords man an opportunity to learn concentration, since he must marshal his forces each time in order to withstand the temptation.

2. *God can't be tempted by evil.* Evil is not one of the realities; it is the natural man's reaction to life. Man has free will.

3. *Father of lights.* God as universal principle, which is as unvarying in its application as any mathematical principle that is derived from it.

4. *turning shadow.* A shadow falls on the side of an object that is removed from the light, therefore, in order to enjoy wisdom, intelligence, and understanding, man faces the light (the Father). He constantly contemplates Divine Mind and himself as its expression.

5. *firstfruits of his creatures.* In the perfect manifestation, ideal man is the first fruit to ripen, being the largest and finest on the tree.

## Hearing and Doing the Word (Meekness)

1:19 So, then, my beloved brothers, let every man be swift to hear, slow to speak, and slow to anger;[1] 1:20 for the anger of man doesn't produce the righteousness of God. 1:21 Therefore, putting away all filthiness[2] and overflowing of wickedness, receive with humility the implanted word,[3] which is able to save your souls[2].

1:22 But be doers of the word, and not only hearers, deluding your own selves.[4] 1:23 For if anyone is a hearer of the word and not a doer, he is like a man looking at his natural face in a mirror; 1:24 for he sees himself,[5] and goes away, and immediately forgets what kind of man he was. 1:25 But he who looks into the perfect law[6] of freedom, and continues, not being a hearer who forgets, but a doer of the work, this man will be blessed in what he does.

1:26 If anyone among you thinks himself to be religious while he doesn't bridle his tongue, but deceives his heart, this man's religion is worthless.[7] 1:27 Pure religion and undefiled before our God and Father is this: to visit the fatherless and widows in their affliction, and to keep oneself unstained by the world.

1. *slow to anger.* As long as he gives way to anger, man cannot enter into the consciousness of universal life and develop towards the perfection of spiritual unity. Anger limits him to a narrow personal standard.

2. *putting away all filthiness.* After we have emptied our minds of material thoughts, through denial, and have affirmed the truth of our being, we then have put the law of Divine Mind into action in our consciousness, we feel an inner urge to do something for the development of our souls and for the good of our fellow man; then, to fulfill the law, we perform the outer act.

3. *implanted word.* The word of Truth that is spoken into the ideal creation by the voice of God. Truth is therefore innate in man, and its manifestation waits only upon his recognition of its presence and his active cooperation with God in all his ways. It is the Logos, whose office in man is explained in the book of John. It is the word of God planted as a seed in the mind of man. We become conscious of the implanted word by cleansing our thoughts of impurity and wickedness, and by making ourselves meek and obedient and receptive to the Spirit of truth.

4. *deluding your own selves.* The hearer who is not a doer is self-deluded because man does not develop according to his passive thinking and understanding, but according to what he applies to both. To hear and understand Truth without trying to apply it practically is to shun spiritual reality and become withered fruit on the tree of life.

5. *for he sees himself.* Many people delude themselves by filling their minds with knowledge for the mere pleasure of learning. There is much running to and fro, reading books, listening to lectures, and many other ways of storing up wisdom, which is not used. People are hungering for Truth, and they often gorge their intellects with more than they can digest. We accomplish nothing of enduring spiritual value. Whatever we accomplish without divine guidance is of no more permanence than the reflection of ourselves that we see in a mirror, which lasts only while we stand before it.

6. *But he that looks into the perfect law.* How James pictures the outworking of the law.

7. *this man's religion is worthless.* Many people accept Jesus' definition, "God is Spirit," but their descriptions of God are material, showing that they do not have true understanding of the character of God. "God is Spirit," and all his creations are spiritual. Man, his image and likeness, is spiritual. The manifest or Adam man is not the direct creation of God, but the formed expression of the image and likeness, that is Jehovah God. In thinking of ourselves, we should always remember that our real ego is Spirit and that personality represents a degree of evolution of this spiritual idea or word implanted in us from the beginning.

---

Fillmore Study Bible annotations compiled by Rev. Mark Hicks

**World English Bible Footnotes:**

[1] v1:2. The word for "brothers" here and where context allows may also be correctly translated "brothers and sisters" or "siblings."

[2] v1:21. or, preserve your life.

# JAMES 2

## Warning against Partiality

2:1 My brothers, don't hold the
faith of our Lord Jesus Christ of glory
with partiality. 2:2 For if a man with a
gold ring, in fine clothing, comes into
your synagogue[3], and a poor man
in filthy clothing also comes in; 2:3
and you pay special attention to him

who wears the fine clothing, and say, "Sit here in a good place;" and you tell the poor man, "Stand there," or "Sit by my footstool;" 2:4 haven't you shown partiality among yourselves, and become judges with evil thoughts? 2:5 Listen, my beloved brothers. Didn't God choose those who are poor in this world to be rich in faith, and heirs of the Kingdom which he promised to those who love him? 2:6 But you have dishonored the poor man. Don't the rich oppress you, and personally drag you before the courts? 2:7 Don't they blaspheme the honorable name by which you are called?

2:8 However, if you fulfill the royal law, according to the Scripture, "You shall love your neighbor as yourself,"[4] you do well. 2:9 But if you show partiality, you commit sin, being convicted by the law as transgressors. 2:10 For whoever keeps the whole law, and yet stumbles in one point, he has become guilty of all. 2:11 For he who said, "Do not commit adultery,"[5] also said, "Do not commit murder."[6] Now if you do not commit adultery, but murder, you have become a transgressor of the law. 2:12 So speak, and so do, as men who are to be judged by a law of freedom. 2:13 For judgment is without mercy to him who has shown no mercy. Mercy triumphs over judgment.

## Faith without Works Is Dead

2:14 What good is it, my brothers, if a man says he has faith, but has no works? Can faith save him? 2:15 And if a brother or sister is naked and in lack of daily food, 2:16 and one of you tells them, "Go in peace, be warmed and filled;" and yet you didn't give them the things the body needs, what good is it? 2:17 Even so faith, if it has no works, is dead[1] in itself.

2:18 Yes, a man will say, "You have faith, and I have works." Show me your faith without works, and I by my works will show you my faith. 2:19 You believe that God is one. You do well. The demons also believe, and shudder. 2:20 But do you want to know, vain man, that faith apart from works is dead? 2:21 Wasn't Abraham our father justified by works, in that he offered up Isaac his son on the altar? 2:22 You see that faith worked with his works, and by works faith was perfected;[2] 2:23 and the Scripture was fulfilled which says, "Abraham believed God, and it was accounted to him as righteousness;"[7] and he was called the friend of God. 2:24 You see then that by works, a man is justified, and not only by faith. 2:25 In like manner wasn't Rahab the prostitute also justified by works, in that she received the messengers, and sent them out another way? 2:26 For as the body apart from the spirit is dead, even so faith apart from works is dead.

1. *faith, if it has no works, is dead.* The question of the relation between faith and works has never been settled. Some theologians contend that a man can be saved by faith alone, while others are sure that it takes works to complete the salvation. But there is diversity of opinion as to the character of the works. [TruthUnity note: Metaphysical Christianity provides an elegant answer to this fundamental controversy in Christian thought. For Paul, Luther and most of Protestantism, works is a work of the law, like circumcision. For James, works is a work of charity, like feeding the poor. For Charles Fillmore, works is an expression in the outer of the inner work of faith. The law of mind action is active here: Faith, if it is founded on true spiritual understanding, always expresses itself in works.]

2. *by works faith was perfected.* There are two kinds of faith; one is founded on intellectual perception of spiritual things

and the other on true spiritual Understanding. The first is not naturally followed by works, while the second, by virtue of the law under which it exists, completes itself in works. Paul describes this true faith in Heb. 11, and in all the examples given, works resulted. There was no question whatever of the absence of works. Whoever has this spiritual faith must manifest it in some way. This faith is Substance and brings forth fruit, as naturally as a rich soil produces a crop. But let no man say what the character of works from spiritual faith shall be. Those who perceive from the intellect claim that the evidence of faith is in such outer works as clothing and feeding the bodies of men, while the spiritually wise see a much greater need in clothing their naked souls.

---

Fillmore Study Bible annotations compiled by Rev. Mark Hicks

**World English Bible Footnotes:**

[3] v2:2. or, meeting

[4] v2:8. Leviticus 19:18

[5] v2:11. Exodus 20:14; Deuteronomy 5:18

[6] v2:11. Exodus 10:13; Deuteronomy 5:17

[7] v2:23. Genesis 15:16

# James 3

## Taming the Tongue

3:1 Let not many of you be teachers, my brothers, knowing that we will receive heavier judgment. 3:2 For in many things we all stumble. If anyone doesn't stumble in word, the same is a perfect man,[1] able to bridle the whole body also.[2] 3:3 Indeed, we put bits into the horses' mouths so that they may obey us, and we guide their whole body. 3:4 Behold, the ships also, though they are so big and are driven by fierce winds, are yet guided by a very small rudder, wherever the pilot desires. 3:5 So the tongue is also a little member, and boasts great things.

See how a small fire can spread to a large forest! 3:6 And the tongue is a fire. The world of iniquity among our members is the tongue, which defiles the whole body, and sets on fire the course of nature, and is set on fire by Gehenna.[8] 3:7 For every kind of animal, bird, creeping thing, and thing in the sea, is tamed, and has been tamed by mankind. 3:8 But nobody can tame the tongue. It is a restless evil, full of deadly poison. 3:9 With it we bless our God and Father, and with it we curse men, who are made in the image of God. 3:10 Out of the same mouth comes forth blessing and cursing. My brothers, these things ought not to be so. 3:11 Does a spring send out from the same opening fresh and bitter water? 3:12 Can a fig tree, my brothers, yield olives, or a vine figs? Thus no spring yields both salt water and fresh water.

1. *If anyone doesn't stumble in word, the same is a perfect man.* It is everyone's responsibility to control one's own life, harmonize one's will with the divine will, and exercise dominion over oneself, one's environment, and one's circumstances. One of the distinctive marks of such a person is poise, which results from one's being in complete command of one's thoughts and words.

2. *able to bridle the whole body also.* Words are able to bridle the whole body because every word has back of it an idea, and the power of the word is primarily in that idea. Added power is given by the speaker according to his realization of oneness with the idea and the force of his thought. Words are made active in the body by being received by the mind and carried into the body through the subconscious by thought. Constructive words that renew the body are made part of the body consciousness by prayer and meditation.

## Two Kinds of Wisdom

3:13 Who is wise and understanding among you? Let him show by his good conduct that his deeds are done in gentleness of wisdom. 3:14 But if you have bitter jealousy and selfish ambition in your heart, don't boast and don't lie against the truth. 3:15 This wisdom is not that which comes down from above, but is earthly, sensual, and demonic. 3:16 For where jealousy and selfish ambition are, there is confusion and every evil deed. 3:17 But the wisdom that is from above❶ is first pure, then peaceful, gentle, reasonable, full of mercy and good fruits, without partiality, and without hypocrisy. 3:18 Now the fruit of righteousness is sown in peace❷ by those who make peace.

1. *the wisdom that is from above* By invoking the "wisdom that is from above" before speaking, we can learn to speak only words that express purity, peace, gentleness, reason, mercy, goodness, steadfastness, and singleness of mind. This places depth of meaning into life through our words.

2. *And the fruit of righteousness is sown in peace* Harmony is indispensable if we are to influence others to follow the true way of life in unity of spirit.

Fillmore Study Bible annotations compiled by Rev. Mark Hicks

**World English Bible Footnotes:**

[8] v3:6. or, Hell

# James 4

## Friendship with the World

4:1 Where do wars and fightings among you come from? Don't they come from your pleasures that war in your members? 4:2 You lust, and don't have. You kill, covet, and can't obtain. You fight and make war. You don't have, because you don't ask. 4:3 You ask, and don't receive, because you ask with wrong motives,(1) so that you may spend it for your pleasures.(2) 4:4 You adulterers and adulteresses, don't you know that friendship with the world is enmity with God? Whoever therefore wants to be a friend of the world makes himself an enemy of God. 4:5 Or do you think that the Scripture says in vain, "The Spirit who lives in us yearns jealously"?

4:6 But he gives more grace. Therefore it says, "God resists the proud, but gives grace to the humble."(3)[9]

4:7 Be subject therefore to God. But resist the devil, and he will flee from you.(4) 4:8 Draw near to God, and he will draw near to you. Cleanse your hands, you sinners; and purify your hearts, you double-minded. 4:9 Lament, mourn, and weep. Let your laughter be turned to mourning, and your joy to gloom. 4:10 Humble yourselves in the sight of the Lord, and he will exalt you.

1. *You ask, and don't receive, because you ask with wrong motives.* But Jesus says, "You ask and you receive not because you ask amiss" (ASV). In other words, you ask in a begging attitude, you're pleading and supplicating for something, something which is already the reality of your being. You see, interestingly enough, if you look up the word, "Ask," in both the Hebrew and the Latin or the Greek root words as they are translated from the scriptures, you find that the strongest connotation is to claim or demand. Not to beg, but to claim. You ask for electricity when you walk into a room by claiming it, by turning on the switch. The power is already there, but you claim it. The Old Testament says, "Concerning the work of my hands, command ye me." Now this is a vital realization of truth, you see. You ask for light by getting out into the sun, or by raising the shades. You ask for air by lifting up the window. You ask for health and for life by accepting it, by claiming it, by demanding it. You don't have to beg God to hear you because God, as far as you're concerned, is the healing principle that is ever present and has nothing whatever to do except to be perfect life and health within you. — Eric Butterworth, Practical Metaphysics, Prayer.

2. *so that you may spend it for your pleasures.* Nor will crying and beseeching bring spiritual understanding. Hundreds of people have tried this method, and have not received that for which they earnestly but ignorantly sought. They have not received, because they did not know how to take that which God freely offered. Others have sought with selfish motives this spiritual understanding, or the power it would give them. "Ye ask, and receive not, because you ask amiss, that ye may spend it in your pleasures" (or to serve selfish ends) — Emilie Cady, Lessons in Truth, Spiritual Understanding.

3. *gives grace to the humble.* This grace is realized by those who are small in their own eyes, in so far as the lesser self is concerned. cf I Pet. 5:5.

4. *resist the devil, and he will flee from you.* "The devil" is a state of consciousness built by man when he has no explanation for the negative experiences in his life, and when he feels that there must be something outside of himself that caused them. In such a state of consciousness we are apt to view "the world" and "the flesh" as part of the outside forces that are causing us unhappiness. "The devil" in our life is the will faculty being used in the wrong direction, resulting in adverse states of consciousness that in turn produce inharmonies in our manifest life. Jesus' command was to "resist not evil" (Matt. 5:39 A.V.), but we also read in James 4:7, "resist the devil, and he will flee from you." If we attempt to fight conditions that are not good, we only succeed in binding them closer to us. On the other hand, if we do not do positive mental work to handle the adverse states of consciousness ("the devil") we will find ourself letting them rule our life. The "resistance" referred to in the quotation from James is the firm stand that we take in refusing to allow wrong beliefs to become our master. Through denial of them we prepare the way for the Truth in the same way that Jesus said, "Get thee hence, Satan [our adverse thought] ... Thou shalt worship the Lord thy God, and him only shalt thou serve" (Matt. 4:10). Overcoming "the devil" is only possible through understanding that the only presence and power in our life is God. "To this end was the Son of God manifested, that he might destroy the works of the devil" (I John 3:8). Only as we show forth (manifest) our Son-of-God self, the Christ,

are we able to remove the error conditions that have been set up by our own adverse states of consciousness ("the devil").

— Unity Correspondence Lesson series 2, lesson 5, annotation 12

## Warning against Judging Another

4:11 Don't speak against one another, brothers. He who speaks against a brother and judges his brother, speaks against the law and judges the law. But if you judge the law, you are not a doer of the law, but a judge. 4:12 Only one is the lawgiver, who is able to save and to destroy. But who are you to judge another?

## Boasting about Tomorrow

4:13 Come now, you who say, "Today or tomorrow let's go into this city, and spend a year there, trade, and make a profit." 4:14 Whereas you don't know what your life will be like tomorrow. For what is your life? For you are a vapor, that appears for a little time, and then vanishes away. 4:15 For you ought to say, "If the Lord wills, we will both live, and do this or that." 4:16 But now you glory in your boasting. All such boasting is evil. 4:17 To him therefore who knows to do good, and doesn't do it, to him it is sin.

---

Fillmore Study Bible annotations compiled by Rev. Mark Hicks

**World English Bible Footnotes:**

[9] v4:6. Proverbs 3:34

# James 5

## Warning to Rich Oppressors

5:1 Come now, you rich, weep and howl for your miseries that are coming on you.❶ 5:2 Your riches are corrupted and your garments are moth-eaten. 5:3 Your gold and your silver are corroded, and their corrosion will be for a testimony against you, and will eat your flesh like fire. You have laid up your treasure in the last days.❷ 5:4 Behold, the wages of the laborers who mowed your fields, which you have kept back by fraud, cry out, and the cries of those who reaped have entered into the ears of the Lord of Armies[10]. 5:5 You have lived delicately on the earth, and taken your pleasure. You have nourished your hearts as in a day of slaughter. 5:6 You have condemned, you have murdered the righteous one. He doesn't resist you.

1. *your miseries that are coming upon you.* How does injustice affect the doer of injustice? It hardens his spirit, making him impervious to the needs of his fellows. It narrows his vision, giving him no insight into the mind and heart of another, and leaving him marooned in his own selfishness. He lays up his treasure "in the last days," since his opportunities to practice justice and righteousness are continually diminished, until he becomes incapable of fellow feeling.

2. *laid up your treasure in the last days.* What is the proper care of money? Since money is a medium of exchange, it should be kept in circulation where it can do most good. Used aright, with vision and originality, money produces material wealth and often produces immaterial wealth, such as good will, at the same time.

## Patience in Suffering

5:7 Be patient therefore, brothers,
until the coming of the Lord. Behold,
the farmer waits for the precious
fruit of the earth, being patient over
it, until it receives the early and late
rain. 5:8 You also be patient. Establish
your hearts, for the coming of the
Lord is at hand.

5:9 Don't grumble, brothers,
against one another, so that you
won't be judged. Behold, the judge
stands at the door. 5:10 Take,
brothers, for an example of
suffering(1) and of patience, the
prophets who spoke in the name of
the Lord. 5:11 Behold, we call them
blessed who endured. You have
heard of the patience of Job, and
have seen the Lord in the outcome,
and how the Lord is full of
compassion and mercy.

5:12 But above all things, my
brothers, don't swear, neither by
heaven, nor by the earth, nor by any
other oath; but let your "yes" be
"yes," and your "no," "no;" so that you
don't fall into hypocrisy.[11]

1. *for an example of suffering.* Why do we invoke divine power in suffering? Because suffering quickly exhausts our human resources, so that we awaken to the need of a higher help than our own. Because we need divine power more urgently, we look to God more often in suffering than in joy.

## The Prayer of Faith

5:13 Is any among you suffering? Let
him pray. Is any cheerful? Let him
sing praises. 5:14 Is any among you
sick? Let him call for the elders of
the assembly, and let them pray over
him, anointing him with oil in the
name of the Lord, 5:15 and the prayer
of faith(1) will heal him who is sick,(2)
and the Lord will raise him up.(3) If
he has committed sins, he will be
forgiven. 5:16 Confess your offenses
to one another, and pray for one
another, that you may be healed.
The insistent prayer of a righteous
person is powerfully effective. 5:17
Elijah was a man with a nature like
ours, and he prayed earnestly that
it might not rain, and it didn't rain
on the earth for three years and six
months. 5:18 He prayed again, and the
sky gave rain, and the earth brought
forth its fruit.

5:19 Brothers, if any among you
wanders from the truth, and
someone turns him back, 5:20 let him
know that he who turns a sinner from
the error of his way will save a soul
from death, and will cover a
multitude of sins.

1. *and the prayer of faith.* The act of mentally taking that which is desired. Je-

sus said, "All things whatsoever ye pray and ask for, believe that ye receive them, and ye shall have them" (Mark 11:24). "We believe that the prayer of faith will save the sick, resurrect the body from "trespasses and sins," and finally overcome the last enemy, death."—Statement of Faith #13.

2. *will heal him who is sick.* This is a very definite and wonderful promise. According to the record, it was undoubtedly acted upon by the disciples and proved to be very effective for hundreds of years. That this mighty promise still stands is proved by unnumbered thousands of Jesus' followers today. Faith healing through prayer has become a practice founded on principles that never fail when rightly applied. Those who seek the kingdom of God and His righteousness are having all things added, as promised. When we "take with us words" (Hos. 14:2) and attempt to go into God's presence, our faith in Him is the power that swings wide open the gate that leads into the inner kingdom. —Charles and Cora Fillmore, *Teach Us To Pray*, Healing Through The Prayer of Faith

3. *and the Lord will raise him up.* It is found by those who have faith in the power of God that the prayer for health is the most quickly answered. The reason for this is that the natural laws that create and sustain the body are really divine laws, and when man silently asks for the intervention of God in restoring health, he is calling into action the natural forces of his being. Doctors agree that the object of using their remedies is to quicken the natural functions of the body. But medicine does not appeal to the intelligent principle that directs all the activities of the organism, hence it fails to give permanent healing.—Charles Fillmore, *Jesus Christ Heals*, The Omnipotence of Prayer.

---

Fillmore Study Bible annotations compiled by Rev. Mark Hicks

**World English Bible Footnotes:**

[10] v5:4. Greek: Sabaoth (for Hebrew: Tze'va'ot)

[11] v5:12. TR reads "under judgment" instead of "into hypocrisy"

# Peter's First Letter

Execution of Ignatius of Antioch, reputed to have been killed in Rome under the emperor Trajan, depicted in the Menologion of Basil II, an illuminated manuscript prepared for the emperor Basil II in c. 1000. Public Domain.

## Introduction to Peter's First Letter

During Jesus' ministry, He foretold that His followers would be called upon to endure persecution, and the New Testament indicates that His predictions were fulfilled during the early period of Christian history, as already mentioned in these lessons. However, these persecutions raised a serious problem for the leaders of the early church. The leaders were continually asking: How can the Christian converts be persuaded to stand steady in the face of such appalling conditions and not abandon their faith? What can be done to strengthen wavering Christians? It was in an effort to solve this problem that several New Testament books were written. Two of these books will now be considered.

Peter, accompanied by Silvanus (Silas) and Mark, arrived at Rome about A.D. 62, and suffered martyrdom in that city about A.D. 67. Shortly before his martyrdom, Peter dispatched an important letter to the Christian groups in Asia Minor. This letter is now known as the First Epistle of Peter. It was written in Greek by Silvanus, from the Aramaic dictation of Peter—the word Babylon, of course, indicating the city of Rome, where the Epistle was probably written. (See I Pet. 5:12-13.) The main purpose of the Epistle was to strengthen the faith of the Christian converts, and to encourage them to hold steady in face of the severe persecutions. The writer placed emphasis on several important points.

First: The converts were to regard persecution as a cleansing process, such as was used to refine precious metals; for this would eventually work out to their advantage. They were to recognize that they were "born anew .. . to an inheritance which is imperishable, undefiled, and unfading, kept in heaven for you" (I Pet. 1:3-4). But in the meantime they would be called upon "to suffer various trials, so that the genuineness of your faith, more precious than gold . . . may redound to praise and glory and honor at the revelation of Jesus Christ" (I Pet. 1:6-7).

Second: Converts were also to remember that they had an important mission to fulfill, and for this purpose they had been richly endowed by God. "You are a chosen race, a royal priesthood, a holy nation, God's own people, that you may declare the wonderful deeds of him who called you out of darkness into his marvelous light" (I Pet. 2:9). God had given them a special revelation and even in face of this persecution, they must fulfill their mission.

Third: Converts were enjoined to rejoice in their sufferings, and to regard persecution as a privilege. Did not Christ suffer? In their sufferings they were sharing in the experiences of their Lord. "Beloved, do not be surprised at the fiery ordeal which comes upon you to prove you, as though something strange were happening to you. But rejoice in so far as you share Christ's sufferings, that you may also rejoice and be glad when his glory is revealed" (I Pet. 4:12-13).

Fourth: Converts were further encouraged to hold steady in times of persecution by repeated assurances regarding the return of the Lord. Persecution would endure only for a brief period, and then the Lord would set all things right. "The end of all things is at hand" (I Pet. 4:7); "And when the chief Shepherd is manifested you will obtain the unfading crown of glory" (I Pet. 5:4); "And after you have suffered a little while, the God of all grace .. . will himself restore, establish, and strengthen you" (I Pet. 5:10).

In addition to the above, Peter also called upon the converts to conduct all their daily activities in accord with Christian principles. It will be noted that Peter's instructions are couched in terms of apostol ic authority. Apparently he recognized that the Christian life would form the best answer to all accusations directed against the Christians. Moreover, the example thus set might be the means of winning many further converts to Christianity, even from the ranks of their persecutors!

**Metaphysical Notes:** Metaphysically, Peter symbolizes the spiritual faculty of faith, as was explained in the first lesson of this series. Faith has been defined as "the perceiving power of the mind," or that deep inner knowing which enables us to recognize reality, despite appearances. However, in the Epistles of Peter, most references to faith also indicate what may be termed a loving, wholehearted trust in Jesus Christ. Christians were urged to rely upon His ability to strengthen and sustain them, and to bring them safely through every trial or difficulty that might arise. Two important aspects of faith are especially stressed in the First and Second Epistles of Peter.

First: Faith as an Antidote for Fear. This aspect of faith is brought out very clearly in the First Epistle of Peter. During the early days of the persecutions, the Christians were beset by fears of many kinds, for at any moment they might be arrested, tortured, and put to death. The writer of this Epistle assured them that they would be "guarded through faith"; and he further promised them that "as the outcome of your faith you obtain the salvation of your souls" (II Pet. 1:5-9). This makes stirring reading. When studying such passages, the student should recognize that while these assurances were originally given to the early church, they have present-day application. Times and circumstances may have changed, but faith still remains as a most effective antidote for fear.

Second: Faith as a Sustaining Power. As already noted. Second Peter was written when Christians were becoming wearied with their long waiting for the return of the Lord. Many of them had become quite discouraged, and were about to give up. Therefore the writer of Second Peter sought to encourage the Christians to hold on just a little longer, for the Lord would surely appear. In this effort, the writer pointed out that if faith was to accomplish its sustaining work, it must be strengthened and enriched; and then he gave what may be termed seven important steps for the development of faith. He urged the Christians to "make every effort to supplement your faith with virtue, and virtue with knowledge, and knowledge with self-control, and self-control with steadfastness, and steadfastness with godliness, and godliness with brotherly affection, and brotherly affection with love." He then assured them that "if you do this you will never fall," and "there will be richly provided for you an entrance into the eternal kingdom of our Lord and Savior Jesus Christ" (II Pet. 1:5-11).

It should be noted that all these encouraging words were addressed to "those who have obtained a faith of equal standing with ours in the righteousness of our God and Savior Jesus Christ" (II Pet. 1:1). This would indicate that, as well as meeting the needs of the hard-pressed Christians of the early church, the teaching also has present-day application. We may strengthen our faith by following the seven steps indicated above. In this way faith will become a great sustaining power to uphold us at all times, no matter how difficult the situation nor how hard pressed we may be. Faith will sustain us today, just as it sustained the Christians of the early church. Another New Testament writer gives us the assurance that "this is the victory that overcomes the world, our faith" (I John 5:4). The closing admonition in Second Peter forms an appropriate closing for this lesson:

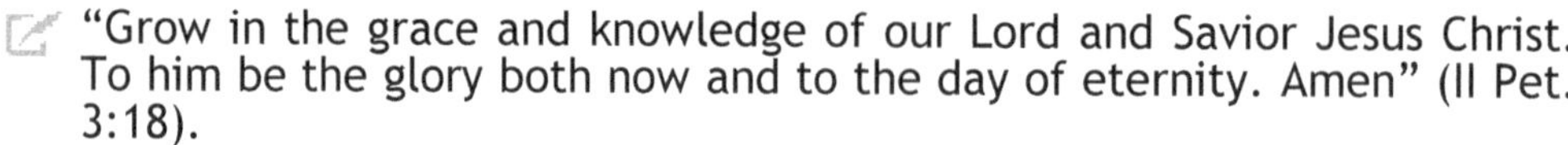

"Grow in the grace and knowledge of our Lord and Savior Jesus Christ. To him be the glory both now and to the day of eternity. Amen" (II Pet. 3:18).

Introduction to *Peter's First Letter* by Herbert J. Hunt, former Dean of Bible Studies for the Unity School of Christianity.

**From Simon to Peter.** Metaphysically, in consciousness, Peter is our spiritual faculty of faith. In our journey of spiritual transformation, our faith faculty's original nature (name) is that of hearing and receptivity

(Simon); we have an ability to discern Truth. But as we follow and are disciplined in the Word of Truth and the Spirit (Jesus), our hearing and receptivity are given a new nature (name), Cephas (Peter), which is Greek for the word rock, and so "our Peter" represents a faith in God that is strong, unwavering, and enduring. This faith is a necessary foundation for the building up of spiritual consciousness, the church of Christ in the individual. Peter (faith) was one of the first disciples that Jesus called. Faith is one of the first spiritual faculties to be called into expression by everyone who would follow Jesus in the overcoming life. (MBD/Peter)

**The significance of our faith (Peter).** The central theme of the message and lessons of both First & Second Peter is faith; as if Peter is writing about the importance of Peter! A metaphysical view of these Letters is a revelation of how faith works in and through our soul and opens the way for the Christ consciousness to be established therein. Faith is the key that opens the door of the kingdom of the heavens within us.

**Summary overview of 1st Peter.** Our faith (Peter) writes to remind us of three key themes:

1. Suffering will happen, therefore, practice separation (denials) from the continuous stream of thoughts, appearances, and conditions manifesting outside and within us (in this life we are strangers and aliens in a foreign land);
2. Your true identity ... you are a child of God and your true home is in the Presence of God (affirmations);
3. A life of holiness & submission ... remain committed to a life of inner and outer steadfastness, holiness, submissive willingness, and perseverance, that you may be able to cultivate a state of consciousness receptive to the Truth and Spirit, thus ensuring your spiritual progress (meditation/prayer, waiting for and obeying your Inner Guidance).

Our faith would remind us to desire and effort to cultivate holiness and faith in God's Word and Spirit, Power and Presence, for this is the way by which we are able to face any adversity (adversarial thoughts or conditions) along our journey.

Introduction to *Peter's First Letter* by Mary Salama.

# First Peter 1

## Let Your Faith Arise

1:1 Peter, an apostle of Jesus
Christ, to the chosen ones who are
living as foreigners in the Dispersion
in Pontus, Galatia, Cappadocia, Asia,
and Bithynia, 1:2 according to the
foreknowledge of God the Father, in

sanctification of the Spirit, that you may obey Jesus Christ and be sprinkled with his blood:[1] Grace to you and peace be multiplied.

1. *Be sprinkled with His blood.* The life contained in God's Word. Therefore, it is spiritual energy that purifies and redeems man by pouring into his life currents a new and purer stream. This divine energy cleanses the consciousness of dead works to enable man to serve the living God (RW/blood of Christ)

## A Living Hope

1:3 Blessed be the God and Father
of our Lord Jesus Christ, who
according to his great mercy became
our father again to a living hope[1]
through the resurrection of Jesus
Christ from the dead, 1:4 to an
incorruptible and undefiled
inheritance that doesn't fade away,
reserved in Heaven for you, 1:5 who
by the power of God are guarded
through faith for a salvation ready
to be revealed in the last time. 1:6
Wherein you greatly rejoice, though
now for a little while, if need be,
you have been put to grief in various
trials, 1:7 that the proof of your faith,
which is more precious than gold that
perishes even though it is tested by
fire, may be found to result in praise,
glory, and honor at the revelation
of Jesus Christ-- 1:8 whom not having
known you love; in whom, though
now you don't see him, yet believing,
you rejoice greatly with joy
unspeakable and full of glory-- 1:9
receiving the result of your faith, the
salvation of your souls.

1:10 Concerning this salvation, the
prophets sought and searched
diligently, who prophesied of the
grace that would come to you, 1:11
searching for who or what kind of
time the Spirit of Christ, which was
in them, pointed to,[2] when he
predicted the sufferings of Christ,
and the glories that would follow
them. 1:12 To them it was revealed,
that not to themselves, but to you,
they ministered these things, which
now have been announced to you
through those who preached the
Good News to you by the Holy Spirit
sent out from heaven; which things
angels desire to look into.

1. *A living hope.* Hope is the expectation of good in the future. It is a quality (good as far as it goes) of sense mind because it is subject to time. Faith is the certain knowledge that our good is ours right now. It is of God; it goes beyond time and space (RW/hope). Both faith and hope spring up spontaneously in our heart on contemplation of Christ Jesus. [In the Hebrew, "hope" has several meanings, including "wait expectantly; be patient; sink down; twist together; to loose; a cord or rope." Thus we can say that to have "a living hope" is to maintain a state of consciousness that expects the good, is patient, is willing to loosen from self-reasonings, sink down, and "stay roped" to the Truth.]

2. *Who or what kind of time the Spirit of Christ, which was in them, pointed to.* [Metaphysically, salvation is always imminent.] From the spiritual viewpoint there is no such thing as time in the way that man has come to regard it. With God a thousand years are as one day and one day is as a thousand years. ... People have gone insane ... trying to calculate by literal interpretation of Scripture the date on which the world would come to an end, not discerning the spiritual meaning of these writings. All this comes from believing man's idea of time to be a reality. Eternity is not an endless number of years, and things that are spiritual and eternal cannot be measured by days and months and years. (MBD/time).

## Holiness and Purity Metaphysically Understood

1:13 Therefore, prepare your minds for action,[1] be sober and set your hope fully on the grace that will be brought to you at the revelation of Jesus Christ-- 1:14 as children of obedience, not conforming yourselves according to your former lusts as in your ignorance, 1:15 but just as he who called you is holy, you yourselves also be holy in all of your behavior;① 1:16 because it is written, "You shall be holy; for I am holy."[2]

1:17 If you call on him as Father,② who without respect of persons judges according to each man's work, pass the time of your living as foreigners here in reverent fear:③ 1:18 knowing that you were redeemed, not with corruptible things, with silver or gold, from the useless way of life handed down from your fathers, 1:19 but with precious blood, as of a faultless and pure lamb, the blood of Christ; 1:20 who was foreknown indeed before the foundation of the world, but was revealed at the end of times for your sake, 1:21 who through him are believers in God, who raised him from the dead, and gave him glory; so that your faith and hope might be in God.

1:22 Seeing you have purified your souls④ in your obedience to the truth through the Spirit in sincere brotherly affection, love one another from the heart fervently:⑤ 1:23 having been born again, not of corruptible seed, but of incorruptible,⑥ through the word of God, which lives and remains forever. 1:24 For,

"All flesh is like grass,
and all of man's glory like the flower in the grass.
The grass withers, and its flower falls;
1:25 but the Lord's word endures forever."[3]

This is the word of Good News which was preached to you.

1. *Just as he who called you is holy, you yourselves also be holy in all of your behavior.* We must develop single-mindedness, must think creatively or constructively (gird up the loins of his mind), must be earnest in his work (be sober) and must keep his thoughts on what he wishes to accomplish. [We know we can] become one with the Divine, as Jesus was because the Christ is revealed to us as an indwelling presence, in whom there is a union of love, wisdom, power, faith, and prescience that can cause the divine to be manifested in us, as we faithfully express it.

2. *If you call on him as Father.* While it is true that God, Divine mind, the principle of life, law, is no respecter of persons, we turn to Him as to a father, because through His Son Jesus Christ we are assured that in His love and wisdom He looks beyond our imperfections and sees us as His sons.

3. *Living as foreigners here in reverent fear.* What fear, if any, is legitimate for us to entertain? We should never surrender to fear. However, in taking thought for our progress in understanding we may consider the fear of falling short in our realization legitimate, since it spurs us on to renewed efforts to realize the Christ.

4. *Seeing you have purified your souls.* The deep purity and mighty strength of the Christ Mind are made manifest in us as we develop spiritually. Instead of consciously and unconsciously tempting one another in sense ways, these qualities in each will incite in others holy aspirations to fulfill the law of righteousness (RW/purity of the Christ Mind).

5. *Love one another from the heart fervently.* The greatest power that man wields is the power of love, a faculty of both mind and heart. Until he learns the lesson of disinterested service to his fellow men (unfeigned love of the brethren), he cannot express the Christ love in its strength and purity.

6. *Not of corruptible seed, but of incorruptible.* The corruptible body is that which is subject to decay. When it is transformed into the spiritual body, it becomes incorruptible and is forever enduring (RW/corruptible). See "This corruptible must put on incorruption" (I Cor. 15:53).

Fillmore Study Bible annotations compiled by Mary Salama.

**World English Bible Footnotes:**

[1] v1:13. literally, "gird up the waist of your mind"
[2] v1:16. Leviticus 11:44-45
[3] v1:25. Isaiah 40:6-8

# First Peter 2

## You are a Living Stone!

2:1 Putting away therefore all wickedness, all deceit, hypocrisies, envies, and all evil speaking, 2:2 as newborn babies, long for the pure milk of the Word,❶ that you may grow thereby, 2:3 if indeed you have tasted that the Lord is gracious:❷ 2:4 coming to him, a living stone,❸ rejected indeed by men, but chosen by God, precious. 2:5 You also, as living stones, are built up as a spiritual house,❹ to be a holy priesthood, to offer up spiritual sacrifices, acceptable to God through Jesus Christ. 2:6 Because it is contained in Scripture,

"Behold, I lay in Zion a chief
cornerstone, chosen, and
precious:
He who believes in him will
not be disappointed."[4]

2:7 For you who believe therefore is the honor, but for those who are disobedient,

"The stone which the builders
rejected,
has become the chief
cornerstone,"[5]

2:8 and,

"a stone of stumbling, and a rock
of offense."[6]

For they stumble at the word, being disobedient, to which also they were appointed. 2:9 But you are a chosen race, a royal priesthood, a holy nation, a people for God's own possession, that you may proclaim the excellence of him who called you out of darkness into his marvelous light: 2:10 who in time past were no people, but now are God's people, who had not obtained mercy, but now have obtained mercy.

1. *as newborn babies, long for the pure milk of the Word.* When the true light from Heaven shines into the consciousness, the soul instinctively turns away from all thought of evil, and, as naturally as a newborn babe, demands its milk.

2. *if indeed you have tasted that the Lord is gracious.* One of the first signs that the soul has tasted of the true fruits of Spirit is the tendency to affirm the enduring goodness of Spirit. Such affirmations broaden, deepen, and strengthen our nature so that shortcomings in others are readily overlooked; forgiveness, grace, and mercy are exercised towards the undeserving; generosity flows forth [effortlessly]; we bless and become a blessing to all, and we even seek the highest possible good of the offender.

3. *coming to Him, a living stone.* This

stone refers to the indwelling Christ, which is the keystone of our character (MBD/stone), and it is upon this pure understanding (white stone) that we are to build up and develop our true Christ self (RW/stone).

4. *built up as a spiritual house.* Each member of the church is a "living stone" in the spiritual house of God. According to the measure that we "live the life," we are elect and precious in the sight of God. To the extent that we make spiritual sacrifices for humanity's sake [and for the sake of our own spiritual progress], so also in that same degree we open the way to receive the rich gifts of the [Presence and Power of God].

## Practicing Truth is True Freedom

2:11 Beloved, I beg you as
foreigners and pilgrims, to abstain
from fleshly lusts,[1] which war
against the soul; 2:12 having good
behavior among the nations, so in
that of which they speak against you
as evil-doers, they may by your good
works, which they see, glorify God in
the day of visitation. 2:13 Therefore
subject yourselves to every
ordinance of man for the Lord's
sake:[2] whether to the king, as
supreme; 2:14 or to governors, as sent
by him for vengeance on evil-doers
and for praise to those who do well.
2:15 For this is the will of God, that by
well-doing you should put to silence
the ignorance of foolish men:[3] 2:16
as free, and not using your freedom
for a cloak of wickedness, but as
bondservants of God.[4] 2:17 Honor all
men. Love the brotherhood. Fear
God. Honor the king.

1. *as foreigners and pilgrims, to abstain from fleshly lusts.* Our Spirit-led will (Paul) makes this request of us, for it is through our clean living that we keep our own soul in peace, as well as protect others, who may judge our faith by our outer expressions and may be influenced by those expressions, for either good or evil.

2. *subject yourselves to every ordinance of man for the Lord's sake.* Our ultimate allegiance is to Truth, and our sense of responsibility to it binds us to observe the rules of good citizenship. Each individual realizes within himself freedom to obey of his own volition the commands of his worldly superiors freedom to honor others, to love those of like mind with himself; to "fear God" (or understand the inevitability of divine law), and to "honor the king" (or render due respect to those in authority over him). It is right for the individual not to waste his energies in futile opposition. He should put them forth where their weight will be felt. When an order is established, the individual only upsets himself by struggling alone to overturn it. He who stands alone should keep himself at peace with others.

3. *by well-doing you should put to silence the ignorance of foolish men.* Each of us may silence their own ignorance by well-doing and gaining wisdom in making a study of their own form of expression; this is the better use of our energies.

4. *as bondservants of God.* "Bondservants of God" are they whose conscience holds them to the right course of conduct; these are the freest of all people since the bonds are within their own consciences. Our ultimate allegiance is to Truth, and our sense of responsibility to it binds us to observe the rules of good citizenship.

## A Household Code for Attaining Glory and Patience[1]

2:18 Servants, be in subjection to
your masters with all fear; not only
to the good and gentle, but also to
the wicked. 2:19 For it is
commendable if someone endures
pain, suffering unjustly, because of
conscience toward God. 2:20 For what
glory is it if, when you sin, you
patiently endure beating? But if,
when you do well, you patiently

endure suffering,② this is
commendable with God. 2:21 For to
this you were called, because Christ
also suffered for us, leaving you[7] an
example, that you should follow his
steps,③ 2:22 who did not sin, "neither
was deceit found in his mouth."[8]
2:23 Who, when he was cursed, didn't
curse back. When he suffered, didn't
threaten, but committed himself to
him who judges righteously; 2:24 who
his own self bore our sins in his body
on the tree, that we, having died
to sins, might live to righteousness;
by whose stripes you were healed.
2:25 For you were going astray like
sheep; but now have returned to the
Shepherd and Overseer[9] of your
souls.④

1. *Household Code.* A social media meme which encouraged Stoicism for keeping a peaceful order in Roman and Greek households. Later inserted in Christian scripture to defend the Jesus movement from pagan criticism of disorderly egalitarianism. See metaphysical interpretations at Ephesians 5:22-6:9, Colossians 3:18-4:1, Titus 2:1-10 and 1 Peter 2:18-3:1-8.

2. *glory is . . . patiently endure suffering.* This is the same as Jesus' teaching of the "second mile," namely, that we should be willing to do more than could humanly be asked or expected of us in order to prove our claim to the divine nature. Patience that has its roots in principle does not break, when one bears undeserved suffering.

3. *For to this you were called . . . follow His steps.* When we choose to follow our inner Christ, like Jesus, we must expect that the path of proving our allegiance to Principle will take us through tests of various kinds; Spiritual strength and transmutation are not demonstrated otherwise.

4. *now have returned to the Shepherd and Overseer of your soul.* The Holy Spirit of God is the One, True Shepherd of our souls. We find our way back to the kingdom and to our Shepherd by keeping our minds open and obedient to this pure Spirit life, and by keeping our consciousness free from all guilt and guile.

---

Fillmore Study Bible annotations compiled by Mary Salama and Mark Hicks.

**World English Bible Footnotes:**

[4] v2:6. Isaiah 28:16

[5] v2:7. Psalm 118:22

[6] v2:8. Isaiah 8:14

[7] v2:21. TR reads "us" instead of "you"

[8] v2:22. Isaiah 53:9

[9] v2:25. "Overseer" is from the Greek episkopon, which can mean overseer, curator, guardian, or superintendent.

# First Peter 3

## Wives and Husbands, Metaphysically Understood①

3:1 In like manner, wives,② be in subjection to your own husbands; so that, even if any don't obey the Word, they may be won by the behavior of their wives without a word; 3:2 seeing your pure behavior in fear. 3:3 Let your beauty be not just the outward adorning of braiding the hair, and of wearing jewels of gold, or of putting on fine clothing; 3:4 but in the hidden person of the heart, in the incorruptible adornment of a gentle and quiet spirit, which is in the sight of God very precious. 3:5 For this is how the holy women before, who hoped in God also adorned themselves, being in subjection to their own husbands: 3:6 as Sarah obeyed Abraham, calling him lord, whose children you now are, if you do well, and are not put in fear by any terror.

3:7 You husbands, in like manner, live with your wives according to knowledge,[3] giving honor to the woman, as to the weaker vessel, as being also joint heirs of the grace of life; that your prayers may not be hindered.

1. A continuation of the Household code explained in the previous chapter.

2. *wives.* Taking a wife represents a unification of the I AM with the affections (RW/wife).

3. *husbands . . . live with your wives according to knowledge.* Spiritually, marriage represents the union of two dominant states of consciousness. When we open the door of the mind by consciously affirming the presence and power of the divine I AM in our midst, there is a marriage or union of the higher forces in being with the lower and we find that we are quickened in every part; the life of the I AM has been poured out for us (RW/marriage).

## Suffering for Doing Right

3:8 Finally, be all like-minded, compassionate, loving as brothers, tenderhearted, courteous, 3:9 not rendering evil for evil,[1] or reviling for reviling; but instead blessing; knowing that to this were you called, that you may inherit a blessing.[2] 3:10 For,

"He who would love life,
and see good days,
let him keep his tongue from evil,
and his lips from speaking
deceit.
3:11 Let him turn away from evil, and
do good.
Let him seek peace, and
pursue it.
3:12 For the eyes of the Lord are on
the righteous,
and his ears open to their
prayer;
but the face of the Lord[3] is
against those who do
evil."[10]

3:13 Now who is he who will harm you, if you become imitators of that which is good? 3:14 But even if you should suffer for righteousness' sake, you are blessed. "Don't fear what they fear, neither be troubled."[11] 3:15 But sanctify the Lord God in your hearts; and always be ready to give an answer to everyone who asks you a reason concerning the hope that is in you, with humility and fear: 3:16 having a good conscience;[4] that, while you are spoken against as evildoers, they may be disappointed who curse your good manner of life in Christ. 3:17 For it is better, if it is God's will, that you suffer for doing well[5] than for doing evil. 3:18 Because Christ also suffered for sins once, the righteous for the unrighteous, that he might bring you to God; being put to death in the flesh, but made alive in the spirit; 3:19 in which he also went and preached to the spirits in prison, 3:20 who before were disobedient, when God waited patiently in the days of Noah, while the ship was being built. In it, few, that is, eight souls, were saved through water. 3:21 This is a symbol of baptism, which now saves you--not the putting away of the filth of the flesh, but the answer of a good conscience toward God, through the resurrection of Jesus Christ, 3:22 who is at the right hand of God, having gone into heaven, angels and authorities and powers being made subject to him.

1. not rendering evil for evil. *Compared to our higher, spiritual-self, our personal-self reacts—both to others as well as to our own selves—directly, returning good for good, evil for evil. Only as our understanding of Principle, our love of Divine rightness, and our desire to spiritually transform grow and increase, will we be able to respond to negativity (our own and others') with Truth and love. Blessing evil is more successful than fighting it. Jesus proved this to be true by befriending publicans and sinners and converting them to right living.*

2. *that you may inherit a blessing.* Unless we acknowledge blessings we remain unconscious of them, and so we miss the joy they are capable of affording us. In accordance with the law that we reap as we have sown, we "inherit" the blessing that we bestow. By blessing our circumstances regardless what they may be, and by blessing others regardless of their attitude, we set in motion the causes that bring blessings into our own life. Doing good brings good to us in the form of a mind that is at ease, a good conscience, and an untroubled outlook on life.

3. *the eyes, ears, face of the Lord.* The "Lord" is the omnipotent I AM. The "eyes of the Lord" and "His ears" are the perceptive powers of the I AM, which know and perceive our right motives, thoughts, and acts. The "face of the Lord" is the awareness of the I AM principle, which embraces the Divine both within us and within our environments.

4. *having a good conscience.* A good (guilt-free) conscience is a great blessing because it creates constructive effects in our life, instead of accumulating negations to be overcome.

5. *It is better . . . that you suffer for doing well.* The joy and good conscience that come from well-doing are a reward in and of themselves, and that even though we may experience suffering, this suffering cannot reduce or destroy these inner rewards. On the other hand, evil (acting against our own good conscience) inflicts its own penalty, so that when we suffer for evil-doing, we are in fact doubly punished.

---

Fillmore Study Bible annotations compiled by Mary Salama and Mark Hicks.

**World English Bible Footnotes:**

[10] v3:12. Psalm 34:12-16

[11] v3:14. Isaiah 8:12

# First Peter 4

## Practice Living Differently

4:1 Forasmuch then as Christ suffered for us in the flesh, arm yourselves also with the same mind;(1) for he who has suffered in the flesh has ceased from sin; 4:2 that you no longer should live the rest of your time in the flesh for the lusts of men, but for the will of God. 4:3 For we have spent enough of our past time doing the desire of the Gentiles,[2] and having walked in lewdness, lusts, drunken binges, orgies, carousings, and abominable idolatries. 4:4 They think it is strange that you don't run with them into the same excess of riot, blaspheming: 4:5 who will give account to him who is ready to judge the living and the dead.[3] 4:6 For to this end the Good News was preached even to the dead, that they might be judged indeed as men in the flesh, but live as to God in the spirit.

4:7 But the end of all things is near.[4] Therefore be of sound mind, self-controlled, and sober in prayer. 4:8 And above all things be earnest in your love among yourselves, for love covers a multitude of sins. 4:9 Be hospitable to one another without grumbling. 4:10 As each has received a gift, employ it in serving one another, as good managers of the grace of God in its various forms. 4:11 If anyone speaks, let it be as it were the very words of God. If anyone serves, let it be as of the strength which God supplies, that in all things God may be glorified through Jesus Christ, to whom belong the glory and the dominion forever and ever. Amen.

1. *arm yourselves also with the same mind.* The greatest discovery of any age is the power of thought. Thought is that process in mind by which substance is acted upon by energy directed by intelligence. Thus three factors are involved in every thought: substance, energy, intelligence. Spirit is not thought, but lies back of thought. Thought is the first emanation of Spirit. Thought is movement of ideas in mind. One of the laws of thought is that of like attracting like. "Birds of a feather flock together." So kindred thoughts gravitate together by a law Divine and universal.

2. *the desire of the Gentiles.* There are many thought atmospheres in this realm in which we live. Two grand divisions are recognized by Christian writers: the Gentile thought and the Israel thought. The Gentile thought is the outer, the senses, and the Israel thought the inner, the spiritual.

3. *to judge the living and the dead.* The "dead" are those thoughts unconscious of Truth. The "living" are those thoughts just awakened, but not fully enlightened. The "judge" is Truth itself, with which every thought in consciousness must align and harmonize.

4. *the end of all things is near.* This is the dissolution in mind of that realm that believes in the reality of material things and conditions. When the Truth enters the consciousness, a great change begins in our viewpoint. The reality of body and its environments gradually dissolves in thought and we see the end of earth. Then our minds become truly sound, and we are sober and prayerful.

## Recycle Your Suffering!

4:12 Beloved, don't be astonished at the fiery trial which has come upon you,[1] to test you, as though a strange thing happened to you. 4:13 But because you are partakers of Christ's sufferings, rejoice; that at the revelation[2] of his glory you also may rejoice with exceeding joy. 4:14 If you are insulted for the name of Christ, you are blessed;[3] because the Spirit of glory and of God rests on you. On their part he is blasphemed, but on your part he is glorified. 4:15 For let none of you suffer as a murderer, or a thief, or an evil doer, or a meddler in other men's matters. 4:16 But if one of you suffers for being a Christian, let him not be ashamed; but let him glorify God in this matter. 4:17 For the time has come for judgment to begin with the household of God. If it begins first with us, what will happen to those who don't obey the Good News of God? 4:18 "If it is hard for the righteous to be saved, what will happen to the ungodly and the sinner?"[12] 4:19 Therefore let them also who suffer according to the will of God in doing good entrust their souls to him, as to a faithful Creator.

1. *don't be astonished at the fiery trial which has come upon you.* All adverse experiences come about under law. In the light of cause and effect, nothing is strange or mysterious; everything is understandable. On the positive note, smooth sailing leaves our faith untried, tending it to become inactive from disuse, thus, challenges, when faced aright, strengthen and arouse our faith to its highest pitch of effectiveness.

2. *rejoice ... at the revelation.* To suffer as a Christian means that when we find ourselves reaping the fruit of error, we study to understand the inner cause. Instead of holding others responsible for what has happened to us, we use suffering to clarify our understanding of the Law and we affix the lesson in our subconsciousness through the heightened emotion thus aroused, so that we may not have to repeat the experience.

3. *If you are insulted for the name of Christ, you are blessed.* Why? Because such occasions are powerful opportunities for our transmutation. We are blessed because we are being given an opportunity to subordinate our individual will to the general good, to affirm the Truth we know (that God uses all things for good, that God is faithful, etc.), to practice concentrating our thoughts on the love and power of God that is at work in us and through us, and because such insults are living proof that the Spirit of the Christ is ascending in us!

---

Fillmore Study Bible annotations compiled by Mary Salama.

**World English Bible Footnotes:**

[12] v4:18. Proverbs 11:31

# First Peter 5

## Are You Tending Your Flock of Thoughts?

5:1 I exhort the elders among you, as a fellow elder, and a witness of the sufferings of Christ, and who will also share in the glory that will be revealed. 5:2 Shepherd the flock of God which is among you, exercising the oversight, not under compulsion, but voluntarily, not for dishonest gain, but willingly; 5:3 neither as lording it over those entrusted to you, but making yourselves examples to the flock. 5:4 When the chief Shepherd is revealed, you will receive the crown of glory that doesn't fade away.

5:5 Likewise, you younger ones, be subject to the elder.❶ Yes, all of you gird yourselves with humility, to subject yourselves to one another; for "God resists the proud, but gives grace to the humble."[13] 5:6 Humble yourselves therefore under the mighty hand of God,❷ that he may exalt you in due time; 5:7 casting all your worries❸ on him, because he cares for you.

5:8 Be sober and self-controlled.❹ Be watchful. Your adversary the devil, walks around like a roaring lion,❺ seeking whom he may devour. 5:9 Withstand him steadfast in your faith, knowing that your brothers

who are in the world are undergoing
the same sufferings. 5:10 But may the
God of all grace, who called you to
his eternal glory by Christ Jesus,
after you have suffered a little while,
perfect, establish, strengthen, and
settle you. 5:11 To him be the glory
and the power forever and ever.
Amen.

1. *be subject to the elder*. The "elder" we are to be subject to and obey is Christ; our One Master, Teacher, and Lord. And we must "gird ourselves with humility" because humility is essential to Chris-likeness.

2. *Humble yourselves therefore under the mighty hand of God*. Try to align ourselves with the Divine Law so as to express the wisdom, love, and power of the Holy Spirit. We are not to follow our personal leading but to depend on Divine leading.

3. *casting all your worries*. In order to cast all our anxiety upon God we need faith (Peter). Faith gives us the courage to meet life in a serene spirit, knowing that whatever may come, we shall be able to extract good from the experience by meeting it in the name and through the power of Jesus Christ.

4. *Be sober and self-controlled. Be watchful*. These inner states are to be applied over of our own thoughts and tendencies rather than upon others. Caring about and watchfulness over our inner life is the "shepherding of our flock" and is consistent with casting all our care or anxiety upon God, growing in us a faith to trust Divine Mind to be equal to our emergencies.

5. *a roaring lion*. The adversarial devil that "walks around like a roaring lion" is doing so, first and foremost, in our consciousness. This "lion" is anything that seeks to and succeeds at weakening our faith in the good. As seekers of spiritual transmutation, we must guard against anything that would "devour the Truth" from us, and so we must, at all times, remain mentally sober, self-controlled, watchful, and

## Greet States of Babel With a Kiss of Love

5:12 Through Silvanus, our faithful
brother, as I consider him, I have
written to you briefly, exhorting, and
testifying that this is the true grace
of God in which you stand. 5:13 She
who is in Babylon,[1] chosen together
with you, greets you; and so does
Mark, my son. 5:14 Greet one another
with a kiss of love.[2] Peace be to you
all who are in Christ Jesus. Amen.

1. See

2. *she who is in Babylon*. To be "in Babylon" is to be in a state of confusion or mixture. Whether on the level of the outer physical, the senses, or on the mental/consciousness, Babylon is a chaotic condition. There are times when we find ourselves in the confusion of the senses and its thoughts are so strong that they seem to have us in complete subjugation. Such cases symbolize captivity in Babylon. (MBD/Babylon)

3. *Greet one another with a kiss of love*. [To kiss is "to put together; to touch gently; to handle; to be equipped with," and so a kiss represents the concept of "fastening together or arranging things in order". Such a "contemplative kissing" practice also has the added benefit of building up our faith (Peter) that we may more easily greet every arising past memory, current circumstance, and future longing with a kiss.]

Fillmore Study Bible annotations compiled by Mary Salama.

**World English Bible Footnotes:**

[13] v5:5. Proverbs 3:34

# PETER'S SECOND LETTER

Douce Apocalypse - False prophet causes men to be marked. Public Domain.

## INTRODUCTION TO PETER'S SECOND LETTER

This Epistle, like First Peter, deals with the persecutions, and the main theme is somewhat similar to that of First Peter. A deeper description of this problem is in Introduction to First Peter. However, there are many marked differences between the two Epistles, and the following special features connected with the Second Epistle of Peter should be carefully noted.

**Date and Authorship:** This Second Epistle seems to have been written somewhere between A.D. 120 and A.D. 150. But since Peter was martyred about A.D. 67, it is apparent that Peter could not have been the writer of this Epistle. The suggestion has been made that, around the date mentioned above, someone who was well versed in the teachings and traditions of Peter wrote what may be termed a revised edition of First Peter. In this, which we now term the Second Epistle, the writer emphasized Peter's earlier teachings regarding faith, and then he added his own views concerning the Second Coming of the Lord, hoping thereby to strengthen the faith of the hardpressed Christians. Just what those views were will be explained below.

**The Main Problem:** When Second Peter was written, the main problem still had to do with the persecutions but in this instance the problem was intensified. In the earlier days, Christians had been encouraged to hold steady by the promise of the Lord's speedy return. However, many years had now passed by, and still there was no sign of the Lord's coming. Many Christians were becoming wearied by this long period of waiting, and some of them were abandoning all hope of relief from the persecutions. "Where is the promise of his coming?" they cried; "For ever since the fathers fell asleep, all things have continued as they were from the beginning of creation" (II Pet. 3:4). Thus the Christians were suffering, not only from the persecutions—which continued with unabated fury—but also from the weariness of waiting, together with the tragic suspicion that somehow they had been forsaken by their beloved Lord.

**The Suggested Solution:** In the period covered by First Peter, the important question was: How can Christians be persuaded to hold steady in face of persecution? In the later period, when Second Peter was written, the problem had shifted somewhat, and it was then a matter of getting Christians to hold on to their belief in the Second Coming of the Lord, despite the long delay. The writer of Second Peter attempted to explain this delay by reminding his readers of a teaching which would be familiar to many Jewish Christians. The Jewish rabbis frequently proclaimed that "With the Lord one day is as a thousand years, and a thousand years as one day." (See Psalms 90:4 and II Peter 3:8.) In other words, God takes no account of what men call "time." Thus the writer of Second Peter indicated that there was no real delay in the Lord's coming. The Lord would surely appear at the divinely appointed moment, but in the meantime Christians must show their faith by waiting patiently for His return. The writer of this Second Epistle then advanced a further idea—which may appear somewhat in the nature of an anticlimax. There was a possibility, he suggested, that the Lord's return was purposely delayed in order to give unconverted persons an opportunity to repent and become Christians. However, the writer continued to aver that the Lord would surely come, at His own appointed time—and then woe betide all those who had opposed the work of the Lord's kingdom!

**A Further Problem:** At the time when Second Peter was written, a considerable amount of erroneous teaching had made its way into the various Christian groups of Asia Minor, and elsewhere. This was not an entirely new development, for references to this are to be found in several of the earlier writings. The writer of Second Peter sought to eradicate this false teaching by a twofold effort. First, he recalled and emphasized the earlier teachings of Peter, reminding his readers how the Apostle said, "We did not follow cleverly devised myths when we made known to you the power and the coming of our Lord Jesus Christ" (II Pet. 1:16). Second, he incorporated a lengthy section from a letter written much earlier by Jude (one of the "Brethren of the Lord"), in which all forms of false teaching were denounced in no uncertain terms. The writer of Second Peter thus used the authority and teaching of Peter and Jude to strengthen his condemnation of these false teachers and their teaching. For purposes of study it will be well at this time to compare Jude 4-16 with II Peter 2:1-18, and Jude 17-23 with II Peter 3:2-7.

**Metaphysical Notes:** See Introduction to First Peter.

Introduction to *Peter's Second Letter* by Herbert J. Hunt, former Dean of Bible Studies for the Unity School of Christianity.

When our faith (Peter) is so awakened, it has capacity to perceive for us and so serve as a "faithful" inner warning system. In this Letter, our awakened faith is writing to alert us of the dangers of new teachings that may infiltrate our souls (the Church) and how we may be able to identify and deal with spiritual counterfeits, or how to avoid them altogether. In 2nd Peter, our faith (Peter) writes to remind us of three key themes:

1. True Christian faith: Our faith manifests as a manner of life or "our lifestyle." By adhering to the Word of Truth and the guidance of Spirit we not only make progress along our journey of spiritual transmutation, but we are also enlightened so that we can more quickly identify error and false teachings. Holding fast to the Truth and putting it into practice holds us fast on the path of transformation.
2. Warnings against false teachers: Jesus appointed but one teacher in His school: the Spirit of truth, the Comforter in every man. "But the Comforter, even the Holy Spirit, whom the Father will send in my name, he shall teach you all things, and bring to you remembrance all that I said unto you" (John 14:25). Therefore, whether external (teachings, appearances, circumstances, pressures), or internal (emotions, feelings, thoughts, images, memories, expectations), we are to beware of "false teachers" by always bringing our minds back to the One Teacher, for He "will keep in perfect peace the one whose mind is stayed on Him" (cf. Isaiah 26:3). (RW/teacher).
3. The promise of the Lord's return: A promise is like a seed, it is a potentiality, contains power and possibility. The Word and Spirit of God stand the test of time as reliable promise-seed keepers for us along our journey of spiritual transmutation, for the return of our Inner Lord; the awakening of our Inner Christ. Let us trust in this promise and no matter what we may have to endure, let us make of our lives and minds a manger, always ready for the birth of our next Higher Consciousness.

Introduction to *Peter's Second Letter* by Mary Salama.

# Second Peter 1

## Salutations of Grace, Peace, and True Knowledge

1:1 Simon Peter, a servant and
apostle of Jesus Christ, to those who
have obtained a like precious faith
with us in the righteousness of our
God and Savior, Jesus Christ: 1:2
Grace to you and peace be
multiplied(1) in the knowledge of
God(2) and of Jesus our Lord,

1. *Grace to you and peace be multiplied.* Grace and peace grow in our hearts

through our increase of God or Christ consciousness.

2. *in the knowledge of God.* It is only when we sit at the feet of our own Lord in the silence that we come forth radiant with the true knowledge, that of Spirit (RW/knowledge).

## Elect the Truth, Consistently!

1:3 seeing that his divine power has granted to us all things that pertain to life and godliness, through the knowledge of him who called us by his own glory and virtue; 1:4 by which he has granted to us his precious and exceedingly great promises; that through these you may become partakers of the divine nature,❶ having escaped from the corruption that is in the world by lust. 1:5 Yes, and for this very cause adding on your part all diligence, in your faith supply moral excellence; and in moral excellence, knowledge; 1:6 and in knowledge, self-control; and in self-control patience; and in patience godliness; 1:7 and in godliness brotherly affection; and in brotherly affection, love. 1:8 For if these things are yours and abound, they make you to be not idle nor unfruitful to the knowledge of our Lord Jesus Christ. 1:9 For he who lacks these things is blind, seeing only what is near, having forgotten the cleansing from his old sins. 1:10 Therefore, brothers,[1] be more diligent to make your calling and election sure.❷ For if you do these things, you will never stumble. 1:11 For thus you will be richly supplied with the entrance into the eternal Kingdom of our Lord and Savior, Jesus Christ.

1:12 Therefore I will not be negligent to remind you of these things, though you know them, and are established in the present truth. 1:13 I think it right, as long as I am in this tent, to stir you up by reminding you; 1:14 knowing that the putting off of my tent comes swiftly, even as our Lord Jesus Christ made clear to me. 1:15 Yes, I will make every effort that you may always be able to remember these things even after my departure.

1. *partakers of the divine nature.* By "availing ourselves of the promises" and through exercising the spiritual qualities of diligence, faith, virtue, knowledge, self-control, patience, godliness, brotherly kindness, and love we learn to express the divine nature and in this way we "partake" of it or make it our own.

2. *make your calling and election sure.* The Christ calls us by arousing in us desire after the glory and virtue of the perfect life. Our election is our voluntary choice of the Christ way and the dedicating of all our energies to following it. We "make our calling and election sure" by consistently and diligently expressing the qualities that we, on our part, have added to our knowledge of the Christ; by our making use of perseverance and a high degree of devotion and intelligence.

## Your Inner Experiences are Real!

1:16 For we did not follow cunningly devised fables, when we made known to you the power and coming of our Lord Jesus Christ, but we were eyewitnesses of his majesty.❶ 1:17 For he received from God the Father honor and glory, when the voice came to him from the Majestic Glory, "This is my beloved Son, in whom I am well pleased."[2] 1:18 We heard this voice come out of heaven when we were with him on the holy mountain.

1:19 We have the more sure word of prophecy; and you do well that you heed it, as to a lamp shining in a dark place, until the day dawns, and the morning star arises in your hearts:❷ 1:20 knowing this first, that no prophecy of Scripture is of private interpretation. 1:21 For no prophecy ever came by the will of man: but holy men of God spoke, being moved by the Holy Spirit.

1. *we were eyewitnesses of his majesty.* In these three verses Peter was explaining that the experiences of the followers of Jesus were not fairy stories or fables, but were realities. [This means that] we need not accept the account of the Transfiguration only in a metaphysical sense. We have the testimony of eye-witnesses to the event, though we are free to accept it as either an objective occurrence or a subjective experience or both. We may interpret it in the way that it is most helpful to us.

2. *the morning star arises in your hearts.* The morning star heralds the coming of light and the glory of the sun. The mind also has its star of promise, which is the arising inner conviction of our Divine sonship and of our ability to accomplish whatever we undertake (RW/star).

---

Fillmore Study Bible annotations compiled by Mary Salama.

**World English Bible Footnotes:**

[1] v1:10. The word for "brothers" here and where context allows may also be correctly translated "brothers and sisters" or "siblings."

[2] v1:17. Matthew 17:5; Mark 9:7; Luke 9:35

# Second Peter 2

## Deceptive Thoughts and Emotions Carry Their Own Punishment

2:1 But false prophets also arose❶ among the people, as false teachers will also be among you, who will secretly bring in destructive heresies, denying even the Master who bought them, bringing on themselves swift destruction. 2:2 Many will follow their immoral[3] ways, and as a result, the way of the truth will be maligned. 2:3 In covetousness they will exploit you with deceptive words: whose sentence now from of old doesn't linger, and their destruction will not slumber.

2:4 For if God didn't spare angels when they sinned, but cast them down to Tartarus[4], and committed them to pits of darkness, to be reserved for judgment; 2:5 and didn't spare the ancient world, but preserved Noah with seven others, a preacher of righteousness, when he brought a flood on the world of the ungodly; 2:6 and turning the cities of Sodom and Gomorrah into ashes, condemned them to destruction, having made them an example to those who would live ungodly; 2:7 and delivered righteous Lot, who was very distressed by the lustful life of the wicked 2:8 (for that righteous man dwelling among them, was tormented in his righteous soul from day to day with seeing and hearing lawless deeds): 2:9 the Lord knows how to deliver the godly out of temptation[2] and to keep the unrighteous under punishment for the day of judgment; 2:10 but chiefly those who walk after the flesh in the lust of defilement, and despise authority.

Daring, self-willed, they are not afraid to speak evil of dignitaries; 2:11 whereas angels, though greater in might and power, don't bring a railing judgment against them before the Lord. 2:12 But these, as unreasoning creatures, born natural animals to be taken and destroyed, speaking evil in matters about which they are ignorant, will in their destroying surely be destroyed, 2:13 receiving the wages of unrighteousness; people who count it pleasure to revel in the daytime, spots and blemishes, reveling in their deceit while they feast with you; 2:14 having eyes full of adultery, and who can't cease from sin; enticing unsettled souls; having a heart trained in greed; children of cursing; 2:15 forsaking the right way, they went astray, having followed the way of Balaam the son of Beor, who loved the wages of wrong-doing; 2:16 but he was rebuked for his own disobedience. A mute donkey spoke with a man's voice and stopped the madness of the prophet.

2:17 These are wells without water, clouds driven by a storm; for whom the blackness of darkness has been reserved forever. 2:18 For, uttering great swelling words of emptiness, they entice in the lusts of the flesh, by licentiousness, those who are indeed escaping from those who live in error; 2:19 promising them liberty, while they themselves are bondservants of corruption; for a man is brought into bondage by whoever overcomes him.

2:20 For if, after they have escaped the defilement of the world through the knowledge of the Lord and Savior Jesus Christ, they are again entangled in it and overcome, the last state has become worse for them than the first. 2:21 For it would be better for them not to have known the way of righteousness, than, after knowing it, to turn back from the holy commandment delivered to them. 2:22 But it has happened to them according to the true proverb, "The dog turns to his own vomit again,"[5] and "the sow that has washed to wallowing in the mire."[3]

1. *But false prophets also arose.* Our inner false prophets are those deceptive thoughts that have been built up by error and selfish desires. Outwardly they present the appearance of being truthful and open; inwardly they are ravenous for personal sensation and worldly gain. Whether a thought is false or true, the Law is: "By their fruits ye shall know them." Constructive, spiritual thoughts always yield a bountiful harvest of good, therefore the motive back of every thought should be watched prayerfully. Under the analysis of Truth all deception is brought into the light and the fact that the fruit is error reveals the motive to be error. The tree (motive) should be cut down and cast into the fire (denied) (MBD/false prophets).

2. *the Lord knows how to deliver the godly out of temptation.* [Our inner Christ knows how to bring forth the good through tailor-made "temptations," that come to serve along our journey of spiritual transmutation.]

3. *The sow that has washed to wallowing in the mire.* See Matthew 7:6 (*neither cast your pearls before the swine*). Metaphysically, swine (the sow) are "swinish" thoughts that belong to the sense, animal plane. Like swine, these thoughts have a tendency to be narrowly focused, return to the same mental feeding pits, and go about repeatedly (MBD/Hezir).

Fillmore Study Bible annotations compiled by Mary Salama.

**World English Bible Footnotes:**

[3] v2:2. TR reads "destructive" instead of "immoral"

[4] v2:4. Tartarus is another name for Hell

[5] v2:22. Proverbs 26:11

# Second Peter 3

## The Promise of the Lord's Coming

3:1 This is now, beloved, the second letter that I have written to you; and in both of them I stir up your sincere mind by reminding you; 3:2 that you should remember the words which were spoken before by the holy prophets, and the commandments of us, the apostles of the Lord and Savior: 3:3 knowing this first, that in the last days mockers will come,[1] walking after their own lusts, 3:4 and saying, "Where is the promise of his coming? For, from the day that the fathers fell asleep, all things continue as they were from the beginning of the creation." 3:5 For this they willfully forget, that there were heavens from of old, and an earth formed out of water and amid water, by the word of God; 3:6 by which means the world that then was, being overflowed with water, perished. 3:7 But the heavens that now are, and the earth, by the same word have been stored up for fire, being reserved against the day of judgment and destruction of ungodly men.

3:8 But don't forget this one thing, beloved, that one day is with the Lord as a thousand years,[2] and a thousand years as one day. 3:9 The Lord is not slow concerning his promise, as some count slowness; but is patient with us, not wishing that any should perish, but that all should come to repentance. 3:10 But the day of the Lord will come as a thief in the night; in which the heavens will pass away with a great noise, and the elements will be dissolved with fervent heat, and the earth and the works that are in it will be burned up.

3:11 Therefore since all these things will be destroyed like this, what kind of people ought you to be in holy living and godliness, 3:12 looking for and earnestly desiring the coming of the day of God, which will cause the burning heavens to be dissolved, and the elements will melt with fervent heat? 3:13 But, according to his promise, we look for new heavens and a new earth,[3] in which righteousness dwells.

1. *mockers will come*. See The Letter of Jude and the commentary on verse 16. Peter's Second Letter incorporates much of the Letter of Jude and what is translated here as *mockers* is translated *murmurers and complainers* in Jude.

2. *one day is with the Lord as a thousand years*. Often quoted by metaphysicians, such as (1) Charles Fillmore in Mysteries of Genesis, *Chapter 1: Spiritual Man*: A "day," as the term is used in Genesis 1. There is no reason to believe that these days were

twenty-four hours in length. They simply represent periods of development or degrees of mind unfoldment. (2) Unity Correspondence Course, *Lesson 11 Judgement and Justice*: Spiritual enlightenment reveals that "days" are symbols of the state and the action of universal Mind. These Biblical texts about judgment have nothing to do with "time," The "day of judgment" is no specific date, because every day is a "judgment day," for every thought, feeling, and action brings its own reaction or judgment, its own experience in the manifest realm. (3) Russell Kemp in Live Youthfully Now, *God Gives Us Life, Not Age:* Is there any power in the mere passage of time to make human beings lose their youth? God gives you your life, and the calendar on the wall has no power over God's life.

3. *new heavens and a new earth.* See Revelation 21:1. Metaphysically, heaven is a state of consciousness in which the soul and body are in harmony with Divine Mind. (MBD/heaven) Similarly, earth is also a condition of mind, representing the consciousness of the physical body. (RW/earth)

## The Ultimate Encouragement

3:14 Therefore, beloved, seeing
that you look for these things, be
diligent to be found in peace,[1]
without blemish and blameless in his
sight. 3:15 Regard the patience of our
Lord as salvation;[2] even as our
beloved brother Paul also, according
to the wisdom given to him, wrote to
you; 3:16 as also in all of his letters,
speaking in them of these things. In
those, there are some things that are
hard to understand, which the
ignorant and unsettled twist, as they
also do to the other Scriptures, to
their own destruction. 3:17 You
therefore, beloved, knowing these
things beforehand, beware, lest
being carried away with the error of
the wicked, you fall from your own
steadfastness. 3:18 But grow in the
grace and knowledge of our Lord and
Savior Jesus Christ.[3] To him be the
glory both now and forever. Amen.

1. *be diligent to be found in peace.* A person who has active faith in God and forms constructive thought habits will find that peace is becoming their natural state of mind.

2. *Regard the patience of our Lord as salvation.* Self-discipline or faithful expression of the Spirit of truth under all conditions, no matter how negative, is the price of overcoming the world.

3. *grow in the grace and knowledge of our Lord and Savior Jesus Christ.* Through study, meditation, prayer, practice, and devotion to the Christ ideal we feed on Truth and we grow in all that is comprised in Truth. This includes grace and knowledge.

---

Fillmore Study Bible annotations compiled by Mary Salama.

# John's First Letter

Byzantine illumination depicting John dictating to his disciple, Prochorus (c. 1100). Wikipedia. GNU Free Documentation License.

## Introduction to John's First Letter

When discussing the Epistle of James, brief reference was made to certain "false prophets" and their teaching. Following the passing of James, this erroneous teaching became a serious problem for the early church. These false prophets combined certain Jewish, Christian, and pagan beliefs, and claimed that in the process they had attained a higher understanding of spiritual things; and they persuaded many Christian converts to accept their teaching. As a result of this "falseprophet" activity, some Christian converts placed emphasis on asceticism—avoiding things material and seeking to separate themselves from the world; while others took the opposite course of licentiousness, using all material things without discrimination, and practicing all varieties of immorality. All this constituted a very serious problem for the Christian leaders. Thus it came about that several New Testament epistles were written in an effort to counteract this activity, and to warn Christian converts against erroneous ways of thinking and living. These epistles include The Three Letters of John and The Letter of Jude.

While the writer's name of The Letter of John not actually mentioned, this Epistle is usually regarded as the work of the Apostle John. After the fall of Jerusalem in A.D. 70 and the break-up of the Apostolic Council, John journeyed to Ephesus, and became the head of the Christian church in that city. John at that time was also regarded as the presiding elder, or bishop, of the Christian groups in the western area of Asia Minor.

The main purpose of this letter was addressing the "false prophets," who sought to introduce into the Christian groups some heretical teachings regarding the person of Jesus Christ. This caused some Christians to think of Jesus as a phantom. They began to deny the reality of His earthly manifestation, and regarded Him as only a temporary manifestation of Deity. The Epistles of John were written in an effort to counteract all these false teachings, with the writer placing great emphasis upon the reality of Jesus Christ, and declaring that He had indeed "come in the flesh" (I John 4:2).

Introduction to *John's First Letter* by Herbert J. Hunt, former Dean of Bible Studies for the Unity School of Christianity.

# FIRST JOHN 1

## The Word of Life

1:1 That which was from the beginning,[1] that which we have heard, that which we have seen with our eyes, that which we saw, and our hands touched, concerning the Word of life[2] 1:2 (and the life was revealed, and we have seen, and testify, and declare to you the life, the eternal life, which was with the Father, and was revealed to us); 1:3 that which we have seen and heard we declare to you, that you also may have fellowship[3] with us. Yes, and our fellowship is with the Father, and with his Son, Jesus Christ. 1:4 And we write these things to you, that our joy may be fulfilled.

1. *That which was from the beginning.* All first principles.

2. *The Word of life* "The life was revealed" (ASV, manifested) in Jesus [the Word], and it must be manifested in us all before the new heaven and the new earth can appear. Everyone must have a part in this work and must undertake to discharge his part gladly and joyfully.

3. *Fellowship.* Fellowship implies that people are of one mind or have a community of interest. Fellowship with God brings a realization that the universal life, energy and power are accessible to us.

## God Is Light

1:5 This is the message which we have heard from him and announce to you, that God is light,[1] and in him is no darkness[2] at all. 1:6 If we say that we have fellowship with him and walk in the darkness, we lie, and don't tell the truth. 1:7 But if we walk in the light, as he is in the light, we have fellowship with one another,[3] and the blood of Jesus Christ, his

Son, cleanses us from all sin.❹ 1:8 If
we say that we have no sin, we
deceive ourselves, and the truth is
not in us. 1:9 If we confess our sins,
he is faithful and righteous to forgive
us the sins, and to cleanse us from
all unrighteousness. 1:10 If we say that
we haven't sinned, we make him a
liar, and his word is not in us.

1. *God is light.* In the mental world light represents clarity of vision, intelligence, understanding, or wisdom, according to the degree of its manifestation. The inability to understand life and live it intelligently and fully is at the root of man's shortcomings.

2. *In him is no darkness.* Darkness is merely the absence of light. God is Spirit, the all-knowing Principle of being. Darkness is ignorance, the absence in consciousness of the all-knowing Principle of being.

3. *Fellowship with one another.* Right conduct actuated by the wisdom and knowledge of Divine Mind makes us all one, and this oneness is true fellowship.

4. *Cleanses us from all sin.* Sin is a failure on the part of man to apprehend and acknowledge the mind of God. We are forgiven in the measure in which we open our heart to divine love and drop from our thoughts all condemnation of ourselves and of others.

---

Fillmore Study Bible annotations by Mark Hicks.

# First John 2

## Christ Our Advocate

2:1 My little children, I write these
things to you so that you may not
sin. If anyone sins, we have a
Counselor[1]❶ with the Father, Jesus
Christ, the righteous. 2:2 And he is
the atoning sacrifice[2]❷ for our sins,
and not for ours only, but also for
the whole world. 2:3 This is how we
know that we know him: if we keep
his commandments. 2:4 One who says,
"I know him," and doesn't keep his
commandments, is a liar, and the
truth isn't in him. 2:5 But whoever
keeps his word, God's love has most
certainly been perfected in him.❸
This is how we know that we are in
him: 2:6 he who says he remains in
him ought himself also to walk just
like he walked.

1. *Counselor (ASV, Advocate).* The "Counselor" the truth that perfect goodness, perfect love and wisdom, and the power to make these manifest reside within man, and can be reckoned and realized by him when he is inspired by the thought that such things are possible to him. The spirit of this truth must lay hold of him and arouse him to faith in his possibilities before the Advocate can he said to be active.

2. *Atoning sacrifice (ASV, propitiation for our sins).* When anyone "sins" or goes contrary to the divine law, the Christ consciousness is available to him, and if he enters into it and puts himself again in harmony with divine law he "propitiates" the law. In this universal consciousness the sins of "the whole world" may be swallowed up and done away with.

3. *God's love has most certainly been perfected in him.* What other quality in us is perfected by our keeping the divine law? Love. "Whoso keepeth his word, in him verily hath the love of God been perfected." Love makes obedience easy.

## A New Commandment

2:7 Brothers, I write no new commandment to you, but an old commandment which you had from the beginning. The old commandment[1] is the word which you heard from the beginning. 2:8 Again, I write a new commandment to you, which is true in him and in you; because the darkness is passing away,[2] and the true light already shines.[3] 2:9 He who says he is in the light and hates his brother, is in the darkness even until now. 2:10 He who loves his brother remains in the light, and there is no occasion for stumbling in him. 2:11 But he who hates his brother is in the darkness, and walks in the darkness, and doesn't know where he is going, because the darkness has blinded his eyes.

2:12 I write to you, little children,<br>
because your sins are forgiven<br>
you for his name's sake.<br>
2:13 I write to you, fathers,<br>
because you know him who is<br>
from the beginning.<br>
I write to you, young men,<br>
because you have overcome<br>
the evil one.<br>
I write to you, little children,<br>
because you know the Father.<br>
2:14 I have written to you, fathers,<br>
because you know him who is<br>
from the beginning.<br>
I have written to you, young men,<br>
because you are strong, and<br>
the word of God remains<br>
in you, and you have<br>
overcome the evil one.

2:15 Don't love the world, neither the things that are in the world. If anyone loves the world, the Father's love isn't in him. 2:16 For all that is in the world, the lust of the flesh, the lust of the eyes, and the pride of life, isn't the Father's, but is the world's. 2:17 The world is passing away with its lusts, but he who does God's will remains forever.[4]

1. *The old commandment.* The old commandment to love God with our whole heart, mind, soul, and strength, interpreted in a new way to meet the needs of a new age and to include the commandment to love our neighbor as ourselves.

2. *The darkness is passing away.* The darkness in our mind that takes the form of distrust, hatred, and suspicion, all of which prevent us from understanding one another and working together toward a common goal.

3. *The true light already shines.* The light of Truth or divine understanding that causes the darkness to pass away.

4. *He who does God's will remains forever.* We make life an expression of the divine will by loving others instead of condemning and criticizing them. In turn, Divine Love obliges us to be our best, to allow those who love us to see our ideal side.

## Warning Against Antichrists

2:18 Little children, these are the end times, and as you heard that the Antichrist[1] is coming, even now many antichrists have arisen. By this we know that it is the final hour. 2:19 They went out from us, but they didn't belong to us; for if they had belonged to us, they would have continued with us. But they left, that they might be revealed that none of them belong to us. 2:20 You have an anointing from the Holy One, and you know the truth. 2:21 I have not written to you because you don't know the truth, but because you know it, and because no lie is of the truth. 2:22 Who is the liar but he who denies that Jesus is the Christ? This is the Antichrist, he who denies the Father and the Son. 2:23 Whoever denies the Son, the same doesn't have the Father. He who confesses the Son has the Father also. 2:24 Therefore, as for you, let that remain in you which you heard from the beginning. If that which you heard from the beginning remains in you, you also will remain in the Son, and in the Father. 2:25 This is the promise which he promised us, the eternal life.

2:26 These things I have written to you concerning those who would lead you astray. 2:27 As for you, the anointing which you received from him remains in you, and you don't need for anyone to teach you. But as his anointing teaches you concerning all things, and is true, and is no lie, and even as it taught you, you will remain in him.

2:28 Now, little children, remain in him, that when he appears, we may have boldness, and not be ashamed before him at his coming. 2:29 If you know that he is righteous, you know that everyone who practices righteousness is born of him.

1. *Antichrist.* That which denies or opposes the idea that the Christ dwells in and is the true self of each individual (against Christ; the meaning of *anti* is opposite, against, contrary to). Those who make the indwelling Spirit of truth their guide and authority will not be deceived by false claims made either by individuals or by institutions. The way to safety is to trust the Spirit of truth continually for protection from false ideas. The "man of sin" is the carnal mind in each individual, and it always opposes and misrepresents the Truth; sometimes it poses as an angel of light and Truth. Every one who overcomes this inner adversary will be saved from all deception that may be practiced by anybody or anything that claims the place of the Lord Jesus Christ. The overthrow of the "man of sin" is promised; to obtain fulfillment of that promise we have only to keep ourselves one with the Spirit of truth. (MBD/Antichrist)

---

Fillmore Study Bible annotations by Mark Hicks.

**World English Bible Footnotes:**

[1] v2:1. Greek Parakleton: Counselor, Helper, Intercessor, Advocate, and Comfortor.

[2] v2:2. "atoning sacrifice" is from the Greek "hilasmos," an appeasing, propitiating, or the means of appeasement or propitiation--the sacrifice that turns away God's wrath because of our sin.

# First John 3

## Children of God

3:1 Behold, how great a love the Father has bestowed on us, that we should be called children of God! For this cause the world doesn't know us, because it didn't know him. 3:2 Beloved, now we are children of God,[1] and it is not yet revealed what we will be. But we know that, when

he is revealed, we will be like him;[2]
for we will see him just as he is.
3:3 Everyone who has this hope set
on him purifies himself, even as he
is pure. 3:4 Everyone who sins also
commits lawlessness. Sin is
lawlessness. 3:5 You know that he was
revealed to take away our sins, and
in him is no sin. 3:6 Whoever remains
in him doesn't sin. Whoever sins
hasn't seen him, neither knows him.

3:7 Little children, let no one lead
you astray. He who does
righteousness[3] is righteous, even as
he is righteous. 3:8 He who sins is of
the devil[4], for the devil has been
sinning from the beginning. To this
end the Son of God was revealed,
that he might destroy the works of
the devil. 3:9 Whoever is born of God
doesn't commit sin, because his seed
remains in him; and he can't sin,
because he is born of God. 3:10 In this
the children of God are revealed, and
the children of the devil. Whoever
doesn't do righteousness is not of
God, neither is he who doesn't love
his brother.

1. *We are children of God.* The offspring of spiritual parentage is spiritual in its nature.

2. *We will be like him.* We manifest the Christ Spirit only as we enter into it consciously and think, live, and act in that Spirit. We become like that which we express or manifest; therefore as we manifest the Christ we become like the Christ.

3. *Righteousness.* A state of harmony established in consciousness through the right use of God-given attributes. It leads directly to eternal life. Truth working in consciousness brings forth the perfect salvation of the whole man—Spirit, soul, and body—and righteousness (right relation) is expressed in all his affairs. (RW/righteousness)

4. *Devil.* The "devil" signifies the mass of thoughts that have been built up in consciousness through many generations of earthly experiences and crystallized into what may be termed human personality, or carnal mind. Another name of the "devil" is sense consciousness; all the thoughts in one that fight against and are adverse to Truth belong to the state of mind that is known to metaphysicians as the Devil. (MBD/Devil)

## Love One Another

3:11 For this is the message[1] which
you heard from the beginning, that
we should love one another; 3:12
unlike Cain, who was of the evil one,
and killed his brother. Why did he
kill him? Because his works were evil,
and his brother's righteous. 3:13 Don't
be surprised, my brothers, if the
world hates you. 3:14 We know that
we have passed out of death into
life, because we love the brothers.
He who doesn't love his brother
remains in death.[2] 3:15 Whoever
hates his brother is a murderer, and
you know that no murderer has
eternal life remaining in him. 3:16 By
this we know love, because he laid
down his life for us. And we ought to
lay down our lives for the brothers.
3:17 But whoever has the world's
goods, and sees his brother in need,
and closes his heart of compassion
against him, how does the love of
God remain in him?

3:18 My little children, let's not love
in word only, neither with the tongue
only, but in deed and truth. 3:19 And
by this we know that we are of the
truth, and persuade our hearts
before him, 3:20 because if our heart
condemns us, God is greater than our
heart, and knows all things. 3:21
Beloved, if our hearts don't condemn
us, we have boldness toward God;[3]
3:22 and whatever we ask, we receive
from him, because we keep his
commandments and do the things
that are pleasing in his sight.

3:23 This is his commandment, that
we should believe in the name of

his Son, Jesus Christ, and love one
another, even as he commanded. 3:24
He who keeps his commandments
remains in him, and he in him. By this
we know that he remains in us, by
the Spirit which he gave us.

1. *For this is the message.* The chief thought running through this epistle is that of the inner conviction of the reality of the Christ, the foundation hope of the Christian faith.

2. *He who doesn't love his brother remains in death.* Death, metaphysically understood,is the selfish personal consciousness that keeps us from feeling love for others. "We know that we have passed out of death into life, because we love the brethren." When we leave personal consciousness behind, we enter into the consciousness of eternal life or life universal.

3. *We have boldness toward God.* That confidence or assurance comes to us only as we overcome the habit of condemning ourselves. As we leave this form of negation behind us we gain power to demonstrate the law.

---

Fillmore Study Bible annotations by Mark Hicks.

# First John 4

## Testing the Spirits

4:1 Beloved, don't believe every
spirit, but test the spirits, whether
they are of God, because many false
prophets[1] have gone out into the
world. 4:2 By this you know the Spirit
of God: every spirit who confesses
that Jesus Christ has come in the
flesh is of God, 4:3 and every spirit
who doesn't confess that Jesus Christ
has come in the flesh is not of God,
and this is the spirit of the antichrist,
of whom you have heard that it
comes. Now it is in the world
already. 4:4 You are of God,[2] little
children, and have overcome them;
because greater is he who is in you
than he who is in the world. 4:5 They
are of the world. Therefore they
speak of the world, and the world
hears them. 4:6 We are of God. He
who knows God listens to us. He who
is not of God doesn't listen to us. By
this we know the spirit of truth, and
the spirit of error.

1. *False prophets.* Deceptive thoughts that have been built up by error, selfish desires. Outwardly they present the appearance of being candid and open; inwardly they are ravenous for personal sensation and worldly gain. In order to attain their end they deceive even "the elect."

2. *You are of God.* The offspring of spiritual parentage is spiritual in its nature. See v3:2.

## God Is Love

4:7 Beloved, let us love one
another, for love is of God; and
everyone who loves is born of God,
and knows God. 4:8 He who doesn't
love doesn't know God, for God is
love. 4:9 By this God's love was
revealed in us,[1] that God has sent
his one and only Son into the world

that we might live through him. 4:10 In
this is love, not that we loved God,
but that he loved us, and sent his
Son as the atoning sacrifice[3] for our
sins. 4:11 Beloved, if God loved us in
this way, we also ought to love one
another. 4:12 No one has seen God at
any time. If we love one another,
God remains in us, and his love has
been perfected in us.

4:13 By this we know that we
remain in him and he in us, because
he has given us of his Spirit. 4:14 We
have seen and testify that the Father
has sent the Son as the Savior of the
world. 4:15 Whoever confesses that
Jesus is the Son of God, God remains
in him, and he in God.② 4:16 We know
and have believed the love which
God has for us.

God is love, and he who remains
in love remains in God, and God
remains in him. 4:17 In this love has
been made perfect among us, that
we may have boldness in the day of
judgment, because as he is, even so
are we in this world. 4:18 There is no
fear in love; but perfect love casts
out fear,③ because fear has
punishment. He who fears is not
made perfect in love. 4:19 We love
Him, because he first loved us. 4:20 If
a man says, "I love God," and hates
his brother, he is a liar; for he who
doesn't love his brother whom he has
seen, how can he love God whom he
has not seen? 4:21 This commandment
we have from him, that he who loves
God should also love his brother.

1. *By this God's love was revealed (ASV, manifested) in us.* God love is manifested in man through the Christ or supermind.

2. *God remains in him, and he in God.* Jesus Christ was the perfect expression of God's perfect ideal man. Whoever sees in the life and works of Jesus Christ the full expression of the Christ consciousness is awakening to the that consciousness, and becomes aware of the universal presence of Spirit, in which the race lives, moves, and has its being.

3. *Perfect love casts out fear.* To follow principle, regardless of consequences and even without considering consequences, and to do right even when it works to our apparent disadvantage, is the perfect expression of love. Then we "have boldness in the day of judgment." Then we have no fear that the course we choose may prove the wrong one. We trust the Christ wisdom to show us the way, and we follow it wholeheartedly and confidently knowing that all things work together for good.

Fillmore Study Bible annotations by Mark Hicks.

**World English Bible Footnotes:**

[3] v4:10. "atoning sacrifice" is from the Greek "hilasmos," an appeasing, propitiating, or the means of appeasement or propitiation--the sacrifice that turns away God's wrath because of our sin.

# First John 5

## Faith Conquers the World

[5:1] Whoever believes that Jesus is the Christ is born of God.[1] Whoever loves the father also loves the child who is born of him. [5:2] By this we know that we love the children of God, when we love God and keep his commandments. [5:3] For this is the love of God, that we keep his commandments. His commandments are not grievous. [5:4] For whatever is born of God overcomes the world. This is the victory that has overcome the world: your faith. [5:5] Who is he who overcomes the world, but he who believes that Jesus is the Son of God?

1. *is born of God.* Only the spiritual recognizes that which is Spirit. He who believes that the perfect manifest man is sprung from the one source thereby proves himself to he divine.

## Testimony concerning the Son of God

[5:6] This is he who came by water and blood, Jesus Christ; not with the water only, but with the water and the blood. It is the Spirit who testifies, because the Spirit is the truth.[1] [5:7] For there are three who testify[4]: [5:8] the Spirit, the water, and the blood;[2] and the three agree as one. [5:9] If we receive the witness of men, the witness of God is greater; for this is God's testimony which he has testified concerning his Son. [5:10] He who believes in the Son of God has the testimony in himself. He who doesn't believe God has made him a liar, because he has not believed in the testimony that God has given concerning his Son. [5:11] The testimony is this, that God gave to us eternal life, and this life is in his Son. [5:12] He who has the Son has the life.[3] He who doesn't have God's Son doesn't have the life.

1. *The Spirit is the truth.* "Spirit" is a name for God. Spirit is synonymous with Mind; therefore we know God, Spirit, as Mind, the one Mind or intelligence of the universe.

2. *The Spirit, the water, and the blood.* Christ is the Word of God, and the life of the Word must he a form of energy far transcending any life current that inheres in blood. Blood represents life, but it is only the vehicle that carries life through the body, not the life itself.

3. *He who has the Son has the life.* A person who realizes the presence of the indwelling Christ has all the qualities of the ideal, including the will, patience, vision, intelligence, faith, and courage to express the will of the Father in his daily thought and conduct.

## Epilogue

[5:13] These things I have written to you who believe in the name of the Son of God, that you may know that you have eternal life,[1] and that you may continue to believe in the name of the Son of God.

[5:14] This is the boldness which we have toward him, that, if we ask anything according to his will, he listens to us. [5:15] And if we know that he listens to us, whatever we ask, we know that we have the petitions

which we have asked of him. 5:16 If
anyone sees his brother sinning a sin
not leading to death, he shall ask,
and God will give him life for those
who sin not leading to death. There
is a sin leading to death. I don't say
that he should make a request
concerning this. 5:17 All
unrighteousness is sin, and there is a
sin not leading to death.

5:18 We know that whoever is born
of God[2] doesn't sin, but he who was
born of God keeps himself, and the
evil one doesn't touch him. 5:19 We
know that we are of God, and the
whole world lies in the power of the
evil one. 5:20 We know that the Son
of God has come, and has given us
an understanding, that we know him
who is true, and we are in him who
is true, in his Son Jesus Christ. This is
the true God, and eternal life.

5:21 Little children, keep
yourselves from idols.

1. *That you may know that you have eternal life.* To express perfect love proves that one has entered into eternal life, since whatever is perfect is destined to endure.

2. *born of God* See v.5:1

---

Fillmore Study Bible annotations by Mark Hicks.

**World English Bible Footnotes:**

[4] v5:7. Only a few recent manuscripts add "in heaven: the Father, the Word, and the Holy Spirit; and these three are one. And there are three that testify on earth"

# JOHN'S SECOND LETTER

Second state of the Isenheim Altarpiece, Colmar, Unterlinden Museum. Public Domain.

## INTRODUCTION TO JOHN'S SECOND LETTER

See the Introduction to John's First Letter by Dr. Hunt for an overview of The Three Letters of John and The Letter of Jude.

In the opening verse, the term *elder* has reference to the writer of this Epistle (the Apostle John), who was then presiding elder, or bishop, of the Christian church at Ephesus, with Jurisdiction over other Christian groups in that area. The phrase "to the elect lady and her children" clearly refers to a Christian church—probably at Pergamum—with the converts designated as the "children." The closing verse, "The children of your elect sister greet you," is easily recognized as a reference to the church at Ephesus.

This short letter was written to warn the Christian converts against the false prophets and their erroneous doctrines, and follows a similar line of thought to that of the First Epistle, only in abbreviated form. While this message is quite brief, it is also very emphatic. Note how the writer urges the converts to keep clear of these erroneous doctrines. He says: "Look to yourselves, that you may not lose what you have worked for . . . Any one who goes ahead and does not abide in the doctrine of Christ does not have God" (verses

8-9). It would appear that John was planning to make a visit to this church in the near future, and he felt that a "face to face" explanation of the dangers involved would be more effective. Apparently, some other matters also needed straightening out, "so that our joy may be complete."

Introduction to *John's Second Letter* by Herbert J. Hunt, former Dean of Bible Studies for the Unity School of Christianity.

# Second John 1

## Truth and Love

1:1 The elder, to the chosen lady and her children, whom I love in truth;[1] and not I only, but also all those who know the truth; 1:2 for the truth's sake, which remains in us, and it will be with us forever: 1:3 Grace, mercy, and peace[2] will be with us, from God the Father, and from the Lord Jesus Christ, the Son of the Father, in truth and love.

1. *Love in truth.* The love of the Christ is an affirmative force that leads us to think unselfishly of others and to see the Christ in them. Spiritual love enables us to disregard the personal self and act from the high level of principle instead of the low level of personality.

2. *Grace, mercy, and peace.* Grace is good will; favor; disposition to show mercy (RW/grace). Jesus taught a new understanding of divine law. He acknowledged mechanical cause and effect, but he knew it was possible to "fulfill the law" by transcending its strictly mechanical repetition. This can be done only by certain changes of consciousness. One of these changes is to let go of the insistence of "even-exchanges" in life all the time. Another change is to be willing to forgive sin instead of insisting on punishment for sin. Grace is the name given to the aspect of divine law which does not deal in "even-exchanging," but in the increase of good through greater giving. Ed Rabel - Metaphysics 1, The Divine Paradox, Law/Grace.

## Perfect spiritual man is made manifest in the flesh

1:4 I rejoice greatly that I have found some of your children walking in truth,[1] even as we have been commanded by the Father. 1:5 Now I beg you, dear lady, not as though I wrote to you a new commandment, but that which we had from the beginning, that we love one another. 1:6 This is love, that we should walk according to his commandments. This is the commandment, even as you heard from the beginning, that you should walk in it.

1:7 For many deceivers have gone out into the world, those who don't confess that Jesus Christ came in the flesh. This is the deceiver and the Antichrist.[2] 1:8 Watch yourselves, that we don't lose the things which we have accomplished, but that we receive a full reward. 1:9 Whoever transgresses and doesn't remain in the teaching of Christ, doesn't have God. He who remains in the teaching, the same has both the Father and the Son.[3] 1:10 If anyone comes to you, and doesn't bring this

teaching, don't receive him into your
house, and don't welcome him, 1:11
for he who welcomes him
participates in his evil works.

1. *walking in truth.* Living according to principle in thought, word, and act.

2. *the deceiver and the Antichrist.* The Christ of perfect spiritual man is made manifest in the flesh of each individual to the extent that he identifies himself through the I AM with that which is perfect and enduring. He who does not admit that "the Word is made flesh" in this fashion is himself deceived and in turn deceives others, as does the antichrist. [The issue here was those who taught docetism.]

3. *has both the Father and the Son.* He has both principle and its mode of expression, that is, mind and thought.

## Final Greetings

1:12 Having many things to write
to you, I don't want to do so with
paper and ink, but I hope to come to
you, and to speak face to face, that
our joy[1] may be made full. 1:13 The
children of your chosen sister[2] greet
you. Amen.

1. *Joy* The happiness of God expressed through His perfect idea-human beings (RW/joy).

2. *The children of your chosen sister.* [A reference to congregants of a sister church]

---

Fillmore Study Bible annotations compiled by Mark Hicks

# John's Third Letter

Wall painting (1st century AD) from Pompeii depicting a multigenerational banquet. Museo Archeologico Nazionale, Naples. Public Domain.

## Introduction to John's Third Letter

See the Introduction to John's First Letter by Dr. Hunt for an overview of The Three Letters of John and The Letter of Jude.

This is a brief personal letter, written by the Apostle John, and addressed to a highly esteemed friend named Gaius. It is interesting to note that a man bearing this same name was closely associated with Paul during his ministry at Ephesus. (See Acts 19:29.) However, this Epistle of John was not written until many years after Paul's ministry at Ephesus, so the two men mentioned could scarcely have been the same. The Gaius mentioned in this Epistle was apparently a wealthy and influential layman, having membership in one of the "seven churches of Asia."

John's main purpose in writing this little Epistle was to secure the support of Gaius in connection with a controversy that had arisen between the apostle and a church leader named Diotrephes. Apparently Diotrephes had acted contrary to instructions, and was also seeking to repudiate the authority of

John, who was then the bishop, or presiding elder of the Christian churches in that area. John states that he had written a letter to Diotrephes, which had been disregarded. John further charges that Diotrephes "likes to put himself first, does not acknowledge my authority . . . he is ... prating against me with evil words . . . refuses himself to welcome the *brethren*, and also stops those who want to welcome them and puts them out of the church." The word brethren, as used here, would refer to some traveling evangelists of those days.

Two possible reasons for Diotrephes' strange conduct may be suggested. About that time (A.D. 100), some Christian churches in that area were making changes in organization, and the controversy mentioned in the Epistle may represent some breakaway from the old patterns. However, what seems more likely is that Diotrephes had come under the influence of the false prophets mentioned in connection with John's other Epistles, and this led to the break between Diotrephes and John. Possibly this is why John hesitated to "write with pen and ink"; preferring to make a fact-finding visit, and assure himself the support of Gaius, before taking any drastic steps in dealing with Diotrephes. The Demetrius mentioned was, in all probability, the bearer of this Epistle.

Introduction to *John's Third Letter* by Herbert J. Hunt, former Dean of Bible Studies for the Unity School of Christianity.

# THIRD JOHN 1

## Calling Forth Redemption of the Body

1:1 The elder to Gaius[1] the beloved, whom I love in truth.[2]

1. *Gaius*. Greek: of the earth; earthy man; exulting; rejoicing; gladness; Lord. Metaphysically, the acceptance by the body consciousness (of the earth, earthy man) of the truth pertaining to the divine law, or Lord. This acceptance of Truth by the seemingly earthy phase of man's being works with Paul (the activity of the word of Truth) in bringing about the redemption of the body; great gladness and rejoicing are thus realized by the individual. (MBD/Gaius)

2. *love in truth*. Divine love in the heart of man, expressed in love of all that is good, right, and true, as well as in love of all people. He who loves in accordance with Truth sees the ideal side of everyone with whom he comes in contact. To see as God sees is to love as God loves, without stint or reservation. Human love is personal rather than universal in its scope.

## Gaius Commended for His Hospitality

1:2 Beloved, I pray that you may
prosper in all things and be healthy,
even as your soul prospers.[1] 1:3 For
I rejoiced greatly, when brothers
came and testified about your truth,
even as you walk in truth. 1:4 I have
no greater joy than this, to hear
about my children walking in truth.

1:5 Beloved, you do a faithful work
in whatever you accomplish for those
who are brothers and strangers.[2] 1:6
They have testified about your love
before the assembly. You will do well
to send them forward on their
journey in a manner worthy of God,
1:7 because for the sake of the Name
they went out, taking nothing from
the Gentiles.[3] 1:8 We therefore ought
to receive such, that we may be
fellow workers for the truth.

1. *Be healthy, even as your soul prospers.* The Scriptures give spirit, soul, and body as constituting all of man. Spirit is I AM, the same in character as Divine Mind, or God. Soul is man's consciousness—that which he has apprehended or developed out of Spirit; also the impressions that he has received from the outer world. Soul is both conscious and subconscious. Body is the form of expression of both spirit and soul. In its invisible forces it expresses Spirit, and in its seeming materiality it pictures the limitations of soul. When man puts out of consciousness all limitations and realizes the perfection of Spirit, his body will be perfect; in other words the salvation of the soul results in the redemption or spiritualization of the body. (MBD/soul)

2. *For those who are brothers and strangers.* Whoever helps strangers without expectation of reward and without expectation of seeing them again has a better chance to express the Christ Spirit than the one who extends help to those well known to him. We make no distinction between our treatment of strangers and our treatment of friends. To us they are all one in Christ Jesus.

3. *Taking nothing from the Gentiles.* Spiritual love shows us that accident, chance, and events classed as happenings are "Gentiles," and if we are faithful to Principle, we do not allow any of these things to operate as causes in our life.

## Diotrephes and Demetrius

1:9 I wrote to the assembly, but
Diotrephes,[1] who loves to be first
among them, doesn't accept what we
say. 1:10 Therefore, if I come, I will
call attention to his deeds which he
does, unjustly accusing us with
wicked words. Not content with this,
neither does he himself receive the
brothers, and those who would, he
forbids and throws out of the
assembly.

¶ 1:11 Beloved, don't imitate that
which is evil, but that which is
good.[2] He who does good is of God.
He who does evil hasn't seen God.
1:12 Demetrius[3] has the testimony of
all, and of the truth itself; yes, we
also testify, and you know that our
testimony is true.

1. *Diotrephes.* ("trained by Zeus") is a symbol of personal exaltation active in consciousness. This state of mind keeps man from entering spiritual consciousness.

2. *Imitate ... that which is good.* Imitation of the good is best for those who have not yet developed power to form original conceptions of the good and the initiative to execute them. Until we are moved by the Spirit within us to original action, we cannot do better than take Jesus Christ as our model and do good as He did and as He taught others to do.

3. *Demetrius.* ("belonging to Demeter," "grain") symbolizes substance.

## Final Greetings

1:13 I had many things to write to
you, but I am unwilling to write to
you with ink and pen;[1] 1:14 but I hope
to see you soon, and we will speak
face to face. Peace be to you. The
friends greet you. Greet the friends
by name.

1. *I am unwilling to write to you with ink and pen.* See Dr. Hunt's Introduction above.

---

Fillmore Study Bible annotations by Mark Hicks.

# The Letter of Jude

Jude Thaddaeus the Apostle. Detail of the mosaic in the Basilica of San Vitale. Ravena, Italy. Gianni Careddu CC BY-SA 4.0.

## Introduction to The Letter of Jude

See the Introduction to John's First Letter by Dr. Hunt for an overview of The Three Letters of John and The Letter of Jude.

**The Author:** The writer of this Epistle declares himself to be "Jude [or Judas], a servant of Jesus Christ and brother of James" (Jude 1:1). In all probability Jude was a brother of Jesus, and was converted after Jesus' resurrection (as was James) when he then became a member of the Jerusalem council. There is a tradition that following the martyrdom of James (about A.D. 66), Jude became the presiding elder of the Apostolic Council at Jerusalem. This would account for his reference to James, as mentioned above, and also for the authoritative tone of this little Epistle. It is noteworthy that Jude makes use of illustrative material drawn from the apocryphal books of Enoch and the Assumption of Moses. The Epistle of Jude was probably written shortly after A.D. 70, and may have been addressed to the Christian groups in the Holy Land and Syria.

**Purpose of the Epistle:** The writer states that he had planned to write a pastoral letter, dealing with some important phases of Christian teaching, but the arrival of some disturbing news caused him to change the subject matter of his Epistle. He recognized that the pressing need was not for doctrinal discussions, but rather for a message of warning and exhortation. Apparently, some of the false prophets had gained entrance into the churches, and the Gospel message was being replaced by erroneous teaching and open invitations to licentious practices. The purpose of this Epistle, therefore, was to denounce these false prophets and their teaching, hoping that this timely action would win back the erring converts and restore the true Christian teaching to the churches.

**Metaphysical Notes:** Jude is usually regarded as symbolizing the activity of renunciation, or elimination. This symbology will be readily understood when recalling the main purpose of Jude's Epistle—which was to eliminate, or cast out, the false prophets and their erroneous teachings from the Christian church. There are times when we also are called upon to cast out some false prophets from our consciousness. These "false prophets" are the erroneous thoughts and conditions that take up their abode in our mind and body; and just as the false prophets wrought havoc in the early church, so do these erroneous thoughts and conditions tend to wreck our health, happiness, and peace of mind. If we are to function harmoniously, the "Jude" within us must be brought into action. But, we may ask, how is this to be accomplished? How can we cast out these erroneous thoughts and conditions from our consciousness? Seeking an answer to this question, we should note that the work Jude sought to accomplish corresponds, very largely, with the activity of denial. Erroneous thoughts and conditions may be denied out of existence, thus bringing a thorough cleansing to our consciousness.

Introduction to *The Letter of Jude* by Herbert J. Hunt, former Dean of Bible Studies for the Unity School of Christianity.

Jude is called "Judas the brother of James" in Luke 6:16 and Acts 1:13. Metaphysically, the name means praise Jehovah and it is the same as Judah and Judas, metaphysically interpreted as our power of life. However the same person is called Thaddaeus in Matthew 10:3. Metaphysically, Thaddaeus is our power of elimination. This double interpretation can lead us to say that this is a letter from our Elimination-Praise faculty.

The Letter of Jude is a letter from our elimination and praise faculty to a church where ungodly ideas had crept in. The letter from Jude provides four things in response: encouragement to charge forward in our faith-fullness to our Spiritual Cause and aim; reminds us of times we fell in the past and the judgments/corrections that followed; instructs and invites us to keep ourselves in the love of God as we await, and ends in a statement of Truth (Doxology) about the nature and keeping-power of God.

The message of this letter, metaphysically, is to be in a continual state of inner work; to both eliminate (Jude) every arising error thought (ungodly men) and to praise (Judah) God in and for everything. When we use the two together, they have a synergistic effect to amplify, support, and strengthen one another.

Because we live in a world (outer and inner) whose default seems to tend to disorder, continual ordering and organizing of the mind is needed. This constant "state of Jude/Judah" not only protects the mind from the "creeping in of ungodly thoughts," but it also supports our spiritual/inner life work that we may attain our greatest goal and hope: the transformation of mind, spiritual ascension.

Error thoughts (ungodly men) are never far from our minds and they require a lot of energy from us. In dealing with these thoughts, our precious Life Energy (Judah) is best conserved by prevention (praise), which works together with cure (elimination), because the more you praise, the more you will be able to detect error thoughts at their onset and quickly pray or praise them away (eliminate them).

And when our best efforts fail, we can trust that God will always give us the precise righteous adjustments (mercy) we need in order to "recover us" back to the right track on our journey of the transformation of mind and spiritual ascension.

Introduction to *The Letter of Jude* by Mary Salama.

# Jude 1

## Salutation

1:1 Jude,[1] a servant of Jesus
Christ, and brother of James, to
those who are called, sanctified by
God the Father, and kept for Jesus
Christ: 1:2 Mercy to you and peace and
love be multiplied.[2]

1. *Jude (Thaddaeus).* See introduction for Jude/Thaddaeus. Metaphysically, Thaddaeus represents the faculty of elimination in man. In the body the eliminative center is situated in the lower part of the back. It is just as necessary that one should learn to let go of thoughts, conditions, and substances in consciousness, body, and affairs, when they have served their purpose and one no longer needs them, as it is that one should lay hold of new ideas and new substances to meet one's daily requirements. Therefore it is very necessary that the eliminative faculty be quickened in one, and a right balance between receiving and giving, laying hold and letting go, be established.

2. *mercy, peace, love.* Mercy: Christlike treatment toward the suffering; the important point in desiring to be merciful is righteous adjustment, as this results in true overcoming (RW/mercy). Peace: Harmony and tranquillity derived from awareness of the Christ consciousness (RW/peace). Love: The pure essence of Being that binds together the whole human family (RW/love). Mercy is multiplied to the one who shows mercy to others in thought, word, and deed. Through remaining peaceful and peaceable even under stress one realizes greater peace. The same rule holds good as regards love.

## Occasion of the Letter

1:3 Beloved, while I was very eager to write to you about our common salvation, I was constrained to write to you exhorting you to contend earnestly for the faith which was once for all delivered to the saints.[1] 1:4 For there are certain men who crept in secretly, even those who were long ago written about for this condemnation: ungodly men, turning the grace of our God into lasciviousness, and denying our only Master, God, and Lord, Jesus Christ.

1. *Faith which was once for all delivered to the saints.* Our firm faith in the power of the Holy Spirit to bring us into the kingdom.

## Judgment on False Teachers

1:5 Now I desire to remind you, though you already know this, that the Lord, having saved a people out of the land of Egypt, afterward destroyed those who didn't believe. 1:6 Angels who didn't keep their first domain, but deserted their own dwelling place, he has kept in everlasting bonds under darkness for the judgment of the great day. 1:7 Even as Sodom and Gomorrah, and the cities around them, having, in the same way as these, given themselves over to sexual immorality and gone after strange flesh, are set forth as an example, suffering the punishment of eternal fire.

1:8 Yet in like manner these also in their dreaming defile the flesh, despise authority, and slander celestial beings. 1:9 But Michael, the archangel, when contending with the devil and arguing about the body of Moses, dared not bring against him an abusive condemnation, but said, "May the Lord rebuke you!" 1:10 But these speak evil of whatever things they don't know. What they understand naturally, like the creatures without reason, they are destroyed in these things. 1:11 Woe to them! For they went in the way of Cain, and ran riotously in the error of Balaam for hire, and perished in Korah's rebellion. 1:12 These are hidden rocky reefs in your love feasts when they feast with you, shepherds who without fear feed themselves; clouds without water, carried along by winds; autumn leaves without fruit, twice dead, plucked up by the roots; 1:13 wild waves of the sea, foaming out their own shame; wandering stars, for whom the blackness of darkness has been reserved forever.

1:14 About these also Enoch, the seventh from Adam, prophesied, saying, "Behold, the Lord came with ten thousands of his holy ones, 1:15 to execute judgment on all, and to convict all the ungodly of all their works of ungodliness which they have done in an ungodly way, and of all the hard things which ungodly sinners have spoken against him." 1:16 These are murmurers and complainers,[1] walking after their lusts (and their mouth speaks proud things), showing respect of persons to gain advantage.

1. *These are murmurers and complainers.* This entire passage is about false prophets who will appear as murmurers and complainers. A false prophet refers to anything in life which makes promises but does not keep them. False prophets abound in the world. They can be found in religion, in business, in the arts, and in human relationships. They are not necessarily "wicked," but they are false. They do not produce the results they promise. How can we recognize a false prophet from a true one? By the results in people's lives. "Thus you will know them by their fruits." Examples of false prophets: (1) All negative emotions, (2) One-sided opinions, (3) Negative thinking, (4) Belief that anything can be a finality (5) Seeking revenge, (6) The belief that "more" equals "better". (USRS Bible Interpretation, Lesson 4 Matt. 5-7).

## Warnings and Exhortations

1:17 But you, beloved, remember the words which have been spoken before by the apostles of our Lord Jesus Christ. 1:18 They said to you that "In the last time there will be mockers, walking after their own ungodly lusts." 1:19 These are they who cause divisions, and are sensual, not having the Spirit. 1:20 But you, beloved, keep building up yourselves❶ on your most holy faith, praying in the Holy Spirit. 1:21 Keep yourselves in the love of God,❷ looking for the mercy of our Lord Jesus Christ❸ to eternal life. 1:22 On some have compassion, making a distinction, 1:23 and some save, snatching them out of the fire with fear, hating even the clothing stained by the flesh.

1. *keep building up yourselves.* On the faith that God is all good and that we as sons of God are fundamentally good and upright. With faith in spiritual reality as a foundation, one builds up the superstructure of character and constrictive living day by day. Faith grows stronger only as it is acted upon.

2. *Keep yourselves in the love of God.* By loving godliness in others as well as expressing it ourselves habitually; to love "the things of God" is to love God.

3. *mercy of our Lord Jesus Christ.* The loving-kindness and charity that we extend to others, when we are consciously one with the Christ.

## Benediction

1:24 Now to him who is able to keep them[2] from stumbling,❶ and to present you faultless before the presence of his glory in great joy, 1:25 to God our Savior,❷ who alone is wise, be glory and majesty, dominion and power, both now and forever. Amen.

1. *keep them from stumbling.* To keep us from stumbling requires that we keep our thoughts stayed on both love and wisdom given us by the Christ Spirit.

2. *to God our Savior.* Salvation is an awareness of the "glory, majesty, dominion, and power" of the Christ life in us; a complete absorption in spiritual life and power.

---

Fillmore Study Bible annotations by Mary Salama

**World English Bible Footnotes:**

[1] v1:1. or, Judah

[2] v1:24. TR and NU read "you"

# THE REVELATION TO JOHN

Old Orthodox Apocalypse Wall-painting from medieval Osogovo Monastery, Republic of Macedonia. Public Domain.

## INTRODUCTION TO THE REVELATION TO JOHN

The theme of the book of Revelation is the redemption and the ascension of human beings from the natural to the divine plane of existence. Ed Rabel, in his audio series of metaphysical interpretations, says that the meaning of the book refers to the reality of the living presence of Jesus Christ and the meaning of the universal Christ spirit in each of us.

Many persons regard Revelation as a closed book: "This is too deep for me!" "Difficult to understand!" "So many terrible events recorded!"—and many other similar comments regarding Revelation are frequently heard. And, from a casual glance at the contents of the book, it would appear that such comments are fully justified. Thus it happens that while other books of the New Testament are given careful consideration, Revelation, for many persons, remains unread. However, it will be recalled that during the course of these lessons, several other books of the New Testament have appeared difficult at first reading; but such difficulties soon vanish when proper background information is supplied. May this not also apply to

Revelation? Indeed, some background information is absolutely essential for the study of Revelation, and without such help it is likely to remain forever a closed book. But when we know why Revelation was written, and when it was written; and when we realize how its message imparted new strength and courage to the hard-pressed Christians of early days, then it becomes a truly readable and inspiring book. Moreover, when Revelation is properly understood, its thrilling message will be seen as applying not only to the early Christians, but also to many of our present-day problems.

The following notes should help readers of the New Testament to gain a better understanding and appreciation of this book called " Revelation."

*Title of the book:* Readers of the New Testament are familiar with the title Revelation. However, the Greek word Apocalypse is often applied to Revelation, and in some translations this is used as a title for the book. The word *Apocalypse* means a brief vision or disclosure of certain phases of Truth, or some forthcoming events. The veil that covers the future is momentarily drawn aside, and the writer describes what he was privileged to witness. Thus the word *revelation* clearly indicates the character of the book. Incidentally, it should be noted that the Revised Standard Version correctly states that this is the "Revelation to John," rather than "of John," as given in most translations.

*The author:* In the opening verse of Revelation, the author mentions his name—"John"—and this is usually regarded as indicating the Apostle John. However, from time to time this apostolic authorship has been questioned, mainly on account of the marked dissimilarity between Revelation and the Fourth Gospel. Even as early as the third century, some theologians pointed out that the style and subject matter of these two books clearly indicated that they could not have been produced by the same writer. Nevertheless, since Revelation was written some thirty-five years before the Gospel of John, there is a possibility that the writer's experiences during the intervening years produced a complete change of viewpoint. A change of this sort is noticeable in Paul's Epistles, as pointed out in Lesson Seven of this course. Could not a somewhat similar change have taken place with the Apostle John? The New Testament indicates that John was somewhat of a "firebrand" in his earlier days, for Jesus renamed him "Boanerges," meaning "Son of thunder." This new name was given after John and his brother sought to call down fire from heaven upon some offending Samaritans. (See Luke 9:52-56.) Moreover, John had witnessed the destruction of Jerusalem by the Romans in A.D. 70; and shortly after his arrival in Ephesus, he had been arrested and imprisoned on the Isle of Patmos (probably about A.D. 80). All this would readily account for the mental attitude revealed in this apocalyptic writing. In later years John apparently attained a calmer state of mind, plus a deeper understanding of Jesus' teaching—all leading to a complete change of style and subject matter, as seen in John's Gospel. In all probability, Revelation was written at Ephesus, shortly after John's release from his imprisonment, as mentioned above,about A.D.85.

*Purpose of the book:* This book was written in an effort to encourage the hard-pressed Christians to hold steady in their faith. The early church placed great emphasis upon the return of the Lord, and this hope enabled the Christians to endure persecution. But with the passing of the years, the persecutions grew in intensity, with the Christians suffering severely, and many of them being called upon to endure martyrdom. Small wonder, therefore, that they were asking, "Where is the promise of his coming?" (II Peter 3:4); while others, in their intense agony, were crying: "O Sovereign Lord . . . how long before thou wilt judge and avenge our blood on those who dwell upon the earth?" (Rev. 6:10). The writer of Revelation, therefore, made answer: "Behold, he is coming with the clouds, and every eye will see him" (Rev. 1:7); and this was confirmed by the declaration from the Lord, "Behold, I come quickly" (Rev. 3:11 A.V.). Thus the persecuted Christians were assured that if they would remain steadfast—maintaining their faith, even in the midst of persecutions—their Lord would surely deliver them, punishing their persecutors, and opening the way for faithful Christians to receive the reward of "a new heaven and a new earth" (Rev. 21:1). The book therefore brought a message of hope, inspiring the early Christians with new courage; and it thus played an important part in preserving Christianity from extinction.

*The apocalyptic viewpoint:* In order to understand Revelation, or any similar book, it is absolutely necessary to have some knowledge of what is frequently termed "the apocalyptic viewpoint." Modern readers are accustomed to think in terms of gradually improving conditions. Indeed, many of our present-day laws and activities are directed toward this much-desired end. In ancient times—especially among Jewish people—the opposite attitude prevailed. Many outstanding teachers and writers openly proclaimed that the prevailing evil conditions were destined to become worse, and all man's efforts towards improvement were in vain. Here was the one gleam of hope: when evil conditions had reached their lowest point, and when man had exhausted all his strength, courage, and endurance, then the Lord Himself would intervene and usher in an entirely new state of affairs. Thus the saying arose, "Man's extremity is God's opportunity." Early Christians were taught to rejoice in their intensified troubles, since all this indicated that the time of divine intervention must be at hand. This "apocalyptic viewpoint" constitutes the key not only to Revelation, but also to several Old Testament books, such as Ezekiel, Joel, and Daniel, besides many apocalyptic books not included in our present Bibie.

*Use of symbols:* An outstanding characteristic of Revelation is its extensive use of symbols. This is noticeable in all apocalyptic literature. It should be noted that these symbols were used not only to represent persons, places, or events, but also for purposes of concealment. All apocalyptic books, including Revelation, were produced during periods of oppression and persecution. Indeed, apocalyptic books are frequently referred to as "tracts for troubled times"! The apocalyptic writers sought to encourage their readers by freely predicting the speedy overthrow of the oppressors and persecutors. However, a message of this type could not be given in plain language. Such a procedure would speedily bring about the arrest and execution of the author and all persons associated with him. Hence the message was couched in symbolic terms, and other devices of concealment were used; so that while the message would be readily understood by those persons "in the know," it would be meaningless to outsiders. In Revelation there are frequent references to "Babylon" and its overthrow, whereas the author was actually predicting the downfall of Rome. Several Roman emperors also figure in the story, but their identity is concealed through the use of symbols. These and many other references would be readily understood by the author and readers of Revelation; but the Roman censors would be hoodwinked, regarding the book as indicative of deranged mentality.

This extensive use of symbols raises a rather important question: How may we distinguish between what the author intended as symbolic, and what he regarded as literal happenings, connected for the most part with the future? For example: In Revelation there are frequent references to "earthquakes." (See Rev. 6:12; Rev. 8:5; Rev. 11:19.) But was the author here symbolically indicating a shake-up of government, with the summary deposing of persons in high places? Or was he predicting a physical catastrophe, with the wrecking of cities and countryside, and loss of life and property? Similarly, there are references to "plagues," "fire," and so on. Present-day readers may ask whether these are to be regarded as symbolic, or are to be taken literally. There is no general rule for making a distinction between the symbolic and the factual. However, a careful study of the context reveals that, in most instances, such references are to be regarded as symbolic. As already mentioned, the entire book is of symbolic character. When literal happenings of this sort appear to be indicated, it should be recognized that this represents the apocalyptic writer's idea of divine intervention. In those days, storms, earthquakes, and all catastrophic happenings were regarded as "acts of God," and these would represent what was deemed fitting punsihment for the oppressors and persecutors.

Present-day evaluation: Revelation is a very important book, and it should be studied from several different viewpoints.

*(1) As literature:* The Book of Revelation is an outstanding piece of literature, and it ranks high among the great books of the world. It is written in what may be termed the dramatic style, with the various episodes arranged in climactic order. The writer was an expert literary craftsman, excelling in description, action, suspense, and climax; he demonstrates his ability to hold the full attention of his readers from the opening chapter until the closing words. The term dramatic as here used does not infer that the book was written for stage production. It refers, rather, to the arrangement of the various episodes, and the many spectacular scenes presented in the book.

*(2) As history:* While the book itself cannot be regarded as historical, yet it deals with many actual happenings during New Testament times. It reveals the intensity of the persecutions directed against the early Christians, and indicates how they were enabled to hold steady during those agonizing times. Furthermore, the symbology used clearly depicts the activities of several Roman emperors, and other historical happenings. Sometimes questions are raised regarding the type of activities recorded in Revelation. Many of these appear to be of the vengeful type, and there is very little indication of the love and forgiveness usually associated with the Christian teaching. However, it should be recognized that Revelation follows along lines of apocalyptic teaching, rather than the Christ way as shown in the Gospels.

*(3) As prophecy:* Some writers regard Revelation as predicting certain dire happenings which are to take place in the distant future. Thus in certain quarters the book has been classified as "history written beforehand"—with the actual fulfillment taking place at the "end of the world." In this connection, two points should be carefully considered: (a) The author of Revelation distinctly states that the events recorded "must soon take place . . . for the time is near" (Rev. 1:1-3). Furthermore, there are the oft-repeated promises of Jesus, "Behold, I come quickly . . ." (Rev. 3:11 A.V.). (b) The

main theme of Revelation concerns the overthrow of the Roman persecutors, and this "overthrow" actually took place with the conversion of the Emperor Constantine in A.D. 312-313. At that time the emperor made the declaration that Christianity should be the recognized religion throughout the Roman Empire. True, this overthrow did not come about exactly as predicted in Revelation, but it did take place, and to this extent the prophecy was fulfilled. From the historical viewpoint, the events recorded in Revelation would now appear to deal with the past, rather than with things yet to come. However, from a metaphysical viewpoint, the past, present, and future are depicted in Revelation.

*(4) Regarding interpretation:* Revelation presents quite a number of possibilities in regard to interpretation, and many interesting suggestions have been made from time to time. However, since Revelation contains so much symbology, it would appear that the most helpful interpretation is to be found along metaphysical lines. In this way, many of the scenes depicted in Revelation may be regarded as symbolic presentations of the trials and difficulties that we encounter on the journey from mortal consciousness to spiritual consciousness. Mainly, these trials and difficulties act as a cleansing process—getting rid of mortal ideas, in order that they may be replaced by spiritual ideas. Thus the recorded happenings in Revelation find their counterparts in human experience. Some events thus depicted may have reference to past experiences, while others indicate overcomings yet to be made. This method of interpretation will be followed in this lesson.

Before entering upon a detailed study of the events recorded in Revelation, an outline will be given, with the various episodes arranged in climactic order, so that the student may get a clear picture of the entire book, and also see the relationship of each section to the whole story. Following this, each section will be discussed in order, so that all details may become clear, and thus form a basis for the metaphysical interpretation which follows.

OUTLINE OF
THE REVELATION TO JOHN

- Introduction (Rev. 1:1-3.)
- Prologue Vision of the Son of Man (Rev. 1:4-20.)
- Episode 1 (Rev. 2:1; 3:22.): Seven letters to the Churches of Asia (Minor)
- Episode 2 (Rev.4:1;8:1.): The Seven Seals. (Brief Interlude: Rev. 7:1-17)
- Episode 3 (Rev. 8:2; 11:19.): The Seven Trumpets. (Brief Interlude: Rev. 10:1; 11:13)
- Episode 4 (Rev. 12:1; 14:20.): Three Great Portents.
- Episode 5 (Rev. 15:1; 16:21.): The Seven Plagues.
- Episode 6 (Rev. 17:1;20:14.): Overthrow of "Babylon."
- Episode 7 (Rev. 21:1; 22:5.): A New Heaven and Earth.
- Epilogue Warning, and Benediction. (Rev. 22:6-21.)

Introduction to *The Revelation to John* by Herbert J. Hunt, former Dean of Bible Studies for the Unity School of Christianity.

# Revelation 1

## Introduction and Salutation

1:1 This is the Revelation① of Jesus Christ,② which God gave him to show to his servants the things which must happen soon,③ which he sent and made known by his angel[1]④ to his servant, John,⑤ 1:2 who testified to God's word,⑥ and of the testimony of Jesus Christ, about everything that he saw.

1:3 Blessed is he who reads and those who hear the words of the prophecy, and keep the things that are written in it, for the time is at hand.⑦

1:4 John, to the seven assemblies⑧ that are in Asia: Grace to you and peace, from God, who is and who was and who is to come; and from the seven Spirits⑨ who are before his throne; 1:5 and from Jesus Christ, the faithful witness, the firstborn of the dead, and the ruler of the kings of the earth. To him who loves us, and washed us from our sins by his blood;⑩ 1:6 and he made us to be a Kingdom,⑪ priests[2] to his God and Father; to him be the glory and the dominion⑫ forever and ever. Amen.

1:7 Behold, he is coming with the clouds, and every eye will see him, including those who pierced him. All the tribes of the earth will mourn over him. Even so, Amen.

1:8 "I am the Alpha and the Omega,[3]"⑬ says the Lord God,[4] "who is and who was and who is to come, the Almighty."

1. *Revelation.* An unveiling, a disclosure of Truth, making known that which is hidden. (RW/revelation)

2. *Jesus Christ.* Jesus is the name that represents an individual expression of the Christ idea. Jesus Christ is the form of the name that is commonly applied to the man of Galilee who demonstrated perfection. Christ, or perfect-man idea existing eternally in Divine Mind, is the true, spiritual, higher self of every individual. (MBD/Christ)

3. *must happen soon.* When these people who wrote the books of the Bible wrote those books, they were attempting to solve problems of their day. Frank Guidici, The Book of Revelation Revealed, Segment 8.

4. *angel.* messenger of God (MBD/angel)

5. *John.* The great truth contained in this book is revealed through the disciple, John. After traveling the rocky, barren path of a pioneer soul, who has cleared a way to the inner kingdom, the outworkings of Spirit from the depths of being were revealed to him, in the truth he has lovingly given to humanity. John,the revelator, represents that quality in humanity which discerns both the spiritual and the evolutionary laws that are involved in creation.

6. *God's word.* God in His capacity as creative power, and includes all the potentialities of Being. (MBD/word)

7. *the time is at hand.* Divisions of time signify degrees of unfoldment. (MBD/time)

8. *to the seven assemblies.* Historically understood, John names the seven churches in Asia. And that means in Asia Minor. These are churches, some of which were established by Paul when he was bringing the message to the gentiles. And apparently these were key churches during that time. He's addressing himself to these churches. (Giudici, Segment 9. Metaphysically, the number [seven] representing fullness in the world of phenomena; seven always refers to the divine law of perfec-

tion. (MBD/seven)

9. *the seven Spirits.* Signifies the natural human redeemed or rounded out; seven is the number of fulfillment in the natural. (MBD/Sardis)

10. *blood.* Spiritual principles that rest on pure ideals. (RW/blood)

11. *he made us to be a kingdom.* We are Christ consciousness. The realm of divine ideas. (RW/kingdom)

12. *dominion.* This supreme authority comes as man realizes his oneness with the Father. (RW/dominion)

13. *I am the Alpha and the Omega.* "There is but one presence and one power in the universe and in my life, God the good omnipotent. God is all there ever really was, is now and ever shall be." This is the recurrent and the eternal message of Jesus Christ, of the Christ spirit in every man and it speaks through the author of our book of Revelation. (Ed Rabel, The Book of Revelation, Introduction) "The key to the mystery of life. Everything has its origin in an idea or a thought, whether it is a person, a possession, or the universe, and it has its completion, the manifestation of that thought form. Let me say that again. Everything has its origin in an idea or God thought, as its completion in the manifestation of that thought form." Eric Butterworth, Podcast 15, The Alpha and the Omega.

## A Vision of Christ

1:9 I John, your brother and partner with you in the oppression, Kingdom,① and perseverance② in Christ Jesus, was on the isle that is called Patmos③ because of God's Word and the testimony of Jesus Christ. 1:10 I was in the Spirit④ on the Lord's day, and I heard behind me a loud voice,⑤ like a trumpet 1:11 saying, "[5]What you see, write in a book and send to the seven assemblies[6]:⑥ to Ephesus, Smyrna, Pergamum, Thyatira, Sardis, Philadelphia, and to Laodicea."

1:12 I turned to see the voice that spoke with me. Having turned, I saw seven golden lampstands.⑦ 1:13 And among the lampstands was one like a son of man,[7]⑧ clothed with a robe reaching down to his feet, and with a golden sash around his chest. 1:14 His head and his hair were white as white wool, like snow. His eyes were like a flame of fire. 1:15 His feet were like burnished brass, as if it had been refined in a furnace. His voice was like the voice of many waters. 1:16 He had seven stars⑨ in his right hand. Out of his mouth proceeded a sharp two-edged sword. His face was like the sun shining at its brightest. 1:17 When I saw him, I fell at his feet⑩ like a dead man.

He laid his right hand on me, saying, "Don't be afraid. I am the first and the last, 1:18 and the Living one. I was dead, and behold, I am alive forevermore. Amen. I have the keys of Death and of Hades[8]⑪. 1:19 Write therefore the things which you have seen, and the things which are,⑫ and the things which will happen hereafter; 1:20 the mystery of the seven stars which you saw in my right hand, and the seven golden lampstands. The seven stars are the angels[9] of the seven assemblies. The seven lampstands are seven assemblies.

1. *Kingdom.* The kingdom of heaven is the realm of divine ideas, producing their expression, perfect harmony. Christ consciousness. (RW/kingdom)

2. *perseverance (ASV, patience).* An attitude of mind characterized by poise, inner calmness, and quiet endurance, especially in the face of trying conditions. Patience has its foundation in faith, and it is perfected only in those who have unwavering faith in God. (RW/patience)

3. *Patmos.* The island to which John was banished. It is a rocky island in the Aegean Sea. This was where John received his vision. Metaphysically, Patmos is a place in consciousness where we realize through Spirit that the fleshly or carnal man produces nothing. When we are in Spirit the body is physically quiet; all sensation is

primarily from the Spirit. So far as the I AM or spiritual is concerned the physical is as a rock, void of sensation or activity. When we still the outer we get the inspiration of Spirit within us. (MBD/Patmos)

4. *in the Spirit.* Being "in the Spirit" refers to the inspiration that comes to one when one has entered into the Lord or master degree of the mind.

5. *I heard behind me a loud voice.* Spirit is the "*still small* voice" in every man that hears and blesses and uplifts. Spirit is made manifest as perfect wholeness through the illumined mind. What John heard was a *loud* voice that sounded like a trumpet. It is the Logos or Word of God(RW/voice)

6. *the seven assemblies.* The seven churches have been interpreted different ways: (1) Charles Fillmore referred to them as the faculties of the divine natural man. "Seven is the number of the complete natural man. Twelve is the number of the complete spiritual man. We have first that which is natural and then that which is spiritual, as Paul says. In other words, we complete the natural man. John the Baptist comes right out of the natural world. Then comes the Christ man with his five additional fundamental faculties of mind." (Unity Archives, Chas. Fillmore Papers, 3026-24-886); (2) Ed Rabel interprets the seven assemblies as "seven great centers of intelligent worship, within our developing spiritual consciousness. They are called churches by the author because they are in reality, a legitimate part of our worship of God and of our personal spiritual development." Ed Rabel, The Book of Revelation, Chapter 1.

7. *seven golden lampstands.* The seven quickened and redeemed nerve centers in the human body. When the seven nerve centers in the organism are quickened, purified, and transmuted into Spiritual Intelligences, they may be compared to relay batteries, through which the Divine Live, Love and Intelligence manifest.

8. *son of man.* Metaphysically, Christ is the one and only complete, ideal man in the mind of the everywhere present God (MBD/Son-of-God). Frank Guidici comments that John pictures Jesus in seven parts: lamp stands, one like a Son of Man, clothed with a long robe, and with a golden girdle round his breast, his head and his hair were white as wool. This is a symbolic picture of Jesus that ties into the seventh chapter of the Book of Daniel. There, it ties into the apocalyptic thrust and also ties into the type of Messiah that the Jewish people were looking for at that time. Frank Guidici, The Book of Revelation Revealed, Segment 9.

9. *seven stars.* The seven stars of the right hand are our sevenfold powers of as human beings in intelligent action (see above annotation on *seven assemblies*), and the countenance as the sun is our strength: the wisdom and warmth of Divine Mind poured forth in unlimited splendor.

10. *I fell at his feet (ASV, right hand)* The side of Truth, the side of power (RW/right).

11. *I have the keys of Death and of Hades.* Sheol in Greek, Hades is the unseen world, or the abode of the dead. Generally, translated as hell. In reality, however, the word has reference to the grave or the pit. Metaphysically, Hades refers to the outer darkness, the realm of sense, in contrast to the inner or luminously spiritual. The keys of death and of Hades is the message of eternal life and I AM dominion through the Christ. As Jesus overcame so can we: *In Christ shall all be made alive.* (MBD/Hades)

12. *and the things which are.* Thoughts lowered in vibration to the level of sense perception. The things that appear are the formulations of man's ideas of himself. (RW/things)

Fillmore Study Bible annotations compiled by Rev. Jim Ernstsen and Rev. Lisa Herklotz.

**World English Bible Footnotes:**

[1] v1:1. or, messenger (here and wherever angel is mentioned)

[2] v1:6. Exodus 19:6; Isaiah 61:6

[3] v1:8. TR adds "the Beginning and the End"

[4] v1:8. TR omits "God"

[5] v1:11. TR adds "I am the Alpha and the Omega, the First and the Last."

[6] v1:11. TR adds "which are in Asia"

[7] v1:13. Daniel 7:13

[8] v1:18. or, Hell

[9] v1:20. or, messengers (here and wherever angels are mentioned)

# Revelation 2

## Speaking to Our Desire

2:1 "To the angel of the assembly in Ephesus[1] write:

"He who holds the seven stars in his right hand, he who walks among the seven golden lampstands[2] says these things:

2:2 "I know your works, and your toil and perseverance, and that you can't tolerate evil men, and have tested those who call themselves apostles, and they are not, and found them false. 2:3 You have perseverance and have endured for my name's sake, and have[10] not grown weary. 2:4 But I have this against you, that you left your first love.[3] 2:5 Remember therefore from where you have fallen, and repent and do the first works; or else I am coming to you swiftly, and will move your lampstand out of its place, unless you repent. 2:6 But this you have, that you hate the works of the Nicolaitans,[4] which I also hate. 2:7 He who has an ear, let him hear what the Spirit says to the assemblies. To him who overcomes I will give to eat of the tree of life,[5] which is in the Paradise[6] of my God.

1. *the assembly in Ephesus.* Metaphysically, this church stands for our desire nature. In reading this letter, we find that the desire nature of us is the first thing about us which becomes activated in the process of worship. Desire and appeal which are the meanings of the word, truth has caused your consciousness to desire more of God and more of God's good. Your desire for more of God and more of his good has become a church of worship within your soul, which the book of Revelation calls by its Greek name, Ephesus. (Ed Rabel)

2. *golden lampstands.* Receptacles of spiritual light.

3. *first love.* The first love that we feel for the things of God, when all our faculties are turned into higher channels. In his "first love" we are full of enthusiasm and zeal for Truth, God's word has power, and we are able to prove our faith in various ways.

4. *Nicolaitans.* Historically, a heretical sect that was not very popular with the Christians during that time. Metaphysically, those with mixed spiritual thoughts. (MBD/Nicolaitans)

5. *To him who overcomes I will give to eat of the tree of life.* The eternal life of God is within each of us. When we consciously realize the presence of this life in every part of our organism we are eating of the tree of life. (RW/eat)

6. *Paradise.* Paradise means pleasure grounds, *Elysium*, region of surpassing beauty, Garden of Eden. It is a place in which all the elemental forces of Being are at the disposal of the soul that believes in the supremacy of the good. (MBD/Paradise)

## Speaking to Our Spiritual Substance

2:8 "To the angel of the assembly in Smyrna[1] write:

"The first and the last, who was dead, and has come to life says these things:

2:9 "I know your works, oppression, and your poverty (but you are rich), and the blasphemy of those who say they are Jews, and they are not, but are a synagogue of Satan. 2:10 Don't be afraid of the things which you are about to suffer. Behold, the devil is about to throw some of you into prison, that you may be tested; and you will have oppression for ten days. Be faithful to death, and I will give you the crown of life. 2:11 He who has an ear, let him hear what the Spirit says to the assemblies. He who overcomes won't be harmed by the second death.[2]

1. *the assembly in Smyrna.* Smyrna (myrrh, flowing, distilling) is substance. When all of our faculties are reinforced by spiritual substance, our spirit is one of unconquerable endurance and staying power. It is the invisible, intangible reality containing all potential of forms. It is not material, but it is the essence out of which all material can be distilled. We are then developing what we call the true prosperity consciousness, which is the purpose of the church of Smyrna within us.

2. *He who overcomes won't be harmed by the second death.* When we are established in a true prosperity consciousness, based upon spiritual understanding of God's laws and God's substance, the comings and goings of outer forms of things will no longer hurt us. We do not feel damaged or cheated when certain forms of things change or are removed. When we really understand that God's spiritual substance fills every part of our lives, every moment of our lives, then we never feel separated from the true Source of our good. (Herbert Hunt, USRS Bible Interpretations.)

## Speaking to Our Intelligence

2:12 "To the angel of the assembly in Pergamum[1] write:

"He who has the sharp two-edged sword says these things:

2:13 "I know your works and where you dwell, where Satan's throne is. You hold firmly to my name, and didn't deny my faith in the days of Antipas my witness, my faithful one, who was killed among you, where Satan dwells. 2:14 But I have a few things against you, because you have there some who hold the teaching of Balaam, who taught Balak to throw a stumbling block before the children of Israel, to eat things sacrificed to idols, and to commit sexual immorality. 2:15 So you also have some who hold to the teaching of the Nicolaitans likewise[11]. 2:16 Repent therefore, or else I am coming to you quickly, and I will make war against them with the sword of my mouth. 2:17 He who has an ear, let him hear what the Spirit says to the assemblies. To him who overcomes, to him I will give of the hidden manna,[2][12] and I will give him a white stone,[3] and on the stone a new name[4] written, which no one knows but he who receives it.

1. *the assembly in Pergamum.* Pergamum means "strongly united; closely knit" representing the intellectual consciousness in us (strongly united, closely knit, tough texture, elevated, height, citadel); Pergamum is intelligence. More specifically, it stands for the cooperation of our intellect in the whole process of spiritual unfoldment. (Herbert Hunt)

2. *I will give of the hidden manna.* The "hidden manna" is the inner substance, that which comes down out of heaven. We eat of it by affirmation; we affirm that we are fed by the one living substance. As

our intellect becomes more spiritualized, we will somehow make contact with a new source of nourishment for our whole being, a type of nourishment which is hidden to ordinary thinking.

3. *I will give him a white stone.* An ancient custom was to hand to an acquitted prisoner a white stone signifying his starting life afresh and free from stigma. Metaphysically, the "white stone" signifies for each of us a fresh start in life, free from tension, upsets, disappointments, and resentments of the past. (LIT Correspondence School, Lesson 9, Annotation 6)

4. *a new name.* The "new name" is our individual concept of self and of God which is is a little different from that of any other person's. No other knows it, for it is peculiar to each of us. It would mean nothing to any one else. Also, it is ever changing, as the our concept of God and of ourself changes.

## Speaking to Our Faculty of Faith

2:18 "To the angel of the assembly in Thyatira[1] write:

"The Son of God, who has his eyes like a flame of fire, and his feet are like burnished brass, says these things:

2:19 "I know your works, your love, faith, service, patient endurance, and that your last works are more than the first. 2:20 But I have this against you, that you tolerate your[13] woman, Jezebel,[2] who calls herself a prophetess. She teaches and seduces my servants to commit sexual immorality, and to eat things sacrificed to idols. 2:21 I gave her time to repent, but she refuses to repent of her sexual immorality. 2:22 Behold, I will throw her into a bed, and those who commit adultery with her into great oppression, unless they repent of her works. 2:23 I will kill her children with Death,[3] and all the assemblies will know that I am he who searches the minds and hearts. I will give to each one of you according to your deeds. 2:24 But to you I say, to the rest who are in Thyatira, as many as don't have this teaching, who don't know what some call 'the deep things of Satan,' to you I say, I am not putting any other burden on you. 2:25 Nevertheless, hold firmly that which you have, until I come. 2:26 He who overcomes, and he who keeps my works to the end, to him I will give authority over the nations. 2:27 He will rule them with a rod of iron,[4] shattering them like clay pots;[14] as I also have received of my Father: 2:28 and I will give him the morning star. 2:29 He who has an ear, let him hear what the Spirit says to the assemblies.

1. *the assembly in Thyatira.* Metaphysically, Thyatira is the intense desire of the soul for the higher expressions of life (burning incense, inspired, perfume). Zeal is the central thought represented by this church; it is also connected with power and faith. (MBD/Thyatira)

2. *Jezebel.* The animal soul, unbridled passions of sense consciousness. The animal soul is connected with the animal nature; it also becomes connected with the spiritual, and the individual becomes zealous for both the sense and the spiritual. Metaphysically, this is to commit fornication or adultery, the mixing spiritual thoughts so that they come into action. (MBD/Jezebel)

3. *I will kill her children with Death.* The end of errors, sicknesses, pains, and the thousand and one inharmonies and discords that come about because of our zealous desire to do things apart from wisdom.

4. *a rod of iron.* The rod represents spiritual power and life and of mastery, a symbol of our Christ dominion. When we have gained the Christ mastery, it is expressed in our thoughts as order and strength and in our body as life. (MBD/rod)

Fillmore Study Bible annotations compiled by Rev. Jim Ernstsen and Rev. Lisa Herklotz.

**World English Bible Footnotes:**

[10] v2:3. TR adds "have labored and"

[11] v2:15. TR reads "which I hate" instead of "likewise"

[12] v2:17. Manna is supernatural food, named after the Hebrew for "What is it?". See Exodus 11:7-9.

[13] v2:20. TR, NU read "that" instead of "your"

[14] v2:27. Psalm 2:9

# Revelation 3

## Speaking to Our Dominion and Joy

3:1 "And to the angel of the
assembly in Sardis[1] write:

"He who has the seven Spirits of
God, and the seven stars says these
things:

"I know your works, that you have
a reputation of being alive, but you
are dead.[2] 3:2 Wake up, and keep
the things that remain, which you
were about to throw away, for I have
found no works of yours perfected
before my God. 3:3 Remember
therefore how you have received and
heard. Keep it, and repent. If
therefore you won't watch,[3] I will
come as a thief, and you won't know
what hour I will come upon you. 3:4
Nevertheless you have a few names
in Sardis that did not defile their
garments. They will walk with me
in white,[4] for they are worthy. 3:5
He who overcomes will be arrayed
in white garments, and I will in no
way blot his name out of the book
of life,[5] and I will confess his name
before my Father, and before his
angels. 3:6 He who has an ear, let
him hear what the Spirit says to the
assemblies.

1. *The assembly in Sardis.* Sardis was the capital city of ancient Lydia and one of the important cities of the Persian Empire. Sardis is in modern day Turkey's Manisa Province. Metaphysically, Sardis refers to that place within you where you are able to, in a sense, gather yourself and exercise the spiritual power, dominion, and authority which is yours and exercise it in a positive, constructive, and beneficial way. (Ed Rabel/Revelation/Sardis)

2. *you have a reputation of being alive, but you are dead.* A mixing of praise and criticism within one statement. They indicate that the Christ Mind judges that we have been using our individual power and dominion in an only slightly satisfactory way. We are divine, and yet our individual power and dominion is remaining dormant for the most part. (USRS Bible Interp/Rev 5)

3. *watch.* A persistent looking toward the fulfillment of divine ideals. (RW/watch)

4. *walk with me in white.* White garments is a symbol of both clean feeling about one's self, and a pure, non-negative attitude connected with self-control. (USRS)

5. *blot his name out of the book of life.* To have a feeling of being useless in God's world. A feeling of suffering a loss of individuality. (USRS)

## Speaking to Our Love Thoughts in Consciousness

3:7 "To the angel of the assembly in Philadelphia[1] write:

"He who is holy, he who is true, he who has the key of David,[2] he who opens and no one can shut,[3] and who shuts and no one opens, says these things:

3:8 "I know your works (behold, I have set before you an open door, which no one can shut), that you have a little power, and kept my word, and didn't deny my name. 3:9 Behold, I give of the synagogue of Satan,[4] of those who say they are Jews, and they are not, but lie. Behold, I will make them to come and worship before your feet, and to know that I have loved you. 3:10 Because you kept my command to endure, I also will keep you from the hour of testing, which is to come on the whole world, to test those who dwell on the earth. 3:11 I am coming quickly! Hold firmly that which you have, so that no one takes your crown. 3:12 He who overcomes, I will make him a pillar in the temple of my God,[5] and he will go out from there no more. I will write on him the name of my God, and the name of the city of my God, the new Jerusalem, which comes down out of heaven from my God, and my own new name. 3:13 He who has an ear, let him hear what the Spirit says to the assemblies.

1. *the assembly in Philadelphia.* Philadelphia is a city in ancient Lydia, Asia Minor. The Greek word for brotherly love. Metaphysically, the church represents our faculty of love or the assembly of love thoughts in consciousness. (MBD/Philadelphia)

2. *key of David.* He who has the "key of David" is the I AM. This I AM in its highest aspect is Christ. (MBD)

3. *no one can shut.* Wherever you are, whatever you are doing in any time, place, or circumstances, you will always have opportunities open for your love nature to give and receive some kind of love. (Ed Rabel/Revelation/Philadelphia)

4. *the synagogue of Satan.* If the "I AM" love thoughts are dominated by selfishness they become "the synagogue of Satan." (MBD/Philadelphia)

5. *a pillar in the temple of my God.* That state of inner peace, poise, and stability, which comes from correctly thinking about and giving and receiving the pure love. ( Ed Rabel)

## Speaking to Our Faculty of Judgment

3:14 "To the angel of the assembly in Laodicea[1] write:

"The Amen, the Faithful and True Witness, the Head of God's creation, says these things:

3:15 "I know your works, that you are neither cold nor hot. I wish you were cold or hot. 3:16 So, because you are lukewarm,[2] and neither hot nor cold, I will vomit you out of my mouth. 3:17 Because you say, 'I am rich, and have gotten riches, and have need of nothing;'[3] and don't know that you are the wretched one, miserable, poor, blind, and naked; 3:18 I counsel you to buy from me gold refined by fire, that you may become rich; and white garments, that you may clothe yourself, and that the shame of your nakedness may not be revealed; and eye salve to anoint your eyes, that you may see. 3:19 As many as I love, I reprove and chasten. Be zealous therefore, and repent. 3:20 Behold, I stand at the door and knock.[4] If anyone hears my voice and opens the door, then I will come in to him, and will dine with him, and he with me. 3:21 He who overcomes, I will give to him to sit down with me on my throne,[5] as I also overcame, and sat down with my Father on his throne. 3:22 He who has an ear, let him hear what the Spirit says to the assemblies."

1. *the assembly in Laodicea.* Laodicea is a city in ancient Phrygia, Asia Minor, about forty miles from Ephesus. Metaphysically, the church represents the faculty of judgment in each person. It is the phase of judgment which bases its decisions on outer seemings and intellectual reasonings. (MBD/Laodicea)

2. *because you are lukewarm.* Criticism pertaining to our lack of true discernment, and our human reluctance and fear about making personal decisions. (Ed Rabel/Revelation/Laodicea)

3. *have need of nothing.* It is foolish for us to become too sure of the infallibility and complete self-sufficiency of our human judgment on its current level of development. No matter how good our judgment may have begun to be, human judgment still needs constant help from a higher source. (Rabel)

4. *I stand at the door and knock.* If we, as individuals, open our mind and heart to the Christ Mind, ask for it to enter, it will do so. (Rabel)

5. *sit down with me on my throne.* Good judgment is always called a throne, and we are told here by the Christ Mind that if we want to sit on the throne, we are aware of our own high state of inner good judgment. Through judgment, check your motive, make sure that your motive for evaluating anything, and for making any decision, is to do what is right and best. (Rabel)

Fillmore Study Bible annotations compiled by Rev. Jim Ernstsen and Rev. Lisa Herklotz.

# Revelation 4

## The Soul in a Higher State of Consciousness

4:1 After these things I looked and saw a door opened in heaven,[1] and the first voice that I heard, like a trumpet speaking with me, was one saying, "Come up here, and I will show you the things which must happen after this."

4:2 Immediately I was in the Spirit. Behold, there was a throne set in heaven, and one sitting on the throne[2] 4:3 that looked like a jasper stone and a sardius. There was a rainbow around the throne, like an emerald to look at.[3] 4:4 Around the throne were twenty-four thrones. On the thrones were twenty-four elders sitting, dressed in white garments, with crowns of gold on their heads.[4] 4:5 Out of the throne proceed lightnings, sounds, and thunders. There were seven lamps of fire burning before his throne, which are the seven Spirits of God. 4:6 Before the throne was something like a sea of glass, similar to crystal. In the midst of the throne, and around the throne were four living creatures[5] full of eyes before and behind. 4:7 The first creature was like a lion, and the second creature like a calf, and the third creature had a face like a man, and the fourth was like a flying eagle. 4:8 The four living creatures, each one of them having six wings,[6] are full of eyes around and within. They have no rest day and night, saying, "Holy, holy, holy[15] is the

Lord God, the Almighty, who was and
who is and who is to come!"

4:9 When the living creatures give
glory, honor, and thanks to him who
sits on the throne, to him who lives
forever and ever, 4:10 the twenty-four
elders fall down before him who sits
on the throne, and worship him who
lives forever and ever, and throw
their crowns before the throne,
saying, 4:11 "Worthy are you, our Lord
and God, the Holy One,[16] to receive
the glory,[7] the honor, and the
power, for you created all things,
and because of your desire they
existed, and were created!"

1. *saw a door opened in heaven.* The scene shifts from earth to heaven. John has spoken to our earthly faculties. He now elevates our attention to our higher state of consciousness as a represented by heaven. (Frank Guidici/Revelation-4)

2. *a throne set in heaven, and one sitting on the throne.* The great symbol which describes the sense of the presence of God. Knowing that this presence is One requires metaphysical thinking for comprehension. God is ONE but not in the sense of one object, one person, or one being. God is ONE in the true meaning of oneness itself. (USRS Bible Interp/Rev 8)

3. *like an emerald to look at.* Precious jewels and rainbows have the appearances they have because of the effects of light. Without the radiance of light, we could not perceive the preciousness of jewels nor the beauty of a rainbow. Equating this idea with the description of the God presence, we are able to perceive God's presence only as there is light in our consciousness. Light is the biblical symbol of living intelligence and spiritual awareness. (USRS)

4. *twenty-four elders sitting, dressed in white garments, with crowns of gold on their heads.* Our twelve powers have a powerful beneficial action on our own inner nature, and outwardly into our life conditions and affairs. This two-fold direction of their benefits is symbolized in the number twenty-four. *Clad in white garments:* imbued with pure power; *wore crowns of gold:* increase greatly in value to our spiritual unfoldment; *elders:* find expression in a very stable and mature manner. (USRS)

5. *four living creatures.* The four main aspects of human nature. *lion*: our physicality, the physical body; *calf*: our subjective and emotional nature, the emotional or astral body; *man*: our mental or intellectual nature, the mental body; *eagle*: our inspirational and intuitive nature, the etheric body. (USRS)

6. *six wings.* Wings symbolize freedom from material limitation. (RW/wings)

7. *glory.* The realization of divine unity; the blending and merging of man's mind with God-Mind (RW/glory)

---

Fillmore Study Bible annotations compiled by Rev. Jim Ernstsen and Rev. Lisa Herklotz.

**World English Bible Footnotes:**

[15] v4:8. Hodges/Farstad MT reads "holy" 9 times instead of 3.

[16] v4:11. TR omits "and God, the Holy One,"

# Revelation 5

## A Vision of Overcoming in the Soul

5:1 I saw, in the right hand of him
who sat on the throne, a book
written inside and outside, sealed
shut with seven seals.[1] 5:2 I saw a
mighty angel proclaiming with a loud
voice, "Who is worthy to open the
book, and to break its seals?" 5:3 No
one in heaven above, or on the
earth, or under the earth, was able
to open the book, or to look in it.[2]
5:4 And I wept much, because no one
was found worthy to open the book,
or to look in it. 5:5 One of the elders
said to me, "Don't weep. Behold, the
Lion[3] who is of the tribe of Judah,
the Root of David,[4] has overcome;[5]
he who opens the book and its seven
seals." 5:6 I saw in the midst of the
throne and of the four living
creatures, and in the midst of the
elders, a Lamb standing,[6] as though
it had been slain, having seven horns,
and seven eyes, which are the seven
Spirits of God, sent out into all the
earth. 5:7 Then he came, and he took
it out of the right hand of him who
sat on the throne. 5:8 Now when he
had taken the book, the four living
creatures and the twenty-four elders
fell down before the Lamb, each one
having a harp, and golden bowls full
of incense, which are the prayers of
the saints. 5:9 They sang a new song,
saying,

"You are worthy to take the book,
and to open its seals:
for you were killed,
and bought us for God with
your blood,
out of every tribe, language,
people, and nation,
5:10 and made us kings and priests to
our God,
and we will reign on earth."

5:11 I saw, and I heard something
like a voice[7] of many angels around
the throne, the living creatures, and
the elders; and the number of them
was ten thousands of ten thousands,
and thousands of thousands; 5:12
saying with a loud voice, "Worthy is
the Lamb who has been killed to
receive the power, wealth, wisdom,
strength, honor, glory, and blessing!"

5:13 I heard every created thing
which is in heaven, on the earth,[8]
under the earth, on the sea, and
everything in them, saying, "To him
who sits on the throne, and to the
Lamb be the blessing, the honor, the
glory, and the dominion, forever and
ever! Amen![17]"

5:14 The four living creatures said,
"Amen!" The [18]elders fell down and
worshiped.[19]

1. *a book written inside and outside, sealed shut with seven seals.* The book, as used here, refers to our own individual self, or the sum total of our present development of consciousness. The seals on the book represent barriers to our process of insight. (Ed Rabel/Revelation/Chapter 5)

2. *No one in heaven above, or on the earth, or under the earth, was able to open the book, or to look in it.* Most persons are not yet capable of full insight into themselves because of the presence of certain mental or emotional barriers, or blocks, seals. (Ed Rabel)

3. *the Lion.* Jesus Christ purified His substance and His life and lifted them up until His life became a pure stream of divine life to cleanse us. The 5th chapter of Revelation reveals the full inner meaning of the atonement, of Jesus Christ's redeeming work on earth. If we understand it fully we shall understand the inner working of the divine principle in its redeeming work in our whole being. (MBD/lion)

4. *the Root of David.* Jesus was descended from David. That's an important point that's made throughout the New Testament in the genealogy of Jesus, it's recorded in both Matthew and Luke. He's descended from the House of David. Because the belief developed that the Messiah was to come through the House of David. (Frank Guidici/Revelation-5)

5. *has overcome.* To correct thoughts that fall short of the divine ideal. (RW/overcome)

6. *a Lamb standing.* The lamb of Revelation stands for the gentle, kind, and forgiving nature of our inner Christ self. The Christ self of us is completely and totally harmless, absolutely understanding and forgiving, and mighty with a power, which cannot be measured. Only in this Christ-awareness, the lamb of God of you, can you or I ever gain insight into our whole nature, which leads to that eventual, priceless blessing called self-understanding. (Ed Rabel)

7. *voice.* The power center in the throat controls all the vibratory energies of this organism. It is the open door between the formless and the formed worlds of vibrations pertaining to the expression of sound. Every word that goes forth receives its specific character from the power faculty. Therefore, the voice is the most direct avenue of expression of consciousness. (RW/voice)

8. *in heaven, on the earth.* See annotation for 4:1.

Fillmore Study Bible annotations compiled by Rev. Jim Ernstsen and Rev. Lisa Herklotz.

**World English Bible Footnotes:**

[17] v5:13. TR omits "Amen!"

[18] v5:14. TR adds "twenty-four"

[19] v5:14. TR adds "the one living forever and ever"

# Revelation 6

## The Chemicalization in Consciousness

6:1 I saw that the Lamb opened one
of the seven seals,1 and I heard one
of the four living creatures saying, as
with a voice of thunder, "Come and
see!" 6:2 And behold, a white horse,
and he who sat on it had a bow.2 A
crown was given to him, and he came
forth conquering, and to conquer.

6:3 When he opened the second
seal, I heard the second living
creature saying, "Come!" 6:4 Another
came forth, a red horse. To him who
sat on it was given power to take
peace from the earth,3 and that
they should kill one another. There
was given to him a great sword.

6:5 When he opened the third seal,
I heard the third living creature
saying, "Come and see!" And behold,
a black horse, and he who sat on
it had a balance in his hand.4 6:6 I
heard a voice in the midst of the four
living creatures saying, "A choenix[20]
of wheat for a denarius,5 and three
choenix of barley for a denarius!
Don't damage the oil and the wine!"

6:7 When he opened the fourth

seal, I heard the fourth living
creature saying, "Come and see!" 6:8
And behold, a pale horse, and he who
sat on it, his name was Death.[6]
Hades[21] followed with him.
Authority over one fourth of the
earth, to kill with the sword, with
famine, with death, and by the wild
animals of the earth was given to
him.

6:9 When he opened the fifth seal,
I saw underneath the altar the souls
of those who had been killed for the
Word of God, and for the testimony
of the Lamb which they had. 6:10 They
cried with a loud voice, saying, "How
long, Master, the holy and true, until
you judge and avenge our blood[7] on
those who dwell on the earth?" 6:11
A long white robe was given to each
of them. They were told that they
should rest yet for a while,[8] until
their fellow servants and their
brothers,[22] who would also be
killed even as they were, should
complete their course.

6:12 I saw when he opened the sixth
seal, and there was a great
earthquake.[9] The sun became black
as sackcloth made of hair, and the
whole moon became as blood. 6:13
The stars of the sky fell to the earth,
like a fig tree dropping its unripe figs
when it is shaken by a great wind.
6:14 The sky was removed like a scroll
when it is rolled up. Every mountain
and island were moved out of their
places. 6:15 The kings of the earth, the
princes, the commanding officers,
the rich, the strong, and every slave
and free person, hid themselves in
the caves and in the rocks of the
mountains. 6:16 They told the
mountains and the rocks, "Fall on us,
and hide us from the face of him
who sits on the throne, and from the
wrath of the Lamb, 6:17 for the great
day of his wrath has come; and who
is able to stand?"

1. *seven seals, horse.* These openings represent the gaining of insight into our own individual nature which comes to us when we let the Christ spirit become the directive power in our search for true inner understanding. Each seal opens a new facet of ourself to our own understanding. The four horsemen are symbols of very strong influences which are currently very active in human beings' consciousness.(Ed Rabel/Revelation/Chapter 6)

2. *a white horse, and he who sat on it had a bow.* The white horse and rider is our awareness of Christ within. This comes before all else, conquers all else and remains after all else has come and gone. Christ within is king of all our world-the inner world, heaven and outer world, earth. If we ride the white horse, which represents our spiritual nature and if we give power to our spiritual nature, then everything will be just fine in our life. (Ed Rabel) and (Frank Giudici/Revelation 6)

3. *a red horse. To him who sat on it was given power to take peace from the earth.* The red horse and rider stand for all our tendencies toward violence. Red in the Bible is the color which symbolizes passions and violence and this is a very active tendency in human nature. Those of us who give power to the red horse, who let emotions rule, which represents the emotional nature, don't lead a very peaceful life. (Rabel) and (Giudici)

4. *a black horse, and he who sat on it had a balance in his hand.* The black horse and rider symbolize the intellectual nature. If we're too intellectual in life then we have to balance it with emotion, with love. Riding the black horse all the time can make us too intellectual, and turn us off to people. (Rabel) and (Giudici)

5. *I heard a voice in the midst of the four living creatures saying, "A choenix of wheat for a denarius".* This saying indicates thoughts of anxiety.

6. *a pale horse, and he who sat on it, his name was Death.* The pale horse and rider stand for the belief in the inevitability of death. Riding the pale horse is the one who wants to live his life on a physical basis, giving power to outer things, material wealth. Until the truth behind it is fully understood, this pale horse and rider will continue to play havoc with our human attitude toward the meaning of life. (Rabel) and (Giudici)

7. *"How long, Master, the holy and true, until you judge and avenge our blood".* Words of old disappointments and unhappy memories of being mistreated. These memories in us want to be assured that God's law of divine justice works. They

need to be released from our subconscious (under the altar). (USRS Bible Interp/Rev 9)

8. *They were told that they should rest yet for a while.* The assurance from the Christ Mind that God's law of divine compensation (justice) is always working, no matter how things may outwardly seem. (USRS)

9. *there was a great earthquake.* The imagery of this sixth vision is so complex that it seems to defy analysis but it describes the process of God's Law of Divine Justice and Compensation always working for our benefit. The earthquake symbolizes seeming chaos and confusion in our lives that becomes our greatest compensations and rewards. All of this upheaval that must take place is not just on an earthly level, it's on a universal level. So everything is affected. The writer brings this idea out by painting these tremendous things that are going to happen here. These also picture the idea of divine intervention. These are all acts of God. (Rabel) and (Giudici)

---

 Fillmore Study Bible annotations compiled by Rev. Jim Ernstsen and Rev. Lisa Herklotz.

**World English Bible Footnotes:**

[20] v6:6. A choenix is a dry volume measure that is a little more than a litre (a little more than a quart).

[21] v6:8. or, Hell

[22] v6:11. The word for "brothers" here and where context allows may also be correctly translated "brothers and sisters" or "siblings."

# Revelation 7

## The Four Corners of Consciousness [1]

7:1 After this, I saw four angels
standing at the four corners of the
earth, holding the four winds of the
earth, so that no wind would blow on
the earth, or on the sea, or on any
tree. 7:2 I saw another angel ascend
from the sunrise, having the seal of
the living God. He cried with a loud
voice to the four angels to whom it
was given to harm the earth and the
sea, 7:3 saying, "Don't harm the earth,
neither the sea, nor the trees, until
we have sealed the bondservants of
our God on their foreheads!" [2] 7:4 I
heard the number of those who were
sealed, one hundred forty-four
thousand, [3] sealed out of every tribe
of the children of Israel: [4]

7:5 of the tribe of Judah were
sealed twelve thousand,
of the tribe of Reuben twelve
thousand,
of the tribe of Gad twelve
thousand,
7:6 of the tribe of Asher twelve
thousand,
of the tribe of Naphtali twelve
thousand,
of the tribe of Manasseh twelve
thousand,
7:7 of the tribe of Simeon twelve
thousand,
of the tribe of Levi twelve
thousand,
of the tribe of Issachar twelve

thousand,
7:8 of the tribe of Zebulun twelve thousand,
of the tribe of Joseph twelve thousand,
of the tribe of Benjamin were sealed twelve thousand.

1. This chapter describes how we are saved; by bringing all our faculties into spiritual consciousness and dwelling in it. When this consciousness is complete, we are wholly at one with God and Christ. After the 6 seals are opened, and before the 7th is opened, there is a shift, an interlude which comes into the picture. The four winds at the four corners of the earth, believed to be harmful, are held back as there is a pause in the action.(Frank Guidici, Revelation 7)

2. *Sealed the bondservants of our God on their foreheads!* Historically, when they were performing emperor worship and bringing their sacrifices and offerings to the emperor, then they received a mark. He's contrasting this mark by saying that those who are faithful to God are going to have their foreheads sealed, but in a very special way.

3. *One hundred forty-four thousand.* A wide number of people, 12 times 12: The 12 tribes and the 12 apostles. Seven represents fullness in the world of phenomena; twelve is the number of fulfillment in the spiritual (MBD/seven).

4. *Israel.* Israel as a nation, in its highest significance, symbolizes spiritual consciousness. The thoughts that have been wrought in Truth and righteousness make the spiritual mind, or spiritual consciousness (MBD/Israel).

## The Multitude from Purified Thoughts

7:9 After these things I looked, and
behold, a great multitude,(1) which
no man could number, out of every
nation and of all tribes, peoples, and
languages, standing before the
throne(2) and before the Lamb,(3)
dressed in white robes,(4) with palm
branches in their hands. 7:10 They
cried with a loud voice, saying,
"Salvation be to our God, who sits on
the throne, and to the Lamb!"

7:11 All the angels were standing
around the throne, the elders, and
the four living creatures;(5) and they
fell on their faces before his throne,
and worshiped God, 7:12 saying,
"Amen! Blessing, glory, wisdom,
thanksgiving, honor, power, and
might, be to our God forever and
ever! Amen."

7:13 One of the elders answered,
saying to me, "These who are arrayed
in white robes, who are they, and
from where did they come?"

7:14 I told him, "My lord, you know."

He said to me, "These are those
who came out of the great
tribulation. They washed their robes,
and made them white in the Lamb's
blood.(6) 7:15 Therefore they are
before the throne of God,(7) they
serve him day and night in his
temple.(8) He who sits on the throne
will spread his tent(9) over them. 7:16
They will never be hungry, neither
thirsty any more;(10) neither will the
sun beat on them, nor any heat; 7:17
for the Lamb who is in the midst
of the throne shepherds them, and
leads them to springs of waters of
life. And God will wipe away every
tear from their eyes."

1. *A great multitude, which no man could number.* As people, those who through the Christ consciousness have overcome the tribulations that are common to all humankind. The multitude was "out of every nation and of all tribes and peoples and tongues." More metaphysically, the great multitude is a host of purified thoughts-thoughts that have passed through the "refiner's fire" and have come out cleansed of the consciousness of sin.

2. *Throne.* The focal point within the soul where the power of unselfish love, purified life-all the constructive forces of Spirit-have gained such a foothold that they

form a nucleus or basis from which Spirit exercises its dominion.

3. *Lamb* The lamb is the pure, innocent sinless life of God, poured into the race consciousness through Jesus Christ.

4. *Robes.* The robes are the vital aura surrounding the body, which is redeemed and made white through a realization of the Christ Life, as the one purifying energy and substance. The palms are symbols of the victory of purity over sin.

5. *Angels, elders, four living creatures.* Angels represent the original, unlimited thoughts of God; the elders are the redeemed faculties and the four living creatures are the purified elemental forces.

6. *Washed their robes, and made them white in the Lamb's blood.* The blood of the Lamb is the life of Christ, and the robes are the thoughts in which humans "clothe" their ideas. When our thought life is cleansed by the Christ Spirit, we are indeed an overcomer.

7. *Throne of God.* The center of thought in Divine Mind.

8. *Serve him day and night in his temple.* The body is the temple of God, and the purified thoughts carry on all of the bodily activities under the divine law.

9. *Tent (Tabernacle, ASV).* Where we dwell in the universal substance of Being (MBD/tabernacle).

10. *They will never be hungry, neither thirsty any more.* It is an indication of the change that takes place in humankind's consciousness, when the material outlook is dropped and spiritual realm is realized. It does not refer to physical death. ... This describes the condition we will achieve when all our thoughts are purified and raised to spiritual consciousness.

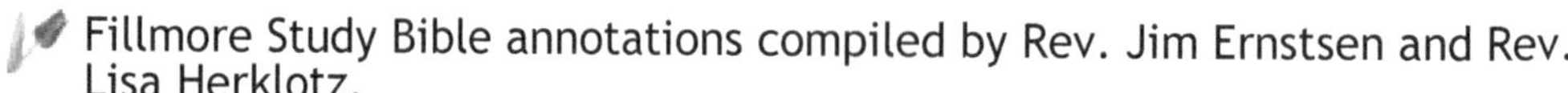

Fillmore Study Bible annotations compiled by Rev. Jim Ernstsen and Rev. Lisa Herklotz.

# Revelation 8

## Silence, then Thunder

8:1 When he opened the seventh
seal, there was silence in heaven(1)
for about half an hour. 8:2 I saw the
seven angels who stand before God,
and seven trumpets(2) were given to
them. 8:3 Another angel came and
stood over the altar, having a golden
censer. Much incense was given to
him, that he should add it to the
prayers of all the saints on the
golden altar which was before the
throne. 8:4 The smoke of the
incense,(3) with the prayers of the
saints, went up before God out of
the angel's hand. 8:5 The angel took
the censer, and he filled it with the
fire of the altar, and threw it on
the earth. There followed thunders,
sounds, lightnings, and an
earthquake.(4)

1. *Silence in heaven.* Metaphysically, a state of consciousness entered into for the purpose of putting man in touch with Divine Mind (RW/silence). Here we have the grand climax to the narrative concerning the opening of the seven seals and also have symbolized the climax of all the steps leading to full self-understanding. The final and greatest step in self-discovery is achieved in the realization of how to become still, how to find silence within. This is a mark of the high spiritual development. It places a person in heaven, because true silence occurs only in heaven, and it results in miracles on earth (Ed Rabel, The Book of Revelation, chapter 8).

2. *Seven trumpets.* Metaphysically, the seven seals can represent the process of denial. We'll see that in order to bring a

demonstration into our life we deny, then we affirm something, and then the demonstration occurs. The seven seals in a very general way are the denial process. The seven trumpets are the Affirmation. (Giudici, Revelation 8)

3. *Smoke of the incense.* The smoke in the incense going up represents what was traditionally done in the temple. During times of prayer, they burned incense and this was symbolic of prayers going up to God (Giudici).

4. *Thunders, sounds, lightnings, and an earthquake.* All of these things are manifestations of God. Any time the fire and loud noises are brought out in the scripture, it means the activities are manifestations of God (Giudici).

## Afflictions are Partial❶

8:6 The seven angels who had the seven trumpets prepared themselves to sound. 8:7 The first sounded, and there followed hail and fire, mixed with blood, and they were thrown to the earth.❷ One third of the earth was burnt up,[23] and one third of the trees were burnt up, and all green grass was burnt up.

8:8 The second angel sounded, and something like a great burning mountain was thrown into the sea.❸ One third of the sea became blood, 8:9 and one third of the living creatures which were in the sea died. One third of the ships were destroyed.

8:10 The third angel sounded, and a great star fell from the sky, burning like a torch, and it fell on one third of the rivers, and on the springs of the waters.❹ 8:11 The name of the star is called "Wormwood." One third of the waters became wormwood. Many people died from the waters, because they were made bitter.

8:12 The fourth angel sounded, and one third of the sun was struck, and one third of the moon, and one third of the stars; so that one third of them would be darkened, and the day wouldn't shine for one third of it, and the night in the same way. 8:13 I saw, and I heard an eagle,[24] flying in mid heaven,❺ saying with a loud voice, "Woe! Woe! Woe for those who dwell on the earth, because of the other voices of the trumpets of the three angels, who are yet to sound!"

1. These visions describe only part of the Earth and its inhabitants to be afflicted at any given time. This fact symbolizes an important metaphysical point. Only a certain part of a person's being can suffer; not one's entire being. And only a portion of one's existence can be afflicted at any given time; not one's whole life. This may seem scant comfort, but at least it offers some comfort. Forms of earthly suffering, such as pain, disappointment, depression, anxiety, grief, lack, etc.; even though these hurt part of the man (1/3 of the earth), they do not and cannot harm the whole man. The Real Self of a person is always higher and greater than any part of himself that is suffering. And, eventually, new good can be brought forth even from suffering. (USRS Bible Interpretation, Revelation Lesson 9).

2. *Earth.* Metaphysically speaking, the earth represents the consciousness of the physical body (RW/earth).

3. *Sea.* The universal sensate thought of the race, which is to be dissolved and cast into the bottomless pit of nothingness (MBD/sea).

4. *Springs of water.* Water represents material cleansing, and fire represents spiritual cleansing (MBD/water).

5. *Heaven.* A state of consciousness in harmony with the thoughts of God. Heaven is everywhere (RW/heaven).

Fillmore Study Bible annotations compiled by Rev. Jim Ernstsen and Rev.

Lisa Herklotz.

**World English Bible Footnotes:**

[23] v8:7. TR omits "One third of the earth was burnt up"

[24] v8:13. TR reads "angel" instead of "eagle"

# Revelation 9

## Afflictions are Temporary

9:1 The fifth angel sounded, and I saw a star from the sky which had fallen to the earth. The key to the pit of the abyss was given to him. 9:2 He opened the pit of the abyss, and smoke went up out of the pit, like the smoke from a[25] burning furnace. The sun and the air were darkened because of the smoke from the pit. 9:3 Then out of the smoke came forth locusts on the earth, and power was given to them, as the scorpions of the earth have power. 9:4 They were told that they should not hurt the grass of the earth, neither any green thing, neither any tree, but only those people who don't have God's seal on their foreheads. 9:5 They were given power not to kill them, but to torment them for five months. Their torment was like the torment of a scorpion, when it strikes a person. 9:6 In those days people will seek death, and will in no way find it. They will desire to die, and death will flee from them. 9:7 The shapes of the locusts were like horses prepared for war. On their heads were something like golden crowns, and their faces were like people's faces. 9:8 They had hair like women's hair, and their teeth were like those of lions. 9:9 They had breastplates, like breastplates of iron. The sound of their wings was like the sound of chariots, or of many horses rushing to war. 9:10 They have tails like those of scorpions, and stings. In their tails they have power to harm men for five months. 9:11 They have over them as king the angel of the abyss. His name in Hebrew is "Abaddon,"[26] but in Greek, he has the name "Apollyon."[27] 9:12 The first woe is past. Behold, there are still two woes coming after this.

9:13 The sixth angel sounded. I heard a voice from the horns of the golden altar which is before God, 9:14 saying to the sixth angel who had one trumpet, "Free the four angels who are bound at the great river Euphrates!"

9:15 The four angels were freed who had been prepared for that hour and day and month and year, so that they might kill one third of mankind. 9:16 The number of the armies of the horsemen was two hundred million[28]. I heard the number of them. 9:17 Thus I saw the horses in the vision, and those who sat on them, having breastplates of fiery red, hyacinth blue, and sulfur yellow; and the heads of lions. Out of their mouths proceed fire, smoke, and sulfur. 9:18 By these three plagues were one third of mankind killed: by the fire, the smoke, and the sulfur, which proceeded out of their

mouths. 9:19 For the power of the
horses is in their mouths, and in their
tails. For their tails are like serpents,
and have heads, and with them they
harm. 9:20 The rest of mankind, who
were not killed with these plagues,
didn't repent of the works of their
hands, that they wouldn't worship
demons, and the idols of gold, and
of silver, and of brass, and of stone,
and of wood; which can neither see,
nor hear, nor walk. 9:21 They didn't
repent of their murders, nor of their
sorceries,[29] nor of their sexual
immorality, nor of their thefts.

1. These symbolic visions in chapter eight and nine are temporary disasters. None afflict the earth permanently. This is true of all suffering. It is always temporary. Suffering may be a part of a cycle within a person's life, but it does not become a person's life. A person's life is eternal, and nothing that occurs as a part of that life, however, is eternal. Events and conditions are always temporary, and this is especially so regarding any form of suffering experience. Forms of earthly suffering such as pain, sadness, depression, anxiety, sorrow, lack, even though these do hurt part of the man and part of his life, 1/3 of the earth and its inhabitants, they do not and cannot harm the whole man and his whole life. Part of a person is always higher and greater than whatever may be going on in any part of him or any part of his life. (Ed Rabel The Book of Revelation 9).

2. *His name in Hebrew is "Abaddon," but in Greek, he has the name "Apollyon".* Metaphysically, the name refers to destroyer; destruction. In Exodus and Joel, as well as in Revelations, locusts represent great destructive power. They quite commonly came up like great armies and ate every living plant in their path; also, the leaves and the branches of the trees. So Abaddon must stand for the error belief in utter destruction of life and form. The true life principle can never be destroyed; only the outer form of man's belief in materiality is destructible. So long as man believes in materiality or destruction, the outer destruction of forms will take place. (MBD/abaddon).

---

Fillmore Study Bible annotations compiled by Rev. Jim Ernstsen and Rev. Lisa Herklotz.

**World English Bible Footnotes:**

[25] v9:2. TR adds "great"

[26] v9:11. "Abaddon" is a Hebrew word that means ruin, destruction, or the place of destruction

[27] v9:11. "Apollyon" means "Destroyer."

[28] v9:16. literally, "ten thousands of ten thousands"

[29] v9:21. The word for "sorceries" (pharmakeia) also implies the use of potions, poisons, and drugs

# Revelation 10

## The Angel with the Little Scroll

10:1 I saw a mighty angel coming
down out of the sky, clothed with a
cloud. A rainbow was on his head.
His face was like the sun, and his

feet like pillars of fire. 10:2 He had in his hand a little open book.[1] He set his right foot on the sea, and his left on the land. 10:3 He cried with a loud voice, as a lion roars. When he cried, the seven thunders uttered their voices.[2] 10:4 When the seven thunders sounded, I was about to write; but I heard a voice from the sky saying, "Seal up the things which the seven thunders said, and don't write them."[3]

10:5 The angel who I saw standing on the sea and on the land lifted up his right hand to the sky, 10:6 and swore by him who lives forever and ever, who created heaven and the things that are in it, the earth and the things that are in it, and the sea and the things that are in it, that there will no longer be delay, 10:7 but in the days of the voice of the seventh angel, when he is about to sound, then the mystery of God is finished, as he declared to his servants, the prophets. 10:8 The voice which I heard from heaven, again speaking with me, said, "Go, take the book which is open in the hand of the angel who stands on the sea and on the land."

10:9 I went to the angel, telling him to give me the little book.

He said to me, "Take it, and eat it up. It will make your stomach bitter, but in your mouth it will be as sweet as honey."[4]

10:10 I took the little book out of the angel's hand, and ate it up. It was as sweet as honey in my mouth. When I had eaten it, my stomach was made bitter. 10:11 They told me, "You must prophesy again over many peoples, nations, languages, and kings."

1. *He had in his hand a little open book.* The little book stands for the letter of truth teaching in the form of a body of knowledge, which can be learned (Ed Rabel The Book of Revelation 10).

2. *When he cried, the seven thunders uttered their voices.* Here he sees another mighty angel who appears with a scroll in his hand and the angel speaks and seven thunders boom, which means another series of judgements is about to come (Giudici, Revelation 10).

3. *Seal up the things which the seven thunders said, and don't write them.* The writer is told to seal, not reveal, because these must be revealed at the right time (Giudici).

4. *Take it, and eat it up. It will make your stomach bitter, but in your mouth it will be as sweet as honey.* Metaphysically, to eat is to appropriate, to become conscious of the food that "abideth unto eternal life," and to use it (RW/eat). When our perceptive faculties first come in contact with the teachings they often make sweet and beautiful impressions . But knowledge digested into consciousness can often become difficult, or bitter, when we find ourselves involved in challenging, or unpleasant life situations. Having to work with truth can be a bitter effort, sweet to the mouth, bitter in the belly, but it is only when the truth teachings become the inner effort, which can be bitter, that the truth nourishes us, and strengthens us, and causes us to become more and more conscious of our own perfection (Rabel).

---

Fillmore Study Bible annotations compiled by Rev. Jim Ernstsen and Rev. Lisa Herklotz.

# Revelation 11

## The Two Witnesses[1]

11:1 A reed like a rod was given
to me. Someone said, "Rise, and
measure God's temple, and the altar,
and those who worship in it.[2] 11:2
Leave out the court which is outside
of the temple, and don't measure
it,[3] for it has been given to the
nations. They will tread the holy city
under foot for forty-two months. 11:3
I will give power to my two
witnesses,[4] and they will prophesy
one thousand two hundred sixty
days, clothed in sackcloth." 11:4 These
are the two olive trees and the two
lampstands, standing before the Lord
of the earth. 11:5 If anyone desires to
harm them, fire proceeds out of their
mouth and devours their enemies. If
anyone desires to harm them, he
must be killed in this way. 11:6 These
have the power to shut up the sky,
that it may not rain during the days
of their prophecy. They have power
over the waters, to turn them into
blood, and to strike the earth with
every plague, as often as they desire.
11:7 When they have finished their
testimony, the beast that comes up
out of the abyss will make war with
them,[5] and overcome them,[6] and
kill them.[7] 11:8 Their dead bodies will
be in the street of the great city,
which spiritually is called Sodom and
Egypt, where also their Lord was
crucified. 11:9 From among the
peoples, tribes, languages, and
nations people will look at their dead
bodies for three and a half days, and
will not allow their dead bodies to be
laid in a tomb. 11:10 Those who dwell
on the earth rejoice over them, and
they will be glad. They will give gifts
to one another, because these two
prophets tormented those who dwell
on the earth. 11:11 After the three and
a half days,[8] the breath of life from
God entered into them, and they
stood on their feet. Great fear fell
on those who saw them. 11:12 I heard
a loud voice from heaven saying to
them, "Come up here!" They went up
into heaven in the cloud, and their
enemies saw them. 11:13 In that day
there was a great earthquake, and a
tenth of the city fell. Seven thousand
people were killed in the
earthquake, and the rest were
terrified, and gave glory to the God
of heaven. 11:14 The second woe is
past. Behold, the third woe comes
quickly.

1. The 11th chapter is representative of an inner work, something that will take place in each one as we are being transformed into the perfect image and likeness of God (MBD/witnesses). After dealing with the interpretation of Revelation up to this point, a student might understandably get a bit weary with so much reference to difficulties and suffering. For a time, most souls go through cycles of existence in which the goal of all their efforts is simply to get what they think they want, and avoid as much trouble and pain as is humanly possible. This can be the goal of life for many persons. Some may spend whole lifetimes never growing beyond this goal. But some persons grow beyond this point and begin to see that self-seeking and finding ease and pleasure are not the highest goals to seek in life. Many Truth students come to realize that *Spiritual Understanding* is the most worthwhile of all goals. Then the direction of that person's life begins to turn away from certain past preoccupations and grows into new realizations. In studying metaphysical Bible interpretation, we are attempting to learn and understand Truth which will take us out of many of the old habits and limitations of mechanical existence. While we know that the nature of life, the essence of life, and the purpose of life are GOOD, we also reconcile ourselves to the fact that there are many factors yet within life which we still react to as NOT GOOD. And it is to help us receive more light on certain of these fac-

tors that our Bible, and especially the book of Revelation, so often deals with difficult or unpleasant subjects. (USRS Bible Interpretation, Revelation Lesson 10)

2. *Measure God's temple, and the altar, and those who worship in it.* This has to do with the inner court and relates to the faithful. The faithful are to be measured and to be saved (Giudici, Revelation 11). Things are sometimes measured to find out not their size but their true value (MBD/witnesses).

3. *Leave out the court which is outside of the temple, and don't measure it.* This refers to the outer court of the temple and to the unfaithful...those who are kept outside the inner sanctum (Giudici, Revelation 11).

4. *I will give power to my two witnesses.* The two witnesses would stand for our good intentions and our positive attitudes. These two qualities of our consciousness, when they are alive and working, bear witness to our faith in God and to our devotion to the truth of Jesus Christ. Our good intentions, our positive attitudes, the two witnesses (Ed Rabel The Book of Revelation 11). Just below the heart is the seat of judgment; so metaphysically these witnesses have power to discern and judge the thoughts and intents of the heart, and to cause a drought to come into the earth or carnal consciousness, and plagues of different kinds, as well as fire to purify and put away error thoughts that oppose the Truth (MBD/witnesses).

5. *The beast that comes up out of the abyss will make war with them.* The beast of Revelation is the metaphysical symbol of negativeness and violence still in existence in human nature. This negativeness comes from the abyss. There is no bottom to it, which means there is no basis of reality to it; there is no real substance to it. The bottomless pit symbolizes the enigma of unreality brought into an appearance of reality, of nothingness being cast into a mold of somethingness. (USRS Bible Interpretation, Revelation Lesson 11).

6. *And overcome them.* The beast of Revelation must be some race error thought that has gained great ascendancy through the power of people's belief in it. This thought for a time keeps the witnesses from continuing their work, and they remain seemingly inactive. "They that dwell on the earth" (the carnal mind) rejoice, for they think that they are free to go on in their old error, sense ways, and not be brought into judgment for them; but in a very short time the word comes into greater activity than ever, with renewed power. (MBD/witnesses).

7. *And kill them.* When sudden uprisings of negativeness come from that mysterious somewhere, bottomless pit in us, often, these two factors are its first victims. Good intentions can be ruined, and positive attitudes can go dead. The two witnesses can be killed (Rabel, The Book of Revelation 11).

8. *After the three and a half days, the breath of life from God entered into them, and they stood on their feet.* Good intentions that are based on truth can never really die out in us. Positive attitudes based on truth can never really die out in us. Negativeness may emerge and seem to conquer these servants of the Lord in us for a spell, but life returns to them and they take an active place once more in our consciousness on a higher level than ever before (Rabel, The Book of Revelation 11).

## The Rounding Out of Our Spiritual Perceptive Faculties

11:15 The seventh angel sounded,[1]
and great voices in heaven followed,
saying, "The kingdom of the world
has become the Kingdom of our Lord,
and of his Christ. He will reign
forever and ever!"

11:16 The twenty-four elders,[2] who
sit on their thrones before God's
throne, fell on their faces and
worshiped God, 11:17 saying: "We give
you thanks, Lord God, the Almighty,
the one who is and who was[30];
because you have taken your great
power, and reigned. 11:18 The nations
were angry, and your wrath came,
as did the time for the dead to be
judged, and to give your
bondservants the prophets, their
reward, as well as to the saints, and
those who fear your name, to the
small and the great; and to destroy
those who destroy the earth."

11:19 God's temple that is in heaven was opened, and the ark of the Lord's covenant[3] was seen in his temple. Lightnings, sounds, thunders, an earthquake, and great hail followed.

1. *The seventh angel sounded.* The sounding of the seventh angle represents the rounding out and completing of our spiritual perceptive faculties in Christ. This heralds the coming of the kingdom of the Christ. The good news is, the kingdom of the Christ is coming, but there is still the third woe to deal with (Giudici, Revelation 11).

2. *The twenty-four elders.* The assembling of the "elders of Israel signifies a drawing together in conscious unity of all the intelligent directive powers of the spiritual self, to the standard of peace and harmony. This process may take place without the conscious mind's understanding its import. The whole consciousness is made up of objective and subjective thoughts and their results. Like a chemical solution, they go through changes on the subjective side that are observed in their outer appearance only, and but dimly understood (MBD/elders).

3. *The ark of the Lord's covenant.* The Ark of the Covenant, sacred ark, or ark of the testimony, represents the original spark of divinity in man's being It is a covenant, or agreement, of the Father with the son that He shall inherit all that the Father has. This original spiritual spark is a very sacred, holy thing, because upon its development depends man's immortality. It is represented as occupying the most holy place in the temple and as being protected and cared for with great devotion. All that man is has been brought forth from this central spark, yet the sense-conscious man often neglects it and ignores its very existence (MBD/ark).

---

Fillmore Study Bible annotations compiled by Rev. Jim Ernstsen and Rev. Lisa Herklotz.

**World English Bible Footnotes:**

[30] v11:17. TR adds "and who is coming"

# Revelation 12

## The Threat to Our Spiritual Awakening

12:1 A great sign was seen in heaven:[1] a woman clothed with the sun,[2] and the moon under her feet, and on her head a crown of twelve stars. 12:2 She was with child. She cried out in pain, laboring to give birth. 12:3 Another sign was seen in heaven. Behold, a great red dragon,[3] having seven heads and ten horns, and on his heads seven crowns. 12:4 His tail drew one third of the stars of the sky, and threw them to the earth. The dragon stood before the woman who was about to give birth, so that when she gave birth he might devour her child. 12:5 She gave birth to a son,[4] a male child, who is to rule all the nations with a rod of iron. Her child was caught up to God, and to his throne. 12:6 The woman fled into the wilderness,[5] where she has a place prepared by God, that there they may nourish her one thousand two hundred sixty days.

1. *Heaven.* Heaven is the realm of conscious harmony, a consciousness of peace in mind, body, and soul. Since we are free to think what we will, discordant thoughts may enter heaven. When this takes place, our harmony is disrupted and there is "war in heaven."

2. *A woman clothed with the sun.* The woman described here symbolizes our own illumined and consecrated feeling nature. The child she is to deliver refers to our feeling nature blooming forth or giving birth to a higher and finer development of our own nature. To successfully become a finer and better person in every way often does involve certain kinds of travail, or creative suffering. This always occurs in our feeling nature, the woman. But it is of short duration and quickly resolves itself into the most rewarding of all events for any human being: the new birth of his better self (Ed Rabel, The Book of Revelation 12).

3. *A great red dragon* This beast stands for our human tendency toward error and negativeness. This tendency constantly appears as a threat to our growth and spiritual unfoldment and development of consciousness (Rabel). Self-depreciation causes man to accuse himself of being inherently evil and incapable of achieving his divine stature as a son of God. This form of negation is satanic in its origin and nature and has a demoralizing effect on man.

4. *She gave birth to a son.* Once our new birth begins, it must succeed, and it will continue. The new human-child is our improved self and is under divine guidance, protection, and spiritual nourishment during the whole glorious process (Rabel).

5. *The woman fled into the wilderness.* Divine love gives our feeling nature protection and strength and feeds it, and enables us to continue this great process of self-evolution into greater and finer being and higher and ever higher awareness in consciousness (Rabel).

## Divine Inspiration Defeats Self-Condemnation

12:7 There was war in the sky.(1)
Michael and his angels made war on
the dragon. The dragon and his
angels made war. 12:8 They didn't
prevail, neither was a place found
for him any more in heaven. 12:9 The
great dragon was thrown down,(2) the
old serpent, he who is called the
devil and Satan, the deceiver of the
whole world. He was thrown down
to the earth,(3) and his angels were
thrown down with him. 12:10 I heard a
loud voice in heaven,(4) saying, "Now
is come the salvation, the power,
and the Kingdom of our God, and
the authority of his Christ; for the
accuser of our brothers has been
thrown down, who accuses them
before our God day and night. 12:11
They overcame him because of the
Lamb's blood, and because of the
word of their testimony. They didn't
love their life, even to death. 12:12
Therefore rejoice, heavens, and you
who dwell in them. Woe to the earth
and to the sea, because the devil
has gone down to you, having great
wrath, knowing that he has but a
short time."(5)

1. *There was war in the sky.* Metaphysically this battle is taking place in consciousness, in truth (Giudici, Revelation 12). The archangel Michael is the leader of the heavenly army that wars against the dragon. Metaphysically, Michael is divine inspiration, and a realization of the all-conquering power of God; also a Godlike or perfect state of being (MBD/Michael).

2. *The great dragon was thrown down.*The dragon is another name for Satan. The Idea of Satan assumes various forms in man's consciousness, but, as an idea of power, it originally had a legitimate place in divine order. It is when power is turned to selfish or destructive ends that the great dragon is "cast down to the earth." Frank Giudici comments that once the battle is won in consciousness, by getting our thoughts straight, then it's going to manifest itself on Earth, at the right time, and in the right way (Giudici).

3. *To the earth.* Metaphysically speaking, the earth represents the consciousness of the physical body (RW/earth).

4. *I heard a loud voice in heaven.* The "great voice" from Heaven symbolizes the beginning of the reign of Christ, through whom comes salvation. When we free the mind from Satan, the resurrection of the

body (salvation from the earth, or mortal concept of the body) into the consciousness of immortality follows, for Christ is "the resurrection and the life."

5. *The devil ... has but a short time.* In a literal sense the time is relatively short compared with eternity. Metaphysically, man soon tires of discord and inharmony and longs for peace, that he may have by claiming his heritage as a son of God through the Christ. When he asserts his better nature, the Devil's reign over him is soon at an end.

## Humanity's Two Wings

[12:13] When the dragon saw that he
was thrown down to the earth, he
persecuted the woman who gave
birth to the male child. [12:14] Two
wings of the great eagle were given
to the woman,❶ that she might fly
into the wilderness to her place, so
that she might be nourished for a
time, and times, and half a time,
from the face of the serpent. [12:15]
The serpent spewed water out of his
mouth after the woman like a river,
that he might cause her to be carried
away by the stream. [12:16] The earth
helped the woman, and the earth
opened its mouth and swallowed up
the river which the dragon spewed
out of his mouth. [12:17] The dragon
grew angry with the woman, and
went away to make war with the rest
of her seed,❷ who keep God's
commandments and hold Jesus'
testimony.

1. *Two wings of the great eagle were given to the woman.* Charles Fillmore adopted the symbol of the winged globe from F.B. Dowd's *The Temple of the Rosycross.* It represents the relation existing between Spirit, soul and body. Soul gives wings to the body. Spirit is the enveloping principle, like the atmosphere in which both soul and body exist, and from which they draw their original inspiration. The winged globe is also a symbol of the earth and the soul. The earth has soul, as have its products of every description. All exist in the luminiferous ether, the *anima mundi*, the divine mother. When the people of the earth lift up their thoughts to God, the Animus Dei or directive Spirit, then the planet takes wings into a higher radiation of universal life—the mortal puts on immortality (James Teener, 1939 Dissertation 43).

2. *The dragon ... went away to make war with the rest of her seed.* Historically, Satan [the dragon] is representing the Roman Empire since in the writer's time, it was the Roman Empire that was persecuting the faithful, through emperor worship. They were made to go and bring offerings to the emperor, receiving a slip of paper or a mark on the had that verified they had performed their obligation (Giudici, Revelation 12).

---

Fillmore Study Bible annotations compiled by Rev. Jim Ernstsen and Rev. Lisa Herklotz.

# Revelation 13

## The First Beast: Blasphemy and the Loss of Authority

[13:1] Then I stood on the sand of the sea. I saw a beast coming up out of the sea,❶ having ten horns and seven heads. On his horns were ten crowns, and on his heads, blasphemous names.❷ 13:2 The beast which I saw was like a leopard, and his feet were like those of a bear, and his mouth like the mouth of a lion. The dragon gave him his power, his throne, and great authority. 13:3 One of his heads looked like it had been wounded fatally. His fatal wound was healed, and the whole earth marveled at the beast. 13:4 They worshiped the dragon, because he gave his authority to the beast, and they worshiped the beast, saying, "Who is like the beast? Who is able to make war with him?" 13:5 A mouth speaking great things and blasphemy was given to him. Authority to make war for forty-two months was given to him. 13:6 He opened his mouth for blasphemy against God,❸ to blaspheme his name, and his dwelling, those who dwell in heaven. 13:7 It was given to him to make war with the saints, and to overcome them. Authority over every tribe,❹ people, language, and nation was given to him. 13:8 All who dwell on the earth will worship him, everyone whose name has not been written from the foundation of the world in the book of life of the Lamb who has been killed. 13:9 If anyone has an ear, let him hear. 13:10 If anyone has captivity, he will go. If anyone is with the sword, he must be killed.[31] Here is the endurance and the faith of the saints.

1. *I saw a beast coming up out of the sea.* In this chapter we are introduced to the concept of the Antichrist. If God has a messiah, which is Jesus, then according to the author, the devil also has a messiah, the Antichrist. Historically, this will be a leader who personifies evil (the Roman Empire). Metaphysically, this is the loss of true authority and blasphemy.

2. *Blasphemous names.* Many of the Roman emperors thought that they were manifestations of God, so they took upon themselves divine titles. This assumption of divine authority was seen as blasphemous (Giudici, Revelation 13).

3. *Blasphemy against God.* Slowness, sluggishness, stupidity of speech: hence, speaking evil, reviling, slandering. One significance of blasphemy is the tendency in our own mind to fear that we can go too far in spiritualizing our thought and its environment (MBD/blasphemy).

4. *Authority over every tribe.* Rightful power; mastery; or dominion. "For he taught them as having authority" (Mark 1:22). The Spirit of truth is the one and only authority in the study of Truth (John 16:13). (RW/authority). "Meantime, whilst the doors of the temple stand open, night and day, before every man, and the oracles of this truth cease never, it is guarded by one stern condition; this, namely; it is an intuition. It cannot be received at second hand. Truly speaking, it is not instruction, but provocation, that I can receive from another soul." (Ralph Waldo Emerson, Divinity School Address)

## The Second Beast: Officials and Priests Under an Emperor

13:11 I saw another beast coming up out of the earth.❶ He had two horns like a lamb, and he spoke like a dragon.❷ 13:12 He exercises all the authority of the first beast in his presence. He makes the earth and those who dwell in it to worship the first beast,❸ whose fatal wound was healed. 13:13 He performs great signs, even making fire come down out of the sky to the earth in the sight of people. 13:14 He deceives my own people who dwell on the earth because of the signs he was granted to do in front of the beast; saying to those who dwell on the earth, that they should make an image to the beast who had the sword wound and lived. 13:15 It was given to him to give breath to it, to the image of the beast, that the image of the beast should both speak, and cause as many as wouldn't worship the image of the beast to be killed. [13:16] He causes all, the small and the great, the rich and the poor, and the free and the slave, to be given marks on their right hands, or on their foreheads; [13:17] and that no one would be able to buy or to sell, unless he has that mark, the name of the beast or the number of his name. [13:18] Here is wisdom. He who has understanding, let him calculate the number of the beast, for it is the number of a man. His number is six hundred sixty-six.④

1. *I saw another beast coming up out of the earth.* Historically, the second beast has to do with the Roman officials who were under the emperor and their priests (Frank Giudici, Revelation 13).

2. *He had two horns like a lamb, and he spoke like a dragon.* The two horns are affirmations and denials (RW/horns) but their message was evil.

3. *He makes the earth and those who dwell in it to worship the first beast.* Metaphysically, the Beast worshipers stand for the strange tendency in human nature where they become so impressed with the many appearances of error and negativeness in life that in a sense, they begin to worship it (Ed Rabel, The Book of Revelation 13).

4. *His number is six hundred sixty-six.* The Beast may be a numeric reference to Nero Caesar, the emperor who is known for persecuting Christians, feeding them to the lions. Scholars tell us that when you take Hebrew letters and write them out numerically, the name Neron Caesar comes to 666. The numerical number for Jesus in Greek works out to 888. In between 666 and 888 we have 777 or perfection. 666 falls below the ideal of fulfilment or perfection. 888 rises above perfection (Giudici).

Fillmore Study Bible annotations compiled by Rev. Jim Ernstsen and Rev. Lisa Herklotz.

**World English Bible Footnotes:**

[31] v13:10. TR reads "If anyone leads into captivity, into captivity he goes. If anyone will kill with the sword, he must be killed with a sword." instead of "If anyone has captivity, he goes away. If anyone is with the sword, he must be killed."

# Revelation 14

## The Pure in Consciousness Sing a New Song

[14:1] I saw, and behold, the Lamb standing on Mount Zion, and with him a number, one hundred forty-four thousand,① having his name, and the name of his Father, written on their foreheads. [14:2] I heard a sound from heaven, like the sound of many waters, and like the sound of a great thunder. The sound which I heard was like that of harpists playing on their harps. [14:3] They sing a new song② before the throne, and before the four living creatures and the elders. No one could learn the song except the one hundred forty-four thousand, those who had been redeemed out of the earth. [14:4] These are those who were not defiled with

women, for they are virgins.[3] These are those who follow the Lamb wherever he goes. These were redeemed by Jesus from among men, the first fruits to God and to the Lamb.
[14:5] In their mouth was found no lie, for they are blameless.[32]

1. *One hundred forty-four thousand.* Metaphysically, this is the opposite of 666 the number of the beast. These 144,000 are named as the redeemed. 12 stands for wholeness and perfection. 12 also stands for the powers of mankind. 12 times 12 stands for the 12 powers in us, combined with wholeness and perfection in manifestation (Ed Rabel, The Book of Revelation 14).

2. *They sing a new song.* Those who turn to the Christ within, those who are willing to work with a concept of God as absolute good and know that life is good, they will sing a new song. Changing our consciousness we put ourselves in tune with absolute good as if it were a new song (Frank Giudici, Revelation 14).

3. *Not defiled with women, for they are virgins.* "Not defined with women" is an unfortunate, literal association of women with sensuality. Metaphysically understood, virginity is a state of consciousness, and this passage refers to those discussed in the previous chapter who are not blasphemous. Like the ten (women) virgins in Matt. 25:113, these represent the *senses who are pure*. They are five in number, but have a twofold action—five in the inner realm, and five in the outer world. The way to supply oil for the lamps of the virgins, even of the foolish ones, is to affirm that the life source, Spirit, from which comes the power of hearing, smelling, feeling, seeing, and tasting, is not material but spiritual (MBD/virgins). Annie Rix Militz adds "The comparison which Jesus makes between the two kinds of followers of Truth is again made in the parable of the Ten Virgins. The foolish man who hears and does not, is like the foolish virgins who had their lamps but were unprovided with sufficient oil. Many are now hearing the words of Christ and are expecting to demonstrate all that he did, even to the overcoming of death. But how can we do all the works unless we obey all the directions?" (The Sermon On The Mount-An Interpretation 133).

## Three Proclamations of Good News

[14:6] I saw an angel flying in mid heaven,[1] having an eternal Good News to proclaim to those who dwell on the earth, and to every nation, tribe, language, and people.
[14:7] He said with a loud voice, "Fear the Lord, and give him glory; for the hour of his judgment has come. Worship him who made the heaven, the earth, the sea, and the springs of waters!"

[14:8] Another, a second angel, followed,[2] saying, "Babylon the great has fallen, which has made all the nations to drink of the wine of the wrath of her sexual immorality."

[14:9] Another angel, a third, followed them,[3] saying with a great voice, "If anyone worships the beast and his image, and receives a mark on his forehead, or on his hand,
[14:10] he also will drink of the wine of the wrath of God, which is prepared unmixed in the cup of his anger. He will be tormented with fire and sulfur in the presence of the holy angels, and in the presence of the Lamb.
[14:11] The smoke of their torment goes up forever and ever. They have no rest day and night, those who worship the beast and his image, and whoever receives the mark of his name.
[14:12] Here is the patience of the saints,[4] those who keep the commandments of God, and the faith of Jesus."[5]

[14:13] I heard the voice from heaven saying, "Write, 'Blessed are the dead who die in the Lord from now on.'"

"Yes," says the Spirit, "that they may rest from their labors; for their works follow with them."

1. *I saw an angel flying in mid heaven.* The first angel, or eternal gospel, has an eternal Good News: God is about to reveal himself, in contrast to worshiping the ember. He speaks of the eternal gospel. This is just building up this whole idea that he's involved in here, that we are to worship God, who is about to reveal himself (Frank Giudici, Revelation 14).

2. *A second angel followed.* The second angel uses Babylon to refer to Rome. Why does he use Babylon? Because the people remember very well their ancestors' time of Babylonian captivity, so Babylon comes to be a symbol for captivity and is simply a reference to Rome, not literally to Babylon but to Rome. Saying that Babylon has fallen is a reference to Rome. Identifying the inequities of the Roman empire (Giudici).

3. *Another angel, a third, followed them.* The third angel warns against worship of the beast. If you worship the beast, you will be punished. The beast, once again, is symbolic of the Roman Empire (Giudici).

4. *The patience of the saints* An attitude of mind characterized by poise, inner calmness, and quiet endurance, especially in the face of trying conditions. Patience has its foundation in faith, and it is perfected only in those who have unwavering faith in God (RW/patience).

5. *The faith of Jesus.* Jesus did not claim an exclusive supernatural power, which we usually accredit to Him. He had explored the ether energy, which He called the "kingdom of the heavens"; His understanding was beyond that of the average man. However, He knew and said that other men could do what He did if they would only have faith. He encouraged His followers to take Him as a pattern for faith and to use the power of thought and word. Divine healing is due to the application of the same law that Jesus used. In most instances, He demanded faith on the part of those He healed; and with this faith as a point of mental and spiritual contact, He released the latent energy in the atomic structure of the ones in need of healing, and they were restored to life and health (RW/faith of Jesus).

## Heralding the Coming Kingdom of Christ

14:14 I looked, and behold, a white
cloud; and on the cloud one sitting
like a son of man,[33] having on his
head a golden crown, and in his hand
a sharp sickle.❶ 14:15 Another angel
came out from the temple, crying
with a loud voice to him who sat on
the cloud, "Send forth your sickle,
and reap; for the hour to reap has
come; for the harvest of the earth is
ripe!" 14:16 He who sat on the cloud
thrust his sickle on the earth, and the
earth was reaped.

14:17 Another angel came out from
the temple which is in heaven. He
also had a sharp sickle. 14:18 Another
angel came out from the altar, he
who has power over fire, and he
called with a great voice to him who
had the sharp sickle, saying, "Send
forth your sharp sickle, and gather
the clusters of the vine of the earth,
for the earth's grapes are fully ripe!"
14:19 The angel thrust his sickle into
the earth, and gathered the vintage
of the earth, and threw it into the
great winepress of the wrath of
God.❷ 14:20 The winepress was
trodden outside of the city, and
blood came out from the winepress,
even to the bridles of the horses,
as far as one thousand six hundred
stadia.[34]

1. *And in his hand a sharp sickle.* God is ready to reap His harvest, to reveal Himself, have this great conflict between the powers of good and evil, to set his kingdom up on earth. ... We see the heralding of the coming of the Christ, the kingdom of the Christ, denial and affirmation produces that kind of demonstration, a real realization within us of our own Christ consciousness, or Christ in dwelling ... our ability to achieve Christ consciousness (Frank Giudici, Revelation 14).

2. *Gathered the vintage of the earth, and threw it into the great winepress of the wrath of God.* Memorialized by Julia Ward Howe in *The Battle Hymn of the Republic*: "He is trampling out the vintage where the grapes of wrath are stored; He hath loosed the fateful lightning of His ter-

ible swift sword: His truth is marching on."

Fillmore Study Bible annotations compiled by Rev. Jim Ernstsen and Rev. Lisa Herklotz.

**World English Bible Footnotes:**

[32] v14:5. TR adds "before the throne of God"

[33] v14:14. Daniel 7:13

[34] v14:20. 1600 stadia = 296 kilometers or 184 miles

# Revelation 15

## Truth: A Sea of Glass Mixed With Fire

15:1 I saw another great and
marvelous sign in the sky: seven
angels having the seven last plagues,
for in them God's wrath is finished.[1]
15:2 I saw something like a sea of glass
mixed with fire, and those who
overcame the beast,[2] his image,[35]
and the number of his name,
standing on the sea of glass, having
harps of God. 15:3 They sang the song
of Moses, the servant of God, and the
song of the Lamb,[3] saying,

"Great and marvelous are your
works, Lord God, the
Almighty!
Righteous and true are your
ways, you King of the
nations.
15:4 Who wouldn't fear you, Lord,
and glorify your name?
For you only are holy.
For all the nations will come
and worship before you.
For your righteous acts have
been revealed."

15:5 After these things I looked,
and the temple of the tabernacle of
the testimony in heaven was
opened.[4] 15:6 The seven angels who
had the seven plagues came out,
clothed with pure, bright linen, and
wearing golden sashes around their
breasts.

15:7 One of the four living creatures
gave to the seven angels seven
golden bowls full of the wrath of
God, who lives forever and ever. 15:8
The temple was filled with smoke
from the glory of God, and from his
power. No one was able to enter into
the temple, until the seven plagues
of the seven angels would be
finished.

1. *Seven angels having the seven last plagues, for in them God's wrath is finished.* A reference to getting close to the end of the time of destruction, close to the time of deliverance, like the darkest hour before the dawn (Frank Giudici, Revelation 15).

2. *I saw something like a sea of glass mixed with fire, and those who overcame the beast.* The sea represents the clarity of Truth and its omnipresence. Those who have overcome self ("the beast") stand be-

side this sea (clear perception of Truth) and behold their possibilities of infinite perfection realized.

3. *They sang the song of Moses, the servant of God, and the song of the Lamb.* The song of Moses is sung right after the Israelites were freed from Egypt, so the identification is made with deliverance (Giudici). Both are songs of praise. Combined, the two songs render new praise and glory to God, the Holy One. They symbolize the truth that eventually all men will come to recognize God as supreme ruler and realize their oneness in Christ.

4. *The temple of the tabernacle of the testimony in heaven was opened.* Historically, the Tent, or the Tabernacle, was the early temple that Moses and his people would set up in the wilderness. This is another reference to Moses and the idea of deliverance. This temple is not earthly but set in Heaven and means that everything is all set in Heaven or in consciousness (Giudici).

Fillmore Study Bible annotations compiled by Rev. Jim Ernstsen and Rev. Lisa Herklotz.

**World English Bible Footnotes:**

[35] v15:2. TR adds "his mark,"

# Revelation 16

## The Bowls of God's Wrath[1]

16:1 I heard a loud voice out of the temple, saying to the seven angels, "Go and pour out the seven bowls of the wrath of God on the earth!"[2]

16:2 The first went, and poured out his bowl into the earth, and it became a harmful and evil sore on the people who had the mark of the beast, and who worshiped his image.

16:3 The second angel poured out his bowl into the sea, and it became blood as of a dead man. Every living thing in the sea died.

16:4 The third poured out his bowl into the rivers and springs of water, and they became blood. 16:5 I heard the angel of the waters saying, "You are righteous, who are and who were, you Holy One, because you have judged these things. 16:6 For they poured out the blood of the saints and the prophets, and you have given them blood to drink. They deserve this." 16:7 I heard the altar saying, "Yes, Lord God, the Almighty, true and righteous are your judgments."

16:8 The fourth poured out his bowl on the sun, and it was given to him to scorch men with fire. 16:9 People were scorched with great heat, and people blasphemed the name of God who has the power over these plagues. They didn't repent and give him glory.

16:10 The fifth poured out his bowl on the throne of the beast, and his kingdom was darkened. They gnawed their tongues because of the pain, 16:11 and they blasphemed the God of heaven because of their pains and

their sores. They didn't repent of
their works.

16:12 The sixth poured out his bowl
on the great river, the Euphrates.[3]
Its water was dried up, that the way
might be made ready for the kings
that come from the sunrise. 16:13 I
saw coming out of the mouth of the
dragon, and out of the mouth of the
beast, and out of the mouth of the
false prophet, three unclean spirits,
something like frogs; 16:14 for they are
spirits of demons, performing signs;
which go forth to the kings of the
whole inhabited earth, to gather
them together for the war of that
great day of God, the Almighty.

16:15 "Behold, I come like a thief.
Blessed is he who watches, and keeps
his clothes, so that he doesn't walk
naked, and they see his shame." 16:16
He gathered them together into the
place which is called in Hebrew,
Megiddo.[4]

16:17 The seventh poured out his
bowl into the air. A loud voice came
forth out of the temple of heaven,
from the throne, saying, "It is done!"
16:18 There were lightnings, sounds,
and thunders; and there was a great
earthquake, such as was not since
there were men on the earth, so
great an earthquake, so mighty. 16:19
The great city was divided into three
parts, and the cities of the nations
fell. Babylon the great was
remembered in the sight of God, to
give to her the cup of the wine of
the fierceness of his wrath. 16:20 Every
island fled away, and the mountains
were not found. 16:21 Great
hailstones, about the weight of a
talent,[36] came down out of the sky
on people. People blasphemed God
because of the plague of the hail, for
this plague is exceedingly severe.

1. Once again, these plagues are an identification with the time of Moses. The people knew that during the time of Moses, when the plagues came, it meant that deliverance was right at hand. Because shortly after the plagues hit, then what happened? Then the Israelites were able to flee Egypt. The writer was telling us now with these plagues, these seven plagues, deliverance once again is almost at hand. He places it in the context of this great battle at Armageddon that's supposed to take place. (Frank Giudici, Revelation 16)

2. *Go and pour out the seven bowls of the wrath of God on the earth!* Destruction and plagues poured out over the Antichrist. The first five plagues are reminiscent of five plagues inflicted on the Egyptians in the time of Moses. (Giudici)

3. *The sixth poured out his bowl on the great river, the Euphrates.* These plagues are an identification with the time of Moses. The people knew that during the time of Moses, when the plagues came, it meant that deliverance was right at hand. The writer is telling us with these seven plagues, deliverance once again is almost at hand. (Giudici)

4. *He gathered them together into the place which is called in Hebrew, Megiddo.* The great battle between God and the beast is to take place at Armageddon (Giudici). Metaphysically, Armageddon represents that place within our consciousness where there is a struggle between our choice of following negative impulses or practicing truth thinking. The battle of Armageddon is that inner struggle, and this struggle ceases only with the victory in favor of truth thinking (Ed Rabel, The Book of Revelation 16).

---

Fillmore Study Bible annotations compiled by Rev. Jim Ernstsen and Rev. Lisa Herklotz.

**World English Bible Footnotes:**

[36] v16:21. 1 talent is about 34 kilograms or 75 pounds

# Revelation 17

## The Great Whore and the Beast

17:1 One of the seven angels who had the seven bowls came and spoke with me, saying, "Come here. I will show you the judgment of the great prostitute who sits on many waters,[1] 17:2 with whom the kings of the earth committed sexual immorality, and those who dwell in the earth were made drunken with the wine of her sexual immorality."[2] 17:3 He carried me away in the Spirit into a wilderness. I saw a woman sitting on a scarlet-colored animal, full of blasphemous names, having seven heads and ten horns. 17:4 The woman was dressed in purple and scarlet, and decked with gold and precious stones and pearls, having in her hand a golden cup full of abominations and the impurities of the sexual immorality of the earth. 17:5 And on her forehead a name was written, "MYSTERY, BABYLON THE GREAT, THE MOTHER OF THE PROSTITUTES[3] AND OF THE ABOMINATIONS OF THE EARTH." 17:6 I saw the woman drunken with the blood of the saints, and with the blood of the martyrs of Jesus. When I saw her, I wondered with great amazement. 17:7 The angel said to me, "Why do you wonder? I will tell you the mystery of the woman, and of the beast that carries her, which has the seven heads and the ten horns. 17:8 The beast[4] that you saw was, and is not; and is about to come up out of the abyss and to go into destruction. Those who dwell on the earth and whose names have not been written in the book of life from the foundation of the world will marvel when they see that the beast was, and is not, and shall be present.[37] 17:9 Here is the mind that has wisdom. The seven heads are seven mountains, on which the woman sits. 17:10 They are seven kings. Five have fallen, the one is, the other has not yet come. When he comes, he must continue a little while. 17:11 The beast that was, and is not, is himself also an eighth, and is of the seven; and he goes to destruction. 17:12 The ten horns that you saw are ten kings who have received no kingdom as yet, but they receive authority as kings, with the beast, for one hour. 17:13 These have one mind, and they give their power and authority to the beast. 17:14 These will war against the Lamb, and the Lamb will overcome them, for he is Lord of lords, and King of kings. They also will overcome who are with him, called and chosen and faithful." 17:15 He said to me, "The waters which you saw, where the prostitute sits, are peoples, multitudes, nations, and languages. 17:16 The ten horns which you saw,[5] and the beast, these will hate the prostitute, and will make her desolate, and will make her naked, and will eat her flesh, and will burn her utterly with fire. 17:17 For God has put in their hearts to do what he has in mind, and to be of one mind, and to give their kingdom to the beast, until the words of God should be accomplished. 17:18 The woman whom you saw is the great city, which reigns over the kings of the earth."

1. *The great prostitute who sits on many waters.* Rome (through a veiled reference to Babylon) (Frank Giudici, Revelation 17).

2. *The kings of the earth committed sexual immorality.* Metaphysically: those times when in our human thinking, we put our thought of *I am*, into our negative emotions [fornication] (Ed Rabel, The Book of Revelation 17).

3. *The mother of the prostitutes [harlotry].* Those who involve themselves in emperor worship were guilty of idolatry, or playing the role of prostitute [harlot] (Rabel)).

4. *The beast.* The emperor of Rome, most likely Nero who persecuted the early Christians (Rabel)).

5. *The ten horns which you saw.* The other Roman emperors will turn on Rome and destroy it (Rabel)).

---

Fillmore Study Bible annotations compiled by Rev. Jim Ernstsen and Rev. Lisa Herklotz.

**World English Bible Footnotes:**

[37] v17:8. TR reads "yet is" instead of "shall be present"

# Revelation 18

## The Fall of Babylon

18:1 After these things, I saw another angel coming down out of the sky, having great authority. The earth was illuminated with his glory. 18:2 He cried with a mighty voice, saying, "Fallen, fallen is Babylon the great,[1] and she has become a habitation of demons, a prison of every unclean spirit, and a prison of every unclean and hateful bird! 18:3 For all the nations have drunk of the wine of the wrath of her sexual immorality, the kings of the earth committed sexual immorality with her, and the merchants of the earth grew rich from the abundance of her luxury."

18:4 I heard another voice from heaven, saying, "Come out of her, my people, that you have no participation in her sins, and that you don't receive of her plagues, 18:5 for her sins have reached to the sky, and God has remembered her iniquities. 18:6 Return to her just as she returned, and repay her double as she did, and according to her works. In the cup which she mixed, mix to her double. 18:7 However much she glorified herself, and grew wanton, so much give her of torment and mourning. For she says in her heart, 'I sit a queen, and am no widow, and will in no way see mourning.' 18:8 Therefore in one day her plagues will come: death, mourning, and famine; and she will be utterly burned with fire; for the Lord God who has judged her is strong. 18:9 The kings of the earth, who committed sexual immorality and lived wantonly with her, will weep and wail over her, when they look at the smoke of her burning, 18:10 standing far away for the fear of her torment, saying, 'Woe, woe, the great city, Babylon, the strong city! For your judgment has come in one hour.' 18:11 The merchants of the earth weep and mourn over her, for no one buys their merchandise any more; 18:12 merchandise of gold, silver, precious stones, pearls, fine linen, purple, silk, scarlet, all expensive wood, every vessel of ivory, every vessel made of most precious wood, and of brass, and iron, and marble; 18:13 and cinnamon, incense, perfume, frankincense, wine, olive oil, fine flour, wheat, sheep, horses, chariots, and people's bodies and souls. 18:14 The fruits which your soul lusted after have been lost to you, and all things that were dainty and sumptuous have perished from you, and you will find them no more at all. 18:15 The merchants of these things, who were made rich by her, will stand far away for the fear of her torment, weeping and mourning; 18:16 saying, 'Woe, woe, the great city, she who was dressed in fine linen, purple, and scarlet, and decked with gold and precious stones and pearls! 18:17 For in an hour such great riches are made desolate.' Every shipmaster, and everyone who sails anywhere, and mariners, and as many as gain their living by sea, stood far away, 18:18 and cried out as they looked at the smoke of her burning, saying, 'What is like the great city?' 18:19 They cast dust on their heads, and cried, weeping and mourning, saying, 'Woe, woe, the great city, in which all who had their ships in the sea were made rich by reason of her great wealth!' For in one hour is she made desolate.

18:20 "Rejoice over her, O heaven,[2] you saints, apostles, and prophets; for God has judged your judgment on her." 18:21 A mighty angel took up a stone like a great millstone and cast it into the sea, saying, "Thus with violence will Babylon, the great city, be thrown down, and will be found no more at all. 18:22 The voice of harpists, minstrels, flute players, and trumpeters will be heard no more at all in you. No craftsman, of whatever craft, will be found any more at all in you. The sound of a mill will be heard no more at all in you. 18:23 The light of a lamp will shine no more at all in you. The voice of the bridegroom and of the bride will be heard no more at all in you; for your merchants were the princes of the earth; for with your sorcery all the nations were deceived. 18:24 In her was found the blood of prophets and of saints, and of all who have been slain on the earth."

1. *Fallen, fallen is Babylon the great.* The beginning of a lament over the destruction of Rome (Frank Giudici, Revelation 18). Metaphysically, All of the products of negative emotions (Babylon), or abominations, shall be reduced back into harmlessness, or nothingness. Our soul shall be cleansed of the abomination of negative emotions and their harmful results. Further, all negative emotions in us fail to survive in the long run. Every negative emotion, Babylon, carries its own seal of doom for itself. (Ed Rabel, The Book of Revelation 18).

2. *Rejoice over her, O heaven.* Metaphysically, while some may hate the thought of losing their anger over something, we will rejoice and give thanks that a great, freeing, cleansing, purifying has actually taken place deep within our soul. (Rabel)).

Fillmore Study Bible annotations compiled by Rev. Jim Ernstsen and Rev. Lisa Herklotz.

# REVELATION 19

## The Rejoicing in Heaven

19:1 After these things I heard something like a loud voice of a great multitude in heaven, saying, "Hallelujah! Salvation, power, and glory belong to our God: 19:2 for true and righteous are his judgments. For he has judged the great prostitute, who corrupted the earth with her sexual immorality, and he has avenged the blood of his servants at her hand."

19:3 A second said, "Hallelujah! Her smoke goes up forever and ever." 19:4 The twenty-four elders and the four living creatures fell down and worshiped God who sits on the throne, saying, "Amen! Hallelujah!"

19:5 A voice came forth from the throne, saying, "Give praise to our God, all you his servants, you who fear him, the small and the great!"

19:6 I heard something like the voice of a great multitude, and like the voice of many waters, and like the voice of mighty thunders, saying, "Hallelujah! For the Lord our God, the Almighty, reigns! 19:7 Let us rejoice and be exceedingly glad, and let us give the glory to him. For the marriage of the Lamb has come,[1] and his wife has made herself ready." 19:8 It was given to her that she would array herself in bright, pure, fine linen: for the fine linen is the righteous acts of the saints.

19:9 He said to me, "Write, 'Blessed are those who are invited to the marriage supper of the Lamb.'" He said to me, "These are true words of God."

19:10 I fell down before his feet to worship him. He said to me, "Look! Don't do it! I am a fellow bondservant with you and with your brothers who hold the testimony of Jesus. Worship God, for the testimony of Jesus is the Spirit of Prophecy."

1. *For the marriage of the Lamb has come.* A marriage, symbolizing the return of Jesus and his union with his faithful followers. Metaphysically: the Lamb refers to Jesus and the bride in this instance means the faithful followers (Frank Giudici, Revelation 19).

## The Rider on the White Horse

19:11 I saw the heaven opened, and behold, a white horse, and he who sat on it is called Faithful and True.[1] In righteousness he judges and makes war. 19:12 His eyes are a flame of fire, and on his head are many crowns. He has names written and a name written which no one knows but he himself. 19:13 He is clothed in a garment sprinkled with blood. His name is called "The Word of God." 19:14 The armies which are in heaven followed him on white horses, clothed in white, pure, fine linen. 19:15 Out of his mouth proceeds a sharp, double-edged sword, that with it he should strike the nations. He will rule them with an iron rod.[38] He treads the winepress of the fierceness of the wrath of God, the Almighty. 19:16 He has on his garment and on his thigh a name written, "KING OF KINGS, AND LORD OF LORDS."

1. *I saw the heaven opened, and behold, a white horse, and he who sat on it is called Faithful and True.* The conquering hero, the rider on the white horse. Metaphysically, the rider represents our spiritual nature, that of our triumphant Christ nature (Frank Giudici, Revelation 19).

## The Beast and Its Armies Defeated

19:17 I saw an angel standing in the sun. He cried with a loud voice, saying to all the birds that fly in the sky, "Come! Be gathered together to the great supper of God,[39] 19:18 that you may eat the flesh of kings, the flesh of captains, the flesh of mighty men, and the flesh of horses and of those who sit on them, and the flesh of all men, both free and slave, and small and great." 19:19 I saw the beast, and the kings of the earth, and their armies, gathered together to make war against him who sat on the horse, and against his army. 19:20 The beast was taken, and with him the false prophet who worked the signs in his sight, with which he deceived those who had received the mark of the beast and those who worshiped his image. These two were thrown alive into the lake of fire that burns with sulfur.❶ 19:21 The rest were killed with the sword of him who sat on the horse, the sword which came forth out of his mouth. All the birds were filled with their flesh.

1. *The beast was taken, and with him the false prophet... These two were thrown alive into the lake of fire that burns with sulfur.* The battle has been won. Metaphysically: When we're working with negative thoughts, we eliminate them from our consciousness in stages. (Frank Giudici, Revelation 19).

---

Fillmore Study Bible annotations compiled by Rev. Jim Ernstsen and Rev. Lisa Herklotz.

**World English Bible Footnotes:**

[38] v19:15. Psalm 2:9

[39] v19:17. TR reads "supper of the great God" instead of "great supper of God"

# Revelation 20

## The Thousand Years❶

20:1 I saw an angel coming down out of heaven, having the key of the abyss and a great chain in his hand. 20:2 He seized the dragon,❷ the old serpent, which is the devil and Satan, who deceives the whole inhabited earth, and bound him for a thousand years, 20:3 and cast him into the abyss, and shut it, and sealed it over him, that he should deceive the nations no more, until the thousand years were finished. After this, he must be freed for a short time. 20:4 I saw thrones, and they sat on them, and judgment was given to them. I saw the souls of those who had been beheaded for the testimony of Jesus, and for the word of God, and such as didn't worship the beast nor his image, and didn't receive the mark on their forehead and on their hand. They lived, and reigned with Christ for the thousand years. 20:5 The rest of the dead didn't live until the thousand years were finished. This is the first resurrection. 20:6 Blessed and holy is he who has part in the first resurrection. Over these, the second death has no power, but they will be priests of God and of Christ, and will reign with him one thousand years.

1. This is the aftermath of Armageddon. Sometimes known as The Millennium. A 1000 year span where the Earth will be free of all evil (a release of all negative thoughts.)

2. *He seized the dragon, the old serpent, which is the devil and Satan, who deceives the whole inhabited earth, and bound him for a thousand years.* Satan, bound a thousand years, stands for those periods in our life when we are not being tormented and deceived by our own negative thinking. When we enjoy the blessed freedom to learn and grow in consciousness through prayer, meditation, and truth thinking, these periods of spiritual freedom can last a thousand years, that is, for an unlimited, unspecified time, as long as negative thinking is held in check. (Ed Rabel, The Book of Revelation 20).

## Satan's Doom

20:7 And after the thousand years, Satan will be released from his prison,[1] 20:8 and he will come out to deceive the nations which are in the four corners of the earth, Gog and Magog, to gather them together to the war; the number of whom is as the sand of the sea. 20:9 They went up over the breadth of the earth, and surrounded the camp of the saints, and the beloved city. Fire came down out of heaven from God, and devoured them. 20:10 The devil who deceived them was thrown into the lake of fire and sulfur, where the beast and the false prophet are also. They will be tormented day and night forever and ever.

1. *And after the thousand years, Satan will be released from his prison.* We hold the Devil, or negative thinking, in check for a while, we keep our thoughts in check, but then we let Satan on earth once again... our practice slips and we start again. (Frank Giudici, Revelation 20)

## The Dead Are Judged

20:11 I saw a great white throne, and him who sat on it, from whose face the earth and the heaven fled away. There was found no place for them. 20:12 I saw the dead, the great and the small, standing before the throne, and they opened books. Another book was opened, which is the book of life. The dead were judged out of the things which were written in the books, according to their works.[1] 20:13 The sea gave up the dead who were in it. Death and Hades[40] gave up the dead who were in them. They were judged, each one according to his works. 20:14 Death and Hades[41] were thrown into the lake of fire. This is the second death, the lake of fire. 20:15 If anyone was not found written in the book of life, he was cast into the lake of fire.

1. *Another book was opened, which is the book of life. The dead were judged out of the things which were written in the*

*books, according to their works.* The last judgment. Metaphysically, judgment day is always taking place within our own consciousness. We, in our humanity, are the ones who criticize and condemn each other and ourselves. God does not judge us (Frank Giudici, Revelation 20).

Fillmore Study Bible annotations compiled by Rev. Jim Ernstsen and Rev. Lisa Herklotz.

**World English Bible Footnotes:**

[40] v20:13. or, Hell

[41] v20:14. or, Hell

# Revelation 21

## The New Heaven and the New Earth[1]

21:1 I saw a new heaven and a new earth: for the first heaven and the first earth have passed away, and the sea is no more.[2] 21:2 I saw the holy city, New Jerusalem, coming down out of heaven from God, made ready like a bride adorned for her husband. 21:3 I heard a loud voice out of heaven saying, "Behold, God's dwelling is with people, and he will dwell with them, and they will be his people, and God himself will be with them as their God. 21:4 He will wipe away from them every tear from their eyes. Death will be no more; neither will there be mourning, nor crying, nor pain, any more.[3] The first things have passed away."

21:5 He who sits on the throne said, "Behold, I am making all things new." He said, "Write, for these words of God are faithful and true." 21:6 He said to me, "It is done! I am the Alpha and the Omega, the Beginning and the End. I will give freely to him who is thirsty from the spring of the water of life. 21:7 He who overcomes, I will give him these things. I will be his God, and he will be my son. 21:8 But for the cowardly, unbelieving, sinners, abominable, murderers, sexually immoral, sorcerers,[42] idolaters, and all liars, their part is in the lake that burns with fire and sulfur, which is the second death."

1. The temporal powers have been dealt with, and the present age has been brought to a close, after all evil (error) has been eliminated. Then comes the New Jerusalem, the birth of a new consciousness.

2. *I saw a new heaven and a new earth: for the first heaven and the first earth have passed away, and the sea is no more.* The sea was considered to be the great divider of mankind. The sea separates us. Now there's no separation. We are all one. We are all together (Frank Giudici, Revelation 21).

3. *He will wipe away from them every tear from their eyes. Death will be no more; neither will there be mourning, nor crying, nor pain, any more.* Heaven and earth brought together. Heaven coming down and earth coming up to meet it, and all become one. Metaphysically: there is no death. There is no weeping anymore.

There is no crying or mourning or pain (Giudici).

## Vision of the New Jerusalem

21:9 One of the seven angels who had the seven bowls, who were loaded with the seven last plagues came, and he spoke with me, saying, "Come here. I will show you the wife, the Lamb's bride." 21:10 He carried me away in the Spirit to a great and high mountain, and showed me the holy city, Jerusalem, coming down out of heaven from God, 21:11 having the glory of God. Her light was like a most precious stone, as if it was a jasper stone, clear as crystal; 21:12 having a great and high wall; having twelve gates, and at the gates twelve angels; and names written on them, which are the names of the twelve tribes of the children of Israel. 21:13 On the east were three gates; and on the north three gates; and on the south three gates; and on the west three gates. 21:14 The wall of the city had twelve foundations, and on them twelve names of the twelve Apostles of the Lamb. 21:15 He who spoke with me had for a measure, a golden reed, to measure the city, its gates, and its walls. 21:16 The city lies foursquare, and its length is as great as its breadth. He measured the city with the reed, Twelve thousand twelve stadia[43]. Its length, breadth, and height are equal. 21:17 Its wall is one hundred forty-four cubits,[44] by the measure of a man, that is, of an angel. 21:18 The construction of its wall was jasper. The city was pure gold, like pure glass. 21:19 The foundations of the city's wall were adorned with all kinds of precious stones. The first foundation was jasper; the second, sapphire[45]; the third, chalcedony; the fourth, emerald; 21:20 the fifth, sardonyx; the sixth, sardius; the seventh, chrysolite; the eighth, beryl; the ninth, topaz; the tenth, chrysoprasus; the eleventh, jacinth; and the twelfth, amethyst. 21:21 The twelve gates were twelve pearls. Each one of the gates was made of one pearl. The street of the city was pure gold, like transparent glass. 21:22 I saw no temple[1] in it, for the Lord God, the Almighty, and the Lamb, are its temple. 21:23 The city has no need for the sun, neither of the moon, to shine, for the very glory of God illuminated it, and its lamp is the Lamb. 21:24 The nations will walk in its light. The kings of the earth bring the glory and honor of the nations into it. 21:25 Its gates will in no way be shut[2] by day (for there will be no night there), 21:26 and they shall bring the glory and the honor of the nations into it so that they may enter. 21:27 There will in no way enter into it anything profane, or one who causes an abomination or a lie, but only those who are written in the Lamb's book of life.

1. *I saw no temple.* The temple in Jerusalem had always been a connecting link between man and God, but now we realize that God dwells with man. There is no separation. There's no need for a temple as Heaven and Earth has always been one. (Frank Giudici, Revelation 21).

2. *Its gates will in no way be shut.* Anyone who wants can come in and out. Diversity and inclusivity are now part of our consciousness. All people are one. (Giudici).

Fillmore Study Bible annotations compiled by Rev. Jim Ernstsen and Rev.

Lisa Herklotz.

**World English Bible Footnotes:**

[42] v21:8. The word for "sorcerers" here also includes users of potions and drugs.

[43] v21:16. 12,012 stadia = or 2,221 kilometers or 1,380 miles. TR reads 12,000 stadia instead of 12,012 stadia.

[44] v21:17. 144 cubits is about 65.8 meters or 216 feet

[45] v21:19. or, lapis lazuli

# Revelation 22

## The River of Life 1

22:1 He showed me a[46] river of
water of life, clear as crystal, 2
proceeding out of the throne of God
and of the Lamb, 22:2 in the middle
of its street. On this side of the river
and on that was the tree of life,
bearing twelve kinds of fruits,
yielding its fruit every month. The
leaves of the tree were for the
healing of the nations. 22:3 There will
be no curse any more. The throne of
God and of the Lamb will be in it,
and his servants serve him. 22:4 They
will see his face, and his name will
be on their foreheads. 22:5 There will
be no night, and they need no lamp
light; for the Lord God will illuminate
them. They will reign forever and
ever.

22:6 He said to me, "These words
are faithful and true. The Lord God
of the spirits of the prophets sent his
angel to show to his bondservants the
things which must happen soon."

22:7 "Behold, I come quickly.
Blessed is he who keeps the words of
the prophecy of this book."

1. New Jerusalem and the New Heaven come down and become one. There is no separation from God. There is no need for a temple. There's no more sea, the great divider of humankind. There's no more death. There's no pain or mourning. There's no weeping. Everything is beautiful and is one.

2. *He showed me a river of water of life, clear as crystal.* All negative thinking is the cause of the negative experiences that we see in life. Anything negative can and will be thrown away creating our own heaven. (Frank Giudici, Revelation 22).

## Epilogue and Benediction

22:8 Now I, John, am the one who
heard and saw these things. When I
heard and saw, I fell down to worship
before the feet of the angel who had
shown me these things. 22:9 He said
to me, "See you don't do it! I am
a fellow bondservant with you and
with your brothers, the prophets,
and with those who keep the words
of this book. Worship God." 22:10 He
said to me, "Don't seal up the words

of the prophecy of this book, for the time is at hand. [22:11] He who acts unjustly, let him act unjustly still. He who is filthy, let him be filthy still. He who is righteous, let him do righteousness still. He who is holy, let him be holy still."

[22:12] "Behold, I come quickly. My reward is with me, to repay to each man according to his work. [22:13] I am the Alpha and the Omega, the First and the Last, the Beginning and the End. [22:14] Blessed are those who do his commandments, that they may have the right to the tree of life,[1] and may enter in by the gates into the city. [22:15] Outside are the dogs, the sorcerers, the sexually immoral, the murderers, the idolaters, and everyone who loves and practices falsehood. [22:16] I, Jesus, have sent my angel to testify these things to you for the assemblies. I am the root and the offspring of David; the Bright and Morning Star."

[22:17] The Spirit and the bride say, "Come!" He who hears, let him say, "Come!" He who is thirsty, let him come. He who desires, let him take the water of life freely. [22:18] I testify to everyone who hears the words of the prophecy of this book, if anyone adds to them, may God add to him the plagues which are written in this book. [22:19] If anyone takes away from the words of the book of this prophecy, may God take away his part from the tree of life, and out of the holy city, which are written in this book. [22:20] He who testifies these things says, "Yes, I come quickly."

Amen! Yes, come, Lord Jesus.

[22:21] The grace of the Lord Jesus Christ be with all the saints. Amen.

1. *Blessed are those who do his commandments, that they may have the right to the tree of life.* We are divine. And in our ideal state we are immortal beings with a right to our eternal divinity. (Ed Rabel, The Book of Revelation 22).

---

Fillmore Study Bible annotations compiled by Rev. Jim Ernstsen and Rev. Lisa Herklotz.

**World English Bible Footnotes:**

[46] v22:1. TR adds "pure"

# APPENDICES